SEVENTH EDITION

Business Marketing Management

A Strategic View of Industrial and Organizational Markets

SEVENTH EDITION

Business Marketing Management

*A Strategic View of Industrial
and Organizational Markets*

Michael D. Hutt
Arizona State University

Thomas W. Speh
Miami University

Harcourt College Publishers

Fort Worth   Philadelphia   San Diego   New York   Orlando   Austin   San Antonio
Toronto   Montreal   London   Sydney   Tokyo

Publisher   Mike Roach
Acquisitions Editor   Bill Schoof
Market Strategist   Beverly Dunn
Developmental Editor   Jana Pitts
Project Editor   Katherine Dennis
Art Director   Carol Kincaid
Production Manager   Lois West

Cover design: The Art Source with photos from EyeWire and PhotoDisk.

ISBN: 0-03-029179-8
Library of Congress Catalog Card Number: 00-10531

Address for Domestic Orders
Harcourt College Publishers, 6277 Sea Harbor Drive, Orlando, FL 32887-6777
800-782-4479

Address for International Orders
International Customer Service
Harcourt, Inc., 6277 Sea Harbor Drive, Orlando, FL 32887-6777
407-345-3800   (fax) 407-345-4060   (e-mail) hbintl@harcourt.com

Address for Editorial Correspondence
Harcourt College Publishers, 301 Commerce Street, Suite 3700, Fort Worth, TX
76102

Web Site Address
http://www.harcourtcollege.com

Harcourt College Publishers will provide complimentary supplements or supplement packages to those adopters qualified under our adoption policy. Please contact your sales representative to learn how you qualify. If as an adopter or potential user you receive supplements you do not need, please return them to your sales representative or send them to: Attn: Returns Department, Troy Warehouse, 465 South Lincoln Drive, Troy, MO 63379.

Printed in the United States of America

0 1 2 3 4 5 6 7 8 9 048 9 8 7 6 5 4 3 2 1

Harcourt College Publishers

To Rita
and
To Michele, Scott, Michael, and Betsy

The Dryden Press Series in Marketing

Assael
Marketing

Bateson and Hoffman
Managing Services Marketing:
Text and Readings
Fourth Edition

Blackwell, Blackwell, and Talarzyk
Contemporary Cases in Consumer
Behavior
Fourth Edition

Blackwell, Miniard, and Engel
Consumer Behavior
Ninth Edition

Boone and Kurtz
Contemporary Marketing
Tenth Edition

Boone and Kurtz
Contemporary Marketing 1999

Churchill
Basic Marketing Research
Fourth Edition

Churchill
Marketing Research:
Methodological Foundations
Seventh Edition

Czinkota and Ronkainen
Global Marketing

Czinkota and Ronkainen
International Marketing
Sixth Edition

Czinkota and Ronkainen
International Marketing Strategy:
Environmental Assessment and Entry
Strategies

Dickson
Marketing Management
Second Edition

Dunne and Lusch
Retailing
Third Edition

Ferrell, Hartline, Lucas, Luck
Marketing Strategy

Futrell
Sales Management:
Teamwork, Leadership, and Technology
Sixth Edition

Ghosh
Retail Management
Second Edition

Hoffman
Marketing: Best Practices

Hoffman and Bateson
Essentials of Services Marketing
Second Edition

Hutt and Speh
Business Marketing Management:
A Strategic View of Industrial
and Organizational Markets
Seventh Edition

Ingram, LaForge, Avila, Schwepker,
and Williams
Professional Selling:
A Trust-based Approach

Ingram, LaForge, Avila, Schwepker,
and Williams
Sales Management:
Analysis and Decision Making
Fourth Edition

Lindgren and Shimp
Marketing: An Interactive Learning System

Krugman, Reid, Dunn, and Barban
Advertising: Its Role in Modern Marketing
Eighth Edition

Oberhaus, Ratliffe, and Stauble
Professional Selling: A Relationship Process
Second Edition

Parente
Advertising Campaign Strategy: A Guide
to Marketing Communication Plans
Second Edition

Reedy
Electronic Marketing

Rosenbloom
Marketing Channels: A Management View
Sixth Edition

Sandburg
**Discovering Your Marketing
Career CD-ROM**

Schaffer
Applying Marketing Principles Software

Schaffer
The Marketing Game

Schellinck and Maddox
**Marketing Research: A Computer-Assisted
Approach**

Schnaars
MICROSIM

Schuster and Copeland
**Global Business: Planning for Sales and
Negotiations**

Sheth, Mittal, and Newman
**Customer Behavior: Consumer Behavior
and Beyond**

Shimp
**Advertising and Promotions: Supplemental
Aspects of Integrated Marketing
Communications**
Fifth Edition

Stauble
Marketing Strategy: A Global Perspective

Talarzyk
Cases and Exercises in Marketing

Terpstra and Sarathy
International Marketing
Eighth Edition

Watson
Electronic Commerce

Weitz and Wensley
**Readings in Strategic Marketing Analysis,
Planning, and Implementation**

Zikmund
Exploring Marketing Research
Seventh Edition

Zikmund
Essentials of Marketing Research

Harcourt College Outline Series

Peterson
Principles of Marketing

Special challenges and opportunities confront the marketer who intends to serve the needs of organizations rather than households. Business-to-business customers represent a lucrative and complex market worthy of separate analysis. A growing number of collegiate schools of business in the United States, Canada, and Europe have added industrial or business marketing to their curricula. In addition, a large and growing network of scholars in the United States and Europe is actively engaged in research to advance theory and practice in the business marketing field. Both the breadth and quality of this research has increased markedly during the past decade.

The rising importance of the field can be demonstrated by several factors. First, because more than half of all business school graduates enter firms that compete in business markets, a comprehensive treatment of business marketing management appears to be particularly appropriate. The business marketing course provides an ideal platform to deepen a student's knowledge of the competitive realities of the global marketplace, relationship management, cross-functional decision-making processes, supply chain management, product quality, and related areas. Such core content areas strike a responsive chord with corporate recruiters and squarely address key educational priorities established by the American Assembly of Collegiate Schools of Business (AACSB).

Second, the business marketing course provides a perfect vehicle for examining the special features of high-technology markets and for isolating the unique challenges that confront the marketing strategist in this arena. High-tech markets represent a rapidly growing and dynamic sector of the world economy and a fiercely competitive global battleground, but yet, often receive only modest attention in the traditional marketing curriculum. Electronic (e) commerce also falls squarely into the domain of the business market. In fact, the market opportunity for e-commerce in the business-to-business market is estimated to be ten times larger than the opportunity that exists in the business-to-consumer market.

Third, the Institute for the Study of Business Markets (ISBM) at Pennsylvania State University has provided important impetus to research in the area. ISBM has become a major information resource for researchers and practitioners and has assumed an active role in stimulating and supporting research on substantive business marketing issues.

Three objectives guided the development of this edition:

1. *To highlight the similarities between consumer goods and business-to-business marketing and to explore the points of departure in depth.* Particular attention is given to market analysis, organizational buying behavior, relationship management, and the ensuing adjustments required in the marketing strategy elements used to reach organizational customers.

2. *To present a managerial rather than a descriptive treatment of business marketing.* Whereas some descriptive material is required to convey the dynamic nature of the business marketing environment, the relevance of the material is linked to business marketing management decision making.

3. *To integrate the growing body of literature into an operational treatment of business marketing management.* In this text, relevant work is drawn from organizational buying behavior, procurement, organizational behavior, logistics, strategic management, and the behavioral sciences, as well as from specialized studies of business marketing strategy components.

The book is structured to provide a complete and timely treatment of business marketing while minimizing the degree of overlap with other courses in the marketing curriculum. A basic marketing principles course (or relevant managerial experience) provides the needed background for this text.

New To This Edition

Although the basic objectives, approach, and style of the first six editions have been maintained, several changes and additions have been made that reflect both the growing body of literature and the emerging trends in business marketing practice. Specifically, the following distinctive features are incorporated into the seventh edition:

- Two new chapters that capture dramatic changes in business practice: "E-Commerce Strategies for Business Markets" and "Supply-Chain Strategies for Business Markets."

- New and expanded treatment of customer relationship management strategies for business markets and enriched coverage of strategic alliance management.

- A timely treatment of strategy formulation in fast-paced, high-technology markets.

- New coverage of brand equity and strategies for managing high-technology products.

- Extensive coverage of new product and service development, including strategies for discontinuous innovation.

- Contemporary business marketing strategies and challenges illustrated with two types of vignettes: "Inside Business Marketing" and "Ethical Business Marketing."

Organization of the Seventh Edition

The needs and interests of the reader provided the focus in the development of this volume. The authors' goal is to present a clear, timely, and interesting examination of business marketing management. To this end, each chapter provides an overview, highlights key concepts, and includes several carefully chosen examples of contemporary business marketing practice as well as a cogent summary and a set of provocative discussion questions.

The book is divided into six parts with a total of 18 chapters. Part I introduces the distinguishing features of the business marketing environment. Careful examination is given to each of the major types of customers, the nature of the procurement function, and the forces that encircle buying decisions in organizations. Relationship management establishes the theme of Part II, in which chapter-length attention is given to customer relationship management, electronic commerce, and supply chain management. By creating two new chapters and thoroughly updating the core content, this section provides a timely and comprehensive treatment of relationship management strategies for business markets. After this important ground is established, Part III centers on the techniques that can be applied in assessing market opportunities: market segmentation and demand analysis, including sales forecasting.

Part IV centers on the planning process and on designing marketing strategy for business markets. Recent work drawn from the strategic management and strategic marketing areas provides the foundation for this section. This edition provides expanded treatment to the challenges and enticing opportunities that confront the strategist in high-technology industries. Special emphasis is given to the defining characteristics of successful high-tech firms and to the interfacing of marketing with other key functional areas such as manufacturing, research and development, and customer service. This functionally integrated planning perspective serves as a focal point in the analysis of the strategy development process. Here at the core of the volume, a separate chapter provides an integrated treatment of strategy formulation for the international market arena. Next, each component of the marketing mix is examined from a business marketing perspective. Adding further depth to this core section are the chapters on managing product innovation and managing services for business markets.

Part V examines techniques for evaluating business marketing strategy and performance. It provides a compact treatment of marketing control systems and uses the balanced scorecard as an organizing framework for marketing profitability analysis. Special attention is given to the critical area of strategy implementation in the business marketing environment. Part VI includes a collection of cases tailored to the business marketing environment.

Cases

Part VI includes 17 cases, 9 of which are new to this edition. These cases, of varying lengths, isolate one or more business marketing problems. Included among the new selections for this edition are two cases that raise provocative issues and illustrate the best practices of leading-edge firms such as Cisco Systems and IBM. Other cases new to this edition provide students with a variety of business marketing strategy applications. A *Case Planning Guide*, which keys the cases to relevant text chapters, provides an organizing structure for Part VI.

Teaching Package

A comprehensive and thoroughly updated *Instructor's Manual, Test Bank, and Transparency Masters* are available to include suggestions for course design and support materials for teaching each chapter. Guidelines are provided for end-of-chapter discussion questions, and suggestions are provided for case use and analysis. The *Instructor's Manual* for the seventh edition also provides a list of candidate readings especially suited to the business marketing course and a series of cooperative learning exercises to spark in-class involvement and discussion. Several hundred objective test questions are found in the manual, and a comprehensive set of essay questions is included to allow instructors to tailor exams to their particular needs. A total of 62 transparency masters are available.

A *computerized test bank* for Windows is also available with this edition.

A new marketing business-to-business web site on the Internet enhances the way business-to-business marketing can be taught. The web site will provide the latest information about "what's new" and "what's cool" in marketing business-to-business. Links to other related sites and much more are planned for the site.

Distance Learning

For professors interested in supplementing classroom presentations with online content or who are interested in setting up a distance learning course, Harcourt College Publishers, along with WebCT, can provide you with the industry's leading online courses.

WebCT facilitates the creation of sophisticated Web-based educational environments by providing tools to help you manage course content, facilitate online classroom collaboration, and tracking your students' progress. If you are using WebCT in your class but not a Harcourt Online Course or textbook, you may adopt the *Student's Guide to the World Wide Web and WebCT* (ISBN 0-03-045503-0). This manual gives step-by-step instructions on using WebCT tools and features.

In conjunction with WebCT, Harcourt College Publishers also offers information on adopting a Harcourt online course, WebCT testing service, free access to a blank WebCT template, and customized course creation. For more information, please contact your local sales representative. To view a demo of any of our online courses, go to webct.harcourtcollege.com.

The Harcourt College Publishers will provide complimentary supplements or supplement packages to those adopters qualified under our adoption policy. Please contact your local sales representative to learn how you may qualify. If as an adopter or potential user you receive supplements you do not need, please return them to your sales representative or send them to:

Attn: Returns Department
Troy Warehouse
465 South Lincoln Drive
Troy, MO 63379

Acknowledgments

The development of a textbook draws upon the contributions of many individuals. First, we would like to thank our students and former students at Arizona State University, Miami University, the University of Alabama, and the University of Vermont. They provided important input and feedback when selected concepts or chapters were class-tested. We would also like to thank our colleagues at each of these institutions for their assistance and support.

Second, we express our gratitude to several distinguished colleagues who carefully reviewed the volume and provided incisive comments and valuable suggestions that improved the seventh edition. They include: Kenneth Anselmi, *East Carolina Univer-*

sity; James Comer, *University of Cincinnati*; Troy Festervand, *Middle Tennessee State University*; Jonathan Hibbard, *Boston University*; George John, *University of Minnesota*; Richard Plank, *Western Michigan University*; and Constantine Polychroniou, *University of Cincinnati.*

We would also like to express our continuing appreciation to others who provided important suggestions that helped shape earlier editions: Joseph A. Bellizzi, *Arizona State University–West* Campus; Paul D. Boughton, *Saint Louis University*; Michael R. Czinkota, *Georgetown University*; S. Altan Erdem, *University of Houston–Clear Lake*; Srinath Gopalakrishna, *University of Missouri, Columbia*; Paris A. Gunther, *University of Cincinnati*; Jon M. Hawes, *University of Akron*; Jay L. Laughlin, *Kansas State University*; J. David Lichtenthal, *Baruch College*; Gary L. Lilien, *Pennsylvania State University*; Lindsay N. Meredith, *Simon Fraser University*; Richard E. Plank, *Western Michigan University*; Bernard A. Rausch, *Illinois Institute of Technology*; David A. Reid, *The University of Toledo*; Paul A. Roobol, *Western Michigan University*; Beth A. Walker, *Arizona State University*; Elizabeth Wilson Woodside, *Louisiana State University*; James F. Wolter, *Grand Valley State University*; Lauren K. Wright, *California State University–Chico*; and John M. Zerio, *American Graduate School of International Management.*

We are especially indebted to three members of the Board of Advisors for Arizona State University's Center for Services Marketing & Management. Each served as a senior executive sponsor for a funded research study, provided access to the organizations, and contributed valuable insights to the research. Collectively, these studies sharpened the strategy content of the volume. Included here are Michael Daniels, *IBM*; Dana Becker Dunn, *Lucent Technologies*; and Merrill Tutton, *AT&T*. We would also like to express our gratitude to Richard C. Munn, Chairman and Founder, and David C. Munn, President and CEO, of *the Information Technology Services Marketing Association (ITSMA)* for allowing us to use two of its best-practices cases in the volume. Since its founding in 1994, ITSMA has become the recognized leader in advancing the state-of-the art of services marketing in high-technology firms.

The talented staff of The Dryden Press displayed a high level of enthusiasm and deserves special praise for their contributions in shaping this edition. In particular, Bill Schoof provided valuable advice and direction for this edition. In turn, our developmental editor, Jana Pitts, kept us on schedule and added spirit to the process; and our project editor, Katherine Dennis, provided a steady hand and superb production assistance. We also want to extend our thanks to others at Dryden who contributed their special talents to this edition, including Carol Kincaid, art director; Lois West, production manager; and Beverly Dunn, marketing manager.

Finally, but most importantly, our overriding debt is to our wives, Rita and Michele, whose encouragement, understanding, and expertise were vital to the completion of this edition. Their involvement and dedication are deeply appreciated.

Michael D. Hutt
Thomas W. Speh

Michael D. Hutt, (Ph.D., Michigan State University) is the Earl and Gladys Davis Distinguished Professor of Marketing at Arizona State University. He has also held faculty positions at Miami University (Ohio) and the University of Vermont.

Dr. Hutt's teaching and research interests are concentrated in the areas of business-to-business marketing and strategic marketing. His current research centers on the cross-functional role that marketing managers assume in the formation of strategy. Dr. Hutt's research has been published in the *Journal of Marketing, Journal of Marketing Research, Sloan Management Review, Journal of Retailing, Journal of the Academy of Marketing Science,* and other scholarly journals. He is also the co-author of *Macro Marketing* (John Wiley & Sons) and contributing author of *Marketing: Best Practices* (The Dryden Press).

Assuming a variety of leadership roles for American Marketing Association programs, he recently co-chaired the 1996 Faculty Consortium on Strategic Marketing Management. He is a member of the editorial review boards of the *Journal of Marketing, Journal of Business-to-Business Marketing, Journal of Business & Industrial Marketing, Journal of Strategic Marketing,* and the *Journal of Business Research.* Dr. Hutt has consulted on marketing strategy issues for firms such as IBM, Motorola, Lucent Technologies, AT&T, Arvin Industries, ADT, and Black-Clawson, and for the food industry's Public Policy Subcommittee on the Universal Product Code.

Thomas W. Speh, Ph.D., is the James Evans Rees Distinguished Professor of Distribution and Director of the Warehousing Research Center at Miami University (Ohio). Prior to his tenure at Miami, Dr. Speh taught at the University of Alabama.

Dr. Speh has been a regular participant in professional marketing and logistics meetings and has published articles in a number of academic and professional journals, including the *Journal of Marketing, Journal of the Academy of Marketing Science, Journal of Business Logistics, Journal of Retailing, Journal of Purchasing and Materials Management, I.C.C. Practitioner's Journal,* and *Industrial Marketing Management.* He was the recipient of the Beta Gamma Sigma Distinguished Faculty award for excellence in teaching at Miami University's School of Business and of the Miami University Alumni Association's Effective Educator award.

Dr. Speh has been active in both the Warehousing Education and Research Council (WERC) and the Council of Logistics Management (CLM). He has served as president of WERC and as a member of the executive committee for both WERC and CLM. Dr. Speh has been a consultant on strategy issues to such organizations as Xerox, Procter & Gamble, Burlington Northern Railroad, Sara Lee, J. M. Smucker Co., and Millenium Petrochemicals, Inc.

Erin Anderson, *INSEAD*

Steven R. Ash, *Franklin University*

Guarab Bhardwaj, *Babson College*

Jan Willem Bol, *Miami University, (Ohio)*

Eric Cannell, *University of Illinois, Champaign-Urbana*

John B. Gifford, *Miami University, (Ohio)*

Michael Gilbertson, *Augustine Medical, Inc.*

Peter G. Goulet, *University of Northern Iowa*

H. Michael Hayes, *University of Colorado at Denver*

Roger A. Kerin, *Southern Methodist University (Edwin L. Cox School of Business)*

Robert B. Leavitt, *ITSMA, Lexington, Massachusetts*

Ken Manning, *Gonzaga University*

Charles Manz, *Arizona State University*

Daniel J. McCarthy, *Northeastern University*

Jakki J. Mohr, *University of Montana*

Richard C. Munn, *ITSMA, Lexington, Massachusetts*

David W. Rosenthal, *Miami University, (Ohio)*

William Rudelius, *University of Minnesota*

Frank Shipper, *Salisbury State University*

Alan J. Stenger, *Pennsylvania State University*

Julian W. Vincze, *Rollins College (Crummer Graduate School of Business)*

Brian Wansink, *University of Illinois*

James E. Weber, *St. Cloud State University*

Paula Schmidt Weber, *St. Cloud State University*

CONTENTS IN BRIEF

Preface ix

PART I
The Environment of
Business Marketing
1

Chapter 1
A Business Marketing Perspective 3

Chapter 2
The Business Market:
Perspectives on the Organizational Buyer 30

PART II
Managing Relationships
in Business Marketing
85

Chapter 3
Organizational Buying Behavior 55

Chapter 4
Relationship Strategies for Business Markets 87

PART III
Assessing Market
Opportunities
171

Chapter 5
E-Commerce Strategies for Business Markets 111

Chapter 6
Supply Chain Management 139

PART IV
Formulating Business
Marketing Strategy
223

Chapter 7
Segmenting the Business Market 173

Chapter 8
Organizational Demand Analysis 194

Chapter 9
Business Marketing Planning: Strategic Perspectives 225

Chapter 10
Business Marketing Strategies for Global Markets 252

Chapter 11
Managing Products for Business Markets   278

Chapter 12
Managing Innovation and New Industrial Product Development   305

Chapter 13
Managing Services for Business Markets   329

Chapter 14
Managing Business Marketing Channels   355

Chapter 15
Pricing Strategy for Business Markets   383

Chapter 16
Business Marketing Communications: Advertising and Sales Promotion   408

Chapter 17
Business Marketing Communications: Managing the Personal Selling Function   432

PART V

Evaluating Business Marketing Strategy and Performance
457

Chapter 18
Controlling Business Marketing Strategies   459

Cases
482

Index
695

CONTENTS

PART I

The Environment of
Business Marketing
1

Chapter 1

A Business Marketing Perspective   3

Business Marketing   4

Business Marketing Management   5

Business Markets Versus Consumer-Goods Markets   5

Marketing's Cross-Functional Relationships   7

Characteristics of Business Markets   9

Business and Consumer Marketing: A Contrast   11

Smucker: A Consumer and Business Marketer   11

INSIDE BUSINESS MARKETING:
Business-to-Business (B2B) E-Commerce   12

Distinguishing Characteristics   13

A Relationship Emphasis   14

The Supply Chain   14

The Internet and the Supply Chain   15

Build to Order   17

Procurement Trends and the Supply Chain   18

Managing Relationships in the Supply Chain   18

INSIDE BUSINESS MARKETING:
Career Profile: Managing Relationships at IBM   19

Business Market Customers   19

Commercial Enterprises as Consumers   20

Classifying Goods for the Business Market   21

Entering Goods   21

Foundation Goods   23

Facilitating Goods   23

Business Marketing Strategy   25

Illustration: Manufactured Materials and Parts   25

Illustration: Installations   25

Illustration: Supplies   25

A Look Ahead   26

Summary   28

Discussion Questions   28

Chapter 2

The Business Market: Perspectives on the Organizational Buyer   30

Commercial Enterprises: Unique Characteristics   32
Distribution by Size   32
Geographical Concentration   32
Classifying Commercial Enterprises   33
The Purchasing Organization   33
Goals of the Purchasing Function   34
Strategic Procurement   35
INSIDE BUSINESS MARKETING:
  The Supply Chain for McNuggets   36
How Purchasing Managers Evaluate Performance   41
INSIDE BUSINESS MARKETING:
  ISO 9000: The International Quality Standard   42
ETHICAL BUSINESS MARKETING:
  Globalization Requires New Ground Rules   44
Supplier Evaluation: Implications for the Marketer   44
Governments: Unique Characteristics   45
Influences on Government Buying   45
Understanding Government Contracts   45
Telling Vendors How to Sell: Useful Publications   46
Purchasing Organizations and Procedures: Government   46
Federal Buying   48
INSIDE BUSINESS MARKETING:
  Jet Fighter Contract: A Flyoff Determines the Winner   49
A Different Strategy Required   49
The Institutional Market: Unique Characteristics   50
Institutional Buyers: Purchasing Procedures   50
Dealing with Diversity: A Market-Centered Organization   52
Summary   52
Discussion Questions   54

Chapter 3

Organizational Buying Behavior   55

The Organizational Buying Process   56
New Task   58
Straight Rebuy   59
Modified Rebuy   63
Forces Shaping Organizational Buying Behavior   67
Environmental Forces   67
Organizational Forces   69

Organizational Positioning of Purchasing 70

INSIDE BUSINESS MARKETING:
  Targeting Buying Influentials: A Web Strategy 72

Group Forces 73

ETHICAL BUSINESS MARKETING:
  Close Buyer–Seller Relationships Pose New Ethical Threats 75

Individual Forces 77

INSIDE BUSINESS MARKETING: Best Practices for Customer
  Satisfaction in Business Marketing Firms 80

The Organizational Buying Process: Major Elements 81

Summary 82

Discussion Questions 83

PART II

Managing Relationships
in Business Marketing
85

Chapter 4

Relationship Strategies for Business Markets 87

Relationship Marketing 88

Types of Relationships 89

Value-Adding Exchanges 89

Nature of Relationships 90

Strategic Choices 90

Buyer-Seller Connector 90

Information Exchange 91

Operational Linkages 91

Legal Bonds 92

Cooperative Norms 92

Relationship-Specific Adaptations by the Seller or Buyer 92

Market and Situational Factors 92

Customer Evaluation of Suppliers 93

INSIDE BUSINESS MARKETING:
  Understanding the Customer's Business—The Key to Success 94

Managing Buyer-Seller Relationships 94

Transactional Exchange 94

Collaborative Exchange 94

Strategy Guidelines 95

Relationship Marketing Strategies 96

Capturing Relationship Data 96

Account Selection 98

Developing Account-Specific Product Offerings 98

Implementing Relationship Strategies 100

Evaluating Relationship Strategy Outcomes 101

INSIDE BUSINESS MARKETING: World Class Leaders 102

Strategic Alliances 102

Benefits of Strategic Alliances | 102
Alliance Management Challenges | 103
Determinants of Alliance Success | 104
INSIDE BUSINESS MARKETING:
   The Internet Helps Cisco Systems Serve Customers | 105
The Social Ingredients of Alliance Success | 107
Summary | 109
Discussion Questions | 109

Chapter 5

E-Commerce Strategies for Business Markets | 111

Defining E-Commerce | 113
Key Elements Supporting E-Commerce | 114
The Internet and World Wide Web | 114
Intranets and Extranets | 116
The Strategic Role of E-Commerce | 117
E-Commerce As a Strategic Component | 118
What the Internet Can Do | 118
Crafting an E-Commerce Strategy | 120
Delineating E-Commerce Objectives | 120
Specific Objectives of Internet Marketing Strategies | 122
Internet Strategy Implementation | 124
The Internet Product | 124
INSIDE BUSINESS MARKETING:
   AMP's Search Engine Makes Finding Products Easy | 128
Channel Considerations with Internet Marketing | 131
The Internet as a Channel Alternative | 133
The Impact of the Internet on Pricing Strategy | 134
The Internet and Customer Communications | 135
The Internet's Expanding Role | 136
Summary | 137
Discussion Questions | 137

Chapter 6

Supply Chain Management | 139

The Concept of Supply Chain Management | 141
Partnerships: The Critical Ingredient | 142
**Supply Chain Management: A Tool for
   Competitive Advantage** | 143
Supply Chain Management Goals | 144
Benefits to the Final Customer | 146

The Financial Benefits Perspective 147

The SCM Improvement Perspective 147

Information and Technology Drivers 147

**Successfully Applying the Supply Chain
Management Approach** 150

*INSIDE BUSINESS MARKETING: Supply Chain Management
Delivers the Office Furniture On Time* 151

Successful Supply Chain Practices 151

**Logistics as the Critical Element in Supply
Chain Management** 153

Distinguishing between Logistics and
Supply Chain Management 154

Managing Flows 155

Timely Logistics Support 155

A Source of Competitive Advantage 155

Sales-Marketing-Logistics Integration 156

Just-in-Time Systems 156

Total-Cost Approach 157

Calculating Logistics Costs 159

Activity-Based Costing 159

Total Cost of Ownership (TCO) 159

Business-to-Business Logistical Service 159

Logistics Service Impacts on the Customer 160

Determining the Level of Service 160

Logistics Impacts on Other Supply Chain Participants 161

Business-to-Business Logistical Management 163

Logistical Facilities 163

Transportation 164

Inventory Management 165

Logistics Information Systems 167

Third-Party Logistics 167

*INSIDE BUSINESS MARKETING:
Case Corporation Constructs a Logistics Model for the Future* 168

Summary 169

Discussion Questions 170

PART III

**Assessing Market
Opportunities**
171

Chapter 7

Segmenting the Business Market 173

Business Market Segmentation Requirements and Benefits 174

Requirements 175

Evaluating the Competitive Environment 175

Evaluating the Technological Environment 176

INSIDE BUSINESS MARKETING: Segmentation at Cisco.com   177
Benefits   177
Bases for Segmenting Business Markets   178
Macrolevel Bases   179
Illustration: Macrosegmentation   183
Microlevel Bases   183
INSIDE BUSINESS MARKETING: Strategy is Revolution   186
Illustration: Microsegmentation   188
A Model for Segmenting the Organizational Market   189
Choosing Market Segments   189
Making a Commitment   191
Implementing a Segmentation Strategy   191
Summary   191
Discussion Questions   192

Chapter 8

Organizational Demand Analysis   194

Organizational Demand Analysis   195
Using the Internet for Business Marketing Research   195
The Role of Market Potential in Planning and Control   198
The Role of the Sales Forecast   200
Applying Market Potential and the Sales Forecast   201
Determining Market and Sales Potentials   202
Statistical Series Methods   202
INSIDE BUSINESS MARKETING:
DeepCanyon.com—A Valuable Resource for Market Analysis   203
Market Research   205
The Essential Dimensions of Sales Forecasting   208
General Approaches to Forecasting   208
The Forecasting Time Frame   210
Forecasting Methods   210
INSIDE BUSINESS MARKETING:
Forecasting Accuracy Depends on . . .   211
Qualitative Techniques   211
Quantitative Techniques   214
ETHICAL BUSINESS MARKETING:
The Wrong Way to Use Forecasting   217
Using Several Forecasting Techniques   218
Technique Selection   219
Summary   220
Discussion Questions   220
Exercises   221

PART IV

Formulating Business
Marketing Strategy
223

Chapter 9

Business Marketing Planning: Strategic Perspectives 225

Market-Driven Organizations 226

Capabilities of Market-Driven Organizations 227

Dimensions of Market-Driven Management 228

Assessing Competitive Advantage 231

Sources of Advantage 231

Figures of Merit 233

Positions of Advantage 233

Converting Skills and Resources into Superior Positions 234

Marketing's Strategic Role 235

The Hierarchy of Strategies 235

Strategy Formulation and the Hierarchy 237

Creating Strategy in High-Technology Industries 239

Discontinuous Innovation Strategies 240

Marketing's Cross-Functional Relationships 244

Cross-Functional Connections 244

Functionally Integrated Planning:
The Marketing Strategy Center 246

The Business Marketing Planning Process 248

The Marketing Plan 248

Summary 249

Discussion Questions 250

Chapter 10

Business Marketing Strategies for Global Markets 252

Drivers of Globalization 254

Market Factors 254

Economic Factors 257

Environmental Factors 257

INSIDE BUSINESS MARKETING:
Innovative Solutions for the Environment 258

Competitive Factors 258

International Market-Entry Options 259

Exporting 259

Contracting 260

Strategic Alliances 261

Joint Ventures 262

Multidomestic versus Global Strategies 264

ETHICAL BUSINESS MARKETING:
Bribery and Differing Business Practices 265

International Strategy and the Value Chain 266
Evolution of International Marketing Strategy 269
INSIDE BUSINESS MARKETING:
Iridium: A Global Satellite Phone System that Didn't Fly 270
Pre-Internationalization 270
Phase One: Initial International Market Entry 271
INSIDE BUSINESS MARKETING:
Global Account Management at IBM 272
Phase Two: Local Market Expansion 273
Phase Three: Global Orientation 274
Summary 275
Discussion Questions 276

Chapter 11

Managing Products for Business Markets 278
Core Competencies: The Roots of Industrial Products 279
Identifying Core Competencies 280
Sustaining the Lead 280
INSIDE BUSINESS MARKETING:
The Meaning of Market Influence 282
From Core Products to End Products 282
Exploiting Selected Core Competencies 283
Product Quality 284
Meaning of Quality 284
Meaning of Value 285
Value in Use 286
Product Support Strategy: The Service Connection 286
Product Policy 287
Types of Product Lines Defined 287
Defining the Product Market 289
Assessing Global Product-Market Opportunities 290
INSIDE BUSINESS MARKETING: High-Growth Market Blues 292
Planning Industrial Product Strategy 292
Product Positioning 292
Determinant Attributes 293
Strategy Matrix 293
Managing Products in High-Technology Markets 294
Managing a High-Tech Brand 294
Isolating Technology Adopters 298
The Technology Adoption Life Cycle 299
INSIDE BUSINESS MARKETING:
The Gorilla Advantage in High-Tech Markets 300

Summary	302
Discussion Questions	303

Chapter 12

**Managing Innovation and New Industrial
    Product Development**   305

The Management of Innovation	306
Patterns of Strategic Behavior	307
INSIDE BUSINESS MARKETING: The Angels of Silicon Valley	309
Bringing Silicon Valley Inside	309
Managing Technology	311
Classifying Development Projects	311
A Product Family Focus	312
Innovation Winners in High-Technology Markets	312
INSIDE BUSINESS MARKETING:	
Patching: The New Corporate Strategy in Dynamic Markets	313
The New Product Development Process	314
What Drives a Firm's New Product Performance?	316
Sources of New Product Ideas	317
Cross-Functional Barriers	319
A Team-Based Process	321
Quality Function Deployment	322
Determinants of New Product Performance	
and Timeliness	323
The Determinants of Success	324
INSIDE BUSINESS MARKETING:	
From Bullet-Point Plans to Strategic Stories at 3M	325
Determinants of Product Success for Japanese Companies	325
Fast-Paced Product Development	326
Summary	327
Discussion Questions	327

Chapter 13

Managing Services for Business Markets	329
Business Services: Role and Importance	330
Product Support Services	331
Pure Services	333
Business Service Marketing: Special Challenges	333
INSIDE BUSINESS MARKETING: You've Got Too Much Mail!	334
Services Are Different	334
Tangible or Intangible?	334

Simultaneous Production and Consumption 336

Service Variability 336

Service Perishability 337

Non-Ownership 337

Service Quality 337

Dimensions of Service Quality 338

Customer Satisfaction and Loyalty 338

Zero Defections 339

Return on Quality 340

Marketing Mix for Business Service Firms 340

Segmentation 340

Service Packages 341

Pricing Business Services 343

Services Promotion 345

Services Distribution 347

INSIDE BUSINESS MARKETING:
Caterpillar's Close Connections with Global Customers 349

Developing New Services 349

Scenarios for Success and Failure 351

Summary 353

Discussion Questions 354

Chapter 14

Managing Business Marketing Channels 355

The Business Marketing Channel 356

Direct Distribution 357

INSIDE BUSINESS MARKETING: IBM Uses the Internet to
Collaborate with Channel Partners and Build Customer Loyalty 358

Indirect Distribution 358

Many Channels Are Often Required 359

E-Channels 359

Participants in the Business Marketing Channel 361

Distributors 361

INSIDE BUSINESS MARKETING:
Distributor Alliances Respond to Changing Customer Needs 362

Manufacturers' Representatives 364

Channel Design 365

Stage 1: Channel Objectives 366

Stage 2: Channel Design Constraints 367

Stage 3: Pervasive Channel Tasks 367

Stage 4: Channel Alternatives 369

Stage 5: Channel Selection 372
Channel Administration 373
Selection of Channel Members 374
Motivating Channel Members 374
INSIDE BUSINESS MARKETING:
   Champion Distributor: W. W. Grainger, Inc. 376
Conflict: The Need for Relationship Management 377
International Business Marketing Channels 378
Domestic Intermediaries 378
Foreign-Based Intermediaries 379
Company-Organized Sales Force 380
Summary 381
Discussion Questions 382

Chapter 15

Pricing Strategy for Business Markets 383
The Meaning of Price in Business Markets 384
Benefits 385
Costs 386
INSIDE BUSINESS MARKETING:
   Create Value-Based Sales Tools 387
The Industrial Pricing Process 387
Price Objectives 388
Demand Determinants 388
Cost Determinants 393
Competition 396
INSIDE BUSINESS MARKETING:
   The Price/Performance Engine in High-Technology Marketing 397
Pricing Across the Product Life Cycle 399
ETHICAL BUSINESS MARKETING:
   On Ethics and Pricing at Raytheon 400
Pricing New Products 400
Tactical Pricing 402
Legal Considerations 403
Competitive Bidding 403
Closed Bidding 404
Open Bidding 404
Strategies for Competitive Bidding 404
Summary 406
Discussion Questions 407

Chapter 16

**Business Marketing Communications:
  Advertising and Sales Promotion** 408

The Role of Advertising 409
Integrated Communication Programs 409
Advertising: Enhancing Sales Effectiveness 410
Advertising: Increased Sales Efficiency 411
Advertising: Creating Awareness 411
What Business-to-Business Advertising Cannot Do 412
Managing Business-to-Business Advertising 412
Defining Advertising Objectives 412
Written Objectives 412
Determining Advertising Expenditures 414
Developing the Advertising Message 416
Selecting Advertising Media for Business Markets 417
Direct Marketing Tools 419
INSIDE BUSINESS MARKETING:
  The Expanding Role of Internet Marketing 422
The Power of Internet Marketing Communications 422
Integrate the Internet into Media Plans 422
Capture the Economies of the Internet 422
Make Real-Time Changes 423
Create "Unlimited Shelf Space" for Products 423
Reach Customers on a Global Scale 423
Build One-to-One Relationships with Customers 423
Measuring Advertising Effectiveness 424
Measuring Impacts on the Purchase Decision 424
The Measurement Program 424
Managing Trade Show Strategy 425
Trade Shows: Strategy Benefits 426
Trade Show Investment Returns 426
Planning Trade Show Strategy 427
Trade Show Objectives 427
Selecting the Shows 427
Managing the Trade Show Exhibit 428
Evaluating Trade Show Performance 428
INSIDE BUSINESS MARKETING:
  Using High Tech to Pursue Trade Show Leads 430
Summary 430
Discussion Questions 431

Chapter 17

**Business Marketing Communications:
Managing the Personal Selling Function**   432

**Foundations of Personal Selling: An Organizational
Customer Focus**   433

Organizational Buying Behavior   434

The Internet: Transforming the Selling Process   435

Relationship Marketing   437

Relationship Quality   438

Enhancing Customer Relationships with the Internet   439

Managing the Sales Force   439

Organizing the Personal Selling Effort   440

Organizing to Serve National Accounts   441

Sales Administration   443

*INSIDE BUSINESS MARKETING: From National
to Global Account Management at Hewlett Packard*   444

ETHICAL BUSINESS MARKETING: Ethics in Selling   449

Models for Industrial Sales Force Management   449

Deployment Analysis: A Strategic Approach   450

Customer Relationship Management Systems   451

Summary   454

Discussion Questions   455

PART V

**Evaluating Business
Marketing Strategy
and Performance**
457

Chapter 18

Controlling Business Marketing Strategies   459

The Balanced Scorecard   460

Financial Perspective   461

Customer Perspective   462

Internal Business Process Perspective   463

Learning and Growth Perspective   464

Marketing Strategy: Allocating Resources   466

Guiding Strategy Formulation   466

The Marketing Control Process   467

Informal Control Affects Behavior   467

Control at Various Levels   468

Strategic Control   468

Annual Plan Control   469

Efficiency and Effectiveness Control   471

Profitability Control   471

Feedforward Control   474

Implementation of Business Marketing Strategy   475

The Strategy-Implementation Fit   475

INSIDE BUSINESS MARKETING:
    ABC Analysis Says, "Change the 80-20 Rule to 20-225"   476

Implementation Skills   476

The Marketing Strategy Center: An Implementation Guide   477

Looking Back   479

Summary   480

Discussion Questions   480

Cases   482

Case Planning Guide   482

**Cisco Systems—Building and Marketing the
    Global Networked Business**   483

S. C. Johnson's Professional Division   509

**Southwestern Ohio Steel Company, L.P:
    The Matworks Decision**   518

Roscoe Nondestructive Testing   530

Nypro Inc.: Strategy for Globalization   538

IBM Corporation: Anatomy of a Branding Campaign   560

W. L. Gore & Associates, Inc.—1996: A Case Study   580

Barro Stickney, Inc.   604

Beta Pharmaceuticals: Pennsylvania Distribution System   609

Wind Technology   615

SAP AG (1995)   622

**Augustine Medical, Inc.: The Bair Hugger®
    Patient Warming System**   631

Ohmeda Monitoring Systems   642

BWI Kartridg Pak   658

Ace Technical   677

Ethical Dilemmas in Business Marketing   692

Name Index   695

Subject Index   701

I

The Environment of Business Marketing

1

A Business Marketing Perspective

The business market poses special challenges and significant opportunities for the marketing manager. This chapter introduces the complex forces that are unique to the business marketing environment. After reading this chapter, you will understand

1. the dynamic nature of the business marketing environment as well as the basic similarities and differences between consumer-goods and business marketing

2. the underlying factors that influence the demand for industrial goods

3. the nature of buyer-seller relationships in the supply chain for a product

4. the types of customers in this important market

5. the basic characteristics of industrial products and services

Business Marketing

Business marketers serve the largest market of all; the dollar volume of transactions in the industrial or business market significantly exceeds that of the ultimate consumer market. In the business market, a single customer can account for an enormous level of purchasing activity. For example, the General Motors' purchasing department spends more than $85 billion annually on industrial products and services—more than the gross domestic products of Ireland, Portugal, Turkey, or Greece. The 1,350 professional buyers at General Motors each spend more than $50 million annually.[1] Others, such as General Electric (GE), Du Pont, and International Business Machines (IBM), spend more than $60 million per day on purchases to support their operations.[2] Indeed, all formal organizations—large or small, public or private, profit or not-for-profit—participate in the exchange of industrial products and services, thus constituting the business market.

Business markets are "markets for products and services, local to international, bought by businesses, government bodies, and institutions (such as hospitals) for incorporation (for example, ingredient materials or components), for consumption (for example, process materials, office supplies, consulting services), for use (for example, installations or equipment), or for resale. . . . The only markets not of direct interest are those dealing with products or services which are principally directed at personal use or consumption such as packaged grocery products, home appliances, or consumer banking."[3] The factors that distinguish business marketing from consumer marketing are the nature of the customer and how that customer uses the product. In business marketing, the customers are organizations (businesses, governments, institutions).

Business firms buy industrial goods to form or facilitate the production process or use as components for other goods and services. Government agencies and private institutions buy industrial goods to maintain and deliver services to their own market: the public. Industrial or business marketing (the terms can be used interchangeably) accounts for more than half the economic activity in the United States, Canada, and most other nations. More than 50 percent of all business school graduates join firms that compete directly in the business market. The heightened interest in high technology markets—and the sheer size of the business market—has spawned increased emphasis on business marketing management in universities and corporate executive training programs.[4]

This book explores the special opportunities and challenges that the business market presents and identifies the new requirements for managing the marketing function in this vital sector of the global economy. The following questions establish the theme of this first chapter: What are the similarities and differences between consumer-goods marketing and business marketing? What customers constitute the business market?

---

[1] Gregory L. White, "How GM, Ford Think Web Can Make Splash on the Factory Floor," *Wall Street Journal*, (December 3), 1999, p. A1.

[2] Ann Millen Porter, "Big Spenders: The Top 250," *Purchasing*, 6 (November 1997), pp. 40–51.

[3] Prospectus for the Institute for the Study of Business Markets, College of Business Administration, the Pennsylvania State University.

[4] J. David Lichtenthal, "Business-to-Business Marketing in the 21st Century," *Journal of Business-to-Business Marketing* 12 (1,2 1998), pp. 1–5 and Michael D. Hutt and Thomas W. Speh, "Business Marketing Education: A Distinctive Role in the Undergraduate Curriculum," *Journal of Business-to-Business Marketing* 12 (1,2 1998), pp. 103–126.

How can the multitude of industrial goods be classified into manageable categories? What forces influence the behavior of business market demand?

Business Marketing Management

Many large firms that produce goods such as steel, production equipment, or computer-memory chips cater exclusively to business market customers and never directly interact with their ultimate consumers. Other firms participate in both the consumer-goods and the business markets. The introduction of laser printers and personal computers brought Hewlett-Packard, historically a business-to-business marketer, into the consumer market. Conversely, lagging consumer markets prompted Sony Corporation to expand to the business market by introducing office automation products. Both companies had to reorient their marketing strategies dramatically because of the significant differences between the buying behavior exhibited in the consumer versus the business markets.

Products like cellular phones, office furniture, personal computers, and software are purchased in both the consumer and the business markets. What distinguishes business marketing from consumer-goods marketing is the *intended use of the product* as well as the *intended consumer.* Sometimes the products are identical, but a fundamentally different marketing approach is needed to reach the organizational buyer.

Business Markets versus Consumer-Goods Markets

The basic task of management cuts across both consumer-goods and business marketing. Marketers serving both sectors can benefit by rooting their organizational plan in a *market orientation*, which requires superior proficiency in understanding and satisfying customers.[5] Such market-driven firms demonstrate

- a set of values and beliefs that places the customers' interests first;[6]

- the ability to generate, disseminate, and productively use superior information about customers and competitors;[7]

- and the coordinated use of interfunctional resources (for example, research and development, manufacturing).[8]

Distinctive Capabilities   A close examination of a market-driven firm will reveal two particularly important capabilities: market sensing and customer linking.[9] First, the **market-sensing capability** concerns how well the organization is equipped to

---

[5] George S. Day, "The Capabilities of Market-Driven Organizations," *Journal of Marketing* 58 (October 1994): pp. 37–52.

[6] Rohit Deshpande, John U. Farley, and Frederick E. Webster Jr., "Corporate Culture, Customer Orientation, and Innovativeness in Japanese Firms: A Quadrad Analysis," *Journal of Marketing* 57 (January 1993): pp. 23–37.

[7] Ajay K. Kohli and Bernard J. Jaworski, "Market Orientation: The Construct, Research Propositions, and Managerial Implications," *Journal of Marketing* 54 (April 1990): pp. 1–18.

[8] John C. Narver and Stanley F. Slater, "The Effect of a Market Orientation on Business Profitability," *Journal of Marketing* 54 (October 1990): pp. 20–35.

[9] Day, "Capabilities of Market-Driven Organizations," pp. 37–52.

continuously sense changes in its market and to anticipate customer responses to marketing programs. Market-driven firms spot market changes and react well in advance of their competitors (for example, Coca-Cola in the consumer-goods market and 3M in the business market). Second, the **customer-linking capability** comprises the particular skills, abilities, and processes that an organization has developed to create and manage close customer relationships.

Consumer-goods firms, such as Procter and Gamble, demonstrate these capabilities in working with powerful retailers like Wal-Mart. Here, multifunctional teams in both organizations work together by sharing delivery and product movement information and by jointly planning promotional activity and product changes. While evident in manufacturer-reseller relations in the consumer-goods market, strong customer-linking capabilities are crucial in the business market where close buyer-seller relationships prevail.

Partnering for Increased Value   A business marketer becomes a preferred supplier to major customers such as Citigroup, Texas Instruments, or Motorola by working closely as a partner, developing an intimate knowledge of the customer's operations, and contributing unique value to that customer's business. Business marketing programs increasingly involve a customized blend of tangible products, service support, and ongoing information services both before and after the sale. Market-driven firms place a high priority on customer-linking capabilities and closely align product decisions—as well as delivery, handling, service, and other supply-chain activities—with the customer's operations. For a firm like Motorola to deliver maximum value to its customers, it must receive maximum value from its suppliers. For instance, Motorola's Paging Products Group could not have achieved its 60 percent global market share without the cost, quality, technology, and other advances contributed by its suppliers.[10]

Creating the Value Proposition[11]   Business marketing strategy must be based on an assessment of the company, the competitor, and the customer. A successful strategy focuses on identifying those opportunities in which the firm can deliver superior value to customers based on its distinctive competencies. From this perspective, marketing can be best understood as the process of defining, developing, and delivering value.

Market-driven firms attempt to match their resources, skills, and capabilities with particular customer needs that are not being adequately served. By understanding customer needs, marketing managers can define value from the customer's perspective and convert that information into requirements for creating satisfied customers. In turn, a firm's capabilities and skills determine the degree to which the company can meet these requirements and provide greater value than its competitors.

Given many strategic paths, the **value proposition** signals the chosen direction by specifying how the organization proposes to deliver superior value to customers. The value proposition is an important organizing force in the firm because it directs all employees to focus on customer requirements, and it provides the means for the firm to position its offerings in the minds of customers.

---

[10]Jordan D. Lewis, *The Connected Corporation: How Leading Companies Win through Customer-Supplier Alliances* (New York: The Free Press, 1995), p. 3.

[11]Frederick E. Webster Jr., *Market-Driven Management: Using the New Marketing Concept to Create a Customer-Oriented Company* (New York: John Wiley & Sons, Inc., 1994), p. 60.

Marketing's Cross-Functional Relationships

Rather than operating in isolation from other functional areas, the successful business marketing manager is an integrator—one who understands the capabilities of manufacturing, research and development (R&D), and customer service and who applies these strengths in developing marketing strategies that are responsive to customer needs.[12] Close and tightly integrated cross-functional relationships underlie the strategy success stories of firms such as Hewlett-Packard and 3M. As firms adopt leaner and more agile structures and emphasize cross-functional teams, the business marketing manager assumes an important and challenging role in strategy formation.

Business marketing success depends to a large degree on such functional areas in the firm as engineering, R&D, manufacturing, and technical service. Planning in the industrial setting thus requires more functional interdependence and a closer relationship to total corporate strategy than planning in the consumer-goods sector. B. Charles Ames points out that "changes in marketing strategy are more likely to involve capital commitments for new equipment, shifts in development activities, or departures from traditional engineering and manufacturing approaches, any one of which would have companywide implications."[13] All business marketing decisions—product, price, promotion, and distribution—are affected, directly or indirectly, by other functional areas. In turn, business decisions in R&D and in manufacturing and procurement, as well as adjustments in the overall corporate strategy, are influenced by marketing considerations. Business marketing planning must be coordinated and synchronized with corresponding planning efforts in R&D, procurement, finance, production, and other areas (see Figure 1.1).

Cross-Functional Working Relationships[14]   A day in the life of a business marketing manager centers on building relationships with customers *and* in forging one-to-one relationships with managers in other functional areas within the firm. By building effective cross-functional connections, the marketer is ideally equipped to respond to the changing needs of customers. Key drivers of effective cross-functional working relationships are described and illustrated in the words of managers.

- **Communication**—the free and open exchange of ideas and information between managers to clarify goals.

  Market Manager: *I think what made the interaction effective was a free flow of thoughts and suggestions back and forth. John [R&D manager] and I equally contributed to the development of the agenda to make sure we had covered the appropriate topics to evaluate market opportunity.*

- **Perspective Taking**—the willingness and ability of a manager to consider the point of view of another functional area, the customer, or the firm.

---

[12] Michael D. Hutt, "Cross-Functional Working Relationships in Marketing," *Journal of the Academy of Marketing Science* 23 (fall 1995): pp. 351–357.

[13] B. Charles Ames, "Trappings vs. Substance in Industrial Marketing," *Harvard Business Review* 48 (July/August 1996): pp. 95–96.

[14] Edward Bond, Matt Meuter, Beth Walker, and Michael Hutt, "Diagnosing Marketing's Effective and Ineffective Cross-Functional Working Relationships," unpublished working paper, Arizona State University, 1999.

FIGURE 1.1

BUSINESS MARKETING PLANNING:
A FUNCTIONALLY INTEGRATED PERSPECTIVE

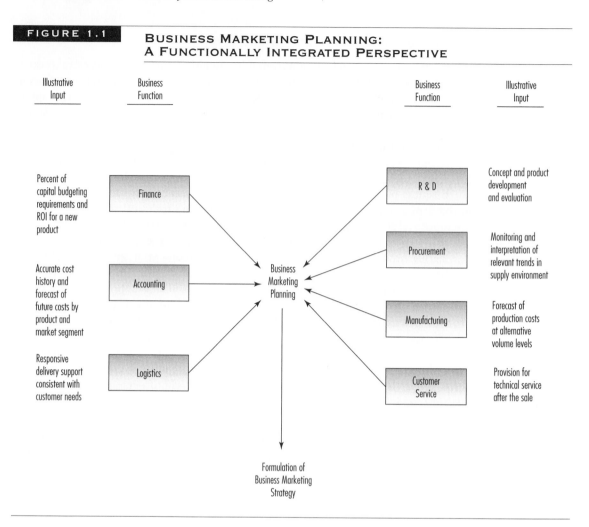

Market Manager: *In the past, R&D managers were concerned with their schedules and their group. But this R&D manager asks: "What does the customer need? What does the market need? When do they need it?" I can't say enough about him.*

- **Responsive Behavior**—the promptness, follow-through, and initiative that a manager demonstrates in handling a request.

R&D Manager: *Mary* [market manager] *got right back to me and quickly solved my problem. It kept us right on schedule with the project.*

Manufacturing Manager: *She doesn't just see a breakdown and say, "Oh, we have a breakdown," and spend two weeks talking about it. She looks for a solution.*

- **Compatibility**—the common ground or shared goals that can unite managers who represent different functional areas.

Marketing manager: *Both of us* [R&D and marketing] *seemed to agree without effort. We both agreed on our basic business philosophy—the need for a more market-based approach versus a focus on technology. Once we agreed, we knew we could take incremental steps in doing more joint planning, in doing more regular communications, to basically foster this approach.*

Reputationally-Effective Managers   A business marketing manager is judged to be **reputationally effective** when he or she is responsive to the needs, demands, and expectations of managers across functions. Reputationally-effective managers use both formal and informal communication channels to build a web of close working relationships; they are sensitive to the perspectives of other functional areas, and they are prompt and thorough in responding to requests from other units. Provided below is a profile of a reputationally-effective manager at a *Fortune* 500, high-technology firm. This manager works in Denver but makes frequent visits to the firm's headquarters in New Jersey. A colleague in marketing observes:

> He has a tremendous network of people to work and solve problems with. He doesn't sit out there in Denver. He was out here visiting yesterday and we were walking down the hall and I was stunned at how many people knew him. . . . He gets things done because he has really good personal relationships with a lot of people and he has a network—he really understands the mechanisms that you have to deal with in order to get things done.

Characteristics of Business Markets

Business marketing and consumer-goods marketing are different. A common body of knowledge, principles, and theory applies to both consumer and business marketing, but because their buyers and markets function quite differently, they merit separate attention. Consumer and business marketing differ in the nature of markets, market demand, buyer behavior, buyer-seller relationships, environmental influences (economic, political, legal), and market strategy. Yet, the potential payoffs are high for the firm that can successfully penetrate the business market. The nature of the demand for industrial products poses unique challenges—and opportunities—for the marketing manager.

Derived Demand   **Derived demand** refers to the direct link between the demand for an industrial product and the demand for consumer products: *the demand for industrial products is derived from the ultimate demand for consumer products.* Consider the materials and components that are used in a Harley-Davidson motorcycle. Some of the components are manufactured by Harley-Davidson, but the finished product reflects the efforts of over 200 suppliers or business marketers who deal directly with the firm. In purchasing a Harley-Davidson motorcycle, the customer is stimulating the demand for a diverse array of products manufactured by business marketing firms—such as tires, electrical components, coil springs, aluminum castings, and other items.

Fluctuating Demand   Because demand is derived, the business marketer must carefully monitor demand patterns and changing buying preferences in the household consumer market, often on a worldwide basis. For example, a decline in mortgage rates can spark an increase in new home construction and a corresponding increase in appliance sales. Retailers generally respond by increasing their stock of inventory. As appliance producers, like Maytag, increase the rate of production to meet the demand, business marketers that supply these manufacturers with items such as motors, timers, or paint experience a surge in sales. A downturn in the economy creates the opposite result. This explains why the demand for many industrial products tends to *fluctuate* more than the demand for consumer products.

Stimulating Demand   Some business marketers must not only monitor final consumer markets, but also develop a marketing program that reaches the ultimate consumer directly. Aluminum producers use television and magazine ads to point out the convenience and recycling opportunities that aluminum containers offer to the consumer—the ultimate consumer influences aluminum demand by purchasing soft drinks in aluminum, rather than plastic, containers. Over 4 billion pounds of aluminum are used annually in the production of beverage containers. Similarly, Boeing promotes the convenience of air travel in a media campaign targeted to the consumer market to create a favorable environment for longer-term demand for its planes; Du Pont advertises to ultimate consumers to stimulate the sales of carpeting, which incorporates their product.

Price Sensitivity   Demand elasticity refers to the responsiveness of the quantity demanded to a change in price. Demand is elastic when a given percentage change in price brings about an even larger percentage change in the quantity demanded. Inelasticity results when demand is insensitive to price—for example, when the percentage change in demand is less than the percentage change in price. Consider the demand for electronic components that is stimulated by companies making digital cameras. As long as final consumers continue to purchase these cameras and are generally insensitive to price, manufacturers of the equipment are relatively insensitive to the price of electronic components. At the opposite end of the spectrum, if consumers are price sensitive when purchasing soup and other canned grocery products, manufacturers of soup will be price sensitive when purchasing metal cans. Thus, the derived demand indicates that the demand for metal cans is price elastic.

Final consumer demand has a pervasive impact on the demand for products in the business market. By being sensitive to trends in the consumer market, the business marketer can often identify both impending problems and opportunities for growth and diversification.

A Global Market Perspective   According to Michael E. Porter, "In international markets, innovations that yield competitive advantage anticipate both domestic and foreign needs."[15] Indeed, the relevant unit of analysis in an increasing number of industries today is not the domestic but the worldwide market position. The accelerating demand for industrial goods in the international market and the dramatic rise in competition—from Western Europe, Japan, the Pacific Rim (with Korea, Taiwan, Hong Kong, and Singapore becoming active players), and nearby industrialized countries (notably India and Brazil)—necessitate a global perspective on competition. Meanwhile, Eastern Europe will likely evolve into an important customer and source of world industrial competition in the years ahead.

A complete picture of the business market must include a horizon that stretches beyond the boundaries of the United States. The demand for many industrial goods and services is growing more rapidly in many foreign countries than in the United States. Countries like Germany, Japan, Korea, and Brazil offer large and growing markets for many business marketers. Countless small firms and many large ones—such

---

[15] Michael E. Porter, "The Competitive Advantage of Nations," *Harvard Business Review* 68 (March/April, 1990): p. 74.

as General Electric (GE), 3M, Intel, Boeing, Dow Chemical, Lucent Technologies, and Motorola—derive a significant portion of their sales and profits from international markets. For example, Motorola is helping China leapfrog one stage of industrial evolution for which Western nations have invested billions of dollars—the need to tie every home and business together with copper wire. Motorola's pagers and cell phones provide valuable solutions to customers in an unwired world, and the firm's sales in China and Hong Kong exceed $3 billion annually.[16]

John F. Welch Jr., chairman and CEO of GE, spawned a strategic redirection that has provided GE with world market-share leadership in nearly all of its major businesses. He offers this challenging profile for competing successfully in the global market.

> The winners . . . will be those who can develop a culture that allows them to move faster, communicate more clearly, and involve everyone in a focused effort to serve ever more demanding customers. To move toward that winning culture, we've got to create what we call a "boundaryless" company. We no longer have the time to climb over barriers between functions like engineering and marketing. . . . Geographic barriers must evaporate. Our people must be as comfortable in Delhi and Seoul as they are in Louisville or Schenectady. The lines between the company and its vendors must be blurred into a smooth, fluid process with no other objective than satisfying the customer and winning in the marketplace.[17]

Business and Consumer Marketing: A Contrast

Many consumer-goods companies with a strong reputation in the consumer market decide to capitalize on perceived opportunities in the business market. The move is often prompted by a maturing product line, a desire to diversify operations, or the strategic opportunity to profitably apply R&D or production strength in a rapidly growing business market. Procter and Gamble Company (P&G), departing from its packaged consumer-goods tradition, is using its expertise in oils, fats, and pulps to diversify into fast-growing industries.

The J. M. Smucker Company operates successfully in both the consumer and the business markets. Smucker, drawing upon its consumer product base (jellies and preserves), produces filling mixes used by manufacturers of yogurt and dessert items. Marketing strawberry preserves to ultimate consumers differs significantly from marketing a strawberry filling to a manufacturer of yogurt. Key differences are highlighted in the following illustration.

Smucker: A Consumer and Business Marketer

Smucker reaches the consumer market with a line of products sold through a range of retail outlets. New products are carefully developed, tested, targeted, priced, and promoted for particular segments of the market. To secure distribution, the firm employs food brokers who call on both wholesale- and retail-buying units. The company's own

---

[16]Melanie Warner, "Motorola Bets Big on China," *Fortune*, 27 (May 1996): pp. 116–124.

[17]"Today's Leaders Look to Tomorrow," *Fortune*, 26 (March 1990): p. 30; see also Betsy Morris, "Robert Goizueta and Jack Welch: The Wealth Builders," *Fortune*, 11 (December 1995): pp. 80–102.

INSIDE BUSINESS MARKETING

Business-to-Business (B2B) E-commerce

While business-to-consumer (B2C) Internet firms like Amazon.com and eBay may be more visible and attract more attention, B2B e-commerce *already* generates nearly ten times more revenue and explosive growth is anticipated. For example, Forrester Research expects B2B e-commerce to reach $2.7 *trillion* by 2004, compared to $108 *billion* for B2C e-commerce. For example, firms like Dell Computer, Cisco Systems, and Intel each generate millions of dollars of Internet sales each day from business customers.

Other B2B firms include Commerce One (http://www.commerceone.com/), which uses an entirely new business model known as an "e-commerce hub" or an "e-commerce" portal. Similar to the approach that eBay follows for consumers, the basic idea of an e-commerce hub is to leverage the power of the Internet to aggregate huge numbers of business buyers and sellers. Clients like Motorola can use Commerce One's Buy Site to purchase operating resources such as office supplies, computer equipment, and maintenance items from its supplier network. In addition, purchasing managers at Motorola can use Commerce One's procurement software to track the purchasing record of employees, automatically track approval requests for purchases, and significantly reduce administrative costs.

A sampling of additional B2B Internet companies is provided below:

Ariba, like Commerce One, centers on e-procurement of operating resources.
http://www.ariba.com/corp/home

VerticalNet aggregates buyers and sellers in more than 47 industries or "vertical markets."
http://www.verticalnet.com/

EarthWeb provides content to information technology managers, including advertising, education and training, job posting, and reference books.
http://www.earthweb.com/

Chemdex brings together multiple suppliers in the chemical industry to serve the needs of research chemists.
http://www.chemdex.com/

FreeMarkets creates online auctions for large purchasing organizations in over 50 product categories.
http://www.freemarkets.com/

RoweCom provides a Web-based storefront that *Fortune*-1000 companies and academic libraries can use to order and manage the acquisition of magazines, journals, and books for employees, students, and faculty.
http://www.rowecom.com/

Exodus Communications is a leading provider of Internet systems and network management solutions for enterprises with mission-critical Internet operations.
http://www.exodus.net/

SOURCE: Garrett Becker, "Internet: The Best E-Commerce Stocks to Buy Now," *Yahoo! Individual Investor Online* (October 1, 1999): pp. 1-4.

---

sales force reaches selected larger accounts. Achieving a desired degree of market exposure and shelf space in key retail-food outlets is essential to any marketer of consumer food products. Promotional plans for the line include media advertising, coupons, special offers, and incentives for retailers. Pricing decisions must reflect the nature of demand, costs, and the behavior of competitors. In sum, the marketer must manage each component of the marketing mix: product, price, promotion, and distribution.

The marketing mix takes on a different form in the business market. Attention centers on manufacturers that potentially could use Smucker products to produce other goods; the Smucker product will lose its identity as it is blended into yogurt, cakes, or cookies. Once Smucker has listed all the potential users of its product (for example, large food processors, bakeries, yogurt producers), the business marketing manager attempts to identify meaningful market segments that Smucker can profitably serve. A specific marketing strategy is developed for each market segment.

When a potential organizational consumer is identified, the company's sales force calls directly on the account. The salesperson may begin by contacting a company president but, at first, generally spends a great deal of time with the R&D director or the product development group leader. The salesperson is thus challenged to identify the **key buying influentials**—those who will have power in the buying process. Senior-level Smucker executives may also assist in the selling process.

Armed with product specifications (for example, desired taste, color, calories), the salesperson returns to the R&D department at Smucker to develop samples. Several months may pass before a mixture is finally approved. Next, attention turns to price, and the salesperson's contact point shifts to the purchasing department. Because large quantities (truckloads or drums rather than jars) are involved, a few cents per pound can be significant to both parties. Quality and service are also vitally important.

Once a transaction is culminated, the product is shipped directly from the Smucker warehouse to the manufacturer's plant. The salesperson follows up frequently with the purchasing agent, the plant manager, and other executives. Product movement and delivery information is openly shared and close working relationships develop between managers at Smucker and key decision makers in the buying organization. How much business can Smucker expect from this account? The performance of the new consumer product in the marketplace will determine this. The demand for industrial goods is, as noted, derived from ultimate consumer demand. Note also the importance of (1) developing a close and continuing working relationship with business market customers, and (2) understanding the requirements of the total range of buying influentials in the target company.

Distinguishing Characteristics

The foregoing illustration spotlights some of the features that differentiate business marketing strategy from consumer-goods marketing strategy. The business marketer emphasizes personal selling rather than advertising (TV, newspaper) to reach potential buyers. Only a small portion of the business marketer's promotional budget is likely to be invested in advertising, most commonly through trade journals or direct mail. This advertising, however, often establishes the foundation for a successful sales call. The industrial salesperson must understand the technical aspects of the organization's requirements and how those requirements can be satisfied, as well as knowing who influences the buying decision and why.

The business marketer's product also includes an important service component. The organizational consumer evaluates the quality of the physical entity and the quality of the attached services. Attention centers on the total package of benefits the consumer will receive. Price negotiation is frequently an important part of the industrial buying/selling process. Products made to particular quality or design specifications must be individually priced. Business marketers generally find that direct distribution to larger customers strengthens relationships between buyer and seller. Smaller accounts can be profitably served through intermediaries—manufacturers' representatives or industrial distributors.

As the Smucker example has illustrated, business marketing strategies differ from consumer-goods marketing strategies in the relative emphasis given to certain elements of the marketing mix. It is important to note that the example also highlights fundamental differences between the buyers in each market. In an organization, a variety of individuals influence the purchase decision. Several major questions confront Smucker's business marketing manager: Who are key participants in the purchasing process? What is their relative importance? What criteria does each apply to the decision? Thus, the business marketer must understand the *process* that an organization follows in purchasing a product and identify which organizational members have roles in this process. Depending on the complexity of the purchase, this process may span many weeks or months and may involve the participation of several members of the organization. The business marketer who becomes involved in the purchase process early may have the greatest chance for success.

A Relationship Emphasis

Relationships in the business market are often close and enduring. Rather than constituting the end result, a sale signals the beginning of a relationship. By convincing a large food processor such as General Foods to use its product, Smucker initiates a potential long-term business relationship. More than ringing up a sale, Smucker creates a customer! To maintain that relationship, the business marketer must develop an intimate knowledge of the customer's operations and contribute unique value to the customer's business. **Relationship marketing** centers on all marketing activities directed toward establishing, developing, and maintaining successful exchanges with customers.[18] Building one-to-one relationships with customers is the heart of business marketing.

The Supply Chain

Figure 1.2 further illuminates the importance of a relationship perspective in business marketing by considering the chain of suppliers involved in the creation of an automobile. Consider Honda and Ford. At its Marysville, Ohio, auto assembly plant, Honda spends more than $5 billion annually for materials and components from some 300 North American suppliers.[19] These expenditures by the 300-member purchasing staff at Honda of America represent 80 percent of the firm's annual sales. Similarly, Ford relies on a vast supplier network, including firms such as TRW and Johnson Controls, to contribute half of the more than 10,000 parts of a typical Ford car. The relationships between these auto producers and their suppliers fall squarely into the business marketing domain. Similarly, business marketers such as TRW rely on a whole host of others farther back on the supply chain for raw materials, components, and other support. Each organization in this chain is involved in the creation of a product, marketing processes (including delivery), and support and service after the sale. In performing these value-creating activities, each also affects the quality level of the Honda or Ford product. Michael Porter and Victor Millar observe that "to gain competitive advantage over its rivals, a company must either perform these activities at a lower cost or perform them in a way that leads to differentiation and a premium price (more value)."[20]

---

[18] Robert M. Morgan and Shelby D. Hunt, "The Commitment-Trust Theory of Relationship Marketing," *Journal of Marketing* 58 (July 1994): pp. 20–38.

[19] Kevin R. Fitzgerald, "For Superb Supplier Development: Honda Wins!" *Purchasing*, 21 (September 1995): pp. 32–40.

[20] Michael E. Porter and Victor E. Millar, "How Information Gives You Competitive Advantage," *Harvard Business Review* 63 (July/August 1985): pp. 149–160; see also Michael E. Porter, *Competitive Advantage* (New York: The Free Press, 1985).

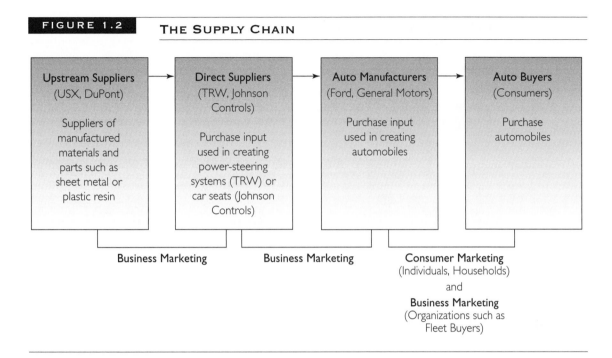

FIGURE 1.2	THE SUPPLY CHAIN

The Internet and the Supply Chain [21]

The Internet is transforming the way in which firms are managing the supply chain. Ford, General Motors (GM), and DaimlerChrysler are moving all of their purchases online—from office supplies to component parts to production equipment. For example, Ford's purchasing group spends $80 billion annually and works with thousands of suppliers around the world. Initially, Ford planned to manage these purchases through Auto-Xchange, a market site created by a joint venture between Ford and Oracle Corporation (see Figure 1.3). A similar supply chain initiative was planned by GM with its TradeXchange market site. As DaimlerChrysler planned a third market, the three firms surprised the global business community by announcing that they were joining forces to create a single auto parts exchange run through the Internet. The combined exchange is expected to handle $240 billion in annual spending by the three auto producers. In addition, a major portion of the $500 billion that the suppliers to the automakers spend each year will flow through the exchange. The combined exchange represents the world's largest Internet business.

A Virtual Marketplace   By creating a virtual marketplace, the firms hope to create a number of powerful advantages. First, each of the auto companies makes hundreds of thousands of individual purchases each year, and the average costs associated with creating a purchase order is $150.[22] By replacing triplicate forms with online purchases, the cost of a purchase order drops to $30 or less, yielding billions of dollars of

---

[21] This section is based on Gregory L. White, "How GM, Ford Think Web Can Make Splash on the Factory Floor," pp. A1, A8, and Robert Guy Matthews, Karen Jacobs, Susan Warren, and Dean Starkman, "Big Three Auto Makers Plan Net Exchange," *Wall Street Journal*, 28 February 2000, pp. A3 and A16

[22] "E-Procurement: The Transformation of Corporate Purchasing," *Fortune*, 6 December 1999, p. S58.

FIGURE 1.3   AUTO EXCHANGE

SOURCE: http://fsn.ford.com/Auto-Xchange/

---

savings to the automakers. Second, both Ford and GM want their suppliers to use the web site to make their own purchases. For example, a supplier that "provides suspension parts to GM might use GM's virtual marketplace to get a more favorable price on steel by piggybacking on the automakers' enormous purchasing power."[23] Third, a market site creates a global electronic forum that advances the efficiency and effectiveness of the supply chain. In essence, then, a virtual marketplace:

- enables a firm and its supply chain community to transact business and access information (for example, production schedules, delivery dates) in real time

- simplifies purchasing processes and reduces purchasing costs

- allows suppliers to work with a manufacturer, like Ford, on new product design (for example, sharing engineering drawings)

- leverages the buying power of the supply chain to reduce the cost of raw materials, products, and services.

---

[23] White, "How GM, Ford Think Web Can Make Splash," p. A1.

FIGURE 1.4	DELL COMPUTER

SOURCE: Courtesy, Dell Computer Corporation.

Build to Order

Dell Computer has excelled with a fast-paced build-to-order approach that involves taking customer orders online, orchestrating production tailored to each customer, and forging a one-to-one relationship with the customer after the sale (see Figure 1.4). The auto industry is turning to Michael Dell, the company founder, for advice concerning how to make their businesses look like his.[24]

Inspired by Dell's success, Ford CEO Jacques Nasser, envisions a future where customers will order online and factories will build to order, eliminating billions of dollars of inventory costs (for example, large stocks of vehicles on hand); dealers will report warranty problems live from the service shops so plants can correct any assembly-line problems immediately; and suppliers will tightly control inventory at Ford plants, in the same way that Wal-Mart gives suppliers like Procter & Gamble responsibility for stocking its shelves.[25] By integrating the supply chain, Ford's newly

---

[24] Gary McWilliams and Joseph B. White, "Dell to Detroit: Get Into Gear Online," *Wall Street Journal*, (1 December 1999): p. B1.

[25] White, "How GM, Ford Think Web Can Make Splash," p. A8.

created market site, Auto-Xchange, provides an important first step in capturing this vision.

Procurement Trends and the Supply Chain

The search for improved quality and superior performance have spawned a significant shift in the purchasing practices of automakers such as Chrysler and Honda, as well as those of other leading-edge firms like Compaq and Motorola. To develop profitable relationships with organizational customers, business marketers must be attuned to these changes. Rather than relying on competitive bidding and dealing at arms-length with a large number of suppliers, a new approach to purchasing has been adopted in many industries. This approach is characterized by:[26]

- longer-term and closer relationships with fewer suppliers (for example, over the past decade, the number of suppliers utilized by Motorola, Delta Air Lines, Chrysler, and IBM have been reduced by 60 percent or more)

- closer interactions among multiple functions—manufacturing, engineering, and logistics as well as sales and purchasing—on both the buying and selling sides (for example, through computer links with its suppliers, Motorola can change specifications and delivery schedules)

- supplier proximity to allow just-in-time delivery and to facilitate closer working relationships targeted at improving product and service quality along the supply chain (for example, Johnson Controls, a producer of auto seats and trim, operates ten plants near its major customers, which include Ford, Toyota, and General Motors.

Managing Relationships in the Supply Chain

The trends in procurement place a premium on the supply-chain management capabilities of the business marketer. IBM spends 85 percent of its purchasing dollars with fifty suppliers.[27] Of particular importance to IBM is the quality of engineering support that it receives from suppliers. IBM actively seeks supplier partners that will contribute fresh ideas and leading-edge technology to attract buyers of future IBM products.

To effectively initiate and sustain a profitable relationship with a customer like IBM or Chrysler, the business marketer must carefully manage the multiple linkages that define the relationship. Given these new marketing requirements, Frank V. Cespedes emphasizes the importance of "concurrent marketing" among the groups that are most central to customer contact efforts: product, sales, and service units.[28] In his view, recent market developments place more emphasis on the firm's ability to:

- generate timely market knowledge by segment and by individual account;

- customize product service packages for diverse customer groups; and

---

[26] Frank V. Cespedes, *Concurrent Marketing: Integrating Products, Sales, and Service* (Boston: Harvard Business School Press, 1995), pp. 14–18.

[27] James Carbone, "Reinventing Purchasing Wins Medal for Big Blue," *Purchasing*, 16 (September 1999): pp. 45–46.

[28] Cespedes, *Concurrent Marketing*, chap. 2.

Career Profile: Managing Relationships at IBM

Brad Bochart is a client executive with IBM in southern California and is responsible for nineteen large customer accounts that operate within the financial services industry (for example, banks, and investment companies). He joined IBM in January, 1997 after receiving a B.S. degree in marketing from Arizona State University. Brad's training at IBM involved two components: (1) six months of courses on topics such as business etiquette, territory management, business finance, and negotiation and sales skills; and (2) six months of training to learn more about his assigned industry-financial services.

As a Client Executive, it is my job to build market share within this Industry, develop key strategic relationships with the CEOs and key managers on their staff, as well as to continuously learn about their business and industry. Ultimately, the goal is to produce long-term partnerships with each of these accounts. I am the point-man for IBM for each of my clients and it is my job to understand their business strategies and the Information Technology (IT) tactics that they are using to support these strategies. Once this understanding is achieved,

I then bring together the IBM resources that will directly support their IT and business strategies. Along with this, I must develop key internal relationships with various IBM consultants, product specialists, and business partners with the objective of using these relations to provide solutions to my customers and strengthen IBM's position across each account.

What I enjoy the most is the responsibility and authority that the job provides. I also enjoy the opportunity to call on and talk with the various CEOs who lead the organizations that I serve. To date, I have had the opportunity to golf with five different CEOs. I take great pleasure in understanding their businesses as well as how they are run. Most of all, I enjoy listening: how they think, how they run their day-to-day schedules, how they deal with critical issues, or how they balance their personal and professional lives. Lastly, I enjoy my colleagues at IBM and I enjoy representing the IBM Company.

SOURCE: Interview with Brad Bochart, October 5, 1998. Reprinted from Czinkota et. al, *Marketing—Best Practices* (Fort Worth, TX: The Dryden Press, 2000), p. 185.

- capitalize on local field knowledge from sales and service units to inform product strategy in real time.

Developing and nurturing close, long-term relationships is an important goal for the business marketer. Built on trust and demonstrated performance, such strategic partnerships require open lines of communication between multiple layers of the buying and selling organizations. Given the rising importance of long-term, strategic relationships with both customers and suppliers, organizations are increasingly emphasizing relationship management skills. Since these skills reside in people rather than in organizational structures, roles, or tasks, marketing personnel with these skills will become valuable assets to the organization.[29]

Business Market Customers

Business market customers can be broadly classified into three categories: (1) commercial enterprises, (2) governmental organizations, and (3) institutions. Each will be

---

[29] Frederick E. Webster Jr., "The Changing Role of Marketing in the Corporation," *Journal of Marketing*, 56 (October 1992): p. 14. See also, Joseph P. Cannon and William D. Perreault, Jr., "Buyer-Seller Relationships in Business Markets," *Journal of Marketing Research*, 36 (November 1999): pp. 439–460.

explored in Chapter 2. However, the supply-chain concept provides a solid foundation for introducing the commercial customers that constitute the business market.

Commercial Enterprises as Consumers

Commercial enterprises can also be divided into three categories: (1) users, (2) original equipment manufacturers (OEMs), and (3) dealers and distributors.

Users   Users purchase industrial products or services to produce other goods or services that are, in turn, sold in the business or consumer markets. User customers purchase goods—such as computers, photocopiers, or automated manufacturing systems—to set up or support the manufacturing process. When purchasing machine tools from GE, an auto manufacturer is a user. These machine tools do not become part of the automobile but instead help to produce it.

Original Equipment Manufacturers (OEMs)   The OEM purchases industrial goods to incorporate into other products sold in the business or ultimate consumer market. For example, Intel Corporation produces the microprocessors that constitute the heart of Compaq's personal computer. In purchasing these microprocessors, Compaq would be classified as an OEM.

Dealers and Distributors   Dealers and distributors include those commercial enterprises that purchase industrial goods for resale (in basically the same form) to users and OEMs. The distributor accumulates, stores, and sells a large assortment of goods to industrial users, assuming title of the goods purchased. Handling billions of dollars worth of transactions each year, industrial distributors are growing in size and sophistication. The strategic role assumed by distributors in the business market is examined in detail in Chapter 14.

Overlap of Categories   The three categories of commercial enterprises are not mutually exclusive. Their classification is based on the intended purpose that the product serves for the customer. Ford is a user when purchasing a machine tool for the manufacturing process, but the same company is an OEM when purchasing radios to be incorporated into the ultimate consumer product.

A marketer must have a good understanding of the diverse organizational consumers in the business market. Properly classifying commercial customers as users, OEMs, or dealers or distributors is an important first step to a sharpened understanding of the buying criteria that a particular commercial customer uses in evaluating an industrial product.

Understanding Buying Motivations   Consider the different types of commercial customers that purchase a particular industrial product such as electrical timing mechanisms. Each class of commercial customer views the product differently because each purchases the product for a different reason.

A food processing firm such as Pillsbury buys electrical timers for use in a high-speed canning system. For this customer, quality, reliability, and prompt and predictable delivery are critical. Whirlpool, an OEM that incorporates the industrial product directly into consumer appliances, is concerned with the impact of the timers on the quality and dependability of the final consumer product. Since the timers will be needed in large quantities, the appliance manufacturer is also concerned about the producer's production capacity and delivery reliability. Finally, an industrial distributor is most interested in matching the capability of the timing mechanisms to the needs of customers (users and OEMs) in a specific geographical market.

Classifying Goods for the Business Market[30]

Having classified the customers that constitute the business market, we must now ask what type of goods they require, and how each type is marketed. One useful method of classifying industrial goods is to ask the following question: How does the industrial good or service enter the production process, and how does it enter the cost structure of the firm? The answer enables the marketer to identify those who are influential in the organizational buying process and to understand how to design an effective business marketing strategy. In general, industrial goods can be divided into three broad categories: entering goods, foundation goods, and facilitating goods (see Figure 1.5).

Entering Goods

Entering goods are those that become part of the finished product. This category of goods consists of raw materials and manufactured materials and parts. Their cost is an expense item that is assigned to the manufacturing process.

Raw Materials Observe in Figure 1.5 that raw materials include both farm products and natural products. Raw materials are processed only to the level required for economical handling and transport; they basically enter the production process of the buying organization in their natural state. AT&T purchases substantial quantities of copper, gold, and silver to be used in making telephone and communication equipment. McDonald's uses over 700 million pounds of potatoes each year and dictates the fortunes of many farmers in that segment of agriculture. In fact, when attempting to introduce a raspberry sorbet, McDonald's found, to its surprise, that not enough raspberries were being grown![31]

Manufactured Materials and Parts In contrast to raw materials, manufactured materials and parts undergo more initial processing. Component materials such as textiles or sheet steel have been processed before reaching a clothing manufacturer or automaker but must be processed further before becoming part of the finished product that the consumer buys. Both Ford and G.E. spend more than $900 million annually on steel. Component parts, on the other hand, include small motors, motorcycle tires, and automobile batteries; they can be installed directly into another product with little or no additional processing. For example, Black & Decker spends $100 million each year on plastic parts and Sun Microsystems spends more than $200 million on displays and monitors.

---

[30] Data on the dollar purchases of particular products by selected customers are drawn from Anne Millen Porter and Elena Epatko Murphy, "Hey Big Spender . . . The 100 Largest Industrial Buyers," *Purchasing*, 9 (November 1995): pp. 31–42.

[31] James Brian Quinn, *Intelligent Enterprise: A Knowledge and Service Based Paradigm for Industry* (New York: The Free Press, 1992), p. 20.

FIGURE 1.5   ## CLASSIFYING GOODS FOR THE BUSINESS MARKET

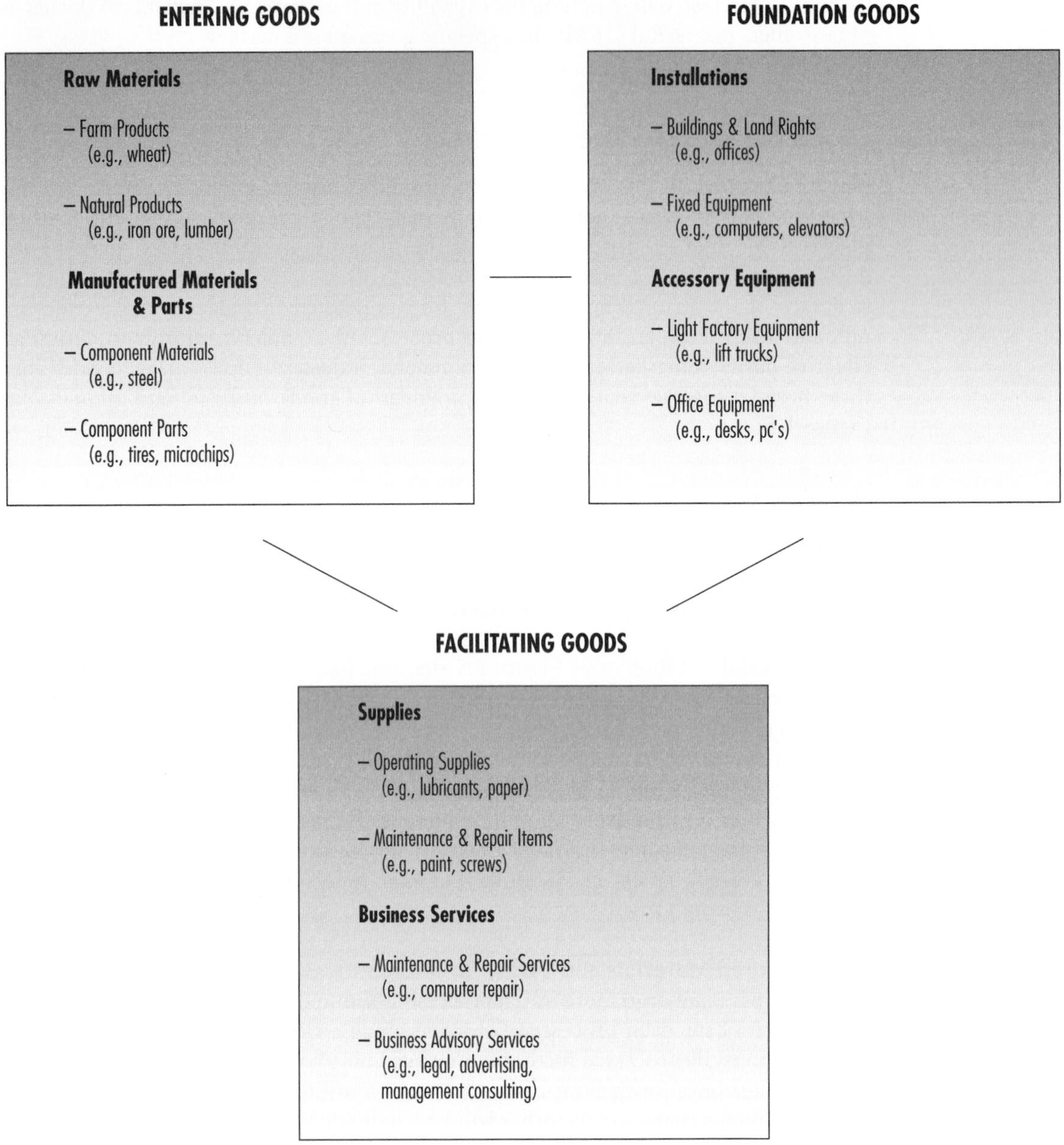

ENTERING GOODS

Raw Materials

— Farm Products
   (e.g., wheat)

— Natural Products
   (e.g., iron ore, lumber)

**Manufactured Materials
& Parts**

— Component Materials
   (e.g., steel)

— Component Parts
   (e.g., tires, microchips)

FOUNDATION GOODS

Installations

— Buildings & Land Rights
   (e.g., offices)

— Fixed Equipment
   (e.g., computers, elevators)

Accessory Equipment

— Light Factory Equipment
   (e.g., lift trucks)

— Office Equipment
   (e.g., desks, pc's)

FACILITATING GOODS

Supplies

— Operating Supplies
   (e.g., lubricants, paper)

— Maintenance & Repair Items
   (e.g., paint, screws)

Business Services

— Maintenance & Repair Services
   (e.g., computer repair)

— Business Advisory Services
   (e.g., legal, advertising,
   management consulting)

SOURCE: Adapted from Philip Kotler, *Marketing Management: Analysis, Planning, and Control*, 4th ed. (Englewood Cliffs, N.J.: Prentice-Hall, 1980), p. 172, with permission of Prentice-Hall, Inc.

Foundation Goods

The distinguishing characteristic of foundation goods is that they are capital items. As capital goods are used up or worn out, a portion of their original cost is assigned to the production process as a depreciation expense. Foundation goods include installations and accessory equipment.

Installations   Installations include the major long-term investment items that underlie the manufacturing process, such as **buildings and land rights** and **fixed equipment**. Large computers and machine tools are examples of fixed equipment. The demand for installations is shaped by the economic climate (for example, favorable interest rates) but is driven by the market outlook for a firm's products. In the face of strong worldwide demand for its microprocessors, Intel is building new plants, expanding existing ones, and making significant investments in capital equipment. A typical semiconductor chip plant costs at least $1 billion to build, with equipment accounting for $600 million of the cost, while the land and building account for the rest.[32]

Accessory Equipment   Accessory equipment is generally less expensive and short-lived compared to installations, and is not considered part of the fixed plant. This equipment can be found in the plant as well as in the office. Portable drills, personal computers, and fax machines illustrate this category.

Facilitating Goods

Facilitating goods are the supplies and services (see Figure 1.5) that support organizational operations. Because these goods do not enter the production process or become part of the finished product, their costs are handled as expense items.

Supplies   Virtually every organization requires **operating supplies,** such as printer cartridges, paper, or business forms, and **maintenance and repair items,** such as paint and cleaning materials. These items generally reach a broad cross-section of industrial users. In fact, they are very similar to the kinds of supplies that consumers might purchase at a hardware or discount store.

Services   "As the service sector has grown to embrace 80 percent of all U.S. employment, specialized service firms have become very large and sophisticated relative to the scale and expertise that individual staff and service groups have within integrated companies."[33] To capture the skills of these specialists and to direct attention to what they do best, many firms are shifting or "outsourcing" selected service functions to outside suppliers. This opens up opportunities for firms who provide such services as computer support, payroll processing, logistics, food operations, and equipment maintenance. These specialists possess a level of expertise or efficiency that organizations can

---

[32] Dean Takahashi, "Makers of Chip Equipment Beginning to Share the Pain," *Wall Street Journal*, (14 August 1996): p. B6.

[33] James Brian Quinn, "Strategic Outsourcing: Leveraging Knowledge Capabilities," *Sloan Management Review*, 40 (summer 1999): p. 9.

FIGURE 1.6   FAO SCHWARZ

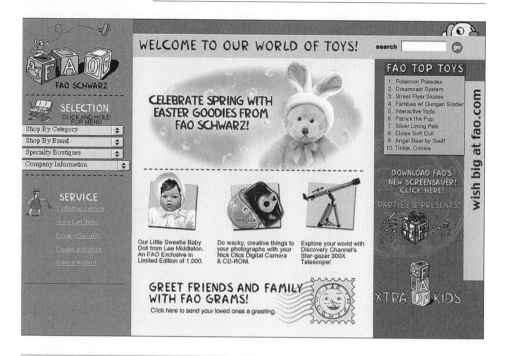

SOURCE: http://www.fao.com/

profitably tap. For example, Cisco Systems turned to Federal Express to coordinate the movement of parts through its supply chain and on to the customer. By merging the parts shipments in transit for a single customer, the desired product can be assembled at the customer's location, never spending a moment in a Cisco warehouse.[34] Business services include **maintenance and repair support** (for example, machine repair) and **advisory support** (for example, management consulting or information management). Like supplies, services are considered expense items.

Moreover, the explosive growth of the Internet has increased the demand for a range of electronic commerce services from web site design to the complete hosting of an e-commerce site. Firms such as Sun Microsystems, Hewlett-Packard, Intel, and IBM, along with powerful new entrants like US Web, provide a range of e-commerce services to customers, large and small, around the world (see Figure 1.6). The Internet also provides a powerful new channel for delivering technical support, customer training, and management development programs. In turn, the Internet provides the opportunity to manage a particular activity or function from a remote location. To illustrate, IBM manages the procurement functions for United Technologies Corporation via the web.[35]

---

[34]Douglas A. Blackman, "Overnight, Everything Changed for Fed Ex: Can It Reinvent Itself?" *Wall Street Journal*, (4 November 1999): pp. A1, A16.

[35]Ira Sager, "Inside IBM: Internet Business Machines," *Business Week E.Biz*, (13 December 1999): pp. ED21–23.

Business Marketing Strategy

Marketing pattern differences reveal the significance of a goods classification system. A marketing strategy appropriate for one category of goods may be entirely unsuitable for another. Often, entirely different promotional, pricing, and distribution strategies are required. The physical nature of the industrial good and its intended use by the organizational customer dictate to an important degree the requirements of the marketing program. Some strategy highlights follow.

Illustration: Manufactured Materials and Parts

Recall that manufactured materials and parts enter the buying organization's own product. Whether a part is standardized or customized will often dictate the nature of marketing strategy. For custom-made parts, personal selling activities assume an important role in marketing strategy and the product is the critical factor in making a sale. Standardized parts are typically purchased in larger quantities on a contractual basis, and the marketing strategy centers on providing a competitive price, reliable delivery, and supporting services. Frequently, industrial distributors are used to achieve responsive delivery service to smaller accounts.

For manufactured materials and parts, the marketer's challenge is to locate and accurately define the unique needs of diverse customers, uncover key buying influentials, and adjust the marketing program to serve these customers profitably.

Illustration: Installations

Installations were classified earlier as foundation goods because they are capital assets that affect the buyer's scale of operations. Here the product itself is the central force in marketing strategy, and direct manufacturer-to-user channels of distribution are the norm. Less costly, more standardized installations such as lathes may be sold through marketing intermediaries.

Once again, personal selling is the dominant promotional tool. The salesperson works closely with prospective organizational buyers. Negotiations can span several months and involve the top executives in the buying organization, especially for buildings or custom-made equipment. Customer buying motives center on economic factors (such as the projected performance of the capital asset) and emotional factors (such as industry leadership). A buyer may be quite willing to select a higher-priced installation if the projected return on investment supports the decision. The focal points for the marketing of installations include a strong personal selling effort, effective engineering and product design support, and the capability to offer a product that provides a higher return on investment than its competition. Initial price, distribution, and advertising play lesser roles.

Illustration: Supplies

The final illustration centers on a facilitating good: supplies. Again we find different marketing patterns. Most supply items reach a broad market of organizational customers from many different industries. Although some large users are serviced directly, a wide variety of marketing intermediaries are required to cover this broad and diverse market adequately.

The goal of the business marketer is to secure a place on the purchasing function's list of preferred or pre-approved suppliers. Importantly, many firms are adopting Internet-based purchasing systems to dramatically streamline the process that employees follow in buying supplies as well as other operating resources.[36] From the desktop, an employee simply logs on to the system, selects the needed items from an electronic catalog of suppliers that have been pre-approved by the purchasing function, and sends the order directly to the supplier.

For supplies, the marketer's promotional mix includes catalog listings, advertising, and, to a lesser extent, personal selling. Advertising is directed to resellers (industrial distributors) and final users. Personal selling is less important for supplies than it is for other categories of goods with a high unit value, such as installations. Thus, personal selling efforts may be confined to resellers and large users of supplies. Price may be critical in the marketing strategy, since many supply items are undifferentiated. By providing the proper product assortment, timely and reliable delivery, and competitive prices, the business marketer may be able to develop a long-term contractual relationship with a customer.

A Look Ahead

The chief components of the business marketing management process are shown in Figure 1.7. Business marketing strategy is formulated within the boundaries established by the corporate mission and objectives. A corporation determining its mission must define its business and purpose, assess environmental trends, and evaluate its strengths and weaknesses. Building e-commerce capabilities and transforming these capabilities into offerings that provide superior customer value constitute vital corporate objectives at leading organizations. Corporate objectives provide guidelines within which specific marketing objectives are formed. Business marketing planning must be coordinated and synchronized with corresponding planning efforts in R&D, procurement, finance, production, customer service, and other areas. Clearly, strategic plans emerge out of a bargaining process among functional areas. Managing conflict, promoting cooperation, and developing coordinated strategies are all fundamental to the business marketer's interdisciplinary role.

The business marketing management framework (Figure 1.7) provides an overview of the five major parts of the volume. This chapter introduced some of the features that distinguish industrial from consumer-goods marketing while the next chapter explores the major types of customers that comprise the business market: commercial enterprises, governmental units, and institutions. The remaining chapter in Part I examines the organizational buying process and the myriad forces that affect the organizational decision maker.

Relationship management provides the theme of Part II, which first examines the specific strategies that business marketers can follow in developing relationships with business market customers. Attention then turns to the special opportunities that

---

[36] Ravi Kalkota and Marcia Robinson, *e-Business: Road Map for Success* (Reading, Mass: Addison-Wesley, 1999), pp. 237–251.

FIGURE 1.7   A FRAMEWORK FOR BUSINESS MARKETING MANAGEMENT

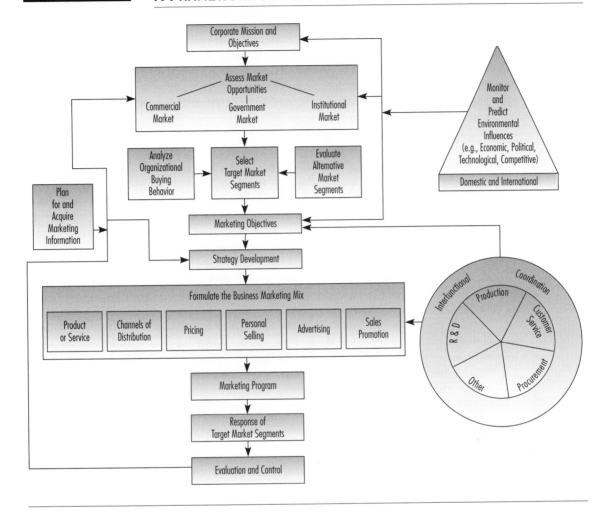

e-commerce strategies present for forging relationships with customers and coordinating activities with supply chain partners. Part III turns to the selection of target segments and specific techniques for measuring the response of these segments.

Part IV centers on designing business marketing strategy. Each component of the marketing mix is treated from a business marketing perspective. Special attention is also given to the marketing of services. Formulation of the business marketing mix (see Figure 1.7) requires careful coordination with such functional areas in the firm as R&D and production. The processes of monitoring and controlling the marketing program are analyzed in Part V. A central theme is how business marketing management seeks to minimize the discrepancy between expected and actual results in target markets by planning for and acquiring relevant and timely marketing information.

Summary

The business market offers significant opportunities and special challenges for the marketing manager. Market-driven firms in the business market demonstrate superior skills in understanding and satisfying customers. They also possess strong market-sensing and customer-linking capabilities. Although a common body of knowledge and theory spans all of marketing, important differences exist between consumer and business marketing, among them the nature of markets, demand patterns, buyer behavior, and buyer-seller relationships.

The dramatic rise in competition on a worldwide basis requires a global perspective of markets. To secure a competitive advantage in this challenging environment, business market customers are developing closer, more collaborative ties with fewer suppliers than they have used in the past, using the Internet to promote efficiency and real-time communication across the supply chain, and demanding quality and speed from their suppliers to an unprecedented degree. These important trends in procurement place a premium on the supply-chain management capabilities of the business marketer. Business marketing programs increasingly involve a customized blend of tangible products, service support, and ongoing information services both before and after the sale. Relationship management constitutes the heart of business marketing.

The diverse organizations that make up the business market can be broadly divided into (1) commercial enterprises, (2) governmental organizations, and (3) institutions. Because purchases made by these organizational consumers are linked to goods and services that they generate in turn, derived demand is an important and often volatile force in the business market. Industrial goods can be classified into three categories, based on how the product enters the cost structure and the production process of the buying organization: (1) entering goods, (2) foundation goods, and (3) facilitating goods. Specific categories of goods may require unique marketing programs.

Discussion Questions

1. A recent study found that General Motors had higher costs than Ford or Chrysler because it produced more auto parts itself instead of buying them from outside suppliers. What factors might contribute to this cost disparity? What decision rules might be applied by an automaker in determining what to make versus what to buy from suppliers?

2. Du Pont, one of the largest industrial producers of chemicals and synthetic fibers, spends millions of dollars annually on advertising its products to final consumers. For example, Du Pont invested more than one million dollars in a TV advertising blitz that emphasized the comfort of jeans made of Du Pont's stretch polyester-cotton blend. Since Du Pont does not produce jeans or market them to final consumers, why are large expenditures made on consumer advertising?

3. What are the chief differences between consumer-goods marketing and business marketing? Use the following matrix as a guide in organizing your response:

	Consumer –Goods Marketing	Business Marketing
Customers		
Buying Behavior		
Buyer/Seller Relationship		
Product		
Price		
Promotion		
Channels		

4. Explain how a company such as GE might be classified by some business marketers as a user customer but by others as an OEM customer.

5. Spending a day in the life of a marketing manager would demonstrate the critical importance of relationship management skills as that manager interacts with employees of other functional areas and, indeed, with representatives from both customer and supplier organizations. Explore the strategic significance of such relationships.

6. Auto executives are enamored with the success that Dell Computer has achieved with its "build to order" model. A computer is built to the customer's precise specifications *after* the order is received. Is the approach feasible for Ford or GM? To succeed, what changes would be required in the way in which the automakers manage the supply chain?

7. Consumer products are frequently classified as convenience, shopping, or specialty goods. This classification system is based on how consumers shop for particular products. Would this classification scheme apply equally well in the business marketing environment?

8. Evaluate this statement: "The ways that leading companies manage time in the supply chain—in new product development, in production, in sales and distribution—are the most powerful new sources of competitive advantage."

9. Evaluate this statement: "The demand for major equipment (a foundation good) is likely to be less responsive to shifts in price than that for materials, supplies, and components." Do you agree or disagree? Support your position.

10. Many firms are shifting selected service functions to outside suppliers. For example, Lucent Technologies, the Bell Labs equipment company, recently outsourced its information management function to IBM. What factors would prompt such a decision and what criteria would a customer, like Lucent Technologies, emphasize in choosing a supplier?

2

The Business Market: Perspectives on the Organizational Buyer

The business marketer requires an understanding of the needs of a diverse mix of organizational buyers drawn from three broad sectors of the business market—commercial enterprises, government (all levels), and institutions—as well as from an expanding array of international buyers. After reading this chapter, you will understand

1. the nature and central characteristics of each of these market sectors.

2. how the purchasing function is organized in each of these components of the business market.

3. the need to design a unique marketing program for each sector of the business market.

The vast business market is characterized by tremendous diversity. Many goods commonly viewed as household consumer products generate significant demand in the business market. For example, cooking oil is a common grocery item that also enjoys a huge market in the business marketing arena. In fact, estimates place the total business market usage of cooking oil at somewhere close to 400 million gallons annually. Firms, such as Procter & Gamble, that have established brands of cooking oil displayed on supermarket shelves for final consumers, also serve the business market. Why? Cooking oil is bought by *commercial firms*—manufacturers of food products (frozen foods, breaded fish, and so forth), fast-food restaurant chains, airline meal-preparation contractors, hotel restaurant operators, and business firms that furnish food for their employees; *institutions*—schools, hospitals, and universities (educational institutions, including schools, colleges and universities, sell more than $17 billion of food annually, whereas health-care institutions exceed $23 billion in annual food sales); and *governments*—federal, state, and local (the U.S. Army is the single largest food-service organization in the world, and various officer and NCO clubs serve nearly $1 billion in food each year). Beyond the borders of the United States, international customers, such as food manufacturers, restaurant chains, and health-care units, also represent a sizable market. The magnitude of the food-service market and its importance to manufacturers of cooking oil is illustrated by its annual sales volume: over $300 billion![1]

Requirements for product quality are as diverse as the types of buyers in the food-service market. For a small, elegant restaurant, how long the cooking oil lasts and its effect on the taste of the food will be critical factors, so the highest-quality oil will be purchased. A school district will be responsive to cost and concentrate on finding the lowest-priced oil. The Marriott Corporation, which operates a major in-flight meal-preparation business for the airlines, will pay close attention to product availability (that is, the reliability of delivery service) as well as the cost and quality. Each of the three types of business market customers—commercial firms, institutions, and governments—have unique characteristics and special needs that must be understood by the business marketer.

The channels of distribution as well as the product characteristics and packaging configurations for deep-frying oils reflect the diversity of the business marketer's customers and of their requirements. For commercial firms in the food-processing industry, purchases of deep-frying oil are made directly from the manufacturer. A processor of frozen fish who is a significant user of deep-frying oil will buy standard grade oil in railroad-car quantities. Some large food processors utilize fryers that have the capacity for 1,000 pounds of oil.

Each of the three business market sectors—commercial firms, institutions, and governments—have identifiable and unique characteristics that must be understood by the business marketer. A significant first step in creating successful marketing strategy is to isolate the unique dimensions of each of the major sectors of the business market. How much market potential does each sector represent? Who makes the purchasing decision? The answers provide a foundation upon which the marketing manager can formulate marketing programs that respond to the specific needs and characteristics of each business market sector.

---

[1] Michael Bartlett, "Restaurants and Institutions' 1996 Annual Forecasts," *Restaurants and Institutions*, (1 January 1996): p. 18.

Commercial Enterprises: Unique Characteristics

Commercial enterprises include manufacturers, construction companies, service firms (for example, hotels), transportation companies, selected professional groups (for example, dentists), and resellers (wholesalers and retailers purchasing equipment and supplies for use in their operations). Manufacturers are the most important commercial customers: the 250 largest purchase over $1.2 trillion of goods and services annually.[2]

Distribution by Size

A startling fact about the study of manufacturers is that there are so few of them. Available evidence suggests that there are approximately 387,000 manufacturing firms in the United States.[3] And though only 36,000 manufacturing firms (9.3 percent) employ more than 100 workers each, this handful of firms ships more than 75 percent of all products manufactured in the United States. Because of this concentration, the business marketer normally serves *far fewer but far larger* customers than a consumer-product marketer. For example, Intel sells microprocessors to a few large manufacturers, like Dell and Gateway, who, in turn, target millions of potential computer buyers. Clearly, these large buyers can be very important to the business marketer. Because each large firm has such vast sales potential, the business marketer will often tailor a marketing strategy for each customer. Smaller manufacturing firms also constitute an important segment for the business marketer. In fact, almost two-thirds of all manufacturers in the United States employ fewer than twenty people.[4] Because the organizational buyer in smaller firms has different needs and often a different orientation, the astute marketer will adjust the marketing program to the particular needs of this market segment.

Geographical Concentration

Distribution of industrial firms by size is not the only form of concentration important to the business marketer: Manufacturers are also concentrated geographically. More than one-half of the manufacturers are concentrated in eight states: California, New York, Ohio, Illinois, Michigan, Texas, Pennsylvania, and New Jersey. Most large metropolitan areas are lucrative business markets. Geographical concentration of industry, however, means only that a large potential volume exists in a given area; the requirements of each buyer may still vary significantly.

Geographic concentration has some important implications for the formulation of marketing strategy. First, firms can concentrate their marketing efforts in areas of high market potential and make effective use of a full-time personal sales force in these markets. Second, distribution centers in large-volume areas can ensure rapid delivery to a large proportion of customers. Finally, firms may not be able to tie their salespeople to specific geographic areas because many large buying organizations entrust to one

---

[2]"Who Spends How Much on What?" *Purchasing* 127 (November 4, 1999), pp. 52–53.

[3]U.S. Department of Commerce, Bureau of the Census, *Statistical Abstract of the United States, Report #859, Establishments, Employees and Payroll: 1992* (Washington, D.C., 1992).

[4]U.S. Department of Commerce, Bureau of the Census, *Annual Survey of Manufacturers, Statistics for Industry Groups* (Washington, D.C., 1994), p. 3–5.

individual the responsibility for purchasing certain products and materials for the entire company.

For example, the Kroger Company, a huge supermarket chain, has centralized purchasing in Cincinnati for store supplies and fixtures. Thus, everything from paper bags to display cases are purchased in Cincinnati for distribution to individual stores. A paper-bag salesperson whose territory includes all retail stores in Tennessee and Arkansas cannot be very effective against a competitor who maintains a sales office in Cincinnati. The marketer requires an understanding of how a potential buyer's purchasing organization is structured.

Classifying Commercial Enterprises

Marketers can gain valuable strategy insights by identifying the needs and requirements of different types of commercial enterprises or business customers. The **North American Industrial Classification System (NAICS)** organizes business activity into meaningful economic sectors and identifies groups of business firms that use similar production processes.[5] The NAICS is a result of the North American Free Trade Agreement (NAFTA); it provides for standardization among Canada, Mexico, and the United States in the way that economic data are reported. Every plant or business establishment is assigned a code that reflects the primary product produced at that location. The new system, which includes traditional industries while incorporating new and emerging technology industries, replaces the Standard Industrial Classification (SIC) system that was used for decades.

Figure 2.1 illustrates the building blocks of the system. Observe that the first two digits identify the economic sector and as more digits are added, the classification becomes finer. For example, all business establishments that create, disseminate, or provide the means to distribute information are included in the Information sector: NAICS Code 51. Nineteen other economic sectors are included in the system. More specifically, U.S. establishments that produce paging equipment are assigned an NAICS Code of 513321. The six-digit codes are customized for industry subdivisions in individual countries, but at the five-digit level they are standardized across the three countries.

Using the Classification System   If a manager understands the needs and requirements of a few firms within a classification category, requirements can be projected for other firms that share that category. Each group should be relatively homogeneous in terms of raw materials required, component parts used, and manufacturing processes employed. The NAICS provides a valuable tool for identifying new customers and for targeting profitable segments of business buyers.

The Purchasing Organization

Every firm, regardless of its organizational characteristics, must procure the materials, supplies, equipment, and services necessary to operate the business successfully. On average, more than half of every dollar earned from sales of manufactured products

---

[5] U.S. Census Bureau, "1997 Economic Census: What's New?" *The Official Statistics*, www.census.gov.pub.epcd/www.ec97new.html (World Wide Web site; cited 27 September 1996).

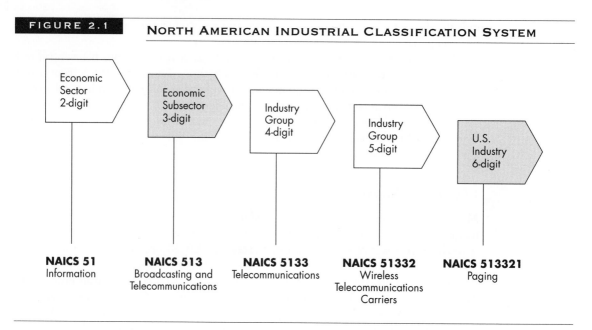

FIGURE 2.1 **NORTH AMERICAN INDUSTRIAL CLASSIFICATION SYSTEM**

Economic Sector 2-digit	Economic Subsector 3-digit	Industry Group 4-digit	Industry Group 5-digit	U.S. Industry 6-digit
NAICS 51 Information	**NAICS 513** Broadcasting and Telecommunications	**NAICS 5133** Telecommunications	**NAICS 51332** Wireless Telecommunications Carriers	**NAICS 513321** Paging

SOURCE: Reprinted from Michael R. Czinkota, et al, *Marketing, Best Practices* (Fort Worth, TX: The Dryden Press, 2000), p. 183.

is spent on the materials, supplies, services, and equipment needed to produce the goods.[6] For example, Ford spends nearly $80 billion annually in the business market. When a customer buys a $24,000 sports utility vehicle from Ford, the auto maker has already spent more than $12,000 to buy steel, paint, glass, fabric, aluminum, and electrical components to build that product. How goods and services are purchased depends on such factors as the nature of the business, the size of the firm, and the volume, variety, and technical complexity of items purchased. Rarely do individual departments within a corporation do their own buying. Procurement is usually administered by an individual whose title is manager of purchasing, purchasing agent, director of purchasing, or director of procurement.

The day-to-day purchasing function is carried out by buyers, each of whom is responsible for a specific group of products. Organizing the purchasing function in this way permits buyers to acquire a high level of technical expertise on a limited number of items. As products and materials become more sophisticated, buyers must become more knowledgeable about material characteristics, manufacturing processes, and design specifications. Frequently, a sizable group will be employed to conduct research, evaluate materials, and perform cost studies.

Goals of the Purchasing Function

To address the needs of business customers of all types, the marketer requires an understanding of the goals that purchasing managers seek and how the purchasing function contributes to the objectives of the organization (see Table 2.1). The purchasing decision maker must juggle a number of different objectives that often clash.

---

[6]"Who Spends How Much on What?" p. 52.

TABLE 2.1	THE GOALS OF PURCHASING
Goal	**Description**
Uninterrupted Flow of Materials	Provide an uninterrupted flow of the materials, supplies, and services required to operate the organization.
Manage Inventory	Minimize the investment in inventory.
Improve Quality	Maintain and improve quality by carefully evaluating and choosing products and services.
Developing and Managing Supplier Relationships	Find competent suppliers and forge productive relationships with supply chain.
Achieve Lowest Total Cost	Purchase required products and services at lowest total cost.
Reduce Administrative Costs	Accomplish the purchasing objectives at the lowest possible level of administrative costs.
Advance Firm's Competitive Position	Improve the firm's competitive position by reducing supply chain costs or capitalizing on the capabilities of suppliers.

SOURCE: Adapted with modifications from Michael R. Leenders and Harold E. Fearon, *Purchasing and Supply Management* (11th ed. Chicago: Irwin, 1997), pp. 34–37 and Robert J. Duffy, "Trail Blazing," *Purchasing Today* (April 1999), pp. 45–52.

For example, the lowest-priced component part is unacceptable if quality standards are not met, or if the delivery arrives two weeks late! In addition to protecting the cost structure of the firm, improving quality, and keeping inventory investment to a minimum, purchasing assumes a central role in managing relationships with suppliers. Here purchasing assumes a central role in supply chain management.

Supply chain management is a technique for linking a manufacturer's operations with those of all of its strategic suppliers and its key intermediaries and customers. The approach seeks to integrate the relationships and operations of both immediate, first-tier suppliers, and those several tiers back in the supply chain, in order to assist second, third, and fourth-tier suppliers in meeting requirements like quality, delivery, and the timely exchange of information. Firms that embrace supply chain management also solicit ideas from key suppliers and involve them directly in the new product development process. By managing supply chain costs and linking supplier capabilities to new product development, the purchasing function is advancing corporate performance in many organizations.

Strategic Procurement[7]

Leading-edge organizations like Dell Computer, General Electric, and Honda demonstrate the critical role that purchasing can assume in creating profit opportunities in their industries. To illustrate, Honda, long recognized for purchasing excellence and its ability to sustain customer loyalty, was able to reduce by 20 percent the costs of

[7] This section is based on Matthew G. Anderson and Paul K. Katz, "Strategic Sourcing," *The International Journal of Logistics Management* 9, no. 1 (1998), pp. 1–13.

INSIDE BUSINESS MARKETING

The Supply Chain for McNuggets

Purchasing managers at McDonald's Corporation have worked closely with suppliers to develop a sophisticated model to reduce the cost of chicken. The model isolates how various feed mixes affect weight gain in chickens and suppliers are able to optimize chicken weight gain in response to changing food prices.

McDonald's also closely manages and tightly coordinates its supply chain from hatchery to processor and into the restaurants. "McDonald's explicitly orders hatcheries to place eggs in anticipation of the sales forecast for chicken products. Product movement through the supply base is so well orchestrated that a supplier can confidently place the eggs in the hatcheries seventy-five days before McDonald's expects to sell the chicken as McNuggets."

SOURCE: Timothy M. Laseter, *Balanced Sourcing: Cooperation and Competition in Supplier Relationships* (San Francisco: Jossey-Bass Publishers, 1998), p. 14.

external purchases that are embodied in the current Accord. A senior purchasing executive at Honda described how it was done:

> The first thing we did was compile a big list of every possible way we could remove costs from the 1998 Accord; most of them, in fact, came from suppliers' work with purchasing and engineering. We studied each idea, prioritized them according to their likelihood of success, and then just started focusing our work on developing them.[8]

Understanding the Total Cost   To unlock savings and growth opportunities, the purchasing function must develop a keen understanding of the total cost and value of a good or service to the firm. Such an approach requires purchasing managers to consider not only the purchase price but an array of other considerations, including

- the factors that drive the cost of the product or service in the supply chain, such as transportation,
- the costs of acquiring and managing products or services,
- quality, reliability, and other attributes of a product or service over its complete life cycle,
- the value of a product or service to a firm and its customers.

Fundamental to this total system cost perspective is the concept of total cost of ownership. "**Total cost of ownership** considers both supplier and buyer activities, and costs over a product's or service's complete life cycle."[9] For example, buying a higher quality product and paying a premium price could be justified because the initial purchase cost will be offset by fewer manufacturing defects, lower inventory requirements, and lower administrative costs. The total cost of ownership means understanding a range of cost-value relationships associated with individual purchases.

---

[8]Timothy M. Laseter, *Balanced Sourcing: Cooperation and Competition in Supplier Relationships* (San Francisco: Jossey-Bass Publishing, 1998), p. 224.

[9]Anderson and Katz, p. 3.

Levels of Procurement Development   In capturing cost savings through improved procurement, Matthew Anderson and Paul Katz, Mercer Management Consulting, suggest that firms operate at different levels of development and emphasize different pathways to cost reduction and revenue enhancement (see Figure 2.2). Ranging from the least to the most developed, these approaches include (1) Buy for Less, (2) Buy Better, (3) Consume Better, and (4) Sell Better. Note that the most developed strategy—Sell Better—ties purchasing activities directly to strategy. Here procurement builds supplier relationships that ultimately enhance the growth and the market strength of the organization.

Level 1—Leveraged Buy (Buy for Less)   Many firms demonstrate level 1 procurement practices and achieve cost savings by centralizing decision-making authority, which permits the consolidation of volume and by selecting suppliers that provide the best prices and terms.

Level 2—Linked Buy (Buy Better)   The next level of procurement development is triggered when the procurement organization takes an external view of the supply chain and develops mutually beneficial relationships with suppliers. Cost savings are achieved by streamlining the bidding process, optimizing delivery and information flows, and making stable commitments to enable efficient production by suppliers. Incremental cost savings of 5 to 25 percent result from moving from level 1 to level 2.

Level 3—Value Buy (Consume Better)   The goal of level 3 is to advance the performance of the procurement function by optimizing the life cycle costs and value of products and services. Value analysis, complexity management, and early supplier involvement in product design provide the means through which buyers and suppliers can uncover added value.

- **Value analysis** is a method of weighing the comparative value of materials, components, and manufacturing processes from the standpoint of their purpose, relative merit, and cost in order to uncover ways of improving products, lowering costs, or both. For example, Ferro Corporation developed a new coating process that allows Maytag to paint a refrigerator cabinet in ten minutes compared to the old process that took three hours.[10] The new process provided significant cost savings for Maytag.

- **Complexity management** seeks cost reductions by simplifying the design of products or by using standardized component parts in products and across product lines. For example, Ford found that one variation in an interior color can trigger changes in fifty or sixty different parts that then have to match that color (for example, fabric, visors, and coat hooks).[11] By reducing complexity, important savings can be realized. Such savings were achieved by reducing the variety of floor carpets used in Ford vehicles from fourteen to five, trunk carpets from eleven to one, and cigarette lighters from fifteen to one. Complexity management can also involve the outsourcing of production or assembly tasks to supply chain partners. Rather than supplying a single

---

[10] Elizabeth Baatz, "How Purchasing Handles Intense Cost Pressure," *Purchasing* 127 (October 8, 1999), pp. 61–66.
[11] Roberta J. Duffy, "Trail Blazing," *Purchasing Today* (April 1999), pp. 51–52.

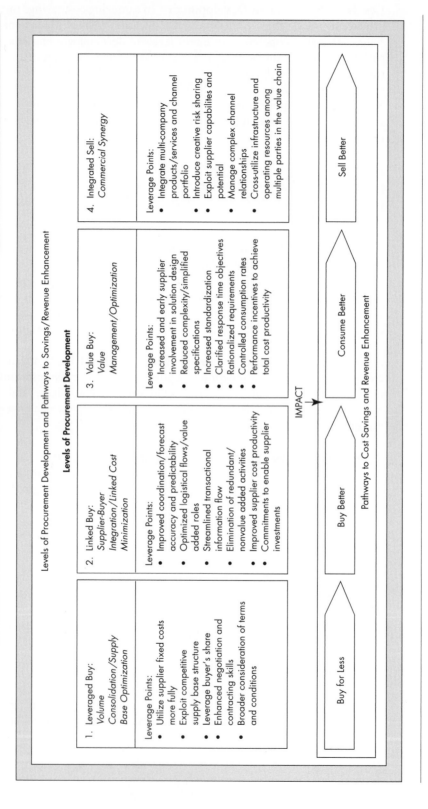

FIGURE 2.2 LEVELS OF PROCUREMENT DEVELOPMENT AND PATHWAYS TO SAVINGS/REVENUE ENHANCEMENT

Levels of Procurement Development and Pathways to Savings/Revenue Enhancement

Levels of Procurement Development

1. Leveraged Buy:
   Volume Consolidation/Supply Base Optimization

   Leverage Points:
   - Utilize supplier fixed costs more fully
   - Exploit competitive supply base structure
   - Leverage buyer's share
   - Enhanced negotiation and contracting skills
   - Broader consideration of terms and conditions

2. Linked Buy:
   Supplier-Buyer Integration/Linked Cost Minimization

   Leverage Points:
   - Improved coordination/forecast accuracy and predictability
   - Optimized logistical flows/value added roles
   - Streamlined transactional information flow
   - Elimination of redundant/nonvalue added activities
   - Improved supplier cost productivity
   - Commitments to enable supplier investments

3. Value Buy:
   Value Management/Optimization

   Leverage Points:
   - Increased and early supplier involvement in solution design
   - Reduced complexity/simplified specifications
   - Increased standardization
   - Clarified response time objectives
   - Rationalized requirements
   - Controlled consumption rates
   - Performance incentives to achieve total cost productivity

4. Integrated Sell:
   Commercial Synergy

   Leverage Points:
   - Integrate multi-company products/services and channel portfolio
   - Introduce creative risk sharing
   - Exploit supplier capabilities and potential
   - Manage complex channel relationships
   - Cross-utilize infrastructure and operating resources among multiple parties in the value chain

IMPACT →

Buy for Less → Buy Better → Consume Better → Sell Better

Pathways to Cost Savings and Revenue Enhancement

SOURCE: Reprinted from Matthew G. Anderson and Paul B. Katz, "Strategic Sourcing," *The International Journal of Logistics Management*, 9, no. 1 (1998), p. 4, Figure 3. Website at www.ijlm.org.

item like a muffler, Ford might ask a supply chain partner to provide a complete exhaust system.

- To capture fresh ideas, technologies, and cost savings, leading purchasing organizations emphasize **early supplier involvement in new product development.** At firms like Boeing, Harley-Davidson, Maytag, and Honda, key suppliers actively contribute to the new product development process from the design stage to the product's introduction, often spending months on-site collaborating with the development team.

By using these methods, Level 3 savings opportunities can be substantial but vary with the nature of the product, capabilities of the suppliers, and the strength of buyer–seller relationships.

Level 4—Integrated Sell (Sell Better) Level 4 development applies to those situations where specific product and service choices made by the purchasing organization have a significant impact on revenue and also involve a high degree of business risk. For example, the investments that a telecommunications firm, like AT&T, makes in technology products that form its infrastructure will have a major impact on the future of the firm. Under such conditions, choosing the right technologies and sharing the risks with important suppliers are crucial to the success of AT&T's corporate strategy. Purchasing professionals, who are highly skilled and possess knowledge of the industry, are required to achieve this advanced level of procurement development which unites purchasing decisions with corporate growth strategies.

Segmenting Purchase Categories Each firm purchases a unique portfolio of products and services. Leaders in procurement are giving increased attention to segmenting total purchases into distinct categories and sharpening their focus on those purchases that have the greatest impact on revenue generation or present the greatest risk to corporate performance. From Figure 2.3, observe that various categories of purchases are segmented based on procurement complexity and the nature of the impact on corporate performance (that is, revenue impact/business risk).

Which Purchases Impact Performance? Procurement complexity considers factors such as the technical complexity, the scope of supply chain coordination required, and the degree to which life cycle costs are relevant. The revenue impact/business risk dimension considers the degree to which a purchase category can influence customers' perceptions of value. For example, purchasing managers at Ford decided that some components are important to brand identity, such as steering wheels, road wheels, and other highly visual parts.

Purchasing managers can use a segmentation approach to isolate those purchase categories that have the greatest impact on corporate revenues.

> For example, the procurement of advertising services could have tremendous risk implications relative to customer perceptions of value, while office supplies remain a cost issue. Or, in the high-tech arena, the procurement of a new generation of semiconductor technology may essentially be a bet on the company's future.[12]

---

[12] Anderson and Katz, p. 7.

| FIGURE 2.3 | SEGMENTING THE BUY |

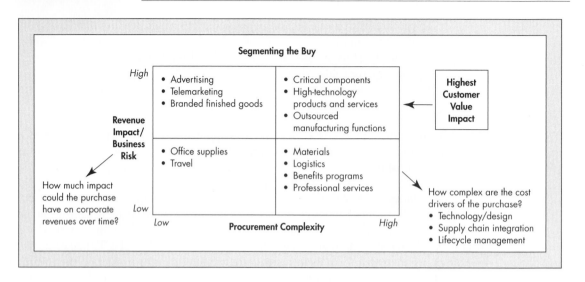

SOURCE: Reprinted from Matthew G. Anderson and Paul B. Katz, "Strategic Sourcing," *The International Journal of Logistics Management*, 9, no. 1 (1998), p. 7, Figure 8. Website at www.ijlm.org.

Business marketers should assess where their offerings are positioned in the portfolio of purchases that a particular organization makes. This will vary by firm and by industry. The revenue and profit potential for the business marketer is greatest in those purchasing organizations that view the purchase as strategic—high revenue impact and high customer value impact. Here the marketer can contribute offerings that are directly tied to the strategy of the customer organization. If the business marketer can become a central component of the customer's supply chain, the impact is significant: an attractive, long-term relationship in which the supplier is viewed as an extension of the customer's organization. For categories of goods that are viewed as less strategic by purchasing organizations (for example, office supplies), the appropriate marketing strategy centers on providing a complete product assortment, competitive pricing, timely service support, and simplified ordering. By understanding how customers segment their purchases, business marketers are better equipped to target profitable customer groups and develop customized strategies.

Purchasing on the Internet   Like consumers who are shopping at Amazon.com, purchasing managers are able to use the Internet to find new suppliers, communicate with current suppliers, or place an order. Forrester Research projects that the dollar volume of business-to-business electronic commerce will be ten times larger than that of business-to-consumer e-commerce.[13] While providing a rich base of information, purchasing over the Internet is also very efficient: it is estimated that purchase orders processed over the Internet cost only $5, compared to the current average purchase order cost of $100. For example, IBM is moving all of its purchasing to the Internet and expects to save over $240 million. Beyond operational efficiencies and lower cost,

---

[13] Mark A. Brunelli, "Consultants See Big Future for e-commerce," *Purchasing* 127 (October 21, 1999), p. S83.

FIGURE 2.4	GE MEDICAL SYSTEMS

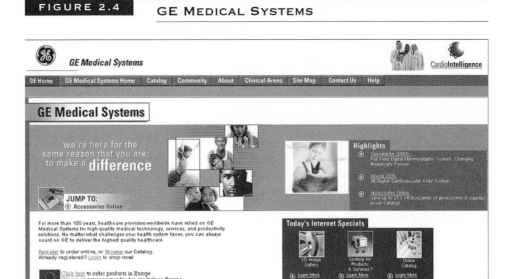

SOURCE: http://www.ge.com/medical/index.html, December 19, 1999.

John Patterson, IBM vice-president of production procurement, sees the Internet as a strategic tool that can be used for supply chain management:

> I believe that the Web creates the platform upon which strategic relationships can be built. It takes a lot of effort and energy to have meaningful strategic relationships with suppliers 12,000 miles away. But with the Web you can have your engineers get together with suppliers' engineers, you can have video conferencing sessions, data exchanges, and engineering drawing exchanges. I don't think there is any future without the Web relationship with suppliers.[14]

Purchasing managers are increasingly turning to the Internet to research the global marketplace for suppliers, materials, technology trends, market trends, sharing information, and coordinating activities. These factors promote efficiency and effectiveness in the supply chain by reducing cycle time, lowering inventory levels, and lowering costs. General Electric is representative of many companies that are using the Internet for purchasing and as a centerpiece of its corporate strategy. For example, GE Medical Systems uses the Internet to manage relationships with its suppliers and provides an online catalog, daily Internet specials, and a host of services for its customers—purchasing managers at hospitals and healthcare facilities worldwide (see Figure 2.4).

How Purchasing Managers Evaluate Performance

Once a contract is awarded to a supplier, actual performance must be evaluated. Buyers rate supplier performance in assessing the quality of past decisions, in making

---

[14]James Carbone, "There's Lots More to the Web than Click and Buy," *Purchasing* 127 (October 21, 1999), p. S76.

INSIDE BUSINESS MARKETING

ISO 9000: The International Quality Standard

Located in Geneva, Switzerland, the International Standards Organization (ISO) was created to promote the development of a series of product and service standards that would be recognized by eighty-nine member nations, including the United States. Products produced by companies that have attained ISO 9000 certification flow freely across national boundaries and are no longer subjected to individual national standards. ISO 9000 identifies the basic attributes of a manufacturer's quality management program and specifies procedures and approaches to ensure that products and services are produced in accordance with the process standards specified by the firm. For certification, an independent audit organization verifies that (1) procedures are in place to measure quality,

(2) a review process has been established to monitor quality, and (3) qualified personnel are available to implement these policies.

Many organizational buyers in Europe use ISO 9000 certification as a screening device for identifying potential suppliers. Because of its growing acceptance as a standard of quality assurance, ISO 9000 has also been adopted by many industries in the United States, including the auto industry. Note that ISO 9000 standards are not product standards (for example, the Good Housekeeping Seal of Approval)—they only ensure that a quality system is employed by the supplier.

SOURCE: Wade Ferguson, "Impact of the ISO 9000 Series Standards on Industrial Marketing," *Industrial Marketing Management* 25 (July 1996): pp. 305–310.

---

future vendor selections—and as a negotiating tool to gain leverage in buyer–seller relationships. Many purchasing organizations provide quarterly performance ratings to suppliers over the Internet. The specific method and the scope of the rating system vary by industry and firm.[15] However, the most widely used approach is the weighted-point plan.

The Weighted-Point Plan In the weighted-point plan, the buying organization weights each performance factor according to its relative importance. Quality might be given a weight of 40; service, 30; and price, 30. This system alerts the business marketer to the nature and importance of the evaluative criteria used by a particular organization. The marketer's total offering can then be adjusted to fit the organization's needs more precisely.

Observe in Figure 2.5 how DaimlerChrysler AG "grades" suppliers of electronic components. Under this program, suppliers can be awarded a total of 100 points, including up to 40 points for quality, 25 points for pricing, 25 points for delivery, and 10 points for technical assistance. Note that a number of dimensions are evaluated for each performance factor. For example, the quality rating is determined by the following factors:

- The supplier's defect rate
- Conformance to a statistical quality audit (SQA) of the supplier's manufacturing plant in which purchasing and engineering inspect manufacturing processes and controls
- The performance of samples provided by the supplier
- The responsiveness of the supplier to quality problems

---

[15] For example, see Larry C. Giunipero and Daniel J. Brewer, "Performance-Based Evaluation Systems," *International Journal of Purchasing and Materials Management* 29 (winter 1993), pp. 35–41; see also Mary Siegfried Dozbaba, "Critical Supplier Relationships," *Purchasing Today* (February 1999), pp. 22–29.

FIGURE 2.5   HOW DAIMLERCHRYSLER GRADES SUPPLIERS

SUPPLIER RATING CHART:

Supplier Name: _____   Commodity: _____
Shipping Location: _____   Annual Sales Dollars: _____

Quality 40%	5 Excellent	4 Good	3 Satisfactory	2 Fair	1 Poor	0 N/A
Supplier defect rates						
SQA program conformance						
Sample approval performance						
Responsiveness to quality problems						
Overall rating						
Delivery 25%						
Avoidance of late or overshipments						
Ability to expand production capacity						
Engineering sample delivery performance						
Response to fluctuating supply demands						
Overall delivery rating						
Price 25%						
Price competitiveness						
Absorption of economic price increases						
Submission of cost savings plans						
Payment terms						
Overall price rating						
Technology 10%						
State-of-the-art component technology						
Sharing research development capability						
Capable and willing to provide circuit design services						
Responsiveness to engineering problems						
Overall technology rating						

Buyer: _____   Date: _____
Comments: _____

SOURCE: Courtesy DaimlerChrysler AG.

Working with other departments, such as engineering and production control, purchasing calculates a performance score for each supplier. In the pricing area, DaimlerChrysler is giving increased attention to the cost savings plans submitted by the supplier.[16] Detailed records are kept of the number of proposals each supplier makes and the dollar savings that they generate. By focusing on continual improvement, suppliers can improve their profitability and increase the amount of sales they

[16]Jeffrey H. Dyer, "How Chrysler Created an American Keiretsu," *Harvard Business Review* 74 (July/August 1996), pp. 52–56; see also Gregory E. Benson, "Value Can Be Measured," *Purchasing Today* (November 1998), p. 14.

ETHICAL BUSINESS MARKETING

Globalization Requires New Ground Rules

The practice of "sourcing"—using cheap foreign labor to make goods that are sold to domestic buyers—has moved up the political agenda, increasing the pressure on companies to be more accountable for the labor and human rights records of their overseas suppliers. Some well-known firms have taken a strong stand by publishing definitive policies regarding the use of foreign labor. All companies that use "sourcing" will need to consider the cost of setting and maintaining standards against the impact on corporate image of being perceived as a bad-or-uncaring player. The heart of the issue regarding "sourcing" is the link between the plight of domestic and overseas workers, and some firms have introduced codes of conduct that set standards for working conditions in foreign manufacturing facilities.

A shining example is the approach taken by Levi Strauss & Co. Levi Strauss operates in many countries and diverse cultures. Special care is taken in selecting contractors in those countries where goods are produced to ensure that products are being made in a manner that is consistent with the company's values and reputation. The company has adopted a set of global sourcing guidelines that establish the standards contractors must meet to ensure that practices are compatible with corporate values. For instance, the guidelines ban the use of child and prison labor, stipulate environmental requirements, and establish that working hours cannot exceed 60 hours per week, with at least one day off in seven.

SOURCE: Adapted from: Robert D. Hass, "Ethics in the Trenches." *Across the Board* 31 (May 1994). pp. 12–13 and Ken Cottrill, "Global Codes of Conduct," *Journal of Business Strategy* 17 (May/June 1996), pp. 55–59.

---

generate from DaimlerChrysler. Those scoring 91 points or higher make the preferred supplier list. It is important to note that only 300 of DaimlerChrysler's 1,000 electronics suppliers achieve this distinction, and they receive more than 80 percent of the firm's $350 million annual budget for electronic components. Suppliers scoring 83 to 90 points continue to be used, but to a lesser degree than preferred suppliers. Those scoring 70 to 83 points are placed in a marginal category and risk being eliminated from the supplier roster unless they work with DaimlerChrysler to improve. Suppliers scoring less than 70 points are usually dropped automatically.

The weighted-point plan is more objective and flexible than the categorical method. The buying organization can adjust the weights of various performance factors to meet particular needs. Likewise, the method forces the organizational buyer to define the key attributes of a supplier.

Supplier Evaluation: Implications for the Marketer

Business marketers must be sensitive to the evaluation criteria of organizational buyers and to how these criteria are weighted. Many criteria may be factored into a buyer's ultimate decision: quality, service, price, company image, and capability. Buyers' perceptions are also critical. When products are perceived as highly standardized, price assumes more importance. On the other hand, when products are perceived as unique, other criteria may dominate. The price of a product cannot be separated from the attached bundle of services and other intangible values.

Economic criteria assume significant importance in many industrial buying decisions,[17] especially the anticipated costs associated with buying, storing, and using the

---

[17] Donald R. Lehmann and John O'Shaughnessy, "Decision Criteria Used in Buying Different Categories of Products," *Journal of Purchasing and Materials Management* 18 (spring 1982), pp. 9–14.

product. By contrast, product performance criteria evaluate the extent to which the product is likely to maximize performance. Economic criteria are important in the purchase of standard products of simple construction with standard applications. Performance criteria are more important in the evaluation of complex products or novel applications. The marketer who secures a new account must be prepared to pass frequent performance tests.

To this point, the discussion has centered on one sector of the business market—commercial enterprises—and the role the purchasing function assumes. Attention now turns to the government market.

Governments: Unique Characteristics

Federal (1), state (50), and local (87,000) **government units** generate the greatest volume of purchases of any customer category in the United States. Collectively, these units spend over $1.3 trillion in goods and services each year—the federal government accounts for $500 billion and states and local government contribute the rest.[18] Governmental units purchase from virtually every category of goods and services—office supplier, personal computers, furniture, food, health care, and military equipment. Business marketing firms, large and small, serve the government market. In fact, 25 percent of the purchase contracts at the federal level are with small firms.[19]

Influences on Government Buying

Another level of complexity is added to the governmental purchasing process by the array of influences on this process. In federal, state, and large city procurement, buyers report to and are influenced by dozens of interested parties who specify, legislate, evaluate, and use the goods and services. Clearly, the range of outside influences extends far beyond the originating agency.

Understanding Government Contracts

Government purchasing is also affected by goals and programs that have broad social overtones, including compliance, set-asides, and minority subcontracting. The **compliance program** requires that government contractors maintain affirmative action programs for minorities, women, and the handicapped. Firms failing to do so are barred from holding government contracts. In the **set-aside program,** a certain percentage of a given government contract is "set aside" for small or minority businesses; no others can participate in that proportion of the contract. The **minority subcontracting program** may require that major contractors subcontract a certain percentage of the total contract to minority firms. For example, Ohio law requires that 7 percent of all subcontractors on state construction projects be minorities. The potential government contractor must understand these programs and how they apply to the firm.

Most government procurement, at any level, is based on laws that establish contractual guidelines.[20] The federal government has set forth certain general contract

---

[18] U.S. Department of Commerce, Bureau of the Census, *Statistical Abstract of the United States: 1995* 11th ed., (Washington, D.C. 1995), p. 297.

[19] Stephanie N. Mehta, "Small Firms Are Getting More Government Contracts," *Wall Street Journal* (27 April 1995), p. B2.

[20] Michael R. Leenders and Harold E. Fearon, *Purchasing and Supply Management* 11th ed., (Chicago: Irwin 1997), pp. 537–566.

provisions as part of the federal procurement regulations. These provisions include stipulations regarding product inspection, payment methods, actions as a result of default, and disputes, among many others.

Without a clear comprehension of the procurement laws, the vendor is in an unfavorable position during the negotiation phase. The vendor particularly needs to explore the advantages and disadvantages of the two basic types of contracts:

1. *Fixed-price contracts.* A firm price is agreed to before the contract is awarded, and full payment is made when the product or service is delivered as agreed.

2. *Cost-reimbursement contracts.* The vendor is reimbursed for allowable costs incurred in performance of the contract and is sometimes allowed a certain number of dollars above cost as profit.

Each type of contract has built-in incentives to control costs or to cover future contingencies.

Generally, the fixed-price contract provides the greatest profit potential, but it also poses greater risks if unforeseen expenses are incurred, if inflation increases dramatically, or if conditions change. For example, inflation and unanticipated development problems resulted in a $60 million loss for a defense contractor producing the first twenty fighter planes for the Navy. However, if the seller can reduce costs significantly during the contract, profits may exceed those estimated when the contract was negotiated. Cost-reimbursement contracts are carefully administered by the government because of the minimal incentives for contractor efficiency. Contracts of this type are usually employed for government projects involving considerable developmental work for which it is difficult to estimate efforts and expenses.

To overcome the inefficiencies of both the cost-reimbursement contract (which often leads to cost overruns) and the fixed-price contract (which can discourage firms from bidding because project costs are uncertain), the government often employs incentive contracts. The incentive contract rewards firms when their actual costs on a project are below target costs, and it imposes a penalty when they exceed target costs.

Telling Vendors How to Sell: Useful Publications

Unlike most customers, governments often go to great lengths to explain to potential vendors exactly how to do business with them. For example, the federal government makes available such publications as *Doing Business with the General Services Administration, Selling to the Military,* and *Selling to the U.S. Air Force.* Government agencies also hold periodic seminars to orient businesses to the buying procedures used by the agency. The objective is to encourage firms to seek government business.

Purchasing Organizations and Procedures: Government

Government and commercial purchasing are organized similarly. However, governments tend to emphasize clerical functions because of the detailed procedures the law requires. Although the federal government is the largest single industrial purchaser, it does not operate like a single company but like a combination of several large companies with overlapping responsibilities and thousands of small independent units.[21] The federal government has more than 15,000 purchasing authorities (departments, agencies, and so on). Every government agency possesses some degree of buying influence or authority. Federal government procurement is divided into two categories: defense and nondefense.

Defense Procurement   The Department of Defense (DOD) spends a large proportion of the federal government's total procurement budget. The DOD's procurement operation is said to be the largest business enterprise in the world. The end of the cold war signaled a new era for the DOD: It must achieve the mission more efficiently and effectively with a smaller force.

Each DOD military division—Army, Navy, and Air Force—is responsible for its own major purchases. However, the Defense Logistics Agency (DLA) procures billions of dollars worth of supplies used in common by all branches. The DLA's budget for procurement exceeds $10 billion annually.[22] The purposes of the DLA are to obtain favorable prices through volume purchasing and to reduce duplication of purchasing within the military. Defense-related items may also be procured by other government agencies, such as the General Services Administration (GSA). In fact, the DOD is the GSA's largest customer. Under current agreements between the GSA and the DOD, the military purchases through the GSA many items such as cars, desks, office machines, and hand tools.[23] Also, many supplies for military-base operations are procured locally.

Nondefense Procurement   Nondefense procurement is administered by a wide variety of agencies, including cabinet departments (for example, Health and Human Services, Commerce), commissions (for example, the Federal Trade Commission), the executive branch (for example, the Bureau of the Budget), federal agencies (for example, the Federal Aviation Agency), and federal administrations (for example, the GSA). The Department of Commerce centralizes the procurement of supplies and equipment for its Washington office and all local offices. The Department of the Interior, on the other hand, instructs each area and district office of the Mining Enforcement and Safety Administration to purchase mine-safety equipment and clothing locally.

Like the DLA, the GSA centralizes the procurement of many general-use items (for example, office furniture, pens, light bulbs) for all civilian government agencies. The Federal Supply Service of the GSA is like the purchasing department of a large diversified corporation because it provides a consolidated purchasing, storing, and distribution network for the federal government. The Federal Supply Service purchases many items commonly used by other government agencies, including office supplies, small tools, paint, paper, furniture, maintenance supplies, and duplicating equipment. In some cases, the GSA operates retail-like stores, where any federal buyer can go to purchase equipment and supplies. The GSA has enormous purchasing power, buying more than $14 billion of products and services annually.[24]

---

[21] Ibid., pp. 552–559.

[22] Leslie Kaufman, "The Top Government Purchasers: Defense Logistics Agency–Supply Budget Bucks Downward Trend," *Government Executive* 26 (August 1994): p. 113.

[23] U.S. General Services Administration, "Doing Business with the GSA" (Washington, D.C., 1996).

[24] Jack Sweeny, "GSA Contracts to Include Services," *Computer Reseller News*, (8 April 1996): p. 113.

Under the Federal Supply Schedule Program, departments within the government may purchase specified items from an approved supplier at an agreed-upon price. This program provides federal agencies with the sources of products such as furniture, appliances, office equipment, laboratory equipment, and the like. Once a supplier has bid and been approved, the schedule may involve an indefinite-quantity contract for a term of one to three years. The schedule permits agencies to place orders directly with suppliers. Like corporate purchasing units, the GSA is using the Internet to streamline purchasing processes and to facilitate communication with suppliers (see www.gsa.gov).

Federal Buying

The president may set the procurement process in motion when he signs a congressional appropriation bill, or an accountant in the General Accounting Office may initiate the process by requesting a new desktop computer. Business marketers can identify the current needs of government buyers by consulting *Commerce Business Daily (CBD)*. The *CBD*, published by the Department of Commerce, lists all government procurement proposals, subcontracting leads, contract awards, and sales of surplus property. A potential supplier has at least thirty days prior to bid opening in which to respond. By law, all intended procurement actions of $10,000 or more, both civilian and military, are published in the *CBD*. Copies of the *CBD* are available at various government field offices as well as local public libraries.

Once a procurement need is documented and publicly announced, the government will follow one of two general procurement strategies: formal advertising (also known as open bid) or negotiated contract.

Formal Advertising   **Formal advertising** means the government will solicit bids from appropriate suppliers; usually, the lowest bidder is awarded the contract. This strategy is followed when the product is standardized and the specifications straightforward. The interested supplier must gain a place on a bidder's list (or monitor the *CBD* on a daily basis—which suggests that a more effective approach is to get on the bidder's list by filing the necessary forms available from the GSA Business Service Centers). Then, each time the government requests bids for a particular product, the supplier receives an invitation to bid. The invitation to bid specifies the item and the quantity to be purchased, provides detailed technical specifications, and stipulates delivery schedules, warranties required, packing requirements, and other purchasing details. The bidding firm bases its bid on its own cost structure and on the anticipation of competitive bid levels.

Procurement personnel review each bid for conformance to specifications. Contracts are generally awarded to the lowest bidder; however, the government agency may select the next-to-lowest bidder if it can document that the lowest bidder would not responsibly fulfill the contract. On balance, formal advertising allows free and open competition. In addition, the government has fairly good assurance that there is no collusion and that it has obtained the lowest possible price.

Negotiated Contract Buying   A negotiated contract is used to purchase products and services that cannot be differentiated on the basis of price alone (such as complex scientific equipment or R&D projects) or when there are few suppliers. There may be

INSIDE BUSINESS MARKETING

Jet-Fighter Contract: A Flyoff Determines the Winner

Boeing and Lockheed Martin are locked in a battle for the largest military contract in history—supplying the U.S. military and the Royal Navy with the next-generation fighter jet. Each company is developing a fighter to meet the desired military specifications. Signaling a shift in policy, the Pentagon is making cost as important as performance in choosing the prime contractor. Boeing and Lockheed Martin have been asked *not* to build the best plane they can, but the best the Government can afford—both in terms of the initial price per plane and in maintenance costs over

time. The winning firm will supply jet fighters to the military for the next two or three decades.

In choosing the contract winner, the Pentagon will stage a flyoff where each of the firms will demonstrate the performance of its plane. After the contest, the Pentagon will conduct thorough analyses of cost and performance data before picking the winner of this lucrative contract.

SOURCE: Leslie Wayne, "Dogfight Over a Must-Win Contract," *The New York Times*, (15 August 1999): Section 3, p. 1 and pp. 10–11.

some competition, because the contracting office can conduct negotiations with several suppliers simultaneously.

Obviously, negotiation is a much more flexible procurement procedure; the government buyers may exercise considerable personal judgment. Procurement is based on the more subjective factors of performance and quality as well as on price. The procurement decision for the government is much like that of the large corporation: Which is the best possible product at the lowest price, and will the product be delivered on time? Usually, extensive personal selling by the potential contractor is required to convince the government that the firm can perform. The selling effort should include negotiating favorable terms and reasonable payment dates as well as investigating future contracts for which the company may want to bid.

In an effort to streamline government negotiation and buying procedures, some agencies are changing competitive source-selection rules. For example, one new approach is to allow oral proposals.[25] Using this method, each bidding team is called into a conference room and given a set amount of time to convince observers why it can do the best job on a contract. This speeds up the process of negotiation and bidding, and allows for an effective exchange of information. It also challenges the business marketer to carefully craft the presentation and to effectively deliver it to the government procurement team.

A Different Strategy Required

A marketer positioned to sell to the government has a much different marketing strategy focus than does a firm that concentrates on the commercial sector. The government seller emphasizes (1) understanding the complex rules and standards that must be met; (2) developing a system to keep informed of each agency's procurement plans; (3) generating a strategy for product development and R&D that facilitates the firm's response to government product needs; (4) developing a communications strategy that

---

[25] "Federal Acquisition Guide: Bidding Farewell to Old Ways," *Government Executive* 28 (February 1996): p. 5A.

focuses on how technology meets agency objectives; and (5) generating a negotiation strategy to secure favorable terms regarding payment, contract completion, and cost overruns due to changes in product specifications.

The Institutional Market: Unique Characteristics

Institutional customers comprise the third sector of the business market. Institutional buyers make up a sizable market—total expenditures on public elementary and secondary schools alone exceed $400 billion, and national health expenditures exceed $850 billion.[26] Schools and healthcare organizations make up a sizable component of the institutional market, which also includes colleges and universities, libraries, foundations, art galleries, and clinics. On one hand, institutional purchasers are similar to governments in that the purchasing process is often constrained by political considerations and dictated by law. In fact, many institutions are administered by government units—schools, for example. On the other hand, other institutions are privately operated and managed like corporations; they may even have a broader range of purchase requirements than their large corporate counterparts. Like the commercial enterprise, institutions are ever cognizant of the value of efficient purchasing.

Institutional Buyers: Purchasing Procedures

Diversity is the key element in the institutional market. For example, the institutional marketing manager must first be ready to respond to a school purchasing agent who buys in great quantity for an entire city's school system through a formal bidding procedure, and then respond to a former pharmacist who has been elevated to purchasing agent for a small rural hospital.

Healthcare institutions provide a good example of the diversity of this market. Some small hospitals delegate responsibility for food purchasing to the chief dietitian. Although many of these hospitals have purchasing agents, the agent cannot place an order unless it has been approved by the dietitian. In larger hospitals, decisions may be made by committees composed of a business manager, purchasing agent, dietitian, and cook. In still other cases, hospitals may belong to buying groups consisting of many local hospitals, or meal preparation may be contracted out. In an effort to contain costs, purchasing executives at large hospitals are adopting a supply chain focus and using sophisticated supplier evaluation methods like their counterparts in the commercial sector. Because of these varied purchasing environments, successful marketers usually maintain a separate marketing manager, staff, and sales force in order to tailor marketing efforts to each situation.

For many institutions, once the budget for a department has been established, the department will attempt to spend up to that budget limit. Thus, institutions may buy simply because there are unused funds in the budget. A business marketer should carefully evaluate the budgetary status of potential customers in the institutional segment of the market.

Because many institutions face strong budgetary pressures, they often outsource segments of their operations to specialists in order to enhance efficiency and effec-

---

[26] U.S. Department of Commerce, Bureau of the Census, *Statistical Abstract of the United States: 1995*, pp. 109, 150.

tiveness. School districts may look to third-party contractors to purchase food and supplies and to manage their meal service operations. For example, in Los Angeles, Marriott Corporation manages food service operations at the city's charter schools, while in Chicago, three different contract companies each operate ten food preparation departments.[27] Many universities have turned over operation of their bookstores, beverage contracts, and management of their student unions to outside contractors. Business marketers must carefully analyze and understand the operational strategy of their institutional customers. Frequently, extensive sales and marketing attention will have to be focused on the third-party contract operators.

Multiple Buying Influences   The institutional market offers some unique applications for the concept of multiple buying influences (discussed in Chapter 1). Many institutions are staffed with professionals—doctors, professors, researchers, and others. In most cases, depending on size, the institution will employ a purchasing agent and, in large institutions, a sizable purchasing department or materials management department. There is great potential for conflict between those responsible for the purchasing function and the professional staff for whom the purchasing department is buying. The purchasing department is in constant contact with suppliers and can challenge restrictive specifications, can secure information on market availability, and can arrange for product demonstrations from several major suppliers. However, many staff professionals resent losing their authority to buy from whom they wish. Business marketing and sales personnel, in formulating their marketing and personal selling approaches, must understand these conflicts and be able to respond to them. Often, the salesperson must carefully cultivate the professional staff in terms of product benefits and service while developing a delivery timetable, maintenance contract, and price schedule to satisfy the purchasing department.

Group Purchasing   An important factor in institutional purchasing is group purchasing. Hospitals, schools, and universities may join cooperative purchasing associations to obtain quantity discounts. Universities affiliated with the Education and Institutional Purchasing Cooperative enjoy favorable contracts established by the Cooperative and can purchase a wide array of products directly from vendors at the low negotiated prices. The Cooperative spends more than $100 million on goods annually. Cooperative buying allows institutions to enjoy lower prices, improved quality (through improved testing and vendor selection), reduced administrative cost, standardization, better records, and greater competition.

   Hospital group purchasing represents a significant market exceeding $10 billion. Group purchasing has become widely accepted: More than one-third of public sector hospitals in the United States are members of some type of affiliated group. Most hospital group purchasing is done at the regional level through hospital associations. However, for-profit hospital chains, which are a growing factor in the healthcare field, also engage in group buying. For example, a multihospital system with a $1 billion operating budget spends $300 to $500 million a year on medical supplies and purchased services. By channeling purchases through group purchasing organizations, these large buyers are reaping significant savings.[28]

---

[27] Susie Stephenson, "Schools," *Restaurants and Institutions* 106 (1 August 1996), pp. 60–64.

[28] Timothy L. Chapman, Ajay Gupta, and Paul O. Mange, "Group Purchasing Is Not a Panacea for U.S. Hospitals," *The McKinsey Quarterly*, No. 1 (1998), p. 160.

Group purchasing poses special challenges for the business marketer. The marketer must be in a position to develop not only strategies for dealing with individual institutions but also unique strategies for the special requirements of cooperative purchasing groups and large hospital chains. The buying centers—individual institution versus cooperative purchasing group—may vary considerably in composition, criteria, and level of expertise. For the purchasing groups, discount pricing will assume special importance. Suppliers who sell through purchasing groups must also have distribution systems that effectively deliver products to individual group members. And even though vendors have a contract with a large cooperative association, they must still be prepared to respond individually to each institution that places an order against the contract.

Institutional Purchasing Practices   In many respects the purchasing practices of large institutions are similar to those of large commercial firms. However, there are some important distinctions between institutional and commercial purchasing. The policies regarding cooperative buying, preference to local vendors, and the delegation of purchasing responsibility for food, pharmaceuticals, and a variety of other items are of particular importance. It is just these characteristics that the business marketer must understand in order to carefully develop a sales and communication strategy for this prospective institutional customer.

Dealing with Diversity: A Market-Centered Organization

Because each sector of the business market is unique, many firms have built market specialization into the marketing organization. To illustrate, the industrial products area of the J. M. Smucker Company is organized around market sectors. The institutional, military, and industrial markets are each managed by different individuals, each thoroughly knowledgeable about one particular market.

One form of a market-centered organizational scheme is illustrated in Figure 2.6. Observe that a market manager supervises and coordinates the activities of three market specialists. Each market specialist examines the buying processes, the product preferences, and the similarities and differences between customers in one sector of the business market. Such an analysis enables the market specialist to further categorize customers within a particular sector into meaningful market segments and to design specialized marketing programs for each segment. A market-centered organization provides the business marketer with a structure for dealing effectively with diversity in the industrial market.

Summary

A large market awaits the business marketing manager. The market can be divided into three major components: commercial enterprises, governments (federal, state, and local), and institutions. Recently, business marketers have seen their market horizons broadened to a global level. The marketer requires an understanding of the unique characteristics and the structure of the purchasing function in each sector.

Commercial enterprises include manufacturers, construction companies, service firms, transportation companies, selected professional groups, and resellers. Of these,

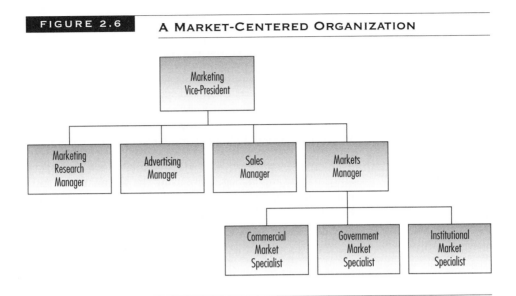

FIGURE 2.6 **A MARKET-CENTERED ORGANIZATION**

manufacturers account for the largest dollar volume of purchases. Furthermore, although the majority of manufacturing firms are small, buying power is concentrated in the hands of relatively few large manufacturing establishments, which are also concentrated geographically. Commercial enterprises, such as service establishments and transportation or utility companies, are more widely dispersed. The purchasing process is administered by a purchasing manager or purchasing agent. In larger firms, the purchasing function has become quite specialized, placing heavy demands on the industrial salesperson who must match the expertise of potential buyers. Rather than devoting exclusive attention to "buying for less," leading organizations tie purchasing activities directly to corporate strategy. Purchasing managers rely on tools such as value analysis to make informed decisions, use a weighted-point approach to evaluate supplier performance, and develop close working relationships with those suppliers who comprise the supply chain.

Many marketers find dealing with the government sector of the industrial market frustrating. However, government is the largest consumer in the United States. The diligent marketer who acquires an understanding of the procurement laws and of the varying contracts employed by the government can find a lucrative market. Federal buying follows two general procurement strategies: formal advertising or negotiated contract. The formal advertising approach, frequently followed for standardized products, involves the solicitation of bids from appropriate suppliers. Negotiated contracts are employed for unique requirements and are typified by discussion and bargaining throughout all phases of the contract.

Diversity is the characteristic that typifies the institutional market. Institutional buyers are somewhere between commercial enterprise and government buyers in terms of their characteristics, orientations, and purchasing processes. Cooperative purchasing—a unique aspect of this segment—necessitates a special strategic response by potential suppliers. Many business marketers have found that a market-centered organization provides the specialization required to meet the needs of each sector of the market.

Discussion Questions

1. Some purchasing organizations center on "buying for less" while others seek to consume better. Explain.

2. Honda of America relies on 400 suppliers in North America to provide more than 60 percent of the parts and materials for the Accord. What strategies could a business marketer follow in becoming a new supplier to Honda? What criteria would Honda consider in evaluating suppliers?

3. Segmentation is a tool that marketers use to identify target markets. Increasingly, purchasing managers are using the segmentation approach to determine which suppliers are most critical to the goals of the organization. Explain.

4. Compare and contrast the two general procurement strategies employed by the federal government: (1) formal advertising and (2) negotiated contract.

5. Institutional buyers fall somewhere between commercial enterprises and government buyers in terms of their characteristics, orientation, and purchasing process. Explain.

6. Explain how the decision-making process that a university might employ in selecting a new computer would differ from that of a commercial enterprise. Who would be the key participants in the process in each setting?

7. Fearing red tape and mounds of paperwork, Tom Bronson, president of B&E Electric, has always avoided the government market. A recent discussion with a colleague, however, has rekindled Tom's interest in this business market sector. What steps should B&E Electric take to learn more about this market?

8. Why have some industrial firms moved away from product-centered organizations and toward market-centered organizations?

3

Organizational Buying Behavior

The organizational buyer is influenced by a wide array of forces inside and outside the organization. Knowledge of these forces provides the marketer with a foundation on which to build responsive business marketing strategies. After reading this chapter, you will understand

1. the decision process that organizational buyers apply as they confront differing buying situations and the resulting strategy implications for the business marketer.

2. the individual, group, organizational, and environmental variables that influence organizational buying decisions.

3. a model of organizational buying behavior that integrates these important influences.

4. how a knowledge of organizational buying characteristics enables the marketer to make more informed decisions about product design, pricing, and promotion.

Market-driven business firms continuously sense and act on trends in their markets. Consider the Automotive Supply Division of Johnson Controls, Inc.—a leading unit that supplies auto interiors (including seats, dashboards, headliners, and instrument panels) to manufacturers.[1] The striking success of the firm rests on the close relationships that its sales reps and marketing managers have formed with design engineers and purchasing executives in the auto industry. To illustrate, some of Johnson Controls' salespersons work on-site with design teams at Ford, GM, or Chrysler plants. To provide added value to the new product design process, the firm also invests over $2 million annually in market research on the needs and preferences of auto buyers—the customer's customer! For example, based on extensive research about how young children spend their time in cars, Johnson Controls developed the Playseat. The product pulls out of the backseat armrest and is essentially a table that acts as a car playground for children. By staying close to the needs of auto buyers, Johnson Controls became the preferred supplier to design engineers who are continually seeking innovative ways to make auto interiors more distinctive and inviting.

Understanding the dynamics of organizational buying behavior is crucial for identifying profitable segments of the organizational market, for locating buying influences within these segments, and for reaching these organizational buyers efficiently and effectively with an offering that responds to their needs. Each decision the business marketer makes is based on a probable response of organizational buyers. This chapter explores the key stages of the organizational buying process and isolates the salient characteristics of different purchasing situations. Next, attention will turn to the myriad forces that influence organizational buying behavior. Knowledge of how organizational buying decisions are made provides the business marketer with a solid foundation for building responsive marketing strategies.

The Organizational Buying Process

Organizational buying behavior is a process rather than an isolated act or event. Tracing the history of a procurement decision in an organization uncovers critical decision points and evolving information requirements. In fact, organizational buying involves several stages, each of which yields a decision. Likewise, the composition of the decision-making unit can vary from one stage to the next as organizational members enter and leave the procurement process.

Table 3.1 presents a model of the eight-stage sequence of activities in the organizational buying process.[2] Recognition of a problem or of a potential opportunity triggers the purchasing process. For example, the firm's manufacturing equipment becomes outmoded or a salesperson initiates consideration of a product by demonstrating opportunities for improving the organization's performance. During the procurement process, many small or incremental decisions are made that ultimately translate into the final selection of a supplier. To illustrate, a quality-control engineer might unknowingly establish specifications for a new production system that only

---

[1] Andy Cohen, "In Control," *Sales & Marketing Management*, 151 (June 1999), pp. 32–38.

[2] The discussion in this section is based on Patrick J. Robinson, Charles W. Faris, and Yoram Wind, *Industrial Buying and Creative Marketing* (Boston: Allyn and Bacon, Inc., 1967), pp. 12–18; see also Morry Ghingold and David T. Wilson, "Buying Center Research and Business Marketing Practice: Meeting the Challenge of Dynamic Marketing," *Journal of Business & Industrial Marketing*, 13, No. 2, 1998, pp. 96–108.

TABLE 3.1	THE BUYGRID FRAMEWORK FOR ORGANIZATIONAL BUYING SITUATIONS

	Buying Situations		
Buying Stages	**New Task**	**Modified Rebuy**	**Straight Rebuy**
1. Problem Recognition			
2. Determination of characteristics and quantity of needed item			
3. Description of characteristics and quantity of needed item			
4. Search for and qualification of potential suppliers			
5. Acquisition and analysis of proposals			
6. Evaluation of proposals and selection of supplier(s)			
7. Selection of an order routine			
8. Performance review			

NOTE: The most complex buying situations occur in the upper left portion of the buygrid framework and involve the largest number of decision makers and buying influences.

SOURCE: Adapted from the Marketing Science Institute Series, *Industrial Buying and Creative Marketing*, by Patrick J. Robinson, Charles W. Faris, and Yoram Wind. Copyright 1967 by Allyn and Bacon, Inc., Boston.

supplier A can meet. This type of decision early in the buying process will dramatically influence the favorable evaluation and ultimate selection of supplier A.

Some research suggests that the eight stages in the model of the buying process may not progress sequentially and may vary with the complexity of the purchasing situation. However, the model provides important insights into the organizational buying process. Certain stages may be completed concurrently; the process may be reoriented at any point by a redefinition of the basic problem; or the process may be discontinued by a change in the external environment or in upper-management thinking. The organizational buying process is shaped by a host of internal and external forces such as changes in economic or competitive conditions or a basic shift in organizational priorities.

Organizations that have significant experience in purchasing a particular product will approach the decision quite differently than first-time buyers. Therefore attention must center on buying situations rather than on products. Three types of buying situations have been delineated: (1) new task, (2) modified rebuy, and (3) straight rebuy.[3] As illustrated in Table 3.1, each type of buying situation must be related to the eight-stage buying process.

---

[3] Robinson, Faris, and Wind, *Industrial Buying and Creative Marketing*, chap. 1; see also Erin Anderson, Wujin Chu, and Barton Weitz, "Industrial Purchasing: An Empirical Exploration of the Buyclass Framework," *Journal of Marketing* 51 (July 1987): pp. 71–86; and Morry Ghingold, "Testing the 'Buygrid' Buying Process Model," *Journal of Purchasing and Materials Management* 22 (winter 1986): pp. 30–36.

New Task

In the **new-task** buying situation, the problem or need is perceived by organizational decision makers as totally different from previous experiences; therefore a significant amount of information is required for decision makers to explore alternative ways of solving the problem and to search for alternative suppliers.

When confronting a new-task buying situation, organizational buyers operate in a stage of decision making referred to as **extensive problem solving.**[4] The buying influentials and decision makers lack well-defined criteria for comparing alternative products and suppliers, but they also lack strong predispositions toward a particular solution. In the consumer market, this is the same type of problem solving an individual or household might follow in buying a first home.

Buying Decision Approaches[5]   Two distinct buying decision approaches are used: judgmental new task and strategic new task. The greatest level of uncertainty confronts firms in **judgmental new task** situations because of the technical complexity of the product, the difficulty of evaluating the alternatives, or the unpredictable aspects of dealing with a new supplier. Consider purchasers of a special type of production equipment who are uncertain about the model or brand to choose, the suitable level of quality, and the appropriate price to pay. For such purchases, the buying activities include a moderate amount of information search and a moderate use of formal tools in evaluating key aspects of the buying decision.

Even more effort is invested in all buying activities for **strategic new task** decisions. These purchasing decisions are of extreme importance to the firm—strategically and financially. If the buyer perceives that a rapid pace of technological change surrounds the decision, search effort is increased, but is concentrated in a shorter time period.[6] Long-range planning drives the decision process. To illustrate, a large health insurance company placed a $600,000 order for workstation furniture. The long-term impact on the work environment shaped the six-month decision process and involved the active participation of personnel from several departments.

Strategy Guidelines   The business marketer confronting a new-task buying situation can gain a differential advantage by participating actively in the initial stages of the procurement process. The marketer should gather information on the problems facing the buying organization, isolate specific requirements, and offer proposals to meet the requirements. Ideas that lead to new products often originate not with the marketer but with the customer.

Marketers who are presently supplying other items to the organization ("in" suppliers) have an edge over other firms; they can see problems unfolding and are familiar with the "personality" and behavior patterns of the organization. The successful business marketer carefully monitors the changing needs of organizations and is prepared to assist new-task buyers.

---

[4]The levels of decision making discussed in this section are drawn from John A. Howard and Jagdish N. Sheth, *The Theory of Buyer Behavior* (New York: John Wiley and Sons, 1969), chap. 2.

[5]The discussion of buying decision approaches in this section is drawn from Michele D. Bunn, "Taxonomy of Buying Decision Approaches," *Journal of Marketing* 57 (January 1993): pp. 38–56.

[6]Allen M. Weiss and Jan B. Heide, "The Nature of Organizational Search in High Technology Markets," *Journal of Marketing Research* 30 (May 1993): pp. 230–233.

Straight Rebuy

When there is a continuing or recurring requirement, buyers have substantial experience in dealing with the need, and they require little or no new information. Evaluation of new alternative solutions is unnecessary and unlikely to yield appreciable improvements. Thus, a **straight rebuy** approach is appropriate.

Routine problem solving is the decision process organizational buyers employ in the straight rebuy. Organizational buyers have well-developed choice criteria to apply to the purchase decision. The criteria have been refined over time as the buyers have developed predispositions toward the offerings of one or a few carefully screened suppliers. In the consumer market, this is the same type of problem solving that a shopper might use in selecting thirty items in twenty minutes during a weekly trip to the supermarket. Indeed, many of the buying decisions that are made each day in organizations are routine. For example, organizations of all types are continually buying operating resources—the goods and services needed to run the business, such as computer and office supplies, maintenance and repair items, and travel services. Ford alone spends more than $15 billion annually on operating resources.[7]

Buying Decision Approaches   Research suggests that organizational buyers employ two buying decision approaches: causal and routine low priority. **Causal purchases** involve no information search or analysis and the product or service is of minor importance to the firm. The focus is simply in transmitting the order. In contrast, **routine low priority** decisions are somewhat more important to the firm and involve a moderate amount of analysis. Describing the purchase of $5,000 worth of cable to be used as component material, a buyer aptly describes this decision process approach:

> On repeat buys, we may look at other sources or alternate methods of manufacturing, etc. to make sure no new technical advancements are available in the marketplace. But, generally, a repeat buy is repurchased from the supplier originally selected, especially for low dollar items.

For routine purchases or straight rebuys, the Internet is being used to streamline the purchasing process. To this end, firms are adopting electronic (e) procurement systems, joining trading communities or turning to electronic marketplaces that have been designed specifically for their industry (for example, chemical).

Electronic Purchasing   Once a supplier is selected and added to the approved list that will guide future buying, most purchasing organizations recognize the value of moving routine purchasing activities directly to employees. Indeed, employees across the organization routinely order a diverse array of items that can be classified as **operating resources** or nonproduction goods.

While production goods (i.e., entering goods) include the raw materials or component parts embodied in the finished product, operating resources are items that organizations of all types need to run day-to-day operations. Included here are computer-related capital equipment; maintenance, repair, and operating (MRO) supplies;

[7] Ravi Kalkota and Marcia Robinson, *e-Business: Roadmap for Success* (Reading, Mass.: Addison Wesley, 1999), pp. 237–238.

and travel services. In the United States alone, organizations spend $1.4 trillion dollars annually on operating resources—from personal computers and spare parts for factory equipment to office furniture and travel.[8] Even today, however, many organizations continue to manage these huge expenditures through paper-based processes that are costly to administer and frustrating for employees to navigate. Electronic (e) purchasing applications provide a solution that employees embrace.

Buy-Side Requisitioning Process[9]   Buy-side requisitioning software enables individual employees to buy online while the company retains control of the purchasing process. Leading suppliers of e-procurement software are enjoying explosive growth and include Ariba, Incorporated (www.ariba.com), Commerce One, Incorporated (www.commerceone.com), and Oracle Corporation (www.oracle.com). By tying the corporate intranet to suppliers' Web-based commerce sites, buy-side software routes employee purchase requests internally before turning them into firm orders. This e-procurement solution allows a company to channel purchases to preferred suppliers, reduce administrative overhead, capture favorable quantity discounts, and significantly reduce operating resource costs.

Here's how the requisitioning process works (see Figure 3.1):

- *Secure Personal Log-in*–Each employee is given a secure personal log-in code that contains a user profile (for example, job title, expenditure limits). These profiles are used to customize the presentation so employees can order those catalog items that they are authorized to purchase.

- *Browse Authorized Supplier Catalogs and Select Products*–Employees use search and browse capabilities to review multiple supplier catalogs. Only contracted products and prices are shown. Purchasing administrators can add details to steer employees to preferred products or to identify products that require approval prior to purchase.

- *Requisition/Order Creation*–Requisitions are created online and can include products from one or more suppliers.

- *Approval Routing*–Internal purchase controls ensure that employees cannot purchase restricted items or place orders beyond certain limits (for example, dollar amount per order). Once submitted, a requisition is routed for approval based on an organization's purchasing policies.

- *Order Submission/Fulfillment*–If more than one supplier is involved, the requisition is broken down into one purchase order per supplier and is automatically routed to each supplier.

- *Order Tracking and Receipt*–Employees are notified via e-mail of internal approval status, order acknowledgment from the supplier, shipment status, and delivery date.

To simplify and streamline the procurement of operating resources, firms such as Motorola, Bristol-Myers Squibb, and Cisco Systems use buy-side e-procurement applica-

---

[8] Mark Vigoroso, "Buyers Prepare for Brave New World of e-Commerce," *Purchasing* 127 (April 22, 1999), pp. S4–S12.
[9] This section draws on Ravi Kalkota and Marcia Robinson, *e-Business: Roadmap for Success*, pp. 246–250.

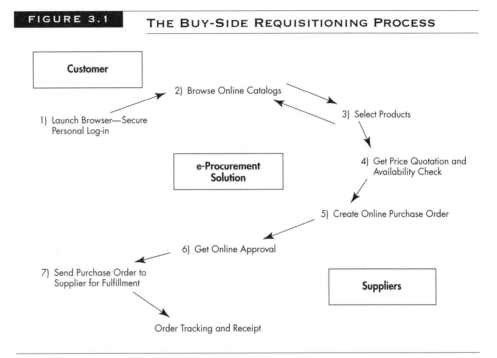

| FIGURE 3.1 | THE BUY-SIDE REQUISITIONING PROCESS |

SOURCE: Adapted from Ravi Kalkota and Marcia Robinson, *e-Business: Roadmap for Success* (Reading, MA: Addison-Wesley, 1999), p. 248.

tions. By offering a self-service system for employees, purchasing managers can move away from transaction management, retain control of the entire purchasing process, and give central attention to supply chain management. However, these buy-side systems are expensive to implement and have been used only by large firms with significant financial resources.[10] In response, online trading communities have been formed to accommodate a more diverse population of buyers and sellers.

Online Trading Communities   Like eBay has done in the business-to-consumer market, an opportunity exists to leverage the power of the Internet to aggregate large numbers of buyers and sellers and create online trading communities. Here a third party links buyers and sellers by efficiently distributing market information.[11] Buyers can participate without making a sizable investment in buy-side procurement software. For example, Commerce One created an open business-to-business marketplace portal for electronic commerce—called MarketSite (see Figure 3.2). This fee-per-transaction network enables buyers and sellers to connect seamlessly and conduct transactions online. By using MarketSite (www.marketsite.net), the catalog content (offerings) of a business marketer are available to buying organizations that are members. Orders are transmitted directly to the supplier, reducing selling and order processing costs for the seller. Trading communities also create e-commerce opportunities for smaller firms.

To effectively serve members of a trading community, business marketers should seize the opportunity to provide buyers with rich product information, like technical

---

[10] Mark Vigoroso, "Electronic Commerce: Lots of Interest, Little Action," *Purchasing* 127 (March 25, 1999), pp. 43–48.

[11] Ibid., pp. 47–48.

| FIGURE 3.2 | MARKETSITE.NET |

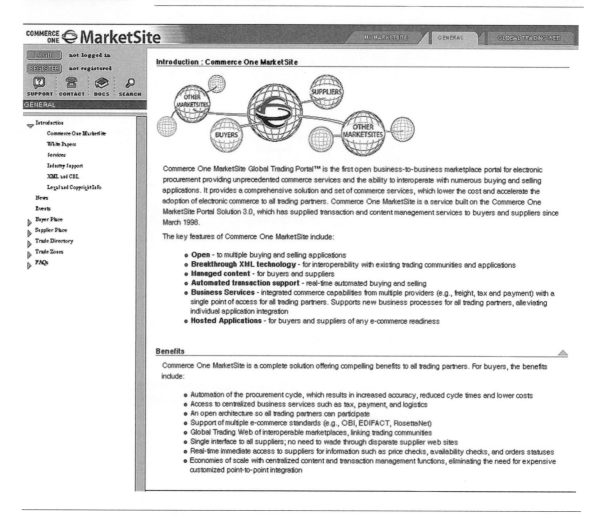

SOURCE: www.marketsite.net/ January 18, 2000.

specifications and repair and maintenance bulletins. Experts suggest that buyers will recognize those suppliers that provide higher levels of product and service quality.[12]

Industry-Specific Marketplaces   An alternative business model that is growing in popularity is the aggregated supply site, or electronic marketplace. Here a third party firm brings together the catalogs from multiple suppliers in a vertical industry (for example, steel or chemicals) in one site. These sites are designed to bring together the particular products that buyers will require from a particular industry to satisfy their needs. Industry exchanges, or electronic marketplaces, have been developed for chemicals, steel, paper, hospital suppliers, plastics, and other industry niches. For example,

---

[12] Ibid., p. 48.

E-Chemicals (www.e-chemicals.com) is an electronic marketplace for chemicals that lists twenty suppliers, including Dow Chemical and Du Pont, more than 1,000 products, and several hundred registered customers.[13] For suppliers, an electronic marketplace, like E-Chemicals, offers a low-cost sales channel to reach and efficiently serve small customers. For buyers, the electronic marketplace provides a one-stop purchasing solution—twenty-four hours a day, seven days a week. Looking ahead, electronic marketplaces will continue on an explosive growth path. By 2004, Forrester Research expects these e-marketplaces to capture 53 percent of all online business trade.

Strategy Guidelines The purchasing department handles straight rebuy situations by routinely selecting a supplier from a list of approved vendors and then placing an order. As organizations shift to electronic procurement systems, purchasing managers retain control of the purchasing process for these routine purchases while allowing individual employees to directly buy online from approved suppliers.[14] Employees use a simple point-and-click interface to navigate through a customized catalog detailing the offerings of approved suppliers, and then order required items. Individual employees like the self-service convenience and purchasing managers can direct attention to more critical strategic issues. Marketing communications should be designed to reach not only purchasing managers but also individual employees who are now empowered to exercise their product preferences.

The marketing task appropriate for the straight rebuy situation depends on whether the marketer is an "in" supplier (on the list) or an "out" supplier (not among the chosen few). An "in" supplier must reinforce the buyer–seller relationship, meet the buying organization's expectations, and be alert and responsive to the changing needs of the organization.

The "out" supplier faces a number of obstacles and must convince the organization that significant benefits can be derived from breaking the routine. This can be difficult because organizational buyers perceive risk in shifting from the known to the unknown. The organizational spotlight shines directly on them if an untested supplier falters. Testing, evaluations, and approvals may be viewed by buyers as costly, time-consuming, and unnecessary.

The marketing effort of the "out" supplier rests on an understanding of the basic buying needs of the organization: information gathering is essential. The marketer must convince organizational buyers that their purchasing requirements have changed or that the requirements should be interpreted differently. The objective is to persuade decision makers to reexamine alternative solutions and revise the preferred list to include the new supplier. For example, Savin challenges Xerox buyers to consider the benefits that they will receive if they switch to its office products (see Figure 3.3).

Modified Rebuy

In the **modified rebuy** situation, organizational decision makers feel that significant benefits may be derived from a reevaluation of alternatives. The buyers have experience in satisfying the continuing or recurring requirement, but they believe it worthwhile to seek additional information, and perhaps to consider alternative solutions.

---

[13] Steve Lohr, "Big Blue Casts Itself as Big Brother to Business on the Web," *The New York Times*, (22 September 1999), p. 50.
[14] Mark Vigoroso, "Buyers Prepare for Brave New World of e-Commerce," pp. S4–S16.

| FIGURE 3.3 | SAVIN VERSUS XEROX: AN AD URGING BUYING INFLUENTIALS TO CONSIDER A SWITCH |

WHAT SAVIN IS DOING TO MAKE XEROX YOUR X-DOCUMENT OUTPUT COMPANY.

You-know-who would have you believe that they're the first and last word in digital document solutions. At Savin, we're working hard to make you believe otherwise.

After all, at Savin we too have the forward-thinking, award-winning technology essential to boosting productivity in today's digital offices. Like our fast, versatile, connectable digital imaging systems that allow you (or your workgroup) to print, sort, duplex and staple—right from your desktop. And full-color digital imaging systems that turn electronic documents into brilliant hard copy.

But that's where similarities end. Because while it would appear that Xerox has dedicated themselves to becoming the biggest document company on the planet, at Savin we're dedicating ourselves to becoming the fastest, most responsive, most easy to work with name in the business. With smart, energetic, highly-trained Savin professionals willing to do whatever it takes to give you the satisfaction and service you deserve.

To find out x-actly what we'll do to win you over, contact us at **1-800-234-1900** or www.savin.com.

WE'VE GOT WHAT IT TAKES TO WIN YOU OVER™
SAVIN CORPORATION, 333 LUDLOW ST., STAMFORD, CT 06904

BTA 1999 CHANNEL'S CHOICE AWARD DIGITAL CONNECTED PRODUCTS

©1999 Savin Corporation

Xerox® is a trademark of XEROX CORPORATION.

SOURCE: Courtesy, Savin Corporation.

Several factors may trigger such a reassessment. Internal forces include the search for quality improvements or cost reductions. A marketer offering cost, quality, or service improvements can be an external precipitating force. The modified rebuy situation is most likely to occur when the firm is displeased with the performance of present suppliers (for example, poor delivery service).

Limited problem solving best describes the decision-making process for the modified rebuy. Decision makers have well-defined criteria, but are uncertain about which suppliers can best fit their needs. In the consumer market, college students buying their *second* computer might follow a limited problem solving approach.

Buying Decision Approaches   Two buying decision approaches typify this buying class category. Both give strong emphasis to the strategic objectives and long-term needs of the firm. The **simple modified rebuy** involves a narrow set of choice alternatives and encompasses a moderate amount of both information search and analysis. Buyers concentrate on the long-term relationship potential of suppliers.

The **complex modified rebuy** involves a large set of choice alternatives and is characterized by little uncertainty. The range of choice enhances the negotiating strength of the buyer. The importance of the decision motivates buyers to actively search for information, apply sophisticated analysis techniques, and carefully consider long-term needs. This decision situation is particularly well-suited to a competitive bidding process. For example, some firms are turning to *online* auctions, where the buying organization allows multiple suppliers to bid on a contract, with downward price pressure being exerted throughout the process.[15] To participate, suppliers must be prepared to meet defined product characteristics as well as quality and service standards. An innovator in this area—FreeMarkets—creates customized business-to-business online auctions for large buying organizations like United Technologies Corporation (see Figure 3.4). Rather than specialized products or services where a close working relationship with the supplier is needed, auctions tend to be used for commodities and standardized parts.

Strategy Guidelines   In a modified rebuy, the direction of the marketing effort depends on whether the marketer is an "in" or an "out" supplier. An "in" supplier should make every effort to understand and satisfy the procurement need and to move decision makers into a straight rebuy. The buying organization perceives potential payoffs from a reexamination of alternatives. The "in" supplier should ask why, and act immediately to remedy any customer problems. The marketer may be out of touch with the buying organization's requirements.

The goal of the "out" supplier should be to hold the organization in modified rebuy status long enough for the buyer to evaluate an alternative offering. Knowing the factors that led decision makers to reexamine alternatives could be pivotal. A particularly effective strategy for an "out" supplier is to offer performance guarantees as part of the proposal.[16] To illustrate, the following guarantee prompted International Circuit Technology, a manufacturer of printed circuit boards, to change to a new supplier for plating chemicals: "Your plating costs will be no more than x cents per square foot or we will make up the difference."[17] Given the nature of the production process, plating costs can be easily monitored by comparing the square footage of circuit boards moving down the plating line with the cost of plating chemicals for the period. Pleased with the performance, International Circuit Technology now routinely reorders from this new supplier.

Strategy Implications   Although past research provides some useful guidelines, great care must be exercised in forecasting the likely composition of the buying center for a particular purchasing situation.[18] The business marketer should attempt to

---

[15] Mark Vigoroso, "Are Internet Auctions Ready to Gear Up?" *Purchasing* 127 (February 11, 1999), pp. 85–86.

[16] Mary Siegfried Dozbaba, "Critical Supplier Relationships: Converting Higher Performance," *Purchasing Today* (February 1999), pp. 22–29.

[17] Somerby Dowst, "CEO Report: Wanted: Suppliers Adept at Turning Corners," *Purchasing* 101 (29 January 1987): pp. 71–72.

[18] Donald W. Jackson Jr., Janet E. Keith, and Richard K. Burdick, "Purchasing Agents' Perceptions of Industrial Buying Center Influence," *Journal of Marketing* 48 (fall 1984): pp. 75–83.

FIGURE 3.4

AD TOUTING THE BENEFITS OF ONLINE AUCTIONS FOR ORGANIZATIONAL BUYERS

SOURCE: Courtesy, FreeMarkets, Inc.

identify purchasing patterns that apply to the firm. For example, the classes of industrial goods introduced in Chapter 1 (such as foundation goods versus facilitating goods) involve varying degrees of technical complexity and financial risk for the buying organization.

The business marketer must therefore view the procurement problem or need from the perspective of the buying organization. How far has the organization progressed with the specific purchasing problem? How does the organization define the task at hand? How important is the purchase to the organization? The answers will direct and form the business marketer's response and also provide insight into the composition of the decision-making unit.

| FIGURE 3.5 | FORCES INFLUENCING ORGANIZATIONAL BUYING BEHAVIOR |

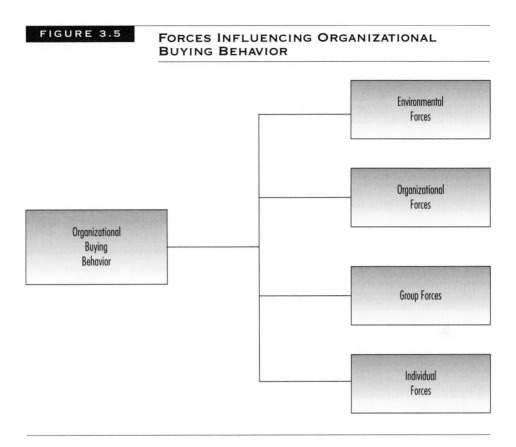

Forces Shaping Organizational Buying Behavior

The eight-stage model of the organizational buying process provides the foundation for exploring the myriad forces that influence a particular buying decision by an organization. Observe in Figure 3.5 how organizational buying behavior is influenced by environmental forces (for example, the growth rate of the economy); organizational forces (for example, the size of the buying organization); group forces (for example, patterns of influence in buying decisions); and individual forces (for example, personal preferences).

Environmental Forces

A projected change in business conditions, a technological development, or a new piece of legislation can drastically alter organizational buying plans. Among the types of environmental forces that shape organizational buying behavior are economic, political, legal, and technological influences. Collectively, such environmental influences define the boundaries within which buyer–seller relationships develop in the business market. Particular attention will be given to selected economic and technological forces that influence buying decisions.

Economic Influences   Because of the derived nature of industrial demand, the marketer must also be sensitive to the strength of demand in the ultimate consumer market. The demand for many industrial products fluctuates more widely than the general economy. Firms that operate on a global scale must be sensitive to the economic conditions that prevail across regions. For example, as the U.S. economy moves out of a recession, the European or Asian economy may continue to sputter. A wealth of political and economic forces dictate the vitality and growth of an economy.

The economic environment influences an organization's ability and, to a degree, its willingness to buy. However, shifts in general economic conditions do not affect all sectors of the market evenly. For example, a rise in interest rates may damage the housing industry (including lumber, cement, and insulation) but may have minimal effects on industries such as paper, hospital supplies, office products, and soft drinks. Marketers that serve broad sectors of the organizational market must be particularly sensitive to the differential impact of selective economic shifts on buying behavior.

Technological Influences   Rapidly changing technology can restructure an industry and dramatically alter organizational buying plans. Notably, the World Wide Web "has forever changed the way companies and customers (whether they be consumers or other businesses) buy and sell to each other, learn about each other, and communicate."[19]

The rate of technological change in an industry influences the composition of the decision-making unit in the buying organization. As the pace of technological change increases, the importance of the purchasing manager in the buying process declines. Technical and engineering personnel tend to be more important to organizational buying processes in which the rate of technological change is great. Recent research also suggests that buyers who perceive the pace of technological change to be more rapid will (1) conduct more intense search efforts and (2) spend less time on their overall search processes.[20] Allen Weiss and Jan Heide suggest that "In cost-benefit terms, a fast pace of change implies that distinct benefits are associated with search effort, yet costs are associated with prolonging the process" because the acquired information is "time sensitive."[21]

The marketer must also actively monitor signs of technological change and be prepared to adapt marketing strategy to deal with new technological environments. For example, IBM has embraced the Internet in its products, services, practices, and marketing—from overhauling its large mainframes into Internet computers to refashioning itself as an Internet leader with its giant "e-business" advertising campaign.[22] Because the most recent wave of technological change is as dramatic as any in history, the implications for marketing strategists are profound and involve changing definitions of industries, new sources of competition, changing product life cycles, and the increased globalization of markets.[23]

---

[19] Stewart Alsop, "e or Be Eaten," *Fortune* (November 8, 1999), p. 87.

[20] Allen M. Weiss and Jan B. Heide, "The Nature of Organizational Search in High Technology Markets," *Journal of Marketing Research* 30 (May 1993): pp. 220–233; see also Jan B. Heide and Allen M. Weiss, "Vendor Consideration and Switching Behavior for Buyers in High-Technology Markets," *Journal of Marketing* 59 (July 1995): pp. 30–43.

[21] Weiss and Heide, "The Nature of Organizational Search," p. 221.

[22] Steve Lohr, "Big Blue Casts Itself as Big Brother to Business on the Web," *The New York Times* (September 22, 1999), p. 50.

[23] Rashi Glazer, "Winning in Smart Markets," *Sloan Management Review*, 40 (Summer 1999), pp. 56–69.

Organizational Forces

An understanding of the buying organization is based on the strategic priorities of the firm, the role that purchasing occupies in the executive hierarchy, and the competitive challenges that the firm confronts.

Strategic Solutions   Organizational buying decisions are made to facilitate organizational activities and to support the firm's mission and strategies. A business marketer who understands the strategic priorities and concerns that occupy key decision makers is better equipped to deliver the desired solution. For example, IBM centers attention on how its information technology and assorted services can improve the efficiency of a retailer's operations or advance the customer service levels of a hotel chain. Alternatively, a supplier to Hewlett-Packard will strike a responsive chord with executives by offering a new component part that will increase the performance or lower the cost of its ink-jet printers. To provide such customer solutions, the business marketer requires an intimate understanding of the opportunities and threats that the customer confronts.

Strategic Role of Purchasing   In many firms, purchasing strategy is becoming more closely tied to corporate strategy. To illustrate, purchasing (sourcing) executives at Motorola have a clear understanding of the firm's objectives, markets, and competitive strategies.

> Ask the Paging Products Group's strategic sourcing director Neil MacIver what he knows about its markets, and he is fast to respond: "We know where we are strong and where we are not; we know why we are selling and why not. We go over the numbers in daily meetings. It is inherent in the nature of our jobs that we have to know this."[24]

Compared to traditional buyers, recent research suggests that more strategically oriented purchasing managers are (1) more receptive to information and draw it from a wide variety of sources; (2) more sensitive to the importance of longer-term supplier relationships, questions of price in relation to performance, and broader environmental issues; and (3) more focused on the competencies of suppliers in evaluating alternative firms.[25] Moreover, these purchasing managers are evaluated on performance dimensions that are more tightly linked to strategic performance.

Strategic Priorities in Purchasing   Given rising competitive pressures, purchasing managers are using rigorous cost modeling approaches to identify the factors that drive the cost of purchased goods and services (see Table 3.2). For example, Honda of America reduced the cost of the purchased content that goes into the Accord by setting cost targets for each component—engine, chassis, and so on.[26] Then, purchasing managers worked with suppliers to understand the cost structure of each component,

---

[24]Jordan D. Lewis, *The Connected Corporation: How Leading Companies Win through Customer-Supplier Alliances* (New York: The Free Press, 1995), p. 202.

[25]Robert E. Spekman, David W. Stewart, and Wesley J. Johnston, "An Empirical Investigation of the Organizational Buyer's Strategic and Tactical Roles," *Journal of Business-to-Business Marketing* 2, no. 4 (1995): pp. 37–63.

[26]Timothy M. Laseter, *Balanced Sourcing: Cooperation and Competition in Supplier Relationships* (San Francisco: Jossey-Bass Publishing, 1998), pp. 5–18.

TABLE 3.2	STRATEGIC PRIORITIES IN PURCHASING

Strategic Priority	Description
Modeling the Total Cost of Outside Purchases	Developing a clear grasp of the factors that drive the cost of purchased products and services.
Creating Purchasing Strategies Tied to Corporate Goals	Conducting a rigorous analysis of the supply industry to determine how suppliers can contribute fundamental value to corporate goals.
Building & Sustaining Supplier Relationships	Structuring relationships with key suppliers to achieve mutual dependence and goal congruence.
Integrating the Supply Chain	Managing purchase and flow of materials from suppliers through production and on to customers.
Leveraging Supplier Innovation	Creating value by bringing suppliers directly into the new product development process.

SOURCE: Adapted from Timothy M. Laseter, *Balanced Sourcing: Cooperation and Competition in Supplier Relationships* (San Francisco: Jossey-Bass Publishers, 1998), pp. 5–18.

observe how it is manufactured, and identify ways to reduce costs, add value, or do both.

To secure competitive advantages, purchasing managers are also tying purchasing strategies more directly to corporate goals to increase product quality, accelerate product development, capitalize on new technologies, or respond more quickly to changing customer expectations. Indeed, leading-edge purchasing organizations have learned that these results can only be achieved by building close relationships with suppliers and by using electronic data interchange (EDI) systems or the Internet to align the activities of the supply chain with the needs of customers. For example, IBM is working to get its 10,000 suppliers Internet-capable to automate all purchasing transactions and eliminate paperwork.[27]

As purchasing assumes a more strategic role in the firm, the business marketer must understand the competitive realities of the customer's business and develop a **value proposition**—products, services, ideas—that advances the performance goals of the customer organization. For example, Motorola's Paging Products Group is keenly interested in working with suppliers who can contribute technology or component parts that enhance the value of the firm's product for customers and that strengthen its competitive position.

Organizational Positioning of Purchasing

An organization that centralizes procurement decisions will approach purchasing differently than will a company where purchasing decisions are made at individual user locations. When purchasing is centralized, a separate organizational unit is given authority for purchases at a regional, divisional, or headquarters level. For example,

---

[27]James Carbone, "Reinventing Purchasing Wins the Medal for Big Blue," *Purchasing*, 127 (September 16, 1999), p. 60.

Mead Corporation's centralized purchasing function directs the purchase of common materials used by Mead plants across the United States. IBM, AT&T, 3M, Hewlett-Packard, and Xerox are among other corporations that emphasize centralized procurement. A marketer who is sensitive to organizational influences can more accurately map the decision-making process, isolate buying influentials, identify salient buying criteria, and target marketing strategy for both centralized as well as decentralized organizations.[28]

Centralization of Procurement: Contributing Factors   Why is there a trend toward centralizing purchasing? Several factors contribute to this trend. First, through centralization, purchasing strategy can be better integrated with corporate strategy. For example, the corporate procurement group at Compaq Computer Corporation was established to manage the purchase of strategic commodities, such as microprocessors and memory, on a worldwide basis. The centralized group maintains a close working relationship with fifty strategic suppliers who are fundamental to Compaq's success in the personal computer market.[29]

Second, an organization with multiple plant locations can often achieve cost savings by pooling common requirements. Before the procurement function was centralized at General Motors, 106 buying locations spent more than $10 million annually on nearly 24 million pairs of work gloves, buying over 200 styles from ninety sources. The cost savings generated from pooling the requirements for this item alone are substantial.

Third, the nature of the supply environment also can determine whether purchasing is centralized. If the supply environment is dominated by a few large sellers, centralized buying may be particularly useful in securing favorable terms and proper service. If the supply industry consists of many small firms, each covering limited geographical areas, decentralized purchasing may achieve better support.

Finally, the location of purchasing in the organization often hinges on the location of key buying influences. If engineering plays an active role in the purchasing process, the purchasing function must be in close organizational and physical proximity.

Centralization versus Decentralization   Centralized and decentralized procurement differ substantially.[30] Centralization leads to specialization. Purchasing specialists for selected items develop comprehensive knowledge of supply and demand conditions, vendor options, supplier cost factors, and other information relevant to the supply environment. This knowledge, and the significant volume of business that specialists control, enhances their buying strength and supplier options.

The priority given to selected buying criteria is also influenced by centralization or decentralization. By identifying the buyer's organizational domain, the marketer can generally identify the purchasing manager's objectives. Centralized purchasing units place more weight on strategic considerations such as long-term supply availability and

[28] E. Raymond Corey, *The Organizational Context of Industrial Buyer Behavior* (Cambridge, Mass.: Marketing Science Institute, 1978), pp. 99–112.

[29] James Carbone, "Compaq Uses World Class Suppliers to Stay #1," *Purchasing* 118 (17 August 1995): pp. 34–39; see also, Susan Avery, "Brunswick Saves Big Bucks by Centralizing Services Buy," *Purchasing* 127 (March 25, 1999), pp. 38–41.

[30] Joseph A. Bellizzi and Joseph J. Belonax, "Centralized and Decentralized Buying Influences," *Industrial Marketing Management* 11 (April 1982): pp. 111–115; Arch G. Woodside and David M. Samuel, "Observation of Centralized Corporate Procurement," *Industrial Marketing Management* 10 (July 1981): pp. 191–205; and E. Raymond Corey, *The Organizational Context of Industrial Buying Behavior*, pp. 6–12.

Targeting Buying Influentials: A Web Strategy

National Semiconductor produces components that are used in a wide range of products such as cellular phones. In designing a Web site for the company, Pat Brockett, head of worldwide sales and marketing, emphasized that the initiative should "target design engineers." Why? When engineers are designing new or improved products, they consult parts catalogs, review data sheets provided by preferred suppliers, and order samples that they can try out. "Brockett knew that the person with the most influence over the actual purchasing decision was the design engineer who designed National Semi's chips into the product, not the procurement officer who actually placed the order for the components to be used in building that product."

To better serve these buying influentials, the firm conducted focus groups with design engineers to determine what they wanted and needed

from a Web site. What they found was that design engineers want a site that includes minimal graphics and that is functional and quick. Moreover, they want detailed technical specifications, pricing information, software simulations, and a way to order samples.

By squarely responding to these needs, over 500,000 design engineers visit National Semi's Web site each month to get timely information about the particular products that best fit their special requirements. In turn, when a design engineer visits the site and reviews information about a particular product, that event is captured in the opportunity management system for the salesperson or distributor who serves that particular customer account.

SOURCE: Patricia B. Seybold, *Customers.Com: How to Create a Profitable Business Strategy for the Internet and Beyond* (New York: Times Books, 1998), pp. 88–93.

---

the development of a healthy supplier complex. Decentralized buyers may emphasize more tactical concerns such as short-term cost efficiency and profit considerations. Organizational buying behavior is greatly influenced by the monitoring system that measures the performance of the unit.

Personal selling skills and the brand preferences of users influence purchasing decisions more at user locations than at centralized buying locations. At user locations, E. Raymond Corey points out that "engineers and other technical personnel, in particular, are prone to be specific in their preferences, while nonspecialized, nontechnical buyers have neither the technical expertise nor the status to challenge them"[31] as can purchasing specialists at central locations. Differing priorities between central buyers and local users often lead to conflict in the buying organization. In stimulating demand at the user level, the marketer should assess the potential for conflict and attempt to develop a strategy that can resolve any differences between the two organizational units.

The organization of the marketer's selling strategy should parallel the organization of the purchasing function of key accounts. To avoid disjointed selling activities and internal conflict in the sales organization, and to serve the special needs of important customers, many business marketers have developed national account management programs to establish a close working relationship that, according to Benson Shapiro and Rowland Moriarty, "cuts across multiple levels, functions, and operating units in both the buying and selling organizations."[32] For example, the chief executive

---

[31] Corey, *The Organizational Context*, p. 13.

[32] Benson P. Shapiro and Rowland T. Moriarty, *National Account Management: Emerging Insights* (Cambridge, Mass.: Marketing Science Institute, 1982), p. 8; see also James Boles, Wesley Johnston, and Alston Gardner, "The Selection and Organization of National Accounts: A North American Perspective," *The Journal of Business & Industrial Marketing*, 14, (No. 4, 1999), pp. 264–275.

officers (CEOs) of each of the fifty major suppliers to Compaq Computer Corporation communicate regularly with Compaq's president and CEO. There is also frequent communication between Compaq and its suppliers at all corporate levels.[33] Thus, the trend toward the centralization of the procurement function on the buying side has been matched by the development of national account management programs on the selling side.

Group Forces

Multiple buying influences and group forces are critical in organizational buying decisions. The organizational buying process typically involves a complex set of smaller decisions made or influenced by several individuals. The degree of involvement of group members in the procurement process varies from routine rebuys, in which the purchasing agent simply takes into account the preferences of others, to complex new-task buying situations, in which a group plays an active role throughout the decision process.

The industrial salesperson must address three questions:

- Which organizational members take part in the buying process?

- What is each member's relative influence in the decision?

- What criteria are important to each member in evaluating prospective suppliers?

The salesperson who can correctly answer these questions is ideally prepared to meet the needs of a buying organization and has a high probability of becoming the chosen supplier.

The Buying Center   The concept of the buying center provides rich insights into the role of group forces in organizational buying behavior.[34] The **buying center** consists of those individuals who participate in the purchasing decision and who share the goals and risks arising from the decision. The size of the buying center varies, but an average buying center will include more than four persons per purchase; the number of people involved in all stages of one purchase may be as many as twenty.[35]

The composition of the buying center may change from one purchasing situation to another and is not prescribed by the organizational chart. A buying group evolves during the purchasing process in response to the information requirements of the specific purchase situation. Because organizational buying is a *process* rather than an isolated act, different individuals are important to the process at different times.[36] A

[33] Carbone, "Compaq Uses World Class Suppliers," p. 34.

[34] For a comprehensive review of buying center research, see Wesley J. Johnston and Jeffrey E. Lewin, "Organizational Buying Behavior: Toward an Integrative Framework," *Journal of Business Research* 35 (January 1996): pp. 1–15; and J. David Lichtenthal, "Group Decision Making in Organizational Buying: A Role Structure Approach," in *Advances in Business Marketing*, vol. 3, ed. Arch G. Woodside (Greenwich, Conn.: JAI Press, 1988), pp. 119–157.

[35] For example, see Robert D. McWilliams, Earl Naumann, and Stan Scott, "Determining Buying Center Size," *Industrial Marketing Management* 21 (February 1992): pp. 43–49.

[36] Ghingold and Wilson, "Buying Center Research and Business Marketing Practice," pp. 96–108; see also Gary L. Lilien and M. Anthony Wong, "Exploratory Investigation of the Structure of the Buying Center in the Metalworking Industry," *Journal of Marketing Research* 21 (February 1984): pp. 1–11.

TABLE 3.3	THE INVOLVEMENT OF BUYING CENTER PARTICIPANTS AT DIFFERENT STAGES OF THE PROCUREMENT PROCESS

Stages of Procurement Process for a Medical Supplier

Buying Center Participants	Identification of Need	Establishment of Objectives	Identification and Evaluation of Buying Alternatives	Selection of Suppliers
Physicians	High	High	High	High
Nursing	Low	High	High	Low
Administration	Moderate	Moderate	Moderate	High
Engineering	Low	Moderate	Moderate	Low
Purchasing	Low	Low	Low	Moderate

SOURCE: Adapted by permission of the publisher from Gene R. Laczniak, "An Empirical Study of Hospital Buying," *Industrial Marketing Management* 8 (January 1979), p. 61. Copyright © 1979 by Elsevier Science Publishing Co., Inc.

design engineer may exert significant influence early in the purchasing process when product specifications are being established; others may assume a more dominant role in later phases. A salesperson must define the buying situation and the information requirements from the organization's perspective in order to anticipate the size and composition of the buying center. Again, the composition of the buying center evolves during the purchasing process, varies from firm to firm, and varies from one purchasing situation to another.

Isolating the Buying Situation   Defining the buying situation and determining whether the firm is in the early or later stages of the procurement decision-making process are important first steps in defining the buying center. The buying center for a new-task buying situation in the not-for-profit market is presented in Table 3.3. The product, intensive-care monitoring systems, is a complex and costly purchase. Buying center members are drawn from five functional areas, each participating to varying degrees in the decision process. A marketer who concentrated exclusively on the purchasing function would be overlooking key buying influentials.

Erin Anderson and her colleagues queried a large sample of sales managers concerning the patterns of organizational buying behavior that their salespeople confront on a daily basis. Sales forces that frequently encounter new-task buying situations generally observe that:

> The buying center is large, slow to decide, uncertain about its needs and the appropriateness of the possible solutions, more concerned about finding a good solution than getting a low price or assured supply, more willing to entertain proposals from "out" suppliers and less willing to favor "in" suppliers, more influenced by technical personnel, [and] less influenced by purchasing agents.[37]

---

[37] Anderson, Chu, and Weitz, "Industrial Purchasing," p. 82.

E T H I C A L   B U S I N E S S   M A R K E T I N G

Close Buyer–Seller Relationships Pose New Ethical Threats

When asked to identify the greatest ethical threat confronting purchasing professionals, only a handful of buyers cited gross infractions such as bribes or kickbacks. Instead, most emphasize the risk of becoming too friendly with supplier personnel as relationships with suppliers become more cooperative. If a purchasing manager fails to survey competitive offerings, such friendships can lead to sub-optimal purchasing decisions, and—given the trend toward long-term contracts—the negative consequences of bad decisions can be magnified.

The free flow of strategic information between suppliers and customers raises other ethical issues.

One buyer suggested that using insider information to profit in the stock market is the greatest ethical danger confronting purchasing professionals today. For example, a publicly-held supplier may provide a purchasing manager with a detailed description of a promising new technology months in advance of a public release. An ethical problem emerges if the buyer trades stock based on that knowledge or passes information in the form of a stock tip to friends or family members.

SOURCE: Anne Millen Porter, "Supply Alliances Pose New Ethical Threats," *Purchasing*, 127 (May 20, 1999), pp. 20–22.

By contrast, Anderson and her colleagues found that sales forces facing more routine purchase situations (that is, straight and modified rebuys) frequently observe buying centers that are "small, quick to decide, confident in their appraisals of the problem and possible solutions, concerned about price and supply, satisfied with 'in' suppliers, and more influenced by purchasing agents."[38]

Predicting Composition   A marketer can also predict the composition of the buying center by projecting the impact of the industrial product on various functional areas in the buying organization. If the procurement decision will affect the marketability of a firm's product (for example, product design, price), the marketing department will be active in the decision process. Engineering will be influential in decisions about new capital equipment, materials, and components; setting specifications; defining product performance requirements; and qualifying potential vendors. Manufacturing executives will be included in the buying center for procurement decisions that affect the production mechanism (for example, the acquisition of materials or parts used in production). When procurement decisions involve a substantial economic commitment or impinge on strategic or policy matters, top management will have considerable influence.

Buying Center Influence   Members of the buying center assume different roles throughout the procurement process. Frederick Webster Jr. and Yoram Wind have given the following labels to each of these roles: users, influencers, buyers, deciders, and gatekeepers.[39]

As the role name implies, **users** are the personnel who will be using the product in question. Users may have anywhere from inconsequential to extremely important

---

[38] Ibid.

[39] Frederick E. Webster Jr. and Yoram Wind, *Organizational Buying Behavior* (Englewood Cliffs, N.J.: Prentice–Hall, 1972), p. 77. For a review of buying role research, see J. David Lichtenthal, "Group Decision Making in Organizational Buying," pp. 119–157.

influence on the purchase decision. In some cases, the users initiate the purchase action by requesting the product. They may even develop the product specifications.

Gatekeepers control information to be reviewed by other members of the buying center. The control of information may be accomplished by disseminating printed information, such as advertisements, or by controlling which salesperson will speak to which individuals in the buying center. To illustrate, the purchasing agent might perform this screening role by opening the gate to the buying center for some sales personnel and closing it to others.

Influencers affect the purchasing decision by supplying information for the evaluation of alternatives or by setting buying specifications. Typically, those in technical departments, such as engineering, quality control, and R&D, are significant influences on the purchase decision. Sometimes, individuals outside the buying organization can assume this role. For high-tech purchases, technical consultants often assume an influential role in the decision process and broaden the set of alternatives being considered.[40]

Deciders are the individuals who actually make the buying decision, whether or not they have the formal authority to do so. The identity of the decider is the most difficult role to determine: *buyers* may have formal authority to buy, but the president of the firm may actually make the decision. A decider could be a design engineer who develops a set of specifications that only one vendor can meet.

The **buyer** has formal authority to select a supplier and implement all procedures connected with securing the product. The power of the buyer is often usurped by more powerful members of the organization. The buyer's role is often assumed by the purchasing agent, who executes the administrative functions associated with a purchase order.

One person could assume all roles in a purchase situation or separate individuals could assume different buying roles. To illustrate, as users, personnel from marketing, accounting, purchasing, and production may all have a stake in which information technology system is selected. Thus, the buying center can be a very complex organizational phenomenon.

Identifying Patterns of Influence Key influencers are frequently located outside the purchasing department. To illustrate, the typical capital equipment purchase involves an average of four departments, three levels of the management hierarchy (for example, manager, regional manager, vice president), and seven different individuals.[41] In purchasing component parts, personnel from production and engineering are often most influential in the decision. It is interesting to note that a comparative study of organizational buying behavior found striking similarities across four countries (the United States, the United Kingdom, Australia, and Canada) with regard to the involvement of various departments in the procurement process.[42]

---

[40] Paul G. Patterson and Phillip L. Dawes, "The Determinants of Choice Set Structure in High-Technology Markets," *Industrial Marketing Management*, 28 (July 1999), pp. 395–411.

[41] Wesley J. Johnston and Thomas V. Bonoma, "The Buying Center: Structure and Interaction Patterns," *Journal of Marketing* 45 (summer 1981): pp. 143–156; see also Gary L. Lilien and M. Anthony Wong, "An Exploratory Investigation of the Structure of the Buying Center in the Metalworking Industry," *Journal of Marketing Research* 21 (February 1984): pp. 1–11 and Arch G. Woodside, Timo Liakko, and Risto Vuori, "Organizational Buying of Capital Equipment Involving Persons Across Several Authority Levels," *Journal of Business & Industrial Marketing*, 14, (No. 1, 1999), pp. 30–48.

[42] Peter Banting, David Ford, Andrew Gross, and George Holmes, "Similarities in Industrial Procurement across Four Countries," *Industrial Marketing Management* 14 (May 1985): pp. 133–144.

TABLE 3.4	CLUES FOR IDENTIFYING POWERFUL BUYING CENTER MEMBERS

- *Isolate the personal stakeholders.* Those individuals who have an important personal stake in the decision will exert more influence than other members of the buying center. For example, the selection of production equipment for a new plant will spawn the active involvement of manufacturing executives.

- *Follow the information flow.* Influential members of the buying center are central to the information flow that surrounds the buying decision. Other organizational members will direct information to them.

- *Identify the experts.* Expert power is an important determinant of influence in the buying center. Those buying center members who possess the most knowledge—and ask the most probing questions to the salesperson—are often influential.

- *Trace the connections to the top.* Powerful buying center members often have direct access to the top-management team. This direct link to valuable information and resources enhances the status and influence of the buying center members.

- *Understand purchasing's role.* Purchasing is dominant in repetitive buying situations by virtue of technical expertise, knowledge of the dynamics of the supplying industry, and close working relationships with individual suppliers.

SOURCE: Adapted from John R. Ronchetto, Michael D. Hutt, and Peter H. Reingen, "Embedded Influence Patterns in Organizational Buying Systems," *Journal of Marketing* 53 (October 1989), pp. 51–62.

Past research provides some valuable clues for identifying powerful buying center members (see Table 3.4).[43] To illustrate, individuals who have an important personal stake in the decision, possess expert knowledge concerning the choice at hand, and/or are central to the flow of decision-related information tend to assume an active and influential role in the buying center. Purchasing managers assume a dominant role in repetitive buying situations.

Based on their buying center research, Donald W. Jackson Jr. and his colleagues provide these strategy recommendations:

> Marketing efforts will depend upon which individuals of the buying center are more influential for a given decision. Since engineering and manufacturing are more influential in product selection decisions, they may have to be sold on product characteristics. On the other hand, since purchasing is most influential in supplier selection decisions, they may have to be sold on company characteristics.[44]

Individual Forces

Individuals, not organizations, make buying decisions. Each member of the buying center has a unique personality, a particular set of learned experiences, a specified

---

[43]John R. Ronchetto, Michael D. Hutt, and Peter H. Reingen, "Embedded Influence Patterns in Organizational Buying Systems," *Journal of Marketing* 53 (October 1989): pp. 51–62; see also Ajay Kohli, "Determinants of Influence in Organizational Buying: A Contingency Approach," *Journal of Marketing* 53 (July 1989): pp. 50–65; Daniel H. McQuiston and Peter R. Dickson, "The Effect of Perceived Personal Consequences on Participation and Influence in Organizational Buying," *Journal of Business Research* 23 (September 1991): pp. 159–177 and Jerome M. Katrichis, "Exploring Departmental Level Interaction Patterns in Organizational Purchasing Decisions," *Industrial Marketing Management*, 27 (March 1998), pp. 135–146.

[44]Jackson, Keith, and Burdick, "Purchasing Agents' Perceptions of Industrial Buying Center Influence," pp. 75–83.

organizational function, and a perception of how best to achieve both personal and organizational goals. Importantly, research confirms that organizational members who perceive that they have an important personal stake in the buying decision will participate more forcefully in the decision process than their colleagues.[45] To understand the organizational buyer, the marketer should be aware of individual perceptions of the buying situation.

Differing Evaluative Criteria **Evaluative criteria** are specifications that organizational buyers use to compare alternative industrial products and services; however, these may conflict. Industrial product users generally value prompt delivery and efficient servicing; engineering values product quality, standardization, and testing; and purchasing assigns the most importance to maximum price advantage and economy in shipping and forwarding.[46]

Product perceptions and evaluative criteria differ among organizational decision makers as a result of differences in educational backgrounds, source and type of information exposure, interpretation and retention of relevant information (perceptual distortion), and level of satisfaction with past purchases.[47] Engineers have an educational background different from that of plant managers or purchasing agents; they are exposed to different journals, attend different conferences, and possess different professional goals and values. A sales presentation that is effective with purchasing may be entirely off the mark with engineering.

Responsive Marketing Strategy A marketer who is sensitive to differences in the product perceptions and evaluative criteria of individual buying center members is well equipped to prepare responsive marketing strategy. To illustrate, a research study examined the industrial adoption of solar air-conditioning systems and identified the criteria of importance to key decision makers.[48] Buying center participants for this purchase typically include production engineers, heating and air-conditioning (HVAC) consultants, and top managers. The study revealed that marketing communications directed at production engineers should center on operating costs and energy savings; HVAC consultants should be addressed concerning noise level and initial cost of the system; and top managers are most interested in whether the technology is state-of-the-art. Knowledge of the criteria that key buying center participants employ is of significant operational value to the marketer when designing new products and when developing and targeting advertising and personal selling presentations.

Information Processing Volumes of information flow into every organization through direct mail advertising, the Internet, journal advertising, trade news, word of

---

[45] McQuiston and Dickson, "The Effect of Perceived Personal Consequences on Participation and Influence in Organizational Buying," pp. 159–177.

[46] Jagdish N. Sheth, "A Model of Industrial Buyer Behavior," *Journal of Marketing* 37 (October 1973): p. 51; see also Sheth, "Organizational Buying Behavior: Past Performance and Future Expectations," *The Journal of Business & Industrial Marketing* 11, no. 3/4 (1996): pp. 7–24.

[47] Sheth, "A Model of Industrial Buyer Behavior," pp. 52–54.

[48] Jean-Marie Choffray and Gary L. Lilien, "Assessing Response to Industrial Marketing Strategy," *Journal of Marketing* 42 (April 1978): pp. 20–31. For related research, see R. Venkatesh, Ajay K. Kohli, and Gerald Zaltman, "Influence Strategies in Buying Centers," *Journal of Marketing* 59 (October 1995): pp. 71–82; and Mark A. Farrell and Bill Schroder, "Influence Strategies in Organizational Buying Decisions," *Industrial Marketing Management* 25 (July 1996): pp. 293–303.

mouth, and personal sales presentations. What an individual organizational buyer chooses to pay attention to, comprehend, and retain has an important bearing on procurement decisions.

Selective Processes   Information processing is generally encompassed in the broader term **cognition,** which U. Neisser defines as "all the processes by which the sensory input is transformed, reduced, elaborated, stored, recovered, and used."[49] Important to an individual's cognitive structure are the processes of selective exposure, attention, perception, and retention.

1. *Selective exposure.* Individuals tend to accept communication messages that are consistent with their existing attitudes and beliefs. For this reason, a purchasing agent chooses to talk to some salespersons and not to others.

2. *Selective attention.* Individuals filter or screen incoming stimuli in order to admit only certain ones to cognition. Thus, an organizational buyer will be more likely to notice a trade advertisement that is consistent with his or her needs and values.

3. *Selective perception.* Individuals tend to interpret stimuli in terms of their existing attitudes and beliefs. This explains why organizational buyers may modify or distort a salesperson's message in order to make it more consistent with their predispositions toward the company.

4. *Selective retention.* Individuals tend to store in memory only information pertinent to their own needs and dispositions. An organizational buyer may retain information concerning a particular brand because it matches his or her criteria.

Each of these selective processes influences the way an individual decision maker will respond to marketing stimuli. Because the procurement process often spans several months and because the marketer's contact with the buying organization is infrequent, marketing communications must be carefully designed and targeted.[50] Poorly conceived messages will be "tuned out" or immediately forgotten by key decision makers. Those messages that are deemed important to achieving goals are retained.

Risk-Reduction Strategies   Individuals are motivated by a strong desire to reduce the level of risk in purchase decisions. The perceived risk concept includes two components: (1) uncertainty about the outcome of a decision, and (2) the magnitude of consequences associated with making the wrong choice. Research highlights the importance of perceived risk and the purchase type in shaping the structure of the decision-making unit.[51] Individual decision making is likely to occur in organizational buying for straight rebuys and for modified rebuy situations when the perceived risk is

---

[49] U. Neisser, *Cognitive Psychology* (New York: Appleton, 1966), p. 4.

[50] See, for example, Brent M. Wren and James T. Simpson, "A Dyadic Model of Relationships in Organizational Buying: A Synthesis of Research Results," *Journal of Business & Industrial Marketing* 11, no. 3/4 (1996): pp. 68–79.

[51] Elizabeth J. Wilson, Gary L. Lilien, and David T. Wilson, "Developing and Testing a Contingency Paradigm of Group Choice in Organizational Buying," *Journal of Marketing Research* 28 (November 1991): pp. 452–466.

INSIDE BUSINESS MARKETING

Best Practices for Customer Satisfaction in Business Marketing Firms

Keeping current customers satisfied is just as important as attracting new ones. Firms that have a reputation for delivering high levels of customer satisfaction do things differently than their competitors. The CEOs and presidents of these firms are obsessed with customers. In turn, employees throughout these organizations understand the link between their jobs (the particular tasks they perform) and customer satisfaction. All the divisions of these firms embrace customer satisfaction as a goal, but particular units are given the freedom to customize customer service performance measures to meet their own needs.

These leading-edge firms collect several kinds of customer satisfaction data. They capture overall trends with periodic surveys; they trace particular transactions and secure customer feedback on what could be improved; and they ask customers to rate the quality of the product, the service, and the interaction. Most importantly, these firms actively use the quantitative and qualitative data to inform decision making and to motivate employee performance. Customer satisfaction performance charts are prominently displayed on company walls. Compensation for managers at all organizational levels is tied to customer satisfaction measurements. Organizations that feature the best practices for customer satisfaction comprise managers who are focused on continuous improvement in the processes that create a satisfied customer.

SOURCE: Abbie Griffin, Greg Gleason, Rick Preiss, and Dave Shevenaugh, "Best Practices for Customer Satisfaction in Manufacturing Firms," *Sloan Management Review* 36 (winter 1995), pp. 87–90.

---

low. In these situations, the purchasing agent may initiate action.[52] Modified rebuys of higher risk and new tasks seem to spawn a group structure.

In confronting "risky" purchase decisions, how do organizational buyers behave? As the risk associated with an organizational purchase decision increases:[53]

- The buying center will become larger and will comprise members with high levels of organizational status and authority.

- The information search will be active and a wide variety of information sources will be consulted to guide and support an important purchase decision. As the decision process unfolds, personal information sources (for example, discussions with managers at other organizations that have made similar purchases) become more important.

- Buying center participants will be motivated to invest greater effort and to deliberate more carefully throughout the purchase process.

- Sellers who have a proven track record with the firm will be favored. The choice of a familiar supplier helps reduce the perceived risk associated with a purchase.

Rather than price, product quality and after-sale service are typically most important to organizational buyers when they confront "risky" decisions. When introducing new products, entering new markets, or approaching new customers, the

---

[52] Sheth, "A Model of Industrial Buyer Behavior," p. 54; see also W. E. Patton III, Charles P. Puto, and Ronald H. King, "Which Buying Decisions Are Made by Individuals and Not by Groups?" *Industrial Marketing Management* 15 (May 1986): pp. 129–138.

[53] Johnston and Lewin, "Organizational Buying Behavior: Toward an Integrative Framework," pp. 8–10. See also Puto, Patton, and King, "Risk Handling Strategies in Industrial Vendor Selection Decisions," pp. 89–95.

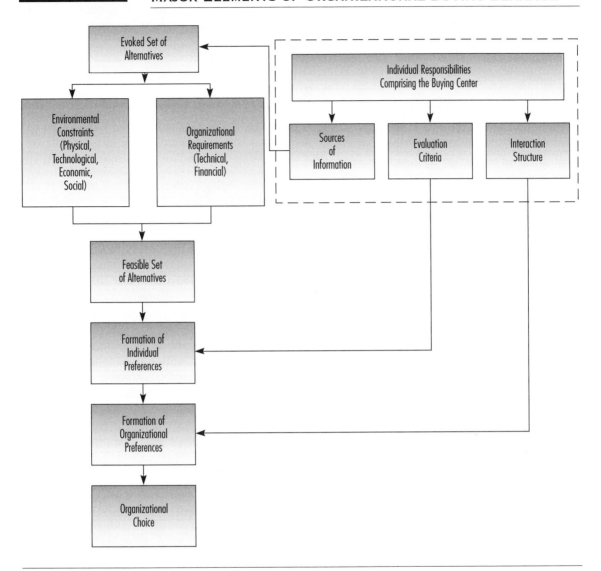

| FIGURE 3.6 | MAJOR ELEMENTS OF ORGANIZATIONAL BUYING BEHAVIOR |

SOURCE: Jean-Marie Choffray and Gary L. Lilien, "Assessing Response to Industrial Marketing Strategy," *Journal of Marketing* 42 (April 1978), p. 22. Reprinted by permission of the American Marketing Association.

marketing strategist should evaluate the impact of alternative strategies on perceived risk.

The Organizational Buying Process: Major Elements

The behavior of organizational buyers is influenced by environmental, organizational, group, and individual factors. Each of these spheres of influence has been discussed in an organizational buying context, with particular attention to how the industrial marketer should interpret these forces and, more important, factor them directly into marketing strategy planning. A model of the organizational buying process is presented in Figure 3.6, which serves to reinforce and integrate the key areas discussed so far in this chapter.[54]

This framework focuses on the relationship between an organization's buying center and the three major stages in the individual purchase decision process:

1. The screening of alternatives that do not meet organizational requirements

2. The formation of decision participants' preferences

3. The formation of organizational preferences

Observe that individual members of the buying center use various evaluative criteria and are exposed to various sources of information, which influence the industrial brands that are included in the buyer's **evoked set of alternatives**—the alternative brands that a buyer calls to mind when a need arises and that represent only a few of the many brands available.[55]

Environmental constraints and organizational requirements influence the procurement process by limiting the number of product alternatives that satisfy organizational needs. For example, capital equipment alternatives that exceed a particular cost (initial or operating) may be eliminated from further consideration. The remaining brands become the **feasible set of alternatives** for the organization, from which individual preferences are defined. The **interaction structure** of the members of the buying center, who have differing criteria and responsibilities, leads to the formation of organizational preferences and ultimately to organizational choice.

An understanding of the organizational buying process enables the marketer to play an active rather than a passive role in stimulating market response. The marketer who identifies organizational screening requirements and the salient evaluative criteria of individual buying center members can make more informed product design, pricing, and promotional decisions.

Summary

Knowledge of the process that organizational buyers follow in making purchasing decisions is fundamental to responsive marketing strategy. As a buying organization moves from the problem recognition phase, in which a procurement need is defined, to later phases, in which suppliers are screened and ultimately chosen, the marketer can play an active role. In fact, the astute marketer often triggers initial awareness of the problem and aids the organization in effectively solving that problem. Incremental decisions made throughout the buying process narrow the field of acceptable suppliers and dramatically influence the ultimate outcome.

---

[54] Choffray and Lilien, "Assessing the Response to Industrial Marketing Strategy," pp. 20–31. Other models of organizational buying behavior include Webster and Wind, *Organizational Buying Behavior*, pp.28–37; and Sheth, "A Model of Industrial Buyer Behavior," pp. 50–56. For a comprehensive review, see Sheth, "Organizational Buying Behavior," pp. 7–24; and Johnston and Lewin, "Organizational Buying Behavior," pp. 1–15.

[55] Howard and Sheth, *The Theory of Buyer Behavior*, p. 26; see also Ronald P. LeBlanc, "Environmental Impact on Purchase Decision Structure," *Journal of Purchasing and Materials Management* 17 (spring 1981): pp. 30–36; and Lowell E. Crow, Richard W. Olshavsky, and John O. Summers, "Industrial Buyers' Choice Strategies: A Protocol Analysis," *Journal of Marketing Research* 17 (February 1980): pp. 34–44.

The nature of the buying process depends on the organization's level of experience with similar procurement problems. It is thus crucial to know how the organization defines the buying situation: as a new task, a modified rebuy, or a straight rebuy. Each buying situation requires a unique problem-solving approach, involves unique buying influentials, and demands a unique marketing response.

A myriad of forces—which can be classified as environmental, organizational, group, and individual—influence organizational buying behavior. First, environmental forces define the boundaries within which industrial buyers and sellers interact, such as the general business conditions or the rate of technological change. Second, organizational forces dictate the link between buying activities and the strategic priorities of the firm and the position that the purchasing function occupies in the organizational structure. Third, the relevant unit of analysis for the marketing strategist is the buying center. The composition of this group evolves during the buying process, varies from firm to firm, and changes from one purchasing situation to another. Fourth, the marketer must ultimately concentrate attention on individual members of the buying center. Each has a particular set of experiences and a unique personal and organizational frame of reference to bring to bear on the buying decision. The marketer who is sensitive to individual differences is best equipped to develop responsive marketing communications that will be remembered by the organizational buyer.

Unraveling the complex forces that encircle the organizational buying process is indeed difficult. This chapter offers a framework that enables the marketing manager to begin this task by asking the right questions. The answers will provide the basis for effective and efficient business marketing strategy.

Discussion Questions

1. Ford revamped the way in which it purchases operating resources such as office, computer, and maintenance supplies. Instead of having employees fill out purchase orders that must be cleared by the boss days later, employees simply log on to an Internet system. They browse through the electronic catalogs of manufacturers, order from a preapproved group of suppliers, and get purchase approval in minutes. What new challenges and opportunities does the e-procurement system present for business marketers who serve Ford?

2. Jim Jackson, an industrial salesperson for Pittsburgh Machine Tool, will call on two accounts this afternoon. The first will be a buying organization that Jim has been servicing for the past three years. The second call, however, poses more of a challenge. This buying organization has been dealing with a prime competitor of Pittsburgh Machine Tool for five years. Jim, who has a good rapport with the purchasing and engineering departments, feels that the time may be right to penetrate this account. Recently, Jim learned that the purchasing manager was extremely unhappy with the poor delivery service provided by the firm's existing supplier. Define the buying situations confronting Jim and outline the appropriate strategy that he should follow in each case.

3. Karen Weber, the purchasing agent for Smith Manufacturing, views the purchase of widgets as a routine buying decision. What factors might lead her to alter this position? More important, what factors will determine whether a particular supplier, such as Albany Widget, will be considered by Karen?

4. Harley-Davidson, the U.S. motorcycle producer, recently purchased some sophisticated manufacturing equipment to enhance its position in a very competitive market. First, what environmental forces might have been important in spawning this capital investment? Second, which functional units were likely to have been represented in the buying center?

5. Brunswick Corporation centralizes its procurement decisions at the headquarters level. Discuss how it would approach purchasing differently than a competitor that decentralizes purchasing across various plant locations.

6. The Kraus Toy Company recently decided to develop a new electronic game. Can an electrical parts supplier predict the likely composition of the buying center at Kraus Toy? What steps could an industrial salesperson take to influence the composition of the buying center?

7. Explain how the composition of the buying center evolves during the purchasing process and how it varies from one firm to another, as well as from one purchasing situation to another. What steps can a salesperson take to identify the influential members of the buying center?

8. Carol Brooks, purchasing manager for Apex Manufacturing Co., read *The Wall Street Journal* this morning and carefully studied, clipped, and saved a full-page ad by the Allen-Bradley Company. Ralph Thornton, the production manager at Apex, read several articles from the same paper but could not recall seeing this particular ad or, for that matter, any ads. How could this occur?

9. Millions of notebook computers are purchased each year by organizations. Identify several evaluative criteria that purchasing managers might use in choosing a particular brand. In your view, which criteria would be most decisive in the buying decision?

10. The levels of risk associated with organizational purchases range on a continuum from low to high. Discuss how the buying process for a risky purchase differs from the process that is triggered for a routine purchase.

II

Managing Relationships
in Business Marketing

4

Relationship Strategies for Business Markets

A well-developed ability to create and sustain successful working relationships with customers and alliance partners gives business marketing firms a significant competitive advantage. After reading this chapter, you will understand

1. the patterns of buyer–seller relationships in the business market.

2. the relationship connectors that are used in different types of buyer–seller relationships.

3. a procedure for designing effective relationship marketing strategies.

4. the critical determinants of success in managing strategic alliances.

The ability of an organization to create and maintain relationships with their most valuable customers is a durable basis for a competitive advantage.[1] On providing superior value to customers, Gary Tooker, vice chairman of Motorola, aptly describes the competitive challenge:

> Fame is a fleeting thing. When the alarm rings tomorrow morning, you'd better get up and understand that your customers expect more from you than they did the day before. You'd better find ways to be better.[2]

A business marketer who wishes to find a place on Motorola's preferred list of suppliers must be prepared to help the firm provide more value to its demanding customers. To this end, the marketer must provide exceptional performance in quality, delivery, and, over time, cost competitiveness. The supplier must also understand how Motorola measures value and how these value expectations can be met or surpassed in the supplier's product and service offering. Building and maintaining lasting customer relationships requires careful attention to detail, meeting promises, and swiftly responding to new requirements.

The new era of business marketing is built upon effective relationship management. Many business marketing firms create what might be called a "collaborative advantage" by demonstrating special skills in managing relationships with key customers or by jointly developing innovative strategies with alliance partners.[3] These firms have learned how to be good partners and these superior relationship skills are a valuable asset in the business market. This chapter explores the types of relationships that characterize the business market. What market and situational factors are associated with different types of buyer–seller relationships? What strategies can business marketers employ to build profitable relationships with customers? What are the special challenges and opportunities that emerge when two firms collaborate in a strategic alliance?

Relationship Marketing[4]

Relationship marketing centers on all activities directed toward establishing, developing, and maintaining successful exchanges with customers and other constituents.[5] The nurturing and management of customer relationships has emerged as an important strategic priority in most firms. Why? First, loyal customers are far more profitable to keep than those customers who are price sensitive and perceive little differences among alternative offerings. Second, a firm that is successful in developing strong relationships with customers secures important and durable advantages that are hard for competitors to understand, copy, or to displace.

---

[1] George S. Day, "Managing Market Relationships," *Journal of the Academy of Marketing Science* 28 (winter 2000), p. 24.

[2] Jordan D. Lewis, *The Connected Organization: How Leading Companies Win through Customer-Supplier Alliances* (New York: The Free Press, 1995), p. 289.

[3] Rosabeth Moss Kanter, "Collaborative Advantage," *Harvard Business Review* 72 (July/August 1994), pp. 96–108.

[4] This section is based on George S. Day, "Managing Market Relationships," pp. 24–30, except when others are cited.

[5] Robert M. Morgan and Shelby D. Hunt, "The Commitment-Trust Theory of Relationship Marketing," *Journal of Marketing* 58 (July 1994), pp. 20–38.

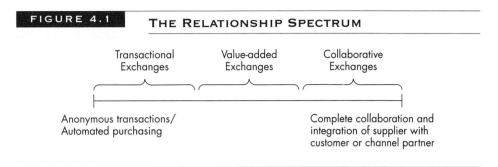

FIGURE 4.1   THE RELATIONSHIP SPECTRUM

Reprinted with permission from George S. Day, "Managing Market Relationships," *Journal of the Academy of Marketing Science* 28 (winter 2000), p. 25. Copyright © 2000, Sage Publications.

Types of Relationships

A business marketer may begin a relationship with General Electric (GE) as a supplier (one of many), move to a preferred supplier status (one of a few), and ultimately enter a collaborative relationship with GE (sole source for particular items). Observe in Figure 4.1 that buyer–seller relationships are positioned on a continuum with transactional exchange and collaborative exchange serving as the end points. Central to every relationship is an exchange process where each side gives something in return for a payoff of greater value. **Transactional exchange** centers on the timely exchange of basic products for highly competitive market prices. George Day notes that such exchanges

> include the kind of autonomous encounters a visitor to a city has with the taxi or bus from the airport, as well as series of ongoing transactions in a business-to-business market where the customer and supplier focus only on the timely exchange of standard products at competitive prices.[6]

Moving across the continuum, relationships become closer or more collaborative. **Collaborative exchange** features very close information, social, and operational linkages as well as mutual commitments made in expectation of long-run benefits. According to James Anderson and James Narus, collaborative exchange involves

> a process where a customer and supplier firm form strong and extensive social, economic, service, and technical ties over time, with the intent of lowering total costs and/or increasing value, thereby achieving mutual benefit.[7]

Value-Adding Exchanges

Between the two extremes on the relationship continuum are value-adding exchanges, where the focus of the selling firm shifts from attracting customers to keeping customers. The marketer pursues this objective by developing a comprehensive

---

[6]Day, "Managing Market Relationships," p. 25.

[7]James C. Anderson and James A. Narus, "Partnering as a Focused Market Strategy," *California Management Review* 33 (spring 1991): p. 96. See also Ven Srivam, Robert Krapfel, and Robert Spekman, "Antecedents to Buyer-Seller Collaboration: An Analysis from the Buyer's Perspective," *Journal of Business Research* (December 1992), pp. 303–320.

understanding of a customer's needs and changing requirements, tailoring the firm's offerings to those needs, and providing continuing incentives for customers to concentrate most of their purchases with them. To illustrate, Dell Computer provides a customized Web page for each of its premier corporate customers that individual employees in the customer organization can access for an array of information and technical support services.

Nature of Relationships

Transactional exchange involves items like packaging materials or cleaning services where competitive bidding is often employed to secure the best terms. Such exchanges are purely contractual arrangements that involve little or no emotional commitment to sustaining the relationship in the future. By contrast, customized, high-technology products—like semiconductor test equipment—fit the collaborative exchange category. While transactional exchange centers on negotiations and an arm's-length relationship, collaborative exchange emphasizes joint problem solving and multiple linkages that integrate the processes of the two parties. Trust and commitment provide the foundation for collaborative exchange.[8] **Relationship commitment** involves the belief by a partner that an ongoing relationship is so important that it deserves maximum efforts to maintain it. In turn, **trust** exists when one party has confidence in a partner's reliability and integrity.

Strategic Choices

Business marketers have some latitude in choosing where to participate along the relationship continuum. However, there are limits imposed by the characteristics of the market and by the significance of the purchase to the buying organization. A central challenge for the marketer is to overcome the gravitational pull toward the transaction end of the exchange spectrum.

> Rivals are continually working to attract the best accounts away; customer requirements, expectations, and preferences keep changing, and the possibility of friction-free exploration of options in real time on the Web conspire to raise the rate of customer defections.[9]

To meet this challenge, managers must learn to forge mutually beneficial relationships with customers by developing a deep understanding of their needs and by providing the product or service solutions that precisely address those needs.

Buyer–Seller Connector [10]

In business markets, there is intense pressure to improve the efficiency and effectiveness of critical functions on both the buying and selling sides. Across the relationship

---

[8]Morgan and Hunt, "The Commitment-Trust Theory," pp. 20–38. See also Patricia M. Doney and Joseph P. Cannon, "An Examination of the Nature of Trust in Buyer-Seller Relationships," *Journal of Marketing* 61 (April 1997), pp. 35–51.

[9]Day, "Managing Market Relationships," p. 25.

[10]Joseph P. Cannon and William D. Perreault Jr., "Buyer-Seller Relationships in Business Markets," *Journal of Marketing Research* 36 (November 1999), pp. 439–460.

| FIGURE 4.2 | SCHEMATIC OVERVIEW OF KEY CONSTRUCTS RELEVANT TO THE PRACTICE OF BUYER–SELLER RELATIONSHIPS |

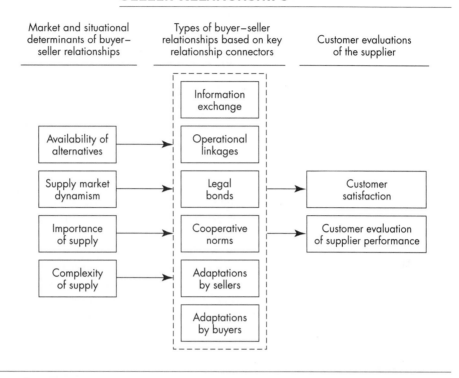

SOURCE: Joseph P. Cannon and William D. Perreault, Jr., "Buyer-Seller Relationships in Business Markets," *Journal of Marketing Research* 36 (November 1999), pp. 442. Reprinted with permission from the *Journal of Marketing Research*, published by the American Marketing Association.

spectrum, different types of relationships emphasize different relationship connectors—the way in which the two parties interrelate and conduct business (see Figure 4.2). **Relationship connectors** reflect the behaviors and expectations of the parties in a particular buyer–seller relationship.

Information Exchange

Information exchange involves the expectation that information will be openly shared in order to benefit both parties. Here the parties are willing to share important, even proprietary, information such as product development plans or cost data. Greater sharing of information can improve product quality and speed product development but the practice may open the door for opportunistic behavior by one of the parties. The open exchange of information is a characteristic of *collaborative* (close) versus *transactional* (distant) exchange.

Operational Linkages

Operational linkages reflect the degree to which the systems, procedures, and routines of the buying and selling firms have been connected to facilitate operations. Such linkages provide the basis for order replenishment or the just-in-time deliveries that

Honda receives each day from suppliers at its Marysville, Ohio production facility. Also, firms like Dell Computer and Cisco Systems are using the Internet to exchange information with customers and to deliver technical support to them.

Legal Bonds

Legal bonds are binding, contractual agreements that define the obligations of both parties in the relationship. While formal contracts are common in the business market, many firms still prefer to operate with a "handshake" agreement. Legal bonds provide protection if something goes wrong but contracts may become liabilities if they reduce the flexibility of the relationship partners in responding to environmental changes.

Cooperative Norms

Cooperative norms reflect the expectations that two exchange partners have about working together to achieve mutual and individual goals. This relationship connector reflects what the two parties believe is appropriate behavior regarding cooperation. High cooperation would be characterized by two parties who treat problems as joint responsibilities, while low cooperation involves a relationship where each of the parties works independently to achieve individual goals. Although the popular press highlights the shift toward buyer–seller cooperation, the trend is not universal. For example, General Motors attempts to achieve cost savings by fostering vigorous supplier competition and arms-length relationships. By contrast, DaimlerChrysler has achieved similar goals by actively cooperating with suppliers and securing valuable cost-saving ideas from them.[11]

Relationship-specific Adaptations by the Seller or Buyer

Relationship-specific adaptations involve investments in processes, products, or procedures that are made to meet the specific needs of an exchange partner. Such relationship-specific investments are common in the business market. For example, Guardian Industries designed a new manufacturing process to provide the expansive windshields used by DaimlerChrysler in its LH series. Buying firms may also adapt to the needs or capabilities of a particular supplier. Dell Computer often designs its personal computers to work with a particular Intel chip. Relationship-specific investments have little value outside a particular relationship; to the extent that these adaptations create value, they increase switching costs.

Market and Situational Factors

Market and situational factors are also important determinants of the form buyer-seller relationships will take in the business market (see Figure 4.2). A buying organization secures needed inputs from the supply market. While a variety of supply market factors may influence the nature of buyer–seller relationships, two are worthy of special attention—supply market dynamism and the availability of alternatives.

---

[11] Jeffrey H. Dyer, Dong Sung Cho, and Wujin Chu, "Strategic Supplier Segmentation: The Next 'Best Practice' in Supply Chain Management," *California Management Review* 40 (winter 1998), pp. 57–77.

Supply Market Conditions   **Supply market dynamism** involves the degree of variability in a firm's supply market. These variations might include factors such as changing technology, frequent price changes, or periodic product shortages. A volatile supply market creates uncertainty and risk for the buying organization. Here the potential risks and rewards of market dynamism can influence the shape of the buyer–seller relationship. Joseph Cannon and William D. Perreault, Jr. observe:

> In such an environment, closer interaction with a particular supplier may create opportunities to learn about and manage future developments. However, such locking-in can create switching costs that make it difficult to change quickly to a superior alternative if, for example, a competing technology offers benefits to the buying firm.[12]

The availability of alternatives also affects the nature of the buyer–seller relationship. The **availability of alternatives** is simply the degree to which alternative sources are available to meet a particular need. The lack of available sources of supply creates uncertainty and prompts the buying firm to seek a close relationship with a supplier. By contrast, readily available alternatives provide market conditions that allow purchasing managers to operate at arm's length with suppliers.

Characteristics of the Buying Situation   Beyond the broader supply market, the characteristics of the buying situation also can create uncertainty for buyers. Some purchases are more complex than others and some of them are far more important to the firm's operations than others. **Complexity of supply** involves the degree of difficulty a purchasing manager has in evaluating purchase choices and supplier performance. When supply needs are complex, the buying firm is likely to opt for a close relationship with a supplier. The **importance of supply** reflects the buying firm's perceptions of the strategic significance of a particular purchase to the organization's objectives. For example, an auto maker might divide purchases into two primary categories: strategic and nonstrategic purchases.[13] Strategic purchases are high-value inputs that relate to the firm's core competencies and that may be useful in differentiating the buying firm's product. At Honda, these are items such as transmission and engine parts, air conditioners, and instrument panels. These components and parts are customized to a particular model and help differentiate the Honda from competing models. Nonstrategic purchases include those items like batteries and tires that are not customized and do not differentiate the model. To optimize the purchasing strategy, buying firms across industries are beginning to segment the supply base: buyers seek a close relationship for strategic purchases and employ a more distant arm's-length approach in procuring nonstrategic items.

Customer Evaluation of Suppliers

Customer evaluations of supplier performance and satisfaction represent the important outcomes of buyer–seller exchange in the business market. Research suggests that more closely coupled buyer–seller relationships generally evoke the highest customer

---

[12] Cannon and Perreault, "Buyer-Seller Relationships," p. 444.

[13] Dyer, Cho, and Chu, "Strategic Supplier Segmentation," p. 68.

INSIDE BUSINESS MARKETING

Understanding the Customer's Business—The Key To Success

To forge a collaborative relationship with a customer, the business marketer requires a deep understanding of the customer's business, its key competitors, and its goals and strategies. In turn, a wealth of communication links are required across the partnering organizations at all levels of management. Salespersons work not only with the purchasing staff, but also have close ties to senior executives. For example, for some of IBM's *Fortune-*500 customers, account executives are direct participants in the customer firm's strategy planning

sessions. Here IBM adds value to the relationship by providing specific recommendations concerning how its products and services can be used to advance the firm's competitive advantage. As a relationship with a large account grows and flourishes, a full-time sales team is often created to serve the needs of that customer. The team is comprised of sales, service, and technical specialists who have extensive knowledge of the customer's industry. Some team members have worked exclusively with a single customer organization for years.

---

evaluations of supplier performance. However, the most closely coupled buyer–seller relationships are not necessarily the most satisfying ones in the eyes of the customer. To illustrate, when a close relationship involves specific adaptations by the customer, satisfaction tends to be lower. In contrast, customer satisfaction with simple exchange relationships nearly rivals the level of satisfaction found in more closely coupled relationships.[14] Such results reflect the differing customer expectations or differing demands placed on suppliers in close versus more distant relationships.

Managing Buyer–Seller Relationships

Buyers and sellers craft different types of relationships in response to market conditions and the characteristics of the purchase situation. To develop specific relationship marketing strategies for a particular customer, the business marketer must understand that some customers will elect a collaborative relationship while others will prefer a more distant or transactional relationship. Figure 4.3 highlights the typical characteristics of relationships at the end points of the buyer–seller relationship spectrum.

Transactional Exchange

Customers are more likely to prefer a **transactional relationship** when there is a competitive supply market featuring many alternatives, the purchase decision is not complex, and the supply market is stable. In turn, customers emphasize a transactional orientation when the purchase is viewed as less important to the organization's objectives. Such relationships are characterized by lower levels of information exchange and are less likely to involve operational linkages between the buying and selling firms.

Collaborative Exchange

Buying firms prefer a more **collaborative relationship** when there are few alternatives, the market is dynamic (for example, rapidly changing technology), and the

---

[14]Cannon and Perreault, p. 454.

FIGURE 4.3	THE SPECTRUM OF BUYER–SELLER RELATIONSHIPS	
	Transactional Exchange ←——→	Collaborative Exchange
Availability of Alternatives	Many Alterations	Few Alternatives
Supply Market Dynamism	Stable	Volatile
Importance of Purchase	Low	High
Complexity of Purchase	Low	High
Information Exchange	Low	High
Operational Linkages	Limited	Extensive

SOURCE: Adapted from Joseph P. Cannon and William D. Perreault, Jr., "Buyer-Seller Relationships in Business Markets," *Journal of Marketing Research* 36 (November 1999), pp. 439–460.

complexity of the purchase is high. In particular, customers seek close relationships with suppliers when the purchase is deemed to be important and strategically significant to the buying organization. Indeed,

> the closest partnerships . . . arise both when the purchase is important and when there is a need—from the customer's perspective—to overcome procurement obstacles that result from fewer supply alternatives and more purchase uncertainty.[15]

Moreover, the relationships that arise for important purchases are the ones that are more likely to involve operational linkages and high levels of information exchange.

Strategy Guidelines

The business marketer manages a portfolio of relationships with customers—some of these customers view the purchase as important and desire a close, tightly connected buyer–seller relationship; other customers assign a lower level of importance to the purchase and prefer a more loosely connected relationship. Given the differing needs and orientations of customers, the first step for the business marketer is to determine which type of relationship matches the purchasing situation and supply market conditions for a particular customer. Second, a strategy must be designed that is appropriate for each strategy type.

[15] Ibid., p. 453.

Finding the Right Match   For collaborative customers, business marketers can sensibly invest resources in order to secure commitments and to directly assist customers with planning. Here sales and service personnel will work not only with purchasing managers in the customer firm, but also with a wide array of managers on strategy and coordination issues. Regular visits to the customer organization by executives and technical personnel can strengthen the relationship. Operational linkages and information-sharing mechanisms should be designed into the relationship to keep product and service offerings aligned with customer needs.

Transaction customers display less loyalty or commitment to a particular supplier, and can easily switch part or all of the purchases from one vendor to another. A business marketer who offers an immediate, attractive combination of product, price, technical support, and other benefits has a chance of winning business from a transactional customer. The salesperson centers primary attention on the purchasing staff and seldom has important ties to senior executives in the buying organization. M. Bensaou argues that it is unwise for marketers to make specialized investments in transactional relationships: [16]

> Firms that invest in building trust through frequent visits, guest engineers, and cross-company teams when the product and market context calls for simple, impersonal control and data exchange mechanisms are overdesigning the relationship. This path is not only costly but also risky, given the specialized investments involved, in particular, the intangible ones (for example, people, information, or knowledge).

Rather than adopting the approach of "one design fits all," the astute marketer matches the strategy to the product and market conditions that surround a particular customer relationship.

Relationship Marketing Strategies

Business marketers often have a portfolio of customers who span the account behavior spectrum: Some emphasize low price and a transaction perspective while others place a premium on substantial service and desire a more collaborative relationship. Indeed, some customers fall somewhat in the middle of the account spectrum and represent accounts that might be effectively upgraded to a level that adds value to the relationship for both parties. To develop responsive and profitable relationship marketing strategies, special attention must be given to five areas: (1) capturing relationship data, (2) selecting accounts, (3) developing account-specific product offerings, (4) implementing relationship strategies, and (5) evaluating relationship strategy outcomes. [17]

Capturing Relationship Data

Accurate customer information provides the foundation for successful relationship marketing strategies. To be useful, the firm's data banks should provide a profile of the history of each customer relationship, identify key decision makers, isolate past

---

[16] M. Bensaou, "Portfolio of Buyer-Seller Relationships," *Sloan Management Review* 40 (summer 1999), p. 43.

[17] This section draws on Anderson and Narus, "Partnering as a Focused Market Strategy," pp. 95–113.

FIGURE 4.4	SALES.COM: A LEADING WEB-BASED PROVIDER OF CUSTOMER RELATIONSHIP MANAGEMENT TOOLS

SOURCE: Courtesy, Siebel Systems, Inc.

purchases across all product lines, and profile the customer's requirements and potential.[18] To capture customer data and transform it into valuable information to guide strategy, business marketers are rapidly adopting customer relationship management software from leading producers such as Oracle Corporation and Siebel Systems. A range of Web-based account management tools are also available to business marketers. To illustrate, Sales.com is an application service provider that provides sales professionals with a complete suite of sales productivity solutions, including account management software licensed from Siebel (see Figure 4.4). Sales.com delivers daily information on key accounts and competitors. Also, a comprehensive sales prospector data base of over 15 million names is provided and enriched by company-specific information from Dunn & Bradstreet.

---

[18] Ian H. Gordon, *Relationship Marketing* (New York: John Wiley & Sons, 1998), pp. 194–216.

Account Selection

Account selection requires a clear understanding of customer needs, a tight grasp on the costs that will be incurred in serving different groups of customers, and an accurate forecast of potential profit opportunities. The choice of potential accounts to target is facilitated by an understanding of how different customers define value. **Value,** as defined by James Anderson and James Narus, refers to "the economic, technical, service, and social benefits received by a customer firm in exchange for the price paid for a product offering."[19] By gauging the value of their offerings to different groups of customers, business marketers are better equipped to target accounts and to determine how to provide enhanced value to particular customers.

The account selection process should also consider profit potential. Because the product is critical to their operations, some customers place a high value on supporting services (for example, technical advice and training) and are willing to pay a premium price for this support. Other customers do not value service support and are extremely price sensitive in making product selection decisions. Frank Cespedes asserts that

> Account selection, therefore, must be explicit about which demands the seller can meet and leverage in dealings with other customers. Otherwise, the seller risks overserving unprofitable accounts and wasting resources that might be allocated to other customer groups.[20]

Developing Account-Specific Product Offerings

To develop customer-specific product offerings, the business marketer should next examine the nature of buyer–seller relationships that characterize the industry. The strategies pursued by competing firms in an industry fall into a range referred to as the **industry bandwidth** of working relationships. Business marketers either attempt to span the bandwidth with a portfolio of relationship marketing strategies or concentrate on a single strategy, thereby having a narrower range of relationships than the industry bandwidth.

Observe in Figure 4.5 how three different industries (corrugated box, fiber drum, and programmable controllers) are positioned on the relationship continuum. Because of the complexity and dynamic nature of the underlying technology, collaborative relations characterize the programmable controller industry. Here the core product can be augmented by a range of services such as the codesign of unique manufacturing systems, installation, training, and maintenance agreements. By contrast, collaborative relations in the fiber drum industry tend to be more focused and center on helping customers adapt their operational procedures (for example, lifting and stacking) to accommodate fiber drums. Because many buyers view the product as a commodity, long-term supply agreements and just-in-time inventory programs represent the only vehicle for collaboration in the corrugated box industry.

---

[19] Anderson and Narus, p. 98.

[20] Frank V. Cespedes, *Concurrent Marketing: Integrating Product, Sales, and Service* (Boston: Harvard Business School Press, 1995), p. 193. See also Don Peppers, Martha Rogers, and Bob Dorf, "Is Your Company Ready for One-to-One Marketing?" *Harvard Business Review* 77 (January/February 1999), pp. 151–160.

TRANSACTIONAL AND COLLABORATIVE WORKING RELATIONSHIPS

(a) Industry Relationship Bandwidths

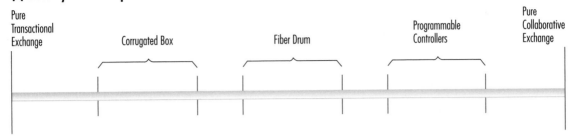

(b) "Flaring Out" from the Industry Bandwidth

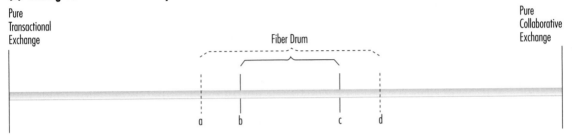

SOURCE: Adapted from James C. Anderson and James A. Narus, "Partnering as a Focused Marketing Strategy," *California Management Review* 33 (spring 1991), p. 97. Copyright © 1991 by the Regents of the University of California. Reprinted by permission of the Regents.

By diagnosing the spectrum of relationship strategies followed by competitors in an industry, a business marketer can tailor strategies that more closely respond both to customers who desire a collaborative emphasis as well as to those who seek a transaction emphasis. The strategy involves *flaring out* from the industry bandwidth in the collaborative as well as in the transactional direction (see Figure 4.5b).

Flaring Out by Unbundling An unbundling strategy can be pursued to reach those customers who desire a greater transaction emphasis. Here related services are unbundled to yield the core product (**a** in Figure 4.5b), which meets the basic price, quality, and availability requirements of customers. For each service that is unbundled, the price is lowered. Augmented services, such as technical assistance and delivery, are each offered, but in a menu fashion, on an incremental price basis. Importantly, the price increments for the entire set of unbundled services should be greater than the price premium sought for the collaborative offering. This reflects the efficiencies involved in providing the complete bundle of services to a collaborative account. This pricing policy is market oriented in that it allows customer firms to choose the product and relationship offering that *they perceive* to provide the greatest value.

Flaring Out with Augmentation At the other extreme, the collaborative offering (**d** in Figure 4.5b) becomes the augmented product enriched with those features valued by the customer firm. Augmented features might include coordinated cost-reduction programs, technical assistance, delivery schedule guarantees, and cooperative advertising. Because collaborative efforts are designed to add value or reduce the costs of exchange between partnering firms, a price premium should be received for the collaborative offering.

Creating Flexible Service Offerings[21]   Business marketers can gain a competitive edge by creating a portfolio of service offerings and then drawing on this portfolio to provide customized solutions for groups of customers or even individual customers. First, an offering should be created that includes the bare-bones-minimum number of services that are valued by all customers in a particular segment of the market. Microsoft Corporation refers to these offerings as "naked solutions." Second, optional services are created that add value to customers by reducing costs or improving the performance of their operations. To meet the needs of particular customers, optional services can then be "custom wrapped" with the core offering to create added value in the relationship.

Baxter International uses flexible service offerings to meet the needs of its hospital customers. For those transactional customers who do business with Baxter on an order-by-order basis, the core offering is emphasized. However, a more elaborate set of services provides the focus of Baxter's strategy with strategic customers—those who have made contractual commitments toward a long-term relationship with the firm. These services create value for the hospitals because they are designed to help them improve their efficiency and financial performance.

Implementing Relationship Strategies

The sales force assumes a central relationship management role in the business market. Technical service and customer service personnel also assume implementation roles that are important and visible within buying organizations. Successful relationship strategies are shaped by an effective organization and deployment of the personal selling effort and close coordination with supporting units, such as logistics and technical service. Some firms divide the sales organization into units that each serve a distinct relationship category such as transactional accounts or strategic accounts. For example, the sales force for Motorola's Semiconductor Group comprises three units: a *strategic market* sales force responsible for 60 partnership accounts, a *geographic* sales force responsible for the thousands of transactional accounts that buy Motorola products, and a *distributor* sales force that serves the needs of resellers of the firm's products.

The strategic market sales force consists of teams of sales representatives, application engineers, quality engineers, and others that are assigned to particular partnership accounts. In contrast, members of the geographic sales force act individually and perform traditional selling tasks. Through a careful screening process, promising transaction accounts are periodically upgraded to partnerships. Finally, the distributor sales force serves channel members that carry Motorola products and assists them in maintaining sound working relationships with this segment of Motorola's customer base.

---

[21] This section is based on James C. Anderson and James A. Narus, "Capturing the Value of Supplementary Services," *Harvard Business Review* 73 (January/February 1995): pp. 75–83. See also James C. Anderson and James A. Narus, "Business Marketing: Understand What Customers Value," *Harvard Business Review* 76 (November/December 1998), pp. 53–67.

Evaluating Relationship Strategy Outcomes

Some relationship-building efforts will fail because the expectations of the parties do not mesh—for example, this occurs when the business marketer follows a relationship approach and the customer responds in a transaction mode.[22] By isolating customer needs and the associated costs of augmented service features, the marketer is better equipped to profitably match the appropriate product offering to the needs of a particular customer.

The goal of a relationship is to enable the buyer and seller to maximize joint value. This points to the need for a formal evaluation of relationship outcomes. For example, Motorola sales executives work closely with their partnership accounts to establish mutually defined goals. After an appropriate period, partnerships that do not meet these goals are downgraded and shifted from the strategic market sales force to the geographic sales force.

Monitoring Relationships An array of factors can damage relationships and business marketers should be particularly sensitive to the signs of stress. Customer requirements may change as a result of changes in the market that the customer organization serves, new competitors in that market, new technology, or continual pressures for cost reduction. For example, under pressure from its competitors, Ford has asked suppliers to cut costs 5 percent per year through the early 2000s.[23] Some suppliers viewed the request as heavy-handed, while others were more constructive. A marketing manager at a leading microcontroller company noted that "Ford's way is cooperative and collaborative." Business marketers must be alert to the changing requirements of customers and be sensitive to the competitive forces that drive buying decisions in customer organizations.

Demonstrating Commitment Relationships with customers can also be damaged by product quality problems, late deliveries, or inadequate service support. Each can pose a serious threat to the relationship and signal a lack of commitment on the part of the marketer. In turn, the customer's definition of value changes over the course of the relationship. As Frederick E. Webster Jr. notes,

> If quality is defined as meeting and exceeding customer expectations, and if the customer's expectations keep increasing as the company improves its performance and competitors make promises of superior value, continuous improvement is an inevitable requirement for survival in the customer relationship.[24]

Business marketers should also continually update the value of their product and relationship offering. Attention here should center on particular new services that might be incorporated into the offering as well as on existing service elements that might be unbundled or curtailed. Working relationships with customer firms are

---

[22] Frederick E. Webster Jr., *Market-Driven Management: Using the New Marketing Concept to Create a Customer-Oriented Company* (New York: John Wiley & Sons, 1994), pp. 166–171.

[23] "Ford to Suppliers: Cut Costs 5%/Year," *Purchasing* 118 (1 June 1995), p. 43.

[24] Webster, *Market-Driven Management*, p. 169.

World-Class Leaders

Many contemporary leaders of organizations have succeeded by focusing on the needs of their own firm and by being the best advocate for their own interest group. Leaders of the future will have to do much more in a borderless world comprising organizations that are removing boundaries. Future leaders will demonstrate a special ability to bring together individuals from diverse functions, disciplines, and organizations to find a common purpose in goals that improve the entire industry and expand the offerings for everyone. Innovative ideas challenge boundaries, create tension, and

present new opportunities. Leaders of the future must be integrators who see beyond obvious differences in functions and organizations, diplomats who can resolve the inevitable "us" versus "them" conflicts, cross-fertilizers who can transfer the best from one place to another, and deep thinkers who can conceptualize new possibilities.

SOURCE: Rosabeth Moss Kanter, "World-Class Leaders: The Power of Partnering," in *The Leader of the Future: New Visions, Strategies, and Practices*, ed. Frances Hesselbein, Marshall Goldsmith, and Richard Beckhard (San Francisco: Jossey-Bass, 1996), pp. 89–98.

---

among the most important marketing assets of the firm. They deserve delicate care and continual nurturing!

Strategic Alliances

Not only do business marketing managers form close relationships with customers, they also develop close bonds with other firms. The traditional management assumption that "good fences make good corporations" has given way to a new philosophy: Firms are stretching their formal boundaries by creating strong ties with other firms.[25] Strategic alliances are assuming an increasingly prominent role in the strategy of leading business firms. **Strategic alliances,** according to George Day, involve "a formal long-run linkage, funded with direct co-investments by two or more companies, that pool complementary capabilities and resources to achieve generally agreed objectives."[26] In contrast, a **joint venture** involves the formation of a separate independent organization by the venture partners.

The driving force behind the formation of a strategic alliance is the desire of one firm to leverage its core competencies by linking them with others who have complementary expertise, thereby expanding the product and geographic scope of the organization. Examples of strategic alliances include the partnerships between AT&T and American Express (unified credit card and calling card), between IBM and Dell (computer service support), among Motorola and Cisco (wireless, Web-enabled handsets).

Benefits of Strategic Alliances

GE has more than 100 strategic partnerships, and its statement of operating objectives points to still more:

---

[25] Rosabeth Moss Kanter, "Becoming PALS: Pooling, Allying, and Linking across Companies," *The Academy of Management Executive* 3 (August 1989), p. 183.

[26] George S. Day, *Market Driven Strategy: Processes for Creating Value* (New York: The Free Press, 1990), p. 272.

To achieve a #1 or #2 global product-market position requires participation in each major market of the world. This requires several different forms of participation: trading technology for market access; trading market access for technology; and trading market access for market access. This "share to gain" becomes a way of life.[27]

Jack Welch, chief executive officer of GE, notes that "Alliances are a big part of this game [of global competition]. . . . The least attractive way to win on a global basis is to think you can take on the world all by yourself."[28] Partners to an alliance seek such benefits as (1) access to markets or to technology (a motivating force for GE); (2) economies of scale that might be gained by combining manufacturing, R&D, or marketing activities; (3) faster entry of new products to markets (for example, when partners with established channels of distribution in different countries swap new products); and (4) sharing of risk.[29] Simply put, there is a tremendous cost—and risk—in a firm's creating its own distribution channels, logistical network, manufacturing plant, and R&D function in every key market in the world. Also, it takes time to develop relationships with channel members and customers and to develop the skills of employees. Alliances provide another option.

Alliance Management Challenges

The value or competitive advantage created by an alliance rests on the joint efforts of the parties. Although offering significant benefits, alliances often fall short of expectations or dissolve. Managing an alliance involves special challenges.

Negotiating the Contract   The alliance contract provides an outline of broad areas of cooperation. While often a lengthy document, the contract cannot begin to cover all the issues and surprises that will spring up once the alliance relationship is initiated. Often, alliance agreements are broadly negotiated by senior executives who turn the final details and day-to-day management of the alliance over to middle managers. The implementation of alliance strategy can be hampered as managers flesh out the details with their counterparts in the partner firm. Painful negotiations often create tension between the parties before things are even under way. A marketing manager who heads an alliance team at a high-tech firm isolated one source of friction that is common in negotiations:

> The thing that took the most time was the question: "What happens when we divorce?" It took us a year to negotiate this thing. Three months to cut the deal and nine months to protect each other's corporate assets when we divide. That's what killed the trust.[30]

[27] General Electric Company, *Operating Objectives to Meet Challenges of the '90s* (Fairfield, Conn.: General Electric Company, 14 March 1988).

[28] Michael Y. Yoshino and U. Srinivasa Rangan, *Strategic Alliances: An Entrepreneurial Approach to Globalization* (Boston: Harvard Business School Press, 1995), p. 3.

[29] Kenichi Ohmae, "The Global Logic of Strategic Alliances," *Harvard Business Review* 67 (March/April 1989), pp. 143–154.

[30] Michael D. Hutt, Edwin R. Stafford, Beth A. Walker, and Peter H. Reingen, "Defining the Social Network of a Strategic Alliance: A Case Study," *Sloan Management Review* 41 (winter 2000), 51–62.

Protecting Core Assets   Many firms are involved in multiple alliances—which can provide an added source of tension to a relationship. Indeed, the partner firm may be a rival or involved in other alliance relationships with competitors. Here the business marketer may find it particularly difficult to strike a balance between trusting one's partner on one hand and protecting the firm's strategic interests and assets on the other. An alliance manager aptly describes the problem:

> We are involved in half a dozen alliances. Some are with rivals and some are not. Our plans call for different levels of information to different alliances. Sometimes I have meetings with different managers from partner firms. It's so hard to keep in mind what can be and cannot be disclosed to different partners. . . . One slip could cause damage.[31]

Linking Systems and Structures   The basic idea behind an alliance is to create added value by effectively linking the core competencies of one firm with those of another. Sometimes things do not work together smoothly. The partner firms may have incompatible systems and decision structures that delay decision making, create inefficiencies, and frustrate alliance personnel, as expressed by one manager:

> Our alliance team is empowered to make decisions—even those that involve significant resources. At the partner firm, they always have to go check with senior executives—follow the channels.

Determinants of Alliance Success

Successful alliances involve a collaborative relationship in which the parties create new value together, rather than an exchange relationship ("you get something back for what you put in"). Rosabeth Moss Kanter emphasizes that "Alliances cannot be controlled by formal systems but require a dense web of interpersonal connections and internal infrastructures that enhance learning."[32]

Developing Close Working Relationships   Observe the interpersonal connections that unite two *Fortune*-500 firms (referred to as Alpha Communications and Omega Financial Services) in an alliance that markets a cobranded credit and calling card targeted to the business market (see Figure 4.6). The lines connect alliance personnel who have *frequent* and *important* communications and who consider the working relationship to be close. These managers are the **core participants** in the work of the alliance in contrast to others who are more loosely connected to the alliance team in each organization (**peripheral participants**). The interpersonal links between the core participants are the circuits through which alliance information flows, decisions are made, and conflicts are resolved.

Boundary-Spanning Connections   Fundamental to the success of the alliance are the working relationships (those connected by the dark lines in Figure 4.6) that

---

[31] Yoshino and Rangan, *Strategic Alliances*, p. 111.

[32] Kanter, "Collaborative Advantage," p. 97.

INSIDE BUSINESS MARKETING

The Internet Helps Cisco Systems Serve Customers

Cisco Systems sells about 80 percent of the routers and other forms of networking gear that power the Internet. In 1999, their revenues approximated $10 billion and they earned over $1.5 billion in profits. Cisco enthusiastically embraces e-business. The company sells large quantities of its complex kits over the Web. Customers place orders through its Web site and suppliers know exactly what materials and components they need to ship to the factory by accessing Cisco's "dynamic replenishment" software through a Web site interface.

Internet applications reach into every part of the company's operations. The equipment that Cisco sells, however good, does not just run the first time out of the box. Customers expect highly customized support and assistance from trained engineers who can deal with the full range of technical problems. Cisco designed its Web site so customers could access the technical information that they would need to solve most routine problems. This allows Cisco's engineering staff to work on

more complicated customer problems. Customers not only go to the Web site to get information; they use it to share their own experiences with both Cisco *and* other customers. Currently, more than 80 percent of customer inquiries are handled online.

Prior to the firm's Internet-based system, almost one-third of all orders contained errors. The Web was used to attack this problem and today over 80 percent of sales come from the Web. Customers select from an electronic catalog, are helped to get their order exactly right, and can track its progress online. The entire process of ordering, contract manufacturing, fulfillment, and payment is automated. Over 55 percent of orders pass through Cisco's system without being touched by anyone. The company estimates it saves over $500 million a year by using the Web.

SOURCE: Adapted from "The Net Imperative," *The Economist*, 26 June 1999, p. 18.

---

span organizational boundaries and unite the partnering firms. These **boundary-spanning** managers (for example, #12 in Alpha and #39 in Omega) have strong communication and friendship links with other managers both within their respective organizations and within the partnering firm. Frequent interactions, the timely exchange of information, and accurate feedback on each partner's actions will minimize misperceptions and strengthen cooperation in an alliance.[33] Likewise, communication among boundary-spanning personnel produces a shared interpretation of goals and common agreement on norms, work roles, and the nature of social relationships.

As close, working relationships develop among the alliance participants, psychological contracts, based on trust and shared goals, replace the formal alliance agreement. **Psychological contracts** consist of unwritten and largely nonverbalized sets of congruent expectations and assumptions held by the parties to the alliance about each other's prerogatives and obligations.[34] By promoting openness and flexibility, these interpersonal bonds can speed alliance progress—decisions can be made quickly, unexpected events can be more readily handled, learning is enhanced, and new possibilities for joint action emerge.

Integrating Points of Contact   Firms that are adept at managing strategic alliances use a flexible approach, letting their alliances evolve in form as conditions change over time; they invest adequate resources and management attention in these relationships,

---

[33] A. Parkhe, "Building Trust in International Alliances," *Journal of World Business* 33 (winter 1998), pp. 417–437.

[34] Peter Smith Ring and Andrew H. Van de Ven, "Developmental Processes of Cooperative Interorganizational Processes" *Academy of Management Review* 19 (January 1992), pp. 90–118.

| FIGURE 4.6 | SOCIAL CONNECTIONS IN AN ALLIANCE |

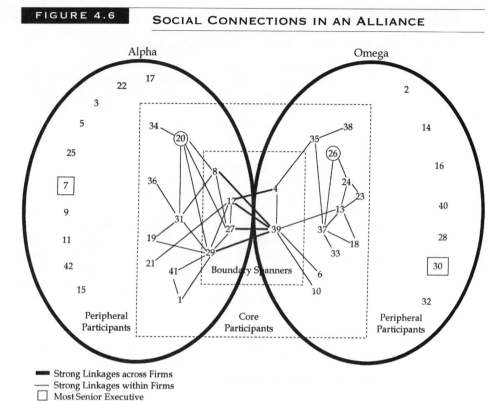

and they integrate the organizations so that the appropriate points of contact and communication are managed. Successful alliances achieve five levels of integration:[35]

1. *strategic integration*, which entails continuing contact among senior executives to define broad goals or discuss changes in each company;

2. *tactical integration*, which brings middle managers together to plan joint activities, to transfer knowledge, or to isolate organizational or system changes that will improve interfirm connections;

3. *operational integration*, which provides the information, resources, or personnel that managers require to carry out the day-to-day work of the alliance;

4. *interpersonal integration*, which builds a necessary foundation for personnel in both organizations to know one another personally, learn together, and create new value; and

5. *cultural integration*, which requires managers involved in the alliance to have the communication skills and cultural awareness to bridge the differences.

---

[35] Kanter, "Collaborative Advantage," pp. 105–107.

Even though significant problems may threaten strategic alliances, a firm that can assemble and manage a portfolio of successful partnerships can secure a competitive advantage in the global market. Indeed, some firms have mastered the art of developing and sustaining successful partnerships. For example, Corning Glass Works is involved in successful partnerships with Dow Chemical, Owens-Illinois, and Eastman Kodak, as well as with partners in France, Great Britain, Australia, West Germany, and China, among others.

The Social Ingredients of Alliance Success[36]

In a strategic alliance, interpersonal relationships matter. The goals of an alliance cannot be realized in practice until many managers in both organizations know one another personally and take coordinated action to create new value together. Indeed, many alliances that appear to make strategic sense fail to meet expectations because little attention is given to cultivating the interpersonal connections and communication patterns that underlie effective collaboration. Strong interpersonal ties must be forged to unite managers in the partnering organizations and continuing boundary-spanning activity is required at multiple managerial levels as a relationship evolves.

Laying the Foundation Alliance negotiations set the tone for the relationship. Smooth alliance negotiations rest on finding the proper balance between the formal, legal procedures that establish detailed contractual safeguards for the parties and the informal, interpersonal processes that are crucial in the successful execution of alliance strategy.

Legal documents that establish an alliance and specify the boundaries in elaborate detail are still not complete and exhaustive. Countless ambiguities become evident as middle managers begin to flesh out the specific elements of the alliance plan. To resolve these issues and move the alliance forward, it is here that personal relationships begin to develop and supplement formal role relationships. Alliance negotiations should be structured in a manner that promotes the development of these interpersonal ties.

Experts suggest that more effective transactions are likely to evolve when managers, rather than lawyers, develop and control the negotiation strategy.[37] In turn, "negotiations appear to go more smoothly when parties from different organizations interact with their role counterparts (for example, managers to managers or lawyers to lawyers)."[38] Interactions between lawyers are largely based on institutionalized professional norms, center on a specific activity, and take place over a relatively short period of time. While a signed agreement culminates the work of the lawyers, manager-to-manager relationships formed during negotiations provide the social structure through which the goals of the alliance can be realized.

Isolating Top Management's Role Beyond establishing joint goals and determining how the alliance fits each firm's total strategy, senior executives define the meaning of the relationship and signal its importance to personnel in the respective firms.

---

[36] This section is based on Hutt, Stafford, Walker, and Reingen "Defining the Social Network of a Strategic Alliance."

[37] Peter Smith Ring and G. Rands, "Sensemaking, Understanding, and Committing: Emergent Transaction Processes in the Evolution of 3M's Microgravity Research Programs," in A. H. Van de Ven, H. Angle, and M. S. Poole, eds., *Research on the Management of Innovation: The Minnesota Studies* (New York: Ballinger/Harper & Row, 1989), pp. 337–366.

[38] Ring and Van de Ven, "Developmental Processes of Cooperative Interorganizational Processes," p. 109.

Top management's involvement in a strategic alliance encompasses much more than merely appointing an alliance manager or project leader. For an alliance-based strategy to succeed, an ongoing level of backing from top management is required.

Executive leadership also assumes a critical role in communicating the strategic role of the alliance and in creating an identity for the alliance within the organization. A senior executive's personal involvement galvanizes support for an alliance throughout the organization. Moreover, direct ties at the top management level across partnering firms spawn organizational commitment and more active involvement between managers at multiple levels of the hierarchy. If visible participation by senior executives is lacking, the members of the alliance team will begin to question the importance of the initiative to their firm and the value of team membership to their careers.

Managing the Information Flow   A firm enters into an alliance to combine its distinctive competencies with those of a partner to create a competitive position that neither could achieve by operating alone. To achieve mutual success, each party must share information and each must learn from the other. However, since alliances often bring together partners who are actual or potential rivals, alliance managers are cautious in managing the outward flow of information and eager to protect the distinctive skills and knowledge that define their firm's competitive standing. To achieve balance, the alliance manager must

> draw the line between the active flow of information that ensures the vitality of the alliance and the unregulated, unmonitored, and unbridled exchange of information that can jeopardize the competitiveness of partners that are also likely to be rivals."[39]

In developing an information management policy, alliance team members should discuss and agree upon the level of confidentiality that should be assigned to different categories of information. Ongoing attention to information management issues is required as an alliance grows in complexity or new personnel join the effort. As information boundaries are defined, however, key alliance personnel must be given appropriate decision-making authority and autonomy to expedite communication and work flows between the firms. An overly restrictive information policy will damage trust, hamper learning, and impede the development of interpersonal relationships across organizations.

Cultivating a Network of Relationships   To achieve alliance goals, a well-integrated communication and work-flow network among managers is required within and across firms. A regular audit of evolving social, work, and communication ties can be a valuable tool for management in gauging the health of an alliance and in spotting problem areas. In reviewing the alliance network, attention first should center on relationship patterns at multiple levels. In particular, connections should be examined among **operating personnel** who require timely access to information and resources; between the **project leaders** who establish the climate for the alliance, craft the strategy, and manage execution; and among **senior managers** who signal the importance of the relationship in their respective organizations, lend critical support at key points, and are central to discussions of new opportunities for successful collaboration.

---

[39] Yoshino and Rangan, *Strategic Alliances*, p. 128.

Summary

Relationships, rather than simple transactions, provide the central focus in business marketing. By demonstrating superior skills in managing relationships with key customers as well as with alliance partners, business marketing firms can create a collaborative advantage.

To develop profitable relationships with customers, business marketers must first understand the different forms that exchange relationships can take. Transactional exchange centers on the timely exchange of basic products and services for highly competitive market prices. By contrast, collaborative exchange involves very close personal, informational and operational connections that the parties develop in order to achieve long-term mutual goals. Across the relationship spectrum, different types of relationships feature different relationship connectors. For example, collaborative relationships that arise for important purchases are the ones that emphasize operational linkages that integrate the operations of the buying and selling organization as well as high levels of information exchange.

Valuable insights into relationship marketing can be secured by examining the time horizon within which a customer makes a commitment to a supplier. Switching costs, the level of perceived risk, and the importance of the purchase provide benchmarks for defining the likely pattern a relationship will follow. The relationship marketing process involves four stages: (1) selecting customer accounts, (2) developing account-specific offerings, (3) implementing relationship strategies, and (4) evaluating relationship strategy outcomes.

The driving force behind the formation of a strategic alliance is the desire of one firm to leverage its core competencies by linking them with another firm that has complementary expertise, thereby creating joint value and new market opportunities. Firms adept at managing strategic alliances are proactive in creating the conditions for mutually beneficial relationships.

Initial negotiations set the tone for the alliance, so they must promote good interpersonal ties. A well integrated communication and work-flow network is required within and across firms. And senior executives' personal involvement galvanizes crucial support. A regular audit of evolving relationship ties can be a valuable tool for gauging an alliance's health.

Discussion Questions

1. The Boeing 777 was the first commercial jet devised by Boeing's "design-build team" that included suppliers and airline managers. Suppliers such as Rockwell International and Honeywell were tied into the process via computer links. When the first 777 came off the assembly line, parts snapped together so precisely that its nose-to-tail measurement was off less than $^{23}/_{1000}$ of an inch from design goals. A senior purchasing executive at Boeing commented that progress was achieved not simply because of the computer links but because of the mutual respect and trust among those who pulled the plans together. What criteria would be important to Boeing in evaluating suppliers? In building a relationship, who would likely be involved on the selling side and on the buying side?

2. Ford develops "collaborative relationships" with some suppliers and "transactional relationships" with other suppliers. What criteria would purchasing executives use in segmenting suppliers into these two categories? Describe the steps that a business marketer might take to move the relationship with Ford from a transaction relationship to a more collaborative one.

3. Some consulting organizations persuasively argue that by properly incorporating suppliers into their product development process, firms can cut their bills for purchased parts and materials by as much as 30 percent. Explore how a buyer–seller partnership might create these cost savings.

4. Concerning buyer–seller relationships, compare and contrast the features of a collaborative relationship versus a transactional relationship in the business market. Describe how the operational linkages might differ by relationship type.

5. Motorola and Hewlett-Packard compete in some markets, are respectively customer and supplier for each other in various markets, share suppliers in several markets, often have the same customers, and have alliances in yet other markets. What steps can be taken by the firms to achieve joint goals, minimize conflicts, and protect their core assets?

6. Discuss the switching costs that Southwest Airlines would incur if they began to phase out their Boeing fleet of airliners with replacements from Airbus Industrie. What steps could Airbus take to reduce these switching costs? How might Boeing counter to strengthen its relationship to Southwest?

7. Describe how an office supply firm may have a core offering of products and services for a small manufacturer and an augmented offering for a university.

8. Knowing how to be a good partner is an asset in the business market. Describe the characteristics of a successful strategic alliance and outline the steps that alliance partners can take to increase the odds that alliance goals will be achieved.

5

E-Commerce Strategies for Business Markets

Leading-edge firms like General Electric are using the Internet to transform the way in which they do business. The Internet provides a powerful platform for conveying information, conducting transactions, delivering innovative services, and building close customer relationships. After reading this chapter, you will understand

1. the nature of e-commerce in business markets.

2. the role that e-commerce can play in a firm's marketing strategy.

3. the key issues involved in designing an e-commerce strategy.

Dell's computer factory on the outskirts of Limerick, on the western coast of Ireland, supplies custom-built PCs to business customers all over Europe. As orders come into the factory via Dell's Web site and call centers, the company relays to its suppliers details of which components it needs, how many and when. Hard drives, motherboards, modems roll in to bays at the back of the building, and roll out as completed computers just a few hours later. Dell is recognized as a leading pioneer in *electronic commerce* (customarily termed e-commerce) because it sells over $15 million worth of computers from its Web site each day! Because Dell's suppliers have real-time access to information about its orders via its corporate *extranet*, they can deliver just enough of the right parts to keep the production line moving smoothly. By plugging suppliers directly into its customer database, Dell ensures that they will instantly know about any changes in demand. By plugging its customers into the supply chain via its Web site, Dell enables them to track the progress of their order from the factory to their office door, thus saving on telephone and fax inquiries. The *Internet's* universal connectivity has enabled Dell to create a three-way "information partnership" with its suppliers and customers by treating them as collaborators who together find ways of improving efficiency and sharing the benefits across the entire chain of supply and demand.[1]

Dell is just one of thousands of business marketers who have integrated the Internet and electronic commerce into their corporate strategies. E-commerce not only speeds up and automates a company's internal processes but, just as importantly, it spreads the efficiency gains to the business systems of its suppliers and customers. E-commerce seamlessly moves data and information over open and closed networks, bringing together previously separate groups inside the organization and throughout the supply chain. The advantages to integrating suppliers and customers in this way are enormous, yet the full potential of the Internet and e-commerce has hardly been tapped in the business-to-business arena.

Data on the scope and size of the Internet provide perspective: the U.S. Internet economy ranked as the world's eighteenth largest economy (ahead of Argentina and behind Switzerland) with revenues of $301.4 billion in 1998.[2] In 1999, a University of Texas study projected the Internet economy to exceed half a trillion dollars, and reflecting the rising importance of the Internet and technology, the Dow Jones Industrial Average added three technology-related firms to the composite Dow Jones Averages while dropping several old-line firms.[3]

According to Forrester Research, in 1998 companies did $43 billion in business with each other over the Internet; by 2004, it will rise to $2.7 trillion, accounting for 9.4 percent of total business-to-business sales.[4] As this huge growth in e-commerce continues, significant opportunities and challenges are raised for almost all firms that market products and services in the business market. Firms that can enter the e-commerce marketplace by leveraging Internet capabilities with information processing, delivery capability, interorganizational collaboration and flexibility may be able to develop important differential advantages in selected market segments. Similarly,

---

[1] "The Net Imperative," *The Economist*, 26 June 1999, p. 11.

[2] *Future Trends*, The Official Newsletter of the Center for Applied Information Technology at the University of Dallas, Newsletter #3 (October 10, 1999).

[3] Sara Nathan, "Internet Economy Soars 68%," *USA Today* (29 October 1999): p. B1.

[4] Michael J. Mandel, "The Internet Economy: The World's Next Growth Engine," *Business Week*, (4 October 1999): p. 86 and Forrester Research Press Release, February 7, 2000.

major challenges confront organizations attempting to formulate an e-commerce strategy. These firms must craft a comprehensive e-commerce strategy, radically transform their traditional business models, and deal with the rapidly changing technology associated with e-commerce.

This chapter examines the nature of e-commerce, the role that it can play in the organization's marketing strategy, the key elements in designing an e-commerce strategy, and the future direction and potential for e-commerce in the business marketing arena.

Defining E-Commerce [5]

To establish a foundation, consider the alternative ways in which e-commerce can be defined. Each is relevant to the business marketer:

1. From a *communications* standpoint, e-commerce is the delivery of information, products/services or payments via telephone lines, computer networks, or any other means.

2. From a *business process* perspective, e-commerce is the application of technology toward the automation of business transactions and work flows.

3. From a *service* perspective, e-commerce is a tool that addresses the desire of firms, customers, and management to cut service costs while improving the quality of goods and increasing the speed of service delivery.

4. From an *online* standpoint, e-commerce provides the capability of buying and selling products and information on the Internet and other online services.[6]

As these definitions suggest, e-commerce is multifaceted and complex. However, the rationale for e-commerce is easy to understand: in certain markets and for selected customers, e-commerce is an approach to doing business that can increase sales volume, lower costs, or provide more real-time information to customers. Ravi Kalakota and Andrew Whinston effectively describe the role of e-commerce for the typical organization:

> Depending on how it is applied, e-commerce has the potential to increase revenue by creating new markets for old products, creating new information-based products, and establishing new service delivery channels to better serve and interact with customers. The transaction management aspect of electronic commerce can also enable firms to reduce operating cost by

---

[5] Some authors and business marketing experts have suggested that the more appropriate term is "e-business," as opposed to "e-commerce." They reason that e-commerce is a broad term that deals with all transactions that are Internet-based, whereas e-business specifically refers to transactions and relationships between organizations. In reality, IBM is given credit for coining the term "e-business" in a major 1997 advertising campaign promoting the notion of *e-business*. The term was new then, but has since become routinely used in the press and marketing campaigns of other companies. This chapter will use the e-commerce term.

[6] Ravi Kalakota and Andrew B. Whinston, *Electronic Commerce* (Reading, MA: Addison-Wesley, 1997); p. 3.

enabling better coordination in the sales, production, and distribution processes (or better supply chain management), and to consolidate operations and reduce overhead.[7]

In short, e-commerce can be applied to almost all phases of business, with the net effect of creating new demand or making most business processes more efficient. E-commerce can be applied to procuring and purchasing products; managing the process for fulfilling customers' orders; providing real-time information on the status of orders, online marketing and advertising; creating online product catalogs and product information data sets; managing the logistics process; and processing the payment of invoices. The applications are limitless, yet not all products and markets can be effectively served through the e-commerce approach. Later in the chapter we will identify those situations that offer the greatest potential for effective application of e-commerce. The different applications of e-commerce are depicted in Figure 5.1. Note that e-commerce can play a pivotal role across all functional areas of the business, yet the most important application from the marketing perspective is how e-commerce facilitates interactions with customers.

Key Elements Supporting E-Commerce

The Internet and World Wide Web

E-commerce is made possible as a result of the development of the Internet and the World Wide Web. The Internet is not new: its roots lie in a collection of computers that were linked together in the 1960s as a project of the Advanced Research Projects Agency and the U.S. Department of Defense.[8] Initially, four mainframe computers from four different universities were linked together to create a network for safe transmittal of data between military computers at different sites. Eventually, other government networks were hooked up to the original network and the system became the Internet.[9]

Until the early 1990s, various government entities controlled access to the Internet. In 1991, the government eased restrictions, and commercial traffic was permitted. By 1995, companies were allowed to provide uncontrolled for-profit Internet access. Growth in Internet use since that time has been phenomenal; by 1999, 6,500 new Web sites were being added to the World Wide Web *every hour*.[10]

The Internet today is a vast collection of computers and computer networks that are interconnected to permit easy communication among them. In physical form, the Internet is composed of computers, wires, routers, and communication links. Lines that carry information on the Internet are leased from telephone companies like AT&T and are connected to computers called "routers" that direct coded data to its destination. The information content on the Internet is located in independently owned, high capacity computers called "servers." These servers are linked to regional networks that, in turn, connect to the basic structure of the Internet.

---

[7] Ibid., p. 5.

[8] Ibid., p. 31.

[9] Ravi Kalakota and Andrew B. Whinston, *Frontiers of Electronic Commerce* (Reading, MA: Addison-Wesley, 1996).

[10] Jolanta Pelika, "E-Services in Practice," *Financial Times Guide to Digital Business* (autumn 1999): p. 9.

FIGURE 5.1	TYPES OF E-COMMERCE

Interorganizational E-Commerce

1. *Supplier management:* helps to reduce the number of suppliers, lower procurement costs, and increase order cycle time.

2. *Inventory management:* instantaneous transmission of information allows reduction of inventory; tracking of shipments reduces errors and safety stock; out-of-stocks are reduced.

3. *Distribution management:* e-commerce facilitates the transmission of shipping documents and ensures the data is accurate.

4. *Channel management:* rapid dissemination of information to trading partners on changing market and customer conditions. Technical, product and pricing information can now be posted to electronic bulletin boards. Production information easily shared with all channel partners.

5. *Payment management:* payments can be sent and received electronically among suppliers and distributors, reducing errors, time, and costs.

Intraorganizationl E-Commerce

1. *Workgroup communications:* e-mail and electronic bulletin boards are used to facilitate internal communications.

2. *Electronic publishing:* all types of company information, including price sheets, market trends, and product specifications can be organized and disseminated instantaneously.

3. *Sales force productivity:* e-commerce facilitates information flow between production and the sales force and the sales force and the customer. Firms gain greater access to market and competitor intelligence supplied by the sales force.

Business-to-Customer E-Commerce

1. *Product information:* information on new and existing products is readily available to customers on the firm's Web site.

2. *Sales:* certain products can be sold directly from the firm's Web site, reducing the cost of the transaction and allowing the customer to have real-time information about their order.

3. *Service:* customers can electronically communicate about order status, product applications, problems with products, and product returns.

4. *Payment:* payment can be made by the customer using electronic payment systems.

5. *Marketing research:* firms can use e-commerce, the Internet, and their own Web sites to gather significant quantities of information about customers and potential customers.

The World Wide Web serves as the nervous system of the Internet by facilitating information sharing and providing a mechanism that integrates all the information and content from Internet servers. The Web's role is to provide the software foundation on which information is created, manipulated, organized, and retrieved on the Internet. Essentially, the Web is the Internet's "library" in that Web sites are the books in the library and Web "pages" are the specific pages in the book. As most people familiar with Internet know, the user begins their exploration of a Web site at the "home page," which is the table of contents for the Web site. The Web is the standard for navigating, publishing information, and executing transactions on the Internet; two aspects are critical—servers and browsers. Servers are the Web "sites" or computers that store the information contained at that site. Browsers, on the other hand, are used to find and view server-based documents.

Intranets and Extranets

The Internet has become a very important element in the marketing strategy of many business marketers; there are, however, two other very important technological elements that are integrated with an Internet strategy. *Intranets* are company-specific, internal Internets. An intranet links documents on the organization's scattered internal networks together. A firm's intranet allows different functions and people to share data bases, communicate with each other, disseminate timely bulletins, view proprietary information, be trained in various aspects of the firm's business, and share about any type of system the company uses to manage their business. For example, Boeing, the largest commercial aircraft manufacturer in the world, maintains a company intranet that is available to more than 200,000 Boeing employees worldwide. One segment of its intranet contains an online course catalog for company educational programs in the areas of supervisor training and quality control. Over 12,000 managers, supervisors, and executives can access this catalog on the company intranet and search for a management course, read a course synopsis, or even play a video or audio clip about a course.[11] Boeing's intranet provides the opportunity to greatly enhance interfirm communications and to assist employees in staying current on matters relevant to the firm.

Extranets, on the other hand, are links that allow business partners such as suppliers, distributors, and customers to connect to a company's internal networks (intranets) over the Internet or through virtual private networks. An extranet is created when two organizations connect their respective intranets for business communications and transactions. The purpose of an extranet is to provide a communication mechanism to streamline business processes that normally take place elsewhere. Hewlett-Packard and Procter & Gamble, for example, have established extranet links to their advertising agencies to speed the review of ad campaigns. Extranets allow business partners to use the Internet by providing a unique password to access the company's intranet. Companies in the printing industry allow customers access to their internal networks to track print jobs as they move through production or to browse databases of images of other media assets.[12] The use of extranets allows the firm to customize information and interaction with each specific customer who is granted access to the company's intranet. Hewlett-Packard offers one of the largest medical sites on the Web. As part of

---

[11] Neal J. Hannon, *The Business of the Internet* (Cambridge, MA: International Thompson Publishing Company, 1998): p. 27.
[12] "Extranets Enhance Customer Relations," *Graphic Arts Monthly* 71 (January 1999): p. 89.

TABLE 5.1	THE "HYPE" AND REALITY OF E-COMMERCE

Hype	Reality
1. E-Commerce enables businesses to bypass channel partners.	1. If existing channels provide key services like shipping, support, training, credit, etc., they are still needed.
2. Businesses can use the Internet as their sole means of acquiring new customers.	2. The Internet extends the firm's reach, most firms in the B-to-B market have not found the Internet an effective way to get new customers. All forms of communication are usually required to acquire a new customer.
3. B-to-B firms with extensive Web sites are able to substantially eliminate their advertising and promotion expenditures.	3. Advertising and promotion are key elements of a Web-based strategy to inform potential prospects about the site. Advertising is still needed to play its typical role of building awareness and recognition.
4. Web sites need to provide all the information that any prospect would ever need.	4. Providing all possible information on a Web site is a great way to provide competitors with all the competitive intelligence they need on your firm.
5. A B-to-B Web site's success is measured by how long a visitor stays.	5. Success of a B-to-B Web site is measured by the successful action it has triggered, not the length of stay. The goal is to provide access to information quickly and accurately.
6. Internet marketing will replace traditional marketing media.	6. The computer cannot achieve many of the functions of traditional media or the benefits of personal iteraction with the customer. Radio didn't replace newspapers and TV didn't replace radio.

SOURCE: Adapted from: Hank Barnes, "Getting Past the Hype: Internet Opportunities for B-to-B Marketers," *Marketing News*, 1 February 1999, pp. 11–12.

their offering, hospital customers have special passwords based on a profile provided by the user that automatically connects that specific user to "special pricing" negotiated through that institution's contracts with the Hewlett-Packard company.[13]

The Strategic Role of E-Commerce

For the business marketer, the crucial question is: what role does e-commerce assume in the firm's overall marketing strategy? One of the great dangers associated with e-commerce is the potential for managers to become enamored with the technological aspects and ignore the strategic elements and the role that e-commerce has in the firm's overall mission. The Internet and, more specifically, e-commerce is just an instrument for accomplishing marketing goals: the need for sound marketing strategy remains. Many companies have made Internet decisions based on the hype and new business models that do not fit their organization, with unfortunate and unprofitable results (see Table 5.1).

---

[13] Curt Werner, "Health Care E-Commerce, Still in Its Infancy, But Growing Fast," *Health Industry Today* 61 (September 1998): p. 9.

E-Commerce as a Strategic Component

The use of e-commerce and, more specifically, the Internet is just like any other element that the business marketer employs to accomplish the firm's mission: it must be focused, based on carefully crafted objectives, and directed at specific target segments. For the marketer, the Internet can be viewed as:

1. a communication device to build customer relationships,

2. an alternative distribution channel,

3. a valuable medium for delivering services to customers,

4. a tool for gathering marketing research data, and

5. a method for integrating members of the supply chain.

In short, the Internet usually does not replace existing channels of distribution; rather it supports or supplements them. In a similar way, it does not eliminate the selling function; rather it facilitates the salesperson's efforts and enhances the effectiveness and efficiency of the sales function.

To be successful, business marketers must integrate the Internet and e-commerce into the "fabric of their traditional business operations, leveraging it as a new communications tool that can increase sales, satisfaction and service levels."[14] Essentially, e-commerce extends a firm's reach, but it does not change the fundamentals of how a firm acquires, responds to, and satisfies its customers. Andy Grove, Chairman of Intel, aptly concludes, "Implementing the new e-commerce model does not mean simply selling something over the Internet, but incorporating the Net into the day-to-day functioning of the company, in particular, as a mode for business-to-business transactions and for building customer relationships."[15]

What the Internet Can Do

Before exploring the strategic elements of e-commerce, let's explore the important benefits that are associated with an effectively developed e-commerce strategy. The Internet is a powerful tool when used properly, and the advantages are significant in terms of more effectively serving customers, communicating useful information, and lowering the cost of doing business.

Enhanced Customer Focus, Responsiveness, and Relationships The Internet allows business marketers to align with their customers on order management and also on product configuration and design, resulting in better customer service and more satisfied customers. Because the Internet creates direct links between customers and factories, corporate buyers can tailor products to meet their exact requirements. Many business marketers now encourage customers to customize products exactly to their specifications right on the Web site.

---

[14]Hank Barnes, "Getting Past the Hype: Internet Opportunities for B-to-B Marketers," *Marketing News* (1 February, 1999): p. 11.

[15]As quoted in David Troy, "E-Commerce: Foundations of Business Strategy," Caliber Learning Systems, http:/www.caliber.com.

Reduced Transaction Costs When customers use the Internet to communicate with suppliers, the supplier is able to provide low-cost access to both order entry and order tracking, twenty-four hours a day, seven days a week. Transactions that do not require in-person services can be handled in a cost-effective manner on a Web site, while the firm can devote more staff to working with higher margin customers requiring personal attention. The result is reduced costs for both types of transactions. Boise Cascade Office Products has deployed an extranet for its largest 600 corporate customers, and its margins have doubled compared to its traditional operations.[16] By automating transactions over the Internet, some companies have reported a decrease in purchasing transaction costs from $150 to $25.[17]

Integration of the Supply Chain The Internet allows companies to electronically link together far-flung constituencies including customers, suppliers, intermediaries, and alliance partners in spite of organizational, geographical, and functional boundaries. All the participants in the supply chain can be linked by a common data base that is shared via the Internet, making the entire value-adding process seamless and more efficient. The key to effective supply chain operations is the sharing of vital information among the participating companies: sales forecasts, production plans, delivery schedules, tracking of finished product shipments through the distribution network, inventory levels at various points in the supply chain, final sales versus plan and the like.

The Internet facilitates the creation, updating, coordinating, and communicating of large amounts of these types of information and makes it readily available to all participants in the supply chain via access to a common Web site. IBM, for example, links 125 suppliers of memory chips, batteries and disc drives via the Internet to a plant in Scotland that produces 15 million personal computers per year.[18] Orders for these items are posted electronically each day on the firm's extranet. Once the suppliers release their components at a nearby service point (warehouse), the payment process is initiated electronically. IBM has been able to increase inventory turnover ten-fold on many components and the suppliers benefit from faster payment and increased coordination of their production process with that of IBM's.

Focus on Core Business The Internet makes it easier for companies to focus on what they do best and spin off or contract out other operations to third parties that are tied to them through the Internet. In this way, the Internet facilitates the development of a "virtual company" that contracts with other firms to perform a variety of functions from manufacturing to warehousing. Boeing developed its latest airplane, the Boeing 777, with a portfolio of relationships among subcontractors and lead customers that were linked electronically.[19] This approach allows Boeing to devote more assets and human resources to the critical area of product design.

Effective Information Availability for Customers Companies that make their product catalog available to customers over the Internet make it easy for customers to

---

[16] N. Venkatraman and John C. Henderson, "Real Strategies for Virtual Organizing," *Sloan Management Review* 40 (winter 1999): p. 39.

[17] Dave Rumar, "Electronic Commerce Helps Cut Transaction Costs, Reduce Red Tape," *Computing Canada* 25 (no. 32, 27 August 1999): p. 24.

[18] "Virtual Auctions Knock Down Costs," *Financial Times Guide to Digital Business*, p. 20.

[19] Venkatraman and Henderson, "Real Strategies for Virtual Organizing," p. 5.

match their needs to products that fill those needs. A number of business marketers provide search engines on their catalog Web sites that allow users to define a set of criteria they desire for a product. Customers usually access an online product database and locate a desired product within their required parameters without navigating through thousands of pages of irrelevant data. Such online data bases are easily updated with a few keystrokes, thus ensuring the timeliness of the data. In addition to the advantages provided by online catalog databases, the Internet Web sites also make it possible for customers to track orders: when their products will be available, estimated ship date and expected date of receipt. The Internet allows customers to transact business anytime they wish: a true twenty-four-hour, seven-day-a-week service.

Reduce Cycle Times   When businesses order PCs on the Web, orders often flow directly to the factory floors of several companies that make the components. Transactions occur in real time. The net effect is to speed the time from order placement to delivery of the finished product. Several automobile manufacturers have seen the development time for new auto models fall from an average of 4 years to 2.5 years. One factor driving the change in new product cycle time is that the manufacturers are in direct contact with suppliers via the Internet or an extranet. Suppliers can more rapidly respond to design changes that the auto makers prescribe. In addition, design work can take place twenty-four hours a day, as suppliers all over the world can integrate their efforts using the Internet. GE's *Trading Process Network*, which links more than 2,500 of their trading partners electronically to streamline the procurement of standardized parts, has reduced procurement cycle time by 50 percent.[20]

Crafting an E-Commerce Strategy

Developing a business-to-business strategy for e-commerce is no different from developing any other type of marketing strategy: it begins with an understanding of the objectives the firm has specified for the e-commerce section of their business and it ends with the delineation of the tactics to be used in support of the strategy. The process begins with an evaluation of the company's products, customers, competitive situation, resources, and operations to better understand how all of these elements will mesh with an e-commerce strategy. Figure 5.2 provides a valuable framework that outlines important strategic and tactical questions that surround e-commerce strategies. Answering these questions will help the business marketing manager to carefully define what the firm hopes to accomplish through an e-commerce strategy as well as to assess several important resource issues associated with strategy implementation.

Delineating E-Commerce Objectives

According to one business marketing manager, "what the Internet can do is limitless, but a company has to decide what the technology means to them and what they have to do with it, then set the business model in place for that."[21] A guiding principle in

---

[20] Ibid., p. 6.

[21] Dana Blankenhorn, "Adding E-Commerce Means Changing Service, Channels, and Procurement," *Business Marketing* 84 (no. 8, August 1999): p. 23.

| FIGURE 5.2 | QUESTIONS TO GUIDE E-COMMERCE STRATEGY FORMULATION |

1. Customers and Markets

What are we already doing on the Internet and how do our activities align with customer needs?

How can we use the Internet to provide better customer service?

How can we use the Internet to make our sales channels more effective?

2. Competitive Threats

How might traditional competitors and e-business startups change market dynamics, take away market share or customers?

Will failure to act now precipitate a crisis within the next two years in any of our lines of business?

Can we ignore the Internet if our competitors are using it to gain attention and pricing advantages?

3. People and Infrastructure

Do our management teams and technical staff have the skills to run an Internet business?

What will it cost to fix weaknesses—exposed by our Internet business strategy—in our processes, infrastructure, and enterprise systems?

What are appropriate business and financial structures for managing Internet business risk?

4. Sources and Operations

Are we blinding ourselves by making assumptions based on our old way of doing business that doesn't fit with the Internet?

What are the Internet-relevant models that match ours, threaten us, or are suitable ways to conduct business?

How can we use the Internet to make supply chains more efficient?

How can we use the Internet to lower our operating costs? How long will it take?

SOURCE: "A CEO's Internet Business Strategy Checklist: The Leading Questions," *Business Technology Journal—Recent Research,* http://gartner112.gartnerweb.com (April 19, 1999).

formulating an Internet strategy is to understand that the Internet and all the associated impressive technology is nothing more than a *tool* for the business marketing strategist to use in satisfying the customer at a profit to the firm. Often, there is a temptation to think that the Internet can eliminate the need for salespeople, reduce expenditures on trade advertising, or totally replace traditional distribution channels and marketing intermediaries. For most firms, the Internet *supplements* the company's traditional marketing strategy, making it more effective or less costly, or both.

In the channels area, for example, many companies find it beneficial to use the Web to support their dealers' e-business efforts by providing Web-based information to them, offering Web co-op advertising dollars and allowing the dealers to build a front-end site onto their own backbone site.[22] Moreover, firms have found that a sales force continues to assume a vital role in forging customer relationships once an Internet strategy is implemented. In fact, the Internet can enhance sales force productivity. For example, PSS WorldMedical is a huge medical products distributor with a sales force of over 700 people. The company developed a closed *Customer Link* system that allows customers to order products online. The system does not replace the sales force; rather sales reps continue to earn commissions on Customer Link sales from their accounts, which frees the salespeople to concentrate more fully on consulting and higher profit capital equipment sales.[23]

Synchronizing the Web with Strategy   Just as important to enhancing effectiveness and efficiency, the Internet is often employed to reach an entirely new or different target market. Many experts consider Dell Computer to be the "poster child for business-to-business e-commerce" because of their legendary success in cost-effectiveness by providing custom-designed personal computers through the Internet.[24] Yet what makes Dell a great Internet marketer is its ability to take its customer-obsessed direct-sales practices and enhance them using the Web. "There isn't anything the company does online that it doesn't do in the physical world. Yet Dell and its customers know that nothing beats the Web for taking care of the 'annoying stuff'."[25] Dell serves as an excellent model for any business-to-business marketer seeking to craft an Internet strategy that is fully synchronized with its traditional salesperson-based strategy. The key to their success is understanding the role of the Internet and its relationship to all other elements of the firm's marketing strategy.

Specific Objectives of Internet Marketing Strategies

The Internet can be effective in providing information as well as in stimulating action by the customer. Internet marketing objectives resemble those that are associated with any type of communication strategy in the business marketplace. The Internet can be used to focus on cognitive objectives like stimulating awareness and knowledge of the company, to create a favorable attitude towards the firm, or to stimulate the buyer to purchase. Note the Web site for "Personalized Post-it Notes" displayed in Figure 5.3. Ads in leading business publications, like *Business Week* and *Fortune*, direct potential customers to this easy-to-navigate site. This site illustrates the objective of creating sales online by making it easy for customers to customize the product to their requirements, to place an order, and to visit "distributor studios" online to create the product. By visiting www.3m.com/notes-on-line you can experience firsthand how

---

[22] Ginger Conlon, "Direct Impact," *Sales & Marketing Management* 151 (December 1999): p. 57.

[23] Curt Werner, "HealthCare E-commerce, Still in Its Infancy, But Growing Fast," *Health Care Industry Today* 61 (no. 9, 1998): p. 10.

[24] Eryn Brown, "Nine Ways to Win on the Web," *Fortune* 139 (no. 10, May 24 1999): p. 114.

[25] Ibid., p. 114.

FIGURE 5.3	3M'S WEB SITE MAKES IT EASY TO PERSONALIZE POST-IT NOTES

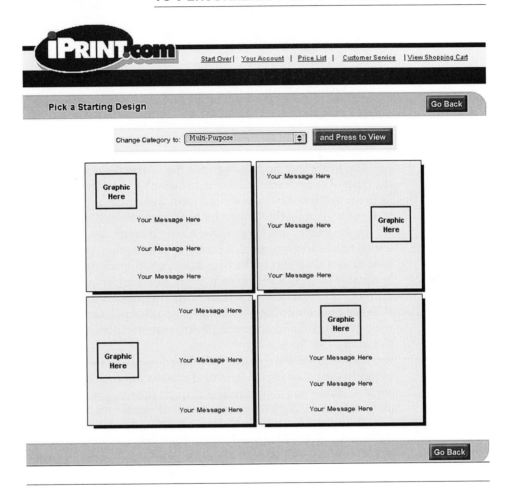

SOURCE: www.3m.com/notes-on-line/ (January 15, 2000), © 3M Company.

easy it is to use this online service. Following are some of the most common objectives that business marketers may have for the e-commerce portion of their business:[26]

1. Target a specific market or group of customers.

2. Build recognition of the company name and brands.

3. Convey a cutting-edge image.

4. Conduct market research.

5. Interact with existing customers and cultivate new ones.

---

[26]Adapted from Neal J. Hannon, *The Business of the Internet* (Cambridge, MA: International Thompson Publishing Company, 1998): p. 210.

6. Provide real-time information on products, services, and company finances to customers and supply chain partners.

7. Sell products and services.

8. Sell in a more efficient manner.

9. Advertise in a new medium.

10. Generate leads for the sales force.

11. Provide a medium for customer service.

12. Build strong relationships with customers.

The firm's specific objectives for the Internet portion of its business will dictate the types of issues it must deal with in formulating its strategy. For example, if the objective is to create new sales volume from an Internet presence, critical attention must be given to creating the systems for handling transactions. Critical issues include making the site easy to use, allowing for speedy transactions, making provisions for secure transactions and protection of customer information, providing readily available information and support of the transaction, creating an after-sale service capability, and being able to logistically move product to customers in a timely and cost-effective manner. There are also important relationship issues that must be considered. If the Web site will cannibalize sales from existing channel members, then the firm must develop a strategy for compensating them, enabling them to participate in other types of transactions, or for phasing them out.

Web sites will vary dramatically based on the objectives. Dow Chemical, for example, has the objective of delivering product information directly to the customer in order to build a one-to-one relationship. At the user's request, Dow will deliver to the user's desktop *News from Dow*, an electronic newsletter customized to individual preferences and needs. Product literature can also be directly downloaded to registered user's desktops. Du Pont, on the other hand, uses the front door of its Web site to show babies, mothers, and athletes to enhance the image of the company.[27]

Internet Strategy Implementation

With the Internet objectives fully delineated, the business marketer is positioned to develop an Internet strategy. As with any marketing process, the Internet strategy must carefully address issues related to product, promotion, channels and pricing. The discussion of the strategy implementation will begin by examining the important product-related dimensions.

The Internet Product

The Internet product is a complex array of physical elements, software, hardware, extranets, intranets, services, and information. The Web site is the major product ele-

---

[27] Ibid., p. 214.

ment associated with a company's e-commerce strategy. Even though e-commerce may include other dimensions, the heart of an e-commerce strategy is the company's Web site, for it is here that all interactions with the customer are most cost-effectively handled.

As indicated, the development of the Web site is predicated on a careful delineation of company objectives and it is rare that a Web site will be developed on the basis of a single objective. Thus, the design of the Web site becomes more complicated as additional objectives are articulated by top management. Another obvious ingredient to the planning process for the Web site are the needs of the targeted Web site visitors. A focus on both dimensions assures that both the company and the customer are accommodated.

Cisco Blazes the Trail   Let's examine some of the important guidelines for creating a successful Web site. A panel of experts was asked to select the top business-to-business Web sites and they selected Cisco Systems' site—"Cisco Connection"—as the very best of the business-to-business sites, noting that Cisco's site (www.cisco.com) "practically defines effective business-to-business Internet marketing."[28] Cisco is the leading technology firm in the area of high-end Internet information processing equipment like routers and hubs. Since more than 80 percent of Cisco's $10 billion in annual sales are generated by its Web site, customers continue to demonstrate their approval. In addition to generating a large sales volume, the site also handles 70 percent of the technical support contacts and about 50 percent of initial marketing contacts. The Cisco Connection contains an unbelievable forty gigabytes of data on 10 million separate pages and it generated over 40 million page views in one month. In one recent month, customers checked the status of orders online 300,000 times. Some of the distinguishing features of Cisco Connection include:[29]

1. Once an order is placed, it drops right into Cisco's enterprise resource planning system and triggers the required activities in the supply chain to immediately manufacture and ship the order.

2. The site opens up information on order status, pricing and product options, so the customer does not have to call a salesperson to receive this information.

3. Three quarters of the sales are to the company's resellers and one quarter are direct to corporate customers.

4. Four world wide advisory boards of about sixty key customers in the United States, Europe, Asia, and Latin America are used to determine what users want and need on the site.

5. Customers can download software from the Web site, which creates huge savings in shipping and postage.

6. Because the customer is able to receive so much information online and also check order status, Cisco estimates that the productivity of sales people and customer service representatives has been increased 15 percent.

---

[28] Matt Roush, "Cisco Makes the Connection," *Business Marketing* 84 (August 1999): p. 23.
[29] Ibid., p. 24.

| FIGURE 5.4 | GUIDELINES FOR DEVELOPING AN EFFECTIVE WEB SITE |

- Anticipate what users want and make it easy for them to find and quick to load

- Create a consistency of look and feel that gives the user a sense of continuity

- Allow the user's needs to drive the content of the site

- Invite users to enter and experience what the site has to offer

- Create a design that is easy to update

- Use color effectively

- Include appropriate fonts that are easy to read

- Provide tools for easy navigation of the site and individual Web pages

- Use graphics and other forms of multimedia effectively

SOURCE: Adapted from Neal J. Hannon, *The Business of the Internet* (Cambridge, MA: The International Thompson Publishing Company, 1998): p. 228.

Successful Web Site Design   To effectively develop a Web site to meet company objectives the designer needs to think like a user—to anticipate how the site will be used and the features that will make it easy to use. Figure 5.4 provides a set of useful guidelines for the business marketer to consider when developing their Web site. Note that most of the suggestions here would apply to any type of communication that a company directs toward its customers.

However, there are some unique elements associated with Web site development, notably tools for navigating the site and making it easy to load. The Web site shown in Figure 5.5 provides a good illustration of several of the principles specified in the guidelines. Iprint (www.iprint.com) allows customers to create customized products such as business cards, stationery and promotional items. The site makes it easy to find the exact product—whether that is Post-it notes or business cards, and it invites the user to click on any one of the products to see how they can be created. What Iprint offers is a start-to-finish automation of the commercial printing process, where the customer can see what their product will look like before it is printed. By scrolling through the different screens in the Web site, you can experience the process a buyer would go through to create their unique business card. The site effectively uses tabs and links from the home page to lead to specialized areas, making it quite user friendly.

To use the Internet as a marketing tool, the Web site should allow customers to easily move along the sales process, provide a quick and easy way to find the product they desire, and determine whether the products fit their needs. If the site can accomplish these goals, then the next function centers on facilitating the financial transaction. Speed, ease of use, and security are central to the goal of completing the sales transaction and meeting the customer's service expectations.

Internet Catalogs   One of the first applications of e-commerce for many business marketers that sell components, materials, and MRO items is to develop an electronic catalog that is available on their Web site. The Inside Business Marketing example

FIGURE 5.5	CREATING CUSTOMIZED POST-IT NOTES

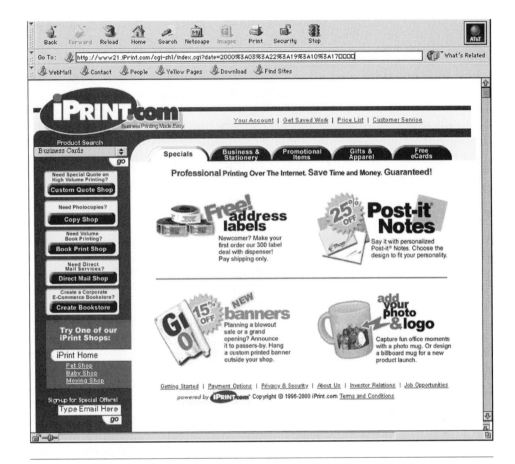

SOURCE: www.iprint.com/ (January 17, 2000) Copyright © 1996–2000 iPrint.com.

featuring AMP is an excellent illustration of the power of an online catalog that facilitates the search process for customers and prospective customers. Rather than leafing through thousands of pages, the user can define exact requirements and easily locate the appropriate item in the catalog. Because AMP has the capability to update the catalog instantaneously, customers are assured they are looking at the most current version of AMP's product offerings. Obviously, there is no way that a print catalog could provide that level of timeliness.

As Chapter 3 indicated, many firms have embraced e-purchasing applications, and have found that electronic purchasing dramatically enhances the effectiveness of buyers and reduces the time and expense spent in searching for operating resources or nonproduction goods. Firms that do not develop Internet catalogs will probably be unable to compete in the future because of the great savings that buyers are able to glean through e-purchasing. Savings in procurement expenses are not the only advantage of Web-based catalogs—a core value of these catalogs is the ability to provide significant technical data in real time. General Electric Plastics (GEP) developed a

INSIDE BUSINESS MARKETING

Amp's Search Engine Makes Finding Products Easy

AMP, Incorporated is the world's leading supplier of electrical connectors and interconnection systems. The firm has operations in 45 countries in every corner of the world and serves customers diverse in language, culture, standards, regulations, product, industry, and market segment. To AMP, with tens of thousands of products serving customers in every major market from the Japanese auto industry to Scandinavian cellular phone manufacturers to American computer makers, effectively and efficiently meeting customer needs is a challenge of massive proportions. To meet these challenging requirements, AMP capitalized on the powerful advantages of e-commerce.

AMP Connect is the company's e-commerce vehicle for interacting with its diverse customer base around the globe. The online catalog of company products describes nearly 90,000 components in eight languages. The site includes a "parametric" search engine whereby users may access information on components by defining a set of characteristics, or parameters. This allows customers to easily locate a desired product without paging through irrelevant data. The online catalog offers a number of efficiencies for AMP: information is made directly available to customers, thereby reducing sales and marketing costs for low-volume customers. The online publishing also eliminates the cost of producing and distributing the catalog in a variety of media such as paper or CD-ROM. Moreover, the entire catalog database can be updated instantaneously so customers and salespeople have access to the most timely and accurate product information.

Since the AMP customer base is global in nature, customers in all parts of the world use the database at their convenience. Further, the online catalog creates a new channel link to customers, supplementing the efforts of the sales force, distributors, and in-house customer service representatives.

SOURCE: Based on Jim Kesseler, "Defining the Future of Business-to-Business Electronic Commerce," *Journal of Global Information Management* 6 (no. 1, 1999): pp. 41–43.

Web catalog to provide continual updates to ever-changing product specifications. Extensive specifications are vital to engineers who use plastics in the design of other products, and GEP's specs were often out of date. The Web site was therefore developed as a searchable repository for all technical specifications and it is updated weekly. When first released, the site contained over 15,000 pages of technical information.[30] GEP's Web site primarily supports existing customers in their search for and use of plastics. Purchase and after-sales service and evaluation are handled by the sales force.

Customer Information Business marketers can provide further value to their customers by using the Internet/extranets to supply collateral and business-building information. They can begin by providing secure account tracking so that authorized persons can find out how much they owe, when their last payment was received, and so forth. They can also let customers know how much they ordered in a previous year, their cost, and even the average annual spending on the same supplies for all companies of the same size and type.[31] Customers can use this information to help plan purchasing and manage their inventories. Another enhancement to a Web site is to add links to other relevant sites. If the customer orders a certain type of paper using the supplier's extranet, the supplier could offer information links to other applications for the same type of paper.

---

[30] Robert M. O'Keefe and Tim McEachern, "Web-Based Customer Decision Support Systems," *Association for Computing Machinery, Communications of the ACM* 41 (no. 3, March 1998): p. 75.

[31] Mark Redwood, "True Potential Goes Far Beyond Online Purchasing," *Purchasing Canada* 25 (no. 14, 9 April 1999): p. 25.

Vertical Hubs, Automated Procurement and Trading Communities Several companies—Ariba, Commerce One, and Oracle for example—offer electronic procurement management systems to their customers. In many of these systems, suppliers are asked to participate by providing electronic catalogs or participating in online auctions. Given the speed with which buyers are turning to electronic buying and the significant advantages it provides, business marketers must carefully examine the role they should play in these systems. If they do not participate, then large volumes of future business may be compromised.

A good example is the approach to procurement taken by General Electric. GE's Trading Partner Network (TPN) acts as a Web-based notice board: suppliers post their catalogs on a master database maintained by TPN. GE buyers can then use a standard Web browser to compare prices or products, and make purchases online (see Chapter 3). A purchase triggers an automatic purchase order and shipment from a supplier. In addition, GE provides an extranet for suppliers that carries a broad range of information on orders, production plans, drawings or anticipated volumes. Supplier scorecards are also posted on the extranet.[32] Clearly, business marketers must be prepared to make their own investments in Internet technology in order to benefit from the type of relationship that programs like TPN imply. Similar to GE, General Motors, Ford, and DaimlerChrysler unveiled plans to set up a massive online bazaar for all the goods and services they buy, and "by the end of 2001 they expect all of the automakers' purchases to go through this site, and they expect all of their suppliers to be actively engaged"[33] (see Chapter 1). Suppliers to the automakers will need to develop processes to adapt their own systems to the automakers' new approach—a strong challenge, given the fact that most suppliers deal with several automobile manufacturers.

Ariba maintains a business-to-business trading community that connects buyers and sellers of low cost office products and operations resources. Ariba has attracted 250,000 suppliers to the system to compete for buyers who will spend $65 billion annually on office products. Buyers on the system are able to make instant price comparisons while suppliers can compete for business that might be very expensive to handle through traditional personal selling efforts.

Vertical Market Sites Electronic forums and communities are emerging to focus on a particular line of product where both sellers and buyers are attracted. In particular, vertical e-marketplaces have emerged and they are designed to serve the needs of a particular industry, such as ChemConnect for the chemical industry; Paper-Exchange.com for the paper industry; XSAg.com for the agricultural industry; and E-Steel for the steel industry. Meanwhile, Boeing has joined with Lockheed Martin Corporation and others to form an electronic marketplace for the aerospace industry where buyers and sellers around the world can conduct business. Similarly, GE Medical Systems Unit, along with other major manufacturers of medical equipment and supplies, are creating an electronic marketplace where hospital buyers can execute and track all of their buying transactions.[34]

---

[32] "Case Study: General Electric," *Financial Times Guide to Digital Business* (autumn 1999): p. 20.

[33] Gregory L. White, "How GM, Ford Think Web Can Make Splash on the Factory Floor," *The Wall Street Journal* (3 December 1999): p. A1 and Robert L. Simison, Fara Warner, and Gregory L. White, "Big Three Car Makers Plan Net Exchange," *The Wall Street Journal* (28 February 2000): p. A3

[34] Ron Winslow, "J&J, Baxter International, Others Plan Internet Concern for Hospital Purchases," *The Wall Street Journal* (30 March 2000): p. B16.

These "communities" enable business buyers to easily locate specific products, materials, and components and to shop around to determine availability, pricing and quality dimensions. Because of the specificity of these online communities, sellers will want to participate in those that align with their products and markets. PlasticsNet (www.plasticsnet.com) is a good example. It is a Web site where buyers and sellers of plastics can link up electronically. Initially it was a trade community and sourcing guide for the plastics industry, but has now evolved into a marketplace for plastics commerce. The site sees more than 90,000 visitors a month and has signed up more than 200 sellers who pay an annual fee of $5,000–$8,000 to have their storefronts and catalogs posted on PlasticsNet.[35] Buyers using PlasticsNet are able to order from multiple suppliers on one purchase order. PlasticsNet's site allows buyers to search by keyword, company, and category of product, as well as view diagrams, pictures, and pricing information. As these new ways to procure products emerge, business marketers should be poised to participate and to rethink the most appropriate strategies for positioning themselves on these vertical buying sites.

New Vertical e-Marketplace Rules   As vertical marketplaces are established across industry sectors, the competitive atmosphere will intensify. Strategists at Forrester Research suggest that successful e-marketplace operators must aggressively link with other sites and develop fresh strategies to[36]

1. *diversify beyond transaction fees.* As online marketplaces multiply, specific market sites will be pushed into competitive market share battles. Such competition will drive down the transaction fees that these e-marketplace operators can charge customers. Specialized services, such as delivery and credit, become the basis of differentiation.

2. *expand by creating alliances with other marketplaces.* Demanding participants will want a marketplace to act as a one-stop shop for a variety of products, but they will also expect highly specialized industry-specific services. For example, e-marketplaces will create point-to-point connections with service specialists like Yellow Freight in logistics or Citigroup in credit.

3. *configure for specific market segments.* Marketplaces serving industries like steel or pharmaceuticals will be unable to treat all buyers alike. Market sites develop deep industry knowledge concerning the needs and preferences of customers. Successful marketplace operators will tailor offerings to particular e-marketplace customer profiles.

Online Auctions   Another important decision for the business marketer is whether to participate in online auctions for business products. A variety of sites currently exist on the Internet that allow purchasers to bid on such items as steel, biological matter, office products, chemicals and plastics, to name just a few. FreeMarkets, Inc. organizes online auctions for suppliers that bid on purchaser contracts for industrial parts, raw materials, and commodities.[37] Currently the firm has arranged transactions

---

[35] Jeffery Davis, "PlasticsNet: The Trading Post," *Business2.0* (September 1999): p. 2.

[36] Verda Lief with Bruce D. Temkin, Kathryn McCarthy, Jeremy Sharrard, and Tobias O. Brown, "e-Marketplaces Reshape the B-to-B Landscape," http://www.forrester.com/ER/Research/Report/Analysis/O,1338,8774,FF.html (4/1/00)

[37] Michael Casey, "Internet Changes the Face of Supply and Demand," *The Wall Street Journal* (18 October 1999): p. B12.

totaling over $1 billion per year and 1,800 suppliers from thirty countries have participated in its auctions. The new marketplaces generated by online auctions of business products tend to empower the buyer and allow them a much wider range of choice. At the same time, business marketers must examine their existing ways of doing business and the relationships that exist with current customers to determine how they will participate in this new approach to buying. When a product is sold at auction, attention centers squarely on pricing and, as a result, on the firm's ability to control cost and efficiencies in its production and marketing processes. In addition, preferred positions they enjoyed with selected customers may be placed in jeopardy as those customers have wider access to more suppliers and potentially lower prices.

Channel Considerations With Internet Marketing

When firms develop an Internet strategy there are several important distribution channel issues to consider. An Internet marketing presence requires the business marketing manager to evaluate the following: the impact on channel efficiencies, the effect on current marketing intermediaries, the ability to rapidly deliver product, the impact on information sharing among channel members, and the need to consider the outsourcing of some key channel functions.

Channel Efficiencies   One of the significant benefits of Internet marketing in the business-to-business arena is the positive impact it can have on efficiency in the channels of distribution. The Internet uses low-cost communications technology to automate several kinds of business transactions. As a result, much of the back-office paper work and tasks required in dealing with channel members that once occupied the time of several employees can now be automated. By linking information systems with channel members through the Web, a firm's intermediaries can more effectively monitor their inventory levels and monitor the flow of goods through their warehouses. Most extranets that link distributors to business marketing firms allow the distributor to examine inventory levels at the manufacturer's warehouse, thus permitting the distributor to tailor orders to inventory availability. The net result is a substantial reduction in inventory costs as well as improved delivery performance to the ultimate customer.

National Semiconductor's Web site links customers, products, and distributors. National's customers who buy through distributors can use National's Web site to search for products and product information and then link directly to the distributor's site to buy.[38] The site serves as a tool to build the National name and to pass on qualified leads to distributors, who have often already negotiated agreements with customers. The Internet approach thereby facilitates distributor sales, and reduces much of the time and effort in answering questions that can be routinely addressed via the Web site.

Impact on Current Intermediaries   Internet strategies pose interesting questions about the structure of a firm's distribution channel. Depending on the nature of the manufacturer's Internet strategy, the role of current channel members may be expanded, unchanged, or dramatically reduced. The key variable is the extent to which

---

[38] Chad Kaydo, "You've Got Sales," p. 32.

the channel member adds value to the process of marketing and physically distributing products. In some instances, the channel members may be called upon to serve target markets that cannot be effectively covered through an Internet approach. There are numerous situations where traditional channel members have been relegated to the role of serving very small niche markets that cannot be efficiently served through direct or Internet marketing approaches. In other instances, channel members have been able to expand their role because of a manufacturer's new Internet strategy. Since many Internet transactions involve one or a few items, a real need exists for someone to handle the process of physically fulfilling orders, and hence a new opportunity is presented to a distributor who can perform this function effectively.

Disintermediation   Because the Internet improves connectivity among firms, it dramatically reduces the cost of communication and coordination in exchange transactions. In a networked channel, firms can bypass intermediaries who have traditionally facilitated the flow of information and goods between firms and their customers. This situation is referred to as **disintermediation,** and there are indications that it is taking hold in several business-to-business sectors. Large travel agencies that sell airline tickets to corporate accounts are experiencing disintermediation as airlines have created their own Web sites that provide as much or more information to the corporate traveler as did the agencies. Itineraries, including hotels, rental cars, and airline tickets can be arranged with the click of a mouse, and payment can be processed through a secure channel right on the Web site. In fact, because of the success of these Internet strategies, the airlines have reduced travel agent commissions substantially, forcing many to either go out of business or focus on leisure travel segments.

Infomediaries   Because the Internet allows the flow of information to be shifted away in both time and space from the physical flow of product in a distribution channel, specialized intermediaries can be used for each of the flows. Again, the pressure is on the traditional intermediary that handled both the physical product and the information component to find an appropriate niche in the channel operations. New intermediaries, referred to as *infomediaries,* have evolved to provide a mechanism for bringing buyers and sellers of selected products and services together over the Internet.[39] For example, in Great Britain, the National Transportation Exchange, (NTE) was set up to use the Internet to connect shippers who have loads they want to move cheaply with fleet managers who have space to fill. Chemdex, an infomediary in the biotechnology and pharmaceutical supplies market, created a single, efficient marketplace on the Internet for all three of the communities it serves—lab scientists, business buyers, and suppliers. It provides immense electronic catalogs, powerful search engines, and information that allows buyers and sellers to effect transactions on over 460,000 lab products. Essentially, Chemdex provides a single point of contact that allows buyers in the fragmented lab supply market to select products based on up-to-the minute prices and product information.

Some traditional channel members have used the Internet to effectively cement their position in the channels in which they operate. Marshall Industries, once a classic distributor of electrical components, has put most of its business on a Web site and transformed itself into an information-based intermediary offering a range of

---

[39]"The Net Imperative," *The Economist,* p. 23.

Internet-based services to over 40,000 customers.[40] Customers are provided everything from technical data sheets to interactive training sessions and product seminars. Marshall also offers "just-in-time" inventory management programs and helps customers run sophisticated marketing campaigns. The underlying lesson to traditional business marketing intermediaries is that they will be successful if they add value somewhere along the supply chain, whether that is in the form of typical services the manufacturer cannot offer or in new, Web-based services.

The Internet as a Channel Alternative

The Internet can be a very effective "channel" of distribution for reaching selected target markets. Rarely do business marketers rely solely on the Internet as their singular approach for contacting customers and consummating sales. Rather, the Internet is but one channel or method for doing business with target markets. At AMP, the large manufacturer of electronic connectors, traditional channels such as the sales force, distributors and in-house customer service representatives are complemented by its Internet electronic catalog. The catalog simply provides another avenue through which customers can do business with the company.[41]

In some cases, the Internet is particularly effective for "distributing" certain types of products like software and reading material. The software industry pioneered the use of the Internet for product distribution. Computer software firms like Netscape and Microsoft take advantage of the new Web distribution channels to sell and distribute software electronically. The advantage of Internet channels is that companies of any size, with very small marketing budgets, can take advantage of the Web to create and distribute new products. Anything that can be digitized can be transmitted over the Internet, which offers numerous advantages to marketers desiring to distribute printed materials. In short, the Internet broadens the reach of marketers, providing them with an efficient channel to serve customers on a global scale.

Digital Channel Advantages   By providing an effective mechanism for contacting potential buyers, the Internet offers some advantages over traditional channels of distribution for business products. According to Judy Strauss and Raymond Frost, the Internet adds value for several reasons:[42]

1. The contact can be customized to the buyer's needs.

2. The Internet provides a wide range of referral sources such as Web pages, search engines, shopping agents, newsgroups, chat rooms, and e-mail.

3. The Internet is always open for business: buyers can contact the site twenty-four hours a day, seven days a week.

Using the Internet, business marketers can create customized solutions for customers. For example, Staples (www.staples.com) offers customized catalogs for its corporate clients. Such a strategy would be costly to implement through traditional channels.

[40] Ibid., p. 24.

[41] Jim Kesseler, "Defining the Future of Business-to-Business Electronic Commerce," *Journal of Global Information Management* 6 (no. 1, January 1999): p. 43.

[42] Judy Strauss and Raymond Frost, *Marketing on the Internet* (Upper Saddle River, NJ: Prentice-Hall, 1997): p. 168.

The Internet provides Staples with unparalleled flexibility in creating just the type of catalog a particular organization desires.

Hewlett-Packard maintains an online store aimed at the small and mid-sized business market.[43] The online store represents the first attempt by Hewlett-Packard to sell directly to the small and mid-size business market rather than going through resellers. This new channel eventually is expected to serve about 10 to 15 percent of the small and mid-size market, and Hewlett-Packard works closely with their established resellers to avoid any conflict as a result of the Internet channel. Customers using the online store are able to order directly from Hewlett-Packard. The typical order is one or two PCs, workstations, printers, or networking units. Generally, small orders are not profitable for Hewlett-Packard resellers, so the direct Internet channel allows them to focus on other markets that have more complex requirements and that usually buy in larger quantities. As this Hewlett-Packard example suggests, the Internet channel, if targeted properly and integrated with traditional channel partners, can be a cost-effective approach for serving selected business market segments.

The Impact of the Internet On Pricing Strategy

The Internet has a pervasive impact on the business marketer's approach to pricing. In many industries, the formation of Internet auctions, hubs, infomediaries, and trading communities has dramatically changed the nature of pricing decisions for the business-to-business marketer. The major impact has been to substantially reduce the marketer's control over price. As Michael Casey suggests, "'market-making' Web sites are shifting the balance of power between buyers and sellers in business-to-business transactions, giving buyers and other firms more control over the cost of raw materials and supplies."[44]

Other sites, called ***industrial communities,*** provide services throughout a wide cross-section of industries that allow purchasers to bid on such items as steel, biological matter or office supplies. The net effect of the Internet agglomeration of sellers of materials and components is to place severe downward pressure on prices. Where sellers may have enjoyed selected geographical advantages due to the lack of close-by competition, the new Internet buying operations have opened up markets to many types of suppliers, with the result being a downward pressure on prices. The net impact is that business marketers of raw materials, components, and supplies that can be priced and sold via the Internet must carefully rethink their pricing approach and develop more effective means for competing on a price-oriented basis.

Price Competition Intensifies   The impact on pricing strategies is highlighted by a recent General Motors strategy to set up massive Internet markets for all the goods and services they buy—everything from paper clips to stamping presses to contract manufacturing.[45] The company expects that all its purchases will go through the site by 2001. GM's intention is to have a global forum where transactions can be completed for all types of supplies and components almost instantaneously. General Motors will encourage suppliers to use the Web sites to make their own purchases or sell excess

[43] Deborah Gage, "HP Opens Up Online Store for Smaller Businesses," *PC Week* (7 June 1999): p. 51.

[44] Casey, "Internet Changes the Face," p. 12.

[45] White, "How GM, Ford Think Web Can Make Splash," p. 1.

inventory. GM expects the prices charged by their suppliers to other customers to be lower, and the company will interpret slow sales figures on its site as a sign the supplier's prices *aren't competitive!* According to GM, "if that's true, we may be looking for a replacement supplier."

As can be seen from this type of system, even greater price pressure is placed on GM suppliers: pressure from GM itself as well as pressure to keep prices low enough to encourage other buyers to purchase from them on GM's Web site. The Internet, because of its ability to provide worldwide linkages to hundreds of suppliers, forces the business marketer to continually explore ways to become more efficient, and to reflect these efficiencies in competitive pricing.

The Internet and Customer Communication

The Internet expands the business marketer's communication capabilities. Providing real-time, up-to-date, low cost information is one of the salient features of an Internet strategy. Within seconds and with a few key strokes, an entire database can be corrected, updated and appended, and the information shared with potential buyers all over the world. The scope of the communications capability of the Internet is illustrated by the different phases of electronic commerce through which companies typically move.[46] At the most basic level of e-commerce, a firm might offer simple *online information*, like their product catalog. Here, access to information is facilitated, and product search capabilities are enhanced. The limitation is the inability to help the user search for information on the basis of predefined criteria—the catalog simply exists in an electronic format. In the next phase of e-commerce, *database publishing*, the user is provided with search capabilities. Using a search engine, the customer can scan the catalog database and target particular requirements. The third phase, *customer self-service*, provides customized information for specific users. Here customers can download search-assisted catalogs and service diagnostics from the system. Information on price and product availability is also provided. The final, and most complex, phase of e-commerce, *transactions*, provides for full transactions, from information gathering to purchase to fulfillment to billing to secure payment, all in a single environment.

Meet the Customer's Requirements Compared to traditional, paper-based approaches, each phase or level of e-commerce represents an improvement in the way in which business marketers interact with their customers and potential customers. Of course, there are many situations where Internet communication merely complements personal contact between buyers and sellers: complex products requiring customer-specific engineering and customization or very high-cost items requiring extensive negotiations and long-term contractual arrangements. For example, Boeing's Web site is used more to describe the company and how it is organized, explain each of its aircraft models, describe and explain the full range of services offered, and delineate how potential buyers can work with the company in creating a product for their specific requirements. However, for many firms that market supplies, standard components, repair parts, and the like, e-commerce provides the greatest potential for reducing transaction costs while advancing the efficiency and effectiveness of marketing communications.

---

[46]Kesseler, "Defining the Future of Business-to-Business Electronic Commerce," p. 43.

To recap, the Internet is just one component of the business marketer's overall strategy: it simply extends the firm's reach and it must be integrated into the overarching strategy the firm uses to reach and interact with its customers. Even at Dell Computer, where the firm operates at the phase-four level of e-commerce—full transaction capability—the Internet is just one approach to the marketplace. According to Michael Dell, Chairman, "we work with customers face-to-face, on the telephone, or over the Internet. Depending on the customer, some or all of those techniques will be used, they're all intertwined."[47]

The Role of the Sales Force   Many firms find that the Internet simply makes sales representatives more effective because they can concentrate on solving customer problems and building customer relationships. The Internet streamlines the sales process and eliminates order-processing details for customers and salespersons alike. While there will be situations where the Internet supplants sales that were once the province of the sales force, Internet strategies generally *support* the efforts of the sales force. The Internet can provide the salesperson with an enormous database of information on customers, products, and competitors. By using these rich information sources, the salesperson can customize presentations, respond to specific customer idiosyncrasies, and effectively respond to competitive challenges. Successful companies have developed approaches for integrating sales force strategies with Internet strategies and for compensating salespeople so that they support online initiatives.[48]

Promotion   To capitalize on the investment in creating and maintaining a Web site, promotions highlighting a site need to be run frequently and in a variety of media to stimulate use. An eighteen-month analysis of small-, medium-, and large-company business-to-business Web sites indicated that the number of hits is directly related to the amount of off-line advertising and sales promotion.[49] Advertising in trade publications and handouts at trade shows and conferences appear to be especially effective in stimulating the use of business Web sites. In addition to promotions and advertising, salespeople must be trained to instruct customers on how to use the Web site and the special features that have been created to provide value to the customer.

The Internet's Expanding Role

The Internet has become such a powerful marketing tool that it will be difficult for any business marketer, regardless of size, to neglect the Internet. Business marketers must focus on the customer and the customer's needs and buying processes, and they must demonstrate how their products and services add value and enhance the customer's profitability. Indeed, corporate buyers continually seek new ways to reduce cost and enhance corporate performance. For business marketers, the Internet provides a powerful vehicle for demonstrating the value of offerings and customizing them for individual customers.

---

[47] *Financial Times Guide to Digital Business*, p. 11.

[48] Stewart Alsop, "E or Be Eaten," *Fortune* 140 (November 8, 1999): p. 87.

[49] Carol Patten, "Marketers Promote Online Traffic Through Traditional Media, With a Twist," *Business Marketing* 84 (August 1999): p. 40.

Summary

Business marketers of all types, whether manufacturers, distributors, or service providers are integrating the Internet and electronic communications into the core of their business marketing strategies. E-commerce is the broad term applied to communications, business processes, and transactions that are carried out through electronic technology—mainly the Internet. E-commerce can be applied to almost any aspect of business, with the intent of making all processes more efficient. The Internet, or the vast collection of interlinked computers and computer networks, is the major vehicle through which business marketers carry out their e-commerce strategies. Based on Internet technologies, an intranet is an internal network that is accessible only to company employees and other authorized users. By contrast, an extranet is a private network that uses Internet-based technology to link companies with suppliers, customers, and other partners. Extranets allow the business marketer to customize information for a particular customer and to seamlessly share information with that customer in a secure environment.

For business marketers, the Internet has been effective as a powerful communication medium, an alternative channel, a new venue for a host of services, a data-gathering tool, and a way to integrate the supply chain. To be successful, the Internet strategy must be carefully woven into the fabric of the firm's overall marketing strategy. The Internet offers important benefits, including reduced transaction costs, reduced cycle time, supply chain integration, information accessibility, and closer customer relationships. To capitalize on the Internet as a strategic tool, the business marketer must center on the special needs of targeted customers.

The e-commerce strategy must be carefully crafted, beginning with a focus on objectives. Once the objectives have been established, an Internet strategy can be formulated. Included in the strategy is a consideration of the product-related dimensions of the Internet offering, the most visible of which is the firm's Web site. Extranets, electronic catalogs, customer information, and vertical hubs must also be integrated into the "product." Several fundamental channel of distribution issues must be evaluated, including the impact of the Internet on present channels and channel partners, channel efficiencies, and the Internet as a separate channel to the market. Pricing issues are also significant, particularly in light of the impact of trading communities and auction sites. Finally, marketing communication strategies consider the extent to which the firm provides transactional capabilities on the Web site and how the Internet strategy is integrated with other promotional vehicles. To an important degree, the Internet provides a powerful medium for developing a one-to-one relationship with customers in the business market.

Discussion Questions

1. How do the different definitions of e-commerce apply to the marketing tasks of a typical business marketer?

2. Describe the structure of the Internet and the major components that facilitate its use in the business marketing environment.

3. What are the different ways a business marketer would employ the Internet, intranets, and extranets to enhance the efficiency and effectiveness of strategy?

4. Comment on the following statement: given the power and pervasiveness of Internet marketing strategies, many business marketers will probably become almost pure Internet marketers in the near future.

5. What are the advantages of Internet marketing strategies compared to traditional strategies?

6. Discuss some of the possible objectives a manufacturer of business jet airplanes might have for the Internet strategy.

7. The Crespy Company makes control systems that regulate large gas turbine engines. Describe the key elements of the "Internet" product the Crespy Company might develop for its customers.

8. Find the Web site of a business marketing company and evaluate how easy it is for a potential customer to move through the Web site and eventually purchase a product.

9. As customers begin to emphasize e-procurement via electronic catalogs, what major challenges are posed for a business marketer of office products?

10. How do electronic vertical hubs and trading communities facilitate the purchasing process?

11. Comment on the following: Internet marketing strategies will eventually wipe out most business-to-business intermediaries.

12. Do you feel that the Internet will result in stiffer price competition in the business-to-business marketplace? Explain.

6

Supply Chain Management

When promised delivery performance is not provided, buyers will search for a new supplier. Organizational buyers assign great importance to supply chain processes that eliminate the uncertainty of product delivery. Supply chain management assures that product, information, service, and financial resources all flow smoothly through the entire value creation process. Business marketers invest considerable financial and human resources in creating supply chains to service the needs and special requirements of their customers. After reading this chapter, you will understand

1. the role of supply chain management in business marketing strategy.

2. the importance of integrating both firms and functions throughout the entire supply chain.

3. the critical role of logistics activities in achieving supply chain management goals.

4. the importance of achieving high levels of logistics service performance while simultaneously controlling the cost of logistics activities.

Intel Corporation, though in an enviable position as the dominant maker of microprocessors, has been busily reinventing the way it moves and stores inventory to minimize the quantity of expensive chips awaiting shipment to customers. Intel is also helping customers in the competitive personal-computer industry to operate with pared-down inventories. Because the average life cycle of a microprocessor has fallen from eight years for the 386 series to less than a year and a half today, Intel must "be able to ship it at today's prices, not tomorrow's, and to know the right amount of new product to build on the right day. Intel's product, ounce for ounce, is more valuable than platinum, and the cost of inventory is a number beyond imagination."[1] Through their new sales-order system, Intel can now monitor inventory levels anywhere in the world and commit products to a customer and deliver them within three days. Customers are electronically linked to Intel so they can minimize the size of their own inventory of chips, and all Intel products are shipped via air from only three warehouses across the globe—Malaysia, the Philippines, and Costa Rica. Through its various improvements in shipping, handling, communication and product tracking, Intel has reduced finished-goods inventory from eight weeks' worth to four weeks' worth. Eventually, Intel hopes to extend its computer links into the inventory systems of the large computer chain stores that sell PCs. Such a system would allow Intel to have instant feedback on what is selling and what products they should be building.

All of these efforts at Intel are part of an innovative approach to tightening distribution processes, bolstering links with suppliers and customers, and integrating production and marketing initiatives that is referred to as **supply chain management (SCM).** As business evolves into the twenty-first century, supply chain management is one of the predominant management approaches driving many organizations.[2] As Robert Derocher and Jim Kilpatrick conclude, "no longer merely the logistics vehicle for the business, the supply chain increasingly is seen as the main conduit for getting product from its source to the ultimate customer. Viewed from this perspective, the supply chain touches almost every function within the organization. As such, it has the greatest impact on customer satisfaction and the greatest potential for improving the bottom line and enabling competitive advantage."[3]

This chapter will describe the nature of supply chain management, explain the important goals associated with it, discuss the factors that lead to successful supply chain strategies, and demonstrate how logistics management is a key driver of supply chain success. Once supply chain management has been defined, the chapter will highlight how the business marketer's logistics processes form the core of the supply chain management strategy. The logistical elements will be described in terms of their interface within the channel of distribution and how they must be integrated to create desired customer service standards. The chapter will then address issues related to the role of logistics in organizational purchasing decisions, the types of logistics services sought by buyers, and the design of effective logistics processes.

---

[1] Stuart F. Brown, "Wresting New Wealth from the Supply Chain," *Fortune* 139 (November 9, 1998): p. 204X.

[2] Peter C. Brewer and Thomas W. Speh, "Using the Balanced Scorecard to Measure Supply Chain Performance," *The Journal of Business Logistics* (spring 2000), p. 75.

[3] Robert P. Derocher and Jim Kilpatrick, "Six Supply Chain Lessons for the New Millennium," *Supply Chain Management Review* (winter 2000): p. 34.

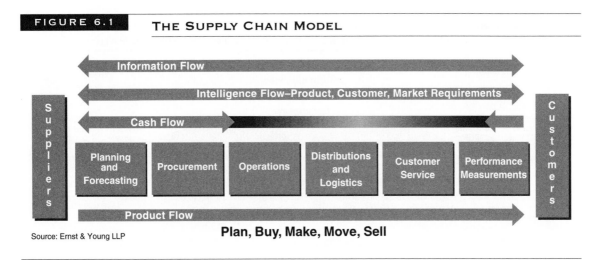

| FIGURE 6.1 | THE SUPPLY CHAIN MODEL |

Source: Ernst & Young LLP

Plan, Buy, Make, Move, Sell

SOURCE: Karl B. Mandrodt, Mary Collins Holcomb, and Richard H. Thompson, "What's Missing in Supply Chain Management?" *Supply Chain Management Review* (fall 1997): p. 81. Reprinted with permission of *Supply Chain Management Review*, a Cahners publication.

The Concept of Supply Chain Management

A supply chain encompasses all the activities associated with moving goods from the raw materials stage through to the end user (for example, a personal computer buyer). A formal definition of supply chain management is:

> Supply chain management (SCM) is the integration of business processes from end user through original suppliers that provides products, services, and information that add value for customers.[4]

The supply chain includes a variety of firms, ranging from those that process raw materials to make component parts or to those engaged in wholesaling. Included also are all types of organizations engaged in transportation, warehousing, information processing, and materials handling. Functions to be executed throughout the supply chain include sourcing, procurement, product design, production scheduling, manufacturing, order processing, inventory management, materials handling, warehousing, and customer service.[5] Successful supply chain management coordinates and integrates all of these activities into a seamless process. Figure 6.1 illustrates the key elements of supply chain management, and highlights the important integration that must take place among a variety of business functions and across several different organizations in the supply chain.

Supply chains should be managed in an integrated manner. Integrated SCM focuses on managing relationships, information, and material flow across organizational borders to cut costs and enhance flow. Firms following the SCM approach look for

[4]Martha C. Cooper, Douglas M. Lambert, James D. Pagh, "Supply Chain Management: More Than a New Name for Logistics," *The International Journal of Logistics Management* 8, no. 1 (Winter 1997): p. 1.

[5]Francis J. Quinn, "A Supply Chain Management Overview," *Supply Chain Yearbook 2000* (January 2000): p. 15.

FIGURE 6.2 SUPPLY CHAIN MANAGEMENT: INTEGRATING AND MANAGING BUSINESS PROCESSES ACROSS THE SUPPLY CHAIN

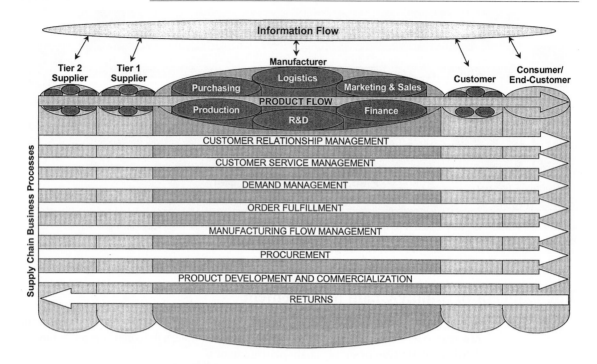

SOURCE: Douglas M. Lambert, Martha C. Cooper, and Janus D. Pagh, "Supply Chain Management: Implementation Issues and Research Opportunities," *The International Journal of Logistics Management* 9, no. 2 (1998): p. 2. Web site at www.ijlm.org.

ways to integrate their logistics, procurement, operations, and marketing functions with other supply chain members so that materials, information, component parts, and finished product flow seamlessly from point of origin to final user at low unit cost and at high levels of service. Leading supply chain-oriented firms focus intensely on monitoring actual user demand, instead of forcing a product into markets that may or may not sell quickly. In so doing, they minimize the flow of raw materials, finished product and packaging materials, thereby reducing inventory costs across the entire supply chain.

Partnerships: The Critical Ingredient

To integrate activities across the supply chain, close working relationships are required. SCM may require that all firms in the supply chain share sensitive and proprietary information about customers, actual demand, point-of-sale transactions, and corporate strategic plans. SCM involves significant joint planning and communication; firms often create teams of personnel that cut across functional and firm boundaries to coordinate the movement of product to market. In other words, achieving the real potential of SCM requires integration not only among departments within the organization, but also with external partners. Figure 6.2 is a comprehensive framework that details the central components of supply chain management. Observe the tight connections that are required among suppliers, manufacturers, and customers to integrate activities to achieve a timely flow of products and information.

Traditional, nonintegrated approaches to managing product and information flows are expensive and time consuming. Such approaches often involve much higher transportation and handling costs; they demand considerable time from salespeople, buyers, and others in the organization. For example, there is often excessive movement of material—one major computer manufacturer reported that some of the components used in its computers had traveled 250,000 miles before they reached the ultimate buyer! Furthermore, traditional transactions processes create excess inventory in the pipeline leading to the customer. In the pharmaceutical industry, firms that have not adopted the supply chain management process incur higher inventory carrying costs and provide lower levels of customer service than their competitors.

Supply chain management seeks to create an "overlap" among participants in the supply chain, where the partners share a long-term commitment and an interwoven relationship not unlike a good marriage.[6] Until some type of partnership is in place, the true benefits of supply chain integration cannot be achieved. A recent study in the United Kingdom demonstrated that when supply chain partnerships exist, superior levels of performance result.[7]

Not only do effective supply chains conduct business as partners, they also openly share information across the supply chain. Intelligence about the customer and what the customer has ordered is transmitted upstream so that every organization in the supply chain has visibility of the information and can respond accordingly. When information is made immediately available to supply chain members, tier 1 and tier 2 suppliers can act immediately, thereby eliminating the delays that created inefficiencies in the past. This allows the supply chain to reduce inventories (safety stocks) and speed up the cash flow process. Figure 6.3 depicts the stages that companies go through when forming inter-company networks. Note that in Stage 3, the "Extended Enterprise," companies have successfully aligned both their internal and external processes. This is the ultimate goal of supply chain management.

Supply Chain Management: A Tool For Competitive Advantage

The supply chain can be a powerful competitive weapon as market leaders like Dell, Grainger, and Hewlett-Packard have demonstrated through the unparalleled success of their supply chain processes. Research by Mercer Management Consulting has found that "best-practice" supply chain management companies typically excel in reducing operating costs, improving asset productivity, and compressing order cycle time.[8] Nucor Incorporated, operating in the mature steel industry, reinvented the traditional steel supply chain and developed a "mini-mill" manufacturing strategy that is highly responsive to customer needs and has fueled an 18 percent compounded annual five year revenue growth rate.[9] As a primary interface point with the customer, supply

[6]James E. Morehouse, "Extending the Enterprise: The Paradigm," *Supply Chain Management Review* (fall 1997): p. 38.

[7]Gwyn Groves and Vassilios Valsamakis, "Supplier-Customer Relationships and Company Performance," *International Journal of Logistics Management* 9, no. 2 (1998): p. 62.

[8]Quinn, "A Supply Chain Management Overview," p. 15.

[9]Robert E. Sabath and David G. Frentzel, "Go for the Growth! Supply Chain Management's Role in Growing Revenues," *Supply Chain Management Review* (summer 1997): p. 17.

FIGURE 6.3	STAGES FIRMS GO THROUGH IN ADOPTING SUPPLY CHAIN MANAGEMET

The Supply Chain Stages

Stage 0 Informal

The lack of functionall policies/processes and basic operations management results in unpredictable product quality and supply.

Stage 1 Functional

Functional orientation sub-optimizes enterprise performance in asset management, cost, and customer satisfaction.

Stage 2 Internal Process Integration

With alignment across all subprocesses and levels of management, operations management processes are integrated and display world-class performance and continuous improvement.

Stage 3 The Expanded Enterprise

There is internal and external process integration, allowing each enterprise to focus on its customers, core competencies, and creating value.

SOURCE: Tom Brunell, "Managing a Multicompany Supply Chain," *Supply Chain Management Review* (spring 1999): p. 49. Reprinted with permission of *Supply Chain Management Review*, a Cahners publication.

chain management can offer value in the form of competitively superior delivery and value-added services, as defined by customers. Best-in-class supply chain management practices provide advantages including 10 to 30 percent higher on-time delivery performance, a 40 to 65 percent (or one-to-two month) advantage in cash-to-cash cycle time, 50 to 80 percent less standing inventory, which all translates into three to six percent of a company's revenue. For a $100 million company, earnings improvements of up to $6 million are achievable by thoroughly adopting supply chain management practices.[10] However, supply chain management, as a source of competitive advantage, should not be seen simply as a means of reducing cost, but also as a means of boosting revenues.[11]

Supply Chain Management Goals

SCM is both a boundary-spanning and function-spanning endeavor. The underlying premise of SCM is that waste reduction and enhanced supply chain performance come

[10] Bill Faherenwald, "Supply Chain: Managing Logistics for the 21st Century," *Business Week*, 28 (December 1998), Special Section p. 3.

[11] Charles Batchelor, "Moving Up the Corporate Agenda," *The Financial Times*, (1 December 1998), p. 1.

only when there is both intrafirm and interfirm functional integration, sharing, and cooperation. Thus, each firm within the supply chain must tear down the functional silos within its organization and foster true coordination and integration of marketing, production, procurement, sales, and logistics. Furthermore, actions, systems, and processes among *all* the supply chain participants must be integrated and coordinated. Firm-wide integration is a necessary, but not sufficient, condition for achieving the full potential benefits of SCM. Integration must be taken to a higher plane, so that functions and processes are coordinated across all the organizations in the supply chain.

Supply chain management is undertaken to achieve four major goals: waste reduction, time compression, flexible response, and unit cost reduction.[12] These goals have been articulated in several contexts associated with SCM, and they speak to the importance of both interfunctional and interfirm coordination.

Waste Reduction   Firms that practice SCM seek to reduce waste throughout the supply chain by minimizing duplication, harmonizing operations and systems, and enhancing quality. With respect to duplication, firms at all levels in the supply chain often maintain inventories. Efficiencies can be gained for the chain as a whole if the inventories can be centralized and maintained by just a few firms at critical points in the distribution process. Similarly, demand planning can be assigned to the particular firm in the supply chain that possesses the best understanding of customers and their ordering patterns. In unintegrated supply chains, personnel, information systems, order selection processes, and various logistics assets are often duplicated at every level, and the redundancies associated with these resources should be candidates for elimination.

A second means to reduce waste is to harmonize operations and systems among supply chain members. Harmonization seeks to achieve uniformity and agreement of operations and systems among the firms. Rather than have two different pallet systems, for example, it makes sense for all supply chain participants to use only one. In this way, they can use common equipment in handling and storing pallet loads and gain leverage for the entire supply chain in dealing with pallet vendors. Another example is for all supply chain entities to use the same system for tracking actual sales, so that all can work from this common software and database in planning production and logistics operations. Harmonized systems create information flow that is timely, relevant, and of high quality, which leads to the elimination of unnecessary activities and more responsive delivery of the product to the ultimate customer.

Finally, maintaining the quality of products, operations, and assets is essential to operating an efficient supply chain. Products that do not meet customer specifications will undermine the tight time requirements associated with just-in-time deliveries. Furthermore, substandard products that must be returned add additional costs to the logistics process. Equipment and facilities that marginally meet requirements may eventually reduce product quality or slow down various processes within the system.

Time Compression   Another critical goal of SCM is the compression of order-to-delivery cycle time. When production and logistics processes are accomplished in less time, all entities in the supply chain are able to operate more efficiently, and a primary result is reduced inventories throughout the system. Time compression also enables

---

[12] Brewer and Speh, "Using the Balanced Scorecard."

supply chain partners to more easily observe and understand the cumulative effect of problems that occur anywhere in the chain and respond quickly. Reduced cycle time also speeds the cash-to-cash cycle for all chain members, thereby enhancing cash flow and financial performance throughout the system. Dell Computer's well-managed supply chain excels on all of these performance dimensions. Time compression means that information and products flow smoothly and quickly, which permits all parties to respond to customers in a timely manner while maintaining minimal inventory.

Flexible Response   The third goal of SCM is to develop flexible response throughout the supply chain. Flexible response in order handling, including how orders are handled, product variety, order configuration, order size, and several other dimensions means that a customer's unique requirements can be met in a cost-effective manner. To illustrate, a firm that responds flexibly can configure a shipment in almost any way (for example, different pallet patterns or different product assortments) and do it quickly without problems for the customer. Flexibility also may mean customizing products in the warehouse to correspond to a customer's need for unique packaging and unitization. The key to flexibility is that individual customer needs are met in a way that the customer views as cost effective and the supply chain views as profitable.

Unit Cost Reduction   The final goal of SCM is to operate logistics in a manner that reduces cost per unit for the end customer. Determine the level of performance desired by the customer and then minimize the costs of providing that service level. The business marketer should carefully assess the balance between level of cost and the degree of service provided. The goal is to provide an appropriate value equation for the customer, which means that cost in some cases will be higher for meaningful enhancements in service. Cost cutting is not an absolute, but the SCM approach is focused on driving costs to the lowest possible level for the service requested. For example, shipping products in full truck load quantities on a weekly basis is less expensive than shipping pallet quantities every day; however, when a customer, like Honda, wants daily deliveries to minimize inventories, the SCM goal is to offer daily shipments at the lowest possible cost. SCM principles drive down costs because they focus management attention on eliminating actions and activities that unnecessarily add cost, such as duplicate inventories, double and triple handling of the product, unconsolidated shipments, and uncoordinated promotions such as special sales.

Benefits to the Final Customer

A well-managed supply chain will ultimately create tangible benefits for customers throughout the supply chain. When the supply chain reduces waste, improves cycle time and flexible response, and minimizes costs, these benefits should flow through to ultimate customers. Thus, a key focus of the supply chain and its members is on monitoring the extent to which the customer is realizing these important benefits and on assessing the factors that may impede their realization.

A supply chain's customer can be viewed on several dimensions, and it is important to focus on each. A producer of electronic radio parts views the radio manufacturer as an absolutely critical customer, but the auto manufacturer that installs the radio in a car is equally, if not more important, and ultimately the final buyer of the automobile must be satisfied. Thus, different demands, desires, and idiosyncrasies of customers all along the supply chain must be understood and managed effectively.

The Financial Benefits Perspective

When the goals of the supply chain partners are being achieved and the benefits are flowing through to customers, supply chain members should experience financial success. The most commonly reported benefits for firms that adopt SCM are lower costs, higher profit margins, enhanced cash flow, revenue growth, and a higher rate of return on assets. Because activities are harmonized and unduplicated, the cost of transportation, order processing, order selection, warehousing, and inventory is usually reduced. A study to validate the correlation between supply chain integration and business success shows that best-practice SCM companies have a 45 percent total supply chain cost advantage over their median supply chain competitors.[13] Cash flows in the supply chain are improved because the total cycle time from raw materials to finished product is reduced. The leading firms also enjoy greater cash flow—they have a cash-to-order cycle time exactly half that of the median company.

Because SCM usually leads to better service, supply chain members often experience a significant growth in revenue. Companies participating in MIT's Integrated Supply Chain Management Program reported a 17 percent revenue increase as a result of SCM initiatives.[14] SCM initiatives, by simultaneously reducing logistics assets and operating costs while increasing revenues, generally create a higher rate of return on assets employed in the supply chain. Improved returns are not automatic and do not necessarily come quickly, but the potential to improve the return on assets is significant for most firms in the chain.

The SCM Improvement Perspective

Supply chains must continually learn and innovate to ensure future profitability. In other words, the world-class benchmarks of supply chain performance in 2005 will be different from those today. Firms following supply chain management prescriptions continuously improve their ability to reduce waste, compress time, respond flexibly, and reduce unit costs in four ways. First, they can redesign the products and processes that span the supply chain in a manner that improves the value delivered to customers. Second, they can more effectively leverage the human knowledge base contained within the supply chain by collaborating inter-organizationally to enhance the value delivered to customers. Third, they can continuously improve the management of supply chain information flows to ensure that all supply chain partners have access to the appropriate information to enable decision making that is accurate, timely, and supportive of customer needs. Finally, each supply chain needs to monitor the external marketplace to ensure that potential threats and/or substitutes do not emerge that redefine the way value is delivered to customers. After all, a supply chain's methods and pace of continuous improvement must always be evaluated relative to the competition.

Information and Technology Drivers

Supply chains could not function at high levels of efficiency and effectiveness without powerful information systems to drive them. Many of the complex Internet supply

---

[13] Rabin, Pittiglio, Todd, and McGrath Special Report, "Integrated Supply Chain Management Benchmarking Study," 1997.

[14] Francis Quinn, "The Payoff," *Logistics Management* 37, no. 11 (November 1997): p. 58.

FIGURE 6.4	EXISTING SOFTWARE APPLICATIONS USED IN SUPPLY CHAIN MANAGEMENT

Application	Function
Enterprise Resource Planning (ERP)	Automate and synchronize day-to-day operations—e.g., finance, human resources, manufacturing, and inventory management.
Advanced Planning and Scheduling	Create production plans and schedules in manufacturing plant. Use constraints and business rules to optimize the schedule.
Demand Planning	Forecast demand and measure forecast accuracy through sophisticated algorithms.
Demand Content	Provide additional information such as point-of-sale or competitor information to facilitate forecasting.
Inventory Planning	Plan inventory required in each distribution point to meet demand.
Manufacturing Execution Systems	Manage shop floor activities in a manufacturing plant.
Warehouse Management Systems	Manage inventory control, product placement, and picking in a warehouse.
Transportation Planning	Optimize freight, select modes, plan routes, and select carriers.
Transportation Content	Supply information that helps optimize the distribution network.
Transportation Execution Systems	Automate transportation operations such as dispatch, shipment reconciliation, and shipment documentation.
Order Management	Automate customer-centric order-fulfillment process.
Component and Supplier Management	Administer data on component parts, suppliers, and the purchasing process. Strategically source parts.

(continued)

FIGURE 6.4	(CONTINUED)
Product Data Management	Categorize product data and manage exchange of data from design and manufacturing.
Strategic Management	Help model the supply chain to make site-selection and market decisions.
Customer Asset Management	Manage the customer interaction life cycle, including sales force automation and customer support.

SOURCE: Steven Kahl, "What's the 'Value' of Supply Chain Software?" *Supply Chain Management Review* (winter 1999): p. 60. Reprinted with permission of *Supply Chain Management Review*, a Cahners publication.

chains maintained by companies like Dell and Cisco (see Chapter 5) could not operate at such high levels without the sophisticated information networks and interactive software that help manage their elaborate networks. The Internet—and Internet technology—is the major tool that business marketers rely upon to manage their lengthy and integrated supply chain systems. In addition, a host of software applications play a key role in helping a supply chain operate at peak efficiency.

Supply Chain Software Generally speaking, supply chain management software applications provide real time analytical systems that manage the flow of product and information throughout the supply chain network of trading partners and customers.[15] As indicated earlier, many functions within the supply chain are coordinated, including procurement, manufacturing, transportation, warehousing, order entry, forecasting and customer service. Much of the software applied to manage the supply chain is focused on each one of the different functional areas. Figure 6.4 includes a list of existing SCM applications, and the list clearly shows the functional orientation of SCM software. However, the trend is to move toward software solutions that integrate several or all of these functions. The result is that firms can work with a comprehensive "supply chain suite" of software that manages flow across the supply chain, while including all of the key functional areas. Several firms producing Enterprise Resource Planning (ERP) software have developed applications that attempt to integrate functional areas and bridge gaps across the supply chain.

SCM software improves the management of existing business processes within the supply chain, but also helps organizations *transform* those processes into competitive advantages. Dell Computer is an excellent example. Dell's build-to-order manufacturing process for PCs was enabled by SCM software applications that support this more flexible and focused manufacturing operation. Having greater control over the flow of materials through the supply chain and more robust technology in the warehouse, an organization can assemble the final PC at the local distribution center. Two benefits accrue to Dell: they are able to apply mass customization to their product line while at

---

[15] Steven Kahl, "What's the 'Value' of Supply Chain Software?" *Supply Chain Management Review* (winter 1999): p. 61.

the same time improve delivery to customers. Enhancements to SCM software that permit inter-organizational integration and build in decision support systems will further enhance the ability of business marketers to operate in the supply chain context in the future.

The Internet   The Internet has allowed business marketers to realize several supply chain related benefits:

- More collaborative, timely product development through enhanced communications between functional departments, suppliers, customers, and even regulatory agencies.

- Reductions in channel inventory and product obsolescence due to closer linkage across the supply chain and better insights into demand signals to drive product schedules.

- Reduction in communication costs and customer support costs with more interactive, tailored support capability inherent with Internet technologies.

- New channel capabilities to reach different customer segments and further exploit current markets.

- Ability to enhance traditional products and customer relationships through customization, driven by Internet connectivity and interactivity.[16]

The most important impact of the Internet on the business-to-business supply chain is the effect it has had on transactional services, that is, the real time exchange of information between an organizations and its suppliers and customers. The transactional services may take the form of either a monetary exchange for a product or service or information exchanged between two entities for decision-making or planning purposes. The SupplyNet program used by Miller SQA as described in the INSIDE MARKETING BOX is an excellent example of how the Internet allows trading partners access to a wealth of internal information that allows them to more effectively interact with their supply chain partners. The Internet permits suppliers to gain real time knowledge of their customer's needs for materials and components, and gives them the lead time necessary to respond to those needs in a timely fashion.

Successfully Applying the Supply Chain Management Approach

The nature of the firm's supply chain efforts will often depend on the nature of the demand for its products. Marshall Fisher suggests that products can be separated into two categories: "functional" items, like paper clips, grease, nuts and bolts, and office furniture, for example, or "innovative" items, like IBM's Thinkpad or other high tech products. The importance of this distinction is that functional items require different supply chains than innovative products.[17] Functional products typically have predictable demand while innovative products do not. The goal for functional products

---

[16] Grieg Coppe and Stephen Duffy, "Internet Logistics: Creating New Customers and Matching New Competition," in John Gattorna, ed., *Strategic Supply Chain Alignment* (Brookfield, VT: Gower Press, 1998): p. 522.

[17] Marshall Fisher, "What Is the Right Supply Chain for Your Product?" *Harvard Business Review* 75 (March/April 1997): p. 106.

Supply Chain Management Delivers the Office Furniture on Time

Herman Miller, a large producer of office furniture, transformed the customer buying experience. Historically, customers for office furniture would wait weeks for their orders—with very little confidence that the promised installation date would be met. To underscore its commitment to the customer, the letters SQA were added to the company name—Miller SQA—meaning Simple, Quick, and Affordable.

SQA involved several supply chain management initiatives. First, a distribution center was established close to the plant that holds supplier-owned inventory. Because material inventory had been consuming 40 percent of production space, this step tripled assembly capacity. With supplier inventory located close by, assembly reliability increased and assembly lead time decreased dramatically.

Second, information systems were adopted to link suppliers into SQA's systems. The firm uses a tool called SupplyNet, that uses Internet technology to open SQA's window to suppliers. Suppliers now see the exact same information SQA sees, when they see it. Suppliers now see customer demand, safety stocks of materials, actual dates required to meet actual customer demand, and the inventory levels of the supplier at the distribution center. The system updates customer demand four times daily, enabling suppliers to adjust their afternoon and night shift schedules.

Third, SQA coordinates direct end-user deliveries in selected markets. Specific delivery dates and times are set. On-board truck tracking technology is used for delivery reporting and truck location status reporting. Often, the truckload includes more than one order, and deliveries must be sequenced. The net impact has been to increase the speed and reliability of the shipment-to-installation cycle. Simply stated, promises made to customers are kept.

A few key performance measures illustrate the success of SQA's supply chain strategy:

On-time shipments average 99.8 percent.

Average lead time from order entry to shipment is less than five days.

Dealers rate SQA as the service performance leader in the industry.

SOURCE: William Buody, "Leveraging Technology for Speed and Reliability," *Supply Chain Management Review* (spring 1999): p. 62.

is to design a supply chain that achieves physical distribution efficiency, that is, it minimizes logistics and inventory costs, and assures low-cost manufacturing. Here, the key information sharing takes place within the supply chain so that all participants can effectively orchestrate manufacturing, ordering, and delivery to minimize production and inventory costs.

Innovative products, on the other hand, have demand that is less predictable and the key concerns are reacting to short life cycles, avoiding shortages or excess supplies, and taking advantage of high profits during peak demand periods. The focus in the supply chain is not minimizing inventory, but deciding where to *position* inventory, along with production capacity, in order to hedge against uncertain demand. The critical task is to capture and distribute timely information on customer demand to the supply chain. When designing the supply chain, concentrate on creating *efficient* processes for functional products and *responsive* processes for innovative products.

Successful Supply Chain Practices

Most successful supply chains have devised approaches for the participants in the supply chain to work together in a partnering environment. Supply chains are not effective and, in reality, are *not* supply chains when the participants have an adversarial

| FIGURE 6.5 | THE SEVEN HABITS OF HIGHLY EFFECTIVE SUPPLY CHAINS |

1. SUPPLY CHAIN QUALITY DEPENDS ON CHANGING BUSINESS PRACTICES WITHIN AND OUTSIDE THE COMPANY

- To correct inefficient processes, suppliers, manufacturers, and customers may all have to alter their practices

- New processes for sharing information, ordering, and communicating are often necessary

2. ELIMINATE ACTIVITIES THAT DO NOT CONTRIBUTE VALUE TO THE END PRODUCT OR SERVICE, OR THAT DUPLICATE EFFORT

- Use activity-based analysis to determine processes and activities that do not contribute value to the end product

- Use electronics to send purchase orders and invoices, thus eliminating activity and costs

3. INTEGRATE DEMAND PLANNING ACROSS ALL ACTIVITIES

- Forecasts of sales to ultimate users should filter back to derive forecasts for raw materials at the start of the supply chain

- Without knowledge of actual ultimate demand, suppliers must guess what will be needed by next-tier customers

4. POOL RISKS AMONG SUPPLY CHAIN PARTNERS

- By positioning inventory close to ultimate users, costs can be reduced, but the entity maintaining the inventory must be compensated in some manner

- Investments by all supply chain partners in demand forecasting systems, all participants can work from a common forecast and reduce uncertainty

5. DISTINGUISH BETWEEN DESIRABLE PRODUCT VARIETY AND COSTLY DUPLICATION

- An effective supply chain must determine the boundary between a product line (mix) that is good for the customer and duplication that is costly and undesirable

- Excessive product lines create huge inventories and pose challenges in tracking and storage; 80/20 analyses will often point out needless duplication

(continued)

FIGURE 6.5	(CONTINUED)

6. IMPROVE ASSET UTILIZATION BY WORKING WITH SUPPLY CHAIN PARTNERS TO ASSURE GOODS ARE PRODUCED AT NEARLY THE SAME RATE THEY ARE CONSUMED

- Surges in capacity are often the result of poor planning or ineffective cooperation between partners

- Sharing of promotional plans and other efforts to smooth out supply cycles make it possible to create production, transportation and warehousing capacity based on a more even level of sales

7. RECOGNIZE HOW AND WHERE CUSTOMER VALUE IS ADDED IN THE SUPPLY CHAIN AND ALIGN REVENUE-GENERATION AND INCENTIVES ACCORDINGLY

- Supply chain partners need to offer each other incentives to "do the right thing" for the supply chain as a whole

- Gain-sharing mechanisms that compensate supply chain participants for activities that are costly, but benefit the entire chain, need to be put in place

SOURCE: Charles L. Troyer, "The 7 Habits of Highly Effective Supply Chains," *Supply Chain Management Review* (summer, 1997), pp. 25–32.

relationship. Supply chain partnerships form the foundation. Several additional dimensions seem to distinguish effective supply chains from less effective ones. Charles Troyer suggests that competent supply chains can be distinguished on the basis of seven important habits. Figure 6.5 summarizes these seven habits and briefly describes the critical elements associated with each. Observe that many of the salient features that define highly-effective supply chains center on integrated operations across supply chain participants, timely information sharing, and delivering value-added services to the customer.

Logistics as the Critical Element in Supply Chain Management

Nowhere in business marketing strategy is the supply chain management approach more important than in the logistics realm. **Logistics** is an imposing and sometimes mysterious term that originated in the military. In business usage, logistics refers to the design and management of all activities (primarily transportation, inventory, warehousing, and communications) necessary to make materials available for manufacturing and to offer finished products to customers in a timely manner. Logistics thus embodies two primary product flows: (1) physical supply, or those flows that provide raw materials, components, and supplies to the production process, and (2) physical distribution, or those flows that deliver the completed product to customers and channel intermediaries.

The flows of physical supply and physical distribution must be coordinated to meet delivery requirements of business customers successfully. The physical supply aspect of logistics requires a business supplier's logistical system to interact with the customer's logistics and manufacturing process. A repair part delivered a few hours late may cost a manufacturer thousands of dollars in lost production time. Although the physical supply dimension of logistics is important, we will concentrate on the physical distribution component because it is the key element of a business marketer's strategy.

Effective business marketing demands efficient, systematic delivery of finished products to intermediaries and industrial users. The importance of this capability to efficiently deliver products has elevated the logistics function to a place of prominence in the marketing strategy of many business marketers. In a recent article, Joseph Fuller, James O'Connor, and Richard Rawlinson effectively capture the essence of the strategic significance of logistics:

> Logistics has the potential to become the next governing element of strategy as an inventive way of creating value for customers, an immediate source of savings, an important discipline on marketing, and a critical extension of production flexibility. Customer needs vary, and companies can tailor logistics systems to serve them better and more profitably.[18]

Distinguishing between Logistics and Supply Chain Management

Logistics is the critical element in supply chain management. In fact, there is considerable confusion over the difference between the discipline of supply chain management and logistics. As our definition of supply chain management stated, SCM is focused on the *integration of all business processes* that add value for customers. Logistics, on the other hand, is focused on *moving and storing activities* as products and information wind their way through the supply chain to customers. Thus, supply chain management is a broader, integrative discipline that includes the coordination of several business processes in addition to logistics.

During the 1990s, the rising importance of time-based competition, rapidly improving information technology, expanding globalization, increasing attention to quality, and the changing face of interfirm relationships combined to cause companies to expand their perspective on the logistics process to include all the firms involved in creating a finished product and delivering it to the ultimate buyer/user on time and in perfect condition. For example, the supply chain for electric motors would include raw material suppliers, steel fabricators, component parts manufacturers, transportation companies, the electric motor manufacturer, the distributor of electric motors, the warehouse companies involved in storing and shipping components and finished products, and the ultimate buyer of the electric motor. Figure 6.6 graphically depicts such a supply chain. The supply chain management concept is an integrating philosophy for coordinating the total flow of a supply channel from supplier to ultimate user. Logistics is critical, however, to business marketers, because regardless of the orientation to the entire supply chain, the firm relies on its logistics system to deliver product to customers in a timely, low-cost manner.

---

[18]Joseph B. Fuller, James O'Connor, and Richard Rawlinson, "Tailored Logistics: The Next Advantage," *Harvard Business Review* 71 (May–June 1993): p. 87.

| FIGURE 6.6 | SUPPLY CHAIN FOR ELECTRIC MOTORS |

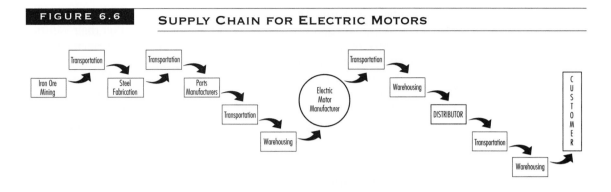

Managing Flows

The significance of the supply chain perspective in logistical management is that the business marketing manager focuses attention on the performance of *all participants* in the supply chain and works to coordinate their efforts to enhance the timely delivery of the finished product to the ultimate user at the lowest possible total logistics cost. Inherent in the supply chain approach is the need to form close *relationships* with the supply chain participants, including vendors, transportation suppliers, warehousing companies, and distributors. The focus of logistics in the supply chain management context for business marketers is the *flow of product* through the supply chain, with *timely information* driving the entire process.

Timely Logistics Support

Owens-Illinois, a major supplier of glass containers, shows how precisely a supplier must tailor its logistics system to customer needs. Owens-Illinois is a primary supplier to the J. M. Smucker Company, the jam and jelly manufacturer. Because of its vast container requirements, Smucker must carefully manage inventory and delivery of glass containers. To reduce container inventory, Smucker maintains only enough glass containers to run the production line for a few hours. The burden of this policy falls directly on Owens-Illinois. First, Owens-Illinois must schedule the production process at its Toledo plant to provide all the inventories Smucker requires. Then, warehouse systems and reliable motor carriers assure that deliveries match Smucker's inventory policy and avoid production interruptions. Consistent delivery performance to Smucker standards is surely an essential ingredient in this long-term supplier–customer relationship. For Owens-Illinois, logistical service may have created the differential advantage.

A Source of Competitive Advantage

In the past, logistics was viewed simply as a cost of doing business and a function whose only goal was higher productivity. Today, logistics is viewed by many companies as a critical strategic weapon because of its tremendous impact on a customer's operation. For many business marketers, logistics is their *primary* marketing tool for gaining and maintaining competitive superiority. These firms typically recognize that logistics performance is an important part of marketing strategy, and they exploit their logistics competencies. Companies that incorporate logistics planning and management into long term business strategies can achieve significant benefits, which create real value for the company.[19] Compaq Computer, the world's leading producer of PCs, estimates it lost almost $1 billion in sales over the course of a year because its laptop and desktop computers weren't available when and where customers were ready to buy them. Compaq has now revamped its logistics system in an effort to make it the "next source of competitive advantage."[20]

Sales–Marketing–Logistics Integration

The rising value of logistics as a strategic marketing weapon has fostered the integration of the sales, marketing, and logistics functions of many business marketers. In progressive firms, unified teams of sales, production, logistics, information systems, and marketing personnel develop integrated logistics programs to offer to potential customers. Sales calls are made by teams of specialists from each area and the teams create tailored logistics solutions to customer problems. United Stationers, one of the largest distributors of office products in the United States, brings operations and sales people together to meet with the company's resellers in an effort to create customer-responsive logistics service. As a result of its efforts, United guarantees customers that orders placed by 7:00 p.m. will be received before noon on the following day. Customers can dial into United's mainframe computer and place orders electronically. The company considers all its logistics people to be part of the sales function. Some firms have taken the integration even further. Baxter Healthcare warehouse workers team up with warehouse personnel at the hospitals that Baxter serves. During visits to the customer warehouse, the Baxter warehouser evaluates the operation, looking for ways to improve packing so shipments will be easier for the customer to unload and unpack. As a result, Baxter warehousers have become salespeople.

Just-In-Time Systems

Many business marketers have realized they have no choice other than to provide almost immediate delivery of their products. The reason is the widespread adoption by U.S. manufacturing firms of the just-in-time (JIT) inventory principle. Under this principle, all suppliers must carefully coordinate delivery of parts and supplies with the manufacturer's production schedule—often delivering products just hours before they are used. The objective of a JIT system is to eliminate waste of all kinds from the production process—requiring the delivery of the specified product at the precise time, and in the exact quantity needed. Importantly, the quality must be perfect—there is no opportunity to inspect products in the JIT process. Because JIT attempts to relate purchases to production requirements, the typical order size shrinks, and more frequent deliveries are required. Increased delivery frequency presents a challenge to the business marketing production and logistics system. However, business

---

[19] Timothy Van Mieghem "Lessons Learned from Alexander the Great," *Quality Progress* (January 1998): p. 42.

[20] Ronald Henkoff, "Delivering the Goods," *Fortune* 128 (November 1994): p. 64.

[21] Bruce Caldwell, "United Stationers' Combination Shot," *Informationweek* (September 1996): p. 48.

marketers will have to meet this challenge as many competitors now compete on the basis of inventory turns and speed to market.[22]

JIT Relationship   A significant effect of JIT purchasing has been the drastic reduction in the number of suppliers utilized by manufacturers. Suppliers who are able to meet customers' JIT requirements will find their share of business growing with the JIT-oriented customer.[23] Meeting JIT requirements often represents a marketing edge, and may mean survival for some suppliers. The relationship that emerges between JIT suppliers and manufacturers is unique and includes operational linkages that unite the buyer and seller. As a result, suppliers find that the relationships are longer lasting and usually formalized with a written contract that may span up to five years.

Speed and Hewlett-Packard's Success   Some business marketers effectively capitalize on their ability to deliver product quickly to customers. The success of Hewlett-Packard in high-margin laser printers is attributed not only to product features and marketing, but also to savvy distribution that has entrenched the company in computer superstores, computer electronic outlets, and office suppliers.[24] Speed is a major element of this company's distribution success. Large retailers like CompUSA and Costco refuse to keep large inventories and demand immediate fulfillment of their orders from vendors. Because Hewlett-Packard can meet these stringent requirements, it has solidified a leading position with its key customers. As such delivery requirements become industry standards, those business firms with effective and efficient logistical systems already in place will enjoy significant marketing advantages. Hewlett-Packard has further revamped their logistics system to simplify the process that moves printers to customers by using an electronic data interchange system to connect customers to its SAP R/3 enterprise resource planning system.[25] Now customers have "visibility" to the company's entire supply chain, allowing them to more effectively plan their own operations.

Elements of a Logistical System   Table 6.1 presents the controllable variables of a logistical system. Almost no decision on a particular logistical activity can be made without evaluating its impact on other areas. The system of warehouse facilities, inventory commitments, order-processing methods, and transportation linkages will determine the supplier's ability to provide timely product availability to industrial users. As a result of poor supplier performance, customers may have to bear the extra cost of higher inventories, institute expensive priority-order-expediting systems, develop secondary supply sources, or, worst of all, turn to another supplier.

Total-Cost Approach

In the management of logistical activities, two performance variables must be considered: (1) total distribution costs, and (2) the level of logistical service provided to customers. The logistical system must be designed and administered to achieve that combination of cost and service levels that yields maximum profits. Logistical costs

[22] Andrew Tanzer, "Warehouses That Fly," *Forbes*, (18 October 1999), p. 121.

[23] Peter Bradley, "Just-in-Time Works, but . . ." *Purchasing* 118 (September 1995): p. 36.

[24] Joe Mullich, "H-P Conquers Channels with Speed," *Business Marketing* 78 (July 1993): p. 44.

[25] Jim Thomas, "Chain Reaction," *Logistics* (May 1999): p. 47.

TABLE 6.1	CONTROLLABLE ELEMENTS IN A LOGISTICS SYSTEM
Elements	**Key Aspects**
Customer service	The "product" of logistics activities, *customer service* relates to the effectiveness in creating time and place utility. The level of customer service provided by the supplier has a direct impact on total cost, market share, and profitability.
Order processing	Order processing triggers the logistics process and directs activities necessary to deliver products to customers. Speed and accuracy of order processing affect costs and customer service levels.
Logistics communication	Information exchanged in the distribution process guides the activities of the system. It is the vital link between the firm's logistics system and its customers.
Transportation	The physical movement of products from source of supply through production to customers is the most significant cost area in logistics, and it involves selecting modes and specific carriers as well as routing.
Warehousing	Providing storage space serves as a buffer between production and use. Warehousing may be used to enhance service and to lower transportation costs.
Inventory control	Inventory is used to make products available to customers and to ensure the correct mix of products is at the proper location at the right time.
Packaging	The role of packaging is to provide protection to the product, to maintain product identity throughout the logistics process, and to create effective product density.
Materials handling	Materials handling increases the speed of, and reduces the cost of, picking orders in the warehouse and moving products between storage and the transportation carriers. It is a cost-generating activity that must be controlled.
Production planning	Utilized in conjunction with logistics planning, production planning ensures that products are available for inventory in the correct assortment and quantity.
Plant and warehouse location	Strategic placement of plants and warehouses increases customer service and reduces the cost of transportation.

SOURCE: Adapted from James R. Stack and Douglas M. Lambert, *Strategic Logistics Management*, 4th ed. (Homewood, Ill.: Richard D. Irwin, 1996).

vary widely for business marketers, depending on the nature of the product and on the importance of logistical service to the buyer. Logistical costs can consume 16 to 36 percent of each sales dollar at the manufacturing level, and assets required by logistical activities can exceed 40 percent of total assets. Thus logistics can have a significant impact on corporate profitability. How, then, can the marketer manage logistical costs?

The **total-cost** or trade-off **approach** to logistical management offers a guarantee that total logistical costs in the firm and within the channel are minimized. The assumption is that costs associated with individual logistical activities are interactive; that is, a decision about one logistical variable affects all or some of the other variables. Management is thus concerned with the efficiency of the entire system rather than with minimizing the cost of any single logistical activity. The interactions among logistical activities (that is, transportation, inventory, warehousing) are described as cost trade-offs, because a cost increase in one activity is traded for a large cost decrease in another activity, the net result being an overall cost reduction.

Calculating Logistics Costs

Activity-Based Costing

The activity-based costing (ABC) technique is used to precisely measure the costs associated with performing specific activities, and then trace those costs to the products, customers, and channels that consumed the activities.[26] This is a powerful tool to use in managing the logistics operations within a supply chain. ABC provides a mechanism to trace the cost of performing logistics services to the customers that use these services, thereby making it easier to assess the appropriate level of customer service to offer. Firms using ABC analysis can obtain more accurate information concerning how a particular customer or a specific product contributes to overall profitability.[27]

Total Cost of Ownership (TCO)

TCO is applied to determine the total costs associated with the acquisition and subsequent use of a given item from a particular supplier (see Chapter 2). The approach identifies costs—often buried in overhead or general expenses—that relate to the costs of holding inventory, poor quality, and delivery failure.[28] A buyer using TCO would explicitly consider the costs that the supplier's logistics system either added to, or eliminated from, the purchase price. Thus, a supplier particularly efficient at logistics might be able to reduce the buyer's inventory costs and the buyer's expenses of inspecting inbound merchandise for damage. As a result, the total cost of ownership from that supplier would be lower than the cost from other suppliers that were not able to rapidly deliver undamaged products. Increasing acceptance of the TCO approach will cause efficiency in logistics operations to become an even more critical element of a business marketer's strategy.

Business-to-Business Logistical Service

Many studies have shown that the importance of logistics service often equals that of product quality as a measure of supplier performance.[29] In many industries a quality product at a competitive price is recognized as a given, and customer service is the key differentiator among competitors. In one industry, for example, purchasing agents begin the buying process by calling suppliers with the best delivery service to see whether

---

[26] Bernard J. LaLonde and Terrance L. Pohlen, "Issues in Supply Chain Costing," *The International Journal of Logistics Management* 7, no. 1 (1996): p. 3.

[27] Thomas A. Foster, "Time to Learn the ABCs of Logistics," *Logistics* (February 1999): p. 67.

[28] Lisa Ellram, "Activity-Based Costing and Total Cost of Ownership: A Critical Linkage," *Journal of Cost Management* 8 (winter 1995): p. 22.

[29] Mary Collins Holcomb, "Customer Service Measurement: A Methodology for Increasing Customer Value through Utilization of the Taguchi Strategy," *Journal of Business Logistics* 15, no. 1 (1994): p. 29.

they are willing to negotiate prices. Similar approaches to vendor selection are evidenced in other situations. Because it is so important to customers, reliable logistics service can lead to higher market shares and profits. A study by Bain and Company showed that companies with superior logistics service grow 8 percent faster, realize a 7 percent price premium, and are twelve times as profitable as firms with inferior service levels. These facts, together with the extensive implementation of just-in-time manufacturing systems, makes it clear that logistical service is important to the organizational buyer.

Logistical service relates to the availability and delivery of products to the customer and can be conceptualized as the series of sales-satisfying activities that begin when the customer places the order and that end with the delivery of the product to that customer. Responsive logistical service advances customer satisfaction and creates the opportunity for closer and more profitable buyer–seller relationships.[30] Logistical service includes whatever aspects of performance are important to the business customer (see Table 6.2). These service elements range from delivery time to value-added services, and each of these elements has the potential to affect production processes, final product output, costs, or all three.

Logistics Service Impacts on the Customer

For the supplier, logistical service translates into product availability. For a manufacturer to produce or for a distributor to resell, industrial products must be available at the right time, at the right place, and in usable condition. The longer the supplier's delivery time, the less available the product; the more inconsistent the delivery time, the less available the product. For example, a reduction in the supplier's delivery time permits a buyer to hold less inventory because needs can be met rapidly. The customer reduces the risk of interruption in the production process. Consistent delivery performance enables the buyer to program more effectively—or routinize—the purchasing process, thus lowering buyer costs. The dramatic impact of consistent delivery cycle performance presents an opportunity for the buyer to cut the level of buffer or safety stock maintained, thereby reducing the inventory cost. However, for many business products, such as those that are low in unit value and relatively standardized, the overriding concern is not inventory cost, but simply having the products. A malfunctioning ninety-five-cent bearing could shut down a whole production line.

Determining the Level of Service

Logistics service is often ranked by buyers right behind "quality" as a criterion for selecting a vendor. However, not all products or all customers require the same level of logistical service. Many business products that are made to order—such as heavy machinery—have relatively low logistical service requirements. Others, such as replacement parts, components, and subassemblies, require extremely demanding logistical performance. Similarly, customers may be more or less responsive to varying levels of logistical service.

---

[30] Arun Sharma, Dhruv Grewal, and Michael Levy, "The Customer Satisfaction/Logistics Interface," *Journal of Business Logistics* 16 (no. 2, 1995): p. 1.

TABLE 6.2	COMMON ELEMENTS OF LOGISTICS SERVICE

Elements	Description
Delivery time	The time from the creation of an order to the fulfillment and delivery of that order includes both order-processing time and delivery or transportation time.
Delivery reliability	The most frequently used measure of logistics service, delivery reliability focuses on the capability of having products available to meet customer demand.
Order accuracy	The degree to which items received conform to the specification of the order. The key dimension is the incidence of orders shipped complete and without error.
Information access	The firm's ability to respond to inquiries about order status and product availability.
Damage	A measure of the physical conditions of the product when received by the buyer.
Ease of doing business	A range of factors including the ease with which orders, returns, credits, billing, and adjustments are handled.
Value-added services	Such features as packaging, which facilitates customer handling, or other services such as prepricing and drop shipments.

SOURCE: Reprinted with permission from Jonathon L. S. Byrnes, William C. Copacino, and Peter Metz, "Forge Service into a Weapon with Logistics," *Transportation & Distribution, Presidential Issue* 28 (September 1987): p. 46.

Some business buyers are far more sensitive to poor service than the majority of buyers. Market segments must be identified on the basis of logistical service sensitivity.[31] For example, buyers of scientific instruments were classified into groups—private firms, government, secondary schools, and so forth. Private firms ranked delivery time more highly than did other groups and secondary schools ranked ordering convenience more highly than did others. Business marketing managers should attempt to isolate segments and to adjust the logistical service offerings accordingly, targeting their service mix to the requirements of product type and customer.

To recap, service levels are developed by assessing customer service requirements. The sales and cost effects of various service levels are analyzed to find the service level generating the highest profits. The needs of various customer segments will dictate various logistical system configurations. For example, when logistical service is critical, industrial distributors can provide the vital product availability (see Figure 6.7), whereas customers with less rigorous service demands can be served from factory inventories.

Logistics Impacts On Other Supply Chain Participants

A supplier's logistical system directly affects a distributor's ability to control cost and service to end users. Delivery time influences not only the customer's inventory

[31] Fuller, O'Connor, and Rawlinson, "Tailored Logistics," p. 93.

FIGURE 6.7 UPS CONVEYS THEIR PROMPTNESS WHEN SERVICE LEVEL IS CRITICAL FOR TARGETED CUSTOMERS

SOURCE: Courtesy, United Parcel Service of America, Inc., © 1999.

requirements but also the operations of channel members. If a supplier provides erratic delivery service to distributors, the distributor is forced to carry higher inventory in order to provide a satisfactory level of product availability to end users.

Inefficient logistics service to the distributors either increases distributor costs (larger inventories) or creates shortages of the supplier's products at the distributor level. Neither result is good. In the first instance, distributor loyalty and marketing efforts will suffer; in the second, end users will eventually change suppliers. 3COM, the firm that makes the Palm Pilot, developed such an effective logistics system that their distributors in Latin America are able to offer the same level of after-sales service available in the United States, allowing 3COM to reach sales levels exceeding $250 million in Latin America in a short time frame.[32] In some industries, distributors are

---

[32] Toby Gooley, "Service Stars," *Logistics* (June 1999): p. 37.

expanding the role they play in the logistics process, which makes them even more valuable to their suppliers and customers. In the chemical industry, for example, the role of distributors is completely transforming as they offer logistics solutions—JIT delivery, repackaging, inventory management—to their customers.[33] The logistics expertise provided by distributors enables their vendors (manufacturers) to focus on their own core competencies of production and marketing.

Business-to-Business Logistical Management

The elements of logistics strategy are part of a system and, as such, each affects every other element. The proper focus is the total-cost view. Although this section treats the decisions on facilities, transportation, and inventory separately, these areas are so intertwined that decisions in one area influence the others.

Logistical Facilities

The strategic development of a warehouse provides the business marketer with the opportunity to increase the level of delivery service to buyers, to reduce transportation costs, or both. Business firms distributing repair, maintenance, and operating supplies often find that the only way to achieve desired levels of delivery service is to locate warehouses in key markets. The warehouse circumvents the need for premium transportation (air freight) and costly order processing by keeping products readily available in local markets.

Serving Other Supply Chain Members   The nature of the business-to-business supply chain affects the warehousing requirements of a supplier. Manufacturers' representatives do not hold inventory while distributors do. When manufacturers' reps are utilized, the supplier will often require a significant number of strategically-located warehouses. On the other hand, a supply chain using distributors will offset the need for warehousing. Obviously, local warehousing by the distributor is a real service to the supplier. A few well-located supplier warehouses may be all that is required to service the distributors effectively.

Outsourcing the Warehousing Function   Operating costs, service levels, and investment requirements are essential considerations regarding the type of warehouse to use. The business firm may either operate their own warehouses or turn over their operation to a "third party"—a company that specializes in performing warehousing services for customers. The advantages of third-party warehousing are flexibility, reduced assets and professional management. The firm can increase or decrease its use of space in a given market, move into or out of any market quickly, and enjoy an operation managed by those who specialize in that business. Third-party warehousing may sometimes supplement or replace distributors in a market.

Many third-party warehouses provide a variety of logistical services for their clients, including packaging, labeling, order processing, and some light assembly. GATX Logistics, a third-party warehouse company based in Jacksonville, Florida,

---

[33] Daniel J. McConville, "More Work for Chemical Distributors," *Distribution* 95 (August 1996): p. 63.

maintains warehouse facilities in a number of major markets. Clients can position inventories in all these markets while dealing with only one firm. Also, GATX can link its computer with the suppliers' computers to facilitate order processing and inventory updating. The GATX warehouse will also repackage products to the end user's order, label, and arrange for local delivery. A business marketer could ship standard products in bulk to the GATX warehouse—gaining transportation economies—and still enjoy excellent customer delivery service. The public or contract warehouse is a feasible alternative to the distributor channel when the sales function can be economically executed either with a direct sales force or with sales reps.

Transportation

Transportation is usually the largest single logistical expense, and with the impact of continually rising fuel costs, its importance will probably increase. Typically, the transportation decision involves the evaluation and selection of both a mode of transportation and the individual carrier(s) that will ensure the best performance at the lowest cost. Mode refers to the type of carrier—rail, truck, water, air, or some combination of the four. Individual carriers are evaluated on rates and delivery performance.[34] The supply chain view is important when considering the selection of individual carriers. Carriers become an integral part of the supply chain process and close relationships are important. One study found evidence that carriers' operating performance improved when they were more involved in the relationship between buyer and seller.[35] By further integrating carriers into the supply chain, the entire supply chain can improve its competitive position. In this section we will consider (1) the role of transportation in industrial supply chains, and (2) the criteria for evaluating transportation options.

Transportation and Logistical Service A business marketer must be able to effectively move finished inventory between facilities, to channel intermediaries, and to customers. The transportation system is the link that binds the logistical network together and ultimately results in timely delivery of products. Efficient warehousing will not enhance customer service levels if transportation is inconsistent or inadequate.

Effective transportation service may be used in combination with warehouse facilities and inventory levels to generate the required customer service level, or it may be used in place of them. Inventory maintained in a variety of market-positioned warehouses can be consigned to one centralized warehouse when rapid transportation services exist to deliver products from the central location to business customers. Xerox is one company that uses premium air freight service to offset the need for high inventories and extensive warehouse locations. The decision on transportation modes and particular carriers will depend on the cost trade-offs and service capabilities of each. It is interesting that in the age of next-day delivery and express air freight services, barges that weave their way through a maze of rivers, lakes, and channels are thriving in the business market.[36] A barge trip that takes seventeen hours would take a train four hours

[34] For example, see James C. Johnson, Donald F. Wood, Danile L. Warlow, and Paul R. Murphy, *Contemporary Logistics*, 7th Edition (Upper Saddle River, NJ: Prentice-Hall, Inc., 1998).

[35] Julie Gentry, "The Role of Carriers in Buyer-Supplier Strategic Partnerships: A Supply Chain Management Approach," *Journal of Business Logistics* 17, no. 2 (1996): p. 52.

[36] Anna Wilde Mathews, "Jet-Age Anomalies, Slowpoke Barges Do Brisk Business," *The Wall Street Journal*, (15 May 1998), p. B1.

and a truck ninety minutes for a similar trip. Although very slow (averaging 15 miles per hour), the barge offers huge cost advantages compared to truck and rail. For products like limestone, coal, farm products and petroleum, the slow and unglamorous barge is an effective logistics tool.

Transportation Performance Criteria **Cost of service** is the variable cost associated with moving products from origin to destination, including any terminal or accessory charges. The cost of service may range from as little as 0.25 cents per ton-mile via water to as high as fifty cents per ton per mile via air freight. The important aspect of selecting the mode of transportation is not cost per se but cost relative to the objective to be achieved. Bulk raw materials generally do not require prepaid delivery service, so the cost of anything other than rail or water transportation could not be justified. On the other hand, although air freight may be almost ten times more expensive than motor freight, the cost is inconsequential to a customer who needs an emergency shipment of spare parts. The cost of premium (faster) transportation modes may be justified by the resulting inventory reductions.

Speed of service refers to the elapsed time to move products from one facility (plant or warehouse) to another facility (warehouse or customer plant). Again, speed of service often overrides the cost of service. Rail, a relatively slow mode used for bulk shipments, requires inventory buildups at the supplier's factory and at the destination warehouse. The longer the delivery time, the more inventory customers must maintain to service their needs while the shipment is in transit. The slower modes involve lower variable costs for product movement, yet they result in lower service levels and higher investments in inventory. The faster modes produce just the opposite effect. Not only must a comparison be made between modes in terms of service, but various carriers within a mode must be evaluated on their "door-to-door" delivery time.

Service consistency is usually more important than average delivery time, and all modes of transportation are not equally consistent. Although air provides the lowest average delivery time, generally it has the highest variability in delivery time relative to the average. The wide variations in modal service consistency are particularly critical in business marketing planning. The choice of transportation mode must be made on the basis of cost, average transit time, and consistency if effective customer service is to be achieved.

In summary, because business buyers often place a premium on effective and consistent delivery service, the choice of transportation mode is an important one—one where cost of service is often secondary. However, the best decision on transportation carriers will result from a balancing of service, variable costs, and investment requirements. The manager must also consider the transportation requirements of ordinary, versus expedited (rush order), shipments.

Inventory Management

Inventory management is the buffer in the logistical system. Inventories are needed in business channels because (1) production and demand are not perfectly matched, (2) operating deficiencies in the logistical system often result in product unavailability (for example, delayed shipments, inconsistent carrier performance), and (3) industrial customers cannot predict their product needs with certainty (for example, because a machine may break down or there may be a sudden need to expand production). Inventory may be viewed in the same light as warehouse facilities and transportation: It is an alternative method for providing the level of service required by customers, and the level of inventory is determined on the basis of cost, investment, service required, and anticipated revenue.

Quality Focus: Eliminate Inventories   Today's prevalent total quality management techniques and just-in-time management principles emphasize the reduction or outright elimination of inventories. Current thinking suggests that inventories exist because of inefficiencies in the system: Erratic delivery, poor forecasting, and ineffective quality control systems all force companies to hold excessive stocks to protect themselves from delivery, forecasting, and product failure. Instead, improved delivery, forecasting, and manufacturing processes should prevent the need to buffer against failures and uncertainty. Information technology involving bar coding, scanner data, total quality processes, better transportation management, and more effective information flow among firms in the supply chain have made it possible to more carefully control inventories and reduce them to the lowest possible levels.

The Internet connectivity that unites the supply chain from an information standpoint has permitted substantial inventory reductions in several industries. In one recent study it was shown that average inventory turnover for manufacturers has increased from eight times per year to more than twelve time per year.[37] Much of the credit for the improvement in inventory turns is attributed to more information sharing among the supply chain members, sophisticated inventory management software, and generally higher levels of coordination in the supply chain. Successful business marketing managers must develop quality processes that in themselves reduce or eliminate the need to carry large inventories, while coordinating and integrating a supply chain system that can function effectively with almost no inventory.

The 80/20 Rule   Most business marketers with extensive product lines know that the great bulk of their products do not turn over very rapidly. This is the 80/20 principle: 80 percent of the sales are generated by 20 percent of the product line. The major implication of the 80/20 principle is that business marketers must manage inventory selectively, treating fast- and slow-moving items differently. If a company has half its inventory committed to products that produce only 20 percent of the unit sales volume, significant gains can be made by reducing inventories of the slow sellers to the point at which their turnover rate approximates that of the fast sellers. This rule applies regardless of how the inventory function is handled in the channel. Thus, suppliers can develop more efficient supply chains and substantially reduce distributor inventory costs by allowing the distributor to cut back inventory on slow-turnover items. Not only will distributor cost performance improve, but enhanced supply chain goodwill should result.

Selective Inventory Strategies   The evaluation of selective inventory strategies depends on the cost and service trade-offs involved. First, inventory of slow movers can be reduced at all locations; the result, however, may be a marked reduction in customer service. As with transportation, one workable alternative is to centralize the slow-moving items at a single location, thereby reducing total inventories. The result is a higher sales volume per unit of product at a given location. In turn, inventories of fast-moving items can be expanded, enhancing their service levels.

---

[37]Thomas W. Speh, *Changes in Warehouse Inventory Turnover* (Chicago: Warehousing Education and Research Council, 1999).

A selective inventory policy must be applied cautiously. Typically, fast-moving items are standardized items that customers expect to be readily available; slow movers are often nonstandardized, and customers expect to wait to receive them. However, there is no rule that all slow-moving items require low service levels. If a slow-moving item is critical in the production process or is needed to repair a machine, an extremely high level of service is required. Thus, a selective inventory policy mandates that both turnover rates and the importance of the product to the customer be evaluated in determining the inventory/transportation system.

Logistics Information Systems

Computer-based information systems play a crucial role in the management of the logistics process. The development of logistics information systems has paralleled the increased awareness among top firms of logistics' potential for providing competitive advantage through value enhancement.[38] The types of information technology that are important in today's environment—for managing sophisticated logistics systems—are electronic data interchange (EDI), warehouse management systems (WMS), order management systems, transportation control systems, and process automation such as bar coding and radio frequency (RF) capabilities.

Information systems control and direct everything that happens in a logistics system, from order placement to measuring customers' satisfaction with service. For example, many firms now place orders electronically through the Internet. Once the vendor receives the order, the computer system will direct a warehouse worker to the requested product in the warehouse (using a warehouse management system (WMS), which is software applied to manage all warehouse internal operations). When the order filler arrives at the proper location, he or she scans the product with a hand-held scanner, transmitting the information to a host computer through a radio frequency (RF) linkup in the warehouse. Inventory records are updated and a computer communication notifies the customer that the order was packed and shipped. An Advance Shipping Notice (ASN) is also transmitted to the customer, specifying exactly what is in the shipment, the transportation carrier, and when it will arrive. This enables the customer to plan production or warehouse schedules before receiving the shipment. These types of information systems help to ensure that a firm meets the logistical needs of its customers and provide the necessary data to manage each element of the logistics process throughout the supply chain.

Third-Party Logistics

An emerging development in performing the logistics process is the utilization of **third-party logistics firms.** These external firms perform a wide range of logistics functions traditionally performed within the organizatin. A study of *Fortune* 500 firms revealed that 60 percent of the responding companies use third-party logistics services.[39] In more than half of the firms using third-party logistics services, the strategic decision to outsource logistics was made by top management. The functions performed by the third-party company can encompass the entire logistics process or

---

[38] Craig M. Gustin, Patricia J. Dougherty, and Theodore P. Stank, "The Effects of Information Availability on Logistics Integration," *Journal of Business Logistics* 16, no. 1 (1995): p. 3.

[39] Robert C. Lieb and Hugh L. Randall, "A Comparison of the Use of Third-Party Logistics Services by Large American Manufacturers, 1991, 1994, and 1995," *Journal of Business Logistics* 17, no. 1 (1996): pp. 306–307.

INSIDE BUSINESS MARKETING

Case Corporation Constructs a Logistics Model for the Future

Case Corporation, an agricultural and construction equipment manufacturer, provides a wonderful example of the types of partnerships that many predict will be the wave of the future in terms of logistics outsourcing. In an effort to speed delivery to customers, improve customer satisfaction, reduce operating costs and working capital requirements, Case Corporation globally integrated its logistics network and outsourced it to a strategic partnership of three logistics providers. Although Case still controls the strategic direction of its logistics system, the alliance of third-party logistics firms will manage all facets of Case's logistics operations.

Managing the flow of raw materials, parts, and finished goods through Case's supply chain is a complex and expensive task. Case products are sold through a network of 4,100 dealers in more than 150 countries. The supply chain includes more than 750 suppliers and sixteen warehousing facilities, with eight manufacturing plants, nine parts depots, and 1,700 dealers in North America. Annually, Case makes more than 800,000 shipments that weigh over 1.6 billion pounds. According to the company's vice president of supply chain management, "Our supply chain management vision is focused on delighting our customers, and covers everything from the order to the delivery of the final product. We believe we are the first in our industry to make significant progress toward that goal. A lot of companies are reengineering their processes, but very few are reengineering their total supply chain."

The strategic alliance to which the logistics operations were outsourced includes: Fritz Companies, Inc., which serves as global integrator of the alliance; GATX Logistics, which will manage off-site warehousing; and Schneider Logistics, Inc., which will have responsibility for transportation and material flow management. The alliance will also provide global data management and logistics support. Case has signed a long-term agreement with each firm in the alliance and all four firms are linked electronically so they can operate "as one" in a virtual response mode. The alliance allows each firm to focus on its unique competencies while Case reaps the benefits of the synergies among the three alliance partners. Case management designed interdependent measures for the alliance that are geared to the success of the supply chain: the partners are dependent on one another to achieve goals and, when goals are reached, all three parties benefit.

SOURCE: Adapted from Leslie Hansen Harps, "Case Corporation Constructs Logistics Model of the Future," *Inbound Logistics*, 16 (October 1996), pp. 24–32.

selected activities within that process. Third parties can perform the warehousing; they may perform the transportation function (a truck line like Schneider National); or they may perform the entire logistics process from production scheduling to delivery of finished products to the customer (for example, Ryder Dedicated Logistics). The use of third parties enables a manufacturer or distributor to concentrate on its core business while enjoying the expertise and specialization of a professional logistics company. The results are often lower costs, better service, improved asset utilization, increased flexibility, and access to leading-edge technology. Recently, some firms have advocated the use of "Fourth-Party Logistics"—firms that own no assets, but serve to manage several third parties that are employed to perform various logistics functions.[40]

Despite the advantages offered by third-party logistics firms, some firms are cautious because of reduced control over the logistics process, diminished direct contact with customers, and the problems associated with terminating internal operations. In

[40]James W. Moore, "Fourth Party Logistics: The New Supply Chain Model Emerges," *Proceedings of the CLM Annual Conference*, (15 October 1999).

analyzing the most effective and efficient way to accomplish logistics cost and service objectives, the business marketing manager should carefully consider the benefits and drawbacks of outsourcing part or all logistics functions to third-party providers. In an interesting application of third-party logistics, Caterpillar (the manufacturer of earth-moving equipment) formed a logistics services company to manage the parts distribution for other manufacturers.[41] The company applies the knowledge gained from its own experiences in distributing 300 families of products that require over 530,000 spare parts. Caterpillar transfers knowledge from the company's internal operations to customers and vice versa.

Summary

Leading business marketing firms demonstrate superior capabilities in supply chain management. Supply chain management is focused on improving the flow of products, information, and services as they move from origin to destination. A key driver to supply chain management is coordination and integration among all the participants in the supply chain, primarily through sophisticated information systems and management software. The goals of reducing waste, minimizing duplication, reducing cost, and enhancing service are the major objectives of supply chain management. Firms successful at managing the supply chain understand the nature of their products and the type of supply chain structure that is required to meet the needs of their customers. Seven important habits describe the key success factors associated with highly effective supply chains. In particular effective supply chains integrate operations, share information, and above all, provide added value to customers.

Logistics is the critical function in the firm's supply chain because logistics directs the flow and storage of products and information. Successful supply chains synchronize logistics with the other functions such as production, procurement, forecasting, order management, and customer service. The systems perspective in logistical management cannot be stressed enough—it is the only way that management can be assured that the logistical function will meet prescribed goals. Not only must each logistical variable be analyzed in terms of its impact on every other variable, but the sum of the variables must be evaluated in light of the service level provided to customers. Logistics elements throughout the supply chain must be integrated to assure smooth product flow. Logistical service is critical in the buyer's evaluation of business marketing firms. Logistical service generally ranks second only to product quality as a desired supplier characteristic.

Decisions in the logistical area must be based on cost trade-offs among the logistical variables and on comparisons of the costs and revenues associated with alternative levels of service. The optimal system produces the highest profitability relative to the capital investment required. Three major variables—facilities, transportation, and inventory—form the basis of logistical decisions faced by the business-to-business logistics manager. The business marketer must monitor the impact of logistics on all supply chain members and on overall supply chain performance. Finally, the strategic role of logistics should be carefully evaluated: logistics can often provide a strong competitive advantage.

---

[41] Peter Marsh, "A Moving Story of Spare Parts," *The Financial Times*, 29 August 1997, p. 8.

Discussion Questions

1. What is supply chain management and what are the types of functions and firms that make up the typical supply chain?

2. Explain how an effective supply chain can create a strong competitive advantage for the firms involved in the supply chain.

3. Explain why cooperation among supply chain participants will determine whether the supply chain will be effective.

4. Explain the different elements of "waste" that exist in supply chains and how supply chain management is focused on eliminating the various elements of waste.

5. Describe the role the Internet plays in enhancing supply chain management operations.

6. Adopting the perspective of an organizational buyer, carefully illustrate how the most economical source of supply might be the firm that offers the highest price but also the fastest and most reliable delivery system.

7. Describe a situation in which total logistical costs might be reduced by doubling transportation costs.

8. A key goal in logistical management is to find the optimum balance of logistical cost and customer service that yields optimal profits. Explain.

9. Explain how consistent delivery performance gives the organizational buyer the opportunity to cut the level of inventory maintained.

10. An increasing number of manufacturers are adopting more sophisticated purchasing practices and more sophisticated inventory control systems. What are the strategic implications of these developments for business marketers wishing to serve these customers?

III

Assessing Market Opportunities

7

Segmenting the Business Market

The business marketing manager serves a market comprising many different types of organizational customers with varying needs. Only when this aggregate market is broken down into meaningful categories can the business marketing strategist readily and profitably respond to unique needs. After reading this chapter, you will understand

1. the benefits of and requirements for segmenting the business market.

2. the potential bases for segmenting the business market.

3. a procedure for evaluating and selecting market segments.

4. the role of market segmentation in the development of business marketing strategy.

A strategist at Hewlett-Packard notes:

> Knowing customers' needs is not enough. . . . We need to know what new products, features, and services will surprise and delight them. We need to understand their world so well that we can bring new technology to problems that customers may not yet truly realize they have.[1]

High-growth companies like Hewlett-Packard succeed by

- selecting a well-defined group of potentially profitable customers;

- developing a distinctive value proposition (product and/or service offering) that meets these customers' needs better than their competitors; and

- focusing marketing resources on acquiring, developing, and retaining profitable customers.[2]

The business market consists of three broad sectors—commercial enterprises, institutions, and government. Whether marketers elect to operate in one or all of these sectors, they will encounter diversity in organizations, purchasing structures, and decision-making styles. Each sector has many segments; each segment may have unique needs and require a unique marketing strategy. The business marketer who recognizes the needs of the various segments of the market is best equipped to isolate profitable market opportunities and to respond with an effective marketing program.

The goal of this chapter is to demonstrate how the manager can select and evaluate segments of the business market. First, the benefits of and the requirements for successful market segmentation are delineated. Second, specific bases upon which the business market can be segmented are explored and evaluated. This section demonstrates the application of key buyer behavior concepts and secondary information sources to market segmentation decisions. Third, a framework is provided for evaluating and selecting market segments. Procedures for assessing the costs and benefits of entering alternative market segments and for implementing a segmentation strategy are emphasized.

Business Market Segmentation Requirements and Benefits

Yoram Wind and Richard N. Cardozo define a **market segment** as "a group of present or potential customers with some common characteristic which is relevant in explaining (and predicting) their response to a supplier's marketing stimuli."[3] In the business market, a select group of customers often accounts for a disproportionate share of a firm's sales and profit. An extensive survey of business-to-business firms

---

[1]David E. Schnedler, "Use Strategic Market Models to Predict Customer Behavior," *Sloan Management Review* 37 (spring 1996): p. 92; see also, Eric von Hippel, Stefan Thomke, and Mary Sonnack, "Creating Breakthroughs at 3M," *Harvard Business Review*, 77 (September–October 1999), pp. 47–57.

[2]Dwight L. Gertz and João P. A. Baptista, *Grow to Be Great: Breaking the Downsizing Cycle* (New York: The Free Press, 1995), p. 54.

[3]Yoram Wind and Richard N. Cardozo, "Industrial Market Segmentation," *Industrial Marketing Management* 3 (March 1974): p. 155; see also Vincent-Wayne Mitchell and Dominic F. Wilson, "Balancing Theory and Practice: A Reappraisal of Business-to-Business Segmentation," *Industrial Marketing Management*, 27 (September 1998), pp. 429–455.

found that the top 20 percent of customers contributed a median 75 percent of sales volume to these firms and that 50 percent of a typical firm's sales came from just 10 percent of its customers.[4] What about profit? When the costs of serving particular customers are isolated, many firms are surprised to learn that a large portion of their current customer base contributes little to profitability. Such patterns demonstrate the importance of choosing market segments wisely.

Requirements

A business marketer has five criteria for evaluating the desirability of potential market segments:

1. *Measurability.* Marketers evaluate the degree to which information on the particular buyer characteristics exists or can be obtained.

2. *Accessibility.* Marketers evaluate the degree to which the firm can effectively focus its marketing efforts on chosen segments.

3. *Substantiality.* Marketers evaluate the degree to which the segments are large or profitable enough to be worth considering for separate marketing cultivation.

4. *Compatibility.* Marketers evaluate the degree to which the firm's marketing and business strengths match the present and expected competitive and technological state of the market.

5. *Responsiveness.* Marketers assess the degree to which segments respond differently to different marketing mix elements, such as pricing or product features.

Thus, the art of market segmentation involves identifying groups of consumers that are sufficiently large, and sufficiently unique, to justify a separate marketing strategy. The competitive environment of the market segment is a factor that must be analyzed.

Evaluating the Competitive Environment

In selecting a market segment, the business marketer is also choosing a competitive environment.[5] In extremely dynamic industries, such as the computer or telecommunications industries, Richard A. D'Aveni emphasizes that "market stability is threatened by short product life cycles, short product design cycles, new technologies, frequent entry by unexpected outsiders, repositioning by incumbents, and radical redefinitions of market boundaries as diverse industries emerge."[6] **Competitive analysis** is the process by which a firm attempts to define the boundaries of its industry, identify competitors, and determine the strengths and weaknesses of its rivals—while anticipating

---

[4] Frank V. Cespedes, *Concurrent Marketing: Integrating Product, Sales, and Service* (Boston: Harvard Business School Press, 1995), pp. 186–188; and William A. O'Connel and William Keenan Jr., "The Shape of Things to Come," *Sales & Marketing Management* 148 (January 1996): pp. 37–45.

[5] Shaker A. Zahra and Sherry S. Chaples, "Blind Spots in Competitive Analysis," *Academy of Management Executive* 7 (May 1993): 7–27.

[6] Richard A. D'Aveni with Robert Gunther, *Hypercompetitive Rivalries: Competing in Highly Dynamic Environments* (New York: The Free Press, 1995), p. 2

their actions. Fundamental to this process is a focus on the strategic intent of current and potential competitors. Here attention is directed to competitors' core competencies and how they can be leveraged in the pursuit of new applications, especially in divergent industries. **Core competencies** are the sets of skills, systems, and technologies through which a company creates uniquely high value for customers.[7] For example, Canon has leveraged its core competencies in fine optics and microelectronics into an impressive range of products: electronic cameras, jet printers, laser fax machines, and color copiers.[8] By examining core competencies, a clearer portrait is provided of Canon's strategic intent across diverse market sectors.

Spotting New Competitors In considering the core competencies of competitors, scenarios of industry change and competitor entry and exit should also be examined. Which firms (current and potential) find this segment attractive? How do we match up with each? When, where, and how will they enter? Put yourself in the shoes of a potential entrant to think creatively about new competition. How could you best attack your own market position? What strategies could be developed now to preempt entrants?[9] This line of inquiry requires challenging one's assumptions about the industry boundaries by probing suppliers' and customers' perceptions of substitutes and industry newcomers.

Business marketing strategists can secure additional insights by examining the particular actions (moves and countermoves) of competitors and by evaluating what they did versus what they could have done. The particular response chosen may reveal how a competitor sees its strengths. In turn, a rapid, visible, and forceful move signals a competitor's strong commitment to a particular market segment.

Evaluating the Technological Environment

The business marketing strategist must also carefully assess the technological environment in which the firm elects to compete. Three features of the technological environment are especially relevant: (1) **product technology** (the set of ideas embodied in the product or service); (2) **process technology** (the set of ideas or steps involved in the production of a product or service); and (3) **management technology** (the management procedures associated with selling the product or service and with administering the business).[10] Changes occurring in any of these areas can lead to less market-segment stability, shifts in traditional product market boundaries, and new sources of competition. To illustrate, technological change is blurring traditional boundaries in the computer, telecommunications, and financial services industries. Kathleen Eisenhardt and Shona Brown observe that

> In turbulent markets, businesses and opportunities are constantly falling out
> of alignment. New technologies, novel products, and services create fresh

---

[7] James Brian Quinn, "Strategic Outsourcing: Leveraging Knowledge Capabilities," *Sloan Management Review*, 40 (summer 1999), pp. 9–21.

[8] C. K. Prahalad and Gary Hamel, "The Core Competence of the Corporation," *Harvard Business Review* 69 (May/June 1990): pp. 79–91.

[9] Paul A. Geroski, "Early Warning of New Rivals," *Sloan Management Review*, 40 (spring 1999), pp. 107–116.

[10] Noel Capon and Rashi Glazer, "Marketing and Technology: A Strategic Coalignment," *Journal of Marketing* 51 (July 1987): pp. 1–14.

INSIDE BUSINESS MARKETING

Segmentation at Cisco.com

Cisco Systems is the world's leader in electronic commerce with more than $5 billion per year in sales coming from its Web site. The heart of the firm's business is selling equipment that directs data around big corporate networks. Small and medium businesses are also a rapidly growing market for corporate data-networking equipment. Cisco also supplies equipment to Internet service providers and telephone companies. For example, 80 percent of the Internet routers, which direct data to the right place on the Net, were produced by Cisco.

Mark Tonnesen, Cisco's director of customer advocacy, describes their segmentation strategy:

We now have a number of different groups of customers and partners, each with very different needs. For example, we have resellers who cater to the small and medium-sized businesses; we have Internet service providers and telcos as customers. There's a big difference between the needs of a small business and that of an Internet utility. So we've reorganized our Web site to serve these different groups.

In order to offer more targeted features to different segments, Cisco refined its customer profiling and then let customers explicitly choose the types of information they need, the products they want to track, and the services they want to access. As customers volunteer more information about their needs, their industries, and the products and services they value, they segment themselves in natural communities with distinct needs and interests. Cisco is then ideally equipped to refine its offerings to appeal to each of these more targeted segments.

SOURCE: Andy Reinhardt, "Meet Mr. Internet," *Business Week* (September 13, 1999), pp. 129–140; and Patricia B. Seybold and Ronni T. Marshak, *Customers.Com* (New York: Times Books, 1998), pp. 322–323.

---

opportunities. . . . As a result, the clear-cut partitioning of businesses into neat, equidistant rectangles on an organizational chart becomes out of date as opportunities come and go, collide and separate, grow and shrink.[11]

Especially in volatile markets, strategists must continually realign the organization to meet changing customer needs and capture promising market opportunities. For example, Hewlett-Packard's printer business was launched on a small scale in 1984, exploded into a major revenue producer for the company, and now extends into digital photography, wireless information distribution, and e-commerce imaging.[12] Such agility has also been a key factor in the success of high-performing companies like 3M, Johnson & Johnson, and Dell Computer.

Benefits

If the requirements for effective segmentation are met, several benefits accrue to the firm. First, the mere attempt to segment the organizational market forces the marketer to become more attuned to the unique needs of customer segments. Second, knowledge of the needs of particular market segments helps the business marketer focus product development efforts, develop profitable pricing strategies, select appropriate channels of distribution, develop and target advertising messages, as well as training

---

[11] Kathleen M. Eisenhardt and Shona L. Brown, "Patching: Restitching Business Portfolios in Dynamic Markets," *Harvard Business Review*, 77 (May–June 1999), p. 82.

[12] Ibid., pp. 72–82.

and deploying the sales force. Thus, market segmentation provides the foundation for efficient and effective business marketing strategies.

Third, market segmentation provides the business marketer with guidelines that are of significant value in allocating marketing resources. Industrial firms often serve multiple market segments and must continually monitor the relative attractiveness and performance of these segments. Research by Mercer Management Consulting indicates that, for many companies, nearly one-third of their market segments generate no profit and 30 to 50 percent of marketing and customer service costs are wasted on efforts to acquire and retain customers in these segments.[13] Ultimately, the costs, revenues, and profits accruing to the firm must be evaluated segment by segment—and even account by account. As market or competitive conditions change, corresponding adjustments may be required in the firm's market segmentation strategy. Thus, market segmentation provides a basic unit of analysis for marketing planning and control.

Bases for Segmenting Business Markets

Whereas the consumer-goods marketer is interested in securing meaningful profiles of individuals (demographics, lifestyle, benefits sought), the business marketer profiles organizations (size, end use) and organizational buyers (decision style, criteria). Thus, the business or organizational market can be segmented on several bases, broadly classified into two major categories: macrosegmentation and microsegmentation.

Macrosegmentation centers on the characteristics of the buying organization and situation, thus dividing the market by such organizational characteristics as size, geographic location, SIC or NAICS category, and organizational structure. For example, more than 350,000 shoppers visit Dell's online store each week and a creative segmentation approach simplifies the buying experience. From Dell's Web site (see Figure 7.1), observe that customers are segmented into large businesses and small businesses; government accounts are split into federal, state, and local; other non-profits are divided into segments such as education and health care. As a result, marketing strategists at Dell can stay tightly focused on serving the special needs of each segment.

In turn, Dell develops a one-to-one relationship with buying organizations through customized and secure Web sites that essentially become a customer-specific store. To illustrate, the service provides employees at Boeing with special price quotes that reflect the volume of purchases that the organization has made. Such innovative practices have been successful: Dell's internet sales are nearly $50 million dollars a day and growing.[14]

In contrast, **microsegmentation** requires a higher degree of market knowledge, focusing on the characteristics of decision-making units within each macrosegment—including buying decision criteria, perceived importance of the purchase, and attitudes toward vendors. Yoram Wind and Richard Cardozo recommend a two-stage approach to business market segmentation: (1) identify meaningful macrosegments, and then (2) divide the macrosegments into microsegments.[15]

---

[13] Gertz and Baptista, *Grow to Be Great*, p. 55.

[14] Gary McWilliams, "Dell Third-Quarter Profit," *The Wall Street Journal*, November 12, 1999, p. B5.

[15] Wind and Cardozo, "Industrial Market Segmentation," p. 155; see also Mitchell and Wilson, "Balancing Theory and Practice," pp. 429–455.

| FIGURE 7.1 | DELL'S ONLINE STORE USES A CREATIVE SEGMENTATION APPROACH TO SIMPLIFY THE BUYING EXPERIENCE |

SOURCE: http://www.dell.com (November 10, 1999)

In evaluating alternative bases for segmentation, the marketer is attempting to identify significant predictors of differences in buyer behavior. Once such differences are recognized, the marketer can approach target segments with appropriate marketing strategy. Secondary sources of information, coupled with data in a firm's information system, can be used to divide the market into macrolevel segments. The concentration of the business market allows some marketers to monitor the purchasing patterns of each customer. For example, a firm that sells industrial products to paper manufacturers is dealing with hundreds of potential buying organizations in the United States and Canadian markets; a paper manufacturer selling to ultimate consumers is dealing with millions of potential customers. Such market concentration, coupled with rapidly advancing marketing intelligence systems, makes it easier for the business marketer to monitor the purchasing patterns of individual organizations.

Macrolevel Bases

Selected macrolevel bases of segmentation are presented in Table 7.1. Recall that these are concerned with general characteristics of the buying organization, the nature of the product application, and the characteristics of the buying situation.

| TABLE 7.1 | SELECTED MACROLEVEL BASES OF SEGMENTATION | |

Variables	Illustrative Breakdowns
Characteristics of Buying Organizations	
Size (the scale of operations of the organization)	Small, medium, large; based on sales or number of employees
Geographical location	New England, Middle Atlantic, South Atlantic, East North Central, etc.
Usage rate	Nonuser, light user, moderate user, heavy user
Structure of procurement	Centralized, decentralized
Product/Service Application	
SIC or NAICS category	Varies by product or service
End Market Served	Varies by product or service
Value in use	High, low
Characteristics of Purchasing Situation	
Type of buying situation	New task, modified rebuy, straight rebuy
Stage in purchase decision process	Early stages, late stages

Macrolevel Characteristics of Buying Organizations   The marketer may find it useful to partition the market by size of potential buying organizations. Large buying organizations may possess unique requirements and respond to marketing stimuli that are different from those responded to by smaller firms. The influence of presidents, vice presidents, and owners declines with an increase in corporate size; the influence of other participants, such as purchasing managers, increases.[16] Alternatively, the marketer may recognize regional variations and adopt geographical units as the basis for differentiating marketing strategies.

Usage rate constitutes another macrolevel variable. Buyers are classified on a continuum ranging from nonuser to heavy user. Heavy users may have different needs than moderate or light users. For example, heavy users may place more value on technical or delivery support services than their counterparts. Likewise, an opportunity may exist to convert moderate users into heavy users through adjustments in the product or service mix.

The structure of the procurement function constitutes a final macrolevel characteristic of buying organizations. Firms with a centralized purchasing function behave differently than do those with decentralized procurement (see Chapter 3). The structure of the purchasing function influences the degree of buyer specialization, the criteria emphasized, and the composition of the buying center. Centralized buyers place significant weight on long-term supply availability and the development of a healthy

[16]Joseph A. Bellizzi, "Organizational Size and Buying Influences," *Industrial Marketing Management* 10 (February 1981): pp. 17–21; see also Arch G. Woodside, Timo Liukko, and Risto Vuori, "Organizational Buying of Capital Equipment Involving Persons Across Several Authority Levels," *Journal of Business & Industrial Marketing*, 14, No. 1 (1999), pp. 30–48.

FIGURE 7.2 AN AD FEATURING TECHNOLOGY FOR E-COMMERCE SOLUTIONS

SOURCE: Courtesy, Sun Microsystems, Inc.

supplier complex. Decentralized buyers emphasize short-term cost efficiency.[17] Thus, the position of procurement in the organizational hierarchy provides a base for categorizing organizations and for isolating specific needs and marketing requirements. Many business marketers develop a national accounts sales team to meet the special requirements of large centralized procurement units.

Product/Service Application   Because a specific industrial good is often used in different ways, the marketer can divide the market on the basis of specific end-use applications. Consider Sun Microsystems (see Figure 7.2). The ad for its net-based

---

[17]Timothy M. Laseter, *Balanced Sourcing: Cooperation and Competition in Supplier Relationships* (San Francisco: Jossey-Bass Publishers, 1998), pp. 59–86.

technologies features e-commerce applications and identifies leading e-commerce sites that are powered by Sun products and services like eBay and Amazon.com. The North American Industrial Classification System (NAICS) or SIC system and related information sources are especially valuable when segmenting the market on the basis of end use. To illustrate, the manufacturer of a component such as springs may reach industries incorporating the product into machine tools, bicycles, surgical devices, office equipment, telephones, and missile systems. Similarly, Intel's microchips are used in household appliances, retail terminals, toys, and aircraft as well as in computers. By isolating the specialized needs of each user group, the firm is better equipped to differentiate customer requirements and to evaluate emerging opportunities.

Value in Use   Strategic insights are also provided by exploring the value in use of various customer applications. Recall our discussion of value analysis in Chapter 4. **Value in use** is a product's economic value to the user relative to a specific alternative in a particular application. The economic value of an offering frequently varies by customer application. Milliken & Company, the textile manufacturer, has built one of its businesses by becoming a major supplier of towels to industrial laundries. These customers pay Milliken a 10 percent premium over equivalent towels offered by competitors.[18] Why? Milliken provides added value, such as a computerized routing program that improves the efficiency and effectiveness of the industrial laundries' pick-up and delivery function.

The segmentation strategy adopted by a manufacturer of precision motors further illuminates the value-in-use concept.[19] The firm found that its customers differed in the motor speed required in their applications and that a new, low-priced machine introduced by a dominant competitor wore out quickly when used in high- and medium-speed applications. The marketer concentrated on this vulnerable segment, demonstrating the superior life cycle cost advantages of the firm's products. A long-term program was also initiated to develop a competitively priced product and service offering for customers in the low-speed segment.

Purchasing Situation   The final macrolevel base for segmenting the organizational market is the purchasing situation. First-time buyers have perceptions and information needs that differ from those of repeat buyers. Therefore, buying organizations are classified as being in the early or late stages of the procurement process, or alternatively, as *new-task*, *straight rebuy*, or *modified rebuy* organizations (see Chapter 3). The position of the firm in the procurement decision process or its location on the buying situation continuum dictates marketing strategy.

These examples illustrate those macrolevel bases of segmentation that business marketers can apply to the organizational market. Other macrolevel bases may more precisely fit a specific situation. A key benefit of segmentation is that it forces the manager to search for bases that explain similarities and differences among buying organizations.

---

[18] Philip Kotler, "Marketing's New Paradigm: What's Really Happening Out There," *Planning Review* 20 (September/October 1992): pp. 50–52.

[19] Robert A. Garda, "How to Carve Niches for Growth in Industrial Markets," *Management Review* 70 (August 1981): pp. 15–22.

Illustration: Macrosegmentation [20]

A business marketer with an innovative technical product sought to become the leader in a market that comprised many small- and medium-sized firms. Based on the purchase decision process, three segments were identified:

1. **First Time Prospects:** Customers who see a possible need for the product and have started to evaluate alternative suppliers—but who have not yet purchased the product.

2. **Novices:** Customers who have purchased the product for the first time within the past three months.

3. **Sophisticates:** Experienced customers who have either purchased the product before and are now ready to rebuy, or who have recently repurchased.

Observe from Table 7.2 that, for this particular business market, the three segments value different benefits. For example, novices seek easy-to-read manuals and technical support hot lines whereas sophisticates want system compatibility and products customized to their needs. The business marketer responded by developing sharply focused marketing strategies for each macrosegment.

Microlevel Bases

Having identified macrosegments, the marketer often finds it useful to divide each macrosegment into smaller microsegments on the basis of the similarities and differences between decision-making units. Often, several microsegments—each with unique requirements and unique responses to marketing stimuli—are buried in macrosegments. To isolate them effectively, the marketer must move beyond secondary sources of information by soliciting input from the sales force or by conducting a special market segmentation study. Selected microbases of segmentation appear in Table 7.3.

Key Criteria For some industrial goods, the marketer can divide the market according to which criteria are assigned the most importance in the purchase decision.[21] Criteria include product quality, prompt and reliable delivery, technical support, price, and supply continuity. The marketer also might divide the market based on supplier profiles that appear to be preferred by decision makers (for example, high quality, prompt delivery, premium price versus standard quality, less-prompt delivery, low price).

---

[20] Thomas S. Robertson and Howard Barich, "A Successful Approach to Segmenting Industrial Markets," *Planning Review* 20 (November/December 1992): pp. 4–11.

[21] David E. Schnedler, "Use Strategic Models to Predict Customer Behavior," pp. 85–92; and Kenneth E. Mast and John M. Hawes, "Perceptual Differences between Buyers and Engineers," *Journal of Purchasing and Materials Management* 22 (spring 1986): pp. 2–6; Donald W. Jackson Jr., Richard K. Burdick, and Janet E. Keith, "Purchasing Agents' Perceived Importance of Marketing Mix Components in Different Industrial Purchase Situations," *Journal of Business Research* 13 (August 1985): pp. 361–373; and Donald R. Lehmann and John O'Shaughnessy, "Decision Criteria Used in Buying Different Categories of Products," *Journal of Purchasing and Materials Management* 18 (spring 1982): pp. 9–14.

TABLE 7.2	**WHAT BUYERS OF INDUSTRIAL PRODUCTS LOOK FOR**		
	First Time Prospects	**Novices**	**Sophisticates**
Dominant theme			
	"Take care of me."	"Help me make it work."	"Talk technology to me."
Benefits sought			
	A sales rep who knows and understands my business	Easy to read manuals	Compatibility with existing systems
	An honest sales rep	Technical support hot lines	Products customized to customer needs
	A vendor who has been in business for some time	A high level of training	Track record of vendor
	A sales rep who can communicate in an understandable manner	Sales reps who are knowledgeable	Maintenance speed in fixing problems
	A trial period		Post-sales support and technical support
	A high level of training		
What's less important			
	Sales rep's knowledge of products and services	An honest sales rep	Training
		A sales rep who knows and understands my business	Trial
			Easy to read manuals
			A sales rep who can communicate in an understandable manner

SOURCE: Adapted from Thomas S. Robertson and Howard Barich, "A Successful Approach to Segmenting Industrial Markets," *Planning Review* 20 (November/December 1992), p. 7.

Illustration: Price versus Service[22]   Signode Corporation produces and markets a line of steel strapping used for packaging a range of products, including steel and many manufactured items. Facing stiff price competition and a declining market share, management wanted to move beyond traditional macrolevel segmentation to understand how Signode's 174 national accounts viewed price versus service tradeoffs. Four segments were uncovered:

1. **Programmed buyers** (sales = $6.6 million): Customers who were not particularly price or service sensitive and who made purchases in a routinized fashion. Product is not central to their operation.

---

[22] V. Kasturi Rangan, Rowland T. Moriarty, and Gordon S. Swartz, "Segmenting Customers in Mature Industrial Markets," *Journal of Marketing* 56 (October 1992): pp. 72–82.

TABLE 7.3	SELECTED MICROLEVEL BASES OF SEGMENTATION
Variables	**Illustrative Breakdowns**
Key criteria	Quality, delivery, supplier reputation
Purchasing strategies	Optimizer, satisficer
Structure of decision-making unit	Major decision participants (for example, purchasing manager and plant manager)
Importance of purchase	High importance . . . low importance
Attitude toward vendors	Favorable . . . unfavorable
Organizational innovativeness	Innovator . . . follower
Personal characteristics	
Demographics	Age, educational background
Decision style	Normative, conservative, mixed mode
Risk	Risk taker, risk avoider
Confidence	High . . . low
Job responsibility	Purchasing, production, engineering

2. **Relationship buyers** (sales = $31 million): Knowledgeable customers who valued partnership with Signode and did not push for price or service concessions. Product is moderately important to the firm's operations.

3. **Transaction buyers** (sales = $24 million): Large and very knowledgeable customers who actively considered the price versus service tradeoffs, but often placed price over service. Product is very important to their operations.

4. **Bargain hunters** (sales = $23 million): Large-volume buyers who were very sensitive to any changes in price or service. Product is very important to their operations.

The study enabled Signode to sharpen its strategies in this mature business market and to gain a clearer understanding of the cost of serving the various segments. Particularly troubling to management was the bargain hunter segment. These customers demanded the lowest prices and the highest levels of service, and had the highest propensity to switch. Management decided to use price cuts only as a defense against cuts made by competitors. Attention was directed instead at ways to add service value to this and other segments.

Fast-Cycle Strategies   Service responsiveness is assuming an increasingly important role in many industrial buying decisions. Business market customers can be surprisingly sensitive to time and are often willing to pay a premium price for responsiveness. George Stalk Jr. and Thomas M. Hout note that "If the customers who are the most sensitive to responsiveness and choice can be locked-up, a time-based competitor

---

INSIDE BUSINESS MARKETING

Strategy Is Revolution

"You can either surrender the future to revolutionary challenges or revolutionize the way your company creates strategy. What is required is not a little tweak to the traditional planning process, but a new philosophical foundation: strategy *is* revolution; everything else is tactics." Gary Hamel, who advanced this bold and intriguing position, offers several paths to industry revolution. For example, a would-be revolutionary might begin completing the following steps:

1. **Reconceiving a product or service.** In every industry, *X* units of dollars buy *Y* units of value. A firm can *radically improve the value equation* as Hewlett-Packard has done in the printer business.

2. **Redefining market space.** Revolutionary strategies go beyond the served market and

focus on the total imaginable market (for example, personal communication devices targeted to business-to-business customers and individuals on a global basis).

3. **Redrawing industry boundaries.** Firms can gain a competitive advantage by compressing the supply chain. For example, Xerox plans to reinvent the way organizations distribute printed materials such as catalogs and user manuals. Why not transmit the information digitally, printing it close to where it is needed?

SOURCE: Gary Hamel, "Strategy as Revolution," *Harvard Business Review*, 74 (July/August 1996): pp. 70–73; see also, W. Chan Kim and Renee' Mauborgne, "Creating New Market Space," *Harvard Business Review*, 77 (January–February 1999), pp. 83–93.

---

secures an almost unassailable and profitable advantage."[23] For example, Atlas Corporation developed a commanding position in the industrial door market by providing customized products in just four weeks, much faster than the industry average of twelve to fifteen weeks. Atlas compressed time by building just-in-time factories and, most important, by automating its entire order entry, engineering, pricing, and scheduling processes. Nearly all incoming orders can be priced and scheduled while the caller is still on the telephone. The faster information, decisions, and materials can flow through an organization, the faster the firm can respond to customer orders or adjust to shifts in market demand and competitive conditions. **Fast-cycle companies** manage both the cycle of industrial activities throughout the organization and the cycle time of the entire delivery system—the number of days it takes to develop a new product or to ship a customer's order.

The marketer can benefit by examining the criteria employed by decision-making units in various sectors of the business market—commercial, governmental, and institutional. As organizations in each sector undergo restructuring efforts, the buying criteria employed by key decision makers also change. For example, the cost pressures and reform efforts in the health-care industry are changing the way in which hospitals buy medical equipment and pharmaceuticals. To reduce administrative costs and enhance bargaining power, hospitals are following the lead of commercial enterprises by streamlining their operations. Also, they are forming buying groups, centralizing the purchasing function, and insisting on lower prices and better service. Reform efforts are likewise moving government buyers to search for more efficient purchasing procedures and for better value from vendors. Those marketers that respond in this challenging environment will be rewarded.

---

[23] George Stalk Jr. and Thomas M. Hout, *Competing Against Time: How Time-based Competition Is Re-Shaping Global Markets* (New York: The Free Press, 1990), p. 102.

Purchasing Strategies Microsegments can be classified according to the purchasing strategy employed by buying organizations. Richard Cardozo has identified two purchasing profiles as satisficers and optimizers.[24]

Satisficers approach a given purchasing requirement by contacting familiar suppliers and placing the order with the first supplier to satisfy product and delivery requirements. **Optimizers** consider numerous suppliers, familiar and unfamiliar, solicit bids, and examine all alternative proposals carefully before selecting a supplier.

These purchasing strategies have numerous implications. A supplier entering the market would have a higher probability of penetrating a decision-making unit made up of optimizers than of penetrating a unit consisting of satisficers who rely on familiar suppliers.

Identifying different purchasing patterns can help the marketer understand differing responses to marketing stimuli. A business marketer who serves the institutional food market, for example, encounters both satisficers and optimizers. Large universities review and test menu alternatives carefully, consult with student committees, and analyze the price-per-unit-cooked before selecting a supplier (optimizers). Restaurants and company cafeterias may follow a different pattern. The restaurant manager, consulting with the chef, selects a supplier that provides the required product quality and delivery (satisficer). Remember that satisficing and optimizing are only two of many purchasing strategies of organizational buyers.

Structure of the Decision-Making Unit The structure of the decision-making unit, or buying center, likewise provides a means of dividing the business market into subsets of customers by isolating the patterns of involvement in the purchasing process of particular decision participants (for example, engineering versus top management). For the medical equipment market, Du Pont initiated a formal positioning study among hospital administrators, radiology department administrators, and technical managers in order to identify the firm's relative standing and the specific needs (criteria) for each level of buying influence within each segment.[25] The growing importance of buying groups, multihospital chains, and nonhospital health-care delivery systems pointed to the need for a more refined segmentation approach.

The study indicates that the medical equipment market can be segmented on the basis of the type of institution and the responsibilities of the decision makers and decision influencers in those institutions. The structure of the decision-making unit and the decision criteria used vary across the following three segments:

- groups selecting a single supplier that must be used by all member hospitals, such as investor-owned hospital chains

- groups selecting a small set of suppliers from which individual hospitals may select needed products

- private group practices and the nonhospital segment

Based on the study, Du Pont's salespersons can tailor their presentations to the decision-making dynamics of each segment. In turn, advertising messages can be more

---

[24]Richard N. Cardozo, "Situational Segmentation of Industrial Markets," *European Journal of Marketing* 14, no. 5/6 (1980): pp. 264–276.

[25]Gary L. Coles and James D. Culley, "Not All Prospects Are Created Equal," *Business Marketing* 71 (May 1986): pp. 52–57.

precisely targeted. Such an analysis enables the marketer to identify meaningful microsegments and respond with finely tuned marketing communications.

Importance of Purchase   Classifying organizational customers on the basis of the perceived importance of a particular product is especially appropriate when the product is applied in various ways by various customers. Buyer perceptions differ according to the impact of the product on the total mission of the firm. A large commercial enterprise may consider the purchase of an office machine routine; the same purchase for a small manufacturing concern is "an event."

Attitudes toward Vendors   The attitudes of decision-making units toward the vendors in a particular product class provide another means of microsegmentation. An analysis of how various clusters of buyers view alternative sources of supply often uncovers opportunities in the form of vulnerable segments being either neglected or not fully satisfied by competitors.

Organizational Innovativeness   Some organizations are more innovative and willing to purchase new industrial products than others. A study of the adoption of new medical equipment among hospitals found that psychographic variables can improve a marketer's ability to predict the adoption of new products.[26] These include such factors as an organization's level of change resistance or desire to excel. When psychographic variables are combined with organizational demographic variables (for example, size), accuracy in predicting organizational innovativeness increases.

   Because products will diffuse more rapidly in some segments than in others, microsegmentation on the basis of organizational innovativeness enables the marketer to identify segments that should be targeted first when new products are introduced. The accuracy of new product forecasting is also improved when diffusion patterns are estimated segment by segment.[27]

Personal Characteristics   Some microsegmentation possibilities deal with the personal characteristics of decision makers: demographics (age, education), personality, decision style, risk preference or risk avoidance, confidence, job responsibilities, and so forth. Although some interesting studies have shown the viability of segmentation on the basis of individual characteristics, further research is needed to explore its potential as a firm base for microsegmentation.

Illustration: Microsegmentation[28]

Philips Lighting Company, the North American division of Philips Electronics, found that purchasing managers emphasize two criteria in purchasing light bulbs: cost and

---

[26] Thomas S. Robertson and Yoram Wind, "Organizational Psychographics and Innovativeness," *Journal of Consumer Research* 7 (June 1980): pp. 24–31; see also Robertson and Hubert Gatignon, "Competitive Effects on Technology Diffusion," *Journal of Marketing* 50 (July 1986): pp. 1–12.

[27] Yoram Wind, Thomas S. Robertson, and Cynthia Fraser, "Industrial Product Diffusion by Market Segment," *Industrial Marketing Management* 11 (February 1982): pp. 1–8.

[28] W. Chan Kim and Renee' Mauborgne, "Creating New Market Space," *Harvard Business Review*, 77 (January–February 1999), pp. 88–89. For other segmentation studies, see Mark J. Bennion Jr., "Segmentation and Positioning in a Basic Industry," *Industrial Market Management* 16 (February 1987): pp. 9–18; Arch G. Woodside and Elizabeth J. Wilson, "Combining Macro and Micro Industrial Market Segmentation," in *Advances in Business Marketing*, ed. Arch G. Woodside (Greenwich, Conn.: JAI Press, 1986), pp. 241–257; and Peter Doyle and John Saunders, "Market Segmentation and Positioning in Specialized Industrial Markets," *Journal of Marketing* 49 (spring 1985): pp. 24–32.

longevity. Philips learned, however, that the price and life of bulbs did not account for the total cost of lighting. Because lamps contain environmentally toxic mercury, companies faced high disposal costs at the end of a lamp's useful life.

New Product and Segmentation Strategy   To capitalize on a perceived opportunity, Philips introduced the Alto, an environmentally friendly bulb that reduces customers' overall costs plus allows the buying organization to demonstrate environmental concern to the public. Rather than targeting purchasing managers, Philips' marketing strategists centered their attention on chief financial officers (CFOs), who embraced the cost savings, and public relations executives, who saw the benefit of purchasing actions that protect the environment. By targeting different buying influentials, a new market opportunity was created. In fact, the Alto has already replaced more than 25 percent of traditional fluorescent lamps used in stores, schools, and office buildings in the United States.

A Model for Segmenting the Organizational Market

Macrosegmentation centers on characteristics of buying *organizations* (for example, size), product application (for example, end market served), and characteristics of the purchasing situation (for example, stage in the purchase decision process). Microsegmentation concentrates on characteristics of organizational decision-making *units*—for instance, choice criteria assigned the most importance in the purchase decision.

Choosing Market Segments

The model in Figure 7.3 combines these macrosegment bases and outlines the steps required for effective segmentation. This approach to organizational market segmentation begins with an analysis of key characteristics of the organization and of the buying situation (macrodimensions)[29] in order to identify, evaluate, and select meaningful macrosegments. Note that the segmentation task is complete at this stage if *each* of the selected macrosegments exhibits a *distinct* response to the firm's marketing stimuli. Because the information needed for macrosegmentation can often be drawn from secondary information sources, the research investment is low.

The cost of research increases, however, when microlevel segmentation is required. A marketing research study is often needed to identify characteristics of decision-making units, as the Philips Lighting case illustrated. At this level, chosen macrosegments are divided into microsegments on the basis of similarities and differences between the decision-making units in order to identify small groups of buying organizations that each exhibit a distinct response to the firm's marketing strategy. Observe in Figure 7.3 that the desirability of a particular target segment depends upon the costs and benefits of reaching that segment. The costs are associated with marketing strategy adjustments such as modifying the product, providing special service support, altering personal selling or advertising strategies, or entering new channels of distribution. The benefits include the short- and long-term opportunities that would

---

[29]Wind and Cardozo, "Industrial Market Segmentation," pp. 153–166; see also John Morton, "How to Spot the Really Important Prospects," *Business Marketing* 75 (January 1990): pp. 62–67.

SOURCE: Adapted by permission of the publisher from Yoram Wind and Richard Cardozo, "Industrial Market Segmentation," *Industrial Marketing Management* 3 (March 1974): p. 156. Copyright 1974 by Elsevier Science Publishing Co., Inc.

FIGURE 7.3   AN APPROACH TO SEGMENTATION OF BUSINESS MARKETS

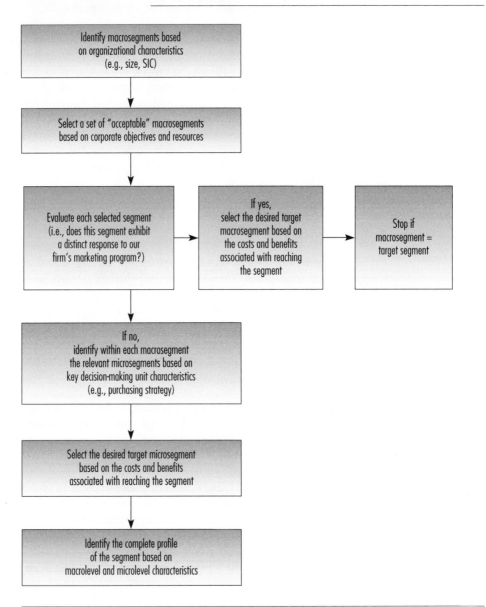

accrue to the firm for tapping this segment. The marketer must evaluate the potential profitability of alternative segments before investing in separate marketing strategies. This requires a process of evaluation that makes explicit the near-term potential and the longer-term resource commitments necessary to effectively serve customers in a segment.

Making a Commitment

Business market segments must be selected with care because of the close working relationship between buyer and seller following the sales transaction. To serve a segment, significant resource commitments may be necessary to provide the level of field sales and customer service support that customers expect.[30] Although producers of consumer goods such as toothpaste can shift from one demographic or lifestyle segment to another relatively quickly, industrial firms may have to realign their entire marketing strategy (for example, retrain salespersons) and alter the manufacturing process to meet the needs of a new market segment. Posttransaction service commitments to the new segment may continue for years. Thus, the decision to enter a particular market segment carries with it significant long-term resource commitments for the business marketer. Such decisions are not easily reversed.

Implementing a Segmentation Strategy

A well-developed segmentation plan will fail without careful attention to how the plan will be implemented. The successful implementation of a segmentation strategy requires attention to the following issues:

- How should the sales force be organized?

- What special technical or customer service requirements will organizations in the new segment have? Who will provide these services?

- Which media outlets can be used to target advertising at the new segment?

- Will adjustments be required in the logistical network in order to meet particular inventory requirements?

- What adaptations will be needed to serve selected international market segments?

The astute business marketing strategist must plan, coordinate, and monitor implementation details. Frank Cespedes points out that "As a firm's offering becomes a product-service-information mix that must be customized for diverse segments, organizational interdependencies increase"[31] and marketing managers, in particular, are involved in more cross-functional tasks. Managing the critical points of contact with the customer is fundamental to the marketing manager's role in the firm.

Summary

The business market contains a complex mix of customers with diverse needs and objectives. The marketing strategist who analyzes the aggregate market and identifies neglected or inadequately served groups of buyers (segments) is ideally prepared for a market assault. Specific marketing strategy adjustments can be made to fit the unique

---

[30] Cespedes, *Concurrent Marketing*, pp. 50–57.

[31] Cespedes, *Concurrent Marketing*, p. 271.

needs of each target segment. Of course, such differentiated marketing strategies are feasible only when the target segments are measurable, accessible, compatible, responsive, and large enough to justify separate attention.

Procedurally, business market segmentation involves categorizing actual or potential buying organizations into mutually exclusive clusters (segments), each of which exhibits a relatively homogeneous response to marketing strategy variables. To accomplish this task, the business marketer can draw upon two types of segmentation bases: macrolevel and microlevel. Macrodimensions are the key characteristics of buying organizations and of the purchasing situation. The SIC and NAICS, together with other secondary sources of information, are valuable in macrolevel segmentation. Microlevel bases of segmentation center on key characteristics of the decision-making unit and require a higher level of market knowledge.

This chapter outlined a systematic approach for the business marketer to apply when identifying and selecting target segments. Before a final decision is made, the marketer must weigh the costs and benefits of a segmented marketing strategy. The market potential of possible target segments must be calculated, and a careful assessment must be made of company versus competitive strengths. Techniques for measuring market potential (opportunity) provide the theme for the next chapter.

Discussion Questions

1. Federal Express believes that its future growth will come from business-to-business e-commerce transactions where customers demand quick and reliable delivery service. Outline a segmentation plan that the firm might use to become the market leader in this rapidly expanding area.

2. Automatic Data Processing, Inc. (ADP) handles payroll and tax filing processing for more than 300,000 customers. In other words, firms outsource these functions to ADP. Suggest possible segmentation bases that ADP might employ in this service market. What criteria would be important to organizational buyers in making the decision to turn payroll processing over to an outside firm?

3. AT&T, Microsoft, Dow Jones, and IBM are all involved in the information business, and all offer equipment and services that enable consumers to access information in an efficient manner. What implications does this raise for competitive analysis and for market segmentation?

4. Firms use their information systems to track what existing customers buy, as well as where and how they buy. A leading management expert suggests that equal attention should be given to noncustomers because they generally outnumber customers. Evaluate this position.

5. Two years ago, Jackson Machine Tool selected four SIC categories as key market segments. A unique marketing strategy was then developed for each segment. In retrospect, Jackson management wonder whether they have been appealing to the right segments of the market. Again this year, sales were up slightly, profits were down rather sharply. They need your help. Outline the approach that you would follow in evaluating the appropriateness of their segmentation.

6. Peter Drucker persuasively argues that traditional accounting systems do not capture the true benefits of automated manufacturing equipment. According to Drucker, such approaches emphasize the costs of *doing* something, whereas the main benefit of automation lies in eliminating—or at least minimizing—the cost of *not doing* something (for example, not producing defective parts that become scrap). Explain how a producer of automated equipment might employ a value-in-use segmentation strategy.

7. Explain why entry into a particular market segment by an industrial firm such as Du Pont often entails a greater commitment than a comparable decision made by a consumer-products company like General Foods.

8. Sara Lee Corporation derives more than $1.5 billion of sales each year from the institutional market (for example, hospitals, schools, restaurants). Explain how a firm such as Sara Lee or General Mills might apply the concept of market segmentation to the institutional market.

9. What personal selling strategy would be most appropriate when dealing with an organizational buyer who is an optimizer? A satisficer?

10. Some firms follow a single-stage segmentation approach, using macrodimensions; others use both macrodimensions and microdimensions. As a business marketing manager, what factors would you consider in making a choice between the two methods?

8

Organizational Demand Analysis

The business marketer confronts the difficult task of predicting the market response of organizational customers. The efficiency and effectiveness of the marketing program rests on the manager's ability to isolate and measure organizational demand patterns and forecast specific levels of sales. Accurate projections of market potential and future sales are among the most significant and challenging dimensions of organizational demand analysis. After reading this chapter, you will understand

1. how the Internet provides a reservoir of business market information.

2. the importance of organizational demand analysis to business marketing management.

3. the role of market potential analysis and sales forecasting in the planning and control process.

4. specific techniques to effectively measure market potential and develop a sales forecast.

To implement business marketing strategy successfully, the business marketing manager must estimate the potential market for the firm's products. Accurate estimates of potential business enable the manager to allocate scarce resources to the customer segments, products, and territories that offer the greatest return. Estimates of market potential also provide the manager with a standard that can be used to assess the firm's performance in the product and market situations targeted. As one management expert suggests, "Without a forecast of total market demand, decisions on investment, marketing support, and other resource allocations will be based on hidden, unconscious assumptions about industrywide requirements, and they'll often be wrong."[1]

Sales forecasting is likewise vital to marketing management. The sales forecast reflects management's estimate of the probable level of company sales, taking into account both potential business and the level and type of marketing effort demanded. Virtually every decision made by the marketer is based on a forecast, formal or informal.

Organizational demand analysis is composed of sales forecasting and market potential analysis, and this chapter explores its role in the planning and control process. First, attention centers on how a business marketing manager can use the Internet to capture valuable information to support decision making. Second, the nature and purpose of both the market potential estimate and the sales forecast are examined and contrasted. Once the groundwork is established, several methods of measuring market potential are described, illustrated, and evaluated. The chapter concludes with an examination of the salient dimensions of sales forecasting, along with selected sales forecasting techniques.

Organizational Demand Analysis

The business marketing manager must analyze organizational demand from two perspectives. First, what is the highest possible level of market demand that may accrue to all producers in this industry in a particular time period? The answer constitutes the market potential for a product. Market potential is influenced by the level of industry marketing effort and the assumed conditions in the external environment. Second, what level of sales can the firm reasonably expect to achieve, given a particular level and type of marketing effort and a particular set of environmental conditions? The answer constitutes the firm's sales forecast. Note that the forecast depends on the level of the firm's marketing effort. Thus, the marketing plan must be developed before the sales forecast. This section examines the significance of both components of organizational demand analysis for business marketing management.

Using the Internet for Business Marketing Research

Whether developed through painstaking marketing research studies or gleaned from existing publications, information exists to support business decisions. Secondary information gathered and published by government agencies, trade associations, trade

---

[1] F. William Barnett, "Four Steps to Forecast Total Market Demand," *Harvard Business Review* 66 (July/August 1988): p. 28. See also John T. Mentzer and Carol C. Bienstock, *Sales Forecasting Management* (Thousand Oaks, CA: Sage Publications, Inc., 1998).

publications, and independent research firms provides a valuable and often inexpensive start to building knowledge of the market. Of the many external sources of business information, secondary data is the principal source of information about a company's competitive and external environment.

The Internet and World Wide Web currently provide the easiest-to-locate information of almost any source for business marketing applications. There are literally thousands of searching sources on the Web and some sites even search the search engines. Nearly every aspect of marketing intelligence that is gathered by business marketers is available on the Internet: competitive information, customer data, economic information, technological trends, and political and legal data. Much of the secondary information found on the Internet is more current than data published in hard copy; it is inexpensive, easy to use, and quick to access. In addition to the multitude of secondary information available, the Internet can also be used to gather primary data—to do surveys via e-mail or through Web pages.

Secondary Data Available to Business Marketers on the Internet   The amount of published data available to business marketers via the Internet is staggering: up-to-date information from over 194 countries is available twenty-four hours a day, seven days a week, and within a matter of seconds. However, just because there is a wealth of data available does not mean that the data is necessarily "good"—such information must be carefully scrutinized by the decision maker to assess its value to the problem at hand. Before using Internet information, the business marketer should assess its quality: how it was gathered, the size of the sample that was used, who provided the information, and the purpose for which the information was collected.

In turn, secondary data published on the Internet may also be out of date. This is a problem that particularly plagues information published by the federal government. For example, the U.S. Census Bureau maintains a huge Web site (www.census.gov) that includes a significant quantity of data from the Census of Manufacturers—data relevant to business marketers—but this information is often two or three years out of date. The Census of Manufacturers is conducted every five years, yet it often takes the Census Bureau two-to-three years to compile and publish the information. Table 8.1 highlights some of the Internet sites that are used by business marketing managers. This table contains a minuscule sample of the total number of sites that might be tapped for useful market or competitive information.

Using the Internet   Table 8.1 illustrates how a manager can use the Internet to monitor almost all the economic statistics of the U.S. government, assess technological trends, analyze competitive strategies, gather data on markets and buyer behavior, evaluate global market opportunities, and investigate almost any business firm in the world. An easy, and often revealing, exercise is to browse the Web sites of major competitors. Competitive Web sites may contain useful information regarding product lines, channel strategy, and pricing. However, sensitive data is usually reserved for customers who are able to enter through the use of an assigned password. Nevertheless, Web sites can contain some very powerful competitive intelligence that is virtually free.

Understanding the Limitations   Keep in mind that there are no standards for the information that is offered on a Web site: the owner has no requirement to provide an evaluation of the site's accuracy. Likewise, there is no review process for publishing

| TABLE 8.1 | EXAMPLES OF BUSINESS-TO-BUSINESS INFORMATION RESOURCES AVAILABLE ON THE INTERNET |

1. www.corporateinformation.com

   A site that offers in-depth information about companies located outside the United States.

2. www.intellifact.com

   This no-cost site provides more than 300,000 company profiles.

3. www.findsvp.com

   This site provides market research on the impact of technological change on businesses and consumers. It covers a variety of industries, including plastics, computers, industrial automation, and software.

4. www.frost.com

   This site is maintained by Frost and Sullivan, a large research firm. It provides market research reports that monitor over 300 industries.

5. www.intelliquest.com

   Intelliquest specializes in providing technology companies with survey-based market research information.

6. www.uspto.gov

   Provides a multitude of information on patent procedures and pending patent applications.

7. www.census.gov

   This is a huge site, which provides a wide range of data gathered and published by the U.S. Census Bureau.

8. www.stat-usa.gov

   The U.S. Department of Commerce provides economic data published by the U.S. government as well as National Trade Data Bank Information for importers and exporters.

9. www.cbd.savvy.com

   The Commerce Business Daily in print form provides a list of the federal government's requests for proposals. The online version includes the same material and is easily scanned.

10. www.dnb.com

    Dun & Bradstreet publish business information on 11 million U.S. private and public businesses and more than 50 million businesses worldwide. D&B Internet Access provides free look-up of both public and private companies and options to order selected D&B reports.

11. www.airsearch.com

    This site is maintained by The Market Research Center and it links the user to almost every product and service category imaginable. It is an excellent source to begin tracking competitors.

12. www.mediametrix.com

    MediaMetrix is a leading marketing information services firm. The firm designs tools that online marketers can use to measure activity on their Web sites.

13. www.liszt.com

    This site catalogs over 66,000 mailing lists.

14. www.infomkt.ibm

    This site searches other search engines and reference sources on the Internet and a variety of business indexes.

15. www.wilsonweb.com/webmarket/

    Articles on Internet marketing are gathered from a wide array of sources and published on this Web site.

Web-based information and anyone can publish what they want. To navigate the Internet wisely, the business marketer should:[2]

1. Learn and evaluate the Web site's author. The government or a well-known firm is more likely to include reliable data than unknown sources.

2. Evaluate the site's credibility. Concerning financial evaluations of companies, a university site is more likely to be unbiased than financial advisory services.

3. Determine how often the site is updated. A site where hyperlinks are inoperative has probably not been updated lately.

4. Validate the information found on the site with other sites or from hardcopy sources in the library.

5. Evaluate the accuracy of numerical data provided by the site: if the numbers don't add up or there are many errors, the data may be questionable.

6. Use many Internet sources, rather than relying on the first site that appears to have comprehensive and detailed data.

Collecting Primary Data on the Internet   As firms become more comfortable with the Internet, they are using it for gathering primary data—that is, information about customer perceptions, behaviors and desires, as well as any other information that may be unavailable from secondary sources. For example, Cisco Systems has developed a "Community of Customers" that it regularly queries for ideas, product preferences, and performance evaluations. The Internet can provide an efficient venue for conducting surveys, running focus groups, and conducting experiments. Compared to traditional approaches, the computer and the Internet simply make it easier and more cost efficient to reach survey respondents. Also, new marketing research companies have been created to take advantage of the Internet's capabilities and they are able to design and execute entire studies by utilizing the Internet and e-mail.

Survey research can be effective over the Internet to gather information easily, quickly, and at low cost. In addition, a large, diverse group of respondents can be reached instantly, data entry errors are reduced, and responses are easy to tabulate. However, the major drawback is the inability to draw a probability sample. If a questionnaire is posted on a Web site, there is no control over who responds; therefore, a manager cannot generalize the results to the broader population of customer organizations. To combat the problem, some firms have used online panels, where respondents are randomly chosen. Using Internet-generated surveys is challenging and the business marketer must use this medium carefully.

The Role of Market Potential in Planning and Control

Market potential is the maximum possible sales of all sellers of a given product in a defined market during a specified time period.[3] Maximum sales opportunities for a

---

[2] Adapted from Judy Strauss and Raymond Frost, *Marketing on the Internet* (Upper Saddle River, NJ: Prentice-Hall, 1997): p. 91.

[3] William E. Cox Jr. and George N. Havens, "Determination of Sales Potentials and Performance for an Industrial Goods Manufacturer," *Journal of Marketing Research* 14 (November 1977): p. 574.

product of an individual company is referred to as **sales potential,** which is the maximum share of market potential an individual company might expect for a specific product or product line.[4]

An example will clarify the nature of potentials. Assume that manufacturers of aircraft engines and parts generated shipments of $9 billion this year. What level of market potential would be expected for the industry next year? Based on commercial airline activity, total volume for the industry next year might be projected to increase by 20 percent. Thus, the aircraft-engine industry has a market potential of $10.8 billion ($9 billion × 1.20). Of this, the aircraft-engine division of General Electric in Cincinnati might expect to obtain 14 percent, based on current market share, anticipated marketing efforts, production capacity, and other factors. General Electric's sales potential is therefore $1.51 billion for next year ($10.8 billion × 0.14).

Potential Represents Opportunity   In most instances, market potentials exceed total market demand, and sales potentials exceed actual company sales volume. Market potential is just that—an opportunity to sell. In the example of aircraft engines and parts, market potential may not be converted to demand for a number of reasons: The government may reduce aircraft defense spending, commercial airlines may postpone aircraft orders if passenger airline travel declines, or a strike against major aircraft manufacturers could reduce their production of jet engines. Similarly, sales potentials are ideals based on an assumed set of circumstances: past market performance; a certain level of competitive activity; and a variety of events, both favorable and unfavorable to the firm. Clearly, a change in competitors' actions, a decline in the general economy, or a reduction in the level and effectiveness of marketing may cause actual sales to fall short of sales potential.

Potentials: Planning and Control by Segment   The primary application of market and sales potential information is clearly in the planning and control of marketing strategy by market segment. Recall from Chapter 7 that *segments* refer to homogeneous units—customers, products, territories, or channels—for which marketing efforts are tailored. Once sales potentials are determined for each segment, the manager can allocate expenditures on the basis of potential sales volume. There is little benefit in spending huge sums of money on advertising and personal selling in segments where the market opportunity is low. Of course, expenditures would have to be based on both potential and the level of competition. Actual sales in each segment can also be compared with potential sales, taking into account the level of competition, in order to evaluate the effectiveness of the marketing program.

Consider the experience of a Cleveland manufacturer of quick-connective couplings for power transmission systems. For more than twenty years, one of its large distributors had been increasing its sales volume. In fact, this distributor was considered one of the firm's top producers. The firm then analyzed the sales potentials for each of its thirty-one distributors. The large distributor ranked thirty-first in terms of volume relative to potential, actualizing only 15.4 percent of potential. A later evaluation revealed that the distributor's sales personnel did not know the most effective way to sell couplings to its large accounts.

---

[4]Francis E. Hummer. *Market and Sales Potentials* (New York: The Ronald Press Company, 1961), p. 8.

Life-Cycle Potential   Market potential is crucial for go/no-go decisions on new products for the business market. The "size of market" has been shown to be a significant screening factor for launching new industrial products. David Kendall and Michael French propose the concept of "life-cycle market potential" as an effective way of analyzing the market size for new industrial products.[5] They suggest that life-cycle market potential is "the greatest number of product adoptions that will eventually occur in a particular market over the product life-cycle, given expected environmental conditions and expected aggregate effects of marketing actions by the industry." The life-cycle measure is useful because it provides realistic boundaries for total sales over the product's life and it is possible to make reasonable estimates of its value. Life-cycle market potential is measured by estimating total annual sales of the generic product class (based on the number of customers and their usage of the product) and scaling down this estimate based on concept tests with potential customers (for example, a market share estimate is multiplied by the estimate of total product class sales). Total sales over the life cycle can then be calculated by estimating repeat purchases and length of time until saturation. This total life-cycle potential then serves as a benchmark to help decide whether the new product should be introduced.

As this discussion demonstrates, market and sales potentials are pivotal in the marketing planning and control process. Therefore, great care must be taken to determine market and sales potential estimates. The business marketing manager must thoroughly understand the various techniques for developing potentials accurately.

The Role of the Sales Forecast

The second component of organizational demand analysis, sales forecasting, likewise poses a significant challenge. The sales forecast answers the question: What level of sales do we expect next year, given a particular level and type of marketing effort? Once potentials have been determined, the business marketing manager can allocate resources to the various elements of the marketing mix. Only after the marketing strategy is developed can expected sales be forecasted. Many firms are tempted to use the forecast as a tool for deciding the level of marketing expenditures. One recent study (which sampled 900 firms) found that slightly more than 25 percent of the respondent firms set their advertising budgets after the sales forecast was developed.[6] Small companies whose budgeting and forecasting decisions were fragmented made up the majority of the firms in this group. Clearly, marketing strategy is a determinant of the level of sales and not vice versa. Figure 8.1 illustrates the position of market potential estimates and the sales forecast in the planning process.

The **sales forecast** represents the firm's best estimate of the sales revenue expected to be generated by a given marketing strategy. The forecast will usually be less than sales potential. The firm may find that it is uneconomical to try to capture all available business. Strong competitors within certain segments may preclude the achievement of total potential sales. Like sales potential data, the sales forecast is an aid in the allocation of resources and in the measurement of performance.

---

[5] David L. Kendall and Michael T. French, "Forecasting the Potential for New Industrial Products," *Industrial Marketing Management* 20, no. 3 (August 1990): p. 177.

[6] Douglas C. West, "Advertising Budgeting and Sales Forecasting: The Timing Relationship," *International Journal of Advertising* 14, no. 1 (1995): pp. 65–77.

| FIGURE 8.1 | THE RELATIONSHIP BETWEEN POTENTIAL AND THE FORECAST |

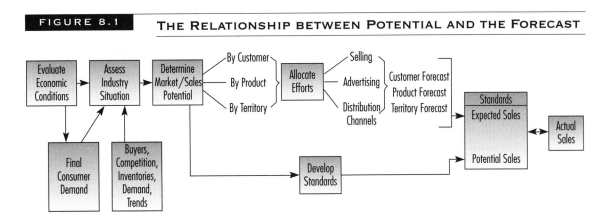

Applying Market Potential and the Sales Forecast

Market potential estimates and sales forecasts complement each other in the marketing planning process. Market potential data are usually vital to sales forecasting: Market potential provides direction as to which opportunities the firm should pursue, and the sales forecast is generated once the level of resources to be applied to each opportunity has been decided. Market potential estimates are used to determine where the firm's attention should be focused, the total and relative levels of expenditure to apply to each opportunity, and the benchmarks for evaluating performance. The sales forecast, in contrast, typically provides direction for making short-run, tactical decisions.

Thus, estimates of actual sales over the next year guide management in planning production, estimating purchasing requirements, setting inventory levels, scheduling transportation and the warehouse work force, estimating working capital requirements, and planning short-term expenditures on promotion and advertising. Two- to five-year projections of sales (based on the analysis of market potential) help guide decision making about plant and warehouse facilities and capital requirements and about channel strategy and structure. In summary, market potential provides guidelines for the general direction the firm will take (in terms of markets and product opportunities) and for budget allocations to those opportunities. The sales forecast directs the timing of short-range tactical expenditures and long-term capital spending.

Supply Chain Links Sales forecasts are critical to the smooth operation of the entire supply chain.[7] Sales forecast data is used to distribute inventory, manage stock levels, and schedule resources for all the members of a supply chain that provide materials, components, and services to a manufacturer. Accurate forecasts go hand in hand with good business practices and effective management policies in directing the entire supply chain process. Specific tools are available to develop accurate estimates of market potential; the business marketer must understand the purposes of alternative techniques as well as their values and limitations.

---

[7] Rosemary Smart, "Forecasting: A Vision of the Future Driving the Supply Chain of Today," *Logistics Focus* 3 (October 1995): pp. 15–16.

Determining Market and Sales Potentials

The secondary data available, whether the product is new or established, the number of potential customers, and the extent of internal company information all play a role in estimating potentials. Estimating market potential requires analysis of variables that relate to, or cause, aggregate demand for the product. It is crucial to find the best measures of the underlying variables so that potential can be measured accurately. This section will examine statistical series methods and survey methods of measuring market and sales potentials.

Statistical Series Methods

Statistical series methods presume a continuing close correlation between the level of product demand and some statistical set (called a statistical series), such as the number of production workers or the value added by manufacturing. Assuming the connection is logical—that is, there is a sound underlying relationship between the two items—then product demand can be projected indirectly by projecting the statistical series. First, the manager must identify specific industries that either use or could use the firm's product. Second, a measure of economic activity is determined for each actual and potential consumer industry. The measure of economic activity is assumed to represent the relative sales volume of each industry. For example, the number of production workers is frequently used as the statistical series representing potential demand. Presumably, the larger the work force in an industry, the greater the potential need for a given industrial product, whether it is a component or capital equipment. Other statistical series used include value added, capital-equipment expenditures, materials consumed, total value of shipments, and total employees and payrolls.

The rationale behind using the single series method is that many industrial products have a variety of applications in a multitude of consuming industries. It would be impractical, if not impossible, to estimate directly all the potential applications of the product as well as the total quantities involved. To make the task of estimating market potential manageable, the analyst turns to information that is easily available—a statistical series. The analyst relates one of these series to the demand for the firm's product. Consider aluminum cans. Secondary data reveal that in a given year, the malt beverage industry spent $2.2 billion on aluminum cans with total shipments amounting to $12 billion. Thus, a relationship between demand for cans and total dollar shipments (the statistical series) can be established. For every dollar of malt beverage sales, eighteen cents in aluminum cans will be used ($2.2 billion/$12 billion = $0.18 per dollar of beverages). Potential for next year could be estimated either for a given region (by determining estimated malt beverage sales in the region for next year) or for another segment of the malt beverage industry (for example, by estimating light beer sales for next year). Past relationships between demand for a product and a statistical series provide a reasonably firm basis for evaluating market potential in various market segments and regions.

Single Series Method   The single series method calculates market potential on the basis of secondary data reflecting the relative buying power of industrial markets. To use this procedure, management must have adequate knowledge of the SIC or NAICS groups that are potential users of a product. Let us consider how this approach may be used to analyze absolute market potential (dollars or units).

INSIDE BUSINESS MARKETING

DeepCanyon.com—A Valuable Resource for Market Analysis

DeepCanyon.com provides a rich source of market information for the marketing manager, including a market calculator, a company locator, and a competitor alert system. For example, the site could be used to identify the cities with the highest density of large pharmaceutical companies. Alternatively, a firm might want to identify potential competitors in the telecommunications market. With the market calculator, you can specify the parameters of the market, calculate the number of organizations in that market, and secure the names of those companies in a matter of minutes. The site is extremely user-friendly and provides an easy-to-follow approach for identifying a particular four-digit SIC industry.

To illustrate, assume that you wanted to identify the number of pharmaceutical and cosmetic firms in the state of California. The DeepCanyon market calculator identifies 472 firms, broken out by city, number of employees, and sales volume. If you were interested in working in the pharmaceutical industry in San Diego, the market calculator indicates that there are 48 potential employers.

Go to www.DeepCanyon.com and click on Market Calculator under the *Cool Tools* heading.

Estimates of absolute market potential for the entire United States, various geographic areas, or specific NAICS groups can be determined with a statistical series using the following approach:

1. Select a statistical series that appears to be related to demand for the product.

2. For each target NAICS industry, determine the relationship of the series to the demand for the product whose potential is being estimated.

3. Forecast the statistical series and its relationship to demand for the desired time frame.

4. Determine market potential by relating demand to future values of the statistical series.

Selecting a Statistical Series   To determine market potential using a statistical series, the analyst must first evaluate which statistical series is best related to the demand for the product. The demand for some products may be highly correlated to the number of production workers—uniforms, hand soap, and some office products are good examples. In other cases, value added or the value of shipments is better correlated to demand. For example, due to the high level of automation in the industry, the demand for metal cans by the beverage industry is more closely related to the value of beverage shipments than to the number of industry production workers.

Important criteria in selecting a statistical series are twofold: (1) data on the series must be available and (2) future estimates of the series should be easier to predict than product demand would be. Many of the statistical series reported by the Department of Commerce in the economic census can be forecasted for one to three years with reasonable accuracy. Private research firms (such as Predicasts and Standard & Poor's), as well as some online data services, develop predictions on many of the series for various industries. In addition, *The U.S. Industrial Outlook*, published by the Department of Commerce, makes short- and long-term projections of employment, sales, and capital spending for a vast array of industries. Thus, if an industrial firm determines that consuming industries could use four units of a product per $1,000 of the consuming

TABLE 8.2	USAGE FACTOR FOR BALL BEARINGS		
Industry	**2001 Bearing Sales to the Industry (in Millions of Dollars)**	**2001 Value of Using Industry Shipments (in Millions of Dollars)**	**Demand factor (Bearings per Dollar of Shipments)**
Motor Vehicles	$1,680	$75,271	$0.022
Trucks and Trailers	39	2,767	0.014

NOTE: Industry values are hypothetical.

industry's output, an estimate of market potential for 2001 could be made by consulting a reference source that forecasts 2001 sales of the consuming industry. Market potential would equal four units multiplied by the estimated 2001 sales (in thousands of dollars) of the consuming industry.

Determining the Relationship between Demand and Statistical Series Once the series has been selected, data on the series must be collected and related to demand in order to develop what might be termed a "demand" or a "usage" factor—that is, the quantity of the product demanded per unit of the statistical series.

One approach is to use the economic census to develop the database for the statistical series, and then relate this to prior levels of demand for the product—either by NAICS code or by geographic region. Assume we wish to estimate market potential for ball bearings in 2001, and that motor vehicles and truck trailers are the primary target markets. The statistical series is value of shipments. To determine the usage or demand factor, we relate past ball bearing demand to the value of shipments in the motor vehicle and truck trailer industry (Table 8.2).

Sales of bearings to the target industries would be gleaned from trade sources, whereas the statistical series, value of shipments, could be found in the economic census. Thus, in motor vehicles, 2.2 cents worth of bearings were purchased for each dollar of shipments. An estimate of market potential in 2001 would be developed by multiplying 0.022 by the projected value of shipments to be made by the motor vehicle industry in that year.

Suppose a manufacturer of plastic resins wants to analyze market potential in four industries with which the firm has never dealt. There is no published data. A short survey of firms in each industry group could be implemented to assess resin purchases and some other statistical series such as production workers. The results would be tallied for each industry group, and a usage factor of resin (pounds) per production worker calculated for each. The result could then be used to forecast market potential in each industry by estimating total production workers in the relevant year and multiplying that by the usage or demand factor. The validity of this approach depends on how well the firms in the sample represent the target industries.

Understanding Limitations Estimating a demand or usage factor this way must take into account the limitations of the approach. The analysis is based on averages; an average consumption of a given component per dollar of output or per production worker is computed. The average may or may not hold true for a particular target industry. Product usage may vary considerably from firm to firm, even in the same industry category. Further, the demand factor is based on historical relationships that may change dramatically; that is, the industry may use more or less of the product as a result of technological change, manufacturing system reconfigurations, or changes in final consumer demand. Nevertheless, carefully derived estimates of the relationship between demand and a statistical series can be powerful tools for measuring market potential.

Forecasting the Statistical Series   Once the relationship of the demand to the series has been documented (the demand or usage factor has been determined), management will estimate future values of the series in one of two ways: by independently forecasting expected values, using their own estimated growth rates; or by relying on forecasts made by government, trade associations, or private research firms. The goal is to project the series forward so that future market potential can be assessed by multiplying the demand factor by the estimated future value of the series.

Future values of the usage factor must also be estimated. The demand or usage factor expresses the relationship between the demand and the series in terms such as "dollar of product per dollar of consuming industry sales" or "pounds of product per production worker." If we are estimating market potential two years into the future, we must ask whether usage of the product per unit of output in the consuming industry will change during that period. Management may want to adjust the demand or usage factor to reflect predicted changes in product usage among the targeted industries. An analysis of production processes, technology, competitive actions, and final consumer demand may be required to adjust the usage factor properly. A good example is found in the plastics industry: The move to lighten automobiles in order to enhance gas mileage would indicate a substantial increase in the "pounds of plastic per automobile" usage factor over the next five years. Similarly, in the beverage industry, aluminum cans are increasingly replacing glass containers, but the pounds of aluminum used per dollar of beverage output may also be declining because lighter aluminum material is being used in the cans.

Determining Market Potential   The final step is the easiest one: The demand or usage factor is multiplied by the forecasted value of the statistical series. Once this stage has been reached, the difficult data and estimation problems have been resolved, and the calculation is routine. Management must be sure that potential is calculated for all relevant market segments. For planning and control purposes, market potential estimates may be required for various customer segments, industry groups, territories, and distribution channels.

In summary, the effectiveness of the single series method of estimating market potential depends on the following: how well the demand or usage factor represents underlying demand, the quality of the data used, the ability to estimate future values of the series and usage factors, and the extent of distortion caused by using averages and gross estimates. This approach is well suited to industrial products that are commonly used. For new products, unique items, and rarely used components, this approach is not appropriate because the data are insufficient. Modifications to the series and considerable management judgment are required to estimate potential. One way to develop better estimates is to use more than one statistical series.

Market Research

To avoid the problems inherent in historical statistical data, firms can use market surveys to gather primary information on future buyer intentions. Market-focused businesses also use focus groups and high-touch techniques such as visiting customers to develop a thorough understanding of the customer's environment and needs.[8]

Surveys   Surveys are also used to generate data to be used with the statistical series. For current applications, it is important to note the use of survey results when estimating market and sales potentials, and when determining the demand or usage factor to be used in the single statistical series approach. The survey method is particularly useful for estimating market potential of new products. Surveys can provide information about whether specific plants are in the market for a new product, about the extent of their needs, and about the likelihood of purchase. Surveys are useful in determining the potential product use by specific industry groups, the plants in each industry that have the greatest potential, and the relative importance of each industry group to total sales. Recall from Chapter 7 that a product's economic value to a user (value in use) can vary by market segment. Surveys can be profitably used to determine the value in use for various customers or market segments. Surveys have also been utilized to evaluate the purchase potential of individual firms.

A complete enumeration of the market can sometimes be made, and the potential volumes for each prospective customer can be summed to arrive at a total market potential. A complete census of the market is warranted when (1) the markets are very concentrated, (2) there is direct sales contact, (3) orders have a relatively high value, and (4) the unit volume is low.[9] The difficulty is collecting data for all potential users of the product. Typically, the sales force is assigned the task of collecting information. Developing information on existing customers is routine, but it becomes more difficult to solicit information from the user who is not a customer. Salespeople often experience difficulties in reaching the individual in a noncustomer firm who has the information they need. They may also be reluctant to allocate a significant amount of time to collecting the data. However, in some industries, buyers are eager to share their annual raw material and component requirements with vendors in order to facilitate vendor planning and therefore assure a continuity of supply. The automobile industry, for example, provides steel suppliers with detailed estimates of its requirements for steel.

Uses and Limitations of Surveys   The survey method is appropriate in estimating the market potential for new products, especially in providing estimates based on objective facts and opinions rather than on executive judgment. In addition, the survey can target specific industries that represent the greatest market potential for new or existing products. Its limitation is the one associated with any survey—the research method used. Nonrepresentative samples and nonresponse bias can distort findings, the wrong person in the respondent companies may fill out the questionnaire, and a small sample size may make sophisticated statistical analysis impossible. A particularly difficult problem is assessing whom to contact. The researcher must invest considerable effort to find the best source of data. It is the responsibility of the marketing manager to resolve the data collection problems and to ensure that the survey design will generate valid results.

Focus Groups   A research technique that is being increasingly applied to business marketing research problems is the **focus group interview.**[10] A focus group consists

[8]Stanley F. Slater and John C. Narver, "Intelligence Generation and Superior Customer Value," *Journal of the Academy of Marketing Science* 28 (winter 2000): pp. 120–127.

[9]William E. Cox Jr., *Industrial Marketing Research* (New York: John Wiley and Sons, 1979), p. 158.

[10]B. G. Yovovich, "Focusing on Consumers Needs and Motivations," *Business Marketing* 76 (March 1991): p. 41.

of between six and twelve people interviewed in an informal group setting. Open-ended questions are used to stimulate group interaction, and a moderator will lead the discussion much like a therapist does in group therapy. Sessions may last up to three hours and are often videotaped so that different managers can evaluate them.

Business marketing focus groups can be effective in uncovering issues, defining the range of opinions on the issue, testing advertising concepts, exploring product needs, and evaluating service perceptions. Standard Register, a business form manufacturer, used a series of focus groups comprising business form buyers to determine buyers' priorities. Before using the focus groups, the firm believed they "were great service people"; however, the focus groups indicated that, although service was the buyers' first priority, Standard Register "had little in terms of service that made them stand out from the crowd."[11] The company quickly created a new customer service management position and initiated a strategy to enhance responsiveness to customers. Generally, focus groups enable researchers to probe issues in greater depth than they could in structured questionnaires. The information can be gathered and analyzed quickly at a relatively low cost. The process is also flexible: The questioning can change direction instantly, and new areas can be explored. Importantly, the data from the focus group session is highly subjective and most experts suggest results should be substantiated through additional quantitative studies.

Customer Visits[12]   Many leading firms, such as Hewlett-Packard, IBM, and Du Pont, include customer visits as an important component of market research. At Hewlett-Packard, customer visits are enthusiastically embraced by project teams and these visits are normally conducted early in the new product development process. The typical visit program includes onsite visits with twenty to forty customer firms by a two-person team—an R&D manager and a product manager. The local Hewlett-Packard sales representative facilitates the visit. Customers are chosen according to a sampling plan and the visitation program is often reinforced with additional market research.

To reap the maximum value from customer visits, the visit should be conducted by a cross-functional team and include well-defined objectives, a careful selection of customers, a discussion guide to structure the visit, and a plan for reporting the results. Customer visits provide a valuable tool for:

- identifying unmet customer needs
- identifying new market opportunities
- learning about the role a product assumes within a customer's operations and strategy
- building customer relationships.

Customer visits give managers a fresh perspective of the market:

It's important to know how our products are being used, and while there are many ways to get that knowledge, the most direct way, the most efficient way

---

[11] Sue Kapp, "Customer Service is Ex-Fighter Jock's Latest Mission," *Business Marketing* 75 (August 1990): p. 19.

[12] This section is based on Edward F. McQuarrie, *Customer Visits: Building a Better Market Focus* (Newbury Park, CA: Sage Publications 1993).

that I know of, is face-to-face with experienced, knowledgeable people talking directly to users in their place of work—not in an artificial environment, but in their place of work.[13] [a manager in a high-technology firm]

The Essential Dimensions of Sales Forecasting

Selection of a sales forecasting technique depends on many factors, including the period for which the forecast is desired, the purpose of the forecast, the availability of data, the level of technical expertise possessed by the company, the accuracy desired, the nature of the product, and the extent of the product line. Evaluations of each factor suggest the limits within which the firm must work in terms of forecasting methods.

General Approaches to Forecasting

A company uses forecasting to plan and attempt to influence its future: The forecast is a major component of the decision-making process.[14] Because all budgets in a company ultimately depend on how many units will be sold, the sales forecast often determines companywide commitments for everything from raw materials and labor to capital equipment and advertising.[15] Various types of forecasts are often required because estimates of future sales are applied to so many activities. A forecast to determine inventory commitments for the next month has to be more precise than one used to set sales quotas, which may differ from expected sales due to their motivational value. A five-year forecast of growth in the machine-tool industry will require a very detailed and sophisticated model incorporating numerous economic variables, whereas a six-month projection of number twenty-eight ball bearing sales may simply require the extrapolation of a trend line. Some firms use *early warning systems* to alert them about changes in market demand for their products.[16] Early warning systems are designed to sample the market in advance of a selling season or period to detect major shifts in demand. The data generated from this early "forecast" are then used to plan operations, production, and the delivery schedule for materials and supplies. The forecasting process may use either a *top-down* or *bottom-up* approach—or a combination of the two.

Top-Down Forecasting   In the **top-down** approach, estimates of the general economy and the industry first give managers a picture of the environmental conditions under which they will be operating. These estimates include evaluations of all economic and industry variables that would influence sales of their products. The database necessary to develop these forecasts might include economic indicators such as Gross Domestic Product (GDP), unemployment, capital expenditures, price indexes, industrial production, and housing starts. A model (that is, a mathematical equation) is created

[13] Ibid., p. 11.

[14] Paul A. Herbig, John Milewicz, and James E. Golden, "The Do's and Don'ts of Sales Forecasting," *Industrial Marketing Management* 22 (February 1993): p. 49.

[15] Geoffrey Lancaster and Robert Lomas, "A Managerial Guide to Forecasting," *International Journal of Physical Distribution and Materials Management* 16 (1986): p. 6.

[16] Paul V. Tiplitz, "Do You Need an Early Warning System?" *Journal of Business Forecasting Methods and Systems* 14 (spring 1995): pp. 8–10.

to link the economic indicators to either industry or product sales. For example, Interroyal, a major supplier of commercial and institutional furniture, uses a forecasting model in which current GDP, construction starts eighteen months earlier, and current P&E expenditures are linked to expected sales of metal office furniture.

The top-down approach will often include econometrics, which refers to large, multivariable, computer-based models of the U.S. economy. Such models attempt to forecast changes in total U.S. economic activity or in specific industries by the use of complex equations that may number more than 1,000 for a single model. Econometric models are available from commercial, university, and bank sources. Chase Econometric Associates, for example, provides clients with a monthly report of more than 200 economic indicators plus current quarter data and data for the next ten quarters.

A drawback of the top-down approach is the gross level at which the forecasts are made. In some cases, the forecasts are too general to be useful. Some experts believe that the top-down approach limits the value of a forecast in developing strategy and may limit the forecast's overall credibility.[17]

Bottom-Up Forecasting   Whereas the top-down approach begins with a macro-level view of the economy and industry and is initiated by upper management, the **bottom-up** method of sales forecasting originates with the sales force and marketing personnel. The logic behind the bottom-up approach is that sales personnel possess a good understanding of the market in terms of customer requirements, inventory situations, and general market trends. Salespeople can also procure economic data from corporate staff so that their projections will be based not only on historical sales data and customer needs but also on economic and industry data.

The bottom-up approach works well when sales are limited to a well-defined industry. Jet aircraft manufacturers are a good example. A firm supplying gaskets for jets knows that there are long lead times in the production of engines and a limited number of producers. Thus, salespeople know almost exactly what will be built in the next one to three years, and by whom. Specific estimates of the gaskets required can be made, so there is little need for an all-encompassing macroeconomic forecast. Although some firms believe salespeople are not realistic enough to create a reliable forecast, they still use sales force input because of its motivational value. One firm asks all 120 salespeople to develop forecasts for their territory that they "can not only live with, but that they could guarantee."[18]

Combination Approach   Rarely are the top-down or the bottom-up procedures used exclusively. The more common approach is to use both, with the marketing executive being responsible for coordinating the estimates. For example, Miracle Adhesives, a marketer of adhesives, sealant, and coatings, develops a sales forecast by polling their territory salespeople in order to estimate sales for the coming year (based on a review of customers and prospects); these forecasts are then reviewed by the divisional sales manager in light of historical sales trends, market trends, economic conditions, and scheduled marketing programs. The final forecast is derived by adjusting the sales force estimates on the basis of the broader economic data.

---

[17] Barbara G. Cohen, "A New Approach to Strategic Forecasting," *The Journal of Business Strategy* 9 (September/October 1988): p. 38.

[18] William Keenan Jr., "Numbers Racket," *Sales and Marketing Management* 147 (May 1995): pp. 64–76.

The Forecasting Time Frame

Sales forecasts may be prepared on a day-to-day basis for inventory control, or an estimate of sales ten years into the future may be needed to plan additional plant and warehouse capacity. The methodologies selected for each of these forecasts would probably differ; each forecasting method is suited for a specific forecasting time frame. In fact, the time horizon for which forecasts are prepared can often serve as a substitute for most of the criteria used to evaluate forecasting techniques. Time horizons reflect such characteristics as the value of accuracy in forecasting, the cost of various methodologies, the timeliness of their results, and the types of data patterns involved in the sales data.[19]

Although the forecasting time frame may range from a year to ten or fifteen years, four basic time frames are common.[20]

1. *Immediate term.*
   Forecasts for this period range from daily to monthly. The purpose is to support operating decisions on such things as delivery scheduling and inventory.

2. *Short term.*
   Short-term forecasts range from one to six months. The time frame may overlap with the immediate and intermediate terms. Short-term forecasts are necessary for planning merchandising and promotion, production scheduling, and cash requirements. The seasonal sales pattern is generally of most interest here.

3. *Intermediate term.*
   This time frame generally ranges from six months to two years. Intermediate-term forecasts are used to set promotional levels, assess sales personnel needs, and set capital requirements. Seasonal, cyclical, and turning points in the sales data are emphasized. Some experts suggest that a sales forecast should span at least five quarters to mitigate the contrived conditions caused by the cyclical calendar year.[21]

4. *Long term.*
   Long-term forecasts extend beyond two years to estimate trends and rates of sales growth for broad product lines. The results are used to make major strategic decisions, including product line changes, capital requirements, distribution channels, and plant expansion.

Forecasting Methods

As discussed, the sales forecast may be highly mathematical or informally based on sales force estimates. Two primary approaches to sales forecasting are recognized: (1) qualitative and (2) quantitative, which includes time series and causal analysis. Each

---

[19] Spyros Makridakis and Steven Wheelwright, "Forecasting: Issues and Challenges for Marketing Management," *Journal of Marketing* 41 (October 1977): p. 30.

[20] Adapted from Robert A. Lomas and Geoffrey A. Lancaster, "Sales Forecasting for the Smaller Organization," *Industrial Marketing Management* 20 (February 1978): p. 37.

[21] Angelo Guadagno, "Mastering the 'Magic' of Sales Forecasting," *American Salesman* 40 (November 1995): pp. 16–23.

Forecast Accuracy Depends on . . .

Time Horizons. The longer the time frame, the more likely patterns and relationships will change, thus invalidating the forecast.

Technological Change. A fast pace of technological change will undermine basic patterns and relationships, resulting in forecasting inaccuracies.

Barriers to Entry. Ease of entrance and exit to market or industry enables new competitors to drastically change established patterns, or disrupt a forecast.

Elasticity of Demand. Products with inelastic demand usually can be forecasted more accurately because they typically are required by the user, and purchases cannot be delayed or eliminated.

Expenditures. Dollars can be invested in the forecasting process to increase its accuracy (for example, better data, more sophisticated techniques), but there is a limit. At some point, the value of marginal changes in accuracy are offset by the additional expenditures on the forecasting techniques.

SOURCE: Adapted from Paul A. Herbig, John Milewicz, and James E. Golden, "The Do's and Don'ts of Sales Forecasting," *Industrial Marketing Management* 22 (February 1993): pp. 51, 52.

---

category contains a variety of techniques; David Georgoff and Robert Murdick maintain that effective forecasting requires an understanding that

> while each technique has strengths and weaknesses, every forecasting situation is limited by constraints like time, funds, competencies, or data. Balancing the advantages and disadvantages of techniques with regard to a situation's limitations and requirements is a formidable but important management task.[22]

Qualitative Techniques

Qualitative techniques, which are also referred to as *management judgment* or *subjective* techniques, rely on informed judgment and rating schemes. The sales force, top-level executives, or distributors may be called upon to use their knowledge of the economy, the market, and the customers to create qualitative estimates of demand. Techniques for qualitative analysis include the executive judgment method, the sales force composite method, and the Delphi method.

The effectiveness of qualitative approaches depends on the close relationships between customers and suppliers that are typical in the industrial market. Qualitative techniques work well for such items as heavy capital equipment or for situations in which the nature of the forecast does not lend itself to mathematical analysis. These techniques are also suitable for new product or new technology forecasts in which historical data are scarce or nonexistent.[23] An important advantage of qualitative approaches is that users of the forecast are brought into the process. The effect is usually an increased understanding of the procedure and a higher level of commitment to the resultant forecast.

---

[22] David M. Georgoff and Robert G. Murdick, "Manager's Guide to Forecasting," *Harvard Business Review* 64 (January/February 1986): p. 111.

[23] A. Michael Segalo, *The IBM/PC Guide to Sales Forecasting* (Wayne, Pa.: Banbury, 1985), p. 21.

Executive Judgment   In a large sample of business firms, the executive judgment method enjoys a high level of usage.[24] The judgment method, which combines and averages top executives' estimates of future sales, is popular because it is easy to apply and to understand. Typically, executives from a variety of departments, such as sales, marketing, production, finance, and purchasing, are brought together to apply their collective expertise, experience, and opinions to the forecast.

The primary limitation of the approach is that it does not systematically analyze cause-and-effect relationships. Further, because there is no established formula for deriving estimates, new executives may have difficulty making reasonable forecasts. The resulting forecasts are only as good as the opinions of the executives. The accuracy of the executive judgment approach is also difficult to assess in a way that allows meaningful comparison with alternative techniques.[25]

The executives' "ballpark" estimates for the intermediate and the long-run time frames are often used in conjunction with forecasts developed quantitatively. However, when historical data are limited or unavailable, the executive judgment approach may be the only alternative. Mark Moriarty and Arthur Adams suggest that executive judgment methods produce accurate forecasts when (1) forecasts are made frequently and repetitively, (2) the environment is stable, and (3) the linkage between decision, action, and feedback is short.[26] Business marketers should examine their forecasting situation in light of these factors in order to assess the viability of the executive judgment technique.

Sales Force Composite   The rationale behind the sales force composite approach is that salespeople can effectively estimate future sales volume because they know the customers, the market, and the competition. In addition, participating in the forecasting process gives sales personnel an understanding of how forecasts are derived and a heightened incentive to achieve the desired level of sales. The composite forecast is developed by combining the sales estimates from all salespeople.

Few companies rely solely on sales force estimates, but usually adjust or combine the estimates with forecasts developed either by top management or by quantitative methods. The advantage of the sales force composite method is the ability to draw on sales force knowledge about markets and customers. This advantage is particularly important for the business market in which buyer–seller relationships are close and enduring. The salesperson is often the best source of information about customer purchasing plans and inventory levels. The method can also be executed relatively easily at minimal cost. An added benefit is that the process of creating a forecast forces a sales representative to carefully review these accounts in terms of future sales.[27]

The problems of sales force composites are similar to those associated with the executive judgment approach: They do not involve systematic analysis of cause and effect, and they rely on informed judgment and opinions. Some sales personnel may overestimate sales in order to look good or underestimate them in order to generate a lower quota. All estimates must be carefully reviewed by management.

[24] Nada Sanders, "Forecasting Practices in U.S. Corporations: Survey Results," *Interfaces* 24 (March/April 1994): pp. 92–100.

[25] Makridakis and Wheelwright, "Forecasting: Issues and Challenges," p. 31.

[26] Mark M. Moriarty and Arthur J. Adams, "Management Judgment Forecasts, Composite Forecasting Models and Conditional Efficiency," *Journal of Marketing Research* 21 (August 1984): p. 248.

[27] Stewart A. Washburn, "Don't Let Sales Forecasting Spook You," *Sales and Marketing Management* 140 (September 1988): p. 118.

To improve the quality of sales force composite estimates, salespeople should be provided with information about major factors that might affect their forecasts, such as economic conditions, political considerations, manufacturing constraints, customer profitability, changes in corporate policy, and so on.[28] Salespeople can provide extremely valuable information for forecasting. When good historical data are not available, the salesperson's experience and judgment become the primary input for forecasting. Sales force estimates are relatively accurate for immediate and short-term projections, but they are not very effective for long-range projections.

Delphi Method   In the Delphi approach to forecasting, the opinions of a panel of experts on future sales are converted into an informed consensus through a highly structured feedback mechanism.[29] As in the executive judgment technique, management officials are used as the panel, but each estimator remains anonymous. On the first round, written opinions about the likelihood of some future event are sought (for example, sales volume, competitive reaction, or technological breakthroughs). The responses to this first questionnaire are used to produce a second. The objective is to provide feedback to the group so that first-round estimates and information available to some of the experts are made available to the entire group.

After each round of questioning, the analyst who administers the process will assemble, clarify, and consolidate information for dissemination in the succeeding round. Throughout the process, panel members are asked to reevaluate their estimates based on the new information from the group. Opinions are kept anonymous, eliminating both "me too" estimates and the need to defend a position. After continued reevaluation, the goal is to achieve a consensus. The number of experts will vary from six to hundreds, depending on how the process is organized and its purpose. The number of rounds of questionnaires will depend on how rapidly the group reaches consensus.

Delphi Application   The Delphi technique is usually applied to long-range forecasting. The technique is particularly well suited to (1) new product forecasts, (2) estimation of future events for which historical data are limited, or (3) situations that are not suited to quantitative analysis. When the market for a new product is not well defined and the product concept is unique, the Delphi technique can produce some broad-gauged estimates.

The Delphi technique suffers from the same problems as any other qualitative approach, but it may be the only way to develop certain types of estimates. However, there are some shortcomings specific to the approach. Assembling a panel of truly independent experts is extremely difficult. Officials in the same firm or individuals in the same profession tend to read the same literature, have similar training and background, and share the same attitudes on the phenomena under study. Some experts refuse to modify their views in light of feedback, thereby negating the consensus-forming process.

Qualitative forecasting is important in the forecasting process. The techniques can be applied to develop ballpark estimates when the uniqueness of the product, the unavailability of data, and the nature of the situation preclude application of quantitative techniques. The accuracy of qualitative forecasts is difficult to measure due to the

---

[28] Herbig, Milewicz, and Golden, "The Do's and Don'ts of Sales Forecasting," p. 54.

[29] Raymond E. Willis, *A Guide to Forecasting for Planners and Managers* (Englewood Cliffs, N.J.: Prentice-Hall, 1987), p. 343.

TABLE 8.3	SUMMARY OF QUALITATIVE FORECASTING TECHNIQUES	
Technique	**Approach**	**Application**
Executive judgment	Combining and averaging top executives' estimates of future sales	Ballpark estimates; new product sales estimates; intermediate and long-term time frames
Sales force composite	Combining and averaging individual salespersons' estimates of future sales	Effective when intimate knowledge of customer plans is important; useful for short and intermediate terms
Delphi method	Consensus of opinion on expected future sales volume is obtained by providing each panelist with the projections of all other panelists on preceding rounds. Panelists modify estimates until a consensus is achieved.	Appropriate for long-term forecasting; effective for projecting sales of new products or forecasting technological advances

lack of standardization. Typically, qualitative estimates will be merged with those developed quantitatively. Table 8.3 summarizes the qualitative approaches.

Quantitative Techniques

Quantitative forecasting, also referred to as *systematic* or *objective* forecasting, offers two primary methodologies: (1) time series and (2) regression or causal. **Time series** techniques use historical data ordered in time to project the trend and growth rate of sales. The rationale behind time series analysis is that the past pattern of sales will apply to the future. However, to discover the underlying pattern of sales, the analyst must first understand all of the possible patterns that may affect the sales series. Thus, a time series of sales may include trend, seasonal, cyclical, and irregular patterns. Once the effect of each has been isolated, the analyst can then project the expected future of each pattern. Time series methods are well suited to short-range forecasting because the assumption that the future will be like the past is more reasonable over the short run than over the long run.[30]

Regression or **causal** analysis, on the other hand, uses an opposite approach, identifying factors that have affected sales in the past and implementing them in a mathematical model.[31] A sale is expressed mathematically as a function of the items that affect it. (Recall the earlier discussion of market potential in which a regression equation was used to project potential based on production workers and on new equipment expenditures.) A forecast is derived by projecting values for each of the factors in the model, inserting these values into the regression equation, and solving for expected

---

[30] Spyros Makridakis, "A Survey of Time Series," *International Statistics Review* 44, no. 1 (1976): p. 63.

[31] Segalo, *Sales Forecasting*, p. 27.

FIGURE 8.2   TREND, CYCLE, AND SEASONAL COMPONENTS
OF A TIME SERIES

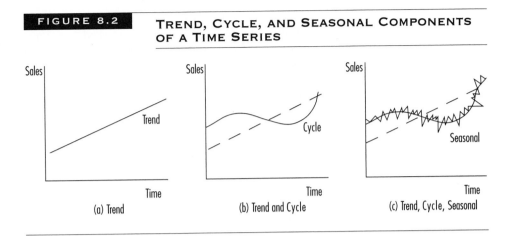

(a) Trend   (b) Trend and Cycle   (c) Trend, Cycle, Seasonal

sales. Typically, causal models are more reliable for intermediate than for long-range forecasts because the magnitude of each factor affecting sales must first be estimated for some future time, which becomes difficult when estimating farther into the future.

A recent study on forecasting methods suggests that the choice of methodology be based on the underlying behavior of the market rather than the time horizon of the forecast.[32] This research indicates that when markets are sensitive to changes in market and environmental variables, causal methods work best whether the forecast is short or long range; time series approaches are more effective when the market exhibits no sensitivity to market and/or environmental changes.

Time Series Analysis   A **time series** is nothing more than a set of chronologically ordered data points. Company sales reported monthly for the past five years are an example. A time series is composed of measurable patterns, and the objective of the analysis is to identify these patterns so that they may be projected. A time series has four components:

- T = Trend
- C = Cycle
- S = Seasonal
- I = Irregular

Figure 8.2 depicts the T, C, and S components of a time series.

The trend indicates the long-term general direction of the data. The trend may be a straight line of the form $y = a + bx$ (see Figure 8.2a); or a curve, $y = ab^x$; or $y = bx + cx^2$. The cycle represents the intermediate term with regular upswings and downswings of the data around the trend. For example, the industrial chemical industry in England shows a fairly regular rise and fall in demand over four- or five-year periods. The cycle variations are shown in Figure 8.2b. The cycle may originate from business

---

[32] Robert J. Thomas, "Method and Situational Factors in Sales Forecast Accuracy," *Journal of Forecasting* 12 (January 1993): p. 75.

cycle movements in the economy as a whole, from business conditions within an industry, from consumer spending fluctuations in finished goods markets, from inventory swings in industry, or from a succession of new product introductions. The cycle is extremely difficult to estimate because reversals need not occur at fixed intervals, and, as a result, the pattern may lack any regularity.

The **seasonal** pattern (depicted in Figure 8.2c) represents regular, recurring movements within the year. Data expressed daily, weekly, monthly, and quarterly may show seasonal patterns, which depend on such factors as seasonality of final consumption, end-of-period inventory adjustments, tax dates, business vacations, pipeline inventory adjustments, and scheduling of special promotions.

The **irregular** component in a time series reflects short-term random movements in the data that do not conform to a pattern related to the calendar. Many factors contribute to such random swings in sales patterns (for example, strikes, competitive actions). Generally, the assumption is that these short-term random effects will average out over a year.

When forecasting future sales volumes, actual sales can be expressed as a combination of all four time series elements:

$$\text{Actual sales} = \text{trend} \times \text{seasonal} \times \text{cycle} \times \text{irregular}$$

To develop a forecast, the analyst must determine each pattern and then extrapolate all four into the future. This requires a significant amount of historical sales information. Once a forecast of each pattern is developed, the sales forecast is assembled by combining the estimates for each pattern.

Regression or Causal Techniques Causal techniques have as their objective the determination of a relationship between sales and a variable presumed to be related to sales; knowledge of the causal variable can be used to determine expected future sales volumes. The method requires a significant amount of historical data to establish a valid relationship. The model mathematically expresses the causal relationship, and the mathematical formula is usually referred to as a regression equation.

A critical aspect of regression analysis is to identify the economic variable(s) to which past sales are related. For forecasting purposes, the *Survey of Current Business* is particularly helpful because it contains monthly, quarterly, and annual figures for hundreds of economic variables. The forecaster can test an array of economic variables from the *Survey* to find the variable(s) with the best relationship to past sales.

As with the statistical series approach, two general rules should be followed in evaluating economic series. First, the economic series (variable) should be logically related to company sales.[33] Forecasters are often tempted to break this rule because they can easily "try out" any number of variables; a variable may be found to be highly correlated to past sales, but with no logical connection. Such spurious relationships are not effective for forecasting future sales because they are usually accidental and may not hold true. Second, it should be easier to forecast the economic variable than to project the sales level. The causal approach develops a sales forecast by establishing the relationship of sales to some other economic variable. Knowledge of this relationship

---

[33] Frank H. Eby and William J. O'Neill, *The Management of Sales Forecasting* (Lexington, Mass.: Lexington Books, 1977), p. 145.

The Wrong Way to Use Forecasting

Sophisticated forecasting approaches, combined with the power of the computer and the ready availability of powerful databases, provide the potential for dramatically enhancing the decision support systems used by business marketers. That potential, however, may go unrealized. In fact, important questions are being raised about the way forecasts are generated and used in the decision-making process. Unrealistic forecasts and the manipulation of computer models are practices that some firms have employed to sway decisions toward some predetermined outcome or to influence viability of a product or brand. In short, it appears that the politics of model building and forecasting deserve as much attention as the technical aspects and objective procedures associated with creating sales and business forecasts.

In some cases, motives other than predicting future sales often politicize the forecasting and modeling process, to the detriment of managerial decision quality. In essence, some firms routinely manipulate elements of the forecasting process. A recent study examined the different ways that forecast results are manipulated or distorted:

1. **Management requests staff revisions.** For example, after reviewing the forecast, a senior manager requests staff to adjust revenue projections to a more favorable level.

2. **Managers make their own revisions.** For instance, a senior manager personally adjusts the forecast developed by the staff.

3. **Management requests "backcasts."** Here a senior manager predetermines an "appropriate" level of revenue, then requests the staff to generate a forecast to support this level.

4. **Incorrect techniques and assumptions are used.** For example, improper assumptions

about industry growth are purposely used in forecasts and models.

5. **Management ignores the forecast.** The forecast produced by a model is dismissed by senior management as being "inaccurate."

6. **The forecast model is incomplete.** Politically sensitive variables are purposely excluded from the computer model.

Interestingly, the study found that the most common manipulation of the forecast process or output was related to adjusting revenue projections to more favorable levels—45 percent of respondents indicated this behavior regularly occurs. The study indicated that highly manipulative firms were characterized by poor training for both management and staff in forecasting techniques, ineffective control systems, high interdivisional politics, and the perception that senior management exhibits "elitist" attitudes. In addition, "highly manipulative" environments are associated with a perception that ethical behavior is not encouraged in the firm.

Because the manipulation of forecast output is unethical and counterproductive, and also leads to negative long-term effects, top management should be encouraged to carefully review the forecast process in their firm. The study's results suggest some solutions: better training for the managers, specification of company codes of conduct, institution of more formalized forecasting procedures that include workable control systems, and programs that will foster positive attitudes among senior managers toward their subordinates.

SOURCE: Based upon Craig S. Galbraith and Gregory B. Merrill, "The Politics of Forecasting: Managing the Truth," California Management Review 38 (winter 1996): pp. 29–43.

is then used to estimate sales by determining future values of the economic variable and the corresponding sales level. If the variable is one for which future projections are either not available or of questionable validity, sales may as well be estimated directly.

To create a sales forecast with causal analysis, the analyst must first determine the mathematical relationship between sales and the causal variable. This relationship is then expressed in the form of a linear equation: $y = a + bx$, where a and b are the coefficients that express the relationship and x represents the causal variable from which estimates are made. Sales are then forecast by inserting estimated future values of x into the equation.

Use of Regression Techniques   Causal models are the most sophisticated forecasting tools. A study found that only 17 percent of firms regularly use regression techniques for forecasting and that 24 percent have never tried them.[34] Regression models are useful to industrial firms projecting final consumer demand for items of which their products become a part. For example, American Can projects motor oil sales based on a regression model that integrates auto registrations, average miles driven per car, average crankcase size, and average interval between oil changes as causal variables. Finally, an important dimension in forecasting is the ability to predict a turning point in the sales series. To the extent that turning points in causal variables can be foreseen, turns in company sales can be predicted.

Limitations   Although causal methods have measurable levels of accuracy, there are some important caveats and limitations. First, as already discussed, the fact that sales and some causal variables are correlated (associated) does not mean that the independent variable (x) caused sales. The independent variable should be logically related to sales.

Second, because both x and y have the same trend pattern, one may be, in effect, correlating only trends, whereas the other components (for example, cyclical and seasonal) are not highly correlated.[35] Thus, regression equations whose variables are highly correlated may be unsuitable for short-range projections in which cyclical and seasonal factors are important.

Third, regression methods require considerable historical data for equations to be valid and reliable, but the data required to establish stable relationships may not be available. Caution must always be used in extrapolating relationships into the future. The equation relates what *has* happened; economic and industry factors may change in the future, making past relationships invalid.

The last, and probably the most crucial, limitation associated with causal methods is the problem of determining future values of independent or causal variables. As we have discussed, before the regression equation can be used to project future sales levels, future values of the independent variables must be determined. Thus, as Spyros Makridakis points out, "what is actually done is to shift the burden of forecasting from that of directly predicting some factor of interest (sales) to another one which attempts to estimate several independent variables before it can forecast.[36] In the final analysis, the quality of the sales forecast generated by regression models will depend on the forecaster's ability to generate valid and reliable estimates of the independent variables.

Using Several Forecasting Techniques

Research on forecasting techniques indicates that improvements in maintaining accuracy can be achieved by combining the results of several forecasting methods.[37] The

[34]Douglas J. Dalrymple, "Sales Forecasting Methods and Accuracy," *Business Horizons* 18 (December 1975): p. 70.
[35]Paul E. Green and Donald S. Tull, *Research for Marketing Decisions*, 3d ed. (Englewood Cliffs, N.J.: Prentice-Hall, 1975), p. 669.
[36]Makridakis, "A Survey of Time Series," p. 62.
[37]See, for example, Essam Mahmaud, "Accuracy in Forecasting, a Survey," *Journal of Forecasting* 3 (April/June 1984): p. 139; and Spyros Makridakis and Robert L. Winkler, "Averages of Forecasts: Some Empirical Results," *Management Science* 29 (September 1983): p. 987.

results of combined forecasts greatly surpass most individual projections, techniques, and analyses by experts.[38] Mark Moriarty and Arthur Adams suggest that managers should use a composite forecasting model that includes both systematic (quantitative) and judgmental (qualitative) factors.[39] In fact, they suggest that a composite forecast be created to provide a standard of comparison in evaluating the results provided by any single approach. Each approach relies on varying data to derive sales estimates. By considering a broader range of factors that affect sales, the combined approach provides a more accurate forecast. Rather than searching for the single "best" technique, business marketers should direct increased attention to the composite forecasting approach.

Besides using several forecasting techniques, firms need to examine several other facets of forecasting in an effort to improve results. Robert Fildes and Robert Hastings found that providing training about sophisticated forecasting techniques, spending more time on improving input data, and making forecasters accountable for their performance are important ways to enhance efforts.[40]

One study (discussed earlier) concluded that when quantitative methods are used, judgmental adjustments are frequently made. Additional research suggests that managers must carefully decide which quantitative forecasts they select for modification through judgmental approaches.[41] When judgmental appraisal fails to identify poor forecasts, the full benefits of revision are unlikely to be achieved.[42] The results of this investigation indicated the managers were indeed effective in selecting the poorer forecasts for judgmental revision and they tended to select forecasts that were underestimated rather than overestimated. Thus, not only did managers typically improve upon forecasts made by a quantitative model, they revised the poorer forecasts. The result is better and more consistent forecasts.

Forecasts developed by interfunctional teams of managers appear to be gaining favor among business marketers. A study of forecasting approaches determined that team-based forecasts appear to be more accurate than other approaches for industry-level and long-range forecasts.[43] Respondents express higher satisfaction levels when a team collectively develops the forecast. These results suggest the necessity for interfunctional development of strategic forecasts.

Technique Selection

Recognizing that all forecasts are subject to error, management must decide on the degree of error that can be tolerated when seeking a forecasting technique.[44] Ultimately, the technique selected should make the "best" use of available data. The selection of a forecasting technique is based on a variety of criteria; choosing the appropriate approach is a demanding task and requires an understanding of the strengths and

---

[38] Georgoff and Murdick, "Manager's Guide to Forecasting," p. 119.

[39] Moriarty and Adams, "Management Judgment Forecasts," p. 248.

[40] Robert Fildes and Robert Hastings, "The Organization and Improvement of Market Forecasting," *I.E.E.C. Engineering Management Review* (fall 1995): pp. 42–43.

[41] Sanders, "Forecasting Practices in U.S. Corporations," pp. 92–100.

[42] Brian P. Mathews and A. Diamantopoulous, "Judgmental Revision of Sales Forecasts: Effectiveness of Forecast Selection," *Journal of Forecasting* 9 (July/September 1990): p. 412.

[43] Kenneth B. Kahn, "The Impact of Team-based Forecasting," *Journal of Business Forecasting* 13 (summer 1994): pp. 18–21.

[44] Lancaster and Lomas, "A Managerial Guide to Forecasting," p. 3.

weaknesses of the available alternatives. The task is an important one because, by using the best available forecasting approach, more accurate predictions for the future can be made. Business marketers who can better anticipate the future gain an important competitive advantage and enhance the efficiency and effectiveness of their operations.

Summary

Estimating market potential and forecasting sales are the two most significant dimensions of organizational demand analysis. Each is fundamental to marketing planning and control. Knowledge of market potential enables the marketer to isolate market opportunity and efficiently allocate marketing resources to product and customer segments that offer the highest return. Measures of market potential also provide a standard against which the manager can monitor performance. Similarly, the sales forecast—the firm's best estimate of expected sales with a particular marketing plan—forces the manager to ask the right questions and to consider various strategies before allocating resources.

The methods for developing estimates of market potential fall into two categories: (1) statistical series methods and (2) market surveys. The marketer must know the strengths and weaknesses of each and understand their appropriateness to a particular marketing environment.

Sales forecasts are developed for various periods, ranging from the immediate (daily or weekly) to the long-term time frame (two or more years), depending on their purpose.

The forecasting techniques available to the business marketer are (1) qualitative and (2) quantitative. Qualitative techniques rely on informed judgments of future sales and include the executive judgment, the sales force composite, and the Delphi methods. By contrast, quantitative techniques have more complex data requirements and include time series and causal approaches. The time series method uses chronological historical data to project the future trend and growth rate of sales. Causal methods, on the other hand, seek to identify factors that have affected sales in the past and to incorporate these factors into a mathematical model.

The essence of good forecasting is to combine effectively the forecasts provided by various methods. The process of sales forecasting is challenging and requires a good working knowledge of the available alternatives described in this chapter.

Discussion Questions

1. Explain how the use of the sales forecast differs from that of an estimate of market potential.

2. What is the underlying logic of statistical series methods used in measuring market potential?

3. What statistical series are provided in the *Economic Census*?

4. Describe how customer visits can be used as a valuable component of market research.

5. Why are market surveys favored over statistical series methods in measuring the market potential for new industrial products?

6. Go to DeepCanyon.com, click on the Market Sizer, and find the number of pharmaceutical firms that are located in the state of New Jersey.

7. The business marketing manager must develop not one but many forecasts over several time frames. Explain.

8. Compare and contrast the sales force composite and the Delphi methods of developing a sales forecast.

9. Although qualitative forecasting techniques are important in the sales forecasting process in many industrial firms, the marketing manager must understand the limitations of these approaches. Outline these limitations.

10. As alternative methods for sales forecasting, what is the underlying logic of (1) time series and (2) regression or causal methods?

11. What are the limitations that must be understood before applying and interpreting the sales forecasting results generated by causal methods?

12. What are the features of the business market that support the use of qualitative forecasting approaches? What benefits does the business market analyst gain by combining these qualitative approaches with quantitative forecasting methods?

EXERCISES

1. The Bol Company manufactures electronic controls for sale to book publishing companies. A primary market is New York State, where past sales volumes have not satisfied management expectations. Last year the firm had sales of $8.2 million to book publishers in New York State, while total U.S. sales to book publishers reached $58.4 million. The following data is gleaned from company and other published sources to evaluate the firm's performance in New York:

Number of Customers in New York State	Total Sales Made by New York State Book Publishers	Total Sales of All Book Publishers
142	$2.2 Billion	$10 Billion

How well did the company perform last year on the basis of sales volume in New York State? Explain your answer.

2. The Stearns Company requires an estimate of total dollar market potential for the purpose of allocating advertising expenditures to the East Coast market. A small-scale study of a sample of customers in each of the firm's SIC groups provides the following data on "valve purchases per dollar of value added":

SIC	Value Purchases /Dollar of Value Added	Total Value Added: East Coast
2992	$0.11	$21,100
3291	0.08	5,600

SIC	Value Purchases /Dollar of Value Added	Total Value Added: East Coast
3541	0.07	48,500
3559	0.05	28,400
3662	0.12	12,500
3679	0.10	17,000

Determine the total dollar market potential for the East Coast market.

IV

Formulating Business Marketing Strategy

9

Business Marketing Planning: Strategic Perspectives

To this point, you have developed an understanding of organizational buying behavior, customer relationship management, market segmentation, and a host of other tools used by managers. All of this provides a perspective that is fundamentally important to the business marketing strategist. After reading this chapter, you will understand

1. the dimensions that characterize market-driven organizations and the importance of this orientation to competitive advantage.

2. the sources of competitive advantage and how they can be converted into superior positions of advantage in the business market.

3. marketing's strategic role in corporate strategy development.

4. important path-breaking strategies for high-technology markets.

5. the multifunctional nature of business marketing decision making.

There is an implicit belief in most large corporations that strategy is the province of senior management. This is not so at GE Capital.[1] At a recent planning session, someone suggested that each of its twenty-eight different businesses assemble a team of lower- to mid-level managers, all under the age of thirty, and give them the task of finding opportunities that their "older managers" had missed. The young teams returned with a number of fresh ideas, including several focused on how GE Capital could capitalize on the Internet. New growth strategies come from new ideas. New ideas often come from new voices. Drawing on the collective strengths of the organization is what strategy formulation is all about.

Regis McKenna summarizes the new role of the marketer in business strategy:

> In a time of exploding choice and unpredictable change, marketing—the new marketing—is the answer. . . . The marketer must be the integrator, both internally—synthesizing technological capability with marketing needs—and externally to bring the customer into the company as a participant in the development and adaptation of goods and services. It is a fundamental shift in the role and purpose of marketing: from manipulation of the customer to genuine customer involvement, from telling and selling to communicating and sharing knowledge; from last-in-line function to corporate-credibility champion.[2]

To meet the challenges brought on by growing domestic and global competition, industrial firms are increasingly recognizing the vital role that the marketing function assumes in the development and implementation of successful business strategies. Effective business strategies share many common characteristics, but at a minimum, they are responsive to market needs, they exploit the special competencies of the organization, and they employ valid assumptions about environmental trends and competitive behavior. Above all, they must offer a realistic basis for securing and sustaining a competitive advantage. This chapter examines the nature and critical importance of strategy development in the business marketing firm.

First, the characteristics that define market-driven organizations are examined, while exploring the meaning and strategic value of this orientation. The sources of competitive advantage are then identified, along with the levers a firm can use to convert these sources into superior positions of advantage in the business market. Special attention is also given to innovation strategies that can transform high-technology markets. Finally, the role that the marketing function assumes in corporate strategy development is presented, with a functionally integrated perspective of business marketing planning. This discussion provides a foundation for exploring business marketing strategy on a global scale—the theme of the next chapter.

Market-Driven Organizations[3]

Leading-edge organizations stay close to the customer and ahead of competition. Peter Drucker notes that "the single most important thing to remember about any

---

[1] Gary Hamel, "Bringing Silicon Valley Inside," *Harvard Business Review*, 77 (September–October 1999), pp. 78–79.

[2] Regis McKenna, Relationship Marketing: Successful Strategies for the Age of the Customer (Reading, Mass: Addison-Wesley, 1991), p. 4.

[3] The discussion in this section draws on George S. Day, *Market Driven Strategy: Processes for Creating Value* (New York: The Free Press, 1990), chap. 14; and Subra Balakrishnan, "Benefits of Customer and Competitive Orientations in Industrial

enterprise is that there are no results inside its walls. The result of a business is a satisfied customer. . . . [I]nside an enterprise there are only cost centers. Results exist only on the outside."[4] A market-driven organization displays a deep and enduring commitment to the principle that the purpose of a business is to attract and satisfy customers at a profit.

George Day suggests that a market-driven organization has a three-level focus that includes

- commitment to a set of processes, beliefs, and values that permeate all aspects and activities, that are

- guided by a deep and shared understanding of consumers' needs and behavior, and competitors' capabilities and intentions, for the purpose of

- achieving superior performance by satisfying customers better than the competitors.[5]

Capabilities of Market-Driven Organizations

Market-driven organizations demonstrate superior market-sensing and customer-linking capabilities.[6]

Market-Sensing as a Distinctive Capability   Market-driven firms are centered on customers—they take an outside-in view of strategy and demonstrate an ability to sense market trends ahead of their competitors. Whereas all organizations scan the environment to spot trends, opportunities, and threats, market-driven organizations approach these activities in a more systematic manner. In market-driven firms, market monitoring is frequent and intensive, customer contact employees actively feed market information to management, knowledge of existing and emerging market segments is extensive, and market information systems make it easy for managers across functions to retrieve comprehensive and timely information.

Customer-Linking as a Distinctive Capability   Market-driven firms demonstrate customer-linking capabilities—they possess special skills for creating and managing close customer relationships. Because of the resource commitments required, special attention is given to the choice of which customers to serve collaboratively (see Chapter 4). Successful collaboration requires a close partnership and joint problem solving. There is also a heightened need for cross-functional coordination and information sharing to work collaboratively with customers. For example, field sales and services units need a deep understanding of their customers' business processes in order to analyze and optimize the value-in-use components of the exchange. In addition, notes Frank Cespedes, "since the buyer is not only purchasing a product but also organizational prowess, field sales and service personnel require more familiarity with their

---

Markets," *Industrial Marketing Management* 25 (July 1996): pp. 257–269; see also Ajay K. Kohli and Bernard J. Jaworski, "Market Orientation: The Construct, Research Propositions, and Managerial Implications," *Journal of Marketing* 54 (April 1990): pp. 1–18.

[4] Peter F. Drucker, "Management and the World's Work," *Harvard Business Review* 66 (September/October 1988): pp. 65–76.

[5] Day, *Market-Driven Strategy*, p. 358.

[6] This section is based on George S. Day, "The Capabilities of Market-Driven Organizations," *Journal of Marketing* 58 (October 1994): pp. 37–52. See also, John C. Narver, Stanley F. Slater, and Brian Tietje, "Creating a Market Orientation," *Journal of Market Focused Management* (2, 1998), pp. 241–255.

own company's business processes across a variety of functional areas."[7] Market-driven firms develop the appropriate structural linkages (for example, teams or liaison units), information systems (for example, joint databases), and management processes (for example, career paths and training programs) to achieve a collaborative advantage and to deliver value and satisfaction to their most important customers.[8]

Dimensions of Market-Driven Management

In a market-driven organization, this orientation is achieved and sustained by making appropriate moves along four interlocking dimensions: (1) shared beliefs and values, (2) organizational structures and systems, (3) strategy development processes, and (4) supporting programs (see Figure 9.1).

1. **Shared beliefs and values.** All decisions within market-driven organizations begin with the customer and the associated opportunities for advantage. Firms such as Federal Express, Dell Computer, Intel, and 3M exhibit these values. Providing superior quality and service on the customer's own terms is a basic value that permeates the entire organization and is continually supported and reinforced by the actions of senior managers. In turn, there is attention to service at every level of value creation in the company. Included here are internal activities that encourage production line employees to appreciate that the customer they must satisfy is the next person on the assembly line.

2. **Organization structure and systems.** Market-driven organizations employ an organization structure that mirrors the segmentation plan of the firm, so that responsibilities for serving each primary market segment are clearly defined. Moreover, the employees closest to the customers are given the power and authority to meet customer needs. Federal Express, with over 40,000 employees in more than three hundred cities worldwide, involves a maximum of only five organizational layers between its nonmanagement employees and its chief operating officer or chief executive officer. Incentive systems emphasize the need to go "to the limit" to insure customer satisfaction.[9]

3. **Strategy development.** Rather than rely on rigid systems geared to the preparation of annual budgets, market-driven firms operate with planning systems that are adaptive, participative, and well grounded in appropriate market information. Adaptive planning is facilitated by the astute blending of information from top-down and bottom-up sources, and is directed to helping the organization learn how to cope with a changing environment. Learning takes place in a participative context, largely occurring in multifunctional teams where operating managers debate, resolve strategic issues, and select strategic options. Managers are encouraged to take informed risks and share information openly within the organization.

---

[7] Frank V. Cespedes, *Concurrent Marketing: Integrating Product, Sales, and Service* (Boston, Mass.: Harvard Business School Press, 1995), pp. 267–270.

[8] Ibid., chap. 10.

[9] James Brian Quinn, *Intelligent Enterprise: A Knowledge and Service Based Paradigm for Industry* (New York: The Free Press, 1992), p. 136.

| FIGURE 9.1 | DIMENSIONS OF MARKET-DRIVEN MANAGEMENT |

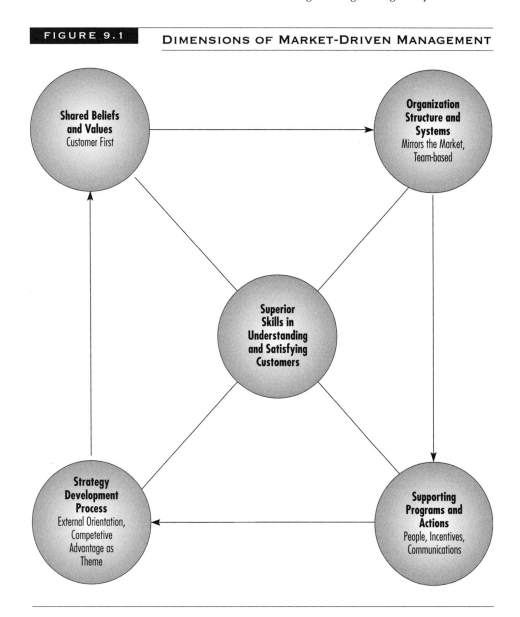

SOURCE: George S. Day, *Market Driven Strategy: Processes for Creating Value* (New York: The Free Press, 1990), p. 358. Reprinted with permission of The Free Press, a division of Simon & Schuster. Copyright © 1990 by George S. Day.

4. **Supporting programs and actions.** A customer-first orientation is deeply ingrained in a market-driven firm and is particularly apparent in each "moment of truth" for the organization—the point of contact between the customer and the organization. At Intel, teams are constantly formed and re-formed around challenging and ambitious projects. Using variants of this system to manage its technological resources, Intel has become a consistent

FIGURE 9.2	3M AD EMPHASIZING ITS POSITION AS AN INNOVATION LEADER

SOURCE: Courtesy of 3M Company.

leader in semiconductor innovation.[10] At 3M, employees are encouraged to champion new products that provide solutions to customer problems, such as its Trizact™ Abrasives that can shape jet engine parts to 1/10,000 of an inch. (see Figure 9.2).

George Day emphasizes the benefits of a customer-first orientation:

> When everyone understands the importance of putting the customer first, while staying ahead of the competition, they have a reason for doing their jobs. Then "quality" becomes an understood dedication rather than an imposed dictum, "fast response" a meaningful innovation rather than a

---

[10] Anil Menon, Sundar G. Bharadwaj, Phon Tej Adidam, and Steven W. Edison, "Antecedents and Consequences of Marketing Strategy Making: A Model and a Test," *Journal of Marketing*, 63 (April 1999), pp. 18–40.

mechanical metric, "market share" an earned result rather than a warlike target. . . .[11]

Assessing Competitive Advantage[12]

Competitive advantage can be examined from the vantage point of competitors or of customers. A competitor-based assessment targets this question: How do our capabilities and offerings compare with those of competitors? Here the focus is on identifying areas where the firm has relative superiority in skills and resources. In contrast, a customer-oriented assessment involves a detailed analysis of customer benefits by segment to identify those actions a company might take to improve performance.

George Day and Robin Wensley point out that

> A competitor-centered perspective leads to a preoccupation with costs and controllable activities that can be compared directly with corresponding activities of close rivals. Customer-focused approaches have the advantage of examining the full range of competitive choices in light of the customers' needs and perceptions of superiority, but lack an obvious connection to activities and variables that are controlled by management.[13]

Observe that a balance of these perspectives is provided in Figure 9.3. Positions of advantage are based on the provision of superior customer value or on the achievement of lower relative costs and the resulting profitability and market share performance. Importantly, positional and performance superiority are derived from relative superiority in the skills and resources that a firm has to deploy. In turn, these skills and resources are an outgrowth of past investments made to enhance a firm's competitive position. To maintain a position of advantage, the firm must erect barriers that make imitation by competitors more difficult. Because these barriers to imitation are continually eroding, the firm must make a continuing stream of investments to sustain or improve the advantage.

Sources of Advantage

A business marketing firm gains a competitive advantage through its superior skills and resources. **Superior skills** are the distinctive capabilities of key personnel that set them apart from the personnel of competing firms. Some of the benefits of superior skills emerge from the ability to perform individual functions more effectively than other firms can. To illustrate, superior engineering may lead to greater reliability in the finished product. Other skills result from the systems and organizational structures that enable a company to adapt faster and more responsively to changing market requirements.

[11] Day, *Market-Driven Strategy*, p. 375.

[12] The discussion in this section draws on George S. Day and Robin Wensley, "Assessing Advantage: A Framework for Diagnosing Competitive Superiority," *Journal of Marketing* 52 (April 1988): pp. 1–20. See also Stanley F. Slater, "The Challenges of Sustaining Competitive Advantage," *Industrial Marketing Management* 25 (January 1996): pp. 47–58.

[13] Ibid., Day and Wensley, p. 2.

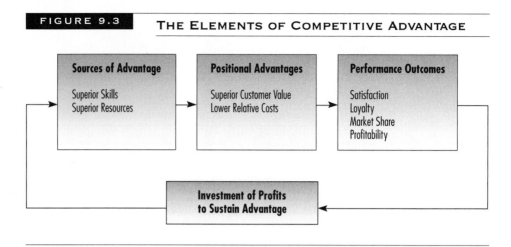

SOURCE: George S. Day and Robin Wensley, "Assessing Advantage: A Framework for Diagnosing Competitive Superiority," *Journal of Marketing* 52 (April 1988): p. 3. Reprinted with permission of the American Marketing Association.

James Brian Quinn emphasizes the importance of a sharp strategic focus:

> Each company should focus its strategic investments and management attention on those core competencies—usually intellectual or service activities—where it can achieve and maintain "best in world" status, i.e., a significant long-term competitive advantage.[14]

To illustrate, Boeing cannot possibly design and manufacture more than a small portion of the many components and subsystems that are embodied in its planes. While producing some systems where it has special expertise, Boeing concentrates on the core competencies of aircraft design, relationships with its worldwide customers, aircraft assembly, and managing the massive logistics systems necessary to support its global procurement program. Experts speculate that Boeing could use its systems expertise and knowledge of air travel to penetrate markets such as air-traffic control and reservation systems.[15]

Superior resources are more tangible requirements for advantage that enable a firm to exercise its capabilities. Included among superior resources are the following elements:

- Number of salespersons and service representatives by territory, region, and market

- Expenditures on advertising and promotional support

- Distribution coverage (number of industrial distributors who carry the firm's products)

---

[14] Quinn, *Intelligent Enterprise*, p. 32.

[15] Andy Reinhardt and Seanna Browder, "Booming Boeing," *Business Week*, (30 September 1996), pp. 118–125.

- Scale of manufacturing facilities and the availability of automated assembly lines

- Expenditures on R&D

Often, competitor analysis centers on making direct comparisons and ranking key competitors on each skill or resource dimension.

Figures of Merit [16]

Benchmarking involves identifying the best practices employed by organizations worldwide, learning about them, and implementing them in the firm. Figures of merit go much further. In defining "best in the world," organizations that use **figures of merit** set a few crucial economic or technical targets that *"if hit, will win"* in competition. "They define economic-performance targets sufficiently above normally expected trend lines to ensure the company has a competitive advantage that will attract customers" away from competitors.[17] For example, Sony has used figures of merit for performance and price to revolutionize the digital-audio recorder, CD-ROM, and other industries.

Positions of Advantage

What we see in the market—from the perspective of customers or competitors—is the positional advantage of a business. This can be achieved by providing the lowest delivered cost or by providing superior customer value.

Lowest Delivered Cost Position   An overall cost advantage is obtained by performing most activities at a lower cost than competitors while offering a comparable product. To illustrate, NUCOR has achieved a low-cost position in the steel industry by making extensive use of scrap metal rather than iron ore and by producing all of its steel using the efficient continuous-casting method. To succeed, a cost strategy must offer an acceptable level of value to customers. If the low-cost position is achieved by providing marginal quality or eliminating desired features, the price discount demanded by customers will more than offset the cost advantage.

Value Superiority   George Day and Robin Wensley explain value superiority in the following way:

> A business is differentiated when some value-adding activities are performed in a way that leads to perceived superiority along dimensions that are valued by customers. For these activities to be profitable, the customer must be willing to pay a premium for the benefits and the premium must exceed the added costs of superior performance.[18]

[16]James Brian Quinn, "Strategic Outsourcing: Leveraging Knowledge Capabilities," *Sloan Management Review*, 40 (summer 1999), pp. 9–21.

[17]Ibid., p. 13.

[18]Day and Wensley, "Assessing Advantage," pp. 3–4.

Dwight Gertz and João Baptista elaborate:

> A company's product or service is competitively superior if, at price equality with competing products, target segments always choose it. Thus, value is defined in terms of customer choice in a competitive context.[19]

There are many ways for a firm to differentiate products and service.

- Provide superior service or technical assistance competence through speed, responsiveness to complex orders, or ability to solve special customer problems

- Provide superior quality that reduces customer costs or improves their performance

- Offer innovative product features that employ new technologies

- Gain broad distribution coverage

Converting Skills and Resources into Superior Positions

Michael Porter proposes that the drivers of positional advantage are those particular skills and resources that have the greatest impact on reducing costs or creating value to customers.[20] There are two principal types: cost drivers and drivers of differentiation.

Drivers of Cost Differences   **Cost drivers** represent the structural determinants of each activity (for example, production) that are largely under a company's control. The principal driver, **economies of scale,** reflects increased efficiency due to size. Large plants cost less per unit to build and operate than smaller plants. Scale effects also apply to many other cost elements such as sales, distribution, research and development, and purchasing.

Learning is a second driver of costs and represents efficiency improvements that result from practice and the exercise of skill and ingenuity in repetitive activities. To illustrate, personnel at Intel learned how to improve the performance of a piece of production equipment and thereby reduced the cost of producing an advanced microchip.

A third cost driver is the extent of **linkages** of activities within a firm. The cost of one activity (for example, inventory) may depend on how another activity is performed (for example, production). To illustrate, closer coordination between purchasing and production may reduce inventory carrying costs. Other drivers of cost that may be important include the rate of capacity utilization, the degree of vertical integration, and the sharing of activities across several business units (for example, a common sales force).

Differentiation   Drivers of differentiation represent the possible underlying reasons why one firm outperforms another on attributes important to customers. Three principal drivers are policy choices, linkages, and timing:

---

[19] Dwight L. Gertz and João P. A. Baptista, *Grow to Be Great: Breaking the Downsizing Cycle* (New York: The Free Press, 1995), p. 128.

[20] Michael E. Porter, *Competitive Advantage: Creating and Sustaining Superior Performance* (New York: The Free Press, 1985).

1. Policy choices concern what activities to perform and how aggressively to perform them. These include product or service features and performance, level of promotion, and the skills and experience of personnel employed in the activity.

2. Linkages among key activities such as coordination between the firm and suppliers can speed product development, while linkages between sales and service can improve the effectiveness of order handling.

3. Timing of entry provides first-mover advantages in a market.

Other drivers of differentiation include location, synergy from sharing a sales force or other activity with another division of the firm, or economies derived from large-scale operations that permit broader market coverage or more responsive service through a number of locations. When activated by an effective strategy, the drivers of differentiation correspond to the sources of advantage that reside in the superior skills or resources of the firm.

Marketing's Strategic Role

Many firms—like Johnson and Johnson, Motorola, and Dow Chemical—have numerous divisions, product lines, products, and brands. Policies established at the corporate level provide the framework for strategy development in each business division to ensure survival and growth of the entire enterprise. In turn, corporate and divisional policies establish the boundaries within which individual product or market managers develop strategy.

The Hierarchy of Strategies

Three major levels of strategy dominate most large multiproduct organizations: (1) corporate strategy, (2) business-level strategy, and (3) functional strategy.[21]

Corporate strategy defines the businesses in which a company will compete, preferably in a manner that utilizes resources to convert distinctive competence into competitive advantage. Essential questions at this level include: What are our core competencies? What businesses are we in? What businesses should we be in? How should we allocate resources across these businesses to achieve our overall organizational goals and objectives? At this level of strategy, the role of marketing is to (1) assess market attractiveness and the competitive effectiveness of the firm, (2) promote a customer orientation to the various constituencies in management decision making, and (3) formulate the firm's overall value proposition (as a reflection of its distinctive competencies, in terms reflecting customer needs) and to articulate it to the market and to the organization at large. According to Frederick Webster Jr., "At the corporate level, marketing managers have a critical role to play as advocates, for

[21]This discussion draws on Frederick E. Webster Jr., "The Changing Role of Marketing in the Corporation," *Journal of Marketing* 56 (October 1992): pp. 1–17. See also, Webster, "The Future Role of Marketing in the Organization," in *Reflections on the Future of Marketing*, ed. Donald Lehmann and Katherine E. Jocz (Cambridge, MA: Marketing Science Institute, 1997), pp. 39–66.

the customer and for a set of values and beliefs that put the customer first in the firm's decision making. . . .[22]

Business-level strategy centers on how a firm will compete in a given industry and will position itself against its competitors. The focus of competition is not between corporations; rather, it is between their individual business units. A **strategic business unit (SBU)** is a single business or collection of businesses that has a distinct mission, a responsible manager, and its own competitors, and that is relatively independent of other business units. The 3M Corporation has defined twenty strategic business units, each of which develops a plan describing how its particular mix of products will be managed to secure a competitive advantage consistent with the level of investment and risk that management is willing to accept. An SBU could be one or more divisions of the industrial firm, a product line within one division, or, on occasion, a single product. Strategic business units may share resources such as a sales force with other business units in order to achieve economies of scale. An SBU may serve one or many product-market units.

For each business unit within the corporate portfolio, the following essential questions must be answered: How can we compete most effectively for the product-market served by the business unit? What distinctive skills can give the business unit a competitive advantage? Similarly, the CEO at GE, Jack Welch, asks his operating executives to crisply answer the following questions:[23]

- Describe the global competitive environment in which you operate.

- In the last three years, what have your competitors done?

- In the same period, what have you done to them in the marketplace?

- How might they attack you in the future?

- What are your plans to leapfrog them?

The marketing function contributes to the planning process at this level by providing a detailed and complete analysis of customers and competitors and the firm's distinctive skills and resources for competing in particular market segments.

Functional strategy centers on how resources allocated to the various functional areas can be used most efficiently and effectively to support the business-level strategy. The primary focus of marketing strategy at this level is to allocate and coordinate marketing resources and activities to achieve the firm's objective within a specific product market.

Managing Three Customer Connections   Marketing is perhaps best understood as the function that manages the three primary connections between the organization and the customer.[24]

- *The customer-product connection.* This involves linking the customer to the focal offering, particularly the knowledge and skills to discover customer needs and connect them to product design.

---

[22] Ibid., p. 11.

[23] Noel M. Tichy and Stratford Sherman, *Control Your Destiny or Someone Else Will* (New York: Doubleday, 1993), p. 26.

[24] Christine Moorman and Roland T. Rust, "The Role of Marketing," *Journal of Marketing*, 63 (Special Issue 1999), pp. 180–197.

- *The customer-service delivery connection.* Included here are the design and delivery actions involved in providing a firm's goods and services to the customer (for example, the performance of frontline sales and customer service employees).

- *The customer-financial accountability connection.* This refers to activities and processes that link customers to financial outcomes (for example, the link between customer satisfaction and profitability or customer retention efforts and financial outcomes).

Strategy Formulation and the Hierarchy [25]

The interplay among the three levels of the strategy hierarchy can be illustrated by examining the collective action perspective of strategy formulation.[26] This approach applies to strategic decisions that (1) cut across functional areas, (2) involve issues related to the organization's long-term objectives, or (3) involve the allocation of resources across business units or product markets. Included here are decisions regarding the direction of corporate strategy, the application of a core technology, or the choice of an alliance partner.

Observe in Figure 9.4 that strategic decision processes often involve the active participation of several functional interest groups who hold markedly different beliefs concerning the appropriateness of particular strategies or corporate goals. Strategic decisions represent the outcome of a bargaining process among functional interest groups (including marketing), each of whom may interpret the proposed strategy in an entirely different light.

Turf Issues and Thought-World Views   Two forces contribute to the conflict that often divides participants in the strategy formulation process. First, different meanings assigned to a proposed strategy are often motivated by deeper differences in what might be called "organizational subcultures." Subcultures exist in an organization when one subunit shares different values, beliefs, and goals than another subunit, resulting in different **thought worlds.** For example, marketing managers are concerned with market opportunities and competitors, while R&D managers view technical sophistication and innovation as means to organizational success. Second, functional managers are likely to resist those strategic changes that threaten their turf. To the extent that the subunit domain defines the individual's identity and connotes prestige and power, the organizational member may be quite reluctant to see the domain altered by a strategic decision.

Negotiated Outcomes   Collective decisions emerge from a process of negotiation and compromise among partisan participants. The differences in goals, thought worlds, and self-interests across participants lead to conflicts concerning what actions

---

[25] Gary L. Frankwick, James C. Ward, Michael D. Hutt, and Peter H. Reingen, "Evolving Patterns of Organizational Beliefs in the Formation of Marketing Strategy," *Journal of Marketing* 58 (April 1994): pp. 96–110; see also Michael D. Hutt, Beth A. Walker, and Gary L. Frankwick, "Hurdle the Cross-Functional Barriers to Strategic Change," *Sloan Management Review* 36 (spring 1995): pp. 22–30.

[26] Orville C. Walker Jr., Robert W. Ruekert, and Kenneth J. Roering, "Picking Proper Paradigms: Alternative Perspectives on Organizational Behavior and Their Implications for Marketing Management Research," in *Review of Marketing*, ed. Michael J. Houston (Chicago: American Marketing Association, 1987), pp. 3–36.

FIGURE 9.4

A COLLECTIVE ACTION PERSPECTIVE OF THE STRATEGY FORMULATION PROCESS

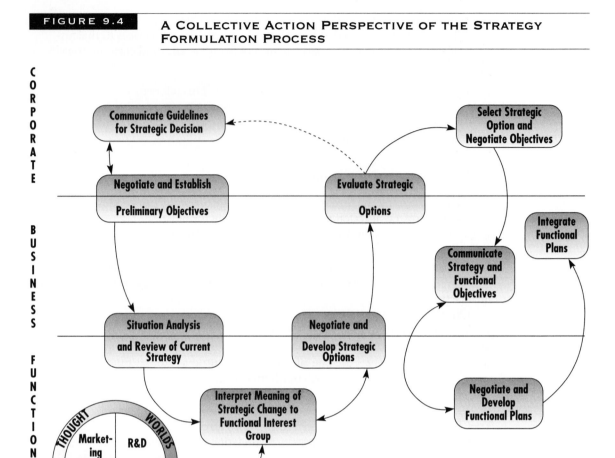

SOURCE: Gary L. Frankwick, James C. Ward, Michael D. Hutt, and Peter H. Reingen, "Evolving Patterns of Organizational Beliefs in the Formation of Strategy," *Journal of Marketing* 58 (April 1994): p. 98. Reprinted with permission from *Journal of Marketing*, published by the American Marketing Association.

should be taken. Choices must be negotiated with each interest group attempting to achieve its own ends. The ultimate outcomes of collective decisions tend to unfold in an incremental manner and depend more on the partisan values and influence of the various interest groups than on rational analysis. A study of a highly-contested strategic decision in a *Fortune* 500 company illustrates the tension that may exist between marketing and R&D.

Two marketing executives describe how the decision was ultimately resolved.[27] According to the marketing manager:

[27] Frankwick, Ward, Hutt, and Reingen, "Evolving Patterns of Organizational Beliefs," pp. 107–108.

> [Marketing] did an extremely effective job of stepping right in the middle of it and strangling it. . . . What has happened is by laying out the market unit concerns and again, refocusing on the fact that we are market-based, basically what Marketing did was force the R&D team into submission where they no longer have the autonomy they once had to go about making decisions—they now get input. And whether it's formal or informal, they definitely get the buy-in of marketing before they move forward on what they're doing now.

According to the vice president of marketing:

> Before I felt it was technology driving the process. Now I feel that technology is partnering with the marketplace. And the reason I feel that way is because we have [marketing people] in place that are working closely with how the technology develops.

Implications for Marketing Managers   In advocating a particular strategic course, marketing managers must be sensitive to the likely response that an initiative may arouse in other functional interest groups. To build pockets of commitment and trust, managers should develop and use a communication network that includes organizational members who have a major stake in the decision. These personal networks can be used by marketing managers to understand the interests of other stakeholders, communicate their own interests clearly and sensitively, and thus diffuse the anxiety of others concerning threats to their turf.

Creating Strategy in High-Technology Industries

Forecasting the future and charting a strategic course are especially difficult in high-technology industries. In dynamic industries, strategic actions will eventually begin to lead or lag behind the strategic intent that was carefully orchestrated by the firm's top management team. Consider the transformation of the computer industry[28] Defined by top management, **strategic intent** represents an ambitious target that a firm is pursuing over the coming decade and emphasizes the distinctive competencies that must be developed to achieve this desired competitive position.[29] As industry dynamics begin to change, some organizational members will see danger ahead and will begin to question the firm's current strategic intent. Often, middle managers and salespersons, who are closest to the customer and openly exposed to the competitive threat, sense the changes first.

Such changes may signal that the firm has reached a **strategic inflection point** in its development—a major crossroad for the firm. Robert Burgelman and Andrew Grove define a strategic inflection point as "the giving way of one type of industry dynamics to another; the change of one winning strategy into another; the replacement of an existing technological regime by a new one."[30]

---

[28]Robert A. Burgelman and Andrew S. Grove, "Strategic Dissonance," *California Management Review* 38 (winter 1996): pp. 8–28.

[29]Gary Hamel and C. K. Prahalad, "Strategic Intent," *Harvard Business Review* 67 (May/June 1989): pp. 63–76.

[30]Burgelman and Grove, "Strategic Dissonance," p. 10.

AN AD SIGNALING INTEL'S NEW STRATEGIC INTENT

intel engineering is at work in our new world-class internet service centers.

take a virtual tour → intel.com/ebusiness   int\el.

© 1999 Intel Corporation. Intel is a registered trademark of Intel Corporation.

SOURCE: Courtesy of Intel Corporation.

For example, Andrew Grove at Intel sees the personal computer industry shifting away from its strict focus on personal computer products toward one that blends communication devices, the Internet, and personal computers.[31] Intel is responding to this initiative with a range of new products and services (see Figure 9.5). Firms that can successfully develop a new strategic intent that capitalizes on the new industry conditions can enjoy a new era of profitable growth. Such results, however, require fundamental change—*discontinuous innovation*.

Discontinuous Innovation Strategies [32]

While incremental innovations are crucial for protecting revenues by growing market share, corporate strategists realize that substantial growth over the long term requires

---

[31] David Kirkpatrick, "Andy Grove: The PC Industry Won't Be the PC Industry," *Fortune* 140 (May 24, 1999), p. 160.

[32] The following is based on Soren M. Kaplan, "Discontinuous Innovation and the Growth Paradox," *Strategy & Leadership*, 27 (March–April 1999), pp. 16–21.

discontinuous innovation. Specifically, **discontinuous innovations** are new products or services that require customers to dramatically change their past behavior, with the promise of gaining equally dramatic new value.[33] Breaking with the past, discontinuous innovation involves "disruptive technologies" that permit entire industries and markets to emerge, transform, or even disappear. To illustrate, Hewlett-Packard's inkjet printer platform represented radical technology that replaced dot-matrix printing, helped spawn the desktop printer industry, and propelled the company into the leadership position of a multibillion-dollar market.

Opportunity Identification Drawing on his work as a strategist at Hewlett-Packard, Soren Kaplan offers a valuable framework that business marketers can use to identify compelling new strategic options that are capable of driving significant growth. The framework rests on two fundamental assumptions. First, discontinuous innovation involves the creation of new forms of customer value within existing or new markets. Second, by introducing discontinuous innovations, firms *create* new competitive space or *displace* existing approaches that are being used to deliver value to customers. Building on these assumptions, four alternative strategies for discontinuous innovation are offered (see Table 9.1). Note that each strategy involves a different approach to opportunity identification and explores a distinct focus.

Strategy One: Radical Cannibalism "**Radical cannibalism** involves replacing one's own successful products or services with fundamentally new technologies or processes, providing a significant leap in customer value."[34] Traditionally, product cannibalism suggests evolutionary change—replacing existing products with new ones that offer next-generation technology. By contrast, radical cannibalism is revolutionary and provides a level of value to customers that far exceeds what has been provided in the past. For example, Kodak, by shifting its core business from chemical-based photography to digital imaging is pursuing radical cannibalism. As it transitions to a digitally focused business, Kodak, however, must sustain or even grow its core business and source of revenue.

Approach To reveal new opportunities, strategists should first consider breakthrough technologies or competitive threats that could be most detrimental to their firm's business. By pondering the organization's demise, new possibilities emerge. Next, attention should be directed to startup companies that may reinvent the industry. Some attractive strategic partners may be identified.

Strategy Two: Competitive Displacement Competitive displacement resembles radical cannibalism but rather than displacing your own products, the focus is on displacing those of your competitors. This strategy involves applying existing competencies to new industries and markets. Often, existing industry competitors are taken by surprise because the new entrant was never considered a potential competitor. In a direct challenge to Kodak, Hewlett-Packard is pursuing a competitive displacement opportunity in digital photography. Hewlett-Packard's PhotoSmart product line— which combines a digital camera, scanner, photo-quality printer with image editing

---

[33] Geoffrey A. Moore, *Inside the Tornado: Marketing Strategies from Silicon Valley's Cutting Edge* (New York: HarperCollins, 1995), p. 13.

[34] Kaplan, "Discontinuous Innovations," p. 17.

	TABLE 9.1	DISCONTINUOUS INNOVATION STRATEGIES	
Strategy	**Approach**	**Focus**	
Radical Cannibalism	Hypothesize obsolescence	What forces could lead to the demise of the business?	
	Scan startups	What emerging technologies could displace the current value you provide to the market?	
Competitive Displacement	Elevate business charter	What is the root end-user need that your business satisfies?	
	Explore tangential industries	How does the fundamental value you provide get satisfied within industries outside of your own?	
Market Invention	Expand customer boundaries	If the entire world represented your customer base, how would you segment your markets and what needs could you satisfy within each segment?	
	Identify systems	What larger systems do your products operate within, and how might you incorporate a larger value set into your offering?	
Industry Genesis	Miniaturize	What value would your technology provide if it were ten–twenty times smaller than it is today?	
	Combine functionality	What unique combinations of technology or functionality might provide a new form of value?	

SOURCE: Soren M. Kaplan, "Discontinuous Innovation and the Growth Paradox," *Strategy & Leadership*, 27 (March–April 1999), p. 19.

and management software—is a direct attempt to displace traditional competitors in the photography industry.

Approach Two methods can be used to identify opportunities in new competitive arenas. First, strategists should elevate the business charter (i.e., the domain) and examine a broader competitive landscape. For example, photography does not fall within the charter of a "computer business," but Hewlett-Packard defines itself as a "communications business." The photography and photocopier markets are logical extensions. Second, direct attention to potential customers that the company does not presently serve. Often, there are opportunities to provide new forms of customer value by applying the firm's competencies in a new way.

Strategy Three: Market Invention The most common approach to corporate growth, market invention involves new products and services that provide customer value within an existing industry. The focus here is on developing logical extensions to the product mix that leverage the firm's competencies. To illustrate, the Chrysler minivan is an example of a market invention strategy; it created a new category in transportation.

Approach Two methods can be used to identify market invention opportunities. First, consider the opportunities that might be revealed by expanding customer boundaries. Competitors converge on a "common definition of who the target customer is when in reality there is a chain of 'customers' who are directly or indirectly involved in the buying decision."[35] To illustrate, Bloomberg—a provider of business information—gained a strong position with brokerages and investment firms by catering to the special needs of *users*—brokers, traders, and analysts. Competitors missed the opportunity because they were focusing on *purchasers*—information technology managers in the financial community.

Second, market invention opportunities can be isolated by understanding the context in which customers use a combination of different products. For example, Hewlett-Packard integrated a fax and printer to provide new value to home offices and small business customers.

Strategy Four: Industry Genesis   Industry genesis results from the introduction of new-to-the-world technology and new forms of customer value. This represents the most challenging discontinuous innovation strategy and presents the most uncertainty and risk. Both the size of the market and the degree to which consumers will adopt the technology are extremely difficult to estimate. Hewlett-Packard has created innovations that spawned new industries (for example, the desktop publishing industry).

Approach   Two strategies that underlie many industry-creating innovations emphasize these goals:

- **Miniaturize:** Provide new value by dramatically reducing the size of products that embody the technology (for example, Sony Walkman).

- **Combine Functionality:** Create new methods by meeting a combination of customer needs in a single product (for example, electronic personal organizers combine computers with pocket calculators and organizers).

A Different Focus for Market Research   Traditional strategy formulation centers on *reducing* uncertainty, but discontinuous innovation involves viewing uncertainty as an opportunity. Likewise, market research cannot precisely forecast the demand for discontinuous innovations because customers rarely understand what is possible.[36] Soren Kaplan observes:

> To underscore this critical point at H-P, we emphasize the importance of achieving "an imaginative understanding of customer needs" when seeking discontinuities. This motto helps market research become a means for exploring, refining, and validating ideas, rather than serving as a "go/no go" decision-making tool.[37]

Culture Is the Key   Two attributes of an organization's culture can aid a firm in transforming itself and adapting to new industry conditions. First, employees should actively contribute to the debate that surrounds the decision. For example, Intel

---

[35] W. Chan Kim and Renee' Mauborgne, "Creating New Market Space," *Harvard Business Review*, 77 (January–February 1999), p. 87.

[36] Clayton M. Christensen, *The Innovator's Dilemma: When New Technologies Cause Great Firms to Fail* (Boston: Harvard Business School Press, 1997).

[37] Kaplan, "Discontinuous Innovations," p. 21.

Corporation's culture actively encourages vigorous debate among employees to thoroughly explore the issues and emphasizes a process that is indifferent to rank. The focus is on finding what is best for the company as opposed to what is best for a particular division or functional area. Intel refers to this mechanism as constructive confrontation. New Intel employees are taught how this feature of the culture has been vital to shaping the firm's success.

Second, the strategic processes of the firm should encourage debate but yield clear decisions that are accepted by the entire organization. Often, executives will accelerate decision making by using a two-step process, called **consensus with qualification.**[38] Executives will discuss an issue and attempt to gain a consensus. However, if consensus appears unlikely, the key manager and the most relevant functional head get together and make the choice, guided by the input of the rest of the group. By taking a realistic view of conflict, consensus with qualification speeds decision making. Kathleen Eisenhardt explains why:

> Most people want a voice in the decision-making process, but are willing to accept that their opinions may not prevail. Consensus with qualification goes one better by giving them added influence when the choice particularly affects their part of the organization.[39]

Marketing's Cross-Functional Relationships

The creation of a boundaryless organization is an important value that underlies G.E.'s current organizational style. To achieve this goal, CEO Jack Welch emphasizes the importance of eliminating artificial barriers—removing the horizontal barriers that divide functional areas, the vertical barriers that come from the formal hierarchy, and the external barriers that prevent close relationships with customers, suppliers, and alliance partners.[40] The restructuring of organizations, the reengineering of business processes, and the search for quicker, more efficient responses to changing customer needs and competitive realities are important strategic priorities in business practice. As firms adopt leaner and more agile structures and emphasize cross-functional teams, the business marketing manager assumes an important and challenging role in strategy formulation.

All business marketing decisions—product, price, promotion, or distribution—are affected, directly or indirectly, by other functional areas. In turn, business decisions in research and development and in manufacturing and procurement, as well as adjustments in the overall corporate strategy, are influenced by marketing considerations. Business marketing planning must be coordinated and synchronized with corresponding planning efforts in R&D, procurement, finance, manufacturing, and other areas.

Cross-Functional Connections

Effective business marketing managers develop close working relationships with their colleagues in manufacturing, R&D, logistics, and other functions. They understand

---

[38] Kathleen M. Eisenhardt, "Speed and Strategic Choice: How Managers Accelerate Decision Making," *California Management Review* 32 (spring 1990): pp. 49–56. See also, Kathleen M. Eisenhardt, "Strategy as Strategic Decision Making," *Sloan Management Review*, 40 (summer 1999), pp. 65–72.

[39] Ibid., Eisenhardt, "Speed and Strategic Choice," p. 50.

[40] "General Electric: The House that Jack Built," *The Economist* (September 18, 1999), pp. 23–26.

TABLE 9.2	FORMULATING BUSINESS MARKETING STRATEGY: VITAL CROSS-FUNCTIONAL CONNECTIONS	
Function	**Contribution to Strategy**	**Support Required from Marketing**
Manufacturing	• Determines the volume, variety, and quality of products that can be marketed • Influences the speed with which the business marketer can respond to changing market or competitive needs	• Accurate and timely sales forecast
R&D	• Provides critical technical direction in new product development process • Remains abreast of competitive technology	• Data on market and competitive trends • Marketing research on product features desired by target segments
Logistics	• Provides on-time accurate shipments to customers • Develops timely order tracking and status reports	• Accurate and timely sales forecasts • Delivery service requirements by customer or segment
Technical service	• Implements post-sale activities such as installation and training • Serves as troubleshooter for customer problems	• Account-specific goals and plans • Promises made to the customer during the selling process

the critical role that each function assumes in the design and execution of strategy and, in turn, what each functional area requires from marketing.

Table 9.2 explores the interrelationships between marketing and four business functions. Observe the significant role that each assumes in the development and implementation of marketing strategy. For example, new product development is the focus of the marketing–R&D interface, from idea generation to performance evaluation of the finished product. The importance of nurturing an effective marketing–R&D interface is reinforced by the sizable investments R&D commands in industrial firms. Motorola, Boeing, and G.E. each spend more than $1 billion annually and IBM more than $5 billion on R&D investments.[41] Successful new product developments depend heavily on marketing research for product features desired by target market segments and for how potential organizational buyers view trade-offs among product attributes. If marketing fails to provide adequate market and competitive information, R&D personnel will be in the precarious position of determining the direction of new product development without the benefit of market knowledge. A successful relationship between marketing and R&D requires that each understands the strengths, weaknesses, and potential contributions of the other. For instance, a promising new product spawned by R&D may fail because the firm lacks the marketing strengths required to penetrate a particular market segment.

---

[41] "In the Labs, The Fight to Spend Less, Get More," *Business Week*, 28 June 1993, pp. 102–104.

Once a new product is developed and manufactured, the logistics and technical services functions assume special significance in strategy implementation. Two factors assigned particular importance by customers are (1) the speed and reliability of delivery service and (2) the quality and availability of technical service after the sale (see Chapter 4). Close coordination between marketing and both of these vital service functions is required to provide the service level that organizational customers expect.

Functionally Integrated Planning: The Marketing Strategy Center [42]

Rather than operating in isolation from other functional areas, the successful business marketing manager is an integrator—one who understands the capabilities of manufacturing, R&D, and customer service and who capitalizes on their strengths in developing marketing strategies that are responsive to customer needs. Marketing managers also assume a central role in strategy implementation.[43] **Responsibility charting** constitutes an approach that can be used to classify decision-making roles and to highlight the multifunctional nature of business marketing decision making. The structure of a responsibility chart is provided in Table 9.3. The decision areas (rows) illustrated in the matrix might, for example, relate to a planned product line expansion. The various functional areas that may assume particular roles in this decision process head the columns of the matrix. The alternative roles that can be assumed by participants in the decision-making process are defined in the following list.[44]

1. *Responsible* (R): The manager takes initiative for analyzing the situation, developing alternatives, and assuring consultation with others and then makes the initial recommendation. Upon approval of decision, the role ends.

2. *Approve* (A): The manager accepts or vetoes a decision before it is implemented, or chooses from alternatives developed by the participants assuming a "responsible" role.

3. *Consult* (C): The manager is consulted or asked for substantive input prior to the approval of the decision but does not possess veto power.

4. *Implement* (M): The manager is accountable for the implementation of the decision, including notification of other relevant participants concerning the decision.

5. *Inform* (I): Although not necessarily consulted before the decision is approved, the manager is informed of the decision once it is made.

Representatives of a particular functional area may, of course, assume more than one role in the decision-making process. The technical service manager may be consulted during the new product development process and may also be held accountable

---

[42] Michael D. Hutt and Thomas W. Speh, "The Marketing Strategy Center: Diagnosing the Industrial Marketer's Interdisciplinary Role," *Journal of Marketing* 48 (fall 1984): pp. 53–61; see also Jeen-Su Lim and David A. Reid, "Vital Cross-Functional Linkages with Marketing," *Industrial Marketing Management* 22 (February 1993): pp. 159–165.

[43] Charles H. Noble and Michael P. Mokwa, "Implementing Marketing Strategies: Developing and Testing a Managerial Theory," *Journal of Marketing*, 63 (October 1999), pp. 57–73.

[44] Joseph E. McCann and Thomas N. Gilmore, "Diagnosing Organizational Decision Making Through Responsibility Charting," *Sloan Management Review* 25 (winter 1983): pp. 3–15.

TABLE 9.3	INTERFUNCTIONAL INVOLVEMENT IN MARKETING DECISION MAKING: AN ILLUSTRATIVE RESPONSIBILITY CHART

Organizational Function

Decision Area	Marketing	Manufacturing	R&D	Logistics	Technical Service	Strategic Business Unit Manager	Corporate Level Planner
PRODUCT							
Design specifications							
Performance characteristics							
Reliability							
PRICE							
List price							
Discount structure							
TECHNICAL SERVICE SUPPORT							
Customer training							
Repair							
PHYSICAL DISTRIBUTION							
Inventory level							
Customer service level							
SALES FORCE							
Training							
ADVERTISING							
Message development							
CHANNEL							
Selection							

Note: Decision role vocabulary: R = responsible; A = approve; C = consult; M = implement; I = inform; X = no role in decision

for implementing service support strategy. Likewise, the marketing manager may be responsible for and approve many of the decisions related to the product line expansion. For other actions, several decision makers may participate. To illustrate, the business unit manager, after consulting R&D, may approve (accept or veto) a decision for which the marketing manager is responsible.

The members of the organization who become involved in the business marketing decision-making process constitute the **marketing strategy center.** The composition or functional area representation of the strategy center evolves during the marketing strategy development process, varies from firm to firm, and varies from one strategy situation to another. Likewise, the composition of the marketing strategy center is not strictly prescribed by the organizational chart. The needs of a particular strategy situation, especially the information requirements, significantly influence the composition of the strategy center. Thus, the marketing strategy center shares certain parallels with the buying center (see Chapter 3).

Managing Strategic Interdependencies   A central challenge for the business marketer in the strategy center is to minimize interdepartmental conflict while fostering shared appreciation of the interdependencies with other functional units. Individual strategy center participants are motivated by both personal and organizational goals. Company objectives are interpreted by these individuals in relation to their level in the hierarchy and the department they represent. Various functional units operate under unique reward systems and reflect unique orientations or thought worlds. For example, marketing managers are evaluated on the basis of sales, profits, or market share; production managers on the basis of manufacturing efficiency and cost-effectiveness. In turn, R&D managers may be oriented toward long-term objectives; customer service managers may emphasize more immediate ones. Strategic plans emerge out of a bargaining process among functional areas. Managing conflict, promoting cooperation, and developing coordinated strategies are all fundamental to the business marketer's interdisciplinary role. By understanding the concerns and orientations of personnel from other functional areas, the business marketing manager is better equipped to forge effective cross-unit working relationships.

The Business Marketing Planning Process

The business marketing planning process is inextricably linked to planning in other functional areas and to overall corporate strategy. It takes place within the larger strategic marketing management process of the corporation. To survive and prosper, the business marketer must properly balance the firm's resources with the objectives and opportunities of the environment. Marketing planning is a continuous process that involves the active participation of other functional areas.

The Marketing Plan

Responsive to both corporate and business unit strategy, the marketing plan formally describes all the components of the marketing strategy—markets to be served, products or services to be marketed, price schedules, distribution methods, and so on. The key components of the marketing planning process are highlighted in Figure 9.6. Note that the planning process format centers on clearly defined market segments, a thorough assessment of internal and external problems and opportunities, specific goals, and courses of action. Business marketing intelligence, market segmentation (Chapter 7), and market potential and sales forecasting (Chapter 8) are fundamental in the planning process.

At a fundamental level, the marketing plan establishes specific objectives by market segment, defines marketing strategy and action programs required to accomplish these objectives, and pinpoints responsibility for the implementation of these

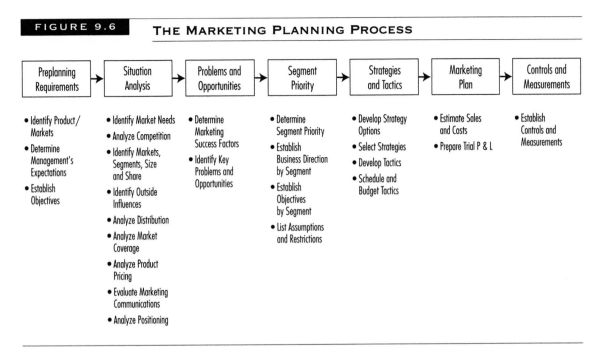

FIGURE 9.6	THE MARKETING PLANNING PROCESS

Preplanning Requirements → **Situation Analysis** → **Problems and Opportunities** → **Segment Priority** → **Strategies and Tactics** → **Marketing Plan** → **Controls and Measurements**

- **Preplanning Requirements**
  - Identify Product/ Markets
  - Determine Management's Expectations
  - Establish Objectives

- **Situation Analysis**
  - Identify Market Needs
  - Analyze Competition
  - Identify Markets, Segments, Size and Share
  - Identify Outside Influences
  - Analyze Distribution
  - Analyze Market Coverage
  - Analyze Product Pricing
  - Evaluate Marketing Communications
  - Analyze Positioning

- **Problems and Opportunities**
  - Determine Marketing Success Factors
  - Identify Key Problems and Opportunities

- **Segment Priority**
  - Determine Segment Priority
  - Establish Business Direction by Segment
  - Establish Objectives by Segment
  - List Assumptions and Restrictions

- **Strategies and Tactics**
  - Develop Strategy Options
  - Select Strategies
  - Develop Tactics
  - Schedule and Budget Tactics

- **Marketing Plan**
  - Estimate Sales and Costs
  - Prepare Trial P & L

- **Controls and Measurements**
  - Establish Controls and Measurements

SOURCE: Howard Sutton, *The Marketing Plan in the 1990s*, report no. 951 (New York: The Conference Board, 1990), p. 10. Reprinted by permission of The Conference Board.

programs. Ultimately, the marketing plan translates objectives and strategies into forecasts and budgets that provide a basis for planning by other functional areas of the firm.

Summary

Guided by a deep understanding of the needs of customers and the capabilities of competitors, market-driven organizations are committed to a set of processes, beliefs, and values that promote the achievement of superior performance by satisfying customers better than competitors do. What sets market-driven firms apart is their ability to continuously sense and act on events and trends in their markets. A business marketing firm gains a competitive advantage through its superior skills and resources. To isolate core competencies, benchmarking provides a valuable tool that goes beyond a mere analysis of competitors. Benchmarking involves identifying the best practices employed by organizations around the world, learning about them, and implementing them in the firm. Positions of advantage—providing the lowest delivered cost or superior customer value—can be secured by effectively managing and deploying the skills and resources of the organization.

Because many industrial firms have numerous divisions, product lines, and brands, three major levels of strategy exist in most large organizations: (1) corporate, (2) business level, and (3) functional. Moving down the strategy hierarchy, the focus shifts from strategy formulation to strategy implementation. Marketing is best viewed as the functional area that manages critical connections between the organization and customers. Firms that operate in high-technology industries must be alert to the rigors that may signal a strategic inflection point—a fundamental change in the basis of competition in the industry. To successfully cope with such change, top management must assess the firm's strategic goals and competencies in light of the new competitive reality. Companies that prosper in high-technology markets demonstrate an ability to transform themselves by adjusting strategic goals, building new competencies, and adapting strategies to the new industry conditions. Discontinuous innovation involves the creation of new forms of customer value within existing or new markets.

Business marketing planning must be coordinated and synchronized with corresponding planning efforts in other functional areas. Strategic plans emerge out of a bargaining process among functional areas. Managing conflict, promoting cooperation, and developing coordinated strategies are all fundamental to the business marketer's role in the firm. A continuous process, marketing planning involves several stages: (1) situation analysis, (2) evaluation of problems and opportunities, (3) formulation of marketing strategy, (4) development of an integrated marketing plan, and (5) measurement and evaluation of results. The result of the planning process is the marketing plan—the formal written description of the marketing strategy. The succeeding chapters will analyze each marketing mix variable.

Discussion Questions

1. Describe the major elements that characterize a market-driven organization and outline the steps a firm might follow in becoming more market driven.

2. Michael Porter proposes that the drivers of positional advantage are those particular skills and resources that have the greatest impact on reducing costs or creating value to customers. Explain.

3. Select a firm such as Federal Express, Apple Computer, IBM, Boeing, G.E., or Caterpillar and assess its competitive advantage. Develop a list of particular skills and resources that are especially important to the selected firm's position of advantage. Give particular attention to those skills and resources that competitors would have the most difficulty in matching.

4. Critique this statement: Positions of advantage tend to erode quickly in high-tech markets. Next, trace the changing fortunes of Apple Computer, Inc. during the past decade.

5. Does the introduction of relatively inexpensive, easy-to-use information appliances by Sony and others signal a strategic inflection point for personal computer makers such as Compaq and key suppliers, like Intel? Explain.

6. Commenting on the decision-making process of his organization, a senior executive noted: "Sometimes the process is bloody, ugly, just like sausage meat being made. It's not pretty to watch but the end results are not too bad." Why do various functional interest groups often embrace conflicting positions during the strategic decision process? How are decisions ever made?

7. When Microsoft Office was introduced, the company created a single product that addressed the spectrum of customer needs—word processing, database management, spreadsheet calculations, and presentations. Which type of discontinuous innovation does this represent?

8. Xerox shifted its goal from being a manufacturer of copier, printer, and facsimile products to becoming a provider of document tools and services that enhance a customer's productivity. Describe how this new strategic intent may call for new strategies and the development of new core competencies.

9. When first tested through market research, the first videocassette recorder, the fax machine, and Federal Express all received negative evaluations from consumers. What role should market research assume when discontinuous innovations are being tested?

10. A day in the life of a business marketing manager will involve interactions with managers from other functions in the firm. First, identify the role that the R&D, manufacturing, and logistics functions assume in the creation and implementation of marketing strategy. Next, describe some of the common sources of conflict that can emerge in cross-functional relationships.

10

Business Marketing Strategies for Global Markets

Business marketing firms that restrict their attention to the domestic market are overlooking enormous international market opportunities and a challenging field of competitors. After reading this chapter, you will understand

1. the forces that drive the globalization of a particular industry.

2. the spectrum of international market-entry options and the strategic significance of different forms of global market participation.

3. the distinctive types of international strategy.

4. the key strategic marketing issues that emerge as a firm's level of participation in international markets expands.

FIGURE 10.1   ERICSSON: A GLOBAL COMPETITOR IN TELECOMMUNICATIONS

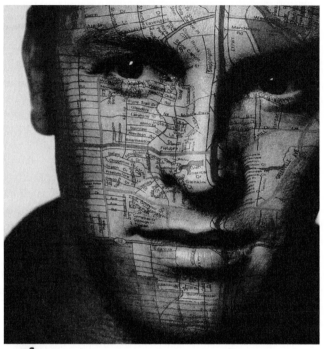

 You are everywhere. Now there's a phone that works everywhere too. The 788 is Ericsson's smallest Go-Everywhere™ tri-mode phone. Which means you get unsurpassed coverage in all 50 states and a phone that fits in your shirt pocket. And as small as the 788 is, it has the ability to store up to 200 numbers, plus voice mail, paging and the ability to vibrate when you get a call. So you can be reached discreetly and still **make yourself heard.**

For more information, visit www.ericsson.com/us/phones. 788 refers to KF 788 and LX 788 models only. ©1999 Ericsson and the Ericsson logo are registered trademarks. Map © by Rand McNally R.L. #99-5-59

  ERICSSON ⧫

SOURCE: Courtesy of Ericsson, Inc.

Motorola is helping the People's Republic of China leapfrog one stage of industrial evolution for which Western nations have invested billions of dollars—the need to tie every home and business together with copper wire. Motorola's pagers and cell phones provide valuable solutions to customers in an unwired world and the firm's sales in China and Hong Kong exceed $3 billion annually. Going forward, the market potential is huge, but the competition will be fierce from rivals such as Sweden's Ericsson and Finland's Nokia.[1] (See Figure 10.1.)

Many large business marketing firms—such as General Electric (G.E.), IBM, Intel, Dow Chemical, Alcoa, Texas Instruments, Boeing, Caterpillar, and Motorola— derive a significant portion of their sales and profits from international markets. These firms also have extensive operating facilities dispersed around the world. For example, in China alone, Motorola employs more than 12,000 people. Likewise, countless small

---

[1] Melanie Warner, "Motorola Bets Big on China," *Fortune,* 27 (May 1996), pp. 116–124; and Erik Guyot, "Foreign Companies Bring China More than Jobs: Motorola's Deal Introduced a Firm to Quality Control," *The Wall Street Journal,* September 15, 1999, p. A26.

firms with less familiar names enjoy strong ties with international customers. In addition to extending a firm's base of operations and thereby enhancing sales and profits, participation in global markets can provide an important pathway to a competitive advantage. Meeting the needs of diverse international customers may speed learning in the firm and spawn improvements in product features and quality.

The discussion in this chapter is divided into three parts. First, attention centers on the factors that are reshaping the way managers think about markets and competitors: the drivers of globalization in an industry. Second, international market-entry options are isolated and described, and, finally, linked to the central strategy questions that must be addressed by firms as their international operations evolve.

Drivers of Globalization

Several forces are driving companies around the world to globalize by expanding their participation in foreign markets. Trade barriers are falling and nearly every product market—computers, fast food, electronic components, nuts and bolts—includes foreign competitors. Maturity in domestic markets is also driving firms to seek global expansion. For example, U.S. companies, nourished by the large home market, have typically lagged behind their European and Japanese rivals in internationalization. Many of these firms are now finding that strong foreign demand can propel future growth.

Business marketers who wish to pursue international market opportunities must first assess the extent of globalization in their particular industry. Some industries are global in character (for example, computers and automobiles), others are moving in this direction (for example, food), while still others remain resolutely national in character (for example, cement). An industry's potential for globalization is driven by market, economic, environmental, and competitive factors (see Figure 10.2).[2] Market factors determine the customers' receptivity to and acceptance of a global product; economic forces determine whether pursuing a global strategy can provide significant cost advantages; environmental forces address the question of whether the necessary supporting infrastructure is in place; and competitive factors can require firms to match the moves of competing firms in other countries.

Market Factors

Singled out most frequently as a major force driving the globalization of markets is the assertion that customer needs are becoming increasingly homogeneous worldwide.[3] When customers in different countries around the world want essentially the same type of product or service, the opportunity exists to market a global product or brand. Whereas global segments with similar interests and response tendencies may be identified in some product markets, considerable debate surrounds the issue of whether this is a universal trend.[4] Some research suggests, however, that compared to

[2] The discussion of these factors draws on George S. Yip, *Total Global Strategy: Managing for Worldwide Competitive Advantage* (Englewood Cliffs, N.J.: Prentice-Hall, 1992), chaps. 1 and 2. See also Yip, "Global Strategy in a World of Nations," *Sloan Management Review* 31 (fall 1989): pp. 29–41; and Christopher H. Lovelock and George S. Yip, "Developing Global Strategies for Services Businesses," *California Management Review* 38 (winter 1996): pp. 64–86.

[3] Theodore Levitt, "The Globalization of Markets," *Harvard Business Review* 61 (May/June 1983): pp. 92–102.

[4] See, for example, Susan P. Douglas and Yoram Wind, "The Myth of Globalization," *Columbia Journal of World Business* 22 (winter 1987): pp. 19–29.

FIGURE 10.2   EXTERNAL DRIVERS OF INDUSTRY POTENTIAL FOR GLOBALIZATION

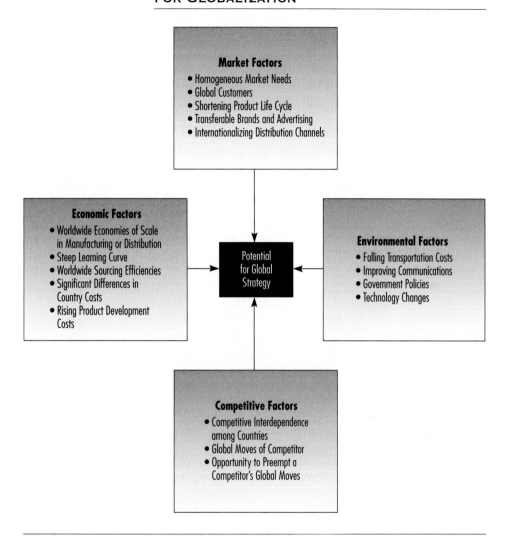

SOURCE: George S. Yip, Pierre M. Loewe, and Michael Y. Yoshino, "How to Take Your Company to the Global Market," *Columbia Journal of World Business* 23 (winter 1988): p. 40. Reprinted with permission.

consumer goods, industrial and high-technology products (for example, computers and machine tools) may be more appropriate for global brand strategies.[5]

In the business-to-business market, firms with multinational operations are particularly likely to have common needs and requirements worldwide. Such global customers search the world for suppliers, but use the purchased product or service in many countries. Citigroup expects many of its suppliers to provide uniform products to its banks and regional offices around the world. The presence of global customers both allows and demands a uniform marketing program—common brand name and

---

[5] Subhash C. Jain, "Standardization of International Marketing Strategy: Some Research Hypotheses," *Journal of Marketing* 53 (January 1989): pp. 70–79.

FIGURE 10.3 GENERAL MOTORS' TAIWAN E-COMMERCE SITE

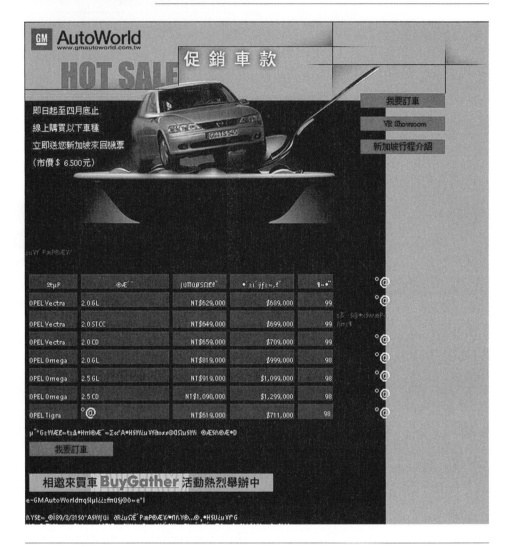

SOURCE: Courtesy of General Motors Corporation.

corporate image—worldwide. Similarly, some channels of distribution may buy on a global or at least on a regional basis, thereby increasing the viability and importance of standardized marketing programs.

By providing a vast spectrum of information, the Internet empowers people around the world, enhancing their ability to learn, communicate, and, of course, shop. For example, General Motors Corporation receives about 150,000 visitors a month at its Taiwan e-commerce site (see Figure 10.3). GM plans to generate 30 percent of its sales in Taiwan through the Internet and change its manufacturing system there to let consumers configure, order, and buy cars online.[6]

---

[6] Fara Warner, "GM Tests E-Commerce Plan in Emerging Markets: In Taiwan, the Auto Maker Prepares to Sell Made-to-Order Cars Online," *The Wall Street Journal*, October 25, 1999, p. B6.

Economic Factors

A single-country market may not be large enough for a firm to realize economies of scale or to warrant the necessary investments in R&D and production equipment. If product standardization is feasible, scale at a given location can be increased by participating in a number of national markets. Similarly, expanded market participation can accelerate the accumulation of learning and experience. Even the largest national markets may be too small to amortize the enormous costs involved in developing a new generation of computers. By developing global or regional products rather than national ones, product development costs can be reduced.

Cost advantages can also be secured by seeking suppliers for components and materials on a worldwide basis. Firms such as Xerox, Ford, and Whirlpool have reduced costs by coordinating the purchase of raw materials across their global manufacturing plants.[7] Finally, global firms can exploit differences in the factor costs and skills across countries. To illustrate, hourly labor costs are twice as high in West Germany as in Spain. A firm might increase productivity or reduce costs by concentrating activities in low-cost countries. Of course, the benefits must be weighed against the dangers of training foreign competitors.

Environmental Factors

Host governments affect globalization potential through trade policies, restrictions, and incentives. The liberalization of trade policies can provide a supportive environment for expanded market participation. The harmonization of trade policies in the European Community (EC); the North American Free Trade Agreement involving the United States, Canada, and Mexico; and the formation of a trading zone in the Pacific Rim are all favorable signs. Christopher Lovelock and George Yip suggest that "with the rise of non-Japan Asia, Latin America, and Eastern Europe, operating in just the 'Triad' of North America, Western Europe, and Japan is no longer sufficient" for a truly global company.[8]

Improvements in telecommunications and in logistical systems have markedly increased a firm's capacity to manage operations on a global scale. The rapid adoption of mobile phones, the Internet, and fax machines, as well as international computer networks, facilitates highly coordinated global strategies. Likewise, more responsive transportation systems, coupled with computerized inventory systems, reduce the time and cost required to move goods to distant markets. For example, the harmonization of trade policies in the European Community speeds the flow of goods across the borders of members, thereby lowering logistics costs.

Protecting the Environment Through increased regulation and legal action, governments around the world have taken a tough stand against firms that follow environmentally irresponsible practices. In turn, consumers are increasingly demanding environmentally friendly products. Leading global companies understand that environmental soundness provides a form of value to customers and other important

[7] Timothy M. Laseter, *Balanced Sourcing: Cooperation and Competition in Supplier Relationships* (San Francisco: Jossey-Bass Publishers, 1998), pp. 1–18.

[8] Lovelock and Yip, "Developing Global Strategies," p. 65.

INSIDE BUSINESS MARKETING

Innovative Solutions for the Environment

Leading strategists suggest that companies that adopt innovative approaches to meet rising environmental standards around the world can gain a competitive edge in the global marketplace.

- Cummins Engine Company developed a low-emission diesel engine for trucks and buses—an innovation that U.S. environmental regulations spurred—and gained a strong position in international markets where similar needs are growing.

- To comply with new regulations to reduce solvent emissions, 3M discovered a way to avoid the use of solvents altogether by coating products with safer, water-based solutions. The company gained an important early-mover advantage over its competitors.

- In response to Japanese law that set standards to make products easier to recycle, Hitachi redesigned its appliances to reduce disassembly time. In the process, the number of parts in a washing machine was reduced by 16 percent and the number of parts in a vacuum cleaner was reduced by 30 percent. Fewer parts make the products not only easier to disassemble, but also to produce in the first place.

SOURCE: Michael E. Porter and Claas van der Linde, "Green and Competitive: Ending the Stalemate, " *Harvard Business Review* 73 (September/October 1995): pp. 120–134 and Forest L. Reinhardt, "Environmental Product Differentiation," *California Management Review*, 40 (summer 1998), pp. 43–73.

---

stakeholders. To succeed, however, a strategy of environmental product differentiation must satisfy three requirements:[9]

- the firm must find, or create, a willingness among customers to pay for environmental quality;

- the business must establish credible information about the environmental benefits of its products; and

- the innovation must be difficult for competitors to imitate.

Competitive Factors

Competitors can raise the globalization potential of their industry by creating competitive interdependence among countries. George Yip contends that this is achieved through the sharing of activities:

> When activities such as production are shared among countries, a competitor's market share in one country affects its scale and overall cost position in the shared activities. Changes in that scale and cost will affect its competitive position in all countries dependent on the shared activities.[10]

A global orientation can prompt firms to make moves to match or preempt individual competitors. As Ford has become more cost efficient by concentrating production

---

[9] Forest L. Reinhardt, "Environmental Product Differentiation," *California Management Review*, 40 (summer 1998), pp. 43–73.

[10] Yip, "Global Strategy in a World of Nations," p. 38.

FIGURE 10.4	SPECTRUM OF INVOLVEMENT IN INTERNATIONAL MARKETING				
Low Commitment					**High Commitment**
Exporting	Contracting	Strategic Alliance	Joint Venture	Multidomestic Strategy	Global Strategy
Low Complexity					**High Complexity**

and by sharing activities, Japanese manufacturers are pressured to enter more markets so that increased production volume will cover costs. Moreover, as Motorola's communication business was threatened in the United States by Japanese competitors, the firm sought to defend its home market while launching a sustained effort to secure markets in Japan. While preserving its market leadership at home, Motorola has also logged some successes in Japan. For example, the Japanese government selected a Motorola design for a cellular telephone component as a national standard.

International Market-Entry Options [11]

A first step in developing effective international marketing strategy centers on understanding the alternative ways that a firm can participate in international markets. The particular mode of entry selected should take into consideration the level of a firm's experience overseas and the stage in the evolution of its international involvement. Figure 10.4 illustrates a spectrum of options for participating in international markets. They range from low-commitment choices, such as exporting, to highly complex levels of participation, such as global strategies. Each is examined in this section.

Exporting

An industrial firm's first encounter with an overseas market usually involves exporting because it requires the least commitment and risk. Goods are produced at one or two home plants and sales are made through distributors or importing agencies in each country. Exporting is a viable entry strategy when the firm lacks the resources to make a significant commitment to the market, wants to minimize political and economic risk, or is unfamiliar with the market requirements and cultural norms of the country.

While preserving flexibility and reducing risk, exporting also limits the future prospects for growth in the country. First, exporting involves giving up direct control of the marketing program, which makes it difficult to coordinate activities, implement strategies, and resolve conflicts with customers and channel members. George Day explains why customers may sense a lack of commitment on the part of the exporter:

> In many international markets customers are loath to form long-run relationships with a company through its agents because they are unsure

---

[11] The following discussion is based on Franklin R. Root, *Entry Strategy for International Markets* (Lexington, Mass.: D. C. Heath, 1987); and Michael R. Czinkota and Ilka A. Ronkainen, *International Marketing*, 2d ed. (Hinsdale, Ill.: The Dryden Press, 1990).

whether the business will continue to service the market, or will withdraw at the first sign of adversity. This problem has bedeviled U.S. firms in many countries, and only now are they living down a reputation for opportunistically participating in many countries and then withdrawing abruptly to protect short-run profits.[12]

Contracting

A somewhat more involved and complex form of international market entry is contracting. Included among contractual entry modes are (1) licensing, (2) franchising, and (3) management contracts.

Licensing   Under a **licensing** agreement, one firm permits another to use its intellectual property in exchange for royalties or some other form of payment. The property might include trademarks, patents, technology, know-how, or company name. In short, licensing involves exporting intangible assets.

As an entry strategy, licensing requires neither capital investment nor marketing strength in foreign markets. This provides a means for a firm to test foreign markets without a major commitment of management time or capital. Because the licensee is typically a local company that can serve as a buffer against government action, licensing also reduces the risk of exposure to government action. With increasing host country regulation, licensing may enable the business marketer to enter a foreign market that is closed to either imports or direct foreign investment.

Licensing agreements do pose some limitations. First, some companies are hesitant to enter license agreements because the licensee may become an important competitor in the future. Second, licensing agreements typically include a time limit. Although terms may be extended once after the initial agreement, additional extensions are not readily permitted by a number of foreign governments. Third, a firm has less control over a licensee than over its own exporting or manufacturing abroad.

Franchising   **Franchising** is a form of licensing in which a parent company (the franchisor) grants another independent entity (the franchisee) the right to conduct business in a specified manner. This right can include selling the franchiser's product or using its name, production, and marketing methods, or a general business approach. Franchising has provided an attractive means for U.S. firms, especially service organizations, to penetrate foreign markets at a low cost and to leverage their skills with local knowledge and entrepreneurial spirit. Foreign government intervention represents a major problem for franchise systems in the international arena. For example, government restrictions on franchising and royalties hindered ComputerLand's Manila store from offering a complete range of services, leading to an eventual split between the company and its franchisee.

Despite such problems, franchising provides a viable foreign market entry alternative for business marketing firms—large and small. To illustrate, Automation Papers Company, a New Jersey-based supplier of high-technology paper products, used franchising to gain exclusive representation by a highly motivated sales force in selected foreign markets. The franchisees receive rights to the firm's trademarks, extensive

---

[12] George S. Day, *Market Driven Strategy: Processes for Creating Value* (New York: The Free Press, 1990), p. 272.

training for local employees, and the benefit of Automation Papers' experience, credit lines, and advertising program.[13]

Other contractual modes of entry have grown in prominence in recent years. **Contract manufacturing** involves sourcing a product from a producer located in a foreign country for sale there or in other countries. Here assistance might be required to ensure that the product meets the desired quality standards. Contract manufacturing is most appropriate when the local market lacks sufficient potential to justify a direct investment, export entry is blocked, and a quality licensee is not available.

Management Contracts To expand their overseas operations, many firms have turned to **management contracts.** In a management contract the industrial firm assembles a package of skills that will provide an integrated service to the client. When equity participation, either in the form of full ownership or a joint venture, is not feasible or is not permitted by a foreign government, a management contract provides a means for participating in a venture. Management contracts have been employed effectively in the service sector in areas such as computer services, hotel management, and food services. Michael Czinkota and Ilka Ronkainen point out that management contracts can "provide organizational skills not available locally, expertise that is immediately available rather than built up, and management assistance in the form of support services that would be difficult and costly to replicate locally."[14]

One specialized form of a management contract is a turnkey operation. This arrangement permits a client to acquire a complete operational system, together with the skills sufficient to allow the unassisted maintenance and operation of the system. Once the package agreement is on line, the system is owned, controlled, and operated by the client. Management contracts provide a means for firms to commercialize their superior skills (know-how) by participating in the international market.

Strategic Alliances

Strategic alliances (treated in Chapter 4) are assuming an increasingly prominent role in the global strategy of many business marketing firms. Frederick Webster Jr. defines strategic alliances as "collaborations among partners involving the commitment of capital and management resources with the objective of enhancing the partners' competitive positions."[15] Strategic alliances offer a number of benefits, such as access to markets or to technology, economies of scale in manufacturing and marketing activities, and the sharing of risk among partners.

Although offering potential, global strategic alliances pose a special management challenge. Among the stumbling blocks that have been isolated are these:[16]

- Partners are organized quite differently for making marketing and product design decisions, creating *problems in coordination and trust.*

---

[13] Czinkota and Ronkainen, *International Marketing*, pp. 392–396. See also Gianni Lorenzoni and Charles Baden-Fuller, "Creating a Strategic Center to Manage a Web of Partners," *California Management Review* 37 (spring 1995): pp. 146–163.

[14] Czinkota and Ronkainen, *International Marketing*, p. 493.

[15] Frederick E. Webster Jr., "The Changing Role of Marketing in the Corporation," *Journal of Marketing* 56 (October 1992): p. 8.

[16] Thomas J. Kosnik, "Stumbling Blocks to Global Strategic Alliances," *Systems Integration Age*, October 1988, pp. 31–39. See also Eric Rule and Shawn Keon, "Competencies of High-Performing Strategic Alliances," *Strategy & Leadership*, 27 (September–October 1998), pp. 36–37.

- Partners that combine the best set of skills in one country may be poorly equipped to support each other in other countries, leading to *problems in implementing alliances on a global scale.*

- The quick pace of technological change often guarantees that the most attractive partner today may not be the most attractive partner tomorrow, leading to *problems in maintaining alliances over time.*

Firms that are adept at managing global alliances choose partners carefully. Observe in Figure 10.5 that potential partners can be evaluated on the basis of their strengths and/or fit across five areas: resources, relationships, reputation, capabilities, and chemistry/culture. This provides a framework for assessing the strengths and weaknesses of a proposed partnership in different-country markets. Once established, effective relationship management skills are needed to coordinate activities, control conflict, and keep alliance strategy centered on the ever-changing customer in the global marketplace.

Joint Ventures

In pursuing international-entry options, a corporation confronts a wide variety of ownership choices, ranging from 100 percent ownership to a minority interest. Frequently, full ownership may be a desirable, but not essential, prerequisite for success in the international market arena. Thus a joint venture becomes a feasible option. The **joint venture** involves a joint-ownership arrangement (between, for example, a U.S. firm and one in the host country) to produce and/or market goods in a foreign market. In contrast to a strategic alliance, a joint venture involves the creation of a new firm. Some joint ventures are structured so that each partner holds an equal share; in others, one partner has a majority stake. The contributions that the partners bring to the joint venture can also vary widely and may include financial resources, technology, sales organizations, know-how, or plant and equipment. Representing a successful relationship is the fifty–fifty joint venture between Xerox Corporation and Tokyo-based Fuji Photo Film Company. Through the joint venture, Xerox gained a presence in the Japanese market, learned valuable quality management skills that improved its products, and developed a keen understanding of important Japanese rivals such as Canon, Inc. and Ricoh Company. This joint venture has thrived for over three decades.[17]

Advantages   Joint ventures offer a number of advantages. First, joint ventures provide the only path of entry into many foreign markets. In most developing countries and even in some developed countries, the governments require firms to either form or accept joint ventures in order to participate in the local market. Second, joint ventures may open up market opportunities that neither partner to the venture could pursue alone. Kenichi Ohmae explains the logic:

> If you run a pharmaceutical company with a good drug to distribute in Japan but have no sales force to do it, find someone in Japan who also has a good product but no sales force in your country. You get double the profit

---

[17]David P. Hamilton, "United It Stands—Fuji Xerox Is a Rarity in World Business: A Joint Venture That Works," *The Wall Street Journal*, 26 September 1996, p. R19.

FIGURE 10.5 WHAT DOES EACH PARTNER BRING TO THE PARTY? A FRAMEWORK FOR EVALUATING STRATEGIC ALLIANCES

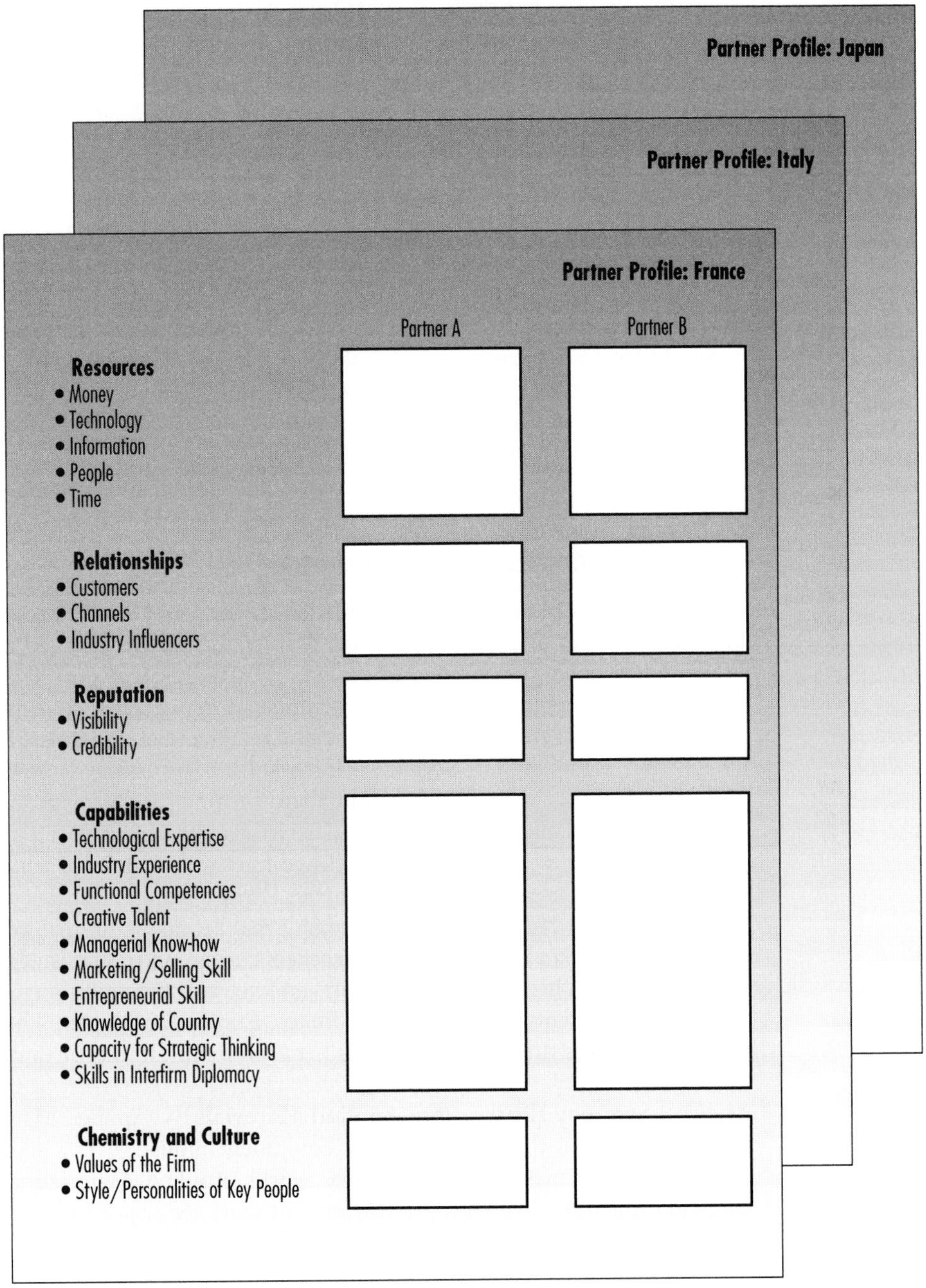

Partner Profile: Japan

Partner Profile: Italy

Partner Profile: France

Partner A   Partner B

Resources
- Money
- Technology
- Information
- People
- Time

Relationships
- Customers
- Channels
- Industry Influencers

Reputation
- Visibility
- Credibility

Capabilities
- Technological Expertise
- Industry Experience
- Functional Competencies
- Creative Talent
- Managerial Know-how
- Marketing/Selling Skill
- Entrepreneurial Skill
- Knowledge of Country
- Capacity for Strategic Thinking
- Skills in Interfirm Diplomacy

Chemistry and Culture
- Values of the Firm
- Style/Personalities of Key People

SOURCE: Rowland T. Moriarty and Thomas J. Kosnik, "High-Tech Marketing Concepts, Continuity, and Change," *Sloan Management Review* 31 (summer 1989): p. 15 by permission of the publisher. Copyright 1989 by the Sloan Management Review Association. All rights reserved.

by putting two strong drugs through your fixed cost sales network, and so does your new ally. Why duplicate such high expenses all down the line? . . . Why not join forces to maximize contribution to each other's fixed costs?[18]

Third, joint ventures may provide for better relationships with local organizations (for example, local authorities) and with customers. By being attuned to the local culture and environment of the host country, the local partner may enable the joint venture to respond to changing market needs and to be more aware of cultural sensitivities.

The Downside Problems can arise in maintaining joint venture relationships. A study suggests that perhaps over 50 percent of joint ventures are disbanded or fall short of expectations.[19] The reasons involve problems with the disclosure of sensitive information, disagreements over how profits are to be shared, clashes over management style, and differing perceptions on the course that strategy should follow. Some experts point to another risk that must be evaluated in considering venture partners. What would happen in the event of a breakup? Michael R. Czinkota and Jon Woronoff warn that companies "must decide whether they really do want to tie up with a knowledgeable partner that could become a troublesome rival at a later date, or whether they would not prefer one that is just a distributor or maybe a manufacturer in a different sector."[20]

Multidomestic versus Global Strategies

The most complex forms of participation in the global arena are multidomestic and global strategies. Multinational firms have traditionally managed operations outside their home country with **multidomestic strategies** that permit individual subsidiaries to compete independently in different-country markets. The multinational headquarters coordinates marketing policies and financial controls and may centralize R&D and some support activities. Each subsidiary, however, resembles a strategic business unit that is expected to contribute earnings and growth to the organization. The firm can manage its international activities like a portfolio.

In contrast, a global strategy seeks competitive advantage with strategic choices that are highly integrated across countries.[21] For example, features of a global strategy might include a standardized core product that requires minimal local adaptation and that is targeted on foreign-country markets chosen on the basis of their contribution to globalization benefits. Major volume and market share advantages might be sought by directing attention to the United States, Europe, and Japan. The value chain concept illuminates the chief differences between a multidomestic and a global strategy.

Global Strategy Illustration: Applied Materials[22] Applied Materials is the global market leader in the semiconductor equipment industry. As a supplier to Intel and semiconductor producers around the world, Applied Materials aptly describes its mission this way: *"We make the systems, that make the chips, that make the products, that*

---

[18] Kenichi Ohmae, "The Global Logic of Strategic Alliances," *Harvard Business Review* 67 (March/April 1989): p. 147.

[19] Arvind Parkhe, "Building Trust in International Alliances," *Journal of World Business*, 33 (winter 1998), pp. 417–437.

[20] Michael R. Czinkota and Jon Woronoff, *Unlocking Japan's Markets: Seizing Marketing and Distribution Opportunities in Today's Japan* (Chicago: Probus, 1991), p. 157.

[21] Yip, "Global Strategy in a World of Nations," pp. 33–35.

[22] *Applied Materials Annual Report, 1998*, pp. 14–19.

Bribery and Differing Business Practices

International marketing managers often face a dilemma when home country regulations clash with foreign business practices. To illustrate, the Foreign Corrupt Practices Act makes it a crime for U.S. firms to bribe a foreign official for business purposes. A number of U.S. firms have complained about the law, arguing that it hinders their efforts to compete in the international market against those competitors who operate under no such anti-bribery laws. Likewise, many managers argue that the United States should not apply its moral principles to other cultures in which bribery and corruption are common. In their view, firms should be free to use the most common methods of competition in the host country. Others counter, however, that if bribes are permitted, a host of unethical business practices will follow.

Jack Welch, General Electric's CEO, insists that G.E.'s policy prohibiting bribes doesn't make it less competitive:

In a global business, you can win without bribes. But you better have technology. That's why we win in businesses like turbines, because we have the best gas turbine. You've got to be the low-priced supplier, but in almost all cases, if you have quality, price, technology, you win—and nobody can sleazeball you.

Instead of offering a long list of rules, or debating the fine points of ethical issues, Welch uses one simple question to address the conscience of every individual G.E. employee directly: "Can you look in the mirror every day and feel proud of what you are doing?"

SOURCE: Michael R. Czinkota and Ilka A. Ronkainen, *International Marketing*, 2d ed. (Hinsdale, Ill.: The Dryden Press, 1990), pp. 112–121; and Noel M. Tichy and Stratford Sherman, *Control Your Destiny or Someone Else Will* (New York: Doubleday, 1993), pp. 111–114.

change the world." Soon after its founding in 1967, the company began selling its systems to emerging chip producers in Japan as well as to its customers in Europe and the United States. Applied Materials was the first semiconductor equipment manufacturer to establish a wholly owned Japanese subsidiary and subsequently added a major technology center there to serve the burgeoning Japanese semiconductor industry.

Regional Technology Centers As the global semiconductor industry continued to expand, Applied Materials added large-scale technology centers strategically located close to its customers. Along with the center in Japan and the main technology development center at its headquarters in Santa Clara, centers have been established in Korea, Taiwan, England, Israel, and Austin, Texas (see Figure 10.6). These centers are equipped with demonstration systems that customers can use in matching Applied Materials' products to particular production requirements. Customers also benefit by having trained technical personnel located near their own facilities (i.e., fabrication plants).

Regional Account Management Organization A regional account management organization was established to serve as the customer's voice, to assess customer needs, and to insure that those needs are satisfied. Comprised of members who are technically knowledgeable and well-versed in local culture and government regulation, each team has overall responsibility for satisfying customers' requirements throughout the world. Applied Materials' global infrastructure and regional account management organization have enabled the firm to sustain and nurture long-established relationships with many of the world's leading semiconductor manufacturers. International customers account for nearly two-thirds of the firm's sales.

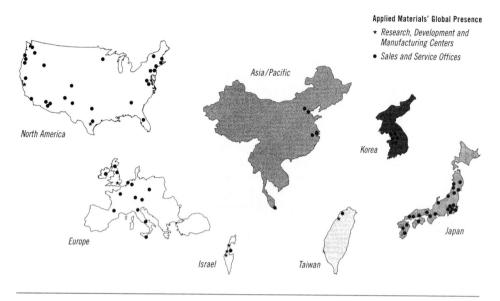

FIGURE 10.6   APPLIED MATERIALS:
THE INFRASTRUCTURE OF A GLOBAL STRATEGY

SOURCE: Courtesy of Applied Materials,Inc.

International Strategy and the Value Chain [23]

To diagnose the sources of competitive advantage, domestic or international, Michael Porter divides the activities performed by a firm into distinct groups. The value chain, displayed in Figure 10.7, provides a framework for categorizing these activities. Primary activities are those involved in the physical creation of the product, the marketing and logistical program, and the service after the sale. Support activities provide the infrastructure and inputs that allow the primary activities to occur. Every activity employs purchased inputs, human resources, and a combination of technologies. Likewise, the firm's infrastructure, including such functions as general management, supports the entire value chain. Porter asserts that "A firm may possess two types of competitive advantage: low relative cost or differentiation—its ability to perform the activities in its value chain either at a lower cost or in a unique way relative to its competitors." [24] A firm that competes in the international market must decide how to spread the activities among countries. Central to this decision is the need to distinguish upstream from downstream activities (see Figure 10.7).

Downstream activities involve those primary activities that are closely tied to the location of the buyer. For example, a business marketer wishing to serve the Japanese market must ensure that a local service network is in place. By contrast, upstream activities (for example, manufacturing and operations) and support activities (for example, procurement) are not tied directly to the buyer's location. Caterpillar, for example, uses

---

[23] Michael E. Porter, "Changing Patterns of International Competition," *California Management Review* 28 (winter 1986): pp. 9–40; see also Porter, *Competitive Advantage: Creating and Sustaining Superior Performance* (New York: The Free Press, 1985).

[24] Porter, "Changing Patterns," p. 13.

FIGURE 10.7   THE VALUE CHAIN: UPSTREAM AND DOWNSTREAM ACTIVITIES

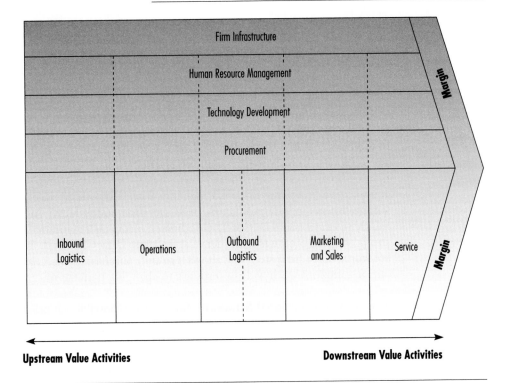

Upstream Value Activities   **Downstream Value Activities**

SOURCE: Reprinted from Michael E. Porter, "Changing Patterns of International Competition," *California Management Review* 28 (winter 1986): p. 16. Copyright 1986 by the Regents of the University of California, reprinted by permission of the Regents.

a few large-scale manufacturing facilities to produce components to meet worldwide demands.

This assessment provides a foundation for valuable strategic insights. Competitive advantage created by downstream activities is largely country-specific: A firm's reputation, brand name, and service network grow out of the firm's activities in a particular country. Competitive advantage in upstream and support activities stems more from the entire network of countries in which a firm competes than from its position in any one country.

Source of Advantage: Multidomestic versus Global   When downstream activities (those tied directly to the buyer) are important to competitive advantage, a multidomestic pattern of international competition is common. In **multidomestic industries,** firms pursue separate strategies in each of their foreign markets—competition in each country is essentially independent of competition in other countries (for example, Alcoa in the aluminum industry, Honeywell in the controls industry).

Global competition is more common in industries in which upstream and support activities (such as technology development and operations) are vital to competitive advantage. A **global industry** is one in which a firm's competitive position in one country is significantly influenced by its position in other countries (for example, Motorola in the semiconductor industry, Boeing in the commercial aircraft industry).

Coordination and Configuration   Further insights into international strategy can be gained by examining two dimensions of competition in the global market: configuration and coordination. **Configuration** centers on where each activity is performed, including the number of locations. Options range from concentrated (for example, one production plant serving the world) to dispersed (for example, a plant in each country—each with a complete value chain).

Coordination refers to how similar activities performed in various countries are coordinated or coupled with each other. If, for example, a firm has three plants—one in the United States, one in England, and one in Japan—how do the activities in these plants relate to one another? Numerous coordination options exist because of the many possible levels of coordination and the many ways an activity can be performed. For example, a firm operating three plants could, at one extreme, allow each plant to operate autonomously (unique production processes, unique products). At the other extreme, the three plants could be closely coordinated, utilizing a common information system and producing products with identical features. Dow Chemical, for example, uses an enterprise software system that allows it to shift purchasing, manufacturing, and distribution functions worldwide in response to changing patterns of supply and demand.[25]

Types of International Strategy   Some of the possible variations in international strategy are portrayed in Figure 10.8. Observe that the purest global strategy concentrates as many activities as possible in one country, serves the world market from this home base, and closely coordinates those activities that must be performed near the buyer (for example, service). Caterpillar, for example, views its battle with the formidable Japanese competitor, Komatsu, in global terms. As well as employing automated manufacturing systems that allow it to fully exploit the economies of scale from its worldwide sales volume, Caterpillar also carefully coordinates activities in its global dealer network. This integrated global strategy gives Caterpillar a competitive advantage in cost and effectiveness.[26] By serving the world market from its home base in Seattle, Washington, and by closely coordinating sales and service activities with customers around the world, Boeing also aptly illustrates a pure global strategy. Airbus Industrie—the European aerospace consortium—is a strong and clever rival that competes aggressively with Boeing for orders at airlines around the world.[27]

Figure 10.8 can be used to illustrate other international strategy patterns. Canon, for example, concentrates manufacturing and support activities in Japan but gives local marketing subsidiaries significant latitude in each region of the world. Thus, Canon pursues an export-based strategy. In contrast, Xerox concentrates some activities and disperses others. Coordination, however, is extremely high: The Xerox brand, marketing approach, and servicing strategy are standardized worldwide.

Michael Porter notes that

International strategy has often been characterized as a choice between worldwide standardization and local tailoring, or as the tension between the

---

[25] Thomas H. Davenport, "Putting the Enterprise into the Enterprise System," *Harvard Business Review*, 76 (July–August 1998), pp. 121–131.

[26] Donald V. Fites, "Make Your Dealers Your Partners," *Harvard Business Review* 74 (March/April 1996): pp. 84–95.

[27] Alex Taylor III, "Blue Skies for Airbus," *Fortune* 140 (August 2, 1999): pp. 102–108.

| FIGURE 10.8 | TYPES OF INTERNATIONAL STRATEGY |

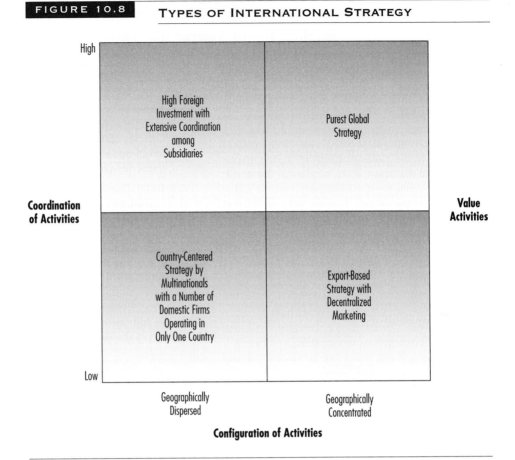

SOURCE: Reprinted from Michael E. Porter, "Changing Patterns of International Competition," *California Management Review* 28 (winter 1986): p. 19. Copyright 1986 by the Regents of the University of California, reprinted by permission of the Regents.

economic imperative (large-scale efficient facilities) and the political imperative (local content, local production) . . . A firm's choice of international strategy involves a search for competitive advantage from configuration/coordination throughout the value chain.[28]

Evolution of International Marketing Strategy[29]

International marketing strategy should be formulated in light of the firm's current position overseas and geared to its vision of growth and future position in worldwide markets. To this point, the chapter has laid a foundation for understanding the forces

---

[28]Porter, "Changing Patterns," p. 25.

[29]This section draws on Susan P. Douglas and C. Samuel Craig, "Evolution of Global Marketing Strategy: Scale, Scope, and Synergy," *Columbia Journal of World Business* 24 (fall 1989): pp. 47–59; and Craig and Douglas, "Developing Strategies for Global Markets: An Evolutionary Perspective," *Columbia Journal of World Business* 31 (spring 1996): pp. 70–81.

INSIDE BUSINESS MARKETING

Iridium: A Global Satellite Phone System that Didn't Fly

Iridium LLC is a company that sought to revolutionize telecommunications by allowing phone calls anytime and from anywhere. Backed by Motorola as the largest investor and a consortium of international backers that included arms of the Chinese and Russian governments, Iridium features a constellation of sixty-six low-orbit satellites that circle the globe enabling, in theory, phone calls from the most remote locations in the world. However, nine months after a high-profile introduction of the system, Iridium had only 20,000 customers—its $100 million international marketing campaign had fizzled. Here's why.

- The space phone is clunky (about one pound), erratic, and expensive—it originally cost $3,000—in a market where consumers are accustomed to pocket-sized handsets.

- The phone was accompanied by a bag of attachments whose functions were difficult for users to understand.

- The international partners, who had responsibility for marketing Iridium's phone and service in their individual countries, failed to build sales teams, create marketing plans, or set up distribution channels.

- Iridium's international ad campaign created more than a million sales inquiries but most global partners did not have a sales force in place to follow up with these interested prospects.

- Iridium's international structure has proved difficult to manage—"the 28 members of the board speak multiple languages, turning meetings into mini-United Nations conferences complete with headsets translating the proceedings into five languages."

Iridium LLC filed for bankruptcy protection; Motorola and the other international partners are restructuring the initiative.

SOURCE: Leslie Cauley, "Losses in Space: Iridium's Downfall: The Marketing Took a Back Seat to Science," *The Wall Street Journal*, August 18, 1999, p. A1.

that shape the competitive advantage of countries and that drive the globalization of markets. In turn, consideration has been given to the array of international market-entry options available to the business marketing firm. For the individual firm, strategy formulation in international markets is an evolutionary process in which the central direction of strategy and the key decisions vary at each successive phase of involvement in international operations.

Figure 10.9 traces the phases in global marketing evolution from the preliminary phase of pre-internationalization through (1) initial entry, (2) local or national market expansion, and (3) globalization. At each phase a number of triggers may prompt movement into a new phase, thereby stimulating a new strategic direction. Those triggers that prompt a company to reassess its current strategy may be external (for example, competitive pressures or industry trends) or internal (for example, management initiative).

Pre-internationalization

A strong domestic orientation may cause a firm to overlook changes that are occurring in target segments and market forces worldwide and to be vulnerable to aggressive foreign competitors. A variety of factors may prompt the domestically oriented firm to reexamine its position, triggering initial entry into international markets. For

| FIGURE 10.9 | PHASES IN GLOBAL MARKETING EVOLUTION |

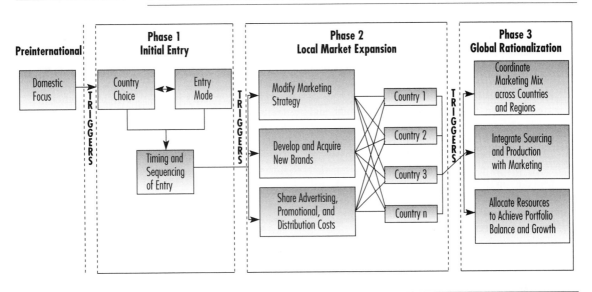

SOURCE: Susan P. Douglas and C. Samuel Craig, "Evolution of Global Marketing Strategy: Scale, Scope, and Synergy," *Columbia Journal of World Business* 24 (fall 1989): p. 50. Reprinted with permission.

example, the domestic market may have become saturated or the firm may wish to diversify risk across a range of countries and product markets.

Phase One: Initial International Market Entry

Given the industrial firm's lack of experience and knowledge in international markets, attention centers on identifying the most attractive market opportunities overseas for its existing (i.e., domestic) products and services. The guiding principle is to extend the geographic base of operations to those international markets that provide the closest match to the firm's current offerings and market conditions. By leveraging its domestic competitive position and core competency internationally, the firm seeks to extend economies of scale by establishing a presence in multiple markets. The key decisions in this phase of initial international market entry are (1) the choice of countries to enter, (2) the timing of entry, and (3) how operations are to be performed in these countries. In addition to selecting an entry strategy, the firm must develop mechanisms for *learning* about international markets and how to operate successfully in specific foreign-country markets.

Choice of Countries   Both risk and opportunities need to be evaluated in choosing which countries to enter. Here the political, financial, and legal risks of entry need to be weighed in relation to the stability and rate of economic growth of a country. Similarly, the size and growth of market potential must be gauged relative to the level of competition and costs of market entry. Difficult trade-offs are common (for example, high growth potential and high country risks or entry costs). Managers are often prone to choose countries where they have had prior contact or experience. To illustrate,

---

INSIDE BUSINESS MARKETING

Global Account Management at IBM

Large computer customers, like General Electric, are demanding more consistent service and support on a worldwide basis. These customers seek suppliers who will provide compatible equipment across international locations, deal with them in a coordinated fashion, and offer consistent and seamless service across countries. To meet the special needs of these important global customers, IBM developed its selected international accounts (SIA) program. Customers are chosen for this program on the basis of revenue potential, the installed base of IBM products across international locations, and the anticipated demand for IBM products and services.

Each SIA is supported by an IBM account manager who is stationed near the customer's headquarters and is responsible for the entire account on a worldwide basis. "SIAs are provided discounts on global purchases based on customer commitment to purchase a particular product volume worldwide (an international volume purchase agreement). The client is allowed to accrue purchases of one product around the world for a volume percentage discount."

SOURCE: George S. Yip and Tammy L. Madsen, "Global Account Management: The Next Frontier in Relationship Marketing," *International Marketing Review*, 13 (no. 3, 1996), p. 32.

Swedish firms tend to enter neighboring countries such as Denmark, Norway, and Finland first and more distant markets such as Brazil, Argentina, and Australia last.[30]

Timing of Entry Should the firm enter a number of country markets simultaneously or, alternatively, should the firm enter one country first to develop a base of experience and then fan out to other countries sequentially? Simultaneous entry might allow the firm to preempt competition by establishing a beachhead in key markets, thereby reducing opportunities for imitation. Multiple market entry may also provide potential scale economies to the firm. Often the determining factor in the decision is the level of resource commitment required to enter a given international market. If, for example, an overseas sales organization must be developed and/or a production facility established, a significant resource commitment is needed.

Mode of Entry Closely intertwined with the evaluation of market potential and country risk is the decision concerning how to operate in a foreign market. The full range of entry modes, presented earlier in the chapter, may be adopted—from exporting, licensing, and contract manufacturing to joint ventures and wholly owned subsidiaries. In high-risk markets, firms can reduce their equity exposure by adopting low-commitment modes such as licensing, contract manufacturing, or joint ventures with a minority share. Although nonequity modes of entry—such as licensing or contract manufacturing—involve minimal risk and commitment, they may not provide the desired level of control or financial performance. Joint ventures and wholly owned subsidiaries provide a greater degree of control over operations and greater potential returns.

The choice of a particular entry mode will also depend on the size of the market and its growth potential. Susan Douglas and Samuel Craig note that

---

[30]Jan Johanson and Finn Wiedershein-Paul, "The Internationalization of the Firm—Four Swedish Cases," *Journal of Management Studies* (October 1975): pp. 305–322.

Markets of limited size surrounded by tariff barriers may be supplied most cost effectively via licensing or contract manufacturing. Where there are potential economies of scale, exporting may, however, be preferred. Then, as local market potential builds up . . . a local production and marketing subsidiary may be established.[31]

Once operations are established in a number of foreign markets, the focus often shifts away from foreign opportunity assessment to local market development in each country. This shift might be prompted by the need to respond to local competitors or the desire to more effectively penetrate the local market. Planning and strategy assume a country-by-country focus.

Phase Two: Local Market Expansion

The expansion effort is generally directed by local management in each country rather than from corporate headquarters. The major objective in this phase is to build strategy on the organizational structure developed in each country in order to leverage assets and to more fully utilize core competencies to foster local market growth. Attention centers on capitalizing on R&D and market knowledge, on sharing production and distribution facilities across product lines, and on identifying opportunities for shared marketing expenditures. While continuing to learn, central attention is given to building a presence in each market.

Decisions   **Economies of scope** are provided if the addition of new products or product variants within a country permit a more effective and efficient utilization of an existing operational structure, such as the distribution network or the sales force. Thus, priority is given to making product and strategy modifications in each country in order to broaden the local market base and reach new segments. Extensions to the product line and new product research may be explored to more precisely meet local preferences. In developing countries, machine tool manufacturers, for example, may consider streamlining and simplifying their products to reach less sophisticated market segments. The costs of initial entry into a country can be substantial, including the costs of establishing relations with distributors, agents, or local authorities, and of gaining familiarity with market conditions and competition. The goal in the local market expansion phase is to capitalize on this resource base by pursuing market development and by realizing economies of scope.

Triggers to a Global Perspective   The country-by-country orientation can yield a patchwork of domestic national businesses. Different marketing strategies are pursued in each country with little or no coordination of operations between countries. The inefficiencies generated by this fragmented system, coupled with external forces that are integrating markets on a global scale, create pressures toward increased coordination across countries. The following factors can trigger this move:

- cost inefficiencies and duplication of effort between the various country operations of the firm

---

[31] Douglas and Craig, "Evolution of Global Marketing Strategy," p. 53.

- opportunities to transfer products, strategies, and experience from one country to another

- emergence of global customers (for example, customers such as G.E. or Citigroup that search the world for suppliers and use the purchased product or service in many countries)

- emergence of global competitors that derive strength from highly coordinated operations worldwide

- improved linkages between the firm's marketing infrastructure units operating in different countries

Phase Three: Global Orientation

In the final phase of internationalization, Douglas and Craig maintain that the country-by-country orientation disappears as "markets are viewed as a set of interrelated, interdependent entities which are becoming increasingly integrated and interlinked worldwide."[32] The firm seeks to capitalize on possible synergies and to take maximum advantage of its worldwide operations. Management attention centers on allocating resources and measuring performance on a global scale, guided by this question: What is the optimal allocation of resources across countries, across product markets, and across target segments to maximize global profits? In this phase, learning and building continue but the central focus is on consolidating the firm's market position to establish a global **leadership** position.

Key Decisions A dual thrust is utilized as a firm adopts a global orientation: (1) improving the efficiency of operations worldwide, and (2) formulating a global strategy for expansion and growth.

Efficiency By coordinating operations across countries and between different functional areas, a firm can reduce worldwide costs in several ways.[33] First, economies of scale can be secured by pooling production, R&D, or other activities for two or more countries. Second, a global firm can reduce costs by moving manufacturing or other activities to low-cost countries. For example, the Mexican side of the U.S.–Mexican border is the site of numerous manufacturing plants established and operated by U.S. companies, but employing Mexican labor. Third, a global firm can reduce costs by exploiting flexibility. A company with manufacturing capability in several countries can move production from one location to another to take advantage of the lowest costs at a particular time. Dow Chemical uses this strategy and examines international differences in exchange rates, tax rates, and transportation and labor costs; production volume for the planning period is then set for each Dow plant. Fourth, efficiency can be enhanced through the coordination across countries of marketing strategies such as brand names, advertising themes, and the standardization of product lines.

Strategy Development A global strategy should define the needs of target segments and determine the geographic configurations of segments. As markets become

---

[32] Ibid., pp. 55–56.

[33] Yip, "Global Strategy in a World of Nations," pp. 33–35.

increasingly international, opportunities for identifying segments that are regional or global in scope, rather than country-specific, are on the increase. In support, expert Kenichi Ohmae notes that

> The market for IBM computers or Toshiba laptops is not defined by geographic borders but by the inherent appeal of the product to users, regardless of where they live. And with the proliferation of trade journals, trade shows, and electronic databases, users have regular access to the same sources of product information.[34]

In fact, IBM has consolidated worldwide advertising with one advertising agency.

The global strategy should also include marketing programs tailored to the needs of the regional and global target segments. Often, the organizational structure must be reshaped to successfully implement strategy on a global scale. For example, some companies—such as Citigroup—that serve multinational corporations have developed a global account management system whereby an executive is given responsibility for ensuring that the needs of a given client are satisfied worldwide. Importantly, the successful implementation of a global strategy requires the establishment of mechanisms to coordinate and control activities and the flows of information and resources across country boundaries and product markets. Firms such as Citigroup and IBM have begun to develop organizational structures that will enable them to compete effectively in the twenty-first century.

Thus, strategy formulation in international markets is an evolutionary process in which the key strategic decisions vary at each phase of involvement in international operations. After initial entry and as experience in the international market builds, the firm can often effectively pursue growth opportunities in selected international markets. This forms a foundation for advancing to the next stage and pursuing the more complex challenges of strategy integration and coordination across country markets.

Summary

In developing international strategy, the business marketer must first assess the globalization potential of the industry. It is driven by market, economic, environmental, and competitive conditions. For example, market forces determine the customers' receptivity to a standardized global product, whereas economic forces dictate whether a global strategy will yield a cost advantage. In turn, the Internet empowers buyers around the world and allows business marketers to develop a one-to-one relationship with customers.

Once a business marketing firm decides to sell its products in a particular country, an entry strategy must then be selected. A range of options are available, including exporting, contractual entry modes (for example, licensing), strategic alliances, and joint ventures. A more elaborate form of participation is represented by multinational firms that employ multidomestic strategies. Here a separate strategy might be pursued in each country served. The most advanced level of participation in international markets is provided by firms that employ a global strategy. Such firms seek competitive

---

[34] Ohmae, "Global Logic of Strategic Alliances," p. 144.

advantage by pursuing strategies that are highly interdependent across countries. Global competition tends to be more common in industries in which primary activities, like R&D and manufacturing, are vital to competitive advantage. Special insights into the international strategy of a firm can be gained by examining *where* activities like manufacturing are performed and *how* such activities are coordinated across countries.

Strategy in the international arena should be tailored to the firm's degree of experience in overseas markets and its vision of growth and future position in markets worldwide. Strategy formulation in international markets is an evolutionary process, in which a firm's involvement in overseas operations may advance through three phases: (1) initial foreign market entry, (2) local or national market expansion, and (3) globalization. The goal of the first phase is to learn about international markets; building a presence in each market is the theme of the second phase; and securing a global leadership position drives the third phase.

Discussion Questions

1. The European aerospace consortium—Airbus—is a strong competitor to Boeing and is climbing toward its long-stated goal of winning 50 percent of the over-100-seat airline market. What criteria would a customer like UPS or British Airways consider in choosing aircraft? What are the critical factors that shape competitive advantage in the airliner market?

2. Leading global firms understand that "environmentally sound" products provide a form of value to customers around the world. For a strategy of environmental segmentation to succeed, what requirements must be met?

3. In introducing a new cellular handset, can Nokia use the same basic advertising message in the United States, Europe, and Asia? Explain.

4. A key premise of the philosophy of global products is that customers' needs are becoming increasingly homogeneous worldwide. Does this trend fit consumer goods more than industrial goods? Does this signal the end of market segmentation strategies?

5. Describe the *competitive* and *economic* factors that are driving the globalization of some industries.

6. A small Michigan-based firm that produces and sells component parts to General Motors, Ford, and Chrysler wishes to extend market coverage to Europe and Japan. What type of market entry strategy would provide the best fit?

7. Global companies must be more than just a bunch of overseas subsidiaries that execute decisions made at headquarters. Using the value chain concept as a guide, compare a global strategy to a multidomestic strategy.

8. Downstream activities in a firm's value chain create competitive advantages that are largely country-specific. Why?

9. The development of effective international marketing strategy should consider the extent of a firm's experience overseas and the stage in the evolution of its international development. Describe the key strategic issues that must

be examined as a firm moves from initial market entry to a more extensive level of involvement in global markets.

10. Hewlett-Packard has scored a major success in the Mexican computer market. Discuss the changes (if any) a firm would have to make in its marketing strategy if it extended its reach beyond the U.S. border into Mexico.

11

Managing Products for Business Markets

The industrial product constitutes the central force in marketing strategy. The ability of the firm to put together a line of products and services that provides superior value to customers is the heart of business marketing management. After reading this chapter, you will understand

1. core products—the tangible link between core competencies and end products.

2. the strategic importance of providing competitively superior value to customers.

3. the various types of industrial product lines and the value of product positioning.

4. how to build a strong high-tech brand.

5. a strategic approach for managing products across the stages of the technology adoption life cycle.

Gary Hamel asserts that "In every industry, there is a ratio that relates price to performance: **X** units of cash buys **Y** units of value. The challenge is to improve that ratio and to do so radically. . . ."[1] Smart marketing means thinking of your company and your product in a fresh way and choosing the way in which you can lead.[2] A business marketer's identity in the marketplace is established through the products and services offered. Without careful product planning and control, marketers are often guilty of introducing products that are inconsistent with market needs, arbitrarily adding items that contribute little to existing product lines, and maintaining weak products that could be profitably eliminated.

Product management is directly linked to market analysis and market selection. Products are developed to fit the needs of the market and are modified as those needs change. Drawing upon such tools of demand analysis as business market segmentation and market potential forecasting, the marketer evaluates opportunities and selects viable market segments, which in turn determines the direction of product policy. Product policy cannot be separated from market selection decisions. In evaluating potential product/market fits, a firm must evaluate market opportunities, determine the number and aggressiveness of competitors, and gauge its own strengths and weaknesses. The marketing function assumes a lead role in transforming the distinctive skills and resources of an organization into products and services that enjoy positional advantages in the market.[3]

This chapter first explores the strategic importance of core competencies—the roots of successful industrial products—and isolates the distinctive skills of leading-edge companies. Second, product quality and value are examined from the customer's perspective and directly linked to business marketing strategy. Third, because industrial products can assume several forms, industrial product line options are described while offering an approach for positioning products and for managing products in high-technology markets.

Core Competencies: The Roots of Industrial Products[4]

You can miss the strength of competitors in the business market by looking only at their product line, in the same way that you can underestimate the strength of a tree if you look only at its leaves. C. K. Prahalad and Gary Hamel offer this analogy: "The diversified corporation is a large tree. The trunk and major limbs are core products, the smaller branches are business units; the leaves, flowers, and fruit are end products. The root system that provides nourishment, sustenance, and stability is the core competence."[5] The success of firms such as 3M, Honda, Canon, Honeywell, Motorola, and others can be traced to a particular set of competencies that each has developed and enriched.

[1] Gary Hamel, "Strategy as Revolution," *Harvard Business Review* 74 (July/August 1996): p. 72.

[2] Regis McKenna, *Relationship Marketing* (Reading, Mass.: Addison-Wesley, 1991), p. 7.

[3] P. Rajan Varadarajan and Satish Jayachandran, "Marketing Strategy: An Assessment of the State of the Field and Outlook," *Journal of the Academy of Marketing Science*, 27 (spring 1999), pp. 120–143.

[4] This discussion is based on C. K. Prahalad and Gary Hamel, "The Core Competence of the Organization," *Harvard Business Review* 68 (May/June 1990): pp. 79–91. See also James M. Higgins, "Achieving the Core Competence—It's As Easy As 1, 2, 3 . . . 47, 48, 49," *Business Horizons* 39 (March/April 1996): pp. 27–32.

[5] Prahalad and Hamel, "The Core Competence," p. 82.

Core competencies are embodied in the superior skills of employees—the technologies they have mastered, the unique ways in which these technologies are combined, and the market knowledge that has been accumulated.[6] Thus, core competencies constitute the collective learning of the organization (see Chapter 9). They focus on the basics of what creates value from the customer's perspective and include both technical and organizational skills. For example, a core competence of Honda is in the design and development of small motors. To apply this competence to one of its products, Honda must ensure that R&D scientists, engineers, and marketers have a shared understanding of consumer needs and of the technological possibilities.

Identifying Core Competencies

Three tests can be applied to identify the core competencies of a firm. First, a core competence provides potential access to an array of markets. Capitalizing on its core competencies in precision mechanics, fine optics, and micro-electronics, Canon is a strong competitor in markets as diverse as cameras, laser printers, fax equipment, and image scanners (see Figure 11.1). Canon appeared to be merely a camera producer at the point it was preparing to become a world leader in copiers.

Second, a core competence should make an important contribution to the perceived customer benefits of the firm's end products. To illustrate, Honda's core competency in small engines is tied directly to important benefits sought by customers: product reliability and fuel efficiency. Honda emphasizes these benefits in its marketing strategy across product lines: motorcycles, automobiles, lawn mowers, snow blowers, and lawn tools.

Third, Prahalad and Hamel point out that "a core competence should be difficult for competitors to imitate. And it will be difficult if it is a complex harmonization of individual technologies and production skills."[7] Even though rivals might acquire the same production equipment or some of the technologies that contribute to a core competence of Motorola, they may encounter severe difficulty in duplicating its internal pattern of coordination and learning. For example, Motorola can produce one of several million different electronic pagers to the exact specifications of an individual customer within two hours of receiving the order.[8]

Sustaining the Lead

McKinsey consultants, Kevin Coyne, Stephen Hall, and Patricia Gorman Clifford suggest that a firm should consider how quickly its best-positioned rival could imitate its competence, assuming it knew how.[9] They suggest that a firm's strategist should consider three questions:

- *How rare is our competence?* **Rareness** involves comparing the competence of your firm to those of other firms across various industries. The fewer

[6] George S. Day, "Marketing's Contribution to the Strategic Dialogue," *Journal of the Academy of Marketing Science* 20 (fall 1992): p. 326.

[7] Prahalad and Hamel, "The Core Competence," p. 84.

[8] James Brian Quinn, *Intelligent Enterprise* (New York: The Free Press, 1992), p. 185.

[9] Kevin P. Coyne, Stephen J. D. Hall, and Patricia Gorman Clifford, "Is Your Core Competence a Mirage?" *The McKinsey Quarterly*, No. 1, 1997, pp. 40–54.

Managing Products for Business Markets • 281

FIGURE 11.1   CORE COMPETENCIES AND SELECTED
PRODUCTS AT CANON

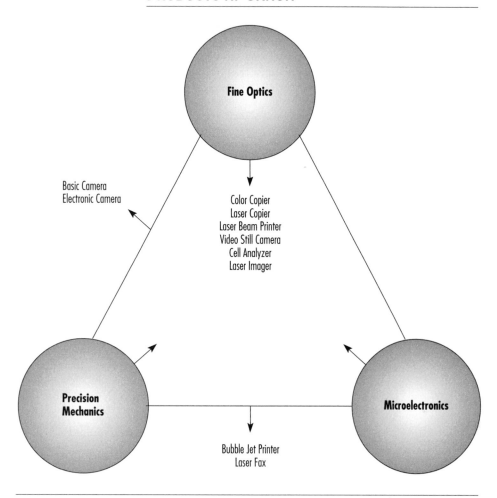

SOURCE: Adapted from C. K. Prahalad and Gary Hamel, "The Core Competence of the Corporation," *Harvard Business Review* 68 (May/June 1990): pp. 75–84.

examples of similar competencies you find, the more likely it is that your firm possesses distinctive capabilities.

Example: High-technology product development and rollout by Cisco Systems.

- *How long will it take your competitors to develop the competence?* Even if a competitor sets out to copy a competence, the advantage will not be eroded immediately. The imitator may need months or years to train personnel, revise policies, and make the multitude of other changes necessary to create and sustain a competence. Particularly difficult and time consuming to replicate are competencies that involve cross-functional processes and include external groups such as important suppliers and leading-edge customers.

Example: Rapid product development process at Sun Microsystems.

The Meaning of Market Influence

C. K. Prahalad, a well-recognized strategy expert, argues that existing measures of market influence, such as market share, center primarily on short-term performance and profitability in an existing market. In his view, strategists must ask this question: What is the appropriate measure of a firm's capacity both to create new businesses—thereby satisfying new customer needs and creating new sources of profit—and to influence the evolution of new industries?

He persuasively argues that core competence share and core product share may provide the best indication of a firm's ability to manage long-term profitable growth. First, the competencies of a firm provide a measure of its capacity to create new

business opportunities. Second, core product share provides a measure of market influence.

Prahalad points to the competencies and core product share of Intel and its influence on the personal computer industry. "Intel is not in the personal computer (PC) assembly business (for example, IBM, Compaq) or purely PC marketing business (for example, Dell, Packard Bell). Intel manufactures a key module. However, Intel's influence in the PC industry is significantly greater than any single PC manufacturer."

SOURCE: C. K. Prahalad, "Weak Signals versus Strong Paradigms," *Journal of Marketing Research* 32 (August 1995): p. iv.

- *Can the source of your advantage be easily understood by your competitors?* Often, the source of a competitor's competence is difficult to pinpoint. For example, skills may be deeply embedded in a company's culture, such as the service responsiveness that is evident in Federal Express's frontline execution strategies. In general, a core competence comprising only a few elements is much easier for a competitor to understand and match than one that relies on the subtle alignment of myriad elements.

  Example: The rich, informal processes and communication networks that guide strategy at 3M.

From Core Products to End Products

Core products—the tangible link between core competencies and end products—are the components or subassemblies that significantly contribute to the value of end products. Although Canon's brand has a small share of the laser printer market (end product), the firm is reputed to hold more than 80 percent world manufacturing share in desktop laser printer "engines" (core product). Similarly, Matsushita has 20 percent of the VCR market, but enjoys a world manufacturing share more than twice as large in key VCR components. Strategy experts suggest that core product share may be a better predictor of profitability than traditional measures of end product market share.[10] By providing core products for a variety of markets, a firm secures the resources and market knowledge to enhance and extend its chosen core competence areas. In turn, the firm can assume a leading role in shaping new applications and developing new end markets.

---

[10] C. K. Prahalad, "Weak Signals versus Strong Paradigms," *Journal of Marketing Research* 32 (August 1995): pp. iii–vi.

FIGURE 11.2	HONEYWELL EMPHASIZING THE FIRM'S CORE COMPETENCIES

Honeywell's control and sensor technologies are often the "secrets" behind our customers' success...

In Space...guiding space flights and keeping satellites in orbit.
In the Air...helping aircraft navigate and fly safely.
In Industry... boosting productivity while protecting the environment.
In Homes & Building... providing comfort, safety and convenience.
In Products...improving performances of appliances, automobiles and other every-day items used at home and work.

Visit our web site to learn the rest of our "secrets"!

Honeywell

www.honeywell.com

Home and Building Control   Industrial Control   Space and Aviation Control

SOURCE: Honeywell, Inc.

Exploiting Selected Core Competencies

Realizing that they cannot dominate in every activity, leading business marketers concentrate their talent and resources on those selected core competencies that will be crucial in serving customers in the future. Honeywell emphasizes its core competencies directly in its advertising and highlights the role that its control and sensor technologies assume in a number of different industries (see Figure 11.2). The 3M company also provides a classic example.[11] The firm's growth for the past several decades has been spawned to a significant extent by its R&D skills in three critical related technologies: adhesives, abrasives, and coating–bonding. In each of these areas, 3M has developed a knowledge base and a depth of skills surpassing those of its major competitors. These historic competencies, coupled with the firm's unique innovation system and entrepreneurial values, have given 3M a continuing stream of successful products: From a producer of sandpaper in the 1920s, historic core competencies have

---

[11] Quinn, *Intelligent Enterprise*, pp. 216–219.

combined to produce Post-it notes, magnetic tape, pressure sensitive tapes, coated abrasives, photographic film, and a wealth of other products.

Product Quality

Increasing global competition and rising customer expectations make product quality and customer value important strategic priorities for marketers. All sectors of the business market are affected. To illustrate, a survey of 700 purchasing managers at the largest U.S. manufacturing companies revealed that more than 75 percent are pressuring suppliers to increase product quality.[12] In turn, the Department of Defense and other governmental units are giving quality an unprecedented level of emphasis in their procurement activities. On a global scale, many international companies insist that suppliers, as a prerequisite for negotiations, meet quality standards set out by the Geneva-based International Standards Organization (ISO). These quality requirements, referred to as **ISO-9000 standards,** were developed for the European Community, but have gained a global following[13] (see Chapter 2). Certification requires a supplier to thoroughly document its quality-assurance program. The certification program is becoming a seal of approval to compete for business not only overseas but also in the United States. For instance, the Department of Defense is employing ISO standards in its contract guidelines. Although Japanese firms continue to set the pace in the application of sophisticated quality-control procedures in manufacturing, significant strides have been made by companies such as Kodak, AT&T, Xerox, Ford, Hewlett-Packard, Intel, General Electric, and others.

The quest for improved product quality touches the entire supply chain as these and other companies demand improved product quality from their suppliers, large and small. For example, General Electric (GE) has an organization-wide goal of achieving Six Sigma quality—that means that a product would have a defect level of no more than 3.4 parts per million.[14] Using the Six Sigma approach, GE measures every process, identifies the variables that lead to defects, and takes steps to eliminate them. GE also works directly to assist suppliers in using the approach. Overall, GE reports that Six Sigma has produced striking results—cost savings in the billions and fundamental improvements in product and service quality.

Meaning of Quality

The quality movement has passed through several stages.[15] **Stage one** centered on conformance to standards or success in meeting specifications. But conformance quality or zero defects will not satisfy a customer if the wrong features are embodied in a product. **Stage two** emphasized that quality was more than a technical specialty and that the pursuit of quality should drive the core processes of the entire business. Particular emphasis was given to total quality management and to measuring customer

---

[12] Anne Millen Porter, "Quality Report: Raising the Bar," *Purchasing*, 127 (January 14, 1999), pp. 44–50.

[13] Wade Ferguson, "Impact of ISO 9000 Series Standards on Industrial Marketing," *Industrial Marketing Management* 25 (July 1996): pp. 325–310.

[14] "Using Six Sigma to Manage Suppliers," *Purchasing*, 127 (January 14, 1999), pp. 90–91.

[15] Bradley T. Gale, *Managing Customer Value: Creating Quality and Service That Customers Can See* (New York: The Free Press, 1994), pp. 25–30.

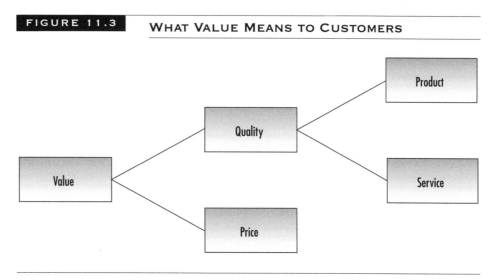

SOURCE: Adapted from Bradley T. Gale, *Managing Customer Value* (New York: The Free Press, 1994), p. 29.

satisfaction. However, customers choose a particular product over competing offerings because they perceive it as providing superior *value*—the product's price, performance, and service render it the most attractive alternative. **Stage three,** then, examines a firm's quality performance relative to competitors and examines customer perceptions of the value of competing products. The focus here is on market-perceived quality and value versus that of competitors. Moreover, attention shifts from zero defects in products to zero defections of customers (i.e., *customer loyalty*). Merely satisfying customers who have the freedom to make choices is not enough to keep them loyal.[16]

Meaning of Value

Strategy experts Dwight Gertz and João Baptista suggest that "a company's product or service is competitively superior if, at price equality with competing products, target segments always choose it. Thus, value is defined in terms of consumer choice in a competitive context."[17] To Bradley T. Gale, "value is simply quality, however the *customer* defines it, offered at the right price."[18] In essence, value equals quality relative to price. Observe in Figure 11.3 that value has two components: quality and price. In turn, quality includes a customer service component. For the service component, business marketing strategists must "recognize that specifications aren't just set by a manufacturer who tells the customer what to expect; instead, consumers also may participate in setting specifications." Frontline sales, and service personnel add value to the product offering by meeting or, indeed, exceeding the customer's service expectations.[19]

[16]Thomas O. Jones and W. Earl Sasser, "Why Satisfied Customers Defect," *Harvard Business Review*, 73 (November–December 1995), pp. 88–99; and Richard L. Oliver, "Whence Customer Loyalty," *Journal of Marketing*, 63 (Special Issue 1999), pp. 33–44.

[17]Dwight L. Gertz and João P. A. Baptista, *Grow to Be Great: Breaking the Downsizing Cycle* (New York: The Free Press, 1995), p. 128.

[18]Bradley T. Gale, *Managing Customer Value*, p. 26.

[19]C. K. Prahalad and M. S. Krishnan, "The New Meaning of Quality in the Information Age," *Harvard Business Review*, 77 (September–October 1999), pp. 109–112.

Value in Use

An industrial product represents the total package of benefits that customers receive when they purchase and use it.[20] This includes the physical and performance attributes of the product; technical assistance provided before the sale; training, maintenance, or repair services provided after the sale; assurance of reliable and timely delivery support; and benefits that the customer derives from the reputation of the seller. Benefits might also include the buyer–seller relationship itself when close interpersonal relationships develop among personnel in the buying and selling organizations. A product is all of the value satisfactions that a customer derives at both an organizational and personal level.[21]

Big Q   Thomas Hogue, vice president of materials and services at Intel Corporation, aptly describes the link between quality and value:

> What I call Big Q (or what others might call "total quality") involves more than product quality. Quality has come to include level of service to the customer, responsiveness to the customer, delivery performance, competitive pricing, comprehension or anticipation of where the customer is going in the marketplace—all of the things that define your worth in the mind of the customer.[22]

Product Support Strategy: The Service Connection

The marketing function must ensure that every part of the organization focuses on delivering superior value to customers. Business marketing programs involve a number of critical components that are carefully evaluated by customers: tangible products, service support, and ongoing information services both before and after the sale. To provide value to customers and to successfully implement these programs, the business marketing firm must carefully coordinate activities among personnel in product management, sales, and service.[23] For example, to customize a product and delivery schedule for an important customer requires close coordination among product, logistics, and sales personnel. Moreover, some customer accounts might require special field-engineering, installation, or equipment support, thereby increasing the required coordination between sales and service units.

Post-purchase service is especially important to buyers in many industrial product categories ranging from computers and machine tools to custom-designed component parts. Responsibility for service support, however, is often diffused throughout various departments, such as applications engineering, customer relations, or service administration. Significant benefits accrue to the business marketer who carefully manages and coordinates product, sales, and service connections to maximize customer value.

---

[20] Frank V. Cespedes, "Once More: How Do You Improve Customer Service?" *Business Horizons* 35 (March/April 1992): pp. 58–67.

[21] Theodore Levitt, *The Marketing Imagination*, new expanded ed. (New York: The Free Press, 1986), pp. 81–85.

[22] Anne Millen Porter, "Intel Corp. Takes on Big Q," *Purchasing* 119 (11 January 1996): p. 54.

[23] Frank V. Cespedes, *Concurrent Marketing: Integrating Product, Sales, and Service* (Boston, Mass.: Harvard Business School Press, 1995), pp. 58–85.

Product Policy

Product policy involves the set of all decisions concerning the products and services that the company offers. Through product policy, a business marketing firm attempts to satisfy customer needs and to build a sustainable competitive advantage by capitalizing on its core competencies. This section explores the types of industrial product lines and the importance of anchoring product management decisions on an accurate definition of the product market. A framework is also provided for assessing product opportunities on a global scale.

Types of Product Lines Defined

Because product lines of industrial firms differ from those of consumer firms, classification is useful. Industrial product lines can be categorized into four types: [24]

1. *Proprietary or catalog products.* These items are offered only in certain configurations and produced in anticipation of orders. Product line decisions concern the addition, deletion, or repositioning of products within the line.

2. *Custom-built products.* These items are offered as a set of basic units, with numerous accessories and options. For example, NCR offers a line of retail work stations that are used by large customers, like Wal-Mart and Seven Eleven stores as well as by smaller businesses (see Figure 11.4). The basic retail work station can be expanded to connect to scanners, check readers, electronic payment devices, and other accessories to meet the particular needs of a business. The firm's wide array of products provides retailers with an end-to-end solution covering the enterprise from data warehousing to the point-of service work station at the checkout. The marketer offers the organizational buyer a set of building blocks. Product line decisions center on offering the proper mix of options and accessories.

3. *Custom-designed products.* These items are created to meet the needs of one or a small group of customers. Sometimes the product is a unique unit, such as a power plant or a specific machine tool. In addition, some items produced in relatively large quantities, such as an aircraft model, may fall into this category. The product line is described in terms of the company's capability, and the consumer buys that capability. Ultimately, this capability is transformed into a finished good. For example, after canvassing airlines around the world, Airbus Industrie detected enough interest in a super jumbo jet to proceed with development.[25]

4. *Industrial services.* Rather than an actual product, the buyer is purchasing a company's capability in an area such as maintenance, technical service, or management consulting. (Special attention is given to services marketing in Chapter 13.)

---

[24] Benson P. Shapiro, *Industrial Product Policy: Managing the Existing Product Line* (Cambridge, Mass.: Marketing Science Institute, 1977), pp. 37–39.

[25] Alex Taylor III, "Blue Skies for Airbus," *Fortune*, 140 (April 1, 1999), pp. 102–108.

FIGURE 11.4	NCR'S WEB SITE PROVIDES RETAILERS WITH AN END-TO-END SOLUTION

All types of business marketing firms confront product policy decisions, whether they offer physical products, pure services (no physical product), or a product-service combination.[26] Each product situation presents unique problems and opportunities for the

---

[26] Albert L. Page and Michael Siemplenski, "Product-Systems Marketing," *Industrial Marketing Management* 12 (April 1983): pp. 89–99.

business marketer; each draws upon a unique type of capability. Product strategy rests on the intelligent utilization of corporate capability.

Defining the Product Market

An accurate definition of the product market is fundamental to sound product policy decisions.[27] Careful attention must be given to the alternative ways customer needs can be satisfied. For example, many different products could provide competition for personal computers. Application-specific products, such as enhanced pocket pagers and smart phones that send e-mail and connect to the Web, are potential competitors. A wide array of information appliances that provide easy access to the Internet also pose a threat. In turn, many firms have developed information networks that enable users to easily access information through inexpensive terminals. This provides users with the option of buying a simple terminal or information appliance, rather than a personal computer. In such an environment, Regis McKenna maintains, managers "must look for opportunities in—and expect competition from—every possible direction. A company with a narrow product concept will move through the market with blinders on, and it is sure to run into trouble."[28] By excluding products and technology that compete for the same end-user needs, the product strategist can quickly become out of touch with the market. Both customer needs and the ways of satisfying those needs change.

Product Market A **product market** establishes the distinct arena in which the business marketer competes. Four dimensions of a market definition are strategically relevant:

1. *Customer function dimension.* The related benefits that are provided to satisfy the needs of organizational buyers (for example, mobile messaging).

2. *Technological dimension.* There are alternative ways a particular function can be performed (for example, cell phone, pager, notebook computer).

3. *Customer segment dimension.* Customer groups have distinct needs that must be served (for example, sales representatives, physicians, international travelers).

4. *Value-added system dimension.* There is a sequence of stages along which competitors serving the market can operate.[29] The value-added system for mobile messaging includes equipment providers, such as Nokia and Motorola, and service providers, like AT&T and American Online (AOL). Analysis of the value-added system may indicate potential opportunities or threats that may arise from possible changes in the system (for example, potential alliances between equipment and service providers).

Planning for Today and Tomorrow Competition to satisfy the customer's need exists at the technology level as well as at the supplier or brand level. By establishing

---

[27] For a complete discussion on market definition, see David W. Cravens, *Strategic Marketing*, 5th ed. (Chicago: Richard D. Irwin, 1997), pp. 89–98.

[28] Regis McKenna, *Relationship Marketing*, p. 184.

[29] George S. Day, *Strategic Market Planning: The Pursuit of Competitive Advantage* (St. Paul, Minn.: West, 1984), p. 73.

| TABLE 11.1 | ASSESSMENT OF GLOBAL PRODUCT-MARKET OPPORTUNITIES |

Product Configuration	Market Needs	
	Same	**Different**
Same	Universal or global product	Market segmentation
Different	Product segmentation	Specialty segmentation (country-tailored product)

SOURCE: Adapted from Jagdish N. Sheth, "Global Markets or Global Competition," *Journal of Consumer Marketing*, 3 (Spring 1986), p. 10.

accurate product-market boundaries, the product strategist is better equipped to identify customer needs, the benefits sought by the market segment, and the turbulent nature of competition at both the technology and supplier or brand levels. Derek Abell offers these valuable strategy insights:

- Planning for today requires a clear, precise *definition* of the business—a delineation of target customer segments, customer functions, and the business approach to be taken; planning for tomorrow is concerned with how the business should be *redefined* for the future.

- Planning for today focuses on *shaping up* the business to meet the needs of today's customers with excellence. It involves identifying factors that are critical to success and smothering them with attention; planning for tomorrow can entail *reshaping* the business to compete more effectively in the future.[30]

Assessing Global Product-Market Opportunities

Because an increasing number of business market sectors—such as the aerospace, telecommunications, computer, agricultural equipment, and automobile industries—include firms that compete on a worldwide basis, an assessment of global product-market opportunities is required. Observe in Table 11.1 that the business marketer has several options in developing an international product strategy. The horizontal dimension represents the similarity in or the difference between market needs across countries, whereas the vertical dimension represents the nature of the product configuration.

A **universal** or **global** product assumes that the needs of organizational customers are the same across countries. This assumption may be valid for some classes of industrial products and for some world markets (for example, Japan, North America, and Western Europe). In fact, some evidence suggests that industrial and high-technology products (for example, computer hardware, airliners, photographic equipment, machine tools, and heavy equipment) may be most appropriate for global product strategies.[31] Customers with multinational operations are particularly likely to have similar

---

[30] Derek F. Abell, "Competing Today While Preparing for Tomorrow," *Sloan Management Review*, 40 (spring 1999), p. 74.

[31] Subhash C. Jain, "Standardization of International Marketing Strategy: Some Research Hypotheses," *Journal of Marketing* 53 (January 1989): pp. 70–74.

requirements worldwide.[32] For example, where the operations are integrated or co-ordinated across national boundaries, as in the case of financial institutions, compatibility of operation systems and equipment may be essential. Consequently, such firms may seek business marketers who can supply their global operations.

Global strategy experts provide three important guidelines for designing successful global products.[33]

1. In examining customer needs around the world, business marketers should search for similarities as well as differences.

2. Global product designers should try to maximize the size of the common global core of the product while also providing for local tailoring around the core.

3. Rather than being adapted from national products later, the best global products are designed with the global market in mind from the start.

Canon's successful entry into the photocopier business emphasized a strategy that exploited the similarities in buyers' needs across country markets. Because of cost considerations, early models could not accommodate all sizes of Japanese paper. Designed as a global product, Canon was willing to give up the ability to precisely meet all needs in its *domestic* market in order to maximize its position in the *global* market.[34]

A **product segmentation** strategy is appropriate when the market needs across countries are the same, but the products must be adapted to fit the local market. Note also from Table 11.1 that a **market segmentation** strategy fits when consumer needs across countries differ, but the product is standardized; other elements of the marketing mix are adapted to reach various target segments. To illustrate, Apple Computer sells a standardized product line worldwide but employs different positioning, promotional, and distribution strategies in each country. Finally, a **specialty segmentation** strategy involves developing tailor-made products for each country. This represents the most extreme form of specialization as market needs vary from country to country.

Susan P. Douglas and Yoram Wind provide this assessment of global product-market strategies:

> A firm's international operations are likely to be characterized by a mix of strategies, including not only global products and brands, but also some regional products and brands and some national products and brands. Similarly, some target segments may be global, others regional and others national. Hybrid strategies of this nature thus enable a company to take advantage of the benefits of standardization, and potential synergies from operating on an international scale, while at the same time not losing those afforded by adaptation to specific country characteristics and consumer preferences.[35]

---

[32] Susan P. Douglas and Yoram Wind, "The Myth of Globalization," *Columbia Journal of World Business* 22 (winter 1987): pp. 19–30.

[33] George S. Yip, *Total Global Strategy* (Englewood Cliffs, N.J.: Prentice-Hall, 1992), pp. 85–102. See also Jean-Phillippe Deschamps and P. Ranganath Nayak, *Product Juggernauts: How Companies Mobilize to Generate a Stream of Market Winners* (Boston: Harvard Business School Press, 1995), pp. 161–162.

[34] Michael E. Porter, "Changing Patterns of International Competition," *California Management Review* 28 (winter 1986): pp. 33–34.

[35] Douglas and Wind, "The Myth of Globalization," p. 28.

INSIDE BUSINESS MARKETING

High-Growth Market Blues

The conventional wisdom that marketers should invest in growth markets is based upon this line of reasoning: In the early phase of a growth market, shares gains are easier and worth more, the experience curve will lead to cost advantages, price pressures will be low, early involvement will provide a technological advantage, and early aggressive entry will deter later entrants. David Aaker and George Day argue that these premises are often shaky. "Numerous firms have entered growth situations only to endure years of painful losses and ultimately an embarrassing, costly, and sometimes fatal exit during a traumatic shakeout phase."

Why do risks often outweigh the rewards of high-growth markets? The authors isolate several factors:

- The number and aggressiveness of competitors is greater than can be supported by the market.

- Adequate distribution may not be available.

- Resources are lacking to maintain a high rate of growth.

- Important success factors change (for example, from product technology to process or production technology) and the firm cannot adapt.

- Technology changes.

- A competitor enters with a superior product or with a low-cost advantage.

- The market growth fails to materialize.

The effective business marketer must challenge the fundamental strategy premises. Aaker and Day point out that "A market is neither inherently attractive nor unattractive because it is experiencing high growth. The real question is whether the firm can exploit the opportunities presented by market growth to gain a competitive advantage."

SOURCE: David A. Aaker and George S. Day, "The Perils of High-Growth Markets," *Strategic Management Journal* 7 (September 1986): pp. 409–421.

Planning Industrial Product Strategy

Formulating a strategic marketing plan for an existing product line is the most vital part of a company's marketing planning efforts. Having identified a product market, attention now turns to planning product strategy. Product positioning analysis provides a useful tool for charting the strategy course.

Product Positioning [36]

Once the product market is defined, a strong competitive position for the product must be secured. **Product positioning** represents the place that a product occupies in a particular market; it is found by measuring organizational buyers' perceptions and preferences for a product in relation to its competitors. Because organizational buyers perceive products as bundles of attributes (for example, quality, service), the product strategist should examine the attributes that assume a central role in buying decisions.

---

[36] This section is based largely on Behram J. Hansotia, Muzaffar A. Shaikh, and Jagdish N. Sheth, "The Strategic Determinancy Approach to Brand Management," *Business Marketing* 70 (fall 1985): pp. 66–69.

| FIGURE 11.5 | DETERMINANT AND NONDETERMINANT ATTRIBUTES |

Attribute

	Determinant		Nondeterminant			
	D_1	D_2	ND_1	ND_2	ND_3	ND_4
Important	x	x	x			
Not Important				x	x	x
Nondifferentiating (SB=COMP)			x	x		
Differentiating (SB>COMP)	x				x	
Differentiating (SB<COMP)		x				x

SB: Sponsor Brand   COMP: Competing Brand

Possible Attribute Types
Determinant:
   D_1—Attribute is important as well as differentiating, but sponsor brand is superior to competing brand (SB>COMP).
   D_2—Attribute is important as well as differentiating, but sponsor brand is inferior to competing brand (SB<COMP).
Nondeterminant:
   ND_1—Attribute is important but not differentiating. Statistically SB and COMP are perceived to be equal (SB=COMP).
   ND_2—Attribute is neither important nor differentiating.
   ND_3—Attribute is differentiating (SB>COMP), but not important.
   ND_4—Attribute is differentiating (SB<COMP), but not important.

SOURCE: Reprinted with permission from Behran J. Hansotia, Muzaffar A. Shaikh, and Jagdish N. Sheth, "The Strategic Determinancy Approach to Brand Management," *Business Marketing* 70 (February 1985): p. 66. Copyright Crain Communications, Inc.

Determinant Attributes

Particular attention should be given to defining those attributes that are determinant —attributes that are both important and differentiating. Figure 11.5 displays the possible types of determinant and nondeterminant attributes. A product manager may find the attributes of his or her brand (see sponsor brand [SB]) in any one of several mutually exclusive categories. In this illustration, only two attributes are determinant; each is considered by organizational buyers to be both important and differentiating. Observe also that another attribute is important but is not differentiating. For example, safety might constitute an attribute that would fit this category in the heavy-duty truck market. Business market customers view safety as being important but may consider the competing products offered by Navistar, Volvo, and Mack Trucks as quite comparable on this dimension. Durability, reliability, and fuel economy might constitute the determinant attributes.

| FIGURE 11.6 | STRATEGY MATRIX |

Brand Difference*

		Increase	Decrease	Maintain
Importance	Increase	$ND_2 \rightarrow D_1$		$ND_3 \rightarrow D_1$
	Decrease			$D_2 \rightarrow ND_4$
	Maintain	$ND_1 \rightarrow D_1$	$D_2 \rightarrow ND_1$	$ND_4 \rightarrow ND_4$ $D_1 \rightarrow D_1$

*NOTE: The brand difference may be positive or negative, depending on whether the sponsor brand or the competing brand is perceived as being superior.

SOURCE: Reprinted with permission from Behran J. Hansotia, Muzaffar A. Shaikh, and Jagdish N. Sheth, "The Strategic Determinacy Approach to Brand Management," *Business Marketing* 70 (February 1985): p. 68. Copyright Crain Communications, Inc.

Strategy Matrix

After defining the key attributes and assessing the firm's competitive standing, particular strategy options can be evaluated by the product manager. Figure 11.6 suggests how the attributes portrayed in Figure 11.5 might be changed. Thus, each cell of the strategy matrix provides possible generic strategies that the product manager could pursue to improve the brand's competitive standing. For example, the upper left cell (increase importance and brand differentiation) is a strategy requiring measures to (1) increase the attribute importance to customers, and (2) increase the difference between the competition and the sponsor brand. Of the attributes displayed in Figure 10.5, D_1 is the attribute most preferred by a product manager—the attribute is important and differentiating, and the sponsor brand is superior to competing brands. Ideally then, the product manager would like to convert attributes wherever possible into the D_1 attribute category. This would require either increasing brand difference (ND_1) or attribute importance (ND_3). Converting ND_2 into D_1 requires increasing both importance and brand difference.

The least-preferred attribute type for the product manager is D_2—attribute is important and differentiating, but the sponsor brand is inferior to competing brands. Here the product manager attempts to convert it into a nondeterminant attribute.

Illustration: Determinacy Analysis The preceding strategic determinacy approach was successfully applied to a capital equipment product at a major corporation. The product that provided the focus of the analysis is sold in three sizes to two market segments: end users and consulting engineers. Through marketing research, fifteen attributes were identified, including such dimensions as reliability, service support, company reputation, and ease of maintenance.

The research found that the firm's brand enjoyed an outstanding rating on product reliability and service support, both attributes generally being determinant for the company against most competitors. To reinforce the importance of both attributes, management decided to offer an enhanced warranty program. Both end users and consulting engineers view warranties as important but not a point of differentiation across competing brands. Management surmised, however, that by establishing a new warranty standard for the industry, the attribute could become determinant, adding to the brand's leverage over competitors. In addition, management felt that the new warranty program might also benefit the brand's reputation on other attributes such as reliability and company reputation.

The study also provided some surprises. Price was not nearly as important to organizational buyers as management had initially believed. This suggested that there were opportunities to increase revenue through product differentiation and service support. Likewise, the research found that the firm's brand dominated all competitors in the large- and medium-sized products, but not in the small-sized products. This particular product had an especially weak competitive position in the consulting engineer segment. Special service support strategies were developed to strengthen the product's standing in this segment. Clearly, determinacy analysis provides a valuable tool for managing products for business markets.

Managing Products in High-Technology Markets

Enticing opportunities and special challenges confront the product strategist in high-technology markets. This section explores two vital elements of high-tech marketing: (1) building a strong brand, and (2) designing marketing strategy during the turbulent life of a high-technology product.

Managing a High-Tech Brand[37]

While consumer-packaged-goods companies like Procter & Gamble, Nabisco, and Nestle have excelled by developing a wealth of enduring and highly profitable brands, a strong brand is also a valuable asset in business markets in general and in high-technology markets in particular. "**Brand equity** is a set of brand assets and liabilities linked to a brand, its name, and symbol that add to or subtract from the value provided by a product or service to a firm and/or to that firm's customers."[38] The assets and liabilities that impact brand equity include brand loyalty, name awareness, perceived quality, and other brand associations, and proprietary brand assets (for example, patents). Along with consumer-goods names such as Coca Cola, McDonalds, or Nike, the world's most valuable brands include high-tech representatives such as IBM, Microsoft, Intel, and Hewlett-Packard.

Strong Brands Promise and Deliver Successful brand management involves developing a promise of value for customers and then ensuring that the promise is kept through the way in which the product is developed, produced, sold, serviced, and

[37] Scott Ward, Larry Light, and Jonathan Goldstine, "What High-Tech Managers Need to Know About Brands," *Harvard Business Review*, 75 (July–August 1999), pp. 85–95.

[38] David Aaker, *Managing Brand Equity* (New York: Free Press, 1991), p. 15. For a comprehensive review, see also John Kim, David A. Reid, Richard E. Plank, and Robert Dahlstrom, "Examining the Role of Brand Equity in Business Markets: A Model, Research Propositions, and Managerial Implications," *Journal of Business-to-Business Marketing*, 5, No. 3, 1998, pp. 65–89.

FIGURE 11.7   HOW HIGH-TECH BRANDS BUILD EQUITY

To build a strong high-tech brand, managers need to answer the following questions:

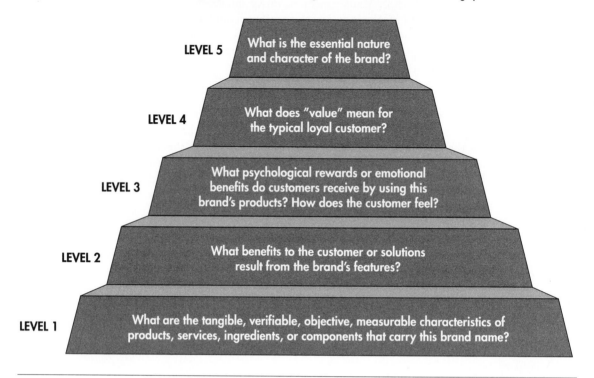

LEVEL 5 What is the essential nature and character of the brand?

LEVEL 4 What does "value" mean for the typical loyal customer?

LEVEL 3 What psychological rewards or emotional benefits do customers receive by using this brand's products? How does the customer feel?

LEVEL 2 What benefits to the customer or solutions result from the brand's features?

LEVEL 1 What are the tangible, verifiable, objective, measurable characteristics of products, services, ingredients, or components that carry this brand name?

SOURCE: Reprinted by permission of the *Harvard Business Review*. From Scott Ward, Larry Light, and Jonathan Goldstine, "What High-Tech Managers Need to Know About Brands," *Harvard Business Review*, 75 (July–August 1999), pp. 85–95. Copyright © 1999 by the President and Fellows of Harvard College; all rights reserved.

promoted. IBM's promise of value is built on its long tradition of superior service and customer support. One major European customer observed: "As long as IBM is in the general price range of competitors, we'll always buy IBM for the service and support. . . ."[39] A **brand,** then, is a distinctive identity that represents an enduring and credible promise of value associated with a particular product, service or organization. Note that emphasis can be placed at the corporate level or at the subbrand level. For high-tech brands, the emphasis is generally at the corporate level (for example, Oracle or IBM). By contrast, Lotus shares brand equity with Domino—a subbrand.

Building Brand Equity   To guide managers in building a strong high-tech brand, Scott Ward, Larry Light, and Jonathan Goldstine developed the brand pyramid (see Figure 11.7). Observe that Level one represents the core product—the tangible product characteristics—while Level two centers on the "solutions" or "benefits" the brand provides. "The first two levels of the pyramid still embody the elements of product competition, not those of brand competition. Competitors can continually match and

---

[39] Ward et al., "What High-Tech Managers Need to Know," p. 89.

FIGURE 11.8 APPLE COMPUTER'S IMAC CAMPAIGN CONVEYS EMOTIONAL BENEFITS TO TARGETED CUSTOMERS

Think different.

SOURCE: Courtesy, Apple Computer, Inc.

leapfrog over one another by offering better and more features and by identifying the benefits of their products for customers."[40]

By providing psychological rewards or emotional benefits to customers, Level three is where a firm can truly differentiate itself from competitors. How do customers feel when experiencing the benefits of the brand? Confident? Productive? Innovative? Brands that reside in the third level are developed and positioned to fulfill a promise of value to selected customers, not simply as technologies in search of a market. Apple Computer, particularly its iMac campaign, comes to mind (see Figure 11.8).

The top two levels of the pyramid suggest that a strong brand provides a promise of value that will attract and hold customers. Level four describes the deeper values (for example, achievement-oriented values or conservative values) that the brand reflects. A strong brand reflects the values of the target customer and this creates and

[40] Ibid., p. 91.

reinforces brand loyalty. The top level of the pyramid captures the personality of the brand. This is the way in which a brand would be described if it had human qualities: friendly, warm, decisive, confident, aggressive. To illustrate, the brand personality of Apple might be described as "fun"; IBM as "confident"; Sun Microsystems as "daring"; and Oracle as "aggressive." Together, Levels four and five of the pyramid isolate the relevant and differentiating character of the brand.

By developing a clearly defined value proposition for customers that is understood across all business functions, strong brand management provides a powerful unifying force throughout the high-tech firm. Externally, a strong brand breeds loyal customers. In the face of swiftly changing technology and in times of uncertainty, buyers will turn to a company that understands their needs—one that they have grown to trust.

Isolating Technology Adopters

After decades of being content with letters, telegrams, and telephones, consumers have embraced fax machines, voice mail, e-mail, Internet browsers, and a range of information appliances. In each case, the conversion of the market came slowly. Once a particular threshold of consumer acceptance was achieved, there was a stampede. Geoffrey Moore defines **discontinuous innovations** as "new products or services that require the end-user and the marketplace to dramatically change their past behavior, with the promise of gaining equally dramatic new benefits."[41] During the past quarter-century, discontinuous innovations have been common in the computer-electronics industry, creating massive new influxes of spending, fierce competition, and a whole host of firms that are redrawing the boundaries of the high technology marketplace.

A popular tool with strategists at high technology firms is the technology adoption life cycle—a framework developed by Geoffrey Moore, a leading consultant to Sun Microsystems, Silicon Graphics, Hewlett-Packard, and others.

Types of Technology Customers   Fundamental to Moore's framework are five classes of customers who constitute the potential market for a discontinuous innovation (see Table 11.2). Business marketers can benefit by putting innovative products in the hands of **technology enthusiasts.** They serve as a gatekeeper to the rest of the technology life cycle and their endorsement is needed for an innovation to get a fair hearing in the organization. Whereas technology enthusiasts possess influence, they do not have ready access to the resources needed to move an organization toward a large-scale commitment to the new technology. By contrast, **visionaries** have resource control and can often assume an influential role in publicizing the benefits of an innovation and giving it a boost during the early stages of market development. However, visionaries are difficult for a marketer to serve because each demands special and unique product modifications. Their demands can quickly tax the R&D resources of the technology firm and stall the market penetration of the innovation.

The Chasm   Truly innovative products often enjoy a warm welcome in an early market comprising technology enthusiasts and visionaries, but then sales falter and often

---

[41] Geoffrey A. Moore, *Inside the Tornado: Marketing Strategies from Silicon Valley's Cutting Edge* (New York: HarperCollins, 1995), p. 13.

TABLE 11.2	THE TECHNOLOGY ADOPTION LIFE CYCLE: CLASSES OF CUSTOMERS

Customer	Profile
Technology enthusiasts (*innovators*)	Interested in exploring the latest innovation, these consumers possess significant influence over how products are perceived by others in the organization but lack control over resource commitments.
Visionaries (*early adopters*)	Desiring to exploit the innovation for a competitive advantage, these consumers are the true revolutionaries in business and government who have access to organizational resources but frequently demand special modifications to the product that are difficult for the innovator to provide.
Pragmatists (*early majority*)	Making the bulk of technology purchases in organizations, these individuals believe in technology evolution, not revolution, and seek products from a market leader with a proven track record of providing useful productivity improvements.
Conservatives (*late majority*)	Pessimistic about their ability to derive any value from technology investments, these individuals represent a sizable group of customers who are price sensitive and reluctantly purchase high-tech products to avoid being left behind.
Skeptics (*laggards*)	Rather than potential customers, these individuals are ever-present critics of the hype surrounding high-technology products.

SOURCE: Adapted from Geoffrey A. Moore, *Inside the Tornado: Marketing Strategies from Silicon Valley's Cutting Edge* (New York: HarperCollins, 1995), pp. 14–18.

even plummet. Frequently, a chasm develops between visionaries who are intuitive and support revolution and the **pragmatists** who are analytical, support evolution, and provide the pathway to the mainstream market. If the business marketer can successfully guide a product across the chasm, an opportunity is created to gain acceptance with the mainstream market comprising pragmatists and conservatives. As Table 11.2 relates, **pragmatists** make the bulk of technology purchases in organizations and conservatives include a sizable group of customers who are hesitant to buy high-tech products but do so to avoid being left behind.

The Technology Adoption Life Cycle

The fundamental strategy for crossing the chasm and moving from the early market to the mainstream market is to provide pragmatists with a 100-percent solution to their problems (see Figure 11.9). Many high-technology firms err by attempting to provide something for everyone while never meeting the complete requirements of any particular market segment. What pragmatists seek is the whole product—the minimum set of products and services necessary to support a compelling reason to buy. Geoffrey Moore notes that "the key to a winning strategy is to identify a simple beachhead of pragmatist customers in a mainstream market segment and to accelerate the formation

The Gorilla Advantage in High-Tech Markets

High-tech companies that can get their products designed into the very standards of the market have enormous influence over the future direction of that market. For example, all PC-based software has to be Microsoft-and-Intel-compatible. All networking solutions must be compatible with Cisco Systems' standards; all printers must be Hewlett-Packard-compatible. This is the essence of gorilla power in high-tech markets that firms such as Microsoft, Intel, Cisco, and Hewlett-Packard enjoy.

The gorilla advantage allows these market leaders to:

- *attract more customers* by enjoying better press coverage and shorter sales cycles just because information technology managers expect it to be the winner.

- *keep more customers* because the cost of switching is high for customers and the cost of entry is high for competitors.

- *drive costs down* by shifting some costly enhancements that customers demand to suppliers while retaining control of the critical components of value creation.

- *keep profits up* because business partners place a priority on developing complementary products and services that make the **whole product** of the market leader worth more to customers than competing products are worth.

The Internet presents an explosive area of growth in many sectors of the high-tech market as firms square off to gain a leadership position in e-procurement, sales force automation, supply chain integration, and Web-focused security. The gorilla games are just beginning!

SOURCE: Geoffrey A. Moore, Paul Johnson, and Tom Kippola, *The Gorilla Game: An Investor's Guide to Picking Winners in High-Technology* (New York: HarperBusiness, 1998), pp. 43–70.

of 100 percent of their whole product. The goal is to win a niche foothold in the mainstream as quickly as possible—that is what is meant by *crossing the chasm*." [42]

The Bowling Alley   In technology markets, each market segment is like a bowling pin and the momentum achieved from hitting one segment successfully carries over into surrounding segments. The bowling alley represents a stage in the adoption life cycle where a product gains acceptance from segments within the mainstream market but has yet to achieve widespread adoption.

Consider the evolution of strategy for Lotus Notes.[43] When first introduced, Notes was offered as a new paradigm for corporatewide communication. To cross into the mainstream market, the Lotus team shifted the product's focus from an enterprisewide vision of corporate communication to specific solutions for particular business functions. The first niche served was the global account management function of worldwide accounting and consulting firms. The solution offered to the customer was enhanced account activity coordination for highly visible products. This led to a second niche—global account management for sales teams where enhanced coordination and information sharing spur productivity.

A Focused Strategy   A logical next step for Lotus was movement into the customer service function where an open sharing of information can support creative solu-

[42] Ibid., p. 22.
[43] Ibid., pp. 35–37.

FIGURE 11.9	THE LANDSCAPE OF THE TECHNOLOGY ADOPTION LIFE CYCLE

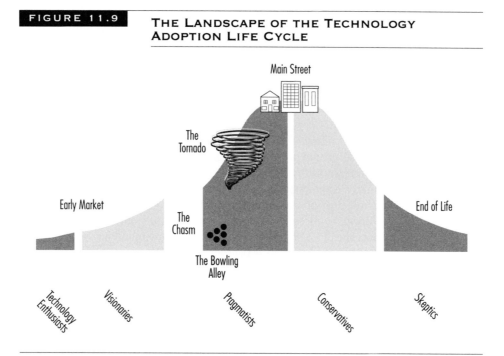

SOURCE: Adapted from Geoffrey A. Moore, *Inside the Tornado: Marketing Strategies from Silicon Valley's Cutting Edge* (New York: HarperCollins, 1995), pp. 19 and 25. Copyright 1995 by Geoffrey A. Moore Consulting Inc. Reprinted by permission of HarperCollins Publishers Inc.

tions to customer problems. Successful penetration of these segments created another opportunity—incorporating the customer into the Notes loop. Note the key lesson here: A customer-based, application-focused strategy provides leverage so that a victory in one market segment cascades into victories in adjacent market segments.

The Tornado While economic buyers who seek particular solutions are the key to success in the bowling alley, technical or infrastructure buyers in organizations can spawn a tornado (see Figure 11.9). Information technology (IT) managers are responsible for providing efficient and reliable infrastructures—the systems through which organizational members communicate and perform their jobs. They are pragmatists and they prefer to buy from an established market leader.

IT professionals interact freely across company and industry boundaries and discuss the ramifications of the latest technology. IT managers watch each other closely—they do not want to be too early or too late. Often, they move together and create a tornado. Because a massive number of new customers are entering the market at the same time and because they all want the same product, demand dramatically outstrips supply and a large backlog of customers can appear overnight. At a critical stage, such market forces have surrounded Hewlett-Packard's laser and inkjet printers, Microsoft's Windows products, and Intel's Pentium microprocessors.

Tornado Strategy The central success factors for the tornado phase of the adoption life cycle differ from those that are appropriate for the bowling alley. Rather than emphasizing market segmentation, the central goal is to gear up production to capitalize on the opportunity that the broad market presents. In its printer business, Hewlett-Packard demonstrated the three critical priorities to emphasize during a tornado:[44]

1. "Just ship"

2. Extend distribution channels

3. Drive to the next lower price point

First, Hewlett-Packard's quality improvement process allowed it to significantly increase production—first with laser printers, and later with inkjet printers—with few interruptions. Second, to extend market coverage, Hewlett-Packard began to sell its laser printers through PC dealer channels and extended its distribution channels for inkjet printers to computer superstores, office superstores, mail order, and, more recently, to price clubs and other consumer outlets. Third, Hewlett-Packard drove down the price points for its printers—moving inkjet printers below $1,000, then below $500, and then well below that. As this example demonstrates, tornado strategy emphasizes product leadership and operational excellence in manufacturing and distribution.

Main Street This stage of the technology adoption life cycle represents a period of aftermarket development. The frantic waves of mass-market adoption of the product begin to subside. Competitors in the industry have increased production and supply now exceeds demand. Moore points out that "The defining characteristic of Main Street is that continued profitable market growth can no longer come from selling the basic commodity to new customers and must come instead from developing niche-specific extensions to the basic platform for existing customers."[45]

Main Street Strategy The goal here is to develop value-based strategies targeted on particular segments of end users. Hewlett-Packard, for example, matches its printers to the special needs of different segments of home office users by offering:

- a compact portable printer for those users who are space-constrained,

- the OfficeJet printer-fax for those who do not yet own a fax, and

- a high-performance color printer for those who create commercial flyers.

Main Street strategy emphasizes operational excellence in production and distribution as well as finely tuned market segmentation strategies. What signals the end of the life for the technology adoption life cycle? A discontinuous innovation appears that incorporates breakthrough technology and promises new solutions for customers.

Summary

The stream of successful products introduced by leading business marketing firms can be traced to a particular set of unique core competencies that each has developed and

---

[44]Ibid., p. 81. See also Stephen Kreider Yoder, "Shaving Back: How H-P Used Tactics of the Japanese to Beat Them at Their Game," *The Wall Street Journal*, 8 September 1994, pp. A1, A6.

[45]Geoffrey A. Moore, *Inside the Tornado*, p. 111.

continually enriched. Core competencies provide access to an array of markets, make an important contribution to the value that customers perceive in a product, and are difficult for competitors to imitate. Conceptualizing a product must go beyond mere physical description to include all the benefits and services that provide value to customers. The unifying goal for the business marketer: *Provide superior market-perceived quality and value versus competitors.* A carefully coordinated product strategy recognizes the role that various functional areas assume in providing value to organizational customers. Special attention should be given to synchronizing the activities among the product management, sales, and service units.

Industrial product lines can be broadly classified into (1) proprietary or catalog items, (2) custom-built items, (3) custom-designed items, and (4) industrial services. Industrial product management can best be described as the management of capability. In monitoring product performance and in formulating marketing strategy, the business marketer can profitably use product positioning analysis. By isolating a product's competitive standing in a market, positioning analysis provides strategy insights to the planner. A product attribute is determinant if it is both important and differentiating.

Rapidly changing high-technology markets present special opportunities and challenges for the product strategist. By developing a strong brand that organizational buyers come to know and trust, the business marketing firm can gain a competitive advantage in the high-tech market. The technology adoption life cycle includes five categories of customers: technology enthusiasts, visionaries, pragmatists, conservatives, and skeptics. New products gain acceptance from niches within the mainstream market, progress from segment to segment like one bowling pin knocking over another, and, if successful, experience the tornado of general, widespread adoption by pragmatists. Importantly, the technology adoption life cycle calls for different marketing strategies at different stages.

Discussion Questions

1. Dell Computer has enjoyed rapid growth and a dominant market position in the computer industry. First, develop a list of what you believe to be the core competencies of Dell. Next, identify which of these core competencies appear to be especially hard for competitors to duplicate.

2. Research in Motion developed BlackBerry—a five-ounce two-pager that gets e-mail messages, includes a calendar, and can fetch stock quotes, flight information, and other data from the Web. Merrill Lynch bought 1,500 of them for employees at its New York City headquarters. Which customer groups should Research in Motion target with this innovative product? Which features of the product should be emphasized in positioning the BlackBerry against competing products?

3. Regis McKenna notes that "No company in a technology-based industry is safe from unanticipated bumps in the night." In recent years, many industries have been jolted by technological change. In such an environment, what steps can a product strategist take?

4. Bradley Gale, managing director of The Strategic Planning Institute, says: "People systematically knock out income statements and balance sheets, but

they often don't monitor the nonfinancial factors that ultimately drive their financial performance. These nonfinancial factors include 'relative customer-perceived quality': how customers view the marketer's offering versus how they perceive competitive offerings." Explain.

5. Distinguish between catalog items, custom-built items, custom-designed items, and services. Explain how marketing requirements vary across these classifications.

6. Describe how a product manager might structure a study to identify the determinant attributes for fax equipment in the university market.

7. A particular product strategy will stimulate a response from the market, and a corresponding response from competitors. Which specific features of the competitive environment should be evaluated by the industrial product strategist?

8. Some industrial product managers argue that their prime function is to market the "capability" of their firm, rather than physical products. Do you agree or disagree? Explain.

9. Moving across the technology adoption life cycle, compare and contrast technology enthusiasts with pragmatists. Give special attention to the strategy guidelines that the marketing strategist should follow in reaching customers that fall into these two adoption categories.

10. Firms like Microsoft, Sony, and Intel have experienced a burst of demand for some of their products. During the "tornado" for a high-tech product, the guiding principle of operations for a market leader is "Just ship." Explain and discuss the changes in marketing strategy that the firm must follow *after* the tornado.

12

Managing Innovation and New Industrial Product Development

The long-term competitive position of most organizations is tied to their ability to innovate—to provide existing and new customers with a continuing stream of new products and services. Innovation is a high-risk and potentially rewarding process. After reading this chapter, you will understand

1. the strategic processes through which product innovations take shape.

2. the characteristics of innovation winners in high-technology markets.

3. the factors that drive a firm's new product performance.

4. the determinants of new product success and timeliness.

Face it: Out there in some garage, an entrepreneur is forging a bullet with your company's name on it. Once the bullet leaves the barrel, you won't be able to dodge it. You've got one option: You have to shoot first. You have to out-innovate the innovators, out-entrepreneur the entrepreneurs."[1]

The long-term health of firms is tied to their ability to provide existing and new customers with a continuing stream of attractive new products. Many firms derive a significant portion of their sales and profits from products introduced in the recent past. But the risks associated with product innovation are high; significant investments are involved and the likelihood of failure is high. With shortening product life cycles and accelerating technological change, speed and agility are central to success in the innovation battle.[2]

This chapter examines product innovation in the business marketing environment. The first section provides a perspective on the management of innovation in the firm. Second, product innovation is positioned within an overall technological strategy for the firm. Third, key dimensions of the new product development process are examined. Attention centers on the forces that drive successful new product performance in the firm. The final section of the chapter explores the determinants of new product success and timeliness.

The Management of Innovation

Management practices in successful industrial firms reflect the realities of the innovation process itself. James Quinn asserts that "Innovation tends to be individually motivated, opportunistic, customer responsive, tumultuous, nonlinear, and interactive in its development. Managers can plan overall directions and goals, but surprises are likely to abound."[3] Clearly, some new product development efforts are the outgrowth of deliberate strategies (intended strategies that become realized), while others result from emergent strategies (realized strategies that, at least initially, were never intended).[4] Bearing little resemblance to a rational, analytical process, many strategic decisions involving new products are rather messy, disorderly, and disjointed processes around which competing organizational factions contend. In studying successful innovative companies such as Sony, AT&T, and Hewlett-Packard, Quinn characterized the innovation process as controlled chaos:

> Many of the best concepts and solutions come from projects partly hidden or "bootlegged" by the organization. Most successful managers try to build some slack or buffers into their plans to hedge their bets. . . . They permit chaos and replications in early investigations, but insist on much more formal planning and controls as expensive development and scale-up proceed.

---

[1] Gary Hamel, "Bringing Silicon Valley Inside," *Harvard Business Review*, 77 (September–October 1999), p. 72.

[2] Kathleen M. Eisenhardt and Shona L. Brown, "Patching: Restitching Business Portfolios in Dynamic Markets," *Harvard Business Review*, 77 (May–June 1999), pp. 72–82; see also Abbie Griffin and Albert L. Page, "An Interim Report on Measuring Product Development Success and Failure," *Journal of Product Innovation Management* 10 (September 1993): pp. 291–309.

[3] James B. Quinn, "Managing Innovation: Controlled Chaos," *Harvard Business Review* 63 (May/June 1985) p. 83.

[4] Henry Mintzberg and James A. Walton, "Of Strategies, Deliberate and Emergent," *Strategic Management Journal* 6 (July/August 1985): pp. 257–272.

But even at these later stages, these managers have learned to maintain flexibility and to avoid the tyranny of paper plans.[5]

Patterns of Strategic Behavior [6]

A planned, deliberate process characterizes the development of some new products whereas a circuitous and chaotic process typifies others. Why? Research suggests that strategic activity within a large organization falls into two broad categories: induced and autonomous strategic behavior.[7]

Induced Strategic Behavior **Induced strategic behavior** is consistent with the firm's traditional concept of strategy and takes place in relationship to its familiar external environment (for example, its customary markets). By manipulating various administrative mechanisms, top management can influence the perceived interests of managers at the middle and operational levels of the organization and keep strategic behavior in line with the current strategy course. For example, the existing reward and measurement systems may direct the attention of managers to some market opportunities and not to others. Examples of induced strategic behavior might emerge around product development efforts for existing markets.

Autonomous Strategic Behavior During any period, the bulk of strategic activity in large, complex firms is likely to fit into the induced behavior category. However, large, resource-rich firms are likely to possess a pool of entrepreneurial potential at operational levels, which will express itself in autonomous strategic initiatives. The 3M Company encourages its technical employees to devote 15 percent of their work time to developing their own ideas. Through the personal efforts of employees, new products are born. For example,

- Art Fry championed Post-it Notes at 3M.
- P. D. Estridge promoted the personal computer at IBM.
- Stephenie L. Kwolck advanced the bulletproof material Kevlar at Du Pont.[8]

Autonomous strategic behavior is conceptually equivalent to entrepreneurial activity and introduces new categories of opportunity into the firm's planning process. Managers at the product-market level conceive of market opportunities that depart from the current strategy course, then engage in product championing activities to mobilize resources and create momentum for further development of the product. Emphasizing political rather than administrative channels, product champions question the firm's current concept of strategy and, states Robert Burgelman, "provide top management with the opportunity to rationalize, retroactively, successful autonomous

---

[5] Quinn, "Managing Innovation," p. 82.

[6] This section is based on Michael D. Hutt, Peter H. Reingen, and John R. Ronchetto Jr., "Tracing Emergent Processes in Marketing Strategy Formation," *Journal of Marketing* 52 (January 1988): pp. 4–19.

[7] Robert A. Burgelman, "A Process Model of Internal Corporate Venturing in the Diversified Major Firm," *Administrative Science Quarterly* 28 (April 1983): pp. 223–244.

[8] Timothy D. Schellhardt, "David and Goliath," *The Wall Street Journal*, (23 May 1996), p. R14.

TABLE 12.1	INDUCED VERSUS AUTONOMOUS STRATEGIC BEHAVIOR: SELECTED CHARACTERISTICS OF THE MARKETING STRATEGY FORMULATION PROCESS	
	Induced	**Autonomous**
Activation of the strategic decision process	An individual manager defines a market need that converges on the organization's concept of strategy.	An individual manager defines a market need that diverges from the organization's concept of strategy.
Nature of the screening process	A formal screening of technical and market merit is made using established administrative procedures.	An informal network assesses technical and market merit.
Type of innovation	Incremental (e.g., new product development for existing markets uses existing organizational resources).	Major (e.g., new product development projects require new combinations of organizational resources).
Nature of communication	Consistent with organizational work flow.	Departs from organizational work flow in early phase of decision process.
Major actors	Prescribed by the regular channel of hierarchical decision making.	An informal network emerges based on mobilization efforts of the product champion.
Decision roles	Roles and responsibilities for participants in the strategy formulation process are well defined.	Roles and responsibilities of participants are poorly defined in the initial phases but become more formalized as the strategy formulation process evolves.
Implications for strategy	Strategic alternatives are considered and commitment to a particular strategic course evolves.	Commitment to a particular strategic course emerges in the early phases through the sponsorship efforts of the product champion.

SOURCE: Adapted from Michael D. Hutt, Peter H. Reingen, and John R. Ronchetto Jr., "Tracing Emergent Processes in Marketing, Strategy Formation," *Journal of Marketing* 52 (January 1988): pp. 4–19.

strategic behavior."[9] Through these political mechanisms, successful autonomous strategic initiatives can become integrated into the firm's concept of strategy.

Product Championing and the Informal Network Several characteristics that may distinguish induced from autonomous strategic behavior are highlighted in Table 12.1. Observe that autonomous strategic initiatives involve a set of actors and evoke a form of strategic dialogue different from those found in induced initiatives. An individual manager, the product champion, assumes a central role in sensing an opportunity and in mobilizing an informal network to explore the technical feasibility and market potential of the idea. A **product champion** is an organization member who creates, defines, or adopts an idea for an innovation and who is willing to assume significant risk (for example, position or prestige) to make possible the successful implementation of the innovation.[10] Senior managers at 3M Company will not commit

---

[9] Robert A. Burgelman, "Corporate Entrepreneurship and Strategic Management: Insights from a Process Study," *Management Science* 29 (December 1983): p. 1352.

[10] Modesto A. Maidique, "Entrepreneurs, Champions, and Technological Innovations," *Sloan Management Review* 21 (spring 1980): pp. 59–70; see also Jane M. Howell, "Champions of Technological Innvation," *Administrative Science Quarterly* 35 (June 1990): pp. 317–341.

INSIDE BUSINESS MARKETING

The Angels of Silicon Valley

"Angels" are wealthy individuals who pool their investments to fund new start-up businesses. Approximately two-thirds of Silicon Valley startups secure their initial funding—usually around $500,000—from angels. In the typical case, each angel invests about $50,000 in the first-round funding of a new business. Many of the ideas that are pitched and funded by angels come from entrepreneurs under the age of thirty. That's why many large corporations are turning to younger employees for fresh strategy ideas. GE Capital, for example, created a team of lower-to-midlevel managers all under thirty in each of its business units and asked them to come up with new opportunities that senior management in the firm had missed. Some new strategic initiatives were born.

Angels review business ideas differently than executives in large corporations would. Take Steve Jurvetson, who funded Hotmail. He views a business plan as a story about an opportunity: "The first thing I ask is, Who will care? What kind of difference will this make? Basically, how high is up? I want to fund things that have just about unlimited upside."

SOURCE: Gary Hamel, "Bringing Silicon Valley Inside," *Harvard Business Review*, 77 (September–October 1999), p. 80.

to a project unless a champion emerges and will not abandon the effort unless the champion "gets tired."

Compared to induced strategic behavior, autonomous initiatives are more likely to involve a communication process that departs from the regular work flow and the hierarchical decision-making channels. The decision roles and responsibilities of managers in this informal network are poorly defined in the early phases of the strategy formulation process but become more formalized as the process evolves. Note in Table 12.1 that autonomous strategic behavior entails a creeping commitment toward a particular strategy course. By contrast, induced strategic initiatives are more likely to involve administrative mechanisms that encourage a more formal and comprehensive assessment of strategic alternatives at various levels in the firm's planning hierarchy.

Bringing Silicon Valley Inside [11]

While corporate leaders strive for innovative ideas and envy the success of Silicon Valley's entrepreneurs, few have considered how they might bring the passion and spirit of the Valley inside—how they might ignite the entrepreneurial energy and focus of their own employees. What drives Silicon Valley are three interconnected markets: a market for ideas, a market for capital, and a market for talent. While ideas, capital, and talent whirl through Silicon Valley at a rapid pace searching for new sources of value, the movement is stifled in most large corporations.

Market for Ideas Gary Hamel, a leading strategy consultant, observes that "the last bastion of Soviet-style central planning can be found in *Fortune* 500 companies—it's called resource allocation." [12] A crucial distinction here is that Silicon Valley is not

---

[11] Hamel, "Bringing Silicon Valley Inside," pp. 71–84.

[12] Ibid., p. 76.

based on resource *allocation* but, instead, on resource *attraction*. Resource allocation is perfectly suited to investments in existing businesses and managing the downside risks whereas resource attraction is about pursuing fresh ideas that will create new businesses and managing the upside—rule-breaking opportunities. To unleash the ideas and passion of employees, large corporations must bring new voices into the opportunity-seeking process, radically changing the conventional belief that strategy is the province of senior managers.

For example, Royal Dutch/Shell, the large oil producer, created a process called GameChanger that gives a panel of employees the ability to allocate $20 million to promising new opportunities. The group meets weekly and has screened over 100 ideas annually from employees throughout the organization. An employee with a promising idea is invited to give a brief presentation to the panel. A favorable review can lead to preliminary funding ($100,000 is the average) ten days later. Four of the five major strategic initiatives launched by Shell in 1999 emerged from the GameChanger process.

Market for Capital   Compared to corporate strategists, venture capitalists in Silicon Valley operate with a different set of expectations about success and failure in funding ideas. Out of several thousand ideas, a venture capitalist might fund ten ideas. Out of the ten, five will fail, three will be a moderate success, one will double the investment, and one will generate 50- to 100-times the investment. Rather than insuring that there are no losers, venture capitalists want to make sure that there is a big winner.

Large corporations often miss the path-breaking idea—the big winner. Why? The typical capital budgeting process in large companies attempts to guarantee no losers. By departing from the current strategy course, creative business ideas pose a risk and seldom make it through a traditional financial screening process. To remedy this problem, a source of funding can be created within the organization that is entirely separate from the traditional capital budgeting process. For example, that's the goal of the GameChanger process at Royal Dutch/Shell—create an innovation-friendly market for capital inside the firm.

Market for Talent   If you do not give your employees truly exhilarating work and solid incentives, Silicon Valley executives know that those workers will jump at the chance to work on the next great thing at another company. To retain talented employees, large corporations need to create an internal market where employees can move freely, move to new jobs that capture their interests or capitalize on their skills. In turn, positive incentives should be provided for employees who are willing to take a risk on an unconventional initiative. At firms like Disney, Monsanto, or Royal Dutch/Shell, employees are given the opportunity to move out of existing businesses into new businesses, or even to nominate themselves for a new venture team.

Gary Hamel notes:

> The bottom line is this: if you have highly creative and ambitious people who feel trapped in moribund businesses, they are going to leave. The only question is whether they leave to join some other company, or whether they leave to join a GameChanger kind of team in your company.[13]

---

[13] Ibid., p. 83.

Managing Technology

Eastman Kodak, Lockheed, IBM, and the management teams of other corporations failed to recognize the major technological opportunity that xerographic copying presented. These firms were among the many that turned down the chance to participate with the small and unknown Haloid Company in refining and commercializing this technology. In the end, Haloid pursued it alone and transformed this one technological opportunity into the Xerox Corporation. Among the "tales of high tech," this will remain a classic. Technological change, Michael Porter asserts, is "a great equalizer, eroding the competitive advantage of even well-entrenched firms and propelling others to the forefront. Many of today's great firms grew out of technological changes that they were able to exploit."[14] Clearly, the long-run competitive position of most industrial firms depends on their ability to manage, increase, and exploit their technology base. This section explores the nature of development projects, the link between technology platforms and product strategy, and the defining attributes of firms that are successful innovators in fast-changing high-technology markets.

Classifying Development Projects

A first step in exploring the technology portfolio of a firm is to understand the different forms that development projects can take. Some development projects center on improving the manufacturing *process*, some on improving *products*, and others on both process and product improvements. All of these represent commercial development projects. By contrast, research and development is the precursor to commercial development. Four types of development projects may be included in a firm's portfolio.[15]

1. **Derivative projects** center on incremental product enhancements (for example, a new feature), incremental process improvements (for example, a lower-cost manufacturing process), or incremental changes on both dimensions.

   Illustration: A feature-enhanced or cost-reduced Canon fax machine.

2. **Platform projects** create the design and components that are shared by a set of products. These projects often involve a number of changes both in the product and in the manufacturing process.

   Illustrations: A common motor in all Black & Decker hand tools; multiple applications of Intel's microprocessor.

3. **Breakthrough projects** establish new core products and new core processes that differ fundamentally from previous generations.

   Illustrations: Computer disks and fiber-optics cable each created a new product category.

---

[14]Michael E. Porter, "Technology and Competitive Advantage," *Journal of Business Strategy* 6 (winter 1985) p. 60; and Tamara J. Erickson, John F. Magee, Philip A. Roussel, and Komol N. Saad, "Managing Technology as Business Strategy," *Sloan Management Review* 31 (spring 1990): pp. 73–83.

[15]This discussion is based on Steven C. Wheelwright and Kim B. Clark, "Creating Product Plans to Focus Product Development," *Harvard Business Review* 70 (March/April 1992): pp. 70–82.

4. **Research and development** is the creation of knowledge concerning new materials and technologies that eventually leads to commercial development.[16]

   Illustrations: Lucent Technologies' development of communications technology that underlies its telecommunications systems used by diverse customers like banks and hotel chains.

A Product Family Focus

A particular technology may provide the foundation or platform for several products. For example, Honda applies its multivalve cylinder technology to power-generation equipment, cars, motorcycles, and lawn mowers.[17] Products that share a common platform but have different specific features and enhancements that are required for different sets of consumers constitute a **product family.**[18] Each generation of a product family has a platform that provides the foundation for specific products targeted to different or complementary market applications. By expanding on technical skills, market knowledge, and manufacturing competencies, entirely new product families may be formed, thereby creating new business opportunities for the business marketing firm.

Strategists argue that a firm should move away from a planning emphasis that centers on single products and focus, instead, on families of products that can grow from a common platform. Consider the Sony Walkman—one of the most successful products of all time. Based on how different customer segments use the product, Sony developed six basic platforms for the Walkman: playback only, playback and record, playback and tuner, and sports. Then, by applying standard design elements such as color and styling, Sony added an assortment of features and distinctive technical attributes to the basic platforms with relative ease.[19]

The move toward a product family perspective requires close interfunctional working relationships, a long-term view of technology strategy, and a multiple-year commitment of resources. While this approach offers significant competitive leverage, Steven Wheelwright and Kim Clark note that companies often fail to make an adequate investment in platforms: "The reasons vary, but the most common is that management lacks an awareness of the strategic value of platforms and fails to create well-thought-out platform projects."[20]

Innovation Winners in High-Technology Markets

In rapidly changing industries with short product life cycles and quickly shifting competitive landscapes, a firm must continually innovate to keep its offerings aligned with the market. The ability of a firm to cope with change in a high-velocity industry is a key to competitive success. Shona Brown and Kathleen Eisenhardt provide an intriguing comparison of successful versus less successful product innovation in the computer

---

[16] Ibid., p. 74.

[17] T. Michael Nevens, Gregory L. Summe, and Bro Uttal, "Commercializing Technology: What the Best Companies Do," *Harvard Business Review* 60 (May/June 1990): pp. 154–163; see also C. K. Prahalad, "Weak Signals versus Strong Paradigms," *Journal of Marketing Research* 32 (August 1995): pp. iii–vi.

[18] Marc H. Meyer and James M. Utterback, "The Product Family and the Dynamics of Core Capability," *Sloan Management Review* 34 (spring 1993): pp. 29–47; see also Dwight L. Gertz and João P. A. Baptista, *Grow to Be Great: Breaking the Downsizing Cycle* (New York: The Free Press, 1995), pp. 92–103.

[19] Kathleen M. Eisenhardt and Shona L. Brown, "Time Pacing: Competing in Markets That Won't Stand Still," *Harvard Business Review*, 76 (March–April 1998), p. 67.

[20] Wheelwright and Clark, "Creating Project Plans," p. 74.

Patching: The New Corporate Strategy in Dynamic Markets

Kathleen M. Eisenhardt and Shona L. Brown contend that traditional corporate planning and resource allocation approaches are not effective in volatile markets. As new technologies, novel products and services, and emerging markets create tempting opportunities, "the clear-cut partitioning of businesses into neat, equidistant rectangles on an organizational chart becomes out of date."

The new corporate-level strategic processes center on managing change and continually realigning the organization to capture market opportunities faster than the competition. Central to this newly defined approach is **patching**—the strategic process used by corporate executives to routinely realign or re-map businesses to changing

market opportunities. Patching can take the form of adding, dividing, transferring, exiting, or combining pieces of businesses. Hewlett-Packard used patching to launch the printer business, create businesses in related products like scanners and faxes, and to develop a second printer business built around ink-jet technology. Patching is less critical in stable markets but a crucial skill when markets are turbulent. Here a small agile unit of the firm can be mobilized quickly to capture fresh market opportunities.

SOURCE: Kathleen M. Eisenhardt and Shona L. Brown, "Patching: Restitching Business Portfolios in Dynamic Markets," *Harvard Business Review*, 77 (May–June 1999), pp. 72–82.

industry.[21] Successful innovators were defined as those firms that were on schedule, on time to the market, and on target in addressing customer needs. The study found that firms with a successful record of product innovation employ different organizational structures and processes than their competitors. In particular, four distinguishing characteristics marked the innovation approach of successful firms.

1. Limited Structure

Creating successful products to meet changing customer needs requires flexibility but successful product innovators combine this flexibility with a few rules that are never broken. First, strict priorities for new products are established and tied directly to resource allocation. This allows managers to direct attention to the most promising opportunities, avoiding the temptation to pursue too many attractive opportunities. Second, managers set deadlines for a few key milestones and always meet them. Third, responsibility for a limited number of major outcomes is set. For example, at one firm, engineering managers were responsible for product schedules while marketing managers were responsible for market definition and product profitability. While successful firms emphasized structure for a few areas (for example, priorities or deadlines), less successful innovators imposed a greater degree of control—lockstep, checkpoint procedures for every facet of new product development—or virtually no structure at all. Successful firms strike a balance by using a structure that is neither so rigid as to stiffly control the process nor so chaotic that the process falls apart.

2. Real Time Communication and Improvisation

Successful product innovators in the computer industry emphasize real-time communication within new product development teams *and* across product teams. Much of the communication occurs in formal meetings but there is also extensive informal

---

[21] This section is based on Shona L. Brown and Kathleen M. Eisenhardt, "The Art of Continuous Change: Linking Complexity Theory and Time-Paced Evolution in Relentlessly Shifting Organizations," *Administrative Science Quarterly*, 42 (March 1997), pp. 1–34.

communication throughout the organization. Clear priorities and responsibilities, coupled with extensive communications, allow product developers to improvise. "In the context of jazz improvisation, this means creating music while adjusting to the changing musical interpretations of others. In the context of product innovation, it means creating a product while simultaneously adapting to changing markets and technologies."[22]

More formally, then, **improvisation** involves activities in which the design and execution of actions approach convergence with each other in time.[23] The shorter the elapsed time between the design and implementation of an activity, the more that activity is improvisational. Successful firms expect constant change and new product teams have the freedom to act. One manager noted: "We fiddle right up to the end" of the new product development process. Real-time communications among members of the product development team, coupled with the limited structure, provide the foundation for such improvisation.

3. Experimentation: Probing into the Future

Some firms make a large bet on one version of the future while others fail to update future plans in light of changing competition. Creators of successful product portfolios did not invest in any one version of the future but, instead, used a variety of low-cost probes to create options for the future. Examples of low-cost probes would include developing experimental products for new markets, entering into a strategic alliance with leading-edge customers to better understand future needs, or conducting regular planning sessions dedicated to the future. In turbulent industries, strategists cannot accurately predict which of many possible versions of the future will arrive. Probes create more possible responses for managers when the future does arrive, while lowering the probability of being surprised by unanticipated futures.

4. Time Pacing

Successful product innovators carefully managed the transition between current and future projects while less successful innovators let each project unfold according to its own schedule. Successful innovators, like Intel, practice **time pacing**—a strategy for competing in fast-changing markets by creating new products at predictable time intervals[24] (see Figure 12.1). Transition processes are carefully choreographed and understood by organizational members. For example, marketing managers might begin work on the definition of the next product while engineering is completing work on the current product and moving it to manufacturing. Time pacing motivates managers to anticipate change and can have a strong psychological impact across the organization. "Time pacing creates a relentless sense of urgency around meeting deadlines and concentrates individual and team energy around common goals."[25]

The New Product Development Process

To sustain their competitive advantage, leading-edge firms such as Canon, Microsoft, and Hewlett-Packard make new product development a top management priority.

---

[22] Ibid., p. 15.

[23] Christine Moorman and Anne S. Miner, "The Convergence of Planning and Execution: Improvisation in New Product Development," *Journal of Marketing*, 62 (July 1998), p. 3.

[24] Eisenhardt and Brown, "Time Pacing: Competing in Markets That Won't Stand Still," pp. 59–69.

[25] Ibid., p. 60.

| FIGURE 12.1 | TIME-PACED INNOVATION AT INTEL: AS ONE IS INTRODUCED, THE NEXT IS IN DEVELOPMENT |

Introducing the Intel® Pentium® III Xeon™ processor. Performance for enterprise servers.

 We're living in a wired world. And since your server is at the heart of it, the power and stability of Intel® Architecture is more important than ever. Specifically designed for today's connected enterprise, the Pentium® III Xeon™ processor is our highest performing processor for servers. Working together with Pentium® III processor-based PCs, it provides the performance and reliability you need to run your critical e-business applications. From back-end database hosting to transaction processing. On UNIX and NT. To learn more about the Pentium III Xeon processor, visit us on the Web. ► www.intel.com/PentiumIII/Xeon

intel. The Computer Inside.™

SOURCE: Courtesy, Intel Corporation.

They directly involve managers and employees from across the organization to speed actions and decisions. Because new product ventures can represent a significant risk as well as an important opportunity, new product development requires systematic thought. The high expectations ascribed to new products are often not fulfilled. Worse, many new industrial products fail. Although the definitions of failure are somewhat elusive, research suggests that 30 to 40 percent of industrial products fail.[26] While there may be some debate over the number of failures, there is no debate over the fact that a new product rejected by the market constitutes a substantial waste to the firm and to society.

This section will center on (1) the forces that drive a firm's new product performance, (2) the sources of new product ideas, (3) cross-functional barriers to successful innovation, and (4) team-based processes employed in new product development. A

[26] Albert L. Page, "Assessing New Product Development Practices and Performances: Establishing Crucial Norms," *Journal of Product Innovation Management* 10 (September 1993): pp. 273–290.

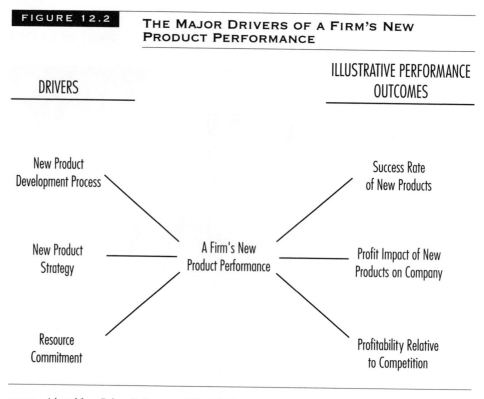

FIGURE 12.2 THE MAJOR DRIVERS OF A FIRM'S NEW PRODUCT PERFORMANCE

SOURCE: Adapted from Robert G. Cooper and Elko J. Kleinschmidt, "Benchmarking Firms' New Product Performance and Practices," *Engineering Management Review* 23 (fall 1995): pp. 112–120.

promising method for bringing the "voice of the consumer" directly into the development process is also explored.

What Drives a Firm's New Product Performance?

A benchmarking study sought to uncover the critical success factors that drive a firm's new product performance.[27] Three factors were identified (see Figure 12.2): (1) the quality of a firm's new product development process, (2) the resource commitments made to new product development, and (3) the new product strategy.

Process Successful companies employ a high-quality new product development process—careful attention is given to the execution of the activities and decision points that new products follow from the idea stage to launch and beyond. The benchmarking study identified the following characteristics among high-performing firms:

- The firms emphasized upfront market and technical assessments before projects moved into the development phase.

---

[27] Robert G. Cooper and Elko J. Kleinschmidt, "Benchmarking Firms' New Product Performance and Practices," *Engineering Management Review* 23 (fall 1995): pp. 112–120; see also, Robert G. Cooper, Scott J. Edgett, and Elko J. Kleinschmidt, "New Product Portfolio Management: Practices and Performance," *The Journal of Product Innovation Management*, 16 (July 1999), pp. 333–351.

- The process featured complete descriptions of the product concept, product benefits, positioning, and target markets before development work was initiated.

- Tough project *go/kill* decision points were included in the process and the kill option was actually used.

- The new product process was flexible—certain stages could be skipped in line with the nature and risk of a particular project.

Detailed upfront homework on the product concept, the likely market response, and the technical feasibility of the product, along with a thorough business and financial assessment, are important dimensions of the process that successful product creators follow.

Resource Commitments   Adequate resources were invested in new product development in top-performing firms. Three ingredients were important here:

1. Top management committed the resources necessary to meet the firm's objectives for the total product effort in the firm.

2. R&D budgets were adequate and aligned with the stated new product objectives.

3. The necessary personnel were assigned and were relieved from other duties so that they could give full attention to new product development.

New Product Strategy   A clear and visible new product strategy was another driver of a firm's new product performance (see Figure 12.2). Successful firms, like 3M, set aggressive new product performance goals (for example, **x** percent of company sales and profit from new products) as a basic corporate goal and communicate it to all employees. In turn, Robert Cooper and Elko Kleinschmidt report that successful firms centered development efforts on clearly defined arenas—particular product, market, and technology domains—to direct the new product program:

> The new product strategy specifies "the arenas where we'll play the game," or perhaps more important, where we won't play . . . what's in bounds and out of bounds. Without arenas defined, the search for new product ideas or opportunities is unfocused. . . .[28]

Sources of New Product Ideas

The business marketer should be alert to new product ideas and to their sources, both inside and outside the company. Internally, the new product ideas may flow from salespersons who are close to customer needs, from R&D specialists who are close to new technological developments, and from top management who know the company's

---

[28] Ibid., p. 117; see also Jean-Marie Choffray and Gary L. Lilien, "Assessing Response to Industrial Marketing Strategy," *Journal of Marketing* 42 (April 1978): pp. 20–31; and Eunsang Yoon and Gary L. Lilien, "New Industrial Product Performance: The Effects of Market Characteristics and Strategy," *Journal of Product Innovation Management* 3 (September 1985): pp. 134–144.

strengths and weaknesses. Externally, ideas may come from channel members, such as distributors or customers, or from an assessment of competitive moves.

Eric von Hippel challenges the traditional view that marketers typically introduce new products to a passive market.[29] His research suggests that the customers in the business market often develop the idea for a new product and even select the supplier to make that product. The customer is responding to the perceived *capability* of the business marketer, rather than to a specific physical product. This points up the need for involving the customers in new product development, and for promoting corporate capability to consumers (idea generators).

Lead Users   Because many industrial product markets for high-technology and, in particular, capital equipment consist of a small number of high-volume buying firms, special attention must be given to the needs of **lead users,** which include a small number of highly influential buying organizations who are consistent early adopters of new technologies.[30] Lead users face needs that will be general in the marketplace, but they confront these needs months or years before the bulk of that marketplace encounters them. In addition, they are positioned to benefit significantly by obtaining a solution that satisfies those needs. For example, if an automobile manufacturer wanted to design an innovative braking system, marketing managers might secure insights from auto racing teams who have a strong need for better brakes. In turn, they might look to a related field like aerospace where antilock braking systems were first developed so that military aircraft could land on short runways.[31]

The Lead User Method   Lead user projects are conducted by a cross-functional team that includes four to six managers from marketing and technical departments; one member serves as project leader. Team members typically spend twelve to fifteen hours per week on the projects, which are usually completed in four to six weeks. Lead user projects proceed through five phases (see Figure 12.3). 3M has now successfully used the lead user method in eight different divisions and support among project teams and divisional managers is strong. For example, the Medical-Surgical Markets Group at 3M used the lead user method to unearth new product ideas and to identify a revolutionary approach to infection control.[32]

Staying Ahead of Customers   Rather than merely asking customers what they want, some firms succeed by leading customers where they want to go before the customers actually know it themselves.[33] To illustrate, Motorola envisions a global communication environment where telephone numbers are attached to people rather than to places, and where a personal communicator allows millions of business travelers to be reached anywhere, anytime. Deep insights into the needs and aspirations of today's and tomorrow's customers is needed to plan the course for innovation. In addition to

---

[29] Eric von Hippel, "Get New Products from Customers," *Harvard Business Review* 60 (March/April 1982): pp. 117–122; see also von Hippel, *The Sources of Innovation* (New York: Oxford University Press, 1988); see also, Gerard A. Athaide and Rodney L. Stump, "A Taxonomy of Relationship Approaches During Technology Development in Technology-Based, Industrial Markets," *The Journal of Product Innovation Management*, 16 (September 1999), pp. 469–482.

[30] Ibid. von Hippel, "Get New Products from Customers," pp. 120–121.

[31] Eric von Hippel, Stefan Thomko, and Mary Sonnack, "Creating Breakthroughs at 3M," *Harvard Business Review*, 77 (September–October 1999), pp. 47–57.

[32] Ibid., p. 56.

[33] Gary Hamel and C. K. Prahalad, "Corporate Imagination and Expeditionary Marketing," *Harvard Business Review* 69 (July/August 1991): pp. 81–92.

FIGURE 12.3	THE LEAD USER METHOD	

Phase	Central Focus	Description
Phase 1	Laying the Foundation	The team identifies target markets and secures support from internal stakeholders for the type and level of innovations desired.
Phase 2	Determining the Trends	The team talks to experts in the field who have a broad view of emerging technologies and pioneering applications in the particular area.
Phase 3	Identifying Lead Users	The team begins a networking process to identify lead users at the leading edge of the target market and to gather information that might contribute to breakthrough products.
Phase 4	Developing & Assessing Preliminary Product Ideas	The team begins to shape product ideas and to assess market potential and fit with company interests.
Phase 5	Developing the Breakthroughs	To design final concepts, the team hosts a workshop bringing together lead users with other in-house managers. After further refinement, the team presents its recommendations to senior management.

SOURCE: Adapted with modifications from Eric von Hippel, Stefan Thomke, and Mary Sonnack, "Creating Breakthroughs at 3M," *Harvard Business Review*, 77 (September–October 1999), p. 52.

providing critical customer feedback to technical personnel, procedures are needed to inform those closest to the customer (marketers) about the coming technological possibilities. Motorola succeeds by educating customers to *what is possible.* Rather than providing precise demand forecasts, "market research acts as a catalyst for developing and enriching new ideas."[34]

Cross-Functional Barriers

Successful new product creation is a collective achievement that requires the energy and commitment of multiple functions (for example, R&D and manufacturing) and stakeholders (for example, suppliers). Three obstacles can damage new product development efforts: turf barriers, interpretive barriers, and communication barriers.[35]

Turf Barriers   New product decisions engage and arouse members who may experience gain or loss. **Turf** includes an area of expertise, or authority, a particular task, or access to resources. Functional units are strongly motivated to defend against loss of status or power. By signaling a new direction for the firm, new product development projects often ignite turf battles among functional units as each competes for resources, information, and support.

---

[34]Soren M. Kaplan, "Discontinuous Innovation and the Growth Paradox," *Strategy & Leadership*, 28 (March/April 1999), p. 20.

[35]This discussion is based on Michael D. Hutt, Beth A. Walker, and Gary L. Frankwick, "Hurdle the Cross-Functional Barriers to Strategic Change," *Sloan Management Review* 36 (spring 1995): pp. 22–30.

Consider the Techno project story: An R&D team at a telecommunications company developed technology that would enable it to fully automate the sales function and introduce a range of new services. In turn, the R&D team wanted to assume the lead role in developing the new products and services. Fearing a declining budget and a loss of control, the marketing unit strongly resisted and a turf battle ensued. Ultimately, the marketing function embraced the technology and introduced a whole host of successful products and services. But months were lost in the development process as the turf squabbles were being settled. Thus, constructive debate and tension across organizational units can speed learning while destructive turf wars stifle it.

Interpretive Barriers In an organization, asserts Deborah Dougherty, "departments are like 'thought worlds': each focusing on different aspects of technology–market knowledge and making different sense of the total."[36] Collaboration across functions is necessary for successful innovation, and differing interpretations are major barriers. Each department has common judgments and procedures that produce a qualitatively different understanding of product innovation.

Figure 12.4 graphs the contrasting views of the Techno project that marketing and R&D managers held at a key milestone in the development process. Recall that the technology would enable customers of a telecommunications firm to order products and services without a salesperson's intervention. Marketing managers had negative opinions of Techno's impact on customer service and selling efficacy. Marketers also saw the sizable investment in Techno as significantly negative and were less enthusiastic than R&D managers about its follow-up opportunities. R&D managers were positive about customer service, the investment, and follow-up opportunities, and less negative about selling efficacy.

Communication Barriers Departments or functional areas develop a shared language that reflects similarities in the way in which members interpret, understand, and respond to information. This language or coding enhances communication within the department. However, organizational members who are unfamiliar with it may find communication with the departmental members difficult.

The new product development process involves a growing network of participants. Research clearly indicates that cooperation and frequent communication among participants is critical to new product success. In particular, interfunctional harmony between marketing and R&D strongly correlates with project success.

Successful Collaboration Underlying an innovative organization's strength is the ability to harmonize technology with a clear understanding of customers' present and future needs.[37] A shared appreciation of each function's distinctive skills contributes to creating competitive advantage. R&D can articulate the technological possibilities, while marketing thoughtfully assesses the possibilities in light of market opportunities and competitive realities. Collaboration creates new, sharper conceptualizations of how technology can profitably serve customers and strengthen competitive advantage.

---

[36]Deborah Dougherty, "Interpretive Barriers to Successful Product Innovation in Large Firms," *Organization Science* 3 (May 1992): p. 179.

[37]For a comprehensive review, see Abbie Griffin and John R. Hauser, "Integrating R&D and Marketing: A Review and Analysis of the Literature," *Journal of Product Innovation Management* 13 (May 1996): pp. 191–215.

FIGURE 12.4   MANAGERS' OPINIONS ABOUT THE
TECHNO PROJECT AT MILESTONE ONE

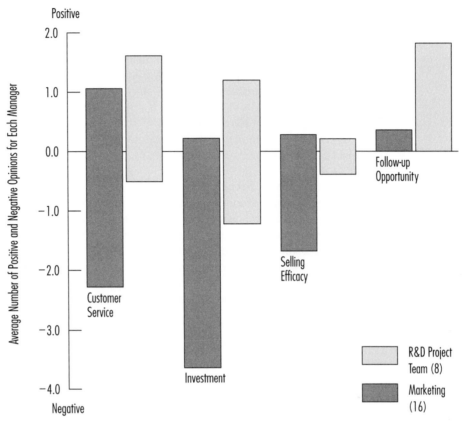

SOURCE: Reprinted from Michael D. Hutt, Beth A. Walker, and Gary L. Frankwick, "Hurdle the Cross-Functional Barriers to Strategic Change," *Sloan Management Review* 36 (spring 1995): p. 25, by permission of the publisher. Copyright © 1995 by Sloan Management Review Association. All rights reserved.

A Team-Based Process

Jon Katzenbach and Douglas Smith offer the following insight regarding teams and performance:

> A **team** is a small number of people with complementary skills who are committed to a common purpose, set of performance goals, an approach for which they hold themselves mutually accountable. The essence of a team is common commitment. Without it, groups perform as individuals; with it, they become a powerful unit of collective performance.[38]

---

[38]Jon R. Katzenbach and Douglas K. Smith, "The Discipline of Teams," *Harvard Business Review* 71 (March/April 1993): p. 112; see also Ravindranath Madhavan and Rajiv Grover, "From Embedded Knowledge to Embodied Knowledge: New Product Development as Knowledge Management," *Journal of Marketing*, 62 (October 1998), pp. 1–12.

To an unprecedented degree, multidisciplinary teams are the preferred structure for organizing the new product development process in business marketing firms.[39] In turn, firms are increasingly turning to *concurrent engineering* to speed new product development and to tighten cross-functional connections (see Chapter 9).

With concurrent engineering, the entire development process is characterized by the constant interaction of a hand-picked interfunctional team whose members work together from start to finish. The team includes experts from marketing, design, manufacturing, R&D, purchasing, and other functional areas. Importantly, key suppliers are involved in the process from the outset to capitalize on their specialized knowledge. The core idea is that the team is responsible for conceptualizing the product correctly up front.[40] Rather than proceeding through highly structured stages, the cross-functional team manages the development process in an integrated manner—it moves as a unit toward a singular objective.

Choosing a Team Structure A business marketing firm should ensure that the structure of its new product development effort matches its strategic priorities and its environment. Research evidence suggests that a firm should match the innovativeness of a new product to the type of organization used to manage its development.[41] Cross-functional teams appear to work best for *new to the world products*—products that are new to the company developing them and to customers using them. Traditional organizational structures can be used when the products are familiar such as *product modifications*—existing products that have been slightly modified.

Quality Function Deployment[42]

Cooperation and communication among marketing, manufacturing, engineering, and R&D are fundamental to greater new-product success and more profitable products. **Quality function deployment,** or **QFD,** is a method used to identify critical customer attributes and to establish a specific link between customer attributes and product design attributes. Cross-functional communication is improved by linking the voice of the customer directly to engineering, manufacturing, and R&D decisions. The approach has been adopted widely by Japanese, U.S., and European firms. The new product development team uses the approach to understand the voice of the consumer and to translate it into the voice of the engineer.

The Voice of the Customer The first task of QFD is to identify customer needs, which are expressions in the customers' own words of the benefits they want the product to deliver. Discussions with customers will often create a lengthy list of needs. Particular attention, however, is given to the five to ten top-level needs or primary needs that set the strategic direction for the product. Small business owners, for example, might seek these attributes in a photocopier: reliable, low cost, compact, quiet, and fast. Research suggests that interviews with twenty to thirty customers should

[39] Page, "Assessing New Product Development Projects," p. 276.

[40] See, for example, Willard I. Zangwill, *Lightning Strategies for Innovation* (New York: Lexington Books, 1993), pp. 231–265.

[41] Eric M. Olson, Orville C. Walker, and Robert W. Ruekert, "Organizing for Effective New Product Development: The Moderating Role of Product Innovativeness," *Journal of Marketing* 59 (January 1995): pp. 48–62.

[42] This section is based on John R. Hauser, "How Puritan-Bennett Used the House of Quality," *Sloan Management Review* 34 (spring 1993): pp. 61–70.

identify 90 percent or more of the customer needs in a relatively homogeneous market segment.[43]

Since some of the customer attributes have more importance to some customers than others, weights are assigned to represent the relative importance of the attributes from the customer's perspective. Such weighting or prioritizing enables the QFD team to balance the cost of meeting a need with the benefit sought by the customer. To guide product design, competitive data on customer perceptions of current products also constitutes a component of QFD. As Abbie Griffin and John Hauser point out, "Knowledge of which products fulfill which needs best, how well those needs are fulfilled, and whether there are any gaps between the best product and 'our' existing product provide further input into product development decisions being made by the QFD team."[44]

The Voice of the Engineer   The strength of QFD comes from translating customer needs into product design attributes. These design parameters should be measurable requirements that are tied to customer attributes (for example, the power of the motor in a photocopier influences the performance speed). Once the design parameters are identified, the QFD team can begin to examine the relationship between a design parameter and a customer attribute. For example, increasing the power of the motor will have a positive impact on the customer attribute "speed," but a negative impact on the customer attributes "low cost" and "quiet." An evaluation of the relationship between design parameters and customer attributes draws on information from customers, engineering experience, and data from designed experiments. Design opportunities that fit customer needs might also be revealed by considering the interrelationships between design parameters.

Using Quality Function Development   QFD provides an important framework for bringing critical information on customer needs together with appropriate engineering data on fulfilling those needs. Rather than yielding design solutions, QFD provides a mechanism for exposing and tackling difficult design trade-offs that inevitably appear in the new product development process. The approach enables the interfunctional product team to develop a common understanding of the design issues. In a head-to-head comparison with a traditional product development process, research indicates that QFD enhances communication among team members.[45] In some applications, QFD has reduced design time by 40 percent and design costs by 60 percent, while maintaining or enhancing design quality.[46]

Determinants of New Product Performance and Timeliness

What factors are most important in determining the success or failure of the new product? Why are some firms faster than others in moving projects through the development process? Let's review the available evidence.

---

[43] Abbie Griffin and John R. Hauser, "The Voice of the Customer," *Marketing Science* 12 (winter 1993): pp. 1–25.

[44] Ibid., p. 5.

[45] Abbie Griffin and John R. Hauser, "Patterns of Communication among Marketing, Engineering and Manufacturing: A Comparison between Two New Product Teams," *Management Science* 38 (March 1992): pp. 360–373.

[46] John R. Hauser and Don P. Clausing, "The House of Quality," *Harvard Business Review* 66 (May/June 1988): pp. 63–73.

The Determinants of Success

Both strategic factors as well as a firm's proficiency in carrying out the new product development process determine new product success.[47]

Strategic Factors   Research suggests that four strategic factors appear to be crucial to new product success. The level of product advantage is the most important. **Product advantage** refers to customer perceptions of product superiority with respect to quality, cost–performance ratio, or function relative to competitors. Successful products offer clear benefits, such as reduced customer costs, and are of higher quality (for example, more durable) than the products of competitors. A study of more than 100 new product projects in the chemical industry illustrates the point. Here, Robert Cooper and Elko Kleinschmidt assert, "the winners are new products that offer high relative product quality, have superior price/performance characteristics, provide good value for the money to the customer, are superior to competing products in meeting customer needs, [and] have unique attributes and highly visible benefits that are easily seen by the customer."[48]

Marketing synergy and technical synergy are also pivotal in new product outcomes. **Marketing synergy** represents the degree of fit between the needs of the project and the firm's resources and skills in marketing (for example, personal selling or market research). By contrast, **technical synergy** concerns the fit between the needs of the project and the firm's R&D resources and competencies. New products that match the skills of the firm are likely to succeed.

In addition to the preceding three factors, an **international orientation** also contributes to the success of product innovation.[49] New products that are designed and developed to meet foreign requirements, and that are targeted at world or nearest-neighbor export markets, outperform domestic products on almost every measure, including success rate, profitability, and domestic and foreign market shares. Underlying this success is a strong international focus in market research, product testing with customers, trial selling, and launch efforts.

Development Process Factors   New product success is also associated with particular characteristics of the development process. **Predevelopment proficiency** provides the foundation for a successful product. Predevelopment involves several important tasks such as initial screening, preliminary market and technical assessment, detailed market research study, and preliminary business/financial analysis. Firms that are skilled in completing these upfront tasks are likely to experience new product success.

Market knowledge and **marketing proficiency** are also pivotal in new product outcomes. As might be expected, business marketers with a solid understanding of market needs are likely to succeed. Robert Cooper describes the market planning for

---

[47] Mitzi M. Montoya-Weiss and Roger Calantone, "Determinants of New Product Performance: A Review and Meta-Analysis," *Journal of Product Innovation Management* 11 (November 1994): pp. 397–417; see also Robert G. Cooper, *Winning at New Products: Accelerating the Process from Idea to Launch* (Reading, Mass.: Addison-Wesley, 1993).

[48] Robert G. Cooper and Elko J. Kleinschmidt, "Major New Products: What Distinguishes the Winners in the Chemical Industry?" *Journal of Product Innovation Management* 10 (March 1993): p. 108. See also, Tiger Li and Roger J. Calantone, "The Impact of Market Knowledge Competence on New Product Advantage: Conceptualization and Empirical Examination," *Journal of Marketing*, 62 (October 1998), pp. 13–29.

[49] Elko J. Kleinschmidt and Robert G. Cooper, "The Performance Impact of an International Orientation on Product Innovation," *European Journal of Marketing* 22, no. 9 (1988): pp. 56–71.

From Bullet-Point Plans to Strategic Stories at 3M

After reviewing countless business plans over several years, Gordon Shaw, executive director of planning at 3M, concluded that the firm's business plans failed to reflect deep thought or to inspire commitment and active support. He suspected that the traditional, bullet-list format of the plans was a major part of the problem. Bullet lists are too generic and fail to convey how the business will win in a particular market. To remedy the problem, he turned to strategic narratives—planning through storytelling. Like a good story, a good strategic plan "defines relationships, cause and effect, and a priority among items—*and those elements are likely to be remembered as a complex whole.*"

In using the approach, a strategist at 3M first **sets the stage** by defining the current competitive, market, and company situation in an insightful and coherent manner. Next, the planner must **introduce the dramatic conflict**—the main challenges or critical issues that provide obstacles to success. Finally, the story must **reach resolution** in a satisfying and compelling fashion. Here a logical and concise argument is provided concerning the specific actions the company can take to overcome the obstacles and win. Narrative plans create a rich picture of strategy, bring critical assumptions to the surface, and provide a central message that can motivate and mobilize employees throughout the organization.

SOURCE: Gordon Shaw, Robert Brown, and Philip Bromiley, "Strategic Stories: How 3M Is Rewriting Business Planning," *Harvard Business Review*, 76 (May–June 1998), pp. 41–50.

a successful product he examined: "Market information was very complete: there was a solid understanding of the customer's needs, wants, and preferences; of the customer's buying behavior and price sensitivity; of the size and trends of the market; and of the competitive situation. Finally, the market launch was well planned, well targeted, proficiently executed, and backed by appropriate resources."[50]

Technical knowledge and **technical proficiency** constitute other important dimensions of the new product development process. When technical developers possess a strong base of knowledge concerning the technical aspects of a potential new product, and when they can proficiently pass through the stages of the new product development process (for example, product development, prototype testing, pilot production, and production start-up), these products succeed.

Determinants of Product Success for Japanese Companies

What factors separate the new product winners from the losers in Japanese companies? X. Michael Song and Mark Parry addressed this intriguing question in a study of nearly 800 new product introductions by Japanese firms.[51] They found that Japanese new product managers view the keys to new product success in much the same way as their North American counterparts. Product advantage was identified as the most important success factor by Japanese managers. Other important success factors include technical and marketing synergy as well as predevelopment proficiency.

Assessing Product Advantage The Japanese study also provides some useful guidelines for assessing potential product advantage. In making this assessment, warn Song and Parry, "managers should consider whether the product offers potential for

---

[50] Cooper, *Winning at New Products*, p. 27.

[51] X. Michael Song and Mark E. Parry, "What Separates Japanese New Product Winners from Losers," *Journal of Product Innovation Management* 13 (September 1996): pp. 422–436.

reducing consumer costs and expanding consumer capabilities, as well as the likelihood that the product offers improved quality, superior technical performance, and a superior benefit-to-cost ratio."[52]

Fast-Paced Product Development

Rapid product development offers a number of competitive advantages. To illustrate, speed enables a firm to respond to rapidly changing markets and technologies. Moreover, fast product development is usually more efficient because lengthy development processes tend to waste resources on peripheral activities and changes.[53] Of course, while an overemphasis on speed may create other pitfalls, it is becoming an important strategic weapon, particularly in high-technology markets.

Matching the Process to the Development Task   How can a firm accelerate product development? A major study of the global computer industry provides some important benchmarks.[54] Researchers examined seventy-two product development projects of leading U. S., European, and Asian computer firms. The findings suggest that multiple approaches are used to increase speed in product development. Speed comes from properly matching the approach to the product development task at hand.

Compressed Strategy for Predictable Projects   For well-known markets and technologies, a **compression strategy** speeds development. This strategy views product development as a predictable series of steps that can be compressed. Speed comes from carefully planning these steps and shortening the time it takes to complete each step. This research indicates that the compressed strategy increased the speed of product development for products that had predictable designs and that were targeted for stable and mature markets. Mainframe computers fit into this category—they rely on proprietary hardware, have more predictable designs from project to project, and compete in a mature market.

Experiential Strategy for Unpredictable Projects   For uncertain markets and technologies, an **experiential strategy** accelerates product development. The underlying assumption of this strategy, explain Kathleen Eisenhardt and Behnam Tabrizi, is that "product development is a highly uncertain path through foggy and shifting markets and technologies. The key to fast product development is, then, rapidly building intuition and flexible options in order to learn quickly about and shift with uncertain environments."[55]

Under these conditions, speed comes from multiple design iterations, extensive testing, frequent milestones, and a powerful leader who can keep the product team focused. Here real-time interactions, experimentation, and flexibility are essential. The research found that the experiential strategy increased the speed of product development for unpredictable projects such as personal computers—a market characterized by rapidly evolving technology and unpredictable patterns of competition.

---

[52] Ibid., p. 422.

[53] See, for example, Robert G. Cooper and Elko J. Kleinschmidt, "Determinants of Timeliness in Product Development," *Journal of Product Innovation Management* 11 (November 1994): pp. 381–417.

[54] Kathleen M. Eisenhardt and Behnam N. Tabrizi, "Accelerating Adaptive Processes: Product Innovation in the Global Computer Industry," *Administrative Science Quarterly* 40 (March 1995): pp. 84–110.

[55] Ibid., p. 91.

Summary

Product innovation is a high-risk and potentially rewarding process. Sustained growth is dependent on innovative products that respond to existing or emerging consumer needs. Effective managers of innovation channel and control its main directions, but have learned to maintain flexibility and expect surprises. Within the firm, marketing managers pursue strategic activity that falls into two broad categories: induced and autonomous strategic behavior.

New product development efforts for existing businesses or market development projects for the firm's present products are the outgrowth of induced strategic initiatives. In contrast, autonomous strategic efforts take shape outside the firm's current concept of strategy, depart from the current course, and center on new categories of business opportunity; middle managers initiate the project, champion its development, and, if successful, see the project integrated into the firm's concept of strategy. To spawn path-breaking innovation, companies should create a vibrant market for ideas, provide a mechanism to fund nontraditional opportunities, and allow talented employees to pursue projects that capture their imagination.

The long-run competitive position of most business marketing firms depends on their ability to manage and increase their technological base. Core competencies provide the basis for products and product families. Each generation of a product family has a platform that serves as the foundation for specific products targeted at different or complementary market applications. Firms that are successful innovators in turbulent markets combine limited structures (for example, priorities, deadlines) with extensive communication and the freedom to improvise current projects. These successful product creators also explore the future by experimenting with a variety of low-cost probes and build a relentless sense of urgency in the organization by creating new products at predictable time intervals (i.e., time pacing).

Effective new product development requires a thorough knowledge of customer needs and a clear grasp of the technological possibilities. Top-performing firms are proficient in executing the new product development process, provide adequate resources to support new product objectives, and develop clear new product strategy. Business marketing firms are emphasizing concurrent engineering and multidisciplinary teams to speed product development, reduce cost, and improve quality. Quality function deployment provides a useful method that the development team can use to link the needs of the customer directly to specific design decisions.

Both strategic factors as well as the firm's proficiency in executing the new product development process are critical to the success of industrial products. Fast-paced product development can provide an important source of competitive advantage for a firm. Speed comes from adapting the process to the new product development task at hand.

Discussion Questions

1. Research by James Quinn suggests that few major innovations result from highly structured planning systems. What does this imply for the business marketer?

2. Compare and contrast induced and autonomous strategic behavior. Describe the role that the product champion assumes in the new product development process.

3. In the Silicon Valley, if an idea has merit, it will attract funding by venture capitalists and it will attract talented employees. What steps can large organizations take to spawn promising new ideas and to better capitalize on the talents of current employees?

4. In fast-changing high-tech industries, some firms have a better record in developing new products than others. Describe the critical factors that drive the new product performance of firms.

5. Rather than planning for and investing in just one version of the future, some firms use low-cost probes to experiment with many possible futures. Evaluate the wisdom of this approach.

6. Hewlett-Packard is working on a health monitoring system. The product features sensors and devices that measure a patient's vital signs in a hospital—or home—and relay data directly to a doctor's computer. What steps can the firm take to ensure that the new product is responsive to customer needs and will be adopted?

7. Getting managers from marketing and R&D "on the same page" is a major challenge during the new product development process. Describe the barriers that often divide functional areas and hamper the new product development process.

8. Describe the process that you would follow in defining the customer needs component of quality function deployment. Assume that the new product in development is an interactive notepad that, when plugged into a telephone, enables people to talk and exchange notes and diagrams.

9. New industrial products that succeed in the marketplace provide clear-cut advantages to customers. Define product advantage and provide an example of a recent new product introduction that fits this definition.

10. Evaluate this statement: "To increase the speed of the new product development process, a firm might follow one strategy for unpredictable projects and an entirely different one for more predictable ones."

13

Managing Services for Business Markets

The important and growing market for business services poses special challenges and meaningful opportunities for the marketing manager. This chapter explains the unique aspects of business services and explores the special role they play in the business market environment. After reading this chapter, you will understand

1. the unique role and distinguishing characteristics of business services.

2. the role that service quality, customer satisfaction, and loyalty assume in service market success.

3. the significant factors that must be considered in formulating a service marketing strategy.

4. how firms are using the Internet to deliver a wide assortment of services.

5. the determinants of new service success and failure.

As General Electric Company faces slow domestic growth and cutthroat price competition abroad for its manufactured items, chairman and CEO Jack Welch is again transforming the global giant.[1] Across GE's business units, Welch sees huge growth by providing specialized services that spring from the firm's core competencies. Take the Medical Equipment Systems unit at GE and its expanding relationship with Columbia/HCA Healthcare Corporation—an operator of a chain of more than 300 hospitals. GE sells medical imaging equipment to Columbia and now services all of the chain's imaging equipment, including that made by GE's competitors. Recently, Columbia turned over the management of all medical supplies to GE—most of these supply items represent products that GE does not produce. As the contract evolved, Columbia executives asked a team of GE managers to help them improve the way Columbia runs hospitals. The consulting and employee training services provided by GE significantly boosted Columbia's productivity and yielded millions of dollars of cost savings.

Similar service initiatives are being launched throughout GE: The aircraft engine unit landed a $2.3 billion, ten-year contract with British Airways to perform engine maintenance; GE's power equipment unit foresees $1 billion dollars in annual new business by operating and maintaining power plants for utilities in the United States and Europe; GE Capital is responding to the growing interest of firms in outsourcing and is competing head-on with IBM and EDS for multimillion-dollar contracts that involve operating computer networks for others.

Given his stunning record of profitable growth at GE, some believe that Jack Welch's aggressive services strategy provides a blueprint for refashioning an industrial company in a post-industrial economy. For example, reengineering expert Michael Hammer sees GE's strategic move as a bellwether: "This is the next big wave in American industry. The product you sell is only one component of your business."[2]

This example demonstrates the important role that services play in the business marketing environment. Indeed, high-tech brands, like IBM or Hewlett-Packard, are built on a promise of value to customers and service excellence is part of the value package that customers demand.[3] Clearly, many equipment manufacturers are now using effective service and support as a core marketing strategy for creating sales growth; moreover, a vast array of "pure service" firms exist to supply businesses and organizations with everything from office cleaning to management consulting and just-in-time delivery service to key customers.

This chapter will examine the nature of business services, the key buying behavior dimensions associated with their purchase, the major strategic elements related to services marketing, and the international environment for business services.

Business Services: Role and Importance

The importance of services marketing is easy to demonstrate: The United States has become a service economy. In fact, fully 80 percent of the employment and 76 percent

---

[1] "General Electric: The House That Jack Built," *The Economist* (September 18, 1999) and Tim Smart, "Jack Welch's Encore: How G.E.'s Chairman Is Remaking His Company—Again," *Business Week*, 28 October 1996, pp. 155–160.

[2] Smart, "Jack Welch's Encore," p. 157.

[3] Scott Ward, Larry Light, and Jonathan Goldstine, "What High-Tech Managers Need to Know About Brands," *Harvard Business Review*, 75 (July–August 1999), pp. 85–95.

of the gross domestic product (GDP) in the United States is accounted for by the service sector.[4] The dramatic growth in the service sector is occurring in both consumer and business markets.

Business services are growing even in regions where manufacturing is in decline. Four factors account for the growth of business services:

1. *E-Business.* Beyond creating new business, the Internet is creating new business models and driving organizations to do business in fundamentally different ways. Customers in the business market spend over $1 billion a day on information technology services to transform important processes like supply chain management, customer service and support, and distribution.[5] To capitalize on this explosive growth, firms such as IBM and Microsoft offer a range of e-commerce products and services to organizations, large and small. (See Figure 13.1.)

2. *Outsourcing.* Organizations of all types are buying more services than in the past. The trend is to outsource functions and services that are not the company's core expertise (like payroll processing, warehousing, or even the entire human resources or information management functions). A blizzard of new application service providers has emerged to meet the needs of large and small customers. For example, a small firm can now access these service marketers through the Internet and outsource applications like accounting, payroll, or in some cases, even selling.[6]

3. *Innovations.* New services, never considered ten years ago, are stimulating increasing services demand. Computer security, remotely delivered computer services, environmental control systems for office buildings, and custom-designed employee training classes are delivered through the Internet.

4. *Manufacturing growth.* Manufacturing output is still growing despite the decline in the number of manufacturing employees. With this growth, the demand for services like logistics, advertising, and information processing continues its upward trend.

Product Support Services

Services in the business-to-business market can be categorized in two distinct groups. The first category is **products supported by services.** In this situation, the wide range of service elements that accompany the physical product are frequently as important as the technical solutions offered by the product itself[7] (see Chapter 11). Some examples of product-service linkages include equipment repair and maintenance, consultation services associated with the sale of computers and other technical products, training programs on the use and application of equipment or customized software, distribution and delivery service, and spare parts. At Otis Elevator, for example, more

---

[4] James Brian Quinn, "Strategic Outsourcing: Leveraging Knowledge Capabilities," *Sloan Management Review*, 40 (summer 1999), pp. 8–9.

[5] *IBM Annual Report, 1998*, p. 42.

[6] Lee Gomes, "Somebody Else's Problem," *The Wall Street Journal* (November 15, 1999), p. R8.

[7] Lauren K. Wright, "Characterizing Successful New Services: Background and Literature Review," Report #9-1985, Institute for the Study of Business Markets, Pennsylvania State University, 25 April 1985, p. 37.

SOURCE: Courtesy Microsoft Corporation.

than 65 percent of its $5 billion in annual sales now comes from service and maintenance. Services also play a key part in the core business of industrial distributors, where up to 25 percent of their revenues come from value-added services.[8]

The business marketing manager must recognize that service activities augment the physical product and can create a differential advantage for the firm in the eyes of organizational buyers. To illustrate, Sun Microsystems provides the computer servers and software for Internet firms like eBay, Inc. and eTrade, Inc. These customers require high-performance systems that can handle millions of simultaneous visitors to their Web sites. Technical problems can frustrate potential customers and competitors are just a click away. A customer, like eBay, turns to Sun for a total solution—a package of hardware, software, and services that will ensure that its Web site will meet or exceed customer expectations. Larry Hamby, president of enterprise services at Sun,

---

[8] "Value-Added Services Equal Greater Revenues," *Industrial Distribution* 85 (January 1996): p. 19.

observes: "You can't compete for mission-critical computing unless you have a solid services offering" to support the customer's strategy.[9]

Pure Services

The second category is pure services, those that are marketed in their own right without necessarily being associated with a physical product. The list of such business services is vast, including insurance, consulting, banking, maintenance services, transportation, market research, information technology management, temporary personnel, security and protection services, and travel booking services. The variety of business services provided and the quantity of services purchased by businesses and organizations is expanding, and services make up a significant percentage of total corporate purchases. A number of factors have contributed to the growth of business services:

1. Companies and other organizations increasingly rely on the services of specialists because of the complexity of economic organization and the costs involved in the division and specialization of labor.

2. Organizations are tying information technology more directly to business strategy. Strategy experts argue that how an organization manages information and knowledge will determine whether it will win or lose, lead or follow.[10] To align information technology with strategy, companies need advice concerning what equipment to buy and continuing guidance concerning how to use it to gain a competitive advantage.

3. Organizations can remain flexible and better control their capital commitment by hiring services that provide "use" without "ownership."

4. Time pressures (long lead time to develop in-house expertise) and lack of available internal resources encourage organizations to focus on a small set of activities—important to customers—that it does best and turn to outside service specialists for the rest.

Current and projected trends in the business environment suggest that these forces will further expand the demand for services and create significant opportunities in the business market.

Business Service Marketing: Special Challenges

The development of marketing programs for both products and services can be approached from a common perspective, yet the relative importance and form of various strategic elements will differ between products and services. The underlying explanation for these strategic differences, asserts Henry Assael, lies in the distinctions between a product and a service:

> Services are intangible; products are tangible. Services are consumed at the time of production, but there is a time lag between the production and

---

[9] Karen Rodriguez, "Sun Spots Lucrative Niche with Services," *The Business Journal of San Jose and Silicon Valley* (October 25, 1999), p. 3.

[10] Thomas H. Davenport and Philip Klahr, "Managing Customer Support Knowledge," *California Management Review*, 40 (spring 1998), pp. 195–208.

INSIDE BUSINESS MARKETING

You've Got Too Much Mail!

Customers now send over 200 million e-mail messages to firms each year. For businesses, e-mail is an inexpensive form of communication that can focus on specific customers and address their particular needs. However, a deluge of e-mails from customers can severely test the customer service function of the firm—openly displaying problems with its internal processes to the world. If an inquiry is not promptly handled, the customer is tempted to call the firm and live phone support is far more expensive ($20 to $50 per call) than e-mail.

Experts suggest that an integrated customer service philosophy should be adopted by companies. Indeed, customer service is much more than an Internet strategy; it's a business strategy. Web-based customer service features should be integrated into a larger strategy that provides several

paths through which consumers can get information about their purchases, answers to their questions, and responses to their present and anticipated needs. In the end, the customer should receive the same level of service on the Web, on the phone, or from a channel member. However, if properly designed and easy to use, many organizations, like Federal Express, have learned that customers prefer the Web for information about order status, special discounts, and package tracking. By transferring its package tracking system to the Web, Federal Express generated brand loyalty and customer satisfaction while dramatically reducing its call center and customer support costs.

SOURCES: Stephen C. Miller, "Anybody in There? Sites Strain to Build in Customer Service," *The New York Times* (September 22, 1999), p. 51 and Timothy Hanrahan, "You've Got Too Much Mail," *The Wall Street Journal* (November 22, 1999), p. R34.

---

consumption of products. Services cannot be stored; products can. Services are highly variable; most products are highly standardized. These differences produce differences in strategic applications that often stand many product marketing principles on their head.[11]

Thus, success in the business service marketplace begins with an understanding of the meaning of *service*.

Services Are Different

There are inherent differences between goods and services, providing a unique set of marketing challenges for service businesses and for manufacturers that provide services as a core offering. Put simply, **services** are deeds, processes, and performances.[12] For example, the core offerings of a management consultant are primarily deeds and actions performed for customers. The most basic, and universally recognized, difference between goods and services is *intangibility*. Services are more intangible than manufactured goods, and manufactured goods are more tangible than services. Because services are actions or performances, they cannot be seen or touched in the same way that consumers sense tangible goods.

Tangible or Intangible?

Figure 13.2 provides a useful tool for understanding the product-service definitional problem. The continuum suggests that there are very few *pure products* or *pure services*.

---

[11] Henry Assael, *Marketing Management: Strategy and Action* (Boston, Mass.: Kent Publishing Company, 1985), p. 693.

[12] Valarie A. Zeithaml and Mary Jo Bitner, *Services Marketing* (New York: McGraw-Hill, 2000), p. 2.

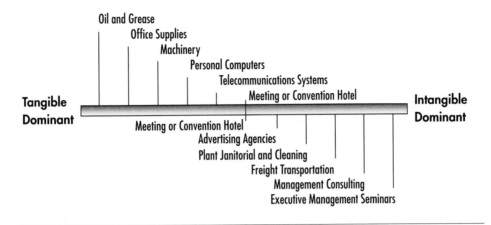

FIGURE 13.2 — BUSINESS PRODUCT-SERVICE CLASSIFICATION BASED ON TANGIBILITY

SOURCE: Adapted from G. Lynn Shostack, "Breaking Free from Product Marketing," *Journal of Marketing* 41 (April 1977): p. 77. Published by the American Marketing Association.

For example, a personal computer is a physical object made up of tangible elements that facilitate the work of an individual and an organization. In addition to the physical design and performance characteristics of the computer, the quality of technical service support is an important dimension of the marketing program. Thus, most market offerings comprise a combination of tangible and intangible elements.

Whether an offering is classified as a good or as a service depends on how the organizational buyer views what is being bought—whether the tangible or the intangible elements dominate. On one end of the spectrum, grease and oil are tangible-dominant, and the essence of what is being bought is the physical product. Management seminars, on the other hand, are intangible-dominant because what is being bought—professional development, education, learning—has few, if any, tangible properties. A convention hotel is in the middle of the continuum because the buyer will receive an array of both tangible elements (meals, beverages, notepads, and so on) and intangible benefits (courteous personnel, fast check-ins, meeting room ambiance, and so forth).

The concept of tangibility is especially useful to the business marketer because many business offerings are composed of product and service combinations. The key management task is to evaluate carefully (from the buyer's standpoint) which elements of the offering dominate. The more the market offering is characterized by intangible elements, the more difficult it is to apply the standard marketing tools that were developed for products. The business marketer must focus on specialized marketing approaches appropriate for services.

The concept also helps the manager to focus clearly on the firm's *total market offering*. In addition, it helps the manager recognize that a change in one of the elements of the market offering may completely change the offering in the view of the customer. For example, a business marketer who decides to hold spare parts inventory at a central location and use overnight delivery to meet customer requirements must refocus marketing strategy. The offering has moved toward the intangible end of the continuum because of the intangible benefits associated with reduced customer inventory and fast transportation. This new "service," which is less tangible, must be carefully

TABLE 13.1	UNIQUE SERVICE CHARACTERISTICS	
Characteristics	**Examples**	**Marketing Implications**
Simultaneous production and consumption	Telephone conference call; management seminar; equipment repair	Direct-seller interaction requires that service be done "right"; requires high-level training for personnel; requires effective screening and recruitment
Nonstandardized output	Management advice varies with the individual consultant; merchandise damages vary from shipment to shipment	Emphasizes strict quality control standards; develop systems that minimize deviation and human error; prepackage the service; look for ways to automate
Perishability: inability to store or stockpile	Unfilled airline seats; an idle computer technician; un-rented warehouse space	Plan capacity around peak demand; use pricing and promotion to even out demand peaks and valleys; use overlapping shifts for personnel
Lack of ownership	Use of railroad car; use of consultant's know-how; use of mailing list	Focus promotion on the advantages of nonownership: reduced labor, overhead, and capital; emphasize flexibility

explained and the intangible results of lower inventory costs must be made more concrete to the buyer through an effective promotion program.

In summary, business services are those market offerings that are intangible-dominant. However, few services are totally intangible—they often contain elements with tangible properties. In addition to the tangibility criterion, business services have other important distinguishing characteristics that influence how they are marketed. Table 13.1 provides a summary of the core characteristics that further delineate the nature of business services.

Simultaneous Production and Consumption

Because services are generally *consumed as they are produced*, a critical element in the buyer–seller relationship is the effectiveness of the individual (the IBM technician, the UPS driver, the McKinsey consultant) who actually provides the service. From the service firm's perspective, the entire marketing strategy may rest on how effectively the individual service provider interacts with the customer. Here the actual service delivery takes place and the promise to the customer is kept or broken. This critical point of contact with the customer is referred to as **interactive** or **real-time marketing**.[13] The recruiting, hiring, and training of personnel assume special importance in business service firms.

Service Variability

Observe in Table 13.1 that the service offering is *nonstandardized*, meaning that the quality of the service output may vary each time it is provided.[14] Services vary in the

[13] Ibid., p. 22.

[14] Valarie A. Zeithaml, A. Parasuraman, and Leonard R. Berry, "Problems and Strategies in Services Marketing," *Journal of Marketing* 49 (spring 1985): p. 34; see also Zeithaml, Berry, and Parasuraman, "Communication and Control Processes in the Delivery of Service Quality," *Journal of Marketing* 52 (April 1988): pp. 35–48.

amount of equipment and labor that are utilized to provide the service. For example, a significant human element is involved in teaching an executive seminar compared to providing overnight airfreight service. Generally, the more labor involved in a service, the less uniform the output. In these labor-intensive cases, the user may also find it difficult to judge the quality before the service is provided. Because of uniformity problems, business service providers must focus on finely tuned quality-control programs, invest in "systems" to minimize human error, and seek approaches for automating the service.

Service Perishability

Generally, services *cannot be stored;* that is, if they are not provided at the time they are available, the lost revenue cannot be recaptured. Tied to this characteristic is the fact that demand for services is often unpredictable and widely fluctuating. The service marketer must carefully evaluate capacity—in a service business, **capacity** is a substitute for inventory. If capacity is set for peak demand, a "service inventory" must exist to supply the highest level of demand. As an example, some airlines that provide air shuttle service between New York, Washington, and Boston offer flights that leave every hour. If, on any flight, the plane is full, another plane is brought to the terminal—even for one passenger. An infinite capacity is set so that no single business traveler will be dissatisfied. Obviously, setting high capacity levels is costly, and the marketer must analyze the cost versus the lost revenue and customer goodwill that might result from maintaining lower capacity.

Nonownership

The final dimension of services shown in Table 13.1 is the fact that the service buyer uses, but *does not own*, the service purchased. Essentially, payment for a service is a payment for the use of, access to, or hire of items. The service marketer must feature the advantages of nonownership in its communications to the marketplace. The key benefits to emphasize are reductions in staff, overhead, and capital associated with a third party providing the service.

Although there may be exceptions to the general prescriptions, these characteristics provide a useful framework for understanding the nature of business services and for isolating special marketing strategy requirements.

Service Quality

Quality standards are ultimately defined by the business customer. Actual performance by the service provider or the provider's perception of quality are of little relevance compared to the customer's perception of the service. "Good" service results when the service provider meets or exceeds the customer's expectations.[15] As a result, many management experts argue that service companies should carefully position themselves so that customers expect a little less than the firm can actually deliver. The strategy: underpromise and overdeliver.

---

[15] "William H. Davidow and Bro Uttal, "Service Companies: Focus or Falter," *Harvard Business Review* 67 (July/August 1989): p. 84.

TABLE 13.2	THE DIMENSIONS OF SERVICE QUALITY	
Dimension	**Description**	**Examples**
Reliability	Delivering on promises	Promised delivery date met
Responsiveness	Being willing to help	Prompt reply to customers' requests
Assurance	Inspiring trust and confidence	Professional and knowledgeable staff
Empathy	Treating customers as individuals	Adapts to special needs of customer
Tangibles	Representing the service physically	Distinctive materials: brochures, documents

SOURCE: Adapted from Valarie A. Zeithaml and Mary Jo Bitner, *Services Marketing* (New York: McGraw-Hill, 2000), pp. 82–85.

Dimensions of Service Quality

Because business services are intangible and nonstandardized, buyers tend to have greater difficulty in evaluating services than in evaluating goods. The inability to depend on consistent service performance and quality may lead service buyers to experience more perceived risk.[16] As a result, buyers utilize a variety of prepurchase information sources to reduce risk. Information from current users (word of mouth) is particularly important. In addition, the evaluation process for services tends to be more abstract, more random, and more heavily based on symbology rather than on concrete decision variables.[17]

Research provides some valuable insights into how customers evaluate service quality. From Table 13.2, note that customers focus on five dimensions in evaluating service quality: reliability, responsiveness, assurance, empathy, and tangibles. Among these dimensions, reliability—delivery on promises—is the most important to customers. High-quality service performance is also shaped by the way in which the service is provided by frontline service personnel. To the customer, service quality represents a responsive employee, one who inspires confidence, and one who adapts to the unique needs or preferences of the customer and delivers the service in a professional manner. In fact, the performance of employees who are in contact with the customer may compensate for temporary service quality problems. (For example, a problem reoccurs in a recently repaired photocopier.)[18] By promptly acknowledging the error and responding quickly to the problem, the service employee may even strengthen the firm's relationship with the customer.

Customer Satisfaction and Loyalty

Four components of a firm's offering and its customer-linking processes affect customer satisfaction:

---

[16] Valarie A. Zeithaml, "How Consumer Evaluation Processes Differ between Goods and Services," in *Marketing of Services*, ed. James H. Donnelly and William R. George (Chicago: American Marketing Association, 1981), pp. 200–204.

[17] Ibid.

[18] Christian Gronroos, "Relationship Marketing: Strategic and Tactical Implications," *Management Decision*, 34, No. 3 (1996), pp. 5–14.

1. the basic elements of the product or service that customers expect all competitors to provide,

2. basic support services, such as technical assistance or training, that make the product or service more effective or easier to use,

3. a recovery process for quickly fixing product or service problems, and

4. extraordinary services that so excel in solving customers' unique problems or in meeting their needs that they make the product or service seem customized.[19]

Leading service firms carefully measure and monitor customer satisfaction because it is linked to customer loyalty and, in turn, to long-term profitability.[20] Xerox, for example, regularly surveys more than 400,000 customers regarding product and service satisfaction using a five-point scale from five (high) to one (low). In analyzing the data, Xerox executives made a remarkable discovery: *very* satisfied customers (a five rating) were far more loyal than satisfied customers. Very satisfied customers, in fact, were *six times* more likely to repurchase Xerox products than satisfied customers.

Customers as Apostles Based on this analysis, Xerox now places a high priority on creating **apostles**—a term describing customers so satisfied that they convert others to a firm's product or service. To create totally satisfied customers, firms like Xerox are upgrading service levels and *guaranteeing* customer satisfaction. These firms, assert Thomas Jones and W. Earl Sasser Jr., also have well-established recovery processes to respond to unhappy customers when service falters. "If a company excels in making amends—that is, in recovering—when failures occur, customers' faith in the company is not just restored, it is deepened, and they become apostles, spreading the good word about the company to potential customers."[21]

Customers as Terrorists While seeking to create apostles, business marketers should strive to avoid creating **terrorists,** a term describing customers so dissatisfied that they speak out against a firm and its product and service. Often, these customers spoke to representatives of the service firm first, but no one responded. They now recount their unpleasant experiences to others.[22]

Zero Defections

The quality of service provided to business customers has a major effect on customer "defections"—customers who will not come back. Service strategists point out that customer defections have a powerful impact on the bottom line.[23] As a company's relationship with a customer lengthens, profits rise—and generally rise considerably.

---

[19]Thomas O. Jones and W. Earl Sasser Jr., "Why Satisfied Customers Defect," *Harvard Business Review* 73 (November/December 1995): p. 90.

[20]The Xerox illustration is based on James L. Heskett, Thomas O. Jones, Gary W. Loveman, W. Earl Sasser Jr., and Leonard A. Schlesinger, "Putting the Service-Profit Chain to Work," *Harvard Business Review* 72 (March/April 1994): pp. 164–174.

[21]Jones and Sasser, "Why Satisfied Customers Defect," p. 96.

[22]Ibid.

[23]Frederick F. Reichheld and W. Earl Sasser, "Zero Defections: Quality Comes to Services," *Harvard Business Review* 68 (September/October 1990): p. 105.

For example, one service firm found that profit from a fourth-year customer is triple that from a first-year customer. Many additional benefits accrue to service companies that retain their customers: They can charge more, the cost of doing business is reduced, and the long-standing customer provides "free" advertising. The implications are clear: Service providers should carefully track customer defections and recognize that continuous improvement in service quality is not a cost, but, say Frederick Reichheld and W. Earl Sasser, "an investment in a customer who generates more profit than the margin on a one-time sale."[24]

Return on Quality

A difficult decision for the business services marketing manager is to determine how much to spend on improving service quality. Clearly, expenditures on quality have diminishing returns—at some point, additional expenditures on service quality do not increase profitability. To make good decisions on the level of expenditures on quality, managers must justify quality efforts on a financial basis, knowing where to spend on quality improvement, how much to spend, and when to reduce or stop the expenditures. Roland Rust, Anthony Zahorik, and Timothy Keiningham have developed a technique for calculating the "return on investing in quality."[25] Under this approach, service quality benefits are successively linked to customer satisfaction, customer retention, market share, and, finally, to profitability. The relationship between expenditure level and customer satisfaction change is first measured by managerial judgment and then through market testing. When the relationship has been estimated, the return on quality can be measured statistically. The significant conclusion is that quality improvements should be treated as investments: They must pay off, and spending should not be wasted on efforts that do not produce a return.

Marketing Mix for Business Service Firms

To meet the needs of service buyers effectively, an integrated marketing strategy is required. First, target segments must be selected, and then a marketing mix must be tailored to the expectations of each segment. The key elements of the service marketing mix include the development of service packages, pricing, promotion, and distribution. Each requires special consideration by the business marketing manager.

Segmentation

As with any marketing situation, development of the marketing mix will be contingent upon the customer segment to be served. Every facet of the service to be offered, as well as the methods for promoting, pricing, and delivering the service, will hinge upon the needs of a reasonably homogeneous group of customers. The process for segmenting business markets described in Chapter 7 will find application in the services market. However, William Davidow and Bro Uttal suggest that customer service segments differ from usual market segments in significant ways.[26]

---

[24] Ibid., p. 107.

[25] Roland T. Rust, Anthony J. Zahorik, and Timothy L. Keiningham, "Return on Quality (ROQ): Making Service Quality Financially Accountable," *Journal of Marketing* 59 (April 1995): pp. 58–70.

[26] Davidow and Uttal, "Service Companies: Focus or Falter," p. 79.

First, service segments are often narrower. This situation reflects the fact that many service customers expect services to be customized. Expectations may not be met if the service received is standardized and routine. Second, service segmentation focuses on what the business buyers expect as opposed to what they need. The assessment of buyer expectations will play a very large role in selecting a target market and developing the appropriate service package. This assessment is critical because so many studies have shown large differences between the ways that customers define and rank different service activities and the ways suppliers define and rank them.[27]

Because expectations play such an important role in determining ultimate satisfaction with a service, service quality expectations can be used to segment business-to-business markets. One study in the mainframe software industry revealed significant differences between "software specialists" (software experts) and "applications developers" (users of software) in the same firm regarding their expectations of new software. The developers (users) had higher expectations regarding the quality of the supplier's equipment, the responsiveness of their employees, and the amount of personal attention provided.[28] The study concluded that different buying center members may well have different perspectives and different expectations of service quality. The business marketer should carefully evaluate the possibility of using service quality expectations as a guide for creating marketing strategy.

Finally, segmenting service markets helps the firm to adjust service capacity more effectively. Segmentation will usually reveal that total demand is made up of numerous smaller, yet more predictable, demand patterns. For a hotel, the demand patterns of a convention visitor, business traveler, foreign tourist, or vacationer can all be forecast individually and capacities adjusted for each segment's demand pattern.

Service Packages

The service package can be thought of as the product dimension of service, including decisions involving the essential concept of the service, the range of services provided, and the quality and level of service. In addition, the service package must consider some factors that are unique to services—the personnel who perform the service, the physical product that accompanies the service, and the process of providing the service.[29] A useful way to conceptualize the service product is shown in Figure 13.3.

Customer-Benefit Concept   Services are purchased because of the benefits they offer, and a first step in either creating a service or evaluating an existing one is to define the **customer-benefit concept**—that is, evaluate the core benefit that the customer will derive from the service. An understanding of the customer-benefit concept will focus the business marketer's attention on those attributes—functional, effectual, and psychological—that must be not only offered but also tightly monitored from a quality-control standpoint. For example, a sales manager selecting a resort hotel for an annual sales meeting is purchasing a core benefit that could be stated as "a successful meeting." The hotel marketer must then assess the full range of service attributes and

---

[27] Ibid., p. 83.

[28] Leyland Pitt, Michael H. Morris, and Pierre Oosthuizen, "Expectations of Service Quality As an Industrial Market Segmentation Variable," *The Service Industries Journal* 16 (January 1996): pp. 1–9. See also Ralph W. Jackson, Lester A. Neidell, and Dale A. Lunsford, "An Empirical Investigation of the Differences in Goods and Services As Perceived by Organizational Buyers," *Industrial Marketing Management* 24 (March 1995): pp. 99–108.

[29] Donald Cowell, *The Marketing of Services* (London: William Heinemann, 1984), p. 73.

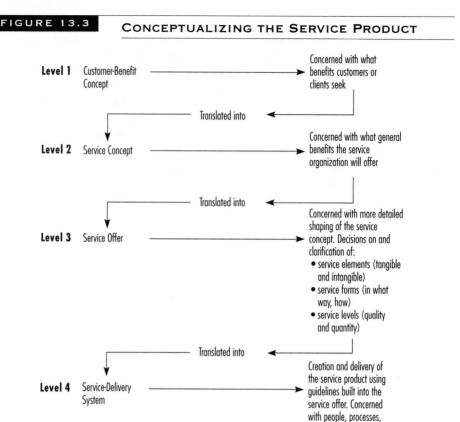

FIGURE 13.3 **CONCEPTUALIZING THE SERVICE PRODUCT**

SOURCE: Adapted from Donald Cowell, *The Marketing of Services* (London: William Heinemann, Ltd., 1984), p. 100. Published by Heinemann Professional Publishing, Ltd.

components necessary to provide a successful meeting. Obviously, a wide variety of service elements will come into play: (1) meeting room size, layout, environment, acoustics; (2) meals; (3) comfortable and quiet sleeping rooms; (4) audiovisual equipment; and (5) staff responsiveness.

As another example, Dun & Bradstreet does not provide its customers with "financial services." Its customer-benefit concept focuses on objective and accurate credit information, security, and even "peace of mind." [30]

Service Concept Once the customer-benefit concept is understood, the next step is to articulate the **service concept,** which defines the general benefits the service company will provide in terms of the bundle of goods and services sold to the customer. The service concept translates the customer-benefit concept into the range of benefits the service marketer will *provide*. For a hotel, the service concept might specify the benefits that it will develop: flexibility, responsiveness, and courteousness in providing meeting rooms; a full range of audiovisual equipment; flexible meal schedules; message services; professional personnel; and climate-controlled meeting rooms.

---

[30] James L. Heskett, *Managing in the Service Economy* (Boston: Harvard Business School Press, 1986), p. 17.

Service Offer   Intimately linked with the service concept is the **service offer,** which spells out in more detail those services to be offered; when, where, and to whom they will be provided; and how they will be presented. The service elements that make up the total service package, including both tangibles and intangibles, must be determined. The service offer of the hotel includes a multitude of tangible elements (soundproof meeting rooms, projection equipment, video players, slide projectors, flip charts, refreshments, heating and air-conditioning, meals) and intangible elements (attitude of meeting room set-up personnel, warmth of greetings from desk clerks and bellhops, response to unique requests, meeting room ambiance). Generally, management will find it easier to manage the tangible (equipment and physical) elements of the service than to control the intangible elements.

Service Delivery System   The final dimension of the service product is the service delivery system—how the service is provided to the customer. The delivery system includes carefully conceived jobs for people; personnel with capabilities and attitudes necessary for successful performance; equipment, facilities, and layouts for effective customer work flow; and carefully developed procedures and processes aimed at a common set of objectives.[31] Thus, the service delivery system should provide a carefully designed blueprint that describes how the service is rendered for the customer.

For physical products, manufacturing and marketing are generally separate and distinct activities; for services, these two activities are often inseparable.[32] The service performance and the delivery system both create the product and deliver it to the customers. This feature of services underscores the important role that people, particularly service providers, play in the marketing process. Technicians, repair personnel, and maintenance engineers are intimately involved in customer contact, and they decidedly influence the customer's perception of service quality. The business service marketer must pay close attention to both people and physical evidence (tangible elements such as uniforms) when designing the service package.

Service Personnel   A first step in creating an effective service package is to ensure that the customer-benefit concept is known, understood, and accepted by all personnel. As Donald Cowell states, "So important are people and their quality to organizations and . . . services that 'internal marketing' is considered to be an important management role to ensure that all staff are customer conscious."[33] In short, the attitudes, skills, knowledge, and behavior of service personnel have a critical impact on the levels of satisfaction that the user derives from the service.

Pricing Business Services

Although product and service pricing policies and strategies share many common threads, the unique characteristics of services create some special pricing problems and opportunities.

Perishability and Managing Demand/Capacity   The demand for services is rarely steady or predictable enough to avoid service perishability. An extremely difficult

---

[31] Ibid., p. 20.

[32] Cowell, *The Marketing of Services*, p. 110.

[33] Ibid.

decision for the business service marketer is to determine the capacity (inventory) of the system: Should it meet peak demand, average demand, or somewhere in between? Pricing can be used to manage the timing of demand and align it with capacity levels.

To manage demand, the marketer may offer off-peak pricing schemes and price incentives for service orders that are placed in advance. For example, resort hotels, crowded with pleasure travelers during school vacations and holidays, develop special packages for business groups during the off-season. Similarly, various utilities may offer significant rate reductions for off-peak usage. It may also be possible, depending on demand elasticity and competition, to charge premium rates for services provided at peak demand periods. It is interesting to note, however, that a recent study of strategies utilized by service firms showed that many service firms do not reduce prices to increase business during slow periods.[34]

Service Bundling   Many business services include a core service as well as a variety of peripheral services. How should the services be priced—as an entity, as a service bundle, or individually? **Bundling** is the practice of marketing two or more services in a package for a special price.[35] Bundling makes sense in the business service environment because most service businesses have a high ratio of fixed costs to variable costs and a high degree of cost sharing among their many related services. Hence the marginal cost of providing additional services to the core service customer is generally low.

A key decision for the service provider is whether to provide pure or mixed bundling.[36] In **pure bundling**, the services are only available in bundled form—they cannot be purchased separately. In **mixed bundling**, the customer can purchase one or more services individually or purchase the bundle. For example, a public warehouse firm can provide its services—storage, product handling, and clerical activities—in a price-bundled form by charging a single rate (eight cents) for each case received by the warehouse from its manufacturer-client. The firm may also market each service separately and provide a rate for each service individually (three cents per case for storage, four cents per case for handling, and one cent per case for clerical). Additionally, a multitude of peripheral services can be quoted on an individual basis: physical inventory count, freight company selection and routing, merchandise return and repair, and so on. In this way, the customer can choose the services desired and pay for each separately.

Attracting New Business   Various bundling strategies can be used to expand sales either by **cross-selling**—selling a new service to customers who buy an existing service—or by attracting entirely new customers. In the cross-selling situation for a public warehouse, current customers (utilizing storage services) may be attracted to a new product-labeling service by the offer of a bundled price that results in a discount on the total cost of the two services. Bundling services in order to attract new customers can be efficient when the service attributes can be evaluated before purchase and when the core service is demand elastic.[37] Thus, noncustomized services, where significant competition exists, would seem to be a fertile environment. Bundling insurance coverage with the rental of an automobile may be effective in attracting new business customers for a car rental firm.

---

[34] Zeithaml, Parasuraman, and Berry, "Problems and Strategies in Services Marketing," p. 41.

[35] Joseph P. Guiltinan, "The Price Bundling of Services: A Normative Framework," *Journal of Marketing* 51 (April 1987): p. 74.

[36] Ibid., p. 75.

[37] Ibid., p. 81.

In the computer service industry, manufacturers are finding that services formerly sold on an ad hoc basis can be sold more effectively if bundled together. Hewlett-Packard is testing a variety of service bundles with customers in order to determine how customers want to buy the services.[38] Clearly, the services, how they are combined, and how the bundle is priced have critical effects on the service firm's success.

Services Promotion

The promotional strategies for services follow many of the same prescriptions as do those for products. However, the unique characteristics of business services pose special challenges for the business marketer.

Communication with Employees   Personnel are vital to many people-based service businesses, and they can have a profound effect on the customer's satisfaction with the service. Internal advertising to employees accomplishes the following:

- Promotes an understanding of the firm's mission and customer service benefit
- Influences them regarding how the service is to be provided
- Motivates them to perform
- Defines management's expectations of them

Some firms, such as Delta Airlines, Marriott Corporation, and IBM, regularly feature employees in their ads. Marketing communications directed to employees are as important as those targeted for potential customers. Such internal communications emphasize the company's purpose, its high standards of service, and the role that each employee assumes in creating satisfied customers (see Figure 13.4).

Keith Murray presents evidence suggesting that managers should train and equip service employees to carry out the service functions and also ensure that they have a clear grasp of the service product and process. A competent employee adds value to the service encounter and enhances customer satisfaction.[39] In turn, service personnel play a critical role in reducing the risk that customers associate with purchasing services, and that role can be enhanced by preparing personnel to offer information that anticipates customer concerns with the service.

Word of Mouth   Service purchases are frequently considered to be riskier than product purchases because it is more difficult for buyers to evaluate quality and value. As a result, buyers are more apt to be influenced by colleagues, peers, and other professionals who have had experience in purchasing and using the service. Promotion must concentrate on the dominant role of personal influence in the buying process and build on word-of-mouth communication. This can be done by[40]

- Persuading satisfied customers to inform others of their satisfaction
- Developing materials that customers can pass on to noncustomers

---

[38] Diane Lynn Kastiel, "Service and Support: High-Tech's New Battleground," *Business Marketing* 73 (June 1987): p. 66.

[39] Keith B. Murray, "A Test of Services Marketing Theory: Consumer Information Acquisition Activities," *Journal of Marketing* 55, no. 1 (January 1991): p. 21.

[40] Cowell, *The Marketing of Services*, p. 171.

FIGURE 13.4	IBM AD FEATURING EMPLOYEES WHO DELIVER E-BUSINESS SOLUTIONS

SOURCE: Courtesy International Business Machines Corporation.

- Targeting opinion leaders in ad campaigns
- Encouraging potential customers to talk to existing customers

Service marketers can capitalize on the satisfaction of current customers and word-of-mouth promotion by featuring customers (and their comments) in advertising. For example, ads for the executive training course by Dale Carnegie regularly feature statements of satisfaction from senior executives at leading corporations. Services marketers also prominently list testimonials and success stories on their Web sites.

Developing Tangible Clues   Service marketers must concentrate either on featuring the physical evidence elements of their service or on making the intangible elements more tangible. Physical evidence plays an important role in creating the atmosphere and environment in which a service is bought or performed, and it influences the customer's perception of the service. Physical evidence is the tangible aspect of the service package, which the business marketer can control. Attempts should be made to translate the image of intangible attributes of a service into something more concrete.

For business service marketers, uniforms, logos, written contracts and guarantees, building appearance, and color schemes are some of the many ways to make their services tangible. An equipment maintenance firm that provides free, written, quarterly inspections helps make its service more tangible. Xerox offers a Total Satisfaction Guarantee that allows customers to return copiers for any reason. The credit card created by car rental companies is another example of an attempt to make a service more tangible. A key concern for the service marketer is to develop a well-defined strategy for managing physical evidence—to enhance and differentiate service evidence through the creation of tangible clues.

Services Distribution

Distribution decisions in the service industry are focused on how to make the service package available and accessible to the user. Direct sale may be accomplished by the user going to the provider (for example, a manufacturer using a public warehouse for storing its product) or, more often, by the provider going to the buyer (for example, photocopier repair). Services can also be delivered over the Internet or sold by intermediaries.

Delivering Services through the Internet   The Internet provides a powerful new channel for a host of services. For example, application service providers serve business market customers by allowing them to rent access to computer software and hardware, often providing the access over the Internet.[41] For example, customers pay USinterworking a fixed monthly fee to run and manage software programs, from basic e-mail to more complex accounting software applications. The software resides on USinterworking servers at remote sites. Customers secure access through the Internet or over telephone links reserved for this purpose.

A Community of Loyal Customers   Leading manufacturers like Hewlett-Packard, Sun Microsystems, Cisco Systems, and countless others, have developed sophisticated Internet strategies to reduce costs, improve service responsiveness, and strengthen relationships with customers. Consider the strategy that Cisco follows. From Figure 13.5, observe that Cisco's Web site provides visitors with information on technology solutions for different types of businesses, technical service and support information, and online customer training. An extensive base of technical knowledge is available to existing or potential customers who can examine the most frequently asked questions and answers by industry category.

Cisco generates more than 75 percent of its product and service sales through its Web site. By providing customers with self-service access to a rich base of information, Cisco saved $550 million per year in customer support costs and reduced the frequency of calls to its call centers. In turn, the company learned something important about Cisco customers—they are anxious to help each other. To illustrate, potential customers who visit the Web site are encouraged to post a question if they are unable to

---

[41]Jon G. Auerbach, "Playing the New Order: Stocks to Watch as Software Meets the Internet," *The Wall Street Journal* (November 15, 1999), p. R28.

FIGURE 13.5 — CISCO SYSTEMS DELIVERS AN ARRAY OF SERVICES ONLINE

SOURCE: Courtesy Cisco Systems, Inc (http://www.cisco.com/) November 22, 1999.

find the information that they require. Often, before Cisco's technical staff could find the answer, another Cisco customer would post a desired response. Many of these customers have completed Cisco's online training and they are anxious to demonstrate their knowledge. By further promoting this sense of community, thousands of technical questions to Cisco each week are now answered by customers.

Patricia Seybold observes:

> Cisco currently receives and processes between 350,000 and 400,000 transactions a month on its Web site. That represents an amazing number of phone calls that no longer have to be made by customers and handled in real time by staff members. And all this is the result of focusing on saving customers time, getting rid of annoyances, and building a community of Cisco users who can help one another out.[42]

---

[42] Patricia B. Seybold with Ronnie T. Marshak, *Customer.Com* (New York: Times Business, 1998), p. 322.

INSIDE BUSINESS MARKETING

Caterpillar's Close Connections with Global Customers

Caterpillar is putting an information system in place that will enable it to deliver a part before customers even realize they need it! The system will monitor the firm's construction equipment or heavy-duty engines after purchase and notify the local dealer when a particular part is beginning to show signs of an impending problem.

Consider this scenario: A component part on a Caterpillar machine, operating at a copper mine in Chile, begins to signal impending failure. A district center, which monitors all Caterpillar machines in the region by remotely reading the sensors on each machine, detects a problem in the making and sends an electronic alert to the local dealer's field technician. Through a portable computer, the technician validates the diagnosis, determines the repair or service required, and the parts and tools that will be needed to complete the job.

The technician can also access Caterpillar's worldwide information system to determine the closest source and to order the part.

Caterpillar plans to have the system fully operational in several years. Most of the pieces are already in place: sensors in the machines; computers that diagnose problems; and an information system that connects Caterpillar's factories, distribution centers, dealers, and large customers. Two pieces are missing: the remote monitoring system and the open sharing of inventories by Caterpillar and its dealers and suppliers. However, a prototype of the monitoring system is already being tested by Caterpillar.

SOURCE: Donald V. Fites, "Make Your Dealers Your Partners," *Harvard Business Review* 74 (March/April 1996): pp. 88–89.

Service Intermediaries Financial services, insurance, lodging, warehousing, and transportation are some of the many services sold through intermediaries. For example, in the freight transportation business, selling agents, brokers, and freight forwarders are some of the typical intermediaries used, generally because they can cost-effectively cover the entire freight service market. In addition, some of these channel members may develop bundles of services from a variety of transportation companies. Thus, a freight forwarder may arrange for a shipment to be moved by three separate modes of transportation—air, rail, and truckline. The forwarder takes care of all arrangements and invoices the customer only once for a single fee.

Franchising As an alternative channel of distribution, franchising has experienced considerable growth in recent years. Such services as office and factory cleaning, car rental, temporary help, employment agencies, uniform rental, and equipment maintenance are now distributed through franchised dealerships. Franchising works best when the service can be standardized (for example, office cleaning). Franchising enables the service provider to expand its market coverage rapidly and to minimize capital investment.

The design of the marketing strategy for a business service must be tailored to those unique factors that are associated with an intangible product. In similar fashion, the marketer developing new service packages must also recognize these important elements. The next section will briefly examine the development of new service packages.

Developing New Services

The conventional process for developing new physical products—exploration, screening, business analysis, development, testing, and commercialization—appears to apply

TABLE 13.3	STEPS FOR ENHANCING THE NEW SERVICE DEVELOPMENT PROCESS

Step	Description
1. Establish a culture for entrepreneurship	Facilitate risk taking and new ideas by creating the proper climate: providing R&D funds, doing customer-need research, allowing employees to voice contrary opinions
2. Create an organization to foster new service development	Assemble a "cast": senior sponsor, who has authority; product champion, who provides continuity and enthusiasm; integrator, who brings the functions together and coordinates them; and referee, who establishes rules for the process and then administers them
3. Test ideas in the marketplace	New ideas must weather the acid test of the marketplace because the service concept is intangible
4. Monitor results	Establish success measures and evaluate against these; track customer reaction
5. Reward risk-takers	Reward those taking good risks, even when they are not consistently successful

SOURCE: Adapted from James L. Heskett, *Managing in the Service Economy* (Boston: Harvard Business School Press, 1986), pp. 86–90.

equally well to services[43] (see Chapter 12). However, the design and introduction of new service offerings has been cited as one of the more difficult challenges for managers in the service sector:

> New product development is inherently more difficult, messier and less successful in the service sector. If a service company perceives a new need and develops a new service, there is less confidence in the result because the service is not subject to the same rigor and predictable outcomes that new products are subject to in the R&D lab. Most service companies focus on geographic extensions of their service or on minor modifications rather than on truly innovative approaches. Innovation in the service sector is the result of trial and error. . . . Service firms have difficulty in linking innovations and imagination to execution of a new offer.[44]

A major stumbling block to creating and launching a new service is the difficulty in "tangibilizing" the service concept. Traditional approaches, such as product prototyping, do not work effectively with services because it is hard to prototype services that are often customized for individual buyers. However, the business service firm can overcome these difficulties by taking steps to improve the new service development process and resulting marketing success. James Heskett offers five steps that a firm can take to improve the new service development process (see Table 13.3). Consistent with

---

[43] Cowell, *The Marketing of Services*, p. 133.
[44] "Service Management: The Toughest Game in Town," *Management Practice*, 7 (fall 1984): p. 8.

| TABLE 13.4 | NEW INDUSTRIAL SERVICE DEVELOPMENT: SCENARIOS FOR SUCCESS AND FAILURE |

Successes

Customized expert service—New services that fully leverage the firm's expert capabilities and resources—in particular, its expert personnel—in providing clients with a customized and high quality service outcome. Success at new service development depends on a high-involvement and innovation-oriented corporate environment.

Planned "pioneering" venture—Pioneering new service ventures aimed at attractive, high volume markets. Key descriptive factors include companies first to market, excellent fit with customer/market segment needs—as well as with the company expertise and resources, tangible evidence used to promote the service, and a detailed and high quality execution of the stages of the new service development (NSD) process.

Improved service experience—Enhanced speed and reliability are essential features of these equipment-based new service offerings. Developers have a good understanding of client needs, they have a reputation for service quality, and they use a fairly planned approach for researching, designing, and marketing the new service product.

Failures

Peripheral, low market potential service—The service offers few real benefits and has only low market potential. It is peripheral to the firm's core line of services and appears to lack any real commitment on the part of the firm. The NSD process is haphazard and companies misuse tangible evidence to feign service quality.

Poorly planned, "industrialized" clone—These are failed "me-too" attempts at "industrializing" complex, equipment-based services. Entering the market long after competitors, the new service projects are deficient in terms of customer orientation, service quality and innovativeness, their fit with corporate capabilities and resources, and the quality of execution of new service development activities.

SOURCE: Ulrike de Brentani, "New Industrial Service Development: Scenarios for Success and Failure," *Journal of Business Research* 32 (February 1995): p. 96. Copyright © 1995. Reprinted by permission of the publisher, Elsevier–Science, Inc.

the discussion of product innovation, it is important to create the proper organizational climate (for example, entrepreneurial culture, championing, taking risks).

Scenarios for Success and Failure [45]

Services depend on the skills and expertise of the people that deliver them; if a new service lies outside the knowledge base of company personnel (no synergy), the quality and delivery of the service may be deficient, resulting in a less than effective experience for the customer. Therefore, when managers screen and select new service ideas, those proposals that score highest on marketing, technical, and operations synergy should be favored.

A recent study tackled these issues: What new service development scenarios do managers in industrial service companies typically pursue, and what factors explain why some are likely to succeed while others fail? Observe in Table 13.4 that three

[45] This section is based on Ulrike de Brentani, "New Industrial Service Development: Scenarios for Success and Failure," *Journal of Business Research* (February 1995): pp. 93–103.

scenarios describe the characteristics of successful situations, while two others characterize failed attempts at developing and launching new business services.

New Service Projects That Succeed   The three successful scenarios differ in terms of the nature of the service initiative, the extent of service innovativeness, and the approach followed in developing and marketing the new service offering. The following profiles highlight key differences.

- **The Customized, Expert Service:** These new services are relatively straightforward and inexpensive but are customized to fit the needs and operating systems of client firms. To respond to a customer's unique requirements, expert personnel are crucial to successful strategy execution. Examples include a customized learning center offered by management consultants and a media planning model developed by a marketing communication firm.

- **The Planned, Pioneering Venture:** These are first-to-market services that are unique, complex, and expensive. A formal and carefully planned new service development process is a distinguishing feature of these service projects. Special attention is given to providing potential customers with tangible evidence that illuminates the benefits of the new service offering for them. Examples of these services include a terminal device linking stockbrokers to multiple information origins developed by a telecommunications firm and a computer-based remote access system developed by a bank to simplify payroll processing by organizations.

- **The Improved Service Experience:** Represented here are equipment-based improvements made to a current service offering that increase the speed and reliability of the service process. Examples include an information systems-based expert production system provided by a computer systems organization and a mutual fund order network developed by a large financial services organization.

All three of these scenarios share certain critical elements that appear to be crucial to the success of new service offerings. Whereas industrial services can take many forms, new service success is closely associated with offerings that respond to market needs; that capitalize on a firm's reputation, skills, and resources; and that issue from a well-managed new service development process.

New Service Projects That Fail   What are the characteristics of new service initiatives that fail in the business market and what can we learn from them? The following two common scenarios for failure are also described in Table 13.4.

- **The Peripheral, Low Market Potential Service:** These new services tend to be peripheral to the firm's core offerings, fail to provide added value to the customer, and enter a market with very limited potential. Failures of this type are common across service sectors in the business market.

- **The Poorly Planned "Industrialized" Clone:** These are complex new services that rely on "hard" technology (that is, equipment) for their production and delivery. Often, these are "me-too" services that offer no real customer benefits or improvements over those of well-entrenched competitors. While many of the new industrial service initiatives fitting this profile were developed by well-established banks and insurance firms, inadequate planning by managers was the key feature distinguishing these failed services from other more successful projects.

Clearly, efforts to improve the efficiency and reliability of services by reducing customer contact and introducing equipment-intensive processes have succeeded in certain sectors of the business market. But, states Ulrike de Brentani, "such development efforts must be accompanied by apparent customer benefits—that is, greater efficiencies and/or superior solutions to problems; a good fit with the capabilities of the developing firm; some competitive advantage in terms of service competitiveness; as well as a set of activities for researching, designing, and launching the new service offerings."[46] Overall, then, the determinants of success for new services closely resemble those found for successful new products (see Chapter 12).

Summary

Business services can be categorized into two segments: pure services, marketed in their own right, and support services, marketed along with goods and equipment. Both segments of the business service market are large, expanding as the world moves toward a service economy. Given the diversity of services, special insights can be secured by classifying business services on a product-service continuum for which the basic underlying factor is tangibility.

Business services are distinguished by their intangibility, linked production and consumption, lack of standardization, perishability, and use as opposed to ownership. Together, these characteristics have profound effects on how services should be marketed. Buyers of business services focus on five dimensions of service quality: reliability, responsiveness, assurance, empathy, and tangibles. Because of intangibility and lack of uniformity, service buyers have significant difficulty in the comparison and selection of service vendors. Service providers must address this issue in the development of their marketing mix.

The marketing mix for business services centers on the traditional elements—service package, pricing, promotion, and distribution—as well as on service personnel, service delivery system, and physical evidence. The goal of the services marketing program is to create satisfied customers. A key first step in creating strategies is to define the customer-benefit concept and the related service concept and offer. Pricing concentrates on influencing demand and capacity as well as on the bundling of service elements. The promotion arena emphasizes developing employee communication, enhancing word-of-mouth promotion, providing tangible clues, and developing interpersonal skills of operating personnel. Distribution is accomplished through direct means, through intermediaries, or by franchising. Firms, large and small, are using the Internet to forge closer relationships with customers and to deliver a vast array of new services.

New service marketing can improve effectiveness by creating an organizational culture that fosters risk taking and innovation. Successful new services respond to

---

[46] Ibid., p. 101.

carefully defined market needs, capitalize on the strengths and reputation of the firm, and issue from a well-planned new service development process.

Discussion Questions

1. Dell Computer recently entered into a strategy alliance with IBM's Global Services division. Under the agreement, IBM will now provide the service support for Dell computers at corporate accounts. Evaluate the benefits of the alliance to Dell and, in turn, to IBM.

2. When a company buys a high-end document processor from Xerox or Canon, they are buying a physical product with a bundle of associated services. Describe some of the services that might be associated with such a product. How can buyers evaluate the quality or value of these services?

3. Critique this statement: "The effective business marketer of technical equipment is the one who successfully develops high-quality services to support the product; the less effective firm focuses on technical solutions offered by the product."

4. Leading service companies, such as AT&T and Federal Express, measure customer satisfaction on a quarterly basis across the global market. Discuss the relationship between customer satisfaction and loyalty.

5. Many firms have a recovery process in place for those situations when their products or services fail to deliver what has been promised to the customer. Illustrate how such a process might work.

6. A new firm has recently been formed to create Web sites and electronic commerce strategies for small businesses. Describe the essential elements to be included in its service product.

7. What is the role of physical evidence in the marketing of a business service?

8. As a luxury resort hotel manager, what approaches might you utilize to manage business demand for hotel space?

9. Critique this statement: "A key dimension of success in services marketing, as opposed to products marketing, is that operating personnel in the service firm play a critical selling and marketing role."

10. What steps could a manager take to enhance the chances of success for a new business service?

14

Managing Business Marketing Channels

The channel of distribution is the marketing manager's bridge to the market. Designing and managing the business marketing channel is a challenging and ongoing task. The business marketer must ensure that the firm's channel is properly aligned to the needs of important market segments. At the same time, the marketer must also satisfy the needs of channel members, whose support is crucial to the success of business marketing strategy. After reading this chapter, you will understand

1. the central components of channel design.

2. the alternative forms of business marketing channels.

3. managerial aids that can be used to evaluate alternative channel structures.

4. the nature and function of industrial distributors and manufacturers' representatives.

5. requirements for managing the existing channel.

Channel Champions, a recent book by Steven Wheeler and Evan Hirsh, aptly describes the vital role that the distribution channels assume in marketing strategy:

> A channel is the essence of the way customers and a business interact—everything about how and where people purchase a product or service and how and where they use that product or service. It is a business's route to its customers and a business's ongoing relationship with its customers . . . When you think in terms of channels you should be thinking of strategy: effective channel management offers the chance to reinvent not just your business but the industry you're in.[1]

The channel component of business marketing strategy has two important and related dimensions. First, the channel structure must be designed to accomplish desired marketing objectives. However, the selection of the best channel to accomplish objectives is challenging because (1) the alternatives are numerous, (2) marketing goals differ, and (3) the variety of business market segments often requires that separate channels must be employed concurrently. The ever-changing business environment requires that the channel structure be periodically reevaluated. Stiff competition, new customer requirements, and the rapid growth of the Internet are among the forces that signal the need for fresh channel strategies. Among the challenges in the design of a distribution channel are specifying channel goals, evaluating constraints on the design, analyzing channel activities, specifying channel alternatives, and selecting channel members. Each requires evaluation.

Second, once the channel structure has been specified, the business marketer must manage the channel to achieve prescribed goals. To administer channel activities effectively, the manager must develop procedures for selecting intermediaries, for motivating them to achieve desired performance, for mediating conflict among channel members, and for evaluating performance. This chapter provides a structure for designing and administering the business marketing channel.

The Business Marketing Channel

The link between manufacturers and customers is the channel of distribution. The channel accomplishes all the tasks necessary to effect a sale and to deliver products to the customer. These tasks include making contact with potential buyers, negotiating, contracting, transferring title, communicating, arranging financing, servicing the product, and providing local inventory, transportation, and storage. These tasks may be performed entirely by the manufacturer, entirely by intermediaries, or may be shared between them. The customer may even undertake some of these functions; for example, customers granted certain discounts might agree to accept larger inventories and the associated storage costs.

At a fundamental level, channel management centers on these questions: *which channel tasks will be performed by the firm and which tasks, if any, will be performed by channel members?* The tasks must always be performed as the product moves from the manufacturer to the customer. Figure 14.1 shows the various ways business marketing

---

[1] Steven Wheeler and Evan Hirsh, *Channel Champions: How Leading Companies Build New Strategies to Serve Customers* (San Francisco: Jossey-Bass Publishers, 1999), p. xxii.

CHANNEL ALTERNATIVES IN THE BUSINESS MARKET

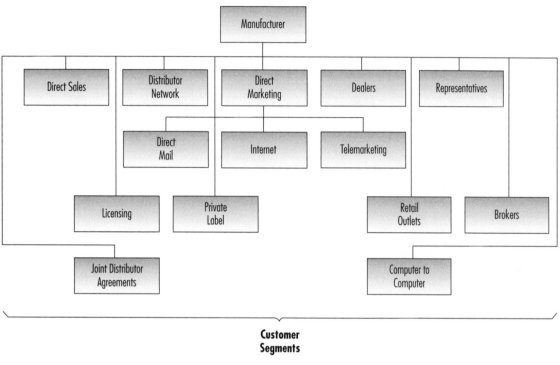

SOURCE: Adapted from David Perry, "How You'll Manage Your 1990s Distribution Portfolio," *Business Marketing* 74 (June 1989), p. 54.

channels can be structured. Some channel structures are **indirect;** that is, some type of intermediary (such as a distributor or dealer) is involved in selling or handling the products. Other channels are **direct;** the manufacturer must accomplish all the marketing functions necessary to create a sale and to deliver products to the customer. The manufacturer's direct sales force and the direct marketing channels are examples.

A basic issue in channel management, then, is how to structure the channel so that the tasks are performed optimally. One alternative is for the manufacturer to do it all.

Direct Distribution

Direct distribution, common in business marketing, is a channel strategy that does not use intermediaries. The manufacturer's own sales force deals directly with the customer, and the manufacturer has full responsibility for performing all the necessary channel tasks. Direct distribution is often required in business marketing because of the nature of the selling situation. The direct sales approach is viable when (1) the customers are large and well defined, (2) the customers insist on direct sales, (3) sales involve extensive negotiations with upper management, and (4) control of the selling job is necessary to ensure proper implementation of the total product package and to guarantee a quick response to market conditions. One recent study found that direct channels result when the end user has a strong need for information service (that is, to explain

INSIDE BUSINESS MARKETING

IBM Uses the Internet to Collaborate with Channel Partners and Build Customer Loyalty

The Internet provides a valuable way for business marketers to collaborate with distributors or other resellers, sharing resources and cooperating on electronic marketing initiatives. An excellent example of this channel outreach program is IBM TeamPlayers (www.ibm-teamplayers.com). This is a program that uses the Web as a communications and information delivery tool to service the channel members (Business Partners) of IBM.

IBM TeamPlayers offers channel members customized direct mail campaigns using mail, fax, and e-mail to reach those customers. The Web site is also an outlet for providing help to channel partners in managing their customer databases, developing Web pages, executing telemarketing campaigns, and more, with IBM acting as a clearinghouse for other needed resources.

The program strengthens IBM's relationship with its channel partners. Moreover, the initiative allows IBM to identify and reach end users through the partners and helps strengthen customer loyalty to both IBM channel members and to IBM itself.

SOURCE: Barry Silverstein, *Business-to-Business Internet Marketing: Five Proven Strategies for Increasing Profits Through Internet Direct Marketing* (Gulf Breeze, FL: MAXIMUM Press, 1999), p. 307.

product use and features for a product like an airplane or a bottling machine) and very minimal needs for logistics services (like lot size, delivery time, or assortments).[2]

Pitney Bowes attributes success in the highly competitive facsimile market to its direct sales efforts. The company only sells direct and only to the top U.S. firms, offering them extra service and the products they require. In fact, two-thirds of its revenue comes from 10 percent of its customers. The firm's strategy is to "concentrate on and service the largest companies in the world with large and growing fax networks."[3] It may take months to make a sale, but deals rarely number less than 10 units; one sale involved 7,000 units to a single customer! Large, complex fax systems require significant amounts of telecommunications expertise, which the Pitney Bowes direct sales force is able to provide.

A direct sales force may include both generalists and specialists. **Generalists** sell the entire product line to all customers; **specialists** concentrate on certain products, certain customers, or certain industries.

Indirect Distribution

Indirect distribution uses one or more types of intermediaries. Business marketing channels typically include fewer types of intermediaries than do consumer-goods channels. Manufacturers' representatives and industrial distributors account for most of the business handled through indirect industrial channels. Indirect distribution is generally found where (1) markets are fragmented and widely dispersed, (2) low transaction amounts prevail, and (3) buyers typically purchase a number of items, often different brands, in one transaction.[4] For example, IBM's massive sales organization

---

[2] Louis P. Bucklin, Venkatram Ramaswamy, and Sumit K. Majumdar, "Analyzing Channel Structures of Business Markets Via the Structure-Output Paradigm," *International Journal of Research in Marketing* 13, no. 1 (1996): p. 84.

[3] "Fax Channels Shift as Market Shrinks," *Purchasing* 114 (18 February 1993): p. 77.

[4] E. Raymond Corey, Frank V. Cespedes, and V. Kasturi Rangan, *Going to Market: Distribution Systems for Industrial Products* (Boston: Harvard University Press, 1989), p. 26.

concentrates on large corporate, government, and institutional customers. Literally thousands of other IBM customers—small- to medium-sized organizations—are served by industrial distributors. These channel partners assume a vital role in IBM's strategy on a global scale.

Many Channels Are Often Required

Various combinations of intermediaries and direct selling may be employed in the business marketing channel. In fact, one manufacturer could use several of the avenues shown in Figure 14.1. The wide array of options reflects the many marketing tasks to be performed and the fact that many business marketers are creating unique channel systems to appeal to a wide variety of customer niches. As business markets evolve, new channel arrangements have been formed to reach every one of the identifiable segments.

Xerox employs a complex channel strategy that includes retail stores, distributors or dealers, and a large direct sales force.[5] Each channel is designed to serve a particular market segment. For example, home office or small business customers are served through the retail store channel while the company sales force serves large corporate and government customers. Distributors cover the vast middle market comprised of a diverse array of medium-sized organizations. Moreover, small and medium-sized customers can purchase some Xerox systems and supplies online through the Xerox Web site. The firm has also developed private extranets (sites) for its largest customers. These customers can use the site to change orders, check delivery status, and make electronic payments. Salespeople continue to work closely with these corporate accounts and receive full commission for sales that come through the Internet. By streamlining the sales process, Valerie Blauvelt, vice president of strategy and market operations at Xerox, estimates that the Web can increase sales productivity by 15 percent.

E-Channels

Many business marketing firms, like Xerox, Dell Computer, Cisco Systems, and National Semiconductor Corporation are emphasizing e-commerce strategies. E-channels can be used by business marketing firms as (1) information platforms, (2) transaction platforms, and (3) as platforms for managing customer relationships.[6] The impact on the business increases as a firm moves from level one to level three.

Level 1: Information Platform   E-channels are widely used as an informational platform. Customers can secure instant information on product specifications and features. The Web site also allows the potential buyer to customize features and options while providing a link to a local distributor or company sales representative.

Level 2: Transactional Platform   The next level of e-channel development provides the potential buyer with additional information plus a mechanism for making transactions. Such systems can be used to get price quotes, place orders, check availability, and access additional services—such as technical support. Cisco Systems—and some other firms—carefully coordinates these online purchases with its distributors. In fact, Cisco requires new customers to work with a distributor or dealer before

---

[5] Chad Kaydo, "Web Masters: You've Got Sales," *Sales & Marketing Management* 151 (October 1999), pp. 36–37.

[6] Wheeler and Hirsh, *Channel Champions*, pp. 192–195.

| FIGURE 14.2 | NATIONAL SEMICONDUCTOR'S WEB SITE: LARGE CUSTOMERS LOG ON TO PRIVATE EXTRANETS WITH TAILORED INFORMATION; OTHER CUSTOMERS CAN RESEARCH PRODUCTS AND LINK DIRECTLY TO DISTRIBUTORS' SITES |

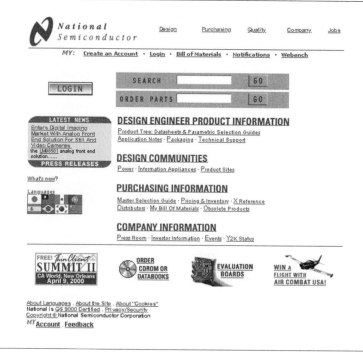

SOURCE: http://www.national.com/ (1/10/00)

purchasing online. This practice allows Cisco to maintain good working relationships with channel members.

Level 3: Platform for Managing Customer Relationships   This advanced level of e-channel development creates an ongoing dialogue with customers that results in improved customer segmentation, more targeted promotions, and more personalized customer care. Importantly, the e-channel strategy must be designed to support the other traditional channels that the firm employs. To illustrate, National Semiconductor serves its largest customers, who account for 60 percent of the firm's revenues, through its direct sales force while the majority of its customers work with a network of distributors (see Figure 14.2).

The e-channel strategy is designed to streamline the sales process and create ongoing dialogue with customers of all types.[7] Salespersons create a private extranet site with tailored information for each of the large customers. Online ordering allows those salespeople to center on managing relationships rather than managing transactions. Likewise, the Web site helps customers who buy from distributors to research products, secure technical information, and link directly to the distributors' sites to order online.

---

[7] Kaydo, "Web Masters," pp. 34–35.

The challenge is determining how to create a channel strategy that blends e-commerce with traditional channels. That means working with field salespeople, inside salespersons, and other channel members—anyone who touches the customer—"to create a seamless buying experience that allows customers to choose the particular channel that best suits their needs."[8]

Participants in the Business Marketing Channel

Use of indirect channels of distribution is common for a wide variety of business products. The quality and performance of the intermediaries have a critical impact on whether the business marketer achieves his or her goals. A channel management strategy begins with an understanding of the various intermediaries that may be utilized in a business marketing channel.

The types of business marketing intermediaries are distributors, manufacturers' representatives (reps), jobbers, brokers, and commission merchants. Distributors and reps handle the vast preponderance of business-to-business sales made through intermediaries. This section of the chapter will emphasize the role of each intermediary in the business marketing channel and the nature of each operation.

Distributors

Industrial distributors are the most pervasive and important single force in distribution channels. U.S. distributors number more than 10,000, with sales exceeding $50 billion. Distributors are heavily used for MRO (maintenance, repair, and operations) supplies, with many industrial buyers reporting that they buy as much as 75 percent of their MRO supplies from distributors. In one study, McGraw-Hill found that only 24 percent of all business marketers sell their products directly to end users exclusively; the remaining 76 percent use some type of intermediary, of which industrial distributors are the most prominent.[9] What accounts for the unparalleled position of the distributor in the industrial market? What role do distributors play in the industrial distribution process?

Distributors are generally small, independent businesses serving narrow geographic markets. Sales average almost $2 million, although some top $3 billion. Net profits are relatively low as a percentage of sales (4 percent); return on investment averages 11 percent. The typical order is small, and the distributors sell to a multitude of customers in many industries. The typical distributor is able to spread its costs over a sizable group of vendors—it stocks goods from between 200 and 300 manufacturers. Orders are generated by a sales force of outside and inside salespersons. **Outside salespersons** make regular calls on customers and handle normal account servicing and technical assistance. **Inside salespersons** complement these efforts, processing orders and scheduling delivery; their primary duty is to take telephone orders. Most distributors operate from a single location, but some approach the "supermarket" status with as many as 130 branches.

Compared to their smaller rivals, large distributors seem to have significant advantages. Small distributors are typically unable to achieve the operating economies

---

[8] Ibid., p. 30.

[9] "Industry Markets Goods through Dual Channels, Says McGraw-Hill Study," *Industrial Distribution* 75 (April 1985): p. 15.

Distributor Alliances Respond to Changing Customer Needs

A major initiative by many U.S. manufacturers has been to simplify the buying process and reduce the costs involved with acquiring MRO (maintenance, repair, and operating) supplies. To accomplish these objectives, manufacturers are entering into integrated supply agreements with limited numbers of MRO distributors. The integrated supply agreement typically states that the buyer will purchase all of a given commodity or group of commodities from the distributor in exchange for a certain level of service and price. It may also specify that activities like anticipating needs and scheduling and disbursing of MRO products be handled by the distributor. This approach usually results in reducing the number of suppliers and holding the remaining distributors responsible for driving costs out of the acquisition process through efficiencies in delivery, invoicing, and selling.

One way that industrial distributors are responding to these important customer demands is through the formation of unique alliances *among themselves.* Distributors that carry dissimilar product lines are banding together to offer customers single-source access to an extremely large array of products along with simplification in the purchasing process, consolidated deliveries, and a single invoice. The alliances function in the following way: Each distributor serves as a preferred supplier for the other distributors in the alliance when an "integrated supply customer" requires access to products not included in the alliance compa-

nies' core offerings. The alliances can take many forms and several different arrangements have been created to deal with specific issues in individual industries.

One significant alliance comprises three of the largest industrial distributors in the United States: Motion Industries, W. W. Grainger, and Ferguson Enterprises. Customers dealing with this alliance have access to more than 1.8 million products carried by the three distributors. Ferguson is one of the largest distributors of pipe, valves, and fittings, carrying over 200,000 items at 228 stocking locations across the country. Motion Industries is the largest U.S. distributor of bearings and power transmission equipment, with 370 locations nationwide and a product line that exceeds one million items. Grainger is a leading nationwide distributor of MRO items whose product line totals almost 100,000 products sold through 342 branches located in all fifty states.

Companies buying MRO supplies can now deal with a distribution alliance able to service a multitude of plant locations with ready access to hundreds of thousands of MRO products not typically found in one distributor's core inventory—and the acquisition process is customer-friendly.

source: Adapted from "Good May Not Be Good Enough," *Purchasing* 119 (9 May 1996): pp. 38–52. See also Adam J. Fein and Sandy D. Jap, "Manage Consolidation in the Distribution Channel," *Sloan Management Review* 40 (fall 1999): pp. 61– 72.

enjoyed by larger firms.[10] The ability of large firms to automate much of their operations enables them to significantly reduce their sales and general administrative expenses, often to levels approaching 10 percent of sales.

Distributor Responsibilities   An industrial distributor's primary responsibilities are shown in Table 14.1. The products that distributors sell—cutting tools, abrasives, electronic components, ball bearings, handling equipment, pipe, maintenance equipment, and hundreds more—are generally those that buyers need quickly to avoid production disruptions. Thus, the critical elements of the distributor's function are to have these products readily available and to serve as the selling arm of the manufacturer.

   Distributors are full-service intermediaries; that is, they take title to the products they sell, and they perform the full range of marketing functions. Some of the more

---

[10] Heidi Elliott, "Distributors, Make Way for the Little Guys," *Electronic Business Today* 22 (September 1996): p. 19.

TABLE 14.1	KEY DISTRIBUTION RESPONSIBILITIES
Responsibility	**Activity**
Contact	Reach all customers in a defined territory through an outside sales force that calls on customers or through an inside group that receives telephone orders
Product availability	Provide a local inventory and include all supporting activities: credit, delivery, order processing, and advice
Repair	Provide easy access to local repair facilities (unavailable from a distant manufacturer)
Assembly and light manufacturing	Purchase material in bulk, then shape, form, or assemble to user requirements

important functions are providing credit, offering wide product assortments, delivering goods, offering technical advice, and meeting emergency requirements. Distributors are valuable not only to their manufacturer-suppliers, but also are generally viewed favorably by their customers. Some purchasing agents view the distributor as an extension of their "buying arms" because of the service, technical advice, and product application suggestions they provide.

Today, many firms have adopted the just-in-time (JIT) concept—the buyer demands that the supplies and components it purchases be delivered on a specified day, at a specific time. The effect of the JIT trend is to move the distributor into a position of prominence in many channel situations because few manufacturers are organized to make JIT deliveries all over the country.

Classification of Distributors   To select the most appropriate distributor for a particular channel, the marketing manager must understand the diversity of distributor operations. Industrial distributors vary according to product lines handled and user markets served. Firms may be ultraspecialized (for example, selling only to municipal water works), or they may carry a broad line of generalized industrial products. However, three primary distributor classifications are usually recognized.

General-Line Distributors   **General-line distributors** cater to a broad array of industrial needs. They stock an extensive variety of products and could be likened to the supermarket in consumer-goods markets.

Specialists   **Specialists** focus on one line or on a few related lines. Such a distributor may handle only power transmission equipment—belts, pulleys, and bearings. The most common specialty is fasteners, although specialization also occurs in cutting tools, power transmission equipment, pipes, valves, and fittings. There is a trend toward increased specialization as a result of increasing technical complexity of products and the need for higher levels of precision and quality control.

Combination House   A **combination house** operates in two markets: industrial and consumer. Such a distributor might carry electric motors for industrial customers and hardware and automotive parts to be sold through retailers to final consumers.

The selection of a distributor will depend upon the manufacturer's requirements. The general-line distributor offers the advantage of one-stop purchasing to the manufacturer's potential customers. If a high level of service and technical expertise is not required, the general-line distributor is a good choice. The specialist, on the other hand, provides the manufacturer with a high level of technical capability and a well-developed understanding of complex user requirements. Fasteners, for instance, are handled by specialists because of the strict quality-control standards that users impose.

The Distributor as a Valuable Asset　The quality of a firm's distributors is often the difference between a highly successful marketing strategy and an ineffective one. Good distributors are prized by customers, making it all the more necessary to strive continually to engage the best in any given market. Distributors often provide the only economically feasible way of obtaining comprehensive market coverage.

In summary, the industrial distributor is a full-service intermediary who takes title to the products sold; maintains inventories; provides credit, delivery, wide product assortment, and technical assistance; and may even do light assembly and manufacturing. Although the distributor is primarily responsible for contacting and supplying present customers, industrial distributors also solicit new accounts and work to expand the market. Products handled by industrial distributors are generally established products—typically used in manufacturing operations, repair, and maintenance—with a broad and large demand.

Industrial distributors are a powerful force in business marketing channels, and all indications point to an expanded role for them. The manufacturer's representative is an equally viable force in the business marketing channel.

Manufacturers' Representatives

For many business marketers who need a strong selling job with a technically complex product, manufacturers' representatives, or reps, are the only cost-effective answer. **Reps** are salespeople who work independently (or for a rep company), represent several companies in the same geographic area, and sell noncompeting but complementary products.

The Rep's Responsibilities　A rep neither takes title to nor holds inventory of the products handled. (Some reps do, however, keep a limited inventory of repair and maintenance parts.) The rep's forte is expert product knowledge coupled with a keen understanding of the markets and customer needs. Reps are usually limited to defined geographical areas; thus, a manufacturer seeking nationwide distribution will usually work with several rep companies.

The Rep–Customer Relationship　Reps are the selling arm for manufacturers—making contact with customers, writing orders, following up on orders, and linking the manufacturer with the industrial end users. Although paid by the manufacturer, the rep is also important to the customers served. Often, the efforts of a rep during a customer emergency (for example, an equipment failure) means the difference between continuing or stopping production. Most reps are thoroughly experienced in the industries they serve; they can offer technical advice while enhancing the customer's leverage with suppliers in securing parts, repair, and delivery. The rep also provides customers with a continuing flow of information on innovations and trends in equipment, as well as on the industry as a whole.

Commission Basis Reps are paid a commission on sales; the commission varies by industry and by the nature of the selling job. Commissions typically range from a low of 4 percent to a high of 18 percent for selected high-tech products. Percentage commission compensation is attractive to manufacturers because they have few fixed sales costs. Reps are paid only when orders are generated. Because reps are paid on commission, they are motivated to generate high levels of sales—another fact appreciated by the manufacturer.

Experience Reps possess sophisticated product knowledge and typically have extensive experience in the markets they serve. Most reps develop their field experience while working as a salesperson for a manufacturer. They are motivated to become reps by the desire to be independent and to reap the substantial monetary rewards possible on commission.

When Reps Are Used

- *Large and Small Firms:* Small- and medium-sized firms generally have the greatest need for a rep, although many large firms—for example, Dow Chemical and Motorola—use them. The reason is primarily economic: smaller firms cannot justify the expense of maintaining their own sales forces. The rep provides an efficient means to obtaining total market coverage, with costs incurred only as sales are made. The quality of the selling job is often very good as a result of the rep's prior experience and market knowledge.

- *Limited Market Potential:* The rep also plays a vital role when the manufacturer's market potential is limited. A manufacturer may use a direct sales force in heavily concentrated business markets where the demand is sufficient to support the expense and use reps to cover less dense markets. Because the rep carries several lines, expenses can be allocated over a much larger sales volume.

- *Servicing Distributors:* Reps may also be employed by a firm that markets through distributors. When a manufacturer sells through hundreds of distributors across the United States, reps may sell to and service those distributors.

- *Reducing Overhead Costs:* Sometimes the commission rate paid to reps exceeds the cost of a direct sales force, yet the supplier continues to use reps. This policy is not as irrational as it appears. Assume, for example, that costs for a direct sales force approximate 8 percent of sales and that a rep's commission rate is 11 percent. The use of reps in this case is often justified because of the hidden costs associated with a sales force. First, the manufacturer does not provide fringe benefits or a fixed salary to reps. Second, the costs of training a rep are usually limited to those required to provide product information. Thus, the use of reps eliminates significant overhead costs.

Channel Design

Channel design is the dynamic process of developing new channels where none existed and modifying existing channels. The business marketer usually deals with modification of existing channels, although new products and customer segments may require entirely new channels. Regardless of whether the manager is dealing with a

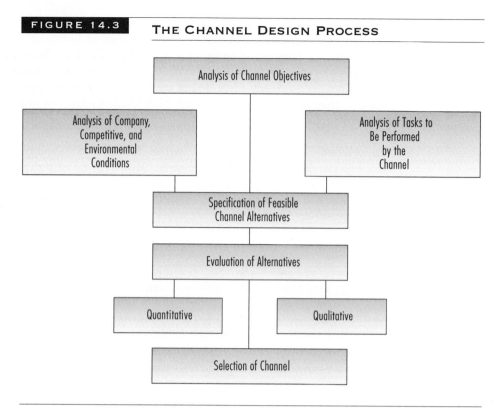

FIGURE 14.3   THE CHANNEL DESIGN PROCESS

SOURCE: Michael D. Hutt and Thomas W. Speh, "Realigning Industrial Marketing Channels," *Industrial Marketing Management* 12 (July 1983): pp. 171–177.

new channel or modifying an existing one, channel design is an active rather than a passive task. Effective distribution channels do not simply evolve; they are developed by management, which takes action on the basis of a well-conceived plan that reflects overall marketing goals.

Channel design is best conceptualized as a series of stages that must be completed so that the business marketing manager can be sure that all important channel dimensions have been evaluated (Figure 14.3). The result of the channel design process is to specify the structure that provides the highest probability of achieving the firm's objectives. Note that the process focuses on channel structure and not on channel participants. **Channel structure** refers to the underlying framework: the number of channel levels, the number and types of intermediaries, and the linkages among channel members. Selection of individual intermediaries is indeed important; it will be examined later in the chapter.

Stage 1: Channel Objectives

Business firms formulate their marketing strategies to appeal to selected market segments, to earn targeted levels of profits, to maintain or increase sales and market share growth rates, and to achieve all this within specified resource constraints. Each element of the marketing strategy has a specific purpose. Thus, whether the business marketer is designing a totally new channel or redesigning an existing one, the first phase of channel design is to comprehend fully the marketing goals and to formulate corresponding channel objectives.

Structure Based on Profits and Strategy Integration   Profit considerations and asset utilization must be reflected in channel objectives and design. For example, the cost of maintaining a salesperson in the field—including lodging, meals, and auto rental—is substantial: the total cost-per-call figure is over $200.[11] For the manufacturer, these costs are somewhat fixed in the short run. The need to commit working capital to these costs might be eliminated by switching from a direct sales force to manufacturers' reps, whose compensation, as a percentage of sales, is totally variable. Of course, many other factors, such as the quality of the selling job, must also be evaluated. Channel structure must be compatible with all marketing strategy elements.

Channel Objectives Reflect Marketing Goals   Specific distribution objectives are established on the basis of broad marketing objectives. Distribution objectives force the manager to relate channel design decisions to broader marketing goals. A manufacturer of industrial cleaning products might have a distribution objective of providing product availability in every county in the Midwest with more than $5 million in market potential. The distribution objective of a supplier of air-conditioning units might be to make contact with industrial plant architects once every month and with industrial contractors once every two months.

Marketing and distribution objectives guide the channel design process and actually limit the range of feasible channel structures. Channel structures need to be developed to reflect both strategic goals (for example, to achieve market share) and efficiency goals (for example, to reduce administrative costs). Generally, management decision models have emphasized effectiveness criteria (strategic issues) and evaluated channel arrangements on the basis of their ability to accomplish certain functions.[12] Both efficiency and effectiveness criteria need to be evaluated when alternative channel arrangements are under investigation. Before the alternative channel structures can be evaluated, the business marketing manager must examine other limitations on the choice of channel structures.

Stage 2: Channel Design Constraints

Frequently, the manager has little flexibility in the selection of channel structures because of trade, competitive, company, and environmental factors. In fact, the decision on channel design may be imposed on the manager. The variety of constraining factors is almost limitless.[13] Figure 14.4 summarizes those factors most relevant to the business marketer.

Stage 3: Pervasive Channel Tasks

Each channel structure will be evaluated on its ability to perform the required channel activities effectively and efficiently. The concept of a channel as a sequence of

---

[11] "The Cost of Doing Business," *Sales & Marketing Management* 151 (September 1999): p. 56.

[12] Jan B. Heide, "Interorganizational Governance in Marketing Channels," *Journal of Marketing* 58 (January 1994): p. 83.

[13] For example, see Louis W. Stern and Frederick D. Sturdivant, "Customer-Driven Distribution Systems," *Harvard Business Review* 65 (July/August 1987): pp. 34–41; and Louis Stern and Adel I. El-Ansary, *Marketing Channels*, 4th ed. (Englewood Cliffs, N.J.: Prentice-Hall, 1992), pp. 202–223.

FIGURE 14.4	FACTORS LIMITING CHOICE OF INDUSTRIAL CHANNEL

1. **Availability of Good Intermediaries**
   Competitors often "lock up" the better intermediaries.
   Established intermediaries are not always receptive to new products.

2. **Traditional Channel Patterns**
   Established patterns of distribution are difficult to violate.
   Large customers may demand direct sales.

3. **Product Characteristics**
   Technical complexity dictates direct distribution.
   Extensive repair requirements may call for local distributors to service the product line.

4. **Company Financial Resources**
   Capital requirements often preclude direct distribution.

5. **Competitive Strategies**
   Direct service by competitors may force all firms to sell direct.

6. **Geographic Dispersion of Customers**
   A widely dispersed market of small customers often requires low-cost representation afforded by intermediaries.

activities to be performed, rather than as a set of channel institutions, is essential to channel design. The business marketing manager must creatively structure the tasks necessary to meet customer requirements and company goals rather than merely accepting existing channel structures or traditional distribution patterns.

How the channel tasks will be assigned among the channel participants will be affected by changes in the technological and business environments. Research by Mini Hahn and Dae Chang suggests that advances in telecommunications systems generally have increased the "power" of manufacturers:

> These systems enable the companies, among other things, to selectively reach a large number of end users, qualify leads and develop prospects, take orders, check inventory, disseminate information, and dispatch customer service. The relative power of producers with respect to both end users and intermediaries is increased because they are able to influence end users directly and to take over many functions of the intermediaries. Distributors in these channels, therefore, fulfill ancillary functions to producers such as following-up the sales call, providing feedback on leads, inventory status, delivery arrangements and other relevant information.[14]

Increasing manufacturer power may diminish the distributor's role in the channel as the manufacturer assumes more channel activities; the distributor's share of profits and revenues could be reduced accordingly.

---

[14]Mini Hahn and Dae R. Chang, "An Extended Framework for Adjusting Channel Strategies in Industrial Markets," *Journal of Business and Industrial Marketing* 7 (spring 1992): p. 36.

Manufacturers' reps typically carry no inventory of their suppliers' products. A manufacturer of semiconductors and microcircuits, upon a careful analysis of required channel activities, may decide that although reps can provide the level of sales service needed, large accounts need emergency local inventories of a few selected micro-circuits. In this case the solution would not be to abandon the rep as a viable channel, but to compensate the rep for carrying a limited inventory of emergency circuits. Analysis of required tasks and a view of the channel as a sequence of activities would lead the firm to a creative solution to the inventory problem.

The backbone of channel design is the analysis of objectives, constraints, and channel activities. Once these are understood, channel alternatives can be evaluated.

Stage 4: Channel Alternatives

Specification of channel alternatives involves four primary issues:

1. The number of levels to be included in the channel (that is, the degree of "directness")
2. The types of intermediaries to employ
3. The number of channel intermediaries at each level of the channel
4. The number of channels to employ

The decisions made for each are predicated upon the objectives, constraints, and activities previously analyzed.

Degree of Directness   The issue of directness concerns whether products will be marketed directly to customers or through intermediaries. The critical aspects of this decision were presented earlier in the chapter.

Assessing Product/Market Factors   The number of channel levels depends on a host of company, product, and market variables. The length of business marketing channels is influenced by availability of capable intermediaries, market factors, and customer characteristics. Market factors include the number of customers, the geographic concentration of customers, and the industry concentration. Customer characteristics include the significance of the purchase as perceived by the customer and the volume potential of a customer. Channel length increases with greater availability of effective intermediaries and with the number of customers; it decreases when the purchase becomes more significant, when customer potential increases, and when market or industry concentration increases.

There is a greater tendency in business than in consumer-goods marketing to sell directly to the customer. However, direct selling is often not feasible. For such products as tools, abrasives, fasteners, pipes, valves, materials-handling equipment, and wire rope, as much as 97 percent of the annual volume moves only through industrial distributors. These products are typically bought frequently, repetitively (straight re-buy), and in small quantities. Instantaneous availability is fundamental; industrial distributors handle such products efficiently.

Types of Intermediaries   A wide array of factors influences the choice of intermediaries, with the tasks they perform being of prime importance. These tasks were carefully detailed for both reps and distributors earlier in the chapter.

A host of product and market conditions also appear to play a role in indicating which type of intermediary will be used. A study by Donald Jackson and Michael d'Amico evaluated the product and market conditions that differed between manufacturer–rep channels and manufacturer–distributor channels.[15] Their findings showed that the manufacturer–rep channel is generally used when:

- the product is not standard but is closer to made-to-order

- the product tends toward technical complexity

- the gross margin is not large

- the market comprises a relatively few number of customers that are concentrated geographically and concentrated in a few industries

- these customers order relatively infrequently and allow fairly long lead times

Use of distributors is associated with the opposite conditions. A review of market and product situations should be made when making the rep versus distributor decision.

A second question concerns whether more than one type of intermediary will be needed to satisfy all target markets. The primary reason for using more than one type of intermediary for the same product is that different market segments require different channel structures. Some firms use three distinct approaches. Large accounts are called on by the firm's own sales force, distributors handle small repeat orders, and manufacturers' reps develop the market that comprises medium-sized firms.

Like size of accounts, differences in purchase behavior may also dictate using more than one type of intermediary. If a firm produces a wide line of industrial products, some may require high-caliber selling to a multitude of buying influences within a single buyer's firm. When this occurs, the firm's own sales force would focus on the more complex buying situations, whereas the distributors would sell standardized products from local stocks.

The Number of Intermediaries   How many intermediaries of each type are required to cover a particular market effectively? The answer is sometimes easy—for example, when a firm distributes through reps. Since reps act as the firm's sales force, it would be pointless for more than one rep to call on a specific customer (unless, of course, each rep specialized in a unique part of the company's product line). The business marketer would select the single best rep organization in each of the geographical areas to be covered.

In the case of distribution through industrial distributors, the company may require two, three, or even more carefully selected distributors in a geographic market to ensure adequate market coverage. The policy of carefully choosing channel members in a particular geographical area is referred to as **selective distribution.** The nature of the product and the purchasing process usually dictate a selective policy. Materials-handling equipment, electric motors, power-transmission equipment, and tools typically fall into the category of straight or modified rebuy situations. The time

---

[15] Donald M. Jackson and Michael F. d'Amico, "Products and Markets Served by Distributors and Agents," *Industrial Marketing Management* 18 (February 1989): p. 33.

spent in evaluating sources for these products is not great, yet the purchase is not always simple and repetitive. The buyer needs advice about applications, maintenance, and repair, and usually demands rapid product delivery, repair, and service. The manufacturer wants to be represented by a distributor that can satisfy these customer requirements. To ensure that distributors will perform the job required and provide proper emphasis to the manufacturer's line, the number of distributors will be limited to a few in a given market.

Generally, the more standardized the products, the more frequently they are purchased, and the smaller their unit value, the greater the number of distributors in a given market. The abrasives manufacturer who requires up to 1,000 general-line distributors is following an intensive rather than a selective distribution policy. An intensive distribution policy is especially appropriate when availability is a requirement. Customers must have a product source near their plants.

The Number of Channels   More than one channel will be required when various market segments are served and when the characteristics of the segment dictate a fundamentally unique approach to distribution.

Channels need to change to match the life cycle position of the product. For example, small office copiers were first sold directly through manufacturers' direct sales forces. The Japanese then began marketing copiers through office equipment dealers, and today these machines are available through a variety of channels—direct, dealers, mass merchandisers, and the Internet. When a product reaches the maturity stage, it may be necessary to find low-cost distributors that offer minimal services and broader market reach.[16] Once in decline, the channel may be contracted to the point of selling through electronic ordering systems and telemarketing. Often the goal in the maturity and decline stages is to create channels that will provide cost-effective market coverage.

Legal Issues   When a firm maintains more than one channel, some accounts may be double-covered, or various channel members may find themselves competing for business. Business marketers often want to reserve large accounts for their own sales force or restrict certain territories for "selected" distributors. There are complex legal issues associated with such restrictions. Channel experts Corey, Cespedes, and Rangan highlight these legal issues:

> The terms and conditions of channel member agreements may require that the reseller do the following:
>
> - Carry the producer's full line
> - Either not stock competing brands or treat them strategically as secondary lines
> - Not solicit business from certain "reserved" accounts, specified classes of trade, and/or beyond the territory in which the reseller is franchised to sell
> - Observe resale price schedules set by the producer
> - Maintain specified inventory levels
> - Meet specified sales quotas

---

[16]"Distribution and the Product Life Cycle," *Sales and Marketing Management* 148 (July 1996): p. 36.

The supplier may secure adherence to these conditions by withholding producer support from nonconforming distributors and by rewarding those that do conform, with resellers resisting such methods of control and sometimes taking legal action against offending suppliers.

In general, the kinds of terms and conditions outlined above and their enforcement are not illegal per se unless they are construed as being "in restraint of trade or commerce." If franchise conditions serve to build and preserve monopoly power as defined by the Sherman Act, and/or if franchise enforcement is carried out through conspiratorial arrangements, both the conditions and the actions to secure adherence are likely to be judged illegal.[17]

The final task facing the business marketing manager is to select the most effective channel structure from among the feasible alternatives.

Stage 5: Channel Selection

Most channel design decisions are only slight modifications of the channel structure in response to changing markets, expanding geographic coverage, new customer requirements, or new products. Selection of the appropriate modification in channel structure may be fairly straightforward; in fact, the range of choices may be quite limited.

Evaluating Alternative Channels   A useful approach to evaluating channel options is provided by Louis Stern and Frederick Sturdivant.[18] The approach, as depicted in Table 14.2, takes into account all the elements of the channel design process as well as important customer requirements. The focus of their approach is to create an "ideal" channel system that fully addresses customer needs; once this system is specified, it is compared to the "feasible" channel system created on the basis of management objectives and constraints. The critical element is to compare both systems on the basis of customer service performance, structure, and costs.

Channel selection is facilitated by looking at "gaps" that may exist between the systems—existing, ideal, and feasible. One of three conclusions could emerge:

1. *All three systems resemble each other.* In this case, the existing system is about as good as it can be. If customer satisfaction is low, the fault is not with the channel design, it is with poor management.

2. *Existing and feasible systems are similar, but differ from the ideal.* Management constraints and objectives may be causing the gap. A careful review is required as specified in step 6 of Table 14.2.

3. *All three systems are different.* If the feasible system lies between the ideal and existing system, the existing system can be changed without sacrificing management goals. Relaxing management constraints might produce even greater benefits.

---

[17] Corey, Cespedes, and Rangan, *Going to Market*, p. 146.

[18] Stern and Sturdivant, "Customer-Driven Distribution Systems," pp. 34–41.

TABLE 14.2	PROCEDURE FOR EVALUATING CHANNEL ALTERNATIVES

Process	Key Analytical Activities
Step 1: Determine customer requirements	Assess desire for sales assistance, locational convenience, one-stop buying, depth of assortment, and the whole range of possible services.
Step 2: Evaluate potential intermediaries	Assess which type of intermediaries are possible, including direct sale.
Step 3: Analyze costs	Involves three dimensions: (1) Is it feasible for the company to satisfy all customer requirements? (2) What types of supplier support are required? (3) What are the costs of the support systems for each type of channel alternative?
Step 4: Specify constraints— create the "bounded" system	Develop management input on key constraints and company long-term objectives. Specify the channel system structure based on these constraints.
Step 5: Compare options	Compare the "ideal system" specified by customers to the "feasible" system specified by constraints and objectives. If an existing channel is being reviewed, compare it to the ideal and feasible systems.
Step 6: Review constraints and assumptions	Use experts—consultants, lawyers, accountants—to evaluate assumptions.
Step 7: Evaluate gaps	If gaps exist between the existing, ideal, and feasible systems, analyze the underlying reasons.
Step 8: Implementation	Modify the ideal system according to objectives and constraints.

SOURCE: Adapted from Louis W. Stern and Frederick Sturdivant, "Customer-Driven Distribution Systems," *Harvard Business Review* 65 (July/August 1987): pp. 34–41.

Qualitative Dimensions The channel decision maker must consider qualitative as well as quantitative factors. Given two channels with nearly similar economic performance, the critical factor may be the degree of *control* that the business marketer can exercise over the channels. Compared to a distributor channel, a rep generally gives the manager more control because the manufacturer maintains title and possession of the goods. The manufacturer may be willing to trade off short-run economic benefits in order to gain long-term control over channel activities.

Adaptation by channel members may be important in the long run. Small, under-capitalized distributors may not be able to respond effectively to new competitive thrusts or to problems caused by economic downturns. The viable alternatives, then, will be to sell direct or to use reps and make products available through a system of public warehouses.

Such factors as intermediary image, financial capacity, sales, and merchandising ability must also be analyzed. And once the channel is designed, it must be administered.

Channel Administration

Once a particular industrial channel structure is chosen, channel participants must be selected, and arrangements must be made to ensure that all obligations are assigned. Next, channel members must be motivated to perform the tasks necessary to achieve channel objectives. Third, conflict within the channel must be properly controlled. Finally, performance must be controlled and evaluated.

Selection of Channel Members

Why is the selection of channel members (specific companies, rather than *type*, which is specified in the design process) part of channel management rather than an aspect of channel design? The primary reason is that intermediary selection is an ongoing process; some intermediaries choose to leave the channel, and others are terminated by the supplier. Thus, selection of intermediaries is more or less continuous. Performance of individual channel members must be evaluated continuously. The manufacturer should be prepared to move quickly, replacing poor performers with potentially better ones. Including the selection process in ongoing channel management puts the process in its proper perspective.

Securing Good Intermediaries   The marketer can identify prospective channel members through discussions with company salespeople and existing or potential customers, or through trade sources, such as *Industrial Distribution* magazine or the *Verified Directory of Manufacturers' Representatives*. Once the list of potential intermediaries is reduced to a few names, the manufacturer will use the selection criteria to evaluate them. For example, the McGraw-Edison Company uses an intensive checklist to compare prospective channel members; the criteria it considers important are market coverage, product lines, personnel, growth, and financial standing.

The formation of the channel is not at all a one-way street. The manufacturer must now persuade the intermediaries to become part of the channel system. Some distributors evaluate potential suppliers just as rigorously as the manufacturers rate them—using many of the same considerations. Manufacturers must often demonstrate the sales and profit potential of their product and be willing to grant the intermediaries some territorial exclusivity.

Firms that effectively use independent manufacturers' representatives often view the rep as a customer; controlling relationships usually do not work well with reps.[19] Business marketing managers must recognize that reps are not employees; rather, they are autonomous entities who are under contract with several companies and answer to several managers. Special efforts will be required to convince the very best rep in a particular market to represent a particular manufacturer's product. Those efforts will often focus on showing the potential rep that the company will be treated as a partner and supported by the manufacturer.

Motivating Channel Members

Distributors and reps are independent and profit oriented. They are oriented toward their customers and toward whatever means are necessary to satisfy customer needs for industrial products and services. Their perceptions and outlook may vary substantially from those of the manufacturers they represent. As a consequence, marketing strategies can fail when managers at the manufacturers' level do not tailor their programs to the capabilities and orientations of their intermediaries. To manage the business marketing channel effectively, the marketer must understand the intermediaries' perspective and devise methods for motivating these intermediaries to perform in a way that will enhance the manufacturer's long-term success. The manufacturer must continually seek support from intermediaries, and the quality of that support will depend on the motivational techniques employed.

---

[19] Sally J. Silberman, "Best Supporting Role," *Sales and Marketing Management* 147 (December 1995): p. 22.

The degree to which a channel member will comply with manufacturer directives appears to be influenced by the intermediary's dependence on the manufacturer.[20] Manufacturers who wish to enhance their ability to affect the decisions and behavior of their channel members should consider strategies that increase the channel member's dependence on them. Such tactics as increasing commissions, encouraging full-line representation, new product introduction, and increased promotion may be effective at increasing the percentage of sales and profits a channel member earns from a given manufacturer, and, as a consequence, strengthening its dependence on the manufacturer.[21]

A Partnership   Channel member motivation begins with the understanding that the channel relationship is a *partnership*. Manufacturers and intermediaries are in business together; whatever expertise and assistance the manufacturer can provide to the intermediaries will improve total channel effectiveness. One study of channel relationships suggested that manufacturers may be able to increase the level of resources directed to their products by developing a trusting relationship with their reps; by improving communication through recognition programs, product training, and consultation with the reps; and by informing the reps of plans, explicitly detailing objectives, and providing positive feedback.[22] Another study of distributor–manufacturer working partnerships recommended similar approaches and also suggested that manufacturers and their distributors engage in joint annual planning that focuses on specifying the cooperative efforts each firm requires of its partner to reach its objectives as well as periodic reviews of progress toward objectives.[23] The net result will be trust and satisfaction with the working partnership as the cooperative relationship leads to meeting performance goals.

Management Aids   Manufacturers often have the size and skill to develop sophisticated management techniques for areas of purchasing, inventory, order processing, and the like, which can be passed on to channel members. Some firms may provide elaborate cost accounting and profitability measurement systems for their distributors in order to assist them in tracking product performance.

Experts Allan Magrath and Kenneth Hardy suggest that a manufacturer should "design a full menu of supports, with sufficient variety to appeal to all its key distributors—small, medium, and large—recognizing that participation in some offerings will vary depending upon the relevance to the particular distributor's size and level of sophistication."[24] The key element is to allow the distributor executives to choose which programs fit their situation.

Dealer Advisory Councils   One way to enhance the performance of all channel members is to facilitate the sharing of information among them. Distributors or reps

[20]Janet E. Keith, Donald W. Jackson, Jr., and Lawrence A. Crosby, "Effects of Alternative Types of Influence Strategies Under Different Channel Dependence Structures," *Journal of Marketing* 54 (July 1990): p. 37.

[21]Ibid., p. 38.

[22]Erin Anderson, Leonard M. Lodish, and Barton A. Weitz, "Resource Allocation in Conventional Channels," *Journal of Marketing Research* 24 (February 1987): p. 95. See also Jan B. Heide and George John, "The Role of Dependence Balancing in Safeguarding Transaction-Specific Assets in Conventional Channels," *Journal of Marketing* 52 (January 1988): pp. 20–35.

[23]James C. Anderson and James A. Narus, "A Model of Distribution Firm and Manufacturing Firm Working Partnerships," *Journal of Marketing* 54 (January 1990): p. 56.

[24]Allan J. Magrath and Kenneth G. Hardy, "Gearing Manufacturer Support Programs to Distributors," *Industrial Marketing Management* 18 (November 1989): p. 244.

INSIDE BUSINESS MARKETING

Champion Distributor: W. W. Grainger, Inc.

W. W. Grainger, Inc. is a leading industrial distributor of maintenance, repair, and operating supplies—MRO items—to the business market. Grainger offers its 1.5 million customers about 210,000 products and its red-covered catalogue (also available in CD-ROM form) contains over 4,000 pages. For example, the catalogue includes more than 4,000 different sizes and types of motors. Moreover, the Grainger catalogue of offerings includes products from over 550 manufacturers. The company has over 1,500 full-time sales representatives and a satellite network linking its 350 local branches. About 80 percent of all U.S. businesses are within a twenty minute drive of a Grainger branch. Each branch provides prompt, round-the-clock deliveries to customers.

Grainger is also pursuing an aggressive Internet strategy through its "digital storefront" (www.

grainger.com). The firm estimates that 20 percent of the traffic on its site occurs after normal business hours and the average order size is twice as large as orders received by phone or fax. Grainger's online business has quickly become one of the highest volume business-to-business sites on the Internet: year 2000 sales will exceed $150 million. The firm has also developed Orderzone.com—a marketplace where business customers can order not just from Grainger but also from leading industrial distributors that carry products from other industry segments.

SOURCE: Barnaby J. Feder, "For This Supplier, the Sum of Its Parts Adds Up to Success," *The New York Times*, 22 September 1999, p. 61 and Douglas A. Blackman, "Selling Motors to Mops, Unglamorous Grainger Is a Web-Sales Star," *The Wall Street Journal*, (13 December 1999), pp. B1, B8.

---

may be brought together periodically with the manufacturer's management personnel to review distribution policies, provide advice on marketing strategy, and supply industry intelligence.[25] Intermediaries can voice their opinions on policy matters and are brought directly into the decision-making process for channel operations. Dayco Corporation uses a dealer council to keep abreast of distributors' changing needs.[26] One month after their meeting, council members receive a written report of suggestions they made and of the programs to be implemented as a result. Generally, Dayco enacts 75 percent of distributor proposals. For dealer councils to be effective, the input of channel members must have a meaningful effect on channel policy decisions.

Margins and Commission In the final analysis, the primary motivating device will be compensation. The surest way to lose intermediary support is to use compensation policies that do not meet industry and competitive standards. Reps or distributors who feel cheated on commissions or margins will shift their selling attention to products generating a higher profit. The manufacturer must pay the prevailing compensation rates in the industry and must adjust the rates as conditions change. Inflation in travel, lodging, and entertainment expenses forces many reps and distributors to seek higher commissions and margins. Although such increases are painful to the manufacturer, rates that are not adjusted fairly usually cause a marked reduction in sales effort.

The compensation provided to intermediaries should reflect the marketing tasks performed. If the manufacturer seeks special attention for a new industrial product, most reps will require higher commissions. The 3M Corporation has an enlightened

---

[25] Doug Harper, "Councils Launch Sales Ammo," *Industrial Distribution* 80 (September 1990): pp. 27–30.

[26] James A. Narus and James C. Anderson, "Turn Your Distributors into Partners," *Harvard Business Review* 64 (March/April 1986): p. 68.

attitude regarding compensation of distributors. According to the firm, "We're studying all the distributors' costs—inventory, sales, and so on—and then we're looking at our costs. Maybe we will want to pay the distributor to assume more of the functions we now do. Or maybe we can absorb some activities back here and reduce the distributors' margin. But somebody has to pay for it. We're trying to come up with a classification system so divisions can have different levels of distributor margins, depending on what services the distributor provides."[27]

Conflict: The Need for Relationship Management

The very nature of a distribution channel—with each member dependent on another for success—can invite conflict among the members. Although realizing the need for cooperation, individual members seek to maximize their autonomy and, hence, their profitability. **Channel conflict** occurs when one channel member *A* perceives another channel member *B* to be preventing or impeding member *A* from achieving important goals.[28]

The opportunities for conflict in business marketing channels are limitless—for example, a manufacturer's refusal to increase reps' commissions, a distributor's refusal to maintain required inventory levels, a manufacturer's use of e-commerce to bypass distributors. Thus, because channel participants have varying goals, varying perceptions of their roles in the channel, and varying evaluations of their spheres of influence, tensions develop that may cause them to perform in ways that damage channel performance.[29] The business marketer must manage conflict through relationship management approaches.[30] Such approaches improve overall channel performance by coordinating relationships among the organizations that make up the channel and by focusing on the creation of long-term, mutually beneficial interactions.

Building Trust Conflict can be controlled through a variety of means, including channel-wide committees, joint goal setting, and cooperative programs involving a number of marketing strategy elements. To compete, business marketers need to be effective at cooperating within a network of organizations—the channel. Successful cooperation results from relationships in which the parties have a strong sense of commitment and trust. Robert M. Morgan and Shelby D. Hunt suggest that relationship commitment and trust develop when (1) firms offer benefits and resources that are superior to what other partners could offer; (2) firms align themselves with other firms that have similar corporate values; (3) firms share valuable information on expectations, markets, and performance; and (4) firms avoid taking advantage of their partners.[31] By following these relationship prescriptions, business marketers and their

---

[27] Howard Sutton, "Rethinking the Company's Selling and Distribution Channels," The Conference Board, Report #885, 1986, p. 6.

[28] Stern and El-Ansary, *Marketing Channels*, pp. 202–223, 283.

[29] Louis W. Stern and James L. Heskett, "Conflict Management in Interorganizational Relations: A Conceptual Framework," in *Distribution Channels: Behavioral Dimensions*, ed. Louis Stern (Boston: Houghton-Mifflin, 1969), pp. 293–294.

[30] For example, see Larriane Segil, *Intelligent Business Alliances* (New York: Random House, 1996) and James C. Anderson and James A. Narus, "A Model of Distributor Firm and Manufacturing Firm Working Partnerships," *Journal of Marketing* 54 (January 1990): pp. 42–58.

[31] Robert M. Morgan and Shelby D. Hunt, "The Commitment-Trust Theory of Relationship Marketing," *Journal of Marketing* 58 (July 1994): pp. 20–38.

channel networks should be able to enjoy sustainable competitive advantages over their rivals and their networks.

International Business Marketing Channels

A variety of channel options are available to a foreign business-to-business marketer. Typically, U.S. business marketers distribute their goods to international markets through three distinct channels (or through some combination of them): [32]

1. *American-based export intermediaries:* Domestic export intermediaries are utilized by smaller companies that lack experience in foreign sales or by firms that are not deeply involved in international marketing.

2. *Foreign-based intermediaries:* Firms that are deeply committed to foreign sales will often use foreign-based intermediaries. This decision depends on the availability of good intermediaries, financial requirements, local customs, desired control, and the nature of the product.

3. *Company-managed and company-organized sales force:* This alternative is pursued by firms heavily involved in international sales. For this approach to be effective, the firm must be strong when providing after-sales service, maintaining delivery reliability, supplying spare parts, and providing many other support services.

Interestingly, international channels of distribution are not clear-cut, precise, or easily defined entities.[33] A necessary step in developing international channels is to understand the functions of intermediaries; international intermediaries are referred to by a multitude of misleading titles. The final section of the chapter will briefly examine these intermediaries and their roles.

To be effective, international business marketers may have to develop a truly global, integrated channel strategy and be willing to invest considerable resources. James Bolt suggests that successful global competitors are companies that, among other things, "develop an integrated and innovative strategy, aggressively implement it and back it with large investments."[34] In the channels realm, a well-conceived distribution structure, utilizing the best intermediaries and backed by the required financial resources, may be a critical element that acts as a barrier to competitors.

Domestic Intermediaries

As the name implies, **domestic intermediaries** are located in the country of the producer. They are convenient to use, but their critical drawback is the lack of proximity to the foreign marketplace. The quality of representation and the access to market information available through domestic intermediaries is limited.

Domestic intermediaries can be broadly distinguished by whether they take title to the goods or not. Nontitle, or agent, intermediaries include **export management**

---

[32] Phillip R. Cateora, *International Marketing*, 5th. ed. (Homewood, Ill.: Richard D. Irwin, 1983), p. 442.

[33] Ibid., p. 581.

[34] James F. Bolt, "Global Competitors: Some Criteria for Success," *Business Horizons* (January/February 1988): pp. 35, 36.

companies (EMCs), manufacturer's export agents (MEAs), and brokers, who are primarily engaged in the selling function, making contact with foreign buyers and negotiating sales. Playing a pivotal role for many small firms, EMCs take over much of the marketing job necessary to reach foreign markets, including responsibility for advertising, credit, and product handling. Agent intermediaries are paid on a commission basis.

The other broad groups of domestic intermediaries are similar to wholesalers—they take title to the products they sell and perform a broad array of marketing functions. **Export merchants** are wholesalers operating in a foreign market. Intermediaries dealing in bulky commodities in foreign markets are referred to as export jobbers. **Trading companies** accumulate, transport, and distribute goods from many countries.[35] Recent legislation in the United States has paved the way for the development of American trading companies (ATCs).[36] Although early success of the ATCs has been limited, they are expected to eventually provide effective one-stop export service.

Foreign-Based Intermediaries

Foreign-based intermediaries offer the advantage of close and constant contact with the marketplace and generally provide a more direct channel to the customer. As with domestic intermediaries, foreign intermediaries are distinguished by whether they take title.

Title-holding intermediaries include distributors, dealers, and import jobbers. The tasks they perform are similar to those with the same name in domestic settings. In similar fashion, nontitle foreign intermediaries include brokers, reps, and factors. **Factors** are similar to brokers, but are also involved in financing the sale, which is complex and cumbersome in many foreign transactions. Essentially, they eliminate the credit risk for both the buyer and the seller.

Selection of a particular type of foreign-based intermediary is dictated by the type of product, margins, and the market conditions.[37] For example, brokers have no inventory and take no risk, whereas importers take title, bear the risk, and guarantee distribution. Consequently, distribution of product through importers will mean a higher landed price for the product because their margins have to be higher to accommodate these risks and additional activities. Whichever type of foreign-based intermediary is used, it may be necessary to creatively structure the initial contract. An importer, for example, may be given a ninety day exclusive contract and agree to buy only 5,000 items. This initial order enables the importer to "test the market." If sales go as expected, large volume commitments can be written into a long-term contract.

Selecting Effective Foreign Distributors Finding effective foreign distributors is a challenging task that requires considerable planning and effort. Because the consequences of selecting the wrong distributor are significant—either because large severance payments may be required or because of missed market opportunities—the business marketing manager should pursue a systematic approach to the selection process. The evaluation of foreign distributors involves identifying both where to go

[35] Cateora, *International Marketing*, p. 590.

[36] Daniel C. Bello and Nicholas C. Williamson, "The American Export Trading Company: Designing a New International Marketing Institution," *Journal of Marketing* 49 (fall 1985): p. 60.

[37] Jack Nadel, "Distribution, the Key to Success Overseas," *Management Review* (September 1987): p. 41.

for information and what to look for.[38] The U.S. Department of Commerce provides two information services: the Agent/Distributor Service and the World Traders Data Report. In addition, private sources like Dun and Bradstreet provide trade directories that list foreign representatives both geographically and by product line. Banks and shipping companies also may be excellent sources of distributor information.

S. Tamer Cavusgil, Poh-lin Yeoh, and Michel Mitri interviewed a large number of international executives to assess the decisive criteria for assessing foreign distributors.[39] Their criteria include thirty-five dimensions that can be grouped into five categories:

1. *Financial and company strength* (for example, management quality, capitalization)

2. *Product factors* (for example, complementary lines, familiarity with the new line)

3. *Marketing skills* (for example, experience with target customers, logistics capability)

4. *Commitment* (for example, investments in sales training, available advertising dollars)

5. *Facilitating factors* (for example, "political" connections, language skills)

The researchers created an expert model (DISTEVAL) that weights the criteria to systematically evaluate potential distributors. They suggest carefully investigating distributors on these dimensions and then supplementing that analysis with actual site visits, a review of the marketing plans of potential distributors, and an evaluation of the distributor's assessment of their own local competition.

Company-Organized Sales Force

The difference between using intermediaries for foreign sales and using a company-organized sales force is complex. The decision, however, is a very important one because managing buyer–seller relationships in the global marketplace is often the key to corporate success in foreign markets.[40] Deeper, more effective relationships with customers are critical as global competition intensifies, product life cycles shorten, quality standards rise, and technological change accelerates. The company sales force gives the company control over the international marketing process but also poses serious challenges and risks due to the foreign environment. Erin Anderson and Anne Coughlan suggest that a company-organized sales force is more likely to be used when one or more of the following exist:

1. The product requires a high service level

2. Competing products are differentiated

---

[38] S. Tamer Cavusgil, Poh-lin Yeoh, and Michel Mitri, "Selecting Foreign Distributors," *Industrial Marketing Management* 24 (August 1995): p. 299.

[39] Ibid., p. 300.

[40] John S. Hill and Arthur W. Allaway, "How U.S.–Based Companies Manage Sales in Foreign Countries," *Industrial Marketing Management* 22 (February 1993): p. 7.

3. There are fewer legal constraints to direct foreign investment

4. The product is closely related to the firm's core product

5. The country's culture is similar to U.S. culture

6. Competitors utilize a company-organized sales force[41]

Anderson and Coughlan also indicate that the decision-making process in international channels is often nonsystematic and often based on little information. One reason for this is that managers operating outside familiar domestic settings have few guidelines to use.

In some foreign markets, business marketers may need a local presence—a plant, a distribution facility, an R&D facility, or a joint venture with a domestic partner in order to participate in the market without substantial penalties (import duties). Many U.S. manufacturers are concerned that the European Community (EC) market may be difficult to penetrate because of possible protectionist initiatives by the members. Investment in manufacturing, channel, and physical distribution operations within the EC may prove effective in guarding against these barriers to EC outsiders.

Consequently, channel strategy may enhance a company's ability to compete in the EC through joint ventures or licensing agreements with existing EC channel intermediaries. These partnerships with local firms would be viewed favorably and may allow the firm to avoid any duties imposed on imported, non-EC goods.

The channel decision in the international arena is a difficult one—made complex by the nature of the unfamiliar setting. However, global competition and worldwide marketing are realities of today's business environment, and the business marketing manager must be prepared to accept the challenge of making an informed and thoroughly deliberated choice.

Summary

Channel strategy is an exciting and challenging aspect of business marketing. The challenge derives from the number of alternatives available to the manufacturer in distributing business products. The excitement results from the ever-changing nature of markets, user needs, and competitors.

Channel strategy involves two primary management tasks: designing the overall structure and managing the operation of the channel. Channel design includes the evaluation of distribution goals, activities, and potential intermediaries. Channel structure includes the number, types, and levels of intermediaries to be used in the channel. A central challenge is determining how to create a channel strategy that effectively blends e-commerce with traditional channels. E-channels can be used as an information platform, a transaction platform, or at the most advanced level, as a platform for managing customer relationships. The primary participants in business marketing channels are distributors and reps. Distributors provide the full range of marketing services for their suppliers, although customer contact and product availability are their most essential functions. Manufacturers' representatives specialize in

---

[41] Erin Anderson and Anne T. Coughlan, "International Market Entry and Expansion via Independent or Integrated Channels of Distribution," *Journal of Marketing* 51 (January 1987): p. 74.

the selling side of marketing, providing their suppliers with quality representation in the market and with extensive product and market knowledge. The rep is not involved with physical distribution, leaving that burden to the manufacturers.

Channel management is the ongoing task of administering the channel structure in order to achieve distribution objectives. Maintaining effective relationships through sound supply chain management approaches is a key ingredient for success in channel management. Selection and motivation of intermediaries are two management tasks vital to channel success. The business marketing manager may need to apply interorganizational management techniques in order to resolve channel conflict. The choice of channels for business marketers competing in overseas markets is both vast and confusing. The manager must choose among domestic and foreign intermediaries and a company sales force.

Discussion Questions

1. Describe how the Internet is reshaping the channel strategy of business marketing firms.

2. An e-commerce expert observed: "You want salespeople to focus less on transactions and more on building and sustaining relationships. In the business-to-business market, that's what the Net allows you to do." Explain.

3. Explain how a direct channel of distribution may be the lowest-cost alternative for one business marketer and the highest-cost alternative for another competing in the same industry.

4. Describe specific product, market, and competitive conditions that lend themselves to (a) a direct channel of distribution, and (b) an indirect channel of distribution.

5. Compare and contrast the functions performed by industrial distributors and manufacturers' representatives.

6. What product/market factors lend themselves to the use of manufacturers' representatives?

7. Often, the business marketer may have very little latitude in selecting the number of channel levels. Explain.

8. Explain how a change in segmentation policy (that is, entering new markets) may trigger the need for drastic changes in the industrial channel of distribution.

9. Both business marketers and distributors are interested in achieving profit goals. Why, then, are manufacturer–distributor relationships characterized by conflict? What steps can the marketer take to reduce the level of conflict and thus improve channel performance?

10. For many years, critics have charged that intermediaries contribute strongly to the rising prices of goods in the American economy. Would business marketers improve the level of efficiency and effectiveness in the channel by reducing as far as possible the number of intermediate links in the channel? Support your position.

15

Pricing Strategy for Business Markets

The price that a business marketer assigns to a product or service is one of many factors scrutinized by the organizational buyer. Pricing decisions complement the firm's overall marketing strategy. The diverse nature of the business market presents unique problems and opportunities for the price setter. After reading this chapter, you will understand

1. the role of price in the cost/benefit calculations of organizational buyers.

2. the central elements of the industrial pricing process.

3. how effective new product prices are established and the need for periodic adjustment of the prices of existing products.

4. strategic approaches to competitive bidding.

A senior executive observed: "Selling only on price—where's the fun in that?" This marketer recognizes that competitive pressure dictates that a firm must demonstrate that it has something unique to offer to customers—something that will provide superior value.[1]

According to Richard D'Aveni, "While the average competitor fights for niches along a common ratio of price and value ('You get what you pay for'), innovative firms can enter the market by providing better value to the customer ('You can get more than what you pay for'). These companies offer lower cost *and* higher quality. This shift in value is like lowering the stick while dancing the limbo. All the competitors have to do the same dance with tighter constraints on both cost and quality."[2] The business marketer must remember this unifying strategic principle: Be better than your very best competitors in providing customer value.[3]

The business marketing manager must blend the various components of the marketing mix into a total offering that responds to the needs of the market and that provides a return consistent with the firm's objectives. Price must be carefully meshed with the product, distribution, and communication strategies of the firm. Thomas Nagle points out that "If effective product development, promotion, and distribution sow the seeds of business success, effective pricing is the harvest. While effective pricing can never compensate for poor execution of the first three elements, ineffective pricing can surely prevent these efforts from resulting in financial success. Regrettably, this is a common occurrence."[4]

The interdependence of price and other strategy components must be recognized before the pricing function can be isolated for analysis. Clearly, there is no single best way to establish the price of a new industrial product or to modify the price of existing products. The price setter must know the firm's objectives, markets, costs, competition, and customer demand patterns—not easy when time is short, information is incomplete, and the competitive business climate is changing rapidly.

This chapter is divided into four parts. First, the special meaning of price is defined in a business marketing context. Second, key determinants of the industrial pricing process are analyzed, and an operational approach to pricing decisions is provided. Third, pricing policies for new and existing products are examined, emphasizing the need to actively manage a product throughout its life cycle. Fourth, price administration (that is, types of price adjustments) is considered, before finally turning to an area of particular importance to the business marketer: competitive bidding.

The Meaning of Price in Business Markets

When members of a buying center select a particular product, they are buying a given level of product quality, technical service, and delivery reliability. Other elements may be important—the reputation of the supplier, a feeling of security, friendship, and other personal benefits flowing from the buyer–seller relationship. Observe in

[1] James C. Anderson and James A. Narus, "Business Marketing: Understand What Customers Value," *Harvard Business Review* 76 (November/December 1998), p. 65.

[2] Richard A. D'Aveni, *Hypercompetitive Rivalries* (New York: The Free Press, 1995), p. 27.

[3] Bradley T. Gale, *Managing Customer Value: Creating Quality and Service that Customers Can See* (New York: The Free Press, 1994), pp. 73–75.

[4] Thomas T. Nagle, *The Strategy and Tactics of Pricing: A Guide to Profitable Decision Making* (Englewood Cliffs, N.J.: Prentice-Hall, 1987), p. 1.

FIGURE 15.1	PRICING ENVIRONMENT: THE RELATIONSHIP BETWEEN BUYER, SELLER, AND COMPETITOR

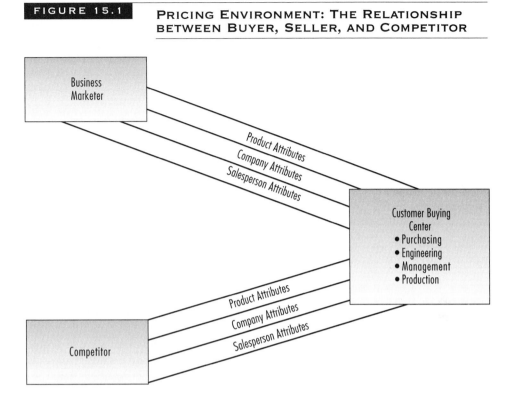

SOURCE: Adapted with modifications from David T. Wilson, "Pricing Industrial Products and Services," Report #9-1986, Institute for the Study of Business Markets, The Pennsylvania State University.

Figure 15.1 that the attribute bundles sought by the buying center may fall into three categories: product-specific attributes (for example, product quality), company-related attributes (for example, reputation for technological excellence), and salesperson-related attributes (for example, dependability).[5]

Thus, the total product (as discussed in Chapter 11) is much more than its physical attributes. Likewise, the *cost* of an industrial good includes much more than the seller's *price*. Pricing decisions and product policy decisions are inseparable and must be balanced within the firm's market segmentation plan.[6]

Benefits

Various market segments, each with unique needs, base their evaluation of a product on dimensions of particular value to them. The benefits of a particular product can be functional, operational, financial, or personal.[7] These benefits are of varying degrees of importance to different market segments and to different individuals within the buying

---

[5] David T. Wilson, "Pricing Industrial Products and Services," Report #9–1986, Institute for the Study of Business Markets, College of Business Administration, The Pennsylvania State University.

[6] Benson P. Shapiro and Barbara B. Jackson, "Industrial Pricing to Meet Customer Needs," *Harvard Business Review* 56 (November/December 1978): p. 125.

[7] Ibid., pp. 119–127.

| TABLE 15.1 | CUSTOMERS' COST-IN-USE COMPONENTS |

Acquisition Costs	+	Possession Costs	+	Usage Costs	=	Total Cost in Use
Price		Interest cost		Installation costs		
Paperwork cost		Storage cost		Training cost		
Transportation costs		Quality control		User labor cost		
Expediting cost		Taxes and insurance		Product longevity		
Cost of mistakes in order		Shrinkage and obsolescence		Replacement costs		
Prepurchase product evaluation costs		General internal handling costs		Disposal costs		

SOURCE: Adapted from Frank V. Cespedes, "Industrial Marketing: Managing New Requirements," *Sloan Management Review* 35 (spring 1994): p. 46.

center. **Functional benefits** are the design characteristics that might be attractive to technical personnel. **Operational benefits** are durability and reliability, qualities desirable to production managers. **Financial benefits** are favorable terms and opportunities for cost savings, important to purchasing managers and controllers. Organizational status, reduced risk, and personal satisfaction are among the **personal benefits** that might accrue to an individual from a particular supplier choice.

Costs

A broad perspective is likewise needed in examining the costs a particular alternative may present for the buyer. When purchasing a product or service, an organizational customer always assumes various costs above and beyond the actual purchase price. Rather than making a decision on the basis of price alone, organizational buyers emphasize the **total cost in use** of a particular product or service.[8] Observe in Table 15.1 that three different types of costs are considered in a total cost-in-use calculation by an organizational customer:

1. **acquisition costs** include not only the selling price and transportation costs, but also the administrative costs of evaluating suppliers, expediting orders, and correcting errors in shipments or delivery.

2. **possession costs** include financing, storage, inspection, relevant taxes and insurance, and other internal handling costs.

3. **usage costs** involve costs associated with the ongoing utilization of the purchased product such as installation, employee training, user labor, field repair, as well as product replacement and disposal costs.

[8] Frank V. Cespedes, "Industrial Marketing: Managing New Requirements," *Sloan Management Review* 35 (spring 1994): pp. 45–60.

INSIDE BUSINESS MARKETING

Create Value-Based Sales Tools

To vividly demonstrate the value of its offering to prospective customers, innovative business marketing firms develop case histories of the savings that current customers have realized. To illustrate, the protective packaging unit of Sonoco Products tracks the savings its customers gain from using its packaging systems. The firm maintains that these packaging systems are stronger, lighter, and smaller than more commonly marketed corrugated-cardboard packaging materials. Customer savings include reduced packaging costs, product damage, shipping costs, and storage costs.

After a customer has used these packaging systems for a year, Sonoco creates a written case history that documents the cost savings for the customer. Salespersons can then draw on these studies when making proposals to other customers. These case studies persuasively demonstrate the cost savings that the potential customer would likely realize in using Sonoco's packaging solutions.

SOURCE: James C. Anderson and James A. Narus, "Business Marketing: Understand What Customers Value," *Harvard Business Review* 76 (November/December 1998), pp. 59–60.

Value-Based Strategies[9]   Aided by sophisticated supplier evaluation systems (see Chapter 2), buyers can measure and track the total cost/value of dealing with alternative suppliers. In turn, astute business marketers can pursue value-based strategies that provide customers with a lower cost-in-use solution. For example, the logistical expenses associated with health-care supplies typically account for 10–15 percent of a hospital's operating costs. Medical products firms, like Becton Dickinson and Company, develop innovative product/service packages that respond to each component of the cost-in-use equation. Such firms can reduce a hospital's acquisition costs by offering an electronic ordering system, its possession costs by emphasizing just-in-time service, and its usage costs by creating an efficient system for disposing of medical supplies after use.

Value-based strategies seek to move the selling proposition from one that centers on current prices and individual transactions to a longer-term relationship built around value and lower total cost in use. The successful implementation of value-based strategies requires close coordination between the product, sales, and service units in the firm (see Chapter 11). Each unit performs activities that ultimately determine the customer's cost in use.

The Industrial Pricing Process

There is no easy formula for pricing an industrial product or service. The decision is multidimensional: The interactive variables of demand, cost, competition, profit relationships, and customer usage patterns each assume significance as the marketer formulates the role that price will play in the firm's marketing strategy. Pertinent considerations, illustrated in Figure 15.2, include (1) pricing objectives, (2) demand determinants, (3) cost determinants, and (4) competition. The additional considerations in the figure—effect on product line and legal implications of a particular pricing decision—are treated later in this chapter.

---

[9]Frank V. Cespedes, *Concurrent Marketing: Integrating Product, Sales, and Service* (Boston: Harvard Business School Press, 1995), pp. 152–160.

FIGURE 15.2   KEY COMPONENTS OF THE INDUSTRIAL
                 PRICING PROCESS

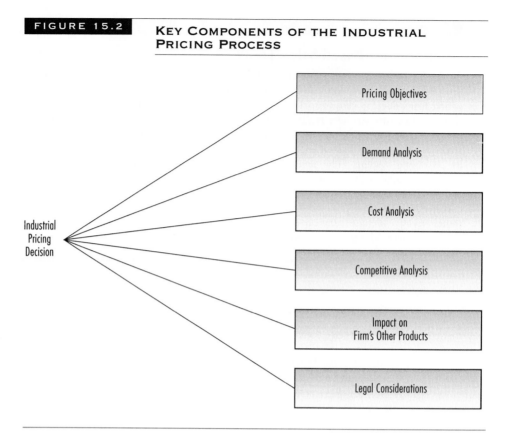

Price Objectives

The pricing decision must be based on objectives congruent with marketing and overall corporate objectives. The marketer starts with principal objectives and adds collateral pricing goals: (1) achieving a target return on investment, (2) achieving a market-share goal, or (3) meeting competition. There are many other potential pricing objectives that extend beyond profit and market-share goals, taking into account competition, channel relationships, and product line considerations.

Because of their far-reaching effects, pricing objectives must be established with care. Each firm faces unique internal and external environmental forces. Contrasting the strategies of Du Pont and Dow Chemical Company illustrates the importance of a unified corporate direction. Dow's strategy focuses first on pricing low-margin commodity goods *low* to build a dominant market share and then on maintaining that dominant share. Du Pont's strategy, on the other hand, emphasizes specialty products that carry a higher margin. Initially, these products are priced at a *high* level, and prices are reduced as the market expands and competition intensifies. Each firm requires explicit pricing objectives that are consistent with its corporate mission.

Demand Determinants

A strong market perspective is fundamental in pricing. The business market is diverse and complex. A single industrial product can be used in many ways; each market segment may represent a unique application for the product and a separate usage level.

TABLE 15.2	ATTRIBUTES OF A TOTAL PRODUCT OFFERING: SOME TRADE-OFFS	
Attribute	**High Level**	**Low Level**
Quality	Impurities less than one part per million	Impurities less than ten parts per million
Delivery	Within one week	Within two weeks
System	Supply total system	Supply chemical only
Innovation	High level of R&D support	Little R&D support
Retraining	Retrain on request	Train on initial purchase
Service	Locally available	Through home office

SOURCE: Irwin Gross, "Insights from Pricing Research," in *Pricing Practices and Strategies*, ed. Earl L. Bailey (New York: The Conference Board, 1978), p. 37. Reprinted by permission of the Conference Board.

The degree of importance of the industrial good in the buyer's end product also varies by market segment. Therefore, potential demand, sensitivity to price, and potential profitability can vary markedly across market segments. To establish an effective pricing policy, attention should center first on the value a customer will place on a product or service. This reverses the typical process that gives immediate attention to the product cost and the desired markup.[10]

Assessing Value[11] How organizational buyers will evaluate the cost/benefit trade-offs of the total offering determines the appropriateness of a particular industrial pricing strategy. Two competitors with similar products may ask differing prices because their total offerings are perceived as being unique by buyers. In the eyes of the organizational buyer, one firm may provide more value than another.

A core pricing issue concerns which attributes of the offering contribute most to its perceived value. Table 15.2 identifies total product offering attributes that have value to buyers and that differ among competitors. Two levels of performance are provided for each attribute. Since higher costs are incurred in providing higher levels of performance on one or more of the attributes, the strategist should assess the relative importance of the attributes to different market segments and should assess the strength of the firm's offering on each of the important attributes vis-à-vis competitors.

The equation in Figure 15.3 highlights how the relative perceived values of two competing offerings are compared. Irv Gross contends that the relative perceived value of offering *A* versus offering *B* "can be thought of as the price differential at which the buyer would be indifferent between the alternatives."[12] As in Figure 15.3, the premium price differential, or perceived relative value, can be broken down into components based on each important attribute: (1) the value of the attribute to the

---

[10] Robert J. Dolan, "How Do You Know When the Price Is Right?" *Harvard Business Review* 73 (September/October 1995): pp. 174–183.

[11] Irwin Gross, "Insights from Pricing Research," in *Pricing Practices and Strategies*, ed. Earl L. Bailey (New York: The Conference Board, 1978), pp. 34–39. See also Valerie Kijewski and Eunsang Yoon, "Market-Based Pricing: Beyond Price-Performance Curves," *Industrial Marketing Management* 19 (February 1990): pp. 11–19; and G. Dean Kortge and Patrick A. Okonkwo, "Perceived Value Approach to Pricing," *Industrial Marketing Management* 22 (May 1993): pp. 133–140.

[12] Gross, "Insights from Pricing Research," p. 35.

FIGURE 15.3 RELATIVE PERCEIVED VALUE OF TWO PRODUCT OFFERINGS

$$
\begin{array}{l}
\text{Relative Perceived} \\
\text{Value of} \\
\text{Offering "A" vs.} \\
\text{Offering "B"}
\end{array}
=
\begin{array}{l}
\text{Price Premium for} \\
\text{Indifference}
\end{array}
=
\left[
\begin{array}{l}
\text{First} \\
\text{Attribute} \\
\text{Value}
\end{array}
\right]
\left[
\begin{array}{l}
\text{Perceived} \\
\text{Performance of} \\
\text{Offering "A" on} \\
\text{First Attribute}
\end{array}
-
\begin{array}{l}
\text{Perceived} \\
\text{Performance of} \\
\text{Offering "B" on} \\
\text{First Attribute}
\end{array}
\right]
+
\left[
\begin{array}{l}
\text{Second} \\
\text{Attribute} \\
\text{Value}
\end{array}
\right]
\left[
\begin{array}{l}
\text{Perceived} \\
\text{Performance of} \\
\text{Offering "A" on} \\
\text{Second Attribute}
\end{array}
-
\begin{array}{l}
\text{Perceived} \\
\text{Performance of} \\
\text{Offering "B" on} \\
\text{Second Attribute}
\end{array}
\right]
$$

SOURCE: Irwin Gross, "Insights from Pricing Research," in *Pricing Practices and Strategies*, ed. Earl L. Bailey (New York: The Conference Board, 1978), p. 38. Reprinted by permission.

---

buyer, and (2) the perception of how competing offerings perform on that attribute. By summing all of the component values, we reach the total relative perceived value of an offering. Thus, product offering *A* may have a total perceived value of $24 per unit, compared to $20 per unit for offering *B*. The $4 premium might be derived from the value that buyers assign to a high level of product quality and a responsive delivery system, and the perceived advantage of offering *A* over others on these attributes.

Strategy Implications of the Cost/Benefit Analysis   By isolating the important attributes and the perceptions that enter into the cost/benefit calculations of organizational buyers, the business marketer is better equipped to establish a price and to shape other elements of the marketing strategy. First, if the firm's performance on a highly valued product attribute is truly higher than that offered by competitors, but the market perceives no differences, marketing communications can be developed to bring perceptions into line with reality. Second, marketing communications may also alter the values that organizational buyers assign to a particular attribute. The importance of an attribute such as customer training might be elevated through marketing communications emphasizing the improved efficiency and safety that training affords the potential buying organization.

Third, the perceived value of the total product offering can be changed by improving the firm's level of performance on attributes that are assigned special importance by organizational buyers. Fourth, knowledge of the cost/benefit perceptions of potential customers presents market segmentation opportunities. For example, good strategy might target those market segments that value the particular product attributes where the firm has a clear competitive advantage.

Elasticity Varies by Market Segment   Price elasticity of demand is a measure of the degree to which customers are sensitive to price changes. Specifically, **price elasticity of demand** refers to the rate of percentage change in quantity demanded attributable to the percentage change in price. Price elasticity of demand is not the same at all prices. A business marketer contemplating an alteration in price policy must understand the elasticity of demand. For example, total revenue (price times quantity) will *increase* if price is decreased and demand is price elastic, whereas revenues will *fall* if the price is decreased and demand is price inelastic. Many factors influence the price elasticity of demand—the ease with which customers can compare alternatives and switch suppliers, the importance of the product in the cost structure of the customer's product, and the value that the product represents to a customer.

Search Behavior and Switching Costs   The price sensitivity of buyers increases — and a firm's pricing latitude decreases — to the degree that: [13]

- organizational buyers can easily shop around and assess the relative performance and price of alternatives. Purchasing managers in many firms use information technology to track supplier prices on a global basis.

- the product represents one for which it is easy to make price comparisons. For example, it is easier to compare alternative photocopiers than it is to compare specialized manufacturing equipment options.

- buyers can switch from one supplier to another without incurring additional costs. As highlighted in Chapter 3, low switching costs allow a buyer to focus on minimizing the cost of a particular transaction.

End Use   Important insights can be secured by answering this question: How important is the business marketer's product as an input into the total cost of the end product? If the business marketer's product has an insignificant effect on cost, demand is likely inelastic. Consider this example:

> A manufacturer of precision electronic components was contemplating an across-the-board price decrease to increase sales. However, an item analysis of the product line revealed that some of its low-volume components had exotic applications. A technical customer used the component in an ultrasonic testing apparatus which was sold for $8,000 a unit. This fact prompted the electronics manufacturer to raise the price of the item. Ironically, the firm then experienced a temporary surge of demand for the item as purchasing agents stocked up in anticipation of future price increases. [14]

Of course, the marketer must temper this estimate with an analysis of the costs, availability, and suitability of substitutes. Generally, when the industrial product constitutes an important but low-cost input into the end product, price is less important than quality and delivery reliability.

When the industrial product input assumes a more substantial portion of the final product's total cost, changes in price may have an important effect on the demand for both the final product and the industrial product input. When demand in the final consumer market is price elastic, a reduction in the price of the end item (for example, a personal computer) that is caused by a price reduction of an industrial component (for example, a microprocessor) generates an increase in demand for the final product (personal computer) and, in turn, for the industrial product (microprocessor).

End Market Focus   Because the demand for many industrial products is derived from the demand for the product of which they are a part, a strong end-user focus is needed. The marketer can benefit by examining the trends and changing fortunes of important final consumer markets. Different sectors of the market grow at differing rates, confront differing levels of competition, and face differing short-term and long-term challenges. A downturn in the economy does not fall equally on all sectors.

---

[13] Dolan, "How Do You Know When the Price Is Right?" pp. 178–179.

[14] Reed Moyer and Robert J. Boewadt, "The Pricing of Industrial Goods," *Business Horizons* 14 (June 1971): pp. 27–34; see also George Rostky, "Unveiling Market Segments with Technical Focus Research," *Business Marketing* 71 (October 1986): pp. 66–69.

Pricing decisions demand a two-tiered market focus—on organizational customers and on final product customers. "All things being equal," comment Reed Moyer and Robert Boewadt, "an industrial supplier will have more success in passing on a price increase to customers who are prospering than to customers who are hard pressed."[15]

Value-Based Segmentation   The value that customers assign to a firm's offering can vary by market segment because the same industrial product may serve differing purposes for various customers. This underscores the important role of market segmentation in the development of profitable pricing strategies. Take Sealed Air Corporation, the innovative supplier of protective packaging materials including coated air bubbles.[16] The company recognized that for some applications of the product, viable substitutes were readily available to buyers. But for other applications, Sealed Air had an enormous advantage—for example, its packaging materials offered superior cushioning for heavy items with long shipping cycles. By identifying those applications where the firm had a clear advantage and understanding the unique value differential in each setting, marketing managers were ideally equipped to tackle product line expansion and pricing decisions and to ignite the remarkable revenue growth that Sealed Air has experienced for nearly two decades.

Methods of Estimating Demand   How can the business marketer measure the price elasticity of demand? Some techniques rely on objective statistical data, others on the intuition and judgment of managers.

Test marketing, as a rule, is considered appropriate only for consumer-goods manufacturers. However, this technique should not be eliminated from the business marketer's repertoire. Industrial products that are sold to a large number of potential users, that have short usage cycles (permitting analysis of repurchase patterns), and that have feasible test market sites lend themselves to test marketing. Most high-priced capital items do not fit this profile; products like industrial paints and maintenance items do.

The **survey approach** can also be used to measure price elasticity, testing for willingness to buy at various prices or price ranges. On occasion, joint research with a consumer-goods customer could be conducted to survey final consumer demand. Because price is only one variable, the survey instrument must also probe for product and service perceptions. It would be useful to ascertain how organizational buyers view price in fundamental cost/benefit trade-offs. This broader perspective is particularly useful in isolating market segments.

When, as often happens, the price setter lacks time and resources, a more informal, subjective approach becomes practical. This technique, drawing upon executive experience, judgment, and customer knowledge, analyzes the relationship of price to other marketing mix variables such as product, promotion, and distribution strategies and a particular competitive setting.

Knowledge of the market is the cornerstone of industrial pricing. A strong market focus, which examines how consumers trade off benefits and costs in their decision making, establishes a base for assigning prices. In this precarious task, the goal is to estimate as precisely as possible the probable demand curve for the firm's product. Knowledge of demand patterns must be augmented by knowledge of costs.

---

[15] Moyer and Boewadt, "The Pricing of Industrial Goods," p. 30.

[16] Dolan, "How Do You Know When the Price Is Right?" pp. 176–177.

FIGURE 15.4 **TARGET COSTING**

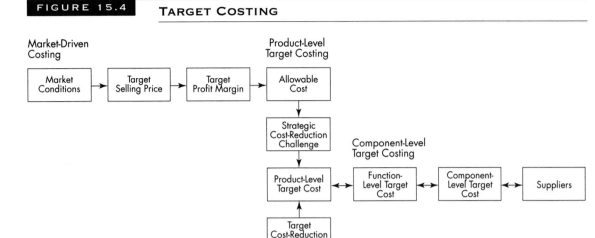

Cost Determinants

Business marketers often pursue a strong internal orientation; they base prices on their own costs, reaching the selling price by calculating unit costs and adding a percentage profit. A strict cost-plus philosophy of pricing overlooks customer perceptions of value, competition, and the interaction of volume and profit. Many progressive firms, such as Canon, Toyota, and Hewlett-Packard (H-P), use target costing to capture a significant competitive advantage in the marketplace.

Target Costing[17]   **Target costing** features a design-to-cost philosophy that begins by examining market conditions: The firm identifies and targets the most attractive market segments (see Figure 15.4). It then determines what level of quality and types of product attributes will be required to succeed in each segment, given a predetermined target price and volume level. To set the target price, the business marketer requires an understanding of the customer's perception of value. "A company can raise selling prices only if the perceived value of the new product exceeds not only that of the product's predecessor, but also that of competing products."[18]

Once the target selling price and target profit margins have been established, the firm calculates the allowable cost. The strategic cost reduction challenge isolates the profit shortfall that will occur if the product designers are unable to achieve the allowable cost. The value of distinguishing the allowable cost from the target cost lies in the pressure that it exerts on the product development team and the company's suppliers.

---

[17] This section is based on Robin Cooper and Regine Slagmulder, "Develop Profitable New Products with Target Costing," *Sloan Management Review* 40 (summer 1999), pp. 23–33.

[18] Ibid., p. 26.

To transmit the competitive cost pressure *it* faces to its suppliers, the firm then breaks down the target price of a new product into a cascade of target costs for each component or function. For example, the major functions of an automobile include the engine, transmission, cooling system, and audio system.

A Profit-Management Tool   Toyota used target costing to reduce the price of its recently modified Camry model and did so while offering as standard equipment certain features that were expensive options on the model it replaced. Similarly, Canon used target costing to develop its breakthrough personal copier that transformed the photocopier industry.[19] Rather than a cost-control technique, Japanese managers who pioneered the approach view target costing as a profit-management tool. As Robin Cooper and W. Bruce Chew assert, "The task is to compute the costs that must not be exceeded if acceptable margins from specific products at specific price points are to be guaranteed."[20]

Classifying Costs[21]   The target costing approach stresses why the marketer must know which costs are relevant to the pricing decision and how these costs will fluctuate with volume and over time; they must be considered in relation to demand, competition, and pricing objectives. Product costs are crucial in projecting the profitability of individual products as well as of the entire product line. Proper classification of costs is essential.

The goals of a cost classification system are to (1) properly classify cost data into their fixed and variable components, and (2) properly link them to the activity causing them. The manager can then analyze the effects of volume and, more important, identify sources of profit. The following cost concepts are instrumental in the analysis:

1. *Direct traceable or attributable costs:* Costs, fixed or variable, are incurred by and solely for a particular product, customer, or sales territory (for example, raw materials).

2. *Indirect traceable costs:* Costs, fixed or variable, can be traced to a product, customer, or sales territory (for example, general plant overhead may be indirectly assigned to a product).

3. *General costs:* Costs support a number of activities that cannot be objectively assigned to a product on the basis of a direct physical relationship (for example, the administrative costs of a sales district).

General costs will rarely change because an item is added or deleted from the product line. Marketing, production, and distribution costs must all be classified. When developing a new line or when deleting an item or adding an item to an existing line, the marketer must grasp the cost implications:

- What proportion of the product cost is accounted for by purchases of raw materials and components from suppliers?

[19] Jean-Phillippe Deschamps and P. Ranganath Nayak, *Product Juggernauts: How Companies Mobilize to Generate a Stream of Market Winners* (Boston: Harvard Business School Press, 1995), pp. 119–149.

[20] Robin Cooper and W. Bruce Chew, "Control Tomorrow's Costs through Today's Designs," *Harvard Business Review* 74 (January/February 1996): pp. 88–97.

[21] Kent B. Monroe, *Pricing: Making Profitable Decisions* (New York: McGraw-Hill, 1979), pp. 52–57. See also Nagle, *The Strategy and Tactics of Pricing*, pp. 14–43.

- How will costs vary at differing levels of production?

- Based on the forecasted level of demand, can economies of scale be expected?

- Does our firm enjoy cost advantages over competitors?

- How does the experience effect impact our cost projections?

Experience Effect   The marketing strategist must also consider the behavior of costs over time. The experience effect is a concept of strategic importance in forecasting costs and, in turn, prices. The experience curve reflects the theory that costs (measured in constant dollars) decline by a predictable and constant percentage each time accumulated production experience (volume) is doubled. Thus, each time accumulated volume is doubled, the unit costs of many products fall, usually by 20 to 30 percent.[22] The experience curve effect encompasses a broad range of manufacturing, marketing, distribution, and administrative costs.

The three major sources of the experience effect are (1) learning by doing, (2) technological improvements, and (3) economies of scale.[23] Figure 15.5 traces the cost experience for steam turbine generators. The cost per megawatt of output of steam generators followed a 70 percent slope (alternatively, a 30 percent reduction in costs for every doubling in production). The sources of the decline in costs resulted from (1) practice in producing units of each size, which followed an 87 percent slope; (2) scale economies derived from building larger (600-megawatt rather than 200-megawatt) units; and (3) technological improvements in such areas as bearings and high-strength steels, which permitted the design of larger units.[24]

Strategic Relevance of Experience   Unfortunately, as experience is gained, costs do not automatically decline. In fact, costs that are not carefully managed will inevitably rise. Experience merely gives management the opportunity to seek cost reductions and efficiency improvements. A thorough effort is needed to exploit the benefits of experience. Product standardization, new production processes, labor efficiency, and work specialization are only a few of the many areas that must be examined to capitalize on the experience effect.

The experience effect can raise a strategic dilemma for the business marketer. Often, the aggressive pursuit of a cost minimization strategy leads to a reduced ability to make innovative product changes in the face of competition.[25] Clearly, any firm following an efficiency strategy must ensure that its product remains in line with the needs of the market. A product that is efficiently produced and carries a low price can survive only if significant market segments emphasize low price as a choice criterion.

The experience effect can be used to project costs and prices. The concept is also valuable when product line modifications are being considered. Often, two or more products in the firm's line share a common resource or involve the same production or distribution activity. With such shared experience, the costs of one item in the

[22] William J. Abernathy and Kenneth Wayne, "Limits of the Learning Curve," *Harvard Business Review* 52 (September/ October 1974): pp. 109–119. See also Staff of the Boston Consulting Group, *Perspectives on Experience* (Boston: Boston Consulting Group, 1972).

[23] George S. Day and David B. Montgomery, "Diagnosing the Experience Curve," *Journal of Marketing* 47 (spring 1983): pp. 44–58. See also George S. Day, *Analysis for Strategic Market Decisions* (St. Paul, Minn: West Publishing Company, 1986), pp. 25–56.

[24] Ralph Sultan, *Pricing in the Electrical Oligopoly*, vols. I and II (Cambridge, Mass.: Harvard Graduate School of Business Administration, 1974), cited in Day and Montgomery, "Diagnosing the Experience Curve."

[25] Abernathy and Wayne, "Limits of the Learning Curve," pp. 109–119.

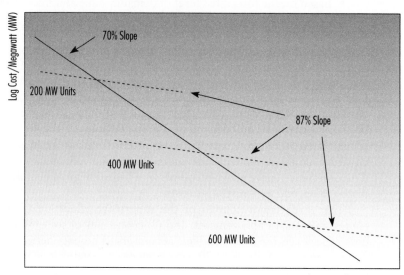

FIGURE 15.5 **COST EXPERIENCE FOR STEAM TURBINE GENERATORS**

SOURCE: George S. Day and David B. Montgomery, "Diagnosing the Experience Curve," *Journal of Marketing* 47 (spring 1983): p. 47. Reprinted by permission of the American Marketing Association.

product line are reduced even more because of the accumulated experience with the other product-line item. For example, the same production operations may be used to produce high-torque motors for oil exploration and low-torque motors for conveyor belts.[26] The marketer that has carefully classified costs is best equipped to take advantage of shared experience opportunities.

Experience curve analysis is relevant when learning, technology, and economies of scale are important in the environment. The business marketer can use experience curve analysis to project potential cost reduction opportunities.

Competition

Competition establishes an upper limit on price. An individual industrial firm's degree of latitude in its pricing decision depends heavily on the product's level of differentiation in the perceptions of organizational buyers. Price is only one component of the cost/benefit equation of buyers; the marketer can gain a differential advantage over competitors on many dimensions other than physical product characteristics—dimensions such as reputation, technical expertise, delivery reliability, and related factors. Regis McKenna contends that "Even if a company manufactures commodity-like products, it can differentiate the products through the service and support it offers, or by target marketing. It can leave its commodity mentality in the factory, and bring a mentality of diversity to the marketplace."[27] In addition to assessing the product's

---

[26] Day and Montgomery, "Diagnosing the Experience Curve," p. 54.

[27] Regis McKenna, *Relationship Marketing* (Reading, Mass.: Addison-Wesley, 1991), pp. 178–179.

The Price/Performance Engine in High-Technology Marketing

The driver behind the rapidly escalating price/performance equation in high-tech products is the semiconductor integrated circuit. Price/performance increased by a power of ten during the decade of the 1970s; it sped to a tenfold increase in seven years during the 1980s; and it has experienced a tenfold increase every 3–5 years in the 1990s. In other words, ten times the performance has been provided at the same price three different times in the 1990s, and the rate of progress is still accelerating.

Firms that compete in this intensely competitive environment cannot rest on past successes—they must prepare for the next tornado. Geoffrey

Moore maintains that infinite improvements in the price/performance of high-tech products generate a rapid series of paradigm shifts. "Each time the underlying constructs that shape the current paradigm are removed, the design trade-offs that characterize its strategy become obsolete, and a new generation of capabilities are enabled." Business marketers who built a position of strength under the old paradigm must switch to the new—or else leave themselves open to attack from new competitors that enter on each new technology wave.

SOURCE: Geoffrey A. Moore, *Inside the Tornado: Marketing Strategies from Silicon Valley's Cutting Edge* (New York: Harper-Collins, 1995).

degree of differentiation in various market segments, one must ask how competitors will respond to particular pricing decisions.

Hypercompetitive Rivalries   Some strategy experts emphasize that traditional patterns of competition in stable environments is being replaced by hypercompetitive rivalries in a rapidly changing environment.[28] In a stable environment, a company could create a fairly rigid strategy designed to accommodate long-term conditions. The firm's strategy focuses on sustaining its own strategic advantage and to establish equilibrium where less dominant firms in the industry accepted a secondary status.

In hypercompetitive environments, successful companies pursue strategies that create temporary advantage and destroy the advantages of rivals by constantly disrupting the equilibrium of the market. For example, Intel continually disrupts the equilibrium of the microprocessor industry sector and Hewlett-Packard stirs up the computer printer business by its consistent drives to lower price points. Moreover, the Internet provides customers with real-time access to a wealth of information that drives the prices of many products lower (see Figure 15.6). Leading firms in hypercompetitive environments constantly seek out new sources of advantage, further escalating competition and contributing to hypercompetition.

Consider the hypercompetitive rivalries in high-technology markets. Firms that sustain quality and that are the first to hit the next lower strategic price point enjoy a burst of volume and an expansion of market share. However, as Geoffrey A. Moore observes, some firms hold off matching the price reduction to sustain profitability:

Fat margins are a habit that is hard to kick. IBM couldn't kick it when Compaq underpriced them, nor could Compaq when Dell underpriced them. Both companies have since reversed their courses, but not before institutionalizing a permanent rival to their core business. Hewlett-Packard, by

[28] D'Aveni, *Hypercompetitive Rivalries*, pp. 149–170.

THE INTERNET FACILITATES COMPARATIVE SHOPPING AND INTENSIVE PRICE PRESSURE

SOURCE: Courtesy, Onsale, Inc.

contrast, has ruthlessly pursued the next lower price point, even as it cannibalized its own sales and margins.[29]

Gauging Competitive Response   To predict the response of competitors, the marketer can first benefit by examining the cost structure and strategy of both direct competitors and producers of potential substitutes. The marketer can draw upon public statements and records (for example, annual reports) to form rough estimates. The experience effect can also be used to assess the cost structure of competition. Competitors that have ascended the learning curve may have lower costs than those just entering the industry and beginning the climb. An estimate of the cost structure is

---

[29] Geoffrey A. Moore, *Inside the Tornado: Marketing Strategies from Silicon Valley's Cutting Edge* (New York: HarperCollins, 1995), pp. 84–85.

TABLE 15.3	SELECTED COST COMPARISON ISSUES: FOLLOWERS VERSUS THE PIONEER
Technology/economies of scale	Followers may benefit by using more current production technology than the pioneer or by building a plant with a larger scale of operations.
Product/market knowledge	Followers may learn from the pioneer's mistakes by analyzing the competitor's product, hiring key personnel, or identifying through market research the problems and unfulfilled expectations of customers and channel members.
Shared experience	Compared to the pioneer, followers may be able to gain advantages on certain cost elements by sharing operations with other parts of the company.
Experience of suppliers	Followers, together with the pioneer, benefit from cost reductions achieved by outside suppliers of components or production equipment.

SOURCE: Adapted from George S. Day and David B. Montgomery, "Diagnosing the Experience Curve," *Journal of Marketing* 47 (spring 1983): pp. 48–49.

valuable when gauging how well competitors can respond to price reductions and when projecting the pattern of prices in the future.

Under certain conditions, however, followers into a market may confront lower initial costs than did the pioneer. Why? Some of the reasons are highlighted in Table 15.3. By failing to recognize potential cost advantages of late entrants, the business marketer can dramatically overstate cost differences.

The market strategy employed by competing sellers is also important here. Competitors will be more sensitive toward price reductions that threaten those market segments they deem important. They learn of price reductions earlier when their market segments overlap. Of course, competitors may choose not to follow a price decrease, especially if their products enjoy a differentiated position. Rather than matching the price cuts of competitors, one successful medical supplies firm promptly reacts to the competitive challenge by enhancing service benefits such as speed of delivery.[30]

The manager requires a grasp of objectives, demand, cost, competition, and legal factors (discussed later) to approach the multidimensional pricing decision. Price setting is not an act but an ongoing process.

Pricing Across the Product Life Cycle

What price should be assigned to a distinctly new industrial product or service? When an item is added to an existing product line, how should it be priced in relation to products already in the line?

---

[30]Robert A. Garda, "How to Avoid a Price War," *The Wall Street Journal*, 10 May 1993, p. A12.

On Ethics and Pricing at Raytheon

Because price negotiations present the opportunity for unfair, unethical, and even illegal behavior, most firms have established a set of business conduct guidelines. The following excerpts from Raytheon's standards of conduct for buying emphasize the importance of fairness in business relationships.

- Raytheon expects its procurement personnel to be fair, do no favors, and *accept no favors.* Accepting kickbacks is a crime—both morally and legally. It is the fastest way for procurement personnel to find the way out the door and for sellers to cease doing business with us.

- The rules apply to all Raytheon employees who influence the buying process.

- Gifts, services, or consideration other than an advertising novelty such as a paper-

weight, key chain, or coffee cup will be returned to the supplier.

- Luncheons with suppliers should not be encouraged. Under some circumstances they are necessary if there is a legitimate business purpose for the get-together. But they should not be a habit. Company facilities should be used wherever possible.

- Raytheon's goal has been to establish a reputation in the marketplace that meets the highest standards of ethical conduct. We want to protect this reputation for both Raytheon and our suppliers.

SOURCE: Robert L. Janson, Linda A. Grass, Arnold J. Lovering, and Robert C. Parker, "Ethics and Responsibility," in *The Purchasing Handbook*, ed. Harold E. Fearon, Donald W. Dobler, and Kenneth H. Killen (New York: McGraw-Hill, 1993), pp. 360–361.

Pricing New Products

The strategic decision of pricing new products can be best understood by examining the policies at the boundaries of the continuum—from **skimming** (high initial price) to **penetration** (low initial price). Consider again the pricing strategies of Du Pont and Dow Chemical. Whereas Du Pont assigns an initial high price to new products in order to generate immediate profits or to recover R&D expenditures, Dow Chemical follows a low price strategy with the objective of gaining market share.

In evaluating the merits of skimming compared to penetration, the marketer must again examine price from the buyer's perspective. This approach, asserts Joel Dean, "recognizes that the upper limit is the price that will produce the minimum acceptable rate of return on the investment of a sufficiently large number of prospects."[31] This is especially important in pricing new products, because the potential profits accruing to buyers of a new machine tool, for example, will vary by market segment, and these market segments may differ in the minimum rate of return that will induce them to invest in the machine tool.

Skimming   A skimming approach, appropriate for a distinctly new product, provides the firm with an opportunity to profitably reach market segments that are not sensitive to the high initial price. As a product ages, as competitors enter the market, and as organizational buyers become accustomed to evaluating and purchasing the product, demand becomes more price elastic. The policy of using skimming at the outset,

---

[31] Joel Dean, "Pricing Policies for New Products," *Harvard Business Review* 54 (November/December 1976): p. 151.

followed by penetration pricing as the product matures, is referred to by Joel Dean as **time segmentation.**[32] A skimming policy enables the marketer to capture early profits, then reduce the price to reach segments that are more price sensitive. It also enables the innovator to recover high developmental costs more quickly.

Robert Dolan and Abel Jeuland demonstrate that during the innovative firm's monopoly period, a skimming policy is optimal if the demand curve is stable over time (no diffusion) and if production costs decline with accumulated volume, whereas a penetration policy is optimal if there is a relatively high repeat purchase rate for nondurable goods or if a durable good's demand is characterized by diffusion.[33]

Penetration   A penetration policy is appropriate when there is (1) high price elasticity of demand, (2) strong threat of imminent competition, and (3) opportunity for a substantial reduction in production costs as volume expands. Drawing upon the experience effect, a firm that can quickly gain substantial market share and experience can gain a strategic advantage over competitors. The viability of this strategy increases with the potential size of the future market. By taking a large share of new sales, experience can be gained when there is a large market growth rate. Of course, the value of additional market share differs markedly between industries and often among products, markets, and competitors within a particular industry.[34] Factors to be assessed in determining the value of additional market share include the investment requirements, potential benefits of experience, expected market trends, likely competitive reaction, and short- and long-term profit implications.

Product Line Considerations   The contemporary industrial firm with a long product line faces the complex problem of achieving balance in pricing the product mix. Firms extend their product lines because the demands for various products are interdependent, because the costs of producing and marketing those items are interdependent, or both.[35] A firm may add to its product line—or even develop a new product line—to fit more precisely the needs of a particular market segment. If both the demand and the costs of individual product line items are interrelated, production and marketing decisions about one product line item inevitably influence both the revenues and costs of the others.

Are specific product line items substitutes or complements? Will a change in the price of one item enhance or retard the usage rate of this or other products in key market segments? Should a new product be priced high at the outset in order to protect other product line items (for example, potential substitutes) and in order to give the firm time to revamp other items in the line? Such decisions require a knowledge of demand, costs, competition, and strategic marketing objectives.

---

[32] Ibid., p. 152.

[33] Robert J. Dolan and Abel P. Jeuland, "Experience Curves and Dynamic Demand Models: Implications for Optimal Pricing Strategies," *Journal of Marketing* 45 (winter 1981): pp. 52–62.

[34] Robert Jacobsen and David A Aaker, "Is Market Share All that It's Cracked Up to Be?" *Journal of Marketing* 49 (fall 1985): pp. 11–22; and Yoram Wind and Vijay Mahajan, "Market Share: Concepts, Findings, and Directions for Future Research," in *Review of Marketing 1981*, ed. Ben M. Enis and Kenneth J. Roering (Chicago: American Marketing Association, 1981), pp. 31–42.

[35] Monroe, *Pricing*, p. 143; see also Robert J. Dolan, "The Same Make, Many Models Problem: Managing the Product Line," in *A Strategic Approach to Business Marketing*, ed. Robert E. Spekman and David T. Wilson (Chicago: American Marketing Association, 1985), pp. 151–159.

FIGURE 15.7	TACTICAL PRICING: THE SUPPORTING INFORMATION SYSTEM

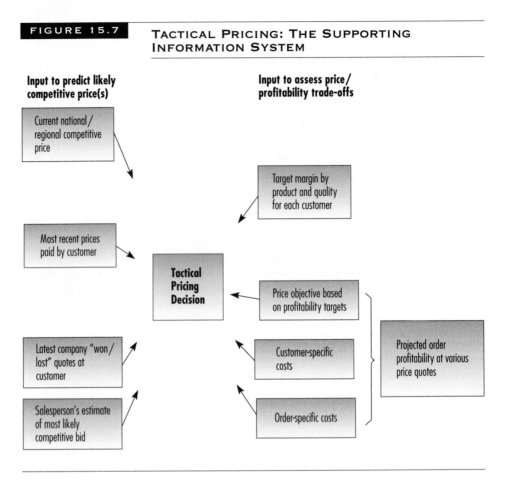

Input to predict likely competitive price(s)

Input to assess price/ profitability trade-offs

Current national/regional competitive price

Target margin by product and quality for each customer

Most recent prices paid by customer

Tactical Pricing Decision

Price objective based on profitability targets

Projected order profitability at various price quotes

Latest company "won/lost" quotes at customer

Customer-specific costs

Salesperson's estimate of most likely competitive bid

Order-specific costs

SOURCE: Adapted with modifications from Robert A. Garda, "Use of Tactical Pricing to Uncover Hidden Profits," *Journal of Business Strategy* 12 (September/October 1991): p. 22. Reprinted with permission by Faulkner and Gray, Inc., 11 Penn Plaza, New York, N.Y. 10001.

Tactical Pricing [36]

Tactical pricing constitutes an important component of price administration and considers the unique customer and order-specific costs of each transaction. Such a customer-specific focus is fundamental in developing and managing successful relationship strategies in the business market. The goal of tactical pricing, asserts Robert Garda, is "to optimize the frequently competing selling objectives of winning orders, maximizing order profitability, building long-term account value, and assuring competitive positioning in the marketplace." [37] Sound tactical pricing issues form a well-developed marketing intelligence system that can provide detailed information by customer. Figure 15.7 provides the information that might be assembled to support a tactical pricing decision for an important customer account. This system aids the price setter in forecasting competitive pricing and in establishing the firm's pricing strategy in line with vivid price/probability trade-offs.

---

[36] Robert A. Garda, "Use of Tactical Pricing to Uncover Hidden Profits," *Journal of Business Strategy* 12 (September/October 1991): pp. 17–23.

[37] Ibid., p. 19.

Win/Loss   An especially valuable tool for gauging the behavior of competitors and customers is **win/loss analysis.** What factors did a salesperson feel were decisive in winning a particular account? In a head-to-head battle with a new competitor, how well did our strategy hold up? Which factors prompt some of our accounts to switch to a competitor? What strategy did a particular salesperson follow who won back a major account? Win/loss analysis also provides insight into how customers define value. Often, contends Bradley Gale, "when the competition wins a battle on price, either the competition has learned to deliver at lower cost than you or the potential customer didn't believe your salespeople when they discussed the quality attributes that *should* have made your product worth more."[38]

The business marketer cannot leave price administration to chance. Discounts must be aligned with the firm's pricing policies and related to the requirements of key market segments. Pricing policies are often based on a defensive, or risk-aversive, perspective rather than on a positive one.[39] For example, industrial firms might offer larger quantity discounts in order to partially offset price increases; opportunities for revising discount schedules may emerge as costs change. Tradition-bound firms can easily overlook creative uses of pricing policies.

Legal Considerations

Since the business marketer deals with various classifications of customers and intermediaries as well as various types of discounts (for example, quantity discounts), an awareness of legal considerations in price administration is vital. The Robinson-Patman Act holds that it is unlawful to "discriminate in price between different purchasers of commodities of like grade and quality . . . where the effect of such discrimination may be substantially to lessen competition or tend to create a monopoly, or to injure, destroy, or prevent competition. . . ." Price differentials are permitted, but they must be based on cost differences or the need to "meet competition."[40] Cost differentials are difficult to justify, and clearly defined policies and procedures are needed in price administration. Such cost justification guidelines are useful not only when making pricing decisions, but also when providing a legal defense against price discrimination charges.

Competitive Bidding

A significant volume of business in the business market is transacted through competitive bidding. Rather than relying on a specific list price, the business marketer must develop a price, or a bid, to meet particular product or service requirements of a customer.

Buying by government and other public agencies is done almost exclusively by competitive bidding. Competitive bidding in private industry is less frequent and is

---

[38] Bradley T. Gale, *Managing Customer Value: Creating Quality and Service that Customers Can See* (New York: The Free Press, 1994), p. 222.

[39] Joseph P. Guiltinan, "Risk-Aversive Pricing Policies: Problems and Alternatives," *Journal of Marketing* 40 (January 1976): pp. 10–15.

[40] For a comprehensive discussion of the Robinson-Patman Act, see Monroe, *Pricing*, pp. 249–267; see also James J. Ritterskamp Jr. and William A. Hancock, "Legal Aspects of Purchasing," in *The Purchasing Handbook*, ed. Harold E. Fearon, Donald W. Dobler, and Kenneth H. Killen (New York: McGraw-Hill, 1993), pp. 529–544.

usually applied to the purchase of nonstandard materials, complex fabricated products where design and manufacturing methods vary, and products made to the buyer's specifications. The types of items procured through competitive bidding are those for which there is no generally established market level. Competitive bids enable the purchaser to evaluate the appropriateness of the prices.[41] Competitive bidding may be either closed or open.

Closed Bidding

Closed bidding, often used by industrial and governmental buyers, involves a formal invitation to potential suppliers to submit written, sealed bids for a particular business opportunity. All bids are opened and reviewed at the same time, and the contract is generally awarded to the lowest bidder who meets desired specifications. The low bidder is not guaranteed the contract—buyers often make awards to the lowest responsible bidder; the ability of alternative buyers to perform remains part of the bidding process.

Open Bidding

Open bidding is more informal and allows suppliers to make offers (oral and written) up to a certain date. The buyer may deliberate with several suppliers throughout the bidding process. Open bidding may be particularly appropriate when specific requirements are hard to define rigidly or when the products and services of competing suppliers vary substantially.

In selected buying situations, negotiated pricing may be employed. Complex technical requirements or uncertain product specifications may lead buying organizations first to evaluate the capabilities of competing industrial firms and then to negotiate the price and the form of the product-service offering. Negotiated pricing is appropriate for procurement decisions in both the commercial and the governmental sectors of the business market (see Chapter 2).

Strategies for Competitive Bidding

Careful planning is fundamental to success in competitive bidding. Planning has three important steps: (1) precise definition of objectives, (2) a screening procedure for evaluating alternative bid opportunities, and (3) a method for assessing the probability of success for a particular bidding strategy.

Objectives   Before preparing a bid for any potential contract, the industrial firm must carefully define its objectives. This helps the firm to decide what types of business to pursue, when to bid, and how much to bid. The objectives may range from profit maximization to company survival. Other objectives might be to keep the plant operating and the labor force intact or to enter a new type of business. The marketer can also benefit by analyzing the objectives of likely bidding rivals.

---

[41] Stuart St. P. Slatter, "Strategic Marketing Variables under Conditions of Competitive Bidding," *Strategic Management Journal* 11 (May/June 1990): pp. 309–317; see also Arthur H. Mendel and Roger Poueymirou, "Pricing," in *The Purchasing Handbook*, ed. Harold E. Fearon, Donald W. Dobler, and Kenneth H. Killen (New York: McGraw-Hill, 1993), pp. 201–227.

TABLE 15.4	**EVALUATION OF A BID OPPORTUNITY**				
		Rating			
Prebid Factors	**Weight**	**High (10)**	**Medium (5)**	**Low (0)**	**Score**
Plant capacity	25	10			250
Degree of experience	20	10			200
Follow-up bid opportunities	15			0	0
Competition	25	10			250
Delivery requirements	15	10			150
Total	100				850

NOTE: Ideal bid score is 1,000; minimum acceptable score is 750.

Screening Bid Opportunities Because developing bids is costly and time-consuming, contracts to bid on should be chosen with care. Contracts offer differing levels of profitability according to the related technical expertise, past experience, and objectives of the bidding firm. Thus, a screening procedure[42] is required to isolate the contracts that offer the most promise (see Table 15.4).

The use of a screening procedure to evaluate contracts has improved the bidding success of business marketers.[43] The procedure has three steps: First, the firm identifies criteria for evaluating contracts. Although the number and nature of the criteria vary by firm and industry, five prebid factors are common:

1. The impact of the contract on plant capacity

2. The degree of experience the firm has had with similar projects

3. Follow-up bid opportunities

4. Expected competition

5. Delivery requirements

Second, once identified, the prebid factors are assigned weights based on their relative importance to the firm (for example, a weight of 25 out of the total of 100 is assigned to plant capacity). The third step is to evaluate each factor, giving it a high (10), medium (5), or low (0) value. In Table 15.4, the contract is evaluated favorably on all factors except follow-up bid opportunities. Summing the product of each factor's weight and rating provides a total score. The business marketer can use this procedure to evaluate alternative potential contracts. The firm may wish to establish a minimum

[42] This method is adapted from Stephen Paranka, "Competitive Bidding Strategy," *Business Horizons* 14 (June 1971): pp. 39–43; see also Stephen Paranka, "Question: To Bid or Not to Bid? Answer: Strategic Prebid Analysis," *Marketing News*, 4 April 1980, p. 16.

[43] For example, see Paul D. Boughton, "The Competitive Bidding Process: Beyond Probability Models," *Industrial Marketing Management* 16 (May 1987): pp. 87–94.

acceptable score before effort will be invested in preparing a bid. Since the bid opportunity evaluated in Table 15.4 yields a score above the cutoff point, a bid would be prepared.

Bidding Strategy   Having isolated a project opportunity, the marketer must now estimate the probabilities of winning the contract at various prices. Assuming that the contract is awarded to the lowest bidder, the chances of the firm winning the contract decline as the bid price increases. How will competitors bid?

In many industries, business marketers confront situations in which the supplier winning the initial contract has the advantage in securing long-term follow-up business. To illustrate, suppliers bidding on contracts to meet 3M's worldwide office equipment needs often provide attractive bids in order to secure an initial relationship with the centralized purchasing unit.[44] Although some immediate profit may be sacrificed, the low bid is seen as an investment that will lead to a continuing stream of profitable follow-up business.

In pursuing this type of bidding strategy, the business marketer must carefully assess the strength of the association between the initial contract and the follow-up business opportunities. For example, the purchase of an office automation system may bond the buyer to a particular seller, thus providing the potential for future business. The costs of switching to another supplier are high because the buyer has made investments in employee training and in new business procedures, as well as in the equipment itself.[45] Such investments create inertia against change. By contrast, for more standardized purchases, such bonding does not occur because the costs of switching to another supplier are quite low for the buyer. In determining the initial bid strategy, the business marketer should examine the strength of the buyer–seller relationship, the probability of securing additional business, and the expected return from that business.

Summary

At the outset, the business marketer must assign pricing its role in the firm's overall marketing strategy. Giving a particular industrial product or service, an "incorrect" price can trigger a chain of events that undermines the firm's market position, channel relationships, and product and personal selling strategies. Price is but one of the costs that buyers examine in the buying process. Thus, the marketer can profit by adopting a strong end-user focus that gives special attention to the way buyers trade off the costs and benefits of various products. Responsive pricing strategies can be developed by understanding the total cost in use of a product for a customer. Value-based strategies can then be designed for particular business market segments.

Price setting is a multidimensional decision. To establish a price, the manager must identify the firm's objectives and analyze the behavior of demand, costs, and competition. Hypercompetitive rivalries characterize the nature of competition in many high-technology industry sectors. Although this task is clouded with uncertainty, the industrial pricing decision must be approached actively rather than passively. For example, many business marketing firms use target costing to capture a

[44] Margaret Nelson, "3M Centralizes Its Office Buy," *Purchasing* 101 (25 June 1987): pp. 62–65.

[45] Barbara Bund Jackson, "Build Customer Relationships That Last," *Harvard Business Review* 63 (November/December 1985): pp. 120–128.

competitive advantage in the business market. Likewise, by isolating demand, cost, or competitive patterns, the manager can gain insights into market behavior and opportunities that have been neglected. Tactical tools, such as win/loss analysis, can be used to refine pricing decisions.

Competitive bidding, a unique feature of the industrial market, calls for a unique strategy. Again, carefully defined objectives are the cornerstone of strategy. These objectives, combined with a meticulous screening procedure, help the firm to identify projects that mesh with company capability.

Discussion Questions

1. A Pac-10 university library recently purchased sixty personal computers from Dell Computer. Illustrate how a purchasing specialist at the university could employ a total cost-in-use approach in evaluating the value of the Dell offering in relation to the value provided by its rivals.

2. Explain why it is often necessary for the business marketer to develop a separate demand curve for various segments of the market. Would one total demand curve be better for making the industrial pricing decision? Explain.

3. Evaluate this statement: To move away from the commodity mentality, companies must view their products as problem solvers, and then sell the product on that basis.

4. Illustrate the process that a firm would follow in using target costing while developing a fax machine for the home office user.

5. The XYZ Manufacturing Corporation has experienced a rather large decline in sales for its component parts. Mary Vantage, vice president of marketing, believes that a 10 percent price cut may get things going again. What factors should Mary consider before reducing the price of the components?

6. Define the *experience effect* (behavior of costs) and explain why it occurs. How does the experience effect relate to strategic pricing decisions?

7. A business marketing manager often has great difficulty in arriving at the optimum price level for a product. First, describe the factors that complicate the pricing decision. Second, outline the approach that you would follow in pricing an industrial product. Be as specific as possible.

8. Rather than time to market, Intel refers to the product development cycle for a new chip as "time to money." Intel's CEO Andrew Grove says that "Speed is the only weapon we have." What pricing advantages issue from a rapid product development process?

9. Describe win/loss analysis and explore the role that it can assume in tactical strategy decisions.

10. Identify a particular industry—like software—that you would describe as hypercompetitive. Who are the key competitors in that industry? What forces are contributing to its rapid rate of change?

16

Business Marketing Communications:
Advertising and Sales Promotion

Advertising supports and supplements personal selling efforts. The share of the marketing budget devoted to advertising is smaller in business than it is in consumer-goods marketing. A well-tailored business-to-business advertising campaign together with a carefully planned promotion program can, however, contribute to the increased efficiency and effectiveness of the overall marketing strategy. After reading this chapter, you will understand

1. the specific role of advertising in business marketing strategy.

2. the decisions that must be made when forming a business advertising program.

3. the business media options, including the powerful role that Internet marketing communication assumes.

4. the methods for measuring business advertising effectiveness.

5. the role of trade shows in the business communications mix and how trade show effectiveness can be measured.

Communication with existing and potential customers is vital to business marketing success. Experience has taught marketing managers that not even the best products sell themselves: The benefits, problem solutions, and cost efficiencies of those products must be effectively communicated to all the individuals who influence the purchase decision. As a result of the technical complexity of business products, the relatively small number of potential buyers, and the extensive negotiation process, the primary communication vehicle in business-to-business marketing is the salesperson. However, nonpersonal methods of communication, including advertising, catalogs, the Internet, and trade shows, have a unique and often crucial role in the communication process.

Consider the valuable role advertising assumes in IBM's corporate strategy. Stretching across print, television, Internet, and radio, IBM has been centering recent attention on a single broad corporate message: e-business (see Figure 16.1). The message is targeted on business strategists, including chief executive officers (CEOs), chief operating officers (COOs), and chief financial officers (CFOs). Maureen McGuire, IBM VP–worldwide integrated marketing communications, described the success of the campaign:

> There's no doubt. We have created the category of e-business. We measure how many people are aware of e-business and what portion attach it to IBM. Our association [with e-business] is four to five times higher than our nearest competitor.[1]

The focus of this chapter is fourfold: (1) to provide a clear understanding of the role of advertising in business marketing strategy; (2) to present a framework for structuring advertising decisions—a framework that integrates the decisions related to objectives, budgets, messages, media, and evaluation; (3) to develop an understanding of each business-to-business advertising decision area; and (4) to evaluate the valuable role that the Internet and trade shows can assume in the promotional mix of the business marketer.

The Role of Advertising

Integrated Communication Programs

Advertising and sales promotion are rarely employed alone in the business-to-business setting, but are intertwined with the total communications strategy—particularly personal selling. Personal and nonpersonal forms of communication interact to inform key buying influencers. The challenge for the business marketer is to create an advertising and sales promotion strategy that effectively blends with personal selling efforts in order to achieve sales and profit objectives. In addition, the advertising and sales promotion tools must be integrated; that is, a comprehensive program of media and sales promotion methods must be coordinated to achieve the desired results.

---

[1] John Evan Frook, "Big Blue Boosts Ad Spending 21 percent to Spread E-Business Message to the Web-Challenged," *Business Marketing* 145 (December 1999): p. 30.

FIGURE 16.1   IBM ADS FEATURE CASE STUDIES OF CLIENTS SOLVING BUSINESS PROBLEMS WITH BIG BLUE'S HELP

SOURCE: Courtesy of International Business Machines, Corp.

Advertising: Enhancing Sales Effectiveness

Effective advertising can make personal selling more productive. John Morrill examined nearly 100,000 interviews on twenty-six product lines at 30,000 buying locations in order to study the impact of business-to-business advertising on salesperson effectiveness.[2] He concluded that dollar sales per salesperson call were significantly higher when customers had been exposed to advertising. In addition to increasing company and product awareness, research indicates that buyers who had been exposed to a supplier's advertisement rated the supplier's sales personnel substantially higher on product knowledge, service, and enthusiasm.[3] A primary role of business-to-business advertising is to enhance the reputation of the supplier.

[2]John E. Morrill, "Industrial Advertising Pays Off," *Harvard Business Review*, 48 (March/April 1970): pp. 4–14.

[3]Ibid., p. 6. For a comprehensive study of the relationship between brand awareness and brand preference, see Eunsang Yoon and Valerie Kijewski, "The Brand Awareness-to-Preference Link in Business Markets: A Study of the Semiconductor Manufacturing Industry," *Journal of Business-to-Business Marketing* 2, (no. 4 1995): pp. 7–36.

Business-to-business advertising also contributes to increased sales efficiency. Increased expenditures on advertising lead to greater brand awareness for industrial products, which translates into larger market shares and higher profits.[4] In one study, a tightly controlled experimental design was used to measure the impact of business-to-business advertising on sales and profits. For one product in the study, sales, gross margin, and net profit were significantly higher with advertising, compared to the pretest period with no advertising.[5] In fact, gross margins ranged from four to six times higher with advertising, compared to the nonadvertising period.

Advertising: Increased Sales Efficiency

The impact of advertising on the overall efficiency of the business marketing program is evidenced in two ways. First, business suppliers frequently need to remind actual and potential buyers of their products or need to make them aware of new products or services. Although these objectives could be partially accomplished through personal selling, the costs of reaching a vast group of buyers would be prohibitive. Carefully targeted advertising extends beyond the salesperson's reach to unidentified buying influentials. A properly placed advertisement can reach hundreds of buying influentials for only a few cents each; the average cost of a business sales call is currently over $200.[6] Sales call costs are determined by the salesperson's wages, travel and entertainment costs, and fringe benefits costs. If these costs total $800 per day and a salesperson can make four calls per day, then each call costs $200. Second, advertising appears to make all selling activities more effective. Advertising interacts effectively with all communication and selling activities, and it can result in higher levels of efficiency for the entire marketing expenditure.

Advertising: Creating Awareness

From a communications standpoint, the buying process can be viewed as taking potential buyers sequentially from unawareness of a product or supplier to awareness, to brand preference, to conviction that a particular purchase will fulfill their requirements, and, ultimately, to actual purchase. Business advertising often creates awareness of the supplier and the supplier's products. Sixty-one percent of the design engineers returning an inquiry card from a magazine ad indicated that they were unaware of the company that advertised before seeing the ad.[7] Business advertising may also make some contribution to creating preference for the product—all very cost effectively. In addition, advertising can create a corporate identity or image. Hewlett-Packard, Dell Computer, IBM, and others use ads in general business publications such as *Business Week* and even television advertising to trumpet the value of their brand and to develop desired perceptions in a broad audience.[8]

---

[4] "New Proof of Industrial Ad Values," *Marketing and Media Decisions*, February 1981, p. 64.

[5] "ARF/ABP Release Final Study Findings," *Business Marketing* 72 (May 1987): p. 55.

[6] "The Cost of Doing Business," *Sales & Marketing Management* 151 (September 1999): p. 56.

[7] Raymond E. Herzog, "How Design Engineering Activity Affects Supplies," *Business Marketing* 70 (November 1985): p. 143.

[8] David A. Aaker and Erich Joachimsthaler, "The Lure of Global Branding," *Harvard Business Review* 77 (November/December 1999): pp. 137–144.

What Business-to-Business Advertising Cannot Do

To develop an effective communications program, the business marketing manager must blend all communication tools into an integrated program, using each tool where it is most effective. Business advertising quite obviously has limitations. Advertising cannot substitute for effective personal selling; it must supplement, support, and complement that effort. In the same way, personal selling is constrained by its costs and should not be used to create awareness or to disseminate information—tasks quite capably performed by advertising.

Generally, advertising alone cannot create product preference; this requires demonstration, explanation, and operational testing. Similarly, conviction and actual purchase can be ensured only by personal selling. Advertising has a supporting role in creating awareness, providing information, and uncovering important leads for salespeople; that is how the marketing manager must use it in order to be effective.

Managing Business-to-Business Advertising

The advertising decision model in Figure 16.2 shows the structural elements involved in the management of business-to-business advertising. First, advertising is only one aspect of the entire marketing strategy and must be integrated with other components in order to achieve strategic goals. The advertising decision process begins with the formulation of advertising objectives, which are derived from marketing goals. From this formulation follows a determination of expenditures necessary to achieve those goals. Then, specific communication messages are formulated to achieve the market behavior specified by the objectives. Equally important is the evaluation and selection of the media used to reach the desired audience. The result is an integrated advertising campaign aimed at eliciting a specific attitude or behavior from the target group. The final, and critical, step is to evaluate the effectiveness of the campaign.

Defining Advertising Objectives

Knowing what advertising must accomplish enables the manager to determine an advertising budget more accurately and provides a yardstick against which advertising can be evaluated. In specifying advertising goals, the marketing manager must realize that (1) the advertising mission flows directly from the overall marketing strategy: advertising must fulfill a marketing strategy objective, and the goal set for advertising must reflect the general aim and purpose of the entire strategy; and (2) the objectives of the advertising program must be responsive to the roles for which advertising is suited: creating awareness, providing information, influencing attitudes, and reminding buyers of company and product existence.

Written Objectives

An advertising objective must specify what is to be achieved and when, must be measurable, and must be realistic.[9] The objective must speak in unambiguous terms of a specific outcome. The purpose is to establish a single working direction for everyone

---

[9]Jack Edmonston, "Practical Tips to Measure Advertising's Performance," *Business Marketing* 81 (April 1996): p. 26.

| FIGURE 16.2 | THE DECISION STAGES FOR DEVELOPING THE BUSINESS-TO-BUSINESS ADVERTISING PROGRAM |

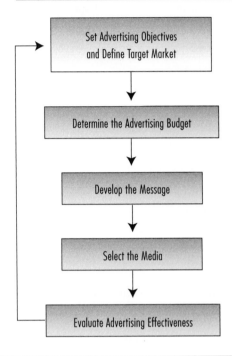

involved in creating, coordinating, and evaluating the advertising program. Correctly conceived objectives set standards against which the advertising effort can be evaluated. A specific objective might be: "to increase from 15 percent (as measured in June 2000) to 30 percent (by June 2001) the proportion of design engineers associating 'lubrication for life' feature with our brand of hydraulic pumps." The objective directs the manager to create a message related to the major product benefit, using media that will reach design engineers. The objective also provides a way to measure accomplishment (awareness among 30 percent of the target audience).

Business advertising objectives frequently bear no direct relationship to specific dollar sales targets. Although dollar sales results would provide a "hard" measure of advertising accomplishment, it is often impossible to link advertising directly to sales. Personal selling, price, product performance, and competitive actions have a more direct relationship to sales levels, and it is almost impossible to sort out the impact of advertising. Thus, advertising goals are typically stated in terms of *communication goals* such as brand awareness, recognition, and buyer attitudes. These goals can be measured; it is presumed that achieving them will stimulate sales volume.

Target Audience   A significant task is the specification of target audiences. Because a primary role of advertising is to reach buying influentials inaccessible to the salesperson, the business marketing manager must define the buying influential groups to be reached. Generally, each group of buying influentials is concerned with distinct product and service attributes and criteria, and the advertising must focus on these.

| TABLE 16.1 | TOP BUSINESS-TO-BUSINESS ADVERTISERS |

Company	Total Advertising Expenditures (millions)
IBM	$293.5
AT&T	288.6
Microsoft	207.4
First Union Corp.	172.0
American Express	168.3
SBC Communications	155.6
MCI Worldcom	137.8
Compaq Computer	136.0
Sprint	130.3
Bell Atlantic Corp.	123.4

SOURCE: Sean Callahan, "High-tech Companies Lead $5.8 Billion Ad Spending," *Business Marketing* 145 (December 1999): pp. 1, 26.

Thus, the objectives must specify the intended audience and its relevant decision criteria.

Creative Strategy Statement A final consideration is the specification of the creative strategy statement. Once objectives and targets are established, the **creative strategy statement** provides guidelines for company and advertising agency personnel on how the product is to be positioned in the marketplace. **Product position** relates to how the target market perceives the product.

For example, if the hydraulic pumps cited earlier currently have an unfavorable product position in regard to lubrication, the firm might use the following creative strategy statement: "Our basic creative strategy is to support a repositioning of the product from that of a reliable pump to a high-performance, reliable self-lubrication pump."

All creative efforts—copy, theme, color, and so forth—as well as media and tactics should be developed to support the creative strategy statement. Effective advertising campaign planning requires objectives upon which to structure media decisions and measure results.

Determining Advertising Expenditures

Collectively, business marketers spend nearly $3 billion on media advertising annually. The leading advertisers are shown in Table 16.1. Note the preponderance of high-tech firms in the top-ten list. Typically, business marketers use a blend of intuition, judgment, experience, and, only occasionally, more advanced decision-oriented techniques to determine advertising budgets. Some of the techniques most commonly utilized by business marketers are rules of thumb (for example, percentage of past years' sales) and the objective-task method.

Rules of Thumb Often, because advertising is a relatively small part of the total marketing budget for business firms, the value of using sophisticated methods for advertising budgeting is not great. In these cases, managers tend to follow simple **rules of thumb** (for example, allocate 1 percent of sales to advertising or match competition spending). Unfortunately, percentage-of-sales rules are all too pervasive throughout business marketing, even where advertising is an important element.

The fundamental problem with percentage-of-sales rules is that they implicitly make advertising a consequence rather than a determinant of sales and profits and can easily give rise to dysfunctional policies. Percentage-of-sales rules suggest that the business advertiser reduce advertising when sales volume declines, just when increased advertising may be more appropriate. Nevertheless, simple rules of thumb will continue to be applied in budget decisions because they are easy to use, and familiar to management.

Objective-Task Method   The task method for budgeting advertising expenditures is an attempt to relate advertising costs to the objective it is to accomplish. Because the sales dollar results of advertising are almost impossible to measure, the task method focuses on the communications effects of advertising, not on the sales effects.

The task method is applied by evaluating the tasks to be performed by advertising, analyzing the costs associated with each task, and summing up the total costs in order to arrive at a final budget. The process can be divided into four steps:

1. Establish specific marketing objectives for the product in terms of such factors as sales volume, market share, profit contribution, and market segments.

2. Assess the communication functions that must be performed in order to realize the marketing objectives and then determine the role of advertising and other elements of the communications mix in performing these functions.

3. Define specific goals for advertising in terms of the measurable communication response required to achieve marketing objectives.

4. Estimate the budget needed to accomplish the advertising goals.

The task method addresses the major problem of the rules-of-thumb methods—funds are applied to accomplish a specific goal so that advertising is a *determinant* of those results, not a consequence. Using the task approach, managers will allocate all the funds necessary to accomplish a specific objective, rather than allocating some arbitrary percentage of sales. The most troubling problem of the method is that management must have some instinct for the proper relationship between expenditure level and communication response. It is difficult to know what will produce a certain level of awareness among business marketing buying influentials. Will twelve, two-page insertions in *Purchasing* magazine over the next six months create the desired recognition level, or will twenty-four insertions over one year be necessary?

Budgeting for advertising must not ignore the political and behavioral aspects of the process. Nigel Piercy's research suggests that attention to budgeting technique is insufficient because organizations operate through structures and processes that are often political in nature.[10] Piercy suggests that what actually determines advertising budgets are the power "interests" in the company and the political behavior of various parties in the budgeting process. An implication of this research is that the manager

---

[10]Nigel Piercy, "Advertising Budgeting: Process and Structure as Explanatory Variables," *Journal of Advertising* 16, no. 2 (1987): p. 34.

may be well-served by focusing considerable attention on the budgetary process as a political activity, and not simply as a technique-driven process.

Passing the Threshold   Several communications are often needed to capture the attention of buyers, which complicates the budgeting decision. Research suggests that a brand must surpass a threshold level of awareness in the market before meaningful additions can be made in its brand preference share. A small advertising budget may not allow the marketer to move the firm's brand beyond a threshold level of awareness and on to preference. Eunsang Yoon and Valerie Kijewski warn that "The communications manager having limited marketing resources will then be in danger of making the mistake of stopping the program prematurely, thus wasting past investment, rather than pressing on to pass the threshold awareness level."[11]

Because the budgeting process is so important to advertising effectiveness, managers must not blindly follow rules of thumb. Instead, they should evaluate the tasks required and their associated costs against industry norms. With clear objectives and proper budgetary allocations, the next step is to design effective advertising messages.

Developing the Advertising Message

Message development is a complex, critical task in industrial advertising. Highlighting a product attribute that is unimportant to a particular buying group is not only a waste of advertising dollars but also a lost opportunity. Both the appeal and the way that appeal is conveyed are vital to successful communication. Thus, creating business-to-business advertising messages involves determining advertising objectives, evaluating the buying criteria of the target audience, and analyzing the most appropriate language, format, and style for presenting the message.

Perception   For an advertising message to be successful, an individual must first be exposed to it and pay attention to it. Thus, a business advertisement must catch the decision maker's attention. Then, once the individual has noticed the message, he or she must interpret it as the advertiser intended. Perceptual barriers often prevent the intended message from being perceived by a receiver. A business advertisement must be successful at catching the decision maker's attention. Yet, even though the individual is exposed to an advertisement, there is no guarantee that the message will be processed. In fact, the industrial buyer may read every word of the copy and find a meaning in it opposite to that intended by the advertiser.

The business advertiser must thus contend with two important elements of perception: attention and interpretation. Buyers tend to screen out messages that are inconsistent with their own attitudes, needs, and beliefs, and they tend to interpret information in the light of those beliefs (see Chapter 3). Unless advertising messages are carefully designed and targeted, they may be disregarded or interpreted improperly. Advertisers must put themselves in the position of the receivers in order to evaluate how the message will appear to them.

Whether an ad uses technical wording appears to have some effect on readers' perceptions of both the industrial product and the ad.[12] Technical ads were shown to create less desire in some readers to seek information because such ads suggest "more

---

[11] Eunsang Yoon and Valerie Kijewski, "The Brand Awareness-to-Preferences Link," p. 32.

[12] Joseph A. Bellizzi and Jacqueline J. Mohr, "Technical Versus Nontechnical Wording in Industrial Print Advertising," in *AMA Educators' Proceedings*, ed. Russell W. Belk et al. (Chicago: American Marketing Association, 1984), p. 174.

difficulty in operation." Therefore, it is important to remember that technical readers (engineers, architects, and so on) respond more favorably to the technical ads, and nontechnical readers respond more favorably to nontechnical ads. From a message development viewpoint, the business advertiser must carefully tailor the technical aspects of promotional messages to the appropriate audience.

Focus on Benefits   An industrial buyer purchases benefits—a better way to accomplish some task, a less expensive way to produce a final product, a solution to a problem, or a faster delivery time. Advertising messages need to focus on the benefits sought by the target customer and to persuade the reader that the advertiser can deliver the benefit. Messages that have direct appeals or calls to action are viewed to be "stronger" than those with diffuse or indirect appeals to action.

Advertisers often tend to concentrate on a physical product, forgetting that the physical product is useless to an industrial buyer unless it solves some problem. Note that the ad for Chemdex in Figure 16.3 is clearly focused on user benefits and solutions. The firm provides an online marketplace that links research scientists to leading suppliers to reduce purchasing costs, streamline the purchasing process, and increase productivity. Note also how potential customers are directed to Chemdex's Web site.

Understanding Buyer Motivations   Which product benefits are important to each group of buying influentials? The business advertiser cannot assume that a standard set of "classical buying motives" applies in every purchase situation. Many business advertisers often do not understand the buying motives of important market segments. The development of effective advertising messages often requires extensive marketing research in order to fully delineate the key buying criteria of each buying influencer in each of the firm's different target markets.

Selecting Advertising Media for Business Markets

Although the message is vital to advertising success, an equally important factor is the medium through which it is presented. Business-to-business media are selected by target audience—the particular purchase decision participants to be reached. Generally, the first decision is whether to use trade publications, direct mail, or both. Selection of particular media also involves budgetary considerations: Where are dollars best spent to generate the customer contacts desired?

Business Publications   More than 2,700 business publications carry business-to-business advertising, for a total exceeding $1 billion. For those specializing in distribution, *Inbound Logistics, Distribution, Logistics Management,* and *Modern Materials Handling* are a few of the publications available. Business publications are either horizontal or vertical. **Horizontal publications** are directed at a specific task, technology, or function whatever the industry. *Advertising Age, Purchasing,* and *Materials Handling Engineering* are horizontal. **Vertical publications,** on the other hand, may be read by everyone from floor supervisor to president within a specific industry. Typical vertical publications are *Glass Industry* or *Manufacturing Confectioner.*

If a business marketer's product has applications only within a few industries, vertical publications are a logical media choice. When many industries are potential users and well-defined functions are the principal buying influencers, a horizontal publication is effective.

FIGURE 16.3	AN AD FOCUSING ON BENEFITS TO USERS AND THAT DIRECTS POTENTIAL CUSTOMERS TO ITS WEB SITE

SOURCE: Courtesy of Chemdex Corporation, © 1999.

Another important aspect of trade publications is **controlled circulation,** which involves free (as opposed to paid) subscriptions, and which is distributed to selected readers in a position to influence buying decisions. Subscribers must provide their title, function, and buying responsibilities, among other information. Thus, the advertiser can tell whether each publication reaches the desired audience.

Obviously, publication choice is predicated on a complete understanding of the range of purchase decision participants and of the industries where the product will be used. Only then can the target audience be matched to the circulation statements of alternative business publications.

Characteristics of an Effective Print Ad   Recent research on the effectiveness of business-to-business print ads provides strong evidence that the marketing strategist should emphasize a "rational approach" in print ads and provide a clear description of the product and the benefits it offers to customers.[13] The effectiveness of ads is also enhanced by detailing product quality and performance information in a concrete and logical manner.

Advertising Cost   Circulation is an important criterion in the selection of publications, but circulation must be tempered by cost. First, the total advertising budget must be allocated among the various advertising tools such as business publications, sales promotion, direct marketing (mail and e-mail), and Internet advertising. Of course, allocations to the various media options will vary with company situation and advertising mission. Allocation of the business publication budget among various journals will depend on their relative effectiveness and efficiency, usually measured in cost per thousand using the following formula:

$$\text{Cost per thousand} = \frac{\text{Cost per page}}{\text{Circulation in thousands}}$$

To compare two publications by their actual page rates would be misleading, because the publication with the lower circulation will usually be less expensive. The cost-per-thousand calculation should be based on circulation to the *target* audience, not the total audience. Although some publications may appear high on a cost-per-thousand basis, they may in fact be cost-effective, with little wasted circulation. Some publications also have popular Web sites that advertisers can use to create integrated marketing communications. AT&T, for example, spends over $10 million annually on Internet advertising. In negotiating with magazines and TV networks, AT&T demands a Web presence as part of the advertising package.[14]

Frequency and Scheduling   Even the most successful business publication advertisements are seen by only a small percentage of the people who read the magazine; therefore, one-time ads are generally ineffective. Because a number of exposures are required before a message "sinks in," and because the reading audience varies from month to month, a schedule of advertising insertions is required. To build continuity and repetitive value, at least 6 insertions per year may be required in a monthly publication, and twenty-six to fifty-two insertions (with a minimum of thirteen) in a weekly publication.[15]

Direct Marketing Tools

Direct mail and e-mail are among the direct marketing tools available to the business marketer. Direct mail delivers the advertising message firsthand to selected individuals. Possible mailing pieces range from a sales letter introducing a new product to a lengthy brochure or even a product sample. Direct mail can accomplish all of the major advertising functions, but its real contribution is in delivering the message to a precisely defined prospect. In turn, direct e-mail can have a substantial impact on creating

---

[13] Ritu Lohtia, Wesley J. Johnston, and Linda Rab, "Business-to-Business Advertising: What Are the Dimensions of an Effective Print Ad?" *Industrial Marketing Management* 24 (October 1995): pp. 369–378.

[14] John Evan Frook, "AT&T Levels Off Spending, Shifts Business Ads' Focus to Products, Services with 'net.working'," *Business Marketing* 145 (December 1999): p. 30.

[15] See Stanton G. Cort, David R. Lambert, and Paula L. Garrett, "Effective Business-to-Business Frequency: New Management Perspectives from the Research Literature," *Advertising Research Foundation Literature Review* (October 1983).

and qualifying customer leads, *if* some important rules are strictly followed: "always seek permission to send e-mail" and "always provide the recipient with the ability to 'opt out'."[16] Attention first will center on direct mail advertising.

Direct mail is commonly used for corporate image promotion, product and service promotion, sales force support, distribution channel communication, and special marketing problems. In promoting corporate image, direct mail may help to establish a firm's reputation of technological leadership. On the other hand, product advertising by direct mail can be used to put specific product information in the hands of buying influentials. Booklets from Kaiser Aluminum explain aluminum's advantages to industrial buyers and specifiers, whereas messages on how to work with aluminum and a quantity/weight calculator are sent to machine operators and shop supervisors.

Direct Mail: Benefits and Requirements   Direct mail also supports the salespeople—providing leads from returned inquiry cards and paving the way for a first sales call. Direct mail can be used effectively to notify potential customers of the location of local distributors. John Deere and Company sent a series of three mailings, by name, to 20,000 farmers who had never purchased their brand, to persuade them to simply visit a John Deere dealer. More than 5,800 farmers did visit a dealer, and purchased more than $35 million worth of Deere equipment over the next three months.[17] In terms of response performance, a typical direct mail package will approximately equal ten to fifty print or broadcast exposures.[18] Finally, direct mail applies to a host of special situations such as identifying new customers and markets, meeting competitor claims, and promoting items that are not receiving enough sales support.

From a cost standpoint, direct mail is efficient when compared to other media. However, direct mail can be a wasteful medium if the prospect lists are so general in nature that it is difficult or impossible to find a common denominator among the prospects. It is a viable advertising medium when potential buyers can be clearly identified and easily reached through the mail. When buying center members have been identified, direct mail is a cost-effective device for making contact with the buying center members. When combined with telemarketing follow-up, even "inaccessible" buying center members can be exposed to promotional efforts.[19]

A direct mail advertisement typically gains the full attention of the reader and therefore provides greater impact than a trade publication advertisement. Industrial buyers usually will at least scan the direct mail promotions sent to them. However, reaching top executives with direct mail may be more difficult. A survey of secretaries of top executives at *Fortune* 500 companies showed that the average executive receives 175 pieces of unsolicited mail each week, and less than 10 percent of this mail is passed on to the executive,[20] who then spends only five minutes a day looking at the seventeen or so pieces of mail. Clearly, the direct mail piece must have effective copy and headlines to grab the attention of both the secretary and the executive.

[16] Barry Silverstein, *Business-to-Business Internet Marketing: Five Proven Strategies for Increased Profits Through Internet Direct Marketing* (Gulf Breeze, FL: MAXIMUM Press, 1999): p. 332.

[17] John D. Yeck, "Direct Marketing Means Accountability," *Business Marketing* 78 (July 1993): p. A4.

[18] Shell R. Alpert, "Testing the 'TOO-Frequent' Assumption," *Business Marketing* 73 (March 1988): p. 14.

[19] Robert D. McWilliams, Earl Naumann and Stan Scott, "Determining Buyer Center Size," *Industrial Marketing Management* 21 (February 1992): p. 48.

[20] Tom Eisenhart, "Breakthrough Direct Marketing," *Business Marketing* 75 (August 1990): p. 20.

Timing of direct mail advertising is also flexible; a new price schedule or new service innovation can be communicated to the buyer as needed. Finally, direct mail makes it easy for the buyer to respond—usually a reply postcard is included or the name, address, and phone number of the local salesperson or distributor are provided.

A Planned Response Package   Most direct mail programs seek some type of response. Often, the potential buyer is asked to return a reply card in order to receive additional information such as a sample or a brochure explaining the benefits and applications of a product. Only one out of every forty raw leads developed from a direct mail campaign may be actually worth a salesperson's attention.[21] As a result, there is often a tendency to adopt a casual approach toward responding to sales leads. However, to realize the potential of direct mail, there must be a formal program to "qualify" each inquiry and respond promptly. Qualification may be accomplished by telephoning the respondent and assessing his or her authority and readiness to purchase. Once the respondent has been qualified, the response program might involve mailing literature to the prospect, referring the prospect to a salesperson, or calling to explain product details. A planned response "package" aims to generate a sale and should include a motivating cover letter, a descriptive brochure, and a reply card that makes it easy to respond.

The Mailing List   The critical ingredient of a direct mail advertising campaign is the list of buying influentials—thus selectivity, although direct mail's primary advantage, is also its greatest challenge. Literally hundreds of mailing lists are available. Mailing lists for business marketing advertising purposes may be (1) circulation lists provided by trade publications, (2) lists provided by industrial directories, (3) lists provided by mailing-list houses (for example, firms specifically engaged in renting industrial mailing lists), and (4) self-generated lists of previous customers and prospects. Information systems are playing an increasing role in maintaining mailing lists. These systems enable the advertiser to supplement the list with sales data and NAISC codes. A catalog published by Standard Rate and Data Service both inventories and describes most of the industrial mailing lists available, often including names of individual executives. However, if the lists are even slightly out of date only company and functional titles (rather than actual names) should be used.

Database Marketing   Effective direct marketing requires application of a concept known as *database marketing*. In essence, database marketing involves knowing a wealth of information about customers and prospects so that the business marketer can direct the appropriate marketing efforts with the correct appeal to the selected target market. Thus, a computer database is built and maintained in the computer that includes a wide range of information on the customer/prospect that can be used to tailor the seller's presentation to that customer/prospect. Based on the success of its database marketing program, IBM has streamlined its sales force, reduced the cost of sales as a percentage of revenue by 50 percent, and seen its sales increase by 12 percent annually.[22] Maintaining and upgrading the database is an ongoing task requiring considerable effort; however, this effort is crucial to effective direct marketing because the information enables the seller to focus on needs and desires relevant to the buyer.

---

[21] John L. DeFazio, "An Inquiry-Based MIS," *Business Marketing* 68 (August 1983): p. 54.

[22] Shari Caudron, "Right on Target," *Industry Week* 245 (2 September 1996): p. 45.

INSIDE BUSINESS MARKETING

The Expanding Role of Internet Marketing

Looking ahead, Internet marketing experts suggest that the entire marketing organization will need to learn new ways of information delivery. Database marketing strategies will revolve around the Internet and e-mail will become an accepted form of external marketing communication. In the future, in-person sales calls will be enhanced or sometimes replaced by Internet conferencing.

Advertising, direct mail, and telemarketing usage could shift dramatically as these media begin to play a more subordinate role to the Internet and the Web. Chances are traditional media will not disappear, but they will follow behind the Internet, relinquishing their leadership position. A primary role of direct mail or direct response advertising may soon be to lead a prospect to a Web response form, an Internet event, or a corporate Web site.

SOURCE: Barry Silverstein, *Business-to-Business Internet Marketing: Five Proven Strategies for Increasing Profits Through Internet Direct Marketing* (Gulf Breeze, FL: MAXIMUM Press, 1999): p. 328.

The Power of Internet Marketing Communications[23]

The Internet provides a powerful medium for enhanced communication with present and potential customers (see Chapter 5). Advertising, direct mail, and telemarketing usage will begin to shift as these media are brought together in an integrated marketing communications program. For example, a primary role of direct mail or direct response advertising may soon be to lead a prospect to a corporate Web site or to an online event, such as a live seminar demonstrating a new product. Internet marketing is assuming an increasingly prominent role in the strategies of business marketing firms because it provides several important benefits.

Integrate the Internet into Media Plans

Successful Internet marketers are integrating the Web with other media. The goal here is to use the right media mix to reach the target audience. Print advertising might be used to generate product awareness and direct mail may continue to generate customer leads. Whenever possible, however, business marketers should use direct mail and media advertising to drive potential customers to their Web site. Also, they should ask prospects and customers to provide e-mail addresses—and request permission to communicate with them via e-mail.

Capture the Economies of the Internet

Internet marketing costs far less than direct mail marketing. With electronic media, there are no printing and mailing lists, no advertising materials to create, or telemarketing calls to make. Once constructed, a Web site can reach one or tens of thousands of prospects for roughly the same cost. Business marketers should explore the cost and performance of a traditional advertising campaign (for example, media and direct mail) versus an Internet-based campaign.

---

[23] This section is based on Barry Silverstein, *Business-to-Business Internet Marketing*, pp. 332–337.

Make Real-Time Changes

While media, direct mail, and telemarketing campaigns might take several weeks to plan and execute, time frames associated with Internet marketing are considerably shorter. For example, e-mail copy can be written and distributed very quickly; Web pages and banner ads can be changed overnight to meet changing market requirements.

Create "Unlimited Shelf Space" for Products

Barry Silverstein, a business-to-business Internet marketing consultant notes: "Only the Internet can act as a virtual warehouse, extending your inventory and presorting an unlimited number of products any time to customers and prospects."[24] For example, on its Web site, Insight Enterprises provides product listings, descriptions, specifications, and real-time pricing for over 45,000 computer-related products.

Reach Customers on a Global Scale

The Internet provides a low-cost medium where any company, regardless of size, can reach global customers with messages, products, and services.

> With no time zones and no meeting protocol, electronic business can be conducted twenty-four hours a day, seven days a week, in every corner of the world—and the Internet marketer need never leave his or her office.[25]

Build One-to-One Relationships with Customers

To form a one-to-one relationship with a customer, the business marketer must treat a particular customer differently based on what was learned about that customer by sales, marketing, service, or other personnel.[26] To succeed, relationship marketing requires the business marketing firm to continually adjust and update its behavior as feedback is received from the customer.

IBM's customer relationship program, called *Focusing on You*, rests on a simple but powerful idea—ask customers what they want and give it to them.[27] By giving the customer the choice, IBM learns about the customer's unique preferences and is better equipped to tailor product and service information to that customer's specific needs. The program relies on e-mail marketing, which is far less costly than direct mail. In fact, IBM found that sending customers traditional printed materials by mail was ten times more expensive than e-mail communications. Moreover, e-mail campaigns often yield higher responses than direct mail campaigns and the results are generated more quickly. For example, one-third of all responses to a particular IBM e-mail campaign were generated in the first twenty-four hours!

---

[24] Ibid., p. 336.

[25] Ibid., p. 336.

[26] Don Peppers, Martha Rogers, and Bob Dorf, "Is Your Company Ready for One-to-One Marketing," *Harvard Business Review* 77 (January/February 1999): pp. 151–160.

[27] Barry Silverstein, *Business-to-Business Internet Marketing*, p. 311.

Measuring Advertising Effectiveness

The business advertiser rarely expects orders to result immediately from advertising. Advertising is designed to create awareness, stimulate loyalty to the company, or create a favorable attitude toward a product. Even though advertising may not directly precipitate a purchase decision, advertising programs must be held accountable. Thus, the business advertiser must be able to measure the results of current advertising in order to improve future advertising and must be able to evaluate the effectiveness of advertising expenditures against expenditures on other elements of marketing strategy.

Measuring Impacts on the Purchase Decision

Measuring advertising effectiveness means assessing advertising's impact on what "intervenes" between the stimulus (advertising) and the resulting behavior (purchase decision). The theory is that advertising can affect awareness, knowledge, and other dimensions that more readily lend themselves to measurement. In essence, the advertiser attempts to gauge advertising's ability to move an individual through the purchase decision process. This approach assumes, correctly or not, that enhancement of any one phase of the decision process or movement from one step to the next increases the ultimate probability of purchase.

A study completed at Rockwell International Corporation suggests that business marketers should also measure the **indirect communication effects** of advertising.[28] This study revealed that advertising affects word-of-mouth communications (indirect effect), and such communications play an important role in buyer decision making. Similarly, advertising was shown to indirectly affect buyers on the basis of its impact on overall company reputation and on the sales force's belief that advertising facilitates their selling tasks. The study suggested that advertising effectiveness measurement include a procedure for tracking and measuring the impact of advertising on the indirect communication effects.

In summary, advertising effectiveness will be evaluated against objectives formulated in terms of the elements of the buyer's decision process as well as some of the indirect communication effects. Advertising efforts will also be judged, in the final analysis, on cost per level of achievement (for example, dollars spent to achieve a certain level of awareness or recognition).

The Measurement Program

A sound measurement program entails substantial advanced planning. Figure 16.4 shows the basic areas of advertising evaluation. The advertising strategist must determine in advance what is to be measured, how, and in what sequence. A pre-evaluation phase is required to establish a benchmark for a new advertising campaign. For example, a pre-evaluation study would be conducted to capture the existing level of awareness a firm's product enjoys in a defined target market. After the advertising campaign, the postevaluation study will examine changes in awareness against this benchmark. Five primary areas for advertising evaluation include (1) markets, (2) motives, (3) messages, (4) media, and (5) results.

---

[28] C. Whan Park, Martin S. Roth, and Philip F. Jacques, "Evaluating the Effects of Advertising and Sales Promotion Campaigns," *Industrial Marketing Management* 17 (May 1988): p. 130.

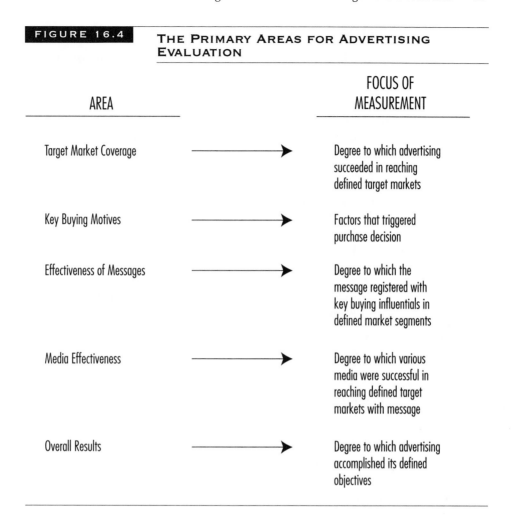

FIGURE 16.4	THE PRIMARY AREAS FOR ADVERTISING EVALUATION

AREA	FOCUS OF MEASUREMENT
Target Market Coverage	→ Degree to which advertising succeeded in reaching defined target markets
Key Buying Motives	→ Factors that triggered purchase decision
Effectiveness of Messages	→ Degree to which the message registered with key buying influentials in defined market segments
Media Effectiveness	→ Degree to which various media were successful in reaching defined target markets with message
Overall Results	→ Degree to which advertising accomplished its defined objectives

The evaluation of business-to-business advertising is demanding and complex, but absolutely essential. Budgetary constraints are generally the limiting factors. However, professional research companies can be called on to develop field research studies. When determining the impact of advertising on moving a decision participant from an awareness of the product or company to a readiness to buy, the evaluations will usually measure knowledge, recognition, recall, awareness, preference, and motivation. Measurements of effects on actual sales are unfortunately not often possible.

Managing Trade Show Strategy

Media and direct mail advertising constitute the cornerstone of most nonpersonal, business-to-business promotional programs. Business advertising funds are designated primarily for trade publication and direct mail, but these are reinforced by other promotional activities such as exhibits and trade shows, catalogs, and trade promotion. Special attention is given here to trade shows—an important promotional vehicle for business markets.

Trade Shows: Strategy Benefits

Most industries stage a business show or exhibition annually to display new advances and technological developments in the industry. The Trade Show Bureau indicates that some 600,000 U.S. firms place displays at trade shows each year and that 80 percent of trade show visitors are classified as "buying influencers."[29] Exhibiting firms spend over $10 billion annually on floor space at expositions in North America.[30] Generally, sellers present their products and services in booths visited by interested industry members. The typical exhibitor will contact four to five potential purchasers per hour on the show floor.

A trade-show exhibit offers a unique opportunity to publicize a significant contribution to technology or to demonstrate new and old products. According to Thomas Bonoma, "For many companies, trade-show expenditures are the major—and for more than a few, the only—form of organized marketing communication activity other than efforts by sales force and distributors."[31] Through the trade show,

- an effective selling message can be delivered to a relatively large and interested audience at one time (for example, more than 30,000 people attend the annual Plant Engineering Show).

- new products can be introduced to a mass audience.

- customers can get hands-on experience with the product in a one-on-one selling situation.

- potential customers can be identified, providing sales personnel with qualified leads.

- general goodwill can be enhanced.

- free publicity is often generated for the company.

The cost of reaching a prospect at a trade show is approximately $160, much lower than the cost of making a personal sales call.[32] Further, trade shows offer an excellent and cost-effective short-term method for introducing a product in new foreign markets.[33] An international trade fair enables a manufacturer to meet buyers directly, observe competition, and gather market research data. The entry time for exporting can easily be cut from six years to six months by attending foreign trade fairs.

Trade Show Investment Returns

A recent study evaluated the impact of a trade show on the sales and profitability of a new laboratory testing device.[34] In a controlled experiment where new product sales

---

[29]"Trade Shows Make More Sense than Ever," *Business Marketing* 77 (November 1992): pp. A7, A8.

[30]Barbara Axelson, "How to Choose the Right Trade Show," *Business Marketing* 84 (April 1999): p. 14.

[31]Thomas V. Bonoma, "Get More Out of Your Trade Shows," *Harvard Business Review*, 61 (January/February 1983): p. 76.

[32]Robert Lapidies, "Internet Strategies for Better Exhibiting," at www.ts.central.com, January 16, 1999.

[33]Brad O'Hara, Fred Palumbo, and Paul Herbig, "Industrial Trade Shows Abroad," *Industrial Marketing Management* 22 (August 1993): p. 235.

[34]Srinath Gopalakrishna, Gary L. Lilien, Jerome D. Williams, and Ian K. Sequeira, "Do Trade Shows Pay Off?" *Journal of Marketing* 59 (July 1995): pp. 75–83.

could be traced to customers both attending and not attending the show, sales levels were higher among attendees. In turn, the proportion of customers buying the product was higher among those who had visited the booth during the show. Importantly, there was a positive return on trade show investment (23 percent) based on incremental profits related to the cost of the trade show. This research is one of the first studies to show that the returns from trade show investments can indeed be measured. Although dramatically enhancing sales effectiveness, trade shows can be extremely costly, and must be carefully planned.

Planning Trade Show Strategy

To develop an effective trade-show communications strategy, managers must address four questions:

1. What functions should the trade show perform in the total marketing communications program?

2. To whom should the marketing effort at trade shows be directed?

3. What is the appropriate show mix for the company?

4. What should the trade show investment–audit policy be? How should audits be carried out? [35]

Answering these questions helps managers crystallize their thinking about target audiences, about results to be expected, and about how funds should be allocated.

Trade Show Objectives

Some of the functions of trade shows in generating sales include identifying decision influencers; identifying potential customers; providing product, service, and company information; learning of potential application problems; creating actual sales; and handling current customer problems. In addition to these selling-related functions, the trade show can be a valuable activity for building corporate image, gathering competitive intelligence, and enhancing sales force morale. Specific objectives are needed to guide the development of trade-show strategy and to specify the activities of company personnel while there. Once specific objectives are formulated, however, the exhibitor must evaluate alternative trade shows in light of the target market.

Selecting the Shows

The challenge is to decide which trade shows to attend and how much of the promotional budget to expend.[36] Clearly, the firm will want to be represented at those shows frequented by its most important customer segments. A useful service is the *Exposition Audit* provided by the Business Publication Audit of Circulation. The audit reports

---

[35] Thomas V. Bonoma, "Get More Out of Your Trade Shows," p. 79.

[36] See Aviv Shoham, "Selecting and Evaluating Trade Shows," *Industrial Marketing Management* 21 (November 1992): pp. 335–341.

registered attendance at trade shows and a complete profile of each registrant's business, job title, and function. Trade Show Central is an Internet site (www.ts.central.com) that provides access to 8,000 trade shows in a searchable database. A wealth of information on each show is provided and exhibitors can promote their presence at the show on the site.

Some firms will use the reports published by Exhibit Surveys, Inc., a company that surveys trade show audiences. Two of the important measures developed by Exhibit Surveys are the **Net Buying Influences** and the **Total Buying Plans.** The first measures the percentage of the show audience that has decision authority for the types of products being exhibited; the second measures the percentage of the audience planning to buy the products being exhibited within the next twelve months. These measures are very useful to the business marketing manager when selecting the most effective shows to attend.

Many firms make a preshow survey of their target prospects in order to learn which trade shows they will attend and what they hope to gain from attending. In this way the exhibitor can prepare its trade show strategy to fit the needs of its potential customers.

Others suggest that a firm rank order various shows based on expected profitability.[37] The expected profitability is computed by calibrating a model of "lead efficiency" using the firm's historical sales lead and lead conversion-to-sale data, gross margin information, and total attendance at past shows. **Lead efficiency** is defined as the number of sales leads obtained at the show divided by the total number of show visitors with definite plans to buy the exhibitor's product or one similar to it.

Managing the Trade Show Exhibit

In an effort to generate interest in an exhibit, business marketing firms run advertisements in business publications profiling new projects to be exhibited at the show. Trade show strategies should also be linked to Internet marketing communications initiatives. This enables many exhibitors to schedule appointments with prospects and customers during the show.

Sales personnel must be trained to perform in the trade-show environment. The selling job differs from the typical sales call in that the salesperson may have only five to ten minutes to make a presentation. On a typical sales call, salespersons usually sell themselves first, then the company, and finally the product. At the trade show, the process is reversed.

There must be a system for responding effectively to inquiries generated at the show. Some business marketers find it effective to use a lap top computer at the show to transmit information to corporate headquarters electronically. Headquarters staff then generate a letter and send out the required information by mail or electronically. When prospects return to their offices after a show, the material is immediately available.

Evaluating Trade Show Performance

The measurement of trade show performance is very important in assessing the success of a firm's trade show strategy. Srinath Gopalakrishna and Gary Lilien present a

---

[37] Srinath Gopalakrishna and Jerome D. Williams, "Planning and Performance Assessment of Industrial Trade Shows: An Exploratory Study," *International Journal of Research in Marketing* 9 (September 1992): pp. 207–224.

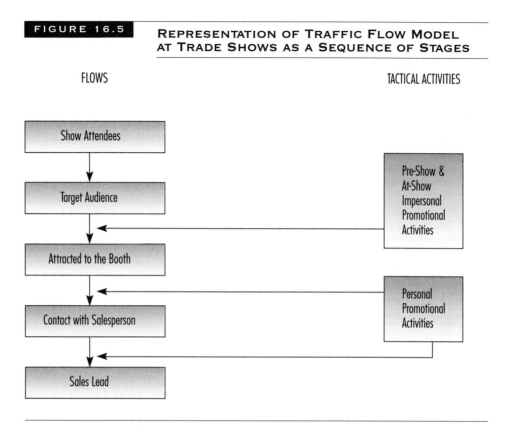

FIGURE 16.5   REPRESENTATION OF TRAFFIC FLOW MODEL
AT TRADE SHOWS AS A SEQUENCE OF STAGES

FLOWS   TACTICAL ACTIVITIES

SOURCE: Srinath Gopalakrishna and Gary L. Lilien, "A Three-Stage Model of Industrial Trade Show Performance,"
working paper #20-1992, Institute for the Study of Business Markets, Pennsylvania State University.

useful framework to assess performance by considering traffic flow through the firm's
booth as a sequence of three stages.[38] Figure 16.5 illustrates the process and the development of three different indices of performance—attraction, contact, and conversion
efficiency for the three respective stages.

An important contribution of this framework is the link between performance indices and key decision variables under the control of the firm. Attraction efficiency is the
proportion of *interested* visitors that the booth is able to attract. Notice that the firm's
target audience is the pool of visitors at the show who are interested in the firm's products, which is usually smaller than the total number of attendees at the show. The booth's
attraction power is a function of booth space (square feet), show promotion, use of
attention-getting techniques, and so on. Similarly, contact and conversion efficiencies
are modeled as a function of the number of booth personnel and their level of training.

For an individual firm, trade show expenditures should be tied to concrete marketing communication goals to secure an adequate return on investment. To this end,
business marketing managers must carefully evaluate each trade show and its associated expenses in terms of the likely sales, profit, and corporate image impacts. As with
all other promotional vehicles, the planning and budgeting for trade shows must focus

[38]Srinath Gopalakrishna and Gary L. Lilien, "A Three-Stage Model of Industrial Trade Show Performance," *Marketing
Science* 14 (winter 1995): pp. 22–42.

INSIDE BUSINESS MARKETING

Using High Tech to Pursue Trade Show Leads

Marketers fail to follow up on roughly 70 percent of leads from all sources, including trade shows. Electronic solutions are now being explored in the trade show arena to dramatically improve the lead management process.

Integrated Leads Management Systems, Inc. (ILMS) is a leader in the application of technology to follow up on leads generated at trade shows. ILMS places touch-screen monitors in an exhibitor's booth to enter data about an attendee's buying authority, buying intentions, budget, and other relevant data. This information is linked with data from the attendee's business card— name, company, address, and phone number— that is fed into the computer via a business card scanner.

Once data has been captured, the exhibitor can distribute the electronic leads via the Internet, fax, or proprietary e-mail. The ILMS system includes a wireless modem that allows for immediate distribution of the leads to the sales force. Use of this technology permits trade show exhibitors to determine if sales materialize, as well as estimate the cost per sales lead. Capturing information in real time and delivery through the Internet is predicted to be the "wave of the future" in lead management strategies.

SOURCE: Adapted from Kate Bertrand, "High Tech Enhancements Fortify Trade Show Leads," *Business Marketing* 81 (February 1996): pp. 1, 4.

on specific objectives. Once these objectives have been determined, the rational approach will then identify the tasks that must be accomplished and the levels of expenditure required.

Summary

Because of the nature of the business-to-business buying process, personal selling is the primary technique for creating sales; advertising supports and supplements personal selling. Yet advertising does perform some tasks that personal selling simply cannot perform. Advertising is able to reach buying influentials to whom sales personnel often do not have access.

Advertising supports personal selling by making the company and product known to potential buyers. The result is greater overall selling success. Effective advertising makes the entire marketing strategy more efficient, often lowering total marketing and selling costs. Finally, advertising can provide information and company or product awareness more efficiently than can personal selling.

Managing the advertising program begins with the determination of advertising objectives, which must be written and which must be directed to a specific audience. Once objectives are specified, funds must be allocated to advertising efforts. Rules of thumb, though common, are not the ideal methods for specifying advertising budgets. The objective-task method is more effective.

Advertising messages are created with the understanding that the potential buyer's perceptual process will influence receptivity to the message. The most effective appeal is one that projects product benefits sought by the targeted buying influential.

Advertising media are selected on the basis of their circulation; that is, how well their audience matches the desired audience of buying influentials. The Internet provides a powerful medium to communicate with target customers. Astute business marketers are integrating the Web with other media. Internet marketing campaigns can be readily changed, provide unlimited shelf space for products, offer a direct path to global customers, and make relationship marketing a reality.

Finally, advertising effectiveness must be evaluated against the communication objectives established for the advertising campaign. Readership, recognition, awareness, attitudes, and intention to buy are typical measures of business-to-business advertising performance.

Trade show visitors tend to be buying influentials and the cost of reaching a prospect here is far lower than through the personal selling vehicle. A carefully planned and executed strategy is needed to secure promising returns on trade show investments. Trade shows are an effective way to reach large audiences with a single presentation, but funds must be allocated carefully.

Discussion Questions

1. Although the bulk of the promotional budget of the business marketing firm is allocated to personal selling, advertising can play an important role in business marketing strategy. Explain.

2. The Hamilton Compressor Company increased advertising expenditures 15 percent in the Chicago market last year, and sales increased 4 percent. Upon seeing the results, Mr. White, the president, turns to you and asks, "Was that increase in advertising worth it?" Outline your reply. (Feel free to include questions that you would ask Mr. White.)

3. Breck Machine Tool would like you to develop a series of ads for a new industrial product. Upon request, Breck's marketing research department will provide you with any data that they have concerning the new product and the market. Outline the approach that you would follow in selecting media and developing messages for the campaign. Specify the types of data that you would draw on to improve the quality of your decisions.

4. Outline how you would evaluate the effectiveness and efficiency of a business firm's advertising function. Focus on budgeting practices and performance results.

5. Explain how a message presented in an industrial advertisement may be favorably evaluated by the production manager, unfavorably evaluated by the purchasing manager, and fail even to trigger the attention of the quality control engineer.

6. Given the rapid rise in the cost of making industrial sales calls, should the business marketer attempt to substitute direct mail advertising or e-mail communications for personal selling whenever possible? Support your position.

7. Describe the role that an Internet strategy might assume in the promotional mix of the business marketer. How can the business marketer use the Web to form close relationships with customers?

8. It is argued that business advertising is not expected to precipitate sales directly. If business advertising does not persuade organizational buyers to buy brand *A* versus brand *B*, what does it do, and how can we measure its impact against expenditures on other marketing strategy elements?

17

Business Marketing Communications: Managing the Personal Selling Function

Business marketing communications consist of advertising, sales promotion, and personal selling. As explored in the last chapter, advertising and related sales promotion tools supplement and reinforce personal selling. Personal selling is the most important demand-stimulating force in the business marketer's promotional mix. Through the sales force, the marketer links the firm's total product and service offering to the needs of organizational customers. After reading this chapter, you will understand

1. the role of personal selling in business marketing strategy.

2. the importance of viewing business marketing management as a buyer–seller interaction process.

3. the nature of the industrial sales management function.

4. the selected managerial tools that can be applied to major sales force decision areas.

John Chambers, president and CEO at Cisco Systems, says that "the customer is the strategy."[1] He began his career in the 1970s as an IBM salesperson. Today, he still spends 40 percent of his time working directly with customers, and believes that the key to Cisco's success comes through continuous customer feedback. In fact, every night, 365 days a year, he receives voice mail updates on ten to fifteen top-tier customer accounts. By developing leading-edge technology and staying close to the customer, Cisco continues on its astonishing growth path.

In the marketing operations of the typical business marketing firm, selling has been a dominant component, as well as a major determinant, of overall company success.[2] Personal selling is dominant in business markets because the number of potential customers is relatively small, compared to consumer markets, and the dollar purchases are large. The importance of personal selling in the marketing mix depends on such factors as the nature and composition of the market, the nature of the product line, and the company's objectives and financial capabilities. Business marketers have many potential links to the market. Some may rely on manufacturers' representatives and distributors, others rely exclusively on a direct sales force. Similarly, each firm must determine the relative importance of the various components of the promotional mix—advertising versus sales promotion versus personal selling.

Across all industries, the cost of an industrial sales call is over $200.[3] Computer firms report much higher costs, whereas chemical producers experience much lower ones. Of course, these figures vary, depending upon a host of company, product, and market conditions. They do indicate, however, that significant resources are invested in personal selling in the business market. To maximize effectiveness and efficiency, the personal selling function must be carefully managed and integrated into the firm's marketing mix. To enhance productivity and to respond to intense competition, sales strategists are employing a host of new approaches and technologies.

Regardless of how a firm implements its sales strategy, the salesperson is the initial link to the marketplace and specific customers. The task of the salesperson is both complex and challenging. To meet all their customer's expectations, salespeople are required to have broad knowledge that extends beyond their own products.[4] They must be able to talk intelligently about competitors' products and about trends in the customer's industry. They must know not only their customer's business but also the business of their customer's customers. This chapter first considers how relevant aspects of organizational buying behavior (Chapter 3) are related to the personal selling process. The chapter then turns to sales force management and the need for defining personal selling objectives, structuring the sales organization, allocating the sales force, and evaluating and controlling sales force operations.

Foundations of Personal Selling: An Organizational Customer Focus

Personal selling is the means through which business marketing strategy is executed. Once the marketer defines target market segments on the basis of organizational

---

[1] Michele Marchetti, "America's Best Sales Forces: Sales to CEO," *Sales & Marketing Management* 151 (July 1999): p. 63.

[2] Thomas R. Wotruba, "The Transformation of Industrial Selling: Causes and Consequences," *Industrial Marketing Management* 25 (September 1996): p. 328.

[3] "The Cost of Doing Business," *Sales & Marketing Management* 151 (September 1999): p. 56.

[4] Martin Fojt, "Becoming a Customer-Driven Organization," *Journal of Services Marketing* 9, no. 3 (1995): pp. 7–8.

characteristics (macrolevel) or the characteristics of decision-making units (microlevel), the sales force is deployed to meet the needs of these segments. The salesperson augments the total product offering and serves as a representative for both seller and buyer. The image, reputation, and need-satisfying ability of the seller firm is conveyed, to an important degree, by the sales force. By helping procurement decision makers to define requirements and match the firm's product or service to requirements, the salesperson is offering not just a physical product but also ideas, recommendations, technical assistance, experience, confidence, and friendship. A large toy manufacturer, for example, evaluates suppliers on the basis of product quality, delivery reliability, price, *and* the value of ideas and suggestions provided by the sales personnel. This buying organization, in fact, openly solicits ideas, and evaluates suppliers formally on the number and quality of these recommendations.

As a representative for the buyer, the salesperson often articulates the specific needs of a customer to R&D or production personnel in the industrial firm. Product specifications, delivery, and technical service are often negotiated through the salesperson. The salesperson serves as an uncertainty absorption point, reducing conflict in the buyer–seller relationship. John Knopp, a regional sales manager at Hewlett-Packard, identifies this trait in high-performing salespersons: "They know how to get special things done for the customer inside or outside the system. When something has to be done outside of normal policies and practices, they find a way to get it done smoothly."[5]

Organizational Buying Behavior

Successful personal selling relies heavily on a recognition of the unique requirements of each organizational customer. Industrial products may have numerous applications; organizational buyers have varying levels of experience and information in purchasing certain products. A sensitivity to how buying organizations vary, coupled with a knowledge of organizational buying behavior, is the foundation for successful personal selling.

A salesperson can benefit by examining a potential buyer organization from several perspectives. First, how would the organization view this specific buying situation—new task, modified rebuy, or straight rebuy? As emphasized in Chapter 3, each buying situation calls for a unique personal selling strategy—the exact form depending on whether the marketer is an "in" or an "out" supplier. Second, what are the environmental, organizational, group, and individual influences on the organizational buying process?

The following considerations contribute to the personal selling task:[6]

1. *Environmental factor identification:* How do business conditions (for example, growth, inflation) or political and legal trends (for example, governmental regulation) affect the industry within which this firm operates?

[5] Thayer C. Taylor, "Anatomy of a Star Salesperson," *Sales and Marketing Management* 136 (May 1986): pp. 49–51.

[6] Richard E. Plank and William Dempsey, "A Framework for Personal Selling to Organizations," *Industrial Marketing Management* 9 (April 1980): pp. 143–149; see also Barton A. Weitz, Harish Sujan, and Mita Sujan, "Knowledge, Motivation, and Adaptive Behavior: A Framework for Improving Selling Effectiveness," *Journal of Marketing* 50 (October 1986): pp. 174–191; and David M. Szymanski, "Determinants of Selling Effectiveness: The Importance of Declarative Knowledge to the Personal Selling Concept," *Journal of Marketing* 52 (January 1988): pp. 64–77.

2. *Organizational factor identification:* Is procurement in this buying organization centralized or decentralized? What are the strategic priorities of this firm? What role can our products and services assume in creating a competitive advantage for this firm?

3. *Buying center identification:* Which organization members are included in the buying center?

4. *Influence pattern identification:* Which buying center members exert the most power in the buying decision? What are the selection criteria of each?

Knowledge of the special competitive challenges that the buying firm faces, how the proposed product/service offering will be applied, how it will influence the cost structure and performance of various departments—these are the insights that enable the marketer to sharply focus personal selling strategy. Empathy with the buyer is the core of a mutually beneficial buyer–seller relationship.

Understanding the Customer's Business   Knowledge of the customers' clients has been shown to be an effective way to create differentiation for a business marketer.[7] By developing a keen understanding of the customer's business and using end-user market research, the salesperson can assist the buying company in creating value-adding services for the buyer's target customers. One study in the machine tool industry showed that successful firms in the industry demonstrated a clear understanding of the changing needs of machine tool buyers.[8] Less successful firms lacked an appreciation of their customers' requirements and did not understand the necessity of developing machine tools that focus on their customers' changing needs.

It appears that many firms are not very effective in understanding their customers' business. A study by *Sales and Marketing Management* revealed that only 20 percent of a sample of more than 400 purchasing managers were satisfied with the salesperson's knowledge about their business.[9] These findings suggest that salespeople should focus more attention on what a customer *really* needs: They should invest sufficient time to develop an in-depth knowledge of the key elements of the customer's business.

The Internet: Transforming the Selling Process

By providing ready access to a wealth of information, the Internet empowers customers and provides them with self-service capabilities that they enthusiastically embrace. They can secure extensive product and service information, compare prices, find solutions to technical problems, watch online seminars and product demonstrations, check the delivery status of orders, receive customer service support, and trouble-shoot special problems. As order processing activities move to the Web, salespersons can center more on relationship building and less on transaction details.

Sales productivity can also be increased by using the Web as an efficient and effective vehicle for communicating with customers on a global scale. For example, business

---

[7] Daniel C. Smith, "Knowledge of Customers' Customers as a Basis for Sales Force Differentiation," *Journal of Personal Selling and Sales Management* 15 (summer 1995): pp. 1–15.

[8] Vivienne Shaw, "Successful Marketing Strategies: A Study of British and German Companies in the Machine Tool Industry," *Industrial Marketing Management* 24 (August 1995): pp. 329–339.

[9] Andy Cohen, "No Deal," *Sales and Marketing Management* 148 (August 1996): p. 51.

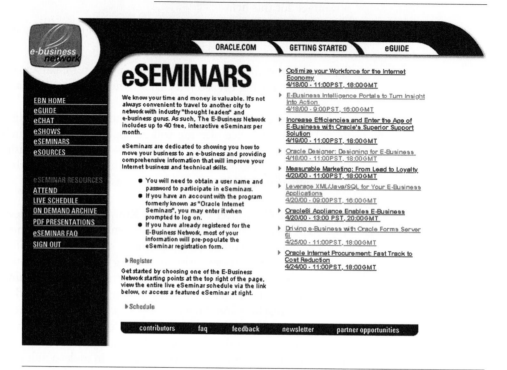

FIGURE 17.1

ORACLE USES ONLINE SEMINARS TO DEMONSTRATE NEW PRODUCTS TO CUSTOMERS AROUND THE GLOBE

SOURCE: Courtesy, Oracle Corporation (www.oracle.com/ebusinessnetwork/esemiars) April 1, 2000.

marketers can hold online seminars to demonstrate new products to customers. Here material can be presented in text, video, and audio forms—taking questions via e-mail. By moving from costly in-person product demonstration seminars to online presentations, dramatic savings can be realized. To illustrate, Oracle Corporation traditionally relied on in-person demonstration seminars that cost $350 per attendee to stage, including special invitations, hotel space, technical support, and more.[10] These seminars were held in over 100 different countries. Today, Oracle does one online seminar for customers around the world. The cost: $1.98 per attendee! (See Figure 17.1)

Barry Silverstein, a leading Internet marketing expert, describes the impact of the Internet on the selling process:

> The salesperson of the future might arrange a virtual meeting over the Web with a prospect, perhaps including live video-conferencing. The prospect, of course, could be anywhere in the world. At this virtual meeting, the salesperson will make eye contact and walk the prospect through a visual presentation on the Web, leading him or her along with live voice. The salesperson will be able to stop at any point and take questions. The salesperson could

---

[10] Matt Richtel, "The Next Waves of Electronic Commerce," *The New York Times*, 20 December 1999, p. C36.

show the prospect video clips of customer testimonials and success stories, or maybe the salesperson will invite the prospect to view and interact with a real-time product demonstration, right then and there.[11]

If a face-to-face meeting is required, the salesperson will use a notebook computer that has presentations and demonstrations pre-loaded. The salesperson might also connect to the Internet and guide the prospect through an online presentation, seminar, or demonstration on the Web.

Relationship Marketing

The trend toward close relationships, or even strategic partnerships, between manufacturers and their suppliers is accelerating in many sectors of the business market. Several forces, highlighted throughout this textbook, support the movement toward closer buyer–seller relationships and away from distant, or even adversarial, relations: rising global competition, the quest for improved quality, rapidly changing technology, and the increased adoption of a just-in-time operations philosophy.[12] Assuming a key role in the relationship marketing program of the firm (see Chapter 4) is the industrial salesperson.

Selling Center   The members of the selling organization who are involved in initiating and maintaining exchange relationships with industrial customers constitute the **organizational selling center**[13] (see Figure 17.2). The needs of a particular selling situation, especially the information requirements, significantly influence the composition of the selling center. Its primary objectives are the acquisition and processing of pertinent marketing-related information and the execution of selling strategies. In many industries, teamwork has emerged as a necessary prerequisite for sales success—often requiring a formal selling team approach that is more structured than the loose coalition of individuals in the selling center.[14] Some firms such as Xerox, Hewlett-Packard, and Du Pont have adopted formal account management teams.

The **organizational buying center** includes those individuals who participate in the purchasing decision and who share the goals and risks arising from that decision. The needs of a particular buying situation dictate the composition of the buying center (see Chapter 3). To illustrate, a new complex buying situation may include several participants representing different functional areas.

Assuming visible roles in this exchange process are the salesperson (selling-center representative) and the purchasing agent (buying-center representative). The salesperson and the buyer each begin the interaction with particular plans, goals, and intentions. The salesperson exchanges information and assistance in solving a

---

[11] Barry Silverstein, *Business-to-Business Internet Marketing: Five Proven Strategies for Increasing Profits Through Internet Direct Marketing* (Gulf Breeze, FL: MAXIMUM Press, 1999): p. 331.

[12] See, for example, Charles O'Neal, "Concurrent Engineering with Early Supplier Involvement: A Cross Functional Approach," *International Journal of Purchasing & Materials Management* 29 (winter 1993): pp. 3–9.

[13] Michael D. Hutt, Wesley J. Johnston, and John R. Ronchetto Jr., "Selling Centers and Buying Centers: Formulating Strategic Exchange Patterns," *Journal of Personal Selling & Sales Management* 5 (May 1985): pp. 33–40; see also J. Brock Smith and Donald W. Barclay, "Team Selling Effectiveness: A Small Group Perspective," *Journal of Business-to-Business Marketing* 1, no. 2 (1993): pp. 3–32.

[14] Dawn R. Deeter-Schmelz and Rosemary Ramsey, "A Conceptualization of the Functions and Roles of Formalized Selling and Buying Teams," *Journal of Personal Selling & Sales Management* 15 (spring 1995): pp. 47–60.

FIGURE 17.2 RELATIONSHIP MANAGEMENT PROCESSES IN BUSINESS MARKETING

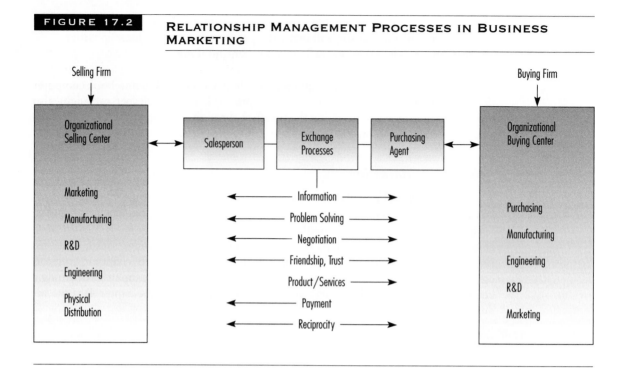

---

purchasing problem for the reward of a sale given by the buyer or by members of the buying center.

In addition to external negotiations with members of the buying center, the industrial salesperson, acting on behalf of the potential customer, is often involved in internal negotiations with other members of the selling center, such as manufacturing or R&D, to ensure a successful exchange relationship with a particular customer. Internal negotiations also occur within the buying center because various members represent the interests of their functional areas in the selection of suppliers. Complex flows of influence characterize buyer–seller interactions in the business market.[15] To ensure maximum customer satisfaction and the desired market response, business marketers must effectively manage the complex web of influences that intersect in buyer-seller relationships.[16]

Relationship Quality

By occupying a position close to the customer and drawing upon the collective strength of the organization, the industrial salesperson is often best suited to perform the role of "relationship manager." For many complex purchase decisions, organizational buyers face considerable uncertainty. From the customer's perspective,

---

[15] Thomas V. Bonoma and Wesley J. Johnston, "The Social Psychology of Industrial Buying and Selling," *Industrial Marketing Management* 7 (July 1978): pp. 213–224; see also Nigel C. G. Campbell, John L. Graham, Alain Jolibert, and Hans Gunther Meissner, "Marketing Negotiations in France, Germany, the United Kingdom, and the United States," *Journal of Marketing* 52 (April 1988): pp. 49–62.

[16] John F. Tanner Jr., "Buyer Perspectives of the Purchase Process and Its Effect on Customer Satisfaction," *Industrial Marketing Management* 25 (March 1996): pp. 125–133.

relationship quality is achieved through the salesperson's ability to reduce this uncertainty. **Relationship quality** comprises at least two dimensions: (1) trust in the salesperson and (2) satisfaction with the salesperson.[17] Confronting the uncertainty often present in complex industrial exchange settings, relationship quality contributes to a lasting bond by offering assurance that the salesperson will continue to meet the customer's expectations (satisfaction), and not knowingly distort information or otherwise damage the customer's interests (trust).[18] As Lawrence Crosby, Kenneth Evans, and Deborah Cowles conclude, "The continuity of interaction that relationship quality provides then creates ongoing opportunities for the seller to identify the customer's unmet needs and propose new business."[19]

Enhancing Customer Relationships with the Internet[20]

Using database technology, business marketers accumulate profile data about each customer's relationship with the firm, capture the names of key buying influentials, track interactions with the customer, and use the data to customize information and the firm's offerings for the customer. To illustrate, IBM has designed a customer contact program called *Focusing on You* that draws on its customer database and uses the Internet as the information delivery vehicle. IBM simply lets customers make the decision concerning the type of information they want to receive and even how they wish to receive it (for example, by e-mail, direct mail, salesperson). Customers complete an Internet profile and the data received is valuable—IBM learns what its customers want firsthand. By providing tailored information, IBM is developing a one-to-one relationship with the customer. The program also enables the salesperson to target the specific priorities that are important to the customer.

This IBM program illustrates how a one-to-one relationship marketing strategy is implemented. The strategy centers on learning about the needs of individual customer organizations. Then, the business marketer uses an individual customer's input and feedback to continually adjust and update its own offerings directed toward that customer. As a result, customer loyalty is enhanced.[21]

Managing the Sales Force

Effective management of the industrial sales force is fundamental to the firm's success. Sales management refers to the planning, organizing, directing, and controlling of

---

[17] Lawrence A. Crosby, Kenneth R. Evans, and Deborah Cowles, "Relationship Quality in Services Selling: An Interpersonal Influence Perspective," *Journal of Marketing* 54 (July 1990): pp. 68–81. See also Jon M. Hawes, Kenneth E. Mast, and John E. Swan, "Trust Earning Perceptions of Sellers and Buyers," *Journal of Personal Selling & Sales Management* 9 (September 1989): pp. 1–8.

[18] Jon M. Hawes, James T. Strong, and Bernard S. Winick, "Do Closing Techniques Diminish Prospect Trust?" *Industrial Marketing Management* 25 (September 1996): pp. 349–360. See also Richard E. Plank, David A. Reid, and Ellen Bolman Pollins, "Perceived Trust in Business-to-Business Sales: A New Measure," *Journal of Personal Selling & Sales Management* 19 (summer 1999): pp. 61–71.

[19] Crosby, Evans, and Cowles, "Relationship Quality in Services Selling," p. 76. For a discussion of specific strategies, see James C. Anderson and James A. Narus, "Partnering as a Focused Market Strategy," *California Management Review* 33 (spring 1991): pp. 91–99.

[20] This section is based on Barry Silverstein, *Business-to-Business Internet Marketing*, pp. 300–303.

[21] Don Peppers, Martha Rogers, and Bob Dorf, "Manager's Tool Kit: Is Your Company Ready for One-to-One Marketing" *Harvard Business Review* 77 (January/February 1999): pp. 151–152.

personal selling efforts.[22] Sales force decisions are tempered by overall marketing objectives and must be integrated with the other elements of the marketing mix. Forecasts of the expected sales response guide the firm in determining the total selling effort required (sales force size) and in organizing and allocating the sales force (perhaps to sales territories). The techniques for estimating market potential and for forecasting sales (discussed in Part III, Assessing Market Opportunities) are particularly valuable in sales planning. Sales management also involves the ongoing activities of selecting, training, deploying, supervising, and motivating sales personnel. Finally, sales operations must be monitored to identify problem areas and to assess the efficiency, effectiveness, and profitability of personal selling units.

This section will consider three strategic components of sales force management: (1) methods for organizing the sales force, (2) the requirements for successful sales force administration, and (3) models that can be employed in deploying the industrial sales force.

Organizing the Personal Selling Effort

How should the sales force be organized? The appropriate form depends on many factors, including the nature and length of the product line, the role of intermediaries in the marketing program, the diversity of the market segments served, the nature of the buying behavior in each market segment, and the structure of competitive selling. The size and financial strength of the manufacturer often dictate, to an important degree, the feasibility of particular organizational forms. The business marketer can organize the sales force by geography, product, or market. Large industrial enterprises that market diverse product lines may employ all three at various points throughout the organizational structure.

Geographical Organization   The most common form of sales organization in business marketing is geographical. Each salesperson sells all the firm's products in a defined geographical area. By reducing travel distance and time between customers, this method usually minimizes costs. Likewise, sales personnel know exactly which customers and prospects fall within their area of responsibility.

The major disadvantage of the geographical sales organization is that each salesperson must be able to perform all of the selling tasks for all of the firm's products and for all customers in a particular territory. If the products have diverse applications, this can be very difficult. A second disadvantage is that the salesperson has substantial flexibility in choosing which products and customers to emphasize. Sales personnel may emphasize those products and end-use applications with which they are most familiar. Of course, this problem can be remedied through training and through capable first-line supervision. Because the salesperson is crucial in implementing the firm's segmentation strategy, careful coordination and control are required to align personal selling effort with marketing objectives.

Product Organization   A product-oriented sales organization is one in which salespersons specialize in relatively narrow components of the total product line. This is

---

[22] A comprehensive treatment of all aspects of sales management is beyond the scope of this volume. For more extensive discussion, see Gilbert A. Churchill Jr., Neil M. Ford, Orville C. Walker Jr., Mark W. Johnston, and John F. Tanner, *Sales Force Management*, 6th ed. (Boston, Mass: McGraw-Hill Companies, 2000).

especially appropriate when the product line is large, diverse, or technically complex and when a salesperson needs a high degree of application knowledge in order to meet customer needs. Furthermore, various products often elicit various patterns of buying behavior. The salesperson concentrating on a particular product becomes more adept at identifying and communicating with members of buying centers.

A prime benefit of this approach is that it enables the sales force to develop a level of product knowledge that enhances the value of the firm's total offering to customers. The product-oriented sales organization may also facilitate the identification of new market segments.

One drawback is the cost of developing and deploying a specialized sales force. A product must have the potential for generating a level of sales and profit that justifies individual selling attention. Thus, a "critical mass" of demand is required to offset the costs. In turn, several salespersons may be required to meet the diverse product requirements of a single customer. To reduce selling costs and improve productivity, some firms have launched programs to convert product specialists into general line specialists who are knowledgeable about all the firm's products and account strategies. Often, as customers learn to use technology, they outgrow the need for product specialists and prefer working with a single salesperson for all products.

Market-Centered Organization The business marketer may prefer to organize personal selling effort by customer type. Owens-Corning Fiberglass Corporation recently switched from a geographical-based sales structure to one that is organized by customer type. Similarly, Hewlett-Packard successfully employed this structure to strengthen its market position in retailing, financial services, and oil and gas exploration.[23] Sales executives at *Fortune* 500 companies that utilize sales teams believe that they are better able to secure customers and improve business results by adopting a more customer-focused sales structure.[24]

By learning the specific requirements of a particular industry or customer type, the salesperson is better prepared to identify and respond to buying influentials. Also, key market segments become more accessible, thus providing the opportunity for differentiated personal selling strategies. The market segments must, of course, be sufficiently large to warrant specialized treatment.

Organizing to Serve National Accounts

To serve large and important customers, an increasing number of business marketers are establishing a national accounts program. The activities of several functional areas in the selling firm, such as design engineering, manufacturing, and logistics, can be carefully integrated to meet special customer needs.

National account management programs have been established by such corporations as Hewlett-Packard, AT&T, Dow Chemical, Union Carbide, Xerox, 3M, and Westinghouse. Why? The concentration of the business market, the trend toward centralized procurement, the rising importance of supply chain management and the ensuing need for close buyer–seller coordination of inventory and logistical support,

[23] Thayer C. Taylor, "Hewlett-Packard," *Sales and Marketing Management* 145 (January 1993): p. 59.

[24] Vincent Alonzo, *Incentive* 170 (September 1996): p. 46.

the increasing complexity of industrial products—these are among the forces that encourage the development of national account management programs.[25]

National Account Management[26]   A distinction can be made between major accounts and national accounts. A **major account** represents a significant amount of potential business. Major accounts are often served through multilevel selling with participation by salespersons, sales and marketing managers, and general managers from the selling organization. Major accounts typically are given separate attention because of their size, rather than because of the complexities of their requirements or organization. **National accounts** are both large and complex, requiring an even more elaborate selling process.

For example, Pitney Bowes' U.S. Business System Division, a producer of mailing, shipping, and copying products, serves more than one million business market customers.[27] The sales force has the following configuration:

- Fifty national account managers serve its 400 largest customers.

- 100 major account managers reach the 1,500 multilocation customers who have centralized procurement.

- 3,500 area sales representatives cover all of its other existing and potential customers (approximately one million).

The complexity that requires a national accounts response can involve three customer dimensions: Customer buying points may be geographically dispersed; several functions (for example, engineering, purchasing, and procurement) are involved in the buying decision; and several autonomous divisions exist within the buying company.

National account management provides a mechanism for responding to these three dimensions of customer complexity. For example, rather than reaching the geographically dispersed plants of the Mead Corporation through geographically dispersed sales offices, a national account management program might be devised to deal with Mead centrally.

Characteristics of National Account Programs   National account management programs vary depending on the company and the industry environment, but they do have some features in common:[28]

1. National accounts are large, relative to other accounts served by the company, sometimes generating more than $50 million in sales revenue each.

2. The national account manager's responsibility often spans multiple divisions in the selling company.

---

[25] Benson P. Shapiro and Rowland T. Moriarty, *National Account Management: Emerging Insights*, Report No. 82–100 (Cambridge, Mass.: Marketing Science Institute, 1982), see also Andy Cohen, "A National Footing," *Sales and Marketing Management* 148 (April 1996): pp. 76–80.

[26] This section is largely based on Shapiro and Moriarty, *National Account Management.*

[27] Howard Sutton, *Rethinking the Company's Selling and Distribution Channels* (New York: The Conference Board, 1986), pp. 10–11.

[28] Benson P. Shapiro and John Wyman, "New Ways to Reach Your Customers," *Harvard Business Review* 59 (July/August 1981): p. 106. See also Arun Sharma, "Who Prefers Key Account Management Programs? An Investigation of Business Buying Behavior and Buying Firm Characteristics," *Journal of Personal Selling & Sales Management* 17 (fall 1997): pp. 27–39.

3. The national account manager's team frequently includes support and operations personnel.

4. The selling activities of the national account manager span several functional areas in the buying company and may involve highly conceptual, financially oriented, systems sales.

Although the organizational structure can vary by company, Benson Shapiro and Rowland Moriarty assert that the common objective of national account management programs is "to provide incremental profits from large or potentially large complex accounts by being the preferred or sole supplier. To accomplish this goal, a business marketer seeks to establish, over an extended period of time, an 'institutional' relationship, which cuts across multiple levels, functions, and operating units in both the buying and selling organization."[29]

National Account Success Research suggests that successful national account units enjoy senior management support; have well-defined objectives, assignments, and implementation procedures; and are staffed by experienced individuals who have a solid grasp of the resources and capabilities of the entire company.[30] Successful national account programs also adopt a strong relationship marketing perspective and consistently demonstrate their ability to meet the customer's immediate and future needs. Barbara Bund Jackson asserts that "Customers making long-term commitments care about longer-term issues: a vendor's general technological capabilities and direction, its financial ability to survive, the staying power of a particular technology, and so on."[31]

Sales Administration

Successful administration of the sales force involves recruiting and selecting salespersons and training, motivating, supervising, evaluating, and controlling the sales force. The industrial firm should foster an organizational climate that encourages the development of a successful sales force.

Recruitment and Selection of Salespersons The recruiting process presents numerous trade-offs for the business marketer. Should experienced salespersons be sought or should inexperienced individuals be hired and trained by the company? The answer is situation-specific; it varies with the size of the firm, the nature of the selling task, the firm's training capability, and its market experience. Smaller firms often reduce training costs by hiring experienced and more expensive salespersons. In contrast, large organizations with a more complete training function can hire less experienced personnel and support them with a carefully developed training program.

A second trade-off is the quantity-versus-quality question.[32] Often, sales managers screen as many recruits as possible when selecting new salespersons. However, this can overload the selection process, thus hampering the firm's ability to identify quality

[29] Shapiro and Moriarty, *National Account Management*, p. 8.

[30] Linda Cardillo Platzer, *Managing National Accounts* (New York: The Conference Board, 1984), pp. 13–19; see also Thomas R. Wotruba and Stephen B. Castleberry, "Job Analysis and Hiring Practices for National Account Marketing Positions," *Journal of Personal Selling & Sales Management* 13 (summer 1993): pp. 49–65; and Andy Cohen, "A National Footing," pp. 76–80.

[31] Barbara Bund Jackson, *Winning and Keeping Industrial Customers* (Lexington, Mass.: Lexington Books, 1985), p. 105.

[32] Benson P. Shapiro, *Sales Management: Formulation and Implementation* (New York: McGraw-Hill, 1977), p. 457.

From National to Global Account Management at Hewlett-Packard

A global account management program was developed by Hewlett-Packard to provide important customers with consistent worldwide service and support. Global accounts are chosen carefully. These customers must generate product and service revenue greater than $10 million, have significant computer purchases across two or three field operations, and be in a global industry segment of importance to Hewlett-Packard.

Once chosen, these customers are served by a global account manager (GAM). GAMs are located near the customer's headquarters and assume full responsibility for directly managing H-P's relationship with the global account. Specifically, GAMs are responsible for:

- worldwide customer sales, support and satisfaction;

- assuring that Hewlett-Packard is perceived as a single company at all customer locations;

- ensuring that adequate resources and personnel are provided to realize the potential identified in the global account;

- building a close working relationship with the senior corporate executives at Hewlett-Packard who are assigned to support the account.

A central feature of Hewlett-Packard's program involves measuring performance on a global account basis rather than on a product or geographic basis. Clear cost and revenue objectives are established for each global account. Moreover, through the program, customers receive globally standardized products and services. Overall, senior executives and Hewlett-Packard's customers believe that the program is extremely successful. Hewlett-Packard is strengthening its relationships with its best customers, increasing revenue per account, reducing costs, and sharing best practices with leading-edge global customers.

SOURCE: George S. Yip and Tammy L. Madsen, "Global Account Management: The Next Frontier in Relationship Marketing," *International Marketing Review* 13 (No. 3, 1996), pp. 33–38.

candidates. Recruiting, like selling, is an exchange process between two parties. Sales managers are realizing that for prospective salespersons, they need to demonstrate the personal development and career opportunities that a career with the firm offers.[33] A poorly organized recruiting effort that lacks closure leaves candidates with a negative impression. A well-organized recruiting effort ensures that candidates fitting the position requirements are given the proper level of attention in the screening process. Thus, procedures must be established to ensure that inappropriate candidates are screened out early, so that the pool of candidates is reduced to a manageable size.[34]

Responsibility for recruiting and selecting salespersons may lie with the first-line supervisor (who often receives assistance from an immediate superior), or with the human resources department, or with other executives at the headquarters level. The latter group tends to be more involved when the sales force is viewed as the training ground for marketing or general managers.

Training To prepare new industrial salespersons adequately, the training program must be carefully designed. Periodic training is required to sharpen the skills of experienced salespersons, especially when the firm's environment is changing rapidly.

[33] Charles Butler, "Why the Bad Rap?" *Sales and Marketing Management* 148 (June 1996): pp. 58–66.
[34] Wesley J. Johnston and Martha C. Cooper, "Industrial Sales Force Selection: Current Knowledge and Needed Research," *Journal of Personal Selling & Sales Management* 1 (spring/summer 1981): pp. 49–53.

Changes in business marketing strategy (for example, new products or market segments) require corresponding changes in personal selling styles. One important trait for successful salespeople is adaptability. A recent study found that adaptable salespeople are effective at identifying cues that signify differences in purchase behavior across differing customer groups.[35]

The salesperson needs a wealth of knowledge about the company, the product line, customer segments, competition, organizational buying behavior, and effective communication skills. All these must be part of industrial sales training programs. Compared to their counterparts, top performing sales organizations train new salespeople in a broader range of areas: market knowledge, communication skills, listening techniques, complaint-handling skills, and industry knowledge.[36]

With the expansion in global marketing, firms need to include a sales training module that examines how to approach and respond to customers of different cultures. The focus of such training would be on the role of intercultural communication in developing global buyer–seller relationships.[37] Effective training builds confidence and motivation in the salesperson, thereby increasing the probability of successful performance. In turn, training helps the business marketer by keeping personal selling in line with marketing program objectives. A successful training effort can reduce the costs of recruiting; many industrial firms have found that salesperson turnover declines as training improves. Clearly, a salesperson who is inadequately prepared to meet the demands of selling can quickly become discouraged, frustrated, and envious of friends who chose other career options. Much of this anxiety—which is especially prevalent in the early stages of many careers—can be alleviated by effective training and capable first-line supervision.[38]

Supervision and Motivation The sales force must be directed in a way that is consistent with the company's policies and marketing objectives. Critical supervisory tasks are continued training, counseling, assistance (for example, time management), and activities that help sales personnel plan and execute their work. Supervision also sets sales performance standards, fulfills company policy, and integrates the sales force with higher organizational levels.

Orville Walker Jr., Gilbert Churchill Jr., and Neil Ford define motivation as the amount of effort the salesperson "desires to expend on each of the activities or tasks associated with his (her) job, such as calling on potential new accounts, planning sales presentations, and filling out reports."[39] The model presented in Figure 17.3 hypothesizes that a salesperson's job performance is a function of three factors: (1) level of

---

[35] John J. Withey and Eric Panitz, "Face-to-Face Selling: Making It More Effective," *Industrial Marketing Management* 24 (August 1995): pp. 239–246.

[36] Adel I. El-Ansary, "Selling and Sales Management in Action: Sales Force Effectiveness Research Reveals New Insights and Reward-Penalty Patterns in Sales Force Training," *Journal of Personal Selling & Sales Management* 13 (spring 1993): pp. 83–90.

[37] Victoria D. Bush and Thomas Ingram, "Adapting to Diverse Customers: A Training Matrix for International Marketers," *Industrial Marketing Management* 25 (September 1996): pp. 373–383.

[38] For a discussion of salesperson turnover, see George H. Lucas Jr., A. Parasuraman, Robert A. Davis, and Ben M. Enis, "An Empirical Study of Salesforce Turnover," *Journal of Marketing* 51 (July 1987): pp. 34–59; and Charles M. Futrell and A. Parasuraman, "The Relationship of Satisfaction and Performance to Salesforce Turnover," *Journal of Marketing* 48 (fall 1984): pp. 33–40.

[39] Orville C. Walker Jr., Gilbert A. Churchill Jr., and Neil M. Ford, "Motivation and Performance in Industrial Selling: Present Knowledge and Needed Research," *Journal of Marketing Research* 14 (May 1977): pp. 156–168. See also Steven P. Brown, William L. Cron, and Thomas W. Leigh, "Do Feelings of Success Mediate Sales Performance-Work Attitude Relationships?" *Journal of the Academy of Marketing Science* 21 (spring 1993): pp. 91–100.

FIGURE 17.3 · DETERMINANTS OF A SALESPERSON'S PERFORMANCE

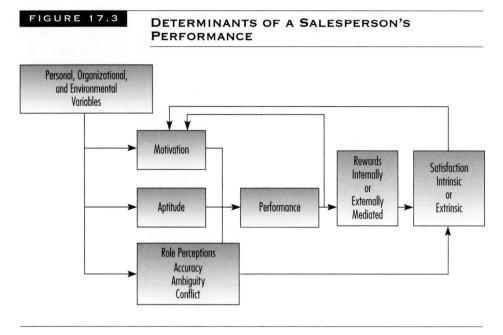

SOURCE: Orville C. Walker Jr., Gilbert A. Churchill Jr., and Neil M. Ford, "Motivation and Performance in Industrial Selling: Present Knowledge and Needed Research," *Journal of Marketing Research* 14 (May 1977): p. 158. Reprinted by permission of the American Marketing Association.

motivation, (2) aptitude or ability, and (3) perceptions about how his or her role should be performed. Each is influenced by personal variables (for example, personality), organizational variables (for example, training programs), and environmental variables (for example, economic conditions). Sales managers can influence some of the personal and organizational variables through selection, training, and supervision.

Motivation to perform is thought to be related strongly to (1) the individual's perceptions of the types and amounts of rewards that will accrue from various degrees of job performance and (2) the value the salesperson places on these rewards. For a given level of performance, two types of rewards might be offered:

1. *Internally mediated rewards:* The salesperson attains rewards on a personal basis, such as feelings of accomplishment or self-worth.

2. *Externally mediated rewards:* Rewards are controlled and offered by managers or customers, such as financial incentives, a raise in salary, or recognition.

The rewards strongly influence salesperson satisfaction with the job and the work environment, which is also influenced by the individual's role perceptions. Job satisfaction is theorized to decline when the salesperson's perception of the role is (1) *inaccurate* in terms of the expectations of superiors, (2) characterized by *conflicting* demands among role partners (company and customer) that the salesperson cannot possibly resolve, or (3) surrounded by *uncertainty* due to a lack of information about the expectations and evaluation criteria of superiors and customers.

Business marketers often utilize formal incentive programs to achieve specified customer service, sales, and profit results. Typically, an incentive program offers rewards for achieving a well-defined goal during a specified time frame. The rewards used in such programs must be well conceived, based on what salespeople value, tied to achieving desired behavior, and recognize both individual and team behavior.[40] Frequently, recognition is a key ingredient in sales incentive programs and may run the gamut from Hewlett-Packard's quarterly award for a salesperson who was particularly astute in converting an objection into an order to the elaborate sales award presentations at IBM.

Organizational Climate and Job Satisfaction[41]   Gilbert Churchill Jr., Neil Ford, and Orville Walker Jr., who contributed the model presented in Figure 17.3, also provide empirical support for some propositions that flow from the model. In examining job satisfaction in a cross section of industrial salespersons, the authors found that role ambiguity and role conflict have a detrimental influence on job satisfaction. Salespersons are likely to experience anxiety and dissatisfaction when they are uncertain about the expectations of role partners or when they feel that role partners (for example, customers, superiors) are making demands that are incompatible and impossible to satisfy.

An effective approach for reducing role ambiguity among new salespeople is a program of training and socialization that offers sufficient information about role expectations and minimizes potential confusion concerning performance requirements. Strategies that reduce role ambiguity are likely to have positive effects on sales performance as well as on job satisfaction.[42] Moreover, a socialization program that provides newly hired salespersons with a realistic picture of their job will strengthen their organizational commitment.[43]

Job Satisfaction: Managerial Implications   Salespersons tend to have a higher level of job satisfaction when (1) they perceive that their first-line supervisor closely directs and monitors their activities, (2) management provides them with the assistance and support needed to meet unusual and nonroutine problems, and (3) they perceive themselves to have an active part in determining company policies and standards that affect them. Job satisfaction also appears to be related more to the substance of the contact between sales managers and salespersons than to its frequency. Also, salespersons appear to be able to accept direction from a number of departments in the organization without a significant negative impact on job satisfaction; unity of command does not appear to be a prerequisite for high morale.

Turnover   Performance and individual differences in achievement motivation, self-esteem, and verbal intelligence may also affect job satisfaction. Richard Bagozzi notes

[40]Katherine Morrall, "Motivating Sales Staff with Rewards," *Bank Marketing* 28 (July 1996): pp. 32–38.

[41]This section is based on Gilbert A. Churchill Jr., Neil M. Ford, and Orville C. Walker Jr., "Organizational Climate and Job Satisfaction in the Salesforce," *Journal of Marketing Research* 13 (November 1976): pp. 323–332. For related discussions, see R. Kenneth Teas and James C. McElroy, "Causal Attributions and Expectancy Estimates: A Framework for Understanding the Dynamics of Salesforce Motivation," *Journal of Marketing* 50 (January 1986): pp. 75–86; William L. Cron, Alan J. Dubinsky, and Ronald E. Michaels, "The Influence of Career Stages on Components of Salesperson Motivation," *Journal of Marketing* 52 (January 1988): pp. 78–92; and Jeffrey K. Sager, Charles M. Futrell, and Rajan Varadarajan, "Exploring Salesperson Turnover: A Causal Model," *Journal of Business Research* 18 (June 1989): pp. 303–326.

[42]Steven P. Brown and Robert A. Peterson, "Antecedents and Consequences of Salesperson Job Satisfaction: Meta-Analysis and Assessment of Causal Effects," *Journal of Marketing Research* 30 (February 1993): pp. 63–77.

[43]Mark W. Johnston, A. Parasuraman, Charles M. Futrell, and William C. Black, "A Longitudinal Assessment of the Impact of Selected Organizational Influences on Salespeople's Organizational Commitment during Early Employment," *Journal of Marketing Research* 27 (August 1990): pp. 333–343.

that "Salespeople tend to be more satisfied as they perform better, but the relationship is particularly sensitive to the level of motivation and positive self-image of the person. Although management may have no direct control over the performance achieved by salespeople, they can influence the level of motivation and self-esteem through effective incentive and sensitive supervisor-employee programs and thereby indirectly affect both performance and job satisfaction."[44]

Research suggests that the leadership behavior of sales managers directly and indirectly influences salespersons' job satisfaction, which in turn affects sales force turnover.[45] In addition, another study indicates that salespeople who are managed by "high performing" sales managers exhibit less role stress and are more satisfied than their colleagues.[46] Although there are some factors that influence job satisfaction and performance beyond the control of sales managers, this line of research points up the importance of responsive training, supportive supervision, and clearly defined company policies that are congruent with the needs of the sales force.

Evaluation and Control   An ongoing sales management responsibility is the monitoring and control of the industrial sales force at all levels—national, regional, and district—in order to determine whether objectives are being attained and to identify problems, recommend corrective action, and keep the sales organization in tune with changing competitive and market conditions.

Performance Measures[47]   Sales managers use both behavior-based and outcome measures of salesperson performance. When a sales force control system is more **behavior-based,** the sales manager monitors and directs the activities of salespeople, uses subjective measures of salesperson behavior to evaluate performance, and emphasizes a compensation system with a large fixed component. Behavior-based selling measures include the salesperson's knowledge of product applications, knowledge of the company's technology, and the clarity of the salesperson's presentations to customers. By contrast, an **outcome-based** sales force control system involves less direct field supervision of salesperson activities, and employs objective measures to evaluate performance and a compensation system with a large incentive component. Sales force outcome measures include sales results, market-share gains, new-product sales, and profit contributions.

Setting Performance Standards   The standards by which salespersons are evaluated offer the means for comparing the performance of various salespersons or sales units (for example, districts), as well as for gauging the overall productivity of the sales organization. Managerial experience and judgment are important in developing appropriate standards. Importantly, the standards must relate to overall marketing

[44] Richard P. Bagozzi, "Performance and Satisfaction in an Industrial Sales Force: A Causal Modeling Approach," in *Sales Management: New Developments from Behavioral and Decision Model Research*, (Cambridge, Mass.: Marketing Science Institute, 1979), pp. 70–91; see also Bagozzi, "Performance and Satisfaction in an Industrial Sales Force: An Examination of Their Antecedents and Simultaneity," *Journal of Marketing* 44 (spring 1980): pp. 65–77.

[45] Eli Jones, "Leader Behavior, Work Attitudes, and Turnover of Salespeople: An Integrative Study," *Journal of Personal Selling & Sales Management* 16 (spring 1996): pp. 13–23.

[46] Frederick A. Russ, Kevin M. McNeilly, and James M. Comer, "Leadership, Decision-Making, and Performance of Sales Managers," *Journal of Personal Selling & Sales Management* 16 (summer 1996): pp. 1–15.

[47] This section is based on David W. Cravens, Thomas N. Ingram, Raymond W. LaForge, and Clifford E. Young, "Behavior-Based and Outcome-Based Salesforce Control Systems," *Journal of Marketing* 57 (October 1993): pp. 47–59.

ETHICAL BUSINESS MARKETING

Ethics in Selling

Here are some common scenarios that a sales person confronts. Consider how you would handle each.

Scenario 1: In an attempt to negotiate the best price, sales rep Bill Smith tries to communicate to purchasing agents that plant capacity is at a very high level because of the popularity of this product. Bill does this even when plant capacity is low.

Scenario 2: Occasionally customers of Bill Smith ask which of his products he recommends for their company. Regardless of real customer need, Bill recommends one of the more expensive items in his product line.

Scenario 3: Industrial sales representative Mary Johnson needs to make a yearly quota of $500,000. During the last month of the year, Mary is $10,000 below quota. Toward the end of the month, Mary is still about $5,000 below quota when she receives an order for $3,000. To make

quota, Mary doubles the order without telling the customer. Mary turns in a $6,000 order and makes quota. Mary decides to tell the customer that the order processing department made the mistake. She figures there is a good chance the customer will accept the double order rather than go to the inconvenience of returning the goods.

As links between their organizations and the customers, salespersons encounter situations that may lead to ethical conflicts. Consider the personal, organizational, and societal stakes that underlie each of these vignettes.

SOURCE: Joseph A. Bellizzi and Robert E. Hite, "Supervising Unethical Salesforce Behavior," *Journal of Marketing* 53 (April 1989): pp. 36–47; see also Shelby D. Hunt and Arturo Z. Vasquez-Parraga, "Organizational Consequences, Marketing Ethics, and Salesforce Supervision," *Journal of Marketing Research* 30 (February 1993): pp. 78–90.

objectives, and they must take into account differences in sales territories, for which the number and aggressiveness of competitors, the level of market potential, and the workload can vary markedly.

Recent evidence suggests that a strict reliance on outcome measures and incentive compensation plans may not produce the desired sales or marketing performance results: "The alleged automatic supervisory power of incentive pay plans has lulled some sales executives into thinking that important sales outcomes could be reasonably accomplished without intense management reinforcement in noncompensation areas."[48] Often, a more balanced approach that assigns a more prominent role to field sales managers and emphasizes behavior-based measures is more effective.[49]

Behavior-based measures also fit relationship selling—an important strategy in the business market. Relationship selling requires salespeople who can relate to a team orientation and who can focus on activities such as sales planning and sales support, as well as on goals such as customer satisfaction.

Models for Industrial Sales Force Management

To this point, our discussion has been concerned with (1) recruiting and selection, (2) training, (3) motivation and supervision, and (4) evaluation and control. Poor decisions in one area can create a backlash in other areas. One critical sales management task remains: deploying the sales force. The objective is to form the most profitable

---

[48] Ibid., p. 56.

[49] Richard L. Oliver and Erin Anderson, "Behavior- and Outcome-Based Sales Control Systems: Evidence and Consequences of Price-Form and Hybrid Governance," *Journal of Personal Selling & Sales Management* 15 (fall 1995): pp. 1–15.

TABLE 17.1	DEPLOYMENT DECISIONS FACING SALES ORGANIZATIONS
Type of Decision	**Specific Deployment Decisions**
Set total level of selling effort	Determine sales force size
Organize selling effort	Design sales districts Design sales territories
Allocate selling effort	Allocate effort to trading areas Allocate sales calls to accounts Allocate sales calls to prospects Allocate sales call time to products Determine length of sales call

SOURCE: Reprinted by permission of the publisher from "Steps in Selling Effort Deployment," by Raymond LaForge and David W. Cravens, *Industrial Marketing Management* 11 (July 1982): p. 184. Copyright © 1982 by Elsevier Science Publishing Co., Inc.

sales territories, deploy salespersons to serve potential customers in those territories, and effectively allocate sales force time among those customers.

Deployment Analysis: A Strategic Approach

The size of the sales force establishes the level of selling effort that can be employed by the business marketer. The selling effort is then organized by designating sales districts and sales territories. Allocation decisions determine how the selling effort is to be assigned to customers, prospects, and products. All these are illustrated in Table 17.1.

Proper deployment requires a multistage approach to find the most effective and efficient means of assigning sales resources (for example, sales calls, number of salespersons, percentage of salesperson's time) across all of the **planning and control units (PCUs)** served by the firm (for example, prospects, customers, territories, districts, products).[50] Thus, effective deployment means understanding the factors that influence sales in a particular PCU, such as a territory.

Territory Sales Response What influences the level of sales that a salesperson might achieve in a particular territory? Eight classes of variables are outlined in Table 17.2. This list shows the complexity of estimating sales response functions. Such estimates are needed, however, to make meaningful sales allocations.

Three territory traits deserve particular attention in sales response studies: potential, concentration, and dispersion.[51] **Potential** (as discussed in Chapter 8) is a measure of the total business opportunity for all sellers in a particular market.

---

[50] David W. Cravens and Raymond W. LaForge, "Sales Force Deployment," in *Advances in Business Marketing*, vol. 1, ed. Arch G. Woodside (Greenwich, Conn.: JAI Press, 1986), pp. 67–112; and LaForge and Cravens, "Steps in Selling Effort Deployment," *Industrial Marketing Management* 11 (July 1982): pp. 183–194.

[51] Adrian B. Ryans and Charles B. Weinberg, "Territory Sales Response," *Journal of Marketing Research* 16 (November 1979): pp. 453–465; see also Ryans and Weinberg, "Territory Sales Response Models: Stability over Time," *Journal of Marketing Research* 24 (May 1987): pp. 229–233.

TABLE 17.2	SELECTED DETERMINANTS OF TERRITORY SALES RESPONSE

1. Environmental factors (e.g., health of economy)

2. Competition (e.g., number of competitive salespersons)

3. Company marketing strategy and tactics

4. Sales force organization, policies, and procedures

5. Field sales manager characteristics

6. Salesperson characteristics

7. Territory characteristics (e.g., potential)

8. Individual customer factors

SOURCE: Adapted from Adrian B. Ryans and Charles B. Weinberg, "Territory Sales Response," *Journal of Marketing Research* 16 (November 1979): pp. 453–465.

Concentration is the degree to which potential is confined to a few larger accounts in that territory. If potential is concentrated, the salesperson can cover with a few calls a large proportion of the potential. Finally, if the territory is geographically **dispersed,** sales will probably be lower due to time wasted in travel. Past research often centered on **territory workload**—the number of accounts. However, Adrian Ryans and Charles Weinberg report that workload is of questionable value in estimating sales response: "From a managerial standpoint, the recurrent finding of an association between potential and sales results suggests that sales managers should stress territory potential when making sales force decisions."[52]

Sales Resource Opportunity Grid Deployment analysis matches sales resources to market opportunities. Planning and control units such as sales territories or districts are part of an overall portfolio, with various units offering various levels of opportunity and requiring various levels of sales resources. A sales resource opportunity grid can be used to classify the industrial firm's portfolio of PCUs.[53] In Figure 17.4, each PCU is classified on the basis of PCU opportunity and sales organization strength.

    PCU opportunity is the total potential that the PCU represents for all sellers, whereas **sales organization strength** includes the competitive advantages or distinctive competencies that the firm enjoys within the PCU. By positioning all PCUs on the grid, the sales manager can assign sales resources to those PCUs that have the greatest level of opportunity and that also capitalize on the particular strengths of the sales organization.

    At various points in deployment decision making, the sales resource opportunity grid is important for screening the size of the sales force, the territory design, and the allocation of sales calls to customer segments. This method can isolate deployment problems or deployment opportunities worthy of sales management attention and further data analysis.

---

[52] Ryans and Weinberg, "Territory Sales Response," p. 464.

[53] LaForge and Cravens, "Steps in Selling Effort Deployment," pp. 183–194.

FIGURE 17.4	SALES RESOURCE OPPORTUNITY GRID

	High	**Low**
High	**Opportunity Analysis** PCU offers good opportunity because it has high potential and because sales organization has strong position **Sales Resource Assignment** High level of sales resources to take advantage of opportunity	**Opportunity Analysis** PCU may offer good opportunity if sales organization can strengthen its position **Sales Resource Assignment** Either direct a high level of sales resources to improve position and take advantage of opportunity or shift resources to other PCUs
Low	**Opportunity Analysis** PCU offers stable opportunity because sales organization has strong position **Sales Resource Assignment** Moderate level of sales resources to keep current position strength	**Opportunity Analysis** PCU offers little opportunity **Sales Resource Assignment** Minimal level of sales resources; selectively eliminate resource coverage; possible elimination of PCU

PCU Opportunity (vertical axis)

Sales Organization Strength (horizontal axis)

SOURCE: Reprinted by permission of the publisher from "Steps in Selling Effort Deployment," by Raymond LaForge and David W. Cravens, *Industrial Marketing Management* 11 (July 1982): p. 187. Copyright © 1982 by Elsevier Science Publishing Co., Inc.

Customer Relationship Management Systems

Effective enterprise resource planning and supply chain management depend heavily on accurate and timely sales forecasts. To meet this challenging requirement, business marketing firms, large and small, are making substantial investments to automate the sales force. The early wave of sales automation tools accompanied the first generation of laptop computers—a laptop provided an important tool for the salesperson in account management, call planning, and sales forecasting.[54] Today, however, sales force automation tools have evolved into sophisticated customer relationship management systems. (See Figure 17.5.)

---

[54] Geoffrey A. Moore, Paul Johnson, and Tim Kippola, *The Gorilla Game: An Investor's Guide to Picking Winners in High Technology* (New York: HarperCollins Publishers, 1998): pp. 252–253.

FIGURE 17.5	IBM CUSTOMER RELATIONSHIP MANAGEMENT SERVICES

Personalizing customer relationships

IBM

IBM Customer Relationship Management Services

Highlights

Approaches customer contact situations as relationship-building opportunities

Integrates customer information from all contact points to create a customer-centric knowledge base

Assesses current processes and suggests ways to integrate sales, marketing and customer service

Employs e-business technologies to expand market presence

Draws on process and industry expertise to identify the best solution for your business

Building customer relationships in a new era
As businesses leverage technology to broaden their market reach and realize their full potential, traditional industry lines begin to blur. Nontraditional competitors find it easier to cross these lines and offer services and products in new markets. At the same time, more sophisticated consumers are using the Internet to seek out companies that can provide them with more personalized services. These new

trends are forcing companies to look for unique ways to service a very demanding customer set.

The effects of globalization, deregulation and competition mean that customer needs must be a priority in order to ensure a company's success. And organizations of all sizes are finding that to satisfy customers, they must transform the sales, marketing and customer service processes into one streamlined,

e-business

SOURCE: Courtesy, IBM Global Services, Route 100, Somers, NY 10589. © International Business Machines Corporation 1999.

Create a Single View of the Customer Customer relationship management **(CRM)** systems are often enterprise software applications that integrate sales, marketing, and customer service functions.[55] The goal of a CRM system is to give all customer-facing departments access to shared customer data in real time. Salespersons, product managers, customer service personnel, and the accounting staff all have the same real-time information on each customer. A CRM system provides a rich history of the performance of individual customer accounts that marketing managers can use in isolating promising customers, deploying the sales force, forecasting sales, and gauging the success of marketing strategies.

InFocus Systems, a multimedia projection vendor, implemented a CRM initiative to improve its ability to track customer relationships and marketing strategy results.[56] Before adopting the system, the sales and marketing staff lacked a unified customer database that could be used by departments across the firm. The CRM system now

---

[55] Ginger Conlon, "No Turning Back," *Sales & Marketing Management* 151 (December 1999): pp. 51–52.
[56] Ibid., p. 56.

allows the firm to conduct customer analysis, evaluate marketing campaigns, and track sales leads. In turn, the performance results were impressive: operating costs were dramatically reduced and revenue per employee nearly tripled. Compaq Computer has also implemented an advanced CRM system.

Compaq Computer's Electronic Sales Force By automating its 225-member sales force in North America, Compaq Computer has recorded impressive gains in revenues per sales rep and other productivity measures. Compaq's CEO describes the system:

> Every workday our reps log into our client/server network with a billion bytes on-line. The database includes a centralized account listing where Compaq people from different departments record their contact with each present and prospective customer. All customers have market segment codes. The system also contains marketing material, technical reports, application stories, and electronic mail. Sales managers and engineering, customer service, and other staffers can scan the network for updates. Reps typically download the material they need for their current day's meetings into a notebook computer or what they call their tool box. . . . They don't have to carry around overhead projectors and transparencies. If they want to leave a brochure or schematic with a client, they just produce one on the laptop computer. . .[57]

Although sales force automation has become a competitive necessity, many salespersons are slow to apply the technology to the selling task. In some cases, the benefits do not meet the sales rep's expectations. Some salespeople find that the greatest help is with nonselling activities like forecasting, billing, and account management—activities that support, but are ancillary to, the main selling mission. Analyzing needs, diagnosing problems, and communicating—the core of the selling process—are often felt to be more "art" than science and, therefore, less amenable to automation.[58] Importantly, the business marketing manager must carefully direct the introduction of technology to the sales force, provide the required training and support, and ensure that the technology is being applied to improve the efficiency and effectiveness of the selling process.

Summary

Personal selling is a significant demand-stimulating force in the business market. Given the rapidly escalating cost of industrial sales calls and the massive resources invested in personal selling, the business marketer must carefully manage this function and take full advantage of available technology to enhance sales force productivity. Business marketers are employing Web-enabled strategies to streamline the sales process, deliver customized information, and develop a one-to-one relationship with

[57] B. Charles Ames and James D. Hlavacek, *Market-Driven Management: Creating Profitable Top-Line Growth* (Chicago: Irwin Professional Publishing, 1997), pp. 138–139.

[58] Kim Harris, "Issues Concerning Adoption and Use of Sales Force Automation in the Agricultural Input Supply Sector," *Agribusiness* 12 (July/August 1996): pp. 317–326.

customers. Recognition of both the needs of organizational customers and the rudiments of organizational buying behavior is fundamental to effective personal selling. Exchange processes often involve multiple parties on both the buying and selling sides—the buying center and the selling center. Likewise, important insights emerge when the industrial salesperson is viewed as a relationship manager. From the consumer's perspective, relationship quality consists of trust in and satisfaction with the salesperson. Developing and sustaining profitable long-term customer relationships is a central goal of the business marketing firm.

Managing the industrial sales force is a multifaceted task. First, the marketer must clearly define the role of personal selling in overall marketing strategy. Second, the sales organization must be appropriately structured—by geography, product, market, or some combination of all three. Regardless of the method used to organize the sales force, an increasing number of business-to-business firms are also establishing a national account sales force so they can profitably serve large customers with complex purchasing requirements. Third, the ongoing process of sales force administration includes recruitment and selection, training, supervision and motivation, and evaluation and control.

A particularly challenging sales management task is the deployment of sales effort across products, customer types, and territories. The sales resource opportunity grid is a useful organizing framework for sales deployment decisions. Likewise, the business marketer can benefit by implementing a customer relationship management (CRM) system. Such tools can aid the sales manager in pinpointing attractive accounts, deploying the selling effort, and building customer loyalty. By capitalizing on advanced information technology and automating the sales force, the sales manager is better equipped to plan, organize, and control selling strategies for the business market and to provide enhanced product-service solutions for customers.

Discussion Questions

1. Relationships in the business market may involve more than the salesperson and a purchasing agent. Often, both a selling team and a buying team are involved. Describe the role that the other team members assume on the selling side.

2. When planning a sales call on a particular account in the business market, what information would you require concerning the buying center, the purchasing requirements, and the competition?

3. Some business marketers organize their sales force around products; others are market-centered. What factors must be considered in selecting the most appropriate organizational arrangement for the sales force?

4. Christine Lojacono started as a Xerox sales rep several years ago and is now a national accounts manager, directing activities for five national accounts. Compared to the field sales representative, describe how the nature of the job and the nature of the selling task differ for a national accounts manager.

5. Explain how a successful sales training program can reduce the costs associated with recruiting.

6. An emerging body of research suggests that role ambiguity and role conflict have a detrimental impact on the job satisfaction of industrial salespersons. What steps can sales managers take to deal with these problems? What role might a management-by-objectives system play in these efforts?

7. To make effective and efficient sales force allocation decisions, the sales manager must analyze sales territories. Describe how the sales manager can profit by examining (a) the potential, (b) the concentration, and (c) the dispersion of territories.

8. Hewlett-Packard Corporation has outfitted all of its 2,000 sales representatives with portable personal computers. Likewise, the firm has implemented a customer relationship management (CRM) system. Early results with the new program suggest that sales force productivity has improved—in some cases, rather significantly. First, describe some specific dimensions of the salesperson's job that lend themselves to such computer support. Second, describe the type of information a Hewlett-Packard salesperson might try to capture and record after a sales call on a particular customer account.

V

Evaluating Business Marketing Strategy and Performance

V

18

Controlling Business
Marketing Strategies

Two business marketing managers facing identical market conditions and possessing equal resources to invest in marketing strategy could generate dramatically different performance results. Why? One manager could carefully monitor and control the performance of marketing strategy, while the other could not. The astute marketer evaluates the profitability of alternative segments and examines the effectiveness and efficiency of the components of the marketing mix so that he or she can isolate problems and opportunities and alter the marketing strategy as market or competitive conditions dictate. After reading this chapter, you will understand

1. a system for converting a strategic vision into a concrete set of performance measures.

2. the function and significance of marketing control in business marketing management.

3. the components of the control process.

4. the specific methods for evaluating marketing strategy performance.

5. the importance of execution or implementation to the success of business marketing strategy.

Michael Dell, CEO of Dell Computer, emphasizes that no advantage is ever permanent: "The only constant in our business is that everything is changing. We need to be ahead of the game."[1]

Managing a firm's marketing strategy is similar to coaching a football team: The excitement and challenge rests in the formulation of strategy. Shall we focus on running or passing? What weaknesses of the opposition can we exploit? How shall we vary our standard plays? So too, the business marketer applies managerial talent creatively when developing and implementing unique marketing strategies that not only respond to customer needs but also capitalize on competitive weaknesses.

However, formulating effective strategy is only half of coaching, or management. A truly great coach devotes significant energy to evaluating team performance during the previous week's game in order to set strategy for the following week. Did our strategy work? Why? Where did it break down? Similarly, a successful marketing strategy depends on evaluations of marketing performance. The other half of strategy planning is **marketing control,** the system by which a firm checks actual against planned performance, evaluating the profitability of products, customer segments, and territories. An effective control system should measure those elements of the business that are key drivers of success in the business environment.[2]

Information generated by the marketing control system is essential for revising current marketing strategies, formulating new strategies, and allocating funds. The requirements for an effective control system are strict—data must be gathered continuously on the appropriate performance measures. Thus, an effective marketing strategy is rooted in a carefully designed and well-applied control system. Such a system must also monitor the quality of strategy implementation. Gary Hamel asserts that "Implementation is often more difficult than it need be because only a handful of people have been involved in the creation of strategy and only a few key executives share a conviction about the way forward."[3]

This chapter presents the rudiments of a marketing control system, beginning with a framework that converts strategy goals into concrete performance measures. Next, the components of the control process are examined. Finally, attention centers on the particular implementation skills that ultimately shape successful business marketing strategies.

The Balanced Scorecard

Measurement is a central element in the strategy process. As new strategies and innovative operating systems are developed to achieve breakthrough results, new performance measures are needed to monitor new goals and new processes. The **balanced scorecard** provides managers with a comprehensive system for converting a company's vision and strategy into a tightly connected set of performance measures.[4] The

---

[1] Kathleen M. Eisenhardt, "Strategy as Strategic Decision Making," *Sloan Management Review* 40 (spring 1999), p. 66.

[2] Robert S. Kaplan and David P. Norton, "Using the Balanced Scorecard as a Strategic Management System," *Harvard Business Review* 74 (January/February 1996): pp. 75–85.

[3] Gary Hamel, "Strategy as Revolution," *Harvard Business Review* 74 (July/August 1996): p. 82.

[4] The discussion in this section is based on Robert S. Kaplan and David P. Norton, *The Balanced Scorecard: Translating Strategy into Action* (Boston: Harvard Business School Press, 1996), chaps. 1–3. See also Kaplan and Norton, "Using the Balanced Scorecard as a Strategic Management System," pp. 75–85.

FIGURE 18.1   THE BALANCED SCORECARD PROVIDES A FRAMEWORK
TO TRANSLATE A STRATEGY INTO OPERATIONAL TERMS

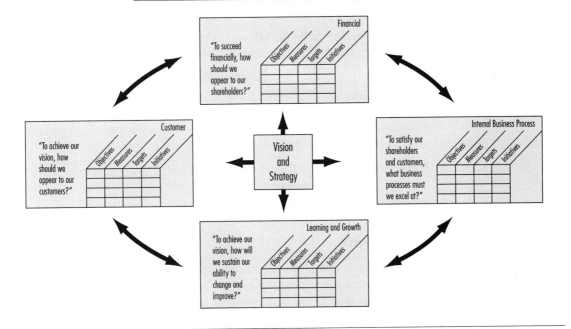

balanced scorecard combines financial measures of *past* performance with measures of the drivers of performance. Observe in Figure 18.1 that the scorecard measures the performance of a business unit from four perspectives: (1) financial, (2) customer, (3) internal business processes, and (4) learning and growth.

The architects of the approach, Robert Kaplan and David Norton, emphasize that "the scorecard should tell the story of the strategy, starting with the long-run financial objectives, and then linking them to the sequence of actions that must be taken with financial processes, customers, and finally employees and systems to deliver the desired long-run economic performance."[5]

Financial Perspective

Financial performance measures allow business marketing managers to monitor the degree to which the firm's strategy, implementation, and execution are contributing to improvements in profitability. The balanced scorecard seeks to match financial objectives to the particular growth and life cycle stages of a business unit. Three stages of a business are isolated and linked to appropriate financial objectives:

---

[5] Kaplan and Norton, *The Balanced Scorecard*, p. 47.

1. **Growth:** business units that have products and services with significant growth potential and that must commit considerable resources (for example, production facilities and distribution networks) to capitalize on the market opportunity

   Financial Objectives: Sales growth rate by segment; percentage of revenue from new product, services, and customers

2. **Sustain:** business units, likely representing the majority of businesses within a firm, that expect to maintain or to perhaps moderately increase market share from year to year

   Financial Objectives: Share of target customers and accounts; customer and product line profitability

3. **Harvest:** mature business units that warrant only enough investment to maintain production equipment and capabilities

   Financial Objectives: Payback; customer and product line profitability

Customer Perspective

In the customer component of the balanced scorecard, the business unit identifies the market segments that it will target (see Chapter 7). Those segments supply the revenue stream that will support critical financial objectives. Marketing managers must also identify the value proposition—how the firm proposes to deliver competitively superior value to the target customers and market segments.[6] Customers derive value from the total offering—the product, supporting services, and the reputation of the supplier (see Chapter 11). Figure 18.2 presents the core customer outcome measures that are used to monitor performance in each target segment. The customer perspective complements traditional market share analysis by tracking customer acquisition, customer retention, customer satisfaction, and customer profitability.

A Customer Profitability Focus   In addition to measuring the share of business a firm does with a particular customer, attention should also center on the profitability of that business. Activity-based accounting systems (discussed later in this chapter) provide a valuable tool for managers in measuring individual customer profitability. As Kaplan and Norton affirm, "A financial measure, like customer profitability, helps keep customer-focused organizations from being customer-obsessed."[7] When customer profitability is examined, managers may be surprised by the results. For example, one industrial firm found that 225 percent of its net income was derived from less than 20 percent of its customer accounts. Seventy percent of its customers provided break-even returns, and 10 percent were significant money losers.[8]

When the customer profitability measures indicate that certain targeted customers are unprofitable, further analysis is required in order to choose an appropriate response. Importantly, new customer accounts may differ from long-standing ones.

---

[6] Frederick E. Webster Jr., *Market-Driven Management: Using the New Marketing Concept to Create a Customer-Oriented Company* (New York: John Wiley & Sons, 1994), p. 60.

[7] Kaplan and Norton, *The Balanced Scorecard*, p. 71.

[8] Robert S. Kaplan, "Kanthal (A)," Case No. 9–190–002 (Boston: Harvard Business School Press, 1990), cited by Frank V. Cespedes, *Concurrent Marketing Marketing: Integrating Product, Sales, and Service* (Boston: Harvard Business School Press, 1995), p. 192.

FIGURE 18.2   THE CUSTOMER PERSPECTIVE—CORE MEASURES

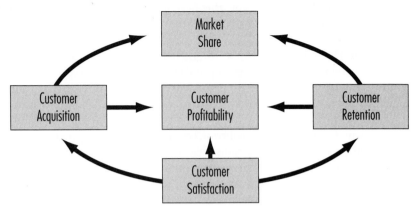

Market Share	Reflects the proportion of business in a given market (in terms of number of customers, dollars spent, or unit volume sold) that a business unit sells.
Customer Aquisition	Measures in absolute or relative terms, the rate at which a business unit attracts or wins new customers or business.
Customer Retention	Tracks, in absolute or relative terms, the rate at which a business unit retains or maintains ongoing relationships with its customers.
Customer Satisfaction	Assesses the satisfaction level of customers along specific performance criteria within the value proposition.
Customer Profitability	Measures the net profit of a customer, or segment, after allowing for the unique expenses required to support that customer.

Newly acquired customers, who are unprofitable now but represent future growth prospects, may be valuable on the basis of **lifetime profitability.** However, unprofitable long-standing customers require action. Profitability might be restored for these customers by developing more efficient processes for producing and delivering these products and services. If infeasible, then price increases may be required for the products and services that these customers use extensively.

Internal Business Process Perspective

To develop the value proposition that will reach and satisfy targeted customer segments and to achieve the desired financial objectives, critical internal processes must be developed and continually enriched. This constitutes the focus of the internal business process perspective. Processes that are critical to the creation of customer value include the innovation process (Chapter 12), operations processes involved in delivering products and services (Chapter 14), and postsale service processes (Chapters 11 and 13). Leading firms seek the best global practices for managing the control processes of their businesses.

Market-Driven Capabilities   Market-driven organizations develop superior processes in two areas: market sensing and customer linking[9] (see Chapters 1 and 9). **Market sensing** involves the processes for gathering, interpreting, and using market information. These well-developed processes enable market-driven firms to sense market trends and to act on information in a more comprehensive and proactive manner than their rivals. By contrast, **customer-linking** processes include the well-defined procedures and systems that a firm uses to achieve collaborative customer relationships. Customer-linking processes are cross-functional in nature, difficult for competitors to imitate, and are designed to provide the product-service solutions that targeted customers desire.

Building Blocks   George S. Day argues that market-sensing and customer-linking capabilities provide the foundation for building a market-driven organization:

> The overall objective is to demonstrate a pervasive commitment to a set of processes, beliefs, and values, reflecting the philosophy that all decisions start with the customer and are guided by a deep and shared understanding of the customer's needs and behavior and competitors' capabilities and intentions, for the purpose of realizing superior performance by satisfying customers better than competitors.[10]

Learning and Growth Perspective

The fourth component of the balanced scorecard, **learning and growth,** isolates the infrastructure that the organization must develop to achieve long-term goals. The three principal drivers of organizational learning and growth are employee capabilities, information system capabilities, and the organizational climate for employee motivation and initiative. To achieve desired performance goals in the other areas of the scorecard, key objectives must be achieved on measures of employee satisfaction, retention, and productivity. Likewise, front-line employees, like sales or technical service representatives, must have ready access to timely and accurate customer information. However, skilled employees who are supported by a carefully designed information system will not contribute to organizational goals if they are not motivated or not empowered to do so. Many firms, such as Federal Express and Southwest Airlines, have demonstrated the vital role that motivated and empowered employees assume in securing a strong customer franchise.

A Market-Driven, Entrepreneurial Culture   Stanley Slater suggests that a well-developed learning capability is required to develop and sustain a competitive advan-

---

[9]George S. Day, "The Capabilities of Market-Driven Organizations," *Journal of Marketing* 58 (October 1994): pp. 37–52. See also George S. Day, "Managing Market Relationships," *Journal of the Academy of Marketing Science* 28 (winter 2000), pp. 24–30.

[10]Ibid., p. 45.

FIGURE 18.3 HEWLETT-PACKARD EMPHASIZES ITS CULTURE FOR INNOVATION

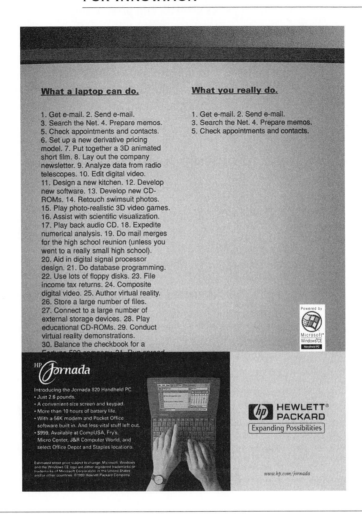

What a laptop can do.

1. Get e-mail. 2. Send e-mail.
3. Search the Net. 4. Prepare memos.
5. Check appointments and contacts.
6. Set up a new derivative pricing
model. 7. Put together a 3D animated
short film. 8. Lay out the company
newsletter. 9. Analyze data from radio
telescopes. 10. Edit digital video.
11. Design a new kitchen. 12. Develop
new software. 13. Develop new CD-
ROMs. 14. Retouch swimsuit photos.
15. Play photo-realistic 3D video games.
16. Assist with scientific visualization.
17. Play back audio CD. 18. Expedite
numerical analysis. 19. Do mail merges
for the high school reunion (unless you
went to a really small high school).
20. Aid in digital signal processor
design. 21. Do database programming.
22. Use lots of floppy disks. 23. File
income tax returns. 24. Composite
digital video. 25. Author virtual reality.
26. Store a large number of files.
27. Connect to a large number of
external storage devices. 28. Play
educational CD-ROMs. 29. Conduct
virtual reality demonstrations.
30. Balance the checkbook for a

What you really do.

1. Get e-mail. 2. Send e-mail.
3. Search the Net. 4. Prepare memos.
5. Check appointments and contacts.

HP *Jornada*

Introducing the Jornada 820 Handheld PC.
• Just 2.6 pounds.
• A convenient-size screen and keypad.
• More than 10 hours of battery life.
• With a 56K modem and Pocket Office
software built in. And less-vital stuff left out.
• $999. Available at CompUSA, Fry's,
Micro Center, J&R Computer World, and
select Office Depot and Staples locations.

HEWLETT® PACKARD
Expanding Possibilities

www.hp.com/jornada

SOURCE: Courtesy of Hewlett-Packard Company.

tage.[11] Firms such as Johnson & Johnson, Hewlett-Packard, and 3M aptly demonstrate this capability—each has displayed an ability to reinvent itself in order to close performance gaps and seize new and exciting market opportunities (see Figure 18.3). Slater argues that

> Continuous, innovative learning is most likely to occur in firms characterized by a facilitative, empowering style of leadership; a market-driven, entrepreneurial culture in which challenging the status quo is encouraged; and a structure that has flexible processes for communication, coordination, and

---

[11] Stanley F. Slater, "Learning to Change," *Business Horizons* 38 (November/December 1995): pp. 13–20. See also Stanley F. Slater and John C. Narver, "Market Orientation and the Learning Organization," *Journal of Marketing* 59 (July 1995): pp. 63–74.

conflict resolution among its own members and with its learning partners. Companies that possess all three characteristics achieve superior new product success, sales growth, and profitability.[12]

To recap, the balanced scorecard provides a series of measures and objectives across four perspectives: financial, customer, internal-business-process, and learning and growth. By developing mutually reinforcing objectives across these four areas, the scorecard tells the story of a business unit's strategy. Attention now turns to the central role that the control process assumes in business marketing management.

Marketing Strategy: Allocating Resources

The purpose of any marketing strategy is to yield the best possible results to the company. Resources are allocated to marketing in general and to individual strategy elements in particular in order to achieve prescribed objectives. Profit contribution, market share percentage, number of new customers, and level of expenses and sales are typical performance criteria; but regardless of the criteria chosen, four interrelated evaluations are required to design a marketing strategy:

1. How much should be spent on marketing in the planning period? (This is the budget for achieving marketing objectives.)

2. How are marketing dollars to be allocated? (For example, how much should be spent on advertising? On personal selling?)

3. Within each element of the marketing strategy, how should dollars be allocated to best achieve marketing objectives? (For example, which advertising media should be selected? How should sales personnel be deployed among customers and prospects?)

4. Which market segments, products, and geographic areas will be most profitable? (Each market segment may require a different amount of effort as a result of competitive intensity or market potential.)

Guiding Strategy Formulation

Evaluation outcomes provide the foundation for the integration of the market strategy formulation and the marketing control system. Results in the most recent operating period will show how successful past marketing efforts were in obtaining desired objectives. Performance below or above expectations will then signal where funds should be reallocated. If the firm expected to reach 20 percent of the OEM market and actually realized only a 12 percent market share, a change in strategy may be required. Performance information provided by the control system might demonstrate that sales personnel in the OEM market were reaching only 45 percent of potential buyers; additional funds could be allocated to expand either the sales force or the advertising budget.

---

[12] Slater, "Learning to Change," p. 18.

Marketing managers must weigh the interactions among the strategy elements and allocate resources in order to create effective and efficient marketing strategies. In order to develop successful strategies, a system for monitoring past performance is an absolute necessity. In effect, the control system enables management to keep abreast of all facets of performance.

The Marketing Control Process

Marketing control is a process whereby management generates information on marketing performance. Two major forms of control are (1) control over efficient allocation of marketing effort, and (2) comparison of planned and actual performance. In the first case, the business marketer may use past profitability data as a standard against which to evaluate future marketing expenditures. The second form of control alerts management to any differences between planned and actual performance and may also reveal reasons for performance discrepancies.

Informal Control Affects Behavior

It is important to recognize that in every organization, systems of informal controls—unwritten, typically worker-initiated mechanisms designed to influence the behavior of marketing personnel—are in operation, and have the potential to affect how the organization operates.[13] Informal controls include shared values and beliefs that guide behavior norms in the organization (for example, the belief that the customer is always right) as well as standards that might be set by the marketing department, which are monitored and have sanctions applied for noncompliance (for example, sales personnel writing reports during evening hours because the typical 8 to 5 work day is reserved for sales calls). The informal control mechanisms combine with formal control devices (the written, management-initiated mechanisms that influence behavior to support organizational goals) in affecting behavior and the resulting achievement or nonachievement of goals. It has been shown that managers often overemphasize formal control and either misread or ignore the impact of informal controls.

Research by Bernard Jaworski, Vlasis Stathakopoulus, and H. Shanker Krishnan stresses the importance of using combinations of control mechanisms, and suggests that some informal control mechanisms be "managed" to ensure high morale and group cohesiveness.[14] The researchers conclude that managers need to be more aware of the effects of informal controls and their role in shaping them. Clearly, the business marketing manager must recognize that guiding the organization to achieve its goals cannot be accomplished through the use of formal controls alone; the informal control mechanisms must be recognized and managed simultaneously. In either case, management must have an information system that will provide timely and meaningful data.

---

[13] Bernard J. Jaworski, "Toward a Theory of Marketing Control: Environmental Context Control Types, and Consequences," *Journal of Marketing* 52 (July 1988): pp. 23–39.

[14] Bernard J. Jaworski, Vlasis Stathakopoulus, and H. Shanker Kirshnan, "Control Combinations in Marketing: Conceptual Framework and Empirical Evidence," *Journal of Marketing* 57 (January 1993): pp. 57–69.

TABLE 18.1		LEVELS OF MARKETING CONTROL	
Type of Control	**Primary Responsibility**	**Purpose of Control**	**Tools**
Strategic control	Top management	To examine whether the company is pursuing its best opportunities with respect to markets, products, and channels	Marketing audit
Annual plan control	Top management, middle management	To examine whether the planned results are being achieved	Sales analysis; market-share analysis; expense-to-sales ratios; other ratios; attitude tracking
Efficiency and effectiveness control	Middle management	To examine how well resources have been utilized in each element of the marketing strategy to accomplish a specific goal	Expense ratios; advertising effectiveness measures; market potential; contribution margin analysis
Profitability control	Marketing controller	To examine where the company is making and losing money	Profitability by product territory, market segment, trade channel, order size

SOURCE: Adapted from Philip Kotler, *Marketing Management: The Millennium Edition* (Englewood Cliffs, N.J.: Prentice-Hall, 2000), p. 698.

Control at Various Levels

The control process is universal in that it can be applied to any level of marketing analysis. For example, business marketers must frequently evaluate whether their general strategies are appropriate and effective. However, it is equally important to know whether the individual elements in the marketing strategy are effectively integrated for a given market. Further, management must evaluate resource allocation within a particular element; for example, the effectiveness of direct selling versus the effectiveness of industrial distributors. The control system should work in any of these situations. The four primary levels of marketing control are delineated in Table 18.1.

Strategic Control

Strategic control is based on a comprehensive evaluation of whether the firm is headed in the right direction. Strategic control focuses on assessing whether the strategy is being implemented as planned and whether it produces the intended results.[15] Because the business marketing environment is subject to rapid change, existing product/market situations may lose their potential, whereas new product/market matchups provide important opportunities. Philip Kotler suggests that the firm periodically conduct a **marketing audit**—a comprehensive, periodic, and systematic evaluation of the firm's marketing operation that specifically analyzes the market environment and the firm's internal marketing activities.[16] An analysis of the environment assesses company

[15] E. Frank Harrison, "Strategic Control at the CEO Level," *Long Range Planning* 24, no. 6 (1991): p. 78.

[16] Philip Kotler, *Marketing Management: The Millennium Edition* (Englewood Cliffs, N.J.: Prentice-Hall, 2000), pp. 708–709; and Michael P. Mokwa, "The Strategic Marketing Audit: An Adoption/Utilization Perspective," *Journal of Business Strategy* 7 (winter 1986): pp. 88–95.

image, customer characteristics, competitive activities, regulatory constraints, and economic trends. Evaluation of this information may uncover threats that the firm can counter and future opportunities that it can exploit.

An internal evaluation of the marketing system scrutinizes marketing objectives, organization, and implementation. In this way, management may be able to spot situations in which existing products could be adapted to new markets or new products could be developed for existing markets. The regular, systematic marketing audit is a valuable technique for evaluating the direction of marketing strategies.[17]

Strategic Dialogue: Ask Tough Questions!   To offer promise, George Day asserts, a strategic option must meet several tests. "Effective business strategies are formed in a crucible of debate and dialogue between and within many levels of management. The challenge is to encourage realism in the dialogue—so critical decisions are not distorted by wishful thinking and myopic analysis—while not suppressing creativity and risk taking."[18] Day suggests that many strategies fail because the right questions are not asked at the right time during the strategy formulation process. He offers insightful questions (listed in Table 18.2) to guide the analysis of strategy options. These tough questions are fundamental to the strategic control process.

Annual Plan Control

In annual plan control, the objectives specified in the plan become the performance standards against which actual results are compared. Sales volume, profits, and market share are the typical performance standards for business marketers. **Sales analysis** is an attempt to determine why actual sales varied from planned sales. Expected sales may not be realized because of price reductions, inadequate volume, or both. A sales analysis separates the effects of these variables so that corrective action can be taken.

Market share analysis is an assessment of how the firm is doing relative to competition. A machine-tool manufacturer may experience a 10 percent sales gain that, on the surface, appears favorable. However, if total machine-tool industry sales are up 25 percent, an analysis of market share would show that the firm has not fared well relative to competitors.

Finally, **expense-to-sales ratios** are analyses of the efficiency of marketing operations. In this regard, management is concerned with overspending or underspending. Frequently, industry standards or past company ratios are used for standards of comparison. Total marketing expenses and expenses of each strategic marketing element are evaluated in relation to sales. Recall the discussion in Chapter 16 on advertising expenditures, which provided a range of advertising expense-to-sales ratios for industrial firms. These figures provide management with a basis for evaluating the company's performance.

A Framework for Marketing Control   James Hulbert and Norman Toy suggest a comprehensive framework for integrating such measures into a marketing control

---

[17] For example, see Philip Kotler, William T. Gregor, and William Rogers III, "SMR Classic Reprint: The Marketing Audit Comes of Age," *Sloan Management Review* 20 (winter 1989): pp. 49–62; and Mokwa, "The Strategic Marketing Audit," pp. 88–95.

[18] George S. Day, "Tough Questions for Developing Strategies," *Journal of Business Strategy* 7 (winter 1986): p. 68.

| TABLE 18.2 | REVIEWING STRATEGIC OPTIONS: SEVEN TOUGH QUESTIONS |

1. **Suitability: Is there a sustainable advantage?**
   (For example, assess each strategy option in light of the capabilities of the business and the likely responses of key competitors.)

2. **Validity: Are the assumptions realistic?**
   (For example, are assumptions concerning sales, profits, and competitions based on fact?)

3. **Flexibility: Do we have the skills, resources, and commitments?**
   (For example, is there an adequate sales force, advertising budget, and commitment of key personnel?)

4. **Consistency: Does the strategy hang together?**
   (For example, is it internally consistent across the functional areas in the firm?)

5. **Vulnerability: What are the risks and contingencies?**
   (For example, if important assumptions are wrong, what are the risks inherent in each strategy alternative?)

6. **Adaptability: Can we retain our flexibility?**
   (For example, if a major contingency occurs, could the strategy be reversed in the future?)

7. **Financial desirability: How much economic value is created?**
   (For example, relate the attractiveness of expected performance to the probable risk of each option.)

SOURCE: Adapted from George S. Day, "Tough Questions for Developing Strategies," *Journal of Business Strategy* 7 (winter 1986): pp. 60–68.

system.[19] Table 18.3 describes how the framework can identify the factors that caused a variance of actual product profitability from planned profitability. The objective is to isolate the reasons for the differences between planned and actual results (the variances displayed in the last column)—specifically the profit contribution variance.

In this case, management seeks to understand why actual profit contribution was $100,000 less than planned profits. A detailed analysis of the data shows that although total sales were larger than expected (22 million versus 20 million units), the firm failed to achieve its targeted market share. In addition, the firm was unable to maintain its price policy. Management must review its forecasting, considering that the market size was underestimated by 25 percent (40 million versus 50 million). To the extent that marketing strategy allocations are predicated on estimated market size, the firm may have failed to allocate sufficient effort to this market. The variances point to some real weaknesses in the forecasting process.

Because the firm did not share proportionately with its competitors in the market growth, the entire marketing strategy must be reevaluated. Management apparently underestimated the magnitude of price reductions necessary to expand volume. Clearly, annual plan control provides valuable insights into where the plan faltered and suggests the type of remedial action that should be taken.

---

[19]James M. Hulbert and Norman E. Toy, "A Strategic Framework for Marketing Control," *Journal of Marketing* 41 (April 1977): pp. 12–19; see also Nigel F. Piercy, "The Marketing Budgeting Process: Marketing Management Implications," *Journal of Marketing* 51 (October 1987): pp. 45–59.

TABLE 18.3	OPERATING RESULTS FOR A SAMPLE PRODUCT		
Item	**Planned**	**Actual**	**Variance**
Revenues			
Sales (units)	20,000,000	22,000,000	+2,000,000
Price per unit ($)	0.50	0.4773	−0.0227
Total market (units)	40,000,000	50,000,000	−10,000,000
Share of market	50%	44%	−6%
Revenues ($)	10,000,000	10,500,000	+500,000
Variable costs ($0.30 unit) ($)	6,000,000	6,600,000	−600,000
Profit contribution ($)	4,000,000	3,900,000	−100,000

SOURCE: Adapted from James M. Hulbert and Norman E. Toy, "A Strategic Framework for Marketing Control," *Journal of Marketing* 41 (April 1977): p. 13.

Efficiency and Effectiveness Control

Efficiency control examines the efficiency with which resources are being used in each element of marketing strategy (for example, sales force, advertising); effectiveness control evaluates whether the strategic component is accomplishing its objective. A good control system will provide continuing data on which to evaluate the efficiency of resources used for a given element of marketing strategy to accomplish a given objective. Table 18.4 provides a representative sample of the types of data required. Performance measures and standards will vary by company and situation, according to the goals and objectives delineated in the marketing plan.

Recall the extensive discussion in Chapter 8 of techniques and procedures for calculating market potential. Because potential represents the opportunity to sell, it provides an excellent benchmark against which to measure performance. Analysis of performance relative to potential can be made for distribution channels, channel members, and products. The results are sometimes combined with profitability control, the last area of a comprehensive control system.

Profitability Control

The essence of profitability control is to describe where the firm is making or losing money in terms of the important segments of its business. A **segment** is the unit of analysis used by management for control purposes; it may be customer segments, product lines, territories, or channel structures. Suppose an industrial firm focuses on three customer segments: machine tools, aircraft parts, and electronics manufacturers. To allocate the marketing budget among the three segments, management must consider the profit contribution associated with each segment and its expected potential. Profitability control, then, provides a methodology for associating marketing costs and revenues to specific segments of the business.

Profitability by Market Segment Relating sales revenues and marketing costs to market segments improves decision making. More specifically, say Leland Beik and Stephen Buzby:

TABLE 18.4	**ILLUSTRATIVE MEASURES FOR EFFICIENCY AND EFFECTIVENESS CONTROL**

Product

Sales by market segments
Sales relative to potential
Sales growth rates
Market share
Contribution margin
Percentage of total profits
Return on investment

Distribution

Sales, expenses, and contribution by channel type
Sales and contribution margin by intermediary type and individual intermediaries
Sales relative to market potential by channel, intermediary type, and specific intermediaries
Expense-to-sales ratio by channel, etc.
Logistics cost by logistics activity by channel

Communication

Advertising effectiveness by type of media
Actual audience/target audience ratio
Cost per contact
Number of calls, inquiries, and information requests by type of media
Dollar sales per sales call
Sales per territory relative to potential
Selling expenses to sales ratios
New accounts per time period

Pricing

Price changes relative to sales volume
Discount structure related to sales volume
Bid strategy related to new contracts
Margin structure related to marketing expenses
General price policy related to sales volume
Margins related to channel member performance

For both strategic and tactical decisions, marketing managers may profit by knowing the impact of the marketing mix upon the target segment at which marketing efforts are aimed. If the programs are to be responsive to environmental change, a monitoring system is needed to locate problems and guide adjustments in marketing decisions. Tracing the profitability of segments permits improved pricing, selling, advertising, channel, and product management decisions. The success of marketing policies and programs may be appraised by a dollar-and-cents measure of profitability by segment.[20]

---

[20]Leland L. Beik and Stephen L. Buzby, "Profitability Analysis by Market Segments," *Journal of Marketing* 37 (July 1973): p. 49.

Profitability control, a prerequisite to strategy planning and implementation, has stringent information requirements. To be effective, the firm needs a marketing-accounting information system.

An Activity-Based Cost System   The accounting system must first be able to associate costs with the various marketing activities and must then attach these "activity" costs to the important segments to be analyzed. The critical element in the process of determining the appropriate marketing costs associated with a product or customer segment is to trace all costs to the activities (warehousing, advertising, and so on) for which the resources are used and then to the products or segments that consume them.[21] Such an **activity-based cost (ABC) system** reveals the links between performing particular activities and the demands those activities make on the organization's resources. As a result, it can give managers a clear picture of how products, brands, customers, facilities, regions, or distribution channels both generate revenues and consume resources.[22] An ABC analysis focuses attention on improving those activities that will have the greatest effect on profits.

Robin Cooper and Robert Kaplan capture the essence of ABC in the following statement:

> ABC analysis enables managers to slice into the business many different ways—by product or group of similar products, by individual customer or client group, or by distribution channel—and gives them a close-up view of whatever slice they are considering. ABC analysis also illuminates exactly what activities are associated with that part of the business and how those activities are linked to the generation of revenues and the consumption of resources. By highlighting those relationships, ABC helps managers understand precisely where to take actions that will drive profits. In contrast to traditional accounting, activity-based costing segregates the expenses of indirect and support resources by activities. It then assigns those expenses based on the drivers of the activities, rather than by some arbitrary percentage allocation.[23]

ABC System Illustrated   For example, a building supply company used six different channels to reach its industrial customers.[24] Using conventional methods, selling, general, and administrative expenses were assigned to each channel on the basis of the company average (each channel was allocated about 16 percent of sales for SG&A expenses). The original equipment manufacturer (OEM) channel, under this process, was determined to be the worst of the six channel systems with 27 percent gross margin and 2 percent operating margin. Application of activity-based systems for developing SG&A costs showed the OEM channel did not use many SG&A activities—the

---

[21] Robin Cooper and Robert S. Kaplan, "Measure Costs Right: Make the Right Decisions," *Harvard Business Review* 66 (September/October 1988): p. 96. For a related discussion, see Robin Cooper and W. Bruce Chew, "Control Tomorrow's Costs through Today's Designs," *Harvard Business Review* 74 (January/February 1996): pp. 88–97.

[22] Robin Cooper and Robert S. Kaplan, "Profit Priorities from Activity-Based Costing," *Harvard Business Review* 69 (May/June 1993): p. 130. See also, Robin Cooper and Robert S. Kaplan, "The Promise—and Peril—of Integrated Cost Systems," *Harvard Business Review* 76 (July/August 1998), pp. 109–118.

[23] Ibid., Cooper and Kaplan, "Profit Priorities from Activity-Based Costing," p. 131.

[24] Cooper and Kaplan, "Measure Costs Right" pp. 100, 101.

OEMs required no advertising, catalog, or sales promotion expenses. As a result, the OEMs' actual SG&A expenses were only 9 percent of sales, well below the 16 percent average for the six channels. The operating profit, under the new analysis, turned out to be 9 percent, not 2 percent. Clearly, an activity-based costing system provides more accurate information on which to make important marketing decisions and guides management attention to those factors that have the most profound impact on the bottom line.

Hewlett-Packard has also changed its accounting system to an activity-based cost system.[25] The costs of producing a printed circuit board are determined by first evaluating the activities required to produce the board and then costing out each of the activities. For example, because each printed circuit board has diodes inserted into it, the firm analyzes the cost of each insertion. If one insertion costs six cents, then the diode insertion activity can be determined by multiplying $0.06 times the number of diodes. The remaining costs are built up in the same fashion. This costing process creates more accurate costs because the system measures the factors that truly drive costs.

Using the ABC System   An ABC system requires the firm to break from traditional accounting concepts. Managers must refrain from allocating all expenses to individual units and instead separate the expenses and match them to the level of activity that consumes the resources.[26] Once resource expenditures are related to the activities they produce, management can explore different strategies for reducing the resource commitments. To enhance profitability, the business marketing managers will need to figure out how to reduce expenditures on those resources or increase the output those resources produce. For example, a sales manager would search for ways to reduce the number of sales calls on unprofitable customers or find ways to make the salesperson more effective with the unprofitable accounts. In summary, ABC systems enable the business marketing manager to focus on increasing profitability by understanding the sources of cost variability and developing strategies to reduce resource commitment or enhance resource productivity.

Feedforward Control

Much of the information provided by the firm's marketing control system offers feedback on what has been accomplished in both financial (profits) and nonfinancial (customer satisfaction, market share) terms. As such, the control process is remedial in its outlook. Raghu Tadepalli argues that the control system should be forward-looking and preventative, and the control process should start at the same time as the planning process, checking the validity of planning assumptions at each stage.[27] Such a form of control is referred to as *feedforward control*.

Feedforward control involves continuous evaluation of plans, monitoring the environment to detect changes that would support the revision of objectives and strategies. Feedforward control monitors variables other than performance—variables that may change before performance itself changes. The result is that deviations can be

---

[25] Debbie Berlont, Reese Browning, and George Foster, "How Hewlett-Packard Gets Numbers It Can Trust," *Harvard Business Review* 68 (January/February 1990): pp. 178–183.

[26] Cooper and Kaplan, "Profit Priorities from Activity-Based Costing," p. 130.

[27] Raghu Tadepalli, "Marketing Control: Reconceptualization and Implementation Using the Feedforward Method," *European Journal of Marketing* 26, no. 1 (1992): pp. 24–40.

controlled before their full impact has been felt. For example, a manufacturer would want to monitor events that are correlated to sales and that would provide early warnings. Thus, continuous evaluation of late delivery complaints by distributors would cause an adjustment in logistics service if the level of complaints showed an increasing trend. In this way a possible loss of sales precipitated by slow deliveries could be avoided. Feedforward control focuses on information that is prognostic: It tries to discover problems waiting to occur. Formal processes of feedforward control can be incorporated into the business marketer's total control program to considerably enhance its effectiveness. Utilization of a feedforward approach would help ensure that planning and control are treated as concurrent activities.

Implementation of Business Marketing Strategy

Many marketing plans fail because they are poorly implemented. Implementation is the critical link between the formulation of marketing strategies and the achievement of superior organizational performance.[28] **Marketing implementation** is the process that translates marketing plans into action assignments and ensures that such assignments are executed in a manner that will accomplish a plan's defined objectives.[29] Special implementation challenges emerge for the marketing manager because diverse functional areas participate in both the development and the execution of business marketing strategy.

The Strategy-Implementation Fit

Thomas Bonoma asserts that "Marketing strategy and implementation affect each other. While strategy obviously affects actions, execution also affects marketing strategies, especially over time."[30] Although the dividing line between strategy and execution is a bit fuzzy, it is often not difficult to diagnose implementation problems and to distinguish them from strategy deficiencies. Bonoma presents the following scenario:

> A firm introduced a new portable microcomputer that incorporated a number of features that the target market valued. The new product appeared to be well positioned in a rapidly growing market, but initial sales results were miserable. Why? The fifty-person sales force had little incentive to grapple with a new unfamiliar product and continued to emphasize the older models. Given the significant market potential, management had decided to set the sales incentive compensation level lower on the new machines than on the older ones. The older models had a selling cycle one-half as long as the new product and required no software knowledge or support.

> In this case, poor execution damaged good strategy.[31]

---

[28] Charles H. Noble and Michael P. Mokwa, "Implementing Marketing Strategies: Developing and Testing a Managerial Theory," *Journal of Marketing* 63 (October 1999), pp. 57–73 and Nigel F. Piercy, "Marketing Implementation: The Implications of Marketing Paradigm Weakness for the Strategy Execution Process," *Journal of the Academy of Marketing Science* 26 (summer 1998), pp. 190–208.

[29] Kotler, *Marketing Management: The Millennium Edition*, p. 695.

[30] Thomas V. Bonoma, "Making Your Marketing Strategy Work," *Harvard Business Review* 62 (March/April 1984): pp. 69–76.

[31] Ibid., p. 70.

ABC Analysis Says, "Change the 80–20 Rule to 20–225"

Activity-based cost (ABC) analysis highlights for managers where their actions will likely have the greatest impact on profits. The ABC system at Kanthal Corporation led to a review of profitability by size of customer.

Kanthal, a manufacturer of heating wire, used activity-based costing to analyze its customer profitability and discovered that the well-known 80–20 rule (80 percent of sales generated by 20 percent of customers) was in need of revision. A 20–225 rule was actually operating: 20 percent of customers were generating 225 percent of profits. The middle 70 percent of customers were hovering around the break–even point, and Kanthal was losing 125 percent of its profits on 10 percent of its customers!

The Kanthal customers generating the greatest losses were among those with the largest sales volume. Initially, this finding surprised managers, but it soon began to make sense. You can't lose large amounts of money on a small customer. The large, unprofitable customers demanded lower prices, frequent deliveries of small lots, extensive sales and technical resources, and product changes. The newly revealed economics enabled management to change the way it did business with these customers—through price changes, minimum order sizes, and information technology—transforming the customers into strong profit contributors.

SOURCE: Robin Cooper and Robert S. Kaplan, "Profit Priorities from Activity-Based Costing," *Harvard Business Review* 69 (May/June 1993): p. 130. See also, Robin Cooper and Robert S. Kaplan, "The Promise—and Peril—of Integrated Cost Systems," *Harvard Business Review* 74 (July/August 1998), pp. 109–119.

Marketing strategy and implementation affect each other. When both strategy and implementation are appropriate, the firm is likely to be successful in achieving its objectives. Diagnosis becomes more difficult in other cases. For example, the cause of a marketing problem may be hard to detect when the strategy is on the mark but the implementation is poor. The business marketer may never become aware of the soundness of the strategy. Alternatively, excellent implementation of a poor strategy may give managers time to see the problem and correct it.

Implementation Skills

Thomas Bonoma identifies four implementation skills that are particularly important to the marketing manager: (1) interacting, (2) allocating, (3) monitoring, and (4) organizing.[32] Each assumes special significance in the business marketing environment.

Marketing managers are continually *interacting* with others both within and outside the corporation. Inside, a number of peers (for example, R&D personnel) over whom the marketer has little power often assume a crucial role in strategy development and implementation. Outside, the marketer deals with important customers, channel members, advertising agencies, and the like. The best implementers have good bargaining skills and the ability to understand how others feel.[33]

---

[32] Ibid.

[33] Michael D. Hutt, "Cross-Functional Working Relationships in Marketing," *Journal of the Academy of Marketing Science* 23 (fall 1995): pp. 351–357.

The implementer must also *allocate* time, assignments, people, dollars, and other resources among the marketing tasks at hand. Astute marketing managers, says Bonoma, are "tough and fair in putting people and dollars where they will be most effective. The less able ones routinely allocate too many dollars and people to mature programs and too few to richer ones."[34]

Bonoma asserts that marketing managers with good *monitoring* skills exhibit flexibility and intelligence in dealing with the firm's information and control systems: "Good implementers struggle and wrestle with their markets and businesses until they can simply and powerfully express the 'back of the envelope' ratios necessary to run the business, regardless of formal control system inadequacies."[35]

Finally, the best implementers are effective at *organizing*. Sound execution often hinges on the marketer's ability to work with both the formal and the informal networks within the organization. The manager customizes an informal organization in order to solve problems and to facilitate good execution.

The Marketing Strategy Center: An Implementation Guide [36]

Diverse functional areas participate to differing degrees in the development and implementation of business marketing strategy. Research and development, manufacturing, technical service, physical distribution, and other functional areas play fundamental roles. Ronald McTavish points out that "marketing specialists understand markets, but know a good deal less about the nuts and bolts of the company's operations—its internal terrain. This is the domain of the operating specialist. We need to bring these different specialists together in a 'synergistic pooling' of knowledge and viewpoint to achieve the best fit of the company's skills with the market and the company's approach to it."[37] This suggests a challenging and pivotal interdisciplinary role for the marketing manager in the industrial firm.

The marketing strategy center (discussed in Chapter 9) provides a framework for highlighting this interdisciplinary role and for exploring key implementation requirements. Table 18.5 highlights important strategic topics examined throughout this textbook. In each case, nonmarketing personnel play active implementation roles. For example, product quality is directly or indirectly affected by several departments: manufacturing, research and development, technical service, and others. In turn, successful product innovation reflects the collective efforts of individuals drawn from several functional areas. Clearly, effective strategy implementation requires well-defined decision roles, responsibilities, timetables, and coordination mechanisms.

On a global market scale, special coordination challenges emerge when selected activities such as R&D are concentrated in one country and other strategy center activities such as manufacturing are dispersed across countries. Xerox, however, has been

---

[34] Bonoma, "Making Your Marketing Strategy Work," p. 75.

[35] Ibid.

[36] Michael D. Hutt and Thomas W. Speh, "The Marketing Strategy Center: Diagnosing the Industrial Marketer's Interdisciplinary Role," *Journal of Marketing* 48 (fall 1984): pp. 53–61; and Michael D. Hutt, Beth A. Walker, and Gary L. Frankwick, "Hurdle the Cross-Functional Barriers to Strategic Change," *Sloan Management Review* 36 (spring 1995): pp. 22–30.

[37] Ronald McTavish, "Implementing Marketing Strategy," *Industrial Marketing Management* 26 (5 November 1988): p. 10. See also Deborah Dougherty and Edward H. Bowman, "The Effects of Organizational Downsizing on Product Innovation," *California Management Review* 37 (summer 1995): pp. 28–44.

TABLE 18.5									

INTERFUNCTIONAL INVOLVEMENT IN MARKETING STRATEGY IMPLEMENTATION: AN ILLUSTRATIVE RESPONSIBILITY CHART

Decision area	Marketing	Sales	Manufac- turing	R&D	Purchasing	Physical Distri- bution	Tech- nical Service	Strategic Business Unit	Corporate- Level Planner
Product/ service quality									
Technical service support									
Physical distribution service									
National accounts management									
Channel relations									
Sales support									
Product/ service innovation									

NOTE: Use the following abbreviations to indicate decision roles: R = responsible; A = approve; C = consult; M = implement; I = inform; X = no role in decision.

successful in maintaining a high level of coordination across such dispersed activities. The Xerox brand, marketing approach, and servicing procedures are standardized worldwide.[38]

The Marketer's Role   To ensure maximum customer satisfaction and the desired market response, the business marketer must assume an active role in the strategy center by negotiating market-sensitive agreements and by developing coordinated strategies with other members. While being influenced by other functional areas to varying degrees in the marketing decision-making process, the marketer can potentially serve as an influencer in key areas such as the design of the logistical system, the selection of manufacturing technology, or the structure of a materials management system. Such negotiation with other functional areas is fundamental to the business marketer's strategic interdisciplinary role. Thus, the successful business marketing manager performs as an integrator by drawing on the collective strengths of the enterprise to satisfy customer needs profitably.

---

[38]Michael E. Porter, "Changing Patterns of International Competition," *California Management Review* 28 (winter 1986): pp. 9–40.

FIGURE 18.4   A FRAMEWORK FOR BUSINESS MARKETING MANAGEMENT

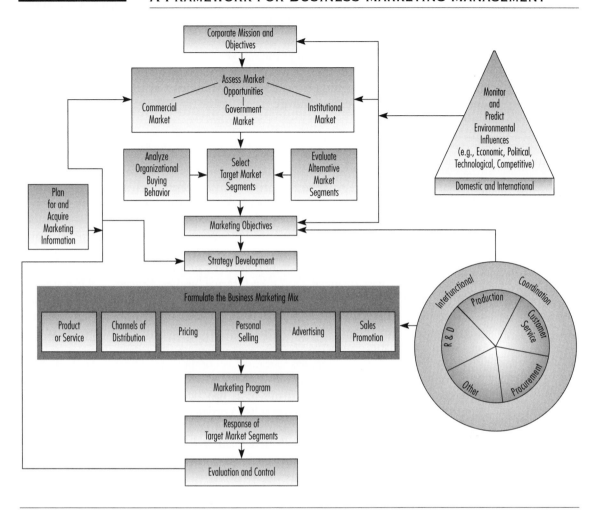

Looking Back

Figure 18.4 synthesizes the central components of business marketing management and highlights the material presented in this textbook. Part I introduced the major classes of customers that constitute the business market: commercial enterprises, governmental units, and institutions. The timely themes of relationship management, e-commerce strategies, and supply chain management provided the focus of Part II. Part III discussed the business marketing intelligence system and the tools for assessing market opportunities; it explored techniques for measuring market potential, identifying market segments, and forecasting sales. Functionally integrated marketing planning provides a framework for dealing with each component of the business marketing mix, as detailed in Part IV.

Once business marketing strategy is formulated, the manager must evaluate the response of target market segments in order to ensure that any discrepancy between planned and actual results is minimized. This chapter, which constitutes Part V, explored the critical dimensions of the marketing control process, which is the final loop in the model presented in Figure 18.4: planning for and acquiring marketing information. Such information forms the core of the firm's management information system; it is derived internally through the marketing-accounting system and externally through the marketing research function. The evaluation and control process enables the marketer to reassess business market opportunities and to make adjustments as needed in business marketing strategy.

Summary

Central to market strategy is the allocation of resources to each strategy element and the application of marketing efforts to segments. The marketing control system is the process by which the industrial firm generates information to make these decisions. Moreover, the marketing control system is the means by which current performance can be evaluated and steps can be taken to correct deficiencies. The balanced scorecard converts a strategy vision into concrete objectives and measures, organized into four different perspectives: financial, customer, internal business process, and learning and growth. The approach involves identifying target market segments, isolating the critical internal processes that the firm must develop to deliver value to customers in these segments, and selecting the organizational capabilities that will be required to achieve customer and financial objectives.

An effective control system has four distinct components. Strategic control, which is operationalized through the marketing audit, provides valuative information on the present and future course of the firm's basic product/market mission. Annual plan control compares annual to planned results in order to provide input for future planning. Efficiency and effectiveness control evaluates whether marketing strategy elements achieve their goals in a cost-effective manner. Finally, profitability control seeks to evaluate profitability by segment.

Many business marketing plans fail because they are poorly executed. Marketing implementation is the process that translates marketing plans into action assignments and ensures that such assignments are executed in a timely and effective manner. Four implementation skills are particularly important to the business marketing manager: (1) interacting, (2) allocating, (3) monitoring, and (4) organizing. Nonmarketing personnel play active roles in the implementation of business marketing strategy. This suggests a challenging and pivotal interdisciplinary role for the marketing manager.

Discussion Questions

1. Discuss why a firm that plans to enter a new market segment may have to develop new internal business processes to serve customers in this segment.

2. Not all customer demands can be satisfied in ways that are profitable to a firm. What steps should be taken by a marketing manager who learns that particular customer accounts—including some long-standing ones—are unprofitable?

3. Describe the relationships between and among the four central perspectives represented in the balanced scorecard: financial, customer, internal business process, and learning and growth.

4. Last December, Lisa Schmitt, vice president of marketing at Bock Machine Tool, identified four market segments that her firm would attempt to penetrate this year. As this year comes to an end, Lisa would like to evaluate the firm's performance in each of these segments. Of course, Lisa turns to you for assistance. First, what information would you seek from the firm's marketing information system in order to perform the analysis? Second, how would you know whether the firm's performance in a particular market segment was good or bad?

5. Susan Breck, president of Breck Chemical Corporation, added three new products to the firm's line two years ago in order to serve the needs of five SIC groups. Each of the products has a separate advertising budget, although they are sold by the same salespersons. Susan requests your assistance in determining what type of information the firm should gather in order to monitor and control the performance of these products. Outline your reply.

6. Assume that the information you requested in question five has been gathered for you. How would you determine whether advertising and personal selling funds should be shifted from one product to another?

7. Hamilton Tucker, president of Tucker Manufacturing Company, is concerned about the seat-of-the-pants approach used by managers in allocating the marketing budget. He cites the Midwest and the East as examples. The firm increased its demand-stimulating expenditures (for example, advertising, personal selling) in the Midwest by 20 percent, but sales climbed only 6 percent last year. In contrast, demand-stimulating expenditures were cut by 17 percent in the East, and sales dropped by 22 percent. Hamilton would like you to assist the Midwestern and Eastern regional managers in allocating their funds next year. Carefully outline the approach you would follow.

8. Delineate the central components of the marketing control process. Describe the role of the control system in formal marketing planning.

9. Using the marketing strategy center concept as a guide, describe how a strategy that is entirely appropriate for a particular target market might fail due to poor implementation in the logistics and technical service areas.

10. Describe how the strategy implementation challenges for a marketing manager working at Du Pont (an industrial firm) might be different from those for a marketing manager working at Pillsbury (a consumer-goods firm).

Case Planning Guide

PAGE	CASE #	CASE TITLE	Relevant Chapters																	
			1	2	3	4	5	6	7	8	9	10	11	12	13	14	15	16	17	18
483	1	Cisco Systems-Building & Marketing the Global Networked Business			★	★	★	★				★	★		★					★
509	2	S. C. Johnson's Professional Division	★	★	★	★														
511	3	Southwestern Ohio Steel Company, L.P.: The Matworks Decision	★	★	★	★														
518	4	Pfizer, Inc. Animal Health Products-A: Market Segmentation and Industry Changes			★				★	★	★									
530	5	Roscoe Nondestructive Testing			★	★			★						★				★	
538	6	Nypro Inc.: Strategy for Globalization				★			★			★								
560	7	IBM Corporation: Anatomy of a Branding Campaign					★					★	★		★			★		
580	8	W. L. Gore & Associates, Inc.—1996: A Case Study									★		★	★						
604	9	Barro Stickney, Inc.														★			★	
609	10	Beta Pharmaceuticals: Pennsylvania Distribution System						★							★					
615	11	Wind Technology							★	★	★		★	★	★			★	★	
622	12	SAP AG (1995)				★			★				★	★					★	★
631	13	Augustine Medical, Inc.: The Bair Hugger ® Patient Warming System											★	★		★	★			
642	14	Ohmeda Monitoring Systems				★	★		★	★	★	★	★	★	★				★	★
658	15	BWI Kartridg Pak							★	★	★	★	★	★						★
677	16	Ace Technical					★				★	★	★	★					★	★
692	17	Ethical Dilemmas in Business Marketing	★	★	★	★														

1

Cisco Systems

Building and Marketing the Global Networked Business

Cisco Systems, the world's leading provider of networking hardware and software for the Internet, has similarly led the way in utilizing electronic networking tools to remake its company in virtually all aspects of business operations.

The networking giant has received extensive publicity for shifting the majority of its sales and support onto the World Wide Web during the past five years. Equally impressive, have been Cisco's efforts to use networked applications to increase efficiency, cut costs, and strengthen relationships with its suppliers, partners, and employees.

"One of the things Cisco has done that is unique is the breadth and depth of our networked applications," says Chris Sinton, Director of the Cisco Connection Online (CCO), the company's centerpiece Web site. "The CCO contains key marketing, training, commerce, and support applications. It is not just a commerce tool or a support tool. It's really a portal for doing business with Cisco on the Internet."

Cisco has increased annual revenues from $1.3 billion in fiscal 1994 to more than $12 billion projected for fiscal 1999 (Figure 1). Services today account for about $1 billion of the total. After initiating online sales in 1996, Cisco now books 77 percent of its product and service orders via its CCO Web site ($28 million per day in May 1999), the majority of which automatically pass right through to its manufacturing partners. The site receives 1.9 million visits each month and Cisco is able to resolve 83 percent of all technical and nontechnical inquiries through the use of interactive agents.

Internally, Cisco's networked applications support everything from filling out travel and expense reports and arranging international conference calls, to processing purchase orders, managing product development and design, and distributing stock options. In all, Cisco estimates that its networked applications save the company approximately $600 million in annual operating costs.

This Best Practice Case Study examines how Cisco has transformed itself into a leading-edge model of a networked business, and how it uses that position to support

This case was written by Robert B. Leavitt, 1999. Best Practice Case Studies provide analysis of a particular company's services marketing strategies and practices, and are presented as educational cases for services marketing professionals. The information in this case study is believed to be reliable but cannot be guaranteed to be correct and complete. The analysis and commentary are the opinions of the author. This case study is the property of ITSMA. Reproduction or disclosure in whole or in part to other parties shall be made only upon the express written consent of ITSMA. © July 1999 ITSMA.

FIGURE 1   CISCO REVENUES 1990–1999

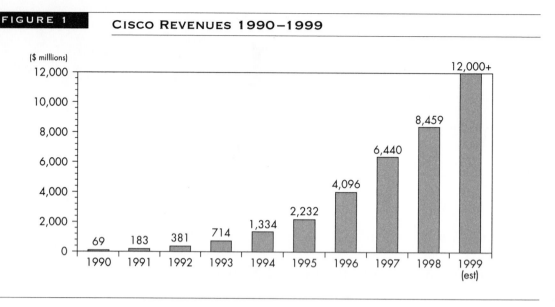

SOURCE: Cisco Systems, 1999

continued growth, rising customer and partner satisfaction, and widely recognized leadership in defining the new wired way of doing business.

Background

When it comes to being a leading player in developing the hardware and software that undergird the Internet, Cisco has always pushed the electronic envelope. Within a year of its founding in 1984, Cisco engineers were using email to bolster customer support. Several years later, the company set up an FTP (File Transfer Protocol) server to provide software upgrades and downloads. By 1992, the company had launched an on-line service, Cisco Information Online (CIO), to provide customers with twenty-four-hour access to product and support information (*See ITSMA's October 1995 Best Practice Case Study on Cisco).

Over the next several years, Cisco developers continued to add features to the CIO. In June 1994, Cisco unveiled a graphical, Web-based version of the system that greatly facilitated customer access. Usage soared as customers flocked to the site to take advantage of such features as technical tips and reports, software downloads, installation notes, bug alerts, and interactive technical assistance. Compared with long waits on the telephone to reach a support engineer, going online proved an immediate hit with the network managers who comprised Cisco's core constituency.

Even so, Cisco's dramatic growth had created a tremendous scaling challenge, especially for a company that prided itself on customer support and satisfaction. The challenge included three fundamental elements:

- Recruiting and training enough skilled engineers and support personnel to keep up with servicing the increasingly large and complex networks of Cisco's customers

Customer Advocacy at Cisco

Cisco may be the only major corporation in America with a Senior Vice President for Customer Advocacy. The position was invented by one of the company's founders, who believed that Cisco would thrive only if customer interests were placed structurally inside the company. Doug Allred, who has held the position since 1993, is responsible for professional services, support, and services for Cisco's customers and partners worldwide, as well as Cisco's internal information and network services (IS). For Allred, as for the company as a whole, supporting the customer and learning from the customer is the essence of corporate strategy. All employees are rated and given bonuses based, in part, on customer satisfaction. Customer feedback mechanisms are legion. CEO John Chambers receives daily updates on fifteen to twenty of Cisco's top customers. As important, the very direction of the company is developed hand in hand with leading customers in an "outside-in" approach. "There is nothing more arrogant than telling a customer, 'Here is what you need to know'" says Chambers. "Most of the time, you are not going to be right."

- Maintaining high-quality customer support, and increasing overall customer satisfaction
- Maximizing return to shareholders in times of
  1. Rapid growth
  2. Technology change
  3. Acquisitions
  4. Shortage of experts

With online usage for technical support growing even faster than the rapid growth of the company as a whole, Cisco executives and managers began thinking of new ways to use the Internet. Doug Allred, Senior Vice President for Customer Advocacy, was a leading force.

"What Allred said," recalls Mark Tonnesen, senior director of Customer Systems, was, "I want our customers to have input into how we support them, how we work with them, and how we do business with them. The only way to do that is to give them complete and open access to not only our processes, but all our technology and systems and how we conduct our own business."

Tonnesen himself made a critical technical breakthrough at about the same time: "We ended up meeting Mark Andreeson who started a company called Mosaic Communications. . . . And it just hit me one day that a Mosaic-like client, with a ubiquitous capability over the Internet, would be the right vehicle. It really was a light bulb thing. I looked at it from a systems standpoint. We should be able to do this with every system, whether we are talking about commerce or support or marketing. . . . Call it luck, call it vision, call it backing into it, whatever; it worked out really well."

Chris Sinton, then in charge of selling Cisco's marketing materials (training kits, brochures, baseball caps, coffee mugs, etc.), realized he could sell his material over the Internet, and was granted a short meeting to pitch his idea to the Executive Staff. "I put together a presentation that had two objectives. The first was, we have marketing products and we can sell them on the Internet, and let me do it. The second was that the Internet and the Web can mean a lot more to our company than a support tool, and we need to take a moment to think about how we are going to organize ourselves so we can really take advantage of this medium."

The meeting was a turning point for Cisco's subsequent transformation. As Sinton explains, "The whole point is that as a company we stopped and said 'look, there's a lot of opportunity here. A lot of people have a lot of good ideas, but who is going to drive this?'" CEO John Chambers and the Executive Staff approved the creation of a new planning group, led by Doug Allred, head of Customer Advocacy, and Don Listwin, head of Marketing. "So we went away as a group and created," recalls Sinton. "We thought we'd need a centralized IT organization for infrastructure. We would need a centralized marketing organization to pull it together for the customer. We'd need to tie the applications developers in better with the central IT infrastructure for the Web. So that's what we did. Then we went back and said 'this is what we want to do,' and the proposal was approved."

Scaling the Business

After its success with online technical support, the next major step was putting information on the Web to help customers review Cisco products and services, and track their orders online. Cisco's growth was pushing its sales and customer service teams to the breaking point. More orders meant more errors; more complicated products and services meant more customer confusion. Phone calls to Cisco's call center to check on orders and request duplicate invoices and other routine information were increasing proportionally to sales volume at some 70 percent annually. Scaling the support infrastructure to handle the growth was becoming impossible. Customer satisfaction levels were acceptable, but not improving.

In order to remain customer focused, the company created a CCO Customer Advisory Board for its new Internet initiative. This group included representatives from a variety of constituencies, such as network engineers, purchasing directors, and marketing managers. As Todd Elizalde, who managed the design of Cisco's online commerce tools, explains, "We tried to keep it at a strategic enough level to have decision makers, but not people so far away from the day-to-day business."

By the end of 1994, the message from the customer was loud and clear: "We need to get information faster. How much do the products cost? How can I configure the order? What's the lead time? When are my products going to arrive?"

"As such," says Elizalde, "the goal of phase one in the commerce area was to scale the business while avoiding the escalation of telephone support—to stop the phone from ringing." Elizalde's team focused on developing relatively simple commerce applications for the Cisco Web site, such as pricing lists that were updated faster than catalogs, and a Status Agent so customers could track their orders. "We wanted to increase satisfaction for customers by getting this information to them faster than if they had to pick up the phone."

A key challenge was working effectively with a nontechnical constituency. According to Elizalde, "When we started, the biggest conversation we had was that most purchasing people, our constituency, didn't even have Web browsers. We had to convince them to get a Web browser, and convince their bosses and management that Internet access was okay for people outside the engineering function."

Building the Model as We Go

From the beginning of the online commerce initiative, Cisco wanted to improve customer satisfaction at every stage of the purchasing process: product and service review, order configuration and submission, monitoring order status, billing and shipping, and even returns.

As purchasing managers began to follow their engineering colleagues to Cisco's Web site, Elizalde's commerce team looked toward a much more ambitious phase two: complete ordering over the Internet. In 1995, this was new territory, and Cisco wanted to demonstrate clear leadership. Says Elizalde, "We did not want to do a 'rip and tear' site where the customer enters an order; it comes across as an email; and someone prints it out and then rekeys it. We really wanted the customer to receive significant benefit in getting information and products much faster. So from day one we had the system designed so that the order would flow right through into our order entry system and not require anyone to touch it. It would get scheduled and dropped into manufacturing as soon as it was ready."

"It's easy to take orders over the Internet," says Chris Sinton. "But it's hard to integrate the ordering system into your backend systems, and into the manufacturing process."

Phase two represented a substantial investment for Cisco. In keeping with the corporate culture, though, the development effort was done by a small team in essentially "skunk works" fashion. "It was one of those things where if you tried to bring in too much of the company, it just would have slowed it down" says Elizalde. "So we kept it extremely focused. We had a couple of business people working on it, and a couple of technology people who pounded out the requirements. We all met with the customers a lot, taking their input into account."

To get that freedom, Elizalde and the development team promised management two things:

- Within twelve months, Cisco would get 30 percent of its product and service revenues via online ordering.

- Within twelve months, the investment would be paid off with a measurable increase in customer satisfaction for anyone using the site.

Making the system work was a significant technical challenge. "The fact that there are very few sites out there even today that have this level of integration is a big differentiator for us, but it's also been a real challenge," says Elizalde. "There is no model or path for us to follow; we're building the model as we go."

Elizalde's confidence that the team could deliver was based on staying close to Cisco's customers. "In the advisory board we had a very good representation of all our customers from around the world, and we really felt after talking to them that one in three were gong to change the way they were going to do business with us. This was not science; there was no big regression analysis. But we felt sure it was doable; we weren't going to mislead the company on that."

Commerce Takes Off

Cisco rolled out its Internetworking Product Center (IPC) in July 1996, a comprehensive suite of interactive commerce applications to allow customers to configure, price, and submit orders online. Previously, Cisco would receive up to 33 percent of its orders with wrong prices or configurations. These often required two or three days of reworking that wreaked havoc with delivery schedules, not to mention chewing up

TABLE 1	BENEFITS OF INTERNET COMMERCE TOOLS
Direct Access	A link to the most current Cisco database information.
Increased Accuracy	Allows faster price quotes and shipments.
Improved Productivity	Reduces ordering errors and delays.
Reduced Costs	Prevents costly order changes and shipping errors.
Reduced Lead Times	Correctly configured orders are sent directly to scheduling.
Order Security	All Internet Commerce Tools contain automatic encryption and password protection.
Self-Service Solutions	Internet Commerce Tools enable a range of customer self-service solutions that is not possible with traditional customer/supplier interactions.

SOURCE: Cisco Systems, 1999

precious staff time. With the IPC, error rates moved close to zero. When customers, for example, chose hardware and software combinations that wouldn't work together, or tried to purchase systems with insufficient memory, the Configuration Agent alerted them to the mistake. When the configuration was approved, the right price appeared automatically.

Additional "commerce agents" allowed customers to check lead times and expected shipping dates for Cisco products, view invoices online, access information on service options and orders, and set up action criteria to automatically receive notifications on Cisco's order status and pricing changes. On the back end, orders were placed directly into Cisco's database and queued for scheduling, reducing lead times by several days (Table 1).

Cisco's streamlined ordering process was an immediate hit. Again, customers rushed to the Web, bypassing the more traditional telephone and fax approach. Online sales totaled $837 millon during the first year of operation, and the company reached its first year goal of moving 30 percent of sales to the Internet several months early (Figure 2).

By the fall of 1997, Cisco estimated that the addition of online ordering to its continually growing online support programs would save the company some $270 million per year in operating expenses, which could be dedicated instead to research and development. From the customer side, gains were equally dramatic. Frank Santefemia, a program manager with Sprint, for example, cited a drop in his error rate for orders from 20 percent to 2 percent. Cellular One standardized the use of Cisco equipment due in large part to the convenience and efficiency of the CCO.

Selling the Sales Force

As online sales took off, a question of compensation for the sales force emerged: If customers simply go to Cisco's Web site to place their orders, would their sales representatives get credit?

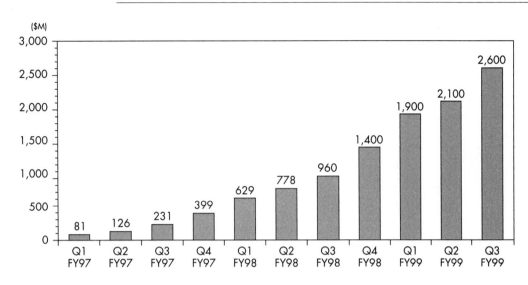

FIGURE 2 **CCO INTERNET COMMERCE REVENUE**

SOURCE: Cisco Systems, 1999

From the beginning, the answer was "yes." Todd Elizalde explains: "This is aimed at getting the order placement process out of the hair of our salespeople and letting them instead focus on really adding value and solving problems with the customer. We wanted them to feel comfortable that if their customer placed an order over the Internet, with or without their knowledge, they would get credit for it. So when they develop a new customer now, they just put them on the CCO and say 'here you go.'"

The shift has been dramatic. Before the CCO, Cisco salespeople spent a lot of their time returning customer calls about order status, figuring out prices for different products, and struggling through ever more complicated network configurations.

Today, customers do most of that work themselves, using the Web site, allowing the sales force to focus much more on building new customer relationships, managing existing accounts in a more proactive fashion, and providing higher value services. The results are increased sales force satisfaction and a 15 percent increase in sales force productivity. In all, Cisco sales per employee are extremely high for the industry at about $650,000.

Integrating the Global Networked Business

With Internet commerce exploding, senior managers throughout the company moved aggressively to shift more of their operations online as well.

On the technical support side, Cisco has continued to use networking and interactive tools to expand its offerings. The company's Electronic Customer Care system

TABLE 2	POST-SALES TECHNICAL SUPPORT ON CCO

Registered Users have twenty-four-hour, seven-day access to critical support tools, including:

- Open Q & A Forum, a powerful search engine for the Cisco support database
- Case Open, Case Query, and Case Update applications for Technical Assistance Center case management
- Bug Toolkit and Internetwork Operating System (IOS) Upgrade Planner, for developing IOS strategies and tactics
- Software updates, upgrades, and release notes
- Technical tips and references, including known problem and workaround reports, installation notes, and case studies

SOURCE: Cisco Systems, 1999

includes a series of features that enable users to solve most of their problems online without any need for Cisco technical staff.

Standard features of the initial early-1990s Cisco Information Online system have grown dramatically. Software downloads in March 1999 totaled about 372,000. In the same period, customers and partners used technical support applications on the Web 380,000 times, compared with only 55,000 calls to the Technical Assistance Center (Table 2).

The Network Analysis Toolkit, which automatically collects critical network information and generates Web-based reports concerning a customer's network performance, represents a more recent advance. As Ethan Thorman, Director of Services Marketing for telecommunications and Internet service providers, explains: "This gives us a window of ongoing visibility into what's going on with the customer's network, helping us dramatically enhance the level of our proactive support."

These interactive tools are helping Cisco move to an even higher level of service where support teams link together the interactive support tools on the Web with electronic network audits and regular design reviews. "When you combine solid network design with solid operational procedures and interactive technical support," says Thorman, "you can then move to guaranteeing network availability because you have covered all the bases. In the service provider world, network availability is the key."

Online Training and Knowledge Development

Cisco now coordinates most of its training initiatives online. Information for all of Cisco's extensive worldwide training activities resides on the CCO, and the site logs more than 18,000 seminar registrations per month. Training documents and kits are available through Cisco's online Learning Store.

To further its online offerings, the company recently unveiled the Cisco Interactive Mentor (CIM), a combination CD-ROM and Web site mentoring program. With the CIM, programmers and network administrators can run simulations of network configuration problems, and gain experience in troubleshooting network problems. It is like having a network lab on a CD. The Web site includes a dedicated technical

TABLE 3	CCO USER TYPES
Guests	Any user receives complete access to the extensive public part of CCO, including news and information about Cisco's products and services, business solutions, technical support, training programs, financial data, employment, partners, and resellers.
Cisco Customers	Cisco customers who have a SMARTnet or Comprehensive support contract with Cisco. Registered customers can access all CCO tools for products and ordering, software planning and downloading, and technical assistance. Customers with an Internet Commerce agreement are able to place and manage orders online.
Cisco PICA Customers	Cisco customers who receive service from an authorized Cisco Partner.
Cisco Partners	Cisco sales partners who have a Reseller, Distributor, or OEM Service Agreement with Cisco.
Premier Resellers	Authorized resellers who have a Reseller Service agreement with Cisco.

SOURCE: Cisco Systems, 1999

assistance center where participants post questions and answers and receive updates for the CD-ROMs.

"One of the things we get a lot of from customers," says Ethan Thorman, "is that they feel they don't have enough knowledge about the rapidly evolving technologies. Frequently they want to outsource elements to Cisco because they simply can't hire and train fast enough to keep pace with the technology."

The knowledge gap represents an opportunity for Cisco to expand its service business, but the company remains focused primarily on product sales. Knowledge development, like all of Cisco's service offerings, is designed first and foremost to support its core focus. Rather than jump on the outsourcing possibilities, Cisco has promoted and developed expanded knowledge transfer initiatives. As Thorman notes confidently, "a knowledgeable customer is much more likely to go with Cisco."

"We also put a lot of energy into developing the knowledge of our channel and professional service partners," says Thorman. "We rely heavily on these partners to help customers overcome the knowledge challenges." (Table 3)

Merge in Transit

At the other end of the supply chain, Cisco used internetworking tools to rationalize complex shipping operations with a new system called Merge in Transit. Because Cisco outsources the majority of its production—a large order from a customer may include parts from many suppliers and locations. "The frustrating part for the customers is that they could be getting fifteen different shipments for their order over a two-month period," says Todd Elizalde. "Customers were telling us they want one single shipment."

The new system works with several major international carriers to coordinate each multipart shipment, virtually merging it, so the products all arrive the same day on the customer's dock. Merge in Transit is especially valuable for Cisco's international partners and customers, who face longer delivery times, different duty rates, and other problems with international shipping.

Organizing Merge in Transit meant bringing together not only a multifunctional team within Cisco—including representatives from customer service, electronic commerce, information systems, manufacturing, and logistics—but also the outside manufacturers and major shippers such as Federal Express. "We had to develop very strong information links with all of them to coordinate this," according to Elizalde. "It's a fabulous project, and no one else is doing this to my knowledge."

Reseller Marketplace

For Cisco's resellers, the company formed the "Reseller Marketplace," a section of the CCO Web site designed to help resellers gain expertise in designing networking solutions for their customers. The site offers full access to Cisco product information, configuration design rules, product comparison tools, and, of course, electronic ordering capabilities.

Because many of the resellers primarily sell PCs and printers, their networking expertise is often limited. As Elizalde explains, "Trying to educate them directly about which Cisco products are appropriate is just not going to scale. So we leverage the Internet to provide them with tools that no other vendors are giving them. . . . The reseller is now in the position of knowing the customer needs a networking solution, and is saying, 'I'm not an expert on that, but I can go on the Cisco site. They have tools that make me look like an expert. Nobody else does that for me.'"

Configuration Express

For service provider customers (telecommunications firms and Internet service providers), Cisco recently created an online "Configuration Express." When service providers create a new Point of Presence (POP) location for local access to the Internet, they normally use technical support personnel to configure the equipment for each individual location. With service providers adding dozens or even hundreds of new locations as they build their services, the onsite technical support is extremely expensive. Cisco's Configuration Express allows the customer to preconfigure all the necessary information via the Internet before the products even ship from Cisco. This enables lesser-paid purchasing staff to coordinate the work, and translates into substantial cost savings for the customer.

Workforce Optimization

Internally, virtually all of Cisco's operations run via an interactive intranet site, the Cisco Employee Connection (CEC). This vast but easy-to-navigate site enables the firm's 18,300 employees to process expense reports, register for and participate in training courses, receive corporate news, access and process human resource documents, sign up for company stock options, and obtain all customer and partner information.

For example, the Managers Access Toolkit gives team managers immediate access to all necessary business information for their staff, including hiring date, salary, stock options, and performance reviews and ratings. It includes tools that show managers their employees' compensation level compared to the median for their grade, and their "walkaway" value with all their stock.

Cisco's Web Viper allows employees not only to search a real-time employee directory, but also to view the reporting relationships and organization charts for each employee—in real time as well.

In all, Cisco estimates it saves more than $35 million annually as a direct result of its networked employee service applications.

Globalizing the CCO

Any company with a Web site is, de facto, "global," since the site is accessible around the world. Functioning effectively in an online global marketplace, however, is rather more complicated. In March 1997, Cisco unveiled a broad range of globalized capabilities for its Cisco Connection Online Web site. These capabilities included:

- Local-Language Content: Translation of selected Web pages and graphics into fourteen languages, including Chinese, French, German, Japanese, Russian, Spanish, and eight others.

- Country-Specific Content: Presentation of country and region-specific information such as local Cisco offices, service and support contacts, certified sales and support partners, seminars, events, and training courses.

- Regional Web Access: Installation of CCO remote distribution servers with local Points of Presence (POPs) around the world so international users can access CCO services through dedicated links in such countries as China, The Netherlands, Japan, and France.

Today, a "Countries/Languages" button on the CCO homepage brings users to a global index page with links to fifty-two Country pages (including the United States), as well as links to nine servers around the world.

Cisco's Mexico homepage, for example, is written in Spanish, and includes links to Cisco offices in Mexico, product and sales information, Cisco partners and distributors, Cisco-related events, and support services. All of that information is provided in Spanish.

In all these ways, Cisco's globalization initiative has greatly enhanced Web functionality for international customers, in terms of faster Internet access, local language information, and more direct linkages to local and regional sales and support networks.

Enhancing Global Performance

Having localized the front-end content of CCO for its worldwide customers and partners, Cisco is now working to add greater integration and even faster performance to its international servers.

Currently, the servers just contain three or four levels of content, and not the more sophisticated technical support or e-commerce applications. These applications reside on the company's main server in San Jose, California, which slows fully interactive operations for users outside the United States.

A November 1998 CCO Advisory Board meeting, for example, highlighted complaints concerning the performance of the CCO's online ordering tools for European customers. Mark Tonnesen explains: "From the customer perspective it's a performance issue, but from our perspective it's a technical issue. You have an e-commerce ordering tool, where do those orders go? They go into your back-end ERP system. Guess what, we only have one and it sits in San Jose."

"So the first step is to put more of the application intelligence on the servers in Europe. This will let the customer do things like validate their shipping address, billing address, contact information, terms and conditions, discount rates. Generally you have to interrogate a customer database somewhere to do all this, so we will push that to the front end. Also they'll be able to do things like check the product configuration and the manufacturability of the order, which typically resides in your manufacturing system. Everything up to the point where you say 'submit this order' we're going to push to the front end. So that will all happen locally, which will be great. But then they hit cement, and there will be a lag time, because to submit the order they have to go back to the San Jose server. We're working right now on an architecture to distribute that as well, we just haven't figured it out yet."

Integration and Customer Focus

"It's very easy, particularly for a large and decentralized company, to deliver a lot of value on their Web site in many different ways but all very stovepiped," according to CCO Director Chris Sinton. "What the customer experiences is disintegration. It's not clear to the customer either that all this value is here, or how to navigate from one value to another value, one application to another."

The sheer scale of Cisco's Web site makes focus and integration an enormous challenge (Figure 3). By the end of May 1999, the CCO included approximately 195,000 files, more than 2,000 separate applications, and some 10 million pages. Chris Sinton and his CCO team are responsible for integrating the work of more than 400 content developers worldwide.

As Sinton explains: "We are putting on the Internet a business process that moves from awareness, information, and interest into planning and designing a network; purchasing it, implementing it, and operating it; and then repurchasing. It's a full spectrum. And it all has to flow in a customer-focused and task-based way. Add in the complexity that we are speaking to different markets: enterprise, service providers, small and medium-sized business, and consumer. We really have to work together on the messages we deliver and on the way the applications come together."

During the first few years, CCO development was driven by the company's functional groups. The technical support group focused on support solutions, content, and applications. The marketing group focused on marketing applications. The commerce and customer service group focused on commerce.

From the customer and partner perspective, this began to cause problems. According to Mark Tonnesen, "The customer was saying, 'look, you have thousands of applications, thousands of pages of content, and it's too confusing. There is too

| FIGURE 3 | THE SCOPE OF CCO |

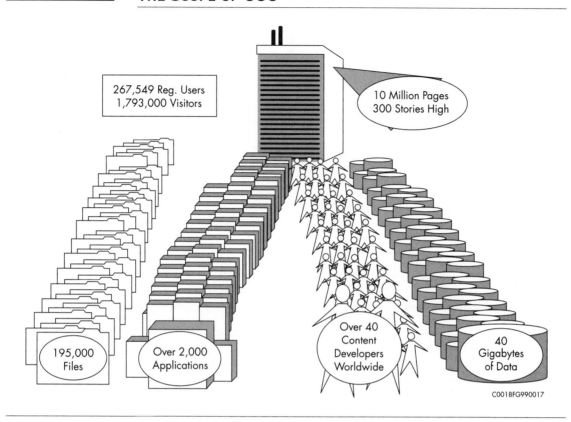

267,549 Reg. Users
1,793,000 Visitors

10 Million Pages
300 Stories High

195,000
Files

Over 2,000
Applications

Over 40
Content
Developers
Worldwide

40
Gigabytes
of Data

C0018FG990017

SOURCE: Cisco Systems, 1999

much there. Why can't you make this custom to me, and speak to my markets, to my challenges?'"

"Let's say you are a large enterprise customer. When you come into CCO you don't want to see one huge silo for commerce and another huge silo for support. You want to see everything in one place for you, the customer-centric view. But that's a very different orientation, strategy and execution."

In 1998, Cisco established the CCO Business Council to provide a formal, cross-functional management team to ensure greater integration and more intense customer and line of business focus for the CCO. With the Business Council, Cisco has taken an important step to revitalize its high-level focus on Web development strategy.

CCO Business Council

The Business Council brings together senior executives representing Cisco's lines of business and major functions, including:

- Service Provider Markets
- Enterprise Markets

FIGURE 4	CCO BUSINESS STRUCTURE

Business	Information Technology

CCO Business Council
Ensure alignment with corporate objectives—Direct Functional Teams—
Endorse Functional proposals—Provide input to Functional Teams—Evangelize CCO direction

Core CCO Internet Solutions Team
Develop strategic direction and initiatives—Direct Functional Teams and execute against plans—
Serve as escalation path—Evangelize CCO direction—Plan, integrate, and coordinate cross-Cisco
projects—Communicate to Business Council—Leverage results of various projects—
Assess new ideas and technologies—Monitor competition—Coordinate with Architecture teams

LOB CCO Teams
Define LOB business and go-to-market strategies—Develop LOB CCO business requirements—
Provide business expertise to CCO Core Team—Integrate CCO plans with business processes—
Create and manage content

CCO Development Teams
Gather requirements—Create project plans—Develop, implement, and enhance applications—
Measure results

SOURCE: Cisco Systems, 1999

- Small and Medium Markets
- Consumer Markets
- Corporate Marketing
- Channels
- Customer Service
- Technical Assistance Center
- Information Technology

The Business Council meets monthly, and maintains oversight responsibility for all CCO development teams.

"Most important," says Chris Sinton, "is the Business Council's mandate to strengthen the integration of the functional and lines of business teams. For example, the head of the commerce function is Todd Elizalde. He develops the vision, strategic direction and initiatives, and shows the company what is possible for his function. Also, he gathers requirements from the customers to make it work for them. But the lines of business are the experts in their markets and their markets' needs for the function.

TABLE 4	CCO BUSINESS COUNCIL SUCCESS FACTORS

The Council will be successful when . . .

- CCO balances the corporate brand and meets individual market needs.
- CCO has a more significant business impact.
- CCO development is prioritized across LoBs (Lines of Business) and functions.
- there is a faster pace for CCO development.
- integration of LoB and functional work is enhanced.

SOURCE: Cisco Systems, 1999

They have to provide requirements back into the function so it works for their markets. It may sound really obvious, but thinking about it, saying it, and doing it are very far apart."

It didn't take long for the Business Council to bring to light duplicative and potentially conflicting initiatives coming from different sides of the business. Dynamic marketing projects for Cisco resellers designed by the channels function conflicted with separate marketing messages and technologies that the small and medium business group had underway for some of the same companies. In wanting to create more personalized "extranets" for Hewlett-Packard, according to Mark Tonnesen, "We found three groups doing the same thing out of three different parts of the organization, all wanting to deliver their system over the CCO Web site. They would have overrun each other and just confused the customer."

The Business Council has succeeded, according to Sinton, because it is top down. "Because we are creating a portal for all types of business interactions and it's all highly cross-functional, it wouldn't work if there is just one function leading it, or just one line of business leading it. You've got to get everyone else to play, from manufacturing to finance to marketing, to customer service. That's not easy to do unless it's top down, and everyone buys into the vision."

Strategic Customization

By mid-1997, the goal of Doug Allred, Senior Vice President of Customer Advocacy, to extend Cisco's information technology systems outward to all the company's customers and partners, had largely been accomplished. The majority of Cisco's sales, support, and marketing interactions were taking place online, and the CCO was contributing substantially to corporate growth, cost savings, and increasing customer satisfaction.

With the Internet, however, yesterday's radical advances are taken for granted today. Although Cisco remained far ahead of the pack in terms of the scale and functionality of its online operations, Internet-based ordering and support were becoming more common.

As the company continued to explore ways to streamline its interactions with customers, Todd Elizalde's group initiated phase three, Integrated Ordering, of its online commerce strategy (Figure 5).

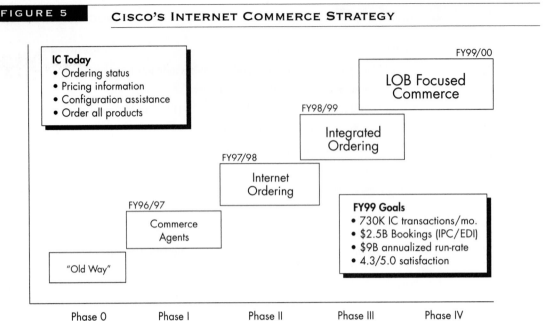

FIGURE 5   CISCO'S INTERNET COMMERCE STRATEGY

SOURCE: Cisco Systems, 1999

The Integrated Ordering, or Integrated Commerce Solution, allows Cisco's largest resellers to fully integrate all the CCO commerce tools—such as price lists, order status tool, and product and network configuration rules—right into their own internal information systems. The goal was to move all the business process savings that Cisco itself already received from online ordering back into their customers' systems as well.

The biggest technical hurdle was dealing with the fact that most of Cisco's customers, not surprisingly, have different Enterprise Resource Planning (ERP) systems. Creating a standard template that any company could use was extremely challenging.

"We sat down with about fifteen customers before coming up with a solution," says Elizalde. "They install a new server behind their firewall, within their Intranet. Once a day it refreshes a set of databases on it that contain our pricing, configuration rules, etc. There is also a series of APIs (Application Program Interfaces) on that server. So the customers integrate the APIs into their internal information system."

Setting up the whole system at the customer's site is obviously not a minor task. Total investment on the partner side is about $50,000 for all hardware and integration costs.

The NEC Test

The first test of the new system was with the NEC Corporation in Tokyo, in late 1997. Elizalde explains: "They had very rigorous demands, and this was a fairly new relationship with Cisco," so both sides had a lot riding on it. But the test proved extremely

FIGURE 6   **CCO INTERNET COMMERCE USAGE HISTORY**

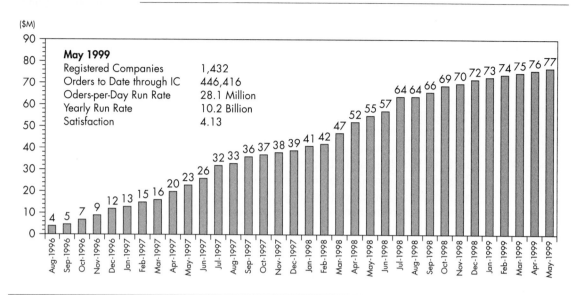

May 1999
Registered Companies	1,432
Orders to Date through IC	446,416
Oders-per-Day Run Rate	28.1 Million
Yearly Run Rate	10.2 Billion
Satisfaction	4.13

SOURCE: Cisco Systems, 1999

successful. "They did an absolutely meticulous integration," says Elizalde, and the extra effort on the Cisco side made it an excellent trial run for moving ahead with phase three.

"The investment generally pays for itself within a year or less," according to Elizalde, "because it cuts so much process out of their purchasing system." NEC itself now submits a full 100 percent of its orders over the Integrated Commerce Solution (ICS)."

With such a large investment, though, Cisco builds in a "structural loyalty" with its customers. Switching costs for the customer to move to another vendor becomes extremely high.

With the NEC system working well, Cisco targeted another twenty customers with which to launch the new system. Mark Tonnesen explains Cisco's strategy: "We're not picking them by revenue, it's more by strategic alliance and relationships. [The group] cuts across the business lines; we have some in small and medium business, some in enterprise, and a large part in service providers. The idea is that we will learn a lot about what to present, what not to present, and how to present it in the different lines."

Keeping the System Running

The overwhelming growth of Cisco's online systems has made infrastructure development an ongoing challenge. "Every estimate you come up with you blow right past it," says Mark Tonnesen. Through most of the 1990s, the company simply added on to the existing architecture with a network of large Sun Solaris Enterprise servers. Although the system "worked," it became increasingly fragile. "We were tending toward a highly mainframe environment," according to Tonnesen, and thus "creating a single point of failure."

One response has been developing more of a "segmented server model." This means that the various main functions of the CCO, such as software distribution, product and service information, and electronic commerce, now all run on separate machines. "By distributing the functions to different environments," explains Tonnesen, "we can better manage and better create redundancy from a cost perspective. Things like high availability, fail-over, and disaster recovery are all facilitated more nicely as the infrastructure is segmented."

As the system has gone global, Cisco has also outsourced a great deal of the international Web hosting to Digital Island, a California-based network support company. Digital Island provides the software and content hosting services for Cisco's non-U.S. servers. Cisco continues to manage the secure portion of the network and infrastructure, but company managers believe it is easier and cheaper to outsource the rest.

In all, Cisco will spend between $10 and $15 million on CCO-related hardware, software, and integration services over the next eighteen months, according to Tonnesen.

Reengineering the basic infrastructure while constantly adding new features to the system is a delicate balancing act. "We have so many ideas, and so many things to do to add functionality to the site," says Tonnesen, "but we also have this infrastructure work we have to do. At the end of the day the customers don't see much benefit for it. They do benefit in terms of performance and reliability, but in terms of features and functionality, $10 million can go a long way in other areas."

"You don't get much credit for infrastructure," Tonnesen notes, "but there is a lot of exposure if you do it wrong."

Cisco's current philosophy with regard to CCO infrastructure is to remain very flexible in terms of technology and partners. "Things change so quickly with technology and with customer expectations," says Tonnesen. "You can invest a couple of million dollars in a technology and then find out that you have to change. That's a lot to throw away. So we're trying to stay very broad-based, very standards-based, very open architecture, and work with a lot of vendors and a lot of partners. We buy solutions in each domain area, but there is no be-all, end-all solution."

Marketing the CCO

"Just because you build it, that doesn't mean they will come," says Chris Sinton. "Marketing the medium" has been a top priority for Cisco since the creation of the CCO.

Given the centrality of the CCO to virtually all Cisco operations, the CCO marketing team is surprisingly small. John O'Donoghue leads the team, which includes six other full-time professionals, plus an administrative assistant and several contract writers. The group has grown substantially, however, as the CCO itself has grown. Four years ago it consisted of just two people.

The group's core mission, according to O'Donoghue, is promoting "new world behavior," working with customers to help and push them to integrate the CCO into all aspects of their routine business operations. "We are trying to change behavior from 'old world,' like faxing in your order, to 'new world,' like ordering online."

FIGURE 7   CCO VISION

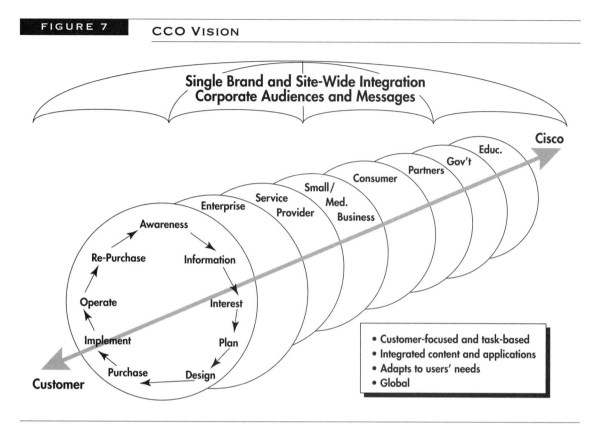

Single Brand and Site-Wide Integration
Corporate Audiences and Messages

Cisco

Educ.

Gov't

Partners

Consumer

Small/
Med.
Business

Service
Provider

Enterprise

Awareness

Re-Purchase   Information

Operate   Interest

Implement   Plan

Purchase   Design

Customer

- Customer-focused and task-based
- Integrated content and applications
- Adapts to users' needs
- Global

SOURCE: Cisco Systems, 1999

Promotion of the CCO has involved a broad range of traditional marketing activities, including organizing seminars, producing white papers, and the creation of a telemarketing program to contact potential customers, generate awareness of and interest in the CCO, and register new users. Needless to say, the team uses the Web as a main vehicle for distributing most of its information, thereby saving thousands of dollars in printing and mailing costs, as well as cutting time in disseminating the information.

Direct email campaigns have proven very effective. As online ordering got underway in 1996, a campaign targeted to registered users of the CCO generated "a high response," according to Chris Sinton. That campaign provided 1,000 leads to a new telesales force of Internet Commerce (IC) representatives. The IC reps followed up with calls to initiate formal Internet Commerce agreements with the customers, enabling them to order online.

Today, CCO customer initiatives are triggered automatically. As soon as a new billing address is entered into the Cisco database, that customer is sent a package outlining the benefits and mechanisms of Internet Commerce. As soon as a customer signs up for a SMARTnet service contract, he or she receives a package on CCO support offerings.

Customizing CCO Marketing

As Cisco continues to focus on customizing CCO for different customers and lines of business, the marketing team stresses customer-based, direct marketing initiatives. "The key is that we are not being stovepiped," says O'Donoghue. "Even though we are releasing new features and functionality all the time, we have to focus on packaging our marketing efforts so we are developing the relationship and not inundating the customer with information they might not think is valuable. . . . We want to get to the point of knowing who they are so well that we can anticipate what they need."

The expansion of the marketing team has focused especially on helping Cisco move beyond its traditional base of enterprise customers. Recently hired program managers focus on the service provider and small and medium-sized business sectors.

The CCO Advisory Board meetings play a central role in the marketing team's program, just as they do for commerce, technical support, and other CCO groups. From the marketing perspective, the meetings provide vital feedback from customers on major complaints, emerging needs, and how they want to be communicated with.

For example, a recent meeting on CCO technical support highlighted the frustration of many engineers that Cisco was sending them too much "marketing fluff," according to O'Donoghue. "The feedback was, 'we like snippets of information. Get to the point and if it is interesting or relates to us, let us know how to get more detailed information.'" From that meeting, the marketing team developed a new online and email newsletter with brief technical notes and live URL links to more detailed presentations. The response, according to O'Donoghue, has been extremely positive.

Marketing Incentives

Many of the demand generation programs rely on incentives. An early program worked in partnership with GTE to help improve Internet access for the customers' purchasing agents. GTE allowed Cisco to offer 20 percent discounts on higher-speed access for customers responding to a Cisco direct marketing campaign. Cisco then offered the discount to customers who made an IC agreement. According to Chris Sinton, this program added two points to the percentage of customers ordering online.

A more recent program included a deal with American Airlines that enabled customers who increased their percentage of online ordering to receive free miles up to the equivalent of a free trip every quarter. The program is targeted specifically at high-volume customers who are not yet using the CCO for a substantial proportion of their orders. "We use the incentive programs to get them engaged," explains O'Donoghue. "When they get used to it and begin to see the advantages, then they adopt it themselves and the incentives aren't needed anymore."

The marketing team organizes a series of incentive programs internally as well. For example, customer service representatives receive "click points" from Netcentives, an outside firm from which they can use to purchase books, CDs, and other products when they sign up customers for new IC purchasing agreements.

TABLE 5	SELLING SOLUTIONS: INTERNET BUSINESS SOLUTIONS GROUP
Industry-Leading Practices	Recommended business and technology practices and models, strategic frameworks, planning tools, and implementation methodologies based on Cisco's own practices.
Network Foundation	Cisco network reference architectures and preconfigured network designs optimized for specific solutions.
Internet Business Solution Application Partners	Relationships with leading software vendors such as BroadVision, InterWorld Corporation, and Open Market.
Internet Business Solution Consulting Partners	Relationships with leading strategic consulting and integration firms, including Cambridge Technology Partners, Ernst & Young, KPMG, and USinternetworking.

SOURCE: Cisco Systems, 1999

Preaching the Gospel

By the end of 1997, Cisco's success in networking its business operations had stimulated a parade of customers through the company's executive briefing center to ask how they could learn from Cisco's example. As Chris Sinton, CCO Director, recalls, "They were coming in and saying, 'we've got your products, love your technology, now tell us how you created e-commerce and e-support.'"

The company responded to the growing interest by creating a new organization called the "Internet Business Solutions Group" (IBSG) (Table 5). A cross between a high-level marketing group and a consulting operation, the IBSG is designed to help customers implement Web-based solutions based on Cisco's best practices.

Officially launched on December 15, 1998, the IBSG combines IT specialists in four separate teams with experts on a variety of industries. The horizontal solutions teams reflect Cisco's disaggregation of the business system into four areas:

- Supply Chain Solutions—R&D and manufacturing
- Commerce Solutions—marketing and sales
- Customer Care Solutions—support
- Workforce Optimization Solutions—employee services

The seven vertical industry teams include the following sectors:

- Financial services
- Health care
- Retail
- Service providers
- Energy and utilities

- Manufacturing

- Public sector

The IBSG represents a major commitment by Cisco to preach the gospel of the Global Networked Business Model. The Group includes about seventy-five people, dwarfing the modest CCO marketing team. Much of the team comes from within Cisco, but the company has also recruited heavily from its target audience.

These team members include senior executives from the major consulting firms and industry leaders such as the Chief Scientist who developed the online banking system for Wells Fargo (now working in the financial services team), and the CIO of BT Concert (on the service providers team).

The group is not designed primarily for direct revenue generation. Sharing best practices does not provide a revenue stream, and most of the consulting revenues pass through to Cisco's partners. There is an incremental revenue stream from additional sales of networking hardware and software, but the primary benefits are more indirect.

- First, the group's effort to solidify relationships with leading software and consulting partners builds the partners' commitment to promote and support Cisco's hardware and software. Already some joint marketing initiatives are underway.

- Second, the higher-level interaction with customers necessitated by the IBSG rebounds to the advantage of Cisco's customer account teams. Typically, the IBSG works directly with top executives such as Vice Presidents for Sales or Marketing, the CIO, or the CFO. Consequently, the account teams become exposed to the senior business executives from their customers, as opposed to the IT executives with whom they normally work.

- Finally, the IBSG helps put Cisco in the role of "trusted advisor" for their customers. By working at the level of "business solutions," Cisco is moving well beyond the simpler role of supplier and supporter of hardware and software. "Where we are headed is providing customers with the ability of getting up and running with Web-based solutions rapidly to improve their business," according to Stephan Cho, head of I-commerce solutions within the IBSG. "We become strategic partners with them, we become their trusted advisor as they think about how to solve their business problems."

Measuring the Results

The success of CCO and related networking initiatives at Cisco can be assessed in at least four ways.

- **Customer Satisfaction.** As most technical and other support queries have shifted from telephone and fax to the Web, average satisfaction ratings on a five-point scale have increased from 3.4 in 1994 to more than 4.3 today, as calculated by an outside contractor. Beyond the hard numbers lies substantial evidence of numerous individual customers choosing Cisco, and expanding their orders from Cisco, due to the convenience and efficiency of the company's online service and support.

- **Facilitating growth.** The integration of networking throughout all of Cisco's operations has played a substantial role in facilitating the company's rapid growth, including revenue growth from $1.3 billion in FY94 to a projected $12 billion in FY99, and employee growth from 2,300 to 18,300 during that same period. Quantitative measurement is impossible, but Cisco managers and outside analysts agree that the rapid scaling of the company's sales, support, manufacturing, partner, and internal operations while maintaining profit margins and increasing customer satisfaction would otherwise have been impossible.

- **Cost savings.** Cisco estimates they would need at least 900 customer service representatives without the CCO, versus about 300 today. The Technical Assistance Center would require an additional 1,000 engineers. In all, the company estimates savings of approximately $600 million in fiscal 1999 via its online systems. This includes more than $80 million for support personnel it would otherwise have to hire and train; $250 million by distributing 90 percent of its software and documentation online; and more than $75 million in supply chain management. Much of this savings has been channeled into Research and Development, which has grown from 9 percent to 12 percent in the last three years.

- **Thought leadership.** This category, too, is impossible to quantify, but there is widespread recognition among Cisco's partners, competitors, and industry analysts that Cisco has taken a clear leadership position in defining and implementing the most ambitious possibilities of networked business operations.

Lessons Learned

Analyzing the CCO story, six lessons emerge to help explain the company's success:

- Customer Focus
- Top-Down Commitment
- Delegation of Authority
- Infrastructure Investment
- Strong Partnerships
- Market the Medium

Customer Focus

Cisco is widely praised for its near-obsession with the customer, and the evolution of the CCO and related online initiatives demonstrates the wisdom of that intense focus. From the beginning, CCO developers put the customer front and center in two fundamental ways. First, the primary goal of Cisco's online efforts has always been to make it easier for its customers to do business. Second, virtually all of the specific developments and improvements have been sustained through constant interaction with customers: from Advisory Board meetings, to extensive seminars and meetings with customers, to usability studies, and online feedback that Cisco managers read on a daily basis.

Top-Down Commitment

From the beginning of the CCO, "the top down focus has never wavered," according to Chris Sinton. Given the complexity of the effort to integrate online systems across all functions and lines of business, this commitment has proven critical to sustaining the pace of innovation and development. Cisco's senior management understood quickly that aggressive internetworking would yield both substantial cost savings and provide a distinct competitive advantage. At the same time, building the "Global Networked Business Model" would serve as an excellent marketing promotion for a way of doing business that would ultimately translate into substantial new sales for Cisco's hardware and software. When integrated corporate commitment was needed to scale CCO to the next level, the company established a senior-level, cross-functional Business Council to ensure continued coherence and momentum with CCO efforts.

Delegation of Authority

While general direction and vision for the CCO came from the top, implementation has largely come from the bottom. Most of the major initiatives resulted from small, skunk works-like projects. As Mark Tonnesen notes, "John Chambers [Cisco CEO] didn't ever approve or disapprove anything about our e-commerce strategy; he didn't even know about it until it was done." Ethan Thorman similarly explains: "I've worked at other companies where every time you wanted to do something new you had to walk through an extensive business case process. How does this fit into the grand strategy? What's your competitive positioning?" At Cisco, "you'll be talking with customers and hear about an important unmet need. Rather than first building a business case, we go and find a customer willing to work with us to test possible solutions and see where it goes. Then we build the business case. And we have the authority to just do this."

Infrastructure Investment

The incredible growth in the CCO and the expectation of continued growth in areas that directly affect Cisco's customers and key business functions have required continual investment in the system. Cisco's "customer listening" mechanism has clearly highlighted the importance of utilizing Internet-related functions and capabilities to enhance business relationships. As such, Cisco has invested roughly $7 million in hardware, software, and support over the last three years to keep the system working, provide better support for its customers, and globalize the CCO to strengthen its international operations. With expectations about the quality of online services constantly rising, Cisco's commitment to substantial and continuing investment in the CCO infrastructure has proven a wise investment.

Strong Partnerships

Throughout the radical overhaul of Cisco's way of doing business, the company is determined to share the benefits as much as possible with its manufacturing and channel partners. Initiatives such as integrated ordering systems, Merge in Transit, and the Resellers Marketplace have strengthened Cisco's relationships, and brought dramatic cost savings, efficiencies, and new opportunities to the partners. The most important example is probably Cisco's rollout of online commerce. Although it could have posed a major threat to Cisco's resellers as a vehicle for direct sales, Cisco worked from the beginning to reassure them that the CCO commerce applications were designed strictly to cut costs on both sides and increase customer service. Today, some 70 percent of Cisco sales continue to come from indirect channels.

Market the Medium

Cisco never relied on the sheer attractiveness of its online offerings to build CCO usage. Rather, they initiated intensive marketing campaigns to promote awareness of the site and help customers and partners take full advantage of its applications. As the site grew, and the company became more focused on lines of business, Cisco added CCO marketing staff to focus on the different lines. When even greater interest developed in Cisco's whole approach to networked business, the company launched a whole new Internet Business Solutions Group to preach the gospel of the new way of doing business and, as a result, drove even more customers to higher-end use of Cisco products and services.

Questions for Discussion

1. Cisco emphasizes customer involvement and feedback in designing and implementing new online features and functions. What mechanisms can be used to gather customer input before launching online offerings?

2. Cisco determined early on that it would not use Internet commerce applications to lessen its reliance on channel partners and resellers. Was that an appropriate decision? Who has been best served by Cisco's strategy? How can or should Internet commerce change relationships with your partners?

3. Cisco created a high-level, cross-functional Business Council to provide direction and ensure overall coherence for the CCO. Is this the best way to manage a mission-critical, company-wide function? Would another management model be more effective?

4. Notwithstanding the clear success of the CCO, one could argue that Cisco has not dedicated adequate resources to marketing the CCO, given the scale and centrality of its operations. Can you think of other marketing initiatives Cisco should consider?

5. Cisco has developed an Internet Business Solutions Group to capitalize on growing interest in the company's own networking initiatives, but the company does not see the group as a profit center in its own right. Should Cisco focus more on developing a consulting practice based on its "Global Networked Business" model?

Acknowledgments

We want to thank Chris Sinton, director of the CCO, for his cooperation and assistance in providing information and contacts for this case study. We also want to thank the following Cisco employees for speaking at length with ITSMA: Todd Elizalde, Director of Internet Commerce; Mark Tonnesen, Senior Director of Customer Systems; Ethan Thorman, Director of Services Provider Services Marketing; John O'Donoghue, Manager, CCO Marketing; and Stephan Cho, Internet Commerce Team, Internet Business Solutions Group.

—Robert B. Leavitt, July 1999

2

S. C. Johnson's Professional Division

S. C. Johnson & Son, Inc. produces a range of well-established consumer products such as PLEDGE furniture polish, GLADE air fresheners, SHOUT laundry soil and stain remover, OFF insect repellant, RAID insecticides, and WINDEX glass cleaner. Each of these brands enjoys a strong position in the market. Through its Professional Division, the firm is also a leading producer of products and services for commercial, industrial, and institutional building maintenance and sanitation. The products include a complete line of specialty formulated cleaners, floor finishes, disinfectants, furniture polishes, and products for insect and odor control.

The Professional Division serves a diverse array of organizations in the business market such as retailers, health-care organizations, and educational institutions. Customers are served directly by the company's sales force or by a large network of distributors. Organizations follow two alternative approaches to building or store maintenance: the job is performed by its own personnel or it is "outsourced" to a building services contractor who regularly brings a trained staff on site to clean the facility.

Maintaining a sparkling and professional appearance is a desired goal in any organization but, for many, a continuing challenge. Consider the heavy store traffic that retailers such as Wal-Mart generate each day or the stream of shoppers who visit a supermarket around the clock. Some retailers spend $100,000 per store each month in cleaning, floor care, and maintenance programs. For large chains with hundreds of stores, this represents a massive expenditure. Included here are the costs of the cleaning products, labor and equipment costs, training expenses, and costs related to regulatory compliance. At a more fundamental level, retail store managers may be even more concerned about other costs—the lost sales that could arise from consumer concerns about cleanliness, food sanitation, or the unsightly appearance of a store. Moreover, there are safety concerns that worry store managers. A slippery floor that causes a shopper to slip and fall may lead to costly legal action against the retailer.

To meet the needs of organizational customers, the Professional Division at S. C. Johnson has developed an array of products and services. For a particular customer, like a supermarket chain, the salesperson will recommend a particular range of products and employee training programs to meet the unique needs of the retailer. Special

This case appears in Michael D. Hutt and Thomas W. Speh, Chapter 6, "Business-to-Business Marketing," of Michael R. Czinkota et al., *Marketing, Best Practices* (Fort Worth, TX: The Dryden Press, 2000), pp. 208–209.

dispensing systems (Solutions Centers) have been developed by S. C. Johnson to assist users in pinpointing the proper dilution level of the company's products to meet different floor-care maintenance tasks. The Professional Division also provides ongoing technical support to a customer. Each year, the unit receives over 30,000 calls from customers on issues that range from product selection for particular types of floor surfaces to environmental or safety queries.

Discussion Questions

1. In purchasing cleaning products and services, which of the following managers might be members of the buying center at a discount retailer, like Wal-Mart or Target: A purchasing executive at the headquarters level, store managers, a merchandising executive, a marketing manager, a maintenance staff supervisor, or maintenance employees? Who would be most influential in the buying decision?

2. Describe how the evaluative criteria employed by the purchasing manager might be different from those that are important to users.

3. Explore how the needs of a health-care organization might differ from the needs of a retailer in purchasing cleaning products and services. What adjustments in marketing strategy might be pursued by the Professional Division in the health-care sector?

3

Southwestern Ohio Steel Company, L.P.: The Matworks Decision

In late March 1994, Dan Wilson, vice president of sales for Southwestern Ohio Steel Limited Partnership (SOSLP), shook his head and laughed out loud. He had just read a letter from Matworks, an important and long-standing customer. The letter requested that SOSLP participate in sponsoring a portion of Matworks' annual sales meeting. (The letter is shown in Figure 1.)

Wilson's first reaction was that the letter was some sort of joke. If this was a bona fide request, it would put him and SOSLP in an uncomfortable position. SOSLP generally did not spend large amounts on any type of promotional activity, and certainly not on individual customers. Undoubtedly, the people at Matworks knew the limited nature of SOSLP's promotional budget. Still, Wilson resolved to consider the letter carefully, since Matworks was an important customer whose request had to be taken seriously.

SOSLP management considered the concept of partnership with customers to be very important. SOSLP customers often had long-standing relationships with the company, having worked together out of mutual respect, loyalty, and good business practice. Matworks was such a customer, dating to the very first days of SOSLP's operation in the 1940s. Whatever decision Wilson made, he did not want to upset the ongoing relationship between the two companies.

Company Background

Bill Wolf founded Southwestern Ohio Steel in 1945 to supply steel to the new General Motors Fisher Body Plant in Hamilton, Ohio. The steel service center bought sheet or coiled steel from local producers and then transported, warehoused, processed, and resold the metal to local users. The basic functions of maintaining inventory, breaking bulk (buying in large quantities and selling in smaller amounts),

This case was written by David W. Rosenthal, Richard T. Farmer School of Business Administration, Miami University. This case is intended as a basis for class discussion rather than to illustrate either effective or ineffective handling of an administrative situation. All individuals and events in the case are real. Certain names have been disguised.

Paid-in-full NACRA members in nonprofit organizations are encouraged to reproduce this case for distribution to their students without charge or written permission. All other rights reserved jointly to the author and the North American Case Research Association (NACRA). Copyright © 1999 by the *Case Research Journal* and David W. Rosenthal.

FIGURE 1   MATWORKS LETTER

MATWORKS, Inc.
1038 Industrial Blvd.
Cincinnati, OH 45201
(513) 231-2200

March 18, 1994

_____*MATWORKS*_____

Mr. Dan Wilson
Southwestern Ohio Steel
903 Belle Avenue
Hamilton, OH 45012

Dear Mr. Wilson:

MATWORKS is planning a very special meeting October 12–16, 1994, in Hilton Head, South Carolina at the Cottages Resort and Conference Center. It will be attended by the top achievers in our sales and service organization who have achieved the *MATWORKS* Peak Club as well as all of the *MATWORKS* executive management staff. We are writing to offer your company a unique marketing opportunity to solidify relationships with *MATWORKS* Regional Vice Presidents, District General Managers, and Sales Representatives in conjunction with this event.

The meeting will mix business and pleasure as a reward for a job well done by our "Peak Performers." We are discussing the possibility of subsidizing our meeting with our larger suppliers. The events that are available for sponsorship are:

1. <u>Carolinas Reception</u> - This Welcome to Hilton Head reception will be held pool side at the Cottages Wednesday evening, October 12.
• Guests receive hats and vests upon arrival
• Southeastern/Carolina decor
• Island band with strolling fiddlers
• Assorted hot and cold regional hors d'oeuvres
• Beer and wine served

Sponsorship $14,000

2. <u>Evening Cruise</u> - Thursday evening, October 13, the *MATWORKS* Peak Club cruises the waters around Hilton Head. Once frequented by galleons and pirates, the waters of Hilton Head are both beautiful and mysterious.
• Cocktails and snacks prior to dinner
• Buffet featuring New York strip steak and swordfish fillet

- Bluegrass band entertains during dinner
- After dinner naturalists will lead wildlife viewing

Sponsorship $25,000

3. <u>Dessert Extravaganza</u> - Following a "Dine Around" on Hilton Head Friday evening, October 14, guests return to the Cottages for a sumptuous dessert buffet and after-dinner cordials.

Sponsorship $6,000

4. <u>Golf Tournament</u> - You may choose to sponsor a golf outing on the famous Jack Nicklaus/Pete Dye Harbortown Golf Course, a regular stop on the PGA Tour. Available the afternoons of Wednesday, October 12 or Thursday, October 13.

Sponsorship $5,000

5. <u>Grand Banquet</u> - The premier event of the entire Peak Club program, the Grand Banquet features:
- Elegant decor - Colonial theme
- Gourmet dinner with veal, beef, or lobster entree
- Wine with dinner
- Peak Club ice sculpture
- Cordials after dinner
- Islands, a contemporary dance band

Sponsorship $30,000

We hope you will consider this exciting opportunity to involve your company with a select group of highly motivated *MATWORKS* representatives. Along with event sponsorship, we would like to talk to you about the display of your company's logo and product and your possible involvement in our business program to provide attendees with a better understanding of our valued business partnership. Linda Lewis, Director of Communications, will be contacting you to discuss your participation in more detail.

Joseph P. Pendleton

Vice President and General Manager

---

intermediate processing, and rapid and accurate delivery were hallmarks of the company and had led to consistent growth.

By 1994, the company had over 500 employees, annual sales of roughly $250 million, and annual shipments of approximately 400,000 tons. SOSLP was widely considered to be one of the industry leaders in technology and service.

Several structural changes impacted the company during the 1970s and 1980s, including a leveraged buy-out by its management. Subsequently, the company was sold to its leading supplier, Armco, Inc. In 1991, Armco, Inc. sold half of SOS to Armco Steel Corporation in Middletown, Ohio, and the other half to Itochu Corporation of Japan. The new company was named Southwestern Ohio Steel Limited Partnership (SOSLP). Neither owner company took an active role in SOSLP's functional management.

SOSLP sold to approximately 500 customers. The top twenty-five customers produced about two-thirds of the company's sales. SOSLP sold to a broad spectrum of industries, thereby limiting the company's exposure to business downturns. In addition to conducting its primary activities and functions SOSLP also operated four subsidiaries:

- SOS Leveling (SOSL) provided state-of-the-art tension leveling services for those customers who required superior flatness.

- SOS Lawrenceburg was a full-service facility located in Lawrenceburg, Tennessee, to serve that region. Transporting steel was expensive; therefore, inventory and delivery services could only be maintained from nearby facilities.

- J. R. Metals (JRM) marketed secondary steel. Secondary steel was steel that did not meet its production standards or had some sort of flaw. Expertise in metallurgy, the ability to correct some of the problems, and superior knowledge of the markets and customers allowed JRM to sell secondary steel profitably.

- Clark Cincinnati, Inc. (Clark), produced metal framing wall studs. Clark employed roughly eighty people and generated sales of approximately $15–$20 million per year.

One of the company's key strengths was its value-added processing. The company bought "master coils" of steel from producers. Master coils were generally forty-eight or seventy-two inches wide and weighed as much as 60,000 pounds. The company provided processing of master coils in a number of ways, such as "cut to length" (providing sheets of a certain size rather than coils); precision slitting (providing coils of a narrower width); and tension leveling (providing very flat sheets of specific sizes). Other strengths included sophisticated market forecasting which enabled the company to purchase at the best possible prices, inventory control, and efficient transportation. SOSLP maintained a fleet of twenty-nine trucks to ensure control over transportation time and delivery schedules.

Industry Background

The steel service center business was generally very competitive. The weight of steel made the cost of shipping over 200 miles prohibitive, thus limiting competition to local suppliers. However, in any given geographical market, there were several competitors, all providing similar products, services, and prices. It was not difficult for a buyer to shop among the various suppliers in a given region. Large customers with established requirements were highly prized targets among the steel service center competitors because their consistent orders made it possible to accurately forecast demand and therefore manage inventory to reduce costs. Similarly, well established service requirements (delivery scheduling, order response time, need for consistent availability of material, dimensional tolerances, etc.) made it possible to measure and demonstrate customer satisfaction and thus justify higher gross margins. Customers varied in their supplier loyalty, some focusing entirely on the steel's price per pound and changing suppliers frequently, others focusing on service and overall cost of operation, thus tending to be more loyal. Competition in the industry was such that an average profit margin was about 3 percent of sales.

Historically, relationships had been an important part of selling in the steel industry. "Wining and dining" the customer had been part of the cost of doing business. Gifts had also been commonplace, and a resort condominium, owned by a senior manager, would be "loaned" to a buyer or customer as a courtesy. However, much of this type of activity had changed over the past two decades. Government regulation such as the Foreign Corrupt Practices Act of 1977 and its revision in the Omnibus Trade Act in the late 1980s had influenced both international and domestic behavior to constrain gifts as a business practice. Increasingly restrictive rulings by the United States Internal Revenue Service requiring that gifts be reported as income had further dampened supplier largesse. In some organizations, even the acceptance of a business lunch or dinner had to be reported.

Tom Wicks, senior sales executive with Ryerson Steel, one of the largest steel companies in the United States, commented on the evolution of the buyer–seller relationship in the industry:

> The industry was much more "free-wheeling" twenty years ago. Expensive dinners and lunches were common. Entertainment was an expected part of the sales job. Competition from the Japanese and the resulting adoption of JIT (just-in-time inventory), cost management, and TQM (total quality management) among American manufacturers put the emphasis squarely on the best business practices. "Buying" business through gifts simply is no longer a big part of the steel industry.

Relationship with Matworks

Matworks was a leading national and international producer of heavy industrial equipment. Its main production facility was located only a few miles from SOSLP, and it had become one of SOS's best customers.

Wilson commented:

> At one time Matworks was our largest customer. The major portion of the raw materials required in manufacturing Matworks' product line is steel, and they buy almost exclusively from us. That goes back a way, too. They buy on a contractual basis. We negotiate a contract with them on a yearly basis and ship according to a schedule. They are pretty good about maintaining that schedule, and so are we.
>
> Over the past few years, though, they have run into trouble. Their sales have been off by quite a bit, and so they haven't been buying as much from us. The recession hit them pretty hard, and the reduction in military spending has affected them as well.
>
> In the eighties they were among our top ten customers in sales. By 1990 they had dropped to twenty-ninth. In 1990 and 1991 they were about fortieth, and last year they were about ninetieth. They have gone from buying

about $2.4 million in 1990 to $770 thousand in 1991 to $1 million in 1992 to only about $672 thousand last year. It is clear that they are having some hard times.

It isn't too difficult to service the account. They have some high expectations regarding the surface finish of the product they receive, but it really isn't anything extraordinary. They are consistent in their demands.

Dan Wilson

Dan Wilson was the vice president of sales for SOSLP. Wilson had begun his work with the company on the processing floor where, as a student, he had worked summers. He had graduated from the business school of a well-known midwestern university in 1982 and had gone into "inside" sales (customer service and telephone sales). He had been very successful in both inside and outside sales and had risen through the sales ranks. He had been promoted to his current position only about a year ago.

In the parable about the tortoise and the hare, Dan would definitely be cast as the tortoise. It wasn't that he was slow, since he accomplished a great deal. Rather, he could be characterized as steady. He was very even tempered and appeared to be careful in his consideration of all of the issues when faced with a decision. In conversations, Dan would often be found doing most of the listening, and when he spoke, his comments were well thought out and, most often, very insightful. At the same time, Dan wouldn't pull any punches. He would give his opinion in as honest and straightforward a manner as he was able. His word was his bond, something that he had reinforced during his tenure at SOSLP.

> Much of customer satisfaction is the management of expectations. Your service can be absolutely terrific, but if you have created the wrong expectations your customer may still be dissatisfied. If you tell your customer, for instance, that the steel will be there by 10:00 A.M. and it arrives at 10:05, it doesn't matter that no other company in the region could have gotten it there before noon! You've failed in your promise. If you promise it by noon and get it there by 10:05, then you are a hero!

The company was known for its honesty and integrity as well. Its roots as a family-owned business and the long-term relationships with many of the customers supported an atmosphere of loyalty and open, cooperative practices. During times of short supply of steel and consequent rising prices, SOSLP had often been known to hold the line on prices for their customers, thus smoothing the ups and downs of the market. The management of the company tended to take a long-term view of business and relationships rather than taking advantage of situations to make a quick buck.

The Current Situation

The letter that Wilson had received had been a shock to him. He had always thought that the relationship with Matworks had been positive and very professional. The negotiations for contracts had been conducted fairly and had provided good value to both parties. The idea of asking for a large donation was clearly something new. Wilson commented, "At the very most we might have a customer call us and ask if we have baseball tickets available for a particular game, but that is about the extent of it!"

SOSLP had no formal policy regarding an expenditure such as that requested by Matworks. SOSLP executives and salespeople occasionally gave a buyer a mug or some other specialty advertising piece. An occasional lunch or tickets to a Cincinnati Reds baseball game were not uncommon, but not the rule, either. The idea of giving one customer $5,000 or more simply was way out of line with normal activity.

SOSLP generally did little advertising or promotion. The sales force, both outside and inside, prided itself on maintaining good communications and relationships with its customers. What little advertising was done was nearly always in the form of direct mail. Wilson estimated that the company spent less than one one-hundredth of a percent of sales on advertising and promotion.

Wilson remarked about the letter:

> You have to give them credit. It takes a lot of guts to ask for something like this. And they didn't do it half-way, either. They went "whole hog." It kind of makes you wonder what they are thinking.
>
> It's kind of funny. We had a situation where we had a golf outing for some of our buyers, just to say, "Thank you." When we finished the outing there were hamburgers and hot dogs and drinks for everyone. I took the young SOSLP guy who organized the thing over to one side and asked him where the food came from, since it wasn't in his budget. He told me not to worry, that he had gotten the company which runs the vending machines in our plant to put up the food. I told him *never, ever, ever* to do that again. I think he got the point.

Wilson could shed no light on what would happen if SOSLP declined to participate. It was obvious from the letter that somebody at Matworks expected their big suppliers to take part in the program. Was this some wild idea that someone at Matworks had hatched to generate whatever funds they could, or did they really expect participation at the levels indicated? What were they willing to do if a supplier failed to support their activities? There was no question in Wilson's mind that some of SOSLP's competitors would jump at the chance to contribute in order to break into the account. The letter indicated that sponsors would have the opportunity to display products, interact with influential executives, and to educate Matworks salespeople, so at least some argument could be made that this was a reasonable business expense.

It seemed to Wilson that the decline in business suffered by Matworks over the past several years had probably put a great deal of pressure on the company's finances. Keeping up the morale of employees would be important under those circumstances, but paying for an annual meeting such as the one described in the letter could be a problem for Matworks.

Wilson had never heard of Linda Lewis prior to this letter, but he had communicated with Joe Pendleton on a number of occasions, and the relationship between the two companies had always been good. The letter made it clear that Linda Lewis would be calling to discuss the matter further and that SOSLP would have to have some response.

Pfizer, Inc. Animal Health Products[1]—A: Market Segmentation and Industry Changes

Jakki Mohr, Associate Professor of Marketing–University of Montana

Sara Streeter, MBA–University of Montana

Kipp Kreutzberg was just putting the finishing touches on his marketing plan for the coming year. As the senior marketing manager of Pfizer's Cow/Calf Division, he was responsible for a full range of animal health products Pfizer marketed to cattle ranchers, including vaccines for both newborn calves and their mothers, medications (for example, de-wormers, anti-diarrheals), and antibiotics (for pneumonia and other diseases). Pfizer positioned its products on the combination of superior science (resulting from its significant R&D efforts) and high-quality production/quality control techniques. Pfizer's pride in its sophisticated research-and-development was shown in its new and useful products for the market. The company invests more in research and development than any other animal health company.

Pfizer had historically segmented ranchers in the cow/calf business on the basis of herd size, as shown in Figure 1.

"Hobbyists" are so-called because, in many cases, these ranchers run their cattle as a sideline to some other job held. For example, a schoolteacher might keep a herd of cattle simply because he grew up on a ranch and couldn't imagine not doing so. In many cases, the hobbyists' ranch income is a minor percentage of their overall income. The average age of hobbyists is 50 years old and 15% hold a college degree. They have been in the cattle business for 26 years and spend 51% of their time with their cattle business.

"Traditionalists'" main livelihood is their cattle operation. The average traditionalist is 51 years old and 26 percent hold a college degree. They have been in the cattle business for 30 years and spend 70 percent of their time with their cattle operation.

[1] Some of the information in this case has been modified to protect the proprietary nature of firms' marketing strategies. The case is intended to be used as a basis for class discussion rather than to illustrate either effective or ineffective marketing strategies.

© Copyright by Jakki J. Mohr, The University of Montana, 1999, All Rights Reserved. Support from The Institute for the Study of Business Markets, Pennsylvania State University, is greatly appreciated.

FIGURE 1	PFIZER MARKET SEGMENTATION, 1998		

Segment	# of Cattle	# of Operations	Percent of National Cattle Inventory
Hobbyist	<100	808,000	50%
Traditionalist	100–499	69,000	36%
Business	500+	5,900	14%

The "Business" segment operations are headed by ranchers who average 53 years of age, 22 percent with a college degree, and 33 years in the business. They spend 80 percent of their time with their cattle. These large ranch businesses are owned either by a family or a corporation.

Pfizer had an extensive network of field sales representatives that visited the ranchers to inform them of products, to offer seminars on herd health, and to sponsor industry activities such as stock shows and 4-H. Time spent with accounts is typically allocated on the basis of volume of product purchased. Ranchers then buy the animal health products they need from either a veterinarian or a distributor/dealer (typically, animal feed stores, and so forth). The field sales reps also call on the vets and distributors/dealers to help them manage inventory and to inform them of new products and merchandising programs.

The Problem: Industry Challenges and Change and a Need to Evaluate Segmentation Practice

As the leader of the marketing team, Kipp recognized that his customers were facing some daunting challenges that would result in significant changes in the industry, changes that would likely reverberate to Pfizer's animal health business. For example, the market share of beef products had declined from 44 percent in 1970 to 32 percent in 1997, while pork and poultry had gained share. The decline in beef consumption was due in part to well-known concerns about cholesterol and fat. In addition, preparation issues also affected the demand for beef, as they did for poultry and pork as well. For example, two-thirds of all dinner decisions are made by a consumer on the same day. Of these same-day decisions, ¾ of the consumers still don't know what they are going to make as late as 4:30 p.m. Obviously, many beef products require cooking and preparation time, which limits consumer selection.

Of course, other types of meat products also require cooking and preparation time. One key difference, however, is that consumers were being bombarded with new products from the poultry and pork industries. For example, in 1997 Tyson Foods introduced stuffed chicken entrees, roasted chicken dinners, Southwest-style blackened fajitas, among a host of other creative products. The names "Tyson" or "Purdue" are well-recognized by the public, unlike most beef products.

Some of the changes that had occurred in the poultry and pork industries were expected to diffuse into the cattle industry. Industry analysts believed that the beef industry would need to develop products that could be more easily prepared, and to develop branded products that consumers could recognize and rely upon for quality and convenience.

In addition, industry analysts believed that the beef industry would need to improve the quality of its products (in terms of more consistent taste and tenderness). Beef quality is assessed based on U.S. production targets for tenderness, juiciness, flavoring, and marbling (fat) of the cuts of beef. The targets are based on two dimensions. The first dimension is based on taste quality (tenderness, juiciness), and specifies that 70 percent of beef production should be rated high quality (choice or prime). The second dimension is based on yield, and specifies that 70 percent of beef cattle should be rated grade 1 and 2 (implying a good amount of beef for the carcass size), with 0 percent poor yield (meaning that the carcass did not yield much meat). Currently, only 25 percent of beef cattle meet these criteria.

One way to improve the percentage meeting these criteria is participation in The Beef Quality Assurance program run through the federal government. This is a voluntary quality control program based on the education, awareness, and training of cattle producers to influence safety, quality, and wholesomeness of beef products. It specifies injection sites (neck versus rump) for shots, a seven-step quality check for cows, method and location of branding, and so forth. Forty percent of ranchers say they have participated in this program in the past two years, of which 67 percent have changed the way they manage their cattle.

In summary, consumer demand for beef products had declined over the years, resulting in a situation of over-capacity, which depressed prices. A flood of imports resulting from the NAFTA regulations further worsened the situation, as did high prices for feed. Most industry analysts were predicting a period of consolidation and alliances. Furthermore, many industry experts expected that beef quality would have to improve and be better marketed and packaged to meet consumers' changing lifestyles.

Kipp wondered how the ranchers, who were the lifeblood of his division's sales, would handle the changes. In reports from the sales representatives out in the field, he knew that the situation was dire for many ranchers. He wondered whether Pfizer's approach to marketing took account of the complicated situation. In particular, the Cow/Calf Division had been segmenting the market of ranchers on the basis of herd size for at least 15 years. In light of the significant challenges posed by industry changes, Kipp wondered whether his team's approach to the marketplace was still a useful one. He wondered whether a different approach to segmenting the market might allow his division to develop more effective marketing strategies, in light of the changes looming on the horizon.

Research Method

In order to provide some insight into the continued viability of segmenting the market on the basis of herd size, Kipp asked Joan Kuzmack, the Manager of Marketing Research for the Livestock Division, to conduct a series of depth interviews with cattle ranchers in the Rocky Mountain/Midwest Region. Depth interviews offer qualitative insights into behavioral and attitudinal differences among cow/calf ranchers. More specifically, the objectives of the research were to:

- Identify the inputs driving ranchers' success as cow/calf producers,
- Identify whether ranchers' values and beliefs about herd management differed by herd size,

TABLE 1	SUMMARY OF TYPES OF RANCHERS INTERVIEWED		
	Hobbyist*	Traditionalist*	Business*
Number of Interviews	3	6	3
Size of herd:			
<100	3		
100–250		2	
251–500		4	
501–1000			2
>1000			1
% of Time Spent With Cattle:			
<80%	2		1
81–90%			
91–99%		1	
100%	1	5	2
% of Income From Cattle:			
<80%	3	2	1
81–90%	2	1	1
91–99%		1	1
100%		1	
Type of Operation: **			
Seed-stock	2	2	
Commercial	1	4	3

*Classifications originally provided by Pfizer.

** *Seed-stock operators* focus on breeding high-quality bulls for use by commercial producers. The bulls are measured by the quality of their offspring. Desirable characteristics include low birth weight, rapid growth, high carcass yield, and grading of choice or better quality meat.

Commercial producers are those who raise calves to sell to feedlots. The feedlots fatten the calves, which are then sold to the packing houses, and on to the retail distribution channel for consumers. In some cases, commercial producers might *retain ownership* of their calves, where the rancher pays the feedlot to feed out the calves, but the rancher himself still owns them. Then, the rancher sells the calves to the packing houses.

- Determine what motivates cow/calf producers in selecting products, and

- Examine ranchers' views about the future.

A stratified random sample was used to select ranchers for interviews. Rocky Mountain and Upper-Midwest ranchers in each of the three groups (Hobbyist, Traditionalist, and Business) were identified, and randomly selected from within those strata. Table 1 provides descriptive statistics on the types and numbers of ranchers interviewed.

Ranchers were asked a variety of questions using a semi-structured questionnaire. The questionnaire focused on their herd management activities, attitudes, values, and beliefs about herd management, and views of the future trends in their industry.

Research Findings

Inputs Driving Ranchers' Success as Cow/Calf Producers

The results from the interviews suggested that commercial producers across all three herd-size categories look for maximum output (weight gain, number of calves) with the minimum inputs. They attempt to improve the quality of their calves through *health and nutrition programs, genetics, and herd culling*. Activities used to manage the herd included vaccinations, nutrition, and breeding programs. Ranchers also strove for uniformity in the calves, typically based on size. These goals in managing the herd are traded off against the cost to do so. As one respondent stated:

> "We strive for the largest amount of production with the least amount of input going in. That's really the only thing we can control at this point with the economy the way it is. We can't control the price that we get for our product, so the only way we can make ends meet is to control the input cost."—Traditionalist

Some ranchers also focused on range management of their grasslands as another objective in managing their operations:

> "Basically I think of us as ranchers, we're in the business of grass managers. We grow grass, and if we don't manage our lands to grow a lot of grass, the right kind of grass, we can't run the cows properly. All the genetics in the world won't be of use without the right grass."—Traditionalist

The degree to which ranchers felt that *health management* was critical to their herds' success varied greatly. Some valued herd health as one of the most important concerns:

> "You start off with the best breeding that you think you can do through bull selection. From there, it goes on with nutrition and herd health. You're expecting more from the cows. You have to put more into them with nutrition and herd health. You can't cut corners on either one of those. Some feeds will be cheaper some years than others, but we stay with the same drugs."—Traditionalist

Others tended to put in the bare minimum on herd health, sometimes because ranchers were uncertain what results the health management programs yielded:

> "We only do the bare minimum on health care. We do more of a preventative maintenance than anything else. We don't do any more than we have to because you can vaccinate for so many things. Our philosophy has been, if you don't need it, don't do it. You can get an awful lot of money in your cows giving them shots of stuff I don't know if you need."—Traditionalist

> "I try to keep them healthy with shots and nutrition. I don't want to skimp on the health of a cow, but if I can save some money by supplementing different things in the ration or with vaccinations . . ."—Hobbyist

Seed-stock producers were seeking "best genetics," a loosely defined goal that commonly focused on breeding bulls that would maximize weight gain in commercial calves. Seed-stock producers consistently used artificial insemination on their cows and kept computer records to track information on their herd. They used software programs provided through the breed association to record animal registry and performance information.

Use of Information in Herd Management

To aid in herd management, most of the ranchers in the Hobbyist and Traditionalist categories collected information on their cows and calves. Information collected on calves included birth date, birth weight, sex, and weaning weight. Information collected on the cows included calving history, mothering ability (temperament and/or milk production), calving ease, and which cows birthed the replacement heifers. This information was typically handwritten in a book of some type. The ranchers maintained an intimate familiarity with their cattle and saw them as individuals.

> "We knew everything there was to know about our cattle. . . . We knew more about our cattle than we did about our family. We could tell you every calf a cow had, pretty much the exact minute she had it every year. I've got little books here that I wrote everything down exactly."—Traditionalist

In the Business category, ranchers collected some information on their cows and calves. This information might be collected on an exception basis, because of the number of head with which the ranchers were working. The ranchers were familiar with their cattle, but not to the same degree demonstrated by the owners of smaller herds.

Some ranchers used a very sophisticated approach to gathering information in order to refine their herd management practices. For example, one pure-bred operation sent some of its calves to a test station where all the calves from various ranches were fed and cared for similarly. This control allowed the rancher to show how well his bulls stacked up to bulls from other ranches in a controlled experiment. Another rancher stated:

> "We've performed quite a few experiments of our own over the years, and still do. I have a fair sense of what a true experiment is with controls and so forth. We get a lot of cooperation from the pharmaceutical industry. We've tested new products such as ear tags. We get a lot of things free as long as we're willing to put in some controls and report on the results. I enjoy that sort of thing. We've had some experiments going for a couple of years on range management. The opportunities are out there if you're cooperative. I think I probably have an advantage because I know how to conduct an experiment. We can get information firsthand from experiments we conduct ourselves. . . . We've changed our method of supplementing cattle in the winter. We're using more expensive supplements that don't rely on salt. We seem to distribute cattle better. I think it worked. It's cheaper in the long run because you have more grass."—Business

Changes made on the basis of the information ranchers collected varied in their sophistication. Some made changes based primarily on judgment and intuition.

> "It's done by eye and is not as scientific as it could be."—Business

> "A lot of times you know in the back of your mind what you want to do with a cow. It's sure nice to have the records, because you go back and refer to it."—Hobbyist

Many of the ranchers did attempt to get information back from the feedlot on their calves in order to assess how well they did after leaving the ranch. In some cases, they also received carcass data, which allowed them to assess weight gain, quality of the meat, and other types of information.

There were isolated, but notable, exceptions to gathering and using information about the herd. One rancher kept no information on his herd, did not attempt to gain new information on herd management practices, and relied strictly on the information "in his head" based on his cumulative years of experience. Another said:

> "It was just a matter of whatever the good Lord gives them when they come out, that's what they are. I can't change that very much."—Hobbyist

The information ranchers gathered was used primarily as a tool in culling the herd. Culling of open cows (not pregnant) or those that were "unsatisfactory producers" usually occurred in the fall. In general, it seemed that changes to herd management were highly judgment-based. Cause-and-effect links for possible problems were hard to establish. For the larger herds, information was not collected on a detailed-enough level to analyze and draw specific conclusions.

> "Where I've got a thousand head, and we've got one full-time employee, we don't track detailed information on a cow-by-cow basis. I've always got a book with me, so when we're working them, I put things down in the book. That information will be put on the computer. After a while you kind of know your cows. It's visual, when you see things you don't like."—Business

Motivations in Selecting Products

Ranchers as a whole were interested in gaining additional information on how to better manage their operations. They read industry trade publications, attended seminars, and talked to neighbors. They were most likely to view information as credible if it came from a local source that was more familiar with specific local conditions. As a whole, it was clear that the person the ranchers trusted most was their veterinarian. The ranchers also found the animal health product firm reps to be a good source of information, but not as credible as the veterinarian.

> "On a drug situation, I wouldn't necessarily trust one person over another, but I would certainly pay attention to my veterinarian. He knows my area and my situation better than the drug rep from the company does. Even though I know the drug rep from that company is going to represent the drugs he sells, I don't necessarily not trust what he says. I just like to have more information about what works in my environment."—Traditionalist

Ranchers bought their animal health products from both veterinarians and supply houses. Price was an important consideration, but not an overwhelming concern.

Ranchers' Views about the Future

The ranchers all expressed concerns about the future. The number one concern among the commercial Hobbyists and Traditionalists was the low prices on their calves. While Business producers, too, were concerned about price for their "outputs" (cattle), they were also concerned about the input side of the equation (expenses). All ranchers noted that with the low prices they were getting for their calves, they couldn't afford to maintain and replace old, dilapidated equipment they were using.

> "It takes a lot of calves to buy a new pickup, when they want about $30K or something."—Hobbyist

> "[My number one concern is] pricing, and not just the price of the product, but the price of what it costs to produce that product. Compare the price of beef with the price of machinery. Calves are bringing what they brought in the '60s, but a tractor costs three times as much."—Traditionalist

In addition, they noted the high price of land. One rancher stated, "the land around here grows houses better than cattle."

Ranchers spoke vehemently against NAFTA, and the influx of cheaper imports.

> "Well, the biggest issue we have right now is NAFTA. NAFTA is probably the worst thing they've come up with. It has lowered our cattle market so bad, it's put a lot of people out of business, driving the prices down so low. It is not fair trade from the standpoint of shipping Australian cattle into Mexico, they become Mexican cattle and come right into the U.S. They can get our top dollar (whatever we're getting here—say 60 cents), but were brought in through Mexico at 30 cents. They flooded the market. They didn't have to make as much, they don't have as much in their cattle. With this R-Calf thing, they're investigating Canada. Let's face it: They're over-running our market. It takes away the supply and demand. It's not just af-fecting us, it's affecting everybody—for example, the beef business, the car business, the timber business."—Traditionalist

Tightening environmental regulations (Endangered Species Act, pesticides, water quality, etc.) also made an impact on the economics of ranching operations.

Increasing market strength of the packers was viewed with fear and trepidation, and also with a sense of increasing helplessness. Ranchers sold their calves to the feed-lots, who in turn sold to the meatpackers. Packer concentration (four packers con-trolled 80 percent of the market) and the packers' perceived ability to set prices (the implication is "collusively") for the industry was a recurring theme. Moreover, fears of vertical integration by the packers, or packers who own their own cattle and feedlots, further worried the ranchers.

> "We have no market for our agriculture products. To back that up, when you've got packers controlling 80% of the cattle and they'll buy cattle for a half-hour in the middle of the week, you either take the offer or you leave it. If you turn them down, pretty soon they won't come back and look at your cattle or price your cattle. This is where we're going to have to have more players in our market or we're going to have to become one of the major play-ers against the packer in supplying food to the consumer. We cannot com-pete with packers that own their own cattle and slaughter their own cattle instead of paying the market value for cattle they don't own. So that's why I say we have no market. The grain is the same way, because basically, the same companies that control the grain control the cattle, Cargill, ConAgra,

ADM. You just look through the hall of mergers. One of these days, if things don't change, we will know the true value of our food when the corporations get it and we're all working for those people. The consumer will find out what the value of it is."—Business

In general, the view among the commercial producers was one of extreme pessimism. They saw a lot of other ranchers going broke (but usually not themselves).

"I think it's all offset by the good things, but sometimes you wonder. You have to wonder about your mentality. You work and you work and you work and you work and you work and then you sell your cows at a loss, and you think 'Why am I doing this?' Either I'm really stupid, or really stubborn." —Traditionalist

"I think the day that the old rancher who gets on his horse at daybreak and gets off his horse at sunset and never sees another human being, and everybody is knocking on his door to buy his calves—those days are through. I hate to admit it, but everywhere you turn, somebody is trying to put you out of business. If it isn't the Bambi-huggers, then it's the prices, and if it isn't that, then somebody's coming along with those brainy ideas. The small producer is really going to have to work at it to stay in business." —Traditionalist

Solutions: Value-Added Marketing, Branded Beef, and Quality

Ranchers were asked about possible solutions to the depressed prices they were facing. Possible solutions discussed in industry publications included value-added marketing, or marketing strategies designed to increase the value and quality customers receive from beef purchases, and a branded beef model. The development of branded beef would require a tracking system from "birth-to-beef" in the supply chain. Such tracking would allow standardized health, quality, and management protocols, as well as improved feedback through the entire production model.

Branded beef production would move the industry from a cost-based (production) model to a value-added model. This change would also necessitate the producers being more closely linked to the feedlots to improve the quality of the beef. Better coordination along the supply chain would ensure an increased flow of information from the consumer to the producer. Alliances between the cow/calf producer and the feedlots would allow ranchers to better track the success of their calves (based on health and weight gain). Such data could allow the ranchers to further improve the genetics of their herd by tracking which cow/bull combinations had delivered the higher-yield calves. As part of these trends, some degree of integration or vertical coordination would occur in the beef industry. Ranchers would need to participate in order to ensure market access for their product. Ranchers would have to think beyond the boundaries of their own ranches.

Most ranchers were familiar with the concepts of value-added marketing and a branded beef model. However, most were dubious about their viability and impact on ranchers' independence.

"I don't know if any kind of marketing at this point is going to get us where we need to be without a change in the price structure of cattle." —Traditionalist

"If there is a demand for high-quality beef, then the market should show it, and the packers will start bidding more for a piece of that quality. There may be some niches somewhere that people can fall into, but it's not going to be the salvation of many ranches. What we need is a mass market. Whatever niche there is is going to be saturated very quickly, and the price will come down. I think the solution is cutting costs. People are eating a tremendous amount of beef, but the production is enormous as well. Numbers are down, but tons are up. The amount of beef being eaten is still quite high. I just think that some people have got to quit producing beef."—Business

"We are concerned about the vertical marketing approach big companies are introducing into the system. Ranchers are very independent-minded people. We are fearful about the control that companies will be able to exert on us."—Traditionalist

Skepticism about value-added marketing is also derived from history: Other programs used in the past to provide a more consistent product to the feedlots, with supporting documentation, had not resulted in noticeable price differences. Of all the information ranchers collected on their herds, only vaccination records seemed to be valued by cattle buyers. Even ranchers with complete histories of their cattle were selling their calves at the same price as ranchers without the information. Hence, the information was not viewed as a way to command a premium for the calves.

"For many years, it seemed like having good health records on the calves didn't matter. One herd would keep excellent records and be real progressive, and the next door neighbor was the exact opposite, and it was the exact same price for both. The local cattle buyers didn't give a premium to keep the records, give the vaccines. . . . There were green tag programs in the '80s (we followed one) where the vet certified you used them (preconditioning records). But the cattle buyers didn't pay a premium for them. They as much as said "We don't care." Today, 10 years later, cattle buyers are starting to ask, will you precondition your calves? Will they be "bunkbroke"? (so when they get to the feedlot, the calves will be trained to go to a feedbunk to eat). Will they be weaned? There's a stress period associated with weaning. So there's more of a focus on those questions now than there has been. But there's still no rule, it's not a given. It's still ambiguous when it comes to marketing the cattle whether the information matters or not [gets a better price for the cattle]."—Traditionalist

The feeling was that price premiums, if any, would accrue to others in the supply chain (e.g., the packers, retailers, and others). Despite that, some with more progressive views noted the need to have more of a consumer-focus in their efforts:

"We need better beef quality if we're going to increase consumption. A lot of the breed associations are concentrating on carcass quality right now. There's measurement, there's selection for marbling and yield on cattle. I think as long as there is a possibility there might be some added value, a person should start working on it a little bit, along with the other production traits. I think it's something to pay attention to."—Traditionalist

"I think in the future, all ranchers are going to have to retain ownership of their cattle more, and follow them closer to the consumer. I think that's part of our problem right now with our packer concentration. The producer's going to have to be a meat producer, and not just sell calves. I think some of our long range goals are going to have to be to get closer to the consumer with our product and know what he wants instead of listening to the packer tell us what he wants."—Business

"The money in agriculture is not in producing it. It's in processing it. This is where more ranchers and farmers have to realize that you can't produce the raw product anymore; you've got to follow it on through."—Business

Ranchers also noted that the idea of consistent quality beef was important.

"I'm expecting to see a change to where quality is more important. I think, down the road, that it's going to be mandatory that you know exactly what your cattle are doing. Those that aren't producing well at the kill floors are going to come back to haunt you."—Business

Interestingly, each of the respondents with whom we spoke felt that the quality of their beef was above-average. However, there was some doubt about whether consistent quality would be easily achieved with range cattle.

"That's going to be pretty tough with cattle. With chickens and hogs, you can throw up a confinement building. One person can control X amount of hogs and turkeys and chickens. But how do you do that with cattle? You can only have so many cattle in one spot because they're bigger and they need more feed. You're going to have to have pasture. It's going to be pretty tough to get everything uniform. There are a lot of small producers with just a few cows around."—Hobbyist

"I'm not convinced that branded products are going to magically save the beef industry. I think we're in competition on a world scale, and we're going to have to cut our costs of production. I think we could get our costs down to about 45 cents per pound of critter sold if we had to. Our total production would go down, but I think our costs would go down more."—Business

Because of the doubts about the viability of moving to a branded beef model, ranchers tended to focus more on controlling the cost of inputs, and weathering the current downturn in the production cycle. One respondent cited earlier summed this up as "striving for the largest amount of production with the least amount of input."

Rancher's Concluding Thoughts

Despite these hardships and concerns, the ranchers were passionate about their love for their lifestyle, feeling that the benefits of living a life on the land outweighed the drawbacks.

"You get up in the morning and go out there, and everything's bright and fresh. We're fortunate in this part of the world that we don't have a lot of

noise from cars and trains. It's gratifying to see what happens when spring turns around, new things start to grow, new animals come into the world. It's pretty special, something that you can't explain to a lot of people because they don't understand what you're talking about. . . . It isn't the highest paying job in the world, but it's got a lot of happiness that money can't buy."
—Traditionalist

They expressed pride in their work, and a sense of ownership for feeding the country's people.

Back to the Segmentation Decision

As Joan perused the findings from the qualitative interviews, she wondered what she would report to Kipp about possible changes in their approach to market segmentation. Joan wondered whether their historical approach to segmenting the market based on herd size was consistent with the changes in the industry and changing needs of ranchers.

Despite the insights gathered, there was a lack of understanding of the various segments of beef consumers and their needs, how brand marketing could affect consumer demand, how alliances within the supply chain could affect the ranchers' situations. Unfortunately, the fragmented nature of the cow/calf producers, combined with their focus on production rather than marketing, meant that the beef industry was not very consumer-focused.

As she pondered how all these pieces fit together, she began to brainstorm new ways to look at the market. She wanted to work with Kipp in developing a plan to maintain Pfizer's market position in light of the changes in the industry.

Discussion Questions:

1. Based on the research findings, evaluate Pfizer's Cow/Calf Team's herd-size segmentation approach.

2. If it doesn't make sense to continue segmenting on the basis of herd size, what variables can be used to segment that more accurately capture differences in the market? What would the resulting segments look like? What segments are most viable for Pfizer?

3. How does the suggested segmentation approach capitalize on changes in the cattle industry? What implications do the industry changes have for Pfizer?

4. How good is the research for drawing conclusions about market segmentation of beef producers?

5. Assuming that support is found for the recommended segmentation approach, how can it be implemented as a marketing strategy?

5

Roscoe Nondestructive Testing

After nine months, Grover Porter, president of Roscoe Nondestructive Testing, Inc. (Roscoe) was beginning to question the success of his new quality improvement program (QIP). Initiated in March 1991, the QIP had produced substantial increases in recent customer satisfaction surveys; however, none of that satisfaction seemed to be fueling a return to growth in either revenue or number of clients. Porter anticipated Roscoe's second down year in a row as the company continued to lose major customers, and he was eager to re-establish the growth that had preceded the last two years of decline.

It was hard to believe that the cyclical downturn in the pulp and paper industry had pushed the boiler inspection business to competing solely on price. Porter still felt that there was room in the industry for a quality service at a fair price, but the ineffectiveness of the QIP had prompted Porter to reconsider adjusting Roscoe's pricing structure.

The Nondestructive Testing Industry

Nondestructive testing (NDT) involves the examination of materials to discover microscopic cracks, corrosion, or malformation, using inspection techniques that do not damage the material under scrutiny. Common inspection techniques include the use of X-rays, ultrasonics, and electrical eddy currents.

NDT is used in a wide variety of applications, including the examination of aircraft parts, tanks and vessels of various shapes and sizes, and welds of all kinds. Roscoe primarily uses ultrasonic thickness measuring devices to determine the thickness of metal plating.

NDT technicians are certified by area of expertise (e.g., ultrasonic) and accumulated skill and experience (Levels I–III). Technicians certified in more than one

This case was prepared by Brian Wansink, University of Illinois, Urbana-Champaign, and Eric Cannell, University of Illinois, Champaign-Urbana as the basis for class discussion rather than to illustrate either effective or ineffective handling of an administrative situation. Copyright © 1993 by Professor Brian Wansink. All rights reserved. No part of this publication may be reproduced, stored in a retrieval system, or transmitted in any form or by any means without permission.

inspection technique are a treasured resource in most firms. They were generally employed by four types of companies:

1. Mom and pop labs usually employ fewer than twenty-five people and provide a single type of inspection service to a small number of customers. These firms are the low-cost providers and are quite willing to bid at cost, simply to keep busy. Many are often tied to a single client who wields considerable control over pricing and delivery.

2. Nation-wide companies have labs around the country and a high degree of name recognition. These firms also provide inspection services to a large number of different industries; however, individual offices usually serve a narrow segment of the market.

3. Specialty firms target very narrow market segments that have specific needs. These firms make large capital investments in the latest inspection equipment and employ the highest skilled technicians. Barriers to entry into these specialized markets are high, so specialty firms have traditionally achieved high levels of profitability.

4. While much larger than the mom and pop labs, regional firms lack the name recognition and market strength of the nation-wide companies. These firms employ up to 150 technicians and have the resources to tackle the largest inspection jobs. Roscoe is a regional firm, operating primarily in the central southern part of the United States.

All in all, management of NDT firms has been historically uninspired, driven mainly by owner-operators who managed to survive the lean years.

History of Roscoe

Roscoe was founded in 1973 by Hans Norregaard, in Roscoe, Louisiana. After thirty years as an NDT technician, Norregaard decided to set up shop for himself amidst many of the pulp and paper mills located in western Louisiana. Roscoe focused on the inspection of large boilers, a service designed to monitor the corrosion of the boiler walls. Inspections conducted every two to three years provided mills with sufficient warning to replace weakened, corroded plates in boiler walls before a catastrophic accident occurred.

In 1980, Norregaard sold the company to National Inspection Services (NIS) for $1.75 million. NIS was a subsidiary of Swanson Industries, a large diversified holding company. At that time, NIS brought in Chad Huerlmann (a Harvard MBA) to manage the company. Huerlmann was eager to own a small business and viewed the Roscoe acquisition as a great opportunity.

The company continued well for four years, until the pulp and paper industry bottomed out again. Hampered by misguided directives and burdened by corporate overhead, Roscoe's low cost position no longer protected it from the growing price pressure facing NDT companies in the pulp and paper industry. Also, Huerlmann failed to establish an effective relationship with the technicians in the company and many resigned or left the NDT industry altogether. By 1984, Swanson Industries decided to divest of NIS completely and Roscoe was once again up for sale.

At that time, Hans Norregaard and a long-time business associate, Grover Porter, decided to get back into the NDT business. Together they bought back Roscoe for about thirty-five cents on the dollar. They were convinced that by offering an improved inspection service for a fair price, they could rebuild the company's reputation and good fortunes.

After dismissing Huerlmann, Hans and Grover began building a new management team for Roscoe. A new controller, Jane Bottensak, was hired away from MQS Inspection. Ted Witkowski, a staff Professional Engineer (PE) out of Texas A&M, who had previously worked for Exxon, was also taken on. Both men thought Ted would bring some much-needed technical backbone to the company. Also, long-time technician, Ed Brown, was promoted to operations manager. Finally, Roscoe began recruiting technicians from the best vocational tech schools in the country.

In 1987, Hans Norregaard retired and Grover Porter became president. Roscoe was back on track.

In 1990, Roscoe encountered a downturn in both revenues and customers. Many mills simply decided not to release bids as often as they used to. While Roscoe always lost some contracts to lower bidders, Porter felt the recent slowdown in the pulp and paper industry exacerbated Roscoe's situation by forcing mills to be more cost conscious. Still, Porter felt that there must be room for the services that Roscoe offered:

> Hans and I have put together a great management team over the last three years and our technicians are some of the best in the industry. Roscoe offers an efficient, quality inspection service and we feel that we can price accordingly.

However, the recent loss of established customers caused Grover Porter to question the validity of Roscoe's purported "high quality" service.

Customer Profiles

Although boiler inspections in pulp and paper mills have been standard practice for many years, mills differed widely on the representative who interacted with Roscoe's inspection team. This contact could be almost anyone from the plant manager down to a purchasing agent. The following descriptions illustrate many of the problems that have plagued Roscoe recently.

George McDonald at the Franklin Paper Company was a typical plant manager who reigned over his plant like a king over his castle. Like any other plant manager, McDonald was primarily concerned about controlling costs and was hostile to the idea of boiler inspections in general. Since inspections could only be conducted during plant shutdowns, McDonald was unhappy about the lost production time:

> Besides the $85,000 inspection fee, my plant is idle during the two days it takes your team to complete the job. At 750 tons per day, I pay an additional opportunity cost of over $330,000 every day you are in my plant. A boiler will last twenty years without exploding and if it wasn't for corporate HQ, I would never bother with the inspections. Besides, the only thing that I ever get out of it is an "OK" and a pile of figures that I can't make head nor tail of.

International Paper's plant in Longview, Texas, was one of the few clients that maintained their own NDT department. As with other mills, the department consisted of only one retired NDT technician who interacted with service providers like Roscoe. Bob Kapala typified the kind of NDT person often found in paper mills. He was friendly and eager to help, but was actually often more of a hindrance. The last thing a technician wanted was someone looking over his [or her] shoulder all the time.

After the inspection was completed, Bob would combine the recent inspection data with a pile of past data and attempt to find trends in corrosion patterns. The fact that different inspection firms provided data in different formats complicated Bob's task.

Jim Bulgrin at the Rockton Paper Mill in Texarkana, Texas, presented a different problem. Bulgrin, a recent graduate of Georgia Tech, had been hired into the mill's engineering services department seven months ago. As one of Roscoe's team supervisors described him, Bulgrin was "as wet behind the ears as a new-born calf." But he was eager to learn and was on top of every detail.

Problems arose when Jim noticed that thickness readings on one section of a boiler were considerably greater than when inspected two years before. After confronting the technicians, who ended up getting very angry, Jim eagerly reported the discrepancy to his boss. It was later discovered that a new plate had been welded onto the boiler in that area, but Roscoe lost the contract with Rockton.

Pulp mill supervisors, like Billy Dunlap at the Lufkin Pulp Mill, were Roscoe's most common contact inside a mill. Dunlap has been cajoling his boiler along for the last fifteen years and did not take easily to anyone mistreating his "baby."

Finally, the inevitable contact is the purchasing representative who files the paperwork with accounting. Lucy Boyle in purchasing at Lufkin was never happy about processing paperwork relating to inspection services:

> Corporate headquarters requires us to file additional paperwork for one-time expenses greater than $50,000. With inspection fees well over $75,000, I end up processing over three times more paperwork than normal. My life doesn't return to normal until the mill goes back on-line.

A Prelude to Action

In January 1991, while attending the Nondestructive Testing Managers Association meeting in Las Vegas, Grover Porter was still struggling with the question of what defined a quality service. As it turned out, one of the speakers in the New Business Segment of the conference presented a talk on the components of service quality. And in that same month, a number of articles describing quality improvement programs at major aerospace inspection firms ran in both the ASNT and AWS Journals.[1]

At the monthly staff meeting in February, Porter discussed his concerns regarding the level of service provided by Roscoe:

> As you all know, we've lost a bunch of accounts in the last few months. I suspect our service quality is not what it should be, and I've been thinking about a quality improvement program. If we don't do something soon, we may be forced to reduce our fees.

---

[1] Trade journals of the American Society of Nondestructive Testing and the American Welding Society.

Bottensak, the controller, nodded her head in agreement and commented that something had to be done:

Let's go for it! None of us needs reminding that 1990 was a bad year, but it looks like this year will be even worse. That's not great for our bonuses!

Ted Witkowski, the staff PE, and Ed Brown, the operations manager, were extremely skeptical. Ted explained:

Look, we have the best trained technicians out there with top of the line equipment. They make some mistakes now and then, but when a boiler inspection requires 20,000 readings, that will happen. Besides, the mill has to look at the readings over an entire area and not just a single point. It's not reasonable to inspect every point twice. The mills couldn't afford the cost or the downtime.

After further discussion, Porter suggested that they first conduct a short customer survey to determine if there were any areas for improvement. No one resisted the idea so Porter spent the weekend composing the survey, and Bottensak pulled together a mailing list of Roscoe customers from the last five years. On Monday morning 357 surveys were dropped in the mail.

The Survey Results

By the first week of March, Porter had collected eighty-two responses. With only three responses returned in the last four days, Porter felt his sample was as big as it was going to get and asked Jane Bottensak to aggregate the results into a single report (Figure 5.1). The next morning, Jane walked into Porter's office with a grin:

Grover, look's like we got something here. I ignored eleven of the responses since they obviously knew nothing about our work. I reckon those surveys didn't even reach the right contact in the mills. Anyway, that left seventy-one responses. I pulled all the results together to determine the frequency distributions and from what I can see it seems our people skills need work. Even our office staff could use some improvement.

Porter was surprised that the accuracy of inspection data and time to completion rated so highly, considering that business was so tough these last months. But then he recalled that the speaker at the NDTMA Conference last month emphasized the importance of the people aspect in service quality.

Unfortunately, Roscoe did not attract the type of people blessed with an abundance of social grace. The environment around a boiler is not pleasant. There is constant noise, grime, and heat. And if there was a reason to climb inside the boiler, the technician . . . [must] struggl[e] through cramped areas with . . . equipment and [a] flashlight. Once out, [the technician's] clothing and equipment were coated with a black muck that not even Ultra Tide could remove. Thus, while technicians survived the conditions on-site, they did not necessarily do so quietly.

FIGURE 5.1	ROSCOE CUSTOMER SATISFACTION SURVEY (MARCH 1991)*

Dear Roscoe Customer,

In an effort to provide you with the best inspection service possible, we would like your opinion of Roscoe and the people who work for us. Simply check the appropriate column on the survey and drop it in the mail within the enclosed stamped envelope. Your cooperation is truly appreciated.

Grover Porter
President

Questions	Poor	Below Average	Average	Above Average	Excellent
On-site inspection team					
Accuracy of inspection data	1.3%	5.9%	15.3%	34.7%	42.8%
Time to complete inspection	2.9	4.8	8.4	45.6	38.3
Knowledge of technicians	1.5	11.5	25.6	33.3	28.1
Willingness to make an extra effort	24.6	26.0	23.6	13.5	12.3
Courtesy of technicians	26.1	30.3	18.7	16.2	8.7
Degree of individualized attention	17.6	29.6	38.2	9.9	4.7
Conveys trust and confidence	9.2	28.3	34.7	23.8	4.0
Organization of team supervisor	4.2	25.6	37.2	29.9	3.1
Accounting department					
Accuracy of billing	3.4	8.3	16.1	55.8	16.4
Promptness of billing	9.8	43.9	21.7	16.5	8.1
Courtesy of staff	6.9	24.7	38.6	13.5	16.3
Willingness to help	22.7	25.6	38.1	8.9	4.7
Overall performance of Roscoe					
Ability to deliver the promised service	2.7	15.6	18.5	39.4	23.8
Variety of services that meet your needs	2.3	13.2	48.8	26.5	9.2
Overall service value for your money	12.7	34.1	43.2	7.8	2.2

*Recorded percentages are the frequency distribution of 71 responses compiled by Jan Bottensak, RNDT's controller. An average was taken for respondents who checked adjacent ratings (i.e., poor and below average).

At the March staff meeting, Porter announced his plans for Roscoe's Quality Improvement Program.

The Quality Improvement Program

The three elements that Porter decided to include in the QIP were initial training, a bonus reward system, and customer surveys at the conclusion of every job. He recognized that the QIP had to be more than a one shot deal to be successful and felt that the proposed combination of training, surveys, and bonuses would establish the lasting, fundamental changes Roscoe needed.

Training was provided by ABS Consultants of Madison, Wisconsin, who specialized in teaching customer contact skills for industrial service companies. Training consisted of guided round table discussions and role playing, through which technicians and office staff explored not only customers' perceptions of Roscoe, but also their perceptions of the customers as well.

ABS also had Ed Brown put together some service guidelines that went beyond the traditional level of service. Brown explained one aspect of the guidelines:

> For example, while on-site, we need to emphasize constant visual inspection of the customer's plant and equipment. If a technician sees some insulation hanging off a section of piping, we expect that person to make a note in [the] report to the client. It doesn't take much time and our customers appreciate the extra effort.

Technicians also earned bonus points that were cashed out at the end of the year for $25 per point. Every time a client requested a particular technician to be part of the on-site inspection team, that person received a bonus point. Also, after each job, the client filled out a customer satisfaction survey. At the end of the year, the surveys were ranked and for each instance that a technician's team was in the top 5 percent, that technician received a bonus point.

Porter also gave a cash bonus to technicians who passed their certification tests and advanced a level. Achieving Level II earned a $150 cash bonus, while reaching Level III earned $500, as this was the most difficult level to achieve. Finally, the customer satisfaction surveys were compiled monthly and the statistics displayed in the shop area.

Another Disappointing Year

Jane Bottensak wrapped up her part of the December staff meeting:

> Well, as I predicted, 1991 is going to be a disappointing year. Revenues were down again and profits were negligible. However, our performance wasn't as bad as I expected, so maybe the quality improvement program was more successful than I thought. But, I think we will still need to re-evaluate our fee structure for the coming year.

Ted Witkowski agreed that the program was a success and commented that Roscoe had a record number of technicians certified at Levels II and III.

Even Ed Brown conceded that customer satisfaction ratings had improved dramatically over the second half of 1991 (Figure 5.2):

> Most of the experienced technicians are excited about the program. They have been around Roscoe a number of years and have established their families in the area. On the other hand, some of the younger folks have not committed as easily. Part of that is the fact that less experienced workers get smaller bonuses, on average. But, also, the younger technicians are more

FIGURE 5.2	ROSCOE CUSTOMER SATISFACTION SURVEYS (NOVEMBER 1991)*				

Questions	Poor	Below Average	Average	Above Average	Excellent
On-site inspection team					
Accuracy of inspection data	1.0%	4.2%	2.1%	24.8%	55.9%
Time to complete inspection	1.4	6.3	7.1	60.0	25.2
Knowledge of technicians	0.9	12.1	20.5	37.4	29.1
Willingness to make an extra effort	11.9	18.2	36.5	27.8	5.6
Courtesy of technicians	9.3	8.9	55.3	16.3	10.2
Degree of individualized attention	2.1	16.7	45.9	30.1	5.2
Conveys trust and confidence	3.8	22.7	39.8	30.6	3.1
Organization of team supervisor	0.0	11.9	31.8	44.7	11.6
Accounting department					
Accuracy of billing	1.5	10.4	19.6	44.2	24.3
Promptness of billing	13.5	33.4	25.6	18.5	9.0
Courtesy of staff	7.9	17.8	33.4	35.1	5.8
Willingness to help	8.6	29.4	30.3	24.6	7.1
Overall performance of Roscoe					
Ability to deliver the promised service	0.0	13.2	23.1	44.2	19.5
Variety of services that meet your needs	7.4	13.5	56.1	15.3	7.7
Overall service value for your money	10.2	31.2	47.1	11.5	0.0

*Compilation of 17 customer satisfaction surveys for inspections completed during November 1991. An average was taken for those respondents who checked adjacent ratings.

mobile and easily move from company to company. Overall, our work force is providing a better service to the customer.

However, regardless of how well the quality improvement program increased customer satisfaction, unless it could support new growth in the company, Grover Porter could only deem the program a failure.

In light of the continued downturn in the pulp and paper industry, Porter felt resigned to restructure the company's pricing policies. And that would mean big changes for Roscoe.

6

Nypro Inc.: Strategy for Globalization

He travelled the world on a motorcycle in 1957 at the age of twenty-six. And that, says CEO Gordon B. Lankton, gave him a "global view" that he has used to guide the growth of his company, Nypro Inc.

Nypro Inc. was one of the world's largest custom injection molders of plastic materials. Founded in 1955 as the Nylon Products Corporation, Nypro's headquarters and main operations were located in the town center of Clinton, Massachusetts, in a completely renovated nineteenth century red brick building, formerly a carpet mill. Gordon Lankton joined the private company in 1962 as general manager and 50 percent owner. He had worked with plastics at DuPont for several years, after graduating with an engineering degree from Cornell. Later in 1969, with company sales at $4 million, he purchased the remaining stock. And although the company continued to grow during the 1970s and 1980s, it was not until the mid-80s that the company hit full stride. Fiscal 1994 marked the company's ninth consecutive year of record revenues and profits as Nypro reported nearly $166 million in consolidated company net sales (see Figure 1 for financial statements). The firm solidified its industry position as one of the largest nonautomotive custom injection molders of plastic parts in the world (Figure 2) Including total sales of all joint ventures, revenues from Nypro's eighteen worldwide molding and assembly operations reached nearly $200 million.

By Daniel J. McCarthy, Northeastern University and Gaurab Bhardwaj, University of Pittsburgh. Management cooperated in the field research of this case, which was written solely for the purpose of stimulating student discussion. The authors thank company executives for their cooperation in developing the case, as well as Professor Sheila Puffer and three anonymous reviewers for their assistance in the development of the manuscript.

| FIGURE 1 | PROFIT LOSS STATEMENTS AND BALANCE SHEETS 1989–1994 |

	1994		1993		1992	
Net Sales	165,983	100.00%	135,829	100.00%	119,856	100.00%
Cost of Sales	126,512	76.22%	104,189	76.71%	93,347	77.88%
Gross Profits	39,471	23.78%	31,640	3.29%	26,509	22.12%
Selling	7,244	4.36%	6,826	5.03%	5,978	4.99%
General & Administration	16,807	10.13%	11,481	8.45%	9,972	8.32%
Research & Development	2,705	1.63%	2,415	1.78%	1,793	1.50%
Total Expenses	26,756	16.12%	20,722	15.26%	17,743	14.80%
Operating Profits	12,715	7.66%	10,918	8.04%	8,766	7.31%
Other Income (Expenses)	647	0.39%	415	0.31%	553	0.46%
Eq. in Net Inc. of Uncon. A	605	0.36%	464	0.34%	202	0.17%
Min. Int. in Loss of Con.	−77	−0.05%	−97	−0.07%	−13	−0.01%
Income Taxes	3,064	1.85%	3,194	2.35%	3,002	2.50%
Net Income	10,826	6.52%	8,506	6.26%	6,506	5.43%

	1991		1990		1989	
Net Sales	100,201	100.00%	96,934	100.00%	84,150	100.00%
Cost of Sales	78,215	78.06%	76,127	78.53%	68,002	80.81%
Gross Profits	21,986	21.94%	20,807	21.47%	16,148	19.19%
Selling	5,546	5.53%	5,037	5.20%	4,202	4.99%
General & Administration	8,035	8.02%	7,446	7.68%	6,018	7.15%
Research & Development	1,005	1.00%	1,131	1.17%	861	1.02%
Total Expenses	14,586	14.56%	13,614	14.04%	11,081	13.17%
Operating Profits	7,400	7.39%	7,193	7.42%	5,067	6.02%
Other Income (Expenses)	915	0.91%	−136	−0.14%	−1,283	−1.52%
Eq. in Net Inc. of Uncon. A	−864	0.86%	−79	−0.08%	−111	−0.13%
Min. Int. in Losses of Con.	152	0.15%	−42	−0.04%	−93	−0.11%
Income Taxes	2,450	2.45%	1,998	2.06%	1,675	1.99%
Net Income	5,153	5.14%	4,938	5.09%	2,545	3.02%

Balance Sheets: Assets

	1994	1993	1992	1991	1990	1989
ASSETS						
Current Assets:						
Cash & short-term investments	7,109	8,731	9,389	7,258	6,329	2,342
Accounts and notes receivable, net allowance for doubtful accounts	27,511	20,551	17,781	16,654	13,795	14,101
Inventories	9,963	6,877	6,984	7,157	7,027	5,689
Mold costs in excess of billing	1,879	3,402	1,108	n/a	n/a	n/a
Prepaid expenses & other current assets	1,057	704	336	228	153	542
Deferred tax assets	1,000	n/a	n/a	n/a	n/a	n/a
TOTAL CURRENT ASSETS	48,519	40,265	35,598	31,297	27,304	22,674

(continued)

FIGURE 1	(CONTINUED)

Balance Sheets: Assets

	1994	1993	1992	1991	1990	1989
NONCURRENT ASSETS						
Investments in & advances to unconstructed affiliates	6,205	5,094	3,013	1,984	2,371	2,759
Restricted bond proceeds	1,976	2,957	n/a	n/a	n/a	n/a
Other noncurrent assets	4,336	2,501	1,899	1,585	1,309	1,121
TOTAL NONCURRENT ASSETS	12,517	10,574	4,912	3,569	3,680	3,880
PROPERTY, PLANT & EQUIPMENT						
Land	1,169	398	55	55	255	146
Building & improvements	27,968	17,360	16,012	12,139	11,520	10,172
Machinery & equipment	57,675	31,125	27,742	23,895	22,888	19,620
Furniture & fixtures	5,495	3,738	3,227	2,542	,145	1,613
Construction in process	6,837	3,995	390	1,812	760	1,014
(Less accumulated depreciation & amortization)	(45,359)	(28,081)	(24,029)	(20,903)	(18,237)	(17,132)
TOTAL PROPERTY, PLANT & EQUIPMENT	53,785	28,535	22,397	19,540	19,331	15,433
TOTAL ASSETS	114,821	79,374	62,907	54,406	50,315	41,987

Balance Sheets: Liabilities

	1994	1993	1992	1991	1990	1989
LIABILITIES & STOCKHOLDERS' EQUITY						
CURRENT LIABILITIES						
Current portion of long-term debt	5,179	1,949	2,223	1,664	2,154	1,515
Notes payable	1,344	625	1,109	1,738	1,279	740
Accounts payable	15,730	9,275	6,926	6,622	5,268	5,321
Accrued liabilities	10,408	11,983	9,277	9,267	8,868	6,622
Mold billings in excess of cost	2,304	2,022	1,689	n/a	n/a	n/a
Income tax payable	682	896	545	540	268	146
TOTAL CURRENT LIABILITIES	35,647	26,750	21,769	19,831	17,837	14,344
NONCURRENT LIABILITIES						
Long-term debt, less current portion	21,342	9,815	8,033	6,393	9,870	11,354
Deferred gain	n/a	185	303	333	350	400
Deferred taxes	1,165	1,030	1,271	1,119	1,053	508
Monthly interests	1,210	1,061	941	884	841	772
TOTAL LIABILITIES	63,988	38,431	32,317	28,560	29,951	27,378
STOCKHOLDERS' EQUITY						
Nonvoting redemption preferred stock, par value $1; authorized 150,000 shares, not all shares issued	130	130	130	115	101	89
Nonvoting convertible preferred stock, par value $1; authorized 50,000 shares, not all shares issued	n/a	n/a	20	20	20	20

(continued)

FIGURE 1   (CONTINUED)

Balance Sheets: Liabilities

	1994	1993	1992	1991	1990	1989
Common stock, par value $1; authorized 1,000,000 shares, issued 422,342 shares	422	422	422	422	422	422
Additional paid-in capital	8,290	6,597	6,830	4,755	3,333	2,616
Retained earnings	48,708	37,882	29,626	23,120	17,967	13,029
Treasury stock, at cost	(6,543)	(4,723)	(6,803)	(2,793)	(1,886)	(1,682)
Cumulative transaction adjustment	(174)	(135)	365	207	407	115
TOTAL STOCKHOLDERS' EQUITY	50,833	40,533	30,590	25,846	20,364	14,609
TOTAL LIABILITIES & STOCKHOLDERS' EQUITY	114,821	79,374	62,907	54,406	50,315	41,987

NOTE: Other Income (Expenses) includes other income, interest expense, and interest income. When using percentages to arrive at 100% you must subtract gross profits, total expenses, and operating profits.

FIGURE 2   TOP TEN NORTH AMERICAN CUSTOM INJECTION MOLDERS

TOP 10

Company	1993 sales	1992 sales
	(figures in millions)	
1. Textron Inc.	$1,000+	$900
2. UT Automotive Inc.	$415	$412.1
3. Decoma International Inc.	$402.2	$308.7
4. Automotive Industries Inc.	$290	$225
5. Owens-Illinois Inc.	$270[E]	$200[E]
6. Worthington Custom Plastics Inc.	$235	$218[E]
7. Becker Group Inc.	$231[E]	$210[E]
8. Lacks Enterprises Inc.	$175	$150
9. Nypro Inc.	$174.9	$148
10. Donnelly Corp.	$170	$150

This 31-page section focusing on the massive custom injection molding industry begins on Page 22 with Plastics News' 1994 ranking of the biggest custom injection molders in North America. For a full alphabetical index of all 474 companies listed, see Pages 18–51. A story on how smaller molders—which make up a large portion of the injection molding industry— fared in 1993 begins on Page 51.

[E] Plastics News and industry estimates

SOURCE: *PLASTICE NEWS*, Cain Communications, Inc., April 18, 1994

The Franchising Decision

In early 1995, Lankton was considering franchising as an additional vehicle for growing the company as it entered the second half of the decade. Lankton amplified his thoughts in comments to the case writers:

> The 1990s will see more manufacturing being franchised. I am seriously considering such a move for Nypro. My objective is to have twenty franchises, starting in the United States, by the year 2000.

As a private company, Nypro's access to capital was always somewhat limited, and franchising, he believed, offered an opportunity for growth which could leverage Nypro's relatively scarce financial resources. Although franchising of manufacturing operations was relatively rare, Lankton felt the future would see a change in the situation. He also believed that Nypro's experience in various forms of partnerships would be invaluable if the company were to begin franchising. Nypro had numerous joint ventures with business partners, each partner sharing ownership in the joint venture companies. It also had numerous strategic alliances with customers and even suppliers. These were agreements by which each party cooperated in various ways for mutual benefit, although no new companies were established in the process. Lankton believed that Nypro's experience with these different types of partnerships, coupled with its plant operations around the world, could provide the foundation for Nypro to successfully lead this change.

With such experience, Lankton believed that working with franchisees would not be very different. He saw Nypro as being similar to McDonald's, the fast-food chain. It had locations in many countries; utilized standardized equipment, processes, and policies; and offered high-quality services from clean efficient plants located near its major customers. He described Nypro's global operations as the most cost-effective, cleanest, most automated, most uniform, and most consistent precision plastic molding plants in the world. He explained further:

> Our global customers want us to be truly global. They want us to use the same machines, the same process control, same mold technology, same procedures, and CAD systems, regardless of where we make their products around the world. Fortunately, information technologies are now available that make this possible and practical.

Lankton understood fully, however, that franchising would not occur without difficulties. He and other managers raised the question of whether Nypro possessed the necessary resources to reach its goals. With equity capital always limited, debt capital was similarly constrained. They also questioned whether Nypro possessed the managerial depth to pursue franchising, as well as to support the 15 percent growth rate which management believed was the company's potential in its present market segments.

Whether the company's highly sophisticated processes could be replicated in franchised operations was another cause for concern among some managers, and many questioned whether suitable franchisees could be found to successfully operate and manage Nypro plants. If any franchise relationships did fail, the franchisee would likely become a competitor, having gained in-depth knowledge and experience about Nypro's core competence. Strategic management analysts have cautioned against this potential risk, stating: "By their very nature, all alliance mechanisms create direct and indirect windows of opportunity for gaining access to a partner's skills, technologies, core competencies, and even strategic direction."[1]

For Lankton himself, committing the company to a new strategic direction of franchising at this point in his career was a cause for his serious reflection. Finally, the decision to franchise was complicated further since the company was also considering focusing more attention on the demanding automotive market, a move which could place serious demands upon its resources.

Lankton felt some pressure to settle the franchising decision so that he and management could focus their efforts on the most promising growth opportunities for the company.

Nypro's Business

"To be the best in the world in precision plastics injection molding, creating value for our customers, employees and communities."

This company mission was formulated at the 1993 managers' conference in Ireland. Lankton estimated that his company had about two-tenths of one percent of the world's custom plastic injection molding market, which positioned the company as one of the largest nonautomotive custom injection molders of plastic parts in the world (Figure 2).

Nypro plants did not manufacture final products, but instead acted as a contract manufacturer for a variety of customers, as a producer of plastic parts and components. The plants, including joint ventures, processed plastic raw material utilizing highly sophisticated, robot-operated plastic injection molding machines. Raw plastic material was purchased from large suppliers such as GE and chemical companies and fed automatically to the machines through a system of pipes. The highly automated machinery was equipped with custom molds which shaped the plastic parts to customer specifications. The finished parts were packaged for delivery to customers.

During fiscal 1994, new company-owned plants had been opened near Chicago, primarily to serve the health care market, and in Oregon to service Hewlett-Packard's needs for printer cartridge components. Joint venture operations were added in China and Wales to better serve the Asian and European markets. By 1995, Nypro had eighteen plastic injection molding plants worldwide, including the United States and Mexico, Asia, Europe, Russia, and the Caribbean, twelve of which were joint ventures (Figure 3). More locations and acquisitions were under consideration, as well as additional joint ventures.

The Plastics Processing Industry

Nypro operated in the highly fragmented and competitive plastics processing industry, a segment of the plastics industry, the largest industry in the world in terms of employment. Although 40,000 plastic custom injection molding companies operated worldwide, almost all were very small in size. The United States had 2,800 molders, while Hong Kong alone claimed 5,000. Firms in this segment of the plastics industry

[1] David Lei and John W. Slocum, Jr. "Global Strategy, Competence-Building and Strategic Alliances," *California Management Review*, Fall 1992, 81–97. Quote on p. 84.

| FIGURE 3 | NYPRO WORLDWIDE LOCATIONS |

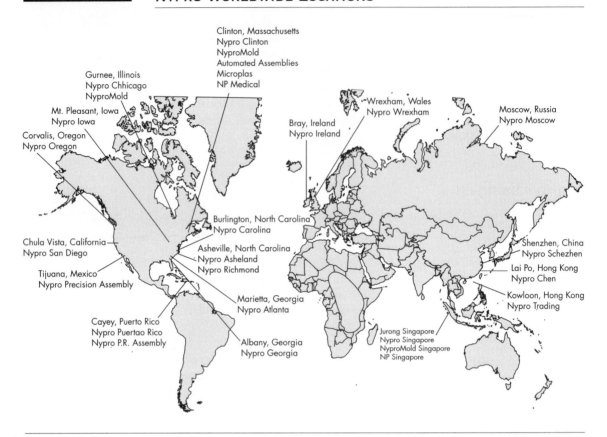

used injection molding machines to produce parts and components to customers' specifications.

The structure of the plastics processing industry made it relatively unattractive in terms of competition and profits. With the large number of companies, price was the primary basis for competition. Barriers to entry were generally low; close physical proximity to customers was required for expected timely delivery and service requirements; and plastics materials suppliers, such as Dow Chemical, Union Carbide, Exxon, and GE, wielded substantial pricing power.

The plastics produced by these companies from petroleum-based materials were polymers that were combined with additives and other ingredients like stabilizers, flame retardants and reinforcing agents. It took the form of pellets, flakes, granule powders, liquid resins, sheeting, and film. These materials were transformed by plastics processing firms like Nypro into finished plastic parts, components, or products. Materials and machinery depreciation usually constituted 30–40 percent of manufacturing costs for injection molders, with labor and packaging constituting the remainder of cost of goods sold.

In pounds, plastic industry sales and production had risen at an annual compound rate of just more than 5 percent during the period from 1985 to 1994. This accounted for about 3 percent of world oil production, and increases in the price of oil were passed on to customers like Nypro. Somewhat slower growth was estimated by experts for 1995 and 1996 due to a buildup in inventories during 1994, as well as a lower rate of economic growth.

Because plastic was cheap, light, corrosion resistant, and easy to fabricate, its use was growing in countless industries producing industrial and consumer goods. Several trends had been noted by industry experts. One, metal substitution, was the engine driving growth, and plastic injection molding companies were expected to grow with the industry. Another was a growing market receptivity to automobiles containing recycled and recyclable parts, resulting in a quest for lighter and more efficient vehicles. A third trend, in consumer goods markets, was the continued growth in plastics use for food, clothing, cosmetics, pharmaceuticals, and entertainment products like compact disks and videocassettes.

In the plastic processing segment in which Nypro competed, industry analysts estimated that approximately 50 percent of output was from independent molding companies, with the other 50 percent belonging to captive in-house molders owned by large producers of plastic parts and products. Customers for companies like Nypro thus faced a make or buy decision with regard to injection molding. To penetrate such companies, independent molders had to offer a combination of price and service that would convince them to "outsource" their injection molding business.

Intensely competitive pricing had, in fact, driven the return on investment from in-house molding below the desired 20–25 percent cutoff points desired by large companies. Many believed they could make better returns by investing in their own products and related operations, rather than in captive injection molding. Further, captive molding operations had difficulty keeping up with rapidly changing injection molding technology. For instance, some custom injection molders such as Nypro had been able to raise productivity by as much as 40 percent, a difficult feat for in-house molders to match.

Few independent molders, however, had developed enough differentiation to attract business away from these in-house molders, although a slight trend away from captive molding had been noted by industry experts. The possibility of customer companies integrating backward into injection molding was not a concern to Lankton, however. He was fond of saying, "Companies are better off sticking to their knitting, including Nypro."

The operations of American and other automobile manufacturing operations located throughout the United States were major customers for a number of large plastic injection molding companies. They were, however, challenging customers. A survey by *Plastic World* in the early 1990s had noted that nearly 80 percent of responding automotive injection molders felt that doing business with the Big Three automakers of Detroit had become even more difficult in recent years. The so-called partnerships had become one-sided, with automakers demanding more quality and service along with constant cost reductions.

Many molders reported late and unpredictable engineering change orders by automakers, unmoldable designs being forced on them, and excessive red tape, in addition to severe pricing pressures. To be competitive, most molders had been forced to invest heavily in areas that would improve operations such as design engineering activities, Just-In-Time (JIT) inventory processes, Statistical Process Control (SPC) and Statistical Quality Control (SQC), while concurrently being pushed to cut prices.

The molders reportedly felt that GM's Saturn division and Japanese plants in the United States were the only ones which operated in true partnerships with molders.

The Japanese, especially, thought out their designs for processability and were more receptive to new ideas while offering more stable schedules, fewer changes, and more secure relationships. However, they preferred to deal with Japanese injection molders. According to one industry source, getting into such companies would be easier if the U.S. molder had a joint venture or business association with a Japanese company.

Nypro's Marketing Strategy

Under Lankton's leadership, Nypro sought customers who demanded top quality and reliability. However, such customers often called for sudden changes in the molder's production schedule. Yet, according to Nypro management, the ability to service this demanding market segment reduced Nypro's worldwide competition from 40,000 firms to less than 100.

Nypro's customers were primarily large corporations in the health care, consumer-industrial, and the electronics-telecommunications market segments. Nypro focused its sales efforts on Fortune 500 companies having the potential of providing at least $1 million in business within two years. By 1994, Nypro had more than forty such accounts (Figure 4).

Among the components that Nypro produced for its customers were handles for "Reach" brand toothbrushes, valves for fire extinguishers, roller clamps to control the flow of intravenous fluids, dental floss boxes, cases for Johnson & Johnson's disposable contact lenses, blood analysis devices, casings for computer floppy disks, plastic components for Gillette's women's sensor razors, and plastic valves for McDonald's soft drink dispensers. Most such customers required that Nypro not only meet demanding product specifications but have the ability to provide production runs in the millions.

Ed Rivera, the business manager for the consumer-industrial segment, described Nypro's success in meeting customer demands:

> Sales of Duracell batteries amount to about five billion units a year, and each battery has a plastic seal that requires an extremely high tolerance due to potential liability from a defective battery which could explode. We have been successful year after year in meeting their requirements.

Regional Nypro plants catered to these large accounts but were free to service smaller local customers that did not meet the corporate "million dollar test," as long as there were no conflicts with the needs of large customers. Like the multinationals, smaller customers had to be financially solid and offer future growth potential for Nypro.

Telecommunication and computer equipment, however, did not use plastic components in such large volumes, but the demanding specifications made the segment attractive to Nypro. In 1994, the company added a new process called NovaPlast, a departure from its high-volume production systems, to specifically address the unique lower volume, small-machine, low-cavitation, high-precision plastic injection molding market segment.

The Health-Care Segment

Nypro's largest market segment was health care, accounting for nearly half of company sales in 1994 (Figure 5). Large customers included Johnson & Johnson, Abbott, and

FIGURE 4	MILLION DOLLAR CUSTOMERS

Nypro Million Dollar Customers

Electronics/ Telecommunications		Health Care		Consumer/Industrial	
Apple	Motorola	Abbott Diagnostics	Eppendorf	Avery Dennison	Polaroid
Canon	Panasonic	Abbott Hospital prods.	Instrumentation Labs	Bendix-JKC	Prestolite
Hewlett-Packard	Verbatim	Abbott Vision	IVAC	Calsonics	Rolodex
IBM	3M	Althin Medical	Johnson & Johnson	Duracell	Scott Sani-Fresh
		Baxter Dade	Marquest	Gillette	Sheaffer
		Baxter Fenwal	3M Health Care	GTE	Siecor
		Baxter IV Systems	Pall Biomedical	HK Cad/ Cam-Gimeli	Techsonic
		Biomérieux	Sandoz	Kidde	Thomas & Betts
		C. R. Bard	Vistakon	Masbac	

FIGURE 5	BUSINESS UNIT SALES

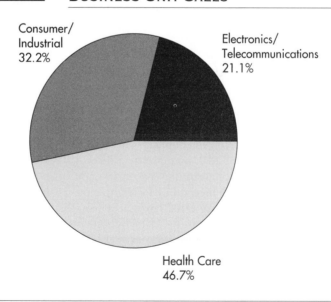

Consumer/Industrial 32.2%

Electronics/Telecommunications 21.1%

Health Care 46.7%

Baxter, each of which provided annual sales in excess of $10 million. Nypro's decision to focus on the health-care industry came about almost accidentally. During the recession of the 1970s, demand for Nypro's services fell in all areas, except health care. Since then, Nypro made a conscious effort to target this industry. As an illustration of overall growth in health care in the early 1990s, annual health-care expenditures were equal to approximately 10 percent of GNP in the United States. Also, cost containment, changing demographics, and a growing concern for controlling the spread of disease provided opportunities for new uses of plastic in health-care products.

To best service this important segment, Nypro utilized a specialized marketing, sales, engineering and manufacturing team, while separate teams served the company's other two major segments. Each was headed by an individual business manager who reported to the vice president of marketing.

Rethinking the Automotive Segment

In contrast to its focus on health-care customers, Nypro had historically chosen not to emphasize service to the automobile manufacturers, in part to avoid competition with the larger plastic injection molders which were dedicated to that industry (Figure 2). By 1994, however, the company did nearly $10 million volume in the industry, but with OEMs (Original Equipment Manufacturers) rather than with the automobile companies.

Lankton explained that automotive companies had generally chosen suppliers primarily on the basis of price rather than high levels of service quality. However, he noted that the automobile companies' *modus operandi* was changing. Automakers were apparently becoming less interested in buying single components, preferring to deal with companies which could deliver more complete assembly-ready units. Nypro was seriously considering putting more emphasis on the automotive segment in 1994 but recognized that this would involve additional investment, risk, and possible changes to its traditional mode of doing business.

Getting Close to the Customer

Although seldom the least expensive supplier, Nypro offered other benefits to its customers. Since most Nypro customers demanded JIT, plant locations depended on where Nypro's customers were located. Customers had the power to dictate delivery times and preferred suppliers who were situated nearby. Most insisted on a delivery schedule of −3 to 0, no more than three days early and zero days late. Locating plants very near major customers also cut freight costs.

As another method of fostering close customer–supplier relationships, Nypro's exceptional quality freed customers from having to inspect products upon delivery. NyproNet, an electronic data interchange (EDI), connected customers to Nypro through a communications network. This technology provided customers with instantaneous access to sixty different pieces of information on production and quality directly from the molding machines, eliminating the need to inspect items upon delivery.

This attention to quality led Nypro's management to pursue the Malcolm Baldrige National Quality Award during 1994. Lankton stated:

> We have been informed that we are one of six finalists in our category with the largest U.S. manufacturing corporations. We are thinking positively.

Joint product and process development, quality management, and reviews of the supplier's operations and training occurred frequently. Nypro engineers often communicated and coordinated developments with customers. Rather than performing much in-house R&D, Nypro instead worked closely with customers on process design. For instance, the disposable lens project with Johnson & Johnson took eight years to develop as teams from both companies worked together with six people form each side meeting every six weeks to perfect the process.

Nypro's customers usually shared with them confidential information about their operations and products and were reluctant to deal with more than one injection molder. Thus, the threat of losing customers to competitors was generally avoided, but backward integration into injection molding by customers was a possibility. Although this was not a major concern to Lankton, he recognized it was a potential threat:

> Our relationship with Johnson & Johnson recognizes that there is always a risk in an alliance, but this sort of partnership is very difficult for our competitors to crack. In fact, the only competition we might face would come from Johnson & Johnson, if they ever decided to make the contact lens molds and produce products in-house.

Company management emphasized that most Fortune 500 companies required that plastic parts for their products be supplied globally. Nypro tried to penetrate these firms at the highest levels to learn where parts were needed and then suggested possible locations where they could be produced. If no Nypro plant was located close enough to the target company, Nypro would offer to build one at a customer-convenient location, as long as they would guarantee Nypro business amounting to $5 million in each of the following five years. Nypro expected to lose up to $1 million in the first year and break even in the second.

After moving to a new location, Nypro sales personnel searched for other potential customers in the area. A major risk in following customers to new locations was that the customer's business could fail. Such a situation occurred in the 1970s in Mexico when one of Nypro's U.S. customers failed to develop a market for its product, and Nypro was forced to abandon the Mexican operations which had been established near that customer. In 1994, however, Nypro re-entered Mexico with a joint venture in Tijuana.

Going Global

During the 1970s and 80s, large corporations had expanded rapidly overseas in search of new markets and lower production costs. This trend convinced Lankton that, as a small manufacturer, Nypro would have to globalize or face the possibility of losing key customers who wanted to deal worldwide with one vendor. Globalization, he felt, would not only provide more business, but also furnish Nypro with immediate access to the latest technologies from around the world. By 1994, however, operations outside the United States still accounted for a relatively small proportion of Nypro's sales, since most of their joint ventures with foreign partners were located in the United States (Figure 6). More recent joint ventures, however, were occurring outside the United States, and global sales were expected to increase rapidly.

Although global customers were served from various Nypro plants, management of customers was coordinated on a centralized basis by the corporate marketing and

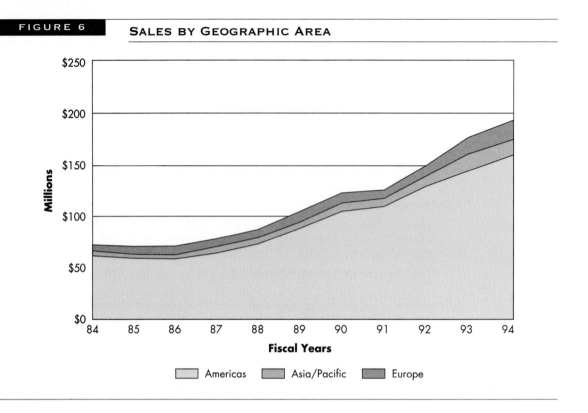

FIGURE 6   **SALES BY GEOGRAPHIC AREA**

sales organization in Clinton, Massachusetts. This coordination also allowed some smoothing of production peaks and valleys among plants by transferring projects from one location to another.

In order to reflect Nypro's global market presence, pricing was also centralized to prevent confusion for large corporate customers. As multinational customers moved to new locations, it was difficult for local general managers to offer full service. To address this, account managers, who reported directly to one of three business segment managers, were assigned to coordinate the servicing of these customers.

However, the beginning of Nypro's global expansion did not go smoothly, but Lankton and other managers acknowledged that the early endeavors had provided a real learning experience for them. In 1975, Nypro started a plant operation in France, but soon after the venture began, Lankton's concern that many French customers were averse to dealing with American businesses proved accurate. The company's operation was losing $700,000 per year by the late 1970s, and Nypro decided to cut costs by trimming the work force. They submitted an action plan to the French Labor Board which deliberated for months before allowing a small number of employees to be discharged. Nypro decided to leave France, but the French Labor Union threatened to intervene. The factory was abandoned and, in the middle of the night, Nypro employees smuggled out the customer-owned molds and sent them to Ireland. Lankton felt that he had learned a lesson and that a partnership with a French company that understood the local business environment would likely have avoided these troubles. He decided that future international expansion would utilize joint ventures, and he believed in equal ownership participation in such alliances.

Using Strategic Alliances

Soon after the French experience, Dennison Manufacturing, one of Nypro's largest customers at the time, with 20 percent of sales (1 percent in 1994), contracted with Nypro to make plastic fasteners for products sold in Japan. Nypro set up operations in Taiwan and within a few years had expanded to Hong Kong. This operation started as a fifty–fifty joint venture partnership and was successful for eight years. After that, however, Nypro managers felt that the molding machines were causing quality problems for American customers and wanted to purchase expensive Swiss-made Netstal machines. When its partner refused to cooperate, Nypro managers realized that a substantial difference existed in management philosophies. They pulled out of active involvement in the Hong Kong venture and kept only 10 percent ownership for investment purposes. This situation was not unusual, since many studies have indicated that the majority of joint ventures are dissolved after a relatively short time. One study of dissolved cross-border alliances also found that one partner bought out the interest of the other nearly 80 percent of the time.[2]

In spite of the difficulties of making alliances work, the French experience had convinced Lankton that such arrangements were critical to the success of globalizing his business. Experts in globalization usually agree and, as one noted: "Globalization mandates alliances, makes them absolutely essential to strategy."[3] Except for Hong Kong, all of Nypro's joint ventures were successful because management understood what it took to make such ventures succeed. They sought 50–50 ownership, carefully aligned their own strategic objectives with those of partners, and achieved tactical integration by bringing together middle-level managers from both companies in joint projects and even on the boards of directors of joint ventures. Lankton himself was always deeply involved in the early stages, seeking cultural as well as strategic and operating integration. One expert on strategic alliances has noted that there are five levels of integration that characterize the most productive alliances.[4]

In 1991, because of the growth potential of Southeast Asia, Nypro built a plant in Singapore which became its Pacific regional headquarters. This operation began as a partnership among three groups, but disagreements arose about strategy and operations. Nypro resolved the situation by buying out one partner, which resulted in a new fifty-five–forty-five joint venture, with Nypro holding the majority position. This unequal proportion was contrary to Lankton's philosophy favoring equal ownership. He explained:

> A fifty-one–forty-nine business partnership is not effective because it is not a free and open relationship between equals. The partner with the lesser stake always would feel like a second-class citizen.

Another venture at odds with equal ownership occurred in 1989 when Nypro entered a joint venture called "Miro" in Russia, with a 20 percent take. The partners were Mikromashina of Moscow, a manufacturer of electrical consumer appliances, and Rotel AG of Switzerland, a supplier of electric motors and household appliances in

---

[2] Bleek and Ernst. "How to Win in Cross-Border Alliances," *Harvard Business Review*, November–December 1991.

[3] Kenichi Ohmae. "The Global Logic of Strategic Alliances," *Harvard Business Review*, March–April 1989, p. 143.

[4] Rosabeth Moss Kanter. "Collaborative Advantage: The Art of Alliances," *Harvard Business Review*, July–August 1994, pp. 96–108.

Europe. At the time, forty East German- and Russian-built injection molding machines were in operation at Mikromashina's plant built in 1982. Nypro planned that Miro would become a world-class plastic injection molding operation. Machines with state-of-the-art technology were to be added in the future to improve Miro's productivity and quality. Computer Aided Design (CAD) and Computer Aided Manufacturing (CAM) techniques were also to be introduced.

Approximately 80 percent of Miro's products were to be sold in Russia for rubles, with the rest to be exported to Europe and North America for hard currency. Russia's political and economic uncertainty made the venture risky but still it made an annual ruble profit of about $100,000 from 1992 to 1994. Earnings in hard currency were not expected in the near term. Lankton commented:

> I am very optimistic about the future of Russia and have strong hopes for our venture there. Getting money out is a problem right now, and there really is no solution to that at present. But we are there for the long term, and as a private company, that is a risk that I am willing to assume. I guess it is obvious that I am an incurable optimist.

Nypro continued its globalization efforts with a modern $4 million plant built as a joint venture in Ireland to take advantage of potential growth expected from the development of the European Union. And in 1993 and 1994, joint ventures were established in China, Wales, and Mexico to serve growing markets in those regions of the world.

Multiple Objectives for Strategic Alliances

Although these enterprises were recent joint ventures, Nypro had utilized this method of growth for decades using various alliances in the United States and elsewhere to achieve different objectives. During the late 1970s and 1980s, for instance, the company had developed many significant strategic alliances with three key partners. The first was with Nestal Maschinen AG of Switzerland in 1979. Nestal wanted to introduce its modern injection molding machines into the U.S. market and approached Nypro because of Nypro's expertise in the plastics processing industry. With the agreement, Nypro gained access to the superior Swiss technology. The Swiss machines were twice as expensive as their U.S. counterparts but were considered by Nypro management to be the best in the world. Initially a fifty–fifty partnership was formed with Nestal, and later two more Nestal partnerships were added in Singapore and North Carolina. Through these relationships, Nypro became Nestal's largest customer and worked with them to expand the market for molding machines as well as to improve the machines themselves.

Also in the late 1970s, Lankton discovered that 70 percent of the injection molding machines in Japan used robots whereas only 5 percent did so in the United States. Nypro then formed a strategic alliance with Sailor Pen Company of Japan, a major manufacturer of robots. Through Sailor Pen's affiliate, Automated Assemblies Corporation, Nypro became the exclusive distributor of Sailor robots in the United States. The alliance made Nypro the U.S. industry leader in automated robotic systems for plastic injection molding machines. Nypro became the first plastic custom injection molder in the United States to robotize operations of all its molding machines. Competition, in contrast, had reached only 15 percent. And by the early 1990s, sales of robots, mostly to its U.S. competitors, generated $10 million in annual sales. The Sailor Pen Co. alliance also led Nypro to new areas in growth. Its molding plant in Iowa was the result of a joint venture between Nypro, Sailor Pen, and Sheaffer Pen to make pen barrels.

A third strategic alliance partner was Japan's Mitsui & Co., one of the world's largest companies. While in college, Lankton had visited Japan where he made contacts and friends who would eventually be instrumental in forming this alliance. One who rose to a top position at Mitsui was assigned to its U.S. operations and proposed a fifty–fifty joint venture to Lankton. Called Amitech, the venture prospered as Nypro helped Mitsui sell their plastic materials to the U.S. processing industry, while Mitsui aided Nypro in forming relationships with Japanese manufacturers which had established plants in the United States. Mitsui dealt with the customers while Nypro ran the factory. The two companies later started other joint ventures in California, North Carolina, and Georgia, primarily to service Japanese companies in these locations.

Utilizing Technology in Operations

Nypro emphasized technology, automation, computers and robotics in its operations in order to achieve high quality as well as efficiency. To facilitate communications throughout its global operations, Nypro in 1992 began developing an extensive wide-area computer network. Computer Integrated Manufacturing (CIM) would eventually be introduced at all the plants in order to form a standardized, cohesive network of operations. The Clinton, Massachusetts, headquarters would have access to detailed information from every Nypro location. Nypro's goal for the 1990s was to computerize everything possible in its operations.

The key component of the CIM system was Statistical Process Control (SPC). Nypro used an advanced, off-the-shelf, on-line SPC system called Quality Alert. This system allowed Nypro to offer its customers products with fewer than five defects per million units. Constant Improvement Teams monitored the processes and developed a continuous stream of product and service innovations. The teams undertook a project with Johnson & Johnson aimed at increasing the yield rate in the production of disposable contact lenses. Initially, components manufactured by Nypro had resulted in a high defect rate by Johnson & Johnson standards. The team worked to identify the cause of the problem and raised the yield by over 20 percent. According to Nypro management, each one-percent decrease in the defect rate resulted in a $1 million increase in Johnson & Johnson's bottom line.

Nypro carried out most production in special "clean rooms" using the latest Computer Aided Engineering (CAE), Computer Aided Design (CAD), and CIM technologies (Figure 7). Health-care products required "clean rooms," but Nypro provided them for virtually all products. R&D at Nypro involved mostly tooling and mold building, as well as improving process and assembly operations. The company also performed R&D on plastic materials used by its customers, as well as in collaboration with suppliers. Nypro also worked closely with customers during product design in order to shorten the time required between product conception and final product design.

FIGURE 7   A NYPRO CLEAN ROOM

8:25 am.
Nymedex, Clinton, Massachusetts, USA
The day shift is in full swing in Nypro's newest multi-level cleanroom at Mymedex. The facility has the capacity for 20 machines with automatic material feed systems below the molding floor level, resulting in a more efficient flow of raw material. The inset photo highlights Nypro's successful achievement of parts-handling robotics and advanced manufacturing techniques in a 175-ton machine equipped with a state-of-the-art high speed, side entry robot.

The company's $200,000 molding machines had an average age of less than six years in 1994, yet had a potential operating life of twenty years. Technical obsolescence, however, sometimes permitted a maximum life of only seven years since Nypro was committed to using the best technology available. Nypro machines diagnostically checked critical variables and self-adjusted every twenty milliseconds. Molding and assembly operations took place at the molding machines through work cell systems in which workers with interchangeable skills were responsible for the entire operation. Robotic take-out devices at every machine placed molded parts on the assembly line in an efficient pattern so that operations downstream did not have to reposition parts. The on-line assembly of parts and components eliminated the need for holding parts inventory or performing batch-type operations.

The individual molds required to produce products were usually owned by customers, but Nypro engineered or built virtually all these molds for its plants at its Clinton, Singapore, and Chicago locations. Tooling demands, however, varied greatly from customer to customer, and toolmakers were thus considered to be among Nypro's most valuable employees. They were relatively scarce and required long periods of training at the Nypro Institute.

Facing Environmental Issues

By the 1980s, environmentalists as well as governments at all levels were concerned about the amount of space discarded plastics occupied in landfills. According to Lankton:

> Plastics have an image problem. Only 8 percent of landfills are taken up with plastics compared to 32 percent for paper. And unlike paper, plastics do not release harmful chemicals into the groundwater. They just stay there like rock.

While explaining this, Lankton referred to Nypro's proactive approach in seeking ways to reduce the environmental impact of plastics. One result was receiving Johnson & Johnson's global award for scrap plastic reduction in 1994. Nypro offered "value analysis" as a service to customers such as Abbott, Baxter, and Johnson & Johnson. Value analysis teams worked on projects with the objective of maximizing the cost effectiveness of the product, as well as minimizing the amount of plastic used in the product in order to reduce waste.

For instance, a joint computer-aided design and engineering project between Nypro and the Diagnostics Division of Abbott Laboratories resulted in the reduction of more than 500,000 pounds annually of medical waste by improving the design and processing of a disposable medical product. The project also reduced incineration bills for scrap plastic without sacrificing product quality and performance. The project team's design and manufacturing technology cut the wall thickness of the product by half and reduced raw material volume by one-third; Nypro boosted its own productivity by 20 percent with these changes. The close relationship between Abbott and Nypro enabled the project to be completed in less than one year and allowed both companies to realize significant cost reductions. Nypro also developed its own molding technologies when conventional computer molding technologies failed to produce desired results. One highly successful project reduced the weight of a medical product by 60 percent.

When possible, plastic scrap was sold in the secondary market for use by other companies. Nypro had as an objective to eliminate all plastic from its waste stream by 1995. To help accomplish this, the company had entered into an agreement with Heat Energy Advanced Technology (HEAT). This Dallas-based company used the waste plastic that Nypro had previously discarded as an alternate energy source in the production of cement. Nypro paid $160 per 1000 pounds of its plastic, plus all freight charges, to eliminate this source of environmental waste. Consistent with its objective, the company's new Chicago and Oregon plants, which opened in 1994, were designed to provide environmentally controlled closed-loop material handling which would eliminate the necessity of plastic scrap going to a landfill.

Emphasizing Human Resources and Sharing Ownership

By 1994 more than 2,400 people were employed worldwide by Nypro. The company culture fostered an entrepreneurial spirit and participative management and attempted to establish uniformity in the operations of all its plants. Company philosophy stressed that employees utilize on-the-spot decision making rather than pushing decisions up the managerial hierarchy. Consistent with this view, the company had no formal organization chart.

Lankton believed that participative human resource policies would enrich the work environment for all employees. The possibility of unionization would also be reduced, and only the Irish plant was unionized. The company's central training center in Clinton, the Nypro Institute, focused on employees learning to take responsibility for their decisions and operations. Seminars and certificate courses were offered in plastic technology, quality control, mold making, management and entrepreneurship. College courses, including an MBA program, were offered in association with local academic institutions.

To provide incentive and career opportunities, company policy stated that at least two-thirds of all management positions be filled from within the company. Lankton admitted that this policy might impede growth if there was a shortage of qualified people. Attempts at hiring outsiders, however, had often failed when new managers could not adapt to the company culture. Added Randy Barko, corporate vice president for marketing and sales, to whom the three business segment managers reported: "Other resources necessary to grow were not as much of a problem as human resources."

As a management development vehicle, each joint venture had its own board of directors that met quarterly and was composed of personnel from each involved operating company, as well as from corporate headquarters. These boards made all major decisions and received regular reports from the general managers of the respective plants. Lankton himself had little to do with the running of these individual operations. As he explained, this structure let managers and other employees participate in top management decisions.

The company management chose these board members from various company functions, selecting employees who were viewed as having good potential for advancement. Boards could be made up of technicians, salespeople, accountants, and engineers, as well as functional and business segment managers. Lankton and other Nypro managers saw this experience as an excellent management development tool.

Turning management of the joint ventures over to others also allowed Lankton to work on attracting new accounts, as well as dealing with important customer issues.

As financial incentives, the company provided a profit-sharing plan and a stock ownership plan. Profit sharing was paid in cash on a quarterly basis to employees. Employees could earn as much as 100 hours of extra pay each quarter. Although Lankton owned most of the company, the stock ownership plan had allowed over 100 employees to own approximately 30 percent of the company's shares by 1994. The stock ownership plan called for five percent of each unit's pre-tax profit to be awarded annually to employees. Eligibility for the plan was decided by a committee made up of the CEO, CFO, administrative head, and the chief engineer, who received recommendations from managers. An employee had to undergo three annual performance evaluations before becoming eligible for recommendation to the committee. When employees left or retired from the company, they were required to sell their stock back to the company at a price based on the average of the last five years' earnings per share multiplied by 12.5. A recently retired senior manager realized a gain of more than $2 million on the stock that he had been granted. Eligibility for this program was opened to all employees worldwide in 1993, with participation based on job performance and years of service.

Looking to the Future

When asked about a successor, Lankton jokingly responded, "I intend to live forever." He added, however, that a succession plan for the company was developed during 1994 by the Succession Planning Committee of the board of directors. Although the succession decision was not fully resolved, internal candidates had been identified. Lankton and the board had also agreed that the company would remain private and ultimately be owned by the employees, consistent with Lankton's vision of a company "reasonably unrestricted by the quarterly earnings syndrome prevalent in many public companies."

Competition, a primary problem for most companies, brought the following response from Lankton:

> I worry less and less about competition. On the other hand, I worry more and more about doing the job right. All I want to do is be the best precision plastics injection molder in the world.

To accomplish this objective, he emphasized the importance of remaining a private company:

> I don't like the quarterly requirement of answering to public stockholders. There is enormous pressure for short-term profit and much of it is ill advised.

Without this pressure, Lankton felt free to do what he believed was necessary for the long-term viability and competitiveness of the company. He planned to continue the company's aggressive growth, but the directions were not yet fully decided. More plant locations and joint ventures were under consideration, following the company's traditional growth path. Franchising was also attractive to Lankton and, as a third route, some managers felt the automotive industry was a segment in which Nypro should compete more aggressively.

When asked about these future directions for the company, some senior managers foresaw a number of issues but spoke again of Lankton's optimism, creativity, and risk-taking attitude. They, as did Lankton, understood that although the company had experienced much success, the future was not without risk.

Revisiting the Franchising Decision

Although the company was seriously considering franchising as a new route for expansion, Nypro's management realized that it was a complex decision. Franchising involved a contract or agreement between a franchisor and franchisee. The agreements specified the roles and responsibilities of both parties, as well as the amount of the franchisee fee, usually paid up front, and the periodic royalty amount, usually expressed as a percent of the franchisee's sales. Agreements varied depending upon the type of business but normally included specifications such as the franchisee's territory, customer categories to be served, required levels of revenue, equipment and supplies to be purchased from the franchisor, and requirements to follow the franchisor's systems and policies. Correspondingly, the responsibilities of the franchisor were also covered including, at least, what specifically was to be franchised, training to be offered, management support to be provided, and the marketing and operations services which the franchisor would offer.

Lankton and other Nypro managers were aware that franchising had grown dramatically during the previous decade. From 1983 to 1993, the number of franchisors in the United States increased from less than 1,900 to 2,900. The gross sales of franchises increased to over $700 billion from just over $100 billion in 1983. On the negative side, however, U.S. Department of Commerce studies showed a 44 percent failure rate among franchisors from the mid-1970s to the late 1980s.

Although all Nypro managers looked forward to Nypro's growth, some questioned the wisdom of franchising. While stating that he would be happy to be the first franchisee, Ed Rivera noted that franchising presented a real dilemma for Nypro. On the one hand, he noted that the nature of the industry was favorable. With 40,000 molders, it was highly fragmented, geographically dispersed, and required locating plants very close to customers, as well as being perceived as having a strong local presence. Also, the scope of product-service offerings required by customers differed at each location and required on-the-spot decision making and entrepreneurial management. He added that Nypro's striking success at standardizing its systems and processes, advanced information technology, and its long experience with joint ventures and other types of partnerships would be significant assets if the company were to begin franchising.

On the other hand, Rivera pointed out, some people in the company felt that franchising would never take off. They argued that in spite of the pluses, it would not be feasible to re-create Nypro in franchises. Nypro was too unique in its culture, operations, technology, and systems, and the farther an operation moved from the core company, the more difficult it would become to mimic this uniqueness.

However, all managers agreed, Ed Rivera continued, that franchises would require stringent controls and frequent contacts to insure consistency like McDonald's and to maintain Nypro's image, culture, and systems in a franchise. Nypro had successfully achieved these objectives with its joint ventures, having a board of directors for each, but no decision had been made on how to do this with franchises. Rivera then expressed the thoughts of many Nypro managers as he wondered aloud, "If we do decide to franchise, how should we bring to bear the controls and consistencies needed to be successful?"

7

IBM Corporation
Anatomy of a Branding Campaign

IBM Global Services, which represents approximately one third of IBM's overall revenues and one third of its workforce, is the largest business and information technology (IT) services provider in the world. Serving both information technology and business professionals, IBM Global Services provides three broad categories of services: business transformation, e-business, and total system management services, which encompass traditional maintenance and support. Including traditional maintenance and support with higher end services, IBM's total service business accounted for 36 percent of corporate revenues in 1998 and some forecasters estimate that all services may account for as much as 46 percent by 2002. IBM's "services" business, which represents the higher-end outsourcing, IT and business consulting, systems integration, etc., has been growing at a 22 percent annual rate compared to industry growth of 13 percent.

This Best Practice Case Study looks at the first-ever major advertising campaign developed and funded directly by IBM's service entity—IBM Global Services. Some of the questions that we set out to answer were: Why did IBM feel that it was important to mount this campaign when from most measures the services business was doing very well? What foundation had to be laid first to support the campaign? What were the steps taken to marshal data (IBM uses the term "fact-based marketing") and sell upper management on the need to fund the campaign? How did the sponsoring team manage executive expectations and sustain management commitment? What was the process of creating the campaign theme and overall campaign strategy? How was the campaign leveraged through integrated marketing in the division and throughout the corporation? How were global issues addressed? And finally, how did IBM measure results?

Many times in the past, IBM corporate advertising has featured services as a key ingredient of the ad content. The campaign—*Solutions for a Small Planet*—is a recent example. There have been individual ads dedicated to services and this author can recall a single ad—probably ten years ago—that featured a pillow on fluffy clouds in a blue sky—with the message, "An IBM maintenance agreement provided a good night's sleep" (for the data processing manager). But there had been nothing of the

This case was written by Richard C. Munn, 1999. Best Practice Case Studies provide analysis of a particular company's services marketing strategies and practices, and are presented as educational cases for services marketing professionals. The information in this case study is believed to be reliable but cannot be guaranteed to be correct and complete. The analysis and commentary are the opinions of the author. This case study is the property of ITSMA. Reproduction or disclosure in whole or in part to other parties shall be made only upon the express written consent of ITSMA. © October 1999 ITSMA.

size, scope and investment level of the new *People* campaign. In ITSMA's view this was a real departure from the past and represented an example worthy of being selected as a Best Practice Case Study.

The Campaign

In early 1999 IBM Global Services launched a $75 million global print advertising campaign featuring simple but striking close-ups of real IBM services employees with the tag line: "*IBM Global Services. People who think. People who do. People who get it.*" followed by a sub tag—*e-business people*. Typically three full-page color ads, each featuring a different individual or small group of individuals as the major graphic element, appear on consecutive pages in major newspapers, business and general interest magazines and computer trade publications. Three pages were used in the early stages of the campaign to make a strong impact and gain readership. As the campaign progressed single-page ads were used, stretching ad dollars.

This advertising highlights real IBM employees, presenting them as e-business people who have significant technical expertise to help customers achieve real business results, and attaching a personality to the brand image that IBM hopes to achieve. Ad copy, which is minimal, typically shows job title, a one-sentence experience profile and a personalized quote or expression, toll free phone number and Web site (for additional information) followed by the campaign tag line. Because of the design of the ad format, local countries can feature their employees, and emphasize different services messages and themes adapted to their particular market situation. See Figure 1.

The campaign was developed after IBM learned through a number of focus groups conducted worldwide that although customers had positive attitudes toward IBM as a computer systems company, they did not know very much about IBM as a service provider. In fact, IBM was being ranked anywhere from second to sixth on an unaided list of biggest service providers—even though its Global Services unit had more revenue than its two nearest competitors (EDS and Fujitsu) combined. The goal of the new campaign was to raise IBM Global Service's profile among potential customers to ensure that IBM would be considered for new services projects (make the short list) and to ensure that customers would get positive reinforcement for selecting IBM. A secondary goal, and not one originally envisioned, was to also reinforce and create a positive impression with present and future employees in an industry where demand for technical skills far outstrips supply.

Starting at the Beginning

There were a number of factors that, given the benefit of hindsight, seemed to provide the nourishment to undertake such a major marketing campaign.

Certainly the atmosphere or culture of the company had changed under Lou Gerstner, the first CEO brought in (April 1993) from the outside. Probably one of the biggest changes was the corporation's new emphasis on marketing. Gerstner had honed his marketing skills at companies such as American Express and RJR Nabisco and consulting firm McKinsey. Abby Kohnstamm, senior vice president, marketing, and IBM's top marketing executive, had also been brought in from the outside. She had been a marketing executive at American Express where Gerstner had been responsible for travel related services earlier in his career. Kohnstamm had been charged with instilling world class marketing disciplines throughout the company.

E-BUSINESS PEOPLE AD FORMAT AND DESIGN OBJECTIVES

Impact
- Insight into brand character
- Arresting images
- Skills expertise

Relevance
- Compelling to customers
- Tangible business results

Approachability
- Honest and direct
- Changing face of IBM

Engaging 'job titles' in thought leadership areas

IBM logo

e-Business People logo

Simplicity
Look and feel, tone.
People who think. People who do. People who get it.™

SOURCE: IBM Global Services, 1999

The creation of a single services entity—IBM Global Services—in December of 1996 set the stage to establish one over-arching brand image rather than what had been seventy-nine different entities. As part of the creation of IBM Global Services, a business blueprint was developed. It outlined a whole different way of doing business under the Global Services umbrella. The blueprint laid out how IBM Global Services would go to market; what competencies were crucial to long term success; what skills were needed and how those skills would be developed or acquired; how disparate services would be segmented and thought of as global offerings; the organizational structure, etc.

Another important factor was the hiring of new marketing leaders by IBM at the divisional level. IBM Global Services was no exception. At the time of the "publication" of the new blueprint model in December 1996, IBM Global Services also began to build the nucleus of a world class marketing operation. At the time this case study was written, IBM Global Services was headed by Sam Palmisano, senior vice president and group executive and member of the IBM Corporate Executive Committee. Mark Elliott had general management responsibility worldwide for all service engagements, marketing, and business development. Phil Juliano, vice president, marketing, reported to Elliott and headed IBM Global Services brand management efforts—including market planning, market intelligence, and integrated marketing communications.

To sum up, here was a situation with a heightened emphasis on marketing; the establishment of a single, large services entity; and new marketing executives at the services unit and corporate levels with fresh ideas to offer IBM. These ingredients all contributed to the strong support by IBM management and IBM Global Services executives for the new $75 million worldwide marketing campaign.

Developing a Value Proposition

One of the many things that Lou Gerstner "brought" to IBM was a heritage of consumer marketing experience. In consumer marketing, brand managers are key to the overall success of a business. They are responsible for the performance of their brand or product line in the marketplace. Procter & Gamble doesn't directly compete with Colgate-Palmolive or Gillette, although battles between Crest (P&G) and Colgate toothpaste, and Oral-B (Gillette) and Colgate toothbrushes, and Scope (P&G) and Colgate mouth rinses are fiercely contested. Brand managers in consumer companies have counterparts in industrial companies known as product line managers or business unit managers. Although the difference in approaching the two responsibilities may be subtle, the consumer brand manager (in ITSMA's opinion) tends to pay more attention to influencing buyer behavior and almost always has a higher percent of overall revenues to spend on marketing. More emphasis gets placed on issues such as "positioning," developing a unique promise of value for the brand; advertising and "message management"; targeting (or segmenting) audiences, promotions, etc.

Whereas the typical consumer goods company has multiple brands and brand managers for each brand, IBM Global Services represents a single brand, but numerous "product" or market segment managers still manage parts of the business. In a consumer goods company the multiple brands can have a very different "look and feel." At IBM, the IBM Global Services "brand" (as well as other "brands" such as Personal Computers, etc.) has to be consistent with the IBM (corporate) brand.

We "IBM watchers" have seen a marked transition over the past five years or so toward managing business lines and product families as brands or sub brands. When IBM Global Services was created a little over two years ago by combining the separate Professional Services (ISSC) division with Availability Services and Network Services, there was a mandate to manage the business as a "brand" and develop an over-arching value proposition. Such a value proposition had to capture the essence of how IBM Global Services "lived and walked their talk" in providing value to customers.

Developing a value proposition is not done lightly. It requires much thought and a deep understanding of customer needs. It takes time to articulate the value proposition and even more time for the organization to "internalize" the value that is being promised.

As IBM Global Services executives started this process in early 1997, they identified a number of themes representing the major needs or concerns of their customers and cited possible intersections with IBM's major strengths. IBM felt that customers wanted their services partner to:

- Focus on delivering real business results

- Have exceptional expertise in the latest information and communications technology

- Have industry knowledge, i.e., experience, in customer's specific industry

- Not only create and design technology solutions, but also ensure they work

- Navigate or guide customers through a very complex landscape

- Very importantly, be a partner they can count on, trust and be confident of a successful outcome

These deliberations led to something like the following as the articulation of IBM Global Services "brand" promise of value or value proposition:

> Customers can count on IBM Global Services people to design and provide strategic technology solutions that produce real business results. Combining unequaled expertise in technology with specific industry experience, IBM Global Services people help customers navigate through complexity.

This value proposition became the foundation for the marketing campaign featured in this Best Practice Case Study, as well as for all marketing, hiring and training strategies. In short, it became the basis for the way people should think about the IBM Global Services' business and act in relation to customers and each other.

"We Didn't Realize IBM Was in the Services Business"

As IBM Global Services conducted research with its customer base to help them develop their value proposition, customers kept saying, "We didn't realize you were in the services business." This was somewhat of a surprise because of IBM's leading market share in the services market. This indicated that in the minds of customers, IBM did not command a commensurate market perception. It had market share; unfortunately, it did not (at this time) have mindshare. Brute strength or serendipity was generating results without the benefit of much "pull" from the marketplace.

A separate piece of research was funded to conduct a brand image and awareness study for services. Approximately 4,000 interviews were conducted worldwide to provide hard data during the third quarter of 1997. What IBM was looking for was a) overall awareness of IBM Global Services as being a potential provider of services, b) whether IBM Global Services was viewed favorably, and finally, c) whether there was intention or consideration to purchase from IBM.

Although results varied by country, in general IBM Global Services clearly had an image and awareness problem.

We asked IBM about the need for such extensive research (4,000 interviews, worldwide). IBM wanted to introduce a discipline it termed "fact based marketing" into its decision making process. Fact based marketing, as opposed to opinion based marketing, relies on solid research and data to guide marketing decision-making. Without this hard data, which means a sizeable number of interviews conducted in a highly rigorous and professional manner, it is very easy to get into opinion arguments, and then the most vocal person sways the group.

The results of the research were presented to senior management near the end of 1997 and the data clearly showed that there was an image and awareness challenge. The question then became, should IBM ignore the challenge or try to do something to correct it? And then, how should IBM deal with it and at what cost?

TABLE 1	WHY IS IT IMPORTANT TO HAVE STRONG MARKET AWARENESS AND IMAGE?

1. If you are number one in actual market share but have the market perception of being only third or fourth, in time your market share will erode. Those with a higher market perception will increase market share.

2. The IT services market place is very dynamic. Other vendors are mounting significant marketing campaigns. It is important to enhance market perception when you have strength and are successful. You can't be complacent.

3. When you are offering mass customized repeatable solutions you have to generate market interest on a broad scale. You can't afford to market one-to-one.

4. When your market perception is strong you have "permission" to grow and expand.

5. If a high percent of your offerings are new, you will be more successful if your market perception is strong.

6. To truly make the IBM Global Services value proposition part of the total IBM e-business effort, an aggressive services-only marketing campaign was necessary.

SOURCE: ITSMA, 1999

Some of the reasons for taking action are summarized in Table 1.

It was agreed that a pilot marketing campaign should be developed and tested in some selected markets. Senior management in effect said—"Come up with a campaign, run it as a pilot and let's see if we can increase our general awareness, favorability and purchase consideration ratings."

Coming Up with the Campaign Theme, or Getting to Eureka

We were interested in learning how IBM and its ad agency, Ogilvy and Mather, came up with the final advertising approach. See Figure 2, which is typical of the ads now appearing in various business oriented periodicals worldwide.

Was the successful ad campaign version 1.0 or some later version? Was there a "eureka" moment when IBM and the ad agency "knew" they had something good? How did they get to eureka?

As IBM executives recount, "It actually was a eureka moment in slow motion."

The first concept ads that were tested featured all the capabilities that IBM Global Services offered, for example, "Here's all we can do," typical of many ad campaigns from other professional services firms a few years ago. Reactions could be summarized as "interesting but boring," "this wouldn't get me to stop flipping pages," "nothing that grabs me."

A second approach tried to incorporate more of the unique promise of value that IBM had settled on, portraying IBM people technically savvy and trustworthy. These concept ads showed rows and rows of IBMers, almost as a rogue's gallery. Reactions to this approach could be summarized as, "better than the other but who are those people? Are they customers or IBM people?"

The third approach featured individual or small teams of IBMers with copy detailing their accomplishments, what they did, etc. Reactions now were, "I can relate to this." "This is interesting." "I'd stop flipping pages to read this." The feeling at IBM was that "this approach just seemed to click with customers." As a result, the marketing team, the ad agency and IBM corporate marketing (which had been involved during the process) all agreed that this approach was the right one.

Piloting the Campaign

Most consumer goods companies will test market a new product in some carefully selected (secondary) area before launching the product in a major national campaign. In the same way, live stage shows earmarked for Broadway frequently will hold limited engagements in a secondary city in order to iron out the wrinkles before facing very demanding audiences in New York City. IBM pursued a similar strategy with its new marketing campaign, not only to "test" the impact of the new campaign in some qualified markets, but also to help the "buy-in" process by the operating units.

Interestingly IBM chose Canada and the Untied Kingdom (UK) as its test markets. Both represented medium-size markets; one in which IBM had very high market share and brand recognition (Canada) and the other in which IBM would like to be doing better (UK). Both country organizations had solid marketing teams in place that could be counted on to do their parts.

By choosing Canada and the United Kingdom, IBM avoided the frequently voiced criticism by international units that new programs too often originate in the United States and then are rolled out to international regions for implementation, with a no-questions-to-be-asked, just-do-it-this-way, attitude implied.

Prior to the kick-off of the two test market campaigns, the marketing team met with the country general managers and their marketing teams of both Canada and the United Kingdom to go over plans and make sure "everyone was in the same boat." There was also a very comprehensive internal marketing campaign explaining the campaign, the schedule, various roles to be played, and so forth. In addition there was an e-mail message from Sam Palmisano, senior vice president and group executive, IBM Global Services, endorsing the campaign and eliciting support.

The test campaigns started in the United Kingdom in April 1998 and in Canada one month later. In addition to the print campaign in periodicals, both countries also tested versions of the ads placed at major airports, at business stops for trains and subways and even taxis apt to transport business executives.

IBM actually tested two themes or approaches with its marketing campaign. The first series of ads were very traditional, outlining all the things that IBM Global Services did and citing numbers of technical people, support centers, and so on. Customers who viewed these ads were, in the words of an IBM executive, "underwhelmed." There was nothing compelling about the ads and certainly nothing that would cause someone to consider positive action in favor of IBM.

A second series of ads (very close in content and style to the current ads) showed actual IBMers with a description of projects in which the individual specialized and other examples that helped portray the breadth and depth of IBM's services capabilities. What turned out to be a key creative decision was to select and feature a single individual (and occasionally a small group) that the reader would be attracted to and want to learn more about. The individual featured helped to personify a variety of services of the larger IBM Global Services entity.

The reaction to this second approach was like night and day. Those viewing the ads immediately reacted positively and said things like, "That's very interesting. I wish you had told us about that earlier."

$75 Million in Perspective

An article in the Wall Street Journal on February 1, 1999, titled "IBM Aims to Raise Services Unit's Profile," described the campaign, listed the reasons IBM felt the campaign was necessary at that time, and provided other background information. The article also mentioned that this campaign was estimated to cost $75 million. Our first reaction was to the huge cost. We wondered how we could get some perspective on the amount. Was it out of the ordinary or was it "business as usual"?

For comparison purposes, Andersen Consulting is spending $100 million and KPMG $60 million on somewhat comparable campaigns now underway. IBM's services business is considerably larger than those two companies, so the amount of $75 million does not seem to be out of line.

Another comparison that can be made is with participants in ITSMA's annual benchmarking study. According to ITSMA's 1999 Edition Benchmarking Study on Services Marketing Practices, for all participants an average of 1.5 percent of (services) revenues is spent on marketing. For professional services firms, spending on marketing is actually 1.4 percent. Of that amount, approximately 34 percent is devoted to marketing communications (for professional services firms) and of that 34 percent, 65 percent is for non-direct personnel expenses, for example, agency, media, printing, and so on.

IBM Global Services revenues reached $29.4 billion in 1998. We estimate their revenue will approach $35 billion in 1999.

Comparing the $75 million to our own benchmarking and industry competitors, we conclude that the IBM Global Services marketing investment is significant but not out of line with the industry.

Another measure of reasonableness is to compare spending on this campaign with total IBM spending on advertising. The Wall Street Journal article states that IBM plans to spend $600 million on advertising in 1999. This services campaign represents one-eighth of that amount, which again seems reasonable given the fact that services account for 36 percent of total revenues and is one of the fastest growing parts of IBM.

In talking with Phil Juliano, vice president, marketing, IBM Global Services we get the impression that in spite of ITSMA's test of reasonableness, this amount did represent a major commitment by IBM Global Services and an amount far larger than any similar campaign in the past. This campaign, because of its cost and the fact that it was indeed global, was very much a significant departure for IBM management.

How Long Does/Should It Take to Establish a Strong Market Brand?

We were interested in gauging how long it might take to establish a strong market brand. What should be the expectations of senior management who hold the purse strings and are anxious to see results?

Part of that answer rests in the ad campaign schedule and a judgment as to what the "legs" (or reasonable length) of the campaign might be before it gets stale.

The IBM Global Services Brand Team was able to convince upper management that the campaign had to be conducted in a sustained manner. That doesn't necessarily mean *an unlimited campaign*, but it does recognize that it takes an extended time to achieve the desired impact.

IBM (and a number of other companies) had a history of "flighting" their advertising; that is, running a campaign for six weeks and then taking four weeks off.

SAMPLING OF ADS FROM IBM CAMPAIGN

SOURCE: IBM Global Services, 1999

FIGURE 2	SAMPLING OF ADS FROM IBM CAMPAIGN (CONT.)

SOURCE: IBM Global Services, 1999

FIGURE 2   SAMPLING OF ADS FROM IBM CAMPAIGN (CONT.)

SOURCE: IBM global Services, 1999

FIGURE 2   SAMPLING OF ADS FROM IBM CAMPAIGN (CONT.)

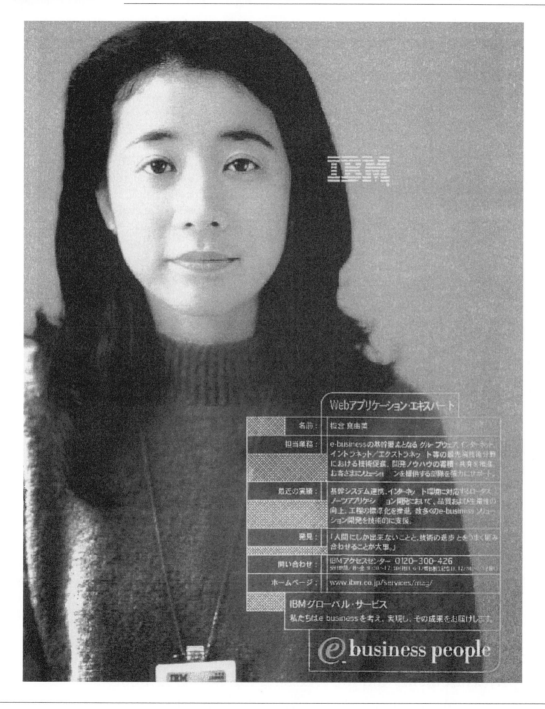

SOURCE: IBM global Services, 1999

Or starting a campaign, getting some results and then getting tired of the campaign or ending funding. In both cases, whatever progress had been made gets shut off prematurely.

With the current advertising, pilot campaigns began in the United Kingdom and Canada in late 1998, but the full campaign did not start until early 1999. The campaign was continued in both the United Kingdom and Canada and rolled out in the United States and France in early 1999, in Japan in April, and with other major markets and countries scheduled later. IBM's feeling is that this campaign, because of its format, can have a life expectancy of eighteen to twenty-four months and possibly longer.

In the first year the goal was to reach 95 percent of IBM's target market (business professionals and IT professionals) with a frequency of fourteen ad impressions. The campaign was designed to have an introductory phase of approximately three months with heavy levels of advertising—for example, three consecutive right hand pages in a magazine such as *Business Week*. After the introductory phase, IBM would place one ad insertion (rather than three) in magazines such as *The Economist* or *Fortune* in order to stretch the advertising dollars once the original message had been established.

Leveraging the Marketing Campaign

To reinforce and leverage other IBM advertising, this campaign is tightly linked to the corporate e-business campaign on television and in business media. There is also a graphic consistency with other IBM campaigns, in which the same type font, logos and e-business tag lines are used. Phil Juliano said that IBM wanted to integrate on two different levels: first, so that it does not conflict with anything another IBM brand unit is doing. In fact this campaign complements the e-business *tools* ads with e-business *people* featured in the IBM Global Services ads. Second, this campaign acts as a proof point to the broader e-business message from IBM. In other words—"here are some of the IBM people who can make e-business work."

The synergy that IBM is striving for is to have its target audience not only understand IBM's offerings but to develop a preference for IBM products and people, including its scalable servers, database and software tools, PCs, the intellectual capital found in its processes, the technical and business skills of its people—all combined to provide e-business solutions.

IBM is also leveraging the ad campaign in direct marketing (mail), in various collateral (see Figure 3), at events such as trade shows and user group meetings, and most importantly on its Web site. Visitors can complete a simple needs assessment and receive a diagnostic to identify specific business needs that IBM can help address. For their time, they will also receive a complimentary copy of a white paper commissioned from International Data Corporation (IDC) entitled *Business Beyond 2000: New Game, New Rules.*

Early Measurements and the Decision for Global Rollout

Although the IBM Global Services brand team believed the campaign would be successful, they were honest with management and admitted, "We don't really know if this is going to work; we think it will, and have built in measurements to our pilot test plan. We will report back when we have some real data."

| FIGURE 3 | IBM'S INTEGRATED MARKETING MESSAGE |

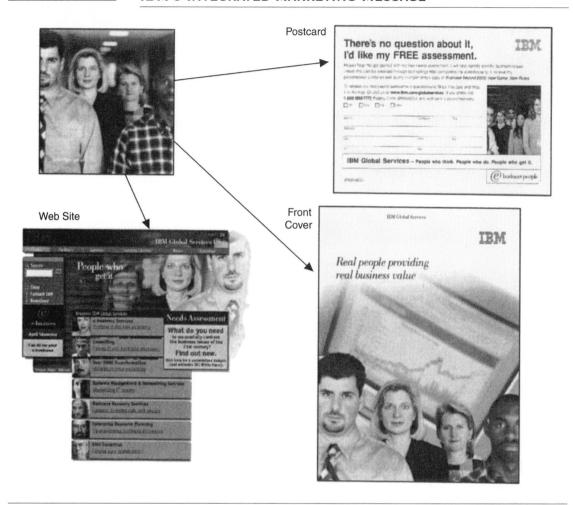

SOURCE: IBM Global Services, 1999

The measurement plan was based upon the concept of using the campaign to help move prospects through the sales qualification process (from Awareness of IBM to Favorable Impression of IBM and finally to Purchase Consideration) to produce candidates that would consider IBM Global Services in their next purchase decision. (See Figure 4.)

As part of the measurement process, researchers asked:

- When you think of all the firms that you could turn to for information technology services (e.g., outsourcing, systems integration, e-business services, etc.) which would you consider? Or, when you think of information technology services firms, what is the first company that comes to mind?

- Which of those firms do you think would be the most effective suppliers for you (or view most positively); which ones wouldn't be considered (or viewed

FIGURE 4	MOVING THE NEEDLES

Awareness   Favorable Impression   Purchase Consideration

SOURCE: ITSMA, 1999

negatively)? Or, how would you rate IBM on a scale of one to ten (where one = very unfavorable and ten = very favorable)?

- Who would be your first choice if you had a need today? Or, how would you rate IBM as your first choice on a scale of one to ten (where one = very unlikely and ten = very likely)?

Other questions that researchers asked drilled down further to gain insight on such issues as:

- How does IBM rate as having superior IT services skills?
  - . . . as a provider of innovative solutions?
  - . . . as someone that you would consider as a strategic consultant?
  - . . . as a team player who works well within your organization?
  - . . . as someone who can lead you through the complexities of the IT landscape?

Answers to questions such as these would help IBM determine whether the pilot campaign was achieving the desired impact.

To determine how effective the pilot tests were, it was important to establish a baseline. Approximately two weeks before the test campaigns launched in Canada and the United Kingdom, IBM contracted with market research firms in both countries to ask target prospects those questions. As was expected (and the reason for the campaign) IBM's ratings were very low.

A print campaign typically takes a number of months (three to six) before you can see an impact. With TV and radio and very high frequency ads results are apparent sooner.

IBM chose to measure results much sooner and then every ninety days to monitor progress. Part of this decision was to have early data to use for IBM's fall planning schedule. The decision on going forward had to be made in the September/October time period and this provided only about eight weeks to determine if there were positive results.

What the data showed (in both countries) was that IBM's *awareness* level had risen dramatically. The *favorability* rating was more mixed but in general it was heading upwards. *Purchase consideration* also increased considerably. These results were in keeping with the dynamics of moving prospects through a sales qualification process. You start by getting awareness. Then you get favorability and finally, you get purchase consideration. The leading indicator for IBM was whether the campaign would raise awareness, and here results were very positive. Favorability showed good movement and that was also positive. Purchase consideration was also quite positive.

Some other measurements that the marketing team made were whether the campaign improved the understanding among IBM Global Services personnel as to the new value proposition, the mission, their role as team members, etc. They found that within two months of beginning the campaigns in both countries there were significant improvements. The "troops" were "buying in."

They also measured Web site "hits" and found a dramatic improvement—a tenfold increase in the visits to the IBM Global Services site.

Impact on Morale and Recruiting—Unexpected Benefit

One other, unexpected benefit of the campaign was the impact it had on the morale of services personnel and on IBM's recruiting efforts. Because the campaign featured actual IBM employees who personified IBM's capabilities and commitment, it resonated with employees and other technically skilled people. Once the campaign started, IBM could almost feel improvement in the morale of the first line personnel.

IBM Canada had participated for a number of years in a large job fair in the July/August time frame. The pilot test of the new ad campaign had been running for about one month then, and people approached IBM recruiters with ads torn out of magazines, asking how they could "become one of the people" in the ads. In past years, IBM had attracted 1,000 job prospects at this fair. This year there were 3,000. Although the campaign was aimed at business prospects, it also turned out to be an excellent recruitment ad and IBM found that it was helping to raise morale of this very important asset base of skilled technical people.

Educating Senior Management (Marketing Internally)

One of the more important critical success factors for the marketing team was to educate senior management. These executives hold the purse strings and are responsible for business results. By nature they have strong opinions, are prepared to make decisions and want to see results quickly. One of the strategies that the marketing team used was to do solid homework before bringing a case forward. They used the term "fact-based marketing" (as opposed to opinion-based marketing) to describe what they did. Fact-based marketing relies on solid research and data to guide marketing decision-making.

After IBM Global Services acknowledged the awareness problem as a result of doing customer research to help develop their value proposition, the marketing team funded a research project that called for 4,000 customer interviews all over the world.

BUILDING A "POWER BRAND" IS ANALOGOUS TO DESIGNING AND BUILDING A HOME

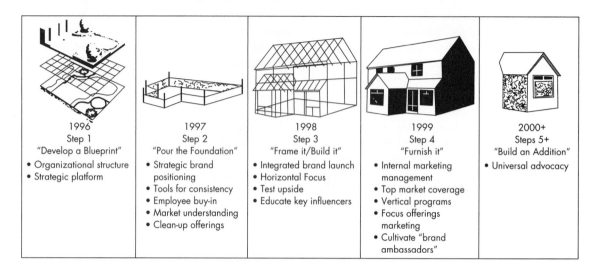

1996 Step 1 "Develop a Blueprint"	1997 Step 2 "Pour the Foundation"	1998 Step 3 "Frame it/Build it"	1999 Step 4 "Furnish it"	2000+ Steps 5+ "Build an Addition"
• Organizational structure • Strategic platform	• Strategic brand positioning • Tools for consistency • Employee buy-in • Market understanding • Clean-up offerings	• Integrated brand launch • Horizontal Focus • Test upside • Educate key influencers	• Internal marketing management • Top market coverage • Vertical programs • Focus offerings marketing • Cultivate "brand ambassadors"	• Universal advocacy

SOURCE: IBM Global Services and ITSMA, 1999

A very credible research partner also conducted these interviews in a rigorous manner (using solid methodology). Four thousand is a lot of interviews. The result, however, was to provide strong data—not just in the United States but also in most other major markets—that management could trust. A business case could now be made based upon solid data rather than opinions or feelings.

This fact-based marketing approach continued through the pilot tests in the United Kingdom and Canada. All pilot test results were shared with the IBM Global Services executive leadership at the 1998 fall planning session. This executive group included Sam Palmisano, the group executive heading Global Services, his top finance executive and the heads of the three major geographies—Americas, Asia/Pacific and Europe/Middle East/Africa. The marketing team in effect said, "We test marketed this approach and it succeeded."

The executive group felt the case had been strongly made and it was now time to put some serious money behind the campaign—in this case, $75 million.

As IBM Global Services executives were kept informed, the team also made sure that IBM Corporate Marketing was kept in the loop. This helped ensure that this campaign was integrated into corporate marketing campaigns and corporate marketing had an opportunity to voice concerns or objections early in the game.

The group came up with a creative metaphor—building a new home—to help senior management understand the length of time and the importance of sustained commitment to building a successful brand. See Figure 5.

Once the property has been selected and purchased, work begins with an architect or design-build firm to design the house and produce the necessary "blueprints" so that work can progress. After the site work has been completed the next step is to "pour the foundation" and then the house is "framed/built." Before anyone moves in, many "finishing" details must be completed. The house then has to be "furnished." Often, after moving in, the owner decides to "build an addition" to increase the enjoyment of the home. This process can take three to four years.

The real enjoyment for the homeowner comes after moving in and then doing small projects to enhance the overall pleasure he/she derives from the house. This can span a lifetime. The better the foundation steps the more the enjoyment. The same things can be said for building a strong brand. Once the "house is built" the benefits come from the marketplace accepting and viewing you as a preferred solution provider, and your costs of marketing decrease and ease of doing business increases.

ITSMA's Perspective

There were many "very right" things that IBM did in mounting this campaign. First, the campaign had a solid underpinning. A "blueprint" for the division was developed and this in turn formed the basis for the articulation of a value proposition for all of IBM Global Services. The creative process (eureka in slow motion) involving the ad agency and IBM Global Services marketing people produced what we judge to be a very effective campaign concept with strong readership appeal. We think the attention paid to educate (selling) senior management, keeping other parts of the organization (corporate marketing, representative international groups, etc.) involved, (what we might think of as integral marketing) was outstanding, and the use of fact-based marketing was a key ingredient in the campaign's ultimate success. The side benefit of raising employee morale and helping to attract more qualified applicants for technical positions was another strong plus. Applying a disciplined measurement system to track impressions helped to keep the "target" in mind and provided real data to judge effectiveness. Finally, integrating the campaign themes and images into other elements of the marketing mix reinforced the campaign and leveraged marketing investments.

The proof of the pudding, however, is whether or not the campaign raised awareness, got IBM Global Services on the "short list" of prospects considering a services provider and raised IBM's win/loss and sole-source selection ratios. We gather from IBM executives that the early feeling is that the campaign is having a very positive impact.

Independently, ITSMA conducted a multi-client Brand Awareness study during the spring of 1999. As part of this study ITSMA asked study respondents, without prompting, to name all the firms they were *aware* of that provide Web-based technology solutions, Internet consulting, or e-commerce business solutions. We later asked what firm would they most likely call for a Web-based technology, e-commerce, or Internet solution—the *preference* question. Table 2 shows these results.

The race for mindshare in the e-commerce space is wide open. At the time of this research, IBM was in the leading position among vendors and has made a significant investment in mass-marketing advertising. We would expect its position to strengthen.

Issue Questions

In the interest of using this case study for education and professional development of services marketing staff, the following questions can be used to stimulate thought and discussion:

1. Flowchart the sequence of events leading up to worldwide rollout of the *People* campaign. Was there an appropriate order to events that helped in

TABLE 2	BRAND AWARENESS—SPRING 1999	
N=300	**"Unaided Awareness"** %	**"Preference"** %
IBM Global Services	17	12
Andersen Consulting	4	n/a
EDS	3	1
Microsoft	3	2
Netscape	2	1
PricewaterhouseCoopers	2	1
Oracle	2	1
Hewlett-Packard	1	n/a
Ernst & Young	1	n/a
Arthur Andersen	1	n/a
US Web/CKS	1	n/a
Lotus	1	n/a
CSC	1	n/a
Broadvision	1	n/a
Sun	n/a	1
Internal Staff	13	17
Other	27	13
Don't know/refused/none	44	51

SOURCE: ITSMA Professional Services and E-Business Solutions Brand Awareness Study, 1999

building success for the campaign? How long did the overall process take and how long did certain elements and milestones take?

2. What did IBM do to build senior management and other geography management confidence in the campaign approach?

3. IBM chose to have one brand for all of Global Services. What are the pros and cons of having one versus multiple brands within Global Services?

4. How could IBM's "fact based marketing" approach be adapted to your situation.

5. Careful consideration was given to eliciting the buy-in from international groups. What do you think of what IBM did?

6. What do you think of IBM's measurement system? Can you suggest any improvements?

7. What would be indicators that the campaign has "run out of legs" and needs to be changed? What might be the next evolutionary step?

Acknowledgements

I would like to thank the marketing team of IBM Global Services, for spending considerable time detailing steps of the campaign development and providing helpful insights.

—Richard C. Munn, October 1999

About ITSMA

Information Technology Services Marketing Association (ITSMA) is a research-based, professional association dedicated to advancing the state of the art of services marketing n the information technology industry. In addition to the organization's educational and professional development events, ITSMA conducts best practices and benchmarking research on services marketing activities. ITSMA has over 135 corporate members from all segments of the information technology industry.

8

W. L. Gore & Associates, Inc.—1996: A Case Study

"To make money and have fun."
—W. L. Gore

The First Day on the Job

Bursting with resolve, Jack Dougherty, a newly minted M.B.A. from the College of William and Mary, reported to his first day at W. L. Gore & Associates on July 26, 1976. He presented himself to Bill Gore, shook hands firmly, looked him in the eye, and said he was ready for anything.

Jack was not ready, however, for what happened next. Gore replied, "That's fine, Jack, fine. Why don't you look around and find something you'd like to do?" Three frustrating weeks later he found that something: trading in his dark blue suit for jeans, he loaded fabric into the mouth of a machine that laminated the company's patented GORE-TEX®[1] membrane to fabric. By 1982, Jack had become responsible for all advertising and marketing in the fabrics group. This story is part of the folklore of W. L. Gore & Associates.

Today the process is more structured. Regardless of the job for which they are hired, new Associates[2] take a journey through the business before settling into their own positions. A new sales Associate in the fabrics division may spend six weeks rotating through different areas before beginning to concentrate on sales and marketing. Among other things the newcomer learns is how GORE-TEX fabric is made, what it can and cannot do, how Gore handles customer complaints, and how it makes its investment decisions.

This case was written by Frank Shipper, Department of Management and Marketing, Franklin P. Perdue School of Business, Salisbury State University, Salisbury, Maryland; and Charles C. Manz, Department of Management, College of Business, Arizona State University, Tempe, Arizona. Copyright 1996 by Frank Shipper. All rights reserved.

[1] GORE-TEX is a registered trademark of W. L. Gore & Associates.

[2] In this case the word "Associate" is used and capitalized because in W. L. Gore & Associates' literature the word is always used instead of employees and is capitalized. In fact, case writers were told that Gore "never had 'employees'—always 'Associates.'"

Anita McBride related her early experience at W. L. Gore & Associates this way:

Before I came to Gore, I had worked for a structured organization, and for the first month it was fairly structured because I was going through training and this is what we do and this is how Gore is and all of that. I went to Flagstaff for that training. After a month I came down to Phoenix and my sponsor said, "Well, here's your office; it's a wonderful office" and "Here's your desk," and walked away. And I thought, "Now what do I do?" You know, I was waiting for a memo or something, or a job description. Finally after another month I was so frustrated, I felt, "What have I gotten myself into?" And so I went to my sponsor and I said, "What the heck do you want from me? I need something from you." And he said, "If you don't know what you're supposed to do, examine your commitment, and opportunities."

Background

W. L. Gore & Associates evolved from the late Wilbert L. Gore's experiences personally, organizationally, and technically. He was born in Meridian, Idaho, near Boise, in 1912. By age six, according to his own account, he was an avid hiker in the Wasatch Mountain Range in Utah. In those mountains, at a church camp, he met Genevieve, his future wife. In 1935, they got married—in their eyes, a partnership. He would make breakfast and Vieve, as everyone called her, would make lunch. The partnership lasted a lifetime.

He received both a bachelor of science in chemical engineering in 1933 and a master of science in physical chemistry in 1935 from the University of Utah. He began his professional career at American Smelting and Refining in 1936. He moved to Remington Arms Company in 1941 and then to E. I. Du Pont de Nemours in 1945. He held positions as research supervisor and head of operations research. While at Du Pont, he worked on a team to develop applications for polytetrafluoroethylene, referred to as PTFE in the scientific community and known as "Teflon" by Du Pont's consumers. (Consumers know it under other names from other companies.) On this team Wilbert Gore, called Bill by everyone, felt a sense of excited commitment, personal fulfillment, and self-direction. He followed the development of computers and transistors and felt that PTFE had the ideal insulating characteristics for use with such equipment.

He tried many ways to make a PTFE coated ribbon cable without success. A breakthrough came in his home basement laboratory while he was explaining the problem to his nineteen-year-old son Bob. The young Gore saw some PTFE sealant tape made by 3M and asked his father, "Why don't you try this tape?" Bill then explained that everyone knew that you cannot bond PTFE to itself. Bob went on to bed.

Bill Gore remained in his basement lab and proceeded to try what everyone knew would not work. At about 4:00 A.M. he woke up his son, waving a small piece of cable around and saying excitedly, "It works, it works." The following night father and son returned to the basement lab to make ribbon cable coated with PTFE. Because the breakthrough idea came from Bob, the patent for the cable was issued in Bob's name.

For the next four months Bill Gore tried to persuade Du Pont to make a new product—PTFE coated ribbon cable. By this time in his career Bill Gore knew some of the decision makers at Du Pont. After talking to a number of them, he came to realize that Du Pont wanted to remain a supplier of raw materials and not a fabricator.

Bill and his wife, Vieve, began discussing the possibility of starting their own insulated wire and cable business. On January 1, 1958 their wedding anniversary, they founded W. L. Gore & Associates. The basement of their home served as their first facility. After finishing dinner that night, Vieve turned to her husband of twenty-three years and said, "Well, let's clear up the dishes, go downstairs, and get to work."

Bill Gore was forty-five years old with five children to support when he left Du Pont. He put aside a career of seventeen years, and a good, secure salary. To finance the first two years of the business, he and Vieve mortgaged their house and took $4,000 from savings. All their friends told them not to do it.

The first few years were rough. In lieu of salary, some of their employees accepted room and board in the Gore home. At one point eleven Associates were living and working under one roof. One afternoon, while sifting PTFE powder, Vieve received a call from the City of Denver's water department. The caller indicated that he was interested in the ribbon cable, but wanted to ask some technical questions. Bill was out running some errands. The caller asked for the product manager. Vieve explained that he was out at the moment. Next he asked for the sales manager and finally, the president. Vieve explained that they were also out. The caller became outraged and hollered, "What kind of company is this anyway?" With a little diplomacy the Gores were able eventually to secure an order for $100,000. This order put the company on a profitable footing and it began to take off.

W. L. Gore & Associates continued to grow and develop new products, primarily derived from PTFE. Its best known product would become GORE-TEX fabric. In 1986, Bill Gore died while backpacking in the Wind River Mountains of Wyoming. He was then Chairman of the Board. His son Bob continued to occupy the position of president. Vieve remained as the only other officer, secretary-treasurer.

The Operating Company

W. L. Gore & Associates has never had titles, hierarchy, or any of the conventional structures associated with enterprises of its size. The titles of president and secretary-treasurer continue to be used only because they are required by the laws of incorporation. In addition , Gore has never had a corporate-wide mission or code of ethics statement; nor has Gore ever required or prohibited business units from developing such statements for themselves. Thus, the Associates of some business units who have felt a need for such statements have developed them on their own. When questioned about this issue, one Associate stated, "The company belief is that (1) its four basic operating principles cover ethical practices required of people in business; (2) it will not tolerate illegal practices." Gore's management style has been referred to as unmanagement. The organization has been guided by Bill's experiences on teams at Du Pont and has evolved as needed.

For example, in 1965 W. L. Gore & Associates was a thriving company with a facility on Paper Mill Road in Newark, Delaware. One Monday morning in the summer, Bill Gore was taking his usual walk through the plant. All of a sudden he realized that he did not know everyone in the plant. The team had become too big. As a result, he established the practice of limiting plant size to approximately 200 Associates. Thus was born the expansion policy of "Get big by staying small." The purpose

FIGURE 8.1   INTERNATIONAL LOCATIONS OF W. L. GORE & ASSOCIATES

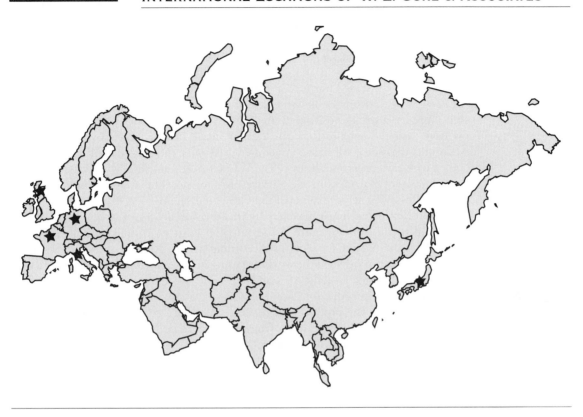

of maintaining small plants was to accentuate a close-knit atmosphere and encourage communication among associates in a facility.

In 1995, W. L. Gore & Associates consisted of over forty-four plants worldwide with approximately 6,000 Associates. In some cases, the plants are grouped together on the same site (as in Flagstaff, Arizona, with ten plants). Overseas Gore's facilities are located in Scotland, Germany, France, and Italy, and the company has two joint ventures in Japan (see Figure 8.1) Gore manufactures electronic, medical, industrial, and fabric products. In addition, it has numerous sales offices worldwide including Eastern Europe and Russia.

Gore electronic products have been found in unconventional places where conventional products will not do—in space shuttles, for example, where Gore wire and cable assemblies withstand the heat of ignition and the cold of space. In addition, they have been found in fast computers, transmitting signals at up to 93 percent of the speed of light. Gore cables have even gone underground, in oil drilling operations, and underseas, on submarines that require superior microwave signal equipment and no-fail cables that can survive high pressure. The Gore electronic products division has a history of anticipating future customer needs with innovative products. Gore electronic products have been well received in industry for their ability to last under adverse conditions. For example, Gore has become, according to Sally Gore, leader in Human Resources and Communications, ". . . one of the largest manufacturers of ultrasound cable in the world, the reason being that Gore's electronic cables' signal transmission is very, very accurate and it's very thin and extremely flexible and has a very, very long flex life. That makes it ideal for things like ultrasound and many medical electronic applications."

In the medical arena, GORE-TEX–expanded PTFE has been considered an ideal replacement for human tissue in many situations. In patients suffering from cardiovascular disease the diseased portion of arteries has been replaced by tubes of expanded PTFE—strong, biocompatible structures capable of carrying blood at arterial pressures. Gore has a strong position in this product segment. Other Gore medical products have included patches that can literally mend broken hearts by sealing holes, and sutures that allow for tissue attachment and offer the surgeon silk-like handling coupled with extreme strength. In 1985, W. L. Gore & Associates won Britain's Prince Philip Award for Polymers in the Service of Mankind. The award recognized especially the life-saving achievements of the Gore medical products team.

Two recently developed products by this division are a new patch material that is intended to incorporate more tissue into the graft more quickly and GORE™ RideOn®[3] Cable System for bicycles. According to Amy LeGere of the medical division, "All the top pro riders in the world are using it. It was introduced just about a year ago and it has become an industry standard." This product had a positive cash flow very soon after its introduction. Some Associates who were also outdoor sports enthusiasts developed the product and realized that Gore could make a great bicycle cable that would have 70 percent less friction and need no lubrication. The Associates maintain that the profitable development, production, and marketing of such specialized niche products are possible because of the lack of bureaucracy and associated overhead, Associate commitment, and the use of product champions.

The output of the industrial products division has included sealants, filter bags, cartridges, clothes, and coatings. The specialized and critical applications of these products, along with Gore's reputation for quality, have had a strong influence on industrial purchasers. This division has introduced Gore's first consumer product—GLIDE®[4]—a dental floss. "That was a product that people knew about for a while and they went the route of trying to persuade industry leaders to promote the product, but they didn't really pursue it very well. So out of basically default almost, Gore decided, Okay they're not doing it right. Let's go in ourselves. We had a champion, John Spencer, who took that and pushed it forward through the dentist's offices and it just skyrocketed. There were many more people on the team but it was basically getting that one champion who focused on that product and got it out. They told him it 'Couldn't be done,' 'It's never going to work,' and I guess that's all he needed. It was done and it worked," said Ray Wnenchak of the industrial products division. Amy LeGere added, "The champion worked very closely with the medical people to understand the medical market like claims and labeling so that when the product came out on the market it would be consistent with our medical products. And that's where, when we cross divisions, we know whom to work with and with whom we combine forces so that the end result takes the strengths of all of our different teams." Bob Winterling of the Fabrics Division explained,

> The product champion is probably the most important resource we have at Gore for the introduction of new products. You look at that bicycle cable.

---

[3] GORE RideOn is a registered trademark of W. L. Gore & Associates.

[4] GLIDE is a registered trademark of W. L. Gore & Associates.

That could have come out of many different divisions of Gore, but it really happened because one or two individuals said, "Look, this can work. I believe in it; I'm passionate about it; and I want it to happen." And the same thing with GLIDE floss. I think John Spencer in this case—although there was a team that supported John, let's never forget that—John sought the experts out throughout the organization. But without John making it happen on his own, GLIDE floss would never have come to fruition. He started with a little chain of drug stores here, Happy Harry's I think, and we put a few cases in and we just tracked the sales and that's how it all started. Who would have ever believed that you could take what we would have considered a commodity product like that, sell it direct for \$3–5 apiece. That is so un-Gorelike it's incredible. So it comes down to people and it comes down to the product champion to make things happen.

The Gore fabrics division has supplied laminates to manufacturers of foul weather gear, ski wear, running suits, footwear, gloves, and hunting and fishing garments. Firefighters and U.S. Navy pilots have worn GORE-TEX fabric gear, as have some Olympic athletes. The U.S. Army adopted a total garment system built around a GORE-TEX fabric component.

GORE-TEX membrane has nine billion pores randomly dotting each square inch and is feather light. Each pore is 700 times larger than a water vapor molecule, yet thousands of times smaller than a water droplet. Wind and water cannot penetrate the pores, but perspiration can escape. As a result, fabrics bonded with GORE-TEX membrane are waterproof, windproof, and breathable. The laminated fabrics bring protection from the elements to a variety of products—from survival gear to high-fashion rainwear. Other manufacturers, including 3M, have brought out products to compete with GORE-TEX fabrics. The toughest competition came from firms that violated the patents on GORE-TEX. Gore successfully challenged them in court. In 1993, the basic patent on the process for manufacturing ran out. Nevertheless, as Sally Gore explained,

> What happens is you get an initial process patent and then as you begin to create things with this process you get additional patents. For instance, we have patents protecting our vascular graft, different patents for protecting GORE-TEX patches, and still other patents protecting GORE-TEX industrial sealants and filtration material. One of our patent attorneys did a talk recently, a year or so ago, when the patent expired and a lot of people who were saying, Oh, golly, are we going to be in trouble! We would be in trouble if we didn't have any patents. Our attorney had this picture with a great big umbrella, sort of a parachute, with Gore under it. Next he showed us lots of little umbrellas scattered all over the sky. So you protect certain niche markets and niche areas, but indeed competition increases as your initial patents expire.

Gore, however, has continued to have a commanding position in the active wear market.

To meet the needs of a variety of customer needs, Gore introduced a new family of fabrics in the 1990s. (Table 8.1). The introduction posed new challenges. According to Bob Winterling,

TABLE 8.1	GORE'S FAMILY OF FABRICS			
Brand Name	**Activity/ Conditions**	**Breathability**	**Water Protection**	**Wind Protection**
GORE-TEX®	Rain; snow; cold; windy	Very breathable	Waterproof	Windproof
Immersion™ Technology	For fishing and paddle sports	Very breathable	Waterproof	Windproof
Ocean Technology	For offshore and coastal sailing	Very breathable	Waterproof	Windproof
Windstopper®	Cool/cold; windy	Very breathable	No water resistance	Windproof
GORE DRYLOFT™	Cold; windy; light precipitation	Extremely breathable	Water resistant	Windproof
Activent™	Cool/cold; windy; light precipitation	Extremely breathable	Water resistant	Windproof

We did such a great job with the brand GORE-TEX that we actually have hurt ourselves in many ways. By that I mean it has been very difficult for us to come up with other new brands, because many people didn't even know Gore. We are the GORE-TEX company. One thing we decided to change about Gore four or five years ago was instead of being the GORE-TEX company we wanted to become the Gore company and that underneath the Gore company we had an umbrella of products that fall out of being the great Gore company. So it was a shift in how we positioned GORE-TEX. Today GORE-TEX is stronger than ever as it's turned out, but now we've ventured into such things as WindStopper®[5] fabric that is very big in the golf market. It could be a sweater or a fleece piece or even a knit shirt with the WindStopper behind it or closer to your skin and what it does is it stops the wind. It's not waterproof; it's water resistant. What we've tried to do is position the Gore name and beneath that all of the great products of the company.

Bill Gore knew that products alone did not a company make. He wanted to avoid smothering the company in thick layers of formal "management." He felt that hierarchy stifled individual creativity. As the company grew, he knew that he had to find a way to assist new people and to follow their progress. This was particularly important when it came to compensation. W. L. Gore & Associates developed its "sponsor" program to meet these needs. When people apply to Gore, they are initially screened by personnel specialists. Those who meet the basic criteria are given interviews with other Associates. Before anyone is hired, an Associate must agree to be his or her sponsor. The sponsor is to take a personal interest in the new Associate's contributions, problems, and goals, acting as both a coach and an advocate. The sponsor tracks the new Associate's progress, helping and encouraging, dealing with weaknesses, and concentrating on strengths. Sponsoring is not a short-term commitment. All Associates

---

[5] WindStopper is a registered trademark of W. L. Gore & Associates.

have sponsors and many have more than one. When individuals are hired initially, they are likely to have a sponsor in their immediate work area. If they move to another area, they may have a sponsor in that work area. As Associates' commitments change or grow, they may acquire additional sponsors.

Because the hiring process looks beyond conventional views of what makes a good Associate, some anomalies have occurred. Bill Gore proudly told the story of "a very young man" of eighty-four who walked in, applied, and spent five very good years with the company. The individual had thirty years of experience in the industry before joining Gore. His other Associates had no problems accepting him, but the personnel computer did. It insisted his age was forty-eight. The individual success stories at Gore have come from diverse backgrounds.

An internal memo by Bill Gore described three roles of sponsors: helping a new Associate get started on a job, seeing that an Associate's accomplishments are recognized, and ensuring that an Associate is fairly paid. A single person can perform any one or all three kinds of sponsorship.

In addition to the sponsor program, Bill Gore articulated four guiding principles:

1. Try to be fair.

2. Encourage, help and allow other Associates to grow in knowledge, skill, and scope of activity and responsibility.

3. Make your own commitments, and keep them.

4. Consult with other Associates before taking actions that may be "below the water line."

The four principles have been referred to as Fairness, Freedom, Commitment, and Waterline. The waterline terminology is drawn from an analogy to ships. If someone pokes a hole in a boat above the waterline, the boat will be in relatively little real danger. If someone, however, pokes a hole below the waterline, the boat is in immediate danger of sinking.

The operating principles were put to a test in 1978. By this time word about the qualities of GORE-TEX fabric was being spread throughout the recreational and outdoor markets. Production and shipment had begun in volume. At first a few complaints were heard. Next some of the clothing started coming back. Finally, much of the clothing was being returned. The trouble was that the GORE-TEX fabric was leaking. Waterproofing was one of the major properties responsible for GORE-TEX fabric's success. The company's reputation and credibility were on the line.

Peter W. Gilson, who led Gore's fabrics division, recalled: "It was an incredible crisis for us at that point. We were really starting to attract attention; we were taking off—and then this." In the next few months, Gilson and a number of his Associates made a number of those below-the-waterline decisions.

First, the researchers determined that oils in human sweat were responsible for clogging the pores in the GORE-TEX fabric and altering the surface tension of the membrane. Thus, water could pass through. They also discovered that a good washing could restore the waterproof property. At first this solution, known as the "Ivory Snow solution," was accepted.

A single letter from "Butch," a mountain guide in the Sierras, changed the company's position. Butch described what happened while he was leading a group: "My parka leaked and my life was in danger." As Gilson noted, "That scared the hell out of us. Clearly our solution was no solution at all to someone on a mountain top." All the products were recalled. Gilson remembered: "We bought back, at our own expense, a fortune in pipeline material—anything that was in the stores, at the manufacturers, or anywhere else in the pipeline."

In the meantime, Bob Gore and other Associates set out to develop a permanent fix. One month later, a second generation GORE-TEX fabric had been developed. Gilson, furthermore, told dealers that if a customer ever returned a leaky parka, they should replace it and bill the company. The replacement program alone cost Gore roughly $4 million.

The popularity of GORE-TEX outerwear took off. Many manufacturers now make numerous pieces of apparel such as parkas, gloves, boots, jogging outfits, and wind shirts from GORE-TEX laminate. Sometimes when customers are dissatisfied with a garment, they return them directly to Gore. Gore has always stood behind any product made of GORE-TEX fabric. Analysis of the returned garments found that the problem was often not the GORE-TEX fabric. The manufacturer "had created a design flaw so that the water could get in here or get in over the zipper and we found that when there was something negative about it, everyone knew it was GORE-TEX. So we had to make good on products that we were not manufacturing. We now license the manufacturers of all our GORE-TEX fabric products. They pay a fee to obtain a license to manufacture GORE-TEX products. In return we oversee the manufacture and we let them manufacture only designs that we are sure are guaranteed to keep you dry, that really will work. Then it works for them and for us—it's a win–win for them as well as for us," according to Sally Gore.

Organizational Structure

W. L. Gore & Associates has been described not only as unmanaged, but also as unstructured. Bill Gore referred to the structure as a lattice organization (see Figure 8.2). The characteristics of this structure are:

1. Direct lines of communication—person to person—with no intermediary.

2. No fixed or assigned authority.

3. Sponsors, not bosses.

4. Natural leadership defined by followership.

5. Objectives set by those who must "make them happen."

6. Tasks and functions organized through commitments.

The structure within the lattice is complex and evolves from interpersonal interactions, self-commitment to group-known responsibilities, natural leadership, and group-imposed discipline.

Bill Gore once explained the structure this way: "Every successful organization has an underground lattice. It's where the news spreads like lightning, where people can go around the organization to get things done." An analogy might be drawn to a structure of constant cross-area teams—the equivalent of quality circles going on all

FIGURE 8.2	THE LATTICE STRUCTURE

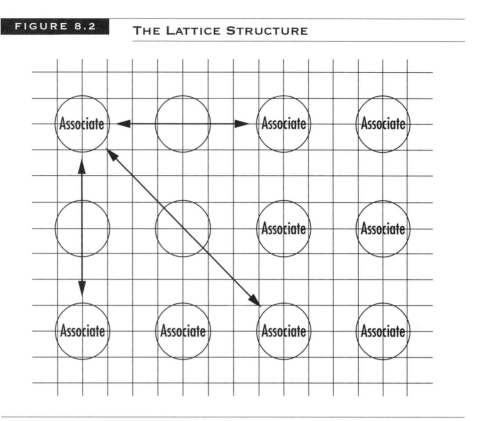

the time. When a puzzled interviewer told Bill that he was having trouble understanding how planning and accountability worked, Bill replied with a grin: "So am I. You ask me how it works? Every which way."

Outsiders have been struck by the degree of informality and humor in the Gore organization. Meetings tend to be only as long as necessary. As Trish Hearn, an Associate in Newark, Delaware, said, "No one feels a need to pontificate." Words such as "responsibilities" and "commitments" are commonly heard, whereas words such as "employees," "subordinates," and "managers" are taboo in the Gore culture. This is an organization that has always taken what it does very seriously, without its members taking themselves too seriously.

For a company of its size, Gore has always had a very short organizational pyramid. As of 1995 the pyramid consists of Bob Gore, the late Bill Gore's son, as president and Vieve, Bill Gore's widow, as secretary-treasurer. All the other members of the Gore organization were, and continue to be, referred to as Associates.

Gore has never had any managers, but it has always had many leaders. Bill Gore described in an internal memo the kinds of leadership and the role of leadership as follows:

1. The Associate who is recognized by a team as having a special knowledge, or experience (for example, this could be a chemist, computer expert, machine operator, salesman, engineer, lawyer). This kind of leader gives the team *guidance in a special area.*

2. The Associate the team looks to for coordination of individual activities in order to achieve the agreed upon objectives of the team. The role of this leader is to persuade team members to *make the commitments* necessary for success (commitment seeker).

3. The Associate who proposes necessary objectives and activities and seeks agreement and team *consensus on objectives*. This leader is perceived by the team members as having a good grasp of how the objectives of the team fit in with the broad objective of the enterprise. This kind of leader is often also the "commitment seeking" leader in 2 above.

4. The leader who evaluates relative contribution of team members (in consultation with other sponsors), and reports these contribution evaluations to a compensation committee. This leader may also participate in the compensation committee on relative contribution and pay and *reports changes in compensation* to individual Associates. This leader is then also a compensation sponsor.

5. The leader who coordinates the research, manufacturing, and marketing of one product type within a business, interacting with team leaders and individual Associates who have commitments regarding the product type. These leaders are usually called *product specialists*. They are respected for their knowledge and dedication to their products.

6. *Plant leaders* who help coordinate activities of people within a plant.

7. *Business leaders* who help coordinate activities of people in a business.

8. *Functional leaders* who help coordinate activities of people in a "functional" area.

9. *Corporate leaders* who help coordinate activities of people in different businesses and functions and who try to promote communication and cooperation among all Associates.

10. *Entrepreneuring Associates* who *organize new teams* for new businesses, new products, new processes, new devices, new marketing efforts, new or better methods of all kinds. These leaders invite the other Associates to "sign up" for their project.

It is clear that leadership is widespread in our lattice organization and that it is continually changing and evolving. The situation that leaders are frequently also sponsors should not confuse that these are different activities and responsibilities.

Leaders are not authoritarians, managers of people, or supervisors who tell us what to do or forbid us doing things; nor are they "parents" to whom we transfer our own self-responsibility. However, they do often advise us of the consequences of actions we have done or propose to do. Our actions result in contributions, or lack of contribution, to the success of our enterprise. Our pay depends on the magnitude of our contributions. This is the basic discipline of our lattice organization.

Many other aspects of the Gore culture have been arranged along egalitarian lines: parking lots with no reserved parking spaces except for customers and disabled workers or visitors; dining areas—only one in each plant—set up as focal points for Associate interaction. As Dave McCarter of Phoenix explained: "The design is no accident. The lunchroom in Flagstaff has a fireplace in the middle. We want people to like to be here." The location of a plant is also no accident. Sites have been selected on the basis of transportation access, a nearby university, beautiful surroundings, and climate appeal. Land cost has never been a primary consideration. McCarter justified the selection by stating: "Expanding is not costly in the long run. The loss of money is what you make happen by stymieing people into a box."

Bob Gore is a champion of Gore culture. As Sally Gore related,

> We have managed surprisingly to maintain our sense of freedom and our entrepreneurial spirit. I think what we've found is that we had to develop new ways to communicate with Associates because you can't communicate with 6,000 people the way that you can communicate with 500 people. It just can't be done. So we have developed a newsletter that we didn't have before. One of the most important communication mediums that we developed, and this was Bob Gore's idea, is a digital voice exchange which we call our Gorecom. Basically everyone has a mailbox and a password. Lots of companies have gone to e-mail, and we use e-mail, but Bob feels very strongly that we're very much an oral culture and there's a big difference between cultures that are predominantly oral and predominantly written. Oral cultures encourage direct communication, which is, of course, something that we encourage.

Not all people function well under such a system, especially initially. For those accustomed to a more structured work environment, there can be adjustment problems. As Bill Gore said: "All our lives most of us have been told what to do, and some people don't know how to respond when asked to do something—and have the very real option of saying no—on their job. It's the new Associate's responsibility to find out what he or she can do for the good of the operation." The vast majority of the new Associates, after some initial floundering, have adapted quickly.

Others, especially those who require more structured working conditions, have found that Gore's flexible workplace is not for them. According to Bill for those few, "It's an unhappy situation, both for the Associate and the sponsor. If there is no contribution, there is no paycheck."

As Anita McBride, an Associate in Phoenix, noted: "It's not for everybody. People ask me do we have turnover, and yes we do have turnover. What you're seeing looks like utopia, but it also looks extreme. If you finally figure the system, it can be real exciting. If you can't handle it, you gotta go. Probably by your own choice, because you're going to be so frustrated."

In rare cases an Associate "is trying to be unfair," in Bill's own words. In one case the problem was chronic absenteeism and in another, an individual was caught stealing. "When that happens, all hell breaks loose," said Bill Gore. "We can get damned authoritarian when we have to."

Over the years, Gore & Associates has faced a number of unionization drives. The company has neither tried to dissuade Associates from attending an organizational meeting nor retaliated when flyers were passed out. As of 1995, none of the plants has been organized. Bill believed that no need existed for third-party representation under the lattice structure. He asked the question, "Why would Associates join a union when they own the company? It seems rather absurd."

FIGURE 8.3

SARAH CLIFTON

SUPREME COMMANDER

1505 NORTH FOURTH STREET
FLAGSTAFF, ARIZONA 86001
PHONE: 602-774-0611
TWX 910-972-0969

Overall, the Associates appear to have responded positively to the Gore system of unmanagement and unstructure. Bill estimated the year before he died that "the profit per Associate is double" that of Du Pont.

The lattice structure has not been without its critics. As Bill Gore stated, "I'm told from time to time that a lattice organization can't meet a crisis well because it takes too long to reach a consensus when there are no bosses. But this isn't true. Actually, a lattice by its very nature works particularly well in a crisis. A lot of useless effort is avoided because there is no rigid management hierarchy to conquer before you can attack a problem."

The lattice has been put to the test on a number of occasions. For example, in 1975, Dr. Charles Campbell of the University of Pittsburgh reported that a GORE-TEX arterial graft had developed an aneurysm. If the bubble-like protrusion continued to expand, it would explode. Obviously, this life-threatening situation had to be resolved quickly and permanently.

Within only a few days of Dr. Campbell's first report, he flew to Newark to present his findings to Bill and Bob Gore and a few other Associates. The meeting lasted two hours. Dan Hubis, a former policeman who had joined Gore to develop new production methods, had an idea before the meeting was over. He returned to his work area to try some different production techniques. After only three hours and twelve tries, he had developed a permanent solution. In other words, in three hours a potentially damaging problem to both patients and the company was resolved. Furthermore, Hubis's redesigned graft went on to win widespread acceptance in the medical community.

Some outsiders have had problems with the idea of no titles. Sarah Clifton, an Associate at the Flagstaff facility, was being pressed by some outsiders as to what her title was. She made one up and had it printed on some business cards: SUPREME COMMANDER (see Figure 8.3). When Bill Gore learned what she did, he loved it and recounted the story to others.

Eric Reynolds, founder of Marmot Mountain Works Ltd. of Grand Junction, Colorado, and a major Gore customer, raised another issue: "I think the lattice has its problems with the day-to-day nitty-gritty of getting things done on time and out the door. I don't think Bill realizes how the lattice system affects customers. I mean after you've established a relationship with someone about product quality, you can call up one day and suddenly find that someone new to you is handling your problem. It's frustrating to find a lack of continuity." He went on to say: "But I have to admit that I've personally seen at Gore remarkable examples of people coming out of nowhere and excelling."

When Bill Gore was asked if the lattice structure could be used by other companies, he answered: "No. For example, established companies would find it very difficult to use the lattice. Too many hierarchies would be destroyed. When you remove titles and positions and allow people to follow who they want, it may very well be someone other than the person who has been in charge. The lattice works for us, but it's always evolving. You have to expect problems." He maintained that the lattice system worked best when it was put in place in start-up companies by dynamic entrepreneurs.

Research and Development

Like everything else at Gore, research and development has always been unstructured. Even without a formal R&D department, the company has been issued many patents, although most inventions have been held as proprietary or trade secrets. Any Associate could ask for a piece of raw PTFE (known as silly worm) with which to experiment. Bill Gore believed that all people had it within themselves to be creative.

One of the best examples of Gore inventiveness occurred in 1969. At the time, the wire and cable division was facing increased competition. Bill Gore began to look for a way to straighten out the PTFE molecules. As he said, "I figured out that if we ever unfold those molecules, get them to stretch out straight, we'd have a tremendous new kind of material." He thought that if PTFE could be stretched, air could be introduced into its molecular structure. The result would be greater volume per pound of raw material with no effect on performance. Thus, fabricating costs would be reduced and profit margins would be increased. Going about this search in a scientific manner, Bob Gore heated rods of PTFE to various temperatures and then slowly stretched them. Regardless of the temperature or how carefully he stretched them, the rods broke.

Working alone late one night after countless failures, Bob in frustration stretched one of the rods violently. To his surprise, it did not break. He tried it again and again with the same results. The next morning Bob demonstrated his breakthrough to his father, but not without some drama. As Bill Gore recalled: "Bob wanted to surprise me so he took a rod and stretched it slowly. Naturally, it broke. Then he pretended to get mad. He grabbed another rod and said, 'Oh the hell with this,' and gave it a pull. It didn't break—he'd done it." The new arrangement of molecules not only changed the wire and cable division, but led to the development of GORE-TEX fabric.

Bill and Vieve did the initial field-testing of GORE-TEX fabric the summer of 1970. Vieve made a hand-sewn tent out of patches of GORE-TEX fabric. They took it on their annual camping trip to the Wind River Mountains in Wyoming. The very first night in the wilderness, they encountered a hail storm. The hail tore holes in the top of the tent, and the bottom filled up like a bathtub from the rain. Undaunted, Bill Gore stated: "At least we knew from all the water that the tent was waterproof. We just needed to make it stronger, so it could withstand hail."

The largest medical division began on the ski slopes of Colorado. Bill was skiing with a friend, Dr. Ben Eiseman of Denver General Hospital. As Bill Gore told the story: "We were ready to start a run when I absentmindedly pulled a small tubular section of GORE-TEX out of my pocket and looked at it. 'What is that stuff?' Ben asked. So I told him about its properties. 'Feels great,' he said. 'What do you use it for?' 'Got no idea,' I said. 'Well give it to me,' he said, 'and I'll try it in a vascular graft on a pig.' Two weeks later, he called me up. Ben was pretty excited. 'Bill,' he said, 'I put it in a pig and it works. What do I do now?' I told him to get together with Pete Cooper in our Flagstaff plant, and let them figure it out." Not long after, hundreds of thousands of people throughout the world began walking around with GORE-TEX vascular grafts.

Gore Associates have always been encouraged to think, experiment, and follow a potentially profitable idea to its conclusion. At a plant in Newark, Delaware, Fred L. Eldreth, an Associate with a third grade education, designed a machine that could wrap thousands of feet of wire a day. The design was completed over a weekend. Many other Associates have contributed their ideas through both products and process breakthroughs.

Even without an R&D department, innovations and creativity continued to work very well at Gore & Associates. The year before he died, Bill Gore claimed that "the creativity, the number of patent applications and innovative products is triple" that of Du Pont.

Associate Development

Ron Hill, an Associate in Newark, noted that Gore "will work with Associates who want to advance themselves." Associates have been offered many in-house training opportunities, not only in technical and engineering areas but also in leadership development. In addition, the company has established cooperative education programs with universities and other outside providers, picking up most of the costs for the Gore Associates. The emphasis in Associate development, as in many parts of Gore, has always been that the Associate must take the initiative.

Products

Gore's electronic products division has produced wire and cable for various demanding applications in aerospace, defense, computers, and telecommunications. The wire and cable products have earned a reputation for unequaled reliability. Most of the wire and cable has been used where conventional cables cannot operate. For example, Gore wire and cable assemblies were used in the space shuttle *Columbia* because they could stand the heat of ignition and the cold of space. Gore wire was used in the moon vehicle shuttle that scooped up samples of moon rocks, and Gore's microwave coaxial assemblies opened new horizons in microwave technology. Back on earth, Gore's electrical wire products helped make the world's fastest computers possible because electrical signals could travel through them at up to 93 percent of the speed of light. Because of the physical properties of the GORE-TEX material used in their construction, the electronic products have been used extensively in defense systems, electronic switching for telephone systems, scientific and industrial instrumentation, microwave communications, and industrial robotics. Reliability has always been a watchword for Gore products.

In medical products, reliability is literally a matter of life and death. GORE-TEX expanded PTFE proved to be an ideal material for combating cardiovascular disease. When human arteries have been seriously damaged or plugged with deposits that interrupt the flow of blood, the diseased portions can often be replaced with GORE-TEX artificial arteries. Because the patient's own tissues grow into the graft's open porous spaces, the artificial portions are not rejected by the body. GORE-TEX vascular grafts, produced in many sizes to restore circulation to all areas of the body, have saved limbs from amputation, and saved lives. Some of the tiniest grafts have relieved pulmonary problems in newborns. GORE-TEX–expanded PTFE has been used to help people with kidney disease. Associates have also developed a variety of surgical reinforcing membranes, known as GORE-TEX cardiovascular patches, which can literally mend broken hearts by patching holes and repairing aneurysms.

Through the waterproof fabrics division, Gore technology has traveled to the roof of the world on the backs of renowned mountaineers and adventurers facing extremely harsh environments. Because the PTFE membrane blocks wind and water but allows sweat to escape, GORE-TEX fabric has proved ideal for those who work or play hard in foul weather. Backpackers have discovered that a single lightweight GORE-TEX fabric shell will replace a poplin jacket and a rain suit, and dramatically outperform both. Skiers, sailors, runners, bicyclists, hunters, fisher[s], and other outdoor enthusiasts have also become big customers of garments made of GORE-TEX fabric. GORE-TEX sportswear, as well as women's fashion footwear and handwear, have proved to be functional as well as attractive. Boots and gloves, for both work and recreation, became waterproof thanks to GORE-TEX liners. GORE-TEX garments have even become standard items issued to military personnel. Wet suits, parkas, pants, headgear, gloves, and boots have kept the troops warm and dry in foul weather missions. Other demanding jobs have also received the protection of GORE-TEX fabric, with its unique combination of chemical and physical properties.

The GORE-TEX fibers, like the fabrics, have ended up in some pretty tough places, including outer protective layer of a NASA spacesuit. In many ways, GORE-TEX fibers have proved to be the ultimate synthetic. They have been impervious to sunlight, chemicals, heat, and cold. They are strong and uniquely resistant to abrasion.

Industrial filtration products, such as GORE-TEX filter bags, have reduced air pollution and recovered valuable solids from gases and liquids more completely than alternatives—and they have done so economically. In the future they may make coal-burning plants completely smoke free, contributing to a cleaner environment.

Gore's industrial products division has developed a unique joint sealant—a flexible cord of porous PTFE—that can be applied as a gasket to the most complex shapes, sealing them to prevent leakage of corrosive chemicals, even at extreme temperature and pressure. Steam valves packed with GORE-TEX have been sold with a lifetime guarantee, provided the valve is used properly.

Compensation

Traditionally, compensation at W. L. Gore & Associates has taken three forms: salary, profit sharing, and an Associate's Stock Ownership Program (ASOP).[6] Entry level

---

[6] Similar legally to an ESOP (Employee Stock Ownership Plan). Again, Gore simply has never allowed the word "employee" in any of its documentation.

salary has been in the middle for comparable jobs. According to Sally Gore: "We do not feel we need to be the highest paid. We never try to steal people away from other companies with salary. We want them to come here because of the opportunities for growth and the unique work environment." In the past, Associates' salaries have been reviewed at least once a year and more commonly twice a year. The reviews are conducted by a compensation team at each facility, with sponsors for the Associates acting as their advocates during the review process. Prior to meeting with the compensation committee, the sponsor checks with customers or Associates familiar with the person's work to find out what contribution the Associate has made. In addition, the evaluation team considers the Associate's leadership ability and willingness to help others develop to their fullest.

Profit sharing follows a formula based on economic value added (EVA). Sally Gore had the following to say about the adoption of a formula:

> It's become more formalized and, in a way, I think that's unfortunate because it used to be a complete surprise to receive a profit share. The thinking of the people like Bob Gore and other leaders was that maybe we weren't using it in the right way and we could encourage people by helping them know more about it and how we made profit share decisions. The fun of it before was people didn't know when it was coming and all of a sudden you could do something creative about passing out checks. It was great fun and people would have a wonderful time with it. The disadvantage was that Associates then did not focus much on, "What am I doing to create another profit share?" By using EVA as a method of evaluation for our profit share, we know at the end of every month how much EVA was created that month. When we've created a certain EVA, we then get another profit share. So everybody knows and everyone says, "We'll do it in January," so it is done. Now Associates feel more part of the happening to make it work. What have you done? Go make some more sales calls, please! There are lots of things we can do to improve our EVA and everybody has a responsibility to do that.

Every month EVA is calculated and every Associate is informed. John Mosko of electronic products commented, ". . . (EVA) lets us know where we are on the path to getting one [a profit share]. It's very critical—every Associate knows."

Annually, Gore also buys company stock equivalent to a fixed percent of the Associates' annual income, placing it in the ASOP retirement fund. Thus, an Associate can become a stockholder after being at Gore for a year. Gore's ASOP ensures Associates participate in the growth of the company by acquiring ownership in it. Bill Gore wanted Associates to feel that they themselves are owners. One Associate stated, "This is much more important than profit sharing."

Commitment has long been considered a two-way street. W. L. Gore & Associates has tried to avoid layoffs. Instead of cutting pay, which in the Gore culture would be disastrous to morale, the company has used a system of temporary transfers within a plant or cluster of plants and voluntary layoffs.

Marketing Strategy

Gore's marketing strategy has focused on three assumptions: that it can offer the best-valued products to a marketplace, that people in that marketplace appreciate what it manufactures, and that Gore can become a leader in that area of expertise. The operating procedures used to implement the strategy have followed the same principles as other functions at Gore.

1. Marketing a product requires a leader, or *product champion*. According to Dave McCarter: "You marry your technology with the interests of your champions, since you've got to have champions for all these things no matter what. And that's the key element within our company. Without a product champion, you can't do much anyway, so it is individually driven. If you get people interested in a particular market or a particular product for the marketplace, then there is no stopping them.

2. *A product champion is responsible for marketing the product through commitments with sales representatives.* Again, according to Dave McCarter: "We have no quota system. Our marketing and our sales people make their own commitments as to what their forecasts have been. There is no person sitting around telling them that is not high enough, you have to increase it by 10 percent, or whatever somebody feels is necessary. You are expected to meet your commitment, which is your forecast, but nobody is going to tell you to change it. . . . There is no order of command, no chain involved. These are groups of independent people who come together to make unified commitments to do something and sometimes when they can't make those agreements . . . you may pass up a marketplace, . . . but that's OK, because there's much more advantage when the team decides to do something."

3. *Sales Associates are on salary, not commission.* They participate in the profit sharing and ASOP plans in which all other Associates participate.

As in other areas of Gore, individual success stories have come from diverse backgrounds. Dave McCarter related one of these successes:

I interviewed Sam one day. I didn't even know why I was interviewing him actually. Sam was retired from AT&T. After twenty-five years, he took the golden parachute and went down to Sun Lakes to play golf. He played golf a few months and got tired of that. He was selling life insurance.

I sat reading the application; his technical background interested me. . . . He had managed an engineering department with 600 people. He'd managed manufacturing plants for AT&T and had a great wealth of experience at AT&T. He said, "I'm retired. I like to play golf but I just can't do it every day so I want to do something else. Do you have something around here I can do?" I was thinking to myself, "This is one of these guys I would sure like to hire but I don't know what I would do with him." The thing that triggered me was the fact that he said he sold insurance and here is a guy with a high degree of technical background selling insurance. He had marketing experience, international marketing experience. So, the bell went off in my head that we were trying to introduce a new product into the marketplace that was a hydrocarbon leak protection cable. You can bury it in the ground and in a matter of seconds it could detect a hydrocarbon like gasoline. I had a couple of other guys working on the product who hadn't been very successful with marketing it. We were having a hard time finding a customer. Well, I thought that kind of product would be like selling insurance. If you think about it, why should you protect your tanks? It's an insurance policy that things are not leaking into the environment. That has implications, big time monetary. So, actually, I said, "Why don't you come back Monday? I have just the thing for you." He did. We hired him; he went to work, a very energetic guy. Certainly a champion of the product, he picked right up on it, ran with it single handed. . . . Now it's a growing business. It certainly is a valuable one too for the environment.

In the implementation of its marketing strategy, Gore has relied on cooperative and word-of-mouth advertising. Cooperative advertising has been especially used to promote GORE-TEX fabric products. Those products are sold through a number of clothing manufacturers and distributors, including Apparel Technologies, Lands End, Austin Reed, Timberland, Woolrich, North Face, Grandoe, and Michelle Jaffe. Gore has stressed cooperative advertising because the Associates believe positive experiences with any one product will carry over to purchases of other and more GORE-TEX fabric products. Apparently, this strategy has paid off. When the Grandoe Corporation introduced GORE-TEX gloves, its president, Richard Zuckerwar, noted: "Sports activists have had the benefit of GORE-TEX gloves to protect their hands from the elements. . . . With this handsome collection of gloves . . . you can have warm, dry hands without sacrificing style."

The power of informal marketing techniques extends beyond consumer products. According to Dave McCarter: "In the technical end of the business, company reputation probably is most important. You have to have a good reputation with your company." He went on to say that without a good reputation, a company's products would not be considered seriously by many industrial customers. In other words, the sale is often made before the representative calls. Using its marketing strategies Gore has been very successful in securing a market leadership position in a number of areas, ranging from waterproof outdoor clothing to vascular grafts.

Environmental Forces

Each of Gore's divisions have faced some environmental forces. The fabric division was hit hard when the fad for jogging suits collapsed in the mid-1980s. The fabric division took another hit from the recession of 1989. People simply reduced their purchases of high-end athletic apparel. By 1995, the fabric division was the fastest growing division of Gore again. The electronic division was hit hard when the mainframe computer business declined in the early 1990s. By 1995, that division was seeing a resurgence for its products partially because that division had developed some electronic products for the medical industry. As can be seen, not all the forces have been negative. The aging population of America has increased the need for health care. As a result, Gore has invested in the development of additional medical products and the medical division is growing.

Financial Information

As a closely held private corporation, W. L. Gore has kept its financial information as closely guarded as proprietary information on products and processes. It has been estimated that Associates who work at Gore own 90 percent of the stock. According to Shanti Mehta, an Associate, Gore's returns on assets and sales have consistently ranked it among the top 10 percent of the Fortune 500 companies. According to another source, W. L. Gore & Associates has been doing just fine by any financial measure. For 35 straight years (from 1961 to 1995) the company has enjoyed profitability and positive return on equity. The compounded growth rate for revenues at W. L. Gore & Associates from 1969 to 1989 was more than 18 percent discounted for inflation.[7] In 1969, total sales were about $6 million; by 1989, the figure was $600 million. As should be expected with the increase in size, the percentage increase in sales has slowed over the last five years (Figure 8.4). Gore financed this growth without long-term debt unless it made sense. For example, "We used to have some industrial revenue bonds where, in essence, to build facilities the government allows banks to lend you money tax free. Up to a couple of years ago we were borrowing money through industrial revenue bonds. Other than that, we are totally debt free. Our money is generated out of the operations of the business, and frankly we're looking for new things to invest in. I know that's a challenge for all of us today," said Bob Winterling. *Forbes* magazine estimates Gore's operating profits for 1993, 1994, and 1995 to be $120, $140, and $192 million, respectively (Figure 8.5).

When asked about cost control, Sally Gore had the following to say:

> You have to pay attention to cost or you're not an effective steward of anyone's money, your own or anyone else's. It's kind of interesting, we started manufacturing medical products in 1974 with the vascular graft and it built from there. The Gore vascular graft is the Cadillac or BMW or Rolls Royce of the business. There is absolutely no contest, and our medical products division became very successful. People thought this was Mecca. Nothing had ever been manufactured that was so wonderful. Our business expanded enormously, rapidly out there [Flagstaff, Arizona] and we had a lot of young, young leadership. They spent some time thinking they could do no wrong and that everything they touched was going to turn to gold. They have had some hard knocks along the way and discovered it wasn't as easy as they initially thought it was. And that's probably good learning for everyone somewhere along the way. That's not how business works. There's a lot of truth in that old saying that you learn more from your failures than you do from your successes. One failure goes a long way toward making you say, Oh, wow!

Acknowledgments

Many sources were helpful in providing background material for this case. The most important sources of all were the W. L. Gore Associates, who generously shared their time and viewpoints about the company. They provided many resources, including internal documents, and added much to this case through sharing their personal experiences as well as ensuring that the case accurately reflected the Gore company and culture.

---

[7] In comparison, only 11 of the 200 largest companies in the *Fortune* 500 had positive ROE each year from 1970 to 1988 and only 2 other companies missed a year. The revenue growth rate for these 13 companies was 5.4 percent compared with 2.5 percent for the entire *Fortune* 500.

| FIGURE 8.4 | GROWTH OF GORE'S SALES VS. GROSS DOMESTIC PRODUCT |

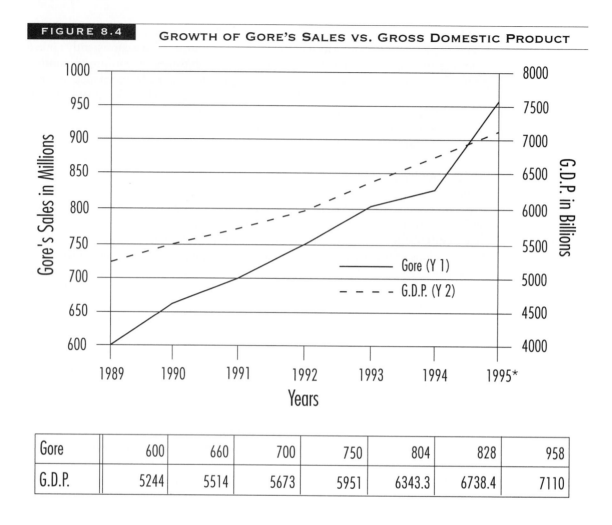

Gore	600	660	700	750	804	828	958
G.D.P.	5244	5514	5673	5951	6343.3	6738.4	7110

Note: *Estimated G.D.P. for 1995

Excerpts from Interviews with Associates

The first excerpt is from an Associate that was formerly with IBM and has been with Gore for two years:

Q. What is the difference between being with IBM and Gore?
A. I spent twenty-four years working for IBM and there's a big difference. I can go ten times faster here at Gore because of the simplicity of the lattice organization. Let me give you an example. If I wanted to purchase chemicals at IBM (I am an industrial chemist), the first thing I would need to do is get accounting approval, then I would need at least two levels of managers' approval, then a secretary to log in my purchase and the purchase order would go to Purchasing where it would be assigned a buyer. Some time could be saved if you were willing to "walk" the paperwork through the approval

FIGURE 8.5   OPERATING AND NET PROFITS OF W.L. GORE & ASSOCIATES

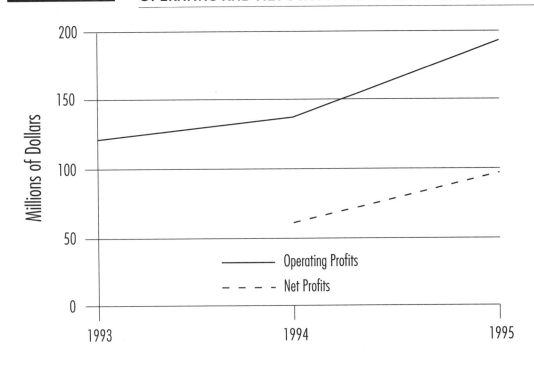

	1993	1994	1995
Operating Profits	120	140	192
Net Profits	N.A.	60	96

Data from *Forbes* Annual Report on the 500 Largest Private Companies in the U.S.

process, but even after computerizing the process, it typically would take one month from the time you initiated the purchase requisition till the time the material actually arrived. Here they have one simple form. Usually, I get the chemicals the next day and a copy of the purchase order will arrive a day or two after that. It happens so fast. I wasn't used to that.

Q. Do you find that a lot more pleasant?

A. Yeah, you're unshackled here. There's a lot less bureaucracy that allows you to be a lot more productive. Take Lab Safety for example. In my Lab at IBM, we were cited for not having my eyewash taped properly. The first time, we were cited for not having a big enough area taped off. So we taped off a bigger area. The next week the same eyewash was cited again, because the area we taped off was three inches too short in one direction. We retaped it and the following week, it got cited again for having the wrong color tape. Keep in mind that the violation was viewed as serious as a pail of gasoline next to a lit Bunsen burner. Another time I had the dubious honor of being selected the functional safety representative in charge of getting the function's labs ready for a Corporate Safety Audit. (The function was a third level in the pyramidal organization: (1) department, (2) project, and (3) function.) At the same time I was working on developing a new surface mount package. As it turned out, I had no time to work on development, and the function spent a lot of time and money getting ready for the Corporate Auditors who in the end never showed. I'm not belittling the importance of Safety, but you really don't need all that bureaucracy to be safe.

The second interview is with an Associate who is a recent engineering graduate:

Q. How did you find the transition coming here?
A. Although I never would have expected it to be, I found my transition coming to Gore to be rather challenging. What attracted me to the company was the opportunity to "be my own boss" and determine my own commitments. I am very goal oriented, and enjoy taking a project and running with it—all things that you are able to do, and encouraged to do within the Gore culture. Thus, I thought, a perfect fit!

However, as a new Associate, I really struggled with where to focus my efforts—I was ready to make my own commitments, but to what?! I felt a strong need to be sure that I was working on something that had value, something that truly needed to be done. While I didn't expect to have the "hottest" project, I did want to make sure that I was helping the company to "make money" in some way.

At the same time, though, I was working for a plant that was pretty typical of what Gore was like when it was originally founded—after my first project (which was designed to be a "quick win"—a project with meaning, but one that had a definite end point), I was told "Go find something to work on." While I could have found something, I wanted to find something with at least a small degree of priority! Thus, the whole process of finding a project was very frustrating for me—I didn't feel that I had the perspective to make such a choice, and ended up in many conversations with my sponsor about what would be valuable. . . .

In the end, of course, I did find that project—and it did actually turn out to be a good investment for Gore. The process to get there, though, was definitely trying for someone as inexperienced as I was—so much ground would have been gained by suggesting a few projects to me and then letting me choose from that smaller pool.

What's really neat about the whole thing, though, is that my experience has truly made a difference. Due in part to my frustrations, my plant now provides college grads with more guidance on their first several projects. (This guidance obviously becomes less and less critical as each Associate grows within Gore.) Associates still are choosing their own commitments, but they're doing so with additional perspective, and the knowledge that they are making a contribution to Gore—which is an important thing within our culture. As I said, though, it was definitely rewarding to see that the company was so responsive, and to feel that I had helped to shape someone else's transition!

Bibliography

Aburdene, Patricia, and John Nasbit. *Re-inventing the Corporation*. New York: Warner Books, 1985.

Angrist, S. W. "Classless Capitalists." *Forbes*, 9 May 1983, pp. 123–124.

Franlesca, L. "Dry and Cool." *Forbes*, 27 August 1984, p. 126.

Hoerr, J. "A Company Where Everybody Is the Boss." *Business Week*, 15 April 1985, p. 98.

Levering, Robert. *The 100 Best Companies to Work for in America*. (See the chapter on W. L. Gore & Associates, Inc.) New York: Signet, 1985.

McKendrick, Joseph. "The Employees as Entrepreneur." *Management World*, January 1985, pp. 12–13.

Milne, M. J. "The Gorey Details." *Management Review*, March 1985, pp. 16–17.

Price, Kathy. "Firm Thrives without Boss." *Arizona Republic*, 2 February 1986.

Posner, B. G. "The First Day on the Job." *Inc.*, June 1986, pp. 73–75.

Rhodes, Lucien. "The Un-manager." *Inc.*, August 1982, p. 34.

Simmons, J. "People Managing Themselves: Un-management at W. L. Gore Inc." *The Journal for Quality and Participation* (December 1987): pp. 14–19.

"The Future Workplace." *Management Review*, July 1986, pp. 22–23.

Trachtenberg, J. A. "Give Them Stormy Weather." *Forbes*, 24 March 1986, pp. 172–174.

Ward, Alex. "An All-Weather Idea." *The New York Times Magazine*, 10 November 1985, sec. 6.

Weber, Joseph. "No Bosses, and Even 'Leaders' Can't Give Orders." *Business Week*, 10 December 1990, pp. 196–197.

"Wilbert L. Gore." *Industry Week*, 17 October 1983, pp. 48–49.

9

Barro Stickney, Inc.

Introduction

With four people and sales of $5.5 million, Barro Stickney, Inc. (BSI) had become a successful and profitable manufacturers' representative firm. It enjoyed a reputation for outstanding sales results and friendly, thorough service to both its customers and principals. In addition, BSI was considered a great place to work. The office was comfortable and the atmosphere relaxed but professional. All members of the group had come to value the close, friendly working relationships that had grown with the organization.

Success had brought with it increased profits as well as the inevitable decision regarding further growth. Recent requests from two principals, Franklin Key Electronics and R. D. Ocean, had forced BSI to focus its attention on the question of expansion. It was not to be an easy decision, for expansion offered both risk and opportunity.

Company Background

John Barro and Bill Stickney established their small manufacturers' representative agency, Barro Stickney, Inc., ten years ago. Both men were close friends who left different manufacturers' representative firms to join as partners in their own "rep" agency. The two worked very well together, and their talents complemented each other.

John Barro was energetic and gregarious. He enjoyed meeting new people and taking on new challenges. It was mainly through John's efforts that many of BSI's eight principals had signed on with BSI. Even after producing $1.75 million in sales this past year, John still made an effort to contribute much of his free time to community organizations in addition to perfecting his golf score.

Bill Stickney liked to think of himself as someone a person could count on. He was thoughtful and thorough. He liked to figure how things could get done, and how they could be better. Much of the administrative work of the agency, such as resource allocation and territory assignments, was handled by Bill. In addition to his contribution of $1.5 million to total company sales, Bill also had a Boy Scout troop and was

SOURCE: This case was written by Tony Langan, B. Jane Stewart, and Lawrence M. Stratton Jr., under the supervision of Professor Erin Anderson of the Wharton School, University of Pennsylvania. The writing of the case was sponsored by the Manufacturers' Representatives Educational Research Foundation. The cooperation of the Mid-Atlantic Chapter of the Electronic Representatives Association (ERA) is greatly appreciated.

interested in gourmet cooking. In fact, he often prepared specialties to share with his fellow workers.

A few years later, as the business grew, J. Todd Smith (J.T.) joined as an additional salesperson. J.T. had worked for a nationally known corporation, and he brought his experience dealing with large customers with him. He and his family loved the Harrisburg area, and J.T. was very happy when he was asked to join BSI just as his firm was ready to transfer him to Chicago. John and Bill had worked with J.T. in connection with a hospital fund-raising project, and they were impressed with his tenacity and enthusiasm. Because he had produced sales of over $2 million this past year, J.T. was now considered eligible to buy a partnership share of BSI.

Soon after J.T. joined BSI, Elizabeth Lee, a school friend of John's older sister, was hired as office manager. She was cheerful and put as much effort into her work as she did coaching the local swim team. The three salespeople knew they could rely on her to keep track of orders and schedules, and she was very helpful when customers and principals called in with requests or problems.

Most principals in the industry assigned their reps exclusive territories, and BSI's ranged over the Pennsylvania, New Jersey, and Delaware area. The partners purchased a small house and converted it into their present office located in Camp Hill, a suburb of Harrisburg, the state capital of Pennsylvania. The converted home contributed to the familylike atmosphere and attitude that was promoted and prevalent throughout the agency.

Over the years, in addition to local interests, BSI and its people had made an effort to participate in and support the efforts of the Electronics Representative Association (ERA). A wall of the company library was covered with awards and letters of appreciation. BSI had made many friends and important contacts through the organization. Just last year BSI received a recommendation from Chuck Goodman, a Chicago manufacturers' rep who knew a principal in need of representation in the Philadelphia area. The principal's line worked well with BSI's existing portfolio, and customer response had been quite favorable. BSI planned to continue active participation in the ERA.

Each week BSI held a five o'clock meeting in the office library where all members of the company shared their experiences of the week. It was a time when new ideas were encouraged and everyone was brought up to date. For example, many customer problems were solved here, and principals' and members' suggestions were discussed. An established agenda enabled members to prepare. Most meetings took about sixty to ninety minutes, with emphasis placed on group consensus. It was during this group meeting that BSI would discuss the future of the company.

Opportunities for Expansion

R. D. Ocean was BSI's largest principal, and it accounted for 32 percent of BSI's revenues. Ocean had just promoted James Innve as new sales manager, and he felt an additional salesperson was needed in order for BSI to achieve the new sales projections. Innve expressed the opinion that BSI's large commission checks justified the additional effort, and he further commented that J.T.'s expensive new car was proof that BSI could afford it.

BSI was not sure an additional salesperson was necessary, but it did not want to lose the goodwill of R. D. Ocean or [its] business. Also, while it was customary for all principals to meet and tacitly approve new representatives, BSI wanted to be very sure that any new salesperson would fit into the close-knit BSI organization.

Franklin Key Electronics was BSI's initial principal and had remained a consistent contributor of approximately 15 percent of BSI's revenues. BSI felt its customer base was well suited to the Franklin line, and it had worked hard to establish the Franklin Key name with these customers. As a consequence, BSI now considered Franklin Key relatively easy to sell.

A few days previously, Mark Heil, Franklin's representative from Virginia, perished when his private plane crashed, leaving Franklin Key without representation in its D.C./Virginia territory. Franklin did not want to jeopardize its sales of over $800,000 and was desperate to replace Heil before its customers found other sources. Franklin offered the territory to BSI and was anxious to hear the decision within one week.

BSI was not familiar with the territory, but it did understand that there were a great number of military accounts. This meant there was a potential for sizable orders, although a different and specialized sales approach would be required. Military customers are known to have their own unique approach to purchase decisions.

Because of the distance and the size of the territory, serious consideration was needed as to whether a branch office would be necessary. A branch office would mean less interaction with and a greater independence from the main BSI office. None of the current BSI members seemed anxious to move there, but it might be possible to hire someone who was familiar with the territory. There was, of course, always the risk that any successful salesperson might leave and start his or her own rep firm.

In addition to possibilities of expanding its territory and its sales force, BSI also wanted to consider whether it should increase or maintain its number of principals. BSI's established customer base and its valued reputation put them in a strong position to approach potential principals. If, however, BSI had too many principals, it might not be able to offer them all the attention and service they might require.

Preparation for the Meeting

Each member received an agenda and supporting data for the upcoming meeting asking them to consider the issue of expansion. They would be asked whether BSI should or should not expand its territory, its sales force, and/or its number of principals. In preparation, they were each asked to take a good hard look at the current BSI portfolio and to consider all possibilities for growth, including the effect any changes would have on the company's profits, its reputation, and its work environment.

It was an ambitious agenda: one that would determine the future of the company. It would take even more time than usual to discuss everything and reach consensus. Consequently, this week's meeting was set to take place over the weekend at Bill Stickney's vacation lodge in the Pocanos starting with a gourmet dinner served at 7 P.M. sharp.

Before the meeting, Bill Stickney examined the sources of BSI's revenue and the firm's income for the previous year. He also estimated the future prospects for each of BSI's lines, considering each line's market potential and BSI's level of saturation in each market. Finally, he estimated the costs of hiring a new employee both in the current sales territory and in the Washington/Virginia area. Immediately before the meeting, Elizabeth finished compiling Bill's data into four figures (see page 608).

Figure 9.1 evaluates the amount of sales effort (difficulty in selling) necessary to achieve a certain percentage of sales in BSI's portfolio (return). Difficulty in selling is measured by the level of marketing investment required for growth. Stickney's estimates are shown on the vertical axis. Return for this investment is measured by the

| FIGURE 9.1 | RETURN VERSUS DIFFICULTY IN SELLING |

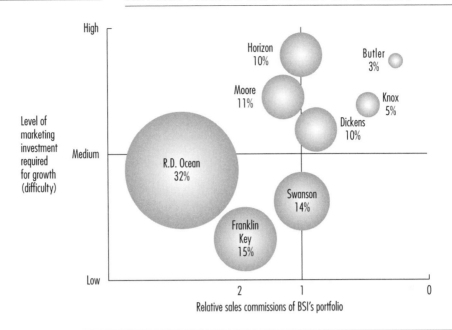

relative sales commissions as a percent of BSI's portfolio shown on the horizontal axis. If BSI's time were evenly divided among its eight principals, each would receive 12.5 percent of the agency's time. The x-axis shows each principal's time allocation as a proportion of 12.5 percent of the "par" time allocation. The area of each ellipse reflects each principal's share of BSI's commission revenue.

Bill Stickney presented the following additional comments as a result of his research:

1. Swanson's products are being replaced by the competition's computerized electronic equipment, a product category the firm has ignored. As a result, the company is losing its once prominent market position.

2. Although small amounts of effort are required to promote Ocean's product line to customers in the current sales territory, Ocean is extremely demanding of both BSI and other manufacturer's representative firms.

3. According to a seminar at the last ERA meeting, the maximum safe proportion of a rep firm's commissions from a single principal should be 25–30 percent. Also, at the meeting, one speaker indicated that if a firm commands 80 percent of a market, it should focus on another product or expand its territory rather than attempt to obtain the remainder of the market.

4. The revenue for investment for the manufacturer's representative firm comes from one or more of several sources. These sources include reduced forthcoming commission income, retained previous income, and borrowed money from a financial institution. Most successful firms expand their sales force or sales territory when they experience income growth and use the investment as a tax write-off.

FIGURE 9.2

BARRO STICKNEY, INC., ESTIMATION OF COST OF ADDITIONAL SALES REPRESENTATIVE

Compensation Costs for New Sales Representative

Depending on the new sales representative's level of experience, BSI would pay a base salary of $15,000–$25,000 with the following bonus schedule:

  0% firm's commission revenue up to $500,000 in sales
20% firm's commission revenue first $0.5 million in sales over $500,000
25% firm's commission revenue for the next $0.5 million in sales
30% firm's commission for the next $0.5 million in sales
40% firm's commission sales above $2 million

Estimate of Support Costs[1] for the New Representative[2]

Search applicant pool, psychological testing, hiring, training,[3] flying final choice to principals for approval[4]	$28,000
Automobile expenses, telephone costs, business cards, entertainment promotion	22,000
Insurance, payroll taxes (social security, unemployment compensation)	16,000
Total expenses	$66,000

Incremental Expenses for New Territory

Transportation (additional mileage from Camp Hill to Virginia)	$ 2,000
Office equipment and rent (same regardless of headquarter's location)	4,000
Cost of hiring office manager[5]	18,000
Total increment expenses	$24,000

[1]Rounded to the nearest thousand. [2]In current territory. [3]Excludes the lost revenue from selling instead of engaging in this activity (opportunity cost). [4]Although rep agencies are not legally required to show prospective employees to principals, it is generally held to be good business practice. [5]Discretionary.

FIGURE 9.3

BARRO STICKNEY, INC., STATEMENT OF REVENUE (TOTAL SALES REVENUE 1988, $5.5 MILLION)

Principal	Estimated Market Saturation	Product Type	Sales/ Commission Rate	Share of BSI's Portfolio	Commission Revenue
R. D. Ocean	High	Components	5.00%	32%	$96,756
Franklin Key	High	Components	5.00	15	45,354
Butler	Low	Technical/computer	12.00	3	9,070
Dickens	Low	Components	5.00	10	30,236
Horizon	Medium	Components	5.50	10	30,237
Swanson	High	Components	5.25	14	42,331
Moore	Medium	Consumer/electronics	5.25	11	33,260
Knox	Low	Technical/communications	8.50	5	15,118

FIGURE 9.4

BARRO STICKNEY, INC., STATEMENT OF INCOME (FOR THE YEAR ENDING DECEMBER 31, 1988)

Revenue

Commission income	$302,362

Expenses

Salaries for sales and bonuses (includes Barro Stickney)	130,250
Office manager's salary	20,000
Total nonpersonnel expenses[1]	128,279
Total expenses	$278,529

Net income[2] $ 23,833   (7.9% of revenue)

[1]Includes travel, advertising, office supplies, retirement, automobile expenses, communications, office equipment, and miscellaneous expenses.
[2]Currently held in negotiable certificates of deposit in a Harrisburg bank.

10

Beta Pharmaceuticals: Pennsylvania Distribution System

Jack Sexton, manager of logistics planning, walked out of his boss's office with a frown on his face. He had just learned that the top management of his company, Beta Pharmaceutical, had been taking a closer look at cost levels in the company's distribution system. In particular, high transportation costs resulting from frequent minimum-size LTL (less than truckload) shipments to customers and low-volume resupply shipments to the smaller warehouses were beginning to raise eyebrows. Total warehousing and material-handling costs had also been questioned.

When he got back to his office, Mr. Sexton sat back and thought the problem over. He recalled that the present plant, warehouse, and customer configuration had evolved during a period of high-growth years, without the systematic development of a master distribution plan. Warehouse location and customer service decisions were based mainly on marketing-centered recommendations, competitive pressures, and customer desires. Customer order frequency and shipment size had been largely in the control of the customer. Basically, Beta believed that to achieve and maintain industry leadership, it was necessary to meet customer demand 100 percent of the time. Thus the cost of customer service, inclusive of distribution, had historically been very high.

Several days later Mr. Sexton settled on a course of action. Calling in a logistics consulting firm, HLW and Associates, he asked that a pilot study be conducted to evaluate a portion of the present product logistics system for cost-service effectiveness. The state of Pennsylvania was determined to be a "typical" subsystem within the national distribution network and was designated by Mr. Sexton as the focal point for the study.[1] An outline of the study proposal is shown in Figure 10.1.

Background

The Company

Beta Pharmaceuticals is a multidivisional manufacturer and distributor of a diversified line of medical care products. Manufacturing, sales, and distribution facilities are

---

This case was prepared by Harvey Boatman, Paul Liguori, and Gary Wiser under the direction of Professor Alan J. Stenger, The Pennsylvania State University.

[1]Pennsylvania represents a "mini model" of the total system in that it contains a three-warehouse configuration, two customer service areas, a customer service representative, and a dollar demand pattern consistent with the rest of the national system.

FIGURE 10.1   **PROJECT DESCRIPTION**

Project: How should Beta Pharmaceuticals distribute products to customers in the state of Pennsylvania?

Background: Beta currently distributes products to customers from public warehouses in Pittsburgh, Harrisburg, and Philadelphia.

- Cartage carriers are used in the three metropolitan areas.
- Common carriers are used in the balance of the state.
- Customers (hospitals) order both in patterns and randomly.
- Shipments are made within 24 to 48 hours of order receipt.
- Shipment sizes are small, from under 100 pounds to a few thousand pounds.
- The full product line is stocked in Philadelphia and Pittsburgh, but only a partial line is stocked in Harrisburg.
- Distribution costs are a significant element of total costs.

Objective: Determine the best method to distribute products to customers, considering the effects on:

- Distribution costs (freight and handling).
- Levels of customer service.
- Inventory levels.

Scope: The scope of the project should be restricted to the state of Pennsylvania to keep it manageable.

- Inventory policies and methods of replenishing warehouses should be ignored. However, the relationship between aggregate inventory levels and warehouse volume must be recognized.
- Customer order patterns can be assumed to be controllable within certain limits, to be defined. Customer contact will not be allowed.
- The number and location of warehouses should be determined.
- Methods of delivery should be determined, including such alternatives as (1) direct shipment or (2) scheduling of customer orders for pooled delivery, including contact with carriers for rates and feasibility.

---

located throughout the world, with major operations existing in Europe, Africa, South America, Australia, Asia, Canada, and the United States. Products include intravenous solutions, artificial organs, disposable medical devices, clinical testing and diagnostic supplies and equipment, blood collecting and storage equipment, prescription drugs, and industrial and medical enzymes.

Beta has twelve production or research facilities in the United States, and markets its products through five customer-service or distribution-center regions. The company employs 13,600 persons throughout its worldwide system.

The backbone of Beta's strong marketing position in the hospital supply industry is a well-funded R&D program. New products, as well as improvements to existing products, are constantly being developed and exploited as a key element in market strategy and industry leadership. As a result of this philosophy, Beta increased the 1994 expenditures for research and development by 25.7 percent over 1993 for a total dollar investment of $46.7 million.

The aggressive competitive stance, supported by resourceful research and development, effective quality control, and customer-oriented distribution, has enabled the company to build a sixteen-year compound growth rate in sales and earnings per share of 20 percent. Its 1994 sales were $855.9 million, which represented a 27.7 percent increase over 1993. Earnings per share for 1994 were $1.95, a 23.4 percent increase over 1993.

The Distribution System

The current distribution system used by Beta within the state of Pennsylvania makes use of three public warehouses: Philadelphia, Pittsburgh, and Harrisburg. From these three warehouses, Beta is able to serve most of its customers in forty-nine of the sixty-seven counties in Pennsylvania: this service is supplemented by shipments from nearby out-of-state warehouses or by carload shipments direct from a Beta plant. The distribution responsibilities of the three Pennsylvania warehouses include shipments to out-of-state customers as well as to the Pennsylvania customers.

Beta maintains either a company-salaried customer service representative or a warehouse employee at each warehouse to handle orders and customer inquiries. Whenever an order is received, company policy dictates that it be filled and tendered to a carrier within forty-eight hours. Orders are received either electronically or by phone, direct at the warehouse or at company headquarters in Chicago. The forty-eight-hour service goal starts at the point the order is received within the Beta system.

Once the warehouse receives the order, two possibilities exist. If the items are in stock, a bill of lading is cut and the freight is tendered to a common carrier or a cartage carrier. Of those shipments tendered to common carriers, 95 percent are delivered by the second morning. This means a maximum order filling time—including transportation—of four days 95 percent of the time. If the customer is located within the commercial zone of the city and a cartage carrier can be used, total time from order receipt by Beta to delivery to the customer is reduced to two days 95 percent of the time.

When sufficient stock is not available, the warehouse representative will contact the regional distribution center to which the warehouse is assigned. The regional distribution center will review the inventory levels of the surrounding warehouses and assign the order to one of these warehouses. Transportation cost is used as the basis for which warehouse should receive the order. If the item is not available in any of the surrounding warehouses, it will be back-ordered and expedited from a production facility. Since Beta wants to maintain high customer service levels, every attempt is made to maintain inventories high enough to avoid the need of back ordering to Chicago.

The majority of Beta's customers are hospitals. As such, they have limited storage space. They also cannot afford to wait very long after ordering items because their inventory averages approximately one week's demand. Since Beta is the major supplier of medical products in the Pennsylvania area, it falls upon them to provide hospitals with the required service. Traditional performance and marketing pressure have forced Beta into the position of maintaining inventory for its customers. However, very few of the shipments made by Beta are on a life-or-death basis for a patient.

Preliminary Findings and Plans of the Consultants

Beta's present distribution system is structured around basic customer service objectives. Competitive stress and rapid growth contributed to the piecemeal development of the present structure, wherein the customer sets the rules. This resulted in a number of marginal, close-to-the-customer warehouses. Warehouse-to-customer shipments are made without consideration of economic order quantities or potential savings to be recognized by shipping in consolidated lots. Many customers avoid assuming inventory responsibility and cost by ordering frequently, often at random intervals and in varying order quantities. Beta provides twenty-four-hour delivery to all customers within the commercial zone of each warehouse, and forty-eight-hour delivery to other customers. This situation has necessitated the establishment of safety stock of nearly 100 percent at most warehouses.

The piecemeal pattern of development has presented coordination problems at the corporate level. Many problems common to several areas are still handled on an individual basis at the local level. Rarely is the experience and information gained at one point generalized for the benefit of other areas of the system. The nearly exclusive use of public warehouses compounds this situation, particularly when quality control, damage, or liability become the question. The use of public warehouses also complicates the information-gathering process as well as making the control aspects of inventory more difficult to handle.

Even though growth potential remains high for Beta, a plateau has been reached in many areas. For example, the climb to leadership in the medical products industry has been achieved; a reputation for high standards, effective quality control, and an understanding for the specialized problems experienced by hospitals has been established; an impressive record of innovation and responsible research and development has been compiled. In essence, Beta has created a "pull" situation, in the marketing sense, for the products bearing the Beta trademark.

Beta presently has good information potential. Most operations-related facts are collected in the present system, but unfortunately those items not lost due to pure volume are presented in a manner that makes their usefulness limited and suspect. Feedback and information update is slow and complicated under the present system of hand tallies, verbal order placement at each warehouse, and conflicting loyalties (due to the nearly exclusive use of public warehouses). Control at the warehouse level is shaky at best.

The Pennsylvania Subsystem

The following information is available for the Pennsylvania subsystem:

1. *Monthly demand for Pennsylvania customers.* A computer printout for March 1995 gives demand by customers for each of Beta's major product lines. It shows how many bills of lading were cut and the number of cases per product line on each bill. Every order shipped within the state of Pennsylvania is included, with coded identification of which warehouse filled the order. There is a considerable amount of overlap in the territory served by various warehouses. Out-of-state warehouses appear throughout the printout, indicating service to cities also serviced by the Pennsylvania warehouses. The monthly

demand information gives no indication of the timing throughout the month for the orders. It is easy to identify how many shipments a customer received but not when they were received. Finally, there is no indication that March 1995 was a typical month in terms of demand level. A quarterly demand schedule was requested but not provided. As a result, the assumption that March 1995 is a typical month had to be made.

2. *Quarterly transportation cost.* This is a summary of the air and truck costs incurred by each of Beta's warehouses on an outbound basis by product line only. It does show total pieces and weight of each product line shipped by air and truck, but it does not break total cost down past a total for air and truck. Since the total cost is a three-month figure for all shipments out of a warehouse, an average cost would not truly reflect the intrastate rate levels.

3. *March payments to carriers.* Beta provided a list of the total billings for transportation charges paid to carriers in March 1995. The charges are broken down by product line pieces and weight. The list is not very useful because it is for bills paid in March, not for shipments made during March. Also, no information was provided concerning the number of shipments each carrier handled or the destination of these shipments.

4. *Warehouse throughput.* Beta was able to provide estimates of the average monthly throughput in terms of total cases for the three Pennsylvania warehouses, as follows:

Philadelphia:	50,000 cases
Pittsburgh:	35,000 cases
Harrisburg:	9,000 cases

Warehouse capacity in both Philadelphia and Pittsburgh is large enough to handle the entire throughput of Harrisburg should that location be eliminated. Average monthly throughput would be useful in evaluating the methods of warehouse replenishment.

5. *Warehouse cost.* The three Pennsylvania facilities are public warehouses. Under the contract agreements with Philadelphia and Harrisburg, a single charge is assessed for each carton that comes into the warehouse. There is no annual rental fee, no quantity discount, and no penalty for falling below a minimum level. The single rate per carton includes storage, handling, stenciling, and anything else the warehouse people might have to do to the case. The charge in Philadelphia is 44 cents per case, while the Harrisburg charge is forty-three cents per case. Pittsburgh, which does not have the same type of arrangements, pays an average of forty-six cents per case. There is no indication of how this figure would vary with different inventory levels. An additional ten cents per case is assigned by Beta to each case handled through the Pittsburgh warehouse due to the presence of a Beta customer service representative in that city.

6. *Warehouse replenishment policy.* Beta will not retain a warehouse unless it can be replenished at least once a month in carload quantity. The information provided by Beta concerning actual replenishment schedules is very sketchy. Philadelphia and Pittsburgh are replenished on a carload basis once a week.

However, no information was available as to how many cars per week were used, whether they get the 40,000-pound or the 60,000-pound carload rate, or whether additional demand would also move at carload rates. If Harrisburg is eliminated, inbound freight costs to Philadelphia and Pittsburgh will change. The Harrisburg replenishment schedule was stated to be once every two to three weeks and once a month.

7. *Average inventory level.* Both Philadelphia and Pittsburgh hold six weeks' demand in inventory, whereas Harrisburg holds eight weeks' demand in inventory. These figures were unfortunately subject to some uncertainty.

8. *Truck rates.* Evaluating configuration changes in the current system requires a comparison of total cost for both the present and proposed systems. Costing out a system requires a close estimate of the transportation costs generated by that system. In light of the restrictions of a linear programming algorithm in terms of homogeneous product and potential system requirement of over 2,000 rates, weighted rate per county was used. Since the three Pennsylvania warehouses service forty-nine counties in Pennsylvania, forty weighted rates were obtained. A weighted rate assumes that all freight destined to a specific county is going to the one city where the major customers' demand is located. By selecting the city having the maximum flow of freight, variation from the actual rates is minimized. The weight break to that city is computed in terms of the average weekly tonnage coming into the entire county. This requires that a maximum of four shipments per month be allowed for any county. After one rate for each commodity group was established, the four rates were combined into one weighted rate, based on the percentage of the total weekly tonnage that the product line accounted for.

Propose several ways in which the Pennsylvania distribution system might be improved.

11

Wind Technology

Kevin Cage, general manager of Wind Technology, sat in his office on a Friday afternoon watching the snow fall outside his window. It was January 1991 and he knew that during the month ahead he would have to make some difficult decisions regarding the future of his firm, Wind Technology. The market for the wind profiling radar systems that his company designed had been developing at a much slower rate than he had anticipated.

Wind Technology

During Wind Technology's ten-year history, the company had produced a variety of weather-related radar and instrumentation. In 1986 the company condensed its product mix to include only wind-profiling radar systems. Commonly referred to as wind profilers, these products measure wind and atmospheric turbulence for weather forecasting, detection of wind direction at NASA launch sites, and other meteorological applications, (i.e., at universities and other scientific monitoring stations). Kevin had felt that this consolidation would position the company as a leader in what he anticipated to be a high-growth market with little competition.

Wind Technology's advantages over Unisys, the only other key player in the wind-profiling market, included the following:

1. The company adhered stringently to specifications and quality production.

2. Wind Technology had the technical expertise to provide full system integration. This allowed customers to order either basic components or a full system, including software support.

3. Wind Technology's staff of meteorologists and atmospheric scientists provided the customer with sophisticated support, including operation and maintenance training and field assistance.

4. Finally, Wind Technology had devoted all of its resources to its wind-profiling business. Kevin believed that the market would perceive this as an advantage over a large conglomerate like Unisys.

Ken Manning, Gonzaga University, and Jakki Mohr, University of Montana. © 1990 by Jakki Mohr.

616 • Case Eleven

Wind Technology customized each product for individual customers as the need arose; the total system could cost a customer from $400,000 to $5 million. Various governmental entities, such as the Department of Defense, NASA, and state universities, had consistently accounted for about 90 percent of Wind Technology's sales. In lieu of a field sales force, Wind Technology relied on top management and a team of engineers to call on prospective and current customers. Approximately $105,000 of their annual salaries was charged to a direct selling expense.

The Problem

The consolidation strategy that the company had undertaken in 1986 was due in part to the company's purchase by Vaitra, a high-technology European firm. Wind Technology's ability to focus on the wind-profiling business had been made possible by Vaitra's financial support. However, since 1986 Wind Technology had shown little commercial success, and due to low sales levels the company was experiencing severe cash flow problems. Kevin knew that Wind Technology could not continue to meet its payroll much longer. Also, he had been informed that Vaitra was not willing to pour more money into Wind Technology. Kevin estimated that he had from nine to twelve months (until the end of 1991) in which to implement a new strategy with the potential to improve the company's cash flow. The new strategy was necessary to enable Wind Technology to survive until the wind-profiler market matured. Kevin and other industry experts anticipated that it would be two years until the wind-profiling market achieved the high growth levels that the company had initially anticipated.

One survival strategy that Kevin had in mind was to spin off and market component parts used in making wind profilers. Initial research indicated that, of all the wind-profiling system's component parts, the high-voltage power supply (HVPS) had the greatest potential for commercial success. Furthermore, Kevin's staff on the HVPS product had demonstrated knowledge of the market. Kevin believed that by marketing the HVPS, Wind Technology could reap incremental revenues, with very little addition to fixed costs. (Variable costs would include the costs of making and marketing the HVPS. The accounting department had estimated that production costs would run approximately 70 percent of the selling price, and that 10 percent of other expenses—such as top management direct-selling expenses—should be charged to the HVPS.)

High-Voltage Power Supplies

For a vast number of consumer and industrial products that require electricity, the available voltage level must be transformed to different levels and types of output. The three primary types of power supplies include linears, switchers, and converters. Each type manipulates electrical current in terms of the type of current (AC of DC) and/or the level of output (voltage). Some HVPS manufacturers focus on producing a standardized line of power supplies, while others specialize in customizing power supplies to user's specifications.

High-voltage power supplies vary significantly in size and level of output. Small power supplies with relatively low levels of output (under 3 kV)[1] are used in commu-

---

[1]V (kilovolt): 1,000 volts.

nications equipment. Medium-sized power supplies that produce an output between 3 and 10 kV are used in a wide range of products, including radars and lasers. Power supplies that produce output greater than 10 kV are used in a variety of applications, such as high-powered X rays and plasma-etching systems.

Background on Wind Technology's HVPS

One of Wind Technology's corporate strategies was to control the critical technology (major component parts) of its wind-profiling products. Management felt that this control was important since the company was part of a high-technology industry in which confidentiality and innovation were critical to each competitor's success. This strategy also gave Wind Technology a differential advantage over its major competitors, all of whom depended on a variety of manufacturers for component parts. Wind Technology had successfully developed almost all of the major components and the software for the wind profiler, yet the development of the power supply had been a problem.

To adhere to the policy of controlling critical technology in product design (rather than purchasing an HVPS from an outside supplier), Wind Technology's management had hired Anne Ladwig and her staff of HVPS technicians to develop a power supply for the company's wind-profiling systems. Within six months of joining Wind Technology, Anne and her staff had completed development of a versatile power supply which could be adapted for use with a wide variety of equipment. Some of the company's wind-profiling systems required up to ten power supplies, each modified slightly to carry out its role in the system.

Kevin Cage had delegated the responsibility of investigating the sales potential of the company's HVPS to Anne Ladwig because she was familiar with the technical aspects of the product and had received formal business training while pursuing an MBA. Anne had determined that Wind Technology's HVPS could be modified to produce levels of output between 3 and 10 kV. Thus, it seemed natural that if the product was brought to market, Wind Technology should focus on applications in this range of output. Wind Technology also did not have the production capabilities to compete in the high-volume, low-voltage segment of the market, nor did the company have the resources and technical expertise to compete in the high-output (+ 10 kV) segment.

The Potential Customer

Power supplies in the 3–10 kV range could be used to conduct research, to produce other products, or to place as a component into other products such as lasers. Thus, potential customers could include research labs, large end-users, original equipment manufacturers (OEMs), or distributors. Research labs each used an average of three power supplies; other types of customers ordered a widely varying quantity.

HVPS users were demanding increasing levels of reliability, quality, customization, and system integration. *System integration* refers to the degree to which other parts of a system are dependent upon the HVPS for proper functioning, and the extent to which these parts are combined into a single unit or piece of machinery.

Anne had considered entering several HVPS market segments in which Wind Technology could reasonably compete. She had estimated the domestic market

FIGURE 11.1   HVPS MARKET SEGMENTS IN THE
3–10 KV RANGE

Application	Forecasted Annual Growth (%)	Level of Customization/ Level of System Integration*	Synergy Rating†	Percentage of $237 Million Power Supply Market††
General/University laboratory	5.40	Medium/medium	3	8%
Lasers	11.00	Low/medium	4	10
Medical equipment	10.00	Medium/medium	3	5
Microwave	12.00	Medium/high	4	7
Power modulators	3.00	Low/low	4	25
Radar systems	11.70	Low/medium	5	12
Semiconductor	10.10	Low/low	3	23
X-ray systems	8.60	Medium/high	3	10

*The level of customization and system integration generally in demand within each of the applications is defined as low, medium, or high.

†Synergy ratings are based on a scale of 1 to 5; 1 is equivalent to a very low level of synergy and 5 is equivalent to a very high level of synergy. These subjective ratings are based on the amount of similarities between the wind-profiling industry and each application.

††Percentages total 100 percent of the $237 million market in which Wind Technology anticipated it could compete.

NOTE: This list of applications is not all-inclusive.

potential of these segments at $237 million. To evaluate these segments, Anne had compiled growth forecasts for the year ahead and had evaluated each segment in terms of the anticipated level of customization and system integration demanded by the market. Anne felt that the level of synergy between Wind Technology and the various segments was also an important consideration in selecting a target market. Figure 11.1 summarizes this information. Anne believed that if the product was produced, Wind Technology's interests would be best served by initially selecting only one target market on which to concentrate.

Competition

To gather competitive information, Anne contacted five HVPS manufacturers. She found that the manufacturers varied significantly in terms of size and marketing strategy (see Figure 11.2). Each listed a price in the $5,500–$6,500 range on power supplies with the same features and output levels as the HVPS that had been developed for Wind Technology. After she spoke with these firms, Anne got the feeling that Wind Technology could offer the HVPS market superior levels of quality, reliability, technical expertise, and customer support. She optimistically believed that a one-half percent market share objective could be achieved the first year.

FIGURE 11.2	COMPETITOR PROFILE (3–10 KV RANGE)				
Company	**Gamma**	**Glassman**	**Kaiser**	**Maxwell***	**Spellman**
Approximate annual sales	$2 million	$7.5 million	$3 million		$7 million
Market share	1.00%	3.00%	1.50%		2.90%
Price†	$5,830	$5,590	$6,210	$5,000–$6,000	$6,360
Delivery	12 weeks	10 weeks	10 weeks	8 weeks	12 weeks
Product customization	No	Medium	Low	Medium	Low
System integration experience	Low	Low	Low	Medium	Low
Customer targets	Gen. lab.	Laser	Laser	Radar	Capacitors
	Space	Medical	Medical	Power mod.	Gen. lab.
	Univ. lab.	X-ray	Microwave	X-ray	Microwave
			Semiconductor	Medical equip.	X-ray

*Maxwell was in the final stages of product development and stated that the product would be available in the spring. Maxwell anticipated that the product would call in the $5,000–$6,000 range.

†Price quoted for an HVPS with the same specification as the "standard" model developed by Wind Technology.

Promotion

If Wind Technology entered the HVPS market, it would require a hard-hitting, thorough promotional campaign to reach the selected target market. Three factors made the selection of elements in the promotion mix especially important to Wind Technology: (1) Wind Technology's poor cash flow, (2) the lack of a well-developed marketing department, and (3) the need to generate incremental revenue from sales of the HVPS at a minimum cost. In fact, a rule of thumb used by Wind Technology was that all marketing expenditures should be about 9 to 10 percent of sales. Kevin and Anne were contemplating the use of the following elements:

1. **Collateral Material.** Sales literature, brochures, and data sheets are necessary to communicate the product benefits and features to potential customers. These materials are designed to be (1) mailed to customers as part of direct-mail campaigns or in response to customer requests, (2) given away at trade shows, and (3) left behind after sales presentations.

   Because no one in Wind Technology was an experienced copywriter, Anne and Kevin considered hiring a marketing communications agency to write the copy and to design the layout of the brochures. This agency would also complete the graphics (photographs and artwork) for the collateral material. The cost for 5,000 pieces (including the 10 percent markup for the agency) was estimated to be $5.50 each.

2. **Public Relations.** Kevin and Anne realized that one very cost-efficient tool of promotion is publicity. They contemplated sending out new product announcements to a variety of trade journals whose readers were part of Wind

FIGURE 11.3	TRADE PUBLICATIONS		

Trade Publication	Editorial	Cost per Color Insertion (1 page)	Circulation
Electrical Manufacturing	For purchasers and users of power supplies, transformers, and other electrical products.	$4,077	35,168 nonpaid
Electronic Component News	For electronics OEMs. Products addressed include work stations, power sources, chips, etc.	$6,395	110,151 nonpaid
Electronic Manufacturing News	For OEMs in the industry of providing manufacturing and contracting of components, circuits, and systems.	$5,075	25,000 nonpaid
Design News	For design OEMs covering components, systems, and materials.	$8,120	170,033 nonpaid
Weatherwise	For meteorologists covering imaging, radar, etc.	$1,040	10,186 paid

NOTE: This is a partial list of applicable trade publications. Standard Rate and Data Service lists other possible publications.

Technology's new target market. By using this tool, interested readers could call or write to Wind Technology, and the company could then send the prospective customers collateral material. The drawback of relying too heavily on this element was very obvious to Kevin and Anne—the editors of the trade journals could choose not to print Wind Technology's product announcements if their new product was not deemed newsworthy.

The cost of using this tool would include the time necessary to write the press release and the expense of mailing the release to the editors. Direct costs were estimated by Wind Technology to be $500.

3. **Direct Mail.** Kevin and Anne were also contemplating a direct-mail campaign. The major expenditure for this option would be the purchase of a list of prospects to whom the collateral material would be mailed. Such lists usually cost around $5,000, depending upon the number of names and the list quality. Other costs would include postage and the materials mailed. These costs were estimated to be $7,500 for a mailing of 1,500.

4. **Trade Shows.** The electronics industry has several annual trade shows. If they chose to exhibit at one of these trade shows, Wind Technology would incur the cost of a booth, the space at the show, and the travel and incidental costs of the people attending the show to staff the booth. Kevin and Anne estimated these costs at approximately $50,000 for the exhibit, space, and materials, and $50,000 for a staff of five people to attend.

5. **Trade Journal Advertising.** Kevin and Anne also contemplated running a series of ads in trade journals. Several journals they considered are listed in Figure 11.3, along with circulation, readership, and cost information.

6. Personal Selling.

a. Telemarketing (Inbound/Inside Sales).[2] Kevin and Anne also considered hiring a technical salesperson to respond to HVPS product inquiries generated by product announcements, direct mail, and advertising. This person's responsibilities would include answering phone calls, prospecting, sending out collateral material, and following up with potential customers. The salary and benefits for one individual would be about $50,000.

b. Field Sales. The closing of sales for the HVPS might require some personal selling at the customer's location, especially if Wind Technology pursued the customized option. Kevin and Anne realized that potentially this would provide them with the most incremental revenue, but it also had the potential to be the most costly tool. Issues such as how many salespeople to hire, where to position them in the field (geographically), and so on, were major concerns. Salary plus expenses and benefits for an outside salesperson were estimated to be about $80,000.

Decisions

As Kevin sat in his office and perused the various facts and figures, he knew that he would have to make some quick decisions. He sensed that the decision about whether to proceed with the HVPS spin-off was risky, but he felt that to not do something to improve the firm's cash flow was equally risky. Kevin also knew that if he decided to proceed with the HVPS, there were a number of segments in that market in which Wind Technology could position its HVPS. He mulled over which segment appeared to be a good fit for Wind Technology's abilities (given Anne's recommendation that a choice of one segment would be best). Finally, Kevin was concerned that if they entered the HVPS market, that promotion for their project would be costly, further exacerbating the cash flow situation. He knew that promotion would be necessary, but the exact mix of elements would have to be designed with financial constraints in mind.

---

[2] *Inbound* refers to calls that potential customers make to Wind Technology, rather than *outbound*, in which Wind Technology calls potential customers (i.e., solicits sales).

12

SAP AG (1995)

Honeymoon Over?

SAP AG, located in Walldorf, Germany, has become recognized as the world's leader for client-server business applications software. With fiscal year 1994 revenues exceeding US$1 billion, a 66 percent increase over 1993, SAP became the first business applications software manufacturer in history to reach the billion dollar revenue level.[1] SAP's phenomenal growth was attributed to the demand for its R/3 System, designed for client-server networks of personal computers (PCs), which was an adaptation of its prior successful R/2 System, designed for mainframe computers. SAP software had over the last few years enjoyed extraordinary success as major companies throughout the globe became customers. However, recently, SAP had been receiving criticism from users in both the United Kingdom and Germany over the large costs of implementation and chronic project overruns. Dennis Keeling, a well-known accounting software analyst, said: "SAP never realized R/3 would take off so fast and was not aware of some of the complexities of implementing it. The honeymoon is over."[2]

Establishing SAP AG

SAP was formed in 1972, when four young employees of IBM in Germany, Dieter Hopp, Hasso Plattner, Hans Werner Hector, and Klaus Tschira, quit because funding for their proposal was turned down. They began by working long hours on borrowed computers and grew a customer at a time. "We had a vision, and we stuck to it," said Hasso Plattner, vice chairman and technology chief of SAP (and member of the board of directors).[3] Although SAP is headquartered in a small town near Heidelberg, the corporate culture is not traditional. Instead, it typifies the entrepreneurial spirit of

This case is intended to be used as a basis for class discussion rather than as an illustration of either effective or ineffective handling of the situation. This case was prepared by Julian W. Vincze, Crummer Graduate School of Business, Rollins College. Copyright © 2000 Julian W. Vincze.

[1] "SAP Surpasses Billion Dollar Revenue Mark; Revenues up 66%, Net Income Jumps 92%," *Business Wire*, February 1, 1995.

[2] Julia Vowler, "Germany: SAP's Honeymoon Comes to an End—SAP Software," *Computer Weekly*, April 6, 1995.

[3] Greg Steinmetz, "German Firm Grows, Silicon-Valley Style," *Wall Street Journal*, April 11, 1995.

its founders; for example, employees wear sandals and can choose their own hours. Mr. Plattner recalls that early in his career he interviewed at Siemens, the huge electronics company, before taking a lesser job with IBM's German subsidiary. He said: "I knew right during the interview that I could never work for Siemans. It was like the post office."[4]

Market Share Growth

When Mr. Plattner and the others began SAP, their idea was to offer standardized computer programs for accounting, finance, and other business applications. Their first product, the R/2 System, was directed at mainframe computer users and met with respectable success. SAP's growth over the period 1972–1991 was an exercise in determination and ingenuity. With the introduction of its R/3 System in 1991, however, SAP made the jump from mainframes to PCs. By 1995, its R/3 package accounted for more than half of total sales. SAP was a closely held organization, which had at least 81 percent of ordinary share capital (and 74 percent of voting rights) in the hands of SAP directors or members of their families (who were involved in a joint voting rights pool.)[5] In response to rapid growth, SAP had continually added new employees worldwide to support the demands of its expanding multinational enterprise. By year end 1994, SAP had twenty-eight international subsidiaries, the largest of which was its U.S. subsidiary, employed a total of 5,044 individuals, and serviced more than 4,300 client companies located in forty-one countries who used SAP software to manage complex financial, manufacturing, sales, and human resources requirements. "The 1994 figures are impressive proof that we have gained the leading position in the worldwide market for standard applications software," said Dieter Hopp, chairman of the executive board. "The high level of investment in our systems is paying off, both for our customers and for the company."[6]

Financial Results

1994 was an outstanding year for SAP in every respect. The total revenue figure of US$1.1 billion consisted of the following categories: product sales revenues of $805 million, consulting and training revenues of $305 million, and other revenues of $20 million. For the first time, SAP's domestic revenues were less than from outside Germany as follows: German revenues up 19 percent to $412 million, while outside revenues, which represent 64 percent of total revenues, were up 48 percent. Klaus P. Besier, chief executive officer and president of SAP America, said: "It was an incredible year for SAP. . . . R/3 was one of the first client-server applications suites [systems] to come to market, and the subsequent growth has exceeded even our ambitious expectations."[7] SAP's financial success was evident in that total revenue had doubled every two years or so, while profits had been increasing at double-digit rates for a

---

[4] *Ibid.*

[5] "Germany: SAP Announces 74 percent of Voting Rights Are Held in Pool," *Boersen Zeitung*, April 6, 1995.

[6] "SAP Surpasses Billion Dollar Revenue Mark; 1994 Revenues Up 66 percent, New Income Jumps 92 percent," *Business Wire*, February 1, 1995.

[7] *Ibid.*

FIGURE 12.1	SOFTWARE SUCCESS STORY

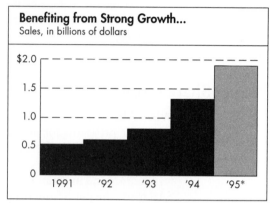

SAP Leads the Market...
Leading vendors of client/server applications based on
1994 world-wide sales, in millions of dollars

	1993	1994
SAP	$180	$603
Lotus	190	270
Oracle	118	149
Microsoft	69	120
PeopleSoft	38	105
Computer Associates	71	90

Benefiting from Strong Growth...
Sales, in billions of dollars

*Projection

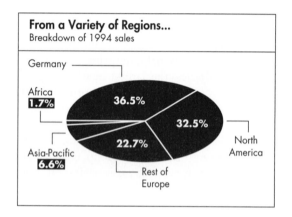

From a Variety of Regions...
Breakdown of 1994 sales

Germany 36.5%
Africa 1.7%
Asia-Pacific 6.6%
22.7%
32.5%
North America
Rest of Europe

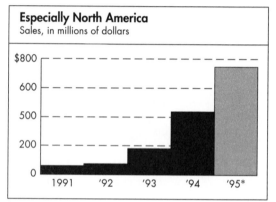

Especially North America
Sales, in millions of dollars

*Projection

NOTE: Sales figures converted from German marks at current exchange rate.
SOURCES: SAP, International Data Corp., Paribas Capital Markets

number of years—up a remarkable 92 percent in 1994.[8] (For more detailed results, the reader should refer to Figures 12.1 and 12.2.)

Product Policy

After approximately twenty years of first development and then fine-tuning, SAP's R/2 System for mainframe computer users in accounting, finance, sales, and other business applications became an industry standard and the basis of SAP's growth into a global competitor. However, SAP recognized the trend toward using PCs in business networks and in the early 1990s allocated sufficient resources to convert the R/2 System for mainframe computers into the R/3 System for client-server business applications.

[8] "Germany: SAP Likely to Be Dominant on Software Market in Future," *Top-Business*, March 1, 1995.

FIGURE 12.2

Income Statement (in 000s DM)	1944	1993	1992	1991
Net sales revenue	1,831,143	1,101,734	831,178	707,103
Cost of goods sold	420,820	299,089	205,683	173,847
Gross income	1,321,661	740,860	561,725	486,112
Depreciation and amortization	88,662	61,785	63,770	47,144
Other operating expenses	1,413,568	917,520	719,975	556,678
Operating income	471,575	184,214	111,203	150,425
Interest income	25,161	31,618	29,962	9,989
Other miscellaneous income	16,087	32,838	25,849	14,481
Reserves (increase/decrease)	−260	−227	−2,080	0
Interest expense	1,749	1,272	1,178	633
Pretax income	457,334	247,625	167,916	174,262
Income taxes	176,160	101,311	40,675	50,983
Minority interests	920	546	899	421
Net income	280,254	145,768	126,342	122,858

Balance Sheet Summary	1994	1993	1992	1991
Cash and equivalents	347,225	433,873	433,006	145,745
Net receivables	623,181	347,717	223,420	199,931
Inventories	4,936	5,497	2,126	1,177
Prepaid expenses	13,385	9,301	13,358	8,285
Other current assets	17,831	14,144	14,934	6,487
Total current assets	1,006,558	837,532	686,844	361,625
Miscellaneous investments	162,610	28,763	20,368	12,763
Property, plant, and equipment	827,835	663,395	549,456	429,657
Accumulated depreciation	313,352	244,007	194,660	144,918
Other miscellaneous assets	51,072	40,004	36,142	16,188
Total Assets	**1,749,729**	**1,306,185**	**1,080,079**	**667,221**
Accounts payable	115,916	53,553	43,358	33,501
Current notes payable	47,189	25,442	17,341	13,598
Income taxes payable	41,849	33,642	26,206	16,252
Other current liabilities	41,447	28,426	18,765	13,003
Total current liabilities	246,401	141,063	105,670	76,354
Long-term debt	21,946	1,000	1,000	1,000
Provisional risks/charges	222,659	135,743	63,607	74,603
Deferred taxes and other liabilities	22,339	19,362	12,349	7,366
Total liabilities	513,345	297,168	182,626	159,323
Reserves and minority interests	2,588	1,199	622	543
Common stock	506,153	100,000	100,000	85,000
Capital surplus	137,837	528,976	528,976	243,976
Retained earnings	589,806	378,842	267,855	178,379
Common shareholders equity	1,233,796	1,007,818	896,831	507,355
Total Liability and Equity	**1,749,729**	**1,306,185**	**1,080,079**	**667,221**

The R/3 System was compatible with most popular hardware, software, and database platforms and hit the market at the height of the downsizing frenzy. "R/3 was written from the bottom up more than three years ago and cost us US$200 million," said Trevor Salomon, SAP's business development manager. "It is not just a mainframe port."[9] R/3's three-tier architecture puts the end-user software on the client PC, the application software on one server, and the associated database on a separate server. "Unlike other client-server products, we have a dedicated application server so you can increase the number of applications and modules but you still only need the one database," said Mr. Salomon.[10]

Release 2.2 Announced

In mid-1994, SAP announced a significant new release of the R/3 System.[11] Release 2.2 incorporated functionality that had not been slated for delivery until 1995. Release 2.2 completed the line of R/3 client-server software by including new business processes and industry-specific capabilities that addressed information management requirements of manufacturing logistics, sales and distribution, and finance departments. In addition, the manufacturing applications were enhanced to provide extended functionality for both repetitive and discrete manufacturers. Release 2.2 also had logistics application enhancements for the packaged-goods industry, corporate resource planning, and integrated supply-chain management. Additionally, Release 2.2 included a powerful component for integrated credit management and significantly extended electronic data information functionality.

For example, human resources (HR) applications could now be linked to optical archiving, which was necessary for payroll accounting functions within U.S. companies. Another enhancement of R/3 Release 2.2 was a new configuration management component within the logistics application that provided a turn-key solution for companies whose product lines included a wide range of product variations such as automobile parts manufacturers. The configuration management function enabled manufacturers to optimize their entire business process chain—from sales to production—and to monitor the process through a powerful order-control function. It also allowed manufacturers to react flexibly to customer orders, to reduce lead times between order and delivery, and to constantly improve product quality. For manufacturers who produced hundreds or thousands of standardized products per day, a new repetitive manufacturing component allowed users to create plans based on quantities and periods. Called the *MRP II planning run procedure*, it was a user-friendly planning table that plotted production qualities per period, allocated production lines, and carried out interactive resource leveling so that users had more flexibility in scheduling than was available traditionally with order/batch manufacturing methods. And MRP II had extensive simulation options that allowed plans to be easily altered as conditions changed. It also had a cross-application function for managing bill-of-material "explosion" numbers, which make it possible to track the paths of individual parts (often a federal government supplier requirement).

---

[9] "Germany: SAP's Honeymoon Comes to an End—SAP Software," *Computer Weekly*, April 6, 1995.

[10] *Ibid.*

[11] "SAP Announces Significant New Release of Its Industry-Leading Client/Server Applications; Version 2.2 Incorporates Functionality Slated for 1995 but Available Today," *Business Wire*, August 29, 1994.

Packaged-goods industry users of Release 2.2 would be able to increase the efficiency of their sales activities through flexible customer hierarchies for graded rebate agreements and enhanced pricing functions for promotions and sales campaigns, while the credit management component allowed fully dynamic credit control from order acceptance to invoicing. The new activity-based costing module supported business reengineering processes and had additional functions for electronic banking based on international standards and enhanced U.S. tax processing. But perhaps the most significant aspect of R/3 Release 2.2 was that it would be available in the Microsoft Windows 3.1 help system WinHelp. This feature would allow users online access to over 100 manuals contained in the R/3 System documentation library. Access was simplified by pull-down menus and key word retrieval functions. This online documentation would give users an intelligent applications link for moving directly from any business process to the appropriate chapter in the R/3 System documentation for assistance.

Changed Strategy

During SAP's earlier growth periods it had used a marketing strategy that had relied heavily on technically up-to-date product features, explained appropriately to potential customers by its direct sales teams and backed up by technical experts and brochures with detailed and thorough explanations of product features, all priced at the high end of competitiveness. This could be described as a direct sales approach, which is standard in the industry. SAP's growth outside Germany followed a similar direct sales approach but adapted to a network of international subsidiaries. For example, the SAP American subsidiary was headquartered in Philadelphia, had a Technology Development Center in Foster City, California, a number of regional headquarters such as the one in Westchester, Illinois (Midwestern region), and within each region sales office such as the Minneapolis office that opened March 1 of 1995. SAP's Minneapolis office opened with twenty-five employees, including consultants and support staff, but had plans for expansion to fifty employees by year's end. The office featured a classroom for hands-on training and two state-of-the-art demonstration rooms with multimedia capabilities. Demonstrations include a range of hardware platforms loaded with SAP's software to educate customers and sales partners on core business needs and processes and how SAP products affected those processes. "The new office offers Minneapolis-based SAP customers greater local service and support," said Scott Martin, district director. "We are aggressively responding to the needs of our customers in the Midwestern region by offering, in Minneapolis, resources that will complement those available through our regional headquarters."[12]

However, in 1994 SAP announced a change in its sales strategy. The new sales strategy was to concentrate on larger customers. SAP's own sales teams in its German language region (and later worldwide) would continue to service existing clients and group customers, but in the future SAP would concentrate its sales efforts on companies with between DM200 million and DM250 million in sales revenue. This meant that small and medium-sized companies would by serviced indirectly and in cooperation with sales partners. SAP would designate and certify sales partners who would

---

[12] "SAP Open Minneapolis Office," *Business Wire*, March 1, 1995.

cease selling their own software (or software from SAP's competitors) in order to concentrate on selling and providing services for SAP's R/3 System.[13] Customers with between DM50 million and DM200 million in sales and a workforce of between 100 and 1500 would be serviced by certified sales partners who had already been working closely with SAP and who would receive a 40 percent margin on sales made to ultimate customers. SAP believed that customer organizations would benefit because they would have a one-stop shop for software solutions and support from an SAP sales partner experienced in working with small and medium-sized firms. Mr. Hopp observed that SAP would only consider as partners those companies which could show they had already made a name for themselves with standard solutions, that had a satisfied customer base, that had their own sales and service structure, that had sufficient competent staff, and of special importance, that had a sound financial base. SAP would provide its sales partners with support, marketing, sales activities, free initial employee training, and a free R/3 System. And although SAP was not planning on capital linkups with its sales partners, it was reported to be investing DM26 million in this program in order to attract partners who were capable of reaching previously unserviced customer areas both geographically and in terms of business activities.[14]

Difficulties Experienced

Although SAP had enjoyed recent successes as major companies throughout the globe signed up for its R/3 System, it also had been criticized by U.K. and German customers about the high costs of implementation and about chronic project overruns. SAP's response was to fight back, especially against accusations that the R/3 System was not capable of performing the tasks desired by users who wanted to unify all their disparate systems and downsize off the mainframe. SAP sued a German magazine for libel and issued a written denial of allegations that it received payoffs from computer hardware manufacturers when SAP recommended such hardware products to customers. However, some industry observers believed the real issue may have been rampant overenthusiasm about SAP's R/3 System. Chris Cadman, of Input, a U.K. market research company, said: "Everyone was carried away with euphoria."[15]

Because R/3 had a three-tier architecture (noted above) whereby end-user software was on the client PC and the application software on one server and the associated database on a separate server, this could prove to be a disadvantage to some users. Accounting software analyst Dennis Keeling said: "It's not easy distributing the database, because R/3 has a centralized configuration, like a mainframe, even though it runs on Unix."[16] This feature made R/3 less scalable than many users expected and made it less suitable for deploying across multiple small departmental units of an organization. However, Chris Knight, European Information Technology manager at pharmaceutical company Syntex and chairman of the R/3 users' technical group (organized by SAP), noted that "few packages of this complexity could run well on a

[13] "Germany: SAP Almost Triples Profit in First Nine Months 1994," *Handelsblatt*, October 21, 1994.

[14] "Germany: SAP Targets Small and Medium-Sized Firms in Bid for Further Growth," *Handelsblatt*, February 14, 1994.

[15] "Germany: SAP's Honeymoon Comes to an End—SAP Software," *Computer Weekly*, April 6, 1995.

[16] *Ibid.*

distributed database."[17] However, other industry observers believed that the major concern about the R/3 System was flexibility—or lack of it—and its impact on implementing the software. David Lyons, chairman of the SAP users' group and R/3 project manager at Unilever, said: "You have to accept that you must map the organization to the software, not vice versa."[18] Mr. Lyons believed that such adjustments were worth it, that the kind of business changes required were trivial, and that the real implementation issue was one of managing the business, not the system. Because R/3's database table structures were very sophisticated, implementors had to be certain to understand them; otherwise, mistakes were easily made. In addition, R/3, like many software products, worked best in organizations with a stable structure, something that in the current business environment of re-engineering and downsizing was not always possible.

Users also might encounter change-related problems when software was upgraded. Mr. Knight said: "That's our biggest problem. For example, moving from R/3 Release 2.1 [to 2.2] required a new version of Oracle. It took us 5 days to export, reorganize, and reimport the tables, which is unacceptable, even though we got more functionality."[19] With SAP due to launch R/3 Release 3.0 in the fall of 1995, current users realistically may be concerned with change-related costs and problems. Current R/3 users also were concerned that the goal of having a unified all-encompassing software application covering all activities of the firm was not easily achieved. Mr. Keeling noted: "They are running into problems because of the complexity of integrating the modules, which is not straightforward, and needs tremendous detailed analysis. This is often underestimated when the software is purchased."[20] However, perhaps it is the very complexity of implementing R/3 that has been one of the reasons for its popularity. R/3's complexity may have encouraged the sales partners and other consultants to push R/3 to corporate users in order to collect ongoing consulting fees.

However, regardless of the implementing complexities, SAP had come under attack from users for failing to provide them with adequate technical and implementation support. The question facing SAP was whether customers who had been euphoric over R/3 would now become disillusioned? And what would disillusioned customers do? SAP's competitors such as Dun & Bradstreet and Oracle Financials probably were eager to help out any disillusioned SAP customers, especially those who wanted to start with a small system and later build it into a much larger one.

Questions

1. What were the key success factors in SAP's growth strategy for the period 1971 through 1990?
2. What if anything changed in the key success factors when SAP introduced the first version of R/3 in 1991?
3. When SAP announced a change in strategy to target larger customers for its own sales teams and to certify what it called sales partners, who would

---

[17] *Ibid.*

[18] *Ibid.*

[19] *Ibid.*

[20] *Ibid.*

then service small and medium-sized customers? How did this alter SAP's marketing mix? Was this a change in sales strategy or a change in marketing strategy?

4. What is the role of SAP's product policy component in its 1995 marketing strategy? Will this change in the foreseeable future?

5. Is the honeymoon over for SAP?

6. What marketing strategy or tactical actions would you recommend that SAP take in 1995 and in subsequent years?

13

Augustine Medical, Inc.: The Bair Hugger® Patient Warming System

In July 1987, Augustine Medical, Inc. was incorporated as a Minnesota corporation to develop and market products for hospital operating rooms and postoperative recovery rooms. The first two products the company planned to produce and sell were a patented patient warming system designed to treat postoperative hypothermia in the recovery room and a tracheal intubation guide for use in the operating room and in emergency medicine.

By early 1988, company executives were actively engaged in finalizing the marketing program for the patient warming system named Bair Hugger® Patient Warming System. The principal question yet to be resolved was how to price this system.

The Bair Hugger® Patient Warming System

The Bair Hugger® Patient Warming System is a device designed to control the body temperature of postoperative patients. Specifically, the device is designed to treat the hypothermia (a condition defined as a body temperature of less than 36 degrees Centigrade or 96 degrees Fahrenheit) experienced by patients after operations.

Medical research indicates that 60 to 80 percent of all postoperative recovery room patients are clinically hypothermic. Several factors contribute to postoperative hypothermia. They are (1) a patients exposure to cold operating room temperatures (which are maintained for the surgeons' comfort and for infection control), (2) heat loss due to evaporation of the fluids used to scrub patients, (3) evaporation from the exposed bowel, and (4) breathing of dry anesthetic gases.

The Bair Hugger® system consists of a heater/blower unit and a separate inflatable plastic/paper cover, or blanket. A photo of the system is shown in Figure 13.1. The heater/blower unit is a large, square, box-like structure that heats, filters, and blows air through a plastic cover. An electric cord wraps around the back of the unit

This case was prepared by Professor Roger A. Kerin, Edwin L. Cox School of Business, Southern Methodist University, Michael Gilbertson, Augustine Medical, Inc. and Professor William Rudelius, University of Minnesota, as a basis for class discussion and is not designed to illustrate effective or ineffective handling of administrative situations. Certain names and data have been disguised. The assistance of graduate students Ann Christensen, Joanne Perty, and Laurel Wichman of the University of Minnesota is appreciated. The cooperation of Augustine Medical, Inc. in the preparation of the case is gratefully acknowledged. Copyright by Roger A. Kerin.

FIGURE 13.1   BAIR HUGGER® PATIENT WARMING SYSTEM

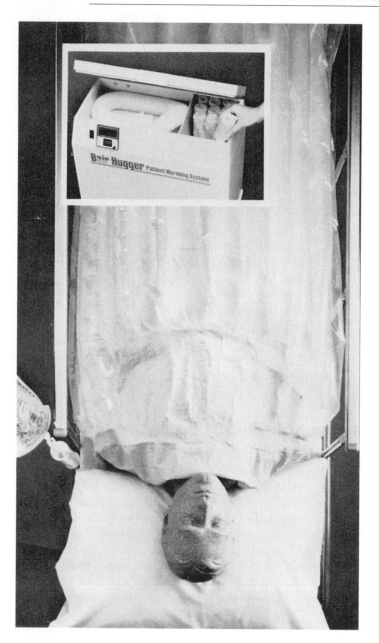

for storage, and the unit is mounted on wheels for easy transport. The blower tubing attaches to the warming cover through a simple cardboard connector strap and can be retracted into the top of the unit for storage. Temperature is set by a dial with four settings on the top of the unit. A top lid opens to a storage bin that holds twelve warming covers for easy access. The disposable warming covers come packaged in eighteen-inch-long tubes. When unrolled, the plastic/paper cover is flat and covers an average-sized patient from shoulders to ankles. The blanket consists of a layer of thin plastic and a layer of plastic/paper material laminated into full-length channels. Small holes punctuate the inner surface of the cover. When inflated through a connection at the feet of the patient, the tubular structure arcs over the patient's body, creating an individual patient environment. The warm air exits through the slits on the inner surface of the blanket, creating a gentle flow of warm air over the patient. The warming time per patient is about two hours.

The plastic cover was patented in 1986; there is no patent protection for the heater/blower unit.

Competing Technologies

Many competing technologies are available for the prevention and treatment of hypothermia. These technologies generally fall into one of two broad types of patient warming: surface warming or internal warming.

Surface-Warming Technologies

Warmed hospital blankets are the most commonly used treatment for hypothermia in recovery rooms and elsewhere. An application of warmed hospital blankets consists of placing six to eight warmed blankets in succession on top of a patient. Almost all patients receive at least one application; it is estimated that 50 percent of the postoperative patients require more than one application. The advantages of warmed hospital blankets are that they are simple, safe, and relatively inexpensive. The main disadvantage is that they cool quickly, provide only insulation, and require the patient's own body heat for regenerating warmth.

Water-circulating blankets are the second most popular postoperative hypothermic treatment. Water-circulating blankets can be placed under a patient, over a patient, or both. If a blanket is placed just under the patient, only 15 percent of the body's surface area is affected. However, hospitals typically place water-circulating blankets either just over the patient or over and under the patient, forming an insulated environment that encloses 85 to 90 percent of the body's surface area. The disadvantages of water-circulating blankets are that they are heavy and expensive and can cause burns on pressure points. Moreover, although a widely used and accepted method of warming, especially for more severe cases of hypothermia, water-circulating blankets are considered only slightly to moderately effective.

Electric blankets are generally unacceptable as a hypothermic treatment because of the risk of burns to the patient and of explosion in areas where oxygen is in use.

Air-circulating blankets and mattresses are not in common use in the United States, although variations on this technology have been used in the past. This technology relies on warmed air flowing over the body to transfer heat to the patient. The advantages of warmed-air technology are that it is safe, lightweight, and theoretically more effective than warmed hospital blankets or water-circulating blankets. Products using this technology are not widely found in the U.S. market, however.

Thermal drapes, also known as reflective blankets, have recently been introduced and are gaining acceptance as a preventive measure used in the operating room. They consist of head covers, blankets, and leggings placed on the uninvolved portions of the patient's body. Their use is recommended when 60 percent of a patient's body surface can be covered. The advantages of this technology are that it is simple, safe, and inexpensive and has been shown to reduce heat loss. The disadvantage is that it merely insulates the patient and does not transfer heat to someone who is already hypothermic.

Infrared heating lamps are popular for infant use. When placed a safe distance from the body and shined on the skin, they radiate warmth to the patient. The advantages of heat lamps are that they are effective and illuminate the patient for observation or therapy. A disadvantage is that since the skin needs to be exposed, modesty prevents widespread use among adults. (They are, however, used in adult skin-graft operations.) Nurses dislike radiant heat lamps and panels because they tend to heat the entire recovery room and are uncomfortable to work under.

Partial warm-water immersion has been used in the past, especially in cases where a patient was deliberately cooled to slow down metabolism. With this method, the patient is placed in a bath of warm water and watched carefully. The advantages of this technology are that it transfers heat very effectively and it is simple. The disadvantages are that the system is inconvenient to set up and requires close monitoring of the patient, which increases labor costs. In addition, water baths must be carefully watched for bacterial growth, and they are very expensive to purchase and use.

Increasing room temperature is the most obvious way to prevent and treat hypothermia, but it is seldom used. The advantages of this method are that it is simple and relatively inexpensive and has been proven effective at temperatures of over 70 degrees Fahrenheit. The disadvantage is that warm room temperatures are not acceptable to the nurses and surgeons who must work in the environment. Furthermore, warm temperatures increase the risk of infection.

Internal-Warming Technologies

Inspiring *heated and humidified air* is a fairly effective internal-warming technique currently being used with intubated patients (those having a breathing tube in the trachea). However, delivery of heated and humidified air by mask or tent to nonintubated patients is not acceptable in postoperative situations, because mask or tent delivery would interfere with observation and communication and, in the case of a tent, might increase the chance of infection. The fact that the patient must be intubated is a disadvantage, since the vast majority of postoperative patients are not intubated.

Warmed intravenous (I.V.) fluids are used in more severe hypothermic cases to directly transfer heat to the circulatory system. Warmed I.V. fluids are very effective because they introduce warmth directly into the circulatory system. The disadvantages of this technology are that it requires very close monitoring of the patient's core temperature and high physician involvement.

Drug therapy diminishes the sensation of cold and reduces shivering but does not actually increase body temperature. Although drug therapy is convenient and makes patients feel more comfortable, it does not warm them and in fact slows their recovery from anesthesia and surgery.

Competitive Products

A variety of competitive products that use the above-mentioned technologies are available (see Figure 13.2). A review of competitors' sales materials and interviews with hospital personnel provided the following breakdown of competitive products.

Warmed Hospital Blankets

For treating adult hypothermia, hospitals use their own blankets, which they warm in large heating units. Many manufacturers produce heating units for hospital use. The cost of laundering six to eight two-pound hospital blankets averages $0.13 per pound. Laundering and heating costs are absorbed in hospital overhead.

Water-Circulating Blankets

Several manufacturers produce water-circulating mattresses and blankets, but Cincinnati Sub-Zero, Gaymar Industries, and Pharmaseal are the major suppliers. Prices of automatic control units that measure both blanket and patient temperatures range from $4,850 to $5,295. Manual control units are priced at about $3,000, although they appear to be discounted by as much as 40 percent in actual practice.

The average life of water-circulating control units is fifteen years. Reusable blankets list at from $168 to $375, depending on quality. Disposable blankets list at from $20 to $26. Volume discounts for blankets can reduce the list price by almost 50 percent.

Water-circulating blankets technology has changed little over the past twenty years except for the addition of solid state controls. There is little differentiation among the products of different firms.

Reflective Thermal Drapes

O. R. Concepts sells a product named the Thermadrape, which comes in both adult and pediatric sizes. Adult head covers list for $0.49 each: adult drapes list for $2.50 to $3.98, depending on size; leggings are priced at $1.50.

Air-Circulating Blankets and Mattresses

Two competitors are known to provide an air-circulating product like the Bair Hugger® Patient Warming system; however, neither is currently sold in the United States. The Sweetland Bed Warmer and Cast Dryer was in use twenty-five years ago but is no longer manufactured. This product consisted of a heater/blower unit that directed warm air through a hose placed under a patient's blanket. The Hosworth-Climator is an English-made product that provides a controlled-temperature microclimate by means of air flow from a mattress. The Climator comes in a variety of models for use in recovery rooms, intensive care units, burn units, general wards, and patients' homes. The model most suitable for postoperative recovery rooms is priced at $4,000. This product could be distributed in the United States sometime in 1988. A summary of representative competitor products and list prices is shown in Figure 2.

The Hospital Market

Approximately 21 million surgical operations are performed annually in the United States, or 84,000 operations per average eight-hour work day. Approximately 5,500 hospitals have operating rooms and postoperative recovery rooms.

Research commissioned by Augustine Medical, Inc. indicated that there are 31,365 postoperative recovery beds and 28,514 operating rooms in hospitals in the

636 • Case Thirteen

FIGURE 13.2   REPRESENTATIVE COMPETITIVE PRODUCTS AND PRICES

Product	List Price	Company	Estimated Size of Company (Sales; employees)	Comments
Blanketrol 200	$2,995/manual unit; $4,895/automatic unit; $165-305/reusable blanket; $20/disposable blanket	Cincinnati Sub-Zero	$10 million; 90 people	Hypothermia equipment is a small part of its overall business.
MTA 4700	$4,735/unit; $139/reusable blanket; $24/disposable blanket	Gaymar Industries	$17 million; 150 people	Hypothermia equipment seems to be a major part of its business.
Aquamatic	$4,479/unit	American Hamilton (division of American Hospital Supply)	$3.3 billion; 31,300 people	Hypothermia equipment is a very minor part of American Hospital Supply's business.
Climator	$4,000/unit	Hosworth Air Engineering, Ltd.	Not available	The company would begin distribution of hypothermia equipment in the United States in 1988.

United States. An estimated breakdown of the number of postoperative hospital beds and the percentage of surgical operations is shown below:

Number of Postoperative Beds	Number of Hospitals	Estimated Percentage of Surgical Operations
0	1,608	0%
1–6	3,602	20
7–11	1,281	40
12–17	391	20
18–22	135	10
23–28	47	6
29–33	17	2
>33	17	2

Given the demand for postoperative recovery room beds, the research firm estimated that hospitals with fewer than seven beds would not be highly receptive to the Bair Hugger® Patient Warming System. The firm also projected that one system would be sold for every eight postoperative recovery room beds.

Interviews with physicians and nurses, followed by a demonstration of the system, yielded a variety of responses:

1. Respondents believed that the humanitarian ethic "to make the patient feel more comfortable" is important.

FIGURE 13.3	SALES LITERATURE FOR THE BAIR HUGGER® PATIENT WARMING SYSTEM

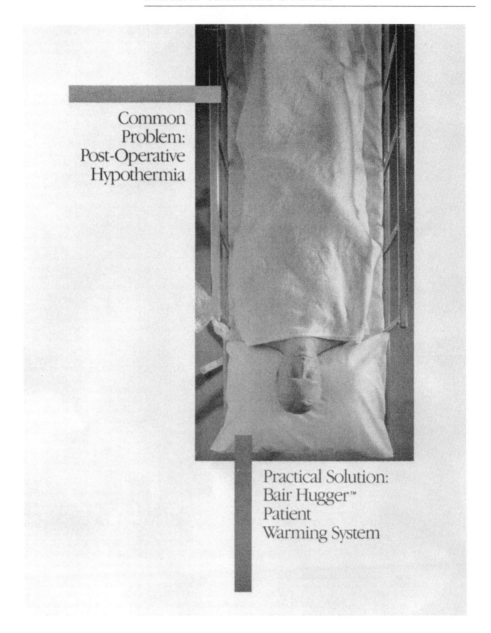

Common
Problem:
Post-Operative
Hypothermia

Practical Solution:
Bair Hugger™
Patient
Warming System

2. Respondents felt that the Bair Hugger® Patient Warming System would speed recovery for postop patients.

3. Respondents wanted to test the units under actual conditions in postoperative recovery rooms. They were reluctant to make any purchase commitments without testing. A typical comment was, "No one today in this market ever buys a pig in a poke."

FIGURE 13.3   (CONTINUED)

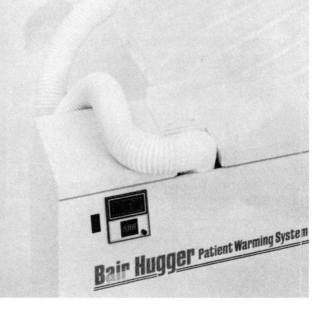

A Warm Welcome for Your Recovery Room Patients

Augustine Medical, Inc.'s new Bair Hugger™ Patient Warming System is the most practical and comforting solution for post-operative hypothermia available today.

Every year more than 10,000,000 hospital patients experience the severe discomfort and vital signs instability associated with post-operative hypothermia. Years later, patients can still vividly recall this discomfort. Augustine Medical's new Patient Warming System is a warm and reliable solution to post-operative hypothermia.

A Practical Solution to Post-Operative Hypothermia

The Bair Hugger™ Patient Warming System consists of a Heat Source and a separate disposable Warming Cover that directs a gentle flow of warm air across the body and provides for safe and comfortable rewarming.

The Bair Hugger Heat Source uses a reliable, high efficiency blower, a sealed 400W heating element, and a microprocessor-based temperature control to create a continuous flow of warm air. There are no pumps, valves or compressors to maintain. Special features include built-in storage space for the air hose, power cord and a convenient supply of disposable Warming Covers. The Heat Source complies with all safety requirements for hospital equipment.

1. PATENTED SELF SUPPORTING DESIGN
   As the tubes fill with air, the Warming Cover naturally arches over the patient's body.

2. TISSUE PAPER UNDERLAYER
   The tissue paper underlayer of the Warming Cover is soft and comfortable against the patient's skin.

3. AIR SLITS
   Tiny slits in the underlayer allow warm air from the Heat Source to gently fill the space around the patient.

4. SHOULDER DRAPE
   The shoulder drape is designed to tuck under the chin and shoulders, trapping warm air under the cover and preventing air flow by the patient's face.

5. DISPOSABLE COVERS
   The disposable Covers prevent cross contamination and reduce laundry requirements.

---

4. Respondents felt that the product was price-sensitive to alternative methods. If the product performed as claimed and demonstrated, purchase was probable by at least one-half of the individuals interviewed. Respondents were very receptive to the notion of using the heater/blower free of charge and only paying for the disposable blankets. Physicians wanted to confer with others who would be responsible for using the product to administer the warming treatment, however, such as the head nurse in postoperative recovery rooms and the chief anesthesiologist.

FIGURE 13.3   **(CONTINUED)**

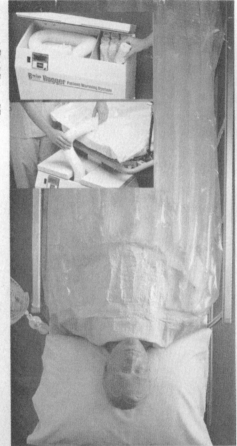

THE BAIR HUGGER™
PATIENT WARMING SYSTEM
IS SO EASY TO USE.
Remove a new Warming Cover
from the storage compartment
and unroll over the patient.

Connect the heater hose to the
inlet of the Warming Cover and
turn on the heater.

6. SIMPLE CONTROLS
A preprogrammed temperature range
and a preset high temperature limit of
110°F make the Bair Hugger safe and
simple to use.

7. INTERNAL WARMING COVER STORAGE
The storage compartment provides a
convenient supply of Warming Covers
ready for immediate use.

8. INTERNAL HOSE STORAGE
The hose retracts into its own
compartment for ready access.

9. LIGHTWEIGHT, COMPACT DESIGN
The Heat Source is designed for
convenience and portability. While in
use, it tucks under the foot of the gurney.
The unit's light weight and small size
make it simple to move and store.

10. BUILT-IN POWER CORD STORAGE
The power cord storage holds up to 12
feet of cord, making the Heat Source
portable and easy to store.

11. 5μ AIR FILTER
The air filter assures dust-free air
circulation through the Bair Hugger
Warming Cover. The filter is simple to
change when necessary.

The Bair Hugger™ Warming Cover:

The Warming Cover consists of a layer of plastic and a layer of tissue
paper laminate bonded together into long tubular channels. The
self-supporting Warming Cover is designed to arch over the patient's
body creating a warm, comfortable environment.

The Warming Cover is convenient to use because no straps, tapes or
other fasteners are required to stabilize the cover and the patient
does not have to be disturbed or moved.

When the Warming Cover is completely inflated, warm air from the
Heat Source exits the tubular channels through slits in the Cover's
soft underlayer, surrounding the patient with a gentle flow of warm air.

FIGURE 13.3   (CONTINUED)

A Warm and Practical Discovery:
Bair Hugger™ Patient Warming System

Post-Operative Hypothermia– A Common Problem

As a practicing anesthesiologist, Dr. Scott D. Augustine observed that there was no practical treatment for the common problem of post-operative hypothermia. An extensive review of post-operative hypothermia revealed several important facts:

- Post-operative hypothermia (T<36°C or <96.7°F) occurs in 60-80% of all post-operative patients (1). This extremely common problem affects more than 10,000,000 surgical patients every year.

- Several factors contribute to post-operative hypothermia including the patient's exposure to cold operating room temperatures, heat loss due to evaporation of fluids used to scrub the patient, evaporation of moisture from exposed bowels, and the breathing of dry anesthetic gases.

- Unlike environmental hypothermia, post operative hypothermia is not usually life threatening. However, it can have serious side effects for older or unstable patients. Negative effects include a decrease in cardiovascular stability and an increase in oxygen consumption of up to 400% during unaided rewarming, as well as severe shivering and significant patient discomfort (2).

- Patients with unstable body temperatures require intensive nursing care, which means higher costs. Recovery room time may also be prolonged due to the instability caused by post-operative hypothermia.

Variety of Treatments–Only One Practical Solution

Many methods have been used to try to warm patients after surgery including warmed hospital blankets, water mattresses and heat lamps (3). Studies have shown, though, that these methods are ineffective.

The most common method of treating hypothermia–heated hospital blankets–does not actively heat the patient. The small amount of heat retained by a cotton blanket quickly dissipates, thereby requiring patients to rewarm themselves. Because multiple blankets are typically used, this method is both inconvenient and time-consuming for nursing staff and produces large amounts of laundry.

Another common method used to try to rewarm post-operative hypothermia patients is the use of a water circulating mattress. Water circulating equipment is heavy, complex, expensive and prone to leakage. While water mattresses have been used for many years, there is no clinical evidence that documents their effectiveness (4, 5). This lack of effectiveness can be explained by the minimal body surface area in contact with the mattress, (only 15%) and the lack of blood flow to this area. The weight of the patient creates a pressure which prevents normal cutaneous blood flow. The heat in the mattress cannot be transported away from the skin and the contact surface becomes an insulator effectively minimizing potential heat transfer to the patient.

New Approach Needed

As Dr. Augustine discussed the problem of post-operative hypothermia with doctors,

nurses, and industry experts he became convinced that a new approach to warming patients was needed. A survey of anesthesiologists showed that most were dissatisfied with the current technology available for treating hypothermia. A new technology was definitely needed.

As a result of his research, Dr. Augustine developed the Bair Hugger™ Patient Warming System. Numerous studies and reports have shown that increased ambient room temperatures will prevent hypothermia (6-10). Indeed, before the advent of air conditioning, the average ambient temperature of the OR was higher and hyperthermia in the peri-operative period was not uncommon. Surgical patients will predictably lose or gain heat depending on the ambient temperature of the surrounding environment. The Bair Hugger™ System simulates a warm room by surrounding the patient in a gentle flow of warm air–A Focused Thermal Environment™

The Bair Hugger™ Patient Warming System combines the convenience and effectiveness of warm air to safely rewarm hypothermic patients. The Warming System's minimal cost is rapidly recovered in saved nursing time, reduced linen expenses and lower overall recovery room costs. There is now a practical and cost-effective solution to post-operative hypothermia.

Two-week Free Trial

To arrange for a free two-week trial of the Bair Hugger™ Patient Warming System, fill out the enclosed reply card or call us collect at (612) 941-8866.

SPECIFICATIONS HEATER/BLOWER UNIT	
Size	26" high x 14" deep x 22" wide
Weight	65 lbs.
Power Requirements	110VAC
Temperature Range	Ambient to 110°F Max
Enclosure	Enameled steel
Displayed Variables	Temperature °F
Power Cable	12 Feet long
Display	.5 inch (1.2 cm) Character LCD
COVERS	
Size	54" x 36"
Weight	8 ounces
Material	Polyethylene and tissue paper laminate.

AUGUSTINE MEDICAL INC.

PRACTICAL SOLUTIONS TO COMMON PROBLEMS IN ACUTE CARE™
10393 West 70th St., Suite 100 Eden Prairie, Minnesota 55344

References: (1) Vaughan MS, Vaughan RW, Cork RC: Anesthesia and Analgesia 60:746-751, 1981. (2) Bay J, Nunn JG, Prys-Roberts C: British Journal of Anaesthesia 40: 398-406, 1968. (3) Kucha DH, Nichols GH, Christ NM, Bynum JW: Military Medicine 139:388-390, 1974. (4) Morris RH, Kumar A: Anesthesiology 36:408-411, 1972. (5) Goundsouzian NG, Morris RH, Ryan JF: Anesthesiology 39:351-353, 1973. (6) Morris RH: Annals of Surgery 173:230-233, 1971. (7) Morris RH, Wilkey BR: Anesthesiology 32:102-107, 1970. (8) Clark RE, Orkin LR, Rovenstine EA: JAMA 154:311-319, 1954. (9) Bigler JA, McQuistow WO: JAMA 146:551, 1951. (10) Harrison GG: Bull AB, Schmidt HJ: British Journal of Anaesthesia 40:398-406, 1960.

---

5. Respondents believed that the pressure to move patients through the operating room and out of postop is greater than in the past. Efficiency is the byword.

6. Capital expenditures in hospitals were subject to budget committee approval. Although the amounts varied, expenditures for equipment over $1,500 were typically subject to a formal review and decision process.

Augustine Medical, Inc.

Augustine Medical, Inc. was founded in 1987 by Dr. Scott Augustine, an anesthesiologist. His experience had convinced him that hospitals needed and desired a new approach to warming patients after surgery. His medical knowledge, coupled with a technical flair, prompted the development of the Bair Hugger® Patient Warming System.

The Bair Hugger® Patient Warming System has several advantages over water-circulating blankets. First, warm air makes patients feel warm and stop shivering. Second, the system cannot cause burns, and water leaks around electrical equipment are not a problem, as they are with water-circulating blankets. Third, the disposable blankets eliminate the potential for cross-contamination among patients. Finally, the system does not require that the patient be lifted or rolled. Augustine's personal experience indicated that all of these features would be welcome by nurses and patients alike. Features and benefits of the Bair Hugger® Patient Warming System are detailed in the company's sales literature, shown in Figure 13.3.

Investor interest in Augustine Medical and the medical technology it provided produced an initial capitalization of $500,000. These funds were to be used for further research and development, staff support, facilities, and marketing. It was believed that this initial investment would cover the fixed costs (including salaries, leased space, and promotional literature) of the company during its first year of operation. The company would subcontract the production of the heater/blower unit and would manufacture warming covers in-house using a proprietary machine. Only minor assembly would be performed by the company.

The Bair Hugger® Patient Warming System would be sold by and through medical products distributor organizations in various regions around the country. These distributor organizations would call on hospitals, demonstrate the system, and maintain an inventory of blankets. The margin paid to the distributors would be competitively set at 30 percent of the delivered (that is, less discounts) selling price on the heater/blower unit and 40 percent of the delivered (discounted if necessary) price on the blankets.

Preliminary estimates from subcontractors and a time-and-motion study on assembly indicated that the direct cost of the heater/blower unit would be $380. The cost of materials, manufacturing, and packaging of the plastic disposable blankets was estimated to be $0.85 per blanket.

The central issue at this time was the determination of the list price to hospitals for the heater/blower unit and the plastic blanket, given the widespread incidence of price discounting. Immediate attention to the price question was important for at least three reasons. First, it was felt that the price set for the Bair Hugger® Patient Warming System would influence the rate at which prospective buyers would purchase the system. Second, price and volume together would influence the cash flow position of the company. Third, the company would soon have to prepare price literature for its distributor organizations and for a scheduled medical trade show, where the system would be shown for the first time.

14

Ohmeda Monitoring Systems

Looking out his office window at the magnificent Front Range of the Colorado Rockies, Joseph W. Pepper, general manager of Ohmeda Monitoring Systems, was deep in thought concerning the future of Finapres®, a relatively new Ohmeda product. Introduced in 1987, the product had not lived up to its expectations. Now, in mid-June 1990, Pepper was considering a number of options. His choice, he knew, would have a significant impact on Ohmeda Monitoring Systems.

Background

Finapres (the name was derived from its use of finger arterial pressure) was the product on the market providing *continuous noninvasive blood pressure monitoring* (CNIBP). As such, it was the only unique product that Ohmeda could offer in 1990.

Originally introduced to the market in 1987, initial results had been disappointing. Its introduction in the United States had been generally unsuccessful. Results in Europe, and internationally, had been somewhat better but still had failed to meet the firm's expectations. Concerns about the product had led Ohmeda to stop shipments on May 1, 1990, pending a review of product problems and the overall situation.

At an all-day meeting on May 23, 1990, marketing research, field sales, and R&D had presented information on the status of Finapres. In particular, R&D had given its assessment as to the likelihood that proposed product changes and improvements would solve some of the product's shortcomings.

The specter of the disappointing initial introduction, and the uncertainty that R&D could improve the product sufficiently to satisfy all the concerns, hung over the decision to commit more funds to the product. An unsuccessful reintroduction would further hurt Ohmeda's credibility, both with customers and with the field sales force. On the other hand, successful reintroduction of Finapres would ensure a strong, and possibly dominant, position in the noninvasive blood pressure monitoring market, plus

---

This case was prepared by Professor H. Michael Hayes and Research Assistant Brice Henderson as a basis for class discussion, rather than to illustrate either effective or ineffective handling of an administrative situation. Copyright © by Michael Hayes, The University of Colorado at Denver.

the possibility of increased sales of other monitoring products, as Finapres was combined with other Ohmeda products into packaged systems.

Subsequently, Pepper had many discussions with his key managers regarding their views of Finapres. In early June he visited a number of Ohmeda customers and distributors in Japan, many of whom were very interested in Finapres. Although there were several unanswered questions, it was up to Pepper to make the key decisions concerning Finapres.

BOC/Ohmeda

Ohmeda Monitoring Systems was a business unit of The BOC Group, a multinational firm, headquartered in Windlesham, Surrey, England. The Group had an international portfolio of what it described as "world-competitive" businesses, principally industrial gases, health care products and services, and high-vacuum technology. The Group operated in some sixty countries and employed nearly 40,000 people.

Health care products and services were provided by BOC Health Care for critical care in the hospital and in the home. Their equipment, therapies, and pharmaceuticals were used in operating rooms (OR), recovery rooms (PACU), intensive care (ICU), and cardiac care (CCU) units throughout the world. Divisions of BOC Health Care were organized around pharmaceuticals, home health care, intravascular devices, and equipment and systems.

Ohmeda Health Care, providing equipment and systems, was an autonomous division of BOC Health Care. It was made up of five major business units, plus a field operations unit. The five business units manufactured products for suction therapy, infant care, respiratory therapy, anesthesia, and monitoring systems. Field operations provided field sales and sales support, worldwide, on a pooled basis to all the business units. (See Figure 14.1 for a partial organization chart of Field Operations.)

A 1985 reorganization had put all business decisions in the hands of the business general managers, and established profit of the business unit as a major performance measure. In 1990, the managers of the business units, and the manager of field operations, reported to the president of Ohmeda Health Care, Richard Leazer, who, in turn, reported to the managing director of BOC Health Care, W. Dekle Rountree.

Ohmeda Monitoring Systems

Ohmeda Monitoring Systems (headquartered in Louisville, Colorado) designed, manufactured, and sold (through the field operations unit) monitoring equipment for a number of segments of the health care industry. It focused its business activities on three classes of products:

- Oximetry products, used to measure oxygen content in arterial blood.

- Gas analysis products, used to measure a patient's respiratory gas levels.

- Noninvasive blood pressure measurement products.

Applications for these products were found in a wide variety of departments within hospitals and other health care facilities. Products were usually sold to the health care

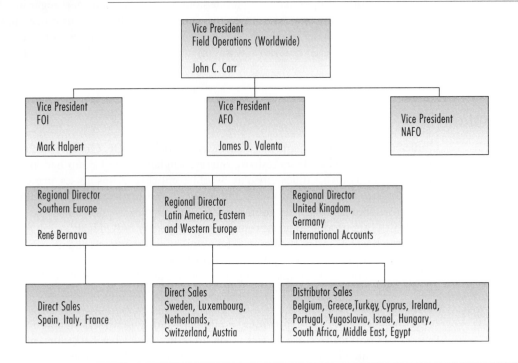

FIGURE 14.1 OHMEDA MONITORING SYSTEMS PARTIAL ORGANIZATION CHART—FIELD OPERATIONS

facility, either directly by the field sales force or by a distributor. Some products, however, were also sold to equipment manufacturers (OEMs) for incorporation in a larger measurement package.

Most Ohmeda oximetry and Finapres products consisted of a "box," containing the hardware, software, and a display unit, and a probe, or cuff, to allow a noninvasive way to measure the parameter of interest. These were of two types, disposable or reusable, and were designed to be attached to the patient's toe, foot, finger, hand, or ear, depending on the application.

Ohmeda had access to Finapres technology by virtue of a worldwide exclusive license, obtained from Research Unit Biomedical Instrumentation TNO (Amsterdam, the Netherlands). Many other technologies had also been acquired, either by license or outright purchase.

Ohmeda estimated the noninvasive monitoring market was $1.2 billion worldwide, with 60 percent of the market in the United States. Overall, its market share was some 15 percent of those segments it served. In selected categories, however, its market share was considerably higher. With considerable variation by country and specific product, Ohmeda estimated the growth rate of its served market at 5–10 percent per year.

The competitive picture for Ohmeda was complex. Its main competitors were U.S.-based firms. Many of its products, however, faced strong competition from European firms. In oximetry there were an estimated twenty-five competitors, although only four had significant shares. Major competitors and estimated market shares were:

Nellcor (U.S.)	50%
Ohmeda (U.S.)	30
Criticare (U.S.)	10
Novametrix (U.S.)	8

In respiratory gases there were an estimated twelve competitors. Major competitors and estimated market shares were:

Datex (Finland)	16%
Ohmeda	15
Siemens (West Germany)	14
Hewlett-Packard (U.S.)	12

In blood pressure measurement only five companies competed. With an 80 percent share, Critikon (U.S.) dominated the noninvasive market with its oscillometric, or noncontinuous, product. Ohmeda's sales of its noninvasive products represented just 2 percent of this market.[1]

Based on pretax operating profits in 1989, Ohmeda's financial situation appeared to be very healthy. There were concerns, however. As Pepper observed:

> We tend to be more financially driven than market driven. Also, we have not been investing heavily in R&D. As a result, our product line is relatively mature and I don't know how much longer we can count on present products for high contribution margins.
>
> Finapres is the only major new product that is close to ready to go. Perfecting Finapres, and successfully reintroducing it, would not only produce direct sales but its uniqueness could also benefit our other monitoring businesses, through integrated packages that included a technology available nowhere else. The sales force in Europe, and also in Asia, is very excited about the product, even with its present deficiencies, and believes that with reasonable improvement it could become a major contributor to sales and profits. In the U.S. there is not the same excitement. There is agreement that if all the product deficiencies could be corrected we would have a real winner, but R&D can't give us any guarantees.

Field Operations

Following the 1985 reorganization of Ohmeda Health Care from a functional organization to the five therapy units, the firm had considered how to organize its field sales operations. Given the complexity of the five product lines, and some desire on the part of the therapy unit managers to have more direct control over the sales forces that represented them, there was considerable support to establish specialized sales forces. There was also support for direct sales, as opposed to extensive use of distributors or dealers. Selling anesthesia equipment, it was argued, was very different than selling patient monitors and other Ohmeda products, both because of product differences and customer buying procedures. Many of Ohmeda's competitors (e.g., Siemens and

---

[1]Market shares were for the U.S. market.

Hewlett-Packard) relied heavily on direct sales, feeling that distributors or dealers could not provide the required level of technical knowledge and service.

Arguing against specialized selling was the belief that it was far more efficient, in terms of time, travel expense, and customer knowledge, to have one salesperson calling on a hospital, rather than three, as was contemplated in one proposed form of organization. Still further, there was great concern about the consequences of terminating distributors or dealers, some of whom had been associated with Ohmeda (or its predecessor companies) for over seventy years. Finally, Ohmeda was aware that Baxter-International, the largest medical supplies and equipment company in the world, had specialized its sales force in 1981 but had subsequently gone back to a general sales organization.

After extensive study, it was decided to continue with a pooled form of sales organization, together with pooled product service, customer service, and finance, all reporting to the vice president of Field Operations. As of early 1990 Field Operations had three principal regional components: NAFO, responsible for sales and service in North America (the United States. and Canada); FOI, responsible for sales and service in Europe, the Middle East, and Latin America; and AFO, responsible for sales and service in Asia, including Japan. Depending on the particular country, sales were all direct, a combination of direct and dealer, or totally through dealers.

Ohmeda recognized the need for making specialized product knowledge, beyond the expertise of the local salesperson, available quickly to the customer. In NAFO it was assumed that such specialized knowledge could be provided by specialists from manufacturing locations. In FOI and AFO it was deemed impractical for specialists to travel from the United States, and product champions were appointed in the major countries. Paid principally on salary (as opposed to the salespeople who were paid on a salary and commission basis), the product champions supported the sales force for their assigned products in a variety of ways. They were available to call on customers with the salespeople. They held product seminars, either for salespeople or for customer groups. In some instances they acted as missionary salespeople, soliciting orders from new customers. In all instances, they provided a focused communication channel between the field and headquarters marketing. It was Ohmeda's view that the product champions had played a major role in assisting the introduction of Finapres in Europe. There was also some concern that not enough manpower was available from headquarters to provide similar support to the field sales force in the United States and Canada.

Health Care Markets

The health care industry was one of the largest, and most rapidly growing, segments of the world economy. While growth was occurring worldwide, the potential for Ohmeda products was greatest in the United States, Europe, Japan, and, generally, in the developed countries of the world. With certain exceptions, the United States tended to lead the world in the development and use of technologically sophisticated health care products. U.S. manufacturers of such products generally felt that the rest of the world followed the U.S. lead in acceptance and use, with countries in Europe following in as little as six months, but with longer delays in other parts of the world.

Hospitals were the principal buyers of Ohmeda products. With some variation, due mainly to government regulations, purchasing practices were very similar in the

FIGURE 14.2	OHMEDA MONITORING SYSTEMS U.S. MARKET SIZE (SALES POTENTIAL IN UNITS, 1990–1992)				
Segment	Potential Sites*	Oximetry	Gas Analysis	Blood Pressure	Saturation
OR/PACU	60,000	26,000	31,000	15,000	HI
ICU/NICU/CCU	78,000	20,000	15,500	9,750	HI
L&D	57,000	10,000	0	4,000	MED
Floors	800,000	15,000	0	2,000	LO
Nonhospital	65,000	10,500	0	200	MED

*Number of physical locations.

developed countries of the world. All purchases of medical equipment required budgetary approval of the hospital administration. Their purchasing influence, however, was generally inversely related to the complexity of the item. Purchase decisions of disposable supplies and gases, for instance, were generally made solely by the hospital purchasing agent, based on the lowest price. By contrast, capital equipment was invariably selected by the hospital's medical specialists and clinical area end-users. Because any machine malfunction was potentially life-threatening, medical specialists were especially concerned with precision, reliability, and safety. In addition, both the sophistication of clinical procedures and the technical expertise and interest of medical specialists were increasing. As a result, the product and clinical knowledge required to sell medical equipment was also increasing.

Ohmeda segmented its market by hospital department or application, as follows:

OR/PACU (Operating Room/Post Anesthetic Care Unit, or Recovery Room)

ICU/NICU/CCU (Intensive Care Unit/Neonatal Intensive Care Unit/Coronary Care Unit)

L&D (Labor and Delivery)

Floors (basically patients' rooms in hospital wards)

Nonhospital (the growing nonhospital segment, which included ambulances, surgicenters, physicians' offices, dental and home care, for oximetry and blood pressure products)

Sales potential varied substantially, depending on the particular segment and the product, as shown in Figure 14.2. Segments outside the United States generally had lower saturation levels than in the United States. As was pointed out, however, saturation levels were not always the best indicator of sales potential. In many instances the replacement markets offered high potential as well.

In the operating room the physician (generally the anesthetist) was the key buying influence for all products. In all other segments decision making was a shared responsibility, as indicated in Figure 14.3. Key buying influences were thought to be influenced by different factors, in order of importance as indicated on page 648:

Physician	Nurse	Technician
Technology	Ergonomics	Serviceability
Ergonomics	Relationship	Technology
Relationship	In-service	
Price/value	Technology	

Administrator	Financial Officer	Materials (Purchasing)
Company reputation	Leasing options	Price/value
Price/value	Total package cost	Total package cost
Revenue generation	Reimbursement	Serviceability

Personal contact with key buying influences by direct sales representatives or distributors was an essential ingredient to securing an order. Key to success, however, were favorable results from experimental trials, particularly of new products, as reported in medical journals. Manufacturers worked closely with the medical community worldwide to identify opinion leaders interested in equipment who were willing to experiment with it and then publish their results in scholarly journals. Most such experiments were reported in English language journals, but these were widely read in non-English-speaking countries.

Finapres®

Modern medicine viewed measurement of arterial blood pressure as essential in the monitoring of patients, both during and after surgery. Traditional monitoring techniques have included both invasive and noninvasive methods. Arterial line monitoring provided continuous measurement but invasion (meaning surgical insertion of a long, small-bore catheter into the radial or femoral arteries) involved the risk of thrombosis, embolism, infections, and nerve injuries. These risks were acceptable when arterial blood samples had to be taken regularly but otherwise were to be avoided.

An oscillometric monitor, such as Critikon's Dinamap, was noninvasive. As commonly used, such a device provided readings automatically every three to five minutes, or on demand. It could provide readings more frequently, but this involved considerable patient pain or discomfort. As normally used, therefore, it could miss vital data due to the time lag of the readings. (Ohmeda sold a noninvasive blood pressure monitor of this type, manufactured for them, but had not promoted it heavily.) Manual methods were noninvasive but were highly dependent on the skill of the clinician and the application of the correct size arm cuff and involved even more time lag.

Finapres Technology

In 1967 a Czech physiologist, Dr. Jan Peñaz, patented a method with which it was possible to measure finger arterial pressure noninvasively. (See Figure 14.4 for a detailed description of the method.) In 1973 the device was demonstrated at the tenth International Conference on Medical and Biological Engineering at Dresden. Subsequently, a group of engineers at the Research Unit Biomedical Instrumentation TNO in the Netherlands became interested in the technology and constructed, first, a laboratory model, and then a model that they felt was clinically and experimentally useful

FIGURE 14.3	OHMEDA MONITORING SYSTEMS BUYING INFLUENCES						
	OR	**ICU**	**NICU**	**PACU**	**CCU**	**Floors**	**L&D**
Probes	P	NTM	NT	NT	NTM	NTM	NT
Blood pressure	P	PNM	PN	PN	PNM	PNM	PN
Gas analysis	P	PTM	PT	PT	—	—	PT
Oximetry	P	NTM	NT	NT	NTM	PNTM	NT

Legend:
 P = Physician   OR = Operating Room
 N = Nurse   ICU = Intensive Care Unit
 T = Technician   NICU = Neonatal Intensive Care Unit
 A = Administrator   PACU = Post Anesthetic Care Unit
 F = Financial officer   CCU = Coronary Care Unit
 M = Materials (purchasing)   L&D = Labor and Delivery

and commercially viable. In 1983 Ohmeda acquired an exclusive license for the Finapres technology.

Finapres and Ohmeda

Although TNO had produced a working model of Finapres, Ohmeda had invested between two and three million dollars in R&D in order to develop a manufacturable box and cuff and to recode the software to conform to Ohmeda protocols. The resultant design could be built largely on existing equipment, although some $100,000 was required for tooling the cuff. Prior to commercial introduction, extensive work was done with opinion leaders to establish the credibility of the product. Favorable test results of clinical studies of Finapres were reported in medical journals, and were widely distributed to the medical profession. Cost of this work, and other market development expenditures, was roughly equivalent to the cost of R&D.

Ohmeda introduced a commercial design of Finapres in 1987 in the United States and in 1988 in Europe and other world markets. The initial offering consisted of a box, a patient interface module that attached to the patient's hand, and three reusable cuffs. It was positioned to compete against invasive measuring products. Although it was expected it would ultimately be offered to the OEM market it was originally introduced directly to the OR market. Priced at approximately $9,500 it was expected to return a contribution margin in excess of 70 percent (generally typical for new and unique products in the health equipment industry). Some price resistance was experienced and the U.S. price was reduced to $8,500, six months after introduction. Disappointingly, U.S. sales through 1989 totaled only 200 units.

In 1988 the product was introduced internationally, at a U.S. equivalent price of $9,600. In contrast to the U.S. introduction, the product was targeted, for direct sale, at a number of segments in hospitals. As in the United States, price resistance was encountered and by 1989 the price had been reduced to approximately the U.S. equivalent of $5,000.

FIGURE 14.4   OHMEDA MONITORING SYSTEMS PRINCIPLES OF OPERATION

Arteries transport blood under high pressure to the tissues. The artery walls are strong and elastic; that is, they stretch during systole (when blood is forced onward by contraction of the heart) and recoil during diastole (dilation of the heart when its chambers are filling with blood). This prevents arterial pressure from rising or falling to extremes during the cardiac cycle, thus maintaining a continuous uninterrupted flow of blood to the tissues. The volume of blood inside the artery increases when it expands and decreases when it contracts. This change in volume is the key phenomenon on which the Peñaz/Finapres technology was based.

In the Finapres system, a cuff with an inflatable bladder was wrapped around the finger (see diagram below). A light source (LED) was directed through the finger and monitored by a detector on the other side. This light was absorbed by the internal structures according to their various densities. The emitted light was an indication of blood volume in the artery. Through a complex servomechanism system, the cuff was inflated, or deflated, to maintain the artery size at a constant level. Thus, cuff pressure constantly equaled arterial pressure and was displayed on the monitor as an arterial waveform and also digitally.

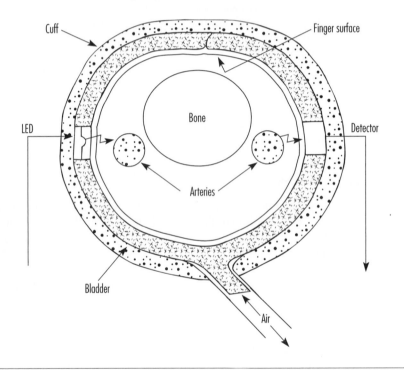

To some extent low sales in the United States were blamed on tactical marketing errors, such as the positioning and price of the product at introduction. There were also some technical problems with the system. Some were cosmetic in nature and easily fixed. Others were more serious, both for the clinicians using the equipment and for Ohmeda. Major problems were the difficulty in applying the cuff properly in order to get an accurate reading, and drift in readings that occurred after several hours of continuous use, a particularly serious problem in OR. Another problem was the inability of the equipment to accurately monitor patients with poor blood circulation.

Results were more promising in Europe. The European medical community had been anxious to get access to Finapres. Much had been written about the Peñaz methodology and the system developed by TNO in the European medical press. The noninvasive aspect of Finapres was particularly attractive. European doctors were less comfortable with arterial line methodology than were their American counterparts. In addition, they tended to be more willing to invest time and effort to learn new technologies and there was less preoccupation with patient throughput than in the United States.

News of the problems experienced in the ORs in the United States had made penetration of the OR segment in Europe difficult. With its broader contacts, the sales force was able to introduce the product to other segments, particularly in CCU and physiology in teaching hospitals, where stability over long periods of time was either not as critical as in OR or where continuous blood pressure monitoring was of paramount importance. With this approach, supported by the willingness of the sales force to train medical personnel in application of the cuff, the company experienced much greater success, selling a total of 700 units in these markets through 1989.

Commenting on results through 1989, Melvyn Dickinson, international marketing manager observed:

> There are significant differences between the hospital markets in the United States and Europe, and in how our sales forces sell to them. In the United States, for example, anesthetic machines, made by one of our sister therapy units, are sold by the same field sales force that sells our monitoring equipment. The U.S. machines are made to more stringent requirements and are much more expensive than those sold in Europe. In addition, they tend to be replaced on a five-year cycle, compared to ten or fifteen years in, say, Italy. As a result, our sales force in the United States tends to really concentrate on the OR market, whereas in Europe the sales force takes a broader approach.
>
> It's also important to recognize that the key influence for OR purchases is an anesthesiologist, for whom blood pressure is just one of many concerns. In other segments of the hospital, the situation is very different. In the CCU, or the cardiac operating theater, blood pressure is of paramount importance. Not all procedures are lengthy, and even when they are, many cardiologists saw value in CNIBP, even though there was drift. For physiological measurements in research hospitals, or in hypertension units, there were even fewer drawbacks, plus the clinicians in these situations were much more inclined to take extra care with application of the cuff.
>
> Beyond these differences, we misread the market in general. It had been our assumption that arterial lines (the term for invasive systems) were the major competitors for Finapres. We priced and positioned Finapres accordingly. Unfortunately, our promotion didn't get this position established in the minds of our customers. As it turned out, many customers viewed the oscillometric machines as our major competitor. For these customers, our original price involved too large a premium, versus the less expensive oscillometric machines. Now there is some real question about going back to the original positioning strategy.

The two years following the introduction of Finapres were characterized by indecision about its future and lack of significant support for the product. Once introduced, Ohmeda required it to be self-supporting, with product improvements made on an ongoing basis financed out of current revenues. When the sales force began to report complaints from the clinicians in the field, it was felt that the major problems were cosmetic, concerning the size of the box and the readability of the screen. Complaints regarding inaccurate readings were thought to result from misapplication of the cuff. Despite some modifications, complaints continued and sales declined. As 1990 began, it was apparent that decisions as to the future of Finapres needed to be made.

Reassessment

Reassessment of Finapres had started with the development of the five-year plan for Ohmeda Monitoring Systems. Subsequently, concerns on the part of the sales force about the commitment to Finapres indicated the desirability of a meeting involving sales force management, product management, and R&D. On May 23, 1990, Joe Pepper convened a meeting of representatives of all three groups, as well as headquarters marketing. The main points that emerged from the meeting were as follows:

- There was general agreement that the market potential for CNIBP was large. There was, however, considerable disagreement as to its exact size. Some estimates of the U.S. market were as large as 7,740 units per year. International estimates were considerably lower. There was general agreement that the largest market segments for Finapres were OR and ICU/CCU. It was the view of Ohmeda's product managers, however, that the focus of the NAFO sales force on the OR market made selling to the ICU/CCU segment difficult.

- It was emphasized that the diffusion of innovation in many instances took a long time. Acceptance of some currently standard medical equipment came only after a number of years. Oximetry, for example, took fourteen years, echocardiography took ten years, and, as it was emphasized, capnometry (CO_2 gas analysis) took forty years to become accepted. However, if Finapres was to ultimately succeed, investment was necessary not only in technological development, but in market development as well.

- The following reasons for lack of success to date were identified:
  — Drift in readings over time.
  — Not accurate for average clinician.
  — Not easy to use.
  — Inadequate alert for misapplied cuff.
  — No alerts for problems with poor circulation.
  — No toe/pediatric/neonatal thumb cuffs.

- Concerns were expressed about:
  — Lack of a research culture.
  — Bottom line/short-term focus.
  — R&D research shortage.

- R&D gave its assessment of time and cost to develop fixes and their likelihood of success:
  — The cause of drift was not certain, but there was a high probability that the problem could be fixed with changes in software, probably in 1990. If this fix worked the cost would be relatively modest.

— Assessing the present cuff as offering 30 percent of ideal requirements, currently contemplated modifications could be expected to improve performance to 40 percent by January 1991, again with relatively modest cost. With a more substantial effort it was expected performance could be improved to 80 percent in two years.

- Noninvasive oscillometric blood pressure machines were not likely to be "thrown out" in favor of Finapres. It was more likely they would be replaced on a normal schedule.

- On the positive side a number of strengths were identified:
  — Patents lasting past the year 2000 (except the U.K. and Germany).
  — Strong distribution, particularly in OR.
  — Technical expertise.
  — Head start over competition.

Following extensive discussion, four options were presented:

1. Stay on the present course. Make sufficient modifications to make it possible to carefully reintroduce the product in selected markets. This approach was estimated to cost $307,000 in R&D expense, generate sales of 820 units through 1994, and have a net present value of $30,000.

2. Stop the project. Taking into account writing off current inventory costs and possible return costs, this approach was estimated to have a negative NPV of $160,000.

3. Make a significant investment in R&D and marketing (including going forward with a mini-Fini, a much smaller version of Finapres that would be targeted at the OEM market). This contemplated a 50 percent penetration of the OR market by 1995, a 50 percent penetration of the ICU market by 1998, and significant penetration of the OEM market. Cumulative sales estimates for this approach were 7,700 units in the United States and 4,000 internationally (through 1995). With projected revenues of $40 million, investment in R&D of $2 million, investment in marketing of $1.2 million, the net present value of this approach through 1995 was estimated to be $2,200,000.

4. Sell the business. There was considerable discussion of this option but the general view was that it was not likely Ohmeda could find a buyer willing to pay any significant amount for the business. In any event, it was unlikely that top management at BOC would approve such a step.

Management Views

Subsequent to the May 23 meeting a number of views were expressed by Ohmeda managers. As John Carr, vice president of Field Operations, saw it:

The international experience with Finapres was more successful for a variety of reasons. The original technology was developed by a European company (TNO) so the European medical community was familiar with the concept. The sales force is more balanced in its approach to the market.

Hence, it was able to exploit niche markets where the device worked very well. The initial sales built confidence. The real key was the use of product champions. The product was given support and attention that it did not receive in the States.

Finapres represented a once-in-five-to-ten-years type of opportunity. It was a significant new technology which didn't seem to fit Ohmeda's culture or annual financial cycle. If the initial effort had been followed by product enhancements, Finapres would have been successful. From here, the only two decisions I see are sell or go.

Similar views were expressed by James Valenta, vice president for Asia (AFO):

Finapres is a great product, which, from my view in the Asian markets, has significant customer appeal. It seems that things were stacked against the product from the beginning. Soon after Finapres was purchased, Ohmeda reorganized. The individual who had pushed to buy the technology moved on to other assignments, which resulted in some lost momentum. Finapres never really had a home, which compounded the problems with the system itself. Had there been a quicker response to feedback from the international sales force, most of what was discussed at the meeting today, the drift issue and the cuff, could have been resolved some time ago. Ohmeda had trouble accepting the fact that there was a problem. The feedback domestically was focused more on cosmetic rather than substantive issues. Changes were made without knowledge of the impact to other parts of the system.

Japan is more technologically oriented, they grasped the idea of the system quickly and easily. Maybe it's just that invasive technology isn't as advanced overseas as in the United States. The doctors in Japan seem more interested in learning about new technology than in the States.

If Ohmeda doesn't want to continue with Finapres, I'll buy it and produce it. I believe in the product that much.

A somewhat different perspective was given by René Bernava, regional director for Southern Europe:

Europe was ready for Finapres. The medical community, especially in Germany, was excited about the studies and papers written about the product. As a whole, European doctors were much less comfortable with arterial monitoring than their American counterparts. Finapres should have been a dazzling success in Europe, but there were problems, both with the product and the way it was marketed.

The technology for Finapres was purchased but not improved. The early version did not work. The project had software problems and lacked leadership. The original plan was to make an inexpensive disposable cuff. With this focus, a cuff that really worked regardless of cost was never developed. Also, the product was introduced at a premium price. That philosophy did not work.

The international sales force felt we had the top technology and wanted to go ahead. The meeting today occurred because we were the most vocal. I went to Dekle (President Dekle Rountree) some time ago and asked him to investigate the product, renew agreements with TNO, and put some money into the project. Some money was forthcoming but it wasn't a continuing process.

As Mark Halpert, vice president for FOI, saw the situation:

There are several reasons Finapres was more successful in Europe and overseas than in the United States. The sales force in Europe sells many products whereas in the United States the sales force only sells Ohmeda products. With the large product line, we developed customer expertise. We know what the customer wants, and we use technical support to help conclude the transactions.

The organization or the medical community in Europe is different also. Anesthesia and monitoring are the same customer. In the United States there are more specialists. The sales force, with its broader coverage and experience, went after other niches rather than anesthesia, where the product had failed in the United States.

The key difference internationally was the product champion. Internationally, the product champion was part of the sales force, thus closer to the customers. In the United States, management served this role. Europe is still enthusiastic about the product. In Germany, just with the 1991 cuff, the product will be a success.

Bonnie Queram was manager of Sales Programs and Administration in NAFO and reported to the vice president of Sales. As she recalled:

Everyone was enthusiastic when Finapres was introduced. It looked easy to sell, although the box was big and clunky. Initially there was a high level of sales activity and orders. Unfortunately, when problems surfaced we tended to focus on cosmetic fixes and sales tapered off in the United States. In contrast, sales held up well in Europe. I developed a questionnaire to find out why. The responses indicated there is a major difference in clinical practice between the United States and Europe. The physicians, for instance, are more down-to-earth there. In contrast to the United States, they are very patient and want to work with the manufacturer, particularly on a new product. The anesthesiologists will spend lots of time in pre-op making sure things like the cuff are OK, whereas in the United States they are very impatient. For these reasons, and a number of others, I concluded that the European experience wouldn't transfer to the United States. Our normal assumption is that we can develop our products for the U.S. market, and then go abroad with the same strategy. This is the one case in a hundred where this assumption doesn't apply.

Bill Belew, a senior product manager in Louisville, had a somewhat different view. According to Belew:

The product problems in Europe and the United States are identical. The only difference is the sales approach. What we need is a complete fix. That will cost in the neighborhood of $2 million, but once we have it we can go after the OR/ICU markets anywhere in the world.

He went on to say:

The May 23 meeting was both good and bad. The potential for the product was reiterated, and we heard the product would not be killed. On the other hand, it didn't sound as if we were going to make the kind of commitment the potential justified. And this was despite information that Nellcor might introduce a CNIBP product in September.

The enthusiasm for Finapres was shared by Lloyd Fishman, director of marketing. He had a number of concerns, however:

I've been watching Finapres evolve since joining Ohmeda two years ago. I think the product has potential to represent as much as 10 percent of our sales, but I was concerned that there was no sense of purpose, no vision, about the product. We were doing lots of "little fixits" without any real sense of our markets or what the product should be. I called the May 23 meeting to see if we couldn't develop such a sense of purpose or vision.

There's no question that we face a complex situation. The markets in the United States and international are very different. The financial orientation of the doctors in the United States rubs off on our sales force and they're much less inclined to sell concept products than in Europe, where the doctors like to work with us on new developments.

Ray Jones had recently joined Ohmeda as R&D group manager and was responsible for the Finapres R&D effort. As he put it:

I think Finapres has lots of potential, but we need to resolve a number of critical issues. For instance, we use finger pressure as a measure of central blood pressure, but we're not sure how closely finger pressure simulates central pressure or how accurately we're measuring finger pressure.

Management would like us to give some performance guarantees, but that's not the nature of R&D. We can, however, identify the key technical and physiological issues and identify milestones with the expectation that we can get data to indicate if the issue is resolvable.

One of the things that would really help would be for marketing to give us some better performance criteria.

Finally, Joe Pepper reflected on his thoughts subsequent to the May 23 meeting, his various discussions with his managers, and his visit to Japan:

I know the people in the organization feel we don't spend enough on R&D. But it's a question of balance. We have been spending over 6 percent of sales on R&D, plus the corporation has a major research facility at Murray Hill, New Jersey, where we do the riskier, blue sky, R&D. In the past our competitors have spent a higher percent of sales on R&D. We estimate that Nellcor, for instance, spent over 10 percent during the last four years. However, we also estimate that they will reduce this in the next four years.

The May 23 meeting was valuable and we got a lot of opinions on the table. One option that was not looked at, however, was to go exclusively with OEMs.

In Japan the product is selling well. The physicians appear more willing to fiddle with the product to make it work. Based on what's going on in Japan, and what is going on in Europe, I wonder if we might not be able to bootstrap their experience back into the U.S. market.

Part of our problem is our whole development process. We've hired some new people, Ray Jones as product development manager and Nick Jensen as a research scientist, but it's going to take them some time to sort out the problems and establish better procedures.

I know John Carr wants us to go with a product that will sell in the United States. Part of the question, though, is how much faith do I put in the numbers?

15

BWI Kartridg Pak

Kartridg Pak (KP) was a mid-sized manufacturer of food processing and packaging equipment located in the Midwest. The firm was a subsidiary of BWI, a British firm which consisted of three divisions comprised of a total of six subsidiaries, all of which manufactured packaging equipment. Kartridg Pak was one of the larger firms in the food packaging machinery industry, with sales between $25 and 30 million in 1992.[1]

Although Kartridg Pak was an established food packaging machinery firm, with four product lines, sales had not been growing as fast as the company would have liked. To continue its own growth, and to keep up with some of its larger competitors, the firm felt it must consider several options, including entry into a new market. Thus, in early 1993, KP was considering entry into the growing vertical form-filled-seal (VFFS) segment of the packaging machinery market. If the firm decided to enter the market it would also have to decide what subsegments to enter, whether to enter de novo or by acquiring an existing firm, and how such a market would fit into its existing organization.

Packaging Machinery

Starting in the middle to late 1980s several important trends began to have a serious impact on consumer packaged goods industries, especially those producing food products: a rising demand for packages which offered the consumer convenience, an increased demand for bulk packaging, and a rising level of environmental consciousness about the role of packaging in reducing resource use and increasing recycling options.

This case was prepared by Peter G. Goulet of the University of Northern Iowa and Bryan R. Hoyt and Carol D. Willenbring of Teikyo Marycrest University. It is intended as the basis for class discussion rather than to illustrate either effective or ineffective handling of an administrative situation. Faculty members in nonprofit institutions may reproduce this case for distribution to their own students without charge or written permission. All other rights reserved jointly to the authors and the Society for Case Research. Copyright ©1996 by the Business Case Journal and Peter G. Goulet, Bryan R. Hoyt, and Carol D. Willenbring.

[1]The actual sales of this firm are unknown because it is a subsidiary of a larger firm. Dun and Bradstreet estimates 1992 sales at $30 million; although parent company financial statements indicate that actual sales may be up to $32 million; although it is possible that some of KP's sales are included in another of the three BWI divisions. Please refer to the financial statements in Figure 15.5.

Firms selling consumer packaged goods, and facing increased pressure on profits, also adopted new packaging techniques to control costs and product quality.

The consumer packaged goods industry consisted of firms producing a wide variety of products with two essential components: the product itself and the package. A package not only contains and protects a product, but also supports shipping and distribution needs. Finally, and perhaps most importantly, a package conveys important information about the product it contains. For these reasons, an important supplier to the packaged goods industry was the industry producing packaging machinery and equipment.

The packaging machinery industry was a fragmented industry serving a variety of market segments. The total value of the U.S. packaging machinery industry shipments, including services and import/export activity, was estimated to be $3.171 billion in 1993, up 6.0 percent from 1992, and it was expected to grow to $3.394 billion in 1994. Industry growth reached an average annual compound rate of 6.4 percent per year between 1987 and 1992. The total value of 1993 shipments included services of $92 million, 4 percent of the total, leaving $3.079 billion of final products. Of the total shipments recorded by the industry in 1993, $670 million were exported. In addition to U.S. production there were imports estimated at $758 million in 1993. The chief export markets are Canada, Mexico, Great Britain, and various European countries. The major countries supplying imports were Germany and Italy. Roughly 23 percent of the value of imports was composed of parts for U.S. affiliates of foreign companies.[2]

Major segments of the packaging machinery industry included strapping machines, bottling and canning equipment, thermoforming equipment, blister packaging machines, code marking equipment, machinery for collating, sorting, and filling, aerosol filling machines, shrink-wrap packagers, testing and quality control equipment, and form-fill-seal machines. Major buyers of equipment in the early 1990s included the food, cosmetics, drug, and chemical industries, as well as producers of liquids. The industry also contained a hybrid segment which included producers of equipment used to package food during its production. (For example, products such as commercially available sandwich spread were packaged, during processing, in flexible tubes.)

The largest single firm in the package machinery industry was the Signode division of Illinois Tool Works (ITW). Signode was a leading supplier of strapping equipment which, by itself, accounted for roughly one-quarter of all industry shipments in 1992. After Signode, only one other U.S. firm, Figgie International, Inc., had sales in excess of $100 million. At least fifty firms had sales of $10 million or less in 1992.

Form-Fill-Seal Segment

The form-fill-seal segment of the packaging machinery industry involved the manufacture of machines that create packages, fill them, and seal them, all in one continuous operation. The package was essentially a bag which could be sealed on four sides or on three sides (top, bottom, and back), or a pillow pouch which was sealed at the top and bottom. These packages were made of various films which ranged from simple cellophane, plastic, or paper to complex, high-barrier films combining paper, various plastics, and/or foil, for example, paper on the outside and foil or plastic on the inside.

---

[2] Data for this section were taken from "Industrial Machinery," *U.S. Industrial Outlook 1994*. Washington, D.C.: U.S. Department of Commerce, 1994, p.17–10.

These barrier films were used for chemicals, liquid and perishable food, or other products which must be protected against leakage or spoilage. In addition, form-fill-seal packages could be injected with air or gas to protect products such as salty snacks from spoilage or damage. Form-fill-seal machines could be designed to operate horizontally (candy bars) or vertically (potato chips, liquid brick packs).

Although the total value of shipments was not known precisely for the various segments of the packaging machinery industry, some estimates placed the market for all types of form-fill-seal equipment at roughly $165 million in 1992 ("Meeting of Minds" 1990). This market was subdivided into horizontal machines, which were used primarily to package dry products, and vertical machines (VFFS) which could be used for both liquid and dry products. The breakdown of sales in these two subsegments was not known exactly. However, given the high percentage of total sales resulting from VFFS machines for the dominant firms in the VFFS market segments, it is likely that the VFFS market was the larger of the two subsegments (see Figure 15.1). Those firms for which sales could be estimated collectively had VFFS sales in excess of $120 million in 1992. In addition, there were other firms for which sales could not be estimated, making the $120 million figure conservative.

The form-fill-seal packaging machinery industry supplied two major customer groups. The first consisted of large producers of food products such as snacks, candy, and frozen foods, as well as certain industrial products producers, that purchased packaging machines and materials and filled their own packages. The second customer group consisted of contract packaging firms hired by food, candy, and other firms not able to afford the machines themselves. The contract firms not only packaged the goods, but also often shipped them to the customers of their clients directly. The industry structure is summarized in Figure 15.2.

The Packaging Industry Environment

Packaging is perhaps the major common feature which characterizes all the major players in the sophisticated world of consumer goods in the United States and other developed economies. The top 100 packaged brands in the United States consumed $12 billion in containers and packaging materials in 1993 (Packaging 1994). The demand for specific types of packaging machinery was derived demand which depends on the demand for the products to be packaged. In addition, machinery demand was also affected by various economic, social, and technological factors.

Consumer Trends

Consumers want packages to perform several functions. According to a survey conducted in 1993, the most important of those functions were keeping the product in good condition up to the time of purchase (95.8 percent) and keeping the remaining product in good condition after it was opened (78.2 percent) (Baum 1994: 40–43). Packages were also expected to inform the customer, make the product more appealing, and dispense the product to the user.

Starting in the 1980s, consumers began to demand increasing convenience in their purchases. There was a sharp growth in the number of products offered in single-serving and convenience packages suitable for microwave cooking, carrying to work, or eating "on the run." Products such as General Foods Lunchables, General Mills

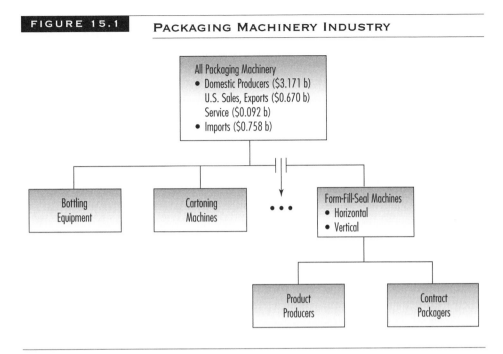

FIGURE 15.1   PACKAGING MACHINERY INDUSTRY

Incredibites granola snacks, and single-serving brick packs of Hi C and other fruit drinks were representative of this trend. However, in the 1990s, consumer attitudes concerning the need for convenient packages changed somewhat. The number of consumers desiring single-serving packages fell by nearly 50 percent. The proportion of consumers who wished to prepare a product in its package or consume it from the package similarly fell from 26 percent of the population to roughly 15 percent (Baum 1994: 41).

While the demand for convenience had abated somewhat, there was evidence of increasing demand for resealable packages. General Foods Post cereals division won an award for its resealable cereal package. Sixty percent of the consumers responding to a 1992 survey reported that they would switch brands to get a resealable package ("Studying the Form" 1992). This trend represented the addition of value to the concept of convenience. Resealable packages reduced spoilage, while permitting consumers to use only what they needed.

In the early 1990s many consumers began to look for the cost savings associated with large bulk packages. Distributors such as Sam's Club and many supermarket chains began to stock an increasing variety of family-size and bulk packaged goods. In addition to value, bulk packaging could reduce package waste, and about one-third of consumers said they would buy bulk packages to achieve waste reduction (Baum 1994: 42).

Economic Factors

The consumer packaged goods segments involving form-fill-seal packages included items such as candy, snack foods, convenience foods in single-serving boil-in-bags, microwave products such as popcorn, single-serving fruit drinks, and premium side dish products. Although convenience foods clearly became a part of everyday life in the 1990s, they were relatively expensive compared to cooking "from scratch." In times of economic weakness, the demand for these foods could decline. Similarly, snack foods, while consumed widely, could not only stress the family budget, but might also be viewed as undesirable by health-conscious families, resulting in reduced sales growth for these foods. These economic factors may have contributed to a rise in bulk size packages. However, while bulk packages were made on form-fill-seal equipment, the number of packaging units was smaller with bulk packages, reducing unit sales growth. Further, after 1989, the number of people who felt packaging was contributing increasingly to product costs rose. By the mid-1990s, more than 80 percent felt they were paying more for packaging in the 1990s than they had been in the past (Baum 1994: 43).

Social Factors

In the late 1980s and through the early and mid-1990s, a growing concern for the state of the natural environment began to exert a strong influence on the packaging industry. A major component of the trash deposited into landfills across the country was packaging material. As landfills began to fill, there was increasing concern over how to dispose of package materials. In one survey, more than half of all consumers felt that foods, cosmetics, and pharmaceuticals were overpackaged (Baum 1994: 42). This led to several critical trends. Consumers wanted packages that could be recycled. A 1990 consumer survey reported that 75 percent of respondents said they were trying to buy products with recyclable packages and recycle the waste material ("Environmental Concern" 1991). In addition, between one-third and one-half of all consumers would buy bulk packages and/or concentrated products, and reject products that appeared to be "overpackaged" to reduce waste (referred to as "source reduction") (Baum 1994: 42).

Technological Factors

The demand for waste reduction, coupled with rising energy costs, encouraged the development of new packaging technologies. In the past many products were packaged in two or three layers of packaging. Many snack foods, for example, often used a simple (form-fill-seal) bag inside a box. However, increasingly, the box and bag were being replaced by a stand-alone bag product with form-fill-seal equipment. Not only did such packages reduce waste by as much as 70 to 80 percent, but they also lowered the use of energy and of natural resources such as trees, the cost of materials, and inventory. Further, stand-alone bags could be shipped in less space than rigid containers which contained more air. This lowered shipping costs and the use of energy resources. Flexible, stand-alone form-fill-seal packages were used for chemicals, household liquids, and other similar products, as well as for food products.

A critical factor affecting expansion in the use of flexible film-based packaging was the development of appropriate films. Although flexible packages provided many benefits, their use could result in reduced shelf life, increased product damage, and other undesirable consequences. These problems were reduced by improvements in film technology. Glass barrier films, complex multilayer laminates, polyolefin, and other materials were emerging as solutions to such problems. However, the new materials were more costly and, because they were difficult to recycle and not readily biodegradable, posed new environmental problems In spite of these drawbacks, the demand for these films was still expected to rise 12 percent per year through 1996, when total film demand was expected to be 11 billion pounds ("Researcher Sees the Demand" 1991).

While some products can be packaged and used without rigid boxes or outer packages, some types of liquids cannot. For these packaging problems, the industry developed the "exchange pouch." This system consisted of a rigid, reusable container which held a pouch of liquid. As the liquid was consumed, only the pouch had to be discarded. It was then replaced with an exchange pouch pierced by a spout inside the rigid container. This system could reduce material costs by as much as 30 percent over more conventional designs.

Important components of the packaging process other than the packaging itself included sterilizing, weighing, measuring, and checking the contents of packages. These additional functions were especially critical for controlling costs, enhancing quality, and reducing contamination, and began to require increasingly sophisticated computer controls and sensor devices.

Product Demand

In general, the packaging of liquid products, especially household cleaning preparations, was expected to create the most demand for flexible packaging through the mid-1990s. Drackett adopted flexible pouch packages for Windex, and firms like Du Pont, S. C. Johnson, Colgate, and Procter & Gamble introduced products in that type of packaging, especially in Canada. It was estimated that North America used 270 billion containers for liquid in 1991 in the dairy, beverage, chemical, food, and personal care markets. Pouches were expected to take as much as 10 percent of this market over the long term ("Pouch Packaging" 1992).

Snack food growth also influenced the demand for flexible packaging. Snack food volume grew at an increasing rate from 1987 to 1991, achieving 6.3 percent growth in dollars and 4.7 percent in volume in 1991, in spite of the onset of a recession. Frozen foods were a mainstay for flexible package demand for some years. However, in 1991 demand fell 3.2 percent, although long-run demand by institutions and bulk purchasers was expected to raise frozen vegetable output later in the decade. Health concerns and other factors also began to slow the growth in candy demand. A survey in *Candy Industry* noted that demand for new candy packaging equipment in 1992 had fallen from 46 percent of the firms surveyed to 20 percent ("Confectioners Bear Out Bulldog Economy" 1992). Pharmaceuticals were also an important source of packaging machinery demand. Their demand grew at just about 6 percent in 1991. Other users of flexible packaging saw their demand rise at roughly 4 percent during the same period.

While the basic product demand for most users of flexible packaging achieved a growth rate only slightly higher than that of the GNP in the early 1990s, the demand for flexible packaging for liquids pushed the overall industry growth rate to 7 percent. Environmental problems with rigid plastic containers caused them to be replaced with flexible packages for many liquids. By some estimates this trend was expected to cause global demand for pouch packages for liquids to rise 25 percent annually through 1996 ("Design May Be the Key" 1992).

International Trends

Consumer packaged goods demand was largely centered in the world's developed economies. However, as the developing world became increasingly integrated with the developed world, consumers in large markets such as the former Eastern Bloc countries and China, for example, were expected to demand more packaged goods, and manufacturers of packaging machinery were expected to see demand for their products rise. In China, the largest untapped market in the world, the demand for food and packaging machinery increased by 250 percent between 1990 and 1991. This type of growth was expected to increase as the Chinese government emphasized food production in its 1991–1995 five-year plan ("China" 1991).

It was expected that many less developed countries, in addition to servicing their domestic markets, would attempt to enhance their stock of hard currency by increasing exports. Lower labor costs gave developing nations a natural price advantage, but to succeed in export markets, these countries needed to raise the quality of their packaging to meet the expectations of their prospective customers. One source estimated that shoddy packaging practices cost China roughly $3.7 billion in lost export earnings in 1989 (Saenz 1990: 12–19). The low quality of packaging in China was attributed to the use of largely obsolete machines and poor materials. Quality control was also often poor, giving further impetus to the demand for sophisticated equipment and technical assistance. While government support for equipment imports was limited in the early 1990s, increasing export activity was expected to force the government to enhance their purchasing levels (Saenz 1990: 18).

Exports of U.S. packaging machinery benefited from the increase in the international demand for packaged goods. Exports by industry firms, reported as $486 million in 1989, were expected to rise to $723 million in 1994, representing growth of more than 8.2 percent per year, compounded. However, United States firms were not the only ones who could satisfy this international demand. In fact, imports of packaging machinery by the United States exceeded exports every year from 1989 through 1994, growing at 4.9 percent per year from $597 million in 1989 to an estimated $795 million in 1994 ("Industrial Machinery" 1994).

The VFFS Equipment Segment

The VFFS segment of the packaging machinery industry was generally competitive. Three of the existing firms were relatively large players in the industry, with total sales of at least $50 million (Figure 15.2). Although the size of packaging machinery producers covered a wide range, in 1991, the average producer had sales of just over $6 million and employed just over sixty workers ("Packaging Machinery" 1992: 1313).

Products and Processes

Packaging machines were generally complex, multifunction products. Because customer needs differed, producers, especially smaller producers, often built machines to customer specifications or modified stock designs to meet special needs. Packaging was critical to customer perceptions of product differentiation, causing innovation to be critical to package machine design. In addition to providing the user the ability to improve products, innovative machines could provide enhanced quality control or lower

FIGURE 15.2	LARGE PACKAGING MACHINERY FIRMS INCLUDING FIRMS SELLING VFFS PACKAGING MACHINERY (DOLLAR FIGURES IN MILLIONS)

Firm	Estimated Firm Sales	Percent of Sales in VFFS	Estimated VFFS Sales
Package Machinery	$63	NA	NA
Woodman/Kliklok	56	<70%	$ 35–40
Hayssen	50	90%	45
Paxall	37	<20%	7
Triangle	18	100%	18
W. A. Lane	7	95%	7
Prodo Pak	5	95%	5
Approximate total VFFS sales			$117–122

SOURCE: This data was estimated from firm sales supplied by *Ward's Business Directory*, and through informed sources in the industry.

the cost of operations, providing the user with competitive advantages. Equipment makers could enhance their own research and development efforts to meet customer needs by forming relationships and alliances with suppliers of machine components or packaging materials, including package films.

In addition to being innovative, it was important that packaging machinery be flexible, providing the user with the ability to use the equipment for more than one product or package size. While the ability to change the equipment quickly from one use to another was critical, it was more important to firms trying to control costs than it was for providing product differentiation for the user, so this factor was not as important as innovation. Flexibility was especially important to contract market customers who provided packaging services to many firms.

The materials used in packaging machinery were similar to those used in other complex machine tools, consisting of various kinds of metal stock, castings, motors, hydraulic cylinders, computer control devices, and related parts. While some of these parts were fairly standard and could be obtained from a variety of suppliers, many critical components were highly sophisticated and could only be obtained from a few key suppliers. In 1988, materials comprised 40 percent of sales. Although some of the equipment required to manufacture packaging machinery was complex, the industry was not, generally speaking, capital-intensive, requiring only 32 percent of the capital equipment employed by the average of all manufacturing firms.

The production processes in much of the packaging equipment industry could be characterized as job shop or batch processes, rather than mass production.[3] Skilled labor was a key component of the production process, making up roughly 31 percent of sales in 1988. Average wages in the industry were relatively high, exceeding the

---

[3] Data in this section is taken from "Packaging Machinery," *Manufacturing U.S.A.*, 2d ed., ed. A. J. Dalway (Detroit: Gale Research, Inc., 1992), pp. 1313–1316.

average for all manufacturing by about 20 percent. This premium was partially offset by productivity, however, as the value added per worker exceeded the average of all manufacturing by 8 percent and the cost per employee was only 53 percent of the manufacturing average.

Since the manufacture of machinery did not require a large capital investment, capital was not really a significant entry barrier in this industry, especially for a larger firm in a related industry. The small size of the typical packaging machinery firm made them popular takeover targets, and many were subsidiaries of larger firms. Although such subsidiaries were not large by themselves, there were substantial resources available to many of them. Much of the equipment used in the manufacture of packaging equipment was fairly standard and could be used by other machinery manufacturers. Thus, exit from this business, like entry, was relatively easy.

Customers and Markets

Because of changing technology and the relatively small size of most packaging equipment producers, successful packaging machinery firms generally tried to focus on one or more market niches, concentrating on product differentiation, rather than cost leadership, as a generic strategy. This factor, which was as important as innovation, required a firm to have a thorough understanding of its customers and a strong research and product development effort to satisfy the needs of those customers. These strategies gave package machinery firms increased pricing flexibility, which was critical to small firms, which experienced lower volumes and had more difficulty covering fixed costs than larger firms. When the number of machinery firms in a given niche was small, customers had fewer choices to satisfy their equipment needs. The market for snack food packaging machines, on the other hand, was very competitive because of the relatively small number of customers in a large, attractive market.

Another critical factor, customer base, was as important as flexibility for every producer. A firm which could capture one or more large customers who were leaders in their product markets could expect growing demand for its equipment, as well as the prospect of maintenance, parts, and technical service business. Postpurchase activities were critical not only for the equipment maker's reputation, but also to support sales, especially since the machines had a relatively long life. Moreover, having leading firms as customers further enhanced the product reputation of the equipment firm, encouraging other customers to buy. While having large customers was important, many producers tried to satisfy specific market niches. Therefore, the growth of these specific market subsegments was also critical.

There were few substitutes for having the appropriate mix of packaging machinery. However, there were alternative ways to package some products, and this could close some niche producers out of markets for substitute types of equipment. Some products could even be packaged by manual labor, although this was rare even for small regional producers. The primary complementary product for the packaging industry was the film used in the packages, and technological changes in film production had a great influence on technological improvements in packaging as a whole. For this reason, long-term relationships between form-fill-seal equipment firms and film producers were relatively common. Each needed the other for success.

Overall, the segmented nature of the package machinery industry, the relatively low barriers to both entry and exit, and the number of small competitors who must fight to stay in business made the rivalry in this industry moderate overall. Rivalry was intensified in certain segments, such as snack foods, where the customer bargaining

| FIGURE 15.3 | EVALUATION OF ATTRACTIVENESS OF VFFS MARKET SEGMENT | |

Attractiveness Factors	Rating	Comments
Market factors		
Size	4.0	Relatively large segment
Growth	4.0	Faster than GNP
Customer bargaining power	3.0	Snacks a problem
Overseas sales potential	4.0	Europe
Price elasticity	3.0	
Environmental factors		
Speed of change	3.0	
Experience curve effects	4.0	Demand high enough
Rapid product innovation	4.0	
Social factors	5.0	High support for VFFS
Regulatory climate	4.0	
Substitutability	3.0	
Competitive factors		
Industry structure	2.0	3 big competitors
Potential for differentiation	5.0	Function of R&D
Competitive stability	3.0	
Average rating	3.6+	

power was relatively strong. In general, the high proportion of variable cost, the relatively low levels of operating leverage, the need for R&D spending, and the lack of pricing flexibility in some markets combined to create stress on the profits of equipment producers.

Attractiveness of the VFFS Market

Figure 15.3 shows the results of an analysis of the overall attractiveness of the VFFS market done by a consultant to the management at Kartridg Pak. A five-point rating scale was used for each factor, with all factors receiving equal weight.

The Competition

As noted in Figure 15.2, there were a number of competitors supplying the VFFS machinery market segment in 1992. Six of these competitors are described below.[4] To clarify Kartridg Pak's evaluation of the prospects in the VFFS market, the firm's

---

[4]This competitive analysis was developed by the company's consultant based on public information, interviews with industry insiders, and the results of an extensive market survey conducted by Kartridg Pak.

consultant suggested that management might enhance its understanding of these competitors by evaluating each in relation to the critical success factors influencing the industry.

Hayssen

Hayssen, a subsidiary of Bemis Company, a major packaging producer, had total sales of about $50 million, with an estimated $45 million in VFFS sales, the highest in the industry. This translated into a market share in excess of 35 percent. The firm served a variety of markets, with 30 percent of its sales overseas. Hayssen's growth was expected to follow the industry, although the percentage of overseas sales was expected to rise to 35 percent by 1994. Approximately 20 percent of its output was for liquid packaging machines, with the other 80 percent composed of machines for packaging dry products. Hayssen was a major innovator, employing over 100 R&D personnel in its headquarters. The firm also prided itself on the flexibility of its machines, a major factor influencing customer purchases. Hayssen's machines could even be adapted for use in both wet and dry packaging. Hayssen had roughly 2,000 customers, including such major producers as Eagle Snacks (Anheuser Busch) and General Mills. The firm had a strong reputation for quality and engineering, although some felt its start-up training was not always up to expectations. Its prices were in line with the industry average base price of $100,000 per machine. It had strengthened its reputation through an exclusive agreement with a leading Japanese scale manufacturer.

Woodman

Woodman was a subsidiary of Kliklok, which also produced packaging machinery. Together, they had sales of $56 million, of which roughly $35 to $40 million was VFFS equipment, giving them a VFFS market share of about 30 percent. They employed about 500 people. Although Woodman produced a variety of packaging machines, including cartoning systems, it had a strong commitment to VFFS machines, especially for the snack market. All of its systems were for the packaging of dry products. Growth was expected to roughly parallel the growth in snack food demand. Woodman was known as an innovative company, with thirty-five people employed in R&D. Its innovative focus was on whole systems—for example, systems that not only packaged the product, but could also put the packages into cases. Although Woodman's machines were not quite as flexible as those of industry leader Hayssen, they did have the latest computerized controls and their machines could be quickly adjusted for a variety of packaging situations. Woodman's major customers included Frito-Lay. Roughly 65 to 70 percent of sales were overseas, although this proportion was expected to decline to about 50 percent by 1994. Woodman's prices, which were a bit higher than the industry average, were supported by product quality and excellent postpurchase training and service. The firm also permitted customers to try a machine before they bought it, adjusting the machine to meet the customer's specific needs.

Triangle

Triangle was an independent firm with $18 million in overall sales, all of which was in the VFFS market. This gave the firm about a 15 percent market share. Triangle focused on the dry segment of the market, concentrating on pouches for convenience foods and other bag-in-a-box applications such as frozen vegetables, cereals, and pastas. Innovation at Triangle concentrated on two areas: making faster machines and developing improved scales for weighing the material to be packaged. Triangle's developments in scale technology enabled it to sell weighing equipment to other package machinery producers. Triangle approached the question of flexibility by supplying a base machine for which options were available to meet customers' specific needs. This flexibility was increased by Triangle's ability to manufacture its own scales. Triangle served over 5,000 customers, the largest of which was General Mills. Only 10 to 15 percent of Triangle's sales were exported, chiefly to Canada and Mexico. The firm enjoyed only modest growth, including growth in exports. Triangle machines were rated as durable and reliable. It differentiated itself through its scale systems and its start-up services.

Paxall

Paxall was a subsidiary of a larger machine manufacturer, Sasib Corporation of America. Although Paxall had overall sales of $37 million, its VFFS sales were only about $7 million, giving the firm a market share of slightly less than 6 percent. Paxall produced VFFS machines for both wet and dry applications, with 60 percent of its sales in the former. Its chief markets were for household products and pharmaceutical applications. Paxall supplied a complete line of equipment, scales, and cartoners. Expectations were that Paxall's strong presence in the liquids markets would permit it to achieve higher than average growth. Paxall's focus in innovation was in the extensive use of sophisticated servomotors and user-friendly computer control systems. These systems were considered superior to older technologies based on air and hydraulic cylinders. However, Paxall was not committing R&D resources to the development of improved VFFS machines. Rather, it was concentrating its efforts on other types of packaging equipment. Paxall produced a considerable number of custom machines. In general, its machines were not as flexible as those of its competitors. Paxall had a large number of accounts, although they did not have any very large customers. Their foreign sales were limited to 5 to 10 percent of the total, and growth was expected to be at about the industry average. Paxall's biggest source of differentiation was its ability to customize its machines for specific customer needs. Although they appeared to have a good reputation among their existing customers, they were not widely known outside this group.

W. A. Lane

W. A. Lane had total sales of $7 million, most of which was in the VFFS segment. It employed only about 60 people. In spite of its size, the firm was the leader in machines for liquid applications, with 100 percent of its business in that area. Because of its concentration in the liquid segment, Lane expected growth to be considerably above average in the next few years. In the last two years Lane had concentrated its R&D on the development of highly flexible machines. Its basic line included machines which could package liquid pouches ranging in size from one ounce to five gallons. This success in innovation greatly improved the firm's reputation for flexibility. Lane had a small customer base with only about 100 customers, several of which were large institutional market packagers. Lane had concentrated primarily on the domestic market, although it expected exports, chiefly to the United Kingdom, to increase to 20 percent of sales by 1994. Lane's chief source of differentiation was found in its expertise for liquid pouch machines, where it was able to command a strong price premium. Its reputation for postpurchase service was also excellent.

Prodo-Pak

Prodo-Pak was the smallest and weakest of the competitors in the VFFS packaging market. It had a market share of only about 5 to 6 percent, with 85 percent of its sales concentrated in the market for liquid applications. Prodo-Pak was not known for innovation, although it had developed machines which provided intermittent motion, allowing more time for sealing the package. This added some flexibility to its machines, along with some ability to make easy changeovers from one application to another. Although it was a small company, Prodo-Pak had numerous customers, mostly small. The firm differentiated itself by having lower prices than its competitors, thereby providing a "bargain" for the small customer who required a relatively unsophisticated machine. Prodo-Pak sold about 20 percent of its output overseas, and sales growth was modest, although future growth might be aided by the firm's concentration on liquid applications. Postpurchase parts service was strong.

Kartridg Pak

As one of the largest subsidiaries of BWI, Kartridg Pak (KP) played a key role in the overall firm's sales, growth, and profitability. With sales of $25 to $30 million (depending on how the sales of Aerofill were allocated between KP and KP Aerofill), KP made up the bulk of the Food Machinery Division of BWI. KP had four main product lines divided into two groups, food equipment and filling equipment. KP's largest product line was the Chub machine. This machine was a highly versatile system for packaging viscous food or industrial products in flexible film. Two major customer groups for this product were meat processors and explosives manufacturers. Available with capacities to 30,000 pounds per hour, KP's chub machines were able to produce packages ranging in weight from one ounce to thirty pounds and ranging in length from two to seventy-two inches.

In addition to the Chub machine, the food equipment line included the Anal-Ray line of fat analyzers. These machines were able to determine, almost instantaneously, the percent of fat in processed meat products. A microprocessor accessory for this machine also calculated the protein and moisture content of meat products. KP's Yieldmaster mechanical deboning systems were designed to remove trimmed or untrimmed meat from the bones of beef, pork, goat, mutton, lamb, poultry, or fish. The fourth product in KP's food equipment line was a smoke generator. This machine produced wood smoke to finish processed meat products. The KP'smoke generator allowed precise control of smoking time, color, and flavor.

The filling equipment product line included two major product groups, aerosol packing equipment and liquid filling equipment. The Aerosol packing equipment included a complete line of machines offering capacities of more than 450 containers per minute. The liquid filling product group included a variety of piston-driven filling machines which filled containers with liquid products in precise amounts. The base machine handled self-supporting containers of up to thirty-two ounces at rates up to twenty-five containers per filling head per minute. A filling machine could be fitted with from three to twenty-four heads, giving a total capacity of over 600 containers per

FIGURE 15.4	EVALUATION OF ATTRACTIVENESS OF KARTRIDG PAK PRODUCT LINES			

Attractiveness Factor	Chub Machine	Anal-Ray	Yieldmaster	Aerosol Products
Market factors				
Size	2.0	4.0	2.0	4.0
Growth	2.0	2.0	2.0	4.0
Customer bargaining power	4.0	3.0	3.0	3.0
Overseas sales potential	4.0	4.0	2.0	3.0
Price elasticity	3.0	4.0	2.0	4.0
Environmental factors				
Speed of change	4.0	3.0	3.0	3.0
Experience curve effects	3.0	3.0	3.0	4.0
Rapid product innovation	3.0	3.0	3.0	3.0
Social factors	2.0	3.0	3.0	2.0
Regulatory climate	2.0	2.0	2.0	1.0
Substitutability	3.0	3.0	3.0	2.0
Competitive factors				
Industry structure	5.0	4.0	4.0	4.0
Potential for differentiation	4.0	4.0	2.0	4.0
Competitive stability	2.0	3.0	3.0	3.0
Average rating	**3.1**	**3.2**	**2.6**	**3.1**
Estimated ranking in sales contribution to KP	1	3–4	3–4	2

minute. A rotary, gravity-driven machine with an available pressurized loading bowl provided an alternative to the piston-driven line.

In addition to these major product lines, KP also supplied testing and other accessory machines and tortilla folders. Figure 15.4 presents the analysis provided by the company's consultant of the market attractiveness of the four major product lines produced by Kartridg Pak. For this analysis each attractiveness factor was given equal weight, and "5" represented a "Very Attractive" rating.

The biggest product line for KP in 1992 was the Chub machine. The strongest aspect of the industry for this product was the relatively small number of competitors. The lack of competition had reduced price sensitivity, compared to the firm's other markets. A slowdown in growth in the 1990s was largely offset by replacement and overseas sales. The company entered the Chinese market and, as a result, KP's overseas sales rose from 30 to 60 percent of the firm's total sales in 1992.

The strongest market served by KP was the market for fat analyzers. Although this market was large, its growth potential was not strong. This slow growth reduced the rate of technological change, permitting the firm to allocate R&D resources elsewhere. However, the reduced risk of obsolescence for customers also served to depress growth in demand.

The weakest market for KP was the market for deboning equipment. This market had low growth and restricted overseas potential. It also offered little opportunity to differentiate or innovate. This reduced technological threats, but also limited the advantage for competitive opportunities.

KP's aerosol line was strong, with good market prospects. The problem in this market was the need to overcome environmental problems associated with traditional propellants. The competitive structure of the aerosol market was favorable, and this market had the potential to become much more attractive if new, safe propellants could be developed. If not, potential users were likely to turn away from traditional pressurized aerosol containers.

Strategies and Issues [5]

Kartridg Pak employed several strategies to enhance its performance and reputation. First and foremost, KP focused on the production of high-quality packaging machines. KP also tried to design products that were relatively easy to use, flexible, and relatively fast. These characteristics were intended to increase customer productivity and allow the customer to reduce costs.

KP's products were distributed through a strong dealer network based on long-term relationships. In addition to its U.S. dealers, KP worked through twenty-three dealers in all parts of the world to distribute its products in Japan and the Far East, South Africa, Europe, Israel, Egypt, and South and Central America. This overseas dealer network, coupled with the firm's recent presence in China and its British parent, had the potential to make the firm a strong international player. The firm's dealer network, coupled with quality replacement parts, had helped it develop a strong reputation for postpurchase service. The firm's service reputation was also supported by a strong technical staff which provided customers with quality installation and a quick startup for new equipment. KP's market success and the resources of BWI provided the firm with a potentially strong financial base.

KP was historically a strong player in its current market niche, the meat segment of the food industry. However, packaging equipment had a relatively long life (some machines lasted twenty years or more). Further, if a machine was not obsolete, or did not reduce its user's competitiveness, its life could often be prolonged through maintenance and repair, especially when quality, factory-built spare parts were available. Both theses factors had resulted in market saturation in this niche, and growth had slowed, reducing the demand for KP's products.

Although KP's dealer network was strong, its sales force was relatively small and all sales personnel were stationed in the home office in Davenport, Iowa. One of the most important considerations in the competitive strength of packaging machine producers was product development and innovation. Because it concentrated on the meat industry, KP tended to focus on accessories and features, rather than significant innovations. Further, some industry insiders felt the firm's strength in its primary market tended to dampen its competitive drive.

---

[5] The information for this section was based largely on a customer survey commissioned by the firm.

BWI Group

Kartridg Pak's parent firm of BWI Group was Barry Wehmiller International PLC (BWI) located in Altrincham, Cheshire, England. BWI was a multiunit packaging machinery company which consisted of six subsidiary companies, divided into three divisions: the Vision Division, the Food Equipment Division, and the General Packaging Division. BWI reported total sales of slightly less than $74,000,000 in 1992 (see the financial statements in Figure 15.5).

The Vision Division consisted of BWI Index which produced vision, inspection, and process control machines for glass and plastic container manufacturers; food, beverage, and pharmaceutical companies; and other producers of consumer goods. These products were used to inspect both the containers and their contents during the packaging process.

The Food Machinery Division of BWI consisted of two subsidiaries: Kartridg Pak and Fords. Fords manufactured filling, sealing, and end-of-line packaging machines for the food, dairy, pharmaceutical, cosmetics, household, and automotive care industries. The product line included cup and tray filling/sealing machines, heat sealing machinery, capping/lidding equipment, and container handling equipment. Kartridg Pak manufactured a range of packaging and process equipment for the food and meat industries. Products included fat analyzers, deboning equipment, Chub packaging machines, smoke generators, and tortilla folders.

The General Packaging Division was BWI's largest division, contributing just over half of the firm's sales and about 35 percent of its profits in 1992. The division consisted of three subsidiaries: Manesty, Dawson, and KP Aerofill. Manesty produced machinery to make tablets and similar products for the pharmaceutical, household products, and confectionery industries. Dawson produced machinery for container handling and bottling for the dairy, brewing, soft drink, food, pharmaceutical, and other industries. KP Aerofill manufactured machines to fill aerosol containers for the cosmetic, pharmaceutical, and health care industries. The product lines included liquid fillers, propellant fillers, testing equipment, and valve assembly and related machines. General Packaging was relatively new and combined existing resources of Kartridg Pak and what was formerly BWI Aerofill.

The Future

As the financial statements in Figure 15.5 illustrate, BWI experienced a number of changes from 1991 to 1992. Growth in Kartridg Pak's primary market, meat processing, slowed dramatically, and both sales and profits for BWI's Food Equipment Division declined in 1992. In late 1992 and early 1993, management began to consider various options to enhance performance.

One strategy considered by KP was entry into new markets. Because of its relative attractiveness, one market considered for entry was the VFFS machinery market. KP felt it had three options:

- *Develop a base machine for the VFFS market in-house.* This option would enable the firm to establish its own name in the market. KP felt it could develop such a machine and seek a competitive advantage based on quality, speed, support, and flexibility. Management felt the new product could be designed and introduced

FIGURE 15.5	SELECTED FINANCIAL INFORMATION FOR BWI AND KARTRIDG PAK FOR FISCAL YEARS JULY 31, 1991, TO JULY 31, 1992

BWI and Kartridg Pak
Income Statement
July 31, 1991–July 31, 1992
(Amounts in Thousands of Pounds)

	1992			1991
Sales		73,699		75,358
Vision division	18,154		17,415	
Food equipment	16,949		17,403	
General packaging	38,596		40,540	
	73,699		75,358	
By origin				
United Kingdom	39,081		44,375	
North America	34,618		30,983	
	73,699		75,358	
By destination				
United Kingdom	22,485		28,434	
Europe	14,269		17,074	
North America	21,683		17,046	
Central and South America	3,560		1,931	
Middle East	2,822		1,569	
Africa	2,529		2,918	
Asia	5,463		5,014	
Australia	888		1,372	
	73,699		75,358	
Cost of sales		49,162		49,139
Gross profit		24,537		26,219
Operating Expenses		18,122		20,091
Distribution costs	5,141		6,950	
Administration				
Depreciation	1,219		1,295	
R&D	2,235		2,531	
Other	9,527		9,315	
	18,122		20,091	
Operating income		6,415		6,128
Vision division	670		(1,633)	
Food equipment	3,489		4,221	
General packaging	2,256		3,540	
	6,415		6,128	
Other (expense)		133		(1,099)
Income before taxes	6,548	5,029		
Taxes		1,594		1,191
Net income		4,954		3,838

Note: To convert these statements to dollars use the following assumptions:

	Year End	Average Last 12 Months
7/31/1991	[Pound]1 = $1.66	[Pound]1 = $1.73
7/31/1992	[Pound]1 = $1.90	[Pound]1 = $1.78

(*continued*)

FIGURE 15.5	(CONTINUED)

BWI and Kartridg Pak
Income Statement
July 31, 1991–July 31, 1992
(Amounts in Thousands of Pounds)

	1992			1991
Current assets	49,332		41,364	
Fixed assets	8,990		10,262	
		58,322		51,626
Current debt	23,764		29,182	
Long-term debt	6,373		5,820	
Equity	28,185		16,624	
		58,322		51,626

Note: To convert these statements to dollars use the following assumptions:

	Year End	Average Last 12 Months
7/31/1991	[Pound]1 = $1.66	[Pound]1 = $1.73
7/31/1992	[Pound]1 = $1.90	[Pound]1 = $1.78

in eighteen to twenty-four months, although some of the company's lower-level personnel felt development time might be significantly less.

- *Acquire an existing liquid-focus manufacturer.* Liquid pouch packaging was the hottest area in the VFFS market. By acquiring an existing liquid-focus firm, entry into this market could be accomplished very quickly. The size of the market, coupled with its projected high growth rates, might reduce potential competitive pressures, at least for the time required to assimilate the acquisition. If KP made such an acquisition, divisional resource limitations might limit the size of the acquisition. Regardless of which firm KP chose to acquire, it was likely some key personnel would have to move to KP's headquarters in Davenport. Failure to attract these people could cause problems with any prospective merger.

- *Acquire an existing dry-focus manufacturer.* This option was attractive because, although expected growth in the dry packaging market was slower than for liquids, the market was bigger, and the immediate gains for KP could be larger.

In addition to the factors noted above, several other considerations might influence the decision to enter the VFFS market. If this market were, in fact, larger than some of the more conservative estimates, other competitors might choose to enter the market. Early in 1993, President Clinton had just been inaugurated and his impact on economic conditions was unknown. Because the companies KP might choose to acquire were privately held or divisions of other companies, they might not be available for acquisition. Furthermore, the cost of such an acquisition might be difficult to estimate. Profits of such firms might range from 2 to 3 percent of sales to 6 to 7 percent after tax. Mature manufacturing firms might command prices ranging from as little as eight times earnings to as much as fifteen times earnings or more.

Another issue faced by KP and its industry competitors was an increasing emphasis on quality. The advent of ISO 9000 (an international process standard related to quality) as a de facto quality standard was forcing firms to make a choice about whether or not to seek conformity with this standard, especially if they wanted to do significant business with major firms in the United States and firms overseas. Seeking ISO 9000 certification was an expensive, time-consuming process. KP and Paxall had started to seek ISO certification by early 1992, although Hayssen had not.

KP had alternatives to entering the VFFS market. It could leave the entry decision to the managers of BWI and concentrate on its existing business. KP's recent gains in sales to China, and the expansion of its overseas markets, especially with the need for development in Eastern Europe, might offer all the opportunities the firm could handle at this point. After all, the effort required to develop a new VFFS machine, or assimilate an acquisition, could be expended to develop the firm's existing markets. Many manufacturing businesses were expanding sales by reengineering their manufacturing and sales organizations and developing strategies based on an increased customer orientation. These firms realized that they could increase their own sales by helping their customers to develop an enhanced competitive position. These options, too, would require resources and KP would have to determine whether it could afford to do any of this. KP had many choices. The firm knew it would probably have to do something. What it should do and when was the question.

References

C. Baum. "Consumers Want It All—and Now." *Packaging*, August 1994, pp. 40–43.

"China to Hold International Food Machine Exposition." Xinhua General News Service, November 21, 1991.

"Confectioners Bear Out Bulldog Economy in Poll." *Candy Industry*, November 1992. pp. 32–38.

"Design May Be the Key to U.S. Business for the Flexible Pouch." *Modern Plastics International*, February 1992, pp. 20–23.

"Environmental Concern: Consumers Say They'll Buy Recyclables, Concentrates." *Packaging*, August 1991, p. 1.

"Industrial Machinery." U.S. Industrial Outlook 1994, Washington, D.C.: U.S. Department of Commerce 1994, p. 17–10.

"Meeting of Minds by Leading Analysts Leads to Realistic Composite Outlook." *Packaging*, April 1990, pp. 32–43.

Packaging. Special Report, January 1994, p. 37.

"Packaging Machinery." In *Manufacturing U.S.A.*, 2d ed., ed. A. J. Dalway. Detroit: Gale Research, Inc., 1992, p. 1314.

"Pouch Packaging." *Modern Plastics International*, June 1992, pp. 30–31.

"Researcher Sees the Demand for Film Hitting 11 Billion Pounds by '96." *Packaging*, August 1991, p. 1.

H. Saenz. "Overwrapped and Underprotected." *The China Business Review*, September/October, 1990.

"Studying the Form." *Packaging Today*, October 1992, pp. 53–58.

16

Ace Technical

In January 1997, Jeff Franklin sat in his office wondering what he should do next. He couldn't believe how rapidly the bar code industry was changing. He had surmounted many challenges thus far and, in many ways, had achieved his goal to succeed as an entrepreneur. But now, the competition was more intense than it had ever been in the past. New rivals were appearing every day hoping to acquire their slice of the market. In addition, a few bar code hardware manufacturers were pursuing vertical integration strategies, limiting the need for intermediary companies like Ace Technical. Could his company successfully continue in the niche he had developed? Was it time to sell?

Jeff hated to admit it, but he had not reviewed his original strategic plan in several years. He had prepared a five-year plan for his company back in 1992. He had been so busy managing his start-up that he scarcely had time to plan for the next week! Rapid growth had forced Ace Technical to deal in a crisis mode for too long, which sometimes resulted in costly errors. This had to stop. He knew that to continue to be a viable, successful company, he had to be able to plan ahead for more than six months at a time.

As he sat contemplating his situation, he started to list the distinctions between his company and the competition. He attributed his success to fast, personal service and ready availability of the latest hardware and software. Jeff reasoned that some of the consolidations actually might have been advantageous for Ace Technical, which strove to provide high-quality personal service. He noted that "larger firms tend to lose touch with their customers. We have developed relationships where we know our customers by first name. I consider that to be one of our key strengths."

Jeff recognized that the future of his company depended on the ability of his employees to continue providing the highest value to their customers. This would only be possible by keeping abreast of technological developments and by moving more

By Paula Schmidt Weber and James E. Weber, State Cloud University, and Steven R. Ash of Franklin University. This case is based upon personal involvement, interviews, and observations. Names and locations have been disguised, but all events and individuals are real. The authors thank the anonymous reviewers for their assistance in the development of this manuscript.

rapidly than his competitors in serving the customers' needs. Growth had been phenomenal, but he wanted to be sure he could keep his company one step ahead of the competition.

Jeff's company, Ace Technical (Ace Tech), based in a suburb of a large, midwestern, metropolitan city, distributed leading edge bar code marking and bar code data collection technologies. Ace Tech purchased bar code products directly from selected manufacturers and in turn sold those products to their customers, who were the end users.

Bar codes are the small series of vertical lines of different widths that appear on many products. These bar codes make unambiguous data entry, identification, and tracking of products and a multitude of other items a reality for many businesses. When an item is purchased, it is scanned at the checkout register. A computer recognizes the identification number of the item, displays the price, and subtracts the item from inventory. Additional inventory can be automatically ordered based upon a previously determined inventory set point. Bar codes are used to both subtract and add items to inventory.

Bar code manufacturing and sales had been a rapidly growing segment of the computer industry. Bar codes had had an enormous impact on numerous sectors in the last decade, and it seemed that potential applications were still just being developed. These new, innovative bar code technologies had a dramatic impact on bar code companies. In addition, while retail uses of bar coding were quite established, Jeff felt that the government, health care, manufacturing, and service industries were relatively underdeveloped markets for bar code implementations. He believed that his prior work experience in computer manufacturing would allow him to develop a unique niche.

Ace Tech's value-added approach included the set-up and servicing of equipment as well as readily providing products customers needed. Thus far, Jeff felt that this strategy had been very successful. However, he realized that no one could have predicted a business based on bar coding thirty years ago. As in many technology-based organizations, success does not necessarily ensure long organizational life; Jeff had every intention of becoming and staying a major player in the data input business. He wanted Ace Tech to always be the knowledge leader in the dynamic bar code market niche.

Ace Tech's mission statement identified the company's goals:

> Our mission is to constantly increase our customers' productivity by providing them with the most advanced automatic data input products and services. Ace Technical focuses solely upon providing unique products and services, which promote a smooth, rapid, and accurate flow of data in business and institutional arenas. Specifically, we provide our customers access to leading edge bar code marking and bar code data collection technologies.

How Ace Tech Came into Being

In early 1990, Jeff Franklin was a quality engineer for a computer manufacturing firm. Jeff, who held a degree in mechanical engineering, enjoyed his job but often didn't feel appreciated and longed for the opportunity to start his own business. To further his

FIGURE 16.1   DECODING THE BAR CODE

What a UPC code says...

The first six digits identify the manufacturer. All of the products the manufacturer makes will begin with the same six digits. The number is assigned by the Uniform Code Council.

The second five digits define the item identification given to that product by the manufacturer. This allows them to make 99,000 products. The 12th digit is a check number.

career goals, Jeff attended a local university in the evenings to obtain his MBA in entrepreneurship. As part of Jeff's final MBA project, he was required to prepare a business plan. Jeff wanted his time in developing the plan to be well spent, so he carefully researched ideas that could possibly be the "right" entrepreneurial venture for him. He had wanted to start a business of his own for many years and had been asking everyone he knew about ideas for starting a business. Jeff had a notebook that was filled with pages and pages of ideas.

His search for the perfect idea ended when a friend who had been a bar code salesman told him how his former employer had more business than he could handle. In fact, the demand for bar code products was so great they were selling themselves. Given this potentially lucrative opportunity, Jeff focused his research on the bar code industry and produced a comprehensive business plan for a start-up business in the wholesale and distribution of bar code products and services. He planned to sell bar code hardware such as bar code scanners and printers, and the labels and software to create bar codes.

The next step was a big one. Jeff stated, "I felt overwhelmed by the amount of work I could see ahead. I was also afraid of trying and failing. But, more overpowering was the fear of not trying at all!"

In the end, Jeff decided the bar code opportunity was worth all the risks. He hoped his MBA had prepared him well for whatever the future might bring.

Jeff founded Ace Technical, in the basement of his duplex, in March 1992. He chose the name "Ace" so that his company would be alphabetically one of the first listings in the yellow pages. He also decided to leave the name generic (Technical) so that he would not inadvertently limit his business opportunities. Jeff felt relieved to be finally taking the step he dreamed of for so long. His start-up funds included $10,000 of personal savings, a $5,000 loan from his father, and $15,000 available from personal credit cards.

As president and sole employee for 1992, Jeff worked twelve–fourteen hours a day, six days a week. He answered the telephone, researched products, made sales presentations, and established accounting and record-keeping practices. Jeff was also tireless in his efforts to establish a customer base. He contacted all his former colleagues, fellow students, and former customers in the computer industry and followed up on all leads. Whenever he was not pursuing customers, Jeff read everything he could about the myriad of bar code products available. He paid the bills by doing janitorial work and other odd jobs at night and on the weekends. Eventually, all his hard work began to pay off.

Jeff made $5,000 in sales the first three months. He purchased bar code equipment on his personal credit card and hoped customers would pay on time. First-year sales (covering a nine-month period) totaled approximately $35,000. While there was no net income the first year, Jeff felt that the groundwork had been laid for a growing customer base.

In the beginning of the second quarter of 1993, Jeff decided Ace Technical was busy enough to support a second employee. So, as had been agreed in February 1992, Jeff sold 45 percent of his shares in Ace Technical to the friend who had recommended he pursue the bar code business. The new co-owner, Dan Brown, had experience in the bar code industry, and Jeff knew he was an exceptional salesperson. Each month, sales doubled those of the previous month, resulting in second-year sales of $510,000. This represented almost a fifteen-fold increase in only a year! Jeff attributed the impressive growth in sales to finally finding the right product mix, better discounts from suppliers, and a more established name.

Jeff noted that, in the beginning, he and Dan tried distributing a variety of products in addition to bar codes. These products included fasteners, company signs, and magnetic boards. They essentially pursued any product customers requested. After a while, Jeff realized that this wasn't working. "This must be a common pitfall for many small businesses," he stated. By mid-1993, Jeff and Dan had found the specific products and suppliers they needed and wanted to service their customers in the manufacturing industry. As Jeff said, "Try a lot of stuff and keep what works!" He believed that philosophy served Ace Tech well.

In 1997, five years after inception, the business had grown to a total of seventeen employees with annual sales of over $6 million. Ace Tech's growth had resulted in a continual barrage of new challenges for Jeff, Dan, and the rest of the company.

Bar Code Technology and Industry Environment

When Jeff started the company in 1992, the bar code industry and bar code technology was relatively new and was experiencing rapid growth. Typical bar code products included scanners, data collectors, printers, software, bar code labels, verifiers, and a variety of accessories.

Bar codes were invented by Norman Joseph Woodland in 1949. Mr. Woodland was a graduate student and instructor at Drexel University. The characteristic vertical line pattern found on bar codes emerged from an adaptation of the Morse code system, with the dots and dashes extended downward to form vertical lines of two different widths. In 1952, Norman Woodland and Bernard Silver were granted a patent on the bar code and set about developing a method of "reading" the code. They used a powerful, 500-watt lightbulb as a light source and a photo-multiplier tube designed for movie sound systems as the reader. The photo-multiplier tube was hooked to an oscilloscope, and when a bar code was "scanned" by using the tube to read the light reflected off the bar code, the oscilloscope produced distinctive patterns.

This first bar code scanner was bulky (the size of a desk), inefficient, and could cause the bar coded paper to smolder under the 500-watt lightbulb. There was also no inexpensive or convenient process to record the data from the oscilloscope. Woodland and Silver sold the patent for bar codes to Philco in 1962. This patent was subsequently resold to RCA.

The next advance in bar code technology occurred in the railroad industry, which was facing problems of how to efficiently and accurately trace freight car movement. In 1967, a design developed by the Sylvania/GTE Applied Research Lab was selected. This clever design utilized a label that indicated the rail car's owner and serial number for each freight car. The label contained horizontal red, white, and blue reflective bars on a nonreflective background and was read by an optical scanning system using white light. Information could be read at any train speed from a post alongside the tracks. However, the excessive cost of the system combined with an economic recession doomed the Sylvania/GTE system's commercial success.

In the next several years, important improvements were made to the Sylvania/GTE system that helped this technology become more popular. A Sylvania engineer quit to found Computer Identics Corporation, which concentrated solely on bar code technology. Colors were removed so that only black and white lines were required, and helium-neon (HeNe) lasers were used to scan the labels. The result was a much smaller and more accurately read label.

In 1969, the first true bar code systems were installed at a GM plant in Pontiac, Michigan, and the General T company in New Jersey. These first bar codes contained only two digits. At that time, two digits were sufficient to keep track of the fewer than 100 items being coded.

In the 1970s, the first large-scale use for bar codes emerged. Several grocery stores tried using bar codes to track cartons at distribution centers and, in 1972, Kroger grocery began an eighteen-month test of bar codes in a Cincinnati store. This adoption was spurred by a study by McKinsey & Company that predicted industry savings of $150 million a year if the system was used. Soon after that, automotive manufacturers began tracking components in factories by using bar code labels. A federal agency, the EPA, was also indirectly influential in the utilization of bar codes. As part of the Clean Air Act, a $10,000 fine was levied for each engine not recorded and made available for inspection. The fines motivated accuracy of engine component tracking.

The large-scale usage of bar codes was also facilitated by the adoption in 1973 of the Universal Product Code (UPC). This twelve-digit bar code permitted end-customers to identify both the manufacturer (the first 6 digits of the code) and the product or particular item (the second five digits of the code). The last digit in the twelve-digit UPC was used as a check-code, to verify that the previous eleven digits had been read correctly. Figure 16.1 contains an example of a bar code and explains what the digits mean.

Over time, numerous bar code formats or *symbologies* were developed. The symbology is a specific look, orientation, and length that the bar code has, and each symbology has constraints associated with it. For instance, in the United States, bar codes had twelve digits; in Europe, they had thirteen. By 1977, there were over forty-five different symbologies, with most aimed at specific applications. These different symbologies were administered by the Uniform Code Council in the United States and Canada and by EAN International in other parts of the world. Bar codes users were required to register their bar codes with their industries and the appropriate administrative agency unless there were no or limited exchange of products, or where the bar code was intended solely for internal use.

The earliest bar codes were referred to as one-dimensional symbologies. They consisted of combinations of long black stripes over varying widths of white background. In the mid-1980s, bar codes were becoming more like portable databases than simple tracking labels. As the trend toward greater amounts of encoded information increased, so did symbologies. The newest bar codes in 1997 were referred to as two-dimensional (2-D) symbologies. These 2-D labels had an appearance of being spotted, or checkered, and could hold up to 2,000 characters as opposed to the fifteen–twenty two character limits on traditional one-dimensional bar codes. As bar codes capabilities evolved, regulation of bar codes evolved as well. The twelve-digit UPC system used for retail sales in the United States was absorbed into a thirteen-digit system, with complete transition required by January 1, 2005. By late 1997, plans for a standardized fourteen-digit system were in progress.

Early helium-neon lasers for scanning bar codes had been replaced by cheaper, more reliable diode or solid-state lasers that emitted a tightly collimated beam of light. Typically the laser was directed toward a mirrored, faceted object that reflected the light through a glass window toward the bar code. As the laser encountered a bar code, light was absorbed by the dark code lines and reflected by each light space between the bars, producing a characteristic pattern of fluctuating reflected light. A photodetector was then used to capture this pattern, which was decoded by a computer that matched each unique pattern to an entry for that bar code. Examples of bar code scanners are shown in Figure 16.2.

In *Using the Bar Code: Why It's Taking Over* (1994), Collins and Whipple gave a number of justifications for the use of bar codes:

1. Instant and continuous availability of operating data, with maximum value for management guidance.

2. Significant reduction in paperwork quantity and time to prepare.

3. Elimination of data entry errors and the multiple costs associated with operating with misinformation (generally accepted error rate for typing is one character per 300 strokes; bar codes have an error rate of one character per one million).

4. Elimination of data verification delay and expense.

5. Accuracy and up-to-date information needed to support JIT and Quick Response concepts accepted by industry.

Bar code customers were quick to recognize the benefits of quick, accurate computer data entry to greatly improve the efficiency of their sales and inventory tracking systems. Sales of bar coding machinery and software totaled $2.5 billion in 1992 and were projected to be $5 billion by the year 2000. In manufacturing, bar codes were used in item or pallet labeling, receiving, work-in-process, shelf/bin storage, inventory, sales and shipping. Other applications included employee time and attendance, patient tracking, and the tracking of different marketing promotional efforts.

FIGURE 16.2   EXAMPLES OF DIFFERENT TYPES OF SCANNERS

**Cordless
Laser Scanner**

**Hand-Held
Batch Terminal**

**2-Dimensional
Bar Code Scanner**

The heavy retail use of bar codes had forced manufacturers in a variety of industry groups that supply retailers to use bar codes. Large industry groups like health care, government, and chemicals were also beginning to require suppliers to bar code their products. Nonretail bar code applications continued to experience a phenomenal growth rate of fifteen–twenty percent annually. In addition, Jeff noted, "Many small businesses too are recognizing the need for bar code technologies in order to increase efficiency and remain competitive."

In addition to traditional inventory management needs, other innovative uses for bar codes emerged. The Masters golf tournament in Augusta, Georgia, used bar codes on the back of each badge to monitor entry and detect invalid badges. There was usually a waiting list of over 5,000 people trying to get to see this tournament, and black market badges went for up to $3,000. The bar code system successfully detected invalid badges, in and out patterns, and arrival and departure times of attendees.

The variety of uses for bar code technology was phenomenal! Essentially, any computer data entry activity was a potential bar code application. Universities used bar codes on student ID cards to track the courses students had taken and what courses they still needed to take. Prisons purchased bar codes to track prisoner education, demerits, and commissary items. Greenhouses and nurseries used bar codes to help keep track of plants. Hospitals were interested in the use of bar code equipment to track patients, patient diagnosis, and patient medications. The news media reported on the use of bar codes to match customers with baggage as they boarded airplanes to increase the safety of air travel.

As with any lucrative market, substitutes for bar codes had also begun to appear. Microchips were being implanted for identification purposes in high-value goods such as cattle and show dogs. As the price of microchips decreased, usage increased. Toyota planned to use microchip identification devices for opening car doors (doors would have no handles). A key advantage to microchips is that their use eliminates the need for direct laser scanning. A microchip anywhere in the vicinity of the scanner can be identified. Magnetic strips offered other substitutes. Interactive identification systems debited accounts for subscribers on toll highways. Other identification systems, which allowed only the correct key to operate an automobile ignition system, were becoming widespread. Overall, competition and rapid technological developments were growing forces influencing the future of the bar code industry.

The continual emergence of new bar code products also made the management of salable inventory and knowledge of product lines a formidable task. Although product life cycles vary, it is not uncommon for bar code products to have an entire life cycle of less than a year. So, despite rapid inventory turnover, numerous changes in product lines due to ever-increasing speed and quality of printers, development of new fonts, and varying service and support levels often resulted in wholesalers' holding an undesirable level of out-of-date inventory. "In addition to these challenges," Jeff said, "customer requests for demonstrations and trial usage periods result in used inventory that needs to be discounted for sale."

Besides the enormous technological change, the entire bar code industry was experiencing considerable change. Buyouts and takeovers of bar code hardware and software manufacturers and associated distributors were common. While this might be expected in a maturing industry, it still caused substantial turmoil. For example, Ace Tech's two largest local competitors were purchased by large public corporations. Jeff noted, "These industry changes resulted in personnel turnover, customer confusion, product line changes, and service lapses."

As manufacturers consolidated, standard applications packages for bar code opportunities were developed. This resulted in increased standardization, consolidation of weaker competitors, stronger profit margins, and continued rapid growth for the remaining firms.

Sales

Over the past five years, Ace Tech had experienced rapid growth. Annual sales figures and employee counts shown in Table 16.1 told the story.

In 1997, Ace tech had a customer base of nearly 1,000 clients. These clients were approximately 60 percent manufacturing concerns, 20 percent software companies, and 20 percent all other. One group that Ace Tech targeted was software companies who developed bar code applications. Their operations provided a steady stream of revenues.

Ace Tech's sales fell into five general product categories: bar code scanners (40 percent), bar code labels and ribbons (30 percent), bar code printers (15 percent), programming, installing, and designing bar code solutions (10 percent), and printer and scanner repair (5 percent). (See Figure 16.3.) This put Ace Tech in the Standard Industrial Classification (SIC) of wholesaler of computers, peripheral equipment, and software (SIC - 5045), although a secondary SIC classification would be 7373 for the 10 percent of their business involving programming, installing, and designing bar code solutions.

The 5 percent segment (repair) was a new growth area for Ace Tech and was a service which few of their competitors offered—and one that Ace Tech felt they provided particularly well. Jeff said, "We found, quite by accident, that we were as good as anybody at repairing equipment. The other bar code companies were reluctant to

| TABLE 16.1 | GROSS SALES AND AVERAGE NUMBER OF EMPLOYEES BY YEAR | | |

Year	Gross Sales	Average Number of Employees
1992	$31,000	1
1993	$510,000	2
1994	$2,500,000	7
1995	$4,100,000	12
1996	$6,300,000	17

provide that service, but we had some people that loved to get their hands on the hardware, so I let them try it. It amazed me to see how well it worked out. I think that this could be another important market niche for us." Ace Tech also considered the development of proprietary hardware/software products to fill specific customer requirements when there were no prepackaged solutions.

The primary service Ace Tech provided their customers was the ready availability of the right equipment. Maintaining a complete, wide-ranging inventory of bar code hardware and supplies was critical to Ace Tech's success. As stated in the mission, Ace Tech was committed to staying at the forefront of data entry technology and to assisting customers in incorporating bar code technology into their organizations. Ace Tech typically sold the hardware and software to clients, but they also provided bar code labels and printing services for clients who were not interested in purchasing their own bar code equipment.

Customer sales information and projected needs were tracked informally and relatively infrequently. Jeff received an annual list of Ace Tech's largest customers. However, he and the rest of the staff reported that they stayed in constant contact with their customers via e-mail and telephone. The administrative software Ace Tech used did not provide products sold by customer, so rapidly obtaining information for a specific customer, as well as analyzing customer purchase patterns, was a problem.

New competitors were appearing constantly. Because of the rapid growth of the bar code industry and the minimal cost of entry, start-ups were vying for a share of the lucrative market. Large public electronic firms were also trying to develop lines of business that would compete with existing technology. Several of Jeff's competitors had been acquired by large corporations in an attempt to expand market share. While those organizations had access to many resources, they had not developed the personal relationships that Jeff and his team had fostered with their customers.

Jeff felt that continued growth was possible by focusing on expanding product sales to the existing customer base and by adding new geographic territories. Jeff believed that long-term growth for Ace Tech would need to come from integrating sales of newly developed scanning and printing equipment with increased customer service and repair of existing equipment. "Our customer's loyalty depends on our product knowledge and the service we can provide." To that end, Ace Tech's staff constantly received training on new products and regularly attended manufacturer training sessions.

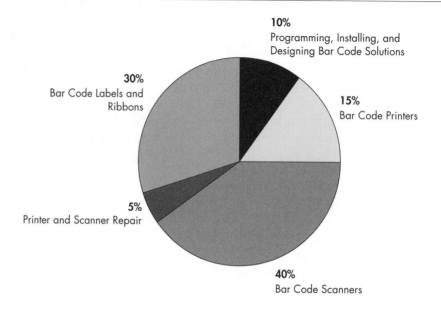

FIGURE 16.3   SALES BY GENERAL PRODUCT CATEGORY

10%
Programming, Installing, and
Designing Bar Code Solutions

15%
Bar Code Printers

30%
Bar Code Labels and
Ribbons

5%
Printer and Scanner Repair

40%
Bar Code Scanners

The company had five independent field sales representatives located in surrounding states. Ace Tech wanted to continue to increase their presence in the Midwest. They planned to add independent sales representatives in five or six additional states. They felt their presence in the Central Time Zone, which offered them a larger core window of accessibility, would help them attract more customers from both coasts. In addition, since many local Midwest competitors had gone national as a result of recent buyouts, Ace Tech's local competition was relatively minimal. They could provide superior service to their customers by focusing primarily on the midwestern region.

Through the Internet, Ace Tech had attracted customers from every state, including Alaska and Hawaii. In addition, they had several Canadian customers and had sold bar code products to customers in Puerto Rico, Barbados, the Philippines, and Mexico.

Internationally, sales were projected to double within the next eight years. Jeff felt the fastest growing market segments for bar code technologies were Latin America and Europe. Jeff and Dan were interested in pursuing these opportunities, but they felt their infrastructure could not cope with the addition of an international business segment. Right now, they were content with responding to demands from international customers without formally pursuing an international marketing effort.

Advertising

Ace Technical had a Web site (see Figure 16.4) and advertised in three national magazines. Many customers expressed interest in buying products over the Internet, but Jeff

FIGURE 16.4   ACE TECHNICAL SERVICES HOME PAGE

Request Ace Catalog

ACE Technical Services

The Bar Code Source

1 800 CALL ACE

Welcome to ACE Technical Services!

We provide our customers access to leading edge bar code marking and bar code data collection technologies. As you discover the enormous advantages of bar code technology, please count on us for the world-class service you deserve.

intranet

Search Ace Tech's Web Site

Contact ACE Technical by E-mail

ACE Technical's Regional Offices

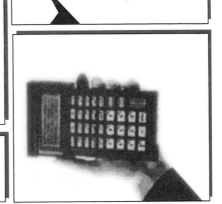

felt the cost to invest in cutting-edge Web-site technology could amount to $20–30,000. This was more of an investment than he and Dan were willing to consider at this time. The option of purchasing via the Internet could possibly upset Ace Tech's existing independent sales representatives, who might lose sales in their territories if customers could order directly from the Internet. Referrals, cold-calls, trade shows, and yellow-page advertising, in that order, were important sources of new customers.

Ace Tech's Employees and Corporate Culture

Jeff insisted, "Top quality, motivated employees are critical to the success of the business." However, good employees were very hard to find, especially at Ace Tech's rate of growth. Jeff and Dan were constantly on the lookout for bright, college-educated people who were very personable. Many new hires at Ace Tech were friends or relatives who had been recommended by an existing employee.

Jeff and Dan's primary concern each day was selling, although increasingly they were distracted by everyday managerial problems. No organizational chart existed, but employees had a good idea of their duties and where they fit within the organization.

Employees at Ace Tech were viewed as associates and treated accordingly. Jeff proudly stated that Ace Tech employees were well compensated with base salary, bonus, and profit sharing. In fact, all seventeen associates, whether in sales (twelve people), technical support (three), accounting (one), or shipping (one), received a base salary plus a bonus based on monthly company sales. Jeff felt that this approach to compensation promoted teamwork and kept everyone focused on meeting customer needs.

Monthly sales goals were progressive throughout the year, with monthly goals being higher at the end of the year (as opposed to an average throughout the year). With annual sales goals that increased by 50 percent from year to year, this graduated process helped to keep morale high, as each month's target was only slightly higher than the previous month's.

Ace Tech promoted a friendly and open office culture. Associates, whose average age was twenty-eight, were allowed to dress casually, play music, and even hold meetings outdoors on nice days. A string of bells was rung in the office for each sale. A company closet contained suits used for formal meetings with clients. Employees enjoyed pizza at the company's expense every Friday if the week's sales goals were met (which was often the case). Ace Tech had a company volleyball team, a lake cabin for use by all associates, and frequent employee gatherings such as riverboat cruises or parties. Rapid growth had made the open culture difficult to maintain. Jeff mentioned that the cabin, intended as a perk for associates, had become a bone of contention. "We have more employees than we have desirable summer weekends."

Each Monday, the entire staff gathered in the early morning for a brief update and discussion of the week's goals and any concerns or issues. At this meeting, associates took turns quizzing each other on the latest developments in the field. In addition, every Monday at noon, one associate was responsible for conducting a technical training session. This might include information on new products, a vendor demonstration, or tips on how to troubleshoot software or hardware problems. The meetings and training sessions helped everyone stay abreast of the many changes in this dynamic industry. Associates commented that the meetings were very informative and inspirational.

Jeff credited the shared sales bonus and the open company culture for a large part of their success. He felt that open communication led to a real synergy that enabled Ace Tech to provide the best service possible to their customers. This open communication style included sharing all information with associates, including financial data on sales and profits.

Generally, decisions at Ace Tech were made by Jeff or Dan after discussion with all involved. While the culture was very open, teams were not used to any great extent. Jeff felt that the use of teams could waste time with too much discussion and not enough results.

Ace Tech did not have a board of directors. Instead, they utilized a not-for-profit service called SCORE (Service Core of Retired Executives), which was offered under the guidance of the Small Business Administration. If Ace Tech was facing an issue where they needed help, they contacted SCORE, who sent out a retired executive, experienced in that area, to meet with them. The company had an accounting firm on retainer but had not yet established a long-term relationship with any law firm.

Internal Technology

Ace Tech had seventeen PCs linked by network software. Each employee had a computer at his desk; three central laser printers were available to all. The administrative system was designed to handle the entire spectrum of needs from inventory to accounting to payroll.

Jeff noted that they were outgrowing their administrative software package and needed to invest in additional software to meet accounting, inventory, and internal reporting needs. Problems with network viruses had caused great concern about the security of their system. In addition, managerial information such as the profitability of specific products, specific customer purchases, sales by area, etc., was not available with the current system.

Jeff said, "My wish list for new software includes the ability to calculate commissions, process returns, track repair orders, produce management reports, and maintain inventory by serial number, just to mention a few." The cost to upgrade was very high in terms of software, hardware, and staff training. Jeff stated, "If we have time to evaluate different packages and free up employees long enough to be trained on a new system, we hope to purchase and install a new system by the end of 1998."

Accounting and Finance

Financial statements from inception through 1996 are shown in Tables 16.2 and 16.3. During that five-year period, Ace Tech's income statement reflects consistent sales growth and rising profits. They had a $900,000 line of credit from a national bank.

The source for additional paid-in-capital was owner reinvestment in the company from their compensation. Current liabilities reflected the high volume of inventory that Ace Tech purchased and warehoused for ready availability for customers.

Ace Tech had one associate whose primary responsibilities were accounting functions. This associate was assisted by other associates on particular tasks such as invoicing and commission payment. Given the breadth of the workload, inventory and accounts receivables were not tightly managed. In addition, short staffing in Ace Tech's

TABLE 16.2	ACE TECHNICAL INCOME STATEMENT				

(In thousands, rounded)

	Dec '92	Dec '93	Dec '94	Dec '95	Dec '96
Sales	$31.0	$510.0	$2,500.0	$4,100.0	$6,300.0
COGS	31.0	377.0	1,900.0	3,200.0	4,600.0
Gross Profit	0.0	133.0	600.0	900.0	1,700.0
Expenses					
Salaries/Commissions	0.0	25.0	374.0	606.0	1,248.0
Rent	0.0	2.0	6.0	8.0	20.0
Utilities	0.3	0.7	2.0	2.0	4.0
Telephone	2.5	6.0	19.0	29.0	49.0
Supplies	0.7	2.0	8.0	9.0	13.0
Advertising	0.7	1.8	21.0	39.0	78.0
Insurance	0.3	0.8	3.0	12.0	20.0
Interest	0.0	1.0	7.0	20.0	22.0
Postage	0.5	2.0	5.0	7.0	9.0
Professional Services	0.0	7.0	14.0	9.0	12.0
Travel	0.0	0.5	23.0	28.0	38.0
Miscellaneous	1.0	1.2	39.0	45.0	81.0
Total Expenses	6.0	50.0	521.0	814.0	1,594.0
Operating Income	(6.0)	83.0	79.0	86.0	106.0
Income Taxes	0.0	19.0	22.0	20.0	31.0
Net Income	(6.0)	64.0	57.0	66.0	75.0

accounting area had sometimes resulted in late payments to suppliers. Ace Tech used an external payroll service.

Office and Warehouse Space

Ace Tech faced an ever-increasing demand for office and warehouse space. The company had moved three times since its inception and had inventory stored in three locations. The result was a logistics nightmare for stocking, packing, distribution, and inventory control. Jeff was searching for solutions to the office and warehouse space issues that could meet the company's needs both now and in the future. One option was to purchase the office building they were currently leasing. Although this provided sufficient space for existing needs, including consolidation of current dispersed storage, there was no extra office or storage space available. However, Jeff had a sentimental attachment to this building which his father had built for use by the construction company that he founded. In considering the purchase option, he was also examining whether to buy the building personally and lease it back to the company or to have Ace Tech purchase the building. Other options were also under consideration,

TABLE 16.3	ACE TECHNICAL BALANCE SHEET				

(In thousands)

	Dec '92	Dec '93	Dec '94	Dec '95	Dec '96
ASSETS					
Cash	$ 0	$ 2	$ 3	$ 36	$ 31
Inventory	1	48	147	341	725
Accounts Receivable	17	161	364	598	882
Fixed Assets	8	9	32	42	62
Total	26	220	546	1,017	1,700
LIABILITIES					
Current Liabilities	$16	$138	$432	$ 817	$1,371
Long-Term Liabilities	7	6	6	7	10
Total Liabilities	23	144	438	824	1,381
Paid-in Capital	9	18	18	38	88
Retained Earnings	(6)	(6)	32	89	156
Year-to-Date Earnings	0	64	58	66	75
Total Capital	3	76	107	193	319
Total Capital & Liabilities	26	220	546	1,017	1,700

including leasing space about 15 miles from the current location. Extra expansion space was available at this location.

The Future

Ace Tech projected sales growth to continue at the impressive rate of 50 percent annually, which Jeff believed would make them approximately number 200 on the Inc. 500 list in 1997. Jeff and Dan were in the process of hiring three additional sales representatives. They were also hoping to establish additional independent sales representatives throughout the midwest. Planned capital investments included office and warehouse space, new administrative software, and the enhancement of their Web site.

As he sat in his office, Jeff pondered how his business had exceeded his expectations. "What is coming in the next five years?" he wondered out loud. "Ace Tech has been very successful, but will doing the things that brought me here continue to guarantee success?" Jeff was proud of what he had accomplished thus far. As he contemplated his situation, he became increasingly sure of only one thing. He knew that he wanted to hold on to the business he had grown. In some ways, he felt like a proud parent who had given birth to the company and wanted to watch it grow and mature even further.

Could an updated strategic plan help Jeff answer his questions and concerns? What would he need to do to formulate a viable plan for the future? What steps could he take to stay ahead of the competition? What would he need to do to stay successful?

17

Ethical Dilemmas in Business Marketing

Individuals in marketing and sales positions are frequently confronted by ethical problems and dilemmas. The scenarios presented below were real situations faced by individuals during their first year on the job after graduation from college. After reading each scenario you should decide what action you would have taken.

1. I presently sell a line of industrial compressors to customers and the standard sales pitch indicates that they are the best for the money available in the market. Unfortunately, I also know that this isn't true. However, they make up 40 percent of my line and I cannot successfully make my quota without selling at least $85,000 worth per month. It's probably okay, because all salespersons say theirs are the best.

   Would you take the same selling approach?

2. My field sales manager drinks excessively and has accompanied me on sales calls hung over and smelling of alcohol. This behavior does not enhance my professional reputation with my customers or the company. I have decided not to say anything, as the field sales manager writes my review and can dramatically influence my success or failure in this, my first selling assignment.

   Would you report the sales manager to upper level management?

3. I am working for a large company which is heavily involved in defense contracts. I have recently been transferred to a new division that builds nuclear weapons. These are weapons of which the public is not aware and of which I do not personally approve. However, our work is entirely legal and classified top secret. I have decided to stay with the company because I find my work challenging and I am not directly involved with any phase of the actual nuclear component of the project.

   If you had similar attitudes, would you stay with the company?

4. I recently had the opportunity to buy a new . . . computer, printer, and software for $1,000 from our MIS Director. He apparently received these items

---

SOURCE: These scenarios were developed by Professor John B. Gifford and Jan Willem Bol, Miami University. They were part of a study of the ethical problems recent business school graduates faced on their first job.

"free" with a large computer order for the company. I would be doing mostly work for the company at home on the computer. I decided to accept his offer and paid him $1,000 cash.

What action would you have taken?

5. After a business dinner with an important client in California, he implied that he wanted to go out and "do the town" plus. . . . Although I wasn't sure what the "plus" might involve, there was a 50/50 chance he wanted an affair on the side. I said I was tired, and retired alone for the evening. I also lost the account which had been a 90 percent sure thing.

What action would you have taken?

6. By coincidence, your salesperson and your distributor are both pitching your product to the same prospect. The distributor, however, does not know this yet. You know that when he finds out he will offer a competitor's product that will most certainly undercut your price. Your salesperson is totally dependent on commission.

Should you ask your salesperson to back off?

7. A buyer for a large government institution (a good prospect with potentially high volume) offers you information about the sealed bids of competitors. You know the practice is questionable, but he is a good friend and no one is likely to find out. Besides, you are below quota, and need the commission badly.

Will you accept his offer?

8. An industrial customer has indicated that our lubricants were priced about 5 percent higher than those being offered by our competition. He indicated that if I would drop my price $7\frac{1}{2}$ percent, he would cancel his order with our competition and buy from me. This will mean a $1,400 commission for me personally. I agreed.

What action would you have taken?

9. As an industrial salesperson, you are in the office of a prospect to provide a verbal price on a project. You and your sales manager have determined that a specific price is the right price for your organization and you believe you will win the contract. However, as the prospect walks out of his office you see a copy of your competitor's proposal on his desk with a substantially lower price. You will need to give him your price now, as he walks back into the room.

Will you change your price?

10. I have a set quota of goods that I must sell every month. Sometimes it becomes necessary to overstock my customers in order to meet my quota. Most of the customers are not very sophisticated, and don't even know how much inventory they should carry.

Is this an appropriate sales tactic?

Names are found within text and in the footnotes.

Aaker, David A., 292, 295, 401, 411
Abell, Derek F., 290
Abernathy, William J., 395
Adams, Arthur J., 212, 219
Adidam, Phon Tej, 230
Allaway, Arthur W., 380
Allred, Doug, 485, 486, 497
Alonzo, Vincent, 441
Alpert, Shell R., 420
Alsop, Stewart, 68, 136
Ames, B. Charles, 7, 454
Anderson, Erin, 57, 74–75, 375, 380–381
Anderson, James, 89, 98–100, 375–377, 384, 387
Anderson, Matthew G., 35–39
Andreeson, Mark, 485
Ash, Steven R., 677–691
Ash, Victoria, 677–691
Assael, Henry, 333, 334
Athaide, Gerard A., 318
Auerbach, Jon G., 347
Augustine, Scott, 641
Axelson, Barbara, 426

Baatz, Elizabeth, 37
Bagozzi, Richard, 447–448
Baldridge, Malcolm, 548
Banting, Peter, 76
Baptista, J. P. A., 174, 178, 234, 285, 312
Barclay, Donald W., 437
Barich, Howard, 183, 184
Barko, Randy, 556
Barnes, Hank, 118
Barnett, William, 195
Barro, John, 604, 605
Bartlett, Michael, 31
Batchelor, Charles, 144
Baum, 662
Becker, Garrett, 12
Beik, Leland L., 472
Belew, Bill, 656
Bellizzi, Joseph A., 71, 180, 416, 449
Bello, Daniel C., 379
Belonax, Joseph J., 71
Bennion, Mark J. Jr., 188

Bensaou, M., 96
Berlont, Debbie, 474
Berry, Leonard R., 336, 344
Betrand, Kate, 430
Bharadwaj, Sundar G., 230
Bienstock, Carol C., 195
Bitner, Mary Jo, 334, 338
Black, William C., 447
Blackman, Douglas A., 24, 376
Blankenhorn, Dana, 120
Blauvelt, Valerie, 359
Bleek, 551
Boatman, Harvey, 609–614
Bochart, Brad, 19
Boewadt, Robert J., 391–392
Boles, James, 72
Bolt, James F., 378
Bond, Edward, 7
Bonoma, Thomas V., 76, 426, 427, 438, 475, 477
Bottensak, Jane, 532, 534–536
Boughton, Paul D., 405
Bowman, Edward H., 477
Boyle, Lucy, 533
Bradley, Peter, 157
Brewer, Daniel J., 42
Brewer, Peter C., 140, 145
Bromiley, Philip, 325
Browder, Seanna, 232
Brown, Dan, 680, 686, 688–689, 691
Brown, Ed, 532, 534, 536
Brown, Eyrn, 122
Brown, Shona L., 176, 177, 306, 312–314
Brown, Steven P., 445, 447
Brown, Stuart F., 140
Brown, Tobias O., 130
Browning, Reese, 474
Brunelli, Mark A., 40
Bucklin, Louis P., 358
Bulgrin, Jim, 533
Bunn, Michele D., 58
Buody, William, 151
Burdick, Richard K., 65, 77, 183
Burgelman, Robert A., 239, 307–308
Bush, Victoria D., 445
Butler, Charles, 444

Buzby, Stephen L., 472
Byrnes, Jonathon L. S., 161

Cadman, Chris, 628
Cage, Kevin, 615–617, 619–621
Calantone, Roger, 324
Caldwell, Bruce, 156
Callahan, Sean, 414
Campbell, Charles, 592
Campbell, Nigel C. G., 438
Cannell, Eric, 530–537
Cannon, Joseph P., 19, 90–91, 93–95
Capon, Noel, 176
Carbone, James, 18, 41, 70, 71, 73
Cardozo, Richard N., 174, 178, 187, 189–190
Carr, John, 654, 657
Casey, Michael, 130, 134
Castleberry, Stephen B., 443
Cateora, Phillip R., 378
Caudron, Shari, 421
Cauley, Leslie, 270
Cavusgil, Tamer, 380
Cespedes, Frank V., 18, 98, 175, 191, 228, 286, 358, 371, 372, 386–387, 462
Chambers, John, 433, 485, 506
Chang, Dae R., 368
Chaples, Sherry S., 175
Chapman, Timothy L., 51
Chew, W. Bruce, 394
Cho, Dong Sung, 92–93
Cho, Stephan, 504
Choffray, Jean-Marie, 78, 82, 317
Christensen, Clayton M., 243
Chu, Wujin, 57, 74, 92–93
Churchill, Gilbert A. Jr., 440, 445, 446, 447
Clark, Kim B., 311, 312
Clausing, Don P., 323
Clifford, Patricia Gorman, 280–281
Clifton, Sally, 592
Clinton, Bill, 675
Cohen, Andy, 56, 435, 442
Cohen, Barbara G., 209
Coles, Gary L., 187
Collins, 682

Comer, James M., 448
Conlon, Ginger, 122, 453
Cooper, Martha C., 141–142, 444
Cooper, Pete, 594
Cooper, Robert G., 316–317, 324, 326
Cooper, Robin, 393–394, 473–474, 476
Copacino, William C., 161
Coppe, Grieg, 150
Corey, E. Raymond, 71, 72, 358, 371, 372
Cort, Stanton G., 419
Coughlan, Anne, 380–381
Cowell, Donald, 342, 343, 345, 350
Cowles, Deborah, 439
Cox, Edwin L., 631–641
Cox, William E. Jr., 198, 206
Coyne, Kevin P., 280–281
Craig, C. Samuel, 269, 271–273
Cravens, David W., 289, 448, 450–452
Cron, William L., 445, 447
Crosby, Lawrence A., 375, 439
Crow, Lowell E., 82
Culley, James D., 187
Czinkota, Michael R., 259, 261, 264, 265

Dahlstrom, Robert, 295
Dalrymple, Douglas J., 218
D'Amico, Michael F., 370
D'Aveni, Richard A., 175, 384, 397
Davenport, Thomas H., 268, 333
Davidow, William H., 337, 340
Davis, Jeffery, 130
Davis, Robert A., 445
Dawes, Phillip L., 76
Day, George S., 5, 88, 89, 90, 102, 226, 227, 229, 230, 231, 233, 259, 260, 280, 289, 292, 395–396, 464, 469–470
De Brentani, Ulrike, 351, 353
Dean, Joel, 400
Deeter-Schmelz, Dawn R., 437
DeFazio, John L., 421
Dempsey, William, 434
Derocher, Robert P., 140
Deschamps, Jean-Phillippe, 394
Deshpande, Rohit, 5
Diamantopoulous, A., 219
Dickinson, Melvyn, 651
Dickson, Peter R., 77, 78
Dolan, Robert, 387, 390–391, 400–401
Donnelly, James H., 338
Dorf, Bob, 423, 439

Dougherty, Deborah, 477
Dougherty, Patricia J., 167, 320
Douglas, Susan P., 254, 269, 271–273, 291
Dowst, Somerby, 65
Doyle, Peter, 188
Dozbaba, Mary Siegfried, 42, 65
Drucker, Peter, 226–227
Dubinsky, Alan J., 447
Duffy, Roberta J., 37
Duffy, Stephen, 150
Dunlap, Billy, 533
Dyer, Jeffrey H., 43, 92–93

Eby, Frank H., 216
Edison, Steven W., 230
Edmonston, Jack, 412
Eiseman, Ben, 593
Eisenhardt, Kathleen M., 176, 177, 244, 306, 312–314, 326, 460
Eisenhart, Tom, 420
El-Ansary, Adel I., 367, 377, 445
Eldreth, Fred L., 594
Elizalde, Todd, 486–487, 489, 492, 496–499
Elliott, Heidi, 362
Ellram, Lisa, 159
Enis, Ben M., 445
Erickson, Tamara J., 311
Ernst, 551
Estridge, P. D., 307
Evans, Kenneth R., 439

Faherenwald, Bill, 144
Faris, Charles W., 56–57
Farley, John U., 5
Farrell, Mark A., 78
Fearon, Harold E., 45
Feder, Barnaby J., 376
Fein, Adam J., 362
Ferguson, Wade, 42, 284
Fildes, Robert, 219
Fisher, Marshall, 150
Fishman, Lloyd, 656
Fites, Donald V., 268, 349
Fitzgerald, Kevin R., 14
Fojt, Martin, 433
Ford, David, 76
Ford, Neil M., 440, 445, 446, 447
Foster, George, 474
Foster, Thomas A., 159
Franklin, Jeff, 677–680, 685–686, 688–691
Frankwick, Gary L., 237, 238, 319, 321, 477
Fraser, Cynthia, 188

French, Michael T., 200
Frentzel, David G., 143
Frook, John Evan, 409, 419
Frost, Raymond, 133, 198
Fry, Art, 307
Fuller, Joseph B., 154, 161
Futrell, Charles M., 445, 447

Gage, Deborah, 134
Galbraith, Craig S., 217
Gale, Bradley T., 284, 285, 384, 403
Garda, Robert A., 182, 399, 401–402
Gardner, Alston, 72
Garrett, Paula L., 419
Gentry, Julie, 164
George, William R., 338
Georgoff, David M., 211, 219
Geroski, Paul A., 176
Gerstner, Lou, 561, 563
Gertz, Dwight L., 174, 178, 234, 285, 312
Ghingold, Morry, 56, 57
Gilbertson, Michael, 631–641
Gilmore, Thomas N., 246
Gilson, Peter W., 587–588
Giunipero, Larry C., 42
Glazer, Rashi, 68, 176
Goizueta, Robert, 77
Golden, James E., 208, 213
Goldstine, Jonathan, 295, 296, 330
Gomes, Lee, 331
Goodman, Chuck, 605
Gooley, Toby, 162
Gopalakrishna, Srinath, 426, 428, 429
Gordon, Ian H., 97
Gore, Bob, 589, 591, 592, 593, 596
Gore, Genevieve (Vieve), 581–582, 589, 593
Gore, Sally, 591, 596, 599
Gore, Wilbert L., 580, 581–582, 586, 588–589, 592–594
Goulet, Peter G., 658–676
Graham, John L., 438
Green, Paul E., 218
Gregor, William T., 469
Grewal, Dhruv, 160
Griffin, Abbie, 320, 323
Gronroos, Christian, 338
Gross, Andrew, 76
Gross, Irwin, 389, 390
Grove, Andrew S., 239
Grover, Rajiv, 321
Groves, Gwyn, 143
Guadagno, Angelo, 210
Guiltinan, Joseph P., 344, 403

Gunther, Robert, 175
Gupta, Ajay, 51
Gustin, Craig M., 167
Guyot, Eric, 253

Hahn, Mini, 368
Hall, Stephen J. D., 280–281
Halpert, Mark, 655
Hamby, Larry, 332
Hamel, Gary, 176, 186, 226, 239,
    279–281, 306, 309–310, 318, 460
Hamilton, David P., 262
Hammer, Michael, 330
Hancock, William A., 403
Hannon, Neal J., 116, 123, 126
Hanrahan, Timothy, 334
Hansotia, Behram J., 292–294
Hardy, Kenneth G., 375
Harper, Doug, 376
Harps, Leslie Hansen, 168
Harris, Kim, 454
Harrison, E. Frank, 468
Hass, Robert D., 44
Hastings, Robert, 219
Hauser, John R., 320, 322, 323
Havens, George N., 198
Hawes, Jon M., 183, 439
Hayes, H. Michael, 642–657
Hearn, Trish, 589
Heath, D. C., 259
Hector, Hans Werner, 622
Heide, Jan B., 58, 68, 367, 375
Heil, Mark, 606
Henderson, Brice, 642–657
Henderson, John C., 119
Henkoff, Ronald, 156
Herbig, Paul A., 208, 213, 426
Herzog, Raymond E., 411
Heskett, James L., 339, 342, 350,
    377
Hill, John S., 380
Hill, Ron, 594
Hirsh, Evan, 356, 359
Hite, Robert E., 449
Hlavacek, James D., 454
Hogue, Thomas, 286
Holcomb, Mary Collins, 141, 159
Holmes, George, 76
Hopp, Dieter, 622, 628
Houston, Michael J., 237
Hout, Thomas M., 186
Howard, John A., 58, 82
Howell, Jane M., 308
Hoyt, Bryan R., 658–676
Hubis, Dan, 592
Huerlmann, Chad, 531–532
Hulbert, James, 469–471

Hummer, Francis E., 199
Hunt, Shelby D., 14, 88, 90, 377
Hutt, Michael D., 7, 77, 103, 106–
    107, 237, 238, 246, 307–308,
    319, 321, 366, 437, 476, 477

Ingram, Thomas, 445, 448

Jackson, Barbara B., 385, 406, 443
Jackson, Donald W. Jr., 65, 77, 183,
    370, 375
Jackson, Ralph, 341
Jacobs, Karen, 15
Jacobsen, Robert, 401
Jacques, Philip F., 424
Jain, Subhash C., 255, 290
Jap, Sandy D., 362
Jaworski, Bernard J., 5, 227, 467
Jayachandran, Satish, 279
Jeuland, Abel, 400–401
Joachimsthaler, Erich, 411
Jocz, Katherine E., 235
Johanson, Jan, 272
John, George, 375
Johnson, James C., 164
Johnson, Paul, 300, 452
Johnston, Mark W., 440, 447
Johnston, Wesley J., 69, 72, 73, 76,
    80–81, 419, 437, 438, 444
Jolibert, Alain, 438
Jones, Eli, 448
Jones, Ray, 656, 657
Jones, Thomas O., 285, 339
Juliano, Phil, 572
Jurvetson, Steve, 309

Kahl, Steven, 149
Kahn, Kenneth B., 219
Kalkota, Ravi, 26, 59, 113–114
Kanter, Rosabeth Moss, 88, 102,
    104, 106, 551
Kapala, Bob, 533
Kaplan, Robert S., 460–463, 473–
    474, 476
Kaplan, Soren M., 240–243, 319
Kapp, Sue, 207
Kastiel, Diane Lynn, 345
Katrichis, Jerome M., 77
Katz, Paul K., 35–39
Katzenbach, Jon R., 321
Kaufman, Leslie, 47
Kaydo, Chad, 131, 359, 360
Keeling, Dennis, 622, 628
Keenan, William Jr., 209
Keiningham, Timothy L., 340

Keith, Janet E., 65, 77, 183, 375
Kendall, David L., 200
Keon, Shawn, 261
Kerin, Roger A., 631–641
Kesseler, Jim, 133, 135
Kijewski, Valerie, 389, 410, 416
Kilpatrick, Jim, 140
Kim, W. Chan, 186, 188, 243
King, Ronald H., 80
Kippola, Tom, 300, 452
Kirkpatrick, David, 240
Kirshnan, H. Shanker, 467
Klahr, Philip, 333
Kleinschmidt, Elko J., 316–317,
    324, 326
Knight, Chris, 628–629
Knopp, John, 434
Kohli, Ajay K., 5, 78, 227
Kohnstamm, Abby, 561
Kortge, G. Deane, 389
Kosnik, Thomas J., 261, 263
Kotler, Philip, 22, 182, 468–469,
    475
Kreutzberg, Kipp, 518–520
Krishnan, M. S., 285
Kuzmack, Joan, 520
Kwolck, Stephenie L., 307

Laczniak, Gene R., 74
Ladwig, Anne, 617–621
Laester, Timothy M., 36, 257
LaForge, Raymond W., 448,
    450–452
Lalonde, Bernard J., 159
Lambert, David R., 419
Lambert, Douglas M., 141–142,
    158
Lancaster, Geoffrey A., 208, 210
Lankton, Gordon B., 538, 542, 543,
    546, 548–551, 555–558
Lapidies, Robert, 426
Laseter, Timothy M., 69, 181–182
LeBlanc, Ronald P., 82
Lee, Elizabeth, 605
Leenders, Michael R., 45
LeGere, Amy, 584
Lehmann, Donald R., 44, 183, 235
Lei, David, 543
Leigh, Thomas W., 445
Levitt, Theodore, 254, 286
Levy, Michael, 160
Lewin, Jeffrey E., 73, 80–81
Lewis, Jordan D., 6, 69, 88
Lewis, Linda, 517
Liakko, Timo, 76
Lichtenthal, J. David, 4
Lieb, Robert C., 167

Lief, Verda, 130
Light, Larry, 295, 296, 330
Liguori, Paul, 609–614
Lilien, Gary L., 73, 76, 78–79, 82, 317, 426, 429
Listwin, Don, 486
Liukko, Timo, 180
Lodish, Leonard M., 375
Loewe, Pierre M., 255
Lohr, Steve, 63, 68
Lohtia, Ritu, 419
Lomas, Robert A., 208, 210
Lovelock, Christopher H., 254, 257
Lucas, George H. Jr., 445
Lunsford, Dale A., 341
Lyons, David, 629

MacIver, Neil, 69
Madhavan, Ravindranath, 321
Madsen, Tammy L., 272, 444
Magee, John F., 311
Magrath, Allan J, 375
Mahajan, Vijay, 401
Mahmaud, Essam, 218
Maidique, Modesto A., 308
Majumdar, Sumit K., 358
Makridakis, Spyros, 210, 212, 214, 218
Mandel, Michael J., 112
Mandrodt, Karl B., 141
Mange, Paul O., 51
Marchetti, Michele, 433
Marsh, Peter, 169
Marshak, Ronni T., 177
Mast, Kenneth E., 183, 439
Mathews, Anna Wilde, 164
Mathews, Brian P., 219
Matthews, Robert Guy, 15
Mauborgne, R., 186, 188, 243
McBride, Anita, 581, 591
McCann, Joseph E., 246
McCarter, Dave, 591, 597
McCarthy, Daniel J., 538
McCarthy, Kathryn, 130
McConville, Daniel J., 163
McDonald, George, 532
McElroy, James C., 447
McGrath, 147
McGuire, Maureen, 409
McKenna, Regis, 226, 279, 289, 396
McNeilly, Kevin M., 448
McQuarrie, Edward F., 207
McQuiston, Daniel H., 77, 78
McTavish, Ronald, 477
McWilliams, Gary, 17, 178
McWilliams, Robert D., 73, 420

Mehta, Shanti, 599
Mehta, Stephanie N., 45
Meissner, Hans Gunther, 438
Mendel, Arthur H., 404
Menon, Anil, 230
Mentzer, John T., 195
Merrill, Gregory B., 217
Metz, Peter, 161
Meuter, Matt, 7
Meyer, Marc H., 312
Michaels, Ronald E., 447
Milewicz, John, 208, 213
Millar, Victor E., 14
Miller, Stephen C., 334
Miner, Anne S., 314
Mintzberg, Henry, 306
Mitri, Michel, 380
Mohr, Jacqueline J., 416, 518–529
Mokwa, Michael P., 246, 468, 475
Monroe, Kent B., 394, 401, 403
Montgomery, David B., 395–396
Montoya, Mitzi M., 324
Moore, Geoffrey A., 241, 298–302, 397, 452
Moore, James W., 168
Moorman, Christine, 236, 314
Morehouse, James E., 143
Morgan, Robert M., 14, 88, 90, 377
Moriarty, Mark M., 212, 219
Moriarty, Rowland T., 72, 184, 263, 442, 443
Morrall, Katherine, 447
Morrill, John E., 410
Morris, Betsy, 11
Morris, Michael H., 341
Mosko, John, 596
Moyer, Reed, 391–392
Mullich, Joe, 157
Murdick, Robert G., 211, 219
Murphy, Elana Epatko, 21
Murphy, Paul R., 164
Murray, Keith B., 345

Nadel, Jack, 379
Nagle, Thomas T., 384
Narus, James, 89, 98–100, 375–377, 384, 387
Narver, John C., 5, 206, 227, 465
Nasser, Jacques, 17
Nathan, Sara, 112
Naumann, Earl, 73, 420
Nayak, P. Ranganath, 394
Neidell, Lester A., 341
Neisser, U., 79
Nelson, Margaret, 406
Nevens, T. Michael, 312
Noble, Charles H., 246, 475

Norregaard, Hans, 531–532
Norton, David P., 460–463

O'Connor, James, 154, 161
O'Donoghue, John, 500, 502
O'Hara, Brad, 426
Ohmae, Kenichi, 103, 262, 264, 275, 551
O'Keefe, Robert M., 128
Okonkwo, Patrick A., 389
Oliver, Richard L., 449
Olshavsky, Richard W., 82
Olson, Eric M., 322
O'Neal, Charles, 437
O'Neill, William J., 216
Oosthuizen, Pierre, 341
O'Shaughnessy, John, 44, 183

Page, Albert L., 288, 315, 322
Pagh, James D., 141–142
Palmisano, Sam, 562, 576
Palumbo, Fred, 426
Panitz, Eric, 445
Paranka, Stephen, 405
Parasuraman, A., 336, 344, 445, 447
Park, C. Whan, 424
Parkhe, A., 105, 264
Parry, Mark E., 325
Patten, Carol, 136
Patterson, John, 41
Patterson, Paul G., 76
Patton, W. E. III, 80
Pelika, Jolanta, 114
Peñaz, Jan, 648–649, 650
Pendleton, Joseph P., 513, 517
Pepper, Joseph W., 642–643, 652, 657
Peppers, Don, 423, 439
Perreault, William D., Jr., 19, 90–91, 93–95
Perry, David, 357
Peterson, Robert A., 447
Piercy, Nigel, 415–416, 470
Pitt, Leyland, 341
Pittiglio, 147
Plank, Richard E., 295, 434, 439
Plattner, Hasso, 622–623
Platzer, Linda Cardillo, 443
Pohlen, Terrance L., 159
Pollins, Ellen Bolman, 439
Porter, Ann Millen, 4, 21, 284, 286
Porter, Grover, 530, 532–534, 537
Porter, Michael E., 10, 14, 234, 266–269, 291, 311, 478

Poueymirou, Roger, 404
Prahalad, C. K., 176, 239, 279–282, 285, 318
Puffer, Sheila, 538
Puto, Charles P., 80

Queram, Bonnie, 655
Quinn, Francis J., 141, 143, 147
Quinn, James Brian, 21, 23, 176, 228, 232, 233, 280, 283, 306–307, 331

Rab, Linda, 419
Rabin, 147
Ramaswamy, Venkatram, 358
Ramsey, Rosemary, 437
Randall, Hugh L., 167
Rands, G., 107
Rangan, U. Srinivasa, 103, 104, 108
Rangan, V. Kasturi, 184, 358, 371, 372
Rawlinson, Richard, 154, 161
Redwood, Mark, 128
Reichheld, Frederick F., 339–340
Reid, David A., 295, 439
Reingen, Peter H., 77, 103, 106–107, 237, 238, 307–308
Reinhardt, Andy, 177, 232
Reinhardt, Forest L., 258
Reynolds, Eric, 592
Richtel, Matt, 436
Ring, Peter Smith, 105, 107
Ritterskamp, James J., Jr., 403
Rivera, Ed., 546
Robertson, Thomas S., 183, 184, 188
Robinson, Marcia, 26, 59
Robinson, Patrick J., 56–57
Rodriguez, Karen, 333
Roering, Kenneth J., 237
Rogers, Martha, 423, 439
Rogers, William III, 469
Ronchetto, John R., 77, 307–308, 437
Ronkainen, Ilka A., 259, 261, 265
Root, Franklin R., 259
Rostky, George, 391
Roth, Martin S., 424
Rountree, Debbie, 655
Rousell, Philip A., 311
Roush, Matt, 125
Rudelius, William, 631–641
Ruekert, Robert W., 237, 322
Rule, Eric, 261
Rumar, Dave, 119

Russ, Frederick A., 448
Rust, Roland T., 236, 340
Ryans, Adrian B., 450–451

Saad, Komol N., 311
Sabath, Robert E., 143
Saenz, 664
Sager, Ira, 24
Sager, Jeffrey K., 447
Samuel, David M., 71
Sanders, Nada, 212, 219
Santefemia, Frank, 488
Sasser, W. Earl, 285, 339–340
Saunders, John, 188
Schellhardt, Timothy D., 307
Schlessinger, Leonard A., 339
Schneedler, David E., 174, 183
Schroder, Bill, 78
Scott, Stan, 73, 420
Segalo, A. Michael, 211, 214
Sequeira, Ian K., 426
Sexton, Jack, 609
Seybold, Patricia B., 177, 348
Shaikh, Muzaffar A., 292–294
Shapiro, Benson P., 72, 287, 385, 442, 443
Sharma, Arun, 160, 442
Sharrard, Jeremy, 130
Shaw, Gordon, 325
Shaw, Vivienne, 435
Sherman, Stratford, 236, 265
Sheth, Jagdish N., 58, 78, 80, 82, 290, 292–294
Shipper, Frank, 580–602
Shoham, Aviv, 427
Shostack, G. Lynn, 335
Siemplenski, Michael, 288
Silberman, Sally J., 374
Silver, Bernard, 680–681
Silverstein, Barry, 358, 420, 422, 423, 436, 437
Simpson, James T., 79
Sinton, Chris, 483, 485–487, 494, 496, 500–503, 506
Slagmulder, Regine, 393
Slater, Stanley F., 5, 206, 227, 231, 465–466
Slatter, Stuart St. P., 404
Slocum, John W., Jr., 543
Smart, Rosemary, 201
Smith, Daniel C., 435
Smith, Douglas K., 321
Smith, J. Brock, 437
Smith, J. Todd, 605, 606
Smith, Todd, 605
Song, X. Michael, 325
Sonnack, Mary, 318–319

Speh, Thomas W., 140, 145, 166, 246, 366, 477
Spekman, Robert E., 69
Spencer, John, 585
Stack, James R., 158
Stafford, Edwin R., 103, 106–107
Stalk, George Jr., 186
Stank, Theodore P., 167
Starkman, Dean, 15
Stathakopoulus, Vlasis, 467
Stephenson, Susie, 51
Stern, Louis W., 367, 372, 373, 377
Stewart, David W., 69
Stickney, Bill, 604, 605, 607–608
Strauss, Judy, 133, 198
Streeter, Sara, 518–529
Strong, James T., 439
Stump, Rodney L., 318
Sturdivant, Frederick D., 367, 372, 373
Sujan, Harish, 434
Sujan, Mita, 434
Sultan, Ralph, 395
Summe, Gregory L., 312
Summers, John O., 82
Sutton, Howard, 249, 377, 442
Swan, John E., 439
Swartz, Gordon S., 184
Sweeny, Jack, 47
Szymanski, David M., 434

Tabrizi, Behnam N., 326
Tadepalli, Raghu, 474
Takahashi, Dean, 23
Tanner, John F., Jr., 438, 440
Tanzer, Andrew, 157
Taylor, Alex III, 287
Taylor, Thayer C., 434, 441
Teas, R. Kenneth, 447
Temkin, Bruce D., 130
Thomas, Jim, 157
Thomas, Robert J., 215
Thomko, Stefan, 318–319
Thompson, Richard H., 141
Thorman, Ethan, 490–491, 506
Tichy, Noel M., 236, 265
Tietje, Brian, 227
Tiplitz, Paul V., 208
Todd, 147
Tonnesen, Mark, 485, 494–495, 497, 499–500, 506
Toy, Norman, 469–471
Troy, David, 118
Troyer, Charles L., 153
Tschira, Klaus, 622
Tull, Donald S., 218

Uttal, Bro, 312, 337, 340
Utterback, James M., 312

Valenta, James, 654
Valsamakis, Vassilios, 143
Van de Ven, Andrew H., 105, 107
Van Meighem, Timothy, 156
Varadarajan, P. Rajan, 279, 447
Venkatesh, R., 78
Venkatraman, N., 119
Vigoroso, Mark, 60–61, 63, 65
Von Hippel, Eric, 318–319
Vuori, Risto, 76, 180

Walker, Beth A., 7, 103, 106–107,
    237, 319, 321, 477
Walker, Orville C., 237, 322, 440,
    445, 446, 447
Walton, James A., 306
Wansink, Brian, 530–537
Ward, James C., 237, 238
Ward, Scott, 295, 296, 330
Warlow, Danile L., 164
Warner, Fara, 256
Warner, Melanie, 11, 253
Warren, Susan, 15
Washburn, Stewart A., 212
Wayne, Kenneth, 395
Wayne, Leslie, 49
Weber, James E., 677–691
Weber, Paula Schmidt, 677–691
Webster, Frederick E., Jr., 5, 6, 19,
    75, 101, 235, 261, 462

Weinberg, Charles B., 450–451
Weiss, Allen M., 58, 68
Weitz, Barton A., 57, 74, 375, 434
Welch, John F. Jr., 11, 103, 244, 330
Wensley, Robin, 231, 233
Werner, Curt, 117, 122
West, Douglas C., 200
Wheeler, Steven, 356, 359
Wheelwright, Steven C., 210, 212,
    311, 312
Whinston, Andrew B., 113–114
Whipple, 682
White, Gregory L., 4, 15, 16, 129,
    134
White, Joseph B., 17
Wicks, Tom, 515
Wiedershein-Paul, Finn, 272
Willenbring, Carol D., 658–676
Williams, Jerome D., 426, 428
Williamson, Nicholas C., 379
Willis, Raymond, 213
Wilson, Dan, 511, 512, 516–517
Wilson, David T., 56, 79, 385
Wilson, Elizabeth J., 79, 188
Wind, Yoram, 56–57, 75, 174, 178,
    188–190, 254, 291, 401
Winick, Bernard S., 439
Winkler, Robert L., 218
Winslow, Ron, 129
Winterling, Bob, 584–585
Wiser, Gary, 609–614
Withey, John J., 445
Witkowski, Ted, 532, 534, 536
Wolf, Bill, 511
Wong, M. Anthony, 73, 76

Wood, Donald F., 164
Woodland, Norman Joseph,
    680–681
Woodside, Arch G., 71, 73, 76, 180,
    188, 450
Woronoff, Jon, 264
Wotruba, Thomas R., 433, 443
Wren, Brent M., 79
Wright, Lauren K., 331
Wyman, John, 442

Yeck, John D., 420
Yeoh, Poh-lin, 380
Yip, George S., 254, 255, 257, 258,
    264, 272, 274, 291, 444
Yoder, Stephen Kreider, 302
Yoon, Eunsang, 389, 410, 416
Yoshino, Michael Y., 103, 104, 108,
    255
Young, Clifford E., 448
Yovovich, B. G., 206

Zahorik, Anthony J., 340
Zahra, Shaker A., 175
Zaltman, Gerald, 78
Zangwill, Willard I., 322
Zeithaml, Valarie A., 334, 336, 338,
    344

Boldfaced page numbers refer to definitions of terms.

Abbott Laboratories, 546–547, 555
ABC system. *See* Activity-based cost
    (ABC) system
ABS Consultants, 536
Ace Technical, 677–691
Acquisition costs, 386
Activity-based cost (ABC) sys-
    tem, 159, **473**–474, 476
Advance Shipping Notice (ASN),
    167
Advanced Research Projects
    Agency, 114
Advertising
    benefit focus of, 417, 418
    budgeting for, 414–416
    business publications and,
      417–418
    business-to-business advertising
      management, 412–421
    buyer motivations and, 417
    case study on, 560–579
    characteristics of effective ads,
      418–419
    costs of, 419
    creative strategy statement and,
      414
    database marketing, 421
    direct mail, 420–421
    direct marketing tools, 419–420
    evaluation of effectiveness of,
      424–425
    formal advertising, 48
    frequency and scheduling for,
      419
    impact on purchase decisions,
      424
    indirect communication and, 424
    integrated communication pro-
      grams, 409
    Internet and, 419, 422–423
    limitations of, 412
    mailing lists and, 421
    media selection for business mar-
      kets, 417–421
    message development for,
      416–417
    objective-task method of budget-
      ing for, 415–416
    objectives of, 412–414
    planned response packages, 421

product awareness and, 411
product perception and,
    416–417
product position and, 414
purchase category segmentation
    and, 39
role of, 409–412
sales effectiveness enhancement
    and, 410–411
target audience for, 413–414, 419
telemarketing and, 429
trade show strategy management,
    425–430
Advisory support, 24
Air Force, 47
Airbus Industrie, 268
Alcoa, 253
Alliances. *See* Strategic alliances
Alpha Communications, 104
Amazon.com, 12, 40, 182
American Airlines, 502
American Can, 218
American Express, 102, 414
American trading companies
    (ATCs), 379
AMP, Incorporated, 127, 128, 133
Anderson Consulting, 567
Angels, 309
Anheuser Busch, 668
Apple Computer, 297–298, 547
Applied Materials, 264–265, 266
Argentina, 112
Ariba, Incorporated, 12, 60
Armco Steel Corporation, 513
Army, 31, 47
ASN. *See* Advance Shipping Notice
    (ASN)
Assembly and light manufacturing,
    363
AT&T, 21, 39, 71, 102, 114, 306,
    414, 419, 441
ATCs. *See* American trading com-
    panies (ATCs)
Atlas Corporation, 186
Auctions, 65, 66, 130–131
Augustine Medical, Inc., 631–641
Australia, 107
Automated Assemblies Corpora-
    tion, 552
Automated procurement, 129

Automation Papers Company, 260–
    261
Autonomous strategic behavior,
    definition of, **307**, 308
Auto-Xchange, 15, 16
Availability of alternatives, 93, 95
Avery Dennison, 547

Bain and Company, 160
Balanced scorecard
    customer perspective and, 462–
      463
    definition of, **460**
    financial perspective and, 461–
      462
    internal business process per-
      spective and, 463–464
    learning and growth perspective,
      464–466
Bar coding, 167, 677–691
Bargain hunters, 185
Barriers to entry, 211
Barro Stickney, Inc., 604–608
Barry Wehmiller International
    PLC (BWI), 673. *See also* BWI
    Kartridg Pak
Baxter International, 100, 547, 555
Beef Quality Assurance, 520
Behavior-based sales force control
    systems, **448**
Bell Atlantic Corp., 414
Bemis Company, 668
Benchmarking, 233
Beta Pharmaceuticals, 609–614
Bidding
    closed bidding, 404
    open bidding, 404
    screening opportunities for,
      404–405
    strategy for, 406
Biomérieux, 547
Black & Decker, 21
Bloomberg, 243
BOC Group, 643
BOC Health Care, 643
Boeing
    business marketing perspectives
      and, 11
    e-commerce and, 116, 129, 135

Boeing (*continued*)
  global markets and, 253, 268
  organizational buying and, 49
  strategy perspectives and, 232, 245
Bolt, James, 378
Bottom-up forecasting, 209
Boundary-spanning connections, 104–**105**, 144–145
Brand, 296
Brand equity, 295, 296–297
Brazil, market growth in, 10
Breakthrough projects, 311
Bribery, 265
Bristol-Myers Squibb, 60
British Airways, 330
BT Concert, 504
Buildings and land rights, 23
Bundling, 344
Business-level strategy, 236
Business market customers, 19–21
Business market planning process, 248–249, 325
Business market research. *See* Market research
Business market segmentation
  bases for, 178–179
  benefits of, 177–178
  case study on, 518–529
  choosing market segments, 189–190
  commitments in, 191
  evaluation of, 175
  fast-cycle strategies and, 185–186
  macrolevel bases of, 179–183
  macrosegmentation and, 178, 183
  microlevel bases of, 183–189
  microsegmentation, 178
  model for segmenting organizational market, 189–191
  new products and, 189
  price versus service and, 184–185
  product/service application, 181–182
  purchasing situation and, 182
  reconceiving products or services and, 186
  redefining market space and, 186
  redrawing industry boundaries and, 186
  requirements of, 174–177
  strategy implementation, 191
  value in use and, 182
Business marketing. *See also* headings beginning Market; Marketing
  buyer-seller connector and, 90–94

characteristics of, 13–14
classifying goods for, 21–24
consumer marketing distinguished from, 4, 5–6, 11–14
cross-functional relationships in, 244–248
diversity in, 31, 52
ethics and, 400, 449, 692–693
goal of, 26
for government agencies, 49–50
key buying influentials, 13
managing buyer-seller relationships and, 94–95
overview of, 4–5
relationship marketing, 14, 88–90
services marketing, 333–334
Business marketing channels
  adaptation by channel members and, 373
  administration of, 373–378
  assessing product/market factors, 369
  channel selection, 372–373
  company-organized sales force for, 380–381
  complex channel strategies, 359
  conflicts in, 377–378
  dealer advisory councils and, 375–376
  design of, 365–373
  direct market channels, 357–358
  distributors and, 361–364
  e-channels, 359–361
  indirect channel structures, 357, 358–359
  intermediaries and, 369–371, 374, 378–380
  international marketing channels, 378–381
  legal issues, 371–372
  management aids, 375
  manufacturer's representatives and, 364–365
  margins and commissions, 376–377
  member selection, 374
  motivation of members, 374–375
  number of channels, 371
  objectives of, 366–367
  overview of, 356–361
  participants in, 361–365
  pervasive channel tasks and, 367–368
  qualitative dimensions and, 373
  selective distribution and, 370–371
  trust building in, 377–378

Business marketing management
  business markets versus consumer-goods markets and, 5
  channel alternatives, 369–372
  components of, 27
  consumer orientation and, 5
  cross-functional relationships and, 7–9
  customer-linking capability, 6
  degree of directness and, 369
  factors limiting choice of channels, 368
  foreign markets and, 10–11
  framework for, 479
  global market perspective, 10–11
  market-sensing capability and, 5–6
  partnering for increase value and, 6
  value proposition creation and, 6
Business marketing strategy. *See* Marketing strategy
Business markets. *See also* headings beginning with Business marketing; Market; Marketing
  characteristics of, 9–11
  definition of, **4**
  derived demand and, 9
  fluctuating demand and, 9–10
  price sensitivity and, 10
  stimulating demand and, 10
Business Publication Audit of Circulation, 427
Business-to-business (b2b) commerce, 12, 150
Business-to-business (b2b) information resources, 197
Business-to-business (b2b) logistical service
  customer impact, 160
  importance of, 159–160
  inventory management, 165–167
  logistical facilities and, 163–164
  outsourcing and, 163–164
  service elements, 160–161, 165
  supply chain participant impact, 161–163
  transportation and, 164–165
Business-to-consumer markets, 61
Business-to-customer e-commerce, 115
Buyers. *See also* Purchasing
  advertising and, 416–417
  bargain hunters, 185
  definition of, **76**
  industrial products and, 184
  price sensitivity of, 390–391
  programmed buyers, 184

relationship buyers, 185
transaction buyers, 185
Buyer-seller connector, 91–93
Buyer-seller relationships, 94–96
Buygrid framework for organizational buying situations, 57
Buying center, 73–76
Buy-side requisitioning process, 60–61
BWI Kartridg Pak, 658–676

C. R. Bard, 547
CAD. *See* Computer Aided Design (CAD)
CAE. *See* Computer Aided Engineering (CAE)
Calsonics, 547
CAM. *See* Computer Aided Manufacturing (CAM)
Cambridge Technology Partners, 503
Canada, 4, 33, 257, 566, 572, 574, 575
Canon, Inc., 262, 268, 279–281, 291, 314–315, 394, 547
Capital expenditures, 208
Capital markets, 310
Case Corporation, 168
Catalogs, 126–128
Caterpillar, 169, 253, 266–267, 268, 349
Causal analysis, **214,** 216–218
Causal purchases, 59
Census Bureau, 196, 197
Census of Manufacturers, 196
Centralization of purchasing, 71–73
Channel Champions (Wheeler and Hirsh), 356
Channel conflict, 377
Channel design, 365
Channel management, 115
Channel structure, 366
Chase Econometric Associates, 209
Chemdex, 12, 132
ChenConnect, 129
Chile, 349
China, 11, 107, 253, 270
Chrysler, 18, 56, 242
CIM. *See* Computer Integrated Manufacturing (CIM)
Cincinnati Reds, 517
Cincinnati Sub-Zero, 635
Cisco Systems
business market channel management and, 359, 360
business marketing perspective and, 12, 24

case study, 483–508
e-commerce and, 125
organizational buying and, 60
organizational demand analysis and, 198
personal selling function and, 433
production management and, 300
relationship strategies and, 102, 105
segmentation and, 177
service management and, 347, 348
supply chain management and, 149
Citigroup, 255, 275
Clark Cincinnati, Inc., 514
Clean Air Act, 681
Closed bidding, 404
Coca-Cola, 6, 295
Cognition, 79
Collaboration, 320
Collaborative advantage, 88
Collaborative exchanges, 89, 91
Collaborative relationships, 94– 95, 99
Columbia/HCA Healthcare Corporation, 330
Combination houses, 363
Commerce Business Daily, 48
Commerce Department, 197, 203, 380, 558
Commerce One, Incorporated, 12, 60, 61
Commercial enterprises
characteristics of, 32–45
classification of, 33
geographical concentration of, 32–33
goals of purchasing function in, 34–35
purchasing organization in, 33–34
size variation of, 32
strategic procurement in, 35–41
Commissions, 376–377
Commitment, 101–102
Communication
advertising's role, 409–412
barriers to, 320
cross-functional working relationships and, 7
definition of, 7
e-commerce and, 115
efficiency and effectiveness control and, 472
goals for, 413

importance of, 409
information flow management, 108
Internet and, 422–423
logistics communications, 158
personal selling function and, 433–455
technology management and, 313–314
working relationships and, 104
Communication barriers, 320
Compaq Computer Corporation, 18, 71, 73, 156, 282, 397, 414, 454
Compatibility, 8–9
Competitive advantage
assessment of, 231–235
benchmarking and, 233
cost drivers and, 234
differentiation and, 234–235
economics of scale and, 234
elements of, 232
figures of merit and, 233
learning and, 234
linkages and, 234
logistics and, 155–156
lowest delivered cost position, 233
positions of advantage, 233–234
sources of, 231–233
superior skills and, 231
supply chain management (SCM) and, 143–150
value superiority, 233–234
Competitive analysis, 175
Competitive displacement, 241–242
Competitive environment
competitive bidding and, 403–406
evaluation of, 175–176
of global environment, 268
industrial pricing process and, 396–399
spotting new competitors, 176
Competitive factors, 255, 258–259
Complex modified rebuy, 65
Complexity management, 37, 39
Complexity of purchase, 95
Complexity of supply, 93
Compliance program, 45
Compression strategy, 326
CompUSA, 157
Computer Aided Design (CAD), 552, 553
Computer Aided Engineering (CAE), 553
Computer Aided Manufacturing (CAM), 552

Computer Identics Corporation, 681
Computer Integrated Manufacturing (CIM), 553
ComputerLand, 260
Concentration, 451
Concurrent engineering, 322
Consensus with qualification, 244
Conservatives, 299, 301
Consumer marketing, 4, 11–14
Contact, as distribution responsibility, 363
Contracts
  cost-reimbursement contracts, 46
  fixed-price contracts, 46
  government contracts, 45
  negotiated contract buying, 48–49
  negotiation of, 103
  psychological contracts, 105
Controlled circulation, 418
Controlling business marketing strategy. *See* Marketing control
Cooperative norms, 92
Cooperative purchasing associations, 51
Copper wire, 253
Core asset protection, 104
Core competencies
  competitors' development of, **281**
  definition of, 176
  exploitation of, 283–284
  identification of, 280
  lead sustenance and, 280–282
  product quality and, 284–285
  rareness and, 280–281
  roots of industrial products and, 279–287
  superior skills and, 280
  value and, 285–286
Core participants, 104
Core products, 282
Corning Glass Works, 107
Corporate culture, 243–244
Corporate strategy, 235
Cost drivers, 234
Cost-reimbursement contracts, 46
Cost-value relationships, 36–37
Costa Rica, 140
Costco, 157
Costs
  acquisition costs, 386
  activity-based costing, 159
  containment of, 50
  industrial pricing process and, 394–395
  Internet and, 119
  logistics and, 157–159, 159

possession costs, 386
pricing strategy and, 386–387
total costs, 36–37, 158, 159
transaction cost reduction and, 119
unit cost reduction, 146
usage costs, 386
Creative strategy statement, 414
Critikon's, 648
Cross-functional working relationships, 7–9
Cross-selling, 344
Cultural integration, 106
Custom-built products, 287
Custom-designed products, 287
Customer-benefit concept, 341
Customer-financial accountability connection, 237
Customer-linking capability, 6, 227–228
Customer-linking process, **464**
Customer-product connection, 236
Customer relationship management systems, 452–**454**
Customer-service delivery connection, 237
Customer visits, 207–208
Customers. *See also* Service management; Services
  as apostles, 339
  balanced scorecard and, 463
  business market customers, 4, 19–21
  case study on, 511–517
  customer satisfaction, 80, 338–339
  customer service, 7, 118–120, 128, 135–136, 158, 160
  Internet customers, 423
  organizational customer focus and, 433–439
  rep-customer relationships, 364
  service delivery and, 347–348
  as terrorists, 339
  zero defection and, 339–340
Customized expert service, 352

DaimlerChrysler AG, 42–44, 92, 129
Dale Carnegie, 346
Database marketing, 421
Database publishing, 135
Dealers and distributors, 20
Decentralization of purchasing, 71–73
Deciders, 76
DeepCanyon.com, 203

Defense Department, 47, 114, 616
Defense Logistics Agency (DLA), 47
Defense procurement, 47
Dell Computer Company
  advertising, 411
  business market channel management, 359
  business market planning, 288
  business marketing perspective and, 12
  e-commerce and, 112, 122, 136
  evaluation of business market strategy and performance, 460
  organizational buying and, 32, 35
  pricing strategy, 397
  product management, 282
  relationship strategies and, 92, 102
  segmentation and, 177–179
  supply chain management, 143, 146, 149
Delphi method, 213–214
Delta Airlines, 18, 345
Demand elasticity, 10, 211
Denmark, 272
Dennison Manufacturing, 551
Department of Commerce *See* Commerce Department
Department of Defense (DOD). *See* Defense Department
Department of Interior. *See* Interior Department
Derivative projects, 311
Derived demand, 9
Determinant attributes, 293
Dickenson and Company, 387
Differentiation, 234–235
"Digital storefronts," 376
Direct mail, 420–421
Direct marketing channels, **357**–358
Direct marketing tools, 419–420
Discontinuous innovations, 241, 298
Disintermediation, 132
Disney, 310
Dispersed territory, **451**
DISTEVAL, 380
Distribution
  alliances and, 362
  assembly and light manufacturing and, 363
  as asset, 364
  channel design, 365–373
  classifications of, 363
  contacts and, 363
  degree of directness and, 369

direct distribution, 357–358
distribution responsibilities, 362–363
e-commerce and, 115, 359–361
efficiency and effectiveness control and, 472
indirect distribution, 357, 358–359
inside salespersons, 361
intermediaries and, 369–371, 374, 378–380
just-in-time (JIT) concept and, 363
legal issues, 371–372
manufacturer's representatives and, 364–365
marketing channels, 356–361
outside salespersons, 361
product availability and, 363
repairs and, 363
selective distribution, 370–371
types of distributors, 361–364
Distributors, 362–363
DLA. *See* Defense Logistics Agency (DLA)
DOD. *See* Defense Department
Domestic intermediaries, 378
Douglas, Susan P., 254
Dow Chemical, 11, 63, 107, 124, 253, 268, 365, 399, 441
Dow Jones Industrial Average, 112
Drackett, 663
Dramatic conflict in business plans, 325
Du Pont
business marketing perspectives and, 4
e-commerce, 124
innovation management, 307
organizational buying behavior and, 63
personal selling perspective and, 437
pricing strategy, 399
segmentation and, 187–188
W. L. Gore and, 581–582, 592
Dun & Bradstreet, 97, 197
Duracell, 547

EAN International, 682
Early supplier involvement in new product development, 39
Early warning systems, 208
EarthWeb, 12
Eastman Kodak, 107, 241
Ebay, Inc., 12, 61, 182, 332

EC. *See* European Community (EC)
E-Chemicals, 63
E-commerce. *See also* Internet
business focus and, 119
business services and, 331
channel considerations, 131–134
customer service and, 118–120, 128, 135–136
cycle times and, 120
definition of, 113–114
demand for, 24
digital channel advantages, 133–134
disintermediation and, 132
electronic catalogs, 126–128
"hype" of, 117
infomediaries and, 132
Internet product and, 124–131
intraorganizational e-commerce, 115
key supporting elements of, 114–117
leaders in, 112
marketing strategies for, 122–124
objectives of, 120–122
online auctions, 130–131
pricing impact of, 134–135
procurement management systems and, 129
promotion and, 136
questions for strategy formulation, 121
sales force and, 136
strategic role of, 117–120
strategy crafting and implementation, 120–136
supply chain and, 119
transaction cost reduction and, 119
types of, 115
vertical market sites, 129–130
Web site design, 126
"E-commerce hub," 12
Economic factors, 255, 257
Economics of scale, 234
EDI. *See* Electronic data interchange (EDI)
Edition Benchmarking Study on Services Marketing Practices, 567
EDS, 330, 561
Education and Institutional Purchasing Cooperative, 51
Efficiency and effectiveness control, 471, 472
80/20 rule, 166
Elasticity of demand. *See* Demand elasticity

Electronic catalogs, 126–128
Electronic commerce. *See* E-commerce
Electronic data interchange (EDI), 70, 167
Electronic publishing, 115
Electronics Representative Association (ERA), 605
EMCs. *See* Export management companies (EMCs)
End products, 282
Endangered Species Act, 525
England. *See* United Kingdom
Entering goods, 21–22
Enterprise Resource Planning (ERP), 149
Entry. *See* Market entry
Environmental factors/forces, 67–68, 255, 257–258
Eppendorf, 547
ERA. *See* Electronics Representative Association (ERA)
Ericsson, 253
Ernst & Young, 503
ERP. *See* Enterprise Resource Planning (ERP)
E-Steel, 129
Ethics, 400, 449, 692–693
ETrade, Inc., 332
European Community (EC), 257, 381
Evaluation
advertising effectiveness, 424–425
alternative marketing channels, 372–373
competitive environment, 175–176
global product-market opportunities, 290–291
market segments, 175
product/market factors for marketing channels, 369
relationship strategy outcomes, 101
sales personnel, 446
strategic alliances, 263
supplier performance, 41–45, 50, 93–94
technological environment, 176–177
trade show performance, 428–430
Evaluative criteria, 78
Evoked set of alternatives, 82
Executive judgment, 212, 214
Exodus Communication, 12
Expense-to-sales ratios, 469

Experiential strategy, 326
Export management companies (EMCs), 378–379
Export merchants, 379
Exporting, 259–260
Exposition Audit, 427
Extensive problem solving, 58
Extranets, 112, 116–117, 360, 497
Exxon, 532

Facilitating goods, 22, 23
Factors, 379
FAO Schwarz, 24
Fast-cycle companies, 186
Fast-cycle strategies, 185–186
Feasible set of alternatives, 82
Federal Express, 24, 228, 334
Federal Supply Schedule, 48
Federal Supply Service, 47
Feedforward control, 474–475
Ferro Corporation, 37
Figgie International Inc., 659
Figures of merit, 233
Financial benefits, 386
Finland, 253
First Union Corp., 414
Fixed equipment, 23
Fixed-price contracts, 46
Flaring out, 99–100
Fluctuating demand, 9–10
Focus group interviews, 206–207
Food-service market, 31
Forces
    environmental forces, 67–68
    group forces, 67, 73–77
    individual forces, 77–82
    organizational forces, 67, 69–70
Ford Motor Company
    business marketing perspective, 14–16, 18, 20, 21
    e-commerce, 129
    global markets, 258–259
    organizational buying, 34, 37, 56, 59
    relationship strategies, 101
Forecasting. *See* Sales forecasting
Foreign Corrupt Practices Act, 265
Foreign labor, 44
Foreign-based intermediaries, 379–380
Forrester Research, 12, 40, 63, 112, 130
Foundation goods, 22, 23
"Fourth-Party Logistics," 168
France, 107
Franchising, 260–261, 349, 542–543, 558–559

Franklin Key Electronics, 604, 606
Franklin Paper Company, 532
FreeMarkets, Inc., 12, 65, 130
French Labor Board, 550
Frito-Lay, 668
Fritz Companies, Inc., 168
Frost and Sullivan, 197
Fuji Photo Film Company, 262
Fujitsu, 561
Functional strategy, 236

Gatekeepers, 76
Gateway, 32
Gaymar Industries, 635
GDP. *See* Gross Domestic Product (GDP)
GE. *See* General Electric Company (GE)
GE Capital, 226
GE Medical Systems, 41, 129
General Accounting Office, 48
General Electric Company (GE)
    business marketing perspective and, 4, 11, 21
    e-commerce, 129
    global markets, 253, 265
    organizational buying and, 35, 41
    relationship strategies and, 89, 103
    service management and, 330
    strategic perspective and, 245
    as supplier, 543–544
General Electric Plastics (GEP), 127–128
General Foods, 660
General line distributors, 363
General Mills, 660–661, 668, 669
General Motors Corporation (GM)
    business marketing perspective and, 4, 15–16, 18
    e-commerce, 129, 134
    global markets, 256
    organizational buying and, 57, 71
    plastics processing industry and, 545
    relationship strategies and, 92, 102–103
    suppliers for, 511
    UPC bar codes and, 681
General Services Commission (GSA), 47
General T, 681
Generalist, 358
Geographical concentration of industry, 32–33
GEP. *See* General Electric Plastics (GEP)

Germany, 10
Gillette, 546, 547
Global industry, 267–268
Global markets
    bribery and, 265
    business marketing channels and, 378–381
    case studies on, 483–508, 538–579
    competitive factors, 255, 258–259
    drivers of globalization, 254–259
    economic factors and, 255, 257
    environmental factors and, 255, 257–258
    evolution of international marketing strategy, 269–275
    global orientation and, 274–275
    joint ventures and, 262, 264
    leadership positions and, 274
    local market expansion and, 273–274
    market factors and, 254–256
    market-entry options, 259–269
    multidomestic versus global strategies, 264
    overview of, 253–254
    phases of international market entry, 271–275
    pre-internationalization, 270–271
    product-market opportunity assessment, 290–291
    spectrum of involvement in international marketing, 259
    strategic alliances and, 261–262
    value chain and, 266–269
Global products, 290–291
GM. *See* General Motors Corporation (GM)
Goods
    accessory equipment and, 23
    classification of, 21–24
    entering goods, 21–22
    facilitating goods, 22, 23
    foundation goods, 22, 23
    installation and, 23
    manufactured materials and parts and, 21
    raw materials and, 21
    services and, 23–24
    supplies and, 23
Government agencies. *See also* specific agencies, such as Defense Department
    advertising and, 48
    business markets and, 4
    characteristics of, 45–50

compliance program, 45
defense procurement, 47
federal buying, 48–49
government contracts, 45–46
influences on buying of, 45
marketing strategies for, 49–50
minority subcontracting program, 45
negotiated contract buying, 48–49
nondefense procurement, 47–48
purchasing organizations and procedures, 46–47
set-aside program, 45
vendor publications, 46–48
Government units, 45
Grainger, 143
Great Britain. *See* United Kingdom
Gross Domestic Product (GDP), 208, 209
Group forces, 67, 73–77
Group purchasing, 51–52
GSA. *See* General Services Commission (GSA)
GTE, 502, 547
Guardian Industries, 92

Harley-Davidson, 9
Hayssen, 668
Health care industry, 631–657
HEAT. *See* Heat Energy Advance Technology (HEAT)
Heat Energy Advance Technology (HEAT), 556
Hewlett-Packard
advertising, 411
business marketing perspectives and, 5, 7, 24
competitors of, 646
e-commerce, 116, 134
evaluation of business marketing strategy and performance and, 465
extranets and, 497
innovation management, 306, 313–315
organizational buying and, 69, 71
organizational demand analysis and, 207
personal selling function and, 437, 441, 444, 447
pricing strategies and, 397
product management, 295, 300–302
segmentation and, 174, 177, 186
service management, 330, 345, 347

strategic perspectives and, 241–243
suppliers of, 543, 547
supply chain management and, 143, 157
High-technology markets
adoption life cycle, 299–302
bowling alley and, 300–301
brand management for, 295–298
customer types, 298–299
discontinuous innovations and, 298
gorilla advantage and, 300
innovation winners in, 312–314
main street and, 302
price/performance drivers in, 397
product management and, 295–302
technology adopters and, 298–299
tornado and, 301–302
HK Cad/Cam-Gimeli, 547
Homogeneity, 254
Honda, 14, 18, 35–36, 69, 92, 93, 279, 280
Honeywell, 267, 279, 283
Hong Kong, 11, 253
Horizontal publications, 417
Housing starts, 208
Human rights, 44

IBM Corporation
advertising, 409–411, 414, 421–422
business market planning and, 245
business marketing perspective and, 4, 18, 19, 24
case study, 560–579
global markets, 253, 272, 275
innovation management, 307
market channel management, 358–359
organizational buying and, 40–41, 68–71
organizational demand analysis and, 207
pricing strategies and, 397
product management, 282, 295, 298
relationship strategies and, 94, 102
service management, 330, 331, 345, 346
suppliers of, 547

supply chain management and, 150
W. L. Gore and, 600–602
IDC. *See* International Data Corporation (IDC)
Idea markets, 309–310
Illinois Tool Works (ITW), 659
ILMS. *See* Integrated Leads Management Systems, Inc. (ILMS)
Immediate term sales forecasting, 210
Importance of purchase, 95
Importance of supply, 93
Improvisation, 314
Indirect marketing channels, **357**
Individual forces, 67, 77–82
Induced strategic behavior, 307, 308
Industrial communities, 134–135
Industrial pricing process. *See also* Pricing strategy
attributes of total product offering, 389
buyer price sensitivity and, 390–391
classification of costs, 394–395
competition and, 396–399
considerations for, 387
cost/benefit analysis strategy implications, 390
cost comparison issues, 399
cost determinants, 393–396
demand determinants, 388–392
demand estimation methods, 392
end market focus and, 391–392
ethics and, 400
experience relevance and, 395–396
gauging competitive response, 398
hypercompetitive rivalries and, 397
key components of, 388
price elasticity of demand and, 390
price objectives, 388
profit-management tools and, 394
target costing, 393–394
value assessment and, 389–390
value-based segmentation and, 392
Industrial production, 208
Industrial products
buyers and, 184
core competencies and, 279–287
determinacy and, 293–295
determinant attributes and, 293

Industrial products (*continued*)
  nondeterminant attributes, 293
  sales resource opportunity grid,
    451
  strategy matrix, 294–295
  strategy planning for, 292–295
Industrial sales force management.
    See also Personal selling; Sales
    force management
  concentration and, 451
  customer relationship manage-
    ment systems, 452–454
  deployment analysis, 450–451
  dispersed territories and, 451
  electronic sales forces, 454
  models for, 449–454
  territory sales response, 450–451
  territory workload and, 451
Industrial services, 287
Industry bandwidth, 98
Industry genesis, 242, 243
Inelasticity, 10
Inflation, 46
Influencers, 76–77
InFocus Systems, 453
Infomediaries, 132
Information
  Internet and, 119–120
  processing of, 78–79
Information exchange, 91, 95
Information platforms, 359
Innovation management
  business services and, 331
  capital markets and, 310
  in high-technology markets,
    312–314
  idea markets and, 309–310
  new product development
    process, 314–323
  overview, 306–307
  patching and, 313
  Silicon Valley and, 309–310
  strategic behavior patterns and,
    307–309
  talent markets and, 310
  technology management and,
    311–314
Inside Business Marketing, 126
Inside salespersons, 361
Installations, 23
Institutions, 4, 50–52
Instrumentation Labs, 547
Integrated Leads Management Sys-
    tems, Inc. (ILMS), 430
Integrated sell, 37, 38
Integrating points of contact, 105–
    107
Intel Corporation

business market planning and,
    228, 234, 243–244
business marketing perspective
    and, 11, 24
global markets, 253
innovation management, 315
organizational buying perspective
    and, 32
product management, 282, 295,
    300, 301
Interaction structure, 82
Interior Department, 47
Intermediaries
  American-based export inter-
    mediaries, 378
  company-managed and company-
    organized sales force, 378
  domestic intermediaries, 378–
    379
  foreign-based intermediaries,
    378, 379–380
  market coverage and, 370–371
  recruitment of, 374
  types of, 369–371
Intermediate term sales forecasting,
    210
International Business Machines.
    See IBM Corporation
International Circuit Technology,
    65
International Conference on Med-
    ical and Biological Engineer-
    ing, 648
International Data Corporation
    (IDC), 572
International markets. *See* Global
    markets
International orientation, 324
International Paper, 533
International Standards Organiza-
    tion (ISO), 42
Internet. *See also* E-commerce
  advertising and, 419
  benefits of, 118–120
  business-to-business (b2b) com-
    merce and, 12
  catalogs on, 126–128
  customer relationships and, 423,
    439
  economy of, 112
  electronic commerce support
    service demand and, 24
  global markets and, 256, 423
  information platforms and, 359
  Internet product, 124–131
  limitation of, 196, 198
  marketing channels and,
    359–361

marketing communications and,
    422–423
  marketing costs and, 422
  marketing research and, 195–198
  online auctions, 65, 66, 130–131
  online trading communities,
    61–62
  operational linkages and, 92
  platform management and,
    360–361
  pricing impact of, 134–135
  purchasing on, 40–41
  real-time changes and, 423
  role of, 136
  service delivery and, 347
  straight rebuys and, 59–63
  supply chain and, 15–16
  supply chain management and,
    150
  trade shows and, 428
  transactional platforms and,
    359–360
  "unlimited shelf space" and, 423
  virtual marketplace and, 15–16
  World Wide Web and, 116
Interorganizational e-commerce,
    115
Interpersonal integration, 106
Interpretive barriers, 320
Interroyal, 209
Intranets, 116–117
Intraorganizational e-commerce,
    115
Inventory. *See also* Business market-
    ing channels; Distribution
  80/20 rule for, 166
  business-to-business logistical
    service and, 165–167
  e-commerce and, 115
  elimination of, 166
  logistics systems and, 158, 167
  selective strategies for, 166–167
  technological management of,
    167
Iridium L.L.C., 270
Irregular components, **216**
ISO 9000 standards, 42, 284, 676
ISO, 42
Israel, 265
Itochu Corporation, 513–514
ITSMA, 560, 563, 567, 577
ITW. *See* Illinois Tool Works
    (ITW)
IVAC, 547

J. M. Smucker Company, 11–14, 52
J. R. Metals, 514

Organizational customer focus (*ctd.*)
  knowledge of customer's business and, 435
  organizational buying behavior and, 434–435
  organizational factor identification and, 435
  personal selling and, 433–439
  relationship marketing and, 437–439
Organizational demand analysis
  definition of, 195
  Internet usage for business marketing research and, 195–198
  market potential and, 198–208
  sales forecast and, 200
Organizational forces, 67
Organizational innovativeness, 188
Organizational selling center, 437
Original Equipment Manufacturers (OEMs), 20, 548
Otis Elevator, 331–332
Outside salespersons, 361
Outsourcing, 50–51, 163–164, 168, 331
Owens-Corning Fiberglass Corporation, 441
Owens-Illinois, 107

P&G. *See* Proctor and Gamble Company (P&G)
Packaging, 158, 658–676
Packard Bell, 282
Paging Products Group, 69
Pall Biomedical, 547
Panasonic, 547
PaperExchange.com, 129
Patching, 313
Paxall, 669
Payment management, 115
PCU opportunity, 451
Penetration, 399
Pentagon, 49
Peripheral participants, 104
Perishability, 343–344
Personal benefits, 386
Personal selling
  electronic sales forces, 454
  industrial sales force management, 449–454
  Internet and, 435–437
  national accounts and, 441–443
  organizational customer focus and, 433–439
  relationship marketing, 437–438
  sales administration, 443–449

sales force management and, 439–449
Perspective taking, 7–8
Pfizer, Inc., 518–529
Pharmaseal, 635
Philippines, 140
Philips Electronics, 188–189
Philips Lighting Company, 188–189
Pillsbury, 20
Pioneering ventures, 352
Pitney Bowes, 358, 442
Planning and control units, 450
Plant and warehouse location, 158
PlasticsNet, 130
Platform management, 360
Platform projects, 311
Polaroid, 547
Possession costs, 386
Potential, as measure, **450**
Prado-Pak, 670
Pragmatists, 299, 301
Predevelopment proficiency, 324
Predicasts, 203
Pre-internationalization, 270–271
Prestolite, 547
Price elasticity of demand, 390
Price indexes, 208
Pricing strategy
  competitive bidding and, 403–406
  costs and, 386–387
  customers' cost-in-use components, 386
  industrial pricing process, 387–399
  legal considerations, 403
  meaning of price in business markets, 384–387
  new product pricing, 399–401
  overview of, 384
  penetration and, 401
  pricing across product life cycle, 399–403
  pricing environment, 385
  product benefits and, 385–386
  product line considerations for, 401
  skimming and, 400
  tactical pricing, 401–403
  time segmentation and, 400
  value-based strategies, 387
Prince Philip Award, 584
Private institutions. *See* Institutions
Process technology, 176
Proctor and Gamble Company (P&G), 11, 17, 31, 116, 295, 663

Product advantage, 324
Product availability, 363
Product champion, 308–309
Product development. *See* New products
Product family, 312
Product management. *See also* New products
  core competencies and, 279–287
  end products, 282
  global products, 290–291
  in high-technology markets, 295–302
  industrial product strategy, 292–295
  lead sustenance and, 280–282
  market definition, 289–290
  market segmentation and, 291
  new product development process, 314–323
  pricing across product life cycle, 399–403
  product line definition, 287–289
  product policy, 287–291
  quality and, 284–285
  segmentation and, 291
  support strategy, 286
  universal products, 290–291
  value and, 285–286
Product market, 289
Product position, 414
Product positioning, 292
Product quality, diversity in requirements for, 31
Product segmentation, 291
Product support services, 331–333
Product technology, 176
Production planning, 158
Products supported by services, 331
Profitability control, 471–474
Project leaders, 108
Proprietary or catalog products, 287
PSS WorldMedical, 122
Psychological contracts, 105
Purchasing
  buying motivations, 20–21
  centralization of, 71–73
  commercial enterprises and, 32–45
  decentralization of, 71–73
  defense procurement, 47
  electronic purchasing, 59–63, 129
  federal buying, 48–49
  goals of purchasing function, 34–35

Japan
  international strategy and, 268
  joint ventures and, 262, 264
  market growth in, 10
  market share advantages and, 264
  quality function deployment (QFD) and, 322
  semiconductor industry and, 265
JIT. *See* Just-in-time (JIT) concept
Job satisfaction, 447
John Deere and Company, 420
Johnson & Johnson, 177, 465, 546–547, 553, 555
Johnson Controls, 14, 18, 56
Joint ventures, 102, 262, 264
Judgmental new task, 58
Just-in-time (JIT) concept, 156–157, 363, 545, 682

Kanthal Corporation, 476
Kartridg Pak (KP), 658–676
Key buying influentials, 13
Kidde, 547
Kliklok, 668
Kodak. *See* Eastman Kodak
Komatsu, 268
Korea, 10, 265
KP. *See* Kartridg Pak (KP)
KPMG, 503
Kroger Company, 33, 681

Lawyers, 107
Lead efficiency, 428
Lead user method, 318, 319
Lead users, 318
Leadership, positions, **274**
Learning, 234
Learning and growth perspective, **464**
Leveraged buys, 37, 38
Levi Strauss & Co., 44
Licensing, 260
Life-cycle potential, 200
Lifetime profitability, 463
Limited problem solving, 64
Linkages, 234
Linked buys, 37, 38
Linking systems and structures, 104
Lockheed Martin Corporation, 49, 129
Logistics
  business-to-business logistical management, 163–169
  business-to-business logistical service, 159–163
  calculation of costs, 159

competitive advantage and, 155–156
cross-functional relationships and, 244, 245
customer impact, 160
definition of, **153**
elements of logistics system, 157, 158
flow management and, 155
"Fourth-Party Logistics," 168
inventory and, 158, 165–167
just-in-time systems, 156–157
logistics information systems, 167
outsourcing and, 163–164, 168
sales-marketing-logistics integration, 156
service elements, 160–161
supply chain impact and, 161–163
supply chain management distinguished from, 154
third-party logistics firms, 167–169
timely logistics support, 155–159
total cost approach and, 157–159
transportation and, 159, 164–165
Long term sales forecasting, 210
Lowest delivered cost position, 233
Lucent Technologies, 11
Lufkin Pulp Mill, 533

Mack Trucks, 293
Macrolevel of business market segmentation, 179–183
Macrosegmentation, 178, 183
Mailing lists, 421
Maintenance and repair items, 23
Maintenance and repair support, 24
Maintenance, repair, and operations. *See* MRO (maintenance, repair, and operations)
Malaysia, 140
Management contracts, 261
Management judgment, 211
Management technology, 176
Managing innovation. *See* Innovation management
Managing technology. *See* Technology management
Manufactured materials and parts, definition of, 21
Margins, 376–377
Market demand forecasting, 195
Market-driven entrepreneurial culture, 464–466

Market-driven organizations
  capabilities for, 227–228
  customer values and, 228
  customer-linking capability and, 227
  dimensions of, 229
  management dimensions of, 228–231
  market-sensing capabilities and, 227
  organizational scheme for, 52, 53, 228
  strategic perspectives for, 226–227
  strategy development of, 228
  supporting programs and actions of, 229–231
  three-level focus for, 227
Market entry. *See also* New products
  barriers to, 211
  contracting and, 260–261
  efficiency and, 274
  exporting, 259–260
  franchising and, 260–261
  global market and, 259–269, 271–275
  international market entry, 271–273
  key decisions for, 274
  leadership position and, 274
  licensing and, 260
  local market expansion and, 273–274
  mode of, 272–273
  phases of international market entry, 271–275
  pre-internationalization, 270–271
  strategy development and, 274–275
  timing of, 272
Market factors, 254, 255
Market influence, 282
Market invention, 242–243
Market orientation, 5
Market potential
  determination of, 202–208
  life-cycle potential, 200
  market research and, 205–208
  as opportunity, 199
  role in planning and control, 198–200
  segmented planning and control, 199
  single series method for calculating, 202–203
  statistical series methods of determining potential, 202–205

Market research
  customer visits as, 207–208
  discontinuous innovations and, 243
  focus groups, 206–207
  Internet usage for, 195–198
  market potential and, 205–208
  primary data, 198
  secondary data, 196
  surveys, 206
Market Research Center, 197
Market segment. *See also* Business market segmentation; Segment
  definition of, **174**–175
  momentum of, 300–301
  profitability by, 471–473
Market segmentation, 291
Market sensing, 464
Market-sensing capability, 5–6, 227
Market share, 463
Market share analysis, 469
Marketing. *See also* headings beginning Business market
Marketing audit, 468
Marketing control
  annual plan control, 469–470
  balance scorecard and, 460–466
  definition of, **460**
  effects of informal control, 467
  efficiency and effectiveness control, 471
  feedforward control, 474–475
  formulation guidance, 466–467
  framework for, 469–470, 479
  implementation skills and, 476–477
  levels of, 468
  marketer's role, 478
  marketing strategy center and, 477–478
  process of, 467
  profitability control, 471–474
  questions for, 470
  resource allocation, 466–467
  strategic control, 468–469
  at various levels, 468–475
Marketing implementation, 475
Marketing proficiency, 324–325
Marketing strategy. *See also* Marketing control
  basis of, 6
  business-level strategy, 236
  collective action perspective on, 238
  competitive displacement and, 241–242
  controlling business marketing strategies, 459–480

corporate culture and, 243–244
corporate strategy, 235
discontinuous innovation strategies, 240–244
flowchart for, 249
formulation of, 237–239
functional strategy, 236
functionally integrated planning, 246–248
hierarchy of strategies, 235–237
for high-technology industries, 239–244
implementation of, 475–478
industrial products and, 292–295
industry genesis and, 242
international marketing strategy, 269–275
managing strategic interdependencies, 248
market invention, 242–243
market segmentation and, 191
marketing plan, 248–249
negotiated outcomes and, 237–239
opportunity identification, 241
overview of, 25–26
pricing strategy, 386–387
radical cannibalism and, 241, 242
resource allocation, 466–467
responsive marketing strategy, 78
strategic business units (SBUs) and, 236
strategic inflection point, 239
strategic intent, 239
strategy-implementation fit, 475–476
thought worlds and, 237
three-customer connections' management, 236–237
Marketing strategy center, 477–478
Marketing synergy, 324
MarketSite, 61, 62
Marmot Mountain Works Ltd., 592
Marquest, 547
Marriott Corporation, 31, 51, 345
Marshall Industries, 132–133
Masbac, 547
Masters golf tournament, 683
Materials handling, 158
Matsushita, 282
Matworks, 515–517
Maytag, 37
McDonald's, 21, 36, 295, 542, 546
McGraw-Hill, 361
MCI Worldcom, 414
McKinley & Company, 681
McKinsey, 561
Mead Corporation, 71, 442
MediaMetrix, 197

Medical Equipment Systems, 330
Medical-Surgical Markets Group, 318
Mercer Management Consulting, 37, 143, 178
Mexico, and NAFTA, 33, 257
Microlevel bases of business market segmentation
  attitudes toward vendors and, 188
  decision-making unit structure, 187–188
  fast-cycle strategies and, 185–186
  importance of purchase and, 188
  key criteria and, 183
  organizational innovations and, 188
  price versus service, 184–185
  purchasing strategies for, 187
Microsegmentation, 178, 188–189
Microsoft Corporation
  advertising and, 414
  e-commerce, 133
  innovation management, 314–315
  product management, 295, 300, 301
  relationship strategies and, 100
  service management, 331–332
Mikromashina, 551, 552
Miller SQA, 150, 151
Milliken & Company, 182
"Mini-mills," 143
Mining Enforcement and Safety Administration, 47
Minority subcontracting program, definition of, **45**
Miracle Adhesives, 209
Mitsui & Co., 553
Mixed bundling, 344
Modified rebuys
  buying decision approaches for, **64**–65
  complex modified rebuys, 65
  definition of, **63**
  limited problem solving for, 64
  simple modified rebuy, 65
  strategy guidelines for, 65–66
Momentum, 300–301
Monsanto, 310
Mosaic Corporation, 485
Motorola
  business market perspectives and, 11, 12, 18
  business market planning, 245
  global markets, 253, 270
  organizational buying and, 60, 70
  product management, 279–280

relationship strategies and, 88, 100, 102
  suppliers of, 547
MRO (maintenance, repair, and operations), 361
Multidomestic industries, 267
Multidomestic strategies, 264

Nabisco, 295
NAFTA. *See* North American Free Trade Agreement (NAFTA)
NAICS. *See* **North American Industrial Classification System (NAICS)**
"Naked solutions," 100
NASA, 615
National account, 442
National Inspection Services (NIS), 531
National Semiconductor Corporation, 72, 131, 359, 360
National Transportation Exchange (NTE), 132
Navistar, 293
Navy, 46, 47
NCR, 288
NDT. *See* Nondestructive testing (NDT)
NDTMA. *See* Nondestructive Testing Managers Association (NDTMA)
NEC Corporation, 498
Negotiated outcomes, 237–239
Nellcor, 646
Nestal Maschinen AG, 552
Net Buying Influences, 428
Netscape, 133
New competitors, 176
New products. *See also* Market entry
  collaboration and, 320
  communication barriers and, 320
  concurrent engineering and, 322
  cross-functional barriers and, 319–320
  customer's voice and, 322–323
  development process for, 314–323
  engineer's voice and, 323
  fast-paced product development, 326
  idea sources, 317–319
  international orientation, 324
  interpretive barriers and, 320
  Japanese companies and, 325–326
  lead users and, 318, 319
  leading customers and, 318–319
  marketing proficiency and, 324–325

marketing synergy and, 324
new product strategy, 317
new to the world products, 322
performance drivers for, 316–317
predevelopment proficiency, 324
pricing of, 399–401
process employment and, 316–317
product advantage and, 324
product modifications and, 322
quality function deployment (QFD) and, 322–323
resources commitments and, 317
segmentation strategy and, 189
success determinants, 324–326
team-based processing and, 321–322
technical proficiency and, 325
turf barriers and, 319–320
New service development, 349–353
New-task buying situation, **58**
NIS. *See* National Inspection Services (NIS)
Nokia, 253
Nondefense procurement, 47–48
Nondestructive Testing Managers Association (NDTMA), 533, 534
Nondestructive testing (NDT), 530–537
Nondeterminant attributes, 293
Non-strategic purchases, 93
North American Free Trade Agreement (NAFTA), 33, 257, 520, 525
North American Industrial Classification System (NAICS), 33, 34, 178, 182, 202–203
NTE. *See* National Transportation Exchange (NTE)
NUCOR, 233
Nucor Incorporated, 143
Nylon Products Corporation, 538
Nypro Inc., 538–559

OEMs. *See* Original Equipment Manufacturers (OEMs)
Ogilvy and Mather, 565
Ohmeda Health Care, 645
Ohmeda Monitoring Systems, 642–657
Omega Financial Services, 104
Omnibus Trade Act, 515
Online auctions, 65, 66, 130–131
Online trading communities, 61–62
Open bidding, 404

Operating personnel, 108
Operating resources, 59
Operating supplies, 23
Operational benefits, 386
Operational integration, 106
Operational linkages, 91–92, 95
Opportunity identification, 241
Optimizers, 187
Oracle Corporation, 60, 97, 298, 436
Order processing, 158
Order-to-delivery time, 145–146
Organizational buying center, 437
Organizational buying process
  buyers and, 76
  buygrid framework for, 57
  buying center, 73–76
  centralization of purchasing, 71–73
  decentralization of purchasing, 71–73
  deciders and, 76
  economic influences on, 68
  environmental forces affecting, 67–68
  evaluative criteria and, 78
  evoked set of alternatives and, 82
  feasible set of alternatives and, 82
  forces affecting, 67–82
  gatekeepers and, 76
  group forces and, 73–77
  individual forces and, 77–82
  influencers and, 76–77
  informational processing and, 78–79
  interaction structure and, 82
  isolation of buying situation, 74–75
  modified rebuys, 63–66
  new-task buying situation, 58
  organizational forces affecting, 69–70
  overview, 56–57
  predicting composition, 75
  purchasing positioning, 70–77
  requisitioning steps, 60
  risk-reduction strategies and, 79–82
  straight rebuy, 59–63
  strategies in purchasing, 69–70
  technological influences on, 68
  types of buying situations, 57–66
Organizational customer focus
  buying center identification and, 435
  influence pattern identification and, 435
  Internet and, 435–437

government agencies and, 45–50
group purchasing, 51–52
industrial products, 184
institutional purchasing procedures, 50–52
key criteria of, 183
levels of procurement development, 37–39
macrolevel characteristics of buying organization, 180–181
microsegment purchasing strategies, 187
modified rebuys, 63–66
new-task purchasing, 59
nondefense procurement, 47–48
on Internet, 40–41
optimizers and, 187
organization of, 33–34, 46–47
organizational buying process, 56–83
performance impact and, 39–40
positioning of, 70–77
price versus service, 184–185
satisficers and, 187
segmentation and, 39, 40, 182
service versus price, 184–185
straight rebuys, 59–63
strategic priorities of, 69–70
strategic procurement, 35–41, 93
supplier performance evaluation and, 41–45, 50
supply chain purchasing trends, 18
total costs and, 36
Pure bundling, 344

QFD. *See* Quality function deployment (QFD)
QIP. *See* Quality improvement program (QIP)
Qualitative techniques for sales forecasting, 211–213
Quality function deployment (QFD), 322
Quality improvement program (QIP), 535–536
Quick Response concept, 682

R. D. Ocean, 604–606
Radical cannibalism, 241, 242
Radio frequency (RF), 167
Rareness, 280–281
Raw materials, 21
Raytheon, 400
Reconceiving products or services, 186

Redefining market space, 186
Redrawing industry boundaries, 186
Regression techniques, **214,** 216, 218
Relationship buyers, 185
Relationship connectors, 91
Relationship marketing
  account selection, 98
  account-specific product offering development and, 98–99
  buyer-seller relationship, 90–96
  capturing relationship data, 96–97
  collaborative exchange and, 89
  commitment demonstration, 101–102
  definition of, **14,** 88
  evaluation of strategy outcomes, 101
  flaring out, 99–100
  flexible service offering creation, 100
  monitoring relationships, 101
  nature of relationship and, 90
  organizational customer focus and, 437–439
  strategic alliances and, 102–108
  strategic choices and, 90
  strategies for, 96–101
  transactional exchange and, 89
  types of relationships, 89
  value-adding exchanges and, 89–90
Relationship quality, 439
Relationship-specific adaptation, 92
Repairs, 363
Reps, 364–365, 376
Reputationally-effective managers, 9
Requisitioning process, 60
Research. *See* Market research
Research & Development (R&D), 7, 244, 245, 247, 312
Resolution of business plans, 325
Resource allocation, 466–467
Response behavior, 8
Responsibility charting, 246, 247
Responsive marketing strategy, 78
RF. *See* Radio frequency (RF)
Ricoh Company, 262
Risk-reduction strategies, 79–82
RJR Nabisco, 561
Rockton Paper Mill, 533
Rolodex, 547
Roscoe Nondestructive Testing, 530–537
Rotel AG, 551

Routine low priority decisions, **59**
Routine problem solving, 59
RoweCom, 12
Royal Dutch/Shell, 310
Rules of thumb, 415
Russia, 270
Ryder Dedicated Logistics, 168, 211
Ryerson Steel, 515

S. C. Johnson, 509–510, 663
Sailor Pen Company, 552, 553
Sales analysis, 469
Sales and Marketing Management, 435
Sales.com, 97
Sales force composite, 212–213, 215
Sales force management. *See also* Personal selling
  evaluation of personnel, 446
  geographical organization and, 440
  industrial sales force management, 449–454
  market-centered organizations and, 441
  monitoring sales force, 448
  national accounts and, 441–443
  organization climate and, 447
  organizing personal selling effort and, 440–441
  performance measures, 448
  performance standards establishment, 448–449
  personal selling and, 439–449
  product organization and, 440–441
  recruitment, 443–444
  sales administration, 443–449
  supervision and motivation, 445–447
  training, 444–445
  turnover and, 447–448
Sales forecasting
  barriers to entry and, 211
  bottom-up forecasting, 209
  causal techniques, 214, 216–218
  combination approach, 209, 218–219
  definition of, 195
  Delphi method, 213–214
  dimensions of, 208–210
  early warning systems, 208
  expenditures and, 211
  irregular components and, 216
  macroeconomic forecasting, 209
  market potential application for, 201

Sales forecasting (*continued*)
methods of, 210–220
qualitative techniques for, 210–214
quantitative techniques, 214–218, 280
role of, 200
seasonal patterns and, 216
supply chain links and, 201
techniques selections, 219–220
technological change and, 211
time frame and, 210, 211
time series techniques, 214, 215–216
top-down forecasting, 208–209
wrong way to use, 217
Sales organization strength, 451
Sales potential. *See* Market potential
Sales resource opportunity grid, 451, 452
Sam's Club, 661
Sandoz, 547
SAP AG, 622–629
Sasib Corporation of America, 669
Satisficers, 187
Savin, 63
SBC Communications, 414
SBU. *See* Strategic business unit (SBU)
Schneider Logistics, Inc., 168
Schneider National, 168
SCM. *See* Supply chain management (SCM)
SCORE (Service Core of Retired Executives), 689
Scott Sani-Fresh, 547
Sealed Air Corporation, 392
Seasonal patterns, **216**
Segment, 471. *See also* Business market segmentation; Market segment
Segmenting purchase categories, 39, 40
Selective attention, 79
Selective distribution, 370–371
Selective exposure, 79
Selective perception, 79
Selective retention, 79
Senior managers, 108
Service concept, 342
Service Core of Retired Executives (SCORE), 689
Service management. *See also* Services
bundling services, 344
business service marketing, 333–334
customer loyalty and, 338–339
customer segmentation, 340–341

customized expert service, 352
delivery system for services, 343
demand/capacity management, 343–344
distribution of services, 347–349
franchising, 349
improved service experience, 352
"industrialized" clones, 352–353
intermediaries and, 349
marketing mix for business service firms, 340–349
new business attraction, 344–345
new service development, 349–353
non-ownership and, 337
perishability and, 343–344
personnel and, 343
pioneering ventures, 352
pricing business services, 343–345
product support services, 331–333
promotion of services, 345
pure services and, 333
quality of services and, 337–340
return on quality and, 340
role of business services, 330–337
service concept, 342
service offer, 343
service packages, 341–343
service perishability and, 337
service variabilities and, 336–337
simultaneous production and consumption and, 336
tangible clue development, 346–347
unique service characteristics and, 336
zero defection and, 339–340
Service offer, 343
Services. *See also* Service management
business services, 330–337
definition of, **334**
as facilitating good, 23–24
industrial services, 287
intangibility of, 334–336
product support services, 331–333
tangibility of, 334–336
technical service support, 245, 335
Set-aside program, 45
Setting the stage in business plans, 325
Sheaffer, 547, 553
Short-term sales forecasting, 210

SIC. *See* Standard Industrial Classification (SIC)
Siebel Systems, 97
Siecor, 547
Siemen's, 645–646
Signode Corporation, 184–185, 659
Silicon Valley, 309–310
Simple modified rebuy, 65
Single series method, 202–203
Skeptics, 299, 301
Skimming, 399–400
Smucker Company, 11–14, 52
Software
business applications software, 622–630
for supply chain management, 148–150
Sony Corporation, 5, 306, 312
SOSLP. *See* Southwestern Ohio Steel Company, L.P. (SOSLP)
"Sourcing," 44
Southwestern Ohio Steel Company, L.P. (SOSLP), 511–517
SPC. *See* Statistical Process Control (SPC)
Specialist distributors, **363**
Specialists, 358
Specialty segmentation, 291
Sprint, 414, 488
SQC. *See* Statistical Quality Control (SQC)
Stage one quality movement, **284**
Stage two quality movement, **284**
Standard & Poors, 203
Standard Industrial Classification (SIC), 33, 178, 202
Standard Rate and Data Service, 421
Standard Register, 207
Staples, 134
Statistical Process Control (SPC), 545, 553
Statistical Quality Control (SQC), 545
Statistical series methods
definition of, 202
determination of market potential and, 205
forecasting and, 205
limitations of, 204–205
relationship with demand, 204
selection of, 203–205
single series method, 202–203
Steel industry, 143
Straight rebuy
buying decision approaches to, 59
buy-side requisitioning process, 60–61

definition of, **59**
electronic purchasing and, 59–63
industry-specific marketplaces
and, 62–63
online trading communities and,
61–62
strategy guidelines for, 63
Strategic alliances
benefits of, 102–103
boundary-spanning connections,
104–105
case study on, 552–553
contract negotiation and, 103
core asset protection, 104
definition of, **102**
evaluation of, 263
global markets and, 261–262
information flow management
for, 108
integrating points of contact,
105–107
linking systems and structures,
104
management challenges for, 103–
104
networking and, 108
problems in coordination and
trust with, 261
problems in implementing alliances on a global scale with,
262
problems in maintaining alliances
over time with, 262
social connections in, 106
social ingredients of, 107–108
success determinants, 104–107
top management's role in,
107–108
working relationship development, 104
Strategic behavior, 307–309
**Strategic business unit (SBU),
236**
Strategic control, 468–469
Strategic inflection point, 239
Strategic integration, 106
Strategic intent, 239
Strategic new task, 58
Strategic perspectives
for competitive advantage, 231–
235
of market-driven organizations,
226–231
marketing's strategic role, 235–
239
Strategy matrix, 294–295
Sun Microsystems, 21, 24, 181–182,
298, 332, 347
Sun Solaris Enterprise, 499

Superior skills, 231, 280
Supplier management, 115
Supplier performance evaluation
cost containment and, 50
implications for marketers, 44–
45
purpose of, 41–42
rating chart, 43
weighted-point plan, 42–44
Supplies, 23
Supply chain. *See also* Supply chain
management (SCM)
build to order and, 17–18
example of, 155
Internet and, 15–16, 119
managing relationships in, 18–19
overview of, 14
purchasing trends and, 18
sales forecasts and, 201
value-creating activities and, 14
Supply chain management (SCM)
application of, 150–153
competitive advantage and,
143–150
concept of, 141–143
customer benefits and, 146
definition of, **35,** 140
financial benefits of, 147
flexibility of response and, 146
improved performance and, 147
Internet and, 150
logistics of, 153–169
operations and systems harmony
and, 145
overview of, 140
partnerships and, 142–143
product quality and, 145
seven habits of highly effective
supply chains, 152–153
technology and, 147–150
time compression and, 145–146
unit cost reduction and, 146
waste reduction and, 145
Supply market dynamism, 93, 95
SupplyNet, 150
Survey approach, 392
Survey of Current Business, 216
Surveys, 206
Swanson Industries, 531
Sweden, 253
Switzerland, 42, 112
Sylvania/GTE Applied Research
Lab, 681

Tactical integration, 106
Tactical pricing, 401–403
Taiwan, 265
Talent markets, 310

Target audience, 413–414, 419
Target costing, 393
TCO. *See* Total cost of ownership
(TCO)
Team, 321
Technical knowledge, 325
Technical proficiency, 325
Technical synergy, 324
Techno, 320, 321
Technology. *See also* E-commerce;
High-technology markets;
Internet
management technology, 176
market strategy in high-technology industries, 239–244
process technology, 176
product technology, 176
and sales forecasting, 211
technological environment evalu-
ation, 176–177
Technology enthusiasts, 298, 299,
301
Technology management
classification of development
projects and, 311–312
experimentation and, 314
innovation winners in high-technology markets and, 312–314
limited structure and, 313
product family focus and, 312
real time communication and
improvisation and, 313–314
time pacing and, 314
Techsonic, 547
Telemarketing, 420
Territory sales response, 450–451
Territory workload, 451
Test marketing, 392
Texas Instruments, 253
Thinkpad, 150
Third-party logistics firms,
167–169
Thomas & Betts, 547
Thought worlds, 237
3COM, 163
3M
business market perspectives and,
6, 7, 11
business market strategy control
and, 465
business marketing channel management, 376–377
business marketing planning,
228, 230, 236
e-commerce, 123
innovation management,
307–309, 317–318, 325
organizational buying behavior
and, 71

3M (*continued*)
personal selling function and, 441
pricing strategy and, 406
product management, 279, 283–284
segmentation and, 177
suppliers of, 547
3M Health Care, 547
Time pacing, 314, 315
Time segmentation, 400
Time series analysis, 214, 215–216
Top-down forecasting, 208–209
Toshiba, 275
Total Buying Plans, 428
Total cost approach, 158
Total cost in use, 386
Total cost of ownership (TCO), 36–37, 159
Total market offerings, 335
Toyota, 18, 394
TPN. *See* Trading Partner Network (TPN)
Trade barriers, 254
Trade Show Bureau, 426
Trade Show Central, 428
Trade shows
evaluation of performance at, 428–430
flow model for, 429
investment returns and, 426–427
lead pursuance and, 430
objectives of, 427
show selection, 427–428
strategy benefits, 426
strategy plan for, 427
trade show exhibit management, 428
TradeXchange, 15
Trading communities, 61–62, 129
Trading companies, 379
Trading Partner Network (TPN), 129
Training, 444–445
Transaction buyers, 185
Transactional exchanges, 89, 91
Transactional platforms, 359
Transactional relationships, 94, 99
Transportation, 159, 164–165
Triangle, 668–669
TRW, 14

Turf, 319
Turf barriers, 319–320
Tyson Foods, 519

Unemployment, 208
Uniform Code Council, 682
Union Carbide, 441
Unisys, 615
Unit cost reduction, 146
United Kingdom, 107, 132, 265, 268, 566, 572, 574
U.S. agencies. *See* specific agencies such as Defense Department
U.S. Industrial Outlook, 203
United Technologies Corporation, 24, 65
Universal Product Code (UPC). *See* UPC bar codes
Universal products, **290**–291
University of Texas, 112
UPC bar codes, 677–691
US Web, 24
Usage costs, 386
Users, 20, 75–76
Using the Bar Code: Why It's Taking Over (Collins and Whipple), 682
USinternetworking, 503
USinterworking, 347

Vaitra, 616
Value
definition of, **98**
meaning of, 285–286
perceived value, 390
perceptions of, 39
value analysis, 37
value buys, 37–38
value superiority, 233–234
value-creating activities, 14
Value-adding exchanges, 89–90
Value-based sales tools, 387
Value chain
coordination and configuration and, 268
international strategies and, 266–269
upstream and downstream activities, 267
Value in use, 182

Value proposition, 6, 70
VCR market, 282
Verbatim, 547
Vertical hubs, 129
Vertical publications, 417
VerticalNet, 12
Virtual marketplace, 15–16
Visionaries, 298, 299, 301
Vistakon, 547
Volvo, 293

W. A. Lane, 669–670
W. L. Gore & Associates, Inc., 580–602
Wall Street Journal, 567
Wal-Mart, 6, 17
Warehouse management systems (WMS), 167
Warehousing, 158
Waste reductions, 145
Web sites, design of, 126
Weighted-point plan, 42–44
Wells Fargo, 504
West Germany, 107
Westinghouse, 441
Whirlpool, 20
Whole product, 300
Win/loss analysis, 402–403
Wind Technology, 615–621
WMS. *See* Warehouse management systems (WMS)
Woodman, 668
Word of mouth promotion, 345–346
World Wide Web, 68, 114, 116. *See also* Internet

Xerox
business market channel management, 359
controlling business market strategy, 477
global markets, 262, 268
organizational buying behavior and, 63, 71
personal selling function and, 437, 441
segmentation and, 186
XSag.com, 129

Japan
  international strategy and, 268
  joint ventures and, 262, 264
  market growth in, 10
  market share advantages and, 264
  quality function deployment
    (QFD) and, 322
  semiconductor industry and, 265
JIT. *See* Just-in-time (JIT) concept
Job satisfaction, 447
John Deere and Company, 420
Johnson & Johnson, 177, 465,
  546–547, 553, 555
Johnson Controls, 14, 18, 56
Joint ventures, 102, 262, 264
Judgmental new task, 58
Just-in-time (JIT) concept, 156–
  157, 363, 545, 682

Kanthal Corporation, 476
Kartridg Pak (KP), 658–676
Key buying influentials, 13
Kidde, 547
Kliklok, 668
Kodak. *See* Eastman Kodak
Komatsu, 268
Korea, 10, 265
KP. *See* Kartridg Pak (KP)
KPMG, 503
Kroger Company, 33, 681

Lawyers, 107
Lead efficiency, 428
Lead user method, 318, 319
Lead users, 318
Leadership, positions, **274**
Learning, 234
Learning and growth perspective,
  464
Leveraged buys, 37, 38
Levi Strauss & Co., 44
Licensing, 260
Life-cycle potential, 200
Lifetime profitability, 463
Limited problem solving, 64
Linkages, 234
Linked buys, 37, 38
Linking systems and structures, 104
Lockheed Martin Corporation, 49,
  129
Logistics
  business-to-business logistical
    management, 163–169
  business-to-business logistical
    service, 159–163
  calculation of costs, 159

  competitive advantage and, 155–
    156
  cross-functional relationships
    and, 244, 245
  customer impact, 160
  definition of, **153**
  elements of logistics system, 157,
    158
  flow management and, 155
  "Fourth-Party Logistics," 168
  inventory and, 158, 165–167
  just-in-time systems, 156–157
  logistics information systems,
    167
  outsourcing and, 163–164, 168
  sales-marketing-logistics integra-
    tion, 156
  service elements, 160–161
  supply chain impact and,
    161–163
  supply chain management distin-
    guished from, 154
  third-party logistics firms,
    167–169
  timely logistics support, 155–159
  total cost approach and, 157–159
  transportation and, 159, 164–165
Long term sales forecasting, 210
Lowest delivered cost position, 233
Lucent Technologies, 11
Lufkin Pulp Mill, 533

Mack Trucks, 293
Macrolevel of business market seg-
  mentation, 179–183
Macrosegmentation, 178, 183
Mailing lists, 421
Maintenance and repair items, 23
Maintenance and repair support,
  24
Maintenance, repair, and opera-
  tions. *See* MRO (maintenance,
  repair, and operations)
Malaysia, 140
Management contracts, 261
Management judgment, 211
Management technology, 176
Managing innovation. *See* Innova-
  tion management
Managing technology. *See* Technol-
  ogy management
Manufactured materials and parts,
  definition of, 21
Margins, 376–377
Market demand forecasting, 195
Market-driven entrepreneurial cul-
  ture, 464–466

Market-driven organizations
  capabilities for, 227–228
  customer values and, 228
  customer-linking capability and,
    227
  dimensions of, 229
  management dimensions of,
    228–231
  market-sensing capabilities and,
    227
  organizational scheme for, 52,
    53, 228
  strategic perspectives for, 226–
    227
  strategy development of, 228
  supporting programs and actions
    of, 229–231
  three-level focus for, 227
Market entry. *See also* New products
  barriers to, 211
  contracting and, 260–261
  efficiency and, 274
  exporting, 259–260
  franchising and, 260–261
  global market and, 259–269,
    271–275
  international market entry, 271–
    273
  key decisions for, 274
  leadership position and, 274
  licensing and, 260
  local market expansion and,
    273–274
  mode of, 272–273
  phases of international market
    entry, 271–275
  pre-internationalization,
    270–271
  strategy development and,
    274–275
  timing of, 272
Market factors, 254, 255
Market influence, 282
Market invention, 242–243
Market orientation, 5
Market potential
  determination of, 202–208
  life-cycle potential, 200
  market research and, 205–208
  as opportunity, 199
  role in planning and control,
    198–200
  segmented planning and control,
    199
  single series method for calculat-
    ing, 202–203
  statistical series methods of de-
    termining potential, 202–205

Market research
  customer visits as, 207–208
  discontinuous innovations and,
    243
  focus groups, 206–207
  Internet usage for, 195–198
  market potential and, 205–208
  primary data, 198
  secondary data, 196
  surveys, 206
Market Research Center, 197
Market segment. *See also* Business
    market segmentation; Segment
  definition of, **174**–175
  momentum of, 300–301
  profitability by, 471–473
Market segmentation, 291
Market sensing, 464
Market-sensing capability, 5–6,
  227
Market share, 463
Market share analysis, 469
Marketing. *See also* headings begin-
    ning Business market
Marketing audit, 468
Marketing control
  annual plan control, 469–470
  balance scorecard and, 460–466
  definition of, **460**
  effects of informal control, 467
  efficiency and effectiveness con-
    trol, 471
  feedforward control, 474–475
  formulation guidance, 466–467
  framework for, 469–470, 479
  implementation skills and,
    476–477
  levels of, 468
  marketer's role, 478
  marketing strategy center and,
    477–478
  process of, 467
  profitability control, 471–474
  questions for, 470
  resource allocation, 466–467
  strategic control, 468–469
  at various levels, 468–475
Marketing implementation, 475
Marketing proficiency, 324–325
Marketing strategy. *See also* Market-
    ing control
  basis of, 6
  business-level strategy, 236
  collective action perspective on,
    238
  competitive displacement and,
    241–242
  controlling business marketing
    strategies, 459–480

corporate culture and, 243–244
corporate strategy, 235
discontinuous innovation strategies, 240–244
flowchart for, 249
formulation of, 237–239
functional strategy, 236
functionally integrated planning,
  246–248
hierarchy of strategies, 235–237
for high-technology industries,
  239–244
implementation of, 475–478
industrial products and, 292–295
industry genesis and, 242
international marketing strategy,
  269–275
managing strategic interdependencies, 248
market invention, 242–243
market segmentation and, 191
marketing plan, 248–249
negotiated outcomes and, 237–
  239
opportunity identification, 241
overview of, 25–26
pricing strategy, 386–387
radical cannibalism and, 241, 242
resource allocation, 466–467
responsive marketing strategy, 78
strategic business units (SBUs)
  and, 236
strategic inflection point, 239
strategic intent, 239
strategy-implementation fit,
  475–476
thought worlds and, 237
three-customer connections'
  management, 236–237
Marketing strategy center, 477–478
Marketing synergy, 324
MarketSite, 61, 62
Marmot Mountain Works Ltd., 592
Marquest, 547
Marriott Corporation, 31, 51, 345
Marshall Industries, 132–133
Masbac, 547
Masters golf tournament, 683
Materials handling, 158
Matsushita, 282
Matworks, 515–517
Maytag, 37
McDonald's, 21, 36, 295, 542, 546
McGraw-Hill, 361
MCI Worldcom, 414
McKinley & Company, 681
McKinsey, 561
Mead Corporation, 71, 442
MediaMetrix, 197

Medical Equipment Systems, 330
Medical-Surgical Markets Group,
  318
Mercer Management Consulting,
  37, 143, 178
Mexico, and NAFTA, 33, 257
Microlevel bases of business market
    segmentation
  attitudes toward vendors and,
    188
  decision-making unit structure,
    187–188
  fast-cycle strategies and, 185–186
  importance of purchase and, 188
  key criteria and, 183
  organizational innovations and,
    188
  price versus service, 184–185
  purchasing strategies for, 187
Microsegmentation, 178,
  188–189
Microsoft Corporation
  advertising and, 414
  e-commerce, 133
  innovation management,
    314–315
  product management, 295, 300,
    301
  relationship strategies and, 100
  service management, 331–332
Mikromashina, 551, 552
Miller SQA, 150, 151
Milliken & Company, 182
"Mini-mills," 143
Mining Enforcement and Safety
    Administration, 47
**Minority subcontracting pro-
    gram,** definition of, **45**
Miracle Adhesives, 209
Mitsui & Co., 553
Mixed bundling, 344
Modified rebuys
  buying decision approaches for,
    64–65
  complex modified rebuys, 65
  definition of, **63**
  limited problem solving for, 64
  simple modified rebuy, 65
  strategy guidelines for, 65–66
Momentum, 300–301
Monsanto, 310
Mosaic Corporation, 485
Motorola
  business market perspectives and,
    11, 12, 18
  business market planning, 245
  global markets, 253, 270
  organizational buying and, 60, 70
  product management, 279–280

relationship strategies and, 88, 100, 102
suppliers of, 547
MRO (maintenance, repair, and operations), 361
Multidomestic industries, 267
Multidomestic strategies, 264

Nabisco, 295
NAFTA. *See* North American Free Trade Agreement (NAFTA)
NAICS. *See* **North American Industrial Classification System (NAICS)**
"Naked solutions," 100
NASA, 615
National account, 442
National Inspection Services (NIS), 531
National Semiconductor Corporation, 72, 131, 359, 360
National Transportation Exchange (NTE), 132
Navistar, 293
Navy, 46, 47
NCR, 288
NDT. *See* Nondestructive testing (NDT)
NDTMA. *See* Nondestructive Testing Managers Association (NDTMA)
NEC Corporation, 498
Negotiated outcomes, 237–239
Nellcor, 646
Nestal Maschinen AG, 552
Net Buying Influences, 428
Netscape, 133
New competitors, 176
New products. *See also* Market entry
collaboration and, 320
communication barriers and, 320
concurrent engineering and, 322
cross-functional barriers and, 319–320
customer's voice and, 322–323
development process for, 314–323
engineer's voice and, 323
fast-paced product development, 326
idea sources, 317–319
international orientation, 324
interpretive barriers and, 320
Japanese companies and, 325–326
lead users and, 318, 319
leading customers and, 318–319
marketing proficiency and, 324–325

marketing synergy and, 324
new product strategy, 317
new to the world products, 322
performance drivers for, 316–317
predevelopment proficiency, 324
pricing of, 399–401
process employment and, 316–317
product advantage and, 324
product modifications and, 322
quality function deployment (QFD) and, 322–323
resources commitments and, 317
segmentation strategy and, 189
success determinants, 324–326
team-based processing and, 321–322
technical proficiency and, 325
turf barriers and, 319–320
New service development, 349–353
New-task buying situation, **58**
NIS. *See* National Inspection Services (NIS)
Nokia, 253
Nondefense procurement, 47–48
Nondestructive Testing Managers Association (NDTMA), 533, 534
Nondestructive testing (NDT), 530–537
Nondeterminant attributes, 293
Non-strategic purchases, 93
North American Free Trade Agreement (NAFTA), 33, 257, 520, 525
North American Industrial Classification System (NAICS), 33, 34, 178, 182, 202–203
NTE. *See* National Transportation Exchange (NTE)
NUCOR, 233
Nucor Incorporated, 143
Nylon Products Corporation, 538
Nypro Inc., 538–559

OEMs. *See* Original Equipment Manufacturers (OEMs)
Ogilvy and Mather, 565
Ohmeda Health Care, 645
Ohmeda Monitoring Systems, 642–657
Omega Financial Services, 104
Omnibus Trade Act, 515
Online auctions, 65, 66, 130–131
Online trading communities, 61–62
Open bidding, 404

Operating personnel, 108
Operating resources, 59
Operating supplies, 23
Operational benefits, 386
Operational integration, 106
Operational linkages, 91–92, 95
Opportunity identification, 241
Optimizers, 187
Oracle Corporation, 60, 97, 298, 436
Order processing, 158
Order-to-delivery time, 145–146
Organizational buying center, 437
Organizational buying process
buyers and, 76
buygrid framework for, 57
buying center, 73–76
centralization of purchasing, 71–73
decentralization of purchasing, 71–73
deciders and, 76
economic influences on, 68
environmental forces affecting, 67–68
evaluative criteria and, 78
evoked set of alternatives and, 82
feasible set of alternatives and, 82
forces affecting, 67–82
gatekeepers and, 76
group forces and, 73–77
individual forces and, 77–82
influencers and, 76–77
informational processing and, 78–79
interaction structure and, 82
isolation of buying situation, 74–75
modified rebuys, 63–66
new-task buying situation, 58
organizational forces affecting, 69–70
overview, 56–57
predicting composition, 75
purchasing positioning, 70–77
requisitioning steps, 60
risk-reduction strategies and, 79–82
straight rebuy, 59–63
strategies in purchasing, 69–70
technological influences on, 68
types of buying situations, 57–66
Organizational customer focus
buying center identification and, 435
influence pattern identification and, 435
Internet and, 435–437

Organizational customer focus (*ctd.*)
   knowledge of customer's business and, 435
   organizational buying behavior and, 434–435
   organizational factor identification and, 435
   personal selling and, 433–439
   relationship marketing and, 437–439
Organizational demand analysis
   definition of, 195
   Internet usage for business marketing research and, 195–198
   market potential and, 198–208
   sales forecast and, 200
Organizational forces, 67
Organizational innovativeness, 188
Organizational selling center, 437
Original Equipment Manufacturers (OEMs), 20, 548
Otis Elevator, 331–332
Outside salespersons, 361
Outsourcing, 50–51, 163–164, 168, 331
Owens-Corning Fiberglass Corporation, 441
Owens-Illinois, 107

P&G. *See* Proctor and Gamble Company (P&G)
Packaging, 158, 658–676
Packard Bell, 282
Paging Products Group, 69
Pall Biomedical, 547
Panasonic, 547
PaperExchange.com, 129
Patching, 313
Paxall, 669
Payment management, 115
PCU opportunity, 451
Penetration, 399
Pentagon, 49
Peripheral participants, 104
Perishability, 343–344
Personal benefits, 386
Personal selling
   electronic sales forces, 454
   industrial sales force management, 449–454
   Internet and, 435–437
   national accounts and, 441–443
   organizational customer focus and, 433–439
   relationship marketing, 437–438
   sales administration, 443–449

sales force management and, 439–449
Perspective taking, 7–8
Pfizer, Inc., 518–529
Pharmaseal, 635
Philippines, 140
Philips Electronics, 188–189
Philips Lighting Company, 188–189
Pillsbury, 20
Pioneering ventures, 352
Pitney Bowes, 358, 442
Planning and control units, 450
Plant and warehouse location, 158
PlasticsNet, 130
Platform management, 360
Platform projects, 311
Polaroid, 547
Possession costs, 386
Potential, as measure, **450**
Prado-Pak, 670
Pragmatists, 299, 301
Predevelopment proficiency, 324
Predicasts, 203
Pre-internationalization, 270–271
Prestolite, 547
Price elasticity of demand, 390
Price indexes, 208
Pricing strategy
   competitive bidding and, 403–406
   costs and, 386–387
   customers' cost-in-use components, 386
   industrial pricing process, 387–399
   legal considerations, 403
   meaning of price in business markets, 384–387
   new product pricing, 399–401
   overview of, 384
   penetration and, 401
   pricing across product life cycle, 399–403
   pricing environment, 385
   product benefits and, 385–386
   product line considerations for, 401
   skimming and, 400
   tactical pricing, 401–403
   time segmentation and, 400
   value-based strategies, 387
Prince Philip Award, 584
Private institutions. *See* Institutions
Process technology, 176
Proctor and Gamble Company (P&G), 11, 17, 31, 116, 295, 663

Product advantage, 324
Product availability, 363
Product champion, 308–309
Product development. *See* New products
Product family, 312
Product management. *See also* New products
   core competencies and, 279–287
   end products, 282
   global products, 290–291
   in high-technology markets, 295–302
   industrial product strategy, 292–295
   lead sustenance and, 280–282
   market definition, 289–290
   market segmentation and, 291
   new product development process, 314–323
   pricing across product life cycle, 399–403
   product line definition, 287–289
   product policy, 287–291
   quality and, 284–285
   segmentation and, 291
   support strategy, 286
   universal products, 290–291
   value and, 285–286
Product market, 289
Product position, 414
Product positioning, 292
Product quality, diversity in requirements for, 31
Product segmentation, 291
Product support services, 331–333
Product technology, 176
Production planning, 158
Products supported by services, 331
Profitability control, 471–474
Project leaders, 108
Proprietary or catalog products, 287
PSS WorldMedical, 122
Psychological contracts, 105
Purchasing
   buying motivations, 20–21
   centralization of, 71–73
   commercial enterprises and, 32–45
   decentralization of, 71–73
   defense procurement, 47
   electronic purchasing, 59–63, 129
   federal buying, 48–49
   goals of purchasing function, 34–35

government agencies and, 45–50
group purchasing, 51–52
industrial products, 184
institutional purchasing procedures, 50–52
key criteria of, 183
levels of procurement development, 37–39
macrolevel characteristics of buying organization, 180–181
microsegment purchasing strategies, 187
modified rebuys, 63–66
new-task purchasing, 59
nondefense procurement, 47–48
on Internet, 40–41
optimizers and, 187
organization of, 33–34, 46–47
organizational buying process, 56–83
performance impact and, 39–40
positioning of, 70–77
price versus service, 184–185
satisficers and, 187
segmentation and, 39, 40, 182
service versus price, 184–185
straight rebuys, 59–63
strategic priorities of, 69–70
strategic procurement, 35–41, 93
supplier performance evaluation and, 41–45, 50
supply chain purchasing trends, 18
total costs and, 36
Pure bundling, 344

QFD. *See* Quality function deployment (QFD)
QIP. *See* Quality improvement program (QIP)
Qualitative techniques for sales forecasting, 211–213
Quality function deployment (QFD), 322
Quality improvement program (QIP), 535–536
Quick Response concept, 682

R. D. Ocean, 604–606
Radical cannibalism, 241, 242
Radio frequency (RF), 167
Rareness, 280–281
Raw materials, 21
Raytheon, 400
Reconceiving products or services, 186

Redefining market space, 186
Redrawing industry boundaries, 186
Regression techniques, **214,** 216, 218
Relationship buyers, 185
Relationship connectors, 91
Relationship marketing
account selection, 98
account-specific product offering development and, 98–99
buyer-seller relationship, 90–96
capturing relationship data, 96–97
collaborative exchange and, 89
commitment demonstration, 101–102
definition of, **14,** 88
evaluation of strategy outcomes, 101
flaring out, 99–100
flexible service offering creation, 100
monitoring relationships, 101
nature of relationship and, 90
organizational customer focus and, 437–439
strategic alliances and, 102–108
strategic choices and, 90
strategies for, 96–101
transactional exchange and, 89
types of relationships, 89
value-adding exchanges and, 89–90
Relationship quality, 439
Relationship-specific adaptation, 92
Repairs, 363
Reps, 364–365, 376
Reputationally-effective managers, 9
Requisitioning process, 60
Research. *See* Market research
Research & Development (R&D), 7, 244, 245, 247, 312
Resolution of business plans, 325
Resource allocation, 466–467
Response behavior, 8
Responsibility charting, 246, 247
Responsive marketing strategy, 78
RF. *See* Radio frequency (RF)
Ricoh Company, 262
Risk-reduction strategies, 79–82
RJR Nabisco, 561
Rockton Paper Mill, 533
Rolodex, 547
Roscoe Nondestructive Testing, 530–537
Rotel AG, 551

Routine low priority decisions, **59**
Routine problem solving, 59
RoweCom, 12
Royal Dutch/Shell, 310
Rules of thumb, 415
Russia, 270
Ryder Dedicated Logistics, 168, 211
Ryerson Steel, 515

S. C. Johnson, 509–510, 663
Sailor Pen Company, 552, 553
Sales analysis, 469
Sales and Marketing Management, 435
Sales.com, 97
Sales force composite, 212–213, 215
Sales force management. *See also* Personal selling
evaluation of personnel, 446
geographical organization and, 440
industrial sales force management, 449–454
market-centered organizations and, 441
monitoring sales force, 448
national accounts and, 441–443
organization climate and, 447
organizing personal selling effort and, 440–441
performance measures, 448
performance standards establishment, 448–449
personal selling and, 439–449
product organization and, 440–441
recruitment, 443–444
sales administration, 443–449
supervision and motivation, 445–447
training, 444–445
turnover and, 447–448
Sales forecasting
barriers to entry and, 211
bottom-up forecasting, 209
causal techniques, 214, 216–218
combination approach, 209, 218–219
definition of, 195
Delphi method, 213–214
dimensions of, 208–210
early warning systems, 208
expenditures and, 211
irregular components and, 216
macroeconomic forecasting, 209
market potential application for, 201

Sales forecasting (*continued*)
  methods of, 210–220
  qualitative techniques for,
    210–214
  quantitative techniques,
    214–218, 280
  role of, 200
  seasonal patterns and, 216
  supply chain links and, 201
  techniques selections, 219–220
  technological change and, 211
  time frame and, 210, 211
  time series techniques, 214,
    215–216
  top-down forecasting, 208–209
  wrong way to use, 217
Sales organization strength, 451
Sales potential. *See* Market potential
Sales resource opportunity grid,
  451, 452
Sam's Club, 661
Sandoz, 547
SAP AG, 622–629
Sasib Corporation of America, 669
Satisficers, 187
Savin, 63
SBC Communications, 414
SBU. *See* Strategic business unit
  (SBU)
Schneider Logistics, Inc., 168
Schneider National, 168
SCM. *See* Supply chain manage-
  ment (SCM)
SCORE (Service Core of Retired
  Executives), 689
Scott Sani-Fresh, 547
Sealed Air Corporation, 392
Seasonal patterns, **216**
Segment, 471. *See also* Business
  market segmentation; Market
  segment
Segmenting purchase categories,
  39, 40
Selective attention, 79
Selective distribution, 370–371
Selective exposure, 79
Selective perception, 79
Selective retention, 79
Senior managers, 108
Service concept, 342
Service Core of Retired Executives
  (SCORE), 689
Service management. *See also* Ser-
  vices
  bundling services, 344
  business service marketing,
    333–334
  customer loyalty and, 338–339
  customer segmentation, 340–341

customized expert service, 352
delivery system for services, 343
demand/capacity management,
  343–344
distribution of services, 347–349
franchising, 349
improved service experience, 352
"industrialized" clones, 352–353
intermediaries and, 349
marketing mix for business service firms, 340–349
new business attraction, 344–345
new service development,
  349–353
non-ownership and, 337
perishability and, 343–344
personnel and, 343
pioneering ventures, 352
pricing business services,
  343–345
product support services,
  331–333
promotion of services, 345
pure services and, 333
quality of services and, 337–340
return on quality and, 340
role of business services,
  330–337
service concept, 342
service offer, 343
service packages, 341–343
service perishability and, 337
service variabilities and, 336–
  337
simultaneous production and
  consumption and, 336
tangible clue development, 346–
  347
unique service characteristics
  and, 336
zero defection and, 339–340
Service offer, 343
Services. *See also* Service
  management
  business services, 330–337
  definition of, **334**
  as facilitating good, 23–24
  industrial services, 287
  intangibility of, 334–336
  product support services,
    331–333
  tangibility of, 334–336
  technical service support, 245,
    335
Set-aside program, 45
Setting the stage in business plans,
  325
Sheaffer, 547, 553
Short-term sales forecasting, 210

SIC. *See* Standard Industrial
  Classification (SIC)
Siebel Systems, 97
Siecor, 547
Siemen's, 645–646
Signode Corporation, 184–185, 659
Silicon Valley, 309–310
Simple modified rebuy, 65
Single series method, 202–203
Skeptics, 299, 301
Skimming, 399–400
Smucker Company, 11–14, 52
Software
  business applications software,
    622–630
  for supply chain management,
    148–150
Sony Corporation, 5, 306, 312
SOSLP. *See* Southwestern Ohio
  Steel Company, L.P. (SOSLP)
"Sourcing," 44
Southwestern Ohio Steel Company,
  L.P. (SOSLP), 511–517
SPC. *See* Statistical Process Control
  (SPC)
Specialist distributors, **363**
Specialists, 358
Specialty segmentation, 291
Sprint, 414, 488
SQC. *See* Statistical Quality Con-
  trol (SQC)
Stage one quality movement, **284**
Stage two quality movement, **284**
Standard & Poors, 203
Standard Industrial Classification
  (SIC), 33, 178, 202
Standard Rate and Data Service,
  421
Standard Register, 207
Staples, 134
Statistical Process Control (SPC),
  545, 553
Statistical Quality Control (SQC),
  545
Statistical series methods
  definition of, 202
  determination of market poten-
    tial and, 205
  forecasting and, 205
  limitations of, 204–205
  relationship with demand, 204
  selection of, 203–205
  single series method, 202–203
Steel industry, 143
Straight rebuy
  buying decision approaches to,
    59
  buy-side requisitioning process,
    60–61

definition of, **59**
electronic purchasing and, 59–63
industry-specific marketplaces
    and, 62–63
online trading communities and,
    61–62
strategy guidelines for, 63
Strategic alliances
benefits of, 102–103
boundary-spanning connections,
    104–105
case study on, 552–553
contract negotiation and, 103
core asset protection, 104
definition of, **102**
evaluation of, 263
global markets and, 261–262
information flow management
    for, 108
integrating points of contact,
    105–107
linking systems and structures,
    104
management challenges for, 103–
    104
networking and, 108
problems in coordination and
    trust with, 261
problems in implementing al-
    liances on a global scale with,
    262
problems in maintaining alliances
    over time with, 262
social connections in, 106
social ingredients of, 107–108
success determinants, 104–107
top management's role in,
    107–108
working relationship develop-
    ment, 104
Strategic behavior, 307–309
**Strategic business unit (SBU),
    236**
Strategic control, 468–469
Strategic inflection point, 239
Strategic integration, 106
Strategic intent, 239
Strategic new task, 58
Strategic perspectives
    for competitive advantage, 231–
        235
    of market-driven organizations,
        226–231
    marketing's strategic role, 235–
        239
Strategy matrix, 294–295
Sun Microsystems, 21, 24, 181–182,
    298, 332, 347
Sun Solaris Enterprise, 499

Superior skills, 231, 280
Supplier management, 115
Supplier performance evaluation
    cost containment and, 50
    implications for marketers, 44–
        45
    purpose of, 41–42
    rating chart, 43
    weighted-point plan, 42–44
Supplies, 23
Supply chain. *See also* Supply chain
        management (SCM)
    build to order and, 17–18
    example of, 155
    Internet and, 15–16, 119
    managing relationships in, 18–19
    overview of, 14
    purchasing trends and, 18
    sales forecasts and, 201
    value-creating activities and, 14
Supply chain management (SCM)
    application of, 150–153
    competitive advantage and,
        143–150
    concept of, 141–143
    customer benefits and, 146
    definition of, **35,** 140
    financial benefits of, 147
    flexibility of response and, 146
    improved performance and, 147
    Internet and, 150
    logistics of, 153–169
    operations and systems harmony
        and, 145
    overview of, 140
    partnerships and, 142–143
    product quality and, 145
    seven habits of highly effective
        supply chains, 152–153
    technology and, 147–150
    time compression and, 145–146
    unit cost reduction and, 146
    waste reduction and, 145
Supply market dynamism, 93, 95
SupplyNet, 150
Survey approach, 392
Survey of Current Business, 216
Surveys, 206
Swanson Industries, 531
Sweden, 253
Switzerland, 42, 112
Sylvania/GTE Applied Research
    Lab, 681

Tactical integration, 106
Tactical pricing, 401–403
Taiwan, 265
Talent markets, 310

Target audience, 413–414, 419
Target costing, 393
TCO. *See* Total cost of ownership
    (TCO)
Team, 321
Technical knowledge, 325
Technical proficiency, 325
Technical synergy, 324
Techno, 320, 321
Technology. *See also* E-commerce;
    High-technology markets;
    Internet
    management technology, 176
    market strategy in high-technol-
        ogy industries, 239–244
    process technology, 176
    product technology, 176
    and sales forecasting, 211
    technological environment evalu-
        ation, 176–177
Technology enthusiasts, 298, 299,
    301
Technology management
    classification of development
        projects and, 311–312
    experimentation and, 314
    innovation winners in high-tech-
        nology markets and, 312–314
    limited structure and, 313
    product family focus and, 312
    real time communication and
        improvisation and, 313–314
    time pacing and, 314
Techsonic, 547
Telemarketing, 420
Territory sales response, 450–451
Territory workload, 451
Test marketing, 392
Texas Instruments, 253
Thinkpad, 150
Third-party logistics firms,
    167–169
Thomas & Betts, 547
Thought worlds, 237
3COM, 163
3M
    business market perspectives and,
        6, 7, 11
    business market strategy control
        and, 465
    business marketing channel man-
        agement, 376–377
    business marketing planning,
        228, 230, 236
    e-commerce, 123
    innovation management,
        307–309, 317–318, 325
    organizational buying behavior
        and, 71

3M (*continued*)
  personal selling function and, 441
  pricing strategy and, 406
  product management, 279, 283–284
  segmentation and, 177
  suppliers of, 547
3M Health Care, 547
Time pacing, 314, 315
Time segmentation, 400
Time series analysis, 214, 215–216
Top-down forecasting, 208–209
Toshiba, 275
Total Buying Plans, 428
Total cost approach, 158
Total cost in use, 386
Total cost of ownership (TCO), 36–37, 159
Total market offerings, 335
Toyota, 18, 394
TPN. *See* Trading Partner Network (TPN)
Trade barriers, 254
Trade Show Bureau, 426
Trade Show Central, 428
Trade shows
  evaluation of performance at, 428–430
  flow model for, 429
  investment returns and, 426–427
  lead pursuance and, 430
  objectives of, 427
  show selection, 427–428
  strategy benefits, 426
  strategy plan for, 427
  trade show exhibit management, 428
TradeXchange, 15
Trading communities, 61–62, 129
Trading companies, 379
Trading Partner Network (TPN), 129
Training, 444–445
Transaction buyers, 185
Transactional exchanges, 89, 91
Transactional platforms, 359
Transactional relationships, 94, 99
Transportation, 159, 164–165
Triangle, 668–669
TRW, 14

Turf, 319
Turf barriers, 319–320
Tyson Foods, 519

Unemployment, 208
Uniform Code Council, 682
Union Carbide, 441
Unisys, 615
Unit cost reduction, 146
United Kingdom, 107, 132, 265, 268, 566, 572, 574
U.S. agencies. *See* specific agencies such as Defense Department
U.S. Industrial Outlook, 203
United Technologies Corporation, 24, 65
Universal Product Code (UPC). *See* UPC bar codes
Universal products, **290**–291
University of Texas, 112
UPC bar codes, 677–691
US Web, 24
Usage costs, 386
Users, 20, 75–76
Using the Bar Code: Why It's Taking Over (Collins and Whipple), 682
USinternetworking, 503
USinterworking, 347

Vaitra, 616
Value
  definition of, **98**
  meaning of, 285–286
  perceived value, 390
  perceptions of, 39
  value analysis, 37
  value buys, 37–38
  value superiority, 233–234
  value-creating activities, 14
Value-adding exchanges, 89–90
Value-based sales tools, 387
Value chain
  coordination and configuration and, 268
  international strategies and, 266–269
  upstream and downstream activities, 267
Value in use, 182

Value proposition, 6, 70
VCR market, 282
Verbatim, 547
Vertical hubs, 129
Vertical publications, 417
VerticalNet, 12
Virtual marketplace, 15–16
Visionaries, 298, 299, 301
Vistakon, 547
Volvo, 293

W. A. Lane, 669–670
W. L. Gore & Associates, Inc., 580–602
Wall Street Journal, 567
Wal-Mart, 6, 17
Warehouse management systems (WMS), 167
Warehousing, 158
Waste reductions, 145
Web sites, design of, 126
Weighted-point plan, 42–44
Wells Fargo, 504
West Germany, 107
Westinghouse, 441
Whirlpool, 20
Whole product, 300
Win/loss analysis, 402–403
Wind Technology, 615–621
WMS. *See* Warehouse management systems (WMS)
Woodman, 668
Word of mouth promotion, 345–346
World Wide Web, 68, 114, 116. *See also* Internet

Xerox
  business market channel management, 359
  controlling business market strategy, 477
  global markets, 262, 268
  organizational buying behavior and, 63, 71
  personal selling function and, 437, 441
  segmentation and, 186
XSag.com, 129